The 1992 MediaGuide

1992 Media Guide

A Critical Review of the Media's Recent Coverage of the World Political Economy

Jude Wanniski
Editor

Peter A. Signorelli
Executive Editor

Patricia M. Koyce
Managing Editor

Richard Doyle
Associate Editor – International

Kathy McNamara
Associate Editor – Financial

Martin S. Krossel
Timothy Meis
Criton Zoakos
Contributing Editors

Ronald deLaRosa
Copy Editor

Danielle DuChamp
Karolyn Necco
Research

Published by:
Polyconomics, Inc., Morristown, N. J.
In association with
Repap Enterprises, Inc., Montreal, Canada

914302

ISSN: 1042-2129
LIBRARY OF CONGRESS CATALOG CARD NUMBER: 87-654448

ISBN: 0-938081-09-8
ISBN: 0-938081-11-X (pbk.)

92 93 94 95 10 9 8 7 6 5 4 3 2 1

The 1992 MediaGuide

TABLE OF CONTENTS

INTRODUCTION

"May you live in interesting times" goes an ancient Chinese proverb, considered by some as being a blessing, by others, a curse. There can be little doubt that for the world, 1991 was the most interesting of times, in both senses of the proverb.

There was Operation Desert Storm, inviting profound anxiety, nervous exhilaration, and euphoric relief as U.S. troops were committed to the first battle engagement of a New World Order. There was the power struggle in Moscow, and the breakup of the Soviet Union amidst the appalling economic disintegration of a one-time superpower. There was, as well, the continuing economic decline of the U.S. against the backdrop of paralyzed, divided national government. There was the dramatic play of national social and cultural conflict brought to searing focus in the Senate confirmation of a Supreme Court Justice. Not only were these stories watershed events in contemporary history, but they will live on as markers in many of our personal lives as well.

While each of these events was powerful enough in its own right, it was the coverage of these stories that enabled them to lodge permanently in our collective consciousness. This is, of course, one of the principal purposes of journalism — to inform — to let us know what is happening, increasingly as it happens. No one can deny that, in terms of sheer volume, the major events of 1991 were covered in more detail than major events ever were before. This is because of the new technology available, as well as an increasing awareness on the part of the global electorate that what happens halfway across the world does indeed have an effect on their own lives. We salute the publishers, producers, editors and other decision-makers in the journalism industry for recognizing this and responding by providing expanded news pages, special sections, and, as in the case of CNN, by literally tracking stories 24 hours a day.

Yet, if one of the purposes of journalism is to inform, another equally vital, if more subjective, purpose is to explain and illuminate, enabling us to understand fully the headlines and news footage and to place them in context. Viewers may now associate the Gulf War with an image of a U.S. bomb falling with near-miraculous accuracy through the open doorway of an Iraqi warehouse. The attempted Soviet coup against Mikhail Gorbachev may conjure up an image of Boris Yeltsin standing defiantly on top of a tank. Anita Hill and Clarence Thomas may now be little more than two telegenic professionals who unwittingly embroiled the nation in a personal dispute.

But what really was the extent of Iraqi casualties in the war? What truly motivated the Soviet coup leaders? What was the full nature of the agenda of the opponents of Justice Thomas? Was war in the Gulf on January 15th inevitable, or could conflict have been averted? Was the Russian Revolution a true revolution, or a power grab by another sector of the Russian political establishment? What did the Thomas nomination portend for the Bush administration's vision of domestic America? How could the White House and Congress remain deadlocked on relief measures as the body economic continued its sickening decline? These are questions that went largely unanswered and unexplored in the mainstream press, perhaps more from shortness of attention than any calculated design.

There were extenuating circumstances, to be sure. This is especially true in the case of Operation Desert Storm, where the press was forced to operate under restrictions that, instead of being unprecedented, sadly seem increasingly the norm for Western governments during times

1

of war. Journalists on the scene in Saudi Arabia found themselves in pool arrangements. Their reports, when they were able to get them out, were subject to censorship by military press officers, who, by some accounts, went so far as to change one-word descriptions of the day's climate. Press blackouts were imposed and lifted with all the vagaries of desert sandstorms. Official briefings were plentiful, especially when things were going especially well or especially not so well, and discerning viewers soon learned to watch the briefings accordingly. The first land battle, for example, was described as both the military equivalent of a "flea" and a victory of historic proportions for the Saudi army. One commander was celebrated for a briefing held on the last day of the war, in which he disparaged Saddam Hussein's abilities as military leader. This same commander's admission that Saddam had "suckered" him on the issue of helicopters at the subsequent cease-fire signing ceremony was seen by a small viewership watching an interview on public TV.

The other important press precedent set during the Gulf War was the coverage from the capital of the enemy. Millions of viewers were riveted to their sets the first night of the war, including Defense Secretary Richard Cheney and Joint Chiefs of Staff Chairman Colin Powell, as network correspondents reported from Baghdad as the city underwent aerial and missile bombardment. The networks, and CNN, continued to provide the view "from the other side of the hill," during the conflict, providing what was to some, unadulterated Iraqi propaganda, to others, vital ground-level intelligence on the effects of the allied bombing, the mood of the Iraqi people, and the shifting of Saddam. After the war, CNN founder Ted Turner would take credit for shortening the conflict.

The assertion may be overblown, but just as overblown was the reaction by segments of both the government and the population to the coverage from Iraq. BBC correspondent John Simpson would write of the efforts of U.S. diplomats, in the days before the expiration of the U.N. deadline, to employ scare tactics in an effort to convince the remaining Western journalists to leave Baghdad prior to its attack. Once the war was underway, aspersions were cast on the patriotism and professionalism of correspondents, such as Simpson and CNN's Peter Arnett, who elected to stay.

Reasoned debate often tends to be one of the first casualties of war, so the important questions raised during Desert Storm surrounding the First Amendment — the people's right to know, the issue of giving aid and comfort to the enemy — remain to be resolved. The *MediaGuide* believes these questions should be resolved in favor of providing the maximum amount of information in the most professional way possible in the minimum amount of time necessary, because it is clear that governments understand the power of the press in the formulation and implementation of policy, even if they do not always understand how to use it most effectively.

The footage of captured allied pilots on Iraqi TV, rather than breaking the coalition's will, for example, only strengthened its resolve, and provided a vivid lesson that presenting the enemy's case is often the way to do him the least aid and cause him the most harm. U.S. officials later admitted that it was fear of the impact of pictures of U.S. forces mauling Iraqi troops that played a large role in the decision not to march on to Baghdad, and that it had been the outcry following the coverage of the plight of the Kurdish refugees that moved Washington to provide humanitarian aid and military protection.

Among the first official acts of the Soviet coup leaders during their short-lived tenure in office was to ban unofficial radio stations and newspapers. They then held a press conference. The shakiness of one of the coup leader's hands was later cited by many Soviets as the first sign that the putsch would not succeed. The press excelled at covering details like this in the aftermath of the coup. We also learned, among other things, that several of the plotters agreed to the original emergency decree while in an advanced state of intoxication, and spent much of the subsequent week in an alcoholic daze. One TV report took us into the KGB laboratory where specimens from the brains of such former leaders as Lenin and Stalin were being faithfully preserved. Fascinating as these footnotes to history are, they do little to advance our understanding of the fundamentals behind the most important year in Soviet history since 1917, when the country was forged through the steel will of the Bolsheviks.

The press followed the Soviet story throughout the year, the problem being that there was more than one story going on. Early in the year, the rising tension between the Baltic republics and Moscow finally escalated into violence, and a world preparing itself for imminent conflict in the Middle East found itself watching Red Army tanks rolling over demonstrators in Vilnius. The press captured the world's outrage, but seemed to focus on two important but secondary elements of the story: the possible involvement or non-involvement by Mikhail Gorbachev in the decision to crack down, and the suspicious timing, coming just days before the expiration of the U.N. deadline for Iraqi withdrawal from Kuwait. While some commentators did note that the tactics used by the Kremlin — the formation of a shadowy "Committee for Public Safety" taking power and declaring a state of emergency — might be the same ones used in the event of a nationwide coup attempt, there was little examination of what that nationwide emergency might actually consist of, the automatic assumption apparently being that any such "emergency" would be little more than a political Potemkin Village.

There were occasional references to concerns about Soviet citizens struggling to eke out an existence, but not until late in the year was there much attention focused on legitimate concerns over what an economic meltdown and violent breakup of the center would actually mean, for both the Soviet people and the world. It was then that these events actually started to happen and there was new-found concern for nuclear weapons in the hands of the breakaway republics and ex-Soviet citizens starving to death in the dark. Too often the Soviet coverage had a "horse race" feel to it, the whole story broken down to Mikhail Gorbachev versus Boris Yeltsin, who, having won a showdown with security forces in the streets of Moscow in March, was elected president of the Russian republic in June. As the year progressed, and Gorbachev and Yeltsin seemed to reach agreement on a new union structure, Gorbachev was seen as moving back toward the left, a movement which culminated on the day of the coup, when Gorbachev's removal was equated with the end of the reform movement and a return to the Cold War. The collapse of the coup was seen as a personal victory for Boris Yeltsin, at least until late in the year, when, confronted with the same seemingly intractable problems as his predecessors, he fell back on a policy of political centralization and economic "shock therapy." The capitalist press watched helplessly along with Western leaders, unable to offer any clear guidance to Moscow on how to make the transition to a market economy without a period of chaos, even cataclysm.

We appreciate the ability of the press to take us up to the barricades and into the besieged Russian parliament building, and we recognize the difficulty of getting into the minds of plotters and conspirators, even though coup stories throughout the year had as many lives as Rasputin. But with few exceptions, we saw little effort to delve into the institutional and societal concerns of what may euphemistically be labeled the "anti-democratic" forces. While the courage of the resisters was breathtaking, and the vision of the Russian people tearing down the statues of Bolshevik icons was inspiring to freedom-loving people everywhere, the resistance was only one side of the story. The other side, the mass of Soviet citizens who took no position on the coup or else supported it, were remarked on almost tangentially. We hold no brief for the coup plotters, who, in one way or another, are receiving their just desserts. But the growing fears of some Soviet democrats, and the growing hope of others, that another coup is coming and may even be necessary, indicates that the press has yet to uncover the last face of the wooden doll of Soviet politics, and reveal if the doll is wearing a face that smiles or frowns.

The role of the press in covering the Gulf War and the historical events in the Soviet Union, are explored in greater detail in the "Major Stories" section of the *MediaGuide* and indeed throughout much of the book.

There were other major developments on the international scene in 1991. Indian leader Rajiv Gandhi was slain on the eve of his country's elections by a bomb blast. In Yugoslavia, ethnic tensions between Serbs and Croats exploded into the worst fighting on the continent since World War II, raising ominous prospects for other nationalist tensions throughout Europe and the former Soviet Union. Anti-immigrant feelings were on the rise in Western Europe. The Pakistani-based Bank of International Credit and Commerce was shut down by the British

Government, but not before prominent citizens and government agencies in many countries, including the U.S., were implicated in the bank's scandalous operations. International concern was heightened over nuclear weapons programs in Israel, Iraq, and most particularly, North Korea. Japan underwent a difficult year as it tried to sort out its role in the new world order, haunted by financial scandal and memories of World War II.

Yet, 1991 was also a year of conciliation and progress, alleviating conflict at times decades old. In perhaps the most dramatic example, months of dogged diplomacy by the U.S. following the Gulf War finally resulted in a Middle East peace conference in Madrid, where Israelis met face-to-face with such long-standing adversaries as the Syrians and Palestinians. While no major breakthrough was immediately apparent, the world could be heartened that at least one new "fact on the ground" — peace talks — had been introduced into the Mideast equation.

President Bush announced unilateral cuts in the U.S. nuclear arsenal and removed elements of the nuclear triad from alert status. In Southeast Asia, the long-standing question of Cambodia seemed to be nearing resolution, albeit one including the Khmer Rouge, with an agreement to end the fighting and hold U.N.-sponsored elections in that star-crossed land. A U.N.-brokered accord was also achieved in El Salvador between the Cristiani government and FMLN. In Angola, the government and UNITA forces agreed to lay down their arms and participate in elections one year hence. The 30-year-old civil war in Ethiopia finally ended, with Col. Mengistu, the "black Stalin," fleeing into exile. It was a year of monumental upheaval in Africa, with the government falling in Somalia and tottering at year's end in Zaire. In Zambia, strongman ruler Kenneth Kaunda peacefully stepped aside when the people voted him out of office. South Africa continued its turbulent path to majority rule.

Haiti, among the most desperately impoverished countries of the hemisphere, saw the election of Rev. Jean-Bertrand Aristide, his subsequent removal in a coup, and an agonizing slide into even deeper economic depression with virtually no credible reporting on why. An increasingly besieged Fidel Castro held on to power in Cuba. In Mexico, the reforms undertaken by President Carlos Salinas de Gortari continued to work their way into that country's surging political economy, offering hope to developing nations around the planet, and North America moved closer to a free-trade agreement. There was continuing discussion of a trade zone of some sort in southeast Asia. Western Europe's movement toward monetary and political unity stumbled, with attendant controversy and angst.

While the media provided individual accounts on the above developments that were often superb, we found ourselves increasingly frustrated by the apparent unwillingness or inability of the media to incorporate the economic dimension of these stories into their day-to-day coverage. Economics was obviously the key element of the Soviet story, for example, with Moscow baffled about how to shed its socialist skin without an economic implosion. The topic seemed too difficult for the Western press corps, which stayed on familiar terrain, highlighting personalities clashing in two-dimensional power struggles. The same shallow treatment of economic woes prevailed in almost all global coverage. Except for one or two major publications, we find the emphasis on the easier, surface aspects of political, security or cultural developments around the world.

Domestically, economics was the major story as well, the backdrop against which all else took place, a fact noted by some of the media some of the time. The recession that began in 1990 turned out to be far more intractable than the nation's political and business leaders had been led to expect by most professional economists. Confusion reigned in Washington as the Republican White House and Democratic Congress jockeyed to avoid blame even as they adjourned for the holidays without legislating any form of relief. The year ended with another dismal Christmas season. President Bush emerged from Desert Storm with historically high public opinion ratings, but those hoping that the President would translate this popularity into a major pro-growth domestic policy were disappointed, as the chief executive preferred to sit tight, motivated apparently by both natural inclination and the advice of his Treasury Secretary.

For the third consecutive year, the financial press treated the partisan struggle over capital gains taxation as a morality play, with seemingly no interest in Federal Reserve Chairman Alan Greenspan's argument that the high level of the tax was a central factor in the real estate depression that threatened the nation's banking system. The only comprehensive analysis we saw anywhere in the nation's press appeared in the November 13 issue of *Investor's Daily.*

Although there is a political election just a year away, for much of 1991 there was a vacuum in political news, with one prominent Democrat after another announcing that they would not challenge the President, depriving the press of the typical "horse-race" coverage devoted to political reporting. Looking ahead to 1992, many editors and network executives promised to provide better coverage than in 1988, when it was felt that they virtually ignored serious discussion of the issues and instead served mainly as conveyers for the "sound-bites" and "photo-ops" of the candidates. While this was encouraging, the networks also announced that they would be scaling back their travel coverage of candidates during the primary season, and that the trend toward decreasing coverage of the party nomination would continue.

There was much discussion of the perceived sour mood of the electorate in 1991, which seemed to be personified by the frightening show of force made by far-right candidate David Duke in the Louisiana gubernatorial race late in the year. Much of the coverage of Duke's campaign, aimed in large part at the resentments felt by lower middle class whites in an increasingly heterogeneous society, offered facile observation that Duke was simply picking up on themes first raised by Richard Nixon in 1968 and used much more extensively by Ronald Reagan in 1980 and George Bush in 1988. More substantive was the debate following Duke's loss, when journalists pondered if, by heavily covering a campaign such as Duke's, the media was not exposing it to the light but rather acting as oxygen to a fire, keeping it alive and helping it grow.

This debate is critical, because recent societal trends projecting an America increasingly at war with itself seemed to intensify during 1991, due no doubt in large part to the weak performance of the economy and attendant belief that the fight is over shrinking resources. Much of the political and cultural debate this year, echoed in the media, had a hard-edged undercurrent that typically comes to those who feel that their backs are to the wall. With the Cold War over, commentators of both the left and right called for the U.S. to "come home" and concentrate on the country's domestic ills, and while many were sincere in their wish to improve the country for all, others struck a much more isolationist tone.

In Congress, such inclusive pro-growth policies as free trade came under increasing attack. On the nation's campuses, free speech and academic freedom were seen by some as being threatened by the "politically correct" movement, while others defended what they saw as hard-won commitments to affirmative action programs for disadvantaged minorities and expansion of the curriculum to include multicultural academics. The national debate had its humorous moments, such as the uproar over a revisionist look at the development of the American West in a special exhibition at the National Gallery or the controversy surrounding the coming 500th anniversary of Christopher Columbus's arrival in what some would call the New World. At other times, the growing fault lines in American society literally took on life-and-death proportions — riots in Washington following an incident between a Hispanic suspect and an African-American police officer, racial violence in Brooklyn's Crown Heights neighborhood after a young boy was accidently struck and killed by a car driven by a Hasidic Jew, or the savage, almost sadistic clubbing of an African-American man by Los Angeles policemen, videotaped by a bystander for all the nation to witness.

It was in this atmosphere that President Bush nominated District of Columbia Circuit Court Judge Clarence Thomas to succeed Thurgood Marshall on the Supreme Court. The nomination of Thomas, an African-American who rose from a background of poverty and racism in the Deep South, touched off a debate both in the legal community, over his professed belief in "natural law" and the growing conservative tilt of the court, and the African-American community. This community gradually split on the nomination, as some were opposed on ideological grounds, while others believed that, ideology aside, it was important to have somebody with Thomas's background and demonstrated character on the highest court in the land.

The Senate Judiciary Committee seemed to mirror the divisions, yet Thomas's confirmation by the full Senate seemed assured. Then, two days before the final vote was scheduled, it emerged that charges of sexual harassment had been leveled at Thomas during the later stages of committee hearings by Anita Hill, an Oklahoma law professor, who had worked for Thomas at both the Department of Education and the Equal Employment Opportunity Commission.

The reaction of some was to strike out at the media through the parties who had originally leaked the charges, but the subterranean pressures in our society that produced both Justice Thomas and the opposition to him had been building for some time, and one believes that if the Thomas hearing hadn't brought the pressure to critical mass, another similar incident would have occurred sooner or later. The fault, in the end, lies not with the process or the media, but with a society increasingly fragmenting into tribes — ideological, economic, ethnic, regional — drawing battlelines and choosing sides. The situation has deteriorated to the point where sober-minded commentators are even suggesting, only half-facetiously, that the country may see another civil war in our lifetime. While it is not the role of the media to prevent this fragmentation, we hope that the media will begin concentrating more on its underlying causes rather than just the symptoms.

We also recognize the media has serious problems of its own. It has struggled with the recession that hit it harder than any in memory. Advertising revenues were down for the print and broadcast media, and many publications saw declines in circulation as well. The largest African-American owned paper in the country, the *Oakland Tribune,* nearly folded. The *New York Daily News,* once the largest-circulation daily newspaper in America, struggled through a crippling strike, saved only by the intervention of British press baron Robert Maxwell. Maxwell's mysterious death later in the year raised new concerns about the future of the *Daily News.*

Network news departments, trapped between declining revenue and the high costs of covering major international stories, continued a recent trend of laying off news-department personnel, including on-air correspondents, and began reducing bureaus both domestically and overseas. Prime-time coverage of the Gulf War reportedly had to be scaled back when advertisers expressed reluctance at placing their commercials in the context of a war. During the weekend of the Hill-Thomas hearings, several networks elected to broadcast baseball games and pro and college football games instead of the hearings. Increasingly, talk was heard that by the end of the decade only two of the three major commercial networks would even survive, or that while three networks would remain, only one or two would continue to carry news on a regular basis.

Network spokesmen argued that viewer needs in the area of news could be met through other sources — CNN was frequently mentioned. While no one will deny that CNN has established itself as a major source of news, especially during times of crisis, not everyone receives cable, or can afford the monthly fee. The networks, who owe a great deal of their respectability to their news departments, still have a responsibility to the public, in whose name they use the airwaves, to keep the public as fully informed as possible.

In addition to the financial difficulties, the media also seemed to offer more egregious instances of poor professional judgement than in recent memory. In April, when an alleged incident of sexual violence occurred at the Kennedy family compound in Palm Beach, Florida, NBC, following the lead of several tabloids, broadcast the name of the accuser. The next day, *The New York Times* also printed the accuser's name, in a story that used unnamed sources to comment critically on the alleged victim's sexual history. During the year both *The New York Times* and *The Washington Post* disciplined reporters for plagiarism, the *Post* going so far as to remove the reporter from its staff. So-called "advocacy journalism" seemed to be gaining greater respectability. While TV news seems to be moving away from the questionable practice of "re-enacting" events, the search for the sensational continues, with one TV newsmagazine going so far as to broadcast a purported exorcism. We await 1992, to see if these incidents were just characteristic of 1991, a most abnormal year in many aspects, or if they portend a worrisome erosion of the standards of the mainstream media.

In the face of the sobering developments outlined above in both the media and the world, we present the seventh annual edition of the *MediaGuide.* Regular readers of the *MediaGuide* will recognize that the basic structure remains the same, with individual journalists and publications changed here and there, as we continue to seek out the finest in news coverage. To new readers, we hope that you find the *MediaGuide* to be an important resource, for both information and enjoyment. Our purpose is to elevate and encourage, not denigrate and attack. When criticism is offered, it is not that of the fanatic of the left or the right searching out "hidden agendas" while seeking to impose agendas of their own, but that of the professional observer, disinterested in that we carry no partisan brief, passionate in that we have a stake in the peace and prosperity of the world, and we recognize the unique role the media can play in bringing about that peace and prosperity.

The global electorate is becoming increasingly empowered. With power comes responsibility, and responsibility, to be exercised intelligently, requires coherent thought that can only come about with an informed view of the world. It is the media that informs and provides that coherence. No other institution can do it. Governments have too large a stake to provide the necessary objectivity, and individuals lack the resources. That is why, even when we despair at the license that takes place in the name of "freedom of the press," we never call into question that freedom itself. Thomas Jefferson once said he would choose newspapers without a government over a government without newspapers. We believe you could not have one without the other, and with that in mind, we now turn our attention to the momentous events of the past twelve months.

AN OVERVIEW OF THE PRINT MEDIA

MAJOR STORIES OF 1991

The Gulf War and the Media

In an assessing the performance of the media in the Persian Gulf War, one can't help but paraphrase Charles Dickens: "It was the best of reporting. It was the worst of reporting."

According to the assistant secretary of defense for public affairs, Pete Williams, writing in a *Washington Post* op-ed 3-17, "the press gave the American people the best war coverage they ever had." Indeed, a Times Mirror poll released around the same time reveals that eight in ten Americans rate the news coverage of the war as "good" (although some polls, less professionally conducted, provided more negative responses). However, "reporters and editors don't believe that. They know they've been had," replies Michael Getler, the assistant managing editor for foreign news at *The Washington Post.* In a *WP* op-ed, "Do Americans Really Want to Censor War Coverage This Way?" 3-17, Getler presents a forceful case for the charge that "the military did a better job controlling the press than the press did carrying out its crucial, cranky function in a democracy." Jonathan Alter, *Newsweek* media reporter, writes in "Clippings from the Media War," 3-11, "News organizations were routed by the military in the battle over access and assaulted by many viewers. . .From beginning to end, this was one of the last places to find a good story. . .Except for some archival footage shot by the military, historians will have no record of most of the actual fighting in this war."

These harsh judgments were not shared by all in the profession (Walter Cronkite, for example, offered critical support for the Defense Department's restrictive ground rules for covering the conflict), but there is more than just a grain of truth in them, and they cannot be dismissed.

On the one hand there is the assertion that no other war was as thoroughly covered by the media as this one, and it is described as "the first televised, real-time war." But closer to reality is the fact that the collection of DoD restrictions on reporters prevented them from really getting close enough to the war to properly cover it. "The Pentagon and US Army Central Command," Getler maintains, "conducted what is probably the most thorough and sophisticated wartime control of American reporters in modern times — they determined what the reporters could see, to whom they could talk, where they could go, what they could tell the public, and when they could tell it. . .Because it all happened so fast and the war ended so happily for the US, the implications of the Pentagon victory over the press may not seem apparent or important. . .But if allowed to stand as a model, the Desert Storm system runs the risk of seriously distorting reality for some uncertain time if the next war is a lot tougher."

This, though, may be a battle that — initially — the media has to fight alone. In fact, along with Saddam Hussein, the media was often referred to as the big loser in the Gulf War. In a poll conducted by Times Mirror shortly after the war began, and while some U.S. journalists were still reporting from Baghdad, Iraq, nearly 80% of Americans supported Pentagon restrictions on journalists covering the war. A majority favored even more restrictions being imposed, and 62% had no objections to bombing the Baghdad hotel where the journalists were staying. ABC's "Good Morning America" asked viewers to phone in their responses to the question "Is the news media doing a responsible and fair job of covering the Gulf War?" 83% of the 62,180 respondents said, "NO!" While the military was enjoying 80% rates of confidence in polls, the same polls revealed about one in five expressing any confidence in the media. The "Saturday Night Live" parody of the press, in which amateurish journalists demanded to know the secret passwords of U.S. soldiers on the front, offers a cutting sense of how low esteem for the profession had become among the populace.

From the very beginning, the chroniclers became a part of the story. This was certainly the case with CNN, especially when correspondent Peter Arnett stayed behind in Baghdad after the 1-15 deadline. As Arnett puts it in a *Washington Post* op-ed, "The Story From Baghdad," 3-17, "I'd go anywhere for a story if there was enough viewer interest and CNN wanted coverage. I'd go to Hell itself for a story if someone important down there wanted to be interviewed. . .Criticism I accept — and expect. It's the labelling that angers me. . .For being in Baghdad when I was, I was. . .labeled a sympathizer." Arnett was referring to the characterization of him made by Sen. Alan Simpson (R-Wyo.). Others, including members of the profession itself, were inclined to advance the same characterization. Generally, though, the profession came to the defense of Mr. Arnett and CNN's decision to keep him in Baghdad filing reports. Sen. Simpson's remarks, for which he later apologized, provoked rancor from the profession, and *WP* correspondent Howard Kurtz writing in "Sen. Simpson Calls Arnett 'Sympathizer,' " 2-8, reminded readers that, one month after a freelance Iranian journalist working for the *London Observer* was hanged in Iraq on phony spying charges, the Senator advised Saddam Hussein that "your problems lie with the Western media and not with the U.S. government. As long as you are isolated from the media, the press — and it is a haughty and pampered press — they all consider themselves political geniuses. That is, journalists do. They are very cynical."

Arnett's safety in Baghdad was always in question, as was, unfairly, his credibility. Reportedly, calls critical of CNN poured into the Defense Department. Peter Arnett was called the "Jane Fonda of Baghdad," and a campaign to persuade CNN into recalling Arnett was initiated by Accuracy In Media, Reed Irvine's ideological media watchdog outfit. But Arnett established early on a procedure to protect his credibility; following delivery of each prepared script, Arnett would engage in a question-and-answer exchange with the CNN anchor, with the Iraqis having no control over the exchange. Arnett abided by their limits on withholding any report that might give details on matters of military security, and "Cleared by Iraqi Censors" appeared on the screen with each of his reports. He also identified the source of his information. Similarly, print accounts also carried notices that their reports were going through Iraqi censorship, and they also utilized information that came from Baghdad radio, the Iraqi government or the country's news service. But sentiment against Arnett's presence in Baghdad ran very high, according to the calls received at DoD denouncing him as a traitor, which underscored a deep and widespread resentment of the media — even though the press later received 80% approval ratings for its "good" coverage of the Gulf War.

Despite the restrictions put on coverage, restrictions which, in part, hampered and weakened effective coverage of the war, the media did turn in a "good" — albeit, very uneven — performance. The first night's reporting, wholly the domain of the electronic media, with Baghdad-based correspondents announcing the commencement of allied bombing of the city, was indeed intensely dramatic. With only CNN's transmittal capacity not closed by the Iraqis, the network's correspondents Peter Arnett, John Holliman and Bernard Shaw continued to

report live from the capital. However, Wednesday night, January 16, with viewers worldwide glued to the television screen, witnessing firsthand an account of the opening stage of the war with Iraq, the hard-news bottom line amounted to little more than announcement of an allied air strike on Iraq, with minimal Iraqi response. It was, in fact, what has been described as "only the illusion of news" rather than the feast of televised news it initially seemed to be. Reporting on the war, from Iraq, settled down into Messrs. Arnett, Holliman and Shaw describing only what they could see from the windows of the Al-Rashid Hotel in the early chaotic hours. Elsewhere, other correspondents interviewed each other and reported over and over, *ad nauseam,* on what they didn't know and were unable to verify, that monotonous routine occasionally broken by views of them scrambling for gas masks as air raid sirens blared outside their quarters. CBS anchor Dan Rather neatly summed up the media's frustration: "There's much more that we don't know than we do know."

On the whole, all the networks lacked pictures of the war, until on Friday, January 18, the Pentagon provided video tapes of precision bombing. Yet, visuals of the war were limited, and for the networks, the war became a talk-show war. Opting to preempt all regularly scheduled viewing for ongoing coverage of the war, the networks had plenty of air time to fill, but not that much with which to fill it. Having established that there is so much that it didn't know, the media proceeded to speculate on what it didn't know. Consequently, the networks turned to various analysts, retired armed forces officer-consultants, strategists, academics, and other journalists. Sometimes, their analyses were fascinating, and, using some hard data and detail provided by the Pentagon, they had an authoritative ring, but in fact, this "reporting" was simply speculation. Verifiable information was sparse, but there was a plethora of questionable information that was nonetheless disseminated to viewers who were famished for fresh news and information. But no one, including the Defense Department and the White House, had any knowledge of just how effective or ineffective the bombing of Iraq might be. No one could answer why the Iraqi air force hadn't engaged the allied planes, nor was there any solid verification of the extent of damage or destruction to the Iraqi air force and other military targets. The media certainly cannot be faulted for that news gap, but it can be faulted for letting drama overcome accuracy, chucking critical judgment, and disseminating misinformation.

Iraq launched SCUD missile attacks on Israel on Day Two of the war, 1-17, and the broadcast networks faced another trial of crisis reporting. Anchors, producers, and editors fell short of their responsibilities. So much of the "news" that came across the screens was simply unfiltered, hair-trigger, instantaneous "reporting." We viewers had to become editors ourselves, distilling and editing information. Worse, the "news" that came across the screens was not so much unedited as it was clearly unverified. Rumor-retailing paraded as news. Dan Rather of CBS News, speaking with correspondent Bill Plante, was the first out of the gate with the most dramatic reporting: "Now the evidence, Bill, is that the Israelis are, as we speak, in the process of retaliating against the Iraqis for the six, at least six, SCUDs that hit Israel." ABC contributed with a report to Peter Jennings from correspondent Dean Reynolds that he was "getting word from, again, a very reliable source that there may have been as many as 20 nerve gas victims taken to a Tel Aviv area hospital this morning. This is the first word, the first hard word, of perhaps unconventional weapons used in this assault this evening." A senior correspondent from the New York news station of CBS, on assignment in Israel, came on live over the phone to Dan Rather to report that official Israeli announcements of a retaliatory air strike against Iraq were being heard on Israeli radio. In fact, he added, sticking his head out the window, Israeli planes can be seen darting toward Iraq right now. CNN's Pentagon correspondent, Wolf Blitzer, also was reporting unverified assertion, claiming that Saddam Hussein's elite corps, the Republican Guard, had been "decimated" by the allied air strikes.

By Saturday, January 19, though, when the second round of SCUDs hit Israel, broadcast correspondents and anchors recovered some professional composure, some even acknowledging the confusion to which they had contributed, and there was evidence that editors were reasserting their traditional roles. Still, erroneous information went out as news — SCUD hits in Jerusalem, although none took place there, or an exaggerated number of hits in Tel Aviv — but the dramatic language was toned down; there was more restraint, less of a rush to present inferences as facts, and a sense of caution was finally emerging. But limited in what they could cover, the media would occasionally succumb to the temptation to over-dramatize. The sound of an air raid siren going off in Saudi Arabia or of an explosion nearby at times was rendered as heralding Armageddon.

At this stage, TV can only lay minimal blame to the difficulties in gaining access to the facts for the electronic media's role in yielding so much confusion and misinformation. More germane to the problem is the very nature of TV itself — its intrinsic capacity for instantaneous reporting. Fact was insufficiently sifted from the material reported, with rumor, error and misinformation being passed on indiscriminately. One might have heard on one network, information being reported that totally contradicted information from another network, or even that contradicted information heard just shortly before on the very same network. At one point, when Iraq poured oil into the Gulf, appalling pictures of cormorants caked with oil, limping ashore, made every network's news reports. (Strangely, these scenes of ecological terrorism provoked more horror than had pictures of gassed Kurdish victims of Saddam Hussein.) But the giant oil slick hadn't reached the Saudi coast when the TV crews were filming the damage. The *Financial Times* would reveale in "Oil Change," 1-28, that the reporters were actually filming the consequences of a much smaller oil slick caused by a refinery fire in the neutral zone between Kuwait and Saudi Arabia during the opening days of the war. *New York Times* reporter Robert E. Tomasson reminded us 1-22 of how the instantaneous nature of TV war reporting can lead to "awkward" situations, as when an Associated Press reporter notified the Zaun family, before the Navy, that their son Jeffrey was a prisoner of the Iraqis. There were, of course, enough of those unforgettable images of war — grieving families of fathers or sons killed in war — some of which were merciless intrusions upon private moments. On NBC's "Sunday Today," for instance, we witnessed a deeply anguished wife, bursting into tears, unable to speak because of her intense sorrow over the death in war of her husband. "Her grief," the reporter stated, "was almost unwatchable," but NBC proceeded to present it for us anyway. All the networks indulged this kind of exploitative "boo-hoo" journalism and non-news touchy-feely topics. CNN had a roving correspondent reporting from Middle America on the "mood" of the nation at war, asking men and women on the street their thoughts, moods, and feelings about what was happening.

By 2-16, we were seeing reported by TV news the imminent end of the Gulf War: "I'm Bryant Gumbel here with Deborah Norville, and on this Friday we greet you with some stunning news, some very hopeful news. Baghdad radio is reporting this morning that Iraq is prepared to withdraw from Kuwait." So began NBC's "Today" show, omitting the Iraqi statement of the long list of conditions attached to the Revolutionary Command Council's. Harry Smith, co-anchor of "CBS This Morning," declared "This war, for a lot of intents and purposes is over. The Iraqis have had the royal snot beaten out of them." Everybody was in the same boat on this one — the administration, the DoD, the families of U.S. soldiers abroad, the average viewer, all were seeing and hearing news develop at the same time — again, unedited and unverified. An egregious example of the medium's eschewal of professional standards is painfully obvious in the report from Baghdad by ABC's Bill Blakemore, in which he reported that "the people here and in other cities have been suffering under siege for a long time. *We've even heard of* [italics added] hospitals being hit in some cases."

David Halberstam offers a thoughtful observation on the TV war in a *NYT* op-ed, "Where's Page 2 in TV News?" 2-21:

> [I]mmediacy does not necessarily mean better, more thoughtful reporting; it is arguable that the lack of satellites and the comparative slowness of the transmission process in the old days permitted the news desks in New York to act less as prisoners of technology than they do today. For if the technology has improved, the editing function, the cumulative sense of judgement — the capacity of network news executives to decide what to use and how to use it, and how to blend the visual and

non-visual — has declined in precise ratio to the improvement in technology. . .We have become terribly dependent upon an instrument of mass communications that feels that the cardinal sin is not so much to be inaccurate as to bore.

On balance, what TV's Gulf reporting revealed is that verification and critical evaluation must take place between the time news is gathered and separated, and when it is actually reported, had shrunk dangerously close to extinction.

Everywhere, the Persian Gulf War was being labeled a TV war, with its advantages in providing dramatic, breaking stories, immediacy, and emotional intensity. But the morning after the initial outbreak of war with Iraq, we were ravenously turning to print, hungry for clarity, perspective, context, the processed and distilled account. We wanted to get our hands around the big picture that the dailies could provide. "Television has been the medium that delivers the news first," *USA Today* editor Peter Prichard tells Debra Gersh of *Editor & Publisher,* "Where's the Beef?" 1-26. "If you want perspective, if you want a complete report, you turn to the newspaper. You can get confused watching television. . .Newspapers are able to show people the next day what happened."

The press differed from the broadcast media in content as well as style, as it is naturally more disposed toward offering greater depth and detail. TV gives us indelible images of the war; the print media gives us a sense of the meaning and context of what is going on there. Newspapers give us processed news, the ability for consumers to look at material, to discriminate, sort, compare and correlate the information, whereas TV is here now and then gone. A cynical comparison likened it to the Monday-morning sports fans who pour over the sports sections, even though they watched the game on TV last night. And, to an extent, the papers were reporting initially "yesterday's news." But the comparison easily breaks down. Watching the war unfold on prime-time TV may be likened to watching the game on TV, only if one likens it to actually hearing the game reported on the basis of what the correspondents can see and hear from their windows. The TV story was still disconnected, bits and pieces of unfiltered news, unpackaged, almost incoherent. Viewers wanted analysis, context, a synthesis that was connected, coherent and that made sense.

On January 18 alone, the *NYT,* for example, published 50 Gulf-related stories and columns. The *Los Angeles Times* Sunday edition, 1-20, weighing in at four pounds, carried 20 war stories in its A section. *The Washington Post* published two extra editions, 1-17, with an increased run of 180,000 papers. *USA Today* increased its press run the same day by 500,000 and published for the first time a Sunday edition, as did *The Washington Times,* which also produced a Saturday run for only the second time in its history, before the paper went to regular weekend editions in the fall. Every paper devoted expanded coverage to the war, reassigning staffers, adding special sections, increasing use of graphics, and it seemed as if there were a veritable information glut. But there really was little hard news, especially detailed information from the front, a condition acknowledged within the press itself. As *E&P's* Debra Gersh reported, 1-26, " 'We're not terribly thrilled with the amount of information coming through,' noted *NYT* foreign editor Bernard Gwertzman, explaining that with preliminary attacks from the air — which by its very nature precludes reporters — the media were not getting very detailed information about what was being hit."

Much of this was the consequence of the new ground rules imposed by the DoD on the media covering Operation Desert Shield, which carried over into Operation Desert Storm. Some of the security guidelines dealt with restrictions on transmission of sensitive military information, and differed little from guidelines accepted by the media from WWII through Vietnam. However, the new addition to the rules required that a reporter qualify for the "pool" system in order to gain access to the frontlines. The "pool" system was limited to a small number of reporters, who were supposed to represent the entire press corps. (There were some 1600 journalists in Saudi Arabia, but the pools permitted no more than 10% of that 1600 to participate at a time.) The pools could go only where the military would take them. All reports from the pool had to be reviewed by an on-site public affairs officer before transmission. A suit was filed by nine publications and four journalists (among them *Harper's, In These Times, Mother Jones, The Nation,* and *The Progressive*) with U.S. District Court in Manhattan against the DoD and others, seeking an injunction against the new policies.

As *NYT* reporter Malcolm W. Browne described it, "Conflicting Censorship Upsets Many Journalists," 1-21: "For the first time since WWII, correspondents must submit to near-total military supervision of their work. . .The Pentagon is clearly eager to be the first to report the most newsworthy information." Browne also includes in the report insight into the military's attitude toward the press, quoting a senior Air Force officer who opened his briefing at Dhahran, Saudi Arabia by telling the assembled reporters: "Let me say up front that I don't like the press. Your presence here can't possibly do me any good, and it can hurt me and my people. That's just so you'll know where we stand with each other." The consequence is succinctly revealed in a dispatch by *WP* military reporter R. Jeffrey Smith, 1-22: "The U.S. military's accounts of the war at the Pentagon and the media center at Riyadh have settled into a routine that provides few facts and more jousting between officials and reporters."

Three weeks later, *WP* reporter Joel Achenbach touched on the limitations the DoD restrictions were imposing on coverage of the war in "Battles Without Bodies," 2-5: "[T]he American news media have not yet produced a single photograph or video image of a dead American soldier. . .even the Iraqi dead are scarcely seen." And a month into the conflict, *NYT* editor Howell Raines was charging a Pentagon, motivated by political concerns, with preventing the press from adequately covering the war. As *NYT* reporter Richard Berke quotes him in a 2-25 report: "The Administration wants to use the legitimate theme of security, in some cases to install a kind of blanket news management that we've never had in this century." A similar condition was in operation for the British press. "The spokesman for the British Defense Ministry claimed," we read in a report from the German weekly *Die Zeit,* " 'We don't have any censorship here.' What the British did do in the Gulf was issue 'orientation assistance' for editors and 'rules of behavior' for reporters." *Die Zeit* expressed a commonly heard judgment made by much of the European media that "all information is coming from the military," which has "made the press a party to the war." And in fact, some British journalists, Robert Fisk of the London *Independent,* for example, did have their dispatches altered by the Ministry of Defense. British military stopped one correspondent from filming a group of British fusiliers accidentally bombed by U.S. planes.

The Pentagon called it "security review," while much of the media called it "censorship." The epitome of this was when *Detroit Free Press* reporter Frank Bruni's characterization of pilots returning from early missions as "giddy" was initially changed by military censors to "proud." Many times, security review resulted in long delays on the transmittal of reporters' dispatches back to the U.S. *NYT* reporter Philip Shenon, with U.S. Armored forces, told AP his military hosts took 72 hours to transmit his dispatches, but one instance of similar stories from the press corps.

Chris Hedges of the *NYT* opted to work outside the system, and wound up having his credentials temporarily lifted for breaking the rules. He reports in *Columbia Journalism Review,* 6/7-91: "Our success [in operating outside the pool system for two months] was due in part to an understanding by many soldiers and officers of what the role of a free press is in a democracy. These men and women violated orders to allow us to do our job." Many of the singular stories of the war came from correspondents who went outside the system. The added nuances of detail in the dispatches on Egyptian troops at the front, by *Wall Street Journal* correspondent Tony Horwitz, which so distinguished his reporting, is but one example. But for so many, being a correspondent at the front meant, as *LAT* reporter Kim Murphy describes it, "sitting in front of a television in Saudi Arabia and taking notes from a briefing." Murphy graphically captures the frustrations of it all in "The Big Story That Got Away," 2-27.

There were very few pictures transmitted during the fighting of wounded or dead U.S. servicemen, and very few of the thousands of dead Iraqi soldiers. The initial accounts of friendly fire deaths were vague and cloudy. Increasingly, an uneasy feeling spread among the press corps in the Gulf and their editors back home that the Pentagon wanted only a sanitized version of the war reported, with correspondents prevented from penetrating the fog hanging over details of the war effort. "Official" reports claimed an 80% accuracy rate for allied bombs dropped on Iraq, with the Pentagon releasing, selectively, videos of successful "smart" bomb hits. But no correspondents could tell us anything about bombs that missed their targets, if all targets were strictly military, if civilian sites were being hit accidentally or otherwise. Nor could they verify the claim of 80% target effectiveness. Efforts to do this were undertaken, notable among them the 1-28 *WP* report by Bob Woodward, in which he reported that the government was reporting only the successes of the allied bombing runs and not disclosing that "important parts of Saddam Hussein's war machine have not yet been significantly hurt." But these were the exceptions.

Large numbers of Iraqi troops surrendered to the allies, but no one did much with the story of what life in the Iraqi trenches was like during the war. Access to the POW camps was denied or restricted. "We're getting only the information the Pentagon wants us to get," stated *Time*'s Washington bureau chief Stanley Cloud. In fact, "each pool member is an unpaid employee of the Department of Defense, on whose behalf he or she prepares the news of the war for the outer world," Malcolm W. Browne wrote in the *NYT Magazine.*

The entire incident at Khafji was a case study of how DoD restrictions guarantee the dissemination of misinformation. Iraqi troops, perhaps in response to increasing harassment by U.S. marine howitzers bombarding their positions nightly, went over the offensive at the Saudi town of Khafji, just south of the Kuwaiti border, 1-29. The reporters who learned of the event and who wanted to move to where the story was taking place were prevented from doing so, with only those journalists assigned to the pool allowed to venture near the area. Initial reports were a muddle, and in fact, even the military brass had its facts wrong. U.S. Army Brigadier General Pat Stevens IV gave an account of the assault at Khafji in which he declared that no Marine ground units were engaged in battle there — this at the very time that video broadcasts of the battle clearly showed U.S. marines engaged in combat. The pool reporters, reporting information given them by their military escorts, were reporting the recapture of Khafji from the Iraqis. But a reporter for the British paper, *The Independent,* operating outside of and in violation of the pool system, headed up to Khafji and reported the real story — the Iraqis were still fighting inside the town. It was at the same time that eleven U.S. marines were killed in an engagement west of Khafji. Initially, no one could confirm the circumstances of their deaths — from Iraqi mortar, in engagements with Iraqi tanks, Iraqi weapons fire, accidental fire by allied forces, a U.S. missile? R. W. Apple, Jr.'s, 2-1 *NYT* dispatch from Dhahran reported Pentagon chief of operations Lieut. Gen. Thomas Kelley stating that "All the marines killed were riding in light armored vehicles that were hit by enemy gunfire." Later, it was established that they'd been killed by friendly fire. In what another journalist describes as "Death by briefing," the press corps was forced into a passive position. So much of the description of the war came primarily from military briefers in the Pentagon and Saudi Arabia that the press lost out to the Pentagon in control over the flow of news.

Coverage of the coalition offensive into Kuwait was severely restricted. The Pentagon intended to maintain its control over the first look at the effort, and DoD Secretary Cheney immediately announced a news blackout — until it became clear how well the allied offensive was doing. Again, some of the best coverage came from those journalists who broke the rules and opted out of the pool system. Michael Kelly's gripping account of the "Highway of Death" *The New Republic* 3-18, and mass surrenders by despondent Iraqi soldiers is a prime example. Bill McKeown of CBS and his crew cut loose from the Saudi unit to which it had been hitched and sped on unescorted into Kuwait City on the heels of routed Iraqi troops and provided graphic coverage of liberated Kuwait. CBS acquitted itself well here, going out on its own and sending back footage of liberated Kuwaitis rejoicing euphorically and of pitiable and desperate Iraqi soldiers surrendering to U.S. forces.

One aspect of the war did involve a deliberate manipulation of the press by the military in efforts to mislead the enemy. As one reporter put it to Gen. Norman Schwarzkopf in a post-assault briefing, reported by *LAT* writer Thomas B. Rosenstiel in "Pentagon Shows Itself Adept at Art of Deception," 3-12: "The chart [of the allied assault] you showed there, was almost the exact reverse of what most of us [in the media] thought was happening." The Pentagon's effort was to keep the press away from the action. Yet there are many occasions when the press discovered information that it voluntarily withheld because its broadcast or publication could hurt allied war efforts or lead to allied casualties. For example, despite the Pentagon's efforts at misinforming on the battle plan, correspondents at CBS, NBC, *The Washington Post* and some other media figured it out, but most of them chose not to report it. Often, though, the military briefings were conducted in such a way as to allow reporters to draw inferences that were helpful to the coalition's intentions of conveying false information to the enemy. But one consequence was that often much of what was reported in the early stages of Operation Desert Shield was misinformation. The likelihood of Iraqi use of chemical weapons, the size and location of allied troop concentrations, the descriptions of formidable Iraqi ground defenses, were among the items of misinformation the media were fed. Numerous graphics in various publications depicted mammoth defensive barriers supposedly erected by the Iraqis that would slow allied assaults and result in high casualty levels. The information on these fortifications came from the military briefings and the press ran with it. But during Operation Desert Storm, Ed Cody, a veteran *Washington Post* foreign correspondent, recalls in a *Financial Times* story by Jimmy Burns, 3-16/17, that he only "saw one trench on the entire trek from the Saudi border to Kuwait City. . .it was one foot deep and it looked like a urination ditch for truck drivers."

It was actually after the liberation of Kuwait and the rout of the Iraqi army that we saw in the print media some of the best and most valuable reporting on the Persian Gulf War. As *WP* political columnist David Broder puts it in "The War Story," 3-20: "War is much more complex than a prizefight and cannot be adequately described or analyzed as it is happening. The best reporters are going back now, when sources can no longer plausibly claim the protection of 'military security' and giving us the reality no one could report at the time." The *WP* provided a gripping account of the bombing of the Iraqi retreat from Kuwait, cutting through the spin control the military put on it, "Spin Control on the 'Highway of Death,' " by Steve Coll and William Branigin with Molly Moore, *WP Weekly* 3-18/24. The *FT,* in collaboration with ABC News/"Nightline," pursued an investigation as to whether an indulgent attitude by the Bush administration toward Iraq facilitated Baghdad's efforts to fund unhindered its illegal arms network, "A Fatal Attraction," by Lionel Barber and Alan Friedman, 5-3. Barton Gellman's report "U.S. Bombs Missed 70% of Time," *WP* 3-16, chagrined the rest of the press corps (and many citizens) who could recall the military's assertion, during the war, of an 80% on-target bombing rate. In fact, the precision-guided bombs that made up so much of the visuals released in Pentagon briefings made up only 7% of U.S. tonnage dropped on Iraqi targets. Gellman produced another blockbuster with "Allied Air War Struck Broadly in Iraq; Officials Acknowledge Strategy Went Beyond Purely Military Targets," 6-23. Here we learn, for the first time, details of Iraq's ruined infrastructure and the devastating straits of ordinary Iraqis as a consequence of the Pentagon's goal of achieving military objectives "by disabling Iraqi society at large." But an examination of the components of this and similar stories reveals that all the factual elements needed to report it earlier were there. The press, though, and not without important resistance, settled for watching and talking to itself as a substitute for reporting on the war. Nationally syndicated military columnist Fred Reed hits upon the psychology of this in an intensely bitter *Washington Times* op-ed, "Capitulation to the Talking Heads," 3-6. Throwing in the towel and giving up on his efforts to cover the war ("I've come halfway around the world to watch CNN?") because to bend to the DoD restrictions seemed an "acquiescence in fraud," Reed uncovers the process by which media succumbed to pressure and retreated from its responsibilities:

...the public had almost no idea what was being done in its name. We were letting the military and the administration tell us how the air campaign was going, what the bombs were hitting and whether the war was working. We saw nothing the military didn't want us to see. . .The process fed upon itself: Because the war seemed to be going well, the public was behind it. Because the public was behind the war, the media hesitated to publish bad news. . .The vital question is whether the nation has a right to know (or, perhaps more important, cares) what its military was doing, a right to hear from those — their children — who were sent to fight. Yet people seem to be. . .impatient with what they see as whining by a spoiled and self-seeking press corps that wasn't getting just what it wanted.

Reed readily acknowledges that the profession is indeed filled with "demanding, wantonly ignorant and excessively [self-] impressed" souls. "The media," he admits, "are indeed backbiters, easily manipulated, readily turned against one another and often foolish." But he strikes a resonantly true chord when he reminds us that "they're all we've got. If we allow a government to be the sole source of information on itself, we're asking for trouble."

The Russian Revolution of 1991

When it comes to Russian regimes, Maxim Natanovitch has seen them come and he has seen them go. Born during the last days of the Romanov dynasty, now in the 100th year of his life, Natanovitch watched the communist system he fought for in 1918 as a Red Guard finally crumble and be swept away by "democratic" forces. Speaking to *Financial Times* correspondent Gillian Tett, in "The Man Who Lived Through it All," 12-27-91, the veteran of the First World War reflected on life in Russia, then and now. "Back in 1917 they said we would have a shining future. Now they say it was all a lie! But how could we have dreamt then that what we started would end like this?"

The story of the Soviet Union in 1991 is basic. In 1991, the Soviet Union ceased to exist. Besides expiring as a territorial entity, one of the largest on the globe, the governing institutions of the Soviet Union also ceased to exist, taking along with them an ideology that at one point ruled over half the world. In 1991, events which, less than a decade ago, would have been dismissed as right-wing fantasy or geopolitical science fiction became a reality, being played out every day in our newspapers and every night on our TV screens.

What happened in the Soviet Union in 1991 was history. We do not, of course, look to the daily press for history, as history, after all, is what happened fifty years ago, not what occurred last night. At times, events seized our attention — the crackdown in Vilnius, the coup attempt in August — at other times events seemed distant, and we left them to the experts to debate the details. We may have won the Cold War in 1991, but we were often preoccupied, with a war in the Middle East or with economic distress and political scandal here at home. Consequently, we were shocked by the events of late August. We were undecided, late in the year, if the break-up of the Soviet Union was a positive development, or a negative one. Did the press fail in its role or did we fail in ours?

Asked once what he thought about the French revolution, Zhou en-Lai replied that it is too soon to tell. It is too soon to tell about the events this year in the former Soviet Union, whether they will mean democracy and stability for that region, or authoritarianism and chaos. "A revolution," the Ayatollah Khomeini once said, "is not about the price of watermelons." It will be up to history to decide if this year's events in the former Soviet Union constituted a genuine revolution. But looking over the news coverage of 1991, one comes away with the impression that in 1991, at least, the story of the Soviet Union, in the end, *was* about the price of watermelons.

The year began with the press expecting the worst, following the dramatic resignation, late in 1990, of Foreign Minister Eduard Shevardnadze, who warned darkly of resurgent hardline forces. Much attention was focused on the Baltic states who were increasingly cutting off ties to the Soviet regime, both political and economic, as *FT* correspondent Leyla Boulton documented in "Estonians Snip Away at the Soviet Economic Net," 12-18-90. One way of cutting the political tie was by resisting the Soviet draft, and early in 1991, Soviet President Mikhail Gorbachev began dispatching Soviet paratroopers to the rebellious republics to round up draft resisters. In "Another Ominous Alarm in Moscow," 1-8, *The New York Times* warned that "Mr. Gorbachev, by allying himself with the forces of order, puts himself and his reforms at their mercy. That raises grave questions about future Soviet relations with the rest of the world."

As the U.S. was preparing for imminent war with Iraq, Soviet forces moved into the Lithuanian capital of Vilnius, 1-13, staging an assault on the republic TV station and tower, and the world saw graphic news footage of civilian demonstrators being cut in half by tanks. Then-*NYT* Moscow bureau chief Bill Keller, in "Soviet Loyalists in Charge After Attack in Lithuania; 13 Killed; Crowds Defiant," 1-14, reported that "The violent action and the ensuing takeover appeared to have the full support of President Gorbachev, who had warned of reprisals if Lithuania failed to back down from its independence claims and who has not commented publicly on the army's attack."

Editorial reaction in the Western press was swift and sharp, with most of the anger directed personally at Gorbachev. The *NYT* contended in "The New Old Face of Tyranny," 1-14, that "When Soviet tanks crush Lithuanian students demonstrating for freedom, the father of glasnost turns his celebrated season of reform into Vilnius Winter," and that "When he uses tanks to crush singing students, and freedom, he instead ignites America's anger and disgust." The *Financial Times,* in "Consequences of Vilnius," 1-14, said that the question now was "what sort of relationships can be maintained with the government and person of President Gorbachev." *The Economist* seemed to know, stating in "Blood on His Hands," 1-19, that "No help, except perhaps some food aid, should go to a government following Mr Gorbachev's present course. The money should be released only to men willing to resume the march to democracy, a free market, the right to independence." *TE's* sentiments were echoed by *The New Republic* in "Gorbachev's Tanks," 2-4.

There was a concentrated effort by some reporters on the ground, though, to draw a distinction between Gorbachev and the "hardliners" with whom he had apparently surrounded himself, in such dispatches as "Gorbachev's Role Called Into Question," 1-14, by then-*FT* Moscow bureau chief Quentin Peel, and "Who Ordered the Assault?" 1-14, by *Los Angeles Times* Moscow bureau chief Michael Parks. The case that the crackdown in the Baltics signaled the end of the lein for *glasnost* and *perestroika* was made by *NYT* columnist William Safire in "Gorby's Black Berets," 1-14, then-*Wall Street Journal* bureau chief Peter Gumbel in "Changing Course," 1-14, and "Resurgent Communists Push for Soviet Crackdown," 2-4; and Peel in "Hardliners Around Gorbachev Fail to Impose Party Line on Baltics," 1-16. "When the Singing Had to Stop," 1-17, was Peel again writing that "[Gorbachev's] problem is that he has been forced to act with the wrong allies. He has thrown in his lot with the military which is one of the last redoubts of blind ideological faith," a point that seemed far less certain in August, when the military shifted support to Boris Yeltsin.

All the talk of resurgent hardliners sent us searching for more information on precisely who they were and what motivated them. We found some answers. Quentin Peel, in "Soviet Union Through the Looking Glass," *FT* 2-18, profiled new Soviet Prime Minister Valentin Pavlov, whose "first actions suggest that he is. . .quite ready to act like a bull in a china shop," but noted that he was pledging price reform and modernization of heavy industry. " 'Don't underestimate Mr Pavlov,' said Mr Boris Fyodorov, his former counterpart as Russian finance minister." Kurt M. Campbell, in "Iron Gnome," *TNR* 3-4, profiled Colonel General Boris Gromov, former commander of Soviet forces in Afghanistan, now number two at the MVD, and observed that "when Soviet intellectuals speak of their fears of a slide toward 'Bonapartism' or even of a military coup, the face they most often conjure up is Gromov's." In the 10 Best selection "The Hard-Liners' Bad Boy Challenges Gorbachev," 2-8, *Washington Post* correspondent David Remnick provides a revealing glimpse at Lt. Col. Viktor Alksnis, leader of the Soyuz faction in the Soviet parliament and one of two colonels singled out by Shevardnadze in his resignation speech. Alksnis expounded further on the necessity of holding the Soviet center together in "Suffering From Self-Determination," *Foreign Policy* Fall 1991.

As the shock waves from the assault on Vilnius subsided, the Western press portrayed Russian politician Boris Yeltsin as Gorbachev's next "challenge," in the words of then-*U.S. News & World Report* Moscow bureau chief Jeff Trimble in "New Yeltsin Challenge," *USNWR* 12-31-90/1-7-91. Indeed, in late February Yeltsin went on national Soviet TV and called upon Gorbachev to resign, *LAT* Moscow correspondent John-Thor Dahlberg capturing the drama of the moment in "Gorbachev Must Go, Yeltsin Says," 2-20. Dahlberg characterized a national vote on unity, 3-7, as a referendum between Gorbachev, who wanted to keep the Union intact, and Yeltsin, who was sympathetic to dissolution-minded republics, in "Soviets Vote in Unity Showdown," 3-18. Gorbachev's desire to hold onto the Union was seen as evidence that he was now an obstacle to reform by many, including *TE* in "Going Yeltsin's Way," 3-23, and *TNR* in "Forced Union," 4-8. At the time we saw only a few voices expressing concern about the possible dangerous consequences of a break-up of the Soviet Union, such as George F. Kennan's sober warning in "Communism in Russian History," *Foreign Affairs* Winter 1990/91.

March saw demonstrations in the streets of Moscow, which the press, in such reports as "Thousands March for Yeltsin," *FT* 3-11, by Anthony Robinson; "Rally Takes Kremlin Terror and Turns it Into Burlesque," *NYT* 3-29, by new Moscow bureau chief Francis X. Clines; and "100,000 Join Moscow Rally, Defying Ban by Gorbachev to Show Support for Rival," *NYT* 3-29, by Serge Schmemann, saw as political victories for Yeltsin. Gorbachev seemed on the verge of eclipse by the man who he had cast out of the Politburo little more than three years earlier. In its 4-8 edition, *USNWR* published the findings of a public opinion poll taken in the Soviet Union during March in which Yeltsin came out ahead of Gorbachev, 70 percent to 14 percent, when respondents were asked whom would they prefer for president of the Soviet Union. If the U.S. was covering this international story as if it were a U.S. presidential campaign, the story still had a uniquely Russian twist. In "The Man Who Saved the Future," *Vanity Fair* 10-91, T.D. Allman recounted how Yeltsin had won the support of striking coal miners in Siberia in May, by stripping down to his underwear and jumping into the Tom River. "Here was a leader who, just like them, could brave the elements, survive them and prevail."

In June, Yeltsin was elected president of the Russian republic by a large margin over his Communist Party opponent. *WP* Moscow bureau chief Michael Dobbs, in "After Election, Russia Faces Uncertain Future," 6-16, predicted that Yeltsin's "populist promises" of better times ahead were unlikely to be kept if he began the transition to a market economy. In "Millennium in Moscow," 6-14, the *WP* observed that "Previously the United States was increasing its leverage on change in the Soviet Union as Mikhail Gorbachev reached out ever more urgently for aid. With Boris Yeltsin now becoming a conspicuous Kremlin alternative, American leverage, if it can be applied skillfully, may increase even more."

The question of U.S. aid to Moscow dominated op-ed pages for much of the year, despite Dimitri Simes's observation in "Gorbachev's Time of Troubles," *Foreign Policy* Spring 1991, that "Events in the Soviet Union have their own dynamics that rarely correspond to American preferences." The debate centered around the concept of a "Grand Bargain," as outlined by Graham Allison and Robert Blackwell in "America's Stake in the Soviet Future," *Foreign Affairs* Summer 1991. Allison and Blackwell, members of the faculty of the John F. Kennedy School of Government, Harvard University, call for "a bargain of Marshall Plan proportions. The terms: substantial financial assistance to Soviet reforms *conditional* upon continuing political pluralization and a coherent economic program for moving rapidly to a market economy." Several months later, in "The Harvard Man and His Plan," *WP* 8-26, Lloyd Grove would portray Allison as more of a salesman than a scholar. "Today he's the quintessential academic entrepreneur — a dominant species in these times of ever scarcer government resources — whose watchwords are not so much 'publish or perish' as they are 'endow or expire.' He's also a super-salesman in the marketplace of ideas, and sometimes just in the marketplace."

The *NYT* quickly became the plan's biggest supporter, championing the concept in such editorials as "A Western Spur to Soviet Reform," 5-24, and "Sticks and Carrots for the Soviets," 6-4, imagining in the latter, "If the aid turns an archenemy into an archally, or even an innocuous neutral state, it would save the U.S. in defense alone many times $3 billion a year — a stroke of genius." However, in "Disarming the Soviets, With Aid," *NYT* 6-18, the paper came out against Defense Secretary Richard Cheney's idea that Western aid to the Soviet Union should be tied to cuts in Soviet military spending: "Tying economic aid to deeper cuts could easily slow the process. Moscow's military-industrial complex will see such demands as blackmail, and stiffen its resistance to economic reform. It would accuse Mikhail Gorbachev of selling out to the West and weakening the Soviet Union."

TE rejected the idea in "How to Help," 5-6, arguing that "You do not need a Marshall plan or 94 blueprints endorsed by the G7 and Harvard University to push a communist economy towards market-driven growth. You just need to get on with the job, which is what Mr Gorbachev has singularly failed to do." *TE* later deconstructed some of the mythology that had grown up around the Marshall Plan in "Doing Well by Doing Good," 6-15. *TNR*, in "Beggar's Opera," 7-1, argued that "Aid to Mr. Gorbachev's regime now would have much the same effect as Western loans to Poland did in the 1970s: the money would be wasted, and talk of it would allow a corrupt despotic regime to think that it could somehow survive without total transformation." The *WP*, in "Aid for the Soviets?" 5-26, argued that massive amounts should not be given now, noting that "the central question is whether the West can do much more to help the Soviets before they have done a great deal more to help themselves," and in "Soviet Aid: The Political Terms," *WP* 6-2, contended that it was entirely appropriate for the U.S. to raise such issues as Soviet defense spending and aid to Cuba when discussing aid. In "Aid Means Transforming, Not Reforming," *WP* 6-5, former national security adviser Zbigniew Brzezinski outlined four "legitimate Western preconditions" of needed changes: "privatization, democratization, self-determination and demilitarization."

Arguing that our "key strategic interest" is centered "on the dismantling of the communist Soviet system that has oppressed its people for 75 years and that has engaged in unremitting expansionism against the free world," Richard Nixon, in "Gorbachev's Crisis — and America's Opportunity," *WP* 6-2, warns that "Some have touted the proposed $100-billion aid package as a 'grand bargain.' But a 'grand con job' sounds like a more appropriate term." *NYT* "Foreign Affairs" columnist Leslie H. Gelb responded in "The Old Trickster," *NYT* 6-5, that "It is great to have the Old Trickster unlimbering the magic that served him so well for so long. Like old times, Mr. Nixon positions himself by misdefining the alternatives as goofy extremes, and as usual the media play along."

While all this was going on, the Soviet economy was deteriorating by the day. The headline for John-Thor Dahlberg's report on Soviet economic performance for 1990, "Soviets Call Economic Output Worst Since 1945," *LAT* 1-27, seemed to say it all. Dahlberg went on to write that "The abysmal economic results for 1990, detailed in a special report from the committee printed in the 'Economy and Life' weekly, give more potent ammunition to Soviet conservative forces demanding a halt, or even a retreat, in economic and political reforms for the sake of social stability." Michael Parks, in "Soviet Ruble Notes Withdrawn in War on Black Market," *LAT* 1-23, noted that the decision to withdraw all 50 and 100-ruble notes "constitutes a major victory for those who advocate a return to central planning." Michael Dobbs, in "Ruble Plan Upsets Many Soviets," *WP* 1-24, deftly evoked the mood in the streets. " 'They told me I could use the money in the toilet,' said [Erburat] Aliev, an Azerbaijani collective farm worker. 'I now can't even buy an air ticket to go home.' " In April an effort at "price reform" raised some prices as much 200 percent. Dahlberg, in " 'Sticker Shock' Jolts Soviets on Eve of Huge Price Boosts,"

LAT 4-2, observed that "For a country whose last major retail price increase came in the 1950s and 1960s under Nikita S. Khrushchev, the consequences of today's Kremlin action are expected to be a colossal shock."

Reports from the Soviet Union took on an increasingly apocalyptic air. *Reader's Digest* Soviet writer David Satter, in "Moscow Believes in Tears," *National Review* 4-29, summed up what we were seeing in daily reports and newscasts: "The Soviet Union is clearly at a turning point in its history, and what happens in the next few months will affect not only its own future shape but the shape of the world. Most Moscow intellectuals now expect that there will be a crackdown." Michael Dobbs, investigating why no socks were available for Moscow consumers in the 10 Best nominee "In Moscow, Running Out of Socks," *WP* 6-22, wrote that the story "is a cautionary tale about the futility of pumping vast sums of money into a hopelessly inefficient economy whose distribution system is still largely controlled by government bureaucrats." Nevertheless, Gorbachev kept trying, bringing his campaign for massive Western aid to such forums as the Nobel Prize ceremony in Oslo and the London Economic Summit, coming away virtually empty-handed. The *NYT* noted tartly in "Bombast at the Summit," 7-18, that "The seven leaders gathered at the economic summit meeting this week in London faced two historic challenges: to jump-start a long-stalled international trade agreement and to help propel the Soviet Union toward a market economy. They responded mainly with wind."

Gorbachev returned to the Soviet Union to stage a summit with President Bush and to prepare to sign a new treaty, which would restructure relations between the national government and the republics. Russian Republic President Boris Yeltsin was already moving to ban party officials from the workplace. Press observers were noting the first early signs of what was directly ahead.

Correctly pegging Gorbachev as "probably the last and surely most unusual of all Soviet leaders," Rowland Evans and Robert Novak, in "Gorbachev's Waning Powers," *WP* 8-2, pick up on a pro-Russian nationalism, anti-Gorbachev letter which appeared in the hardline newspaper *Sovietskaya Rossiya* and was signed by "major personages in the despise-Gorbachev camp," including Deputy Defense Minister Valentin Varennikov and Deputy Interior Minister Boris Gromov. "Their cry came dramatically close to suggesting assassination or a military takeover." David Remnick, in the remarkably prescient "For Gorbachev, It's Back to Facing Intractable Problems," *WP* 8-2, cited the letter as well, and reports that "In stores and markets, ordinary goods regularly double and triple in price. 'This is the sort of financial situation that causes military overthrows in South America,' [economist Vasily] Selyunin said grimly." Remnick went on to observe that the "hard-line opposition seems firm only in its anger and resentment and lacks anything resembling an alternative platform. Even if they could manage a successful coup — and that is highly doubtful — what would the leaders do the next day? Return to a collapsed system? Attract Western cooperation under a Stalinist banner?"

"Ally Who Soured on Gorbachev Warns of a Stalinist-Style Coup," Francis X. Clines reported in the *NYT* 8-17, writing that "Aleksandr N. Yakovlev, an estranged confidant and reform strategist of President Mikhail S. Gorbachev, warned today that party reactionaries were planning a vindictive Stalinist coup d'etat as he quit the Communist Party." Clines described Yakovlev's warning as a "melodramatic flourish," pointed out that he made the same prediction last January, and noted that he "offered no details or names and made no estimate of the hardliners' chances of success." David Remnick took the same low-key approach, writing in "Reformist Yakovlev Quits Communist Party," *WP* 8-17, that "In an interview with the Washington Post earlier this week, Yakovlev said the real danger does not come from the Soviet Army. . .Instead, Yakovlev said that political forces within the party that have opposed radical reform from the start of Gorbachev's leadership in 1985 are still capable of taking advantage of declining economic conditions to stir up anti-Gorbachev anger and organize support."

"Gorbachev Is Ousted in an Apparent Coup by Soviet Armed Forces and Hard-Liners; Accused of Steering Into a 'Blind Alley,'" ran the banner headline in the *NYT* on 8-19. The news had broken on TV the night before, all three networks and CNN offering sketchy reports throughout the night and into the morning, but the banner headline of the country's newspaper of record seem to put the imprimatur of history on the event. Banner headlines continued, in the *NYT* and in other major papers as well, for the rest of that remarkable week, while TV offered expanded coverage. The central image soon became that of Yeltsin standing defiantly on top of a tank, R.W. Apple, Jr. writing in "The Next Chapter," *NYT* 8-22, that the image was "one of those emblematic moments that television can burn into the world's consciousness."

The media, both TV and print, at times gave the impression that the opposition to the coup was a mass revolt, as headlined in David Remnick's story, "Crisis Jolts Masses Out of Passivity and Onto Moscow Streets," 8-21, will attest. Numbers in print differed, at times wildly, on the true number of protestors at the same event. Accounts of crowd sizes in Leningrad, for example, varied between 50,000 cited by Fen Montaigne in "The Takeover Was Doomed When KGB Troops Said No," *Philadelphia Inquirer* 8-25, to 200,000 by the *FT* foreign staff in "Moscow Put Under Curfew as Yeltsin Fears Attack," *FT* 8-21. Crowd sizes outside the Russian parliament building, the crucial night of the August 20, varied from "30,000" cited by Francis X. Clines in "3 Die Near Russian Building; Disarray in Coup Committee," *NYT* 8-21, to "hundreds," cited by Peter Gumbel and Gerald F. Seib in "Democratic Forces Roll Back Soviet Coup," *WSJ* 8-22.

CBS correspondent Bert Quint in Moscow reported, 8-21, that, while thousands of Muscovites had supported Boris Yeltsin, the coup also had support, and the vast majority of Russians had not taken a stand. However, the other reports played up the story line that the failed coup had been a huge victory for Soviet democracy in general and Boris Yeltsin in particular, Michael Parks writing in "Plotters Overlooked Will of Soviet People," *LAT* 8-22, that "Perhaps for the first time since the Russian Czar was overthrown in 1917, the will of the people had overcome raw power." This simplistic image dominated the press coverage of the coup, as if Boris Yeltsin, standing atop a tank in Red Square, was single-handedly staring down the Red Army. Of course, the military had simply shifted its support from Gorbachev to Yeltsin, a fact that took months to get media attention of any kind, as it cut against the earlier media image of the military as a redoubt of "ideological" hardliners.

If the coup opposition was one side of the story, the coup leadership was another, and here there was less data to work from. Michael Dobbs, in "Crowds Mass Against Tanks," *WP* 8-20, referred to Soviet vice president Gennady Yanayev as "a colorless apparatchik" and wrote that "Despite assurances. . .that market-oriented reform will continue, it seems likely that the change of regime will result in a move back toward the discredited command economy." Michael Krepon, president of the Henry L. Stimson Center, wrote in "Who Is Gennady Yanayev?" *WP* 8-21, that "He comes across as a man who cannot be dismissed simply as a party hack trying to survive the sea-change of Soviet politics. He seems to care for the future of his country and the problems it faces. But he is also a purebred creature of the party." Martin Malia, in "The August Revolution," *TNYRB* 9-26, wrote that "With their own careers at stake, all that these people were fighting for was the preservation of the Party, state 'property,' and the Union — which Gorbachev himself had been trying to preserve in his more sophisticated manner."

The *NYT,* in "Gorbachev's Loss, and Ours," 8-20, labeled the coup leaders "members of a discredited Communist old guard," who "lack the legitimacy and the vision needed to succeed." The *WP*, in "The Moscow Coup," 8-20, denounced the coup as well, as "a desperate and despicable throwback to Stalinism by a cabal without the slightest chance of easing the 'chaos and anarchy' it cited in rationalizing its grab." The next day, in "People Have to Free Themselves," 8-21, the *NYT* noted that "The Bush Administration might have fortified Mr. Gorbachev's position by committing itself this summer to the so-called Grand Bargain. The basic idea was to offer substantial aid explicitly linked to measurable reforms. Would such an arrangement have prevented this week's coup? No one can say, though it could have shown the Soviet people a plausible path out of hardship."

Post-mortems on why the coup failed began appearing almost as soon as the last tanks were rolling out of Moscow, and Jim Hoagland, in "Another Round in a Long Struggle," *WP* 8-22, noted that "It was Dostoyevski at the beginning, but the Marx brothers by the end." Bill Keller, in "Plotters Who Had Handcuffs but a Poor Sense of History," *NYT* 8-25, blamed the conspirators for being so "fine tuned to the plodding rhythms of the Five Year Plan." In "How Not to Mount a Coup," *WSJ* 8-29, Peter Gumbel would draw on Gorbachev loyalists who contended that captured conspirator Valentin Pavlov drew a picture of a conspiracy "fueled in large part by fear and alcohol" hatched by desperate bureaucrats who were taken in by Kremlin warnings of an imminent uprising and false reports about Gorbachev's health, and who quickly developed "cold feet" as opposition mounted. In "Anatomy of a Botched Putsch," 8-24, *TE*'s Moscow correspondent blames the failure on the "lack of ruthlessness and planning" on the part of the coup leaders. Alistair Cooke, in "The Fate of the Union," *FT* 10-5/6-91, credited CNN.

The collapse of the coup was quickly followed by Gorbachev's dramatic return to Moscow, his subsequent resignation from the Communist Party, and the resulting dismantling of the Soviet Communist Party and the Soviet Union itself. There was surprisingly little soul-searching on the part of the U.S., through its media, on what the end of the Cold War would mean. Sen. Daniel Patrick Moynihan, in "Totalitarianism R.I.P." *WP* 8-22, ruminated that "Perhaps now, at last we will realize that it is *we* who need to scrutinize *us*. Surely the Soviet democrats will prove themselves. Will that fact penetrate our thick institutional skulls, still lost in the fog of the Cold War?" The *WP* sent David Maraniss to Fulton, Mo., where Winston Churchill ushered in the Cold War with the phrase "iron curtain" back in 1948, for "Iron Curtain Rises in Missouri Town," 9-3, to capture the town's reaction to recent events. Maraniss found respondents ranging from an insurance agent comparing it to "the second coming of Christ" to a leftist college professor coming to grips with the fact the conservatives were right all along about the instability of the Soviet system. Mostly he found professionals more concerned with the local and national economy.

The local and national economy was always the chief concern of the new leaders in Moscow, even as the Soviet Union was breaking apart, with the Baltic states gaining international recognition of their independence in September. Bill Keller, in "Collapse of an Empire," *NYT* 8-27, enumerated a chilling list of questions being raised by the crack-up of the Soviet Union, "From some politicians, the sundering of a nuclear superpower conjured up an alarming future of border wars, the dismembering of a nuclear arsenal, the disintegration of a feeble but integral economy, and the prospect that some of the states-in-the-making would revert to dictatorship." Opinion varied as to what course the U.S. should pursue. William Safire, in "After the Fall," *NYT* 8-29, calls for President Bush to encourage the dissolution of the Soviet Union and the complete abolition of the Communist Party: "With the Soviet monolith broken up and a commonwealth established to negotiate arms reductions, the world will be a far safer place." Charles Krauthammer, on the other hand, argued in "The Only Alternative to Chaos," *WP* 8-30, that Washington should work to aid the center: "Given the fact that what remains of the center is in the control of democrats, and given the fact that the collapsed empire is a nuclear warehouse, we have no interest in a further weakening of the center."

But events in the former Soviet Union seemed to be swirling out of anyone's control. David Remnick in "Critics Assail Soviet Georgia's Ruler," *WP* 9-18, and Leyla Boulton, in "Georgia's Independence Crusade Turns Into Farce," *FT* 9-11, provided solid reports on the growing chaos in that republic under the leadership of President Zviad Gamsakhurdia. In the 10 Best selection "Iran Makes Trade Inroads in Soviet Asian Republics," *LAT* 9-30, Mark Fineman expertly portrays Iran's efforts to fill one growing geopolitical vacuum.

Another vacuum appeared to be developing in Moscow as the economy spun out of control with rubles being printed around the clock. Peter Gumbel, in "Russian Leaders Are Torn Apart by Infighting," *WSJ* 10-7, and Serge Schmemann, in "Soviet 'Democrats' Now Wrestle Over the Spoils," *NYT* 10-8, draw strong portraits of Yeltsin officials, many from Sverdlovsk, unable to cope in the absence of their leader, ostensibly taking time off to write a book. Yeltsin emerged late in the month to introduce "shock therapy" to the Russian economy. John Lloyd, writing in "Yeltsin's Bitter Pill," *FT* 10-29, commented that "The constituent parts of what was the Soviet Union, now thrown back upon their own resources, are about to discover how painful it is to build nations from a political, economic and moral wasteland." In the 10 Best selection "Top Russian Banker Ridicules Monday's Ruble Devaluation," *WSJ* 12-6, Laurie Hays interviewed Georgy Matykhin, chairman of the Board of the Central Bank of Russia, who predicted that the floating of the ruble, scheduled for the start of the new year, would be "something much more destructive than an atomic bomb." The piece was rare in that it suggested genuine debate over economic issues within the new democratic framework.

As the year ended, and Yeltsin forged a new Commonwealth of Independent States out of the ashes of the U.S.S.R., Celestine Bohlen noted, in "Yeltsin Leads a Bold Move to Replace the Soviet Union," *NYT* 12-15, that "Instead of being discouraged by the disarray around him, Mr. Yeltsin seems to thrive on it, reacting quickly and boldly as he tries to mold a solution out of chaos."

In the 10 Best selection "From Resistance of the Few to Revolt of the Masses," *NYT* 9-15, Bill Keller produces another dimension to the good guy/bad guy analysis that we found suffocating in the U.S. press during the August coup, as he wondered "Will the August Revolution be mythologized to suit a new orthodoxy that goes by the name of democracy?" The answer to that question may be one of the major stories of 1992. Meanwhile, Maxim Natanovitch sits alone in his "tiny flat" in the Moscow suburbs, worried about going to the market. "It's very, very bad now — the queues, the prices." As for democracy? "When I see them on television it all seems a bit like before. Like 1917. The leaders are promising people freedom and new ideas and a future. They promise and promise! Only this time they are called democrats!"

The U.S. Political Economy in Recession

Amazing changes swept the global political economy in 1991, requiring unprecedented intellectual rigor and flexibility from the business and financial press corps. Indeed, it was a perplexing year for those journalists used to resting on their laurels and assessing the world from a conventional viewpoint. Too much was changing too fast. It was a period that cried out for fresh ideas and perspectives. Yet, in times of great fluctuation or uncertainty, the human tendency is to cling to the familiar and to run with the pack, a defense mechanism that revealed itself frequently in the year's news reports and analyses, especially those on the U.S. recession. It often seemed that the further the course of events moved away from the results predicted by conventional economics, the more the financial press resorted to catch phrases and hackneyed formulas, and looked for someone or something to blame for their misassessments. There were, of course, many exceptions to this rule, journalists flexible enough to allow the facts to bring them to a new understanding of a topic. Certainly, the best reporters set out on assignments with the conventional wisdom in hand, knowing that unless their preconceptions were destroyed in the reporting process, they had learned nothing new, nothing worth passing on as *news*. But all too often, financial and business journalists simply refused to allow the facts to stand in the way of the story they had envisioned when they began the reporting process.

This fruitless exercise, practiced by so many reporters in this tumultuous year, severely limited the financial press corps' capacity to help us interpret the economic events occurring in the U.S. political economy. Throughout the present recession, many business journalists clung to old-fashioned business cycle theory, with lamentable results. In its 7-1 cover story, *Business Week* argued for a strong economic recovery on the grounds that the recession was more severe than generally thought: "The evidence from past business cycles shows that the deeper the downturn, the sharper the bounceback — and this recession has been nastier than advertised." *Fortune,* meanwhile, argued on 7-15 that the recovery would be strong because "this recession is turning out to be milder, and perhaps briefer, than average." For this reason, *Fortune* added, the economy "will rebound with more vigor over the next year and a half than most forecasters expect — and a good deal more robustly than business is currently bargaining for." Only a few months later we were reading headlines about the possibility of a double dip recession.

Perhaps one reason that the press corps had such a difficult time assessing this recession was that it had never fully explored the roots of the downturn. Most reporters assumed that big deficits and tight monetary policy had led to the decline, but this theory, which slowly but surely became "fact" on the pages of the nation's newspapers, was never actually dissected. In fact, there were indications that tight monetary policy was not the culprit at all. Fed officials pointed out that this was the first time since WWII that the economy had entered a recession when interest rates were falling. And one important indicator of excessively tight monetary policy, the so-called inversion of the yield curve (short-term interest rates turn higher than long-term rates), a phenomenon which took place in the 1974, 1980 and 1982 recessions, did not occur during the 12 months prior to July-August 1990, when the present recession presumably started. On the contrary, the yield curve was positive and rising during those months. Yet the press corps, unsettled by the implications of this data, clung to the familiar, refusing to reassess their preconceptions about the recession. They were, instead, content to rely on conventional wisdom, and to blame the recession on Alan Greenspan. David Rosenbaum was so convinced that the Fed chairman had caused this recession that in "A Second Chance for Greenspan," *The New York Times* 1-18, he asserted "War in the Persian Gulf could give Alan Greenspan a chance to redeem his reputation. . .[A]ll will be forgotten if Mr. Greenspan makes the right decisions in the weeks ahead."

The press corps did not hold President Bush and his economic advisers accountable for a role in the recession until late in the year. Certainly, early in 1991, it was difficult to criticize a president who was leading the nation to victory in the Gulf and enjoying record popularity in the polls. Yet, as the war came to an end, the nation's attention turned homeward where a painful recession still lingered. For a while the press was content with the administration's line that it had a domestic economic plan already in place in the form of the budget pact of 1990. The pact was marketed by the administration as *the* plan to reduce the deficit through tax increases and pay-as-you-go spending caps. Yet, after the accord was passed, the deficit expanded exponentially. Nationally syndicated columnist Warren Brookes, one of the few to consistently scrutinize the deficit numbers, provided some startling figures in "Darman's Deficit Disaster," *The Washington Times* 7-25: "In January of 1990, Mr. Darman forecast that the total budget deficit from fiscal 1991 through fiscal 1995 would be $62.3 billion. In July 1991, just 18 months later, the same five-year figure is projected to be $1,081.9 billion, a 1,637 percent increase."

Despite such appalling data, there was, for the most part, a deafening silence from the press corps on this paradox. Paul Craig Roberts put it this way in his op-ed "Bush's Teflon Deficits," *The Wall Street Journal* 5-6: "This year's U.S. budget deficit is now approaching twice the size of Ronald Reagan's record, and no one has said a word about it. President Bush enjoys a remarkable immunity to the issue that so bedeviled 'the teflon president.' " Indeed, there was scant questioning of why the budget accord wasn't fulfilling its promise, perhaps because this reality flew in the face of the conventional wisdom to which the press corps was clinging. One of the few critiques we saw on the subject was Howard Gleckman's "How the Budget Deal Has Choked Off America's Choices," *BW* 9-16, in which he observed: "Last year's fiscal deal may or may not bring down the deficit, but it guarantees that no matter what happens in the world, the priorities agreed upon last November remain fixed through fiscal 1993. . .All this is just as Budget Director Richard G. Darman had hoped when he dreamed up the spending caps. The scheme gives Bush the equivalent of a line-item veto. Not incidentally, it also gives Darman enormous new power within the Administration." Despite these criticisms, very few mainstream economic reporters would ever hazard to question the budget pact's role in the economic downturn.

Since fiscal stimulus had been disregarded as a policy option by both the administration and a mostly unquestioning press corps, the Federal Reserve was indeed forced to assume the crucial and challenging role of keeping the economy afloat all by itself, not because it had been proven that tight monetary policy had caused the recession, but because no other options were made available. Thus, the journalists following this often enigmatic institution became especially important sources of information. What was truly ironic about the assumption that monetary policy was the only tool to bring us through the recession, was the fact that the man in charge of monetary policy, Federal Reserve Chairman Alan Greenspan, testified before Congress several times in 1991 that certain fiscal policy moves, such as cutting the capital gains tax, could accelerate an economic recovery. But Greenspan's expert remarks did not gel with the press corps' belief that the recession was an inherent part of the business cycle — a purging of the excesses in the system. As a result, many of his important economic observations and recommendations went unreported.

A quick study of the press coverage of Federal Reserve Chairman Alan Greenspan's testimony before the House Budget Committee on 1-22 is quite educational in this regard. During this testimony, Greenspan made his first public statement in support of lowering or eliminating the capital gains tax. It was only a few months earlier that Washington's political wrangling over this issue had practically brought the budget process to a standstill, yet none of the nation's top economic correspondents included the chairman's statements on capital gains in their reports on his testimony — not David Rosenbaum of *The New York Times,* not David Wessel of *The Wall Street Journal,* not James Risen of *Los Angeles Times,* and not John Berry of *The Washington Post.* Business readers who relied on these reporters were completely unaware of Greenspan's consequential statement. Only those who watched the actual testimony on C-SPAN were initially privy to this crucial information. The editorial page of *WSJ* was the first to print Greenspan's remarks on 1-25. But it was not until a week later, when President Bush gave his State of the Union address and appointed Greenspan to head a study on the capital gains issue, that this important piece of information surfaced in news articles. *WSJ*'s Washington bureau, which had not initially mentioned Greenspan's observations, reported on 1-31, following Bush's State of the Union announcement, that "Mr. Greenspan is a partisan in the capital gains debate," in that "Just last week, he told a congressional committee 'I've always been supportive of lowering the capital-gains tax or preferably eliminating it.' " When Greenspan, widely known as one of the most respected economists in the nation, is asked to state his opinions on specific monetary policies, he is not called a "partisan," even though his comments sometimes support the administration's position, but when asked by Congress to state his opinion on the benefits of this specific tax cut, he instantly became a "partisan."

In "Money Supply Pushed Fed to Lower Interest Rates," 1-10, *WSJ*'s Alan Murray reported that the Fed was watching M2 (time deposits at commercial banks plus deposits at non-bank thrift institutions) as a primary indicator of economic health. But despite ease after ease, which brought short-term interest rates to a 14-year low by late summer, the Federal Reserve could not hit its M2 targets. This was a troublesome phenomenon few reporters hazarded to explore. Randall Forsyth at *Barron's* was one of the few to examine the Fed's troubles with M2 in "Global Rate Tug-of-War," 7-29. After researching the topic at length, he deferred to the *Bank Credit Analyst's Interest Rate Forecast* which pointed out that "The Fed has noted that the large spread between savings rates and borrowing cost makes it attractive for consumers to finance their expenditures by running down M2 balances rather than taking out new loans. . .But the drop in the interest rates hasn't pushed down M2's velocity. . .The impact of banking consolidation on financial flows is largely responsible for the decline in velocity, and that suggests that velocity may have suffered a permanent upward shift and could move higher. Therefore, the Fed should be tolerant of money growth in the lower part of its target range as long as disintermediation from the banking system continues."

A month later, Sylvia Nasar of *NYT* penned, "The Fed's Worry Over Money," 8-9, another solid explanation of why M2 was proving to be a shaky monetary indicator: "Since the end of June, the money supply has fallen by around $1 billion. As it happens, consumers have cashed in, on a net basis, some $11 billion worth of C.D.'s. It's not hard to figure out why, either. Rates on C.D.'s above 8 percent last winter, have plunged to around 5.5 percent. These days they are even lower than passbook savings rates. What are consumers doing with their money? They mostly are pouring into mutual funds, that offer higher returns. In recent months, bond mutual funds have swelled by $7 billion a month and stock mutual funds have grown by roughly $4 billion a month. Funds outside the banks, of course, are not counted in the money supply. 'While M-2 stalled, the public's financial assets have continued to expand,' said Robert V. DiClemente, an economist at Salomon Brothers." Nasar was definitely on to something. On 10-9, she followed up with "Money Supply Doesn't Tell All": "[E]verybody is watching the weekly money supply numbers as if the economy's life depended on them. And some people who have been leaning on the Federal Reserve to ease for years, including the Bush Administration, have seized on anemic money growth as a rationale for pressing the Fed to lower short-term rates — already the lowest since 1973 — some more. . .But the relationship between money and the economy is not all that tight. . .and the money supply has sent some spectacularly wrong signals in the past. . .In 1986, while M-2 raced, the economy ground to a halt. In 1987, when M-2 started to crawl, the economy took off. . .No one can ever be sure that stagnant money growth is not a portent of an economic downturn. But simply assuming that it is — and putting pressure on the Fed to crank up the printing presses — carries its own risks."

There was only a handful of reporters who were keeping their eyes on other economic barometers. For example, throughout the year, gold traded within a surprisingly narrow range, but why? John Liscio, commodities editor of *Barron's,* knew something was up, although he couldn't quite put his finger on it. In "Brigitte Bardot, Freddie Krueger and Gold," 4-15, he designated himself as one of the few not to believe that price of gold was on the verge of skyrocketing. One of his sources noted that "The gold market is still called the gold market. But it has totally changed and will not return to its former self." Soon after, in "Operation Money Storm," *WP* 5-13, Rowland Evans and Robert Novak revealed that Fed Gov. Wayne Angell, who had been the lone dissenter on the April 30 vote to lower the discount rate, "insists long-term bond rates will come down only if the Fed sticks to tracking commodities and keeping gold at $350 an ounce." By August we started to read reports about price level targeting, the use of commodity prices, gold especially, as a guide for setting monetary policy. A *WSJ* editorial entitled, "The New Inflationists," 8-7, had this to say: "In the real world, we've always thought the Fed worked best when it targeted not the quantity of money but the price level. The job of monetary policy is to keep prices stable, while the job of fiscal policy is to provide incentives for economic growth." Two months later Malcolm S. Forbes, Jr., proposed the bold question in his "Fact and Comment" column, "Is Gold Guiding the Fed?" 10-14: "There is circumstantial evidence that it is. If true, the implications for the economy are profoundly positive. . .Federal Reserve Chairman Alan Greenspan has long been fascinated by the barbarous relic as a monetary guide. His influential colleague, Governor Wayne Angell, has stated that commodity prices, particularly gold, are the best compass for avoiding inflation and deflation. Angell is said to think the right price for gold is around $350. Thus, when it went below that level, Angell-watchers were not surprised that the Fed cut the discount rate to its lowest level in 18 years."

While monetary barometers may be crucial to our understanding of the economy, they are complex and dry — not the characteristics that make for especially exciting copy. Thus Nasar, Liscio, Forsyth and Forbes's inquisitiveness was the exception rather than the rule. Dissension at the Fed, on the other hand, was the juicy scoop we got from Alan Murray, who made a mountain out of a molehill in "Dispute Flares Up at Fed Over Greenspan's Authority," 4-4, and "Democracy Comes to the Central Bank, Curbing Chief's Power," 4-5, in which he declared that a new assertiveness among the district governors damaged the economy in October '90: "Instead of combating the recession, the Fed's lack of action exacerbated it." He rescinded slightly in "Fed Fight Could Work to Delay Cut in Rates," 4-15, conceding that "The recent flare-up between the presidents and Mr. Greenspan concerned procedure, not policy." *Newsweek*'s Rich Thomas reminded us of the main mission at the Fed in "A Food Fight at the Fed," 4-22, reassuring that differences between the chairman and the regional bank presidents, that had *NYT* and *WSJ* hyperventilating, were "minute." "Few understand that. . .[The Federal Reserve Board's] main aim is to maintain price stability and the value of the dollar." Similarly, John M. Berry at *WP* reported in his well-sourced, "Did Greenspan Face Fed Revolt?" 4-18: " 'I think the whole thing is a tempest in a teapot,' said Robert Black, president of the Richmond Federal Reserve Bank, and supposedly one of the inflation 'hawks' worried that the Fed has been cutting rates too much."

It was frustrating to see so much editorial time and energy wasted on concocting a tempest in a teapot when there was in fact a genuine tempest swirling around the global political economy. As the U.S. economy sank deeper into recession, the Bush administration's economic team, especially Treasury Secretary Nicholas Brady, elevated its pressure on the central banks of other countries to ease. The European press, including the *Financial Times* of London and *The Economist,* came down especially hard after Brady tried to pressure the G7 at its April meeting into a co-ordinated lowering of interest rates. In "The Diminished Fed," 5-4, *The Economist* editorialized that the spectacle was "an unexpectedly ugly sight. . .This will stand as a textbook example of how not to conduct monetary policy. Start with Mr Brady's arguments for a co-ordinated lowering of interest rates. They were dismayingly feeble. He said that global real interest rates are too high, and need to come down to spur economic recovery around the world. This supposes that governments can reliably control, real, long-term interest rates by changing nominal, short-term ones, which is an illusion. . .But put that aside. Just now, the big economies are strikingly unsynchronised. America and Britain are still in recession; they have spare industrial capacity and rising unemployment. Japan and Germany are growing, if anything too quickly; the Bundesbank especially is worried about mounting inflationary pressures at home. The idea of a co-ordinated lowering of interest rates was plainly barmy." And the *FT* opinion writers commented in "G7 Under US Pressure," 4-30: "Rarely can a great power have come to an important meeting with arguments as feeble as those advanced by the US at the meeting of the finance ministers and central bankers of the group of seven industrial countries in Washington over the weekend. But the arguments were not merely indefensible; they were dangerous."

With monetary manhandling at home and abroad failing to bring the U.S. economy out of its slump, the administration became increasingly desperate. The angry anti-tax sentiments that dominated the state elections in November finally brought the nation's tax burden into the media spotlight. At this time, we recalled David Rosenbaum's unsubstantiated and unattributed editorial generalization in such articles as "Greenspan Named for New Term as Chairman of Federal Reserve," *NYT* 7-11: "The nation's largest budget deficit prevents the President or Congress from using tax and spending policies to influence the economy." But even with the press corps' newfound cognizance that fiscal policy was indeed part of the economic landscape, we were still disappointed by the plethora of unrefined economic analysis. On the political implications of the elections, the press corps had the story down. Comparisons to President Hoover and headlines like Robin Toner's "Dark Skies for Bush," *NYT* 11-18, covered the pages of the nation's newspapers and news magazines. But the quality of reporting on the economic aspects of the story varied widely. When the DJIA dropped 120 points on 11-15, the *WSJ* editorial page ran "Economic Incompetents," 11-18, one of the most astute and hard-hitting assessments we saw on the mini-crash: "The proximate cause of Friday's 120-point meltdown in stocks was Congressional reaction to the President's spectacularly inane remark about stimulating the economy by having banks shave interest rates on credit card balances. The underlying cause is the growing perception that even as lusty a beast as the U.S. economy can take only so much punishment from its political masters in Washington. The long and short of it is: The world's most important economy is in the grip of economic incompetents."

Yet, as the tax cut proposals spilled out of Congress and the administration, some well-conceived and others ill-conceived, we found many reporters indiscriminately lumping them all together. For instance, "Suddenly, Everyone Wants to Cut Taxes," *BW* 11-4, by Howard Gleckman and Mike McNamee with Douglas Harbrecht and Paula Dwyer, makes the sweeping generalization that ". . .even if Bush and congressional leaders come to terms on a tax package, economists doubt it will do much to boost growth." Once again, *WSJ*'s editorial page stood out as one of the few sources to differentiate between the deluge of proposals in "Beltway Bond

Traders," 11-8: "Even President Bush said. . .that 'long-term interest rates went through the roof' when the tax-cut talk started. There may be something to this, we concede, for there are tax cuts and tax cuts. Having the government mail everyone in the country under the age of 18 a check for $300 would not help the economy or the markets."

As had happened during the 1990 budget debate, when the press corps bought into the political rhetoric of "fairness" versus "growth" without ever investigating if the two concepts actually had to be mutually exclusive, the reporting on taxation issues often degenerated into a war of words that found a home in the nation's newspapers and magazines. The coverage of the administration's proposal to cut the capital gains tax, widely categorized as "a tax cut for the rich," was especially generic. What was interesting was that, as the press corps categorically dismissed it as a Republican ploy to appease wealthy voters, more and more Democrats were coming out in support of it. In "The Democratic Smorgasbord," 12-1, by Dan Balz of *WP,* we found that "In contrast to past years, Democrats have jumped on the theme of economic growth. . .Not only Tsongas, but Clinton, Cuomo and perhaps Kerrey favor a targeted capital gains tax cut." But, despite growing support in both parties, statistical and historical analysis of this tax cut's strengths and weaknesses was rare, the issue considered more a political story than an economic one. Thomas McArdle was one of the few to break through the rhetoric and examine the issue on its economic merits in his 10 Best selection, "Cap Gain: Cut for All Reasons: Politics Aside, It May Be All-Purpose Antidote," *Investor's Business Daily* 11-13. Backed by quotes from several economists who probe the pros and cons, McArdle pours on the data concluding that "If recent history is any guide, a sizable reduction in the capital gains rate would stimulate the sluggish economy and create jobs, provide direct tax relief to many middle-income Americans and even lower the federal deficit. . .Despite the back-and-forth political debate between conservatives and liberals, the idea of a cap gains tax cut to spur the economy is gaining advocates."

All in all, the media did not come through with the creative ideas and fresh perspectives we sought, or the hard-hitting questions aimed at policymakers that we expected. It was easier and safer to rely on conventional wisdom than it was to ferret out the facts buried beneath the rhetoric. Much of the time, there seemed to be an almost standard recipe for covering the economy — a new statistic, a few economic generalizations to put it into context, a quote from one or two administration officials. In a quintessential example of just how formulaic reporting on the economy could become, two *NYT* articles on 12-18 covering Bush's struggle to formulate an economic policy included the exact same observations, as if they had been pulled from a pool of generic catch phrases appropriate to the story. David Rosenbaum told us in "Bush Out of Options," 12-18: "At one extreme, President Bush is being urged to propose a rebate in income taxes due April 15. This might be good politics, but it is probably bad economics. At the other extreme, Mr. Bush is being counseled to sit tight and ride out the recession. This could be good economics, but it is terrible politics." Nearby Andrew Rosenthal's "In Sharp Reversal, White House Tells of Bleak Economy," 12-18, states: "Some advisers are calling on the President to propose an income tax rebate: good politics but probably bad economics. Others are telling him to ride out the recession: perhaps good economics but terrible politics."

Perhaps. But at year's end, much of the administration's most important work on the economy was left unfinished, and much of the press corps' most important analysis of the recession was left unwritten. Meanwhile, the U.S. electorate continued to deal with the harsh realities of the lingering recession, and continued to search for answers to the political and economic questions raised by this downturn.

THE BEST STORIES AND COLUMNS OF 1991

For the sixth consecutive year, the *MediaGuide* highlights individual efforts by ten print journalists in each of five categories: Business/Financial, Commentary, Foreign, General and Political. Journalists within each category are listed in alphabetical order, *not* in the order in which we might rank them. For this year's edition of the 10 Best, we reviewed almost 2,000 articles, reports and essays, constantly refining the list, to make the final 50 selections. Many were nominated by our contributors over the course of their readings for the book. As in previous years, we have also invited the top tier of editors at each publication we review for the *MediaGuide* to nominate their own selections.

Because we can't possibly read every word of the national press, we can't certify that there were no better columns or articles that appeared during the year. But there are no other award citations in American print journalism where the judges have read as much *at the time of publication* or where the judges consist exclusively of consumers of news, as opposed to professional peers. As a result, some selections were chosen on the basis of timeliness, some because they stand the test of time, still others because they changed or challenged our perspectives, or answered our questions when no one else could. In order to do justice to the work cited, we have added our comments following the citation, further defining the material's distinctiveness.

Business/Financial Reporting

1. **Bacon, Kenneth H.** *The Wall Street Journal.* "Cracking Down: The New Banking Law Toughens Regulation, Some Say Too Much," 11-29. A veteran *Journal* reporter on a variety of Washington economic beats, Bacon took a few years away from the pencil and notebook to edit the work of others in the bureau. This deep and varied experience showed up splendidly when he returned to the trenches, this time covering banking regulation, at a time when the nation's financial institutions were having their gravest problems since the Great Depression. He was clearly the reporter of choice on this beat, as this jewel of a report on the banking law that emerged from Congress will attest. There is nothing sensational here, no personalities dragged through a journalistic torture chamber, but a bread-and-butter account of an issue of immense importance to the newspaper's readers, delivered in classic Dow Jones fashion. We get first a crisp lead of contrasts, what the Bush administration wanted, and what it got instead. We get a broad outline of the legislation's thrust, with Bacon's opinion carrying weight with us because he is so careful in weaving it through his material. Just when we begin to suspect his opening theme will overwhelm the piece, he brings in alternative views from respected sources, especially impressing us with the sharp views of one critic who, nevertheless, "doesn't denounce the bill" entirely. There are shades and nuances from all angles, and just enough detail to satisfy, written with impressive clarity. A future historian forced to cite one source on this issue could do no better than this one.

2. **Beaty, Jonathan and Gwynne, S.C.** *Time.* "The Dirtiest Bank of All," 7-29. It was only a short time after BCCI was seized by regulators that Beaty and Gwynne shocked readers across the country by revealing the extent of this seedy and dangerous bank's dark side. This gripping and widely cited expose blows the lid clean off of BCCI's "black network" which functions as a global intelligence operation and a Mafia-like enforcement squad. "The black network. . .operates a lucrative arms-trade business and transports drugs and gold. According to investigators and participants in those operations, it often works with Western and Middle Eastern intelligence agencies. The strange and still murky ties between B.C.C.I. and the intelligence agencies of several countries are so pervasive that even the White House has become entangled. . . .The bank's intelligence operations and alleged bribery of public officials around the world point to an explanation for the most persistent mystery in the B.C.C.I. scandal: why banking and law-

enforcement authorities allowed the bank to spin out of control for so long." Although most of the sources in the story are mysterious, maintaining anonymity, we understand their concerns about the consequences of going on record: "The black network was the bank's deepest secret, but rumors of its activities filtered through the bank's managerial level with chilling effectiveness. Senior bankers voice fears that they will be financially ruined or maimed — even killed — if they are found talking about B.C.C.I.'s activities."

3. **Coll, Steve.** *The Washington Post.* "BCCI's Abedi: A Courtier's Ruin; Luxury and Largesse Brought Banking Empire's Downfall," 9-1. Not only was this the best profile of BCCI chairman Agha Hasan Abedi that we saw, it also provided an educational window on the cultural aspects of this bank. Coll takes us back to Mahmudabad, India, from which Abedi and nearly all of BCCI's executives fled as young adults to build institutions from scratch in the newly independent Islamic nation of Pakistan in 1947 and 1948. From this clan of people, Abedi built a loyal following strengthened by lavish favoritism. "The patterns suggest that, in some ways, Abedi saw BCCI less as a 20th-century, multinational bank than as a 17th century feudal kingdom with international horizons. ...Abedi's feudal business practices extended to Westerners who came in contact with him. All employees enjoyed exceptional salaries and access to loans that they were not expected to repay. In some cases bank employees made little effort to hide the practice. Records from BCCI's Paris branch show a loan for 1.67 million francs ($280,000) to Lemarche C. Yves, a French national and a BCCI director. Under the heading 'Expected Date of Settlement,' the loan entry states simply, 'Never.' " Also interesting is Coll's sensitivity to how differently South Asians view the bank's downfall: "Pakistanis. . .see Abedi as having tried foolishly to extend to the West the style of business commonplace in his own world but unacceptable abroad. They also see the West's crackdown on BCCI and Abedi as a repetition of colonial attempts to repress great Muslim rulers such as the rajahs of Mahmudabad. When the Bank of England shut down BCCI on July 5 and U.S. prosecutors then indicted the bank's senior executives on fraud charges, it seemed to Pakistanis that another Abedi was being hung out in a cage by the colonials as an example to the local population. To Westerners, that attitude may seem naive and dishonest. To South Asians, it is an article of faith."

4. **Cook, James.** *Forbes.* "Collision Course," 5-13. With the recession reducing public revenues everywhere in the country, state, county and local governments are beginning to say no to the powerful public sector unions. In this vigorous, fast-paced, fact-filled report, a trademark of this veteran business reporter, Cook assembles a dizzying array of numbers in a palatable snapshot style that surrounds this hot topic: "Why are state and local deficits mushrooming while the garbage piles up, the streets become less safe and the kids can't read properly? Where the private sector struggled during the 1980s to become more efficient, learning to do more with fewer people, state and local bureaucracies went in the other direction: doing less with more people." This is not an anti-union editorial, however. Cook is a reporter's reporter, and much of his material in this piece is drawn from interviews with the union leadership. He brings us to a persuasive, unsettling conclusion that the unions are not only after higher wages, but also control of their job descriptions with no interference from taxpayers. Says one public union leader: " 'We want to get involved in what happens to our pension money, how they work out the bond ratings. We want to get involved in making decisions in terms of the tax base, in terms of priorities. We want to play a larger role in the formation of public policy, the formation of national policy as it affects our people.'. . .It was this sort of drive for power by the Labour Party and the unions that controlled it that brought the U.K. to the verge of economic and social bankruptcy. Twelve years of counterrevolution under Tory governments has only partly undone the damage."

5. **Farhi, Paul.** *The Washington Post.* "Waves of the Future," 5-5. This is an outstanding profile of FCC chairman Alfred C. Sikes, "a low-tech kind of guy" with a "high-tech vision of the future" who has the potential to realize the amazing technological imaginings of the communications industry if he can take the reins decisively at the FCC. "Sikes's agency, once a sleepy bureaucratic backwater that regulated long-distance phone rates and handed out radio

and TV licenses, now holds sway over a massive and growing collection of telecommunications businesses — from the phone companies to the broadcast networks to cable TV and satellite communications — and has the power to foster new technologies or hasten the decline of others." In weighing the odds that Sikes will succeed in his quest to "remap much of the communications landscape," Farhi explores the chairman's relationship with Congress, well-funded telecommunication lobbyists, and other FCC members who collectively have the power to override Sikes's vote. Skeptics and critics defer to "an independent-minded group that stunned him recently by voting against his effort to repeal rules that keep ABC, CBS and NBC from selling programs on the TV rerun market. 'I don't think he's in control of much over there,' sniffs one lobbyist. 'He can't dictate results.' " Farhi concludes that as is so often the case in Washington, it will be Sikes's ability to master the game of politics rather than the intricacies of technology that will make or break his efforts to spearhead change. "The chairman may not have figured out how to work his speaker phone, but he could still orchestrate a technological revolution."

6. **Landler, Mark and Dobrzynski, Judith H.** *BusinessWeek.* "Time Warner," cover with Ronald Grover and Mark Lewyn 7-22. The controversial Time Warner rights offering was one of the biggest shareholder stories of the year. "Investors still chafing from Time's rejection of the Paramount bid were now even angrier, branding the new offering coercive. 'This is like Rape Two,' says one major shareholder." Since Landler and Dobrzynski wrote their version of the events, the clearest and most far-reaching we'd seen, the unorthodox rights offering has been restructured to be more orthodox as they predicted in their report, and CEO Steve Ross has secured the long-sought big money deal with Toshiba and C. Itoh which the authors make clear is necessary to help the company make its big debt payment due in 1993. They look back at the original Time Warner merger, pointing out that "the billions more that Ross promised would come from the merger have materialized. And a close look at Time Warner suggests that that's because Ross's and Munro's original rationale for fusing the companies is fundamentally flawed." They explain the particularities of the rights offering that enraged shareholders, they look at the strengths and weaknesses of the divisions of Time Warner's empire, and they look ahead at the pros and cons of specific big-money alliances that the company is going after, including Toshiba. While many reporters used the events to bash Ross for his free-spending ways and cronyism, Landler and Dobrzynski wrote this report about Time Warner shareholders and for Time Warner shareholders, and focused on the aspect of Ross that worries them most: His risky, overarching global vision. "Time Warner is in no imminent danger. But many shareholders of the world's largest communication company are starting to wonder: Is their money being mortgaged on a chimera?"

7. **Loomis, Carol J.** *Fortune.* "Can John Akers Save IBM?" 7-15. Penetrating and hard-hitting when appropriate, appreciative where proper, this was *the* definitive analysis of Big Blue's financial woes in 1991, and a new yardstick for business profiles. Loomis not only masters "IBMspeak" and the company's unique corporate culture, but so effectively does she dissect management's strengths and weaknesses that her assessment will be as instructive to Big Blue executives as it is to IBM shareholders and general business readers. There doesn't seem to be any stone left unturned in the author's reconnaissance. Product pricing, marketing, corporate infrastructure, R&D investments, are all scrutinized in this stellar piece of business journalism packed with revealing and provocative observations from IBM insiders and outsiders, and Loomis herself. On pricing: "The wobbler in IBM's wares is its personal computers, which sell in a soybean-and-sowbelly, price-driven market. They lack the distinctive qualities that might allow them to command the premium prices IBM keeps trying to get." On marketing: "Indeed, the biggest indictment of [CEO John] Aker's management would seem to be that he has failed to fix IBM's marketing problems. . ..Under way is yet one more revamping of U.S. marketing. . ." On corporate infrastructure: "Despite Aker's vigorous efforts to decentralize and drive decision-making authority further down into the company, IBM's bureaucracy still lives and thrives. Almost everyone who deals with the company comes away with a numbing sense

of how slowly it moves, how many people must weigh in on a decision, how the competing interests of one camp in the company must be balanced against those of other camps." As IBM's financial problems mounted and its stock fell during the balance of the year, we frequently recalled this Loomis effort and its insights.

8. **McArdle, Thomas.** *Investor's Business Daily.* "Cap Gain: Cut for All Reasons," 11-13. In 1988, President Bush campaigned on a cut in the capital gains tax. Ever since, the Democratic Congress has blocked the cut on the grounds that it only favors the rich. Not once in this endless debate did we see the financial press seriously examine the issue on its merits, as opposed to the so-called "fairness" argument. *The Wall Street Journal*'s Washington bureau, which should have done the definitive work on the issue, instead sat back and treated it as a political debate. So it was left to the upstart *Investor's Business Daily* to finally deliver the goods, with this fresh and provocative analysis of the economic upside of a capgains tax cut. This was easily the most comprehensive report on this controversial issue that we'd seen all year, with McArdle turning to several economists to discuss the pros and cons, including one, Alan Sinai, who had opposed a cut, but on reexamination decided it would have powerful and positive effects. Wrote McArdle: "If recent history is any guide, a sizable reduction in the capital gains rate would stimulate the sluggish economy and create jobs, provide direct tax relief to many middle-income Americans and even lower the federal deficit. . .Not all fans of the tax cut. . .are the fat cats and right-wing ideologues portrayed in that political smokescreen. Despite the back-and-forth political debate between conservatives and liberals, the idea of a cap gains tax cut to spur the economy is gaining advocates."

9. **McGough, Robert.** *FW.* "Empires of the Sky" and "Wolf at the Gateway," cover 5-14. While most of the airline watchers in the press corps focused on the various company failures, bemoaning the deregulation of the industry, McGough stepped back from the carnage and in an admirably dispassionate way discerned the free-market forces reshaping the industry and the movement toward global liberalization. With vivid, deliberate examples, these two contributions to a ten-article global report invite us to understand airline carriers in terms of international competition, and the fatal outcome of carriers that do not adjust to this emerging new order. In "Empires of the Sky," he gives a broad overview of the many dimensions of this virtually unstoppable transition — from the possibility of multinational airlines, to protectionist and infrastructure barriers that will have to be overcome, to how to get flambe on a Swiss Air flight leaving Islamabad. In a wonderful example of political economy, "Wolf at the Gateway," he examines the privatized British Airways' struggle with the Tory government's market intrusions. Through the eyes of BA's management, we get a unique look at the recasting of Europe's airline marketplace, and the airline's efforts to circumvent the politics that are distorting the natural flow of this process.

10. **Rappaport, Andrew S. and Halevi, Shmuel.** *Harvard Business Review.* "The Computerless Computer Company," 7/8-91. Of all the "big think" pieces on the future of the computer industry that we read in 1991, this was the most significant. Indeed, George Gilder hailed this issue as "the most important HBR published in the last decade. . .Rappaport and Halevi have fathomed the essence of an economic era." These two consultants turn some of the industry's most cherished notions about strategic planning on their head, and tell us that by the year 2000 the most successful computer companies will buy computers rather than build them: "The strategic goal of U.S. companies should not be to build computers. It should be to create persistent value in computing. Increasingly, computers themselves are marginal to the creation of value in computing." The success of Microsoft is used throughout the analysis to exemplify the profitability of this concept. "A computer company is the primary source of computing for its customers. Thus Microsoft, the world's leading developer of systems software for personal computers, is not a "software" company. Microsoft is a computer company. . . .Microsoft thrives because it bridges the gap between power and utility, and it does so in a way that both maintains its proprietary position and leverages rather than replicates the massive capital investments made by less influential hardware companies." The concept is stunning in its simplicity and we cheer the authors for it.

Commentary

1. **Baker, Russell.** *The New York Times.* "Scipio, to Hannibal," 6-25. At the height of the flap over multiculturalism, Baker put it all in perspective for us with his trademark humor. Baker begins with a familial incident over a crossword puzzle, where he expounds on Scipio Africanus, the Second Punic War and Hannibal. "I paid for that knowledge in agonies of mental toil in high school Latin while reading Livy's history of Rome. What a pleasure it was, having it finally pay off like this. . ..This family episode makes me laugh at the latest intellectuals' flareup about how history should be taught in New York schools. Should the approach be 'multicultural'? 'Monogendered'? 'Ethnodynamic'? 'Sexocentrifical'? 'Euromaniacal'? 'Nonsensidaisical'? Take your stand and beg for mercy. It's this year's big fun slanging match for intellectuals, probably because it offers such rich opportunity for venting your most beastly animosities on race, sex and ethnic issues while sounding so utterly, so absolutely, so unbelievably civilized." Baker then applies his own solution: "The question is not what bias should be applied when teaching history, but why our schools seem incapable of teaching any history, biased or otherwise. As now taught, history is neither multicultural or unicultural; it is nocultural. At a time when any teaching of it would be a step forward, we ought to be able to agree that while either the multicultural or the unicultural stuff would be splendid, in the meantime we could use some anycultural history."

2. **Crovitz, Gordon.** *The Wall Street Journal.* "Congress May Regret Trying to Bork Justice Thomas," 10-16. The sheer volume of amateurish blather written about the Hill-Thomas hearings by professional journalists helped make 1991 a non-vintage year by *MediaGuide* standards. Crovitz, a lawyer trained in the Clarence Darrow tradition, now turned journalist, stood like a lighthouse in a midnight hurricane during these events. His "Rule of Law" column lays out a series of facts and assertions that will help historians understand why the American people overwhelmingly sided with Justice Thomas, despite the vast weight of press reportage on Ms. Hill's side, especially by the distaff press. Crovitz opens by clearing away the political slime with a powerful summation of what has been going on: "The ghost of King Henry VIII must have had a chuckle watching the latest use of the anti-legal process he invented to skewer political opponents, the Bill of Attainder. The Senate Judiciary Committee effectively issued a Bill of Attainder against Clarence Thomas by charging him with a crime while denying him any criminal procedure to disprove the claim. The Constitution prohibits legislators from using this ploy to brand a political opponent a criminal, but what's a constitutional right to the senators who were desperate to block Justice Clarence Thomas?" He goes on to detail the careful planning that went into this singular case of character assassination, "a case study of how Washington has become a place where privacy rights and FBI confidentiality mean little."

3. **Grenier, Richard.** *The Washington Times.* "Indian Love Call," *Commentary* 3-91. No American journalist is as encyclopedic in his broad knowledge of history, religion, culture and art as Grenier, who is constantly alert to Hollywood's use of poetic license to advance a leftist political agenda. In this lengthy essay, he treats us to a semi-review of Kevin Costner's "Dances With Wolves," a richly informative account of the way Indians *really* lived during the "Dances" time period, using eyewitness accounts and diaries to buttress his points that the Sioux simply did not live as politically correctly as Costner has portrayed. The author of *Capturing the Culture: Film, Art, and Politics* will not stand for revisionism in any form, and "Dances With Wolves" is no exception. "Costner, naturally, is at great pains to demonstrate that his Buffalo Indians were not inferior to the invading white man, but in fact, were really much superior at doing things that really count. To do so, he simply omits everything from period Indian life that modern film audiences would find repugnant, and lays heavy stress on what he considers its strong point: that Indians, as opposed to the white brutes who replaced them, lived in harmony with nature and were environmentally responsible." Grenier then details some of the Sioux customs omitted or downplayed in the film, such as scalping, self-mutilation as religious rite, polygamy, and torture of prisoners. "Thousands and thousands of accounts, some from

observers quite well-disposed toward them, describe the celebrated Plains tribes as being absolutely merciless, raiding and scalping and murdering and torturing captives for entertainment — at war with their fellow Indians far more than with whites." We loved the movie, but we appreciate Grenier's truths, too.

4. Kinsley, Michael. *The New Republic.* "Liar or Boob?" 10-21. When Robert Bork was denied a Supreme Court seat a few years earlier, the U.S. journalist who counted most in that denial was Anthony Lewis of *The New York Times,* whom the *MediaGuide* congratulated for his razor-sharp, masterful indictments. This year, the single most telling argument against the Clarence Thomas nomination came in this Kinsley column, which sharply challenges the credulity of Thomas, a man with long-held professional positions and ambitions in government and in law, on his assertion that he did not give "serious thought" to the *Roe v. Wade* decision. Many others wrote sappy denunciations of the judge on this point of his testimony, but the lawyer-like, rigorous Kinsley produced this singular commentary that focuses on the debasement of the process, rather than the politics, when discussing Thomas's position on the abortion decision. Clearly, Judge Thomas had permitted his White House "handlers" to program his testimony to a cardboard cutout, the weakness Kinsley exploited: "In his confirmation hearing, Thomas testified under oath that he had never discussed *Roe v. Wade* and had no opinion about it. This was not an offhand comment. Everyone knew in advance that *Roe* was the issue most on senators' minds. Thomas made the remark with malice aforethought (in the legal sense of premeditated design, not evil intent). There are only two possibilities. Either he was lying or he was telling the truth." Kinsley goes on to "consider each possibility impartially." The net effect of this column, we suspect, whether or not Clarence Thomas ever saw it, would cause him to dispatch his White House handlers, speak from his heart, and win confirmation. One might say he owes Kinsley a measure of thanks.

5. Krauthammer, Charles. *Time.* "Must America Slay All the Dragons?" 3-4. At precisely the right moment, when most of us were wondering of America's responsibilities in the new world order, Krauthammer did what he does best: He sorts it all out. Not that he ended all discussion of when America's youth will henceforth be sent off to do battle with another perceived injustice, somewhere in the world. This *Time* essay was simply the best we saw on the reasonable tensions between internationalism and isolationism, and how to think of them in several dimensions that embrace all legitimate concerns. He begins by examining the "false everywhere-nowhere dichotomy [that] is the moral pillar of American isolationism," i.e., that if it is right to spend blood and treasure to deal with dictator X, we must do the same and confront dictator Y, or no neither. "The question is posed constantly. Only the place names change. . ..The answer is breathtakingly simple. Why are American exertions on behalf of the oppressed selective? National interest," dismissing the notion that morality is the overriding consideration. If it was, the United States would "spend itself dry righting every wrong in the world." A clearer way to look at it is that "Every intervention requires a just cause. That doesn't mean that every just cause requires intervention." He then reaches us with a line remarkable for its wisdom and simplicity: "Life presents us with a hierarchy of evils," and common sense tells us we can only deal with them according to a schedule: "Being finite, we are forced to assign them priorities and even, if necessary, tolerate some lesser evil to fight the greater. Was it wrong to have blinked at the enormities of Stalin for the four years that he was needed in the war against Hitler?" He thus allows that "After the gulf crisis, we must be equally nimble in reordering our priorities. We must immediately turn to a vigorous advocacy of Baltic independence. But it would be irresponsible to jeopardize the war effort by doing so during the crisis. War is no time for moral luxuries. The first task of war is winning it. We cannot slay all the dragons at once. There is no dishonor in slaying them one at a time." An extraordinary exercise!

6. Kristol, Irving. *The Wall Street Journal.* "The G.O.P. Message: A State of Disunion," 1-27. The reason we associate grey beards with wisdom is that one expects life is the best teacher, and a long life teaches better than a short one. Too many pundits refuse to learn, assuming that they know it all by the time they have turned forty. Kristol remains clean shaven, but now in his 70s, the Godfather of U.S. neo-conservatism still astonishes and delights us with fresh insight and vision that is the hallmark of an open mind. In this January essay, written at the height of the Persian Gulf War, with President Bush's popularity soaring along with the sense of national pride and mission, Kristol surprises us with this cup of cold water, reminding us that "every war ends, and one can reasonably assume the end will have come before the next presidential election. Domestic issues will remain, and our two political parties will be positioning themselves to address them. Or trying to, anyway, for both parties are in considerable disarray. Both lack a credible agenda to propose to the electorate." His assessment of President Bush's weakness on domestic issues, which would drag his popularity down exactly as Kristol foresaw, rests on the schism within the GOP wrought by the President in 1990: "The public break with his party came with Mr. Bush's abandonment of his commitment to 'no new taxes,' and his acceptance of a budget that was, in effect, written by Congressional Democrats." No less important, Kristol asserts, is Bush's attachment to his own pollsters. "The White House, focusing on the 1992 election, is more and more concerned with the President's popularity. . . .Controversy is something the White House wants to avoid. Its goal is to have Mr. Bush re-elected in 1992 as the 'consensus' president," an impossible goal without leaving the GOP behind, he warns. The essay, which seemed so-so in January, was awesome when read again in December.

7. **Mortimer, Edward.** *Financial Times.* "Reality v Rhetoric in a New World Order," 12-28-90. A genuinely brilliant geopolitical thinker, Mortimer does not flinch at addressing the most difficult, complex topics in his regular *FT* essays, written in London. In this masterful effort, written on the eve of the new year and fighting in the Gulf War, Mortimer contemplates yet another American President sending "yet another massive US expeditionary force across the Atlantic to redress the balance of the old world." Mortimer's ruminations take in much of Twentieth Century political impulses from the New World, including those of Woodrow Wilson and FDR, as he wonders about the shape of a "New World Order." The motivation of this President, he suggests in a marvelous paragraph, may partly be in response "to a strong and continuous strand in American culture: the belief that a supreme sacrifice is worth making only for the sake of a supreme good, and that the projection of American power overseas can be justified only if the effect is to spread worldwide the benefits of American democracy." Paired with the Krauthammer essay cited above, from Washington, this London perspective captures all the dimensions of what it will take to make a New World Order realistic: "If it is to have any chance of success at all, [it] will have to be based on a broader and more genuine sharing of both power and responsibility." As for the Soviet Union, Mortimer simply tosses it off: "It may cease to exist."

8. **Raspberry, William.** Washington Post Writers Group. "Race-based Advantage Is a Detour," *Los Angeles Times* 3-17. Like Irving Kristol, Raspberry continues to develop with age as a pundit who is constantly challenging *his own* assumptions by testing them against the reality of fact. He's become the most important media commentator with an African-American perspective, and this daring foray onto the frontier of race relations is a fine example of why this is so. The year 1991 will be remembered, we think, as a watershed year for black Americans, most exemplified by the changing of the guard at the Supreme Court, to Clarence Thomas from Thurgood Marshall. On the broader canvas, though, was the shifting agenda of younger, more confident black leadership, straining against the Old Guard notion that black advance requires a race-based advantage. Raspberry discusses a transition, using a metaphor of a "product line" to be sold to White Americans: "My own view is not that white people have changed but that our goals have been transformed. We still say we want to be judged by the 'content of our character,' but our agenda is based on the color of our skin." He suggests "another product line based on the ideals we hold in common; equal opportunity, equitably enforced; programs to heal the crippling effects of past discrimination," etc. Raspberry argues the "old model, designed to appeal to white guilt, no longer is selling." He thinks a new model will sell, its chief marketing points being its emphasis on solutions and unambiguous fairness. A watershed idea for Raspberry and an important milestone for race relations in America.

9. **Safire, William.** *The New York Times.* "In Deep Sununu," 6-20, "Sununu Blames the Jews," 6-27, & "B.C.C.I. and Sununu," 10-28. When Safire gets a political target in his crosshairs, he can be merciless, even savage, but always factual and fair. This year he has made a spectator sport of dissecting Bush administration policy and personnel, zeroing in on the hapless chief of staff, hammering at him until he could stand no more. The White House was rocked with "In Deep Sununu," 6-20, in which Safire sent the signal that conservatives are viewing the connection of the chief of staff to their agenda as a serious liability: "John Sununu should be dumped because he lacks a Presidential aide's most essential attribute: political judgement." When Sununu shot back through *The Wall Street Journal* and Evans & Novak, Safire returns fire with "Sununu Blames the Jews," 6-27. Safire, as usual, has the last word: "Thus does John Sununu depart, creating a supernova of bigoted resentment to make himself a household name at his President's expense. Spiro Agnew is alive and well and working near the Oval Office." Continuing the barrage, Safire reveals possible links between "B.C.C.I. and Sununu," 10-28, via the connection between Ed Rogers, Sununu's "right-hand man, political protege and personal press agent," and Sheik Kamal Adham, the former chief of Saudi intelligence accused of being the BCCI's front man, and the $25,000 a month fee being paid to Rogers for "legal expertise as well as 'duties that could border on political.' " Sununu, after the pounding given him by Safire, and the investigations of Charles Babcock and Ann Devroy, resigned late in the year.

10. **Williams, Juan.** The Washington Post. "Open Season on Clarence Thomas." 10-10. A first rate political journalist with a liberal bent, Williams had gotten to know Clarence Thomas while covering the Reagan White House in the 1980s, and had profiled him for the *Post.* As Williams is black, the Beltway's liberal establishment simply assumed he would happily join their lynch mob and began calling him after the nomination asking for dirt on the judge. Instead, Williams wrote this incredible, sulfuric column that stunned the Capital, much as David Broder's 1969 "The Breaking of a President" column, which laced into the "liberal" community for consciously trying to destroy Richard Nixon. Here is the heart of Williams's indictment: "The desperate search for ammunition to shoot down Thomas has turned the 102 days since President Bush nominated him for a seat on the Supreme Court into a liberal's nightmare. Here is indiscriminate, mean-spirited mudslinging supported by the so-called champions of fairness; liberal politicians, unions, civil rights groups and women's organizations. They have been mindlessly led into mob action against one man by the Leadership Conference on Civil Rights. Moderate and liberal senators, operating in the proud tradition of men such as Hubert Humphrey and Robert Kennedy, have allowed themselves to become sponsors of smear tactics that have historically been associated with the gutter politics of a Lee Atwater or crazed right-wing self-promoters like Sen. Joe McCarthy." For just a moment, the mob stopped to glare at Williams, and take down his name. So did we.

Foreign Dispatch

1. **Buchan, David.** *Financial Times.* "A Heath Robinson Design for Europe," 12-12. We were counting on Buchan, our correspondent of choice on the European Community, to provide the most authoritative coverage of the European Union agreement, which the EC had been working toward all year. Buchan did not disappoint, and he offers us a breathtaking analysis of what was, and was not, agreed upon "in the small hours of a cold Maastricht morning," and what it all portends for Europe through the rest of the decade. Deftly characterizing the agreement as "a strange, heterogeneous creature," whose "only solid achievement" is the establishment of procedures to bring about economic and currency union by 1-1-99, the ever-alert Buchan quickly zeroes in on the key issue which European political leaders and EC officials wrestled with right up to the eleventh hour — the question of sovereignty. Would matters such as immigration policy and European defense be handled through inter-government mechanisms or through Community institutions, such as the European Parliament? In his clear, crisp style, Buchan cuts to the heart, revealing that while there was some movement toward integration, such key issues

as security and social policy will remain outside "standard community rules." Buchan then gets us ahead of the curve, disclosing that, in consequence, hybrids, such as a "European Social Community," are being created in an attempt to effect a compromise between Great Britain, intent on protecting its sovereignty, and EC officials such as President Jacques Delors, concerned over the movement of decision-making away from the Community. Thus, "While it may be the biggest step in Community integration in 34 years, the Maastricht treaty will take some selling, even to the most hardened of European enthusiasts." We look forward to reading Buchan's coverage of this sales job.

2. **Crossette, Barbara.** *The New York Times.* "Rajiv Gandhi Is Assassinated in Bombing at Campaign Stop; India Puts Off Rest of Voting," and "A Blast, and Then the Wailing Started," 5-22. It was a year of tumult for India, as that vast country tried to cope with ethnic violence and the legacy of Nehru socialism. The one subcontinent event that made headlines around the world, though, was the assassination of former Prime Minister Rajiv Gandhi. No account of this tragic event was more thorough than these two reports by Crossette, which, combined, are among the finest on-the-scene coverage of a breaking international story that we saw all year. The outgoing New Delhi *NYT* bureau chief accompanied the Indian political leader on what turned out to be his final campaign trip, scoring, with Neena Gopal of *The Gulf News* of Dubai, his last interview as he literally rode to his death in a bulletproof Indian-made Ambassador car, garlanded by well-wisher's flowers. An expert, non-sentimental recounting of Gandhi's troubled political career, "Gandhi Is Assassinated," is a harrowing eye-witness account of the assassination: "This reporter, who was about 10 yards behind Mr. Gandhi, saw only the flash of the blast and the circle of bodies that fanned out from its epicenter." "A Blast. . ." features Gandhi's last interview, a tantalizing glimpse of what might have been had he lived. The son of the late Indira Gandhi speaks of his hopes for making the system more efficient and easing regional and religious tensions, while addressing concerns that some "outside power" might try to cripple India's ascent to regional superpower status by targeting Indian leaders. He also discusses his fatalistic attitude about plunging into crowds, despite the violent nature of Indian politics. " 'I campaigned this way before I was Prime Minister,' he said. 'I'm not Prime Minister now so I'm campaigning this way again.' "

3. **Dempsey, Judy.** *Financial Times.* "In Yugoslavia, the Centre Cannot Hold," 3-18; "Balkan End-Game," 6-27; and "The Awful Shape of Things to Come," 8-6. While we were generally impressed by the coverage of Yugoslavia we saw in the daily press, it was the *FT*'s Judy Dempsey who clearly had the edge on that story. She consistently provides multidimensional coverage of events without losing us in the details. These three reports, each of which appeared at a critical juncture during the crisis, serve as the best picture of the nature of Yugoslavia's complex predicament. There is a singular acuity in these reports that elevate them beyond all other accounts. With "In Yugoslavia, the Centre Cannot Hold," 3-18, she is outstanding on the beginning of the crisis, sharp and clear on the dangerous game Serbian leader Slobodan Milosevic and the military are playing with the office of the presidency, which they hope to fill and then use to protect the communist center without provoking a civil war — "a task which will demand that rationality triumphs over emotionalism." As emotionalism inevitably begins to triumph over rationality, Dempsey, in "Balkan End-Game," 6-27, provides a highly-detailed, very readable account of the next steps for Yugoslavia's republics. We appreciate here the proper attention she pays to the way in which the political crisis is now feeding off an expanding economic malaise. In "The Awful Shape of Things to Come," 8-6, Dempsey comprehensively outlines Milosevic's apparent ambition to carve out a Greater Serbia, but assigns portions of blame for the fighting all around, observing that both Milosevic and Croatian leader Franjo Tudjman are using the crisis to divert attention from a dismal economy: "What is surprising is the way in which the population has tolerated the political ambitions of its leaders at the expense of concentrating on economic renewal."

4. **Fineman, Mark.** *Los Angeles Times.* "Iran Makes Trade Inroads in Soviet Asian Republics," 9-30. The world's "strategic black hole" is developing in Soviet central Asia. In the wake of the center's dissolution, what forces will emerge dominant from the swirling currents there looms as a key strategic question. Fineman, one of the profession's finest chroniclers of developments in the region, provides us with the best report on the new relationships beginning to materialize throughout that area. In this brief but information-laden report, Fineman presents a revealing intelligence briefing on "Iran's overall strategy of economic — and perhaps religious — conquest" by taking advantage of the "fertile ground for a renaissance of Islamic fundamentalism" and filling the trade vacuum created by the end of inter-republic trade. Iran's tactics, he reveals, are to flood the republics of Turkmenistan and Uzbekistan, not with mullahs, but with business representatives. With an unerring eye for the telling detail, Fineman reports on how the Iranians are offering "just a bit of what was labeled 'Islamic propaganda' " along with more secular items such as fruit, toilets, and anti-freeze at trade fairs, in an effort to not only establish cultural links but also tap "into the new nation's strategic reserves of gold and natural gas." Already, reports Fineman, two trade fairs have resulted in "new contracts between Iran and the republics," and an agreement to build a railroad has been concluded. The railroad, Fineman notes, will link Iran to western China. " 'Having conquered the market and established strong relations with Turkmenistan, it will open up all the doors for us to conquer China,' [Iranian official Shahrokh Modarres] said. 'So you see, as these very big changes are happening around us, we are already here.' "

5. **Hays, Laurie.** *The Wall Street Journal.* "Top Russian Banker Ridicules Monday's Ruble Devaluation," 12-6. As Russia moved toward its version of Poland's "shock therapy" of "free market" prices for January 1, 1992, the Western press acted as if all of Moscow was behind the move. For this reason, "Top Russian Banker. . ." stands out, both for resourcefulness and for the valuable glimpse it provides of the thinking at the very top of Boris Yeltsin's economic team at a crucial moment in Russian history. As Yeltsin's implementation of economic "shock therapy" was being applauded by some observers, as evidence that the former Sverdlovsk party leader was finally taking command of the situation, Hays, in an inspired move, scores an interview with Georgy Matykhin, chairman of the Board of the Central Bank of Russia. Matykhin tells her, and through her, the world at large, that the recent devaluation of the ruble is "something ridiculous" and that it is " 'destroying' the country because foreigners are swooping in and buying up materials on the commodity exchanges 'for nothing,' " citing as an example purchase of "a rocket plant for $100 practically." Insisting on maintaining the three-tier system of "official," "commercial," and "tourist," exchange rates, Matykhin expresses surprise when Hays informs him of Deputy Prime Minister Yegor Gaidar's statement that the three-tiered system would be abandoned to make the ruble convertible internally, affording readers a firsthand look at the "dissension and utter confusion in the Russian government," as the country lurches into winter. Matykhin discusses other topics as well, including his plans to bring Russia's banking system in line with the West and his opposition to the recent debt agreement between the G7 and the former republics. However, it is the insight into the critical issue of convertibility and a ruble float — which Matykhin likens to "an atomic bomb" in its powers of destruction — that makes this article such a superior report.

6. **Keller, Bill.** *The New York Times.* "From Resistance of the Few to Revolt of the Masses," 9-15. No international story was more studied, probed, analyzed and discussed than the Soviet Union dissolution, as that country and the Communist Party which led it for 75 years lurched into extinction. Paradoxically, though, the advent of democracy and *glasnost* seemed to make Russia even more mysterious, in many ways, to the Kremlinologists and Russian tea-leaf readers in the press. In this masterful "Week in Review" essay, Keller places the so-called "August Revolution" in perspective. Stepping outside the prevailing conventional appraisal, Keller provides the definitive assessment of the event. He brilliantly documents how, just like the Bolshevik Revolution of 1917, the "August Revolution" is already taking on a mythology of its own. Keller, of course, does not see Boris Yeltsin and his followers as the Bolsheviks *redux.* He

points out that, unlike Lenin's power grab, Yeltsin's legitimacy derives from having won an election, not from having stood on top of an armored vehicle. "One reason the August upheaval has come in for much embellishment," he continues, "is that the victors hope to repair the morale damaged by the explosion of the old myths." In this essay, the wisest commentary we saw on the failed coup attempt and immediate aftermath, Keller provides a salutary reminder that "In reality, August 1991 was less a revolution than a culmination." Even more important, in his precise, discriminating way, he warns that in Russia, more than in most societies, ruling myths tend to take on lives of their own, often controlling their creators. Keller does not know if "the August Revolution [will] be mythologized to suit a new orthodoxy that goes by the name of democracy," it being far too early to tell. But in this essay, we learned what to watch for in order to know in which direction Yeltsin intended to take the country he assumed control of in August 1991.

7. **Randal, Jonathan C.** *The Washington Post.* "Kurds' Spring of Hope Collapses Amid Feelings of Betrayal," 4-3. Like William Safire of the *NYT,* we also believe that Randal's coverage of the plight of the Kurds deserves to be singled out. It was the failed Kurdish uprising which cut through the post-war euphoria like a Scud missile in the night and served notice that Saddam Hussein was unlikely to go quietly into retirement as many were predicting. Randal provided superlative coverage of the Kurdish rebellion from its promising start, inside Iraq, immediately after Saddam's defeat in Kuwait, to its tragic ending in the hills of Turkey. "Kurd's Spring of Hope. . ." is his most outstanding dispatch. Randal captures poignantly the drama of refugees on the move under fire — "shoeless grandmothers, retired civil servants still in ties and business suits, mothers with babes in arm and an old man clutching his heart medicine" — and their bitterness toward President Bush and the United States. While sympathizing with their plight, Randal goes beyond mere pathos to report on how the Kurdish people were let down by their own leaders as much as by Washington and the anti-Saddam coalition. "Supremely overconfident for far longer than warranted by the facts on the ground," Randal reports, Kurdish commanders "at times seemed out of synch" and "looked on rocket-firing helicopter gunships as 'mere terror weapons' against civilians." Most important, Kurdish leaders such as Massoud Barzani forgot "the lessons of the past," and Saddam Hussein's history of ruthlessly crushing challenges to his rule. By his deft rendition of this latest tragic chapter in the star-crossed history of the Kurds, Randal has provided a revealing case study on the ways of the world in the "New World Order."

8. **Remnick, David.** *The Washington Post.* "The Hard-Liners' Bad Boy Challenges Gorbachev," 2-8. When former Soviet Foreign Minister Eduard Shevardnadze resigned in late 1990, he singled out "two mere colonels" as representing the forces of opposition to policies of reform, Nikolai Petrushenko and Viktor Alksnis. Just when we were searching far and wide for insight into the motivations of Russian hardliners, Remnick presents a three-dimensional profile of "the black colonel," giving us the full measure of the man, his beliefs, and the strategic views of a key faction within the hardline opposition. In an interview, Alksnis, the leader of the Soyuz faction in the Soviet parliament, tells Remnick point-blank that "Gorbachev must dissolve the Supreme Soviet and the parliaments of the 15 republics, 'by force if necessary,' and establish a coalition National Salvation Committee to rule the country." Remnick, one of the sharpest correspondents chronicling the fortunes of both reformers and hardliners all year, adroitly observes that Alksnis is, "in a perverse sense, a product of Gorbachev's early reforms," for whom "order, not ideology, is his obsession." Remnick reveals Alksnis's shadowy relationship with such officials as KGB Chairman Vladimir Kryuchkov, Defense Minister Dmitri Yazov and Interior Minister Boris Pugo, all of whom participated in the August coup attempt, an event which Alksnis survived. Remaining in the Soviet parliament, he defended the preservation of the center until the very end, speaking out against the Commonwealth agreement before empty parliament seats. That image may be of a marginal hardliner whom time has passed by, but, as Remnick details, Alksnis has the political astuteness which marks him as a player to be reckoned with down the road: " 'I have no lust for power,' Alksnis said. 'But Gorbachev's time is passing. He no longer has a choice. Either he takes command or he heads to the sideline. There is no time left to wait.' "

9. **Sanger, David E.** *The New York Times.* "A New Car for Malaysia, New Influence for Japan," 3-6. Japan's role in the new world order was a heavily debated subject this year, and much of what we read tended to generate more heat than light on the subject. In "A New Car for Malaysia. . .," Sanger, one of the brighter stars among the constellation of U.S. correspondents in Tokyo, provides a thoroughly objective, thoroughly fascinating case study of how Japan "has gradually transformed itself into the single most important element in [Southeast Asia's] economy," creating a *de facto* regional trading block. Beginning the story with Malaysian Prime Minister Mahathir Mohamad's efforts to spur industrialization of his country, Sanger masterfully recounts how a mixture of patience, diplomacy, and expertise enabled Mitsubishi Corporation to take over the development of Malaysia's would-be national car, the Proton Saga. The story of the Proton Saga includes elements of Malaysian ethnic politics, car design, manufacturing know-how and cultural shock. With professional artistry, Sanger skillfully weaves each of these elements together in a textbook example of superb political economy reportage. We come away from "A New Car. . ." realizing that Japan's regional success is not a case of economic imperialism but rather the result of national governments acting in their own best interests; if the U.S. is feeling shut out, then it has no one to blame but itself. " 'These markets look small, so America decides they are not worth the trouble,' a senior executive of one of Japan's biggest trading houses said. 'That's how you missed Thailand. And 10 years from now, there will be more Thailands.' " Sanger's dispatch gets us ahead of the curve on the story of Asia, not just for 1991 but for the 1990s.

10. **Sheehan, Neil and Sheehan, Susan.** *The New Yorker.* "In Vietnam," 11-18. Neil Sheehan began covering the U.S. involvement in Vietnam back in the early 1960s and was *The New York Times* reporter who obtained the Pentagon Papers, for which he won a Pulitzer Prize in 1972. It was with this impressive professional background that Sheehan returned to Vietnam along with his wife in 1989 to find a society struggling to cope with the legacy of the war and the legacy of the 10 years of economic mismanagement which followed the communist victory in 1975: "The period is seen in retrospect as a time of tyranny and waste, a precipitate attempt to create a visionary socialist state in defiance of reality, a folly that compounded the troubles inherited from the war and drove Vietnam into bankruptcy." Notably, the Sheehans find that "Even with the economic sanctions in effect, the Vietnamese have never said that their economic troubles were principally the fault of outsiders." "In Vietnam" is the story of the perseverance and self-reliance of the Vietnamese people. Sheehan documents how these traits, which enabled them to overcome the military might of France, China, and the U.S., are now being channeled into the program of *Doi Moi,* or renovation. During their travels, the Sheehans speak to former soldiers, ranging from North Vietnamese General Vo Nguyen Giap, the military amateur who engineered the communist victory, to Ly Tong Ba, one of the few South Vietnamese commanders not to cut and run in 1975. Through their stories, and others, the war is fought all over again, in all its tragic glory. In a land where history is such a physical presence, the Sheehans find there is no escape from the past. As U.S. political leaders claim that, with Desert Storm, America can finally put its military defeat in Southeast Asia behind it, the Sheehans explain in this report why the victors of that conflict will always remain "In Vietnam."

General Reporting

1. **Angier, Natalie.** *The New York Times.* "Pit Viper's Life: Bizarre, Gallant and Venomous," 10-15. Angier won a Pulitzer last year for Beat Reporting. Still, when we heard this "Science Times" snake story had been nominated for a 10 Best in general reporting by one of our readers, there was general hooting and snickering. One reading, though, persuaded us that Angier may be in a class by herself, not only fascinated with every detail in the world around her, but also able to fascinate us in the telling. It's something for a reporter to fill up a notebook with facts and figures, but to assemble them as lovingly as Angier does here, writing with fine, stylish confidence, is another matter. "After a few minutes of gingerly petting, the visceral response

subsides and the furious beauty of the creature shines forth. Its body is pure, pulsing muscle, its expression as proud as a prince's." As the Tuesday "Science Times" is becoming a staple for high school students in the *Times* circulation area, it strikes us that gifted writing of this kind can make an enormous contribution in itself to a generation of inquisitive youngsters. The pit viper, "a group that includes diamondback rattlesnakes, cottonmouths, copperheads, sidewinders, and other commonly loathed snakes. . . [are] the most intricate and admirable of all vertebrates, cold-blooded or otherwise." The most fascinating material of all involves the mating habits, of both male and female, which take up the middle third of the article. We quote the opening paragraph of the section, to offer a sense of wonder that Angier can impart: "Following prairie rattlesnakes in Wyoming, scientists have found that during mating season, males embark each morning from their den on a grueling, five-mile, round-trip search for willing females. And as they travel, they crawl in a line so straight it could have been penned by a draftsman. Should they have to deviate from their path to scoot around a pond or boulder, the vipers return to the straight and narrow as soon as possible." It gets even better!

2. **Barry, John.** *Newsweek.* "One Man, Many Tales," with Daniel Pedersen, et al., 11-4, and "Making of a Myth," with Tony Clifton, et al., 11-11. Although other publications made serious and successful attempts to debunk the "October surprise" conspiracy theory (*The New Republic,* "The Conspiracy That Wasn't," Steven Emerson and Jesse Furman, 11-18, and *Human Events,* "The Sick Tale of a 1980 Reagan-Iran Hostage Deal," Herbert Romerstein, 5-25), *Newsweek*'s effort, spearheaded by John Barry, stands out with its rich detail, readability, firsthand interviews and accounts with those who claim to have been involved, and pertinent detail from those records which would seem to disprove the conspiracy. In the first article, Barry sets out to determine the credibility of alleged witness Ari Ben-Menashe, "a leading evangelist for the cult of the October Surprise," and finds his story seriously contradictory in detail, Ben-Menashe insisting he met with then-Vice President George Bush and CIA Director William Casey in Paris, on dates that Secret Service records show would have been impossible. In the second article, Barry assesses flaws in the allegations as well as the strengths, concluding with a memorable piece of evidence: "On July 1, or July 2, 1980, Cyrus Hashemi met with a member of the Iranian leadership at the Ritz Hotel in Madrid. He was, apparently, acting as a go-between for the Carter administration, which was by then desperately seeking some new avenue to reopen the hostage negotiations. (That meeting NEWSWEEK sources say, led to a last-ditch diplomatic initiative by Secretary of State Edmund Muskie in September.) Within a week, according to Bani Sadr's diaries, Bani Sadr was told by the Ayatollah Khomeini's nephew that Iran had been approached by Reagan's men with a proposition on the hostages. The meeting site — Spain — was mentioned. Could it be that the ayatollah's nephew confused Reagan with Carter — and that the whole notion of the October Surprise stems from that simple mistake?"

3. **Broad, William J.** *The New York Times.* "There's a 'Doomsday Rock,' But When Will It Strike?" 6-18. As if we don't have enough to worry about, now we learn from Broad in this "Science Times" report that "Somewhere in space at this moment, hurtling towards the Earth at roughly 16 miles a second, is the doomsday rock." Because of the relentless journalistic efforts of the late Warren Brookes, we now worry less about "Global Warming" than we otherwise might, but Broad handles this "latest" threat to the planet, from errant asteroids with the sock of a billion Hiroshima bombs, with enough detachment to discourage sleepless nights. When it shows up, though, it can "severely disrupt life on Earth upon impact, lofting pulverized rock and dust that blocks most sunlight. Agriculture would virtually end, and civilization could wither and die, just as the dinosaurs and many other forms of life are thought to have been wiped out by a massive object from outer space 65 million years ago." We read of the near misses, and the burgeoning scientific field of asteroid detection and avoidance. Broad assures us that Big Thinkers such as Dr. Edward Teller, the principal developer of the hydrogen bomb, have contemplated the problem. Teller announced, on the occasion of his 81st birthday in 1989, that an asteroid shield would cost less than $100 million to build. A large, threatening asteroid could be observed while it was as much as a year away, Dr. Teller said, allowing a rocket to "send out something to meet it and give it a little sideways shove." As Broad is always accessible, we appreciate this intelligent appraisal.

4. **Dahl, Jonathan.** *The Wall Street Journal.* "Missing in America: A Lost Brother Sends One Man on a Search With Few Guideposts," 3-18. In this astonishing, front-page, personal odyssey, reporter Dahl shares his experience with the *Journal*'s readers on his lengthy search for his runaway brother, how he found him, and what happened. We realize the experience is not one that can be explained away by a theory of some "underclass," but can happen to any U.S. family. This is powerful stuff. We are gripped from the start by the intensity of the lead: "One tense day in August 1982, my brother vanished. Strung out on drugs, Jeff kicked in our parents' car door that afternoon — because they wouldn't give him $35. Years of drug treatment hadn't helped; he had smashed furniture, taken off with the family car and threatened to burn down the house. Afraid and frustrated, my father told his 27-year-old son never to come home. Jeff took Dad at his word. From that day on, we didn't hear from my brother or know if he was dead or alive. My mother was haunted by police photos of a local bank robber resembling Jeff. I imagined by brother, three years my senior, holed up in a crack house. But no one suffered more than our father, who agonized over evicting his son. Shortly before he died in May 1988, Dad made one final wish: Find Jeff." A mix of detective work and reporting follows, and this intimate examination of the drug and homeless subculture is both moving and compelling. The *MediaGuide* staff knew it was a sure-fire 10 Best the morning it appeared.

5. **D'Souza, Dinesh.** *The American Scholar.* "The New Segregation on Campus," Winter. Like the fabled elephant in the living room, which the family pretends not to notice, racial segregation on college campuses is a target hard to miss. Yet, if it were not for this sizzling essay by D'Souza and a similar tract on the March cover of *The Atlantic,* we would suspect the news media of terminal color blindness. Here we are, almost two generations after *Brown vs. Board of Education* and the court-ordered integration of black and white schools, and on the supposedly *most liberal college campuses* black and white students glare at each other across a multicultural divide. What's going on? D'Souza does not have all the answers, but this eye-opener and his book, *Illiberal Education,* would cause a maelstrom on college and university campuses, embarrassing an American intelligentsia that cannot explain the results of social engineering gone awry. He is especially vivid in examining the data on affirmative action admissions, separatist policies and a "Balkanized" environment that would be the cause of considerable debate over the atmosphere on campus, and the education available at the university level. D'Souza seems not anti-multicultural, but anti-separatist: "Somehow Martin Luther King, Jr.'s legacy is being undone by university activists and leaders who claim to be advancing the civil rights cause. But, alas, the only consequence of their policies seems to be the encouragement of bigotry and racial division, which do not bode well for America's future as a multicultural community." At last, some light on the subject.

6. **Lemann, Nicholas.** *The Atlantic.* "The Other Underclass," 12-91. Lemann, author of *The Promised Land,* persuades us with this lengthy essay that he is in a class by himself, the master of sociological journalism. The "other underclass" is not simply about the Puerto Rican subculture in the South Bronx, but about the entire Puerto Rican experience, including a sweeping short history of the island, as a quasi-nation commonwealth, and the impact its unusual relationship with the United States has had on its people, both here and there. We are first surprised to learn that statistically the Puerto Rican underclass of New York City sits beneath the black underclass: "In New York City, black median family income is substantially higher than Puerto Rican, and is rising more rapidly. The black home-ownership rate is more than double the Puerto Rican rate. Puerto Rican families are more than twice as likely as black families to be on welfare, and are about 50 percent more likely to be poor. In the mainland United States, Puerto Ricans have nothing like the black institutional network of colleges, churches and civil-rights organizations; there isn't a large cadre of visible Puerto Rican successes in every field; black politicians are more powerful than Puerto Rican politicians in all the cities with big Puerto Rican populations; and there is a feeling that blacks have America's attention, whereas Puerto Ricans, after a brief flurry of publicity back in *West Side Story* days, have become invisible." From this opening springboard, Lemann takes us on a soaring reconnaissance of the hows and the whys, and we understand a Puerto Rico we thought we knew. This is state of the art, required reading in Sociology 101.

7. **Morrocco, John D.** *Aviation Week & Space Technology.* "Air Strikes Spearhead Mideast War," 1-21. What Morrocco accomplishes in this trim introduction to *Aviation Week*'s Persian Gulf War coverage was the journalistic equivalent to Gen. H. Norman Schwarzkopf's masterminding of allied strategy. Morrocco provides a blueprint for the conduct of the war, without revealing specific strategies or giving away the game. "If sustained, the U.N. coalition's devastating, high-tech air blitz against Iraq may govern much of the war's course, even its outcome. This time, the U.S. Air Force may be able to prove its long-disputed contention that air power can be the decisive factor in waging war and winning it quickly. . .In narrow terms, the world's military establishments will learn a great deal about the efficacy of contemporary tactics and leading edge technology — stealth, night attack and electronic warfare systems, 'smart' and standoff weapons, and immensely complex software." He also predicts that, given the political climate and Bush's excessive rhetoric on Saddam Hussein, "if that means the U.S. military has to conquer Baghdad as well as free Kuwait City, even a devastating air war may not be enough." Though the coalition forces, as it turned out, did not march all the way to Baghdad, we're reminded of General Schwarzkopf's stated desire to do so, and we're impressed accordingly by Morrocco's military and strategic acumen, at least worth this 10 Best equivalent of a ticker tape parade.

8. **Politt, Katha.** *The Nation.* "Media Goes Wilding in Palm Beach," 6-24. Politt's essay on the naming of the alleged victim in the Palm Beach case involving the nephew of Senator Edward Kennedy was simply the best dissection we saw of the press issues and the moral implications. She assembles material from a wide variety of sources to present a damning indictment of the news media, pulling the piece into the reporting category from commentary. *The New York Times,* which lost control of the story in a kind of journalistic Chernobyl, is squarely nailed, particularly Soma Golden, Fox Butterfield, and William Safire, as is NBC's Michael Gartner, and *The Washington Post*'s Richard Cohen. How about this for a lead?: "I drink, I swear, I flirt, I tell dirty jokes. I have also, at various times, watched pornographic videos, had premarital sex, hitchhiked, and sunbathed topless in violation of local ordinances. . . There are other things, too, and if I should ever bring rape charges against a rich, famous, powerful politician's relative, *The New York Times* will probably tell you all about them — along with, perhaps, my name. Suitably adorned with anonymous quotes, these revelations will enable you, the public, to form your own opinion: Was I asking for trouble, or did I just make the whole thing up?" Confronting Cohen's argument that the press should not discriminate against accused males in favor of alleged victims (females), Politt sews it up: "Thus, by some mysterious alchemy, the media, which is perhaps the single biggest promoter of the sexist aura surrounding crimes of violence against women, can redeem itself by jettisoning the only policy it has that eases, rather than augments, the victim's anguish."

9. **Siegel, Barry.** *Los Angeles Times.* "Victims to Victors in Farming," 5-19, and "Family Farm Reaped Gains From Economic Crunch," 5-20. This two-part "Column One" series takes us through the saga of the Schmidt family of Lonsdale, Minnesota. A farming family since 1969, when they began farming "when they barely knew what dirt looked like," the Schmidts would lose their 1,572-acre farm in 1985, to buy more than half of it back from the Traveler's Insurance Co. four years later, at "a fire-sale price." We see very few updates from the heartland on the issue of farming that was so hot a few years back, and so Siegel's definitive examination, replete with pertinent detail and vivid in its recounting, was appreciated greatly. "Thinking back now, talking of the past or reading yellowing minutes of his family farm corporation's annual meetings, Bob Schmidt sometimes flinches. There were good reasons for the rapid expansion and heavy debt burden, he tells himself. But still, certain decisions haunt him." Siegel never loses our attention in this riveting story of loss, and success, providing appropriate context of the changing times which gave rise to the odyssey with a rich flavor that we don't often find. With a sharp eye for detail, Siegel weaves related information throughout about the shifting finances of the region that transforms what is merely a marvelous story into an educational experience. Great journalism from the *LAT.*

10. **Vartabedian, Ralph.** *Los Angeles Times.* "Political Moves in Defense," 3-6; "States Finding California Defense Firms Easy Targets," 3-8; and "Aerospace Moves: Hidden Costs Often Negate Gains," 3-9. On the surface, this three-part "Column One" series, "Losing Clout," looks like a local story, the retrenching of the defense industry in California. Like the preceding Siegel piece, though, Vartabedian delivers a terrific national story from a local angle, here instructing us on the Darwinian pressures on defense contractors in a post-Cold War era of shrinking defense budgets in Washington and the rising cost curve in upscale California. In part one, we find Hughes Aircraft Co. shifting work out of Southern California to remote Southern towns in the congressional districts of powerful members of Congress. "Congress, not the military, is often viewed as 'the customer,' " with Vartabedian also citing production of defense systems and weapons that the services don't want or can't use, an appalling twist on pork-barrelling in an era of huge budget deficits. The material is presented with cold detachment, Vartabedian eschewing the kind of tabloid hype usually associated with exposes of this sort, which makes it all the more effective. There are plenty of names, specifics, and hard-edged quotes. In parts two and three, he assembles marvelous examples of the cost disadvantages driving contractors to places like Orangeburg, S.C., Marietta, Ga., or Salt Lake City. This is "local" journalism at its best, Vartabedian giving the newspaper's readers a clear-eyed understanding of an important dynamic in the world around them.

Political Reporting

1. **Babcock, Charles, and Devroy, Ann.** *The Washington Post.* "Sununu: Frequent Flier on Military Aircraft," 4-21. This dispatch from the *Post*'s investigative reporter and White House correspondent, respectively, was the beginning of the end for Bush's chief of staff. One only had to read the first paragraphs of this scoop to suspect Sununu's days were numbered. "White House Chief of Staff John H. Sununu has used military jets for more than 60 trips over the past two years, in many instances for what appears to be personal or partisan political travel, including flights to Colorado ski resorts, to his home state of New Hampshire and to Republican fundraising events. A presidential spokesman said White House policy requires Sununu to use military planes in order to stay in 'immediate voice contact with the White House at all times.' Neither he nor Sununu's office would say whether any personal or political trips had been reimbursed at full commercial rates, as the policy also requires. That reimbursement rate, in any case, would have covered only a fraction of the flights' actual cost to the government — more than a half million dollars in Sununu's case." The team then gets the detail on the trips that outraged so many inside and outside the Beltway: 27 trips to New Hampshire or Boston; the 1989 sojourn to Vail, when the plane returned to Washington empty and then flew back to pick up Sununu's party three days later, for a total flying time of 16 hours; the Aspen trip which cost more than $30,000, with the commercial coach fare between Aspen and D.C. pegged at $1,076. A sidebar reprints the chief of staff's 1990 travel records which, although the reasons for travel are not listed, are damning in sheer numbers. Sununu, trapped and frustrated by the scrutiny of his behavior that followed, would eventually question Devroy's integrity at a White House press briefing, a judgment error that contributed to his fall.

2. **Cohen, Richard E.** *National Journal.* "The Judge's Trials," 7-13. Senate Majority Leader George Mitchell came out of 1989 seeming the dominant force in the Democratic party. Somehow, in the year and a half that followed, the bloom came off the rose so slowly that it wasn't noticed by anyone directly, until Cohen brought it to our attention, and we soon realized it was the buzz in Washington too. There's nothing remotely demeaning here, simply important subtleties in the mysterious chemistry of power shifts as they relate to policymaking inside the Beltway: "the glow has dimmed on Mitchell's initial aura of command over the Senate and influence within his party. The non-partisan aura and tightly controlled persistence that marked the successes of his first two years as Senate leader have been eroded by the often personal and intractable nature of Senate politics." Based in part on Cohen's book, *Washington at Work: Back*

Rooms and Clean Air, we get intimate detail on the workings of the Senate, and where Mitchell fits in this unique, ever-shifting universe. We also get a trim personality profile of the Senator: "A meticulous politician who prefers not to deal in ambiguities, Mitchell has had to struggle to manage the inherently unmanageable Senate. Despite his influential and public position, Mitchell does not easily reveal himself to outsiders. He rarely engages in public displays of anger or joy. More often, he expresses emotion by a wry grin, a glaring frown or a nervous shake in his leg." Cohen also insightfully notes that Mitchell's "rough sailing in 1991 mirrors the Democratic Party's problems. He has spent nearly as much time refereeing and taking sides in intra-party clashes on domestic and foreign policy issues as he has confronting Bush."

3. **Evans, Rowland, & Novak, Robert.** Creator's Syndicate. "Judicial Armageddon," *The Washington Post* 7-1. The journalistic output of the era's premiere political reporting team is so vast that it stands to reason at least one piece per year would stand out for a *MediaGuide* award, which is usually the case. This report is almost scary in its prescience, the boys seeing around corners in the coming Senate cataclysm over the confirmation of Justice Thurgood Marshall's yet unknown replacement. It opens thus: "Confidence in the White House that President Bush's first Supreme Court appointment, Justice David Souter, is the guaranteed fifth vote to overturn *Roe vs. Wade* promises a Senate confirmation of unprecedented bitterness." And, "Since the White House sees no need to compromise, the prospect is for an Armageddon in the Senate that will exceed in fervor even the Bork struggle." After warming us up with a few quotes from Democratic senators, they deliver the political dazzler of the year: "Thus, with Bush determined to name an anti-abortion conservative, any nominee may end up Borked. That definitely includes Appeals Court Judge Clarence Thomas of Washington, the leading black prospect to replace the court's only black member. Instead of his race protecting him, Bush strategists believe liberals would like to punish conservative Thomas for straying from their own 'politically correct' standard for black thinking. His meager judicial experience might also yield an American Bar Association appraisal branding him barely qualified."

4. **Germond, Jack W., & Witcover, Jules.** *National Journal.* "Tsongas Enters Democratic Vacuum," 3-23. The only two political writers to take seriously the presidential candidacy of former Massachusetts Sen. Paul Tsongas, Germond and Witcover boost him in this extremely savvy column that runs at the pinnacle of President Bush's national popularity. Where dimwit political hacks dismiss Tsongas because he doesn't *look* like a President, or *sound* like a President should [the conventional Democratic favorite is Arkansas Governor Clinton], these veterans see through that nonsense and size him up as just the fellow to break the tired Democratic logjam of business bashing and class warfare, "and start talking about how, together with the federal government, they can help American industry take on the new economic giants." They wisely note polls indicating 77.6% of the public believe the country will still be in recession in the coming year, which foresees President Bush's vulnerability at a moment his popularity is at a Gulf War 91%. "The same poll also found a strong belief that poverty, homelessness and health care will all worsen, and a willingness, by 2-1 or more, to pay higher taxes to cope with these problems. But getting voters to cast their ballots on such issues has been a trick that has eluded recent national Democratic candidates." Tsongas, they suggest, might do it, as he is even willing to support a capital gains tax cut, chiding fellow Democrats for myopia on the subject. At year's end, in a field of six, Tsongas topped the opinion polls in New Hampshire. Good work, boys.

5. **Grove, Lloyd.** *The Washington Post.* "The Israel Lobby, on the March," 6-13, and "The Men With the Muscle," 6-14. These richly detailed dispatches, outlining the inner workings of the American Israel Public Affairs Committee (AIPAC), hit hard by dispelling misconceptions about the lobbying group as much as recounting its history and revealing how it operates. "As the pro-Israel lobby anointed to speak for the major U.S. Jewish organizations — not, as some persist in believing, Israel's registered agent — AIPAC has prospered mightily since its birth 37 years ago. . .[Its] rapid expansion has forced it to cope with a host of competing constituencies — from liberal Democratic Jews to conservative Republican members of Congress, from

American doves to Israeli hard-liners." We get three-dimensional portraits of Tom Dine, the organization's executive director, and Steven Rosen, research director. "If Tom Dine is the bright face AIPAC shows to the world, the man who speaks around the country and testifies to Congress, Steven Rosen, is the lobby's back-room strategist — a planner, schemer and conspiracy theorist. (He would not permit his picture to be taken for this series.)" The ups and downs of AIPAC is a tangled, twisted story, but Grove easily guides us through the thickets and we come away with a superlative sense of the lobby's goals and methodology of a group "grappling with a potential 'New World Order' in which foregone conclusions are a thing of the past."

6. **Klein, Joe.** *New York.* "Ask Not? Don't Ask," 6-3. Klein scores with a superlative essay on the failure of liberalism, as embodied in the slow and steady erosion of the Kennedy legacy, with the life of Senator Edward M. Kennedy a metaphor for the current corrupt state of American liberalism. From Jack to Bobby to Ted, Klein finds there has been a definite change in the message of the liberals and the Democratic party. "[Ted] Kennedy is no dolt — but hardly the sparkling presence his brothers were — overwhelmed by life and fate, is almost enough to lure one toward compassion. Almost, but not quite: His irresponsibility has had consequences. The life of Mary Jo Kopechne, obviously, was one. But, more subtly, the values inherent in his careless way of life and feckless politics have been disastrous for American liberalism and the Democratic Party." Klein uses E. J. Dionne, Jr.'s *Why Americans Hate Politics* as a springboard to define the morality that is so important to the white, working-class voter, a group that has all but deserted the Democratic party, linking this to Kennedy and his effectiveness. "Kennedy's personal behavior not only betrays a not-so-subtle contempt for middle-class values like sobriety and fidelity, it makes it impossible for him to demand *any* reasonable standard of morality from the poor. . ..It's been argued that Kennedy merely followed a well-worn path, adapting his family's liberal politics and sexual flagrance to more modern times. It's been argued that his obsession with 'picking up the fallen standard'. . .led to his brain-dead reflexiveness in love and war. But Kennedy took the family topisms past several key boundaries. He divorced; he broke the law — and most important, he allowed liberalism's essential message to slip from sacrifice for the common good to *entitlement,* from 'Ask not what your country can do for you. . .' to 'You deserve a break today.' " An American tragedy.

7. **Kurtz, Howard.** *The Washington Post.* "Cuomo Sapiens: The Thinking Man's Non-Candidate," 11-14. Media analyst Kurtz skillfully plumbs the depths of the relationship between the press and New York Gov. Mario Cuomo, the perennial presidential contender-but-not-candidate, in this effervescent, diabolically clever treatment of the governor's terminal indecision on what Bush would call "the Presidential thing." "Call it Cuomology, the science of dissecting, analyzing and interpreting the musings, ramblings and offhand comments of the governor of New York. The press has Mario Cuomo right where it wants him, stretched out on the journalistic couch. Merely by saying he would think about running for president, Cuomo has unleashed a tidal wave of speculation that has all but washed away the six declared Democratic candidates. What sane reporter would rather write about Bill Clinton's welfare program when he or she can plumb the inner depths of Cuomo's psyche?" Kurtz, a former New York bureau chief for the *Post,* also surveys his fellow journalists to get additional input, quoting *New York*'s Joe Klein, who defines what sets the New York Governor apart from the pack: "Cuomo is a hell of an interesting human being. Most politicians speak in athletic or military metaphors; he speaks in religious metaphor. It ain't 'we're in the huddle, do I drive up the middle or throw long?' It's 'I'm Saul of Tarsus on the road to Damascus and I'm waiting for the lightning.' " A sparkling political feature, the best we saw on Mario all year, and there were jillions.

8. **Pines, Burton Yale.** *Policy Review.* "Bull Moose Revolt," Winter. While all the country and the world was likening George Bush to Winston Churchill before, during, and after the Persian Gulf War, Pines brings out the eerie parallels between the presidencies of George Herbert Walker Bush and William Howard Taft. Pines makes an original and convincing case that the

two are inextricably linked by the coincidences of history. "Like Taft, Bush was hand-picked by his predecessor. Both were seen as heirs of their predecessors' popular legacies and champions of their successful policies. Both thus took office with enormous reservoirs of good will. The story of Taft's subsequent self-destruction is one of the best known dramas of American history. He surprised, then disillusioned, and finally angered much of his party." Pines then provides a history lesson replete with detail on Taft's fall. While he notes "history, of course, runs no exact replays and too much must not be made of historical parallels," Pines senses and defines early, as did Irving Kristol, the deep-seated discontent that conservatives were feeling with Bush's stewardship, particularly on the tax issue, which he compares here to Taft's disavowal of Roosevelt's stand on tariffs, a comparable economic issue in the early part of the century. Warns Pines, ". . .there will almost surely be a revolt if George Bush and his most senior White House aides continue to repudiate the Reagan legacy as they have done in the last year. . .It can be prevented. But this requires Bush to return to the policies, principles and politics that gave Reagan and then Bush three landslide victories. If Bush and his advisors keep to their current course, they are asking for the one-term presidency of William Howard Bush."

9. **Tumulty, Karen.** *Los Angeles Times.* "Court Path Started in the Ashes," 7-7. Tumulty lost no time in getting to Pin Point, Ga., seemingly within hours after its favorite son, Clarence Thomas, was nominated to the Supreme Court by President Bush. This was, then, the first serious "roots" profile of the judge we saw and, as far as we know, it was not improved upon thereafter. Tumulty scours sources in Pin Point and elsewhere, then crafts a meticulously detailed and remarkably fresh portrait of Thomas, his early life and times. Her opening lines invite us into this superlative story: "The event that would set Clarence Thomas on the extraordinary personal climb that has brought him within one step of the nation's highest court was a freak accident: In the mid-1950s, his toddler brother, Myers, and a cousin set fire to their small wooden house and burned it to the ground. In those ashes died the dismal pattern of life that had awaited 6-year-old Clarence here in Pin Point — a world far removed from the Ozzie and Harriet America of that era. . . Until that fire, Leola Thomas — abandoned by her husband when she was pregnant with Myers, her third child — had been able to get by on her wages, earned by picking the meat from crabs for a nickel a pound at a factory within shouting distance from her children. Suddenly, however, the family was no longer merely poor; it was destitute. Struggle though she did, Leola Thomas was eventually forced to send her two sons to live with her parents." The rest, as they say, is history. "Under the stern eye of his grandfather, young Clarence began to develop the drive and the personal values that today mark his view of life and the law. He thrived under the Roman Catholic nuns of his all-black school, rejected many of their values when he reached college in the turbulent 1960s and found them again when he encountered the writings of leading black conservative Thomas Sowell." It's all there.

10. **Whalen, Bill.** *Insight.* "'92 Race Gets Wilder," 10-14. Whalen's political acumen is evident in this smart, timely assessment of Virginia Gov. L. Douglas Wilder's presidential candidacy, placed here in the context of Democratic racial politics. Much of the political press corps seemed baffled by the cross currents in the black community, a younger generation identifying with growth dynamics, not the welfare plantation, but Whalen was watching and understood. He notes the conventional appraisals of the tensions between Wilder and Jesse Jackson, but refreshingly, Whalen views this in wider parameters than merely Wilder vs. Jackson. "Within the black community, however, there is no doubt that the Wilder candidacy will present a further challenge to the political views of the black establishment. It could turn into a replay of the hearing for Supreme Court nominee Clarence Thomas, in which Thomas, a black judge who served in the Reagan administration, was castigated by civil rights groups for his stand against racial quotas." A quote from conservative black columnist Walter E. Williams ties the material together beautifully: "The Thomas nomination, and perhaps Doug Wilder running, will bring blacks out of the closet who have had long-standing reservations against what the Democratic Party is doing and what black politicians have been doing for a number of years." *The New York Times* could trade six of its political writers for Whalen and still get a bargain.

AN OVERVIEW
OF THE
CANADIAN PRESS

Major Stories

International and Internal Conflicts

As might be expected, the Gulf War dominated Canadian politics in the first two months of 1991, as it did throughout the world. But Brian Mulroney led a nation into war that was more divided than any other over participation in the anti-Iraq coalition. As in the United States, a vigorous parliamentary debate immediately preceded Canada's entry into the conflict. Both opposition parties — the Liberals and the socialist New Democratic Party — were resisting Canada's military participation. But, unlike the United States, there was no coming together, no "rally 'round the flag" effect, once the decision to go to war had been made. While declaring their support for the troops in the Gulf, the opposition made it clear they did not agree with the policy that put them there in the first place. It is hard to understand this hairsplitting distinction.

The debate over the Gulf War played into existing themes in Canadian politics. Ever since Mulroney concluded the Free Trade Agreement with the United States, his opponents have accused him of selling out Canadian independence to the United States. His rush to join the military operations in the Gulf provided more fodder for these critics. Over and over again, political opponents and commentators asserted that there was no vital Canadian interest at stake in the Gulf, and that Mulroney was only going to war because George Bush was telling him to do so.

It was also said that Canada's participation in the war jeopardized its reputation as "peacemaker," an image carefully nurtured by its participation in a number of peace-keeping forces. In a feature in the *Montreal Gazette,* 3-2, foreign affairs analyst Gwynne Dyer took issue with the notion that the participants in Operation Desert Storm violated the spirit of the U.N. Charter, arguing that Canada's image as "peacemaker" remains in its "upholding the rule of law." He wrote, "The truth is that the UN was not created by the peace movement, but by statesmen and soldiers who were the survivors of history's most terrible war. In order to deal with the Saddam Husseins of this world — in a world of 160 sovereign states there are bound to be a few — the UN needed the ultimate right to uphold international law. So they wrote that into the Charter. Everybody accepts the need in our domestic society for a police force that is authorized, in specific circumstances, to use deadly force to uphold the rule of law. The international world is far less law-abiding, so why do so many people have trouble with a UN that uses force?"

One legacy of the Gulf War for the Mulroney government was the so-called Mashat affair. The former Iraqi ambassador to the United States was expelled with the rest of his country's delegation at the outset of the war on January 16th. But instead of heading home, like the rest of the diplomats, Mashat ended up in Vienna, where he applied for landed-immigrant status in Canada. His case was advanced to the Canadian bureaucracy by John Godfrey, who was then the editor of *The Financial Post,* and Allan Gotlieb, a former Canadian ambassador to the United States. Once Mashat was in the country, Godfrey got an exclusive interview, and devoted one of his regular columns to arguing in favor of Mashat's admission. Federal cabinet ministers, and most everyone else, did not agree that Mashat would make a welcome contribution to Canada, portraying Mashat's entry as a mistake. But they refused to accept any personal responsibility. Instead they tried to pass the blame onto subordinates in the civil service, who they accused both of exceeding their authority in permitting Mashat to enter Canada, and of failing to pass information about the case up to their political superiors. A Parliamentary inquiry failed to clear the air, but, quite naturally, the press and the public were skeptical about claims that the ministers involved knew nothing.

In leading a deeply divided nation into war, Brian Mulroney was unable to capitalize on Canada's participation in the Gulf War to boost his personal popularity or that of his ruling Progressive Conservative Party. Indeed, the fall in the government's popularity that began shortly after the Tories were re-elected in 1988, continued during 1991. By midyear, the Progressive Conservative's popularity rating had fallen to 14%, a record low for a governing party, and well below the ratings of the other two traditional national parties. Throughout the year, Mulroney and the Conservatives barely managed to keep ahead of the Reform Party, a conservative protest movement with origins in rural Western Canada. The disillusionment of the public with all three traditional parties and the consequent rise of the Reform Party, was one of the major political stories of the year. The leader of Reform, Preston Manning, began making forays away from his western base into Ontario, where he was greeted by large and enthusiastic crowds. It was partially the popularity of Reform that convinced many analysts that no party would be able to win a majority in the next federal election, and there could be as many as five parties holding seats in the next Parliament.

There are many reasons for the unpopularity of the Prime Minister. Certainly, the poor performance of the Canadian economy was a major factor. The unpopular Goods and Services Tax becoming effective at the beginning of the year was another. The GST itself was a major contributor to Canadian prices being significantly higher than those in the United States. In response to the tax, Canadians crossed the border in increasing numbers to do their shopping in the United States, with considerable economic harm done to commercial enterprises in communities adjacent to the U.S. border. The problems of these merchants became a national issue, largely because most Canadians live within easy driving distance of an American shopping mall. But perhaps just as important was the symbolic dimension, the general sense of malaise in the Canadian economy. And, of course, there was the recession, which many blamed on Mulroney. For opponents of the Free Trade Agreement, the job losses seemed to be the embodiment of their worst concerns, made more urgent by the free trade talks between the United States and Mexico. Effectively, this re-opened the whole free trade debate in Canada.

One should not dismiss the possibility, however, that the media not only reflected public perceptions of Mulroney — but that they helped shape them. In her column, "Public's View Flawed in the Case of the PM," *The Ottawa Citizen* 6-27, Marjorie Nichols contrasted relationships between the leader and the press in the Trudeau and Mulroney eras. "The press were fascinated by Trudeau and all but a few were too intimidated to take him on. In the scrums outside of the House of Commons the conversation was never adoring, but it was inevitably respectful. No more. Reporters now make poisonous remarks about him that should disqualify them as reliable and dispassionate purveyors of public information. The problem with the press pack is that they think they're smarter than Mulroney. Unlike Trudeau, the present Prime Minister does not treat them with contempt and stay up late at night memorizing quotes from obscure philosophers with which to intimidate them." Indeed, this year we continued to see pundits take all manner of cheap shots. Mulroney's integrity and even his loyalty to Canada were frequently called into question. Over the course of the year, we saw many articles that explicitly charged that Mulroney took his marching orders from George Bush, and by implication, ignoring the wishes and the interests of the Canadian people. In a similar vein, but in less flattering language, we have often seen and heard Mulroney referred to as Bush's "lapdog" by various pundits. We have also heard a radio advertisement for electrical appliances, which referred to "the great ripoff in the Mulroney age." But most gratuitous of all was this item in the 8-16 *Toronto Star*'s "Best Bets Tonight" television column. "You might think 'The Case Of The Flying Dinosaur' was a look at the travel expenses of Tory cabinet ministers. Alas not. It's a rerun of a fascinating Nova episode. . ."

Clearly, being anti-Mulroney was "politically correct," and anyone that was even remotely associated with the Prime Minister could expect an especially rough ride from the Canadian press. Nowhere was this more vividly demonstrated than in the John Crispo affair. Crispo, an economist at the University of Toronto, was one of the country's most vocal supporters of the Free Trade Agreement with the United States. He was also highly critical of the role of the press in that debate, alleging that coverage in major media outlets, such as *The Toronto Star* and the Canadian Broadcasting Corporation, was heavily biased in favor of those who opposed the agreement. In April, Brian Mulroney appointed Crispo to the CBC's Board of Directors, and this set off a storm of protests, with most of Canada's prominent journalists joining in.

The *Globe and Mail's* Michael Valpy led the charge against Crispo, devoting no fewer than four columns to the appointment. In one, "Director Has Nothing But Contempt For CBC," he enumerated his criticisms of Crispo, quoting extensively from testimony that Crispo had given at a hearing of the body that regulates radio and television in Canada, the Canadian Radio and Telecommunications Commission. Crispo had admitted having contempt for CBC because of "what I perceive to be deliberate, continued and repeated intellectual dishonesty in virtually all of its news and public affairs programming." Crispo is also quoted as declaring "I have almost come to the conclusion that we have to have co-producers of news and public affairs shows. They have left-wing producers. Hire some right-wing. The CBC couldn't hire them. They wouldn't recognize one if they saw one. Well, I guess they would, because they know what not to hire." Because of these comments, for Valpy, the Prime Minister had made a "scorched earth appointment." His colleague at the *Globe,* Jeffrey Simpson, opposed the appointment because Crispo "hates the CBC." *Toronto Star* columnist Gerald Caplan called the appointment "a horror story" and he said that it showed the government to be "meanspirited, perverse, [and] bloody-minded." Even the *Star's* Dalton Camp, an advisor to this and previous Tory administrations, came out against the appointment, because Crispo had views that were "off-the-wall."

For us, the Crispo affair is important because so many journalists were willing to argue, without any reservation, that Crispo's political views disqualified him from receiving an appointment to the board of directors of a state-owned corporation. We acknowledge that Crispo's statements are often inflammatory and extreme, but no more so than those of many of his detractors. Most of those who argued that Crispo should be disqualified from serving on the board of the CBC because he was critical of the corporation, would probably argue that the boards of private corporations should be composed of individuals who represent a wide variety of interests, such as labor and environmentalists who would be expected to oppose management on many issues. How much greater is the need for diversity on a board of a corporation that is funded by government.

Brian Mulroney was not the only unpopular politician in Canada. Pollsters in 1991 detected a new, and potentially dangerous hostile trend towards all politicians and the political system. One who appeared to be in the eye of the storm throughout 1991 was Ontario Premier Bob Rae. Rae was the first member of the socialist New Democratic Party to head the government of the country's largest and most industrialized province. This alone would have been sufficient for Rae's government to attract more national attention than most provincial regimes, but in its first year in office, the Rae government provided abundant fodder for any would-be critics. Within its first months in office, a number of ministers had been forced to resign because of various forms of unprofessional conduct. In the most interesting of these cases, the Minister of Financial Institutions, Peter Kormos, left the cabinet kicking and screaming, after posing (fully clothed) for the *Toronto Sun's* "Sunshine Boy" feature. Moreover, in its first year the government took a number of initiatives that were widely perceived to be excessive. A virtual ban on Sunday shopping was seen as a major factor driving Canadian consumers south of the border, but most controversial of all was the NDP's budget, featuring a whopping $9 billion deficit, which led to most bond-rating services downgrading Ontario's credit rating. The corporate community essentially went to war with the NDP government. Industrial mogul Conrad Black used the op-ed pages of one of the papers he partially owns, *The Financial Post,* as a platform for his own pro-capitalist views, and for some hard-hitting attacks on the socialists. In one of these, he threatened to do no more business in Ontario until the government changed. Ominously, the appearance of the piece coincided with the moving of the head office of a conglomerate that Black controlled, the Varity Corporation, from Toronto to Buffalo, N.Y. There was also the highly unusual specter of executives with their briefcases and in business suits rallying in front of provincial legislature to protest the economic policies of the Rae government.

Journalists, to a large extent, came to Rae's defense. On numerous occasions, they spoke and wrote of a business conspiracy to undermine the Rae government. In the eye of much of the press it seeded, the NDP government, and only the NDP government, was entitled to have immunity from public criticism. By the end of October, this boosterism had returned some dividends. Two more provinces, British Columbia and Saskatchewan, had elected NDP governments.

The public's dissatisfaction with its leaders probably had a greater impact on efforts to revise the constitution than on any other issue. In 1990, under intense public pressure, the Meech Lake Accord — an agreement between Ottawa and the provinces to provide a framework for constitutional reform — collapsed. One of the prime reasons for the opposition was the perceived lack of public participation in the process. This year in reaction, the federal government and its counterparts in a number of the provinces, established parliamentary committees to involve the public. In Quebec, the Belanger-Campeau Commission, envisioned the provincial government assuming jurisdiction over a number of areas now controlled by Ottawa. At the same time, in the wake of the failure of the Meech Lake Accord in 1990, the ruling Liberal Party declared that if a new constitutional arrangement was not reached with the rest of Canada by September 1992, a referendum on separation would be held. This was worrisome because the Liberals, under Premier Robert Bourassa, were thought to be the one party in Quebec that had the strongest commitment to keeping the province in Canada. Here, it was threatening to initiate a process that could very easily lead to the separation of Quebec from the rest of the country.

For its contribution to this populism, the federal government established the Spicer Commission. Throughout the first half of the year, it organized town meetings around the country to solicit the public's view on constitutional reform. Various panels of "ordinary Canadians" were assembled by the Commission to discuss the country's problems. The proceedings were carried on local cable television stations across the country. Following these hearings convinced us that the constructive role the general public could play in the process of constitutional reform was necessarily a limited one. One writer we saw compared the hearings to a national therapy session and we think that this analogy is appropriate. In general, the participants in the Spicer hearings used them merely to voice their complaints about how the country was being run, without offering any suggestions. Keith Spicer's final report, issued in late June, to a large extent reflected this negativism. The Prime Minister was singled out as being personally responsible for the country's constitutional crisis and there was a call for an ending to policies, such as official bilingualism, which had always been unpopular with the Canadian public. While the Spicer Commission received extensive attention from the press when its public hearings were being held and when its report was being issued, it was interesting for us to see how quickly its findings and recommendations were forgotten. Within weeks of the report's publication, one would have been hard pressed to find any reference to it in the Canadian press.

To us, this only points to the folly of having a constitution written by the general public. It must be framed by individuals who can anticipate how each word may be interpreted by the judiciary. Yet, throughout the first half of 1991, there was much talk about convening a Constitutional Convention to draft a constitution. Those who favored the holding of such a convention usually argued that participants should represent specific groups such as women, aboriginal people, and visible minorities. Much of the press got on the populist constitutional bandwagon during the course of the year. For its issue to mark Canada Day at the beginning of July, *Maclean's* 7-1, brought twelve "ordinary Canadians" from different parts of the country for a weekend retreat where they worked with experts in conflict resolution to arrive at a common vision for Canada. Their sessions were recorded for the private Canadian television network, CTV.

It took the federal government more than a year to develop its own constitutional alternative to the failed Meech Lake Accord. The Constitutional Affairs Minister unveiled the government's proposal at the end of September. Unlike the Meech Lake Accord, which was presented as a take-it-or-leave-it package, the new proposals were presented as a basis for discussion which could be revised in response to the reaction of interested parties. And while the Meech Lake Accord was only produced to deal with Quebec's grievances, the new proposal was much broader. The federal proposal included: an amendment to the Charter of Rights of Freedoms to guarantee property rights; recognition of Quebec's distinctiveness and Canada's linguistic duality; guaranteed aboriginal representation in a reformed Senate; a directly elected Senate with more equitable provincial and territorial representation; a declaration that Canada was an economic union with guarantees to which persons, goods, services and capital would move without barriers based on provincial or territorial boundaries; more provincial control over immigration, culture and job-training; and the creation of a Council of Federation composed of federal, provincial, and territorial appointees to design programs that are funded by different levels of government and to establish national standards for them.

The Daily News

The Globe and Mail

In last year's review, we scoffed at those critics who argued that *The Globe and Mail*'s change in format foreshadowed a decline in the paper's quality. After watching the newspaper in its new format, though, we are, to a large degree, forced to eat our words. Unhappily, the serious economic problems of the Canadian economy squeezed *The Globe and Mail* as well. There were changes in editorial content, and many of them did not improve the paper. Early in 1991, *The Globe and Mail* fired most of its sports staff, and that section was reduced to two pages at the back of the paper. Most of the beat reporters were let go, and the *Globe* relied heavily on wire service reports to cover most sporting events. Most of those who survived the purging of the sports staff wrote columns or features. This is just the most dramatic example of the kind of editorial upheaval that plagued the paper throughout the year. There have been noticeable cutbacks in other areas. The arts coverage has become particularly skimpy. One of the most popular items in the paper was the book review section at the end of the Saturday arts section, which has been reduced to a mere two pages.

There is less local coverage of events in the paper's home base of Toronto. Because the editors take the motto of being "Canada's National Newspaper" seriously, we feel they are almost reluctant to publish too much Toronto news, even in the edition of the paper distributed only in the local market. On most days, there are just one or two pages of Toronto news, with three or four mostly short articles, and a "Toronto in Brief" item containing an equal number of one-paragraph summaries of other local stories. An indication of the extent to which the *Globe* is no longer regarded as a local paper can be seen in the decision of the major theater chains to withdraw local movie ads from the weekday editions. In response, the paper began publishing a daily listing of movies playing at theaters around the Toronto region.

The *Globe* has also gone further than most other newspapers in conceding to the electronic media the job of covering daily events. Excepting the "Report on Business," the editors no longer see the paper's role as being a provider of the definitive daily chronicle of events. Hard news, be it local, national, or international, is now covered in *USA Today*-style fashion; these stories, four to ten paragraphs long, often originate from a wire service. Suffering from a now-serious identity crisis, the *Globe* also has proceeded to transform itself into a daily magazine with its own staff increasingly putting out the kinds of overviews that are usually positioned elsewhere. Indeed, the paper instituted a feature on its front page that uses the term that is almost exclusively used by magazines — "Cover Story." These are very similar to the "Page One" treatments of *The Wall Street Journal.*

The editors were continually tinkering with the paper's format. In February, a "National Classified" page was added to the Saturday "Focus" section, containing everything from political statements from various groups to personal ads. John Dafoe's "The West" column was added to Lysiane Gagnon's "Inside Quebec," and David Olive's "Chronicles of the Week." But on the whole, we find "Focus" inferior to similar sections in other papers. Too many of the features deal with "soft news." In the 9-21 edition, the front page feature deals with surveys of what type of house $200,000 can buy in each major Canadian city. Inside we find items on subjects such as death from overwork in Japan, and how changes in national boundaries are affecting cartography — interesting reading but not exactly the comprehensive analysis of national and international events that one finds, say, in *The New York Times*'s "Week in Review" or *The Washington Post*'s "Outlook," among others.

Unfortunately, the editors, like their counterparts at the CBC, feel that, in order to fulfill the *Globe's* mandate as "Canada's National Newspaper," they somehow must "reflect" each of Canada's regions. The reporters in each of the bureaus across the country are given a regular space to fill, whether something of genuine national interest has happened on their beat or not. This gives the paper a distinctly schizophrenic feel. Thus, we get items like Andre Picard's "Wheelchair Users in Bad Fix Over Repairs," 9-16, in which we are told how the Quebec government's funding policies have driven all but one of Montreal's wheelchair repairmen out of business. A good local story, certainly, but this isn't related to the larger business picture in Canada. On the other hand, a valuable weekly addition to the "op-ed" page has been Pauline Couture's "Quebecois Voices," a weekly sampling of items from the French-Canadian Press. Not only do English-Canadians get their "other side's" view of the ongoing constitutional debate, but Couture, in each of her columns refers to items in the Quebec media that are not directly related to "The Great Canadian Issue."

We continued to appreciate some of the features introduced with the revamped format. The "Social Studies" feature on the "Facts and Arguments" page continues to inform and amuse us with what the *Globe* calls "A Daily Miscellany of Information," which is comparable to the "Index" in *Harper's*. A Wednesday feature on "Religion" was premiered by the new religion editor, Jack Kapica, who formerly was the paper's book editor. Other contributors cover topics such as "Personal," "Principles," "Behavior," and the "Family." We are also often attracted to the "Cross-Currents" column which appears daily at the front of the "Arts" section. This feature investigates the intersections between the arts, politics and social issues. Interestingly, a new regular contributor to "Cross-Currents" is Rick Salutin, who also pens a weekly column on the media. Salutin, a well-known Canadian writer, novelist and essayist who has had frequent flirtations with the underground press and the radical left, has often argued that the *Globe* reflects the views of only the Canadian establishment. Perhaps, with his addition, that perspective is changing.

Actually, in its editorials, the paper espouses a rather moderate form of conservatism. While usually on the free-market side of most economic issues, rarely do we see the bombastic socialist-bashing that is a staple of the opinion in the *Financial Post*. At times, the *Globe* actually supports the left; in a 10-16 editorial, "It's Mr. Harcourt's Turn in British Columbia," the paper endorsed the socialist NDP in a provincial election. This middle-of-the-road approach so frequently employed by the *Globe* is perhaps best exhibited in the stand it took on the medicare issue. In "The Challenges of Medicare Reform," 11-22, the editors argue that the Canadian health insurance is superior to its U.S. counterpart. Yet in "The Health Care Patchwork," 10-14, the *Globe* maintains that the Canadian system is in need of serious reform, as the cost of health care to provincial governments is expanding rapidly. In "GST's Mild Impact on Prices," 7-23, the editorialist notes the inflationary impact of the introduction of the value-added Goods and Services Tax has been as low as the government itself predicted and far less than the government's critics said that it would be. And who have the Canadian people to thank for this fortunate circumstance? Not business, government, or the Consumers Association of Canada, but the magic of the marketplace, according to the *Globe*'s editorial writers.

Throughout the year, the *Globe* opposed the socialist NDP's efforts to include a "social charter," or what one might call an individual bill of economic rights, in the constitution. In one of its editorials, "The Kitchen Sink and the Constitution," 11-12, the editors provided much-needed clarification on the purposes of the constitution, with clear reasoning for not including a social charter in it. "A constitution is a set of rules for the operation of a system of government. It sets out the division of powers between different levels of government, as well as marking the limits of the states on the prerogatives of a free people and the rights of an individual. It is not a wish list for the permanent preservation of whatever government programs a particular subset of society might fancy. Nor can it guarantee merely by so stating, these things which are in a fickle world incapable of guarantee. The dangers in a cluttered constitution are apparent. Germany would like to privatize part of its postal service, but cannot without an amendment to its constitution. Mexico is similarly bound by a constitution provision vesting control for the oil industry in state hands, effectively closing it to foreign investment. Is the ownership of communications utilities and natural resources the stuff of constitutions? Or is it a question of democratic debate?"

The *Globe*'s magazine approach to daily journalism sometimes leaves the paper short-handed and left in the dust in the coverage of major events, as in its coverage of the Gulf War. The paper did not have a Middle East bureau when the fighting broke out, and it was obliged to parachute in reporters from other parts of the globe to cover the hostilities. John Gray, for instance, moved to Israel from his regular beat in Europe. Timothy Appleby, who had been in the Gulf shortly after Iraq's invasion of Kuwait, was recalled to the region from his regular police beat! At least Gray had filed some stories from Israel in 1990. Suddenly depositing reporters in parts of the world where they have no experience does affect the quality of their work. This comes out clearly in Appleby's writing. One month into the Gulf War, he gives us the entirely conventional "Why the U.S. Cannot Win," 2-14, predicting that the U.S. will incur heavy casualties, large protests from the domestic peace movement, and the wrath of the entire Arab world. His 10-5 cover story "Fighting the Criminan Mosaic: Would Ethnic Data Help?" is an illuminating investigation into what proved to be a highly controversial topic: whether police should collect and release to the public statistics that break down criminals by their ethnic origin. The *Globe* did open a bureau in the Middle East later in the year, dispatching Patrick Martin from its editorial board in Toronto to run the bureau from Jerusalem. We threw up our hands later in the year as the game of musical chairs continued — as Gray was shipped off to become the *Globe*'s Moscow correspondent.

Foreign coverage continued to be one of the paper's weaknesses this year, largely due to a shortage of staff and the overworking of the reporters employed at the paper. As with national and local news, the *Globe* sometimes found itself covering "big stories" with short wire dispatches, with its own correspondents weighing in only a day or two later with their own "analysis." After a generally poor year with their foreign correspondence, the *Globe* launched a series of front-page features that showcased the reporters in each of its ten foreign bureaus. Most of them chose "soft news" items for their contribution to this series. From Washington, John Saunders gives us "Mean Streets: Crime With a Capital C," 11-14, an exploration of the inability of that city's police department to deal with the escalating murder rate, but we've heard this all before on "Nightline" and various other television shows originating from the United States. On the other hand, in "Storm Cloud Builds in Europe," 11-21, Paul Koring documents the growth of xenophobia and racism throughout the continent from his perch at the European bureau. The *Globe* also used the series to launch news bureaus in Africa and South America.

In spite of the paper's attempts at comprehensive foreign coverage, the *Globe* is still comparatively weak in its analysis of foreign affairs. The only staffers to write regularly on the subject are John Cruickshank, the paper's managing editor, and Linda Hossie, who this year was named foreign affairs specialist. In the absence of a truly historic event like the Gulf War or a Soviet coup, the excellent national affairs correspondent Jeffrey Simpson stays away from international relations.

It was a "business as usual" year for the "Report on Business" section. Fortunately, we did not see it following the rest of the paper's leap to a magazine format. The "ROB" is still the paper of record on Canadian business, but not by as wide a margin as it held in earlier years. We now find less investigative or in-depth reporting within its pages. To us, the most interesting parts of the "ROB" are the commentaries of Peter Cook and Terrance Corcoran, whose columns run on alternating days. Indeed, more than anyone else on the paper they take firm stands on issues related to business and the economy.

Indeed, the greatest deficiency of the *Globe* is that there are no people like Cook and Corcoran working on the news and editorial sections of the paper. Fairness and objectivity are of course important for newspapers. But this need not be equated with being long-winded and dull. Yet the *Globe* is often both. The style of writing and the choice of subject matter seldom excites or challenges the reader. Herein lies the paper's greatest shortcoming. May the editorial and format changes undertaken by the paper last year remedy this, without shortchanging the reader either information or analysis.

Chairman:	Ken Thomson
Publisher:	A. R. Megarry
Editor-in-Chief:	William Thorsell
Managing Editor:	Timothy Pritchard
Business Editor:	Margaret Wente
Address:	444 Front Street, W. Toronto, Ontario M5V 2S9 (416) 585-5000
Circulation:	1990 — 325,113 1991 — Not Available

The Financial Post

In February 1991, the editor of *The Financial Post,* John Godfrey, helped facilitate the entry of the former Iraqi ambassador to the United States, Mohammed al Mashat, into Canada. Within weeks of his role in the affair being made public, he was replaced by financial columnist Diane Francis, and his role on the paper was reduced to that of columnist. We can only speculate as to why Godfrey was demoted and succeeded by Francis, a superb writer and economic analyst, and for over the remainder of the year we watched Francis put her own distinctive mark on the paper.

Once fully settled in, Francis started making some subtle changes in the paper. In early October, she announced a number of changes to the lineup of columnists, shuffling and adding personnel. A "View from B.C." feature was to be written by a former provincial cabinet minister in British Columbia, Rafe Mair. In the same vein, Jean Pare and Ted Byfield were given regional columns to reflect views in Quebec and the West, respectively. Others added to the columnist fold were Sandra Gotlieb, who wrote a column for *The Washington Post* while her husband was Canada's ambassador to the United States, and Peter Worthington, the conservative Canadian journalist who comes the closest to the U.S.'s Patrick Buchanan. Francis and the *FP* did not settle on anyone to replace its regular Ottawa columnist, Hyman Solomon, who passed away near the end of 1990. Ottawa column duties for the year were shared by Jill Vardy, Allan Toulon, and John Geddes. Neville Nankivell left the editorial board to become editor-at-large, and now files columns from overseas, usually from different locations in Europe. The loss of Andrew Coyne, to the editorial board of *The Globe and Mail* was a big one for *The Financial Post,* but we didn't mind as much with the addition of so many new names and faces. We can only guess from Francis's appointment of so many regional columnists that she plans to make the *FP* that much more relevant to each province, thereby increasing the paper's nationwide importance.

But perhaps the biggest change was in the work of Francis herself. Before she assumed the editor's chair, her column "The Insiders," most often profiled various businesses and executives. This year she has focused almost exclusively on political issues, in particular, socialism and Ontario's NDP government. In a series of articles that ran in the spring, Francis argued strongly that under the new government's welfare proposals, anyone earning under $35,000 per year would be financially better off receiving government assistance, "Developing a Parasite Underclass," 4-19. Along the same lines, in "Landlords Take a Hit in Rae's Ontario," 10-4, she persuasively asserts that revamped rent control policies are bringing about the financial ruin of many small landlords. In most of her columns during the early fall, Francis warned readers in other parts of the country to learn the appropriate lessons from Ontario's experience with a socialist government. The timing of these "warnings" were not accidental. Two western provinces, Saskatchewan and British Columbia were due to hold elections in October; in both instances, it was widely expected that the NDP would unseat an unpopular incumbent administration.

Along with Francis, Conrad Black is *FP's* most outspoken contributor. Being one of the owners of the paper gives Black access to more space than other columnists. His opinion pieces generally cover most of the page in the tabloid-style paper, and because of their length, many are rambling and often lack a coherent theme. But most also contain an insightful observation and it's worth the work to get at his view. For instance, in "Why Won't Our Left-Wing Take a Right Turn," 9-18, he is scathing on the refusal of the Canadian left to repent, when socialists worldwide are reconsidering their position: "In Canada, the fashionable poseurs who were proud of vacationing in Cuba, who bought Ladas but ostensibly departed their deadly cocktail parties if South African sherry or wine lurked on the bar, who were prompted by almost every edition of *The Toronto Star* to demonstrate at the U.S. consulate, who shrilly proclaimed that cruise missile testing and NATO's Euro-missile deportment endangered world peace, have sunk back into the lumpen tory-socialist masses of Canada. They are comparatively silent about international affairs, jubilation over supposed American decline has given way to simpering over American omnipotence, but they are still ascendant in domestic politics. Jane Fonda, Joan Baez, most of the British Labor Party, and the Chicago Seven, and even Regis Debray and H. Rap Brown have recanted. No such morally enhancing rite has blessed Canadian public discussion. Farley Mowet, Stephen Lewis, and John Ralston Saul, who in the '70s and '80s doubled Canada's Gross Clabtrap and Philistinism Product, are apparently unchastened." Wow!

A year ago, we took note of the uniformity of the political leanings of the paper's columnists and even with all the changes in the column lineup in 1991, this uniformity continues to exist. Indeed, Alan Fotheringham is the only staff columnist with political views that are at all to the left of center. Unhappily, we find Fotheringham's musings neither convincing nor especially thought-provoking. Francis must find someone to spice up the columns, so that at least occasionally we can open the pages of the *FP* and be surprised by an opposing viewpoint.

There are those who expressed the "fear" that Black would try to control the editorial policy of the paper that he owns, but we see little evidence of this. There was even editorial criticism of the Varity Corporation. The paper also urged the government to resist any pressure from the United States to remove the protection of "cultural industries" from the Free Trade Agreement, a position we suspect would trouble Black. Of course, one would expect that a paper catering almost exclusively to the businessman and executive would cheer on capitalism and free enterprise, and the *FP* does, as we find in the editorial, "Let's Eat Our Competitive Cake," 8-14: "In truth, applying the combativeness yardstick will neither make us a less socially just society, nor loosen our health-care system, nor lower our environmental standards. The opposite is true. As the collapse of Communist regimes all over Eastern Europe has amply demonstrated, societies which are equally efficient, which heed the rules of the marketplace, are also more environmentally benign and socially just than their authoritarian alternatives." There is, though, a surprising shallowness of analysis throughout the *FP* on the causes of the desperate recession that has wracked the nation all year. We saw no discussion at all on Canada's capital gains tax, for example, among the world's highest since 1989, when coincidently the economic difficulties began in earnest.

The decline in the quality of *The Globe and Mail* should provide opportunity for *FP* to expand its readership. Certainly, domestic business news is covered comprehensively. The tabloid style should be attractive to busy executives with little time to read long stories. There are also regular features on topics, such as real estate, technology, trade, and the oil patch for readers with more specialized interests. But, in our view, there are still gaps in coverage which would prevent the *FP* from seriously challenging *The Globe.*

One of these areas of weakness is the coverage of foreign news. Page two of the paper contains a *Wall Street Journal*-style summary of general news, divided into "Canada," "United States," and "World" sections. Other than that, most general news comes either from wire service stories, or dispatches from the *Financial Times* of London which has an equity stake in the paper. *FP*'s own correspondents concentrate almost entirely on business stories. The paper did publish a special edition on the first Monday of the Gulf War, on a day when the paper usually does not publish. But on the whole, foreign coverage is just not as comprehensive as it is in most quality papers. Another area of weakness is the paper's arts coverage, and though this is not essential to a business tabloid, it does add fullness to the newspaper. Both the *Financial Times* of London and *The Wall Street Journal* provide some arts coverage. In the *FP,* there is only John Burgess' short weekday column which dabbles in both entertainment and society items, a "Timeout" page in the broadsheet weekend editions, featuring short reviews and previews, and a "Summer Reading" feature consisting of excerpts of well-known business books. The contrast between the meager arts coverage and the four-page daily sports section is particularly striking. Apparently, the editors have a fairly myopic view of their readers' interests. Is a businessman or executive more interested in sports than the arts? If they are to have one, why not the other?

What the editors don't seem to realize is that good business newspapers are usually good general newspapers as well. While giving in-depth coverage to business stories, papers like New York's *Wall Street Journal* and London's *Financial Times* are leaders in the coverage of general news. One can rely almost exclusively on these papers to be globally well-informed. The same cannot be said yet of *The Financial Post.* We look forward to seeing in which new directions Diane Francis and Conrad Black may yet point the paper.

Publisher:	Ronald W. Mitchell
Editor:	Diane Francis
Managing Editor:	Fred LeBolt
Address:	333 King Street East Toronto, Ontario M5A 4N2 (416) 350-6300
Circulation:	1990 — 106,000 Daily; 190,000 Weekend 1991 — 100,874 Daily; 180,226 Weekend

The Toronto Star

The Gulf War provided a shot in the arm to the *Toronto Star*'s credibility this year, clearly outdistancing any paper that we saw in the comprehensiveness of its coverage. The paper had its own correspondents at most of the main flashpoints of the war — Saudi Arabia, Jordan, Qatar (where Canadian troops were stationed), Israel, Washington, and Moscow. The *Star*'s Sunday section had a meticulously detailed review of the week's events in the war at important chronological markers such as the war's first 25 days. When the war formally ended, the *Star*'s own reporters and photographers were with the Kurds in the hills of Iraq and Turkey to witness their suffering. So obviously proud was the *Star* of its own coverage, that it sponsored a public symposium on the future of the Middle East that showcased its own correspondents who covered the war.

The comprehensiveness of the paper's international coverage continues to be its strength. Its Sunday "World" section, similar to that of the *Los Angeles Times*' Tuesday "World Report" allows the largest stable of foreign correspondents of any one newspaper in Canada to provide in-depth background and analysis. We look to Moscow correspondent Stephen Handelman for the most intelligent interpretation of the turmoil in the Soviet Union that we saw coming across any foreign desk in Canada. Handelman's work is also available through *The Spectator* of London. And, unlike *The Globe and Mail*, the *Star* does have a full-time correspondent in Eastern Europe, Alan Ferguson, and a full-time "in-house" columnist on international affairs, Richard Gwyn, based in the London bureau. Surprisingly, the *Star* dropped Gwynne Dyer mid-year, a foreign affairs analyst who divided his time between Toronto and Montreal, but we were able to continue following his work in the *Montreal Gazette*.

In spite of this, the *Star* often emulates the look and feel of a tabloid. We're disturbed by how often the pictures of sports figures make it to the front page. Toronto did generate its share of big sports stories this year, with the Blue Jays making it to baseball's American League Championship Series, and the Argonauts signing Heisman Trophy winner Raghib Ishmail and going on to win the Grey Cup, the championship of the Canadian Football League. The *Star* at times creates its own stories as an excuse for putting a color picture of the city's most popular sports figures on the front page, "Alomar's a Hit With Toronto Fans," 10-7, the result of a fan poll conducted by the *Star* to determine the most valuable player on the Blue Jays, for example. More seriously, the front page has been used in morally questionable ways to generate newspaper sales. Quite often we saw color photos there of children or women who had been kidnapped or murdered. Readers, or even those who look casually at the paper, are constantly reminded of the city's most sensational crimes. The headline "Hunting Kayla Clues," 8-5, appears over the picture of a police photographer looking for evidence that might lead to the person that committed the highly-publicized murder of a three-year old girl. In this regard, a strange fusion of infotainment, *The Toronto Star* is something like the *New York Post* combined with *The New York Times*.

The *Star*, though, is best known for its heavy emphasis on commentary. Unfortunately, like the U.S.'s *Washington Times*, the commentary is ideologically rooted in a particular framework, with very little variation. There is now overt advocacy journalism in the *Star*, to the extent that regular columnists use their space to promote the agenda of political groups or parties with which they are associated, without any pretense at reportage or journalism. In such cases, there is no question or discernment of view from the columnist, but instead a mindless spoon-feeding of ideological pap. In previous years, we have made mention of the close relationship between regular contributor Gerald Caplan and the New Democratic Party. This year, with the socialists holding power in the *Star*'s home province of Ontario, he allowed his column to become a propaganda outlet for the provincial government. Similarly, weekly contributor Bruce McLeod, a minister in the United Church, is associated with the peace movement. During the Gulf War, he regularly criticized the coalition's attack on Iraq, emphasizing the effect the bombardment was having on that country's civilian population, which was certainly reasonable enough. But, McLeod did not let up once the fighting was over. As the year went on, we noticed that he repeatedly reprised the theme of coalition responsibility for the suffering of the Iraqi people, with Saddam Hussein having little to do with their plight. The most blatant example was a piece by columnist Doris Anderson, "Women Confront Joe Clark," 8-12, an account of a meeting involving the Minister of Constitutional Affairs and a women's lobby group to which Anderson belonged. Here Anderson offered only empty platitudes such as, "We told him that women have learned to share power and use different forms of decision-making and that these talents would be a decided asset in the present confrontational all-male process." Oh. At best, this is not a very forceful presentation of her view.

As with the columns, the paper's general editorial stance is most definitely left-of-center. The philosophy was perhaps best summarized in an almost full-page op-ed "No More Rambo-ization," 11-28, by Sylvia Fraser, who is identified here as a "Noted Canadian Author." She portrays Canada as being superior to the United States because of Canada's universal health care system, and because Canadian culture has not become commercialized. Yet, many in Canada feel that the Canadian identity is threatened because the Americans seemingly dominate so much of the country's economy and culture. Much of what is in the paper reflects this liberal world view. Two years ago, we commented on how the *Star*'s politics too often made it onto the front page and to the paper's credit, we have been seeing less of this. But occasionally the editor slips, as with the banner headline, "98 Men, 2 Women to Cast Votes Today on Judge Thomas," 10-15, clearly leaving the impression that the Senate is stacked in Clarence Thomas's favor, and is an awfully bigoted boys club to boot.

The editorial board reflects many of these same themes in its work. Nat Laurie, the deputy editor of the editorial page writes in "Capitalism and the Right to Be Poor," 10-10, that gains in productivity achieved by such policies as free trade and deregulation have only resulted in an increase in unemployment and poverty. Because the United States is portrayed as the home of unbridled, decadent capitalism, anyone seen to be friendly to the U.S. risks the wrath of *Star* editorialists, and as might be expected, the prime villain is Brian Mulroney. When the rumor surfaces that the Prime Minister is in the running for the position of U.N. Secretary General, we get "Unsuitable for the Job," 10-23. The editorialist concedes that Mulroney has a number of personal qualities that make him an excellent candidate — he is bilingual, he is a champion of human rights and he led the campaign to impose sanctions against South Africa in the days of apartheid — all politically correct positions, yet, "Mulroney is too closely aligned with U.S. foreign policy to be the kind of leader the U.N. now needs." From Thomas Walkon, a columnist for the *Star,* we get "Bush's Puppet Hunker's for Bigger Stage," 10-23, where he argues pedantically that Mulroney only wants the United Nations position so he can escape certain political defeat at home. Given the paper's overt hostility to everything capitalist, we are not surprised to see the paper ask "Need We Enshrine Right to Property?" 10-5, and come up with a negative answer. The editorialist's reasons for opposing the entrenchment of property rights seems unoriginal and trite. "Entrenching property rights could conceivably affect restrictions on foreign ownership of land and companies, the right of government to expropriate or nationalize property in the public interest, and who knows what else. In this muddled debate, the American experience is not reassuring. It has taken the U.S. courts more than 50 years to narrow down the application of property rights. Initially, they used that protection to overturn most of the New Deal agenda of the 1930s including laws on hours of work, and working conditions."

Similar to the columns and editorials, a high degree of uniformity of opinion continues to exist on the op-ed page of the paper. True, this year a feature was introduced in which the paper solicited opposing views on controversial subjects, and they are run side-by-side on the op-ed page. The feature was started to deal with issues associated with the constitutional debate. Thus, we have "Should Quebec's 'Distinctiveness' Be Entrenched?" 7-5, and, "Should Canada Have Constitutional Veto?" 7-26. Later this particular feature was expanded to deal with other issues. On the eve of the Madrid peace talks, we find a debate between the president of the Canadian Arab Federation and the president of the Jewish Federation of Greater Toronto on "What Chance Peace in the Middle East?" 10-29, but, this only provides appearance of a paper that encourages balanced debate on controversial issues. The format is only used occasionally and used only where the *Star* takes a strong editorial stand. Indeed, we have seen occasions when debates have been set up on matters that are not even on the public agenda. On 11-17, an Islamic theologian and a Rabbi compared Jewish and Islamic ritual slaughter with regards to avoiding pain to animals being killed. But on the whole, it is only those on the left who have any hope of making it on the editorial page — or anywhere else in the paper. And sometimes, it appeared that those with the more extreme positions had a better opportunity of getting their pieces printed. For instance in "Cuba, Haiti, Reveal U.S. Double Standard," 10-11, by Raynier Maharaj, the editor of the a Toronto-based Caribbean newspaper, attributes Cuba's economic problems to the U.S. embargo, rather than the existence of a one-party dictatorship. Our objection is not to socialist opinion, but to its relentlessness, its monopoly of the page that stifles intellectual competition.

The *Star* added little of substance to the reporting and commentary on the ongoing constitutional questions and discussions. Drawing on populist sentiments, the paper came out in favor of a constituent assembly to draw up a new constitution in "A Way Ahead for Canada," 4-20, and in a number of other editorials the *Star* suggested that in order to make the process more broadly based, a body consisting of federal and provincial parliamentarians, from both government and opposition parties, as well as outsiders, who would "reflect the diversity of Canada," be made members of the constituent assembly.

We were encouraged by the slight degree of independence that the *Star* showed from the provincial NDP socialist government, however. When the paper saw legislation it did not like, it came down hard on the ruling party in Ontario. In "A Pro-Union Bias Mars Labor Reform," 11-14, the paper saw some positive elements in the newly-proposed legislation, agreeing with provisions to make collective bargaining more accessible to women, minorities, and part-time workers,though it forcefully argues that the provision that would prevent companies from hiring replacement workers during a strike would force some companies to close down their operations and discourage investors from putting money into Ontario. But rather than attempting to examine the NDP provincial government from a different angle, the *Star* gave us only more leftist pablum. Thomas Walkon, who most closely followed provincial affairs, concluded Bob Rae and the socialists were not paying enough attention to the lessons of Marx, who taught that the poor and disadvantaged in society could not be helped without the fundamental restructuring of the economy. The NDP had once favored such restructuring through greater public ownership of industry, but in an attempt to maintain high levels of electoral support, the NDP had completely stopped discussing the economy.

The *Star* did some good things this year, especially off the foreign desk. But it can only earn our respect by abandoning sensationalism and the pap-like cliches of political correctness. Democracy cannot work, after all, without a variety of opinions from which the electorate can choose.

Chairman:	Beland H. Honderson
Editor:	John Honderich
Managing Editor:	Ian Urquart
Address:	1 Yonge Street Toronto, Ontario M5E 1E6 (416) 367-2000
Circulation:	1990 — 518,441 Daily; 783,443 Saturday; 528,222 Sunday 1991 — 504,597 Daily; 745,936 Saturday; 504,333 Sunday

Major Periodicals

Maclean's

In Canada, you can watch the television news, or you can read *Maclean's,* which styles itself as "Canada's weekly newsmagazine," *a la Time* or *Newsweek.* In either case, you usually get no more than a superficial summation of the news.

Certainly this description would fit much of *Maclean's* coverage of the Gulf War. As might be expected, from the beginning of the year until the fighting ended, some aspect of the war was the featured "Cover Story" in almost every issue. Each story was long, but most often there was little information that was not available earlier. "After Midnight," 1-21, focuses on the last-minute diplomatic efforts to avert fighting. A follow-up, "Preparing for the Worst: Canada Braces Itself for War," 1-21, unfairly depicts a nation in hysteria, particularly on the prospect of increased terrorist incidents as a consequence of hostilities; Canadians rushing out to buy gas masks and build bomb shelters seems an extreme picture at best. In the same issue, we find two articles side-by-side that, respectively, summarize the case for and against going to war, but because the editors refer to the most commonly used arguments on each side, it is virtually assured that the reader will get no fresh insights on the question. "The End of Illusion," 2-4, reflects the end of the euphoria of the first weeks of the war. Similar to the U.S. newsweeklies, *Maclean's* serves up war pictures of POWs and destruction by missiles, with accounts of refugees and their hardships. The same issue brings us "The Outlook After the War," with suggestions that there will be turmoil in the Middle East for years to come. These predictions were made in other places, but none were as unnecessarily bombastic as we found in *Maclean's*.

On the constitutional issue, the magazine's performance was uneven. "Quebec's Deadline," 2-4, is ostensibly about the difficulty that province will have on reaching a consensus on the constitution with the rest of Canada. We get a good survey of the political forces at work within the province, but the article is too long, and it deteriorates into a *People*-style profile of Premier Robert Bourassa. More informative was "Loosening the Grip," 4-8, which looks at how the Canadian federation will change, regardless of what constitutional agreements are reached. Ottawa is committed to widespread deregulation, though at the same time, it seeks "to contain the deficit by restricting the growth in the amount of money that Ottawa sends to the provinces for such services as health, welfare, and higher education. In return, Ottawa will give the provinces the responsibility — and the authority — to restructure and increase their own income taxes if they want to maintain or improve the current level of service. Critics claim that the change will lead to a patchwork federation of have and have-not provinces. In the absence of strong federal leadership, they argue, richer provinces maintain sound medicare systems, among other services, while poorer regions will be able to afford only skeleton health programs." When the federal government introduces its own constitutional proposal, *Maclean's* offered "Brave New Worlds," 7-10, a surprisingly comprehensive review of the proposals and their impact on the country. But *Maclean's* major effort on the constitution was "The People's Verdict," 7-1. Twelve Canadians, selected by a pollster and the magazine's editors, come together to discuss solutions to Canada's constitutional problems; this seems more appropriate to television, and indeed the sessions were recorded and shown on the largest private network, CTV. Unfortunately, the magazine offers only verbosity, including profiles of the participants and the members of the Harvard negotiating team that led the sessions, and a play-by-play description of discussions that were driven more by emotion than reason. The recommendations, for the most part, consisted of motherhood statements, focused on making government more responsive to the will of the people, certainly an admirable sentiment. But *Maclean's* never really addressed whether the job of constitution-writing is best carried out by members of the general public or whether the work would be better done by experts in such areas as constitutional law and Canadian history. The magazine was not alone; Canadian editors were almost unanimous in their faith in some populist form of creating a new constitution.

During the course of the year, there were any number of feature stories on the economy and business. "The Fight to Find a Job," 6-24, focused on the recession by profiling people who had lost their jobs, an exercise done many times before, but in an interesting twist, the magazine also interviewed the former employer of each of the workers interviewed in an attempt to document why specific jobs are being lost. The common factors turn out to be competition from the United States which is aggravated by a high Canadian dollar and the free-trade agreement. Focusing on GM's efforts to improve efficiency and quality at its plants, we found "The Future of the Car," 4-15, to be quite informative, although the profile of GM's Saturn factory disappointed; the lecture on the benefits of "team management" and "worker participation" could have come straight from an MBA. An accompanying story on Japanese auto plants in North America gave a good explanation of why Japanese firms continue to grab larger shares of the American market. As part of a "Special Report," marking the 50th anniversary of Pearl Harbor, the magazine had a series of articles on Japanese economic and social trends in its 11-18 issue. In "Will the Steam Run Out?" we get a good look at the refusal of a younger Japanese generation to accept the traditional "work ethic" and the tension that this is causing with their elders. "The Company

Man" follows one Japanese mid-level manager who is still committed to that "work ethic" and in the process we learn of the many important differences between North American and Japanese corporate practices.

There were a number of features about the increasing popularity of democratic socialism in Canada. "Rating Bob Rae: What Canadians Can Learn From Ontario's Year With the NDP," graced the cover of the 8-26 issue, but disappointingly failed to deliver the promised lesson, with merely a cursory review of the NDP's first ten months in office. After the NDP has just elected provincial governments in Saskatchewan and British Columbia, we get "New Democrats on a Roll," 11-4, *Maclean's* suggesting that the election of three socialist governments in little more than a year does not signal a fundamental shift to the left in the country, but instead is a new manifestation of the historic tendency that Canadians have not allowed the party in power in Ottawa to also control provincial governments. An accompanying piece, "A New National Voice," assesses as very low, the chances that the three governments would form a unified bloc in future constitutional negotiations. The same article contains an interesting survey of the history of enshrining economic and social rights in national constitutions, where we learn that often they cannot be effectively enforced.

Twice this year, *Maclean's* entered the "Political Correctness" controversy. "Goodbye Columbus," 8-5, focuses on the probability that the Vikings reached North America first, and only superficially looks at the debate over whether Columbus should be praised or condemned. Much more to the point, "The Silencers," 5-27, tackles the issue of political correctness directly. In this broad survey of how leftists have managed to stifle all unpopular ideas and behavior, we learn that the "new puritans" have not only targeted alleged racism and sexism, but that they have also broadened the movement to encompass such causes as animal rights and environmentalism.

Occasionally, the cover story profiles a well-known public figure, but often the results are a let down. We were interested to know more about the "The Private Life of Canada's Richest Man," by Peter C. Newman 10-14, an account of the life of publishing baron Ken Thomson, but we were frustrated by the fact that Newman dealt more with Thomson's attachment to his dog and the firm grip he keeps on his household purse strings, than on matters which would genuinely interest readers concerned with public policy or business. We were more satisfied with William Lowther's profile of Gerald Bull, "The Man With the Golden Gun," 4-22, as we learn about the Canadian scientist, who helped Saddam Hussein obtain a "super-gun," and the international arms trade. As with the U.S. newsweeklies, soft news also found its way to *Maclean's* covers this year. Sounding very American, "Mid-Life Panic," 8-19, discussed "The Growing Struggle to Look After the Kids — and Mom and Pop Too." Prince Charles and Princess Diana always attract an audience, so we were not surprised to see them on the cover of the 10-28 issue, when *Maclean's* had an excuse for putting them there, since they were touring Canada at the time. But we can see little newsworthy in "The Olympic Dream," 12-2, a major feature on the Albertville games that simply appears too early, almost three months before the Olympic torch is to be lit.

For serious students of Canadian and international affairs, *Maclean's* is not necessary reading. It does not quite match its U.S. counterparts in the depth of its coverage of the week's events. The columnists, with the exception of Barbara Amiel, Peter C. Newman, and Diane Francis, are easily missed. Our particular peeve is Alan Fotheringham, who went through another year without finding much of anything to say, despite being given the entire back page every week. Rarely going beyond the daily newspaper, and often just as superficial as most television newscasts, *Maclean's* is best for those who just want a review of the news. But the moniker, "McWeekly," as we'd dubbed it last year, is still the best way to describe the magazine — fast, light news for people on the move.

Executive Editors: Alan Walker and Carl Mollins

Editor: Kevin Doyle

Address: Maclean Hunter Building
777 Bay Street
Toronto, Ontario M5W 1A7
(416) 596-5386

Circulation: 1990 — 600,000
1991 — 580,000

Saturday Night

The year 1991 was a year of transition for *Saturday Night*. The magazine signed agreements with six newspapers across the country, for distribution to some of those newspaper's regular subscribers, starting in October. Circulation immediately jumped to 400,000 from 130,000. Editor John Fraser says that this arrangement will allow the magazine to be seen by more readers who have interests and backgrounds that are similar to existing subscribers. Increased mailing costs also led to this arrangement. In most large Canadian cities, *Saturday Night* is now distributed with newspapers that are part of the Southam chain. In Toronto and Southern Ontario, for example, the magazine comes with *The Globe and Mail*. Essentially, the strategy is to put it in the hands of readers with larger incomes and higher levels of education. The hope is, with the resulting increase in advertising revenue, for the first time since 1950, the magazine will be able to be financially self-sufficient, and without the need of a regular subsidy from a benevolent proprietor.

Fraser has written, "Our business is Canada, its people and their politics, their culture, work and amusements, their successes and foibles, their adventures and aspirations. As a publication, our curiosity is not confined by the country's borders any more than Canadians are in their lives, but here is where we are, and here is where we intend to stay." As missions go, that's a tall order to live up to, since general interest magazines are in the process of being permanently squeezed out of the marketplace by increased competition from the electronic media and increased specialization in print journalism.

In spite of an October format change, *Saturday Night* is still committed to offering its regular diet of politics, travel, business, fiction and film. Will the survival plan succeed? We continue to perceive a significant void in Canadian journalism which we feel that *Saturday Night* is perhaps best-suited to fill. There is no publication that specializes in offering comprehensive in-depth commentary and analysis on major political, social, and economic issues — *a la The New Republic* of the U.S.

Each issue has at least one feature that addresses an ongoing major political topic or battle. Over the decades, *Saturday Night* has been able to earn the stature and reputation to attract most of the country's best writers to its pages. Most of the pieces are thoroughly researched, and it is difficult for the regular reader to detect any consistent ideological bias. The magazine deserves credit for consistently keeping its pieces topical, given that stories are planned and written at least three to four months before they appear. We were particularly impressed with Nicolas Regush's "Health and Welfare's National Disgrace," 4-91, which documented the federal government's failure to insure that devices used in medical procedures were safe. The June issue was devoted thoroughly to Canada's constitutional issue, although here the writing was uneven. Francine Pelletier's autobiographical piece on the making of a French-Canadian nationalist is both compelling and informative, but Dalton Camp completely botches a potentially important profile of separatist leader Jacques Perizeau by getting bogged down in a confusing discussion of financial arrangements between Ottawa and the provinces. All of *Saturday Night*'s coverage of the Gulf War went into the May issue. Paul William Roberts had himself smuggled into Iraq during the hostilities, and while his feature, "Dispatch: Into Iraq," includes some graphic descriptions of how ordinary Iraqis suffered, his anti-American slant is entirely conventional and reflects much of what was being written in the Canadian media at the time. We found William Lowther's profile of Dr. Gerald Bull, the Canadian munitions expert who was helping Saddam

Hussein develop a super-gun until he was murdered in Brussels in 1990, far more interesting. Aside from this issue, though, we found less international coverage in the magazine this year, and what there was came not in the form of news articles or analysis, but in the magazine's fine book review section.

There were some interesting business stories, although not enough for our tastes. Peter Foster's "Strange Bedfellows," 3-91, documented how Olympia & York tycoon Paul Reichman tried to bail out Robert Campeau, and how the two men had a falling out after Campeau lost control of his conglomerate. We were also interested in Don Gilmor's "Dangerous Liaisons," 9-91, which documented the collapse of Lester & Orpan Dennys, one of the country's most prestigious publishing houses. *Saturday Night* missed a number of major national stories, though, such as the deterioration of the U.S. economy and the new populism which manifests itself in disillusionment with all politicians, a phenomenon which is occurring not only nationally, but *globally.*

We are most disappointed by the trend to cover politics and economics through the profile of individuals rather than examining public policy issues directly. To do this, like *The Atlantic,* the magazine could try attracting academics for "big think" essays on the major national and internaitonal issues of the '90s. *Saturday Night*'s practice of publishing long pieces provides the potential for covering political, social and economic issues in a much more informative fashion. Now with the security of finding itself delivered with Sunday papers all across the country, the potential can be developed. There's no time like the present.

Editor:	John Fraser
Address:	36 Toronto Street, Suite 1160 Toronto, Ontario M5C 2C5 (416)368-7237
Circulation:	1990 — 109,445 1991 — 403,522

Journalists

Amiel, Barbara. *The Toronto Sun, Maclean's.* (★ ★ ★)
Writing from London, where she is a columnist for *The Times,* Amiel still manages to keep in touch with Canadian affairs, commenting on social trends as well as politics. We find her to be one of the most articulate commentators in Canada. "Standing Up to a Murderous Tyrant," *Maclean's* is an eloquent argument for taking on Saddam Hussein that includes a point-by-point refutation of the arguments of the peaceniks: "True, a number of regions, other than Kuwait, have been invaded or annexed and the West has not fought for them. Demanding that we do not in the name of consistency is foolish. The mere fact that we cannot remedy all the evils in the world because of physical limitations or certain other dangers is absolutely no argument for not remedying the particular evil that is within our power to correct." Amiel postulates intelligently on the reasons for what she considers to be the failure of U.S. foreign policy in the Middle East in "Why Did We Fight the Gulf War?" *Toronto Sun* 7-7: "America seems unable to comprehend that a theocracy does not regard it as a good thing to live in peace with their neighbour, if that neighbour is not part of the same theocratic entity. This is the fallacy behind convening international conferences and the like." She joins the fray over the appointment of John Crispo to the CBC board in "In Defence of Crispo, Fecan, and the CBC," *Maclean's* 4-29, raging effectively about her own association with the CBC: "We were anti-American, anti-big business and pro-feminist and accepted uncritically certain assumptions about the existence of racism and sexism in Canadian society. We took a relentless approach against apartheid and turned a blind eye to the tyrannies in independent Africa." One of Amiel's favorite targets is the modern manifestations of feminism, and she makes her case well in "A Conservative

Feminism," *TS* 6-30: ". . .for years a credo of pseudo-Marxism has hijacked the title of feminism. . .that is collectivist and, in my mind, intrinsically unfair since like many socialist ideas, it reduces all of us to a group rather than seeing us as individuals." And she compels with her complaints of the popularity of individuals to portray themselves as victims to excuse their own behavior in "The Noise of Women's Turmoil," 10-26.

Camp, Dalton. *The Toronto Star.* (★ ½)
Camp continues to disappoint. As a former political insider, we expected compelling commentary, *a la* William Safire, but sometimes Camp's work is rambling, incoherent, and we have trouble digging out the point. In "Those Advocating War Should Keep Silent," 1-13, Camp uses the goofy logic that, for the U.S., the human cost of war will be high, and that true friends should be urging the U.S. to give sanctions a chance to work. He profiles Parti Quebecois leader Jacques Parizeau in "The Plot to Kill Canada," *Saturday Night* 6-91, but this is too long for the little return we get, and Camp, despite his political background, doesn't clearly explain Parizeau's transition from federalist to separatist. He is hard on his own Progressive Conservative Party when they meet in convention in "Time for Mulroney to Reveal If He Is Heading North or South," 8-11, venting his spleen for past sins. Yet we see signs of promise. Using a study that shows Canadians largely ignorant of their history and current politics, Camp hits the mark in "Ignorance of History Bodes Ill for Future," 4-3: "Someone ought to make the distinction between the public having wisdom and having power. Right now people have this backward, believing they are wise in these matters, but powerless, when, in fact, it is the other way round." He is insightful in "Shift Shows PM More Resourceful Than Clever," 4-24, in which he convincingly demonstrates that Mulroney was willing to lower his own profile for the sake of his government. Camp argues convincingly in "PM Has Hard Life Taking It on the Chin," 7-31, that reasons for Mulroney's lack of popularity go beyond the obvious, though he declines to detail what they are, while in "Master Communication Plan Aims to Avoid Meech Trip," 9-28, Camp discerns the differences in the promotion of the Meech Lake Accord and the government's new constitutional proposals. What emerges is a picture of a chastened federal government, willing to submit its new proposals to an examination of Parliament and the public.

Caplan, Gerald. *The Toronto Star.* (½ ★)
With his party in power in Ontario, Caplan's column became a virtual P.R. organ for the socialists, and, in a year that saw the collapse of the Soviet Union, he continued to exhibit tunnel vision by blaming all of the world's problems on the U.S., the "far right" and Western capitalist democracies. At times he seemed completely unhinged. In his "Was Gulf War the Mother of All Deceptions?" 3-3, Caplan charges without evidence that the Gulf War was launched solely to test out the weapons developed during the Reagan administration. "Only Paranoid Fantasy, Or Could It Happen Here?" 4-28, sinks to new depths. Based on a British television movie, in which business interests sabotage a left-wing Labor government, Caplan speculates that the same thing may be going on in Ottawa. There is knee-jerk support for the socialists in "Ontario NDP Shows That It's Come of Age," 9-15, which praises the party's flexibility in deciding not to go ahead with state-run auto insurance, and decries "corporate overreaction to the relatively moderate proposals of the government." Caplan attributes all the problems of African states to its debt to capitalist countries in "Where Hopes for a Better African Future Lie," 9-29, ignoring the lack of representative democratic government as a factor in the misery of Africans and blaming it all on the "neo-quackery of western capitalism." There is more boosterism from the Ontario socialists in "Why the Frenzy? NDP's Listening to Business," 10-13, but he adds an ugly note, implying that businessmen who criticize the NDP are somehow disloyal.

Cook, Peter. *The Globe & Mail.* (★ ★)
Cook improved this year, with especially enlightening dispatches from Eastern Europe and the Soviet Union. In "Economic Battles Cover Gulf to GATT," 2-1, Cook tells us that the Gulf War has exposed deep divisions between European nations that are supposedly preparing to unite politically in 1992. While there has been much criticism over Germany's failure to finance the

68

Gulf War, despite having Europe's strongest economy, Cook reminds his readers that Germany and Europe has undertaken the heavy burden of financing Eastern Europe's recovery. We find clever, sharp commentary on the possibility that the U.S. and Canadian economies may soon be back in "Double Dips, Dead Cats May Be in Recovery's Way," 7-31, using the "dead cats" as a symbol of phony recovery: "In Canada, double dips have occurred in three of the past four recoveries; that is in 1951-54, in 1957-60, and in 1980-82. The only recovery that was not affected followed the recession of 1970." Cook describes with salient detail the anomaly of merger-mania driving up the stock prices of U.S. banks in the face of bad management as evidenced by the growth in non-performing loans in "When Bankers Become Barracudas," 8-15, telling us "The industry is in trouble — severe structural trouble." Uh oh. In "Eastern Europe Gets Full Marx for Disaster," 10-19, Cook graphically describes the impact that industrial pollution has had on the so-called "Black Triangle" of Eastern Europe, that encompasses parts of Germany, Poland, and Czechoslovakia, concluding "The tragic legacy of the past is a system that for 40 years followed the precepts of Karl Marx to the letter and simply ignored the evidence of a polluted environment. Karl Marx taught that, in a Communist state, there would be an indivisible harmony between the works of man and nature."

Corcoran, Terrance. *The Globe & Mail.* (★ ½)
Corcoran is still one of the best defenders of free-market economics in the Canadian press, but, with the Canadian economy a basket case, he spent too little time exploring the reasons for his own analytical inadequacies. At times, he seemed an apologist for the failed economic policies of the Bank of Canada and the Mulroney government. We found him in the "ROB" this year championing such unpopular causes as the inclusion of property rights in the constitution, and the tight money policy of the central bank. "Live From the Economic Free-Fire Zone," 1-18, is a witty parody on CNN's coverage of the bombing of Iraq, describing himself as besieged in the newsroom while a rain of forecasts falls, with the message from the beleaguered columnist: Don't take economists too seriously. "Recession Isn't the Problem; It's the Solution," 2-16, is a page-long column arguing, incorrectly, that the recession will not be deep and will usher in a period of price stability. We've come to expect this type of argument from Corcoran in "Goodbye Ralph Nader: Markers Work," 3-13, but he is less feisty, less convincing than usual. In "Bankruptcy No Way to Protect Wages," Corcoran argues against the notion that proponents of the free markets are reflexively anti-worker. Corcoran provides marvelous commentary on Bell Canada's monopoly in "Hello Operator, Get Me Mr. Marchese," 7-31, taking to task Rosarie Marchese, both P.R. chief of Bell Canada and Ontario Communications Minister: "Ontario doesn't like competition, it doesn't like market forces. Instead, it prefers regulated monopolies, government-planned economic activity and directed technological change. As Lenin once said: 'What is to be done?' " Corcoran does a good job championing the case for the enshrining of property rights in the constitution in "Property Rights Need a New Champion," 11-2: "if a company dumped hazardous chemicals that leeched through the groundwater of a neighboring property, entrenched property rights would leave no doubt that the company is responsible. With property rights there is more certainty of a company's liability — and there is less probability that governments (which have a long history of sanctioning pollution for the sake of jobs and votes) will be prevented from passing laws allowing pollution." Corcoran could do with a dash of humility and a goodly portion of inquisitiveness.

Crane, David. *The Toronto Star.* (★ ½)
The commentary and analysis of the *Star*'s economics editor is often conventional, lining up with the status quo. While he does acknowledge the importance of competition, he seems to feel that competition is best achieved through protectionism. We get "Our Politicians Are Floundering as Industry Loses Global Race," 1-26, as Crane frets over the deficit and the decline of competitiveness in Canadian industry. Crane departs from his usual business turf in "Europe Frets as War Radicalizes Muslims," 2-4, claiming unconvincingly that European governments have wavered on the Gulf issue, because they are fearful of the reaction of the large Arab minorities within their borders. In "Big Shift of Powers May Prove Too Costly for Canada,"

4-6, he decries the tendency of business to endorse constitutional solutions which would see significant transfers of powers from the federal government to the provinces; he points out that in a highly decentralized country, businesses would have to comply with a different set of regulations in each province where they operated. With "Lay Off Our Cultural Industries or Else, Canada Should Tell U.S.," 8-24, Crane urges the government to pull out of the free-trade talks with the U.S. and Mexico, as well as the bilateral pact with the U.S., if the United States does not stop pressuring Canada to remove its protection of publishing and broadcasting industries, an ineffective appraisal. He uses Harvard economist Michael Porter's oatmeal study of Canada to pick up on one of the favorite themes of Canadian nationalists in "High Levels of Foreign Ownership Hampers Our Ability to Compete," 11-26. We are told that Canada needs only that kind of investment where a company bases an entire product line in the country. High-paying jobs, in areas such as research and development go along with this kind of investment. But how do we attract this high value-added investment? Crane doesn't tell us.

Cruickshank, John. *The Globe & Mail.* (★ ★ ½)
A better year for *The Globe*'s Managing Editor who writes the weekly "A World View" column. More frequently we saw Cruickshank turning from the process of international relations to attempt to deal with issues of principle. In "Maybe It's Right But Still It's Crazy," 1-18, he says that those fighting Saddam Hussein are not the Allies, and that Saddam is no Hitler, but the differences are not explained. There is extreme pessimism about the future of Canada in "Is Canada Too Selfish or Indolent to Survive?" 2-1, as Cruickshank judges, "English Canadians would rather accept fragmentation, international irrelevance and utter Americanization than give an understanding hearing to Quebec." "A Leaky Flagship Sailing a Racial Sea," is a thoughtful look at the role of race in world politics. "Okay Let's Talk About Who Gets In," 6-14, is a fine examination of Canada's immigration policy, which Cruickshank portrays as being highly successful. He asserts that instead of focusing on the race and the national or origins of immigrants, the debate should concentrate on the "skills and attitudes" that Canada wants from those coming into the country. We appreciate the perspective in "Let's Put the Money Into the Right Hands," 7-12, as Cruickshank does not share most of his colleagues' enthusiasm for providing aid to the Soviet Union. "Time to Tie the Money to Morality," 10-18, is a ringing endorsement of Mulroney's plan to tie foreign aid to human rights. Cruickshank writes: "Acting together, economic and political reforms could create dramatic improvement in the lives of millions of Africans. However, Western nations, including Canada, must be prepared to do their part in resolving the debt crisis and eliminating the massive subsidies of agriculture and resource production in affluent countries." In "Who Gets Yes, Who Gets No?" 12-13, Cruickshank wades into the debate about which of the states in the Communist empire in Eastern Europe deserves Canadian diplomatic recognition, almost convincing us of the dichotomy by which, according to the existing criteria, Slovenia is far more deserving than the Ukraine, but it is the latter that is being recognized.

Dyer, Gwynne. *The Toronto Star, Montreal Gazette.* (★ ★ ★)
Dyer's byline gradually disappeared from *The Star,* and we saw his work almost exclusively in the *Gazette.* One of the better commentators on foreign affairs in Canada, Dyer focused on areas of the world not in the headlines. In "UN Military Intervention May Not Recur," *Montreal Gazette* 1-28, Dyer makes his case that it may be impossible to assemble another multinational force like the one fighting Iraq, because of deep post-Cold War cuts in arms. Investigating political developments in South Africa, "South Africa Five Years From Now is In View," *MG* 2-16, Dyer tells us that the changing political scene, particularly the repeal of anti-black legislation and the implicit admission by the ANC that it no longer represents all blacks, ensures that it is in the interests of all political factions in the country to work together for the creation of a new political system. He adds: "The greatest danger will come when the present universal recognition of the need for restraint has been eroded by time and a modest degree of success." In "Fading Paternalism Gives Us New Hope," *MG* 6-26, Dyer bubbles over with optimism, and we see signs of Francis Fukuyama's influence in this intriguing discussion of the end of history,

or at least a change in its tenor: "...you have to admit at least that there is something big and systematic going on." Dyer provides a unique profile on contemporary Vietnam, in "Communism Changed Early in Vietnam," *MG* 7-23, maintaining that communism can survive longer in Vietnam than in any other country because economic reform began earlier than in other communist countries, and, because there is a strong authoritarian tradition in Southeast Asia, economic liberalization will not lead to demands for political reform. Hmm. In "Saving a Training Base," *MG* 9-24, Dyer makes a good case for converting an old army camp in Nova Scotia into an international training base for peacekeepers. "Redrawing the Horn," *MG* 11-1, outlines the tension in Africa between drawing borders along colonial and tribal lines, a solid overview.

Fotheringham, Allan. *The Financial Post, The Toronto Sun, Maclean's.* (★ ½)
We still don't understand why Fotheringham is so popular and revered, as he seems to build his career largely on cynicism and politically-correct cliches. We see moderate improvement, but often his style reminds us of Dalton Camp, often rambling, making it difficult to follow his line of thinking. There is nothing new in "Canada No Longer Peacekeeper, Sort Of," *Financial Post* 2-21, as many have told us that Canada's participation in the Gulf War will allegedly damage its noble reputation as a peacekeeper. This column only stands out with its nastiness, as Fotheringham refers three times to the Canadian government as the U.S.'s "lapdog." "PM Should Have Used Axe in Cabinet Shuffle," *FP* 4-23, is vintage Fotheringham, containing random insults of Mulroney and cabinet ministers, but little that informs. His visit to Israel was fodder for several columns: in a standard comparison of the democratic systems in "Democracy Run Amok," *Toronto Sun* 6-12, Fotheringham concludes "No one pretends that Israel should be a model for a multi-party, inevitably coalition government Canada. But Israel does not at the moment think that Israel should be a model for anyone." Surprisingly, when he discusses the Arab-Israeli conflict in "Can Peace Bloom in the Desert?" *TS* 6-6, Fotheringham showed sensitivity to strategic dangers for Israel that are inherent in trading territories for peace. In graphic fashion, he explains how small the distances are in the Mideast, and how this is not necessarily understood by outsiders like Secretary of State Baker who would impose their own settlements on the region. In "Romanow, Harcourt Are Men of Caution," *FP* 10-22, he abandons his usual cynicism to give us a complimentary profile of two new western socialist premiers Roy Romanow and Mike Harcourt. The two men are contrasted favorably with Ontario NDP Premier Bob Rae, who is portrayed more as an idealogue. And, for once, Fotheringham's cynicism seems to be well-placed in a convincing "Going to the Dogs With the Royals," *Maclean's* 11-4, arguing that the retention of the monarchy is a sign of Canada's political immaturity.

Francis, Diane. *The Financial Post, The Toronto Sun, Maclean's.* (★ ★ ½)
On becoming editor of *The Financial Post,* Francis changed the focus of her column, "The Insiders," from a business personalities column to a political column in which she crusaded against socialism; she was a relentless critic of the three NDP governments. "Sorting Out Truth From Fiction," *Maclean's* 1-14, is a counterattack against those that charge that free trade has cost Canada jobs, citing statistics which convince. In "Canada Hates Ottawa, and There's a Start," *Financial Post* 2-14, Francis suggests that English Canadians should develop a unified stand for the upcoming constitutional talks with Quebec, suggesting that this be done by a referendum through which their views would be solicited on a variety of subjects including whether Quebec is wanted in the Confederation and the role of bilingualism in the new Canada. More than any other columnist we saw, Francis took direct aim at Ontario's NDP government, and she was particularly upset by welfare benefits, that in her estimation, were overly generous. In "Developing a Parasite Underclass," *FP* 4-19, she finds that a breadwinner making $37,500 per year ends up only slightly ahead financially of an equivalent head of a family of four who receives government assistance, Francis argues this creates a minimum wage of $18 per hour. In "UI's Burden on Manufacturers," *FP* 9-3, Francis successfully shows that "Unemployment Insurance, as constituted, is wrong-headed and destructive to our economy. So is open-ended

welfare. It is destroying manufacturing in Canada, not free trade. It is also subsidizing tax evasion." With "Time for the Middle Class to Strike Back," *Toronto Sun* 9-8, Francis reasonably articulates the public's frustration with public sector strikes: "Civil servants don't understand. They are working for the public-sector equivalent of Dome Petroleum. They don't understand that they enjoy privileges the rest of us do not, such as job security. What is it worth? What would a middle class guy with a mortgage and two kids in a troubled export industry accept as a pay cut to be guaranteed a job?"

Fulford, Robert. *The Financial Times of Canada.* (★ ★ ★)
Easily the most erudite columnist in Canada, it is disappointing that Fulford's column gets so little exposure in the small-circulation *Financial Times of Canada*. His column is never predictable and always thought-provoking. "High-Tech Advances Have Lowered Our Understanding of War," 2-11, was one of the most original critiques of the media's coverage of the Gulf War that we saw. Fulford argues that the quality of war reporting has deteriorated over the last century. Of William Howard Russell, who covered the Battle of Balaklava in 1854, he writes, "By 34, he considered himself knowledgeable about warfare, so he confidently described the course of the battle. That alone put him a notch above the entire press corps in the Gulf, which seems to include not a single reporter who can speak with authority rather than deferring to military officers on the ground or retired generals at home." When the British magazine *Encounter* ceased publication, Fulford came forward with a thoughtful tribute in "A CIA Encounter That Really Mattered to Those It Touched," 3-4, mourning this forum for important writers and ideas. He makes the good point that "Blaming Civil Servants For al-Mashat Sets Bad Precedent," 6-17, because it undermines the principle of ministerial civil service. In "Fear of Racism Censors the Facts," 8-12, Fulford rejects the idea that collecting crime statistics broken down by race would fuel racial prejudice; insightfully, he argues, that the lack of information could be creating an exaggerated perception of the involvement of the members of some ethnic groups in criminal activity. "Don't Ignore the Constitutional Talks," 10-14, is a plea for ordinary Canadians to become interested in the process of constitutional reform, but, rather than a cheap sentimental appeal, Fulford appeals to civic pride, and responsibility: ". . .in our complacency, we believe profoundly that what has always been ours will always be ours. We grew up with peace, order and good government as our patrimony, and come to think that this condition was our natural right. Actually, it's not. It can be squandered, like any inheritance." But "The Disturbing Pervasiveness of Commercial Television," 7-8, is one of the rare instances in which Fulford totally misses the mark, his criticisms old and tattered.

Gherson, Giles. *The Financial Times of Canada.* (★ ★ ½)
One of the best Ottawa columnists that we see, Gherson focuses on the kind of economic and business issues that rarely make it to the front page, even in the business sections. In "Business Calls for a National Phone Bill," 2-18, Gherson shows how lack of competition in the telecommunications industry is driving businesses that operate national networks out of the country, using the U.S. as a basis for comparison. His points are well taken in "Competition-keen Ottawa Is Long on Talk; Short on Action," 3-11, again comparing the business situation in Canada to the U.S., and smartly contrasting the atmosphere in each that promotes competition, with Gherson questioning Ottawa's fiscal priorities. In "A New Education Agenda's Coming," 4-22, he anticipates a new government initiative in education that would focus on literacy, national standards, and training in the sciences: although there may be some complaints about Ottawa meddling in the province's domain, Gherson smartly advises the Mulroney government to stick to its guns. In "The No-No Bid for a New Child Tax Credit," 5-13, Gherson shows why the introduction of a guaranteed income for families with small children would be good policy and be good for the political fortunes of the Mulroney government, additionally telling us why it will never happen. Gherson provides us with a comprehensive profile of the renegade Reform Party and its leader, in "Preston Manning: The Making of a Maverick," 8-26, presenting Manning as a different kind of political leader who genuinely communicates with his party in the formation of policy. Gherson tells us that "Canada Stands to Lose Big if the GATT Talks

Founder," 10-21, largely because Canada cannot compete in an all-out subsidy war among the world's largest trading blocs, pointing out that all of the country's exporting industries, not just agriculture, are victims of these battles, and therefore, Canada badly needs an agreement that would curb subsidies. In "How Canada's Disenfranchised Can Be Helped by UI Reform," 11-4, Gherson argues that the national Unemployment Insurance Program which now serves as a disincentive for people to return to work quickly, by replacing workers' incomes, should instead focus on the financing of skills, training and manpower upgrading programs.

Goar, Carol. *The Toronto Star.* (★ ½)
National affairs. Although Goar researches her stories well and often deals with off-beat issues, we found her too often blindly falling into the liberal line, her column filled with the standard cliches. "Sour Mood Deepens Recession," 1-10, is a good description of psychological factors that have worsened the recession, but she places all of the blame for public pessimism on the federal government without persuasive argument. "Why Medicare May Not Last the Decade," 2-19, is a well-researched examination of how health care in Canada is publicly financed, but her conclusion that the federal government will stop providing financing, and all national standards will consequently disappear, seems unduly alarmist. More well-researched and thoughtful is her critique of the federal government's economic policies in "Wilson's Harsh Medicine Is No Cure All," 3-7, but her conclusion that the high growth rates and the low inflation and interest rates of the 1950s can never be attained again seems premature. Goar's critique of the Reform Party, "Manning's Ideas Don't Conform With Reality," 4-9, is reasoned and well-argued, observing that "[Manning's] dictum that no federal leader with seats in Quebec has a right to negotiate the national contract is more than a little self-serving. It is also highly divisive. It penalizes national leaders for doing exactly what they are supposed to do; speak for Canadians from all regions and backgrounds." Goar misses the mark badly in " 'Prosperity Agenda' Smacks of Propaganda," 9-10, attacking a government economic proposal that hasn't even been made public yet, she writes "Prosperity implies privilege. It conjures up visions of Rolls Royces and elegant parties and country estates. This is the kind of economics that rich people understand and poor people can only dream of. It divides those who are likely to benefit from an increase in national wealth from those who know they never will." And "Tory MP Is Blind to the Power of Books to Bind a Nation Together," 11-7, is a poorly-argued, cliche-ridden rationalization of the protection of cultural industries. A poor year for Goar.

Gwyn, Richard. *The Toronto Star.* (★ ★)
We were surprised to see Gwyn, the *Star*'s foreign affairs columnist based in London, come out in support of the Gulf War, in "After This We'll Take Arabs Seriously," 1-16. Yet in most other areas he was predictable. In "Iraq Faces Tough List of Coalition Conditions," 2-19, Gwyn incorrectly predicts that, in exchange for peace, Iraq will be forced to get rid of Saddam Hussein and require known terrorists to leave the country. He argues, without convincing, that the fighting in the Gulf War would have been in vain, if it did not lead to an Israeli withdrawal from the West Bank and Gaza in "Will Iraq's Defeat Heal Arab Division?" 3-1. "Moral Landscape Shifts in South Africa," 4-26, contains a refreshingly frank profile of the ANC and concludes "South Africa, for all its past and continuing failings, is the continent's single success story. It's hard to imagine any prospect more unutterably depressing than that South Africa might become like the rest of Africa." While the Soviet coup was still in progress, Gwyn gave us the rather prophetic, "Whatever Happens Gorbachev Era Is Over," 8-21, telling us that "In the face of a determined public, tanks and secret police cannot govern a country. It's quite possible that, faced by unbroken resistance and with the economy deteriorating even faster than it already is, the junta will end up pleading for someone else to take over," predicting that person will not be Gorbachev but Yeltsin. He is over-simplistic in "Time Ripe for Peace Dividend," 9-8, arguing that domestic electoral and economic considerations alone are preventing the United States from making drastic cuts to its military.

Handelman, Stephen. *The Toronto Star, The Spectator.* (★ ★ ½)
Moscow. Probably the paper's top correspondent, and also the correspondent for *The Spectator,* Handelman understood the former Soviet Union better than anyone we see in Canada. Remarkably, he delivers few of the cliches that we see from others there. In "Soviets Caught in Mideast Dilemma," 1-25, he asserts the defeat of Iraq is a defeat for the Soviet Union, because of the degree to which the Soviet supplied Iraq with arms. In "Soviets Red-Faced Over Iraqi Debacle," 3-1, Handelman shows how Iraq's defeat again reveals how poorly the Soviet military and weapons perform. In "The Great Soviet Sell-Off," 6-30, Handelman focuses on a hairdresser's shop in Moscow, and the difficulties that the owners are having in trying to secure ownership, and we're left with the impression that the entrenched communist bureaucracy will continue to be a major impediment to economic reform. A full month before the Soviet coup, and six months before Gorbachev's resignation, we get "Gorbachev's Swan Song?" 7-21, in which Handelman suggests that Gorbachev's fate may have been sealed at the G-7 summit, when he failed to commit himself to a free market and other economic reforms. In "Yeltsin Playing Suicidal Games," 9-27, Handelman warns that Yeltsin's new administration in Russia is being run by people who held senior positions in the old communist regime, and whose commitment to democracy may be somewhat suspect. In "Red But Not Dead," *TS* 10-5, Handelman argues that predictions about the demise of the Communist Party may be premature, and in any case, outlawing it may be counterproductive. He reminds readers that because the party was driven underground in 1905, it was able to regroup and make a comeback in 1917. Ah-hah.

Hepburn, Bob. *The Toronto Star.* (★ ½)
The *Star*'s Jerusalem-based Middle East correspondent has often been accused of being biased, but we find him to be much more balanced than his predecessor, Gordon Barthos. In many of his dispatches we saw a multitude of viewpoints fairly portrayed, and there have been some solid profiles of the Arab countries in the region. Hepburn's "Palestinians Seethe Under Israeli Curfew," 2-1, is quite well-balanced, as we're told how Israel's curfew is making life difficult for the Arabs in the West Bank and Gaza, as well as how Arabs are applauding SCUD falling on Israel. Here, Israeli officials are given the opportunity to explain why the curfews are necessary. The last weekend in June finds Hepburn in Beirut for two features on Lebanon: "Lebanese Pray That Peace Will Last," 6-29, is highlighted by a graphic description of what fifteen years of civil war have done to the city of Beirut; "Guns Are Silent But They're Never Far Away," 6-30, focuses on the problems of disarming the country's militias and points to the apprehension that many have about Syria's role within the country. Hepburn files an informative profile of post-war Kuwait in "War Scars as Deep as Ever in Shell-shocked Kuwait," 7-11. He portrays a people overcome by lethargy, unwilling to put the effort into rebuilding what Iraq had destroyed during the invasion. Hepburn provides a comprehensive survey of Arab-Israeli relations in "Mideast Peace: New Challenge for Mr. New World Order," 9-8, a discussion of not only the coming conflict between the U.S. and Israel over loan guarantees, but also the arrest of "moderate" Palestinian leaders, and Israeli fears brought about by a new Syrian arms buildup.

Johnson, William. *Montreal Gazette.* (★ ★)
Although he writes from Ottawa, Johnson spends much of his time defending the interests of his paper's readership — the English-speaking minority of Quebec. Interestingly, he is a virulent critic of Quebec nationalism, yet a strong supporter of bilingualism. In "Chaput's Dogma Lives on Today," 1-22, Johnson uses the death of a prominent Quebec nationalist, Marcel Chaput, to argue that separatists have been wrong to argue that the French language and culture would disappear if Quebec stayed in Canada. Johnson is convincing in "Important Issue Now Is to Win the Peace," 2-23, written at the time of the Soviet peace proposal, and argues that Bush and the coalition should reject it, as it lets the Iraqi leader off the hook. In a rambling "Spicer Forums' Confused Report Deserves to Be Ignored," 6-28, Johnson still manages to raise the key issue by citing the report itself: "Canadians both inside and outside Quebec admit they are grievously hampered by lack of knowledge: knowledge of our land, history, of our economic reality, of our family citizens. And these are the people asked to propose the form of the new Canada?" In

"World Will Benefit by Aiding Soviet Union," 7-20, Johnson strongly argues that assistance need not necessarily be economic. In "No Need to Push the Panic Buttons," 9-22, he expresses the fear that the federal government's proposals to create an economic union may really be a power grab by the federal government, too easily accepting the government's assurances that there will be many opportunities to fully discuss all proposals. "Telling Tales Out of School," explains the angry reaction to an article by Mordecai Richler in *The New Yorker.* "French Canada was for a very long time a sacred society, with religion and language fused. It was also a society that was assaulted by modernism, by pluralism, and the secular culture of North America. It was defensive, and extremely sensitive to any criticism. Now Quebec has secularized, but it still has the defensive reflexes of a sacred society." In "Canada Has a Lot to Learn from EC Meeting in Mastricht," 12-11, Johnson argues vigorously that Canada has made progress toward constitutional reform more quickly than Europe, and nationalists are incorrect to say that the rest of Canada has not responded to Quebec's demands.

Reguly, Eric. *The Financial Post.* (★ ★ ½)
New York. Although his pieces appear on the "Comment and Opinion" page, he is more of a bread-and-butter writer who concentrates on reporting. Reguly usually sticks to stories on business that often have a Canadian angle. In "Canada Isn't Marketing Its Brainpower," 2-26, he argues that the country isn't promoting its highly skilled labor force and its cheap water supply in its drive to attract new manufacturing jobs. In "Why GATT Would Chill Labatt Deal," 3-5, Reguly shows how GATT may force Canadian provinces to dismantle protective barriers set up for the brewing industry, and how this would make Canadian breweries less attractive to foreign investors. Reguly was identified as a part of a joint team with the *Financial Times* of London and ABC News that uncovered American arms shipments to Iraq just months before the invasion of Kuwait; his own story "White House Allowed U.S. Firms to Arm Iraq," appeared 4-17. In "Water a Precious Commodity to Belzbergs," 9-20, Reguly dissects the last holding that the Canadian financier has in the U.S. The company that Belzberg owns, wants to sell water from under the San Luis Valley in Colorado to urban areas in the Western United States. "Trashy Newspapers Have Strong Appeal," 11-1, is a good profile of one of the healthiest industries in North America — tabloid newspapers. In "Complex Challenge for 'Simple Jeweller,' " 11-22, Reguly traces how Toronto jeweller Irving Gerstein was responsible for the collapse of Zale Corp., the company that he had bought in 1986. The question now, according to Reguly, is whether the fall of Zale's will bring down Gerstein's Canadian business.

Sheppard, Robert. *The Globe & Mail.* (★ ★ ½)
The "Provinces" columnist. He usually provided some new insight but his focus tends to be quite local and limited. For those who follow constitutional affairs, Sheppard provides "Big Brother Isn't So Big Any More," 3-6, arguing strenuously that the government is no longer the senior partner in Confederation, since the responsibilities of the provinces have increased greatly over the past three decades. Sheppard devotes "I'm Trying as Hard as My Parents Ever Did," 6-5, to the views of a reader who challenges the widely-held assumption that the elderly have had an easier economic time than the current generation. "If You Have No. 709, Poor You," 6-13, a profile of the public funding of medical services in Oregon, is the kind of piece that Sheppard typically wrote last year, and we have come to miss. Sheppard argues here that the rising costs of health care to governments will force all of them to examine some form of rationing services, using Oregon's experiment with ranking illness as a case in point quite effectively. In "When a Premier Has a Tunnel Vision," 7-30, he vigorously criticizes Premier Robert Bourassa for pursuing the development of the James Bay II power project, without any apparent concern for the environment or the fate of natives in the affected area in Quebec. Sheppard tells us in "The Long Summer of Our Discontent," 8-26, that Canadians' unhappiness extends well beyond the Prime Minister and other politicians to all the country's institutions, stating only the obvious, although we didn't know that Canadians held beer companies in low esteem until Sheppard mentioned it. In order to control the supply of wheat on the Canadian market during a time of over-production, Sheppard suggests in "How to Make Good Use of a Glut," 10-17, that Canada give some of it away to poor countries without strings attached. Maybe, but he doesn't make the case here.

Simpson, Jeffrey. *The Globe & Mail.* (★ ★ ★)
Still the dean of the Ottawa press corps, Simpson can be counted on to deal with each issue that arises substantively and smartly. With "Reviving the United Nations' Original Version of Keeping the Peace," 1-18, he shows effectively that the U.N. has not abandoned its peacekeeping mandate by participating in the Gulf War; rather, the use of force to challenge aggression was enshrined in the San Francisco Charter. In "Assessing the Position of the United States After the Persian Gulf War," 3-6, he takes on the Canadian commentators who express fear at having a world in which the U.S. is the only superpower, but his discussion could have been stronger, as it's not the knockout punch we'd expected. With the Premier of British Columbia, Bill Vander Zalm, on the political ropes, we get a revealing profile of the man who will probably succeed him in "Taking Stock of the Views of Mr. Harcourt, B.C.'s Premier-in-Waiting," 3-19. Here, the leader of the provincial NDP party is portrayed as more of a Westerner than a socialist. In "School Systems Are Searching for Ways to Measure Student Performance," 7-30, Simpson bemoans the inability of the provinces to collectively develop a standardized test for graduating high school students, and fears that the federal government will enter the field, believing the provinces can do better administering education, making a convincing case. In "Trying to Overcome With a Mishmash Constitutional Approach," 9-25, Simpson hits the nail on the head when he suggests that Canadian politics is dominated by individuals caring only about their own groups, without any concern for the general welfare, echoing Charles Peters of *The Washington Monthly* a year ago. "Tribe, of course, celebrates self by denigrating others, and by recalling all slights, real or imagined, from the recesses of memory and today's headlines. Tribal jealousies are usually rooted in the belief that even though the tribe is doing all right, some other tribe is doing better." Simpson finds substantial agreement on constitutional reform among the three major political parties in "The Hidden Stories Behind the Headlines: Success Is on the Way," 11-8, predicting that the Tories will eventually abandon their proposal to enshrine property rights, in return for the NDP giving up on their insistence that a social charter be included in the constitution.

Stevens, Geoffrey. *The Toronto Star, Montreal Gazette.* (★ ★)
Although his name is not well known, Stevens can be counted on to provide insightful commentary in his column which simultaneously appears in both papers on Sundays. In "It's Time to Reform Our National Symbols," 2-10, Stevens sets forth intriguing suggestions for change, rather than spouting polemics: abolish the monarchy, make the province of Ontario bilingual, and change the provinces to states. With "Some Bad Ways to Put More Women in the House," 6-23, he effectively criticizes the New Democratic Party's plan to set aside a specified number of ridings for women and candidates. Stevens makes some good points in "Canadians Wise to Ignore Out of Touch Party," as he notes how out of touch the ruling Progressive Conservatives are, since their position on many issues is at odds with the feelings of Canadians expressed in public opinion polls. Stevens concedes that the NDP could not win another election in Ontario in "NDP Miracle Exposed as an Accident," 9-8, but he smartly notes the "government has not been as inept as its critics maintain. Viewed in perspective, its mistakes have been more the consequence of inexperience and a shallow talent pool than of wrongheadedness." In "A Federal Election Would Help to Clean the Air," 10-13, Stevens makes a good case for an early vote, as the Prime Minister had just put forward a program for constitutional reform, and an election campaign would force the other party leaders to clearly define their stand on these critical issues. But "Fawning PM Has Lost Influence in Washington," 3-31, is merely a collection of well-worn anti-American cliches: "Mulroney's passion for close relations with the oval office led us into a hasty commitment in the Persian Gulf; into a free trade agreement that has failed to prevent — and may have actually stimulated the de-industrialization of Ontario and Quebec, with nearly 100,000 jobs permanently lost already; [and] into an acid rain agreement that is fatally flawed becase it doesn't provide for independent monitoring of pollution reduction."

Thorsell, William. *The Globe & Mail.* (★ ½)
The paper's editor-in-chief provides a mix of social and political commentary that appears in his column every Saturday. But, as with much of the material we see in the paper, his writing often lacks force and power. In "No 'New Order' Around the Corner, Just a More Powerful Pragmatism," 2-9, Thorsell makes the weak argument that the Iraqi invasion of Kuwait is no different than the U.S. invasion of Panama, but it cannot be compared to Israel's conquering of Arab territories in the 1967 war. In "Defining 'The Nation' Is the Essence of the Canadian Dilemma," 4-27, Thorsell argues rather obviously that the specter of Quebec's separation has forced English Canada to formulate its own identity. Thorsell lamely defends the conservative lending practices of Canadian banks in "Thinking Like a Canadian Is Highly Risky When Talking About Banks," 11-23, making the dubious claim that Canadians are less likely than Americans to loan money for risky ventures because they are more aware of their duty to protect their depositors' money. In "Voice of English Canada Coming Through Loud and Clear," he notes the similarity between the recommendations of the Spicer Commission and the platform of the new Reform Party, extrapolating that government officials and the national press centered in Ottawa will not be able to dismiss English Canada's frustration and demands. Thorsell may not be politically correct but he strikes a sensible note in "Group Dynamics Give Rise to a New View of Morality," 7-6, via the film "Thelma and Louise": "Like the crowd in a summertime melodrama, cinema-goers applaud violence against villainous men by oppressed women — akin to cheering on the innocent damsel in her struggle against the lecherous mortgage-holder. It is morally lazy to accept the murder of a repulsive man who has been prevented from rape but will not say he is sorry. And it is morally careless to applaud two women's assault on a policeman who is doing his duty in tracking them down, and to take delight in the sight of two women shooting at a trucker who makes obscene gestures from the cab of his semi-trailer."

Ward, Olivia. *The Toronto Star.* (★)
After the Gulf War, the focus shifted away from the U.N., and Ward's weekly column was often the only way for us to follow events there. Often facile this year, her column was barely better than nothing. In "Arctic Nuclear Ban in Canada's Interest," 1-7, Ward argues that Canada should support Gorbachev's call for a nuclear test ban. While she naively acknowledges that the Soviet Union has been testing weapons on an Arctic island, she would have us believe that the tests were undertaken without Gorbachev's approval. Ward lists the standard ethical dilemmas of war, making the questions specific to the Gulf, "Nobody's Hands Are Clean in Bloody Warfare," 2-18, but, rather than providing cogent answers, she remains whiny and trite on the horrors of war. In the post-Cold War world, Ward suggests a new but completely impractical role for the U.N. in "Overtures of Peace Rouse U.N. From Coma," 9-30, which amounts to little more than that of world policeman: a new court would be established to deal with "crimes against humanity; crimes against peace; genocide; war crimes; and environmental criminality," and U.N. intervention across international borders. "Mulroney's Bush Ties Don't Sway Diplomats," 10-28, is a mean-spirited attack on the Prime Minister, in which she suggests that, if appointed U.N. Secretary General, Mulroney's friendship with George Bush might lead him to reveal information received in confidence during the course of his work. Ward was well ahead of most of the rest of the press in picking up on the pending repeal of the "Zionism Equals Racism" resolution, and in "U.N. Blew Its Chance to Remedy Mideast Ills," 11-4, she argues forcefully that this resolution and other similar measures directed against Israel may have disqualified the United Nations from taking an active role in the Arab-Israeli peace talks.

Watson, William. *The Financial Post.* (★ ★)
Advice and dissent columnist. Watson is a McGill University economics professor who writes a weekly column that focuses almost exclusively on economic issues. But for an academic, he sometimes relies too much on emotional appeals and not enough on hard data. In "Free Trade Was About Productivity, Not Jobs," 12-28-90, Watson admits that free trade will lead to job losses in the manufacturing sector, but smartly points out that as firms become more efficient, productivity will increase, and so will wages. It is generally assumed that over the past thirty

years, Quebec has been profoundly changed by the development of an entrepreneurial business class, though Watson challenges this perception in "No Wish for Economic Union in Quebec Inc," 2-26, strongly asserting that French Canadian businessmen are inherently protectionist, and therefore unlikely to favor an economic union with the remaining provinces should Quebec separate. Watson gets it right in "Did Gigantes Resign for Right Reasons?" on the resignation of the Ontario's Health Minister, questioning whether Canada's health system needs to be a state-run monopoly, and whether coverage needs to be universal for all the correct economic reasons. The case for "Work of Equal Value Is a Mythical Concept," 5-7, is well made, as he asserts that the determination of what constitutes "equal value" is best made by the marketplace, and not a government commission. Watson may be right when he argues that the federal government has the support of the public in clamping down on wages in the public service sector in "Tories Have Support on PSAC Wage Policy," 9-6, but he is utterly unconvincing as he relies more on unsubstantiated emotion than on a logically reasoned discourse. He is far better in attacking a book by Canadian supernationalist Mel Hurtig, "Free Trade Pact Is Not Betrayal of Canada," 10-24, effectively challenging Hurtig's contention that the pact has hurt Canada's balance of trade, and that foreign investors have been making windfall profits.

Young, Christopher. *Southam News.* (★)
Young, who we see in the *Ottawa Citizen,* is a typical Canadian pack-columnist, his stand on every issue almost entirely predictable. Young was way off the mark in "Will Goals on Gulf Escalate Out of Control?" *The Toronto Star* 1-29, telling us that "Some voices in the U.S. are now expounding a wider agenda than Kuwait, as though the goal of evicting the aggressors was not tough enough. Reinforcing these new objectives is an alarming chauvinism in influential quarters, emphasizing a primary need to prove America's manhood." He is more perceptive in "Reality Is Not Much a Part of Constitutional Considerations," *Montreal Gazette* 3-16, noting that while provincial Liberals ask for more powers for Quebec, statistics reveal that Montreal has the highest unemployment rate in the country. Except for scoring political points, why would any government want what the Liberals are asking for — exclusive provincial jurisdiction over unemployment insurance? In "Gorbachev Wins Another Victory Despite the Odds," *OC* 7-27, Young argues weakly that the Soviet Union has done more for social justice than "Reaganite-Thatcherite-Mulroneyite big-business Toryism" in the West. And with "Elected Senate Might Also Sink to Muckraking," *OC* 10-17, Young uses the excesses of the Senate during the Thomas affair to argue that an elected Senate, approving government appointments, would not be appropriate for Canada.

BROADCAST NEWS

It was a fascinating year to be watching the broadcast industry, with turbulent change in the world and within the industry itself. Newsmen became instant superstars and disappeared just as quickly. It was a year that uninterrupted news coverage would rivet the public for days or weeks on end, the "CNN effect." This was a year for which Walter Cronkite's "picture headline service" was perfectly suited, a year of haunting images: the light show of missiles and anti-aircraft fire over Iraq, the carnage at the Baghdad bunker, Boris Yeltsin waving a Russian flag atop a Soviet tank, the dot obscuring the face of Patricia Bowman at the William Kennedy Smith trial, Clarence Thomas angrily denying Anita Hill's allegations, Anita Hill calmly and succinctly stating them.

For the third consecutive year, the *MediaGuide* offers an appraisal of the broadcast media, defined here as the three major networks — ABC, CBS and NBC — PBS and the cable news stations, CNN and C-SPAN. Broadcast and print share a symbiotic relationship, sharing news and information and helping to establish priorities for coverage and placement. Although the transient quality of television news prevents us from assigning star ratings to broadcast journalists, our methods of evaluation are similar. Our observations are the result of countless hours viewing news programming, occasionally using videotape and transcripts for direct comparisons. Print and broadcast differ in countless ways due to the wide differences in technology employed in each medium. But, as the basic function of each is the same — the dissemination of information in a timely and efficient manner — both should adhere to the same basic principles of journalism. These are accuracy, fairness, balance or objectivity; of course, some programs and correspondents meet these criteria with greater frequency than others. We limit the treatment which follows to the nightly news and Sunday morning programs available on the three networks, public television and the two major cable outlets; these are the primary sources for news in most of America.

With the advent of satellite technology, television became the fastest conduit of news available, with the potential to be the best as well. As we saw with the soaring ratings of CNN during the Persian Gulf War and uninterrupted coverage of the William Kennedy Smith trial, and PBS during the Anita Hill-Clarence Thomas hearings, the public has a genuine craving for raw news and raw information, news in the making. Yet the broadcast media persists in airing journalists interviewing journalists, often in place of substantive reporting. So the public, in order to satisfy its hunger for news and information, must continue to turn to print. Overall, we found the broadcast media's performance in 1991 to be adequate, but just barely. The instantaneous nature of the images presented on news programs has led to a tendency towards instant history; if a broadcaster can't package an event in a 30-second soundbite, he doesn't discuss it at all. This is accepted openly among broadcast journalists. The pit bull of television journalism, ABC's Sam Donaldson, describes his role as a White House correspondent as shallow: " 'I'm talking about very simple, often superficial information, when it comes to the long march of history. . .I don't think it's the job of the reporter to go to a press conference saying, "I'm going to show how smart I am," ' he says. 'It's our job to find out what the president's reaction to the day's news is. . .We're not going to care what Bush has to say [today] five years from now, but it's the story today. And tomorrow my job would be a different story' " ("The Flack Pack," by James Bennet *The Washington Monthly* 11-91). Brit Hume, ABC's current White House correspondent, is equally blunt, calling much of the combativeness of reporters "adversarial posturing": "When members of Congress come in to talk to the press, all you're usually trying to get them to do is get them to make some sharp critical statement about the administration or whoever. The idea that you would seriously challenge any member of Congress to defend his or her position on any issue, and then follow up on the questions, is almost unheard of" ("Brit Hume Fumes on Liberal Biases in Reporting," *The Washington Times* 7-9).

Three Blind Mice author Ken Auletta notes in "Look What They've Done to the News," *TV Guide* 11-9, that "before our eyes, network news is dying. Probable cause of death: both murder *and* suicide." Murder by CNN, Auletta reasons, because of the strains of competing with a global network, and suicide from the increased emphasis on costs. We would add that the networks are indeed committing suicide, but not due to a bottom-line mentality; it is because too little information is being provided to the audience. The nightly newscasts offer journalists who, by their own admission, don't ask enough questions. While this is an indictment also applicable to print, the problem is particularly acute in broadcast; comparatively, print has more physical column inches in which to provide information, whereas the broadcast medium is constricted by the soundbite. The exceptions are the cable stations. CNN is not hampered by a half-hour format, offering news stories that frequently run more than five minutes per story. C-SPAN airs the debates and committee hearings of Congress, with no voiceover, the purest form of news available. Fortunately, during times of crisis in 1991 — the Persian Gulf War, the Soviet coup attempt, the William Kennedy Smith trial, the Anita Hill-Clarence Thomas hearings — broadcast news did provide a wealth of raw data: the news conferences, uninterrupted hearings, the events *as they happened.* But after the crises ended, broadcast news went back to business as usual. And so, we continue to supplement print with broadcast news, simply for the power of images of "a picture headline service."

THE NETWORKS
American Broadcasting Corporation

"World News Tonight"

The long-held internationalist perspective of "World News Tonight" paid off in 1991, proving that a half-hour network news program can compete with the 24-hour news service. "World News Tonight" anchor Peter Jennings had the first news of the initial air attack of the Persian Gulf War due to a live feed from Gary Shepard in Baghdad, 1-16, who noted anti-aircraft fire on the horizon, beating out the other two networks and CNN for the scoop.

Jennings remained his calm, collected self throughout the night and the various crises that would arise during the rest of the year. It was the first evening of the war, though, that we most appreciated his detachment; CBS's Dan Rather was quite distressed, his voice cracking as he announced the beginning of hostilities, and NBC's Tom Brokaw appeared unsure, emphasizing that the reports might be false alarms. Jennings seemed fazed only once, when ABC consultant Lt. Gen. Bernard E. Trainor (ret.) drew an eye-opening parallel: the former *New York Times* Pentagon analyst estimated that, given the number of planes used in the first hours of the operation and the payload they were able to carry, the tonnage of bombs dropped on Kuwait and Iraq was about 18,000 tons, roughly equivalent to that of the bomb dropped on Hiroshima. A numb Jennings could only respond "well, General, keep on with your sums." Jennings acquitted himself well as the feed from Baghdad was lost, turning easily to various maps and experts, despite the foibles of live television. When Jennings tried to compare distances between Baghdad and Riyadh to Baghdad and Teheran in order to evaluate the probability of SCUD attacks on Saudi targets, a cameraman moved the camera to the left, bumping the Iranian city completely off the map. Jennings sighed, "to the right, please," Teheran reappeared, and the anchor finished his calculations. But when the President spoke at 9 p.m. EST, Jennings announced that he wasn't going to try to second-guess or critique Bush, and then proceeded to do just that, reporting, despite all evidence to the contrary in Bush's speech and various reports, that French forces were involved in the first hours.

The following night, 1-17, Jennings kept emphasizing the fact that Pentagon reneged on a promise to brief the press twice daily, noting occasionally "we haven't been briefed yet." (When regular briefings were suspended, 2-24, Jennings predicted that the blackout would worsen the already testy relationship between the press and the Pentagon.) ABC was again first to air a videotape of the bombing of Baghdad, 1-17, from British sister station ITT, with Jennings responding "Good Lord!" to the impressive scene of anti-aircraft fire and tracers flying through the air; Jennings then reran the tape with the commentary added by the ITT correspondent. Trainor and ABC military expert, Anthony Cordesman, explained the different lights and firings, which the anchor unintentionally debased by noting neither had been a pilot. Trainor and Cordesman provided to be assets for the network, explaining strategic developments and possibilities clearly. Cordesman evolved into a military John Madden, drawing chalk lines over maps like a pro. All in all, Jennings's work was steady and collected throughout the war, ABC even running a children's question-and-answer session with Jennings on the war on a Saturday morning, 1-26. Unlike the other two network anchors, Jennings stayed in the studio, his distance from the front lines probably helping him to stay impartial. ABC's coverage generally reflected Jennings's demeanor, refusing to run videotapes of the captured coalition airmen, 1-21, 1-22, the only national news organization to decline.

Jennings turned in a similar performance during the first hours of the Soviet coup attempt, 8-19. Where CBS and Dan Rather led with Hurricane Bob, and NBC and Tom Brokaw led with the word "Chaos!", Jennings was grim, but detached. In discussing the status of Mikhail Gorbachev, Jennings said tautly, "It is assumed he is not free to do what he wants." This special edition of "World News Tonight" ran a full hour, where the other network news broadcasts stayed within their alloted time slot. We depended a great deal on the anchor's experience as the correspondent in Moscow, Sheilah Kast, had only arrived in the Russian capital a few days prior to the coup attempt to staff the bureau during the vacations of the regular correspondents. Much of the Hill-Thomas hearings were aired uninterrupted by anchors and correspondents, who were only seen when recesses were taken. One guest expert on ABC, a female lawyer who would not be expected to be a Thomas supporter, said that the evidence was devastating to Hill's case, 10-12, but Jennings quickly moved on, one of the few hints of bias we saw this year.

The Correspondents

As with the anchors, the Gulf War was the major test for the correspondents. During the first hours, 1-16, Brit Hume at the White House and John McWethy at the State Department did well. Hume professionally reported the drama in the first minutes of confusion, when even Gary Shepard in Baghdad wasn't certain the attack had been launched, but only asserted there was anti-aircraft fire. Hume confirmed suspicions of a coalition strike, reporting that Marlin Fitzwater had been summoned to the Oval Office. Fitzwater, he reported, ran out of his own office down the hallway, responding to the queries of waiting reporters by yelling he'd be back. Minutes later, Fitzwater summoned reporters to the White House briefing room and said simply and soberly, "The liberation of Kuwait has begun." McWethy reported that Secretary of State James Baker and the department were pretty much out of the loop, as diplomatic options had been exhausted. In one of the rare occasions where one journalist interviewing another garnered information, Jennings inquired as to whether diplomacy had failed. McWethy replied, no, as diplomacy had succeeded in putting together and keeping together an international coalition of 28 countries. Diplomacy had failed only with Hussein.

Overseas, Dean Reynolds, son of the late ABC anchor Frank Reynolds, stalwartly reported developments from Tel Aviv, donning his gas mask when the SCUDs were flying. Reynolds, unfortunately, was the one to report for ABC on 1-17 that "we are getting word from, again, a very reliable source that there may have been as many as 20 nerve gas victims taken to a Tel Aviv area hospital this morning. This is the first word, the first hard word, of perhaps unconventional weapons used in this assault this evening." Of course, Reynolds's "very reliable source" was wrong. Forrest Sawyer had memorable moments too, one during a stand-up at the Kuwaiti border, where he had to move several feet in the middle of his report, 2-24, explaining, "We're in the way of a tank." And indeed, a tank was rumbling towards Sawyer and the camera.

On the home front, the reporting of the correspondents remained acceptable. Capitol Hill's Jim Wooten remains palatable, though conventional. Typical is his assessment of the battle over the civil rights bill, 6-5, where he notes that "for better or worse, quotas have become a hot button issue, easily exploited in the quick context of a television commercial," using the Helms-Gantt Senate race as a case in point. Stephen Aug still leaves much to be desired on the economic front, one of the many reporters making assertions on policy that are left unsupported. On 8-20, Aug is flawed in not assessing the overall history when he notes "During the 1930s, the government turned to massive public works projects to pull the nation out of the Great Depression. Government spending on programs like the interstate highway system in the 1950s was also used to help end several recessions." This is simple-minded stuff, as is Aug's determination to tell us several times a year that currency devaluations are good for the economy. He is better, 6-7, investigating further than just the unemployment statistics; Peter Jennings introduces his report, "Economists say that the really important news lies elsewhere in the [government's] report. For the first time in nearly a year, businesses hired more workers instead of firing them." Aug then gives us cogent examples.

The special features of "World News Tonight" continue to attract us, and CBS followed suit with a feature segment of its own. Although "Person of the Week" doesn't have the drama of *Time*'s "Man of the Year," the segment is entertaining enough and sometimes informative. The "American Agenda," though, still needs work. For example, with the "American Agenda," 5-30, Rebecca Chase focused in on the working poor: "This old farmhouse is home to Penny Sheely, her three children and five grandchildren. Penny and her family live on the edge of homelessness." Yet as the camera panned the room, we could see a VCR, a large console television set, a coffee maker, and a microwave. And we see ABC's green side during the 4-1 segment, as Ned Potter laments that "one unfortunate downside to the Gulf War victory has already become clear: gas prices are actually lower than before Iraq invaded Kuwait. That means any hope of higher prices rallying Americans behind a real national energy policy. . .has been dashed once again." Similarly, in the 9-18 segment, Potter notes, "The EPA, which rarely sounds alarmist, says the ozone problem is twice as bad as anyone expected. . .12 million Americans may get skin cancer in the next 50 years. Cataracts and immune disorders will increase. There could even be a threat to the food supply if crops and ocean life are killed by ultraviolet rays." A National Academy of Sciences paper, released 9-6, was far less alarmist and left unreported.

"World News Tonight" is still first in the ratings, garnering 11.6 ratings points (each point equals approximately 1.5 million viewers) for the September 1990 to April 1991 season. It is our first choice as well. Like the other two networks, the news division is restructuring. Unlike the other two networks, ABC is not retrenching. The division got its first executive vice president since David Burke left in 1988. Steven A. Weiswasser will work directly under news president Roone Arledge, and will undoubtedly be a force in the administration of the department. The news division is eager to expand its dominant position, perhaps by adding more prime-time news programming.

Additional News Programming

Jennings, in addition to his anchor duties, is often seen during prime time. It is clear from the ambitious nature of these special reports that ABC is looking to expand. But it is also within these specials that we most clearly see an agenda. Airing the night before the expiration of the U.N. deadline, "A Line in the Sand," 1-14, seems critical of the prospects: one segment explores the lack of an energy policy at length, indicating, apparently, this was to be a war over oil; another is highly critical of Kuwait, as opponents of the regime were interviewed, but not one defender appeared; the final segment, on the military, begins and ends with GIs filling out their wills, and featured military experts, including a Soviet general who helped build the Iraqi war machine, contending that war with Iraq would be long and nasty, despite the predictions of the U.S. air force. Strangely, the theme music for the special was Barber's "Adagio for Strings," coincidentally also the theme for "Platoon." Jennings's follow-up, "A Line in the Sand: What

Did America Win?" 9-12, is oddly timely, airing the same week Saddam Hussein was openly defying the U.N. Jennings's answer is "not much," as he introduces segments on Iraq's continuing defiance (including "never before seen" video of the U.N. inspection team), the arms buildup in the Middle East, the lack of democracy in Kuwait, and the continuing Arab-Israeli conflict centered around the Palestinians and the West Bank. The Israelis come across as Bible-thumping, gun-toting, intolerant fanatics while the Palestinians are moderate, quietly suffering bystanders of historical forces beyond their control. We are happier with the unadulterated news specials. The "National Town Meeting" with Mikhail Gorbachev and Boris Yeltsin, anchored by Peter Jennings and airing in the "Nightline" spot, 9-6, was worth the wait, a fascinating exercise where a Houston Rabbi could ask Yeltsin about anti-Semitism in Russia, and a New York banker could ask Gorbachev how he could have had "those stupid coup plotters" working in his government. No other station had anything remotely this interactive, and we salute ABC for trying something so ambitious.

The "news" value of ABC's prime-time news programming varies in quality. Neither "20/20" nor "Prime Time Live" comes close to "60 Minutes," the perennial standard, but neither truly sinks to the tabloid quality of NBC's "Expose." "20/20" runs excerpts of an exorcism, 4-5, very dramatic, beginning with Barbara Walters intoning "Heaven and Hell — are they real?" and Hugh Downs warning that some scenes may be frightening. The segment, though, never makes clear that the subject, "Gina," was not possessed, but obsessed, having met only two of the four clinical criteria the Catholic Church sets for authentic possession. Background material includes film from "The Exorcist" and a skeptical psychologist who asserts that "Gina's" problem is not demonic, but some extreme form of psychosis or schizophrenia, exaggerated by the priests and her religious mother. Hosts Downs and Walters took this all quite seriously. In closing, Walters noted nervously that nothing was wrong with segment correspondent Tom Jarriel — he was away on assignment. The remainder of the program is equally skippable: high school seniors on spring break. The exorcism segment garnered the program's highest national rating since 1981. Yet we still find quality material on the program. "20/20" was the first program to interview Gen. H. Norman Schwarzkopf, Barbara Walters getting the scoop in a 3-22 segment. We also liked the segment on the hidden children of the Holocaust, 8-9, that was moving without being maudlin. But we rarely tune into "Prime Time Live," as we can stomach neither the inane combativeness of Sam Donaldson, nor the refined fluff of Diane Sawyer. Sawyer offered a goofy appraisal of Demi Moore's provocatively pregnant pose for *Vanity Fair,* 7-18: "It's been about, oh, 15,000 years since a pregnant body was last an object of veneration...when the Jews and the Christians came along, they saw it differently. Women were temptation. The only pregnancy you could celebrate was the one that didn't need sex."

With the combination of the point-counterpoint punch of George Will and Sam Donaldson, interviews with policymakers and the smooth moderation of veteran journalist David Brinkley, "This Week with David Brinkley" is our first choice on Sunday morning. There is a feisty quality of open debate on the program that has yet to be matched by the current mix of "Meet the Press" and "Face the Nation." Sometimes, though, the combative Donaldson oversteps his bounds, and we have to turn the sound off. It's apparent he perceives his role on "This Week" quite differently than his "superficial" role as White House correspondent. We find Sam Donaldson blasting away at Macy's Chairman Edward Finkelstein for his prescription to end the recession, 9-22: "You want to lower taxes? Wouldn't that result in an increased deficit? And haven't we come to believe that that's part of our problem with the country?" Donaldson cuts off Gov. Mario Cuomo, 11-24, interrupting his answer on the state of the U.S. economy by demanding to know what Cuomo is thinking about abortion. When Cuomo objected, saying he was trying to address a more important question, Donaldson responded haughtily that he was the interviewer and he would conduct the interview. Although Donaldson adds less and less to our understanding of the world, Brinkley and Will's intelligent querying of policymakers keeps our attention, and the fireworks over ideology between Will and Donaldson are not to be missed. Brinkley closes the program with his folksy humor, buoyed by his generations of experience as a journalist, taking a marvelous shot at John Sununu, 6-23, at the height of the travel flap: "Buy him a bus...Fix up the inside of his bus with a bed, a bathroom and a little kitchen. He could stop for groceries at the 7-Eleven, and then ride on to some big, important political meeting. If it's in a hotel, he wouldn't even need a room. He could sleep in his bus in the parking lot."

"Nightline" remains the standard for late-night news programming. As with "This Week," the heated exchanges on the program go beyond the sedate debates of "The MacNeil/Lehrer NewsHour" and approach the rough-and-tumble atmosphere of "The MacLaughlin Group." Host Ted Koppel somehow manages to stay unruffled as his guests turn vociferous. The exchange between Sen. Alan Simpson and NPR's Nina Totenberg over the Anita Hill-Clarence Thomas controversy, 10-7, is one example. Said Simpson: "You've been beating the drum on this one almost every day since it started, in the most extraordinary way. Let's not pretend your reporting is objective in here. That just would be absurd." Totenberg shot back: "All I do is report. I don't know who's telling the truth here. There are inconsistencies on both sides. But I do know that I do not appreciate being blamed just because I do my job and report the news." Koppel also follows up: after an hour-long special devoted to the "October surprise," 6-20, he reports at the close of the 6-27 show with information that William Casey, a prime player in the conspiracy theory, could not possibly have been in Paris at the time the alleged meetings occurred. "We have spoken with several men who attended the Anglo-American Conference on the History of the Second World War. William Casey attended that conference at the Imperial War Museum in London." The program acquired a new executive producer, Tom Bettag, formerly with CBS, after Dorrance Smith resigned to become a White House media aide, but suffered no visible ill effects. "Nightline," with its impressive roster of guests and potential for explosive interviews and dialogue, is often a must-see, if you can keep your eyes open that late.

Columbia Broadcasting System

"The CBS Evening News With Dan Rather"

We'd noted last year in our review of the "CBS Evening News" that "increasingly at CBS we see a network in disarray." The situation has not improved. Watching the once-great network news division crumble has been a painful process, prompting such stories as Edwin Diamond's "Eye of the Storm," *New York* 4-15, and Kevin Goldman's "Weak War Coverage Isn't the Only Problem at CBS Evening News," *The Wall Street Journal* 2-7. Producers came and went, Eric Sorenson replacing Tom Bettag as executive producer of the program early in the year, and Susan Zirinsky becoming supervising producer, replacing 30-year CBS News veteran Bill Crawford. Budget cutbacks at CBS hovered near the $150 million mark. Due to a contract with Major League Baseball, the network could only cover portions of the Clarence Thomas-Anita Hill sexual harassment hearings. The contract of China correspondent, John Sheahan, who had been with the network since 1969, was not renewed. The division was publicly criticized for friction between Don Hewitt and the pregnant Meredith Vieira over her "60 Minutes" contract. One of the founding correspondents of "60 Minutes," Harry Reasoner, died suddenly at the age of 68, and the program's producer Don Hewitt and CBS News President Howard Stringer were faced with the challenge of finding potential successors for Reasoner and the other "60 Minutes" correspondents, only one of whom is under age 50. Anxious over the lack of a female star on the CBS roster, once Diane Sawyer departed for ABC and Connie Chung cut her workload, CBS Inc. chairman Lawrence A. Tisch attempted to woo Barbara Walters away from ABC, but was unsuccessful. According to *WSJ* media reporter Kevin Goldman, "CBS's Tisch Sought Barbara Walters for No.3 Network," 7-26, the news department moved beyond the conventional choices in a way that seemed desperate. "CBS is so anxious to land a high-profile woman that it has considered going outside the news ranks. Earlier this year, CBS studied reprising its classic interview series 'Person to Person.' The plan is all but dead, but a favored choice of host was an interesting indication of CBS's thinking: Instead of a CBS News correspondent, some at the network were pushing Candace Bergen, the actress who plays a broadcast journalist on the hit series 'Murphy Brown.' "

As with last year, though, all was not lost for CBS news. Despite all the flaws of CBS's Persian Gulf War coverage, CBS's Bob McKeown was the first journalist in Kuwait to record its liberation. In an exclusive, 9-2, Peter Van Zant was present in the Latvian president's office when he received the official call from Bush informing him that the U.S. is prepared to recognize the independence of the Baltic states. "60 Minutes," after 23 seasons, is still the top-rated evening magazine news program. "48 Hours," hosted by Dan Rather, is gaining in stature, avoiding the fluffy topics that "20/20" often employs. The news division toyed with a news-gathering partnership with Turner Broadcasting. And "The CBS Evening News With Dan Rather," although often occupying last place in the ratings, retains a traditional hard news style; its airing of the first profiles of the Democratic presidential candidates, 9-16 to 9-20, is just one example.

The Gulf War coverage was, at best, imperfect. Dan Rather went to Saudi Arabia for the special series, "Countdown to Confrontation," at 1990's end, and would adopt there a combative, "War is Hell" posture that did not leave him, even after the war ended. "The CBS Evening News" opened 1-16 with Rather informing viewers that Baghdad correspondent Allan Pizzey was reporting flashes on the horizon. We were shocked to hear Rather's voice nearly cracking. After Marlin Fitzwater made the official announcement, the anchor gulped that war "always brings a, a lump, to your throat." Unfortunately, there was no live feed from Pizzey, because CBS lost all contact with its Baghdad team right before the broadcast at 6:30 p.m. EST, and did not regain the link for more than five hours. This meant Rather was reduced to interviewing consultants and correspondents in the studio and in Washington, ordering a sour-looking General Michael Dugan and Bob Schieffer to point out different items of interest on a studio wall map. Rather's somber interview with Fouad Ajami, of Johns Hopkins and *U.S.News & World Report,* gave us some sense of potential realignments in the region, but realistically, as Ajami was careful to note, it would be months before Bush's New Order emerges, if that quickly, and it's clear that the Middle East "will never be the same." Rather later interviewed Walter Cronkite, who expressed disbelief that New Yorkers were still going about their business even though war had broken out. At 10 p.m. EST, a frazzled Lesley Stahl emerged from a briefing and informed us somewhat gratuitously that Bush had made the decision for the use of force several days earlier. Stahl also told us that Bush had invited Rev. Billy Graham to spend the night at the White House. Saudi correspondent Bob Simon kept alleging, bitterly, that the Saudis were abandoning their posts in the oil fields on the border of Kuwait with no confirmation, Rather turning grim at this news. It was not an auspicious start to the war for the heirs of Edward R. Murrow. Rather and the correspondents added little to our knowledge the first night of the war, a sharp disappointment as the network had had six months to prepare for the moment.

"The CBS Evening News" spent the rest of the year playing catch-up, unable to recover from those first fumbled moments of the Persian Gulf War. Once Iraqi missiles were fired at Tel Aviv, 1-17, Rather postulated that this was aimed to blow up the Arab coalition, not an Israeli target, and then proceeded to discuss it with every guest, from the dour-faced Dugan to Fouad Ajami, for the next two hours. That night, Rather would also report incorrectly that the Israelis were retaliating for the SCUD attacks, via a phone call from Jim Jensen in Tel Aviv. Rather's coverage of the Soviet coup attempt was also mushy. The first CBS report came fifteen minutes after ABC briefly outlined the situation at 12:45 a.m. EST, 8-19, both of which followed CNN's bulletin; CBS interrupted local programming with a grim Bill Plante telling viewers unceremoniously that "Soviet President Mikhail Gorbachev has been dumped in a coup." But Rather and CBS News chose to lead the 8-19 newscast with footage of Hurricane Bob, a storm with no geopolitical implications. When Rather did get around to the coup, he only presented interviews with Russians and Latvians around the U.S. to find out what they thought, along with analysis from Princeton Sovietologist Stephen Cohen. Special prime-time programming would supplement this coverage, but the actual newscast was lacking. And sometimes Rather's coverage of these events is just plain goofy. In a mid-morning update, 8-21, Rather announced "One airplane is carrying the coup leaders trying to make their getaway. They're on the run like Thelma and Louise, if you will," describing the escape minutes later as "the coup leaders have already high-diddle-diddled out of here." We give up.

The Correspondents

Baghdad-based correspondent Betsy Aaron turned in a questionable performance during the war; *The New York Times*'s Walter Goodman warned "cautionary signals for the alert viewer" in his assessment, "Broadcasters in the Gulf and What They Merit," 3-4. We find this is an accurate *caveat*. Aaron's reporting seemed to bend with the prevailing wind, often pointing at U.S. culpability: "[Saddam Hussein's speech] drew a captive audience, in hotel lobbies, tea houses, and on the street. All day long, they waited to see if the United States would stop the war," 2-26; "With their city in ruins, what is left on the street is pride. . .the average citizen here is confused by the politics swirling around him. He thinks the Iraqi government has made every concession for a peace with honor. He believes that Iraq is due at least that, and tonight, this [bombing] is what the Allies have to say to the Iraqis," 2-27; "The one thing people have to know is that this man privately, Saddam Hussein, is a hated man," 3-7. But Aaron's work was compensated for by Bob McKeown's intrepid march into Kuwait City. "From this day forward," proclaimed McKeown, "I think history will record Independence Day as February 26 in Kuwait City." The first of two CBS crews into Kuwait, McKeown and his crew made their way to the capital unescorted by the military, and scooped the competition with vivid accounts and interviews. "I've been kissed by more Kuwaiti men tonight than I can count," said McKeown, 2-26. Richard Threlkeld had charge of the second crew, reporting from the border. Pentagon correspondent David Martin observed it seemed as if the mother of all battles had become the mother of all bug-outs. Saudi correspondent Bob Simon's earlier adventure was not so fortunate when he and his crew of three were captured by the Iraqis after going off without a military escort. Missing for 40 days, Simon and his crew would tell their story on "60 Minutes." Exploits such as these, though, were few and far between.

White House correspondent Lesley Stahl moved to "60 Minutes," replacing not Meredith Vieira, but Harry Reasoner. She was succeeded by Susan Spencer, a national correspondent with CBS since 1989 who covered the Perisan Gulf War from Riyadh. Spencer is innocuous enough, but we don't understand why Stahl was not replaced by her number two at the White House, Wyatt Andrews. The remaining reporters are a mixed group. On the Clarence Thomas nomination, Rita Braver offered a reasonable interpretation of the liberal backlash over the event, 7-1: "The thing that has most people worried, though, is the statement he once made about what are called the unenumerated rights, the things like abortion that are not specifically mentioned in the Constitution. And he once talked about how judges should not be roaming unfettered through the Constitution and to some people that means they should not expand those rights, should not expand abortion. I think that's what's behind all this concern." Bruce Morton, though, crosses the line in his commentary, 6-29: "The Warren Court stressed concern for individuals and individuals' rights. . .The Rehnquist Court is much more concerned with the rights of government, the state, authority. Government can tell the difference between good and evil in this philosophy and should encourage one and forbid the other." Oh. Morton offers some free advice to Bush, 4-1, that also seems inappropriate: "Many Eastern Europeans claim that socialism has been a political and economic failure, but here at home, George Bush's domestic policies offer no hope of solutions to our ever-festering social problems. Bush could capitalize on his new-found popularity by bringing some European style social justice to this country." Morton never looks at the implications of such advice. On general assignment, Richard Threlkeld moved from the Gulf to economics, and distinguished himself on neither subject. He alarms us with the prospects of war, predicting the battle deaths of 2,500 Americans in the first 10 days alone, 1-4, and postulating that macho is behind the atrocities of war, 2-8. And Threlkeld just gets it wrong, 9-26, in reporting that "the Census figures confirm what's so evident throughout America in this recession. There are more poor people now than ever," but, in reality, census data shows that while the percentage of people defined as poor rose 0.7 percent, the number of people living in poverty actually declined.

Similarly, Ray Brady is filled with gloom and doom on economics, regardless of the data. He is particularly sensational where he can put a face to the statistics. Brady catalogues the plight of striking workers replaced by those willing to work with flourish, 4-3: "Captain Jim Gulley's family has worked these waters for a hundred years. But a strike pitted him against the management of the tugboat company he helped to build. Gulley and his shipmates were replaced. Out of the work they loved." The remainder of his report is unabashedly pro-union: ". . .as strikes disappear, swamped by a wave of replacment workers, some wonder if a valuable American tradition is also being replaced." Management, in this dispatch, is given one sentence, and the replacement workers none. Dan Rather introduced the 0.3 percent rise in unemployment with drama, 6-7: "Amid all the talk and some evidence of economic recovery, unemployment hit a four-year high." Ray Brady opined, "the unemployment numbers jumped last month partly because of workers like these Massachusetts state employees. They're protesting the cutbacks that pushed them into the ranks of the 370,000 Americans who lost their jobs last month." But only 1,700 jobs of 12,123 jobs *added* by Dukakis were lost in 1991, according to *The Boston Herald*. "CBS Evening News" dropped the nightly stock chart in February, airing the Dow Jones Industrial Averages only when there are major swings in stock prices. "The CBS Evening News With Dan Rather" did add a special feature, perhaps to make it more competitive with ABC's "World News Tonight." The CBS entry, "Eye on America," is a renamed, recycled "American Agenda," and works about just as well.

Additional News Programming

The grandaddy of all television news magazines, of course, is "60 Minutes." One of the last remnants of the glory days of the network, the program is consistently rated in the top 10 weekly, and is unequalled by any of its prime-time competition. "60 Minutes" this year weathered the departure of two correspondents: Meredith Vieira left after becoming pregnant with her second child, and a founding correspondent, Harry Reasoner, died at age 68, three months after retiring. Of the original reporters, only Mike Wallace remains. Lesley Stahl came on board to replace Reasoner early in the fall. "60 Minutes" provides challenges to the conventional wisdom, and relishes exploding myths. Morley Safer, 3-24, does just that in an expose of the civil rights bureaucracy of the EEOC. Safer reported the story of the EEOC discrimination lawsuit against Chicago's Daniel Lamp Co., claiming that no blacks worked at the company. "60 Minutes" established that 11 blacks were working there at the time, and that the majority of the remainder of the small company's employes were Hispanic. What began the company's troubles? As reported by Safer, "[Owner Mike Welbel's] troubles began in February 1989 when a black woman named Lucille Johnson who'd applied for a job was not hired. She filed a complaint with the Chicago office of the EEOC. She claimed she didn't get the job because she was black." "60 Minutes" gets the exclusive on Bob Simon and his 3-man crew's 40 days as POWs in Iraq, 3-3. We get a chilling coda to the week's events in the Soviet Union, 8-25; a Soviet journalist who rose to fame for his critical coverage of the Afghan war provides an alternative view to the euphoric coverage of the failed coup, contrasting the demonstrators standing in front of the Russian Parliament Building with the long lines of consumers snaking around empty Moscow stores, and comparing this to Germany in the early '30s. He then visits communal farms, factories, and hospitals to find nostalgia for the Brezhnev years when, despite all the other problems, food was on the shelves and spare parts were available for the machinery. The reporter tells Mike Wallace that about 80% of the population, the "Soviet 'silent majority,' " either supported the coup attempt or were neutral, and that the reformers have about a year to prove that they can deliver the goods, or they may face another coup. We were moved by Andy Rooney's tribute to the late Harry Reasoner, 8-11. At moments, it seemed the essay was a eulogy for the old times at CBS News, when thoughtful documentaries were produced as regularly as "reality programming," such as "Rescue 911," is now.

Happily, "48 Hours" is beginning to show signs of evolving in the "60 Minutes" tradition. Where Dan Rather appears combative and uncomfortable on the evening newscast, he's a tough, hard-nosed reporter out on the streets for "48 Hours," and the role suits him. We got everything from battered women, 2-6, to marriage and divorce (a 2-hour special edition), 5-22, to gun control, 6-5. As further evidence of the program's seriousness, "48 Hours," 8-21, preempted the scheduled show on adoption, in favor of live reports from Moscow, with dramatic footage of Gorbachev's motorcade driving through eerily lit Moscow streets, interviews with young Soviet journalists who had covered the siege of the Russian parliament building from the inside, profiles of Boris Yeltsin, reports from their White House correspondents up in Maine, and an interview with Zbigniew Brzezinski. On the late night schedule, one side benefit for the CBS News division was the resuscitation of "America Tonight." Scheduled to be cancelled January 18, the program was given new life by the Persian Gulf War. CBS News is also planning the addition of "The Verdict," a series covering the courts, and "Whose Side Are You On?" a program which would debate a controversial topic, such as doctor-assisted suicide, each week. These programs ran in previews during the summer.

The Sunday morning entry from CBS is "Face the Nation," hosted by Lesley Stahl, until her move to "60 Minutes." Stahl, like Sam Donaldson, views her role as combatant rather than interviewer. An adversarial stance is acceptable, but Stahl often turned inappropriately accusatory. A 3-31 program with HHS Secretary Louis Sullivan brought on this diatribe: "There are all these other health issues, and your administration always says we can't throw money at it. But the only solution to solving these unbelievably painful things to watch, poor children, children who die before the age of one, children getting measles again, is money." And when she wasn't crossing swords with her guests, Stahl was just plain mushy. She complained to Brent Scowcroft, 2-17, of the "image" problem in the Persian Gulf: "[The U.S.] is going to come out looking like the bad guys, and the Soviets are going to walk away looking like all they care about is peace and they will have won the hearts and minds of the Arab world, and we will have lost that." Stahl was succeeded by Bob Schieffer, who has yet to make his mark at the network. He has his opportunity on "Face the Nation."

National Broadcasting Co., Inc.

"NBC Nightly News With Tom Brokaw"

The network that once hosted the esteemed "Huntley-Brinkley Report" now appears a victim of tabloidization, despite the kinder, gentler persona of anchor Tom Brokaw and several bona fide news scoops. There were two defining moments that colored the balance of NBC's news coverage. On 4-16, NBC was the only network to air the name and photo of the alleged Palm Beach rape victim, and would continue to do so throughout the trial. As justification, NBC News president Michael Gartner cited the publication of her name in London's *Sunday Mirror* and Palm Beach's *Globe,* arguing that adding her name to a national newscast did not make any difference in preserving her anonymity, a ridiculous extrapolation. *The New York Times* followed suit, citing NBC's broadcast and leaving NBC News to take the heat. Gartner ascribed even nobler motives to *Newsweek,* 4-29: "I'm in the business of disseminating information, not withholding it. Names add credibility; they round out a story," and asserting that the "outing" of rape victims will be "extraordinarily difficult for this generation, but it may perhaps help their daughters and granddaughters." The second incident occurred when "Expose," NBC's news magazine, broadcast a report, 4-28, on Sen. Charles Robb (D-Va.) alleging an affair with a former Miss Virginia/U.S.A. seven years ago and Robb's presence at a 1983 party where cocaine was used. Said *Los Angeles Times* Washington bureau chief Jack Nelson in *The Wall Street Journal,* 4-30: "This is a new low." We agree and hope that NBC can right its course under Gartner before the division acquires the character of Fox's "A Current Affair."

The finances of NBC and its parent company, GE, are also a factor in the generally discouraging atmosphere. Network president Robert C. Wright had to issue a memo in May to nervous affiliates asserting that General Electric had no plans to sell the network. Still, rumors flew in August about a possible sale to Los Angeles developer Marvin Davis. The Gulf War cost

NBC an estimated $37 million to cover, and GE's acquisition of FNN, which merged with CNBC, cost $145 million, not including the $9.5 million in liabilities GE assumed. Perhaps as a result of the unusual cash expenditures, the news division suffered serious cutbacks, inhibiting its news-gathering ability. There were layoffs in Boston, Pittsburgh, London, and Johannesburg, and bureau closings in San Francisco, Miami and Frankfurt. The Barcelona station will close after the Olympics. NBC will pool convention coverage with PBS in an unprecedented agreement to cut costs and expand coverage. But most telling was the closing of the New York bureau. Geraldine Fabrikant reported in *The New York Times,* "NBC Is Closing News Bureau in New York," 7-12, that "a number of NBC News employees said that as the network closed bureaus and laid off people, it was changing from a news-gathering organization to little more than a news-production company that gets its news from outside sources."

Gartner has already begun to redefine the mission of NBC's news division, particularly "NBC Nightly News." The program has developed a populist voice and become more reactive. Instead of being centered on government or international events, Gartner and executive producer Steve Friedman have pioneered the concept of a local national newscast that focuses on local reaction to national events. While the concept is interesting, and the mix lively, the program's content has suffered. For instance, Carl Stern, the Supreme Court correspondent has been demoted from regular on-air status; he will instead submit memos about legal reasoning, and the Supreme Court coverage will center around people's reactions throughout the country. With all these discouraging developments, things can't get much worse for NBC News.

Yet "NBC Nightly News" is palatable. Tom Brokaw is both anchor and managing editor of the program, and his friendly, folksy manner serves him well. It certainly will be appropriate for the kind of concept news show that Gartner and Friedman apparently have in mind. Unfortunately, Brokaw was the anchor most obviously unsettled by the Gulf War. For the first minutes of the crisis, 1-16, after ABC had gotten the scoop, Brokaw kept reporting the events as a false alarm, emphasizing this to the extent that a viewer we contacted was taken aback to find that the attack was the real McCoy. Ten minutes into the broadcast, Brokaw had his confirmation. From Baghdad, Tom Aspell placed the location of the first explosions at the airport and, in his refined British manner, reported the aerial bombardment of Baghdad — "Ohh, that was a big one, right outside the window" — until the line went dead. Brokaw informed viewers that Aspell was an experienced Middle East correspondent, and losing the line was no cause for alarm, reassuring himself as much as his audience. To make things worse, Mike Buettcher was reporting from Dhahran when the air raid sirens went off. Brokaw asked an increasingly worried-looking Buettcher what the drill was, as Buettcher told his camera crew to seek shelter. Then the picture went dead, and Brokaw seemed completely unnerved. He appeared only comforted by the appraisal of Col. H. G. (Harry) Summers, Jr., an NBC consultant for the duration, whose combat record and expertise at the Army War College, Brokaw rightly commended. When Summers said things were going fine, Brokaw's tensely hunched frame relaxed visibly. On day two, 1-17, Brokaw was easily the most visibly nervous of the three network anchors. He was constantly reminding us that there was no word out of Baghdad from the correspondents. He dutifully reported events in Israel, but even the strategically-minded assessments of Harry Summers did not ease his mind. The *Los Angeles Times*'s Robin Wright also turned up as an NBC consultant/expert on the Middle East for the Gulf War, as did General William Odom. But no one could get Brokaw to relax on the air. Watching him became a nerve-wracking experience.

The mood was initially apocalyptic during the Soviet coup attempt as well. Brokaw led with "Chaos!" 8-19. Pentagon correspondent Fred Francis did not help. Initially pictured in his office with scarlet-bound books on the Soviet Union clearly visible on his bookshelf, a grim Francis discussed the situation with Brokaw, correctly identifying the possibility of a faction launching a nuclear strike at a rival faction. But possibility is not probability, and the voiceover by Francis, about the confusion over who was in charge, running over video of nuclear missiles being launched, was inappropriate. Fortunately, we were spared video of the missiles exploding. The rest of the coup coverage was steady and professional, with Brokaw regaining his cool. NBC scored a scoop among the networks, 8-27, when it obtained a homemade video of Gorbachev that his son-in-law had recorded the second night of the attempted takeover, when the Soviet leader, aware of what the coup leaders were telling the world from BBC and VOA broadcasts, decided to set the record straight. The tape has an almost surrealistic quality, as it begins with shots of Gorbachev's granddaughter dancing — they were using a family tape — before a drawn and haggard Gorbachev, dressed in a sweater, appears in the first political "living will," telling of how he was arrested and demanding to be returned to office.

Garrick Utley and Jane Pauley are Brokaw's seconds. While Pauley's presentation is Brokaw's, Utley can barely sit still in his chair. In addition to his tendency towards drama that we noted last year, he insists on talking down to his viewers. We're informed by Utley, 10-19, that "American tax rates today, are, relatively speaking, low. Repeat, low. About half the top rate in the rest of the industrialized world. Our sales taxes are equally low. Fact: the United States is a tax bargain, believe it or not." Utley never bothers to support this facile appraisal with comparisons or data on marginal rates, but instead calls for socialism: "The difference of course is that in other countries, people see their tax money coming back to them to make life more agreeable and secure. In Western Europe, health care for everyone. In Scandinavia, day care centers for mothers and children. In Japan, modern, efficient cities that work." Where Brokaw and Pauley represent everyman, Utley brings to mind an Ichabod Crane-ish schoolmaster. When we see Utley in the anchor chair, we move on. John Chancellor, the program's in-house pundit, doesn't add much to the newscast, his commentaries quirky, relentlessly pompous, and often unsupported. "In the 1980s, the rich got the headlines and the rest of the country got the shaft," he asserts 11-20. He does catch the White House, though, 7-11, commenting on Clarence Thomas's admission that he was a casual pot smoker back in school, and noting the discrepancy between the White House's willingness to overlook Thomas's casual drug use and its tough anti-drug policy, under which casual users face stiff penalties. But, overall, the former anchor's commentary offers little to set the newscast apart from the competition.

The Correspondents

The most recognizable correspondent for "NBC Nightly News" is Capitol Hill reporter Andrea Mitchell, a frequent face on "Meet the Press" as well. Mitchell will generally only put her spin on a story when prompted by the anchor or another correspondent, although we saw this tendency increase more this year than ever before, particularly regarding racial issues. She allows White House counsel C. Boyden Gray no rebuttal of her on-air ravaging of his White House memo on civil rights guidelines, 10-24: "The only problem — [the memo's] claims are dead wrong." The memo, she admits, was only "on the table" for discussion. Mitchell reports, 11-21, that "civil rights advocates believe [the battle over the bill] was only the first shot in a deliberate White House attempt to play the politics of race. The issue is jobs and who gets them — a powerful political issue, especially in hard times." Mitchell names no one to support her assertion. We continue to be impressed by Mitchell's understudy, Henry Champ. His 8-11 dispatch on the wetlands provided balance to the controversy over the definition: ". . .even though the Maryland coast is dotted with farms centuries old, building lots were now being reclassified as wetlands. This wooded lot, with housing on both sides, couldn't get a building permit — all because the new Army Corps of Engineers regulations said land with any amount of water lying on the surface for seven consecutive days, or land with moisture found 18 inches below surface for the same seven days, was to be called wetlands."

NBC's war coverage gave rise to one of the Persian Gulf stars who went back to relative obscurity as soon as the war was over. Arthur Kent, the so-called "SCUD stud," did not particularly impress us with his reporting, and we were left wondering what all the fuss was about. Mike Jensen remains "completely trapped by his conventional readout of events, rarely venturing into uncharted waters," as noted in *The 1991 MediaGuide*. In his dispatch, 1-2, Jensen cites "a lot" of economists, businessmen, and sundry who think we may slip into depression, but he names no names, his opening including only a clip of Gary Shilling for support, Shilling a hopelessly inveterate doomsayer. We were pleased, though, by the steadfast quality of Fred Francis at the Pentagon, who turned up several scoops. Francis stayed on the newsbeat this year, a refreshing change. He discloses that a high-level Iraqi defector has confirmed that gaps in U.S. intelligence allowed much of the still-active nuclear weapons program to escape destruction during the war, 6-25, adding that a recent U.N. delegation was denied access to one particular nuclear facility. Francis updates this, 7-11, with the news that the U.S. could launch air strikes against Iraqi nuclear research targets in seven to ten days, if need be, calling to account Western intelligence sources, who underestimated both Iraqi and Iranian nuclear research abilities. At the height of the tension, Francis was the first to reveal that the U.S. was poised to attack Iraq, if Iraq did not agree to full inspections of weapons sites, 9-18. Iraq backed down.

We see a disturbing tendency for "NBC Nightly News" to use the program as a springboard for advertising. White House correspondent John Cochran, in his report on President Bush's latest defense of John Sununu, 6-19, noted that at least comedians had something else to joke about other than Dan Quayle. NBC then ran a clip of Jay Leno telling a Sununu joke on NBC's "Tonight Show." This plug came after NBC News ran stories related, directly or indirectly, to the NBA championship series, on nights in which the games were aired on NBC. Science correspondent Robert Bazell reported on an upcoming episode of "Quantum Leap," 8-13, in which the main character becomes an ape in a science research lab. The news value? According to Bazell, animal rights activists are applauding the episode, while researchers are worried that viewers will get the wrong idea about the treatment of apes in labs. This trend gets a resounding thumbs down to NBC for allowing its nightly newscast to become a shill for its entertainment programming.

Additional Network Programming

"Expose" is the closest competitor to the news magazines of ABC and CBS, but does not approach the quality of its competition. There was little to "Expose" that was newsworthy, much of it along the lines of the Sen. Chuck Robb story, 4-28. It was a disappointing year for the alternative news programming at NBC. It did run a special, "The Soviet Coup," 8-21, which, while similar to the CBS entry, had one distinguishing characteristic. While both shows made mention of the distressed Soviet economy, only NBC offered a report on the subject, concentrating on the black market, and featuring KGB footage of undercover operations against the marketeers. Sunday's "Meet the Press," the longest-running newsmaker program in the history of television, remains true to founder Lawrence Spivak's vision of the press giving policymakers a live grilling for the electorate to consider. The policymakers include everyone from Cabinet undersecretaries to the vice president, with Richard B. Cheney, 1-27; Richard Darman, 2-3, and George Mitchell, 4-3, among them. The press interrogators are among the most distinguished in Washington: Bob Novak, David Broder, Elizabeth Drew, et al. The mix is one of the most informative and entertaining available, and has been imitated in one aspect or another by every other policymaker talk show on television. In an effort to cut costs, NBC transferred the "Sunday Today" staff to New York, moving "Meet the Press" host Garrick Utley as well. He was replaced by Tim Russert, 12-8, NBC's Washington bureau chief, and former Cuomo strategist. As a politico-turned-journalist, it will be interesting to see what Russert will dish out.

Public Broadcasting System

Although PBS is not necessarily known for its news programming, there was a story this year that belonged part and parcel to public television. Uninterrupted live coverage of the Anita Hill-Clarence Thomas sexual harassment hearings garnered record ratings for PBS. The recesses were filled by interviews with members of the Senate Judiciary Committee that were conducted by Paul Duke, Jr., and NPR reporter Nina Totenberg, who first broke the story of Anita Hill's allegations. That most of the country tuned into PBS or CNN, and stayed there for hours on end, indicates that there is a desire for news in the making. PBS also got a great deal of attention with the "Frontline" expose of the "October surprise." Aired 4-16, the program detailed accusations outlined by Gary Sick in *The New York Times,* 4-15. This was the most notable of the PBS documentaries, and had the most far-reaching implications with its allegations of treason. Ultimately, though, reporter Robert Parry admitted he could find no smoking gun.

PBS also offers the best nightly newscast available. "The MacNeil/Lehrer NewsHour" not only offers an overview of the day's events, but interviews with policymakers, economists, academics, and various experts on the events and pertinent issues of the day. The hour-long program, hosted by veteran journalists Jim Lehrer and Robin MacNeil, is the best possible marriage between the information and overviews of the network news programs and the interviews of the Sunday talk shows. We particularly appreciated the perspectives during the war, MacNeil conducting a roundtable discussion among geopolitical strategist Edward Luttwak, the U.K. Defense Minister Tom King, *Time* national security correspondent Bruce Van Voorst, *New York Times* columnist Leslie Gelb, and two retired U.S. Generals, Fred Hayes of the Marine Corps and John Wickham of the Army, 1-30. After the press flap over pool restrictions, "NewsHour" offered several roundtable assessments of the overall coverage, 2-1 and 2-14. It is on 2-14 that we hear a fine defense of CNN's coverage from CNN VP Ed Turner: "There are no easy answers. We're trying to find them, but that's a real war going on out there. . .we let the conclusions come later. It's an imperfect world, this business of daily and hourly journalism. The truth will come out eventually." It is this type of intelligent perspective that is the steady fare of the "NewsHour." The correspondents, Judy Woodruff and Charlayne Hunter-Gault, are solid interviewers and command our attention on the set or on assignment. We rarely miss a "NewsHour."

The one-two punch of the "NewsHour" and the "Nightly Business Report" that we celebrated last year was terminated early in the year, unfortunately, as WNET in New York moved NBR to a late-night spot. By the time NBR was aired, we'd already gotten detail on the winners and losers in the market from other sources. Subsequently, WNET moved NBR back to its pre-"NewsHour" time slot, and we're much happier with the reams of detail from all the markets that NBR provides rather than the alternative newscasts.

THE CABLE ALTERNATIVE
Cable News Network

As *Time* magazine's man of the year cover would attest, it was Ted Turner's year in the broadcast industry. Although we don't necessarily agree with *Time*'s selection, we cannot dispute the impact CNN has had on the world at large. From the 24-hour coverage of the Persian Gulf War to minute-by-minute updates of the Soviet coup to live coverage of the William Kennedy Smith trial and Anita Hill-Clarence Thomas sexual harassment hearings, CNN had it all.

Despite the fact that ABC had the first reports of the initial air attack on Baghdad, it was CNN's war. Anchor Bernard Shaw, Peter Arnett and John Holliman gave dramatic live reports from the Al-Rashid hotel, 1-16, with Holliman holding a microphone out the window so viewers could hear the bombs exploding. Shaw and Holliman could not resist tweaking the noses of the competition, reassuring the networks that their correspondents were fine in the bomb shelter beneath the hotel, naming the reporters and the networks. Wolf Blitzer noted from the Pentagon, "it would appear to be the real thing." CNN got unintentional plugs from Secretary Dick Cheney, who noted in the first Pentagon briefing at 9:30 p.m. EST, 1-16, that he'd been watching, and from Joint Chiefs Chair Colin Powell who referred to CNN's coverage during a briefing twelve hours later. So many were glued to CNN that the phenomenon grew into something apart from the network: the "CNN effect." After the first days, though, CNN became a lightning rod for criticism, due to the reportage of Peter Arnett, who was allowed to stay in Baghdad long after other journalists were expelled. Arnett was later snookered by a woman screaming in front of the bombed-out bunker, who later turned up at other bomb sites for the BBC and European stations, a mourner for hire. The networks accused CNN of making special concessions to Iraq in return for privileges, and ABC sneered at the cheap emotionalism of CNN's rerunning of the POW video. CNN spokespeople put much of this down to sour grapes on the part of the networks. The accusations became particularly ugly after Arnett scored an exclusive interview with Saddam Hussein, 1-30. CNN VP Ed Turner had the last word on "MacNeil/Lehrer," 2-14: "There are some who try to cast us as un-American or less than patriotic, because we are reporting from the camp of the adversary. I hold the old-fashioned belief that one can be both a journalist and a good American, that you don't have to come down on one side or the other. . .Americans are resilient and tough and they understand that news does not have to be agreeable to be newsworthy." This attitude was further reflected in CNN's coverage of the new famine in Africa, 6-17 to 6-21, a story the networks largely ignored. The Soviet crisis also belonged to CNN. CNN interrupted a business news show with a special report at roughly 11:45 p.m. EST, 8-18. Moscow correspondent Steve Hurst, who made the *big* mistake last year with the "news" of Gorbachev's resignation as Communist Party General Secretary, redeemed himself as he reported, quietly and calmly, on what was known at that time, and continued his professional reporting throughout the coup attempt. CNN had continued to run special reports updating us throughout the night. During the 12:00-12:30 a.m. time slot, CNN broadcast the pre-recorded "World News This Week," striking a note of surreality, as the head of the Institute for U.S.-Canada Studies asserted that the U.S.S.R. had passed the most dangerous phase of political instability. CNN released for home video both its coverage of the war and coup attempt.

Further evidence of CNN's growing clout is found in the defections of journalists to the network. NBC's Mary Alice Williams was rumored to be talking to CNN about returning to the network. Veteran newspaperman Tom Johnson consolidated his power at the network after only a year and a half as CNN's president. David Broder and Jack Germond became political analysts for CNN. Additionally, the BBC announced plans midyear to become the second global television network, via satellite. The estimable "Crossfire" show, with Michael Kinsley usually dueling with the likes of Robert Novak, can sometimes pull us away from PBS's "MacNeil/Lehrer NewsHour." We do love competition.

C-SPAN

A year CNN's senior, C-SPAN is the news junkie's dream come true. Broadcast, like CNN, 24 hours a day, C-SPAN does not offer programming in the traditional sense. Where Turner and CNN really do give us much of what we need to know about the world, C-SPAN gives us the unadulterated news in the U.S. government and the U.K.'s House of Commons, airing debates and committee hearings live and without anchor voiceover, the purest form of news available in the country. It was to C-SPAN that we were riveted during the congressional debate over the use of force in the Gulf, 1-11 to 1-14. It was C-SPAN we (and Wall Street) switched to for Alan Greenspan's testimony throughout the year, as the Fed chairman became instrumental in steering the economy. And we tuned in to C-SPAN again and again to check the progress of legislation affecting the markets, and, of course, to see if Clarence Thomas would be confirmed by the full Senate to the vacant seat on the Supreme Court. C-SPAN, though, offers more than the workings of government, supplementing its coverage with interviews and panel discussions. In an unusual experiment, C-SPAN branched out to provide a week of *Time,* in which C-SPAN's cameras were allowed into *Time*'s editorial offices, and like Congress, simply left running as the editors and sundry at *Time* went about their business, a fascinating exercise.

It was a year of challenges for broadcast news, some met, some missed. Despite dire predictions, most of them on television, it is unlikely that broadcast will replace print anytime soon as the best source of news and information. The programming now simply does not have the sophistication of print, as simple as print can be sometimes. But with broadcast so sorely tested in 1991, and largely remaining an adequate source of news, for the first time we are beginning to see the potential. As we said last year, though, "we won't hold our breath."

PUBLICATIONS

THE PACESETTERS

The New York Times

It used to be that when *The New York Times* found itself embroiled in a controversy, the issues involved rattled the Establishment, posed important constitutional questions, and changed the course of history, as in the case of the Pentagon Papers in 1971. In 1991, however, the *Times* came under attack from all fronts for its tabloid-style handling of a story about an alleged rape victim in a case involving a relative of Senator Edward Kennedy. Both *Times* staffers and long-time readers were shocked and dismayed by the story, Fox Butterfield's "For Woman in Florida Rape Inquiry, a Fast Jump Up the Economic Ladder," 4-17, and publications ranging from *The Economist* to the *National Enquirer* declared open season on the *Times,* with *Time* running an article on the embroglio under the mischievous headline: "Tarting Up the Gray Lady of 43rd Street," 5-6.

Stepping back from the emotions of the moment, though, it is clear that the rape story is symptomatic of the existentialist crisis the paper has been suffering in recent years. The *Times* has always been proud of its reputation as the country's paper of record, enjoying all the power and prestige that position conveys. But as newspaper readership declines, especially among the young, the *Times* runs the risk of becoming a monarch in a country that has moved on to a parliamentary system of government. On a less lofty level, the *Times* was hit hard by the recession of 1990-91, with the New York Times Co. newspaper group suffering a 52% drop in profits in the first quarter of 1991. The financial problems are exacerbated by the astronomically high costs of publishing a newspaper in New York, which almost sank two city tabloids, the *Post* and the *Daily News,* and which has *The Wall Street Journal* nervously awaiting its union contract renewal. As if all this wasn't enough, the Long Island-based tabloid *Newsday* has established beachheads in the outer boroughs and is steadily advancing into Manhattan, laying the groundwork for what some observers feel will be the mother of all circulation battles.

The *Times,* under the guidance of executive editor Max Frankel, who inherited his post just as these problems were developing, is responding vigorously to the various challenges. The *Times* is repositioning itself in the New York marketplace with a greater emphasis on features and local news. In April, an expanded daily sports section was added with much fanfare and more sports stories were featured on the front page, placed right next to the latest developments from the Middle East and the Soviet Union. There is an increased emphasis on city news, and interestingly, unlike other papers, such as *The Washington Post,* which shifted foreign correspondents into the Gulf to cover the story, the *Times,* by and large, sent metropolitan reporters.

Does all this mean an end to the days when the *Times* was more concerned with the political intrigue in Kabul than with municipal politics in the Bronx? We doubt it, although stories about the Bronx may be better written than in the past. The question remains, however, if the *Times*' motto to publish "All the news that's fit to print" will continue to be the paper's standard for journalistic excellence, or its epitaph.

At Home Abroad

The *Times* coverage of the Gulf War was anchored by chief Washington correspondent R. W. Apple, Jr., who landed in Dhahran shortly after hostilities began. Apple, who was the Saigon bureau chief in 1968, drew on that experience. In one of his earliest pieces from the Gulf, "Hueys and Scuds: Vietnam and Gulf Are Wars Apart," 1-23, he marveled at the remarkable breakthroughs in technologies since that time, noting that "A newspaper reporter who spent almost three years in Saigon talked more times to his editors on the first day in Saudi Arabia than he did the entire time he was in Vietnam." Nevertheless, Apple soon discovered that some elements of communication during wartime still hadn't changed since the days of Tet and Westmoreland, and had what *Washington Post* media reporter Howard Kurtz characterized in "Times Pulls Rank in Dhahran Tiff," 2-9, as a "rather unpleasant discussion" with Col. Bill Mulvey, the officer in charge of the Pentagon's Joint Information Bureau.

Apple was apparently upset because the *Times* pool correspondent was idle, leaving the paper with no dispatches from the field. As Kurtz reported it, Mulvey said that Apple had threatened to use his connections in Washington with officers above Mulvey's pay grade in Riyadh and Washington to put Mulvey's career out of commission. In the grand tradition of the press getting the last word, Apple penned a "News Analysis," "Press and the Military: Old Suspicions," 2-4, writing that Mulvey ". . .has lost the confidence of the press corps as the days have rolled by with no major change, and questions have mounted about the fairness of the entire system."

The *Times* coverage of the war did suffer from a lack of on-the-scene reporting from the front lines that we have come to expect; although coverage did pick up once the ground war was underway and the pool system disintegrated. National security correspondent Patrick E. Tyler broke an important story in "Best Iraqi Troops Not Badly Hurt by Bombs, Pentagon Officials Say," 2-6, quoting unnamed "Pentagon officials" to the effect that the intensive air war had failed to "substantially weaken the combat effectiveness of Iraq's elite ground forces in a well-entrenched 'strategic reserve' in northern Kuwait and southern Iraq." The report set off fireworks in Riyadh and Dhahran. Eric Schmitt, in "Iraq Said to Hide Key War Center In a Baghdad Hotel for Foreigners," 2-14, reported that "senior American military officials" had disclosed that the last secure transmission link between Baghdad and its forces in Kuwait was originating from a "two-floor basement 'communications node' in the Rashid Hotel in downtown Baghdad," and that the large presence of civilians, including foreign journalists, prohibited the allies from launching a strike on the site.

Metro reporter John Kifner, in "Mud Is the Strongest Enemy as the 101st Takes Central Iraq," 2-28, offers an evocative dispatch from the Euphrates River Valley on the success of the longest helicopter assault — 170 miles — in military history. Kifner later covered the aftermath of the failed post-war uprising against Saddam in haunting, graphic reports. Another metro reporter, Donatella Lorch, did a fine job in covering newly-liberated Kuwait City.

It was then-metro reporter Chris Hedges, though, who emerged with the most interesting war stories, and whose experience may serve as a paradigm of sorts for the paper's overall coverage. On February 10th, he was detained by U.S. military officials while investigating complaints that Saudi merchants were charging exorbitantly high prices. Several weeks later, covering the liberation of Kuwait City, which he reached before U.S. troops did, Hedges encountered one Kuwaiti woman who asked him his name and then said that she had promised God that she would name her newborn son after the first American she met during Kuwait's liberation. "My boy will be named Chris Hedges Dhubia."

Things turned more serious for Hedges, though, when he ventured into southern Iraq to cover the Shiite revolt following the war and was held captive for five days by Iraqi Republican Guards. Hedges recounted his captivity in two superlative reports nominated for 10 Best consideration in foreign correspondence, "In Growing Disarray, Iraqis Fight Iraqis," 3-10, and "A Reporter in Iraq's Hands: Amid the Fear, Parlor Games," 3-12. Hedges returned from his adventures and reassigned to his old beat, and was soon covering gangster funerals in Queens. Late in the summer, he was named Cairo bureau chief.

There was much reshuffling of the *Times* foreign staff throughout the year, with no net decline in quality in the political reports, but with no serious effort was made to grapple with economic issues. Bill Keller left the Moscow bureau in February, replaced by Francis X. Clines as bureau chief, but returned in August at the time of the coup, scoring a 10 Best selection for foreign reporting for his "Week in Review" analytic, "From Resistance of the Few to Revolt of the Masses," 9-15. Former Bonn bureau chief Serge Schmemann, who received a 1991 Pulitzer Prize for International Reporting for his coverage of German reunification in 1990, returned to Moscow, where he had been stationed previously. *Times* Soviet coverage was also bolstered in August by the brief return of Felicity Barringer, who reported from Leningrad.

New Delhi bureau chief Barbara Crossette was reassigned to Washington, but scored a 10 Best for Foreign Reporting for her coverage of the assassination of Rajiv Gandhi. She was replaced by former Beijing bureau chief Edward Gargan. Former legal affairs correspondent Philip Shenon assumed duties in Bangkok, and global trade reporter Clyde H. Farnsworth was transferred to Toronto. South of the border, Lindsey Gruson is gone from El Salvador, replaced by Shirley Christian, who in turn was replaced in Buenos Aires by former banking reporter Nathaniel C. Nash. We immediately saw a marked improvement in economic coverage of Argentina. New Mexico City bureau chief Tim Golden shows promise in this important beat. Finally, in the key Jerusalem bureau, former Rome bureau chief Clyde Haberman replaced Joel Brinkley. Roger Cohen was originally slated as Brinkley's replacement, but opted instead to take time off to co-author a book on General Schwarzkopf.

Public and Private

When the news of a possible occurrence of rape at the Kennedy family compound in Florida first broke shortly after Easter, regular readers of the *Times* were not surprised to see the story buried in the paper's national news section. The story was more suitable for the tabloid press, after all, than for the respectable *Times*. The story moved to the front page, 4-17, when political correspondent Robin Toner profiled the beleaguered Senator in "For Kennedy, No Escaping a Dark Cloud," noting that "Even many of his critics acknowledge that Mr. Kennedy is one of the most influential Senators on Capitol Hill, perhaps the most visible standard-bearer for liberal causes." Included on the jump page, page A17, was "For Woman in Florida Rape Inquiry, a Fast Jump Up the Economic Ladder," by Boston bureau chief Fox Butterfield with Mary B. W. Tabor, billed by the *Times* on the front page as "A profile of the woman who accused Senator Kennedy's nephew [William Kennedy Smith] of rape."

Readers were shocked, however, by the article, which not only named the alleged victim, but pictured her mother as a social-climber and cast aspirations on the alleged victim's character. Butterfield included quotations from her "friends" on her "wildness" despite a *Times* policy of not publishing negative comments from unnamed sources and published information on her illegitimate daughter and moving vehicle violations. Butterfield and Tabor were literally voyeuristic at the end, offering readers who had the stomach to read that far a peek inside her daughter's bedroom window, an unprecedented low for reporting at the *Times*.

The article appeared the day after NBC News, citing the publication of the alleged victim's name in a British tabloid and the fact that many people in the Palm Beach area were aware of the young woman's identity, had named the alleged victim in a nationwide broadcast. The *Times* stated that while it usually declines to print the names of rape victims, "NBC's nationwide broadcast took the matter of her privacy out of their hands." Despite the *Times* effort to center any controversy around the largely philosophical (and trendy) question over the propriety of publishing the names of rape victims, the character of the article itself quickly came under attack.

The very next day, on the *Times* op-ed page, former Dukakis campaign staffer Susan Estrich (a rape victim herself) wrote in "The Real Palm Beach Story," 4-18, that the *Times* was like a "thoughtful toddler" in following NBC News in "jumping off the Empire State Building," and that while "it is one thing for women to encourage one another to stand up and stand tall. It is another for a news organization to substitute its judgement for the victim's — to decide that keeping up with the competition is more important than humiliating this woman or encouraging others to report rapes." *Times* columnist Anna Quindlen, in "A Mistake," 4-21, wrote that "Any woman reading the *Times* profile now knows that to accuse a well-connected man of rape will invite a thorough reading not only of her own past but of her mother's, and that she had better be ready to see not only her own name but her drinking habits in print."

Quindlen wasn't the only *Times* staffer upset with the article. In "Times Article on Kennedy Accuser Ignites Debate on Journalistic Values," 4-26, William Glaberson reported that "A petition, signed by some 100 Times employees, including many reporters and editors, raised three concerns" about the article, including an " 'outrage about the profile' because of its tone, the lack of a similar piece about Mr. Smith and the publication of the woman's name." Official *Times* comment on this equivalent of a journalistic Chernobyl came in an "Editor's Note," 4-26, which intoned that "The article drew no conclusions about the truth of her complaint to the police. But many readers inferred that its very publication, including her name and detailed biographical material about her and her family, suggested that the Times was challenging her account." The *Times* insisted that "No such challenge was intended," and that "Whenever possible, the Times intends to continue its longstanding practice of withholding the names of sex crime victims while informing its readers in the fullest and fairest ways about major cases."

In the Nation

Investigative political reporting continues to be the weak spot at the Washington bureau, with the paper being scooped this year on such stories as White House Chief of Staff John Sununu's questionable travel expenses and the Clark Clifford-BCCI scandal, the latter story first appearing in the *Times* as a "Washington at Work" profile, "Clark Clifford, Symbol of the Permanent Capital, Is Faced With a Dilemma," 4-5, by legal affairs reporter Neil A. Lewis.

Ironically, the *Times* had the BCCI story back in 1988, but unaccountably never published the report. According to a news brief in *Newsweek,* 9-16: "Times investigative reporter Jeff Gerth traveled to the bank's Luxembourg headquarters and reported on how BCCI had mysteriously escaped regulation worldwide, funded arms deals and forged ties to Clark Clifford's First American Bankshares — all details that would become newsworthy later on. The article languished in the business department before finally being published in altered form this summer. Gerth was never told why the story wasn't published earlier. Business Editor Fred Andrews says he doesn't recall why the article didn't run: 'At the time it was not a bombshell. In hindsight, it looks like a fine piece of work.' "

The *Times* is showing some life on the national security beat, although we were disappointed by State Department correspondent Thomas Friedman's war coverage. Michael R. Gordon continued to show improvement, before taking time off to write a book on the Gulf War. The aforementioned Patrick E. Tyler, coming over from *The Washington Post* late in 1990, is developing into a major talent. The *Times* even took the unprecedented step of profiling a Washington figure who had died four years ago but still continued to cast a shadow over the U.S. intelligence community in Andrew Rosenthal's report on the late William Casey, "A Spy's Bequest: Riddles He Might Love," 8-15. "In a city where many former officials linger in that category called Forgotten But Not Gone, Mr. Casey has accomplished the opposite trick."

Congressional coverage has been uneven in the past, but the paper evidently feels it has shored things up with the addition of Adam Clymer, a veteran whose work this year showed a fresh, youthful enthusiasm. Now departed-Congressional reporter Susan F. Rasky and chief Washington economic correspondent David E. Rosenbaum received the 1991 George Polk for National Reporting for their coverage of the 1990 budget mess. "Meticulously and insightfully, they covered the complex issues, political maneuvering and personalities in the greatest budget debate that has ever taken place in the United States," the awards committee said. Polk Award aside, we still feel Rosenbaum, who often misses the finer points of Beltway policymaking, all but ignored fiscal policy options to deal with the recession, placing the health of the economy solely on the Federal Reserve's shoulders. He will reportedly be transferred to a new beat in 1992.

Washington correspondent Maureen Dowd had a rocky year. In April, she turned in the eyebrow-raising "All That Glitters Is Not Real, Book on Nancy Reagan Says," 4-7, a breathless look at Kitty Kelley's *Nancy Reagan: the Unauthorized Biography.* Kelley's publisher, Simon & Schuster, had sent advance copies to major newspapers with the understanding that stories on the book would not appear until 4-8, the *Times* jumping the gun with a lengthy article devoted to gossipy details about the Reagan's personal lives as unearthed by Kelley. At the time we thought the article was just an editorial glitch, but it turned out to be a harbinger of what was to come. Dowd's coverage of the Clarence Thomas controversy in October was also noticeably partisan, in favor of the woman's movement, in such reports as "Getting Nasty Early Helps G.O.P. Gain Edge on Thomas," 10-15, as first Republicans are ravaged for "battering" the other side with "nasty, personal attacks," and then the Democrats are ravaged for putting up with it.

The Thomas-Hill confrontation received the amount of space and coverage in the *Times* that the paper usually reserves for international crises, offering eight articles on 10-8 alone. The reports varied in quality. Tamar Lewin, in "Professor's Description of Events Called Typical," 10-8, states that "Experts on sexual harassment say that the description Anita Hill gave of Clarence Thomas's advances when she was a personal assistant 10 years ago are almost a model for the kinds of sexual harassment cases that have gone to the Federal courts over the last decade." However, "A Private Person in a Storm," by Roberto Suro 10-11, based on reporting by Suro, Isabel Wilkerson and Felicity Barringer, is as thorough a report on Anita Hill's background as we saw anywhere, the *Times* reporters even speaking to her parents. "Her family and friends point to her rigidly moral upbringing in rural Oklahoma that left her somewhat naive and more than a little idealistic."

The whole issue of sexual harassment in the workplace was given prominent attention, with "Sexual Harassment at Work Is Pervasive, Survey Suggests," by Elizabeth Kolbert 10-11, appearing on the front page. Even the normally sensible editorial page was affected, the *Times* arguing in "Finally, a Proper Hearing," 10-10, that "Though limited in scope to alleged misconduct in the Federal workplace, the inquiry must include a short course on the subject of sexual harassment."

In non-political domestic coverage, science writer Natalie Angier received a 1991 Pulitzer Prize for Beat Reporting for her "compelling and illuminating" articles on molecular biology in 1990, and received a 10 Best selection for General Reporting for her "Science Times" article "Pit Viper's Life: Bizarre, Gallant and Venomous," 10-15. Science writer William J. Broad also won a 10 Best for General Reporting for his report on the possible threat posed by meteorites, "There's a 'Doomsday Rock,' But When Will It Strike?" 6-18. Publishing reporter Edwin McDowell was right on top of one of the year's biggest and strangest industry stories. In "Simon & Schuster Pays $920,000 for a First Novel," 4-11, McDowell wrote how a first-time novelist with an apparent background in the intelligence community had hit the jackpot with a novel on a serial killer by presenting a manuscript with endorsements from such bestsellers as John le Carre, Joseph Wambaugh and Clive Cussler. Le Carre's U.S. agent faxed a copy of the article to the author in London and two days later McDowell reported in "A Spy Novel's Boosters, It Seems, Aren't," 4-13, that in the case of the le Carre and Wambaugh the endorsements had been faked. Simon & Schuster rejected the novel, *Just Killing Time,* several weeks later.

Economic Watch

The *Times* faces several strong competitors in its coverage of finance and Wall Street, primarily from the "Money and Investing" section of *The Wall Street Journal,* but "Business Day" holds its own against the best of them, featuring such talent as Wall Street correspondent Kurt Eichenwald, finance correspondent Leslie Wayne and accounting reporter Alison Leigh

Cowan. The inquisitive Sarah Bartlett, back from authoring a book on KKR, usually follows the Big Apple's budgetary problems, but occasionally weighs in with precise examinations of Wall Street personalities and financial topics.

Floyd Norris, whose most impressive work appears in his Sunday "Market Watch" column, rounds out Wall Street coverage with insightful analyses of the broad financial trends revealing themselves in the Big Board's ups and downs. Also on Sunday, Diana Henriques, authors the perceptive "Wall Street" column, devoted to a brief but in-depth study of a particular company's outlook. Just below Henriques's column, we find Jonathan Fuerbringer's "World Markets" column, which typically highlights an attention-grabbing currency topic, but rarely illuminates the ebb-and-flow of political and economic forces contouring the markets. Isadore Barmash retired this year after 26 years on the retail and fashion beat.

Beyond these specialties, the quality of the section's reporting varies. One area that needs work is the coverage of economics and economic policy. Business editor Fred Andrews seems to be working on this, trying out new talent such as Sylvia Nasar, who joined the page after stints at *U.S.News & World Report* and *Fortune*. Economics correspondent Louis Uchitelle remains very often out of focus, hampered by the two-dimensional belief that there is an inflation/growth tradeoff built into the economy. The "indicator" man in Washington, Robert D. Hershey, Jr., seems to go along with the *Times* indicator fixation. On trade, Keith Bradsher switched from the telecommunications beat early in the year, landing in unfamiliar territory just as important trade issues were unfolding. Consequently, his reports usually only skimmed the issues, lacking the insights we craved.

The "Economics Scene" column is designed to add new dimensions to the section's economic coverage, but under the watch of septuagenarian Leonard Silk and his protege Peter Passell, the column has most often been a vehicle to advance their particular perspective on the economy. Silk, a dyed-in-the-wool Keynesian on domestic economics, allied himself with the easy money crowd this year even when lower short term interest rates were doing next to nothing for the economy. Passell, a Yale-educated Ph.D. who has slowly been assuming responsibility for the column, is neo-Keynesian and only slightly more open to exploring other economic frameworks in the column. He is strong on micro-economics issues, at least.

"Business Day" is placing increasing emphasis on its coverage of the tumultuous banking industry and legislation that affects it. Beginning on 2-17, the section ran a five-part, front-page series called "Banks Under Stress," which examined the upheaval. Steve Lohr, who impressively bounded onto the business pages after several years in London, dazzled us with dependable high-quality explorations and profiles of the banking sector. He also handled much of the paper's BCCI coverage. Also on banking, Michael Quint showed steady improvement, becoming increasingly more probing as the year went on and banking-merger-mania moved into high gear. On banking and S&L legislation, Stephen Labaton, new to the position this year, stands out as a promising up-and-comer.

Regional and foreign correspondents add a national and international dimension to "Business Day." In Chicago, Eric Berg, a competent generalist, proved reliably solid on business stories emanating from the Midwest's financial capital, while Detroit's Doron P. Levin is reliable on the inner-workings of the Big Three automakers. Business stories generated in the Southwest are serviceably tracked by Thomas C. Hayes in Dallas and Bernard Weinraub, who replaced Larry Rohter in Los Angeles. Also regular contributors to the page are foreign correspondents James Sterngold and David E. Sanger in Japan, Steven Greenhouse in Paris and Ferdinand Protzman in Germany, Sanger this year scoring a 10 Best for Foreign Reporting for his report on the Japan's successful auto manufacturing venture in Malaysia, "A New Car for Malaysia, New Influence for Japan," 3-6.

The Sunday "Business" section should be the strongest weekend business section in the country, but this year especially we found the lengthy leads that dominate the front page varying in quality from week to week, often too featurish to be useful. Within the body of the section, however, there are plenty of original articles that go beyond daily reporting to look at business and industry trends, with Peter Lewis's column "The Executive Computer" especially useful, and Floyd Norris's P.1 column a must-read. "Forum," an op-ed page that is still in its formative years, keeps getting stronger, attracting more authoritative and creative business, financial and economic policy thinkers. Claudia Deutsch's "Managing" is always an interesting and quick read, although "The Executive Life" that appears next to it is still mere fluff, even though it is more substantive than it was under Deidre Fanning's stewardship.

Approximately once a quarter, the Sunday business section also runs a special magazine supplement called "The Business World" which mixes articles from the business staff and outside contributors. We were especially impressed this year by Stephen Labaton's "Wall Street's Ambitious Top Cop," cover 3-24, and L. J. Davis's "When A.T.& T. Plays Hardball," cover 6-9. Finally, we applaud the *Times* for its Sunday "World Stockmarket Survey," the best such display anywhere, but we are not happy that "Business Day" dropped the gold price display on page one, substituting the oil price.

On Our Mind

In 1991, for the first time since publication of the *MediaGuide* began, we were dismayed at the poor quality of the editorial columns. The editors are direct in their viewpoints, and this we can appreciate. We also concede their right to an unremitting devotion to Democratic party political positions. In the last several years, though, we had been encouraged by the willingness of the editorialists to seriously engage in debate with legitimate opposing viewpoints. This year, they all too often were back to the bad old habit of issuing manifestos, take it or leave it boilerplate we found exceedingly dull.

The *Times* opposed war with Iraq in early January, calling on Congress, in "The Larger Patriotism," 1-10, not to "confuse patriotism with blind loyalty to the President." Once war began, the paper, in "What the Bombs Said," 1-17, called the aerial bombardment of Baghdad "a just message on behalf of honorable goals." In "State of the War," 1-31, the *Times* applauded the President for limiting his goals in the Gulf to the removal of Iraqi troops from Kuwait and viewed favorably the Baker-Bessmertnykh statement as one that "can be interpreted as opening, if only by a crack, a new door to peace." After the war was over, the *Times,* in " 'This Aggression Will Not Stand,' " 3-1, called the victory a "glowing moment" for the allied forces, and concedes that "The world that overestimated Saddam Hussein also underestimated George Bush. This page, and others who agreed with the President's goals but thought he was pressing too fast, have to acknowledge that his choices at treacherous junctures proved as successful as they were bold."

The *Times* was unsparingly critical of Mikhail Gorbachev early in the year, contending in "The New Old Face of Tyranny," 1-14, that "When he uses tanks to crush singing students, and freedom, he instead ignites America's anger and disgust," and, in "No Aid for a Repressive Moscow," 1-15, calling for the suspension of food and other aid to Moscow. Not surprisingly, the *Times* soon became an ardent supporter of the Grand Bargain approach toward the Soviet Union, in such editorials as "A Western Spur to Soviet Reform," 5-24. However, in "Sticks and Carrots for the Soviets," 6-4, and "Disarming the Soviets, With Aid," 6-18, the *Times* came out against Defense Secretary Richard Cheney's contention that Western aid to the Soviet Union should be tied to cuts in Soviet military spending. In "People Have to Free Themselves," 8-21, the *Times* praised President Bush for his handling of the Soviet crisis so far but comments: "The Bush Administration might have fortified Mr. Gorbachev's position by committing itself this summer to the so-called Grand Bargain. The basic idea was to offer substantial aid explicitly linked to measurable reforms. Would such an arrangement have prevented this week's coup? No one can say, though it could have shown the Soviet people a plausible path out of hardship." In "After the Joy, Winter," 8-25, the *Times* renews its campaign for the Grand Bargain: "It is not to provide charity, but to promote the birth, and ease the birth pains, of a market economy." The paper's views on these matters were indistinguishable from those of the Western bankers and International Monetary Fund.

The *Times* gave the President much lower marks for his domestic policy. In "The Bully Pulpit, Half Empty," 1-2, the *Times* ushered in the third year of the Bush presidency by noting that "... so far Mr. Bush rejects only ambiguity: clever and energetic in foreign policy, clumsy at politics, irresolute about domestic needs." Commenting on claims that a cut in the tax rate on capital gains would help bail out ailing banks by causing real estate prices to rise in "Capital Games," 3-10, the *Times* sniffs that "This claim is even more pathetic than the other rationales. It makes about as much sense attacking Scud missiles in Iraq by carpet bombing the entire Middle East." In "The Many David Dukes," 11-14, the *Times* charged that "Mr. Duke was astute enough to recognize that the Republicans were soliciting racist votes without owning up to it. He is the extreme result of the Republican strategy to play to racial fears."

We were dissatisfied, overall, by the performance of *Times* columnists this year, with new "Foreign Affairs" columnist Leslie H. Gelb ranking as the biggest disappointment. Gelb took up the cause of the Grand Bargain in his columns, more out of reflexive action than reflective thought. His forays into domestic affairs were mostly foam. We got more out of retired columnist Flora Lewis's efforts. We dread the mush of Anna Quindlen. William Safire remains at the head of the pack, turning his not-inconsiderable critical talents to the Bush administration this year, and receiving a 10 Best citation for his efforts on White House Chief of Staff John Sununu, "In Deep Sununu," 6-20, "Sununu Blames the Jews," 6-27, and "BCCI and Sununu," 10-28. "Observer" columnist Russell Baker also scored a 10 Best for his effort on the multicultural movement, "Scipio to Hannibal," 6-25. At the end of the year, "In the Nation" columnist Tom Wicker retired, and word had it that R. W. Apple, Jr., hoped to replace him.

Outside of the regulars, the *Times* op-ed page continues to be a Trafalgar Square for America's chattering class, and we appreciate the wide range of contributors, from former presidents to unemployed TV writers. At times the writers produce something provocative. In "The Election Story of the Decade," 4-15, former national security council staffer Gary Sick advances the thesis that high-ranking Iranian officials stuck a deal with the Reagan-Bush campaign in 1980 to delay the release of the U.S. hostages in exchange for arms supplies from Israel. The account brought the so-called "October Surprise," back into the headlines and the public debate, although it was discredited again by the end of the year. The *Times* op-ed page even ran two major efforts debunking Sick's theories, by two men who would know, former Carter advisor Lloyd Cutler in "The 'October Surprise' Made Unsurprising," 5-15, and Middle Eastern arms merchant Manucher Ghorbanifar, in "Spilling the 'October Surprise,' " 8-28.

More than most issues the debate over Clarence Thomas's nomination to the Supreme Court was fought in the nation's op-ed pages, and the *Times* published essays which both framed the debate and carried it further. In "Clarence Thomas, A Counterfeit Hero," 7-9, Haywood Burns, dean of the CUNY Law School at Queens College and chairman emeritus of the National Conference of Black Lawyers argues that Supreme Court nominee Clarence Thomas "is no role model for poor youth. If he has 'made it,' he has at the expense of betraying those from whom he has come," and that Thomas is a "counterfeit hero," and a "snake." Harvard law professor Laurence H. Tribe, in " 'Natural Law' and the Nominee," 7-15, questions Thomas's professed belief in the doctrine of "natural law" deriving from the "inalienable right 'given man by his Creator' " clause in the Declaration of Independence.

In "I Dare to Hope," 8-25, Maya Angelou, poet and professor of American Studies at Wake Forest, and no friend of conservatism or the Bush administration, writes that she is supporting Clarence Thomas's nomination to the Supreme Court: "Because Clarence Thomas has been poor, has been nearly suffocated by the acrid odor of racial discrimination, is intelligent, well trained, black and young enough to be won over again, I support him." In the most illuminating article we read anywhere on the Thomas debate, we hear from Thomas himself, in "Climb the Jagged Mountain," 7-17, excerpts from a commencement address that he delivered at Savannah State College on June 9th, 1985, in which he spoke of his own experience in overcoming racism while growing up and warns the graduates not to use racism as an excuse for not getting ahead. "Do not be lured by sirens and purveyors of misery who profit from constantly regurgitating all that is wrong with black Americans and blaming those problems on others. Do not succumb to this temptation of always blaming others." We congratulate op-ed editor Michael Levitas for digging out this gem.

Weekend Edition

The *Times* weekly wrap-up of the news, "The Week In Review," continues to feature correspondents recycling the events of the previous week, at times offering some analytical insight, the highlight being the Bill Keller piece on the "August Revolution" cited earlier. *The New York Times Magazine* sets the standard for Sunday magazines. In 1991, though, most of the action in the Sunday *Times* came in the *Book Review.*

Late in the year, the *Book Review* brought down on itself the wrath of Norman Mailer, upset over the assignment of his new novel, *Harlot's Ghost,* to critic John Simon, whom Mailer reportedly labeled the "Adolf Eichmann of theater critics," and the anger of attorney Alan Dershowitz over the assignment of *Den of Thieves* by James B. Stewart to *Hanover Square* author Michael Thomas. In the full-page advertisement "An Open Letter from Alan Dershowitz Concerning a Conflict of Interest Hidden From the Readers of The New York Times Book Review," 10-17, the famous lawyer argued that Thomas is an anti-Semite and disgruntled former employee of Burnham and Company (forerunner of Drexel Burnham) who has a vested personal and professional interest in seeing Milken in particular and Wall Street in general discredited. "When I learned of these facts, I brought them to the attention of *The Book Review* in an effort to have the book reviewed by an objective reviewer. Alternatively, I requested an opportunity to provide 'a box' adjoining the review, which would express my point of view and which would disclose the conflict. *The Book Review* refused to do either, and I have felt compelled to take out this advertisement." We must say we were astonished at the selection of Michael Thomas to review the book, simply because he had compiled a record of venomous attacks on Drexel at *The New York Observer.*

Like Dershowitz, Mailer is never one to duck from a fight, and he promptly fired off a lengthy letter to the *Book Review* editor, "A Critic With Balance," 11-17, claiming that, based on his earlier critique of his novels and his actress-daughter's stage performance, Simon was professionally unqualified to review *Harlot's Ghost.* The editor replies that Simon "wrote a fair and balanced review that met the standards of this newspaper," while Simon dismissed the letter as an "irrelevant hue and cry." Perhaps the most telling comment on all came in a letter from a reader in Maine, published in the 12-15 edition: "The whole episode confirms what I have suspected for some years: you folks in the big city are not getting enough oxygen."

At times in 1991 we could understand that letter writer's feelings. But while the *Times* stumbled on occasion during the year, it remains structurally sound, and the editors seem to be edging closer to striking the right balance between finding fresh, unorthodox approaches to presenting the news and still delivering on substance. In competition with other dailies, with TV news, and with the history and tradition of the *Times* itself, Frankel and his crew remain formidable contenders.

Editor:	Max Frankel
Address:	229 West 43rd Street New York, NY 10036 (212) 556-1234
Circulation:	1990 — 1,000,000 Weekday; 1,700,000 Sunday 1991 — 1,209,225 Weekday; 1,762,015 Sunday

The Wall Street Journal

Still struggling with the fall-out of Wall Street's 1987 market crash, the *Journal* entered its fifth year of austerity in 1991 with new managerial and editorial leadership. On the management side, Peter R. Kann succeeded Warren H. Phillips as parent company Dow Jones' chief executive, becoming the first Dow Jones CEO since WWII not to have served first as managing editor of the *Journal*. On the editorial side, managing editor Norman Pearlstine, the lawyer turned newspaperman, who along with Page One editor James B. Stewart, has encouraged a much more prosecutorial reporting style at the paper, was promoted to executive editor.

Perhaps more far-reaching than this power shift at the top, though, is the subtle fractionalization of the paper's major sections and bureaus. For two decades there has been an intense rivalry between the *Journal's* editorial pages and its news pages. In modest doses, such editorial tensions can serve as a healthy reflection of the journalists' various perspectives and the diverse society which they cover, but when ideological rivalry becomes bitter and exaggerated, as has been increasingly the case at the *Journal*, the cohesiveness of the overall editorial product is likely to be compromised. So divided has the editorial environment become, that we often feel we've purchased several newspapers rather than one. On many of the major issues of the year — the war in the Gulf, the economy, the Clarence Thomas nomination hearings, the break up of the Soviet Union — there were vastly different, sometimes contradictory, positions staked out by Page One, the Washington bureau, the editorial page, and other sections of the paper. While the editorial pages have a mandate to express the opinion of the paper, the news pages are supposed to strive for objectivity, but with bitter ideological rivalry increasingly paramount to reporting, this is not always the case. In one glaring example, Page One and the Washington bureau countered the editorial page's pro-Clarence Thomas stance during the nomination hearings with blatantly pro-Anita Hill reporting, compelling the editorial page in one instance to break its customary silence and reprimand, albeit subtly, the *Journal's* news correspondents in "Thomas Said That? Never Mind," 12-2. The issue was the reporting on Clarence Thomas's statement that he had never discussed *Roe v. Wade,* an alleged comment that badly tarnished the judge's credibility. But as the editorialists point out, the *Journal* reporter's and much of the press corps' interpretation of the nominee's actual comments was plainly irresponsible:

> SENATOR PAT LEAHY: Have you ever had a discussion of Roe v. Wade other than in this room, in the 17 or 18 years it has been there?

> CLARENCE THOMAS: Only, I guess, Senator, in the fact, in the most general sense, that other individuals express concerns one way or the other, and you listen and you try to be thoughtful. If you are asking me whether or not I have ever debated the contents of it, the answer to that is no, Senator.

So Justice Thomas would not promise how he'd rule in a case, but he did have discussions about the abortion case. . . .Still, the day after this testimony page one of the *Washington Post* reported that he 'had not discussed the issue, even in a private setting, in the 18 years since the court decided it.' This newspaper carried a similar account. . . .Credibility was indeed the issue here, but the main issue is how did journalism manage to mangle a remark so badly? Repeating a false claim doesn't make it true, though it makes it harder to find the truth. In a nomination marked by smears large and small, Justice Thomas does not deserve this one, either.

On the economy too, there were often glaring incongruities. While the editorial page consistently advised that a cautious monetary policy accompanied by a pro-growth fiscal policy was the best medicine for a feeble economy, "The Outlook" column on Page One was regularly the forum for reporters' calls for another easing by the Federal Reserve. Even news articles, especially those written by head economic correspondent Alan Murray, are peppered with invectives against inflation hawks, as was his "Fed Banks' Presidents Hold Private Positions but Major Public Role," 8-1.

Coverage of the war in the Gulf and the Middle East peace talks in Madrid also served as an outlet for the paper's different ideological camps. Although the editorial page's hardline against the Arabs has mellowed somewhat in recent years, the page was unable to adjust to the dramatic shifts in the Middle East, and approached the peace talks with such intense, knee-jerk suspicion that negotiation seemed virtually impossible from their perspective. Foreign correspondents Geraldine Brooks and Tony Horowitz, on the other hand, grasped that the year's events had presented a rare historical opportunity for negotiations between Israelis and Palestinians, and in such balanced accounts as "Together, Say Arabs and Israelis, We Could Do Wonders," 10-28, told of the hopes and dreams of ordinary Arabs and Israelis as the Madrid peace talks got under way.

Even on the Soviet Union, ideological passion took precedence over dispassionate logic. The paper's opinionists were so preoccupied with their quest to destroy Mikhail Gorbachev's credibility that when it finally became clear that the president's reign was coming to an end, they gloated over the past, rather than concentrating on the challenges of the future. So distracted were they by their "triumph" that when the new Yeltsin government, struggling to formulate a monetary policy, decided to float the ruble by January 1, 1992, the page sloppily abandoned its stalwart and longstanding defense of a stable currency and in "The Empire Melts," 12-13, supported the float: "Mikhail Gorbachev's once-feared Soviet Union has disappeared with the same anticlimactic suddenness that attended the leave-taking of the wicked witch in 'The Wizard of Oz,' — 'I'm melltiiing!'. . .Government authorities are beginning to let the ruble float rather than trying to maintain the fiction of a fixed exchange rate. . .These are forms of progress toward a free market in goods and currencies." Only three days later, Moscow correspondent Laurie Hays spoke at length with Georgy Matykhin, chairman of the Board of the Central Bank of Russia, and filed a jarring "Top Russian Banker Ridicules Monday's Ruble Devaluation," 12-6, a 10 Best selection, which makes clear that a float would be dire, a consequence that the *Journal's* opinion writers, after years of attacking currency floatations and devaluations, must surely have been cognizant: "For us to have a floating system would be something much more destructive than an atomic bomb," said Matykhin in the article.

But by far the most glaring ideological battle began on 10-2, when the "Marketplace" section ran "Scenes From a Scandal," an excerpt from Page One editor James B. Stewart's new book on Michael Milken and Ivan Boesky entitled *Den of Thieves.* The excerpt presented the thesis that Milken and Boesky, together driven by absolute greed, were conscious partners in criminal schemes to enrich themselves at the expense of the investing public. The piece took up two full pages, including all of page B1, around a line drawing of Milken designed to prepare the *Journal's* three million readers for a profile of evil incarnate. It is important to note, that under Stewart's editorship, reports on Page One have consistently bashed Milken and the junk bond market he popularized. Also, the fact that the U.S. Attorney's office in New York in 1988 and 1989 spoon-fed the *Journal* material that portrayed Michael Milken as the embodiment of white-collar crime, is widely known. The conflicts of interest were profound. So disturbed were we by this corruption of journalistic standards that we critiqued Stewart's account and its abundant inaccuracies in "Insider Reporting," by *MediaGuide* editor Jude Wanniski, which appeared in the 12-2 *National Review.* Editorial page editor Robert L. Bartley and his associate, L. Gordon Crovitz, for years have also tried to counterbalance this trial-by-press by defending the rule of law which abhors such corruptions of the criminal justice system. The publication of Stewart's book is an astonishing event in the long, illustrious history of the *Journal,* its low point by far.

"Page One"

The unprecedented stridency and prosecutorial tone that we criticized the page for last year has been somewhat tempered, although overzealous criticisms not based on fact still appear from time to time. One of the most glaring of the year, "Bad Bets: Many Big S&L Losses Turn Out to Be Due to a Financial Gamble," 8-9, by Charles McCoy, was not only riddled with factual inaccuracies and misinterpretations but was replete with editorial overtones: "In the tough thrift environment of the 1980s, this spiel was as beguiling as fool's gold." Another overly strident piece was George Anders's "LBO Odyssey: Playtex Goes Through 4 Buy-Outs Since 1985, Enriching Top Officer," 12-17, a hatchet job on Joel Smilow of Playtex, whose crime seems to be making money for himself and, in much larger amounts, for his shareholders. To James B. Stewart, too much income is a clear sign of criminal, if not immoral, behavior.

What we find increasingly unsettling, especially in light of the page's convenient role in setting the groundwork for Stewart's book, is the fact that the page is more often becoming a showcase for future authors rather than present day reporters. We now must brace ourselves in approaching articles like "Legend Revisited: Warren Buffett's Aura as Folksy Sage Masks Tough, Polished Man," 11-8, by Ron Suskind, so light on Buffett's business and financial successes and failures, and so heavy on the sordid details of his private life, that we wonder when the book announcement is forthcoming. Late in the year there was even a radio advertisement for the *Journal* that featured a playwright who loved reading the paper because its reports "beg to be part of a feature film." Indeed, Page One's rewrite staff is a talented crew of wordsmiths, and savvy writing is a trademark of the page, but too often the news value of a leder is sacrificed for style or dramatic impact, and when we're asked to make the jump inside, we question if it will really be worth our time. Granted, there are notable exceptions to this rule. When the paper's top talents get hold of Page One's premier space — those correspondents who have the clout to minimize the effects of the rewrite process — they can be counted on to impress us with a near perfect balance of information and style.

The A-hed in column four is the perfect place to showcase the wit and technique of the *Journal's* talented corps of writers. When we have time, we love to sit down for an enjoyable and leisurely read. And although the column's topics are often quirky, they occasionally add unique dimensions to our understanding of the week's major stories. "What's News," in columns two and three, is a synopsis of the day's hard news stories. This serves as a convenient table of contents for readers with little time to page through the paper, but we wonder if these columns could not be bumped inside the paper so that the space on Page One could be used for more in-depth reporting. Column five circulates between five different focuses: "The Outlook," "Tax Report," "Labor Letter," "Business Bulletin," and "Washington Wire." We usually dash through the blurb format of these articles, wondering why the editors don't utilize this space to expand on more important issues. "The Outlook" column is the only full length article that runs in this column, and although the present group of writers rarely reach beyond the conventional to give us a fresh outlook, we think the column could develop into an interesting format if opened up to a wider group of journalists from within the paper.

"Marketplace" and "Money and Investing" Sections

While the Page One struggles for credibility, the "Money and Investing" section of the paper, keeps getting stronger. In 1991, section "C" offered some of the best overall reporting on the Salomon Brothers Treasury auction scandal, and continued to steadily improve its analysis of the markets. In addition to solid reporting on Salomon, Kevin Salwen, who covers regulation and the SEC, has given the section a reputation as the place to turn to for the latest news on the power struggle between the CFTC and the SEC, as well as the power shifts and regulatory changes at other agencies with influence over the markets.

The front page of the section is a strange blend of articles for both unsophisticated and well-seasoned investors. Columns like "Your Money Matters," a primer on different investing strategies aimed at green investors, run next to complex articles on the securities industry. Then there's the page's quarterly practice of dart throwing in which the reporters match their arbitrary stock picks (chosen by the throw of the dart) against the stock picks of a group of professional analysts. We're not sure who the audience for this indulgent exercise is supposed to be. Inside the section, we always read "Heard on the Street," especially when it's written by veteran Roger Lowenstein. We also regularly take a look at James Tanner's analysis of the oil markets and Constance Mitchell's work on the credit markets. While the quality of Mitchell's analysis is far from consistent, we've seen steady improvement in her work this year.

The direction that section "B," known as "Marketplace," is heading is not as distinctly positive as that of the "C" section. We always read the "Enterprise" column which usually appears on page B2 but is getting more play on the front page, and we appreciate the section's strong coverage of marketing, media and advertising topics. The section's dogged coverage of privacy issues with regard to credit reporting agencies has also been admirable. But management issues remain a weak point, Amanda Bennett simply not driven enough to go out and get *the* management stories being produced elsewhere.

Editorial Page

With a distracted editorial-page editor Robert Bartley off writing a book about the supply-side movement, the page has virtually been handed over to the talented but relatively inexperienced Melanie Kirkpatrick. Although Kirkpatrick has shown potential as editorial features editor, she is decidedly not seasoned enough to be solely responsible for the decisions necessary to enhance or even preserve the quality of one of the nation's premier editorial pages. The decline of this distinguished forum has been pronounced, speeded by the extraordinary events of 1991, which called for the hand of a veteran who had navigated history's swift currents before. L. Gordon Crovitz, Paul Gigot and George Melloan, no matter how outstanding they might be as individual columnists, have not been able to uphold the overall excellence of the page with Bartley's attention so scattered.

As a result, the inspiring sagacity which we have come to expect from the editorial writers is no longer the rule. More and more, we are taken back by their hot-headed, knee-jerk stance on major issues. While we still find editorials on the domestic political economy that are fresh and forward-looking, cutting edge analysis is growing scarcer, and editorials on the global political and economic issues are ever more backward-looking and disjointed. With the world's governments and economies changing and becoming interlinked at exponential speed, this is a weakness the *Journal's* editorial page cannot afford to leave unaddressed for very long. The alternative is a swift decline toward obsolescence. The events of 1991, which vaporized many long-held assumptions about the global political economy, and forced journalists, editors and readers to deal with an entirely new set of precepts, made the rigid, formulaic thinking of the *Journal's* editorial writers seem especially dank. Rather than grappling with the complexities of these monumental changes, we found them clinging to the well-defined, black and white parameters of the Cold War. Indeed, unable to grasp that the end of the Cold War also meant an end to an indulgent us vs. them mentality, the page often resorted to a type of sophomoric emotionalism. They gloated over the demise of Mikhail Gorbachev, in such editorials as "Tokyo Etiquette," 4-16, on Gorbachev's trip to Japan; "Prizes for Peace," 6-6, on Gorbachev's Nobel Peace Prize; and "Party and Property," 7-16, on the G-7's struggle to come up with some proposals on the Soviet economic crisis.

As already mentioned, the editorialists were fervent defenders of Clarence Thomas during the ugly confirmation hearings that preceded his appointment to the Supreme Court. But on this topic too, we were often discouraged by their inability to rise above the fray. Although they often provided invaluable insights on the nominee, and the nomination process, they were often so defensive in response to valid questions about the nominee's qualifications that they undermined their many genuine insights in such opinions as "Biden Meets Epstein," 9-12, a gloves-off name calling session which made for riveting copy but failed to impart much information. They were equally jarring, but more high-minded and informative in "The Senate's Tiananmen Square," 10-14: "If Senate Democrats want to validate this ugliness by denying Judge Thomas a seat on the Supreme Court, Americans will now have seen that they are the ones throwing the rope over the tree limb. They will be further degrading themselves and the nation, and will be responsible for whatever dark racial resentment flows in the aftermath of a lynching."

As for its strengths, of which there are many, the page remains the stalwart watchdog of regulatory overreach and budgetary blunders. On economic policy, they were one of the few sources of information to look beyond the press corps' knee-jerk calls for easy money, discerning that a proper balance of fiscal and monetary policy must be struck to sustain a healthy economy. They defended the integrity of the dollar and supported Federal Reserve chairman Alan Greenspan's cautious monetary policy throughout the year. "The New Inflationists," 8-7, was one of the few places we saw mention of price level targeting, an important gauge that the Fed seemed to be relying on more heavily: "In the real world, we've always thought the Fed worked best when it targeted not the quantity of money but the price level. The job of monetary policy is to keep prices stable, while the job of fiscal policy is to provide incentives for economic growth." And when talk of tax cuts consumed Washington following the November elections, the page was one of the few to differentiate between the deluge of proposals in "Beltway Bond Traders," 11-8: "Even President Bush said. . .that 'long-term interest rates went through the roof' when the tax-cut talk started. There may be something to this, we concede, for there are tax cuts and tax cuts. Having the government mail everyone in the country under the age of 18 a check for $300 would not help the economy or the markets. . ."

The editorial writers also continue to throw muscular punches at RICO in such hard-hitting editorials as "Rudy Reversal," 6-4, on the reversal of Robert Wallach's conviction in the Wedtech case. And in a sage and articulate, "The Greed Decade Reversed," 7-22, they lucidly delineate the symbolic importance of the reversal of John Mulheren, Jr.'s insider trading conviction: "The markets of the 1980s did in fact unsettle many honest and fair-minded people. It was a decade of great economic activity and upheaval. . .[But] a 'Decade of Greed' was really never much more than a rhetorical device, a hammer in someone's argument. . .The Giuliani prosecutions validated a moral and political indictment with real indictments. . . .Now nearly all of this has been reversed on appeal. . .Perhaps a less prosecutorial construction of the financial and corporate period of the 1980s is now possible."

One of the biggest changes on the page in 1991 was the passing on of the "Viewpoint" column. The regular rotation of the column between Alexander Cockburn, Hodding Carter and Michael Gartner, gave way to "Counterpoint" which is devoted to a much wider range of authors likely to disagree with the *Journal's* editorials. After a decade with these three liberal columnists, we welcomed the opening of this space to fresh contrary perspectives. The "Counterpoint" column, although off to a shaky start, found its footing by March and is becoming an increasingly important medium for hard-hitting, well-informed debate.

The page's most important regular columnists, George Melloan, Paul Gigot who pens "Potomac Watch," and L. Gordon Crovitz and his "Rule of Law" column, are all outstanding. Melloan was not only the page's most astute observer of the global political economy, but he added a new dimension to the *Journal's* impressive coverage of BCCI, painstakingly drawing a drug-money connection between the bank, close associates of Argentine President Carlos Menem, and Syria's Baath party in the 10 Best nominee, "Drugs — The Argentine Connection," 4-25. On the domestic front, Gigot was as devastating as always in his appraisals of the flaws and foibles of the Bush administration. He proved particularly sharp on the weakness of domestic policymaking at the White House this year in such stand-out columns as, "The Bush-Team's One Man Economic Policy," 2-15, in which he lambastes the administration for its lethargic approach to the domestic economy. Crovitz's elegant discourses on legal matters involving finance and business are brilliantly conceived and outstandingly argued. He was in top form with his work on the legal and constitutional issues surrounding Clarence Thomas's nomination in such articles as "Congress May Regret Trying to Bork Justice Thomas," 10-16.

Less spectacular is Tim W. Ferguson who writes "Business World." After two years with this column, he still hasn't found a steady focus. Similarly, the "Manager's Journal," a hands-on look at workplace issues, is of limited value, varying widely in usefulness and quality according to the manager who fills the space. "The Americas" column, on the other hand, circulates among a wide range of thinkers, and is usually a forum for outstanding analysis of issues that emanate from South and Central America.

The Washington Bureau

There were plenty of important topics for the Washington bureau to sink its teeth into in 1991 — the war, the Thomas nomination, the S&L crisis, the economy, and the kick-off of the 1992 presidential campaign — but, under the undistinguished direction of Albert Hunt, the bureau was rarely a pacesetter on any of these stories. And those exceptions to this rule, we attribute to outstanding individual efforts rather than inspired editorial leadership. In fact, in what has become a steady stream of departures of young, talented reporters, Hunt lost yet another promising up-and-comer in 1991. Paul Duke, Jr., 27, who we cited in last year's *MediaGuide* for his surprisingly polished interpretive skills, departed in the fall.

Even some of the bureau's top talent, Supreme Court reporter Stephen Wermiel, for example, have been left to languish. Wermiel, a three-star reporter in past *MediaGuides*, dropped a startling star and a half this year, his work lacking the clarity and insights we'd come to expect. With the Thomas nomination capturing the nation's attention, it was an especially poor time to fall apart. Much of Wermiel's unimpressive work on the nomination hearings was penned with Justice Department correspondent Paul Barrett, who over the years has proven to be quite comfortable skimming the issues. Their "The Marshall Seat: Bush's Court Nominee, A Black Republican, Is a Deft Political Choice," 7-2, was an acceptable roundup on the judge, but provided little on why Thomas was such a bold nomination, and "Mystery Man: Judge Thomas, Billed as Conservative, May Prove Unpredictable," 7-19, seemed completely unoriginal, a mere regurgitation of facts found elsewhere.

Despite the bureau's overall weakness, it houses some extraordinary individual talent. Four-star reporter Peter Truell is one of the best in the business on the global economy. This year, he not only remained an important source of information on GATT, the G-7 and foreign aid, but his dogged reporting on the BCCI scandal explored unique crevices of this massive international conundrum. For example, "The Fed, Already Under Fire, Must Deal With 2 International Banking Scandals," 4-8, provided insights into how BCCI could shake up the balance of power in Washington. New to banking this year, but a veteran to Beltway politics, Kenneth Bacon has quickly emerged as one of the most consistently discerning reporters on this beat. In a year riddled with labyrinthine legislative banking proposals, his expertise and clarity were a vital resource. He received a 10 Best for "The New Banking Law Toughens Regulation, Some Say Too Much," 11-29, in which he sifts through the details of the banking bill as it finally emerged from Congress, to reveal its draconian regulatory nature. Paulette Thomas is another stand-out at the bureau. Her penetrating work on the S&L debacle won her a 10 Best last year, and three stars in this year's *MediaGuide*. We were especially appreciative of her reports on the regulatory excesses that were developing as policymakers tried to deflect public outrage over the crisis. On the cutting edge was her "Regulators Are Ousting Top Managers in an Effort to Curb Banking Failures," 5-14. Gerald Seib's stateside coverage of the war in the Gulf is discussed more fully under the "The *Journal* Abroad" section, but his overall contribution to the Washington bureau deserves special mention. Seib is one of the best in the press corps at discerning exactly what is at stake as the Bush administration works out various foreign policy positions. His move from general White House reporting to national security issues places this expert reporter on a key beat at a crucial time. With national security reporter Walter Mossberg disappointing us, Seib's move should enhance the bureau's credibility in this important area of reportage.

At the Pentagon, John Fialka not only provided excellent stateside Gulf War coverage, but he crafted other information-laden gems as the world's strategic and military alliances shifted dramatically. For example, on the Soviet Union he gave us the sober and even "Soviet Chaos Upends Strategies for Averting Nuclear Miscalculation," 8-30, in which he revealed that "the Soviet apparatus for ordering a nuclear strike may have been immobilized for much of three days." Also at the Pentagon, Andy Pasztor complemented Fialka's reporting with outstanding politico-military analysis, and Rick Wartzman got even more specific, keeping a sharp eye on the aerospace industry as it dealt with the war and adjusted to a challenging financial environment. Meanwhile, Robert Greenberger kept us focused on the pressures straining and reshaping international relations, but while he handles the lexicon of his beat competently, his moorings in Washington narrow his perspectives on many issues.

Most of the bureau's coverage of Congress is spearheaded by Jeffrey Birnbaum, who thankfully is becoming less reliant on his premier source, Rep. Dan Rostenkowski (D-Ill.), and producing fresher reports with a wider range of sources. While he can ferret out the details on specific developments, we'd like to see him step back more often and take a look at the bigger picture as he did in his effective "Congressional Democrats Choose Tax Fairness, Health Care as Issues on Which to Make a Stand," 7-31, a solid analysis which gives us considerable detail on Democratic infighting. Also on Congress, Jackie Calmes tracks tax legislation. Relatively new to the beat, Calmes has yet to develop the economic acumen necessary to give us definitive analysis, but we were impressed by the political astuteness she revealed in "Budget Pact, Undermined by Global Upheavals, Could Come Under Full-Scale Attack by Spring," 9-18, an intriguing report on the Democratic assaults on the 1990 budget agreement. After years on the congressional beat, we expected more from David Rogers than the commonplace coverage he produced this year. While he touched on the fall-out of the 1990 budget law in "Deficit Law Turns the Budget Debate Into Process of Cutting and Spending," 2-7, he did little probing on this crucial economic issue, a serious shortfall. Following lobbying and campaign finance, Jill Abramson displayed a healthy skepticism and professional detachment from her subject matter, but she seemed a bit uncomfortable with analysis.

Coverage of the economy is handled much better by the editorial page than by the economic reporters at the Washington bureau. Chief economic reporter Alan Murray, a bright political observer, has an irksome tendency to use news reports to sell us his own economic blueprint, an egregious abuse of his journalistic responsibility. Throughout the year, he irresponsibly pounded the Federal Reserve to ease, echoing the demands of the Beltway Keynesians. Murray's bias taints much of the Washington bureau's reports on the economy. Although competent on routine economic topics, David Wessel doesn't seem to break out of the mold when it comes to more far-reaching economic stories, mirroring Murray's prejudices with typically two-dimensional reports. But Wessel did reveal his potential capabilities in "U.S. Statistics on '90 Capital Inflow Are Off to the Tune of $73 Billion," 5-24, where he thoroughly scrutinized the government's statistical mill, and criticized the financial press corps for passively accepting faulty statistics on capital inflows to the U.S. We'd like to see him break with Murray's conventional reporting more often, and stake out more cutting-edge angles like this.

With an election year approaching, the *Journal* fortunately has two talented veterans observing the Washington political scene in James Perry and David Shribman. As the 1992 presidential campaign kicked off, the stand-out profiles of the candidates written by these two savvy reporters were particularly insightful. Perry followed the roller coaster ride of speculation that led up to Cuomo's announcement that he would not run for president with such memorable pieces as "As Cuomo Denies Publicly He Will Run, Many Think He's Privately Preparing," 10-14. Shribman's "Tsongas Kicks Off '92 Presidential Race, Vowing to Start 'Economic Renaissance,'" 5-1, was one of his best, offering a colorful and wonderfully well-rounded portrait of former Sen. Paul Tsongas. The biggest shortfall in the political arena is coverage of the White House, where much of correspondent Michel McQueen's portfolio remained superficial and lifeless. She revealed flashes of potential but often simply recounted the findings of polls as exemplified in "Polled Americans Strongly Support Gulf War, Even Beyond Goals of U.N. Mandate on Kuwait," 1-25, and "Americans, More Optimistic About the Economy, Have Become Less Eager for Federal Remedies," 3-22.

On social policy, Sonia Nazario, who keeps watch on health care and education, has yet to match the work she did on affirmative action two years ago. She has been sent out on so many varied assignments this year that we fear her potential is being quelched by a lack of focus. And, at a time when so many large issues are being debated on the education beat, Gary Putka seldom gets beyond the multitude of statistics on various aspects of the education system. Following housing, urban affairs and civil rights, Timothy Noah has finally settled into the daily grind of the Washington bureau, and is now up to speed on the beat.

The *Journal* Abroad

In a year defined by dramatic global change, the *Journal's* foreign correspondents, hindered by a lack of editorial direction, often seemed painfully out of the loop. While we would be comfortable relying on the *Journal* as our primary source of information on the domestic political economy, we rarely count on the paper as our key source for foreign dispatch. There are too many other newspapers and news magazines keeping a closer eye on the world's political economy. This is not to say that the *Journal* lacks talent overseas; it simply lacks focus. As we said last year, "we saw too many reports in which the correspondent walked into a situation, looked around, picked up a few quotes here and there, and then gave us his or her impressions." With few exceptions, the digging and probing for the political and economic roots of a crisis or development didn't materialize, and we were forced to look elsewhere for more definitive coverage.

On the war in the Gulf, the *Journal* was terribly outclassed by *The New York Times, The Washington Post* and others. Page One broke with tradition to cover the outbreak of war with four rather than six columns, including a rare two-column story. But the most impressive reports came from stateside journalists rather than foreign correspondents. Targeting the *Journal's* investment-minded readers, James Tanner and Allanna Sullivan provide calm, expert reporting on the war's likely impact on oil prices in "Waves of U.S. Planes Attack Iraq as War Breaks Out in Persian Gulf: A Major Oil Glut Offers a Cushion to Global Markets," 1-17. Well seasoned in the politics and economics of petroleum, Tanner, a four-star reporter, would throughout the year provide rich analysis of the shifting sands at OPEC caused by Desert Storm. Filing from Washington, Gerald Seib, who wrote much of the most insightful analysis on the war found in the paper, offered "Waves of U.S. Planes Attack Iraq as War Breaks Out in Persian Gulf: Bush Tells Nation Operation Is Going 'According to Plan,' " 1-17, a powerful and comprehensive report which includes a compelling account of the actual decision to go to war. Even before war was declared, Seib produced some of the more solid overviews of the complicated policy objectives faced by the U.S. during the Middle East crisis. In "U.S. Dilemma: How to Hammer Iraq in a Battle Without Smashing It, Emboldening Iran, Syria," 12-26-90, he thoughtfully addressed the issue of regional stability and balances of power with which the administration was grappling, and in "Shots Not Yet Fired Are Heard Round the World as Gulf Crisis Starts to Reshape Global Alliances," 1-9, he looked over the horizon, suggesting a *quid pro quo* for U.S. action on the Palestinian question would be high on the post-war agenda.

Over in the trenches, Geraldine Brooks and Tony Horwitz traveled from their London base to wander through the Middle East's cities giving us gripping anecdotal narratives of destruction, confusion and shifting attitudes, but only occasionally stepping back for the long view. They are both talented correspondents, but we'd like to see them move beyond their anecdotal style more frequently. We should note, however, that Brooks's reports on the failed Kurdish uprising after the war, and the lack of support they received from the U.S., were truly jarring, at times her descriptions almost too painful to read. "Iraqi Kurds Awaken from Long Nightmare," 3-26, catches the high-water mark of the rebellion, while "As Rebellion Fails, Kurds, Once Again, Flee Cities in Sorrow," 4-3, is riveting on the refugee movement into Turkey. Also, her "The Lost People: In Humiliating Defeat, Can the Palestinians Finally Find Peace?" 3-6, a 10 Best nominee, was a brilliant, historically-rich exploration of the Palestinian people's cultural and political plight. Like Brooks, Horwitz is a talented wordsmith, but he is rarely a cutting-edge reporter. During the war, he gave us pieces like "As Iraqi Missile Falls in Riyadh, Saudi Arabians Discover Patriotism and a Stiffened Will to Fight," 2-13, in which he artfully juxtaposed contradictory reactions and shifts in thinking engendered among the Saudi population by war with Iraq. In his strongest effort of the year, "Saddam's Popularity Reaches Rock Bottom as Iraq's Woes Grow," 7-25, he made his seventh visit to Iraq and discovered widespread discontent with Saddam's rule. At the time, many journalists were following the same trail, but Horwitz was one of the few to tie Sunni dissidence to the depressed Iraqi economy. We'd like to see more of this type of scrutiny in his reports. The other *Journal* voice from the Middle East, Peter Waldman, was passing his first year in Israel during these extraordinary times. He struggled to get his arms around this immense story, but clearly needed some adjustment time.

The events in the former Soviet Union were perhaps even more momentous than those in the Middle East. But where the Gulf War required a type of reporting familiar to journalists schooled in the U.S. war correspondent tradition, the crisis unfolding in the Soviet Union called for a type of reporting less familiar to U.S. foreign correspondents, that of political economy. The *Journal* certainly has reporters capable of this type of highly-sophisticated reporting — Peter Truell, James Tanner, George Melloan, and David Asman come to mind — but none of them are stationed near the Big Bear. Moscow correspondent Peter Gumbel, who is transferring to Paris in 1992, has part of the equation right. Despite his tendency to load articles with a heavy film of analytical projections, he has proven to be fairly strong on the political aspects of the Soviet story. He was on the trail of the hardliners all year with such stories as "Resurgent Communists Push for Soviet Crackdown," 2-4, in which he illuminated the road ahead with a quote from Boris Gidaspov, Leningrad party boss, on "waiting for just the right moment" to reassert the hardline tone: "If I were the party and the KGB, I would keep silent, choose clandestine activity and wait for people to tire of democrats and call for an iron hand." And in "Russian Leaders Are Torn Apart by Infighting," 10-7, he provided one of the better updates we saw on the post-coup government, vividly capturing the vacuum of power increasingly surrounding Boris Yeltsin's regime. But on the equally important economic aspects of the Soviet story, he missed most of the critical turning points. Adi Ignatius, who did not receive high marks for his coverage from Beijing in previous years, is set to replace Gumbel in 1992. His record doesn't indicate that he's up to the demands that will be placed on him in this new position, but he has yet to file from Moscow, so we'll reserve comment. The real promise lies in Laurie Hays, who has the potential to fill the bureau's void of reporting on the new commonwealth's political economy. As mentioned earlier, her pathbreaking reports on the Russian and Republics' unfolding monetary policy was one of the most important dispatches we'd read on the region the entire year. If she can grasp the inseverable juncture between politics and economics that is especially pivotal to the Soviet story, she will undoubtedly emerge as an important voice from Moscow.

As central and eastern Europe face crucial historical junctures on numerous fronts, the area is primarily being covered by one and one-and-a-half star reporters such as Craig Forman and Barry Newman in London. Frederick Kempe in Bonn is the exception. He continues to be superb at presenting a ground level perspective of economic trends, as in his insightful, "New 'Miracle': Germans Avoid Slump With Unusual Tactic: Subsidizing the East," 6-11. But we'd like to see him delve into Germany's struggle with monetary policy as it tries to cope with the immense financial burden of unification, while assuming the monetary leadership of a European Community with its own financial challenges. This determining issue for the EC's future has not been adequately addressed by any of the *Journal's* European reporters. Now editor of *The Wall Street Journal/Europe,* Philip Revzin, spent his final year as Paris bureau chief following European trade issues. Like Kempe, he's weak on the macro-economic forces reshaping the continent's political economy. In his best report of the year, "Hardy Weed: EC's Farm Subsidies That Imperil Trade Have Deep Roots," 5-17, he visits two French farms, one large, one small, to provide valuable insights from the working man on the EC's trade dispute with the outside world over farm subsidies. Roger Thurow picked one of the most turbulent years in the continent's post-war history to transfer from South Africa to Vienna. While his reports generally reflected his sold professionalism, it was clear that he needed time to get acclimated.

If it were not for "Americas" columnist David Asman, an editorial page writer not a foreign correspondent, the *Journal's* coverage of the astonishing economic turnaround south of the border would be decidedly mediocre. Neither Jose de Cordoba, who covers the Caribbean and Central and South America from Miami, nor Thomas Kamm in Rio de Janerio, nor Matt Moffett in Mexico City, have the wherewithal to adequately handle the dramatic monetary and fiscal policy changes being undertaken by the governments in this area of the world. Asman, on the other hand, tracks Latin America's transition to market-oriented economies with an expert eye, passing out praise when progress is made, and no-holds-barred criticism when establishment elites attempt rearguard actions, usually backing up his assessments with reams of information.

Asia's growing economic prowess is also of critical significance to the *Journal's* savvy financial readers. Yet, once again, this region is covered by only a few strong players, the rest of the correspondents producing scattered insights but usually missing the bigger picture. This is a foreboding shortcoming for a world class financial daily. In Tokyo, Marcus Brauchli focused on the key issues of Japan's political economy all year, especially on the workings of the Bank of Japan, but he gave us insufficient information on the intense debate in Tokyo over the questions of growth and inflation. Urban Lehner, also in Tokyo, showed slight improvement this year. He and Christopher Chipello were sharp on what the ascension of Kiichi Miyazawa portends for U.S.-Japanese relations in "With Miyazawa as Japan's Prime Minister, Nation May Strengthen Role in Global Issues," 10-14: "Mr. Miyazawa is capable of the kind of long-distance relationship with the U.S. president that some European leaders have — and of occasionally telling Mr. Bush something he might not want to hear." One bright spot at the bureau, Jacob Schlesinger, a young reporter, is showing a great deal of potential, offering solid reporting and forward-looking analysis on high-tech issues. Following a notable stint in Tokyo, Damon Darlin is handling the Korean beat with increasing confidence and competence, paying particular attention to shifts and new developments in the volatile issue of U.S.-ROK trade relations. Darlin, along with James McGregor, who is more than up to covering the Chinese political economy from Beijing, are by far the *Journal's* most illuminating correspondents in Asia.

It is painfully obvious that the *Journal's* editors depend too heavily on the paper's editorial page to bring the developments of the global political economy into focus. The definitive facts and depth of analysis that we find in the news articles of such papers as *The Journal of Commerce* and *Financial Times* of London, simply aren't regular fare in the *Journal's* overseas reports. As the world's political economies and markets become ever more closely linked, the *Journal,* in its distinctive position as one of the world's premier business and financial papers, simply can't afford to let the competition lead on foreign dispatch.

Publisher:	Peter R. Kann
Executive Editor:	Norman Pearlstine
Editor:	Robert L. Bartley
Managing Editor:	Paul E. Steiger
Address:	200 Liberty Street New York, NY 10081 (212) 416-2000
Circulation:	1990 — 1,935,866 1991 — 1,919,355

The Washington Post

" 'South African sanctions — who gives a rat's ass whether they lift them today or tomorrow? I would like to get it first, but I'm not fooling myself anymore that it's terribly important.' "

With those words to reporter Peter J. Boyer in "The Bradlee Mystique," *Vanity Fair* 9-91, Ben Bradlee, the most famous and one of the most influential newspaper editors in post-war America, served notice that his journalistic pilot-light had gone out. The hunger for scoops, which had marked his tenure at *The Washington Post,* had gone. And in August, Bradlee was gone as well.

The *Post* underwent other major changes in 1991 as well. On May 9, Katherine Graham stepped down as chief executive officer, succeeded by her son, Donald E. Graham, vice president and publisher. Joining Mrs. Graham in her departure was Richard D. Simmons, president and chief operating officer since joining the company in 1981. Alan G. Spoon, president of *Newsweek,* was named as Simmons's replacement.

Will Donald E. Graham and Alan G. Spoon be able to repeat the success of Katherine Graham and Richard D. Simmons? Financially, newspapers across the country are in trouble, although the *Post* seems to be weathering the storm better than most, aided no doubt by the circulation increase brought on by the Gulf War. It's worth noting that Spoon's prior responsibilities included marketing and financing at the *Post* and supervising the company's TV stations. Journalistically, the *Post*'s future is now in the hands of executive editor Leonard Downie, Jr., Bradlee's successor. In his prime, Bradlee was a throwback to the older days of U.S. journalism when "The Front Page" was a documentary, relishing nothing more than a good scoop, and that tradition still seems to be alive at the *Post.*

War Coverage

The *Post* may have been second only to the Pentagon when it came to deploying resources in the Gulf, though it was way ahead of the Pentagon when it came to broadcasting information about the war. If the Pentagon was spooning out information like a headmaster guarding the soup pot at the head of a food line in a Dickensian orphanage, the *Post* was laying it out as if it was the last banquet of the Bourbons. Before the fighting even started, then-"Ombudsman" columnist Richard Harwood, in "Bloviation Blues," 1-13, was moved to write about the paper's coverage of the Gulf crisis in the 1-8 edition that he "read the congressional piece, skimmed the poll data and glanced at the other stuff. It didn't seem vital to eat, in a manner of speaking, the whole thing."

Reading the *Post*'s saturation coverage of the war, we came to understand Harwood's feelings. Each edition featured oceans of ink on the major developments of the previous day, along with a half dozen or so other war-related stories. And this was just the front page and special "War in the Gulf" section. We found ourselves returning to Harwood's 1-13 column: "In these leaner economic times, less space is available to those who would daily replicate 'War and Peace.' This is an opportunity for our newsroom managers. If they seize it they will make better papers, and we will call them by a better name: Editors."

Melting down the *Post*'s Tolstoyian war coverage reveals several major scoops and important articles. Barton Gellman, a superb national security correspondent, broke the news that allied forces had targeted Saddam Hussein himself in "Air Strike Against Saddam Foiled by Storm," 1-25, and, in the much-quoted "U.S. Smart Bombs Missed 70% of Time," 3-16, he divulges figures on the number of bombs dropped during Operation Desert Storm and their effectiveness, or, as he pieced it together, their non-effectiveness. Gellman later produced the most valuable post-war assessment of the damage inflicted on Iraq's civilian infrastructure, "Allied Air War Struck Broadly in Iraq; Officials Acknowledge Strategy Beyond Purely Military Targets," 6-23.

Pentagon correspondent Molly Moore, who covered the ground war from the mobile command post of Lt. Gen. Walter Boomer, produced a superlative report on the liberation of Kuwait, "Allies Take Kuwait City," 2-28, and later recounted her personal experiences in the 10 Best nominee, "Storming the Desert With the General," 4-14. Chief Central America correspondent Lee Hockstader was able to get into Iraq as the war was winding down and filed several reports under Iraqi censorship, but valuable all the same. Jonathan Randal was on top of the Kurd story earlier than virtually any other reporter, and received a 10 Best selection for Foreign Reporting for "Kurd's Spring of Hope Collapses Amid Feelings of Betrayal," 4-3. In "U.S. Scrambled to Shape View of 'Highway of Death,' " 3-11, Steve Coll and William Branigan superbly report on how the U.S. bombing raids on Iraqi soldiers fleeing Kuwait City on 2-26 was as much an operation in public relations as military tactics.

Assistant managing editor Bob Woodward, in "Key Iraqi Assets Said to Survive 10-Day Air War," 1-28, broke the news that the much-ballyhooed air campaign was much less effective than the Pentagon had been letting on. Later in the spring, the *Post* printed excerpts from Woodward's book on the Pentagon during the Bush presidency, *The Commanders,* giving the excerpts front-page treatment, and featuring book-jacket style prose by Haynes Johnson, in the accompanying "Book Says Powell Favored Containment," 5-2.

The *Post* Foreign Service

We remain impressed by the breadth of *Post* international coverage, the paper maintaining a staff that reaches all four corners of the globe, and from which foreign editor David Ignatius can draw in a time of crisis, such as the Gulf War. The standout continues to be Soviet coverage, Moscow bureau chief Michael Dobbs receiving an Overseas Press Club award for best daily newspaper interpretation of foreign affairs for nine articles in 1990 covering the collapse of the Soviet empire. In his best effort of 1991, the 10 Best nominee "In Moscow, Running Out of Socks," 6-22, he is exceptional on the ground level workings of the Soviet economy. David Remnick, who won a $5,000 Livingston Award for Young Journalists for his three-part series on poverty in the Soviet Union in 1990, and who late in 1991 became Edward R. Murrow Fellow at the Council on Foreign Relations, covered the epic events in the former Soviet Union with the touch of a novelist and the eye of a journalist. In the 10 Best selection, "The Hard-Liners' Bad Boy Challenges Gorbachev," 2-8, he offers a memorable profile of Soyuz leader Lt. Col. Viktor Alksnis.

The editors nominated Dobbs's and Remnick's coup coverage for 10 Best consideration, and their dispatches that historic week did have much to recommended them. Post-coup Soviet coverage was highlighted by Fred Hiatt's reports on the Red Army, and in the 10 Best nominee, "Soviet Military Seeks New Focus Amid Uncertainty," 9-1, he is authoritative on the feelings of conscripts on the ground and high-level Defense Ministry officials in Moscow on the existential crisis faced by the largest armed force in the world. Hiatt, along with his wife, Margaret Shapiro, began reporting out of Moscow in August, and the work we've seen from both of them so far looks promising.

Other *Post* foreign correspondents who stood out in 1991 were Warsaw bureau chief Blaine Harden, whose Yugoslavia coverage was especially strong; Jerusalem bureau chief Jackson Diehl, who covered Middle East politics with an insider's feel all year; and New Delhi bureau chief Steve Coll, who scored a 10 Best for Financial reporting for his effort on BCCI founder Agha Hasan Abedi, "BCCI's Abedi: A Courtier's Ruin," 9-1. As the 50th anniversary of Pearl Harbor approached, Tokyo correspondent T.R. Reid had an interview with Japanese Foreign Minister Michio Watanabe at the minister's invitation, "Official Voices Japan's 'Remorse' Over War," 12-4, which created a stir both here and in Japan. If the *Post*'s foreign coverage has any real shortcoming it is in Latin America, particularly Mexico, a beat which increasingly demands a superstar.

Domestic Coverage

Post domestic coverage in 1991 was highlighted by investigative efforts that set off tremors in the White House, the international financial community and Democratic presidential circles. The *Post* unearthed a scandal involving a Washington figure almost as venerable as the Washington monument in "Who Controls First American Bankshares?" 2-3, a lengthy investigative piece by Jim McGee on the role played by "an aggressive and high-flying Persian Gulf bank, the Bank of Credit and Commerce International (BCCI)," in the affairs of the Washington-based First American Bankshares, a bank at which Clark Clifford was chairman of the board. The article carries Clifford's denials of any knowledge of wrongdoing. Several months later, in "Clifford, Altman Earned $9.8 Million Stock Profit," 5-5, McGee and Sharon Walsh reveal that "In 1988, Clark M. Clifford and Robert A. Altman, First American Bankshares Inc.'s top officers earned $9.8 million on the bank's stock in a deal financed by the foreign-owned Bank of Credit and Commerce International (BCCI) after telling federal regulators that BCCI would have no financial relationship with First American and its senior management."

The *Post*'s coverage of BCCI extended beyond First American and Clark Clifford. In "BCCI Clues Went Unheeded Since '84," 9-6, Charles E. Shepard and Anne Swardson provide an exhaustively researched report on how warnings about BCCI — including two CIA reports — went unheeded by federal officials, not out of corruption, but sheer bureaucratic "tunnel vision." Shepard and Swardson take readers step-by-step through the regulatory cracks BCCI fell through and the buck-passing and bureaucratic alibis going on now. Notwithstanding their findings, in the editorial "What the U.S. Knew About BCCI. . .," 9-9, the *Post* states that while bureaucratic jealousies and inertia may be part of the reason, "there are also darker possibilities. BCCI showed a talent for subverting the process of justice in other countries, and may have been working on something similar here."

Not content with having bagged Clark Clifford this year, the *Post* brought home a trophy from the White House as well. In the 10 Best selection for political reporting, "Sununu: Frequent Flyer on Military Aircraft," 4-21, Charles R. Babcock and Ann Devroy are detailed on the then-White House Chief of Staff's use of military aircraft, "in many instances for what appears to be personal or partisan political travel," and personal finances, right down to the $413 he paid in penalty and interest for being delinquent on his New Hampshire property tax. The breathlessly written follow-up report, "Sununu Deems Only 4 Plane Trips 'Personal,' " 4-24, by Babcock and Devroy, is accompanied by a reprint of Sununu's travel record on military aircraft. Babcock and Devroy then put the personal finances of the Sununu family under the microscope one more time in "Figures Show Sununus on Tight Budget," 5-11, an exercise which came off as an invasion of privacy in our view, almost as bad, in its way, as *The New York Times*' now-infamous profile of the accuser in the Palm Beach scandal.

Invasion of privacy was the issue at the heart of the other big political story broken by the *Post* this year, a story which, in effect, derailed one Democratic presidential campaign and seriously damaged another. In "Wilder Says He's Bugged," 6-8, Donald P. Baker reaches Virginia Governor Douglas Wilder in Bonn, where he claims that "someone has been recording conversations from the cellular telephone in his state limousine and passing the information to his Democratic party rival, U.S. Sen. Charles S. Robb (D-Va.)." The very next day the *Post,* with "In '88 Phone Call, Wilder Says Robb 'Is Finished' Politically, Excerpts Show," 6-9, reprints excerpts of a transcript of an evidently wire-tapped cellular call conducted between Wilder and Hampton Roads developer Daniel Hoffler three years ago. In the transcript, Wilder, then Lieutenant Governor, claims that stories appearing in the *Roanoke Times and World-News* and the *Post* about the State Police being ordered to kill investigations of drugs and gambling in Virginia Beach because of Robb's possible involvement, will end Robb's political career. Baker and Kent Jenkins, Jr. note drily that "The verbatim transcript of the Wilder tape provides an insight into the gossipy, cocky governor, familiar to intimates but shielded from the public." Coincidentally (or perhaps not), the transcript appeared on the same day as Juan Williams's *Magazine* profile of Wilder, "One-Man Show," 6-9, Williams documenting how Wilder has assumed his prominent position in U.S. politics while alienating virtually everyone around him. "He acts independently and demands respect for this integrity, but he doesn't necessarily reward others for acting in the same manner."

Not surprisingly, coverage of the biggest domestic political story of the year, Clarence Thomas's nomination to succeed Justice Thurgood Marshall on the Supreme Court, was both broad and deep. Ann Devroy and Sharon LaFraniere provided a valuable glimpse at the high-level decision-making process behind the selection of Thomas in "Danforth's Backing Was Key to President's Choice of Thomas," 7-3. Writing on Thomas's professional life in "Despite Achievements, Thomas Felt Isolated," 9-9, LaFraniere turns up a piece of intelligence which becomes fascinating in retrospect: "Anita Hill, a former special assistant to Thomas at the Education Department and the EEOC, was particularly disturbed by Thomas's repeated, public criticism of his sister and her children for living on welfare. 'It takes a lot of detachment to publicize a person's experience in that way' and 'a certain kind of self-centeredness not to recognize some of the programs that benefitted you,' said Hill, now an Oklahoma law professor. 'I think he doesn't understand people, he doesn't relate to people who don't make it on their own.' "

When Prof. Hill exploded onto the front pages, the *Post* featured saturation coverage, with banner headlines and numerous articles that touched on every related topic — from the low image Congress was creating for itself in the eyes of the country, to the issue of sexual stereotyping for African-American men. The *Post* handled the delicate subject matter well, striking a perfect balance between sensationalization on the one hand, and not reporting essential details on the other. Supreme Court reporter Ruth Marcus, in "Hill Describes Details of Alleged Harassment; Thomas Categorically Denies All Her Charges," 10-12, for instance, is able to convey the nature of the testimony without quoting the most graphic details. We also wish to single out *Post* TV critic Tom Shales for his reviews of the proceedings, a welcomed beacon of sanity in a very insane time.

The *Post* had two major mishaps on the domestic beat this year. In July, Miami bureau chief Laura Parker "left the paper" after "violating Post policies" in a report on a mosquito infestation in Florida that "lifted substantial information from three [Miami] Herald stories, including several quotations, without giving credit," according to *Post* media reporter Howard Kurtz in "Post Apologizes for Plagiarism," 7-13. In "Reporter Leaves Newspaper After Dispute Over an Article," *The New York Times* 7-14, Parker tells a *NYT* reporter that "I made a mistake which I deeply regret. My integrity and ethics have never been questioned in my 16 years in journalism, and I think I was very harshly punished."

In a year of racial tension in the U.S., it should be no surprise that the *Post* would handle stories of urban unrest delicately, but in its coverage of the Mt. Pleasant rioting in early May, some felt that the *Post* may have crossed over the line. The *Post* avoided any mention of the race of the [African-American] female police officer who shot a Hispanic in custody, touching off two nights of rioting, in such reports as in "Police, Youths Clash in Second Night of NW Violence," 5-7, by Carlos Sanchez and Rene Sanchez, who write that the unrest broke out "for the second time since an officer shot a Hispanic man being detained for public drinking."

Editorial

The *Post* has continued its move to the right on foreign policy and continues to support free trade, while remaining resolutely liberal on social issues, the environment, and the domestic economy, a world view which, when one thinks about it, sounds a lot like the type of platform some Democratic centrists believe is necessary for the party to regain the White House. While we often find the positions raised by *Post* editorials interesting, at times they can be tough to slog through, the editorial writer often circling around an issue before zeroing in to give an opinion. We believe that opinions carry more weight when backed by fact, but sharper writing counts too. There is nothing wrong with being opinionated in an editorial. Hemming and hawing is a no-no.

Cautiously hawkish might best describe the *Post*'s editorial view toward the Gulf War. In "The War Begins," 1-17, the *Post* announced that it was supporting the war against Iraq: "There can be no question of the threat Saddam Hussein has posed to the American interest in an orderly world." However, while it supported the President, the *Post* did not issue him a blank check, warning in "Longer, Tougher, Costlier," 1-27, that: "A president who does not again and again explain his purposes and who does not allow the public to check the official version of war against the independent version supplied by the press asks for trouble." Once the fighting ended, the *Post* was effusive in its praise of the administration, singling out President Bush, in "The President's Role," 3-1. "The president and his administration did an exceptional job in a very tough and touchy situation."

117

The *Post* also urged caution when it came to dealing with the epic changes in the Soviet Union. In "Aid for the Soviets?" 5-26, the *Post* argues that massive amounts should not be given now, noting that "the central question is whether the West can do much more to help the Soviets before they have done a great deal more to help themselves." In "The Moscow Coup," 8-20, the *Post* denounces the attempted takeover as "a desperate and despicable throwback to Stalinism by a cabal without the slightest chance of easing the 'chaos and anarchy' it cited in rationalizing its grab."

The *Post* continues to support international free trade, throwing its considerable weight this year behind the Free Trade Agreement with Mexico, calling for approval of the fast-track amendment in sharply written editorials, "Free Trade With Mexico," 3-3; "Labor, Wages and Mexico," 4-17; "Mexican Trade and Jobs," 5-5; and "What Fast Track Means," 5-22, arguing in the 5-5 editorial that free trade "creates jobs and makes countries — including this one — rich." The *Post* editorial page was, if nothing else, consistent on the perceived failings of Reaganomics, agreeing with Sen. Lloyd Bentsen, in "There He Goes Again," 8-19, that "the eight year economic expansion of which the Reagan-Bush administration was so proud was financed by writing billions of dollars in 'hot checks.' "

If the sputtering economy was one of the two major domestic stories of the year, then the nomination of Clarence Thomas to the Supreme Court was the other, and here the *Post* took an editorial stand that was much less doctrinaire, much more thought-out. The *Post* endorsed Thomas in "The Thomas Hearings," 9-15, writing that "Our own sense, on the strength of what we know of his record and the testimony given so far, is that Clarence Thomas is qualified to sit on the court." When Professor Anita Hill and her charges first surfaced in the *Post,* "Waiting for Judge Thomas," 10-8, it observes that "the actual substance of some of Miss Hill's remarks raised questions of consistency and accuracy too." After the weekend of hearings, the *Post* stuck by its endorsement of Thomas, deciding in "The Thomas Nomination," 10-15, that while neither Thomas nor Hill could "conclusively" establish the validity of their claims and counter-claims, "in these circumstances history gives us too many reasons not to act on the unproven word of a single accuser."

The op-ed page remains strong under editor Meg Greenfield's expert direction. *Post* columnists include such heavyweights as David Broder, George F. Will, Evans and Novak, and William Raspberry. The *Post* op-ed page carries considerable influence as well. It has been said that associate editor and senior foreign correspondent Jim Hoagland was the most favored columnist by the White House during the autumn of 1990 as the country headed toward war with Iraq. Hoagland received a 1991 Pulitzer Prize for his "searching and prescient" columns on the growing crises in the Persian Gulf and the Soviet Union.

The *Post* op-ed page continues to be a major forum for national and international movers and shakers. Former secretary of state Henry Kissinger and former national security adviser Zbigniew Brzezinski appeared regularly, writing on the Gulf crisis and the Soviet Union. Other important op-ed contributions included Sen. Sam Nunn's "War Should Be a Last Resort," 1-10, and the widely-noted "Time to Help the Republics," 8-28, in which Senator Bill Bradley calls on the West to provide aid to the individual Soviet republics in normalizing their economic relationship with the outside world after they have met several conditions. White House counsel C. Boyden Gray's op-ed on the apparent administration perspective on the civil rights bill, "Civil Rights: We Won, They Capitulated," 11-14, set off a political firestorm that overshadowed the legislation itself.

The standout effort of the year for the op-ed page of the *Post,* however, was its use as a forum by both sides for the debate over Clarence Thomas's nomination. Evans and Novak received a 10 Best citation for commentary for "Judicial Armageddon," 7-1, which warns, prior to the nomination, that "Bush strategists believe liberals would like to punish conservative [Clarence] Thomas for straying from their own 'politically correct' standard for black thinking."

Civil rights establishment standards for "black thinking" was exhibited in "Thomas: Estranged From His 'Blackness,'" 7-15, by Ronald Waters, chairman of the political science department at Howard University, who argues that black conservatives do not represent the black mainstream, contending that "[Thomas] will be found not to be the 'black' nominee to the court, because 'blackness' ultimately means more than color; it also means a set of values from which Thomas is apparently estranged." NAACP board member Julian Bond, in "My Case Against Clarence Thomas," 9-8, defends the organization's vote against Thomas, rejecting the suggestion that the NAACP owed Thomas its support regardless of his qualifications because of his race.

Thomas received support from people who had known him personally over the years on the *Post*'s op-ed page, including Allan Moore, former principal adviser to Sen. John Danforth, in "The Clarence Thomas I Know," 7-16. In "The NAACP Is Wrong on Thomas," 8-6, Margaret Bush Wilson, a former chairperson of the National Board of Directors of the NAACP, states that Thomas is "intellectually honest." Charles A. Shanor, Thomas's general council at the EEOC, defended Thomas's record there in "Thomas's Record at the EEOC," 9-9.

As the Clarence Thomas confirmation hearings approached and criticism mounted on his "blackness," Colbert I. King, a member of the editorial page staff, wrote scathingly on the penchant of whites in positions of power of "scolding" blacks on their perceived shortcomings in "Whites Judging the Blackness of Blacks," 8-11. In a 10 Best selection for commentary, *Post* political reporter Juan Williams, in "Open Season on Clarence Thomas," 10-10, documents the extra-legal efforts of the liberal establishment to derail the Clarence Thomas nomination.

"Style"

"Style," the *Post* section which perhaps more than anything else exemplified Ben Bradlee's type of journalism, had a bumpy year under the direction of new editor Gene Weingarten. While the section could still provoke outrage on occasion, such as Henry Allen's report on a royal visit to Washington, "Britain's Hat of State, Weathering Gaffes & a Ceremonial Storm," 5-15, which poked fun at protocol in general and the Queen in particular: "Queen Elizabeth II, this fusty cartoon, this upholstered relic in white gloves, this walking logo for a country that looks like a theme park with riots," it was often because of outrageous writing, not ground-breaking reporting. "Style" did score a 10 Best for Political Reporting with Lloyd Grove's two-part series on AIPAC: "The Israel Lobby on the March," 6-13, and "The Men With the Muscle," 6-14.

The leading example of egregious reporting in "Style" this year was "The Case of the Senior Schwarzkopf," 3-4, Martha Sherrill's hatchet job on General H. Norman Schwarzkopf's father, Col. H. Norman Schwarzkopf, and his handling of the Lindbergh kidnapping case when he was New Jersey State Police superintendent. At times "Style" irreverence could be of use. In "The Experts, in Retreat," 2-28, Joel Achenbach ridicules the apocalyptic predictions of the Gulf War made by "experts," and their rationalizations as the war was reaching its rapid conclusion. It was here that much-quoted armchair strategist Edward N. Luttwak made his now-famous admission that he used hypothetical figures for a projected ground war that would advance his own particular policy position, which favored continuation of the air campaign.

Business and Financial Reporting

While the *Post* may not be able to compete with *The Wall Street Journal* and *The New York Times* business section on Wall Street coverage, its roots in Washington put it in the enviable position of having the nation's *political* economy take shape right in its own backyard. Unfortunately, the section doesn't seem to merit the editorial priority it deserves, and we often find it buried in the sports section and filled with newswire pieces. The section is geared more toward a local audience than *NYT*'s business section. On Mondays, the *Post*'s business pages are devoted entirely to "Washington Business." Of course, there's no denying that Washington's local audience is a very influential one, and those financial and economic pieces of interest to a national audience often appear in the *National Weekly* edition. Individual entries on the *Post*'s economic journalists and columnists can be found in the "Financial Reporters and Columnists" section of *MediaGuide*.

Sunday "Outlook"

"Outlook" showed some stirrings of life in editor Jodie Allen's first full year, Allen searching out contributors of various ideological leanings who were willing to grapple with the major issues facing the country at this critical juncture in history. At times we found penetrating insight, but still too often we found recycled conventional wisdom and, in several cases, contributions bordering on the surreal.

Soviet Union commentary was particular strong in "Outlook." Former President Richard Nixon weighed in on the "Grand Bargain" debate in "Gorbachev's Crisis — and America's Opportunity," 6-2, warning that "Some have touted the proposed $100-billion aid package as a 'grand bargain.' But a 'grand con job' sounds like a more appropriate term." Other outstanding "Outlook" essays on the Soviet Union included "If the Kremlin Can't Rule. . ..," 2-3, by George F. Kennan, and "Russia After the Summit: A Long, Cold Winter Ahead," 8-4, by *Post* deputy editor Robert G. Kaiser, which picks up the growing signs of trouble ahead for Gorbachev.

Like other sections in the *Post* during the Gulf War, "Outlook" filled its pages with reams of commentary on Operation Desert Storm and attendant issues. In the best effort, David Ignatius teamed with national security correspondent R. Jeffrey Smith to presciently ask "Gulf War and Postwar: Has Bush Planned for a Future?" 1-13, and found, by-and-large, in this 10 Best nominee, that the answer was "no." The worst effort on the war was Sally Quinn's "Mothers at War: What Are We Doing to Our Kids?" 2-10, touchy-feely journalism of the lowest order, Quinn condemning the military policy of separating service parents from their young children, labeling the policy "shameful and uncivilized."

Patrick J. Buchanan brought his "America First" campaign to "Outlook" in the widely-noted "Now That Red Is Dead, Come Home, America," 9-8: "Powerful as she is, America cannot dictate the shape of the world to come. Nor should we try." In the 10 Best nominee "On the Set: Dallas in Wonderland," 5-19, national security correspondent George Lardner brilliantly deconstructs filmmaker Oliver Stone's conspiratorial look at the assassination of President John F. Kennedy. The one other "Outlook" essay which stuck in our minds was "Mugging and Redemption," 3-10, in which *Congressional Quarterly* reporter Alissa Rubin recounts how she was recently mugged and how the crime "was redeeming — a moment of communion for me and I think, although I will never know for sure, for one of those who mugged me."

In "Bradlee Retiring as Editor of the Post," 6-21, incoming executive editor Leonard Downie, Jr. tells Howard Kurtz that "the paper needs to be more aggressive" on what he calls "accountability reporting — finding out information that is not provided by events or press conferences or political campaigns. I'm going to push real hard for the kind of reporting I began doing here when I was 23 years old." We look forward to seeing how this translates into coverage of the 1992 presidential campaign, as well as the unforeseeable developments both home and abroad.

Managing Editor:	Robert G. Kaiser
Address:	1150 15th Street, NW Washington, DC 20071 (202) 334-6000
Circulation:	1990 — 824,282 Weekday; 1,514,420 Sunday 1991 — 838,902 Weekday; 1,165,567 Sunday

THE DAILY NEWS

Financial Times

The "newsier" the year, the more we appreciate the *Financial Times,* the international business newspaper of record.

FT people argue that the British have a natural edge in what has generally been know as foreign reporting. As an island nation dependent on trade to a much greater degree than was the United States, and once the proud possessor of an empire upon which the sun never set, the British were simply more accustomed to dealing with the entire world than were the Americans who had a relatively self-sufficient continental market. That heritage stands the *FT* and its sister weekly, *The Economist,* in good stead going into the nineties. Now the very term "foreign reporting" seems an anachronism for a newspaper that prints in the U.K., the U.S., Germany and Japan, just as corporations, seeing their revenues and profits come from around the world, are often losing their national identities.

FT prides itself on being "indispensable reading for European executives" and managers, and it cites impressive statistics to underscore its preeminence:

97% of London's professional investors read the *FT;*

86% of Europe's leading money managers read the *FT;*

44% of senior financial managers in major companies read the *FT;*

Over 1 million readers in 155 countries.

But its utility is hardly limited to the continent. *FT* editors appreciate the global context of political economy in a way that gives it a decided edge in its international coverage.

FT also stands apart in its format from its general newspaper rivals in the U.S.. Not merely technical issues, these differences contribute to its strength and its value as a resource. Drawing on its large and very skilled staff and even more extensive network of stringers (295 correspondents), the *FT* covers the globe in an unrivaled fashion. Indeed, the sun never sets on the range of *FT*'s reach. More to the point, the paper prints the news it gathers, whether the stories are three graphs or thirty. On a given day with no shocking major story out of Eastern Europe, for example, it may carry two stories from the Soviet Union and six or eight from other countries. Some may be only four inches long, but that is part of the format's value — it doesn't neglect developments because they aren't long enough to justify a 500-word dispatch.

Staff opinion pieces, on the other hand, tend to be two or three times the length of the standard 750-word U.S. op-ed column. This added length is a challenge, especially in a paper which doesn't encourage writers to pad their work with extensive quotations. Fortunately, the *FT* staff is easily up to it, capable of mixing personalities, culture, economics, politics, geography, finance, history and business to analyze complex developments. The emphasis on economic components of issues is to be expected in a paper with this name, but on the whole, *FT* writers are far more disposed to appreciating financial and economic fundamentals and complexities within the stories they are working. At the same time, it's evident that the correspondents have an intimate feel and understanding of the socio-cultural content of the country on which they are reporting. These qualities elevate *FT*'s coverage above that of its rivals.

A third contribution to its depth in coverage comes from surveys. About twice weekly the *FT* produces a several-page supplement, often an entire separate section, devoted to specific markets, industries, countries or technologies. Written by both staff and outsiders, these in-depth sections often provide the best single distillation and summation on the topic, making them invaluable references for the readers. Additionally, interviews with heads of state have become a regular staple for the paper, *FT* providing far more of these than any other publication we rate.

FT also regularly wades into topics that on occasion might be regarded as dull — EC regulatory proposals, details of GATT, subsidies of European coal or oilseed — with no apologies, and almost no effort to glamorize or personalize. It's a paper for adults.

Section II of the paper, "Companies & Markets," is a rich lode of fresh news on companies around the world, with the *FT* reporters locating their stories and reports in the context of the global economy. The section regularly carries the full range of market reports from the world trading centers, including a host of relevent data on bullion and various currencies. As an example of the skills of *FT* correspondents with synthesis, we cite Alice Rawsthorne's "Design Fashion Starts to Falter," 10-11, in which she seamlessly weaves together recession in the U.K. and U.S., demographics, changing investor attitudes, advertising costs, Japanese buying habits and the effects of rap and acid rock on young consumers to explain why Hermes, Gucci, and Chanel have continued to prosper.

FT provided some of the best editorial commentary anywhere on tasks and perspectives for the European Community, producing a series of especially strong editorials in October. With non-EC states queuing up at the admissions' door, *FT* suggests a way out of the dilemma facing the Community. In "Ever Wider and Deeper," 10-3, it advises that one way to cut through the impasse on the issue may be through the European Free Trade Association: "This would permit the. . .[new applicants] to benefit fully from the single European market, without participating in the Community's political and defence activities." In "The Security of Europe," 10-15, editors address the growing debate between western European countries such as France, who want to see the WEU become the military-security arm of the EC, and other countries such as England, who believe the WEU should become a pillar of NATO: "Both sides are right. It is indeed logical, when a group of states form a community or union with a 'common foreign and security policy' that they should place their armed forces jointly at the service of that policy. But it is equally logical that in doing so they should proclaim their desire to strengthen collectively an alliance to which they already belonged individually."

The editors return to the question of EC enlargement with "The Road to a Wider Europe," 10-23, welcoming the accord between the EC and the European Free Trade Association as "establishing the world's biggest common market." This agreement, they note, will intensify the debate on EC enlargement, not dampen it. It what may be a very prescient warning, the editors caution that the "plethora of exclusions" could lead to overregulation: "The bureaucrats must be wary of the danger that they may end up controlling more trade than they liberate."

The *Financial Times* grew into a much more aggressive paper during 1991 — picking up some of the investigative style of the celebrated teams fielded by the *Sunday Times* of London, but with several curious innovations. Washington staff collaborated with ABC's Ted Koppel and "Nightline" to produce some strong investigations of Washington secrets, including CIA knowledge of missile sales to Iraq and South Africa, and Saddam Hussein's hidden billions, which the paper first traced in its scoop of the "60 Minutes" report. Lionel Barber in Washington, and Alan Friedman on loan from New York to the Washington bureau, worked the story and then worked the TV studio with Koppel — the whole effort for *FT* directed and supported from the top in London, and with *FT* sales increasing in D.C. and New York, so we're told,. We welcome any additional exposure of this highly impressive paper. Especially as *The Wall Street Journal* reduces costs by cutting foreign coverage, the *FT* becomes required reading for the growing number of businesses which cross national borders.

On the unfolding BCCI scandal, the *FT* has been out in front again, culminating in a November series, "Behind Closed Doors," 11-10/17, written by banking editor David Lascelles and, like the rest of the BCCI coverage, showing extremely strong reporting by *FT* staff from around the world. Its highly readable narrative style makes it fast and enjoyable reading, even as it deals with the complexities of treasury fraud and cover-up. If there's another paper that makes such excellent use of its global resources, we can't think of it.

In the Soviet Union, the *FT*'s coverage suffered from the departure of Quentin Peel, whose farewell, "Mutiny Aboard the Ship of State," 4-12, depicted a nation of "drift. . .black despair," before drifting off to Germany himself, though not too far as it turns out. As a major contributor to a survey on Germany, 10-28, Peel saw lessons in the reunification of Germany and the recovery from east German socialism that would instruct leaders of nations and would-be nations to the east. He brought to his new post the insight and geopolitical acuity he displayed in his reports from the U.S.S.R.

Leyla Boulton was spotty on the Soviet Union, often reporting the political rhetoric uncritically, as in "Pavlov Outlines Rescue Plans," 4-23, or "Yeltsin's Long Waiting Game," 3-30/31. She did better as she moved west into the Baltics where she skillfully differentiated the political opinions, "Lithuanians Weigh Prospects of a Bloodbath," 1-21, and detailed new banking and pricing policies in "Estonians Snip Away at the Soviet Economic Net," 12-18. "Soviet Bank Reveals Gold Reserve," 6-25, by Kenneth Gooding, was useful ferreting of proposals within the U.S.S.R. on the relationship of gold to monetary policy. In Poland, Christopher Bobinski reported intelligently on the economic issues facing a communist country moving toward a free economy and the problems it raises both internally and with trade, "Sudden Switch to Hard Currency Trade 'a Mistake,' " 4-5, and "Walesa's Old Comrades Lead Assault on Financial Stringency," 5-21, on the politics of it all.

Judy Dempsey, as always, is strong on details, which she has firmly under control in Eastern Europe. We selected her reports, "In Yugoslavia, the Centre Cannot Hold," 3-18, "Balkan End-Game," 6-27, and "The Awful Shape of Things to Come," 8-6, taken together as one of the year's 10 Best stories in foreign correspondence. Dempsey and Laura Silber have been invaluable sources of fresh, well-developed information on the devolution of Yugoslavia, working all dimensions of this most volatile of the new Europe's crises. *FT* reporters have been in the thick of the action in Eastern Europe over the last several exciting years, and Dempsey's timing was critical again as she provided an eyewitness report of "Army Aircraft Bomb Zagreb," 10-8.

However, the *FT* fell a little short this year of its usual excellence on coverage of the former U.S.S.R. and East bloc. The economy was such a large part of the story there that we are surprised by the less than rigorous attention given to key economic details by some *FT* correspondents. Christopher Bobinski, for example, failed to meet our expectations in his dispatches from Poland, providing insufficient information of tax and monetary policies there. And in the U.S.S.R., John Lloyd seemed inclined to pass along uncritical acclaim for the Yavlinsky Plan, instead of probing for the detail and analysis of the status of Soviet tax and monetary policies. Here is one area where *The Wall Street Journal*'s coverage, with Laurie Hays, outshone the *FT*.

Similarly, the same shortcoming afflicts this year's reporting from the subcontinent. David Housego's skillful analytical ability is apparent in his reconnaissance of Indian politics and national economy, "A Passage to Paralysis," 2-22, about potential economic collapse, as political maneuvering takes center stage. But the effort was inconsistent, and, regrettably, Housego failed to follow through with necessary tax, fiscal and monetary detail on India's economy. Editorially, the *FT,* in "Last Days of the Raj," 5-9, saw Britain's contradictory, mixed legacy of democracy and socialism finally coming to the forefront of the Indian agenda. Enlightenment wasn't universal, however; Joe Rogaly's advice, "Rao's Tough Agenda," 6-25, ranged from silly to downright criminal, in urging the Indian government to bow to the International Monetary Fund and hope for the best, as it steered toward chaos with two devaluations within three days.

Lionel Barber, in his report on Robert Strauss's appointment as U.S. ambassador to Moscow, "Capitalist Insider to Try His Hand in Moscow," 6-8, followed the Washington line labeling this lawyer and lobbyist as a highly successful capitalist, instead of seeing an influence peddler who would be entirely at home among the favor-trading *nomenklatura* of the Soviet Union. A 10-8 editorial-page analysis, "US Budget Goes Back to the Block," demonstrated the depth permitted by doubling the length of U.S. columns. Barber could examine Darman's role in protecting the budget agreement while still having plenty of room for other players and still support his conclusion that Bush will have to address a number of domestic economic concerns in his race for re-election.

In its U.S. coverage, *FT* found little to like about the Bush administration, especially in economics. "Just Say No to Mr Bush," 4-27, was a brutally frank editorial telling Bush to get lost after U.S. attempts to persuade European central bankers to lower interest rates. Anthony Harris, who left Washington last year, returned in print to muse, in "Contrasting Tales of War and Peace," 10-28, that the U.S. was once again leading the way on open borders with its agreement with Mexico and nations south, providing a way for Latin American countries to work out of the debts; European nations, though, rather than rushing to aid Eastern Europe, were worried about the threat of Polish raspberries and other market invaders from the east.

In the Americas, the *FT* is where we first found, sometimes the only place we found, such stories as Leslie Crawford's "Chile Makes US Free Trade Pact a Top Priority," 4-16, or "Shell Oil Announces Big Find in Gulf of Mexico," 5-2, by Deborah Hargreaves. The Mexican economy was under excellent reportorial care from Damian Fraser, as demonstrated in his state-of-the-art business report, "Mexico Succeeds in a Fair Exchange," 5-17, on the privatizing of Telemex. We continue to see excellent advances in *FT*'s coverage of the Americas, not simply compared to the less than rigorous level from a couple of years ago, but also in comparison to the paper's competitors. With the exception of *The Journal of Commerce, FT*'s Latin American coverage is superior to that of any U.S. publication.

FT's correspondents in Africa are among some of the best foreign correspondents anywhere. Julian Ozanne, who has been wounded, imprisoned, expelled and barred from various countries in his reporting journeys across the continent, is our reporter of choice on black Africa, and Patti Waldmeir remains unmatched for superior work out of South Africa. *FT* stringer, Francis Ghiles, knows the Maghreb like the back of his hand and there isn't even any competition around from anywhere else on this beat. Tony Walker's work out of Cairo was especially forceful this year, although Walker still displays a tendency to view political economy through the austerian model of the IMF. Moving east of Cairo during the Gulf crisis and war with Iraq, he produced an especially evocative dispatch from Iraq on the eve of the war, "Baghdad Puts its Faith in a Defensive War — and God," 1-11. Along side observations of increased activity around anti-aircraft installations, Walker apprises us of Saddam Hussein's boasts that God will protect Iraq. In a prescient appraisal, he reports that "While this has pleased Islamic militants, it not clear that it has brought much joy to Iraqi military professionals who must be watching with apprehension the build-up of forces against Iraq."

Victor Mallet is *FT*'s correspondent on the ground in the Middle East and was particularly intrepid in covering the Gulf War, bringing, at times, just the proper hint of skepticism in his dispatches from the front. In "Dash into the Desert Serves Saddam's Political Purpose," 2-1, a questioning survey of the spin control efforts being taken by all sides on the battle for the Saudi border town of Khafji, Mallet smartly notes that "the fighting there has amply demonstrated the maxim that politics and propaganda are as important as troops and tanks." *FT* deployed solid correspondents into that theater, using very knowledgeable stringers from the area and various correspondents from other *FT* departments who possess and display prowess and strong competence in their particular fields. Among them was David Thomas, who lost his life in a tragic accident in the burning oil fields during the Gulf War.

FT "Weekend" edition almost always includes an engaging lead feature that is at least well-written. Even when we find ourselves disagreeing on occasion with the premise of a feature, we often end up reading completely through the item because of an appreciation for its ability to provoke us into re-examining perspectives we may have taken for granted. Such was the case with "The Fate of the Union," by Alistair Cooke, 10-5/6. In this lead essay to a "Weekend" section on the U.S., Cooke draws upon such observers of declining empires as Gibbons to portray a country in steep decline as a sense of anarchy and anomie begins to sweep across the land, with the federal government unable to respond because of the budget deficit. The host of "Masterpiece Theatre" writes that "I believe the feeling is epidemic across the country that daily life, in every sort and size of community, is getting more squalid, expensive and dangerous, and that the US is going or has gone over the peak of what the Spenglers and Toynbees would call its 'maturity.' " Cooke sees three possible courses for the future if the U.S. doesn't get its act together fast: a second civil war, the coming of the man on the white horse, or a return to the socialism of Franklin Roosevelt's first term. Any one of these is facilitated through satellite broadcasting, which, Cooke writes, makes it impossible for a government these days to insist that things are all right.

Finally, the "Observer" column on the editorial page continues to be a generous source of amusing, or entirely nutty, clips to go on the bulletin board at our office, a consistent smile-generator which is the sort of minor pleasure not to be scorned by the reader who has waded through the often depressing news pages to get there.

FT will continue to enjoy a leading edge as a world-class business newspaper because of its appreciation for political economy. Because of it, *FT* correspondents, in general, have an advantage over their rivals in getting beneath the surface to look for and report the salient details and data.Increasingly, *FT* is becoming "indispensable reading" for U.S. executives and managers, as well as their European counterparts.

Editor:	Richard Lambert
Deputy Editor:	Ian Hargreaves
Address:	Number One Southwark Bridge London SE1 9HL United Kingdom 011-4471-873-3000
Circulation:	1990 — 291,531 Worldwide 1991 — 292,000 Worldwide

Investor's Business Daily

ID made a bold and useful change in September, expanding its space for news without sacrificing the concise writing style that makes it a useful and attractive alternative to *The Wall Street Journal.* The paper, with its small staff of experienced reporters, can still be annoyingly uneven, but the quality of the overall product is at least a half-star higher than last year, and evidence toward the end of the year suggests that both editors and reporters are adjusting well to the demands and the potential of the new design. Indeed, more frequently *ID* has been publishing stories that aren't appearing elsewhere.

The big challenge for the paper's reporters, and increasingly the big reward for readers, is the daily lead story which is roughly twice the length of other front page reports. Chuck Freadhoff, a regular on the front page, exemplifies both the problems and promise of *ID*'s new format in his various reports. With Robert Corrigan, he cut through the debate about the U.S. savings rate in an excellent, "Are Americans Saving Enough?" 9-30, pulling apart the statistics for closer scrutiny than we'd seen elsewhere. As *ID* does quite often now, the story carries two intelligent graphs for illustration. In a report showing how school spending has far outstripped educational quality, "Do Schools Need More Money?" 9-20, Freadhoff shatters the money myths and explains where the funds really flow. Unfortunately, because *ID* has a limited travel budget and no overseas staff, Freadhoff also has the unenviable job of covering many international stories from his desk, such as "GATT Talks Start Amid Renewed Optimism," 7-30, which falls into the common *ID* trap of filling space with undiscriminating quotes from unidentified analysts, nine of them alone in this one article.

From Silicon Valley, Sean Silverthorne covers the computer industry with an eye for detail, but at mediocre depth. For example, in "Shootout at PC Corral: Clones Under Attack," 4-25, he could have looked a bit more critically, and more broadly, at those clone companies most vulnerable to price reductions by Apple, Compaq, and IBM. Instead, he runs out of space and crams in comments on smaller companies near the end. He's better in features such as "Potential Pen PC Users Demand New Standard of Ruggedness," 7-23, a strong evaluation of pen computers from a users point of view, which he perks up with a fine bit of humor. When it came to *the* computer story of the year in Armonk, NY, though, Silverthorne was caught off stride. His uncritical reporting of IBM's financial woes, "IBM Reports Yet Another 'Disappointment,' " 6-21, left us searching elsewhere for definitive details and analysis. Contributing to a five-part series on federal research development projects, he takes a stab at industrial policy in "Supercomputers: America's Industrial Policy?" 5-8, but this also fell short of his capabilities, failing to fully examine the key issues and players. Late in the year he was getting assistance on the technology front from other reporters, leaving him free to try his hand at warehouse retailing, where he did an excellent job with "Costco: Warehouse Whirlwind," 10-29.

Kathleen Hay's economic reporting on the U.S. and foreign countries was consistently solid throughout the year, partly because she proved adept at substituting solid research for actual field reporting. On U.S.-German disputes over interest rates, "U.S., Germany Face Off Over Interest Rates," 4-26, and in a number of articles on the Federal Reserve and the U.S. economy, such as "July Loss of 51,000 Jobs Puts Heat on Fed," 8-5, and "Fed Survey Sees Few Signs of Solid Rebound," 8-8, her reporting was thorough, went beyond the immediate "econo-speak" of official reports, and showed a skilled use of sources to enhance her article — something a reporter can do when she knows her topic, and something which many of her *ID* colleagues have still to master. On the international scene, her coverage of the Swedish Social Democrats' downfall, "Election Marks End of the Swedish Model," 9-17, combined heavy research with deft writing to overcome the fact that she could not file from Stockholm.

From Washington, Thomas McArdle kept an eye on the supply-side debate brewing behind the scenes in the Beltway. This was a crucial dispute within the administration that almost no one else in the press corps was following until the very end of the year. Most of McArdle's coverage zeroed in on the politics of the debate rather than the economics, as in "Supply-Side Policy Spurs Debate Decade After Reagan Revolution," 7-30, and "Reminiscences of the Reagan Tax-Cutters," 8-15. With his fresh and provocative "Cap Gain: Cut for All Reasons," 11-13, he proved he also has a sturdy understanding of the economic angles of a capital gains tax cut. This was easily the most objective and fact-filled report on this controversial issue that we'd seen all year, a 10 Best selection. *The Wall Street Journal,* by contrast, never even attempted a comprehensive analysis of this crucial issue to business and finance. Susan Mandel, gearing up for the elections, has provided a number of well written political profiles only occasionally marred by a shortage of firsthand reporting. When committed to ferreting out the facts as she was in "Bill Clinton Stirring Democrats' Excitement," 8-6, the results are excellent, but when she reverts to skimming the surface as she did in "Cuomo: Democratic Asset and Liability," 11-15, the outcome is far less satisfactory. Barbara Benham's "New CFOs May Help Untangle Mess," 8-6, about financial controls in Washington, was a superb synthesis of politics, bureaucracy, and government finance. Far from the corridors of power in Washington, Christine Shenot gave a fresh perspective on a key Beltway debate. Her examination of the positions different business groups have carved out on health reform, "Health Reforms Advance as More Join Cause," 5-29, includes an effective chart showing where the AMA, NAM and the Business Roundtable stand on the issues. In an overview distinguished by its original material on one of the year's most widely-covered stories, she looked at the economics and politics of the major proposals and noted that the whole reform effort still has a long way to go up the learning curve before responsible legislation can be developed.

Publications
The Daily News

ID's primary audience remains the investment community, and the paper continues to run snapshot profiles of individual companies that give us the facts straight up, but sometimes lack the critical edge we find in other publications that allow for longer articles. Reports on investing practices, such as Dana Manning's explanation "A Stop-Loss Order Can Reduce Selling Pain," 7-30, also play well with *ID*'s investment-minded readers. The paper prides itself on providing investment ideas not found in the "Money & Investing" section of the *WSJ*, as it did in an unbylined "Beware: P-E Vigilantes on the Prowl Again," 8-21, which calls into question the oft-used argument by Wall Street analysts, and some *WSJ* reporters, that the market's best stocks are " 'overvalued' based on price-to-earnings ratios." As befits a paper that finds 20 percent of its readers have the title of president or chairman, *ID* also carries a regular Executive Update consisting of both staff articles and summaries from other publications. The page is concise and consistently rewarding in its selection and treatment of topics.

Investment is a numbers game, so *ID* can be expected to understand charting, as it surely does in its stock and financial indicator charts. For those who read the paper for more than its charts, *ID* has also brought its charting skills to stories where it runs graphic displays that are imaginatively conceived, well executed, and supportive of the reporting.

ID has markedly sharpened its focus and enhanced the quality of its product this year, often displaying a valuable synthesis of economic and political news and analysis within a limited amount of space. The editorial staff is working harder and smarter than it did last year, and as a result, the paper is becoming more and more valuable to its readers.

Editor:	Wesley Mann
Address:	1941 Armacost Avenue
	Los Angeles, CA 90025
	(213) 207-1832
Circulation:	1990 — 105,000
	1991 — 118,000

The Journal of Commerce

It was a year of new beginnings at *JC*. More important than the paper's April relocation from Wall Street to new headquarters in the World Trade Center, was the dramatic reshuffling of the paper's management and editorial staff. Following internal complaints that advertising considerations had been compromising editorial integrity, and the departure of editorial director Marc Levinson based on those concerns, parent company Knight-Ridder undertook an investigation of *JC*'s operations spearheaded by Knight-Ridder's vice president for news, Jenny Buckner. According to a report in *Editor & Publisher,* 3-9, the probe revealed that " 'a significant number' of staffers thought barriers between news and advertising were 'insufficient.' " The result of these findings was a staff shake up that included the replacement of editor Robert L. Harris who was succeeded by Scott Bosley, editor of Knight-Ridder/Tribune News service. Bosley, who took the reins on April 1, had worked with *JC* publisher Don Becker at Knight-Ridder's *Detroit Free Press* where Bosley was managing editor. A month after this major announcement, *JC* also named a new managing editor, Howard Abramson, who had been editor of *JC*'s newly acquired *Traffic World* magazine.

Indeed, Knight-Ridder's involvement with *JC* has brought many changes to the paper, most of them positive. In addition to these latest staff changes, a move that surely will enhance the daily's credibility, Knight-Ridder seems to be slowly moving the paper toward a broader editorial mission that will appeal to a larger audience. By virtue of its original mission of following shipping and trade, *JC* writers and editors have long been conditioned to view the world as a single interlinked system of trade and commerce. This places *JC* a step ahead of many other papers that are just now beginning to orient their editorial infrastructure toward the global economy. But *JC,* too, could more fully capitalize on the resources it has in this area. The paper offers a wealth of useful economic and political news briefs, "Poland Devalues Currency as Exports Fall," 5-20, "S. Korea to Float Won After 1992," 6-4, or "France to Boost Capital Gains Tax," 9-19, important tidbits of information that dramatically affect trade and capital flows, and are not regularly found elsewhere. But we don't see this information put to good use within the paper's more extensive articles as often as we'd like. Other papers that spar for business and trade readers, *The Wall Street Journal* and the *Financial Times* of London, recognize the weight of this intelligence with more in-depth explorations. For example, *JC* was one of the few papers to carry the news brief, "Sweden Surprises Markets With Boost in Lending Rate," 11-27, but didn't expand upon this important development which mushroomed a few days later. *FT,* on the other hand, lent the news the proper editorial weight by leading with "Sweden Lifts Bank Rate by Six Points," 12-6, and explored the broader implications of this interest rate move that dramatically affected capital flows in and out of that country.

We suspect that part of the reason for this weakness is that financial editor Gordon Platt does not recognize the significance of these news briefs. Platt, who writes the "Currency Forecast" column, has not proven to us his ability to juggle the complexities that play on world currencies in today's intricately intertwined global political economy. His columns are typically little more than a so-so compilation of generic speculation from a handful of analysts. To be fair, there are occasions when *JC* reporters do explore the effects of monetary and fiscal policy on trade, as Duncan Robinson did in "Soviet Currency Moves May Snare US Ventures in Catch-22," 11-25, which crisply conveys the uncertainties created for U.S. businesses in the Soviet Union following word of Yeltsin's plans to float the ruble. But we'd like to see this type of reporting become the rule rather than the exception. Currency and taxation issues are surely as important to trade and capital flows as the tariff issues which *JC* covers so well.

JC has also benefitted from Knight-Ridder's vast network of reporters stationed throughout the world. Journalists from Knight-Ridder newspapers and Knight-Ridder Financial make frequent appearances, adding dimension to *JC*'s global coverage. For instance, Abudi Zein's news analysis, "War's End Won't Affect New Asia Oil Patterns," 3-5, on the new oil-trading patterns that sprang up in Asia following Iraq's invasion of Kuwait; Don Ward's revelation about how an Iraqi arms dealer twisted the U.S. export program in "Arms Deals with Iraq Could Prove Embarrassing for US," 5-20; Jennifer Lin's eye-opening "Canadians Cross Border to Escape Taxes," 5-6; Julia C. Martinez's informative two-article report on Mexican oil, "Foreign Investment Could Be Key to Mexico's Treasure Chest of Oil," 6-10, and "Lack of Funds Puts Mexican Oil Riches on Hold," 6-11; and Valerie Rice's revealing "US Probe of Japanese Screen Sales Splits Industry," 7-5, are just a few examples.

JC's Editorial/Opinion page is steadily improving under the direction of Leo Abruzzese. The former deputy chief of the Washington bureau took over following Marc Levinson's departure last year, and has done a fine job of developing the page's strengths and subtly expanding its scope. Traditionally, the page has been strong on domestic transport and specific trade issues, but recently we've noticed a sturdier handling of broader economic and trade issues. *JC*'s opinion writers are decidedly free trade and have evinced a keen understanding of the importance of bringing down protectionist trade barriers and moving toward worldwide free trade. They urged Congress to grant the administration fast-track authority in order to enhance the possibility of successfully concluding NAFTA and GATT negotiations in dozens of editorials such as "GATT Talks," 2-25, and "Something to Prove," 7-25.

Staunchly anti-protectionist, *JC*'s opinion writers make clear in "Due Credit," 4-10, that "Japan is not America's economic enemy." In the same vein, anti-subsidy sentiments dominate many editorials such as "No More Subsidies," 6-25, which states frankly, "maritime subsidies don't work," or "Tied Aid Subsidy," 3-12, which warns against the "tempting but ill-advised proposition" of attaching strings to foreign aid in order to force poor countries to buy U.S. products. These themes are solidly adhered to no matter what the country or region — the U.S., the EC, South America, Asia, etc. Just before the EC's historic meetings at Maastricht, the opinion writers offered "The Battle for Europe," 11-25, a solid work of political economy in which they assert that "An ideological battle is under way in the European Community that will determine how business is conducted there in the next century. The struggle pits proponents of open, unfettered competition against supporters of 'national champions' — large companies protected and propped up by European governments so they can better compete in the EC and against Japanese and American corporations. . ..The EC has taken remarkable strides toward a single market and is now considering a common currency and central bank. Compromising those gains by endorsing national champions over competitive markets would give the world good reason to question what the EC is really up to after all."

Although the many op-ed pieces that appear on the page present a wide sampling of perspectives on trade, transportation, economics, regulation, etc., we'd like to see Abruzzese tighten up the standards for these outside submissions as their quality varies widely. In contrast, op-ed pieces by JC correspondents are characteristically strong, and reveal a sturdy grasp of political economy. We appreciate A. E. Cullison's "Asia View," for its incisive insights into business and trade developments in Japan. Washington bureau chief Tom Connors pens a crisp column on news from the capital, Richard Lawrence looks into trade issues around the world in "Trade Scene," and the unbylined "Washington Report" is full of unique little tidbits. Additionally, "Europe View," showcases the acumen of JC's talented European correspondents, Janet Porter, Bruce Barnard and Keith M. Rockwell, with Mark D. Berniker occasionally contributing from the Soviet Union. There are also a few regulars from outside the JC staff who regularly appear, including William Neikirk, a business writer for The Chicago Tribune, and H. Erich Heinemann, chief economist of Ladenburg, Thalman & Co., who has been notable over the years for his forecasting failures.

With JC's comprehensive coverage of shipping, trucking, air transport, railroads, and so on, the opinion writers are expertly equipped to handle transportation editorials, and are clearly pro-deregulation no matter what mode of transportation is being discussed. In "Trucking Roulette," 7-11, and "Market Made Rates," 4-26, the writers commend Congress for endorsing the competitive pricing of the trucking industry that has blossomed over the last decade. On the airline industry, the page favors "Open Markets," 4-23, on a global scale and advises the government that "Playing God," 4-29, through continued regulation of air routes is bad for the airline industry. The billions of dollars hanging on the fate of the transportation bill were also closely tracked in editorials such as "One Step Backward," 5-6, in which they advised policymakers to keep their eye on the most immediate transportation needs, that of maintaining "highways of national significance."

In fact, the opinion writers are very wary of too much government intervention. In "A Troubling Sign," 7-1, they observe that the EC's agreement on the broad harmonization of the sales and excise taxes "carves out a large role for government in the market. With 1992 just around the corner, that is a troubling sign indeed." And on the complex economic hurdles facing the Soviet Union in its quest for a free market economy, the opinion writers were one of the few to challenge economist Grigory Yavlinsky's program in "Yeltsin's Challenge," 8-27, asserting "that, if implemented, [Yavlinsky's plan] will have the same effect in the Soviet Union it had in Poland: soaring prices and widespread unemployment. Mr. Yeltsin will be pressured by his constituents to artificially hike wages to compensate for the higher prices — exactly the wrong response."

As on the news side of JC, the editorial writers need to spend more time exploring how currency and taxation issues affect trade and capital flows. They are perceptive on how tariffs, over-regulation and protectionist legislation can negatively impact trade, but if the paper is to attract a broader audience, financial and economic opinions will have to be more frequent and more bracing. When the page has dabbled in financial topics, the results have been disappointing. Its views on banking regulation and budget policies are decidedly unsophisticated. For instance, "Government Gaffe," 7-22, reveals a lack of understanding of the relationship between the budget, the deficit and taxation, and "Early Warning," 2-7, on proposed banking reform, seems unaware of the risks of seizing banks earlier and forcing them to stash away funds to meet rising capital requirements just as they are struggling with lower profits.

JC's daily trade coverage stands out as some of the best found anywhere. Throughout the year the paper kept us abreast of important developments in GATT negotiations and free-trade talks between the U.S. and Mexico. With regard to the FTA, *JC* was very forward-looking on the Mexico-U.S.-Canada transportation network that would need to be expanded to accommodate increased trade flows. John Boyd's "Mexican Carpets Roll Into Canada by Rail," 3-15, and "Proposed Accord Fuels Expansion of US-Mexican Road, Rail Links," 7-8, by Charles W. Thurston, are just two examples of the type of focused transportation reporting *JC* provided. Taking on broader free-trade issues, international economics correspondent John Maggs, new to the position this year, landed two important interviews with Mexican president Carlos Salinas, "Mexico Aims to Break Unions' Hold on Port," 5-28, and "Salinas Says Free Trade May Be Key to Solving Some of Mexico's Problems," 5-29. The second is the most far reaching, making crystal clear Salinas's pro-growth aspirations and ambitions for the free-trade agreement. Maggs also did a fine job of framing the FTA debate taking place behind the scenes in Congress. His "Gephardt Is Wary of Bush Strategy in Mexico Talks," 8-6, walks us through House Majority Leader Richard Gephardt's concerns about free trade with Mexico, giving us a solid feel for the Democrat's position following fast track approval.

Overseas, *JC*'s network of business reporters rivals the best at any U.S. daily. In Southeast Asia, Mark Magnier inaugurated a new bureau in Singapore, signaling the paper's recognition of the growing economic importance of the region. As the former West Coast editor, Magnier was an inspired choice, but in his first year, it was obvious that he was still struggling to familiarize himself with the terrain. He is straightforward on a Pacific Economic Cooperation Conference in Singapore where Asian self-sufficiency in financing trade was emphasized, "Asia Seen Relying Less on Outside Capital in '90s," 5-28: "Venture capital has become a popular tool for strong regional companies hoping to become Asian multinationals, during a time when global bank capital is drying up." Veteran P.T. Bangsberg, one of the best on the Hong Kong beat, keeps us abreast of the latest investment opportunities and trade-related issues developing in this financial hub of southeast Asia. His reports offer plenty of detail, as in "Hong Kong Traders Fight Protectionism," 3-19, on how local importers are launching a multimillion dollar campaign targeted at the protectionist efforts by the textile industry in the U.S. In "China Hopes Visit by EC Delegation Pays Off in Trade," 10-24, he is sharp on Beijing's efforts to increase trade with Europe as its U.S. market becomes clouded with political tensions, noting that the old argument China used to have with Washington over its trade deficit is already cropping up in Europe.

From Brussels, Bruce Barnard remains clear-eyed on the points of solidarity and conflict as the EC moves toward 1992. His reports provide capable analysis of the obstacles which still remain to European economic and political union, as in "EC Police Start Crackdown," 3-26, in which he applauds the zest with which the antitrust division of the EC is moving to break up monopolies, both private and state-owned: "The commission must keep its nerve as it confronts recalcitrant member states." Analyzing Germany's shift on deep cuts for EC farm subsidies and what it portends for both the EC and the Uruguay Round, "German Concession on GATT May Not Resolve Subsidy Issue," 10-16, he moves this story forward, pointing out that while the French and Irish agricultural ministries "continue to play to the farm gallery," Dublin and Paris, along with Bonn, understand that their best long term economic interests lie in liberalizing international trade. Addressing more immediate European concerns, chief European correspondent Janet Porter is a steady producer of data-filled reports and concise analysis on European ports, charter markets, and other subjects of direct interest to *JC* readers. A sampling of her work shows she is commendably keyed into taxation issues as in "Norway Shippers to Lobby Against Tax Proposals," 4-15, which has all the reasons why the Norwegian shipping industry is opposed to this tax reform plan, although a quote from a government defender of the program would have rounded out the report. Her familiarity with the European shipping industry and its efforts to weather the stormy seas of international trade regulation is exhibited in such dispatches as "Tanker Owners Float Idea for US Pollution Fund," 6-12, in which she reports that the Norwegian Shipowner's Association feels that U.S. pollution liability claims include unlimited liability provisions that are "dangerous and intolerable." From London, Keith M. Rockwell, new to the post this year, has been offering penetrating reports on Europe's move toward integration, his analytic framework firmly grounded on the bedrock principles of free trade and free markets. He is sharp on shifts in the Bonn-Paris axis on Common Agricultural Policy in "EC Marriage of Convenience," 8-6, as Germany has a new interest in a successful completion of the Uruguay Round to help alleviate economic conditions in eastern Germany and Eastern Europe.

JC's coverage of the Soviet Union has shown marked improvement lately. We suspect that the paper's year-old Russian-language monthly tabloid published in Moscow is helping to beef up its access to important contacts in that region of the world. Admirably directed by its highly-specialized editorial mission during the anxious days of the Soviet coup in August, *JC* offered excellent coverage, fully exploring the coup's impact on world trade under the umbrella headline, "Soviet Coup Imperils World Trade," 8-20, which was accompanied by more than a dozen companion pieces on specific trade issues. "US Grain Exports Facing 'Disaster,' " 8-20, by Kevin Commins, gives a crisp, concise update on the plummeting grain prices which followed news of the coup and President Bush's remarks that economic aid and assistance to the Soviet Union would be "on hold." In hindsight, Commins did react perhaps a little too hastily in ringing the alarm bells, but overall this was competent reporting. Richard Lawrence goes into more details on the status of aid to the Soviet Union: "At stake here is a proposed U.S.-Soviet trade agreement, $900 million of U.S. grain export credits, potentially large Export-Import Bank financing of Soviet energy and other projects, relaxed controls on exports to the Soviets, and technical assistance in agriculture, energy and transportation recently proposed by Mr. Bush for the Soviets." Duncan Robinson's "Coup Will Darken Short-Term Outlook for US-Soviet Trade," 8-20, is a very perceptive and level-headed assessment of the international economic implications of the coup: "Most U.S. companies plan to put operations in the Soviet Union on hold only temporarily, calling economic change in the Soviet Union 'irreversible.' " Erich Toll explains the watchful state of the shipping industry in "Ships, Cargo Move Despite Coup; Traders Ponder Eventual Impact," 8-20. On the insurance beat, William Pitt's "Insurers Fear Losses on Soviet Contracts," 8-20, explores the losses that could be incurred by private insurers if contracts between Soviet importers and Western traders are not honored: "Political risks in the Soviet Union that are covered by insurance include repudiation of contracts by public buyers and the confiscation of goods by the Soviet government. Interestingly, it was only in the last year or so that insurers began to curtail their appetites for Soviet political risk, and to restrict their policy terms. . ." Well in advance of the coup, senior correspondent Michael S. Lelyveld was uncovering all kinds of interesting stories on the Soviet Union from his post in Boston. We're not sure where he dug up his leads, but perhaps Boston's international academic community offered a connection. His important scoop on World Bank and IMF meetings with dissident Soviet republics, "World Bank, IMF Met With Rebel Soviet Republics," 2-4, is Lelyveld the sleuth at his best, even though the report is based entirely on anonymous sources. Two days after his equally eye-opening follow-up, "Banks' Meetings With Republics Send a Signal to Gorbachev," 2-6, ran in the paper, a letter-to-the-editor from the Chief of Information and Public Affairs at the World Bank denied his reports, but *JC* stood firmly by Lelyveld's account. Moscow stringer Mark Berniker has also done an admirable job of tracking Soviet developments throughout the year, as in his insightful "Trade Blocs to Become New Soviet Powers," 12-10, written as the Soviet Union was looking perilously close to extinction.

JC is also geared into the prospects for economic growth in South America. In Sao Paulo, Bruce James chronicles the struggle as President Collor continues his efforts to reform the Brazilian economy. Bruce concentrated on how those changes were being played out in the key sectors of trade and maritime transport. We need to hear more from Collor's critics in Bruce's reports, though, if only for the sake of balance. He is straightforward on the resignation of Economic Minister Zelia Cardoso de Mello and the entire top economic team in "Brazil Names Moreira Economic Minister," 5-10, seeing the move as a step forward for the Collor government's efforts to reform the economy and renew relations with international creditors.

North of the border Leo Ryan celebrated a decade as *JC*'s Canadian bureau chief, and his work reflects his experience. He is able to see the trade implications in virtually every story. Informative on what Canadian negotiators are hoping to get as they enter trilateral trade talks with the U.S. and Mexico, he pens "Canada Wants Greater Access to US Contracts," 6-5. And he thoughtfully studies the incendiary debate over cultural and entertainment industries in a free-trade pact in "Canadian Culture Under Siege?" 8-8, observing that "Clearly, Canadians and Americans have different agendas on cultural issues and suffer from a lack of mutual understanding."

Not to be overlooked on the foreign side of *JC* is the paper's coverage of Africa. *JC* is perhaps the only newspaper to seriously track trade and economic developments on this huge continent. Such singular articles as Paula Green's "US Investors Seen Missing the Boat in Portuguese-Speaking Africa," 6-25, provided useful information we simply couldn't find elsewhere.

Similarly, *JC* has developed several other important reporting niches that enhance its role as a unique source of information. The paper's coverage of the insurance industry is the most comprehensive found in the mainstream U.S. press and is matched only by insurance coverage in the *Financial Times* of London. Department editor Janet Aschkenasy has done a fine job of balancing coverage of daily developments and long-term regulatory trends in this far-reaching industry. The department has produced such informative special sections as "Risk & Insurance Management," 4-29, and "Multinational Insurance Review," 12-6. Insurance correspondent Aviva Freudmann is an ace on the ever-shifting regulatory environment to which the insurance industry must adjust, as she exhibits in "Is Government Regulation Necessary?" 3-26, part of a special report, "American Insurers," 3-26, in which she fully examines the debate over "proposed federal roles in setting and enforcing nationwide solvency standards." *JC*'s gradually expanding insurance reporting is a natural outflow of its traditional coverage of maritime insurance, and the paper continues to track specific transportation insurance issues in such articles as William DiBenedetto's "Shipowners, Insurers, Coast Guard Still at Odds on Oil Spill Liability," 12-2.

With Congress mulling over the creation of an office of intermodalism, *JC*'s coverage of this important transportation niche will undoubtedly earn the paper new readers down the road. Along the same lines, the paper has recently delved into coverage of the electronic data interchange (EDI). "CN Weighs Competitive Intermodal Link to US," 1-7, by Michael S. Lelyveld, informs us of the prospects for a new container-on-flatcar and trailer-on-flatcar link between Canadian National and Massachusetts Central Railroad, exemplifying the kind of bread-and-butter issues explored in *JC*'s daily intermodal reports. On the other hand, reports like "EDI: Setting Sights on Far East," 1-23; "Containerization/Intermodalism," 6-27; "Intermodalism," 5-28; and "Transportation & Trade Technology," 12-10, looked more closely at trends shaping the industry.

As *JC* continues to develop unique reporting niches, as well as expands its global trade coverage, we see this sturdy daily becoming an ever-more-important source of information for business leaders and policymakers.

Publisher:	Donald C. Becker
Editor:	Scott Bosley
Address:	2 World Trade Center 27th Floor New York, NY 10048 (212) 837-7000
Circulation:	1990 — 27,000 1991 — 23,200

Los Angeles Times

The newspaper of record West of the Mississippi, the *Los Angeles Times* continues to impress us with its smart mix of local and foreign reporting and spicy commentary. It is apparent, though, that Shelby Coffey and the *Times* are not quite content with that particular mantle and, despite some retrenching due to the recession, are gearing up to take on the East. The largest metropolitan daily in the country, with a wider circulation than either *The New York Times* or *The Washington Post,* correspondents stationed in 27 foreign and 13 domestic bureaus, and a newly redesigned Sunday *Magazine* section, they are well-poised to score points against their Eastern competition.

The paper's phenomenal growth and expanding influence can be attributed to Coffey, the editor for five years, and the publisher since 1989, Times Mirror President David Laventhol. Together they have added sections, such as "World Report," revamped others, and included a more detailed table of contents. Although there is no official national edition yet, the paper is readily available on the day of publication in both New York and Washington. Coffey and Laventhol continue to broaden the paper's readership. *Time* magazine reports that "to ensure the *Times*'s voice is heard in Moscow, the paper hand delivers a digest of news and editorials to top-ranking Soviet officials each day" ("Hello, Sweetheart! Get Me Remake!" Susan Tifft, 4-15). At the same time, there has been considerable cutting back at the *Times,* though not on the editorial end. The *Times* dropped its afternoon edition due to declining readership. Lack of advertising revenue forced the paper to halt distribution to ten central California counties as well as Reno, Tucson, Phoenix and Salt Lake City. This shift away from a Southwestern focus may simply be a practical consideration, a redistribution of resources, as there continues to be many signs that the paper is gearing up for a national assault.

The best evidence we see of this is in the redesign of the *Magazine,* unveiled April 7, 1991. Reversing a decision of six years ago to make the *Magazine* similar to publications such as *People,* the *LAT* is now following a format very much like that of *The New York Times,* its biggest and most prestigious competitor. The change was made primarily to attract upscale advertising, mostly from cosmetic and fashion companies. The most exciting aspect of the changes wrought in the *Magazine,* though, is the editorial shift away from covering local news to events more internationally and nationally flavored. Linda Matthews, who has edited the *Magazine* for two years, is quoted in *The New York Times*: "The mandate I have now is to make the magazine every bit as sophisticated and lively and worldly as the rest of the paper. Before, there was a sense that we could do so little and that every story had to have a Southern California peg, a rule that was applied literally and sometimes laughably" ("Los Angeles Times Revamps Magazine in a Bid for Ads," Richard W. Stevenson, 4-8). We are intrigued and encouraged by what we've seen so far. Paul Ciotti's "The Scud That Hit Greensberg," 5-12, examines in detail the reaction of the Pennsylvania area from which members of the 14th Quartermaster Detachment hail, some of whom were killed in one scud attack; a vivid picture of western Pennsylvania and the horror of war is brought home, along with the evident pride that these people feel for their soldiers. Ronald Brownstein offers an ambitious and perceptive "Beyond Quotas," 7-28, in which he catalogues the new and varied theories on the state of race relations and what it may do to current voting blocs. Even before the changeover in format we saw increased signs of editorial and reportorial muscle-flexing. Celeste Fremon's "Love & Death," 1-27, is the final interview with Bruno Bettelheim before his suicide, and we find him to be articulate and eclectic, but devoid of hope, a corpse waiting to happen; the benefit of 20/20 hindsight gives this a sharp edge. John Johnson takes us inside the world of pornography, "Into the Valley of Sleaze," 2-17, using a dispassionate, non-judgemental eye to give us the sense of the business itself, an excellent account. Also in this issue is Alan Prendergast's "The Long Strange Trip of the U-Haul Family," a *Forbes*ian expose of the Shoen dynastic problems that include murder. These ambitious undertakings are a far cry from even last year's selections, when we complained that "the *Magazine* offered mostly local stories, which, while interesting, weren't quite suited to the new *Los Angeles Times*." Now the *Magazine* is beginning to stand on its own.

The national coverage at the *Times* keeps pace with the national papers. Again there are several 10 Best selections awarded for the *Times*'s national coverage this year. Barry Siegel's two-part "Column One" series on the farm crisis, as seen through the eyes of the Schmidt family, "Victims to Victors in Farming," 5-19, and "Family Farm Reaped Gains from Economic Crunch," 5-20, was superlative, a 10 Best selection in General Reporting. We see very few updates from the heartland on the issue of farming that was so hot a few years back, and Siegel's definitive examination, replete with pertinent detail and vivid in its recounting, was appreciated greatly. On the surface, Ralph Vartabedian's three-part "Column One" series, "Losing Clout," ("Political Moves in Defense," 3-6; "States Finding California Defense Firms Easy Targets," 3-8; and "Aerospace Moves: Hidden Costs Often Negate Gains," 3-9) looks like a local story, the retrenching of the defense industry in California. Like the preceding Siegel piece, though, Vartabedian delivers a terrific national story from a local angle, here instructing us on the Darwinian pressures on defense contractors in a post-Cold War era of shrinking defense budgets in Washington and the rising cost curve in upscale California. The "Losing Clout" series is also awarded a 10 Best in General Reporting. Technically a business reporter based in Washington, Karen Tumulty delivers a knockout profile of then-Supreme Court nominee Clarence Thomas in "Court Path Started in Ashes," 7-7, a 10 Best selection for Political Reporting. Unfortunately, Eric Harrison, out of Chicago, and Stanley Meisler, once both staples of the paper's national coverage, all but vanished.

The Gulf War coverage, due to the omnipresent emphasis on world events at the *Times,* was quite good. From "Column One" to "Calendar," the war pervaded the paper, as was the case with most daily journals. The *Times*'s work, though, was particularly extensive; in addition to the day-by-day dispatches coming from the Middle East, the paper also ran columns almost daily on the war's media coverage, written by Howard Rosenberg, Rick Du Brow and Thomas Rosenstiel. We remember one essay by Rosenstiel on the pool restrictions as being especially useful and balanced, "Information on War Key to Public Trust," 1-24. Rather than taking a line similar to many publications, griping about the pool's unfairness, Rosenstiel clearly draws the line between the public's right to know and the military's right to protect its soldiers, stating plainly that "few journalists think the Pentagon is deliberately deceiving them," and listing the main questions for which the public and reporters would like answers. There were also frequent columns by Col. H. G. (Harry) Summers, Jr., outlining the effectiveness of U.S. strategy; we'd been reading Summers for years, but did not fully appreciate his expertise and experience as an Army veteran and professor at the Army War College until the onset of hostilities in the Persian Gulf.

Few angles were omitted in the blanket coverage that the *LAT* offered. Pentagon correspondent John Broder posed the question, "Will It Be War or Peace in the Mideast?" 1-8, an excellent scenario of how the war will unfold, once forces are unleashed against Iraq, which held up extremely well when war did break out. Stephen Braun and Tracy Wilkinson offer the requisite Hussein profile in the "Column One" "What Sort of Man Is Hussein?" 2-10, the team pulling us all the way through until the final word, even though some of this information is rather well known. Sent overseas from a domestic assignment, Douglas Jehl offered vivid, though anecdotal, accounts of life in the trenches. We liked Jehl's "After Sunset, Rules of War Change Drastically," 2-23, his evocative lead setting the tone: "In 24 hours in the field governed mostly by nature, there is light and then there is almost total blackness. By day, the sprawl of military across acres of sand can sometimes seem all reaching. But in what now resembles homesteads in an uncharted frontier, a plunge into night means baffling disorientation. Camps only next door fade to nothingness as dusk deepens, and soon even adjacent tents become invisible. With rules strictly enforced to ban even a cigarette ember, the desert at night is a void." (Jehl would later be dismissed from the pool after reporting information that 50 military vehicles were missing; though cleared by the censors, this data was deemed detrimental to the service by officials.) The *Times* includes a special edition of "World Report" called "Witness to War," 3-12, in which various photos, charts and experiences of the reporters covering the war — all of whom are listed with photos and location — combine to make a memorable section, beginning with the first days of the invasion and through the cease fire and its aftermath. As always, the op-ed and editorial pages were relatively open-minded, presenting a tapestry of viewpoints for our consideration. The editorial "The Temptation Must Be Resisted," 3-6, makes a good case that the U.S. should not send in troops to aid the Iraqi resistence, offering the idea that Arab or Muslim troops could be sent in to restore order if necessary. "Opinion" offers a strong examination of "What Happens Postwar?" 1-27, including a cautionary tale from Alan Tonelson, former associate editor of *Foreign Policy,* and Leon Hadar, "The Best-Laid Plans of Global Dreamers Are No Match for the Realpolitiks of the Middle East — So Resist Them." The pair quickly deflates Washington's optimistic expectations, predicting that "in the aftermath of this gulf war, what will be most striking about the Middle East will be what has not changed. The depressingly long list of problems that have kept the region a hotbed of violence, hatred and repression will remain: the conflicts between Arabs and Israelis, among Arabs, Kurds and other ethnic minorities and between Sunni and Shiite Muslims; the bitter resentment of Arab populations in resource-poor countries of their oil-saturated gulf cousins; the classic power rivalries embroiling Syria, Iran, Iraq and even Egypt; the competition among the forces of Arab socialism, quasi-Western modernization and Islamic fundamentalism, and, perhaps most important, what might be called the Arab world's pervasive crisis of political legitimacy."

What was most intriguing about the *Times*'s Gulf War coverage was the performance of its correspondents in the war zone. Like many publications, the *Times* pulled foreign reporters off their regular beats and sent them to the Gulf, and there were several surprises. Mark B. Fineman, who covers India so well, was one of the disappointments, writing some excellent early dispatches, then settling for merely so-so reporting. Typical was "New Threat to Baghdad: Diseases," 3-7, in which he highlights the U.N. warning of "deadly epidemics" of cholera, typhoid and meningitis in Baghdad. Moved from his regular assignment in El Salvador, Kenneth Freed displayed panache in tackling the deeper issues of Arab politics in the war's aftermath. In "The Varied Politics of Islam," 3-21, he turns our attention beyond the immediate post-victory political situation and comes to grips with a future challenge to the West, the slow-paced but inexorable cultural shift in the Arab world, whereby the political center of gravity is shifting away from secularism to a broadly-defined Islamic fundamentalism that defies analysis: "As more and more once-autocratic Middle East governments give way to demands for democratic reforms, it is Muslim fundamentalists who often win elections on platforms demanding the ouster of foreign presence and influence and a return to strict Islamic law." Bob Drogin, normally stationed in Manila, was superlative when redeployed to Saudi Arabia a few days before the ground war. We feel the heat with his sobering "On Forgotten Kuwait Road, 60 Miles of Wounds of War," 3-10: "desert sands and wild dogs are taking care of the wounds of war. Here, on a forgotten road hit by anonymous allied air strikes, Iraqi military units sit in gruesome repose, scorched skeletons of vehicles and men alike, black and awful under the sun. And here, far from the smart-bomb videos and 'target rich environment' jargon, the grim reality of war is a horror to behold." Out of Cairo, Kim Murphy tried to evoke the same kind of feeling, but without Drogin's flair, she came across as naive. After the portrayal of the Horrors of War by Goya, we get in Murphy's "Conditions Go From Bad to Worse in Kuwait City," 3-12, a circumstance that would have horrified even the hardiest survivor of the Thirty Years War: "Most Kuwaitis haven't had a hot bath in two weeks. There is no water for laundry or washing dishes or flushing toilets. There are few telephones and no television!" No television?

The foreign bureaus of the *Los Angeles Times* certainly match the best in the English-language press, save for the extraordinary network of bureaus and freelancers at London's *Financial Times.* Richard Boudreaux produced crisp portrayals of the changing political landscape in Managua, although we'd like more of the economic picture. Posted in Mexico City, Juanita Darling branched out from the economic to the political in Mexico, and is quickly becoming one of the key reporters in the country. Joel Havemann in Brussels specializes in European economics, his dispatches useful to anyone doing business there. Scott Kraft offered valuable dispatches from Johannesburg all year with his valuable report on the growing split within the Afrikaner movement between the reformers and the conservatives, "In South Africa, the Latest

Fight Is White Against White," 10-8, typical. From New Delhi, Mark B. Fineman scores with a 10 Best nomination on the historical anomaly, a democratically-elected communist municipal government, "Poverty and Harsh Critics Surround Calcutta's Island of Communism," 3-2, and a 10 Best citation for Foreign Dispatch with the revealing intelligence briefing, "Iran Makes Trade Inroads in Soviet Asian Republics," 9-30.

Teresa Watanabe sends out finely-tuned dispatches on Japanese-American business relations from Tokyo, an increasingly important beat. Michael Parks was again a meticulous observer of the fast-paced changes taking place in Moscow. Superbly analyzing the growing crisis of confidence two months after the coup attempt, "Another Soviet Coup Likely and — Some Say — Welcome," 10-21, he writes that recentc ommentary is speculating that the plotters this time would be second-echelon members of the military, KGB and party, who feel it necessary to "consolidate" the gains made by *perestroika* while restoring political and economic stability. Daniel Williams, in Jerusalem, did an excellent job of analyzing the evolving Israeli political reorientation after the Gulf War; his "Racing to Intercept Arms Control," 3-5, is an excellently written, sophisticated analysis of how Israel intends to counter President Bush's postwar agenda which is centered on control of arms in the region: "Shamir's government is also trying to preempt discussion of mutual arms control. In official Israeli eyes, it is an idea best applied only to Arab states." Out of Rome, William D. Montalbano displays his political acuity in "It's Time for 'Crisis' — so Andreotti Quits," 3-30, as he puts Italy's latest cabinet crisis in perspective: "Americans who associate the idea of crisis with quickened pulses, tough decisions and ailing sirens may have trouble understanding what follows, but here is what has been happening in Rome these soft spring days: All week, politicians of sober mien and myriad political coloration have been meeting over coffee to earnestly inquire of one another whether this is a good time to have a crisis. They decided it is." The *LAT* does indeed span the globe.

In the *Times*'s coverage of world capitals, no city is more important than Washington. The Washington bureau has been headed by veteran correspondent Jack Nelson since 1975, and his stamp goes on nearly everything coming out of the office. While there's no specific bias, there is an ennui in the political correspondence that is endemic, and may stem from Nelson's overlong tenure. Nothing is terribly bad, but nothing is exceptionally good either. With all the excitement evident in the pages of the paper, the disenchantment in the Washington bureau is particularly acute. All journalists in the bureau are competent, certainly, but none have the enthusiasm or analytic skill of a Joe Klein, and the best we see out of the bureau is of an anecdotal nature. White House reporter James Gerstenzang pens an evocative "Bush Strives to Stay Above the Fray," 1-24, examining the methods of relaxation Bush is using to keep himself steady during the Gulf War: "more than once over the past week and well before dawn, a tall, solitary figure and his two dogs could be seen walking the south grounds of the White House. Awakened by the telephone and unable to go back to sleep at 4 a.m. or so, the President of the United States slipped on a coat against the January chill and went for a stroll, spaniels Millie and Ranger at his heels, before heading over to the Oval Office." David Lauter, also at the White House, is meticulous to avoid the bias we've complained about, but his dispatches remain colorless. Veteran reporter William J. Eaton rarely fleshes out his stories on the House, though Senate reporter Sara Fritz fares better with her sharp eye for detail. National correspondent Ronald Brownstein should be in the Washington bureau, but isn't; instead, he is traipsing around the country reporting on Democratic party meetings that almost any reporter could handle. Supreme Court reporter David Savage turned his hand to overviews, replete with background, becoming more competitive with Ruth Marcus of *The Washington Post* and Linda Greenhouse at *The New York Times*. Douglas Jehl departed the bureau for the greener pastures of the Washington bureau of *The New York Times*. Nelson himself had one of his more prolific years, his material as sharp and fresh as we've ever seen it. It is perhaps this attention to his own reporting, and appearances on various journalist talk shows such as "Washington Week in Review," that have distracted him from the business of the bureau. The powers that be in Los Angeles, though, will have to dispel this generally moribund atmosphere in order to move onto the national scene and be considered real players.

We'd wondered how the "Business" section would fare after losing its star Washington correspondent, Tom Redburn, to a Parisian daily late last year, mere months after losing Art Pine to the post of Washington projects editor. While there aren't any reporters of either Pine's or Redburn's caliber now, there are several promising journalists who may yet develop into top-notch reporters. Karen Tumulty in Washington comes to mind, one of the bright lights in the bureau. New to the trade beat, she has quickly proven herself able to manage the details of international trade and interest rate issues. In "The Balancing Act of Reparations: Punishing Iraq Without Ruining It," 2-25, she provides a lucid discussion of the struggle to strike a "difficult balance" that ensures those who suffered at the hands of Iraq receive reparations without bankrupting and further destabilizing this troubled country. In a year of mounting crisis for the insurance and banking sector, Robert A. Rosenblatt reliably kept us abreast of the political scrambling on the issues. Weaving in the broader issues at hand in the seizure of the Bank of New England in "U.S. Seizes Bank Group in 3rd-Biggest Collapse," 1-7, he thoughtfully comments on federally insured deposits and the "too-big-to-fail" doctrine. James Risen, Redburn's successor on the economic and international trade beat, can be facile, but he may simply be a little on the green side. He sticks to the basics in "Greenspan Gets a Second Term as Fed Chairman," 7-11, failing to develop interesting ideas from Greenspan's critics and President Bush; but his "Fed Cuts Discount Rate to 5%," 9-14, is better than most in detailing the latest easing.

The business columns and features vary in quality, but are mostly entertaining and informative, occasionally offering a bit of wisdom or analysis we didn't see elsewhere. Labor columnist Harry Bernstein, while still a mouthpiece for the pro-labor lobby, has nonetheless toned down the vitriol aimed at his ideological adversaries and come up with some useful analysis this year. In "AFL-CIO Should Shun Soviet Battle," 4-9, a level-headed Bernstein advises the AFL-CIO to urge its Soviet counterpart, the miners union, to drop its demand for Gorbachev's resignation: "A more productive approach. . .would create a coalition of U.S. coal industry management and union leaders to offer their advice on mining technology and labor-management relations." Although not as consistent as we'd like, business columnist James Flanigan is struggling to assess more advanced topics this year. His unique analysis of the shrinking trade deficit, "Exports Are Up, but We're 'Winning Ugly,' " 2-17, made us think twice about the positive press we have read on the subject: "Even though a low dollar helps U.S. industry in world markets, you're poorer in many ways. Obviously, your dollar buys less in foreign goods. . .Traditionally, American workers had more to buy with their wages than workers in any other country. . .thanks to imports bought at the expense of the U.S. trade deficit." Bruce Horovitz's skills sharpened considerably this year as he took on numerous marketing and advertising debacles with vigor and insight, giving the *Times* bite in its marketing coverage. Out of Washington, Oswald Johnston still has a long way to go, though he improved somewhat this year, his reports remaining generally formulaic, rarely probing deeper than surface issues. The *LAT* had New York's Paul Richter juggling such a hodgepodge of subjects that he was only infrequently able to showcase his talents in the media and movie industry arena. Also out of New York, Scot Paltrow flitted from topic to topic, and his lack of a specific assignment created a superficiality to his work that we hadn't seen before. Robert Dallos, the airline and transportation correspondent who was competitive with the big league business reporters on this beat, sadly died of a heart attack while vacationing in August.

One of the strengths in the business section of the *Los Angeles Times* is that the paper regularly shares reporters with different newspapers, particularly *The Washington Post,* giving the paper a diversity and versatility in columns and business features. *Times* reporter Carla Lazzareschi is one example, her high tech features and stories appearing occasionally in the *Post.* With "In High-Tech Marriages, Little Bliss," *The Washington Post* 12-30-90, she carefully examines the downside of AT&T's move on NCR Corp., noting that high-tech mergers don't typically work out as planned, but fails to explore AT&T's reasons for forging ahead with the takeover. John Crudele, officially on staff with the *New York Post,* appears in both the *LAT* and *WP,* sometimes adding spice to the pages of each. Business columnist Michael Schrage, who also turns up in the *WP,* impressed us with consistently provocative perspectives on the cutting-edge, looking forward just when it was needed. Panning the latest critical technology list, he gets right to the heart of the matter in his brilliant 10 Best nomination, "Meaningless Lists of 'Critical' Technologies," 5-9: "The problem here is that people are focusing on the technologies rather than on the economic, industrial, governmental and scientific processes that create them."

We value the opinion pages in the *Los Angeles Times* for their diversity as well, with authors and ideologies from Cockburn to Krauthammer. Happily, in this regard, the "Column Left" and "Column Right" has turned into a forum for debate as well as commentary. One example is the exchange between neoconservative Charles Krauthammer and the super-liberal Colman McCarthy. Krauthammer is unrelenting in uncovering Iraqi hypocrisy, "A Cause for Sorrow, but Not Guilt," 2-15: "It indiscriminately attacks Israeli civilians, boasts that it will turn Tel Aviv into a 'crematorium' — then complains of attacks on its civilians. It scorns a dozen U.N. resolutions demanding that it withdraw from Kuwait — then complains that the allied war effort has gone beyond the U.N. mandate for getting it out of Kuwait." McCarthy, on the flip side, postures hysterically that "The U.S. Wages a Coward's War," 2-15, asserting the hackneyed parallel of Baghdad as the modern-day Dresden or Berlin or Hiroshima, which we later found was simply not the case. *Nation* columnist Alexander Cockburn is frequently found in the portside position, as is former *Nation* foreign affairs editor George Black. Black effectively links 17th century white settlers in Connecticut to the Canadian Hydro-Quebec project, as both took resources from the Indians, "Indian Lands, White Man's Real Estate," 10-13; although Black takes awhile to get to his point, it is worth the effort. We find William Raspberry's 10 Best selection for Commentary on the opinion page of the *Times,* "Race-based Advantage Is a Detour," 3-17, a sterling examination of race relations and affirmative action.

The Sunday "Opinion" section is equally varied, including authors of note. We get Fang Lizhi's "Are Human Rights Too Un-Chinese?" 2-3, as he fights against the "double standard with which the United States and other Western countries view Chinese affairs" as well as anyone we've seen, a sterling effort reminding us that China still is as repressive as it has ever been, and is using "the distraction of the war in the Persian Gulf to intensify the repression of those fighting for democracy in China." And we find an excerpt of Dr. Timothy Quill's article from *The New England Journal of Medicine,* on his helping to end a terminally ill patient's life, rather than getting an expert to dissect his decision. "Of Death and Dying: Not a Simple Case of Acute Leukemia," 3-17, is a look inside the case, but leaves us wanting more. "Playing Games With the Court," 7-7, is a crafty appreciation from William Schneider of the administration's smart conceptual strategy for navigating the treacherous political waters surrounding Clarence Thomas, albeit somewhat grudgingly rendered: "The nomination has the potential of dividing rank-and-file blacks and civil-rights leaders. It could set white liberals against blacks. And it could fracture the alliance between civil-rights and women's rights groups."

The editorials remain decidedly liberal, divided almost equally between local issues and international and national subjects. Environmental issues, the drought and California's budget problems were all highlighted this year. But editorial-page editor Thomas Plate, formerly of *Newsday,* and deputy editor Frank Del Olmo, left their mark with a single editorial that reverberated around the country after the beating of Los Angeles motorist Rodney Glen King by the LAPD. "For Chief Daryl Gates, the Moment Has Come," 3-19, was *the* editorial calling for Chief Gates's resignation after the incident. A superlative evaluation of the situation, this was quoted and cited by both print and broadcast news outlets: "Because the King case is a symptom of a larger problem, larger questions must be raised. The problem is that the department is in danger of losing support from significant sections of Los Angeles and the trend must not be permitted to accelerate. 'They hate us and clearly they hate me,' Gates said of his critics, to an applauding crowd of police officers last week as he sought to rally support for his continued incumbency. It's true that there are a small number of Angelenos who do hate cops. But the large majority of law-abiding citizens of this town are deeply sincere in their criticisms and are looking for positive reform. Gates' 'us-against-them' statement is unintentionally revealing and illustrates the flaw at the heart of his command. There should be no 'them,' there should be only one Los Angeles with one police chief concerned with all the people of this city."

As the *Los Angeles Times* continues to creep into the national consciousness, Coffey and Laventhol will undoubtedly seek innovative methods to further define the paper's personality and character. They have come a long way already, taking the paper from a good regional daily to a hovering, ghostlike national presence.

Publisher: David Laventhol

Editor: C. Shelby Coffey, III

Address: Times Mirror Square
                Los Angeles, CA 90053
                (213) 237-5000

Circulation: 1990 — 1,225,189 Weekday; 1,514,096 Sunday
                1991 — 1,242,864 Weekday; 1,576,425 Sunday

USA Today

"Looks great, less filling," should be the rallying cry for the nation's newspaper as it enters its ninth year of publication. The color-coded sections and bright graphics still hold sway over the eye as the mind quickly digests the printed sound-bites. The newspaper equivalent of CNN, *USA Today* can give you the nation while waiting in a hotel lobby or killing time commuting. The paper's curt style was pushed to its limit this year as it skimmed the surface of a number of major stories; from the worsening of the economy, to the moral ambiguities of the Judge Thomas nomination, to the Gulf War.

The paper's founder, Al Neuharth, continues to play a substantial role within the pages, appearing in his "Plain Talk" editorial section. In "Measure the Media by Gulf War Reports," 1-18/20, he rates the best networks and best papers on covering war news. *USA Today* came out ahead of *The New York Times* and *The Los Angeles Times*. This from the man who attributed the paper's success to "Maximum of facts. Minimum of personal prejudices, innuendoes, slanting or cynicism."

One of the nation's most explosive stories arose from the Clarence Thomas Supreme Court nomination hearings, and *USA Today* was caught up in the fray. Senator Specter used "Hill Assured Thomas Would Withdraw 'Quietly,' " 10-9, by Tom Squitieri and Sam Meddis as a key piece of evidence in his attempt to prove Anita Hill perjured herself with a discrepancy in her testimony. Ms. Hill had said she was originally told that Judge Thomas would withdraw privately. Former Senate Judiciary Committee staffer and friend of Hill, Keith E. Henderson assured *USA Today* readers in "No Promises Made to Anita Hill," 10-15, that "at no time did Professor Hill tell me that the Senate staff gave any assurances to her that Judge Thomas would withdraw 'quietly.' " "Testimony Shifts Support to Nominee," 10-14, by Dennis Cauchon, recounts how an unbiased panel, viewing only the testimony footage, overwhelmingly supported Thomas. But the accompanying plethora of pie graphs and opinion polls does little to accentuate the article. In the "Opinion USA" column, "Anguish of the Black Community," 10-15, Wanda Lloyd took aim at the confirmation hearings as a blight on blacks: "Many blacks feel great pride in positive accomplishments of other blacks, but also carry the burden of their race when another errs in a public way." Norman A. Lockman, a guest columnist, intelligently assessed the lopsided racial situation in "When Old Stereotypes Resurface: A Tough Reminder," 10-15: "When the chips are down and all else fails, your enemies, whether they are white or black, can rely on racial stereotypes to bring you down. It's a tough way to be reminded that you are black in America."

The paper's front page slipped from its domestic moorings to set sail for expanded Persian Gulf coverage at the beginning of the year. Though the paper didn't provide us with the expert analysis we craved on the Gulf military action, as did many of the other dailies, it did keep us informed on up-to-the-minute scenario changes that were as close to competing with TV as a newspaper can get. Their "News Roundup" section during the Gulf crisis provided brief, newswire-style blurbs on the conflict next to their corresponding time during the day, e.g., "8:45 a.m./ 4:45 p.m.: Iran News Agency says country is sending emergency food supplies to Iraq." The paper was especially adept in its monitoring of the shifting diplomatic situation, as well as war-zone maneuvering. In the 1-19 extra edition, the paper provides a detailed, color map of how the allied attack might be staged, and the armaments necessary. In hindsight, they pretty much hit the bull's-eye in their assessment.

In an attempt to make the paper as contemporary as its visual counterpart, *USA Today* retained some of the rougher edges on its dispatches, as though they were filed by Peter Arnett, struggling to remain on the air. Don Kirk found himself an unwary front-row viewer of the air attack in "Air Raid Cuts Off Iraq Dispatch," 1-17: "—hold on — Paul, Paul, there's anti-aircraft fire going off right now. It's starting. Paul. . .I'm getting the hell off the phone. . .I'm going. . .bye." The front page, at the onset of the conflict, was consumed almost entirely by Gulf War reports. The news-rich dispatches on Schwarzkopf and Hussein, the calendar of events, military targets, and world reaction were balanced by such human interest pieces as "Until I Get Started There Will Be Fear," 1-29. This piece, by Laurence Jolidon, is more concerned with latrines and rations in the camps than the ensuing conflict. He and Sharen Shaw Johnson co-wrote the light "Poetry Helps Soothe Pain of Separation," 2-12. Bill Nichols shoots higher and captures the bigger picture with the short but precise "80 Iraqi Jets Held by Iran," 1-29, as does Jessica Lee with "Gulf War Postpones Summit," 1-29. The quick report, "Fishing Village Fears Onslaught of Oil," 1-28, by Judy Keen, gives a common man's perspective of the war, this time from fishermen in the Gulf who will suffer from Saddam's vengeance.

The cover stories throughout the rest of the year focused primarily on domestic issues. Too often, though, these reports were finished before we really got into them, glossing over the issue at hand. Instead of comprehensive cohesive reporting, *USA Today* tends to divide a topic, serving different angles in several smaller articles. The blurb "Birth Control Implant Out Next Week," 1-30, by Kim Painter, hardly addresses the subject and "In 2010: Fla., Ark. Hot Spots for Seniors," 1-29, also suffers from a short attention-span format, barely rising above shuffle board-hour chatter.

The foreign stories handled in the front section were considerably better, addressing pertinent news from overseas, important enough to snare part of the front page from sports news. "Refugees Escaping 'Dangers,'" 11-21, by Tom Squitieri and Deborah Sharp, provides a quick sketch of Haitian immigrants, as well as the hypocrisy of President Bush, who condemned Britain's repatriation of Hong Kong refugees while turning Haitians away. "A Narrow Escape From East Timor," 11-21, by Allan Nairn, is the horrific account of a journalist's escape from a massacre in East Timor that would have been better served on the front page, rather than the back of the first section.

Sports continues to flex its muscle at the daily, quite often appearing on the front page. The "Sports" section provides the nation with late-breaking box scores and analyses, no doubt a major reason the sports newspaper "The National" went down swinging this year. On the first day of the Gulf War, "Sports" was just as beefy as the front-section reporting on the largest U.S. military engagement in nearly 20 years.

The "Money" section remains user-friendly in its presentation of economic trends, handling the recession adeptly, but without the sophisticated analysis useful to the serious investor. "Couldn't Ask for Anything Better," 1-18/20, by Gary Strauss, dutifully reports the action on the NYSE the day after the Gulf War began. He doesn't make any unnecessary predictions, but does give some possible scenarios of where the markets might head as a result of the war. John Scheidawind's "Patriot's Fame Shines on Raytheon," 1-22, tied business into the war by discussing the Patriot missile, yet provided little on Raytheon, which makes the weapon. "Proposed Overhaul Gets Cool Reception," 2-6, by Mindy Fetterman and Jim McTague, doesn't really explore the issue of bank reform and why it's necessary to any great degree. As with other "Money" section cover stories, this one needed an accompanying article to complete it. In "Year Later, '80s Seem Decades Ago," 12-31-90, Kevin Anderson and John Hillkirk do some inappropriate editorial '80s bashing: "The hedonistic 1980s — like the 1920s — were marked by selfishness, greed and materialism." Other business stories were handled with a lighter touch, such as David A. Markiewicz "Pepsi's Choice Pays Off, Un-huh," 1-29: "Diet Pepsi took one look at Ray Charles and knew it had the right one, baby."

"*USA Today* hopes to serve as a forum for better understanding and unity to help make the USA truly one nation." Al Neuharth's quotation lodged at the top of the editorial page boldly announces the paper's high aspirations. Although a forum format is presented, the page doesn't always provide the "better understanding" to which it aspires. In its attempt at fairness, the editorial page, under the direction of Karen Jurgensen, gives us "Our View" as well as contrasting viewpoints by guest columnists on current issues in "Opposing View." Too often "Our View" highlights the page's liberal slant, while "Opposing View" is occasionally too far right to be believed, and seems to appear only as a counterweight. "Thomas Nomination: The Answer Is Still 'No,' " 10-15, asserts: "*USA Today*'s editorial board said before the hearings began that Thomas should be rejected, and the week's events have done nothing to reverse that view — or reinforce it." The "Opposing View," "Answer Should Be 'Yes,' " 10-15, by Armstrong Williams, offers this comment: "The U.S. Senate should confirm Thomas to the Supreme Court because he is eminently qualified. . ." Yet the piece centers wholly on his character rather than his qualifications.

The 12-3 "Our View," "This Capital-gains Tax Cut Is No Economic Solution," is a prime example of the editorial page's knee-jerk liberal economic view. Newt Gingrich weighs in on the "Opposing View" with "Capital-gains Cut Is Vital," 12-3. "Pursuit of Palace Tops the Agenda for '91," 1-2, laments with very little credible evidence: "Hard Times: The last 10 years' bills come due with a vengeance. . .We didn't fix the budget when we were best able to. 1991 is the time to show that we've learned the lesson of a decade of fiscal irresponsibility, time to develop the will to live within our means." The 1-22 "Opposing View," "Pressing Gorbachev May Backfire on Us," by George Thompson, takes the Soviet leader's side on the crackdown in the Baltics, grabbing us with this opener: "Just a damn minute, ladies and gentlemen." "Senate Should Slow Down, Extend Thomas Probe," 10-14, advocates delaying the confirmation vote on the eve of that tumultuous event: "If Thomas is confirmed and evidence later emerges that he is the perjurer, impeachment demands will be deafening. They will make this week's hearings look like a sideshow." Other editorials, such as "Bush Must Consult Congress About Gulf," 1-3, cover little ground on major stories, opting instead for the path of least resistance. The balanced "Continue Support for Soviet Reforms," 12-26-90, calls for continued U.S. support of Gorbachev and Soviet reforms: "The Soviets must not turn back now, and we must not turn our backs on the Soviets." On the "American Psycho" controversy, *USA Today* warns in "Book Boycott Could Backfire, Boost Sales," 12-27-90, that "Whatever the book's merits, the author has a right to write. Simon & Schuster have the right to publish, or not. The public has a right to buy, or not, and NOW has a right to call a boycott."

The op-ed section delved into the nation's psyche concerning the Gulf War at the forefront of the year. Occasionally serving up intelligent, pointed discussions, it more often than not catered to the baser aspects of the nation's whims. In the unsubstantiated "A Generation Sent to Mop Up," 1-17, Steve Marmel complains: "thanks to the previous generation's irresponsibility toward the environment, *we're* cleaning up. Thanks to their fiscal irresponsibility, *we're* being taxed to cover their mistakes. And thanks to their energy conservation, *we're* at war." In "Face-Off," 1-21, Nancy Myers and Kate Michelman argue abortion rights, but emotion and morality, not law, is the focus of this glossy discussion. "Iraqi Outrages Show Why War Must Stop," 1-23, by Virginia Olsen Baron in the "Debate" column, offers a totally simplistic view of calling off the war due to POWs: "We don't understand the lessons of the playground. Any mother tries to stop fights at the first sign of trouble."

The op-ed page is also home to "Voices," where a relevant question is proposed and answered in varying degrees of usefulness by Mr. and Mrs. Joe Average. Though not terribly enlightening, it does seem to register the pulse of the nation. The 1-17 query "How do you feel now that war has broken out?" has the flagrantly liberal actor Ed Asner responding: "Although I am generally opposed to war. . ." Other such tabloid fare includes various articles in the "Inquiry" column, such as "Prophecy Clock Is Ticking in Mideast," 1-19, where Barbara Reynold interviews John Walvoord, a professor of systematic theology. The "Inquiry" section also falls prey to being a soapbox as was the case with Jesse Jackson in the 1-23 edition: "our president had drawn the line [in the sand], he was then losing face from what he'd established as this imaginary, rather arbitrary line."

As *USA Today* grows into its first decade, we find it becoming more a part of a busy, time-strapped nation's curriculum than ever before. From its blanket coverage of the Gulf War, to the most newsworthy domestic/political story it broke all year, the Anita Hill perjury accusations, the paper finds mainstream American life inviting and profitable.

Editor:	Peter S. Pritchard
Address:	1000 Wilson Boulevard
	Arlington, VA 22209
	(703) 276-3400
Circulation:	1990 — 1,755,545
	1991 — 1,863,436

The Washington Times

For many of the years we have been reviewing *The Washington Times,* Washington's other daily paper, it has been a case of two steps forward, one step back. Last year we saw progress; 1991 was another year of transition for the newspaper, and we sometimes wonder if the paper will ever get settled. This year saw the inauguration of a Saturday and Sunday edition, the departure of several editors and reporters, and the departure of Arnaud de Borchgrave, the second editor-in-chief since the paper's founding in 1982.

The departure of de Borchgrave and the succession of managing editor Wesley Pruden to the top spot is extremely significant. We noted last year that "Editor-in-chief Arnaud de Borchgrave is the engine behind the push at *WT.* De Borchgrave, who loves foreign news, has a European sense of what a newspaper ought to be — 'interesting' — and is always seeking to stir things up. *WT* reporters and editors reflect that aggressive drive. In a city where *The Washington Post* is so dominant, extra zeal and grit is required to compete. *WT* has been able to go up against competition nationally, breaking key stories, producing impressive numbers of scoops, putting certain issues on the Beltway agenda."

In this transitional year, we saw little of this drive resulting in reportorial excellence. Despite the can-do spirit of the reporters that was evident in many dispatches, there were few scoops, and we have a growing sense that the *Times* is not the player that it was. While Associated Press broke the story of the check-kiting in Congress, for example, it was Paul M. Rodriguez who discovered Speaker of the House Tom Foley was one of the financially negligent, "Foley Admits 1 Float, Orders Ethics Probe," 10-4. The Sununu travel story that helped torpedo the political career of the White House chief of staff was broken by *The Washington Post*'s Ann Devroy and Charles Babcock, "Sununu: Frequent Flier on Military Aircraft," 4-21; the *WT* followed up with such dispatches as Rodriguez's "Girlfriend Gets Discount on Air Aspin," 5-7, with Rodriguez detailing Rep. Les Aspin and Sharon Sarton's trip to Colorado, where Aspin was hospitalized for a heart ailment and after his release was picked up by a military plane. With "Sexual Performers Lucked Into List for New NEA Grants," 1-1, George Archibald stays on the case of John Frohnmayer, Karen Finley and Holly Hughes by exposing new grants and paraphrasing those in the know, who postulate that Frohnmayer is announcing a record list of grants to obscure grants to Finley and Hughes; a solid expose with some effect to be sure, as grants to Finley and Hughes were ultimately rescinded, but this is not a subject of terrific import. This was the way much of the year went for the *Times*. A notable exception is Bill Gertz's "Saddam Close to Nuclear Weapon," 6-11, where he provides the details on disclosures, by a senior Iraqi scientist and defector, to U.S. intelligence sources on Saddam Hussein's plans to construct a nuclear bomb. Gertz provides good background for the story and makes attempts to verify charges. He quoted one official as saying "We didn't touch Saddam's nuclear weapons program. He's still in business."

There has also been considerable editorial turnover this year, apart from de Borchgrave's resignation, that adds to the turmoil at the paper. The promising Supreme Court reporter Dawn Ceol, in her third year with the *Times,* departed abruptly during the Anita Hill-Clarence Thomas sexual harassment hearings. (As reported in *The Washington Monthly* by Katharine Boo, "The Organization Woman," 12-91, Ceol quit after publication of her story on the Sunday testimony was rewritten for the local editions in a manner she considered improper.) Health reporter Jay Mallin left after more than five years with the paper. Rick Marin, the *Times*'s television reviewer, moved on to greener pastures, as did movie critic and feature writer Diana West. Cynthia Grenier, wife of columnist Richard Grenier, ascended to the "Life!" editor posting as John Podhoretz moved to *Insight,* only to resign four months later. Columnist and editorial page editor Tony Snow resigned to become deputy assistant to the President for communications and director of speechwriting at the White House. Even the gossip columnist, Charlotte Hays, decamped in 1991. Certainly April layoffs and the restructuring that occurred at the Washington Times Corp. could not have been encouraging to *WT* staffers, particularly since 25 of the 55 people laid off were editorial employes of *Insight,* the *WT*'s sister publication. Finally, the death in December of syndicated columnist Warren T. Brookes will leave a gaping hole in the "Commentary" section. Brookes, the only reporter to be awarded the top *MediaGuide* rating of four stars each year since the *MediaGuide*'s inception, was unique in his reporting and analytic skills; there was no one else quite like him on any op-ed page.

This is not to say *The Washington Times* did not have its memorable moments in 1991. The addition of a Sunday paper, 9-8, which the editors are clearly attempting to tailor to Washington tastes through marketing surveys, is certainly an important step in competing with the *Post*. In addition to the usual sections published during the week, the *WT* added special sections such as "Food," "Travel," "Arts," and a "Special Report," which focuses on a particular item of note from the preceding week. Also, beginning with the 11-3 issue, *Insight* magazine was inserted as a bonus in all home-delivery and single copy editions of the Sunday edition, and we sense the editors at the *Times* are starting to think of *Insight* as a prototype for a Sunday magazine, if not actually turning the weekly into the Sunday magazine. The launching of the Sunday edition really does indicate to us that the *WT* is at least attempting to remain a serious player in the Washington newspaper game, despite all the fits and starts in its nine-year history.

Another indication of the paper's seriousness was its attention to the international arena, particularly during the Persian Gulf War. Despite its small staff (the *Times* has few foreign bureaus), the *WT* keeps pace by utilizing the resources of freelancers and wire services, such as Reuters and Scripps-Howard, to supplement its own coverage, though not to the level of effectiveness of the *Financial Times*. During the Gulf War, though, the *Times* sent quite a few of its domestic reporters abroad to cover the story, as did many U.S. newspapers. Michael Hedges, normally on the drug beat, filed evocative dispatches, as in "Merry It Isn't, But GIs Take Heart," 12-25-90, a refreshing account of Christmas for U.S. troops in eastern Saudi Arabia, where "many said they preferred to treat Dec. 25 as just another day rather than squander precious emotional reserves thinking about the possibilities of Christmas at home." And with "Mines, Tank Traps Settled in Kuwait," 1-28, traveling with the U.S. 1st Infantry Division, Hedges provides a rounded picture of the VII Corps' tasks and perspectives for clearing Iraq's defenses before allied troops can roll forward. From the Middle East, "Life!" writer

Elizabeth Hickey resorted to features on life in the press pool, "To Military Baby Sitters, Press Proves Wild Bunch," 2-11, and "Reporters: So Many Soldiers, So Little News," 2-12; she makes the most of both, as we get a real sense of how many reporters are simply sitting around waiting for news, as many of us were at the time. And, as with many other papers, the war permeated the pages, not just the daily headlines. Media reporter Don Kowet penned daily "Media Notes" on the performance of the various media outlets for the duration of hostilities; there was no real overview available in these columns, unfortunately, Kowet only bulleting his points. In the "Life!" section, Cathryn Donohoe provided a sprightly, timely feature on the U.S.O., "More Than Doughnuts," 2-7, that's delightful and informative as well.

The foreign correspondents handle themselves adequately, although they rarely turn up scoops for the paper, mostly because, rather than being assigned to countries, they are assigned to continents, and frequently write on foreign subjects while sitting in Washington. While veteran Andrew Borowiec spent less time writing from overseas this year, his daily reports and analytical pieces rarely failed to pick up on key nuances of developments in Europe and the Middle East. In a sharp report on the Damascus Pact, "8 Arab Nations Agree to Become Gulf Watchdogs," 3-7, he is prescient, writing that "The coalition members eventually hope for a 'new world order,'" a concept still blurred by conflicting ideologies and often clashing political ambitions." Long-time *Times* staffer Ed Neilan remains in Tokyo, excelling at capturing the role Japan plays on the world stage, but too often this year he seems to be using a Cold War prism, with important Japanese domestic stories, such as the scandal in the financial market, generally neglected. In "Japan Said to Mull Postwar Aid for Iraq," 2-18, he alertly hooks the story around the possibility that Moscow is apparently drawing Japan into its diplomatic efforts to end the war, quoting one Western diplomat: "[Moscow] might even be seen as being generous with Japan's money." He reports from the Soviet Pacific rim, "Vladivostok Tires of Waiting for Moscow, Looks to Future," 9-23, on how officials there are eager to introduce a market economy to the port city and begin economic development, a quick sketch that still manages to pack a lot of information. Martin Sieff uses an impressive array of sources to compile dispatches on geopolitical subjects. Analyzing the Soviet coup, "Other Shoe Finally Dropped," 8-20, he forcefully argues that the die was cast last fall, when the KGB and the military formed an alliance against further reform. Sieff also draws a contrast between the hardline Marxist coup leaders and *Soyuz* leader Lt. Col. Viktor Alksnis, whom he labels "an economic pragmatist," but fails to fully develop this key point. Foreign editor Marc Lerner makes the most of his slim staff, and further supplements coverage with that of the wire services.

The national coverage at the *Times* is, of course, centered in and around Washington, cataloguing the players and events as much as policy. A good example is investigative reporter George Archibald's "Director of USIA Ordered to Resign," 1-28. The *WT* had reported that U.S. Information Agency Director Bruce Gelb had interfered with Voice of America operations, delaying for a month a new relay station in the Persian Gulf for VOA broadcasts into Iraq and Kuwait and that he had also tried to block interviews last year with Chinese dissident Fang Lizhi after the Tiananmen Square massacre. Four days later, Gelb was told by John Sununu that he had to leave as USIA director. Archibald brings us up-to-date on the story, reporting that the White House has offered to nominate Gelb as U.S. ambassador to Belgium as a face-saving measure. Former Supreme Court reporter Dawn Ceol professionally handles "Pro-Choice Side Angry at Souter," 5-24, and "Court: Public Money Banned for Counseling," a smart review of the Supreme Court decision upholding federal regulations banning use of public money to fund abortion counseling or promotion, with Ceol giving us the straight details on the issue at stake and then providing an important reading on the reaction of pro-choice organizations. In "Lawmakers Play Name Game," 6-6, Major Garrett takes an instructive look at the spin being put on various pieces of proposed legislation to enhance its chances of passage, with examples from civil rights bills (where "the title alone establishes a certain legitimacy"), handgun control ("violence prevention"), education, taxes ("the Working Family Tax Relief Act"), and family leave. A few new names were added to cover Washington doings, J. Jennings Moss, for one, but there was little from the veteran reporters, Frank Murray, among others, that was noteworthy.

The "Life!" section shows signs of modest improvement, despite having had three different editors in the course of the last year. We'd rapped editor John Podhoretz last year for his witless attempts at satire that were beginning to poison the entire section. While "Life!" still can't match the powerful political profiles found in the *Post*'s "Style" section, the writers are beginning to keep pace with some of the lighter, frothier features found in the *Post*. Two writers, whose bylines we'd noted briefly last year, caught our eye in 1991 and kept it. Betsy Pisik updates us on the doings of two fabulous redheads, cartoonist Dale Messick and her brainchild "Brenda Starr, Reporter," in "Glamorous Granny Recalls Her Famous, Daring Strip," 8-2, a charmingly vivid feature: "Back in 1940, women cartoonists were plenty desirable but not on the comics page. 'I would bring my drawings in,' Miss Messick remembers, 'and the editors would toss them aside and say [wolfishly] Let's have lunch.' So Dalia Messick of Gary, Ind., changed her name to the more ambiguous Dale. She mailed her work in to the syndicate. By the time they found out that he was a she, it was too late. 'Brenda Starr' already had caught on — and not just with women. With a happy chuckle, the cartoonist recalls how men used to write, begging for 'a picture of Brenda in a more daring pose. And I sent them a drawing of Brenda going over Niagara Falls in a barrel. Now *that's* daring! And I'd sign it *Miss* Dale Messick.' " Sean Piccoli pokes fun at the Elvis craze that refuses to die, "I Dreamed I Saw Elvis Last Night," 2-12, in an attempt to answer the question, Is Elvis Dead? Piccoli thinks so, but has an awful lot of fun with the question in the process: "Consider this: When you add the numbers contained in the date of Elvis Presley's death, Aug. 16, 1977, you get 2,001. An unremarkable figure except that — brace yourself — Elvis used the theme music for '2001: A Space Odyssey' to open his final concerts!" Cathryn Donohoe, as always, is a staple of "Life!" One of the profession's more accomplished profilers, Donohoe always manages to pull us into reading a feature on a subject that we'd otherwise dismiss. But it's not mere wordsmithery; when we finish we come away richer, because she has again found some new aspect of the human condition to illuminate. Such is the case with Donohoe's "A Promoter of Heroes," 4-24, a profile of Dominique Lapierre, the author who gives spiritual dimension to sufferings, from poverty to AIDS. Podhoretz's successor, Cynthia Grenier, left "Life!" to pursue other projects in November, turning the section over to Kenneth McIntyre, deputy editor since 1990.

The strongest section in *The Washington Times* is surely "Commentary." Editor Mary Lou Forbes brings together the best of conservative opinion for each day's section, and is even beginning to branch out by including moderate liberal commentary such as that of *San Francisco Examiner* Washington bureau chief Christopher Matthews. Like foreign editor Marc Lerner, Forbes relies largely on the syndication services rather than in-house talent, pulling together for "Commentary" the best of Pat Buchanan, Paul Greenberg, Mona Charen, B. J. Cutler, Walter Williams, Thomas Sowell and Georgie Anne Geyer, among other notables. The death of syndicated *Detroit News* columnist Warren T. Brookes will, of course, diminish the stature of the section; he will be missed. Forbes also has a stable of thoroughbred columnists from which to select material: Suzanne Fields, Samuel Francis, Paul Craig Roberts, and the ineffable Richard Grenier. We noted last year that "there doesn't seem to be a formula for 'Commentary,' but Mary Lou Forbes' instincts for finding stimulating ideas from responsible commentators and going for the movers and shakers, seem to work well in keeping the section vibrant, provocative and useful." This is still accurate; Forbes, rather than limiting the section to names, seems to look for ideas, and this method of assimilation works extremely well. With the departure of Tony Snow to the post of chief White House speechwriter, the editorials have gotten a bit soggy. Now under the direction of former *Insight* "Last Word" columnist Tod Lindberg, many editorials contain little fresh reporting, as with "Empowerment for Whom?" 4-25. Using the *National Journal* Robert Guskind-Carol Steinbach article as a source, the editorialist reveals to a somewhat broader audience that, despite HUD Secretary Jack Kemp's leadership, taxpayers are still going to get it in the neck for his big-deal "empowerment" program — "empowerment" for HUD and those in the projects who participate in the homestead plan, and further tax "impoverishment" for the middle class: "But there is a worse aspect to this plan than the creative financing. Taxpayers may have thought they were going to get a deal from selling off public housing: We pay now to restore the units, but once they're sold, we're through with a multibillion-dollar federal housing bureaucracy. But in reality, even as the Bush administration sells the public housing stock, it's planning increased spending on other HUD programs that will more than offset the savings. The housing dole rolls on."

The "Money" section in *The Washington Times* took two steps decidedly backwards in 1991. Business editor Margie Malandro and whatever powers that be at the paper have removed the emphasis from national policy and economics to a pseudo-*U.S.News & World Report* "News You Can Use" format. For instance, Karen Riley, who once detailed doings at Treasury and the Federal Reserve Board, now is a consumer reporter. In these recessionary days, "news you can use" might be of more utility in the short run, but it doesn't tell us much about what is going on in government to deal with the economic situation. The business features are acceptable, certainly, but the complete lack of hard economic news featured anywhere in *The Washington Times* is appalling. This holds them back from becoming a real competitor to the *Post,* the lack particularly acute in the land of politics and policy.

Wesley Pruden, the new editor, has a long way to go with *The Washington Times,* a daily newspaper with clear strengths and weaknesses. At 55, he has plenty of time to work out the paper's problems, and as a long-time staffer, joining the daily a mere three months after its founding, knows the ropes at the *Times.* With a little help from the economy and advertisers, perhaps he can steady its course.

Editor:	Arnaud de Borchgrave
Managing Editor:	Wesley Pruden
Address:	3600 New York Avenue, NE Washington, DC 20002 (202) 636-6000
Circulation:	1990 — 103,420 1991 — 100,000

146

MAJOR PERIODICALS

The American Spectator

With its professed willingness to engage directly in the great debates of the day, both within the conservative movement and the world at large, *The American Spectator* at times seems to be auditioning for a new role, that of *The American Participant.* At other times, *TAS* stands back from the fray and examines where current events fit into the big picture, based on the framework of a legitimate political philosophy of conservatism. It is a conservatism that mixes values from the heartland of America and the intellectual ferment that swept the conservative movement in the late-1970s and 1980s. While *TAS* is not a neo-con publication by any stretch of the imagination, neither does it qualify as a member of the paleo-con species either. Instead, *TAS* occupies an uneasy slot between the two, which perhaps is understandable, given the magazine's history.

Founded in 1924 in a tavern and taken over in 1967 by the "Saturday Evening Club," who renamed it *The Alternative: An American Spectator* and who consequently dropped *The Alternative* from the title in 1977, *TAS* has always evoked an era when political discourse took place over cigars and beer steins and affairs of state were the province of men of letters. Its tone, however, has often been that of the graduate who has seen something of the world and, while he still retains the beliefs of his youth, cannot contain a smirk when one of his older relatives on his mother's side lets loose with an extremism at the Thanksgiving dinner table. Editor-in-chief R. Emmett Tyrrell, Jr.'s decision to move *TAS*'s editorial offices several years ago from Indiana, the Mecca of America conservatism, to the heart of the elite eastern seaboard liberal establishment in the suburbs of Washington, D.C., can be read as both an attempt to inject *TAS* more directly in the political system and an effort to put some physical distance behind his roots, a trait familiar to many graduates.

Tyrrell's efforts to come to terms with Indiana may still be unresolved, as his misguided cover story on Vice President Dan Quayle two years ago illustrated, but when it comes to participating in the political debates of the times, we can report: mission accomplished. *TAS* intervened in the escalating debate between paleo-cons and neo-cons, personified by the growing neo-con criticism of Patrick Buchanan and the debate over funding of conservative intellectual endeavors with all the impact of the U.S. intervening in the border dispute between Iraq and Kuwait.

The intervention came in the provocative cover story "The Conservative Bully Boy," 7-91, by David Frum. Frum, an assistant features editor at *The Wall Street Journal,* vividly portrays Buchanan as both a personification of the darker side of American conservatism that many had thought had been exorcised from the movement forever, and a shameless self-promoter and intellectual lightweight. Frum concedes that Buchanan, in his tirades against "neoconservatives," has focused on the great philosophical divide between conservatives today — between "Big Government" conservatives and traditional "Small Government" conservatives — but that Buchanan's "real message" is evidenced by his stands on segregation, immigration, and the Japanese is "not a message that can be accommodated in any conservatism — Big Government or Small — that seriously hopes to govern a great and diverse country. . ." Frum concludes: "What [Buchanan's] conservatism seeks is to keep its followers constantly on the boil — to keep their checks coming to his newsletter and their eyeballs glued to 'Crossfire.' And Buchanan is doing exactly the right thing to achieve that goal: blowing wind."

TAS editors may have seen the piece as an attempt to clarify the debate within the conservative movement on the issues Buchanan was raising, and the methods by which he was raising them, but for Buchanan's supporters Frum's piece was all too clear. In an obviously heartfelt "Special Correspondence" piece the following month, Robert Novak defends his comrade in the columnist trenches, writing that "Ideologically, Buchanan is no kook but an eloquent and effective spokesman for mainstream conservative causes," and repudiates charges of anti-Semitism on Buchanan's part. In his reply, Frum writes that "It is simply bizarre to suggest — as Robert Novak seems to — that it is unfair to judge a writer by his writings," and points out that he only touched on the issue of Buchanan's alleged anti-Semitism.

Novak was just the beginning. In the September issue, *TAS* published reader reaction to the Frum piece, "Special Correspondence," "The Good, The Bad, and The Ugly," and much of it was ugly. Out of 22 letters, 19 were pro-Buchanan, 2 were pro-Frum, one was mixed. The letters ranged from spirited defenses of such far-right tenets that the late Rev. Dr. Martin Luther King was a communist of dubious character; to far-out letters on the neo-con/paleo-con battle; to open expressions of anti-Semitism, racism, and nativism. One writer stated, "I'm a little weary of the charge of 'denying the Holocaust' being applied to people who, like myself, don't believe 'gas chambers' ever were used or that 6 million Jews were killed." In his response, Frum noted "Unfortunately, as this correspondence shows, Patrick Buchanan has been finding a constituency among the movement's haters."

Tyrrell also became engaged in the other great debate in America's political culture this year, the rising tide of "multiculturalism" on the nation's campuses, writing in "PC People," 5-91, that multiculturalists were "pampered provincials from the 'burbs, and now they are returning American universities to the status of second-rate cow colleges whose attainments in the humanities and in various of the social sciences (sic) are the laughingstock of the world." Tyrrell then announced the formation of "Amnesty in Academia," a "public-service group to protect the rights of university students and faculty," and supplied an address and 800 number for students and faculty who felt that their rights had been violated.

AIA's initial findings were printed in "A Bizarre Province," 11-91. Tyrrell writes that such cases as a University of Texas professor forced to resign for opposing the creation of an Ethnic and Third World Literature concentration for M.A. students and a Harvard pre-law senior who suffered "threats and indignities" for hanging the Confederate stars and bars outside her dorm window as clearly demonstrating that "American higher education, at least in the humanities and among university administrators, has lost touch with the intellectual life of Western Europe, the intellectual aspirations of erstwhile Communist satellites, and, of course, the social and political life of the United States."

While we are not sure that we would go quite that far, we did get a kick out of the submission that won first-prize, a letter from the School of Journalism at the University of Kentucky taking a recent scholarship applicant to task for the "inappropriate" and "thoughtless" use of the word "chairman" in her application letter, and offering to help make up the apparent gap in her education which has failed to prepare her to use "gender inclusive language" in her writing. Tyrrell also writes that some of the cases may be taken to court while others will be handled by "mediation teams" dispatched to the nation's campuses, teams that include Tyrrell and P.J. O'Rourke, "to facilitate better understanding between university administrators and the innocent."

If that facilitation is in the same spirit as O'Rourke's "Joe McCarthy Memorial New Enemies List," 11-91, then we would advise those campuses to begin removing women, children, and all noncombatants from the area now. O'Rourke, in "Commies — Dead But Too Dumb to Lie Down," 11-91, exults that "We rule the world," and urges *TAS* readers to show no mercy to the "intellectual Gulagmongers," through such eminently politically incorrect acts as smoking "great big capitalist-pig chair-leg-sized stogies that smell like barbecuing snow tires" and shooting cats. "Owning a cat is as close as most pinkos come to having a normal personal relationship." Saddam Hussein went easier on occupied Kuwait.

Of course, O'Rourke is always a treat, and we were disappointed that all of his war dispatches appeared in *Rolling Stone,* not that they did not serve a useful function for *RS* readers, but that they might have added an extra dimension to *TAS*'s war coverage. *TAS* did devote three cover stories to the Gulf War. Micah Morrison, in "The Sword and the Shield," 1-91, offered a literate report on Operation Desert Shield, taking us to the front lines in the northern Saudi desert and showing us the fault lines running through Saudi society, but we were getting a sandstorm of such stories elsewhere. Frequent *TAS* contributor Michael Ledeen, in the analytical "We *Are* Number One," 3-91, breathlessly belabored the obvious: "The first two nights of the war showed the awesome difference between a superpower and a regional power;" "One of the dramatic developments in this war has been the change in the behavior of Saudi leadership;" "We are on the verge of fulfilling our destiny as the leader and the inspiration of the Second Democratic Revolution." Such a piece quickly sinks to the bottom of the vast ocean of commentary on the war. Much more appreciated was a superior analysis of Winston Churchill's reflections on the morally bankrupt leadership and disastrous tactics of the First World War, "A Ground War for All Time: Churchill's Forgotten Masterpiece," 4-91, by Algis Valiunas. Appearing just as the ground war was approaching in the Gulf, "Churchill's Forgotten Masterpiece," was *TAS* at its best, drawing on history to provide a stimulating model with which to view contemporary events, from a slightly-off-center perspective.

TAS devoted only one cover to the other major international story of the day — the crisis within the Soviet Union. In "The Empire Strikes Out," 2-91, Adrian Karatnycky, director of research at the AFL-CIO Department of International Affairs, offered a generally upbeat assessment of the nationalist movements within the U.S.S.R., raising the key point that "ethnic violence is in fact a product of acute poverty. . ."

The Soviet Union and Eastern Europe were the subjects of many of the best articles we saw in *TAS* this year. George Szamuely, in "Germany Neither East Nor West," 3-91, cut through the angst of Germany's existential crisis contending that: ". . .it is hard to believe that a mere forty years — thirty, if you count back only to the building of the Berlin Wall — would be long enough to produce two separate states. The truth is that, after a lot of grumbling, most Germans accepted partition as a fact of life." Anne Applebaum, Warsaw correspondent for *The Economist,* offered a sophisticated look at the underlying problems complicating the privatization of state-owned industries in Eastern Europe in "Who Owns Central Europe?" 2-91. Cathy Young's "Soviet Presswatch" continues to be the most informative of the regular features as she keeps us up-to-date on the latest revelations brought about by *glasnost.* In "Taking Care of Business," 3-91, she reports on how developments in the Soviet press foreshadowed the violent crackdown in the Baltics in January, while "Free at Last," 11-91, provides a sophisticated report on the performance of the Soviet press, both official and underground, during the coup attempt and immediate aftermath.

However, much of *TAS*'s analytics on international developments continue to be anchored by former Reagan administration official Michael Ledeen, who often seems more intent on defending policies of the past ten years, such as "Leftist Liars and Ideological Suicide," 10-91, than in looking ahead. The editors are evidently high on Ledeen, feeling that he was on to Gorbachev's shortcomings fairly early, and perhaps he was. But just as observers noted during the Robert Gates confirmation hearings, simply arguing that there was less to Gorbachev than met the Western eye isn't enough to move policy forward. We have to believe, given the vast network of former Reagan administration officials now prowling in the hallways of think tanks and academe, that *TAS* can produce the same mix of intellectually exciting international analysis that it is increasingly achieving in its domestic coverage.

TAS's domestic coverage in 1991 focused more on the Bush administration, often turning to White House watchers in the press corps for cover stories on the President and his top aides. The results were mixed. In "The Mission Thing," 5-91, senior Reuters correspondent Gene Gibbons took a laudatory look at President Bush as "a warrior-President," contending that Bush's background as a World War II pilot gives him a better ability to place national interests above "concern for the suffering of a few unfortunate citizens." The article might have been interesting if Gibbons had examined why a President so skilled at diplomacy turns to force virtually every time he is confronted with a problem overseas. ABC News correspondent Brit Hume's examination of the controversy surrounding the White House Chief of Staff, "John

Sununu's Foolish Pride," 9-91, fails to address what Sununu's air travels has done to his effectiveness. David Brock, in "Not Losing At All Cost: Smooth Jim Baker's Rocky Reign at State," 8-91, launches an all-out assault on James Baker's tenure as Secretary of State, condemning Baker as a "pragmatist," with "no grounding in principle." Brock raises some telling criticisms, but much of his credibility is undercut by his feelings toward the professional officers of the foreign service, whom he views with a near-McCarthyesque contempt as "soft-headed" appeasers.

TAS also resumed covering Vice President Dan Quayle, assuming a cautious approach, as if the Vice President was still a third rail for the magazine. Kevin J. McNamara, in the "Nation's Pulse" column "The Making of a Vice President," 7-91, documented how the nation's political press corps portrayed the Indiana senator as an up-and-comer right up to the day George Bush chose him as a running mate. "Until his nomination to the vice presidency, Washington correspondents praised Quayle with the kind of superlatives that inevitably brought him to the attention of people like, well, George Bush." *TAS* followed up with Thomas Mallon's "Travels With My Veep," 9-91, Mallon self-consciously watching for signs of juvenile behavior as the VP tours a charity hospital and attends the opening of the Quayle hometown museum. Mallon came away impressed by Quayle's political abilities, but questioned his character, writing that Quayle has allowed himself to be turned into "a sweet, miniature creature in a Republican petting zoo."

Social issues remain a key concern to *TAS,* who devoted much attention this year to the on-going debate over the creation of a new domestic policy, keen to the dangers of a resurgent welfare state. Tyrrell set the tone early in the year with "A Memo to George Bush," 2-91, urging the chief executive to match the "old wing" of the Republican party, whose members "get things done," with the "Thatcher Wing," whose members "have the passion, the energy, the numbers, and the ideas that made the Republican Party the power that it was in your first year and a half." House Minority whip Newt Gingrich followed with "Maggie's Magic," 3-11, offering tribute to Margaret Thatcher and contending that American conservatives can learn from her shrewd blend of ideology and political pragmatism.

David Frum, the writer of the Patrick Buchanan piece cited earlier, quickly became the *TAS* pointman on the social debate. The editors feel Frum is a major find, and we agree that he does show potential. In "A Poorhouse Divided," 2-91, he offered a critical study of the history of U.S. anti-poverty programs from the turn of the century settlement houses to the "New Paradigm" and "culturalist" philosophies dividing conservatives today.

The argument boils down to the question: can poverty be eradicated through economic growth, or is it the result of ingrained social traits in certain segments of society? The issue is explored in greater depth in the cover story, "Chronicler Without a Clue," 6-91, in which William Tucker writes on Nicholas Lemann and his new book, *The Promised Land: The Great Black Migration and How It Changed America,* and unintentionally illustrates the contradiction at the core of the conservative response to poverty, claiming that blacks are just the same as anyone else — "what [Lemann] is describing. . .is the urban transformation every ethnic group has experienced" — and that they are fundamentally different as well because of their African heritage. It is the inability to resolve this core contradiction, of which the "new paradigm" and the "culturalist" dispute is the latest version, which has frustrated conservative efforts on this issue. If *TAS* can help resolve the contradiction, it will go a long way toward staking a claim as the premier conservative journal of opinion.

TAS delivered superb coverage on the major domestic political story of the year, the Clarence Thomas nomination to the Supreme Court, due largely to the efforts of "Presswatch" columnist Terry Eastland, who has become required reading for anyone interested in the confluence of government, politics, and the national media, no matter their political persuasion. Writing on the coverage of Thurgood Marshall's retirement and the nomination of Clarence Thomas to replace him in the cover story, "Thomas Linked to Marshall," 10-91, he presciently outlined the stories the press either overlooked or deliberately ignored, including Thomas's days as EEOC chairman. Fully aware of the role the press itself plays in stories like the Hill-Thomas affair, in "Anonymous Chickens," 12-91, he correctly points out that the eleventh-hour effort to derail the nomination through the leaking of Anita Hill's charges is "eerily similar" to an incident he reported over a year ago. In "The Leak That Fizzled," 6-90, he divulged an attempt by Senate staffers to block the nomination of Tim Ryan to head the Office of Thrift Supervision by leaking an FBI report on Ryan's alleged cocaine use to an NBC reporter.

In a peripheral way, *TAS* itself played a role in the Thomas confirmation story, as Thomas's opponents and the press seized on a speech he delivered four years ago in which he spoke highly of an essay by Lew Lehrman on the right-to-life movement which appeared in *TAS* 4-87 as if it were a Rosetta stone for decoding the nominee's beliefs. It generated unusually high interest in *TAS,* as the *TAS* masthead appeared as part of the lead story one night on "ABC Evening News," indicating the possible explosive nature of stories which appear in a publication dedicated to provocative thinking.

Of course, *TAS* can produce duds as well, which is especially true in its regular departments. "The Continuing Crisis" continues to sink into a crisis of its own, Tyrrell's monthly exercise in sophomoric humor becoming increasingly embarrassing, his occasional genuine witticisms far outweighed by tasteless references to various instances of behavioral indecency which, more often than not, reflect badly on members of minorities or holders of political persuasions that Tyrrell does not agree with.

"Capital Ideas" columnist Tom Bethell remains one of a kind, combining conservative preserve-the-status-quo instincts with an innate hostility to government at all levels. At times these feelings collide, as they did in "The Center Folds," 11-91, where Bethell takes potshots at such familiar targets as Eurobureaucrats, pro-abortion rights advocates, and pragmatic Republicans. The latter seem only to rank right up there with evolutionists on Bethell's enemies list. In "California Calamity," 9-91, he unloaded a ferocious barrage at California Gov. Pete Wilson, and his tax-raising, income-redistributive ways: "Socialism may have collapsed in Eastern Europe, but its animating emotions are alive and well in California."

The back-of-the-book departments are a grab bag of columns, features, and essays, from such conservative war horses as Joe Queenan, Vic Gold, Benjamin J. Stein, and Richard Brookhiser. The quality varies, and sometimes a first-rate journalistic effort pops up, as with Jennifer Howard's vivid depiction of Calcutta, "Enduring India," 7-91; and "Out to Lunch With Sendero," 12-91, a memorable look at Shining Path members keeping the faith alive in a Peruvian prison. John Corry, in "The Most Considerate of Men," 7-91, provided a moving appreciation of Jerzy Kosinski.

TAS fails to provide any regular feature devoted to economics, which is puzzling given that the editors evidently feel that economic freedom is one of the most important basic freedoms in the world. We learn how freedom of another sort is constantly being taken to extremes in "Ben Stein's Diary," the former White House speechwriter taking us through his daily rounds of casting calls, TV shoots, and close encounters with New Agers. We are told that Stein's column is one of the most popular that appears in *TAS,* his fans include Manhattan District Attorney Robert Morgenthau, but despite Stein's evident geniality, the feature has begun to take on the traits of the self-centered southern California power brokers and power broker wanna-bes that Stein bemusedly profiles month after month.

The product those power brokers churn out, the "Talkies," are addressed each month by James Bowman, and we share the editor's appreciation for his efforts at finding underlying themes connecting movies which, on the surface, seem unrelated. He produces the occasional misfire — writing on the celebration of 1960's values in recent releases in "Swinging No More," 5-91. In it, he refers to such films as "The Doors" and "Scenes From a Mall" as being hits when in fact they were box office failures, so instead of examining why movies dedicated to 1960's values were such flops in 1991, he criticizes "the jaded children of the Reagan era" for looking at the 1960s as a"Golden Age." In the much more successful "The Banality of '90s Evil," 8-91, he expertly examines how the concept of evil is handled in such lightweight Hollywood concoctions as "Backdraft," "Jungle Fever," and "Robin Hood, Prince of Thieves."

The strength of *TAS* continues to be the book reviews, drawing on a large spectrum of conservative writers to comment on the major non-fiction works of the day, with the occasional work of fiction or influential if obscure non-fiction tome tossed in. There were only several major disappointments here: Michael Ledeen, 5-91, reviewing Iran-contra prosecutor Jeffrey Toobin's book on the investigation, *Opening Arguments: A Young Lawyer's First Case: United States v. Oliver North,* continues his efforts to whitewash the excesses of the Reagan years, dismissing Toobin as being "way out of his depth," and the investigation itself as an act of hypocrisy by a Congress which had "known about the affair the whole time." Reviewing P.J. O'Rourke's bestseller *Parliament of Whores,* 9-91, Daniel Wattenberg defends O'Rourke against his liberal critics instead of simply telling us about this widely-read book on the U.S. government.

As usual, the better reviews were able to put ideological blinders aside and deal honestly with the book itself. Terry Eastland, drawing the assignment of reviewing Ronald Reagan's autobiography *An American Life,* 5-91, found that "the memoir is a poor one — it is bland, uninformative, and even inaccurate," while cautioning that "Contrary to the assessments of some reviewers of this book, it is always a mistake to judge a presidency by a presidential memoir." In an inspired move, the editors assigned *A Question of Character: A Life of John F. Kennedy,* by Thomas C. Reeves to English writer Paul Johnson, who, in the 9-91 issue, provided former British Prime Minister Harold Macmillan's take on Camelot: "Oh,. . .it's rather like watching the Borgia brothers take over a respectable north Italian city."

We always enjoy the annual "Books for Christmas" article. *TAS* soliciting contributions from journalists, politicians, and academics across the political spectrum. The result often is a hilarious and revealing look at the *zeitgeist* of our time. This year was no exception, with the afore mentioned Reeves, for example, nominating *"Johnny, We Hardly Knew Ye": Memories of John Fitzgerald Kennedy*: "For sheer fun, this is hard to beat. It is especially recommended for fans of black comedy and people who believe in Santa Claus." Intriguingly, two separate contributors, academic Richard Pipes and *Vanity Fair* columnist James Wolcott, both nominated an Anthony Trollope novel, *The Eustice Diamonds,* making us wonder if Trollope would be the 19th century British writer of the 1990s much the way Charles Dickens seemed to stage a comeback during the 1980s.

TAS itself has affected many of the trimmings of the late 19th century, both in illustration and in tone, but that may be changing. The world will find a new *TAS* on its newsstands and magazine shelves in 1992, one that has been "downsized" in physical size, so that it will fit more easily on newsstands and magazine racks. This change will affect the editorial content, many of the illustrations gracing the pages will be gone, and the articles themselves may be shorter. The editors are clearly positioning themselves for the decade ahead, where they see a world undergoing tumultuous change which they want to be a part of.

We wish the editors success, well aware of the task before them. Tyrrell and the rest of the "Saturday Evening Club" may have seen themselves filling a vacuum in 1967, and no doubt a need did exist for a conservative publication which was infused with the irreverent spirit, if not the New Left philosophy, of the 1960s. *TAS* seems to be successfully evolving to a new stage, one more compatible with the information glut of the 1990s, when insight and understanding, not political gadflyism, is at a premium. Right now *TAS* has a chance at being one of the last survivors of a great race, redolent of the time when thousands roamed freely across North America.

Editor: R. Emmett Tyrrell, Jr.

Address: 2020 N. 14th St., Suite 750
Arlington, VA 22216
(703) 243-3733

Circulation: 1990 — 39,408
1991 — 35,947

The Atlantic

The Atlantic's quirky, intriguing mix of literary efforts, cultural events and national perspectives persists in drawing us into the monthly. As a magazine mostly comprised of ideas and formulations, there generally is little space spent on practical application, as though the editors see implementation as almost an afterthought. The ideas are usually enough to provoke and stimulate discussion, if not necessarily among Washington policymakers, then surely among the elites of the Eastern seaboard from Boston to D.C.

James Fallows and Nicholas Lemann are the closest thing the monthly has to bonafide stars on the masthead. Both noted and notable for their recent bestsellers on Japan and the war on poverty, respectively, they generally appear in the opening "Reports & Comment" section. Fallows, though, hasn't had the same edge we appreciated several years ago, seemingly changed after his two years in Asia. He reflects on his sojourn in "Real Originals," 1-91, meandering about his point on the beginnings of a possible boom in Malaysia, descriptive and evocative, but with little of import. Fallows is better with "Shut Out," 3-91, as he describes the sorry state of U.S.-Vietnamese relations, prodding the U.S. government on to normalization, and, by his eloquent conclusion, he's made a rather convincing case. "It's natural that we would prefer never to think about Vietnam again. Being involved there did us great harm. So with a kind of unconscious spite we continue a policy that hobbles an entire nation and helps us not at all, mainly because a generation ago we came to grief there. In decency we should stop." Lemann, on the other hand, is continually maturing, honing his theses on poverty on a regular basis, keeping them rather fresh and intelligent. He provides an interesting dissertation on the war on poverty via HUD Sec. Jack Kemp's empowerment ideas, wrapping this up by drawing an eerie historical parallel between the circumstances of Bush's war on poverty and the origins of Jack Kennedy's war on poverty, "Fighting the Last War," 2-91. Nominated by *The Atlantic*'s editors for 10 Best consideration is Lemann's "The Other Underclass," 12-91, in which he examines the Puerto Rican subculture as it relates to the underclass. This is an important discussion in that so few have addressed Hispanic issues in this context: "In New York City, black median family income is substantially higher than Puerto Rican, and is rising more rapidly. The black home-ownership rate is more than double the Puerto Rican rate. Puerto Rican families are more than twice as likely as black families to be on welfare, and are about 50 percent more likely to be poor. In the mainland United States, Puerto Ricans have nothing like the black institutional network of colleges, churches and civil-rights organizations; there isn't a large cadre of visible Puerto Rican successes in every field; black politicians are more powerful than Puerto Rican politicans in all the cities with big Puerto Rican populations; and there is a feeling that blacks have America's attention, whereas Puerto Ricans, after a brief flurry of publicity back in *West Side Story* days, have become invisible." Lemann assembles and examines different historical patterns in an attempt to ascertain the underlying causes of poverty for this group, and though he is ultimately inconclusive, it's a step in assessing the problems that hasn't been taken before, and we're impressed accordingly.

The cover treatments are as diverse and eclectic as any we find, spanning subjects from economics to POWs this year. Robert Reich seems more interested in who's wrong in "The Real Economy," cover 2-91, rather than constructing his own prescription; while there are some good things to be found in this treatment, the textbook language grates. Douglas Wilson offers an intriguing examination of the literary interests of Thomas Jefferson and Abraham Lincoln, "What Jefferson and Lincoln Read," cover 1-91, a treatment that typifies *The Atlantic*, blending the literary and historical to assess the talents and the achievements of the two. A scholarly debate over Shakespeare and the authorship of his plays is found in "Looking for Shakespeare," cover 10-91, *The American Spectator*'s Tom Bethell and the author of *Shakespeare: The Living Record,* Irvin Matus, arguing the point in question in this long, thick discourse. One would have to have a specific interest to slog through this point-counterpoint discussion in its entirety, although the tour of Elizabethan England is interesting enough. Nominated for 10 Best consideration by the editors at *The Atlantic* is *Washington Post* reporter Thomas B. Edsall with Mary D. Edsall's "Race," cover 5-91; the Edsalls draw some interesting lines here, but this is an overlong, esoteric handling of the subject. Joe Klein of *New York* magazine does this much more succinctly, and effectively. The first in an unconventional triad of articles on children and psychology, *The Atlantic*'s "Therapy for Children," by Katharine Davis Fishman appears on the cover 6-91, a treatise on the clinical aspects of child psychotherapy that precedes the exercises in *The New York Times* and *The Progressive*. Writing almost from a consumer's point of view, Fishman occasionally descends into indecipherable jargon ("Sarnoff thinks that Kevin is on the cusp of ludic demise") but much of this is quite understandable. The cover "Waiting for the Weekend," 8-91, by Witold Rybczynski, is reminiscent of the *Utne Reader* in size and scope, as the author postulates that we are becoming enslaved by leisure: "People used to 'play' tennis; now they 'work' on their backhand." We get an amusing history of the weekend and its cultural evolution as well. Like Hugh Sidey at *Time,* William Least Heat-Moon paints a composite portrait of Chase County, Kansas in "Prairy Earth," cover 9-91, vivid and poetic. Equally evocative is William Langewiesche's tour of the Sahara region, "The World in Its Extreme," cover 11-19, nominated for 10 Best consideration by the editors at *The Atlantic*: "Algerians call it the Extreme South, with the same feeling that we put into our 'Far West.' It is the land of more so: drier, fiercer, and wilder, a desert of parched basins and volcanic mountains, of buttes, cinder cones, and confused black rock. You can walk for hours absorbed by the drama of desolation and distance. The view is mesmerizing, like a night sky. The peaks give it depth; the nomads give it scale. It is the central Sahara, a long way to everywhere." H. Bruce Franklin challenges the popular assumptions on "The POW/MIA Myth," cover 12-91, systematically deconstructing the government's case that there are any POWs or MIAs left in Southeast Asia and indicting the film industry for its propagandizing of the idea. Sure to be a controversial effort somewhere along the line, it's an engrossing perspective.

Another cover addressed the question of a New World Order. Formerly of *Foreign Policy,* Alan Tonelson offers his view of "What Is the National Interest?" cover 7-91, nominated by *The Atlantic*'s editors for 10 Best consideration. Tonelson advocates that the U.S. distinguish "between what it must do that is absolutely essential for achieving this more modest set of objectives and those things it might do that are not essential. It must, in other words, begin to think in terms not of the whole world's well-being but rather of purely national interests." This isolationist perspective, however practical it sounds, seems naive: with nuclear warheads positioned all over the globe, it seems the most basic national interest — self-preservation — would be precisely to think in terms of the world's well-being. At the same time, Tonelson postulates that "despite its heightened sensitivity to questions involving resources, the new foreign policy would proceed from an assumption of American strength, not weakness. While conceding that the United States is neither powerful nor wealthy enough to remake the world in its own image, or to achieve security and prosperity for itself by securing these benefits for every country on the planet, it would recognize that America is powerful, wealthy and geopolitically secure enough to flourish without carrying out this ambitious agenda." This brand of hopeful isolationism seems particularly facile in his recommendation for the U.S. to take the credit for world peace while having none of the responsibility and without having to make any effort to secure such a peace. Hmm. A point-counterpoint on the Gulf War follows. Harvard associate dean for international affairs and director of Harvard's Center for International Affairs, Joseph S. Nye, Jr., offers reasons "Why the Gulf War Served the National Interest." The other half, penned by Christopher Layne, former senior fellow in foreign policy studies at the Cato Institute, argues "Why the Gulf War Was Not in the National Interest." Layne, unfortunately, immediately takes a defensive position, arguing against the reasons already presented in the press for going to war, and he doesn't offer his own appraisal of why the war was not in our best interests until the closing pages.

Two covers this year were followed by articles broadening the original premise. We get a preview of Dinesh D'Souza's ideas on "Illiberal Education," 3-91, a discourse of D'Souza's perceptions on multiculturalism and political correctness which helped precipitate a political maelstrom. Longer than many of *The Atlantic*'s essays, D'Souza's cogent, compelling examples inform. Later, Daniel J. Singal outlines "The Other Crisis in American Education," 11-91, proffering ideas for a return to educational excellence through more rigorous curricula, particularly in English and history. His ideas ring true when we think about the state of the public education system. The cover on language seems a rather esoteric selection. In "Quest for the Mother Tongue," 4-91, Robert Wright simply doesn't pique our interest, beginning with "Linguistics has long been a haven for Soviet intellectuals of a contrary sort." More inviting is "The Decipherment of Ancient Maya," by David Roberts, 9-91. A subject also treated in *The New York Times* "Science Times," this is more detailed, particularly on the history of the study of the Mayans, and what the decoding of the language means for such scholarship.

Other articles intrigue us to varying degrees. Wendell Berry's goofy "Out of Your Car, Off Your Horse," 2-91, lists suggestions for a new kind of ecological community: "XXII. What, for a start, might be the economic result of local affection? We don't know. Moreover, we are probably never going to know in any way that would satisfy the average dean or corporate executive. The ways of love tend to be secretive and, even to the lovers themselves, somewhat inscrutable." Suzanne Gordon takes a crack at formulating "A National Care Agenda," 1-91, but, while her ideas of support networks for elder care and child care, among other things, are laudable, there's no practical application here. On a related topic, Regina E. Herzlinger offers another approach to the health care crisis with "Healthy Competition," 8-91, postulating that if employes bought their own health care insurance and plans, the market would be forced to control costs, actually including a reasonable mechanism for doing so, an interesting perspective that needs fleshing out and is surprisingly practical. One of *The Nation*'s theater reviewers, Thomas Disch, examines the state of the Great White Way in "The Death of Broadway," 3-91, a sad lament for changing times in the New York theater district. Disch provides a broad overview here, and we come away informed, though depressed, at the potential for Broadway's demise. We learn the fine points of cement and concrete ("Cement, then, is the bonding agent in concrete; it is not, as is popularly thought, the same as concrete.") in John Sedgwick's "Strong but Sensitive," 4-91. We get a history of concrete, as well as a physical explanation for the crumbling and erosion of concrete roadways. We tour Macedonia through the last century with Robert D. Kaplan, "History's Cauldron," 6-91, Kaplan comparing it to modern-day Lebanon, and using it as a kind of model for projecting and predicting current nationalist turmoil in the region. We're initially dubious about "The UFO Experience," by James S. Gordon, 8-91, but after a far-out opening this turns into a credible examination and summation of different alleged "close encounters." A light evaluation of the press by Norman J. Ornstein is available in "Sexpress," 10-91; rather than evaluating what these titillating items, such as Chuck Robb's indiscretions and Nancy Reagan's less-than-flattering exposure by Kitty Kelley, mean for the direction of the national media, Ornstein lists the examples without saying much about changing standards.

And then, of course, there are the monthly short stories and departments. Joyce Carol Oates turns up with a engrossing "Life After High School," 11-91, evidence of *The Atlantic*'s clout in pursuing and obtaining writers of note for their pages. One needn't be a famous author, however. *The Atlantic* is surprisingly egalitarian in their selections. We enjoy perusing the monthly "Almanac," in which we find varying information on "The Skies," and excerpts from *The Atlantic* from "100 Years Ago," among other things. Like the index in *Harper's,* this page is fun and always worth perusing for pertinent and amusing banter. Edward Sorel and Nancy Caldwell Sorel's "First Encounters" are also worth skimming, as we find the "first encounters" of various personages of note, from Major John Andre and General Benedict Arnold, 5-91, to the origins of the long-standing feud between Bette Davis and Joan Crawford, 9-91.

Cutting a wide swath across journalistic borders, we're consistently amazed that *The Atlantic* is able to seem a whole magazine, so diverse are its contents. But the literate, literary combinations that editor William Whitworth devises continue to attract and entertain elite readers. We're sure *The Atlantic* will remain a staple on the Eastern seaboard, an important guide to some of the cocktail party ideas of the times.

Chairman:	Mortimer Zuckerman
Editor:	William Whitworth
Managing Editor:	Cullen Murphy
Address:	745 Boylston Street Boston, MA 02116 (617) 536-9500
Circulation:	1990 — 450,000 1991 — 450,000

Aviation Week & Space Technology

Celebrating its 75th anniversary in 1991, *Aviation Week & Space Technology* remains the unchallenged leader of defense and aerospace publications, but it is more than merely a leader. It is perhaps best described by a dictum attributed to the journal's chief editor of the 1930s, Edward P. Warner, in the article "Securing the Industry's Foundations," that we find in the 8-12 anniversary issue: "A professional journal is not a static observation post, he said, but an advancing intelligence division."

AWST's superlative reporting and analysis of the Gulf War was easily the very best to be found anywhere in the public domain. This achievement was not accidental, but one that reflects the rising intellectual standards that this journal is imposing on itself. From the outset, in senior military editor John D. Morrocco's "Air Strikes Spearhead Mideast War," 1-21, it understood better than anyone else what had to be watched for in Desert Storm, "the first war of the space age"; and this 10 Best nomination outlined the following watch-list: "In narrow terms, the world's military establishments will learn a great deal about the efficacy of contemporary tactics and leading edge technology — stealth, night attack and electronic warfare systems, 'smart' and standoff weapons, and immensely complex software." Excellent reports such as "USAF Missile Warning Satellites Providing 90-sec. Scud Attack Alert," 1-21; John Morrocco's "Allies Shift Air Attacks to Break Ground Units," 1-28; Senior space technology editor Craig Covault's "Recon Satellites Lead Allied Intelligence Effort," 2-4; "Nighttime CAS to Pose Challenge for Air Units Once Ground War Begins," 2-11; by John Morrocco and "U.S. Tactics Exploit Advances in Avionics, Air-to-Surface Weapons," 2-18, by John Morrocco were replete with almost classified technical and operational intelligence could serve as reference materials on the conduct of high-tech, space-based warfare as defined by Desert Storm.

In the victorious aftermath, thoughtful conclusions were presented by Craig Covault in "Desert Storm Reinforces Military Space Directions," 4-8: "Lessons from the extensive use of military spacecraft in Operation Desert Storm are reinforcing the objectives of advanced U.S. military space technology development already underway," and in John Morrocco's "War Will Reshape Doctrine, But Lessons Are Limited," 4-22, where he concludes that "the conflict validated the U.S. military's Air-Land Battle doctrine," but also cautions that "it will be difficult to draw any conclusions about close air support given the limited scope of the ground war," and that "the lessons not learned from the conflict may prove to be as important as those that were." *AWST*'s war coverage also included two invaluable "scoops" which will be decisive in the way the war's political and military history will be ultimately written. The politically important scoop is found by technical editor Stanley Kandebo in "Tomahawk Missile Excels in First Wartime Use," 1-21, which reveals that "Missiles from U.S. ships in the Mediterranean also may have been used to strike Iraq if Syria allowed the weapons to overfly its territory to reach potential targets," and that "in general, cruise missile-equipped ships and boats are provided with Tomahawk firing solutions prior to leaving port," which suggested the U.S. decision to go to war had been taken long before the U.N. resolution and congressional vote on the use of force. The militarily significant scoop was reported in "Allied Strategists Altered Battle Plans to Compensate for Dugan's Comments," by John Morrocco 7-22, which presents in superb detail that the tactics employed "during the first night of the war, crippled Iraq's air defense network."

Very distinctive also was *AWST*'s treatment of the attempted Soviet coup d'etat, in that it differed drastically from the nearly universal, popular and mistaken view that it was supposedly a military coup. The editorial "The Mastodon's Last Gasp," by Craig Covault 8-26, attributed the failed attempt to "Bolshevik hardliners," and scrupulously avoided blaming the military. Similarly, "Soviet Defense Ministry Rifts Spurred Coup; Instability Lingers," 8-26, highlights the fact that "the entire Soviet military refused to participate in the attempt to oust Gorbachev," and, judiciously declining to join in the premature celebrations for the purported triumph of freedom, cautions us that realities over there "still carry the potential for sparking a civil war in the USSR."

With respect to the great systemic changes in the world's strategic/security equation, *AWST* limited itself, for the most part, to providing superior insights into the changes wrought on the U.S defense budget and, by extension, on the defense/aerospace industry. Typical were "Lower Defense Budgets Forcing Industry to Boost Productivity and Reduce Costs," by congressional editor Trish Gilmartin 3-18; "Naval Aviation Plan Sacrifices Some Capability to Avoid Further Cuts in Aircraft Carriers," by John Morrocco 5-6; "Shift in U.S. Military Strategy Calls for Increasing SAC's Conventional Role," again by Morrocco 5-13; and "Uncertain U.S. Military Needs Hamper Industry Restructuring," also by Morrocco 6-17, which concludes that "Industry is a captive of the same uncertainties that plague Pentagon long-range planning — how to mold a smaller force structure to meet the shifting and often conflicting requirements posed by a changing world order. What is certain is that as the U.S. military budget and force structure shrinks, so will the defense industry that serves it."

Coverage of SDI developments was once again exemplary this year, combining unsurpassed technical evaluations of the results of on-going experimental work, as in "Shuttle Plume Data Advances SDI Warhead Tracking Goal," by Craig Covault 11-18, which identifies "a breakthrough that will help solve two key SDI challenges — detecting and tracking ballistic missile warheads during their space coast phase," with bold political predictions such as that the Soviet Union will ultimately cooperate with the U.S. and move beyond the 1972 Antiballistic Missile Treaty, found in "Gulf War Rekindles U.S. Debate on Protecting Space System Data," by Trish Gilmartin 4-29.

If any of *AWST*'s labors during 1991 are found wanting, it is in the lack of serious effort to study the possibility of major shifts in the American security/strategic relation with Europe and the Far East, even though the magazine has paid serious attention to the growing potential for economic frictions between the U.S. and these two blocs.

On the other hand, *AWST* must be commended for the increasingly evident spirit of an intellectual integrity at the weekly which transcends the cliches of our political culture, and of civil virtue and love of the common good not to be found in your average "industry publication." The former is exemplified in the editorial "Soviet Conversion Is No Panacea," 11-18, which admonishes the Bush Administration to stop making "ridiculous and hypocritical" demands for conversion of the Soviet economy to civilian use. The latter shines through Paul Mann's outstanding political essay "Why Contempt for Politics Damages National Security," 12-24-90, a stirring reminder of our ancient republican virtues, dormant today as "the American polity is ill with one of its chronic bouts of contempt for politics and politicians. . .an expression of contempt for ourselves." Its object is to argue that the [defense/aerospace] "industry's lament about its adversarial relations with the Pentagon and Congress often sound either naive or disingenuous."

Justifiably reluctant to tamper with proven success, *AWST* made virtually no editorial or layout changes. Business editor Nicholas C. Kernstock was dropped from the masthead, production editor Marion L. Reilly was replaced by Karen Andrews and moved on to replace Librarian Mark C. Barghesian. As in the past, its space is organized into distinctive sections with their characteristic rubrics the most permanent of which are "Headline News," "Propulsion Technology," "Aeronautical Engineering," "Air Transport," "Avionics," "Military

Electronics," and "Space Technology." Its standard departments also remained the same in format, but we are getting a higher appreciation of the important function that these unassuming parts of *AWST*'s landscape perform when we read, for instance, in "Washington Roundup," 11-11, under the subtitle "Honesty, Please," that "Strategic Defense Initiative officials are peeved at Israel's refusal to explain publicly what went wrong with the latest Arrow test flight."

In the year ahead, AWST's 76th, the world of aviation, high technology and space exploration will navigate in the unchartered waters of a world without a Soviet Union, without strategic arms races and with emerging challengers in the Pacific and in Europe. is navigating, we have no doubt would be much more perilous were it not for the future contributions that we have the right to expect from this great American publication.

Editor-in-Chief:	Donald Fink
Address:	1221 Avenue of the Americas
	New York, NY 10020
	(212) 512-2000
Circulation:	1990 — 143,310
	1991 — 141,259

Barron's

The year 1991 marked a rite of passage for the Dow Jones & Co. business weekly. Not only did the publication celebrate its 70th anniversary, but after 45 years with the publication, Robert M. Bleiberg, who has served as editor, publisher and, most recently, editorial page editor, announced his retirement. Although the 67-year-old Bleiberg has slowly ceded control over the past few years, his departure will nonetheless reformulate the balance of power at the magazine. Bleiberg has long been a countervailing force against editor Alan Abelson's vitriolic style and strictly bearish outlook. He is also much better on broader economic trends than Abelson whose talents lie in analyzing the value of specific stocks, not evaluating the broader political and economic forces moving the markets. A very competent Thomas G. Donlan now takes the wheel at the editorial page, and although we look forward to watching the page develop under his stewardship, it is yet to be seen if he can balance out Abelson with Bleiberg's same commendable vigor.

Despite all the change this year, the most important question at the weekly remains unanswered — when will Abelson retire? Only two years younger than Bleiberg, he will certainly make the big announcement within the next few years. Abelson's departure, more than anyone else's on the masthead, will mark the end of an era at the publication. Indeed, with his acerbic writing style and authoritarian management technique, Abelson has so dominated the publication's content and tone, that his departure will literally transform the character of *Barron's*. A 5-20 article in the *New York Post* entitled, "Barron's Since '87: Circulation a Bear," by Helen Thorpe, provided plenty of insight into the editor's autocratic style: "Mr. Abelson has taken a particularly active interest in all aspects of Barron's. He abolished group story meetings, preferring to make individual assignments himself. He reads and edits most features. He writes the headlines and even the 'teaser' lines in the table of contents. And he sits down, usually not until Friday, to write his lengthy column on deadline. Some called the result a virtual dictatorship."

With such an overbearing personality presiding over the masthead, it is difficult to speculate as to who might emerge as Abelson's successor. Though lean, the masthead carries some outstanding writers and analysts, and according to the *NYP* article, Abelson said, "there was 'no question' that his own successor would come from within *Barron's* staff. Likely candidates are Kathryn Welling, managing editor, and James Meagher, deputy editor."

In the meantime, *Barron's* continues to struggle with dwindling circulation and a tight budget. The financially strapped publication lost another long-time writer in what has become a small but steady stream of departures. Commodities Editor Richard A. Donnelly left "to take his considerable talents and apply them to other pursuits," according to Abelson. Fortunately, John Liscio has stepped in with his impressive grasp of the commodities markets to fill that void.

The lean times at the publication are showing through in other ways, too. We notice a much heavier reliance on the serviceable Q&A format which can be effective, especially when Kathryn M. Welling is conducting the interview, but can also get long and monotonous. Almost every other issue of *Barron's* now features a Q&A or a Roundtable. By nature, interviews are more effective on television where the interactions between the participants and the intonations in their voices enrich the encounter. In print, however, we get little more than a transcript of the conversations. We would suggest that the editors use this type of format more sparingly.

There is also a growing dependence on freelance contributors, most of whom were apparently educated at the Abelson school of cantankerous journalism which favors caustic commentary over cogent analysis. According to the *NYP* article, Abelson believes irreverence and skepticism are part of *Barron's* mission, which is to define values. This may explain why Abelson and his freelance cronies spend so much time preaching and so little time analyzing the facts. Typical of this style is contributor Benjamin J. Stein who spent yet another year bashing junk bonds even though they were one of the highest yielding investments of the year. In "Sunk by Junk," 4-1, he ignores evidence that insurer First Executive Corp. was in financial trouble well before it bought into junk bonds, and closes his eyes to the suffocating regulatory environment that contributed to the insurer's decline. Ironically, as prospective buyers surveyed the failed insurer's assets later in the year, reports at other publications noted that it was the junk bond portfolio that was attracting buyers and escalating bids. Once again, Stein let reason give way to emotion in "Junk Bunk," 7-1, trying with all his might to debunk the junk bond rally. He asserts that the various junk bond indexes do not accurately measure the downside of junk bond activity, but we don't remember him making a stink about their accuracy last year when junk bonds were still down. These types of inconsistencies weigh heavily on Stein's credibility. We saw a little less of Joe Queenan who never has a positive word to say about anything and much less of Christopher Whalen who spent last year pooh-poohing the stock market rally in Mexico. Since Abelson feels the need to teach investors about "values," we assume that Mexico, like junk bonds, is on his "unvirtuous" investment list, which means that any positive facts about that particular topic are immediately thrown in the wastebasket. But, this year, we did see some recognition of the positive changes taking place south of the border, not from Whalen of course, but from Maggie Mahar in "An Upward Turn South of the Border," 5-13.

As for cover stories, we think Maggie Mahar is one of the best at the weekly with such perceptive and well-researched offerings as "No Mickey Mouse Company," 6-24, in which she makes a convincing argument to Wall Street that Disney still has long-term growth prospects overseas; or her jolting post Soviet coup interview with Soviet economist Vladimir Popov, "Comes the Revolution," cover 8-26, and follow-up report, "Death of an Empire," 9-16, in which Popov asserts that hyperinflation and nationalism are leading the country toward another coup. Another stellar writer and researcher, Thomas Donlan, confronted conventional wisdom in "Riding for a Fall?" cover 10-21. Looking beyond McDonnell Douglas's current prosperity, he challenges Wall Street's blue skies scenario, finding clouds on the company's horizon in its loss of commercial airplane market share to Boeing and Airbus Industrie, and even deeper troubles on the defense side of its business. Eric J. Savitz weighs in with an interesting contrary perspective in "No Miracle Cure," cover 8-5, which asserts that the ever more popular HMOs, may not be the cure-all for soaring healthcare costs that they're cracked up to be. And we respected Jonathan R. Laing's hard-hitting and well-documented assessment of Edward and Peter Bronfman's corporate complex in "Shaky Dominion," 5-6.

Of course, "cover story" is kind of a misnomer for the above articles since Abelson's "Up & Down Wall Street" column is the only work that actually ever appears on page one. Abelson still uses his extensive Wall Street network and decades of experience in market analysis to send stocks for a ride, but his evaluations of the broader forces moving the markets seem less potent each year. As the editor of the magazine that advertises itself at "The official atlas of the road to riches," Abelson's strictly bearish stance has led him to advise his investment readers to take some decidedly bumpy financial routes this year. For example, in his 1-14 column a few days before the coalition forces launched an air attack which kicked off an amazing stock rally, he wrote: "Beware of the ides of January" (a learned reader later pointed out that there are no ides of January). Abelson framed the future in this gloomy fashion: ". . .however enthusiastically the stock market might greet peace or some reasonable facsimile thereof, the celebration would likely be over before you can say hurrah. And, in fact, any upside sprint touched off by favorable news from the Persian Gulf may well prove the market's last hurrah." With such an erroneous assessment of the situation, it was no wonder that Abelson turned his column over to Jonathan Laing when it came time for *Barron's* to engage in damage control in late February amid a record-setting bull market. In the 2-25 "Up & Down Wall Street" column, Laing provided this good-humored reflection: "In retrospect, the so-called Saddam Bull Market wasn't as surprising a development as it seemed. Of course, it's easier to be a Monday morning quarterback some 400 points into a market move." But instead of the earnest reassessment of the business weekly's earlier off-target analysis, Laing slipped into a transparent public relations campaign: ". . .it's now clear that many of the prerequisites were in place for a powerful market blowoff in mid-January. Futures trader Paul Tudor Jones presciently sensed the potential for a market melt-up and verbalized this conviction at the 1991 *Barron's* Roundtable [1-21 issue], just two days before the first Allied attack." Mr. Jones, one of the various Wall Street analysts questioned during Roundtable, had indeed predicted a bull market two days before war broke out, but his remarks were not *published* until several days after both the war and the rally were already in full swing. Abelson was, however, more on target in the fall when the economy did indeed take a turn for a worse. Slowly, it began to dawn on him that easy money would not bring the country out of recession, and that Bush's lack of economic leadership was indeed part of the problem, leading the country toward a "Bush Bear Market," as he called it in his 11-18 column. But it is worth noting that this analysis came only after a 120 point drop in the DJIA on 11-17, a rather obvious indication that things were not going well.

One has to page deep into the center of *Barron's* to find the type of fresh, incisive financial analysis that should command prime space in the publication. In "Current Yield," capital markets editor Randall W. Forsyth weaves together the micro and the macro in a way that Abelson seems unable to do. Forsyth seems much more able to put his finger on the political and economic trends that are affecting the market. He offered the most exceptional insights we'd seen on the Federal Reserve's troubles with M2 targets in "Global Rate Tug-of-War," 7-29.

Commodities editor John Liscio is also emerging as a first rate analyst at the weekly. In "Brigitte Bardot, Freddie Krueger and Gold," 4-15, he designates himself as one of the few not to believe that gold is on the verge of skyrocketing: "Gold bugs are more than twice as dense and 100 times as ornery as silver investors. . .No matter how many times they get buried in the market, they keep coming back, like Freddie Krueger." And his insights are terrific in "Trading Points," 8-5, uncovering why the government's GNP numbers for the second quarter are malarkey because they are based on dubious assumptions that create a mirage of slight growth when in fact more realistic deductions would probably have indicated negative growth. Most impressive, though, was his debunking of California's unemployment figures in "Politically Correct Data?" 10-28, and several follow-up stories in which he uncovered numerous questionable practices that raised yellow flags about the accuracy of the government's unemployment and income statistics.

Buttressing these expert observations from *Barron's* financial analysts are some very strong policy assessments. With Washington editor Shirley Hobbs Schiebla no longer writing her "Potomac Potpourri" or "D.C. Current" column, the editorial page has become the main forum for policy evaluations at the magazine. Robert Bleiberg offers rich, instructive analyses bolstered by his sturdy grasp of history. A reliable watchdog of regulatory overreach, he penned "Regulators' Lynch Mob," 2-4, which applauds Jonathan Eisenberg, a Washington lawyer who wrote a daring, bylined article criticizing a legal decision by the powerful Stanley Sporkin, former head of the Enforcement Division of the SEC: " 'Assigning judge Stanley Sporkin in the Lincoln Savings & Loan case,' caustically wrote Mr. Eisenberg, 'was a bit like assigning Eliot Ness to preside over the trial of Al Capone.' " L. Gordon Crovitz, who writes for the editorial page of *Barron's* sister publication *The Wall Street Journal,* has become a frequent editorial contributor. With an exacting style and a sturdy grasp of legal issues, he strengthened the page with crisp perspectives, including "Federal Anti-Trade Commission," 7-8, and "Clarence Thomas for Justice," 8-26.

With the retirement of Robert Bleiberg, *Barron's* loses an important cornerstone, but it will be the departure of Alan Abelson that will mark the beginning of a new era at *Barron's.* Abelson's irreverent humor will be missed by some, but we think that an editor who believes in stewardship rather autocracy will liberate the publication's expert individual writers, and return *Barron's* to its former esteem.

Editor: Alan Abelson

Address: 200 Liberty Street
               New York, NY 10281
               (212) 416-2762

Circulation: 1990 — 250,789
               1991 — 235,587

BusinessWeek

In a fitting tribute to its potential, *BW* was honored as the best business magazine by *Washington Journalism Review*'s 1991 "The Best in the Business" poll. Editor in chief Stephen B. Shepard explained *BW*'s edge over what he considers the magazine's main competitor, *The Wall Street Journal:* "As a weekly we can be more analytical, interpretive and forward-looking." Indeed, with its weekly format and 239 editors and correspondents all over the world, *BW* is perhaps the best positioned among the major business publications to provide its readers with extensive, full-toned analysis of the global political economy. Unfortunately, for all its resources, *BW* can't seem to see the forest for the trees. We find a multitude of international, political and economic reports on the pages of the McGraw-Hill weekly, but rarely does a single story comprehend the crucial juncture of the three.

We blame this shortcoming not so much on the publication's talented corps of journalists, but rather on a lack of cohesive editorial leadership. Granted, certain department editors have created distinguished, dynamic sections — Information Processing editor John W. Verity, Personal Computers editor Deidre A. Depke, Corporate Finance editor Larry Light and Industries editor Thane Peterson are among the best department editors at the magazine. At the top of the masthead, assistant managing editor Anthony J. Parisi proved that with focused editorial direction, as with the special issue he edited, "The Quality Imperative," 10-25, *BW* can produce an extremely cohesive and distinguished product. But for the most part, those senior editors that share Parisi's broad decision-making powers, and are able to tie things together to make *BW* more than the sum of its parts, have failed to fully capitalize on the individual energies at the business weekly.

In this regard, we have long been critical of William Wolman for his inability to smooth out the discordant voices contributing to *BW*'s extensive coverage of economics and finance. Wolman, an old war horse who still clings to the hoary assumption that the economy revolves around the consumer, *not* the producer, must be held accountable for the magazine's miserable economic coverage. He underwent a title change from editor to chief economist in late 1990, and, indeed, the new designation seems to more appropriately reflect his role at the magazine. But we wonder how this hollow remedy will facilitate *BW*'s economic and financial reporters whose work would certainly improve with stronger editorial guidance. Certainly, Economics editor Karen Pennar is not up to the task. A survey of her work reveals an extremely weak grasp of the political economy.

Following the spring 1991 announcement by the National Bureau of Economic Research that the recession had "officially" begun in July of 1990, Editor Stephen B. Shepard bragged in a 5-3 editor's memo, "A Leading Indicator," that *BW* had in fact called the recession by answering "yes" to the question on its 8-13-90 cover, "Are We in a Recession?" a story spear-headed by Pennar. Nevermind that the report offered little more than generic generalizations such as "Americans feel in their bones that something has gone badly awry," or that the author failed to discern the *reasons* the nation was sliding into recession. We place more stock in cogent analysis than in the ability to correctly answer a multiple choice question.

Pennar paired with Mike McNamee for a follow-up on the state of the economy in "The New Face of Recession," cover 12-24-90. Once again revealing no appreciation of the critical balance between fiscal and monetary policy, the two ignore the economic impact of the austere tax hikes imposed in the fall of 1990, and place blame for the recession squarely on the shoulders of the Federal Reserve: "The economy was prepared for a fall by the middle of 1990, thanks to the Fed's two-year-old policy of trying to slow growth to a 'soft landing.' " It was also the middle of 1990 when President Bush abandoned his "no new taxes" pledge, an important fiscal policy event not mentioned here. What was especially perplexing about Pennar and McNamee's one-sided assessment was that the same issue carried "Dangerous Days for Dick Darman," a pithy account of why conservatives wanted budget director Richard Darman's scalp following the 1990 budget accord: "Darman has emerged from two years of budget battles with his political armor dented and his reputation with conservatives in tatters. And when the budget deal is mentioned now, Bush looks like a man who has just nibbled a bit of bad lobster." With such a racket over the 1990 tax hikes examined in the same issue, we would think top editors would have encouraged Pennar and McNamee to explore the role of fiscal policy in the economic downturn.

Then there's the example of Jeffrey Laderman's "Has the Market Gone Bonkers?" cover 2-25, an upbeat overview of the market euphoria which presents a well-versed description of the technical forces spurring the bull, but doesn't adequately factor in the political and economic news that feeds the market. It's worth noting that Laderman is noticeably more optimistic about an economic recovery than James C. Cooper and Kathleen Madigan in their "Business Outlook" column in the same issue. Laderman asserts that the stock market has proven itself a reliable indicator of economic recovery while Cooper and Madigan dwell on the times when the market has given "false signals."

Indeed, we are not the only readers dissatisfied with *BW*'s muddled economic coverage, as an article in the 6-3 *Barron's*, "Exotic Indicators," tells how one successful economist uses *BW* stories as a contrary indicator to speculate on the future direction of the economically sensitive bond markets. Ironically, a month after this article appeared, *BW* offered one of its most glaring economic misreadings of the year. "A Strong Recovery? Yes, It's Possible," cover 7-1, by Michael J. Mandel and Christopher Farrell *et al,* which tries to buttress the authors' assertion that "the rebound now gathering momentum could turn out to be surprisingly powerful." The only thing that could stall the recovery, the authors observe, would be if the "Federal Reserve could tighten the monetary screws if policymakers believe a stronger-than-expected rebound would spur inflation." There's no mention of the economic drag resulting from the rising tax burden at the state and federal level, even though only four months later high taxes would become a major issue in the November elections. Another major blunder occurred in a 11-25 editorial "Stop Soaking Credit-Card Shoppers," which urges Washington to continue to be tough on banks that carry high credit-card rates. When President Bush announced that he wanted to put a cap on these rates, and Congress tried to rush through legislation on the issue, the DJIA overwhelmingly rejected this anti-competitive measure and fell 120 points in a single day! We wonder if *BW* got the same message as Bush on this misguided policy. Consequently, we had difficulty finding the forward-looking coverage Shepard touted to the *Washington Journalism Review* in either of these pieces.

Even after the tax burden had been discovered as an economic issue at *BW,* in such stories as "Suddenly, Everyone Wants to Cut Taxes," 11-4, by Howard Gleckman and Mike McNamee with Douglas Harbrecht and Paula Dwyer, we were surprised by the unrefined analysis. The authors indiscriminately lumped all tax cuts into one mold, asserting that ". . .even if Bush and congressional leaders come to terms on a tax package, economists doubt it will do much to boost growth." Had the authors studied the specific proposals more closely, and interviewed a wider range of sources on Capitol Hill, they might have discovered that not all tax cuts are created equal.

In that same issue we found another interesting example of the difference an editor can make. Markets and investments editor Gary Weiss introduces "Financing the 90s," 11-4, a special report, with unsubstantiated, blatantly editorial generalizations, mirroring the worst of pack journalism: "Perhaps what we are entering is an Era of Atonement, in which we all must suffer for the reckless lending practices that were endemic during the 1980s." The second article, written by corporate finance editor Larry Light, "The Tightwads Are Running the Show Now," with David Greising 11-4, is much more perceptive. Eschewing most of Weiss's ideological hooey, Light opts to examine the facts which reveal that the below-investment-grade companies "which are the employers of most Americans and are often the incubators for tomorrow's growth" are having trouble finding capital to help them through the recession, a worrisome trend. "Access to capital is emerging as the crucial factor in corporate success." The striking inconsistency in tone and quality between these two articles which appear in the same special report is further evidence of *BW*'s lack of editorial cohesiveness.

The "Economic Viewpoint" column is an island of crisp insights in *BW*'s murky pool of economic appraisals. The column circulates among such fertile minds as the University of Chicago's Gary Becker; supply-sider Paul Craig Roberts, chairman of the Institute for Political Economy; Robert Kuttner, economics correspondent for *The New Republic;* and Alan S. Blinder from Princeton. We regularly turn to this column for articulate, well-developed opinions on the political economy.

Additionally, there were stories written by editors outside of economics department that indirectly gave us insights into the state of the economy via studies of industrial or financial trends. One such cover story, "The Age of Consolidation," cover 10-14, spearheaded by Corporate Strategies editor Brian Bremner with Kathy Rebello, Zachary Schiller and Joseph Weber, thought-provokingly examined whether the growing number of mega-mergers would really make the U.S. more competitive. "Advocates of consolidation argue. . .that the short-term economic pain, and even some increases in domestic pricing and market power, are burdens worth bearing to gird U.S. corporations for the international competitive arena. Unfortunately, the example of at least one oligopoly, the auto industry's Big Three, is hardly a rousing endorsement of this view. Far from using their domestic sway as a springboard for a vigorous assault on foreign markets, our 'national champions' grew so sluggish, complacent, and bloated that they lost their dominance of the home market." Similarly, senior writer John A. Byrne examined how arrogance and complacency can enter the executive suite in his outstanding "CEO Disease," cover 4-1. And senior writer Judith Dobrzynski's "Cutting Loose From Shareholder Activists," 7-8, is a reflective analysis of shareholder activism during the '91 proxy season. Despite gains, she notes that some states' legislative removal of hostile tender offers has had a constraining effect on shareholder activism. Dobrzynski and Mark Landler offered the best analyses we saw of one of the biggest shareholder stories of the year, the controversial Time Warner rights offering. Their 7-22 cover on the offer, "Time Warner," receives a 10 Best award in Business/Financial Reporting.

The high tech industry, another economic powerhouse, is expertly tracked under the editorial guidance of Technology editor Robert Buderi, Information Processing editor John W. Verity, and Personal Computers editor Deidre A. Depke, all strong editors. True to form, this impressive group produced a bundle of cutting-edge cover stories that, with a single thrust, propel us into the future. Among the best offerings this year: "Software Made Simple," cover 9-30, by John W. Verity and Evan I. Schwartz; "I Can't Work This Thing," cover 4-29, by senior writer Bruce Nussbaum and Tokyo bureau manager Robert Neff; "PCs: What the Future Holds," cover 8-12, by Deidre A. Depke and Richard Brandt; and "Computer Confusion," cover 6-10, by John W. Verity with Robert D. Hof, Richard Brandt, Jonathan B. Levine and Gary McWilliams.

Washington coverage is definitely a mixed bag at *BW*. John Carey has struck an effective fusion of his real-world scientific experience and obvious acumen in the area of industrial and scientific policy. In one of his best pieces, "Will Uncle Sam Be Dragged Kicking and Screaming into the Lab?" 7-15, he expertly dissects the great ideological debate over the value of having a U.S. industrial policy: "The larger question is whether 'critical technologies' programs. . .can slow the industrial slide. It may well be that tax policies, environmental regulation, health care costs, the value of the dollar, and industry's own resolve will determine U.S. competitiveness. . ." Howard Gleckman lands many of the big stories at the bureau, and with his solid network of contacts in government policymaking circles, he fills his well-sourced reports with sturdy facts. Beyond the particulars, however, he rarely delivered provocative angles, although we were impressed by "How the Budget Deal Has Choked Off America's Choices," 9-16, in which he reveals just how constrictive the 1990 budget deal is to the economy. Covering the Federal Reserve in a critical year, Mike McNamee compressed a wide range of facts into crisp, compact studies and typically struck an impressive balance of political and economic analysis. "Just When Bank Reform Seemed Almost in the Bag," 9-9, is an incisive and prescient review of why momentum for banking reform is slowing: "some banking lobbyists think that the legislation now taking shape may be worse than the status quo. Says one reform advocate: 'Kill it before it multiplies.' " Bill Javetski also comes through with some strong profiles from the Capitol. In "He's Selling the Free Market to the World," 6-3, Javetski offers a crisp snapshot of Robert Zoellick, the new Under Secretary of State for Economic and Agricultural Affairs, and "the point man for the Bush team's plan to push U.S.-style free markets and democracy into the vacuum left by the crumbling of the Soviet empire." Similarly, Douglas Harbrecht's "The Man Who's Rising as Sununu's Sun Sets," 7-15, was a compact look at how pollster Robert M. Teeter strengthened his power base within the administration following chief of staff Sununu's troubles with lavish travel spending. Two of the cover stories spearheaded by the D.C. bureau, "Race in the Workplace?" 7-8, by Howard Gleckman, Tim Smart, Paula Dwyer, Troy Segal and Joseph Weber, and "The Future of Banking," 4-22, by Catherine Yang, Howard Gleckman and Mike McNamee with Chuck Hawkins, and Peter Coy, were only average journalistic efforts. The first piece is a fairly deep examination of the pros and cons of the effectiveness of Affirmative Action in the workplace, but ends with an unacceptable last paragraph editorializing on the need to continue affirmative action. The second report on banking is enterprising, but the authors ended up trying to tackle too many issues, skimming them all, probing none.

As for Wall Street, the Salomon Brother's treasury auction manipulation was the biggest scandal of 1991, and Markets and Investment editor Weiss landed a big scoop with "Did Somebody Squeeze the Treasury Notes?" 7-1, a revealing investigation of the May 22 Treasury bond auction well before Salomon's wrongdoing at that auction became public. An even harder-hitting investigation, "The Mess at Pru-Bache," cover 3-4, by Chuck Hawkins with Leah Nathans Spiro, received a 10 Best nomination for its careful and responsible probe, which centers around the questionable transactions of James Darr, who headed Pru-Bache's limited partnership unit from 1979 to 1988. "*Business Week*'s investigation suggests that Darr's relationship with some real estate developers may have compromised his responsibility to find the best partnerships to sell Pru-Bache customers. Serious questions also exist about whether Pru-Bache and Prudential properly disclosed these potential conflicts of interest. In fact, Prudential has initiated its own independent investigation." The article is replete with indicting facts, but avoids sweeping generalizations and inappropriate characterizations. One *BW* cover story sure to be read by Wall Street stock analysts was "Hot Growth Companies," 5-27, by Bruce Hager. But the list of the 100 "Best Small Growth Companies" undoubtedly lost some credibility this year after listing K Med Centers Inc. as number 17. A report in *The Wall Street Journal* noted that K Med had sold off the core of its business and had no acquisitions planned for the near future, thus the company didn't have any business whatsoever with which to grow. A spokeswoman for publisher McGraw-Hill responded that the publication "wasn't 'aware they had sold their primary business. If we had known, the company wouldn't have been on the list.' " We expected the long-awaited return of senior writer Anthony Bianco from his book-writing sabbatical to enhance *BW*'s Wall Street coverage. Bianco began chronicling the market's movers and shakers for *BW* when stocks took off in 1982. Over the years we've grown to respect his acumen on the Street's financial titans. But, book promotions must have kept him busy this year as he only wrote a few articles. His outstanding investigation of the dozens of civil charges that imprisoned financier Michael Milken may still face, "Mike Milken's Days in Court Are Far From Over," 4-1, a 10 Best nomination, crystalized the complicated legal issues at hand, observing that "At a minimum, a legal battle royal looms."

On the year's biggest battle, the war in the gulf, *BW* produced three cover stories. The magazine managed to eke out an eight article "War," that hit the stands just after the air attack began. But despite its timeliness, the lead report, "The Gulf: A Special Report," cover 1-28, was disappointing, a simple recounting of logistics with scant examination of the major themes of the conflict. The problem could have been that there were eight reporters listed on the byline, certainly an unwieldy number of perspectives to integrate into one article. Rome bureau chief John Rossant's contribution to the cover, "For Riyadh, a Forced March Into the Real World," forwards some interesting observations about the changes war is forcing on the kingdom, but his reflections are flecked with old-school ideas about Saudi society.

BW's second war-related cover, "Managing the War," 2-4, was better, giving us insights into the war's top manager, Colin Powell:"The only Chairman of the Joint Chiefs with prior service in a top White House job, Powell has the political instincts of a salon diplomat. Those skills could prove crucial to keeping domestic politics from hindering Desert Storm, as it did the military's effort in Vietnam." But still this cover story did not provide enough fresh analysis to distinguish *BW*'s war coverage from the deluge of perspectives found elsewhere. "The High-Tech War Machine," was little more than a descriptive catalog of the instruments of today's high-tech war; much more interesting and relevant to business readers was "This Army Marches on Silicon." "While the Pentagon's smart bombs and Top Gun fighters have grabbed the limelight, a huge array of computer and communications systems may ultimately prove to be the Pentagon's decisive weapon." Least impressive was John Rossant's featurish report from Dhahran, "Aramco Toughs It Out." And for the amount of information we get in "A Drive Through Desert Storm," authors Rossant and Pentagaon correspondent Russell Mitchell should have stayed in their hotel in Dhahran rather than head off into the desert with a mysterious Saudi businessman whose insights are far too general to be of much interest. As on other issues, a lack of editorial cohesiveness showed through in *BW*'s war coverage. Beyond the battlefield, wars are fought within a global political economy. By covering the war primarily as a military event, yet another opportunity to create a synergy between the political, economic and international sections of the publication was missed, as was an opportunity to give *BW*'s war coverage the economic slant fitting of a business publication.

On other major international stories, *BW* is able to tap information from some of the best foreign bureaus at the business weeklies. But we must point out that despite accuracy and timeliness, *BW*'s international coverage is still inconsistent in framing its coverage for a business audience. For instance, the Moscow bureau, managed by Rose Brady, provided a descriptive blow-by-blow of the remarkable events in Moscow surrounding the failed coup d'etat in August. "Yeltsin's Triumph," cover 9-2, by Rose Brady, Patricia Kranz, Peter Galuszka *et al,* more closely resembled coverage from the newsweeklies than the business periodicals. But as the dust settled, the bureau became more reflective, looking toward the political *and* economic horizon in "After the Soviet Union," cover 9-9, by Rose Brady, Peter Galuszka, *et al*: "The newly empowered republics won't necessarily make all the right economic decisions. Eastern Europe's behavior after the Berlin Wall came down stands as a sobering object lesson. When the wall fell, Moscow's former satellites opted for economic self-sufficiency instead of pushing trade among themselves. . .To their long-term economic detriment, they preferred new links to wealthier Western nations." International news editor Galuszka, who often contributes to coverage of the Soviet Union from New York, came closer to the Soviet's key economic issue in "The Ruble Is Dead. Long Live. . .the Ruble?" commentary 10-14, but still didn't seem cognizant of the necessity to stabilize the ruble *before* other economic moves are initiated: "Even though a new currency would do much to end the Soviet economic tailspin, it can't work unless other reforms are well under way on other fronts. Prices need to be freed, the bloated central budget deficit needs to be cut, and millions of unneeded jobs should vanish. The money presses must be shut off." Easier said than done.

In Japan, the big story of 1991 was the country's slowing economy and the securities scandal which ultimately forced Prime Minister Kaifu's resignation. Throughout the year, we were disconcerted by what we perceived as a growing anti-Japan sentiment seeping into *BW*'s coverage of this country, and feared that after an impressive start, manager Robert Neff might be leading the bureau down the slippery slope of Japan bashing. A perfect example was the bureau's post-security scandal cover story, "Hidden Japan," 8-26, by Robert Neff, Ted Holden, and Karen Lowry Miller with Joyce Barnathan: "Foreigners wanting to do business in Japan are getting a good look at the collusive network they're up against. And those stung by Japanese competition back home are now glimpsing what underlies Japanese corporate prowess. The scandals are again raising the troublesome question: Is Japan's economic system compatible with the rest of the world's?" Certainly, we did not notice *BW* making such sweeping generalizations about the U.S. financial system following the Salomon Brothers treasury auction scandal which exploded shortly after Japan's uproar.

On another Asian front, we appreciate bureau chief Dinah Lee's coverage from Hong Kong. Although she rarely writes single byline articles, her solid reports on China and Taiwan such as "Rebuilding a Tiger: Who'll Get the Lion's Share?" with Dirk Bennet, Robert Neff, Joyce Barnathan and "China's Ugly Export Secret: Prison Labor," with Robert Neff, Amy Borrus and Joyce Barnathan, nicely round out *BW*'s coverage of Asia. And when the *BW*'s bureaus team up (without placing *too* many correspondents on the story, that is), we get a glimpse at *BW*'s undeniable potential to deftly cover the international political economy. In "Assembly Lines Start Migrating From Asia to Mexico," with Peter Coy 7-1, Hong Kong bureau chief Dinah Lee and Mexico City bureau chief Stephen Baker work together to give us some fabulous insights into why U.S. manufacturers are increasingly shifting production plants from Asia and China to Mexico.

Europe is more than efficiently covered by *BW* with bureaus in Bonn, Paris, London, Brussels and Rome. Paris bureau manager Stewart Toy seems to spearhead most of the major European stories, while London bureau chief Richard A. Melcher, Brussels bureau manager Jonathan Kapstein, and Rome bureau chief John Rossant primarily play supporting roles. The most important European cover story produced by *BW* this year was "The Battle for Europe," 6-3, by Stewart Toy, Jonathan B. Levine, Mark Maremont and Karen Lowry Miller with Igor Reichlin. This very well-informed report examines the European Community's dilemma over

Japan. On one hand the authors assert that individual European nations crave the Japanese capital that is flooding into industries, but on the other, the EC as a unit fears that a growing Japanese market share could lead to a shake out of less competitive European companies. "The double-edged sword of Japan cuts to the heart of how Europeans want their promised union to evolve. Given this heavy political backdrop, dealing with the Japanese challenge may prove even more wrenching for Europe than it has for America. How the Europeans react will shape not just their own economy but also America's place in the world economic order for decades to come."

Bonn bureau manager John Templeman also lands many plum European assignments, but his contribution to the special cover report "Eastern Europe: A Market Economy Takes Root," "Eastward, Ho! The Pioneers Plunge In," with Ken Olsen, David Greising, Jonathan Kapstein and William Glasgall 4-15, reveals a tendency toward over-generalization. Exploring the increasing amount of western cash pouring into Poland, Hungary and Czechoslovakia, the authors lump the countries together as if interested foreign companies view these aspiring-to-be-free-market economies as a single entity with clone investment climates. In fact, these three countries have pursued different economic policies, especially regarding their currencies, and have ultimately fared quite differently in attracting western capital.

Stephen Baker in Mexico City is emerging as a strong foreign bureau manager, his work steadily improving throughout the year. In a time of great transition south of the border, Baker has captured the new dynamics with such strong reports as "The Friends of Carlos Salinas," 7-22, a rich analysis of President Carlos Salinas' attempts to walk the tightrope between Mexico's power elite, of which he is a member, and the unsettling but lucrative forces of free trade. Also well done was his "As Argentina Strides Ahead, Will Its Neighbors Follow?" 10-7, a short piece that packs a whopper of a message with Argentina's President Menem calling his decision to tie the austral to the dollar the turning point in his successful battle against hyperinflation. North of the border, William C. Symonds has done an admirable job in his first year as Toronto bureau manager.

Overall, *BW* is, as editor Shepard believes, a business magazine with great potential. But until the magazine's top editors establish a more cohesive editorial product, *BW* as a whole will never match the quality of the individual efforts of its best and brightest.

Editor:	Stephen B. Shepard
Chief Economist:	William Wolman
Address:	1221 Avenue of the Americas New York, NY 10021 (212) 512-2000
Circulation:	1990 — 911,386 1991 — 896,803

Chronicles

This stylish and steadfastly paleoconservative "Magazine of American Culture" published by the Rockford Institute is dedicated to defending the traditional culture. We noted last year that "its frankness and candor and its commitment to the 'American nationalist' perspective has frequently provoked ire and acrimonious debate, often within the ranks of conservatives." This is still the case, and as isolationism continues to gain currency in the political arena, the role of *Chronicles* can only increase in importance, particularly as the presidential candidacy of columnist Pat Buchanan highlights such issues in the debate.

Thomas Fleming edits the trim monthly, and it is his column in each issue that draws us in. In the delightful "Divorce — Italian Style," 1-91, Fleming, a champion of "localism and regionalism as the true basis of the American system," discovers that the localist spirit of the old Italian republics is still alive, and he provides us with an incredibly rich picture of a side of Italy rarely perceived, let alone understood, outside of that country, a 10 Best nominee. Still, the fertility of his mind gives us an abundance of food for thought in "Surviving in the New World Order," 4-91, a critique of the limited potentials of the U.S.'s readiness "to assume the responsibilities of empire even under the pleasant guise of a New World Order, which President Bush now describes. . .as the 'rule of law' imposed upon the world — a rule of law that presupposes a sovereign power capable of enforcing it." This perspective is typical of those we find in *Chronicles,* and Fleming consistently promotes this theme. He combines the populism of radical Jeffersonianism with the aristocratic distaste for equality of a John Randolph, and in "America Through the Looking Glass," 6-91, he is especially acute in his observation on the battle between corporativism and populism as the central focus for the remainder of this century. "The Big Lie of Modern American life is that the assimilation process worked. It didn't," Fleming forthrightly maintains in a spirited and thought-provoking "The Broken Promise of American Life," cover 7-91. "What sort of community can be created without the ties of blood, history and faith to bind it together?" He is especially cutting and incisive, using sharp polemical skills to the utmost, in this rebuttal to the notion that assimilation has produced in America "a new culture for the first universal nation." Nominated for 10 Best consideration by the editors at *Chronicles* is Fleming's "America First, 1941/1991," cover 12-91, advocating a return to what Fleming terms "the old federalism" and offering his final word on isolationism: "We cannot be free or prosperous at home, so long as our Presidents continue to gratify their vanity with international power games."

We were pleased, as well, by the contributions of *Washington Times* columnist Samuel Francis. His "Principalities and Powers" column is decidedly belligerent, almost to the point of demagoguery. He perceives as "the fundamental social and political conflict. . .emerging in the United States. . .not between left and right. . .or rich and poor. All these divisions merely feed the main conflict which is between elite and non-elite," he argues in the 1-91 column. In a Sorelian bent, he builds a case for the formulation of a new comprehensive myth by would-be-leaders of the Middle American Revolution, since "mainstream conservatism has nothing to say" to the non-elite. Francis' style is tolerable, but he sounds a bit too much the ideologue in this effort. In a bitter, fiery feature essay selected by editors at *Chronicles* as appropriate to our 10 Best section, "Beautiful Losers," 5-91, Francis develops a scathing assessment of the failure of American conservatism: "Not only has the American right lost on such fundamental issues as the fusion of state and economy, the size and scope of government, the globalist course of American foreign policy, the transformation of the *Constitution* into a meaningless document that serves the special interests of whatever faction can grab it for a while, and the replacement of what is generally called 'traditional morality' by a dominant ethic of constant gratification, but also the mainstream of those who today are pleased to call themselves conservatives has come to accept the premises and often the full-blown agenda of the left."

Other features have also consistently challenged the perspectives of the right, in which *Chronicles* represents a particular faction. A symposium debates the demise of the conservatives, a popular theme this spring that was treated superbly in "Conservative Movement, R.I.P.?" cover 5-91. Associate editor Theodore Pappas takes apart "The New World Order," 9-91, of George Bush, dismantling the arguments of various conservatives in the process: "The New World Order is not, never has been, and never will be about self-determination or sub-sovereignty or about the exercise and propagation of grand schemes or specific doctrines; it is instead — simply and boldly — about the exercise of will and the propagation of American hegemony. It is about power, not principle, and in particular about the power to play Julius Caesar abroad while playing Nero amidst a burning Rome at home." Rather than accepting the conventional notion of an open door immigration policy, a trio of articles stress the strengthening of national boundaries, although Garrett Hardin stresses the exchange of ideas in "Conspicuous

Benevolence and the Population Bomb," 10-91. Jacqueline R. Kasun links population, government and the environment in "A Nation of Davids," and Richard D. Lamm details "The New Wealth of Nations," the "renewable human skills" which bring economic success, rather than necessarily the sole acquisition of natural resources. Another trio, 6-91, outlines the situation in Russia, running completely against the established opinion of the right. In "Jack and Jill, or Why I Am Not a Conservative," Andrei Navrozov urges the broadening of debate over the fate of the Union to include the socialist perspective, rather than discounting it entirely, simply for the sake of ideas. In "Gorbachev and the Market," Yuri Maltsev points out that both *perestroika* and *glasnost* were originally designed to remedy the ills of socialism, not supplant the ideology itself. Here we also find the nationalist bent that runs through so much of the material in *Chronicles,* accompanied by a haunting warning: "More importantly, the United States should not use the opportunity of Soviet weakness as an excuse to attempt to run its own world empire. The attempt will bankrupt America and cause the growth of Soviet-style government here." More typically conservative is Arnold Beichman's appraisal of Gorbachev, "Willing Belief," which rounds out the cover treatment, although there are nuggets here well worth mining: "Yet we now see that Gorbachev's 'reforming zeal' is ebbing fast as the KGB, the military, the party bureaucracy reassert themselves to prevent what would to those pillars of power be the ultimate blow — the dissolution of the Soviet system of rule. Without that dissolution, either Gorbachev's 'reforming zeal' will come to the untimely end or, equally likely, Gorbachev himself will."

As a cultural digest and barometer, *Chronicles* is unequalled. Two covers this year were completely devoted to literature, "Southern Writing," 3-91, and "Western Writing," 11-91. Both examine the intertwining of literary works and the dominant culture through a series of erudite and serious articles. But culture is not ignored the rest of the year. There are learned book reviews in each issue, edited by Chilton Williamson, Jr., that intelligently assess the state of ideology and the progress of history in the U.S. Feature articles often gauge notable events in academia and in the lives of persons of note. For example, Theodore Pappas takes us through the chronicle of the dissertation of Dr. Martin Luther King, Jr., in "A Doctor in Spite of Himself," 1-91. This minute examination was nominated by *Chronicles*'s editors for 10 Best consideration.

Though some may consider *Chronicles* to have a too-narrow focus, one of a nationalistic and isolationist perspective, there's no journal better to expound this point of view. We've attributed much of this in past years to the stewardship of Thomas Fleming. "A Jeffersonian in the tradition of John Randolph and John C. Calhoun, with even some William Jennings Bryan populism thrown in, Fleming keeps the magazine hammering away on behalf of an American nationalist policy based on the old ideals of limited government and free enterprise, combined with the statecraft of the coiled 'Don't Tread on Me' rattlesnake." Intelligent and logical, *Chronicles* has continued to challenge the ideas of the right, serving an important function in the ever-growing struggle over the direction of the U.S. and the world at large.

Editor:	Thomas Fleming
Associate Editor:	Theodore Pappas
Address:	The Rockford Institute 934 N. Main Street Rockford, IL 61103 (815) 964-5054
Circulation:	1990 — 160,000 1991 — 162,000

Commentary

Erudite and invigorating, *Commentary* continues to be a publication we rely on for penetrating analyses of the cultural, political and economic issues of our time. For more than 30 years, Editor-in-Chief Norman Podhoretz has been the heart, soul and brain behind this cerebral monthly. He is an editor who takes intellectual risks in his own writing and through his choice of provocative contributors. When he triumphs, *Commentary* triumphs, and when he stumbles, *Commentary* stumbles with him. As we said last year, "The monthly has never had any hesitation in using strong terms like evil, or truth, beauty and good, and has always insisted that there exists a universal criterion for making those judgements." Indeed, this black and white landscape radiates from Podhoretz's own personal canvass. As one literary critic observed while evaluating Podhoretz's *The Bloody Crossroads* in 1986, his essays "are crisp and well argued — almost too well argued, you feel, since they display some of the limitations as well as the strengths of intellectual neatness." Indeed, this "intellectual neatness" is both the muscle and Achilles' heel of Podhoretz and *Commentary*.

Take for instance, Podhoretz's evocative essay on acquaintance rape, "Rape in Feminist Eyes," 10-91, in which he states: ". . .if everyone has always understood that it was rape when a man used a weapon and/or physical violence or the threat of it to force a woman into sex, whether she had met him previously or not. . .why introduce the new category of date or acquaintance rape? The answer is that this is a way of applying the word 'rape' to a multitude of situations in which. . .'Assailants are more likely to use verbal or psychological coercion to overpower their victims than guns or knives.' Now, if we pause for a moment and remind ourselves that overcoming a woman's resistance by 'verbal and psychological' means has in the past been universally known as seduction, it will immediately become clear that we are in the presence here of nothing less than a brazen campaign to redefine seduction as a form of rape, and more slyly to identify practically all men as rapists." This is decidedly a very tidy, logical argument, but it completely ignores the grey area which is at the core of the debate over "acquaintance rape" as defined by a much larger population than radical feminists. Similarly, Leon R. Kass makes use of his editorial license in "Suicide Made Easy," 12-91, to appraise Derek Humphry's book on how to commit suicide, *Final Exit,* as "evil." More broadly, however, he makes an effective case against "active euthanasia."

At other times, *Commentary*'s "intellectual neatness" translates into a powerful and persuasive strain of conviction. For example, when it comes to black and white historical facts which have been grayed by modern interpretation, *Commentary*'s contributors weigh in strongly, as Richard Grenier did in "Indian Love Call," 3-91, a 10 Best nomination which is merciless on the distortion of history that is rendered in Kevin Costner's film, *Dances With Wolves.* Grenier treats us to an account of Indian life and practices of the time with which Costner's film deals. Also strong was Jerry Muller's "A Neglected Conservative Thinker," 2-91, a rich study of the neglected works of Philip Rieff, which warns of the conflict between the trends of modern intellectuals and the preservation of moral decency: "For Rieff, a morally desirable culture is one in which the system of moral demands is so deeply accepted by individuals that the evil instinctual possibilities of which men are always capable are generally felt to be repugnant: so repugnant that they are not even spoken of directly."

Perspectives on the war in the Persian Gulf garnered much space on the pages of *Commentary* throughout the year. Editor-in-Chief Podhoretz, who came out in favor of war against Iraq's Saddam Hussein in his 11-90 essay, "A Statement on the Persian Gulf Crisis," was also full of conviction in the 1-91 issue which was still on the newsstands when war actually broke out. In "Enter the Peace Party," 1-91, an incisive defense of the Bush administration's precise intentions in the Gulf, he questions the dubious manner in which congressional doves criticized the President: ". . .it was much riskier for the politicians and much harder for the pundits to produce a convincing case of their own for an alternative to military action than to allege disingenuously that no case for military action had yet been made by the President, or to characterize the case he actually had made in derisively reductive terms."

Podhoretz faced his own struggle with the difficult decisions of war while visiting Jerusalem with his family in January. When war ensued a few days after his arrival, he kept a journal of his experiences and his deeply-felt, often conflicting, emotions in "In Israel, With Scuds and Patriots," 4-91:

> All this time I went on writing and speaking of the need to stop Saddam Hussein by force, while half convinced that Bush and Baker would in the end make a deal that would get him out of Kuwait but leave his military machine intact. This 'nightmare scenario' (as some were calling it) depressed me deeply. Yet I could never shake the feeling that while such a settlement would be very bad for America, and also in the long run for Israel, maybe it would not be so bad for me and mine. For if war came, Saddam Hussein would almost certainly deliver on his promise to attack Israel, perhaps even with chemical weapons. And what if, God forbid, something were to happen to my daughter, my grandchildren, my wife?

After bringing us along through the fear and confusion endured as the first scuds hit Tel Aviv, he expresses his clashing emotions — on one hand, a proud American Jew watching Americans man U.S. Patriots to protect Israel, on the other, an unsettled observer who has witnessed Israel permit a foreign country to defend it. From that point, the implicatons of this shift in Israeli defense policy would become an important theme in *Commentary*'s analysis of the war: "By one means or another — whether through an international conference or some alternative mechanism — Bush and Baker are intent on forcing Israel into withdrawing from the territories in favor of a Palestinian state. In preparation for this, they now want to turn Israel into a dependent while demonstrating that the Israelis can rely for their security on an American guarantee."

The most important post-war question to be probed on the pages of *Commentary* was why the U.S. had left Saddam Hussein in power. The U.S.'s arguments about preserving the "territorial integrity" of Iraq was often queried. Elie Kedourie adds new dimension to what he considers the flawed U.S. policy of supporting Iraq to counterbalance Iran in "Iraq: The Mystery of American Policy," 6-91, but he is too hot-headed in his dismantling of the U.S. territorial integrity argument: "Why the integrity of a state with such a continuous record of violence and malfeasance should have been thought worth preserving is quite mysterious." As a result, he fails to examine the dubious precedent the dismantling of the Iraqi state would set. In "How We Helped Saddam Survive," 7-91, Lauri Mylorie, co-author of *Saddam Hussein and the Crisis in the Gulf,* makes her first appearance in *Commentary,* and brings to light a State Department communications ban imposed in June 1988 that stayed in place throughout the war, and thus undermined the Iraqi opposition: "Why did the administration maintain the ban? Part of the explanation lies in its view of Iraq's future. The administration was fixed on promoting a coup within Iraq's ruling elite. As a National Security Council staffer, frantically seeking to abort an inadvertently scheduled meeting with opposition elements, protested, 'you know we don't want to talk to those people. Our policy is to get rid of Saddam, not his regime.' Still, it is not entirely clear how meeting the opposition would have jeopardized the chances of promoting a coup. Such contacts might in fact have helped, as elements in the Iraqi opposition had connections with would-be coup-makers in Baghdad."

Daniel Pipes, director of the Foreign Policy Research Institute, pens "Israel, America & Arab Delusions," 3-91, on the "contradictory positions" taken over Israel's relationship with the U.S. In light of the dramatic recasting of relationships in the Middle East as a result of the war, Pipes' backward-looking essay, which mentions virtually nothing about these changes, seemed terribly stale and out of place. Also far from fresh was Joshua Muravchik's "The End of the Vietnam Paradigm?" 5-91, which was one of many lashings of the Gulf-war doves we saw. On the other hand, "Iraq's German Connection," 4-91, by Michael Ledeen, is a timely compilation of what is known about German businesses' ongoing sale of raw materials and key military hardware to Iraq's weapons establishment, and the German government's closed-eye approach to the available information. Fact after fact does indeed lend credibility to Ledeen's charge of hypocrisy with regard to German foreign minister Hans-Dietrich Genscher's 1-31 comment that "In this situation which threatens Israel's existence, we stand by Israel's side without any reservations." David Bar-Illan, editorial editor of the *Jerusalem Post,* provides a valuable perspective on Israeli's role in the war in "Israel After the Gulf War," 5-91. But the real point of his essay is to make clear that Israel's fate might have been very different if the territories had been relinquished: ". . .had Israel relinquished the 'territories'. . .Saddam Hussein would not have been limited to ineffectual missile attacks from remote bases in Western Iraq. The whole land mass from the Iranian border to the outskirts of Tel Aviv would have become Saddam-land." As with most of his articles, Bar-Illan is heavy-handed with the ideological criticism of U.S. policy toward Israel, asserting that perhaps now the U.S. will "have the courage to realize that seeking a Middle East solution by pressuring Israel to make concessions, instead of by pressing for changes in the Arab world, is like searching for a coin where there is light rather than where it is lost. Such a search may have its moments as the light and shadows play tricks with one's imagination. But it will not produce the coin."

But amid this mostly earnest struggle with the difficult policies of war and diplomacy, something was chipping away at *Commentary*'s reputation as a forum for debate and the exploration of ideas. What seemed to be a vindictive and deliberate campaign to tarnish the reputations of journalists that question or oppose certain Israeli policies was unfolding. While we appreciated such hard-hitting critiques of the media as Andrea Levin's "CNN vs. Israel," 7-91, which documents the Arab bias in CNN's "The Israeli Connection," and John Corry's "TV News & the Neutrality Principle," 5-91, which examines the role of the "new-style neutral journalists" in the Gulf war, we were disconcerted by the knee-jerk accusations of anti-Semitism that littered the pages of *Commentary,* and offended some of its loyal readers. The boiling point came with Joshua Muravchik's diatribe, "Patrick J. Buchanan and the Jews," 1-91, in which Muravchik accuses Buchanan of anti-Semitism. Allan H. Ryskind of *Human Events* was among those disturbed by this attack. In a 5-91 letter to the editor, he cites various pro-Israel statements made by Buchanan over the years and concludes: "I am normally a fan of both Norman Podhoretz and Joshua Muravchik, but, in this case, I believe, they have made a grave error in judgement. Just as Buchanan is quick to assail anyone who challenges the Pope or the Catholic Church — too quick in my mind — so Messrs. Podhoretz and Muravchik are too ready to detect 'anti-Semitism' in people because they have an honest quarrel with Israel and/or the Jewish community on substantive issues."

Another harangue which appeared in *Commentary* was written by David Bar-Illan. His "'60 Minutes' & the Temple Mount," 2-91, a compilation of articles that originally appeared in the *Jerusalem Post,* was much more than a critique of "60 Minutes" correspondent Mike Wallace's scrutiny of the official Israeli version of the Temple Mount riot, it was an outright attempt to discredit Wallace's journalistic credibility: "Like many professed liberals, [Wallace] seems so awed by dictators that he often acts as a public-relations huckster for strongmen." Wallace, who incidentally practices Judaism, responded with "60 Minutes" producer Barry Lando in a 4-91 letter: "[Bar-Illan] is the captive of misapprehensions of any and all reporters who fail to follow the line he sets down. A difference of opinion is fair game, but to republish [Bar-Illan's] ad-hominem slanders is beneath the standard of *Commentary.*" Another reader, who was in fact skeptical of Wallace's report on the Temple Mount riot, also criticized Bar-Illan's stridency: "Those who employ the methods of yellow journalism discredit the causes they set out to defend. . ." We found this intolerance of differing points of view, this neat categorization of journalists as friends of Israel or anti-Semites, especially unjust in light of Podhoretz's own personal struggle with U.S.-Israel policies during his stay in Jerusalem at the start of the war.

The collapse of the Soviet Union was explored from an economic and ideological point of view on the pages of *Commentary.* While Vladimir Bukovsky gives Gorbachev and the U.S. a rather sophomoric lashing in an emotionally-charged "What to Do About the Soviet Collapse," 9-91, Owen Harries, editor of the *National Interest,* looks back at the ironies of the entire Cold War experience in a very intelligent "The Cold War & the Intellectuals," 10-91, a 10 Best selection from the editors: "Even as liberal intellectuals continued to berate capitalism, the political leaders of the social-democratic and labor parties of the world, men subject to the practical test of winning votes in elections, were abandoning socialism and recognizing the superiority of the market economy. Even as the death knell of democracy was being sounded by intellectuals, it was rapidly gaining ground in Europe, Latin America, and Asia."

Published by the American Jewish Committee, *Commentary* strives to examine topics of special interest to the Jewish Community. One of the best offerings of the year, "The Future of American Jewry," 8-91, by Irving Kristol, thoughtfully reflects on how the surge of secular humanism is changing Judaism in the U.S. So thought-provoking was Kristol's essay that the letters section devoted to responses, "Is Secular Humanism Good for the Jews," was featured on the cover of the 12-91 issue. Edward Norden's "Counting the Jews," 10-91, was nominated as a 10 Best by the editors for its frank assessment of the changing realities of Jewish demographics: ". . .numbers in and of themselves do not necessarily a strong or happy or well-adapted people make. Must a smaller Jewish people, redistributed along the above lines, necessarily be a weaker or more neurotic or less capable or consequential one as it begins its next 4,000 years?"

As a rule of thumb, Podhoretz and his hand-picked contributors have a fairly sturdy understanding of political economy. This strength combined with the philosophical bent of the magazine makes for some outstanding coverage of policy issues. For example, Irwin M. Stelzer, a resident scholar at the American Enterprise Institute, offers a brilliant critique of Robert Kuttner's *The End of Laissez Faire: National Purpose and the Global Economy After the Cold War* and Robert B. Reich's *The Work of Nations: Preparing Ourselves for 21st-Century Capitalism* in "Bad Advice for the Democrats," 7-91: "In short, the case that burgeoning world trade and internationalization rob a country as large, wealthy, and powerful as ours of the ability to fashion its own economic destiny is far from proven. What, then, really worries this liberal Democratic duo? As best one can determine from what are, in key places, murky statements, it seems to be that increased international competition makes it difficult to adopt high-cost social-welfare programs, and to levy the taxes to fund them." Also persuasive was "What Everyone 'Knows' About Reaganomics," 2-91, in which Paul Craig Roberts employs an excellent mix of data, detail and analysis as he takes on and demolishes the "convention" that Reaganomics failed.

As in year's past, *Commentary* continues to devote attention to race relations. In "The Question of Black Leadership," 1-91, Arch Puddington, the author of *Failed Utopias,* is a bit heavy handed in his criticism of black leaders for their complacency toward extreme or paranoid voices in the black community. But his criticism of the negative influence of the "white Left" rang in our ears later in the year with the nomination of Judge Clarence Thomas, a black conservative, to the Supreme Court: ". . .It is difficult to think of a more insidious combination of ideologies than state socialism and black nationalism. By teaching that poverty and inequality derive from the class nature of capitalist society, Marxism provides a ready-made rationalization for the plight of the inner city that is at heart subversive of the idea of personal responsibility and hence demoralizing to the individuals. . .and from radicals and liberals of all stripes came the most devastating idea of all: that society was to regard the black criminal, even the violent criminal, as a victim — of racism, poverty, bigoted police — instead of as a predatory menace to individual citizens and to the health of black neighborhoods." With the Affirmative Action debate in high-gear, Chester E. Finn, Jr. penned an articulate discussion of the Bush administration's confused treatment of quotas in "Quotas and the Bush Administration," 11-19. Amid what he perceives as numerous examples of the Bush administration's muddled statements of purpose and bungled opportunities, Finn writes: "In all this confusion, sound values sometimes manage to prevail. But not often enough to arrest the government's slow, twisting passage into that looking-glass world where diversity means uniformity; where uniformity is so important that measuring sticks may be calibrated to different metrics in order to ensure identical outcomes; where color-blindness is suspect and tribalism honored; and where tribe counts for more than personal qualities when it comes to meting out various benefits."

On education, another topic given significant attention by *Commentary,* Barbara Lerner's important and timely contribution to the discussion of educational reform, "Good News About American Education," 3-91, received a 10 Best nomination from the editors for its solid case that educational advancements have occurred in the U.S. because of insistence on a criterion of required standards. Of the many articles we read on education in the press this year, this analysis stands out as one of the few articles that added to our understanding of the issues.

We regularly peruse the "Letters" section of *Commentary* with its lengthy debates and rebuttals over topics previously discussed in the magazine. Functioning as much more than a letters-to-the-editor section, this forum for disputation attests to *Commentary*'s commitment to editorial integrity, giving generous space to those who do not agree with the various positions of the magazine's contributors. Also worth reading is the "Books in Review" section. Podhoretz, who began his professional life as a literary critic, has molded this section into a first-rate forum for literary intellectuals.

Whether you consider *Commentary*'s "intellectual neatness" a virtue or a vice, it is, by a wide range of measures, a magazine that commands respect.

Editor-In-Chief:	Norman Podhoretz
Editor:	Neal Kozodoy
Managing Editor:	Marion Magid
Address:	165 East 56th Street New York, NY 10022 (212) 751-4000
Circulation:	1990 — 30,000 1991 — 35,243

Defense News

We'd wondered privately what kind of psychological effect the post-Cold War world would have on this trim, five-year-old tabloid weekly centered upon and around the defense industry. *Defense News,* happily, never missed a beat in relating information and appraisals of the international arms trade. Rather than being intimidated by the changing framework of the industry, the staff and editors at *DN* seem invigorated by it, bringing to the magazine's pages their own brand of enthusiasm and expertise that is reflected in the weekly's circulation figures and its active competition with the well-established *Aviation Week & Space Technology,* the industry standard that is seventy years *DN*'s senior.

What is most impressive about this youthful upstart is not so much the circulation figures themselves, but the numbers of policymakers and influential figures around the world who receive the magazine. Outside the United States, *Defense News* goes to more than 8,000 state ministers, generals, defense attaches, cabinet secretaries and industry experts in the Middle East, Southeast Asia, and Europe, an extremely impressive array of readers for a magazine barely out of infancy. We attribute much of the weekly's success to founding editor Richard C. Barnard, who moved up last year to the post of executive editor. From that position, Barnard oversees the general operations and long-range planning for *Defense News* as well as the two-year-old *Space News.* Sharon Denny succeeded him as editor, and has continued to govern the weekly wisely, broadening the scope of the magazine by establishing the Brussels bureau a few years back, anchored by Theresa Hitchens, and defining the specific beats of writers in order that they might best pursue expertise in their field.

With the onset of hostilities in the Persian Gulf, *Defense News* had a unique opportunity in its short history. The Persian Gulf War was the first time the weekly actually covered the use of various weapons systems outside a test site or controlled situation. Editor Denny and *DN* did not disappoint. Nearly as well as any other publication available to policymakers, *DN* offered clear, precise appraisals of the technology in action. Caleb Baker, who covers Army issues, offered some of the best descriptions of Iraqi fortifications in "Iraqi Fortifications Will Test Allies," 1-14, including a solid overview of the allied engineer units' training to surmount them. From the European bureau, Giovanni de Briganti contributed to Desert Storm coverage with such items as "European Countries Boost Support to Desert Storm — Opposition Political Leaders Decry NATO Role in Gulf," 1-28, contrasting Germany's dovish attitude to Turkey's enthusiastic support. Robert Holzer's "Contractors Play Key Role in Gulf War Operations," 1-21, is an excellent examination of the reliance of the Armed Forces on civilian contractors to maintain their ever-increasing technically complex equipment. Some of George Leopold's strategic coverage anticipated the daily press by weeks or months, as evidenced by "Arms Controls Experts Eye Multinational Effort to Stabilize Gulf," 2-25. Leopold's solid technical coverage was typified by such items as his "Allied Radar Hunters, Jammers Cloud Skies for Desert Storm," 1-21, reporting how the allied electronic warfare systems " 'made the Iraqis blind and deaf'...[as] allied electronic jamming and radar-hunting aircraft overwhelmed Iraqi communications and air defenses." Barbara Opall's (formerly Amouyal) "Allies Deliver a High-Tech Storm," 1-21, heavily relying on exclusive Air Force sources, reflects the service's authoritative first assessment of the air campaign against Iraq, and attributes "the unusual low rates of attrition at the outset of the war to the precision accuracy of the radar-evading, night-fighting F-117A stealth fighter, the navigation and targeting capabilities of the F-15E and F-111 fighter bombers and a well-coordinated campaign to suppress enemy air defenses."

Yet the war and its aftermath were not really a primary focus for the weekly. There were so many other issues of defense that deserved, and received, considerable attention. Theresa Hitchens, from her posting as Brussels bureau chief, concentrated for the most part, on Western Europe's inchoate endeavors to redefine its security identity between the end of the Cold War and the collapse of the Soviet Union. In "Havel Warns West Against Allowing East Europe Drift," 3-25, she deftly analyzes the broader issues of NATO and EC membership of former Warsaw Pact members on the occasion of Czech President Havel's plea to be accepted by the West as "Our countries are dangerously sliding into a certain political, economic, and security vacuum." Two selections cogently outline the changes of NATO's most basic role in Europe, "Post-Cold War NATO Plans to Key on Reserve Forces," 5-27, and "NATO to Rewrite Nuclear Strategy," 6-3, an important preview outlining the shift from land forces to air, from nuclear weapons to conventional, and from pre-targeting to doctrinal flexibility. The effects of the communist collapse in Moscow are ably discussed in "NATO Rethinks Role After Soviet Breakup," 9-9, in which she notes that "the breakup of the Soviet Union threatens to unravel hard-won consensus among the 16 NATO countries about the future of the alliance, reviving old debates about its military strategy and political role." She is right to keep warning about the potential of a European-U.S. rift in "Army Proposal Divides NATO," co-authored by George Leopold 10-21, and "Europe Sharpens WEU Teeth," 11-18.

For the strictly strategic implications of a changing NATO, EC and Soviet Union, it's Hitchens and Giovanni de Briganti to whom we turn. This year de Briganti pioneered reporting on Europe's growing interest in anti-missile defenses. In "Allies Ponder Bolstered Air Defenses," 2-11, he gives us an exemplary overview of the different efforts and interests of Germany, France, Italy and Spain in anti-tactical ballistic missile systems. He picks up the same theme in "U.S., France Discuss Joint ATBM Program," 9-2, a first-rate scoop leaking the fact that "France should cooperate with the United States to develop an antitactical ballistic missile (ATBM) system, according to a report submitted in early July to French Defense Minister Pierre Joxe." Issues of European moves toward military integration are ably explored in items such as "France to Urge Export Policy Coordination," 4-8; "France, U.K., Want Europe Satellite Network," 6-3;"France, Britain to Probe Joint Development of Antiair Frigate," 7-8;and "Firms Stall RM-5 Development," 8-12.

Coverage of international relations is no longer strictly limited to strategic or political developments in Europe. We had criticized *DN* last year for its Eurocentric approach; today the editors seem to be more open to pursuing a world view, although they've still a long way to go. In her important "U.S.-European Joint Programs Sink to New Low," 6-24, Theresa Hitchens issues a timely warning: A result of the fact that "cooperative programs between the United States and Europe have slid to their lowest point in years," the danger exists that "separate, adversarial [defense] markets" will develop. George Leopold keeps us informed of developments in the global arms environment with dispatches such as "China Markets Missile to Middle East Buyers," 4-8, an excellent treatment of missile proliferation in the Mideast with a focus on the alarming prospects of China's M9 and M11 missile exports. In "U.S.-Japan Relation to Struggle, Report Warns," 8-12, he points out: "None of the U.S. major bilateral relationships have been rendered so vulnerable to domestic pressures by the end of the Cold War as the U.S. relationship with Japan." His "Cold War Leaves Legacy of Instability in Asia," 9-30, is a convincing argument about "growing instability. . .in Asia's Pacific rim" as a result of the end of the Cold War. His stimulating analysis in "Change in China: Military May Hold Reform Key," 10-28, suggests that a regionally fragmented and perhaps pro-reform Chinese army leadership will call the shots, whose "biggest concern related with economic and political reforms is modernization of its outdated conventional forces which have not kept pace with China's small but advanced nuclear arsenal."

One of the strengths of *DN* is the considerable energy international trade reporter David Silverberg applies to covering the international arms bazaar. Though others also till this ground, it is Silverberg to whom we look regularly for the detail necessary in assessing the state of the world in this regard. He painstakingly monitors developments on this beat. In his "U.S. State Department Delays Phase Two of Saudi Arms Sale," 1-7, he analyzes why the decision to delay a $14 billion "second phase of a U.S. arms sale to Saudi Arabia. . .came as little surprise to defense industry." He portrays the tension between State Department and Pentagon in "Baker: U.S. Must Curtail Post-War Gulf Arms Flow," 2-11, which highlights Baker's commitment that "arms control in the Middle East will be one of the major challenges addressed by the United States after the war," as it contrasts with the "Cheney: Conventional Mideast Arms Ban Not in U.S. Interest," 3-25, where Cheney argues that "a ban on conventional arms sales to the Middle East would not be in the interest of the United States or its allies." In "Gulf War Is No Panacea for Defense Firms," 2-18, he cautions that despite the spectacular success of many systems in the Gulf War, "export prospects are not so promising." In "Sales of Armored Vehicles Hinge on Gulf War Outcome," 2-25, he details the state of the world market for armored vehicles and explains how future sales will "depend on how well they perform on the battlefield against Iraq." Israel's pronounced distaste for the Patriot is accounted for in terms of interest in "funding of Israel's own antitactical ballistic missile (ATBM) interceptor, the Arrow," in "Israeli Aversion to Patriot Grows," 4-8. The massive congressional opposition to the arms industry is chronicled in his detailed "Senators Target Mideast Arms Sales," 5-20, and "House Panel Kills Lending Plan," 6-3. In "Official: Firms May Profit From Mideast Sales Curb," 7-22, he describes the types of constraints that Congress prepares for the arms industry "in the effort to restrain arms sales, and a code of conduct that applies not only to the defense industry but other industries as well."

The business perspective *DN* applies is inextricably linked to the international trading of arms. Philip Finnegan, in addition to his continuing focus on SDI and on defense budget issues, contributed numerous very useful analyses of the financial conditions of key defense/aerospace firms — a crucial concern in this year of tumbling budgets and unprecedented changes in defense requirements. Good examples of his studies of the financial status of defense companies are: "Solid, Conservative Martin Marietta Finds Favor With Analysts," 6-3; "Grumman Prospects May Rest on Future of Navy F-14 Fighter," 8-26, and "Analysts Anticipate Turnaround at Boeing Defense Unit," 9-30. In "Boeing, Sikorsky Win LH Competition," 4-8, Caleb Baker offers a good technical discussion of the differences in design of the Light Helicopter that gave Boeing and Sikorsky the edge over the losing team of McDonnell Douglas and Bell. And his

"Technical Glitches Stall Short-Range UAV Effort," 5-6, is a very good report on delays by two teams, one led by Israeli Aircraft Industries and one by McDonnell Douglas, in the unmanned aerial vehicle (UAV) program.

Naturally, the armed services and U.S. defense are not neglected. One of *DN*'s strongest selling points, the weekly steadfastly maintains and cultivates an insider perspective, without seeming spoon-fed by either the military or DoD. The Army's budget and mission redefinition problems are portrayed very effectively by Caleb Baker in such articles as "Despite War, Army to Build No New Tanks," 2-18; "Cheney, Army Secretary Clash on M1 Upgrade," 7-22; and "Funding Shortages Curtail Plans at Special Forces Center," 8-26. Robert Holzer is a well-informed, meticulous writer who enjoys privileged sources of information; he is the person to be consulted about developments in the naval service. In "Navy Struggles to Find Funding for Ailing Aviation," 3-25, he argues that naval aviation's capabilities are being severely reduced and that the "Navy will have to decide whether they will shift funding away from ships and submarines to fund naval aviation." With "Navy Explores Advanced Technology for Future Cruise Missiles," 6-3, Holzer reports on Navy research to add sensors to cruise missiles that would make them more autonomous on the battlefield. "Navy Initiates Long Term Effort to Convert Satellite Links," co-written by Neil Munro 8-12, is a fascinating report on stealthy communications where "Low probability of detection radio networks disguise their radio signals as background static" — only friendly radios with computers that know the pattern can detect the signals. Munro, for his part, can be counted on to keep us informed on issues of command, control, communication and intelligence. His greatest contribution was that he identified from the outset the powerful, growing trend toward intelligence centralization in the U.S. armed services. "DoD Proposal Downgrades Space, Strategic Defense Programs," 1-28, reports on the proposed plan to create a new unified Strategic Command by merging U.S. space command and NORAD with Air Force Strategic Air Command and command of the U.S. Navy's missile carrying submarines. He argues persuasively in "DIA Reshuffle Will Consolidate, Bolster Commands," 6-10, that the Pentagon's intelligence reorganization plan will result in "centraliz[ing] oversight and control of intelligence within the office of Duane Andrews, assistant secretary of command, control, communications and intelligence, and within the multiservice regional commands. . .rather than the services." And Munro emphasizes further in "Role of CINCs Increases as Budget Forces Shift," 9-2, the drift away from the services: "As the service chiefs argue over the allocation of roles and missions needed to justify funding, the multiservice commanders in chief (CINCs) find themselves with significant influence over the internal debates." Along the same lines, Barbara Opall sketches, in "Air Force to Restructure Tactical Forces," 1-14, the Air Force's proposed "restructuring. . .plan [which] calls for the service to operate in peacetime as it does in war with. . .composite wings [that] would include a variety of combat aircraft, along with tankers, electronic warfare, reconnaissance planes and possibly, air transports." And with "AF Planners Advocate Quick-Strike Doctrine," 4-8, she is at the forefront of doctrinal developments, reporting that "Future conflicts involving the U.S. military are likely to be offensive in nature, with U.S. forces using the first minutes of battle to dictate the terms and tempo of war to overwhelm enemy forces."

One of the reporters who first attracted us to the weekly, Debra Polsky, was assigned to special projects. Though her output was reduced considerably, her reporting remained excellent and judicious on a number of highly specific issues, mostly the cutting edge of high-tech military developments such as night vision combat technologies, simulator technologies, chip manufacturing and selective monitoring of the financial health of defense companies. Her "Life-Like Simulators Are Almost Reality for Researchers," 1-28, is an impressive report on the military uses of "virtual reality" computing, probing into "how sophisticated computers can be used to immerse troops in distant battles without sending them into a simulator." In "Air Force Eyes LANTIRN Upgrade," 2-25, and "Army to Evaluate Low-Cost, Lightweight Night Vision Systems," 3-4, she reports on expected future developments in the "complex night vision system being used by U.S. Air Force pilots," and on the Army's pondering the high-tech "designs for low-cost, lightweight night vision systems" that could provide "a helmet-mounted display to allow soldiers to shoot targets at night." A 9-23 three-article survey of advanced research into "the Defense Department's 10-year, $1 billion campaign to develop lightning-fast computer chips," consists of "Production Costs Prohibit MIMIC Chip Proliferation," which argues that "only when a strong commercial market develops can MIMIC (Microwave/Millimeter-wave Monolithic Integrated Circuits) chips become truly affordable," and of "Large MIMIC Market Fails to Bloom," and "Chip Miniaturization Is Sizable Challenge," two brief items that expand nicely on the information contained in their titles.

We find more and more that the staff writers and reporters of *Defense News* are the journalists of record on their particular beats, largely due to the clear chain of command at the weekly and the exact delineation of roles and reporters. *DN* is meticulous in defining the parameters within which a reporter may operate, and thus there is very little that is either repetitious or extraneous in its pages. This young weekly is fast becoming a must read for anyone connected with the defense industry, and, as circulation is beginning to show, anywhere in the world. An impressive year, again.

Executive Editor:	Richard C. Barnard
Editor:	Sharon Denny
Address:	6883 Commercial Drive Springfield, VA 22159-0400 (703) 642-7300
Circulation:	1990 — 35,231 1991 — 38,400

The Economist

The Economist began reprinting its motto in 1991: "to take part in 'a severe contest between intelligence, which presses forward, and an unworthy, timid ignorance obstructing our progress.' " Progress — in the classical liberal sense of free trade and free societies — is what *TE* is all about, and 1991 was a year which saw more than its fair share of progress in that regard, and obstacles as well. The world's premier newsweekly was more than up to taking part in the contest, covering the momentous events of 1991 with tightly-written editorials and articles that were both insightful and informative. Through its use of "humint" — human intelligence resources on the ground throughout the world, including stringers from the better U.S. newspapers — and "comint" — high-tech fax machines and satellites — *TE* is able to provide the freshness of a daily newspaper with the broader prospective of a weekly. "Intelligence" indeed.

"Don't save this face," pleaded *TE* on 1-12, referring to Iraq's ruler, *TE* arguing inside that "A peace that left Saddam Hussein unchallenged in Kuwait would be. . .bad," for a number of reasons. *TE* not shy about the need to protect the world's oil supply while noting the "high principle" of not allowing one country "to over-run and annex another." Consequently, *TE* argued, peace now "would mean accepting a peace that was no peace at all, merely the lull before a bigger explosion." Still, once war arrived, *TE* began looking to what would lie ahead, drawing on Europe's colonial past for a perspective often lacking in U.S. commentary on the war, as most U.S. historical perspective went back no further than the ill-fated involvement in Beirut during the early 1980s.

In "When the Hurly-Burly's Done," 1-19, *TE* warns that "when the war is over, the West cannot impose peace, order and democracy at the point of a gun. That is colonialism, and it doesn't work." Addressing the question of what sort of a post-war "regional security structure" the allies should seek in "On Their Way?" 2-9, it found that "They should at least consider whether the best contribution their armies can make after the war is to pack their bags and go home. . .going home may be the only gesture bold enough to persuade wider Arab opinion that the western world returned to the Middle East to enforce international law, not to reimpose colonialism." *TE* continued this line of thought as the war wound down, warning in "Now, the Peace," 3-2, that the U.S. will not be able to go it alone in dealing with post-war security concerns, but will rather have to welcome in the Soviets, the Europeans, the U.N. "Mr Bush has had his brilliant moment in the Middle East. As in winning this war, he will need to share the burden with others if he is to win a historic peace."

The geopolitical landscape brought about by the war, and the Bush administration's efforts to win "a historic peace" were the subjects of the best international survey we saw in *TE* all year, "Out of Joint," by Peter David, 9-28. David, *TE*'s international editor, writes that the Gulf War has, for the time being, pushed *qawmiyya,* or loyalty to Arab nationalism, aside in favor of *wataniyya,* or loyalty to a particular country, and is superb on the domestic and international pressures and considerations facing the Shamir government as it prepares for the proposed Middle East peace conference. "If, against expectations, it leads on to a formal peace between Israel and the Arabs, it will be because the outside world, with America at its head, has run out of patience with a quarrel that becomes more dangerous as the decades slip by."

TE also closely followed the other major international development in 1991, the political upheaval in the Soviet Union, and was early in announcing that for Mikhail Gorbachev, his time had come and gone. Discussing the West's options after the bloodshed in Vilnius in the leader "Blood on His Hands," 1-19, *TE* writes that "No help, except perhaps some food aid, should go to a government following Mr Gorbachev's present course. The money should be released only to men willing to resume the march to democracy, a free market, the right to independence." In reaction to Soviet Prime Minister Valentin Pavlov's statements that Western banks were plotting to bring down the government by flooding the country with rubles, "Primitive Pavlov," 2-16, argues that the remarks "reveal how the forces of reaction are prevailing in all areas of Soviet policy," and that "Now the sad truth has to be faced. Mr Pavlov was Mr Gorbachev's own choice as prime minister. The buck — or rather the rouble — stops with Mr Gorbachev."

Commenting on Gorbachev's attempt to get a national mandate through a referendum on the survival of the union in "Going Yeltsin's Way," 3-23, *TE* also draws the curtain on the Soviet Union itself, arguing that Gorbachev is "no longer" the right leader for the Soviet Union because of his refusal to abandon two notions; holding the Soviet Union, "the inner empire" intact, and his commitment to communism. As to after Gorbachev: "The mother of all doubts about the Yeltsin alternative is fear of the unknown. That fear is understandable. But it should not be exaggerated into an excuse for keeping an unhappy empire together and unwanted Communists in power."

Not surprisingly, *TE* saw Boris Yeltsin as the big winner of the botched coup attempt, commenting in "Yeltsin's Army," 8-24, that "It will be increasingly to him that Russians, and maybe other Soviet citizens will turn to tackle the difficulties that still beset the Soviet Union," such as dissolving the empire and restoring the economy. "The mending has to start at home: if the next government in Moscow goes for really radical economic policies, it could draw in the cash that really would make a difference: private investment from foreign companies with the expertise and technologies the Soviet Union needs."

TE's emphasis on private, not public, Western monies to bail out the Soviet Union was spelled out in "How to Help," 5-6, a critical appraisal of recent proposals to offer large-scale aid to the Soviet Union in exchange for reform, *TE* commenting that "You do not need a Marshall plan or 94 blueprints endorsed by the G7 and Harvard University to push a communist economy towards market-driven growth. You just need to get on with the job, which is what Mr Gorbachev has singularly failed to do." Unfortunately, *TE* seemed to equate "getting on with the job" with ending price controls and balancing the budgets at the national and republic levels with scarcely a mention of currency convertibility. In "Turn Off the Presses," 10-5, *TE* examines the skyrocketing inflation rate in the Soviet republics, and pronounces, not very helpfully, that "Goods are indeed in acutely short supply, but the remedy for that is a once-and-for-all rise in their price relative to the cost of labour, not an endless upward spiral of both prices and wages." This is simplistic monetarism.

TE provided strong ground-level coverage of events in the ex-Soviet Union (late in the year, the magazine even ran a reader contest to come up with a new name for the territory encompassed by the old U.S.S.R.), highlighted by "Anatomy of a Botched Putsch," 8-24, a succinct wrap-up of the failed coup attempt, with *TE*'s Moscow correspondent blaming the failure on the "lack of ruthlessness and planning" on the part of the coup leaders, and noting that the coup actually started back on June 17, when the leaders attempted to have the Soviet parliament reduce Gorbachev's powers. "Parliament rejected the demand and President Gorbachev, flanked by the defence, KGB and police chiefs, laughingly observed that 'the coup is over.' At last, it really is."

Europe was of course a major story in 1991 as well, and *TE* tried to split the difference between European federalists and British Tories who saw Europe 1992 as encompassing free trade only. In "Playing as One?" 6-29, *TE* observes that "When it works, federalism is an excellent way of accommodating differences within a single system," but that in the case of Europe too many differences remain. Several months later, in "The German Question," 10-12, *TE* urges faster European unity now, while Germany is amenable to limits on sovereignty. "For other Europeans, there is a high cost in accepting the German offer now; they would have to give up chunks of their own sovereignty. But, in the run-up to Maastricht, they must be clear about their choice — between a Europe in which they have more direct influence on Germany (and vice versa); and a Europe in which reunited Germany is free to go, alone, its German way." Commenting on the Maastricht summit in "Europe's Dutch Treat," 12-14, *TE* continues to advocate an "*a la carte*" approach, one in which "EC governments commit themselves only to those dishes that are appropriate to their wealth, geography and traditions."

Asian coverage was strong once again in *TE* this year. The waxing and waning of democratic fortunes in the region were closely charted by *TE* all year. In "Yes, They Do March Together, But Sometimes Out of Step," 6-29, a mini-survey on "freedom and prosperity," *TE* examines the curious existence of the latter in many Asian countries without the presence of the former. Offering a roundup of the Asian reaction to the failed Soviet coup in "Feeling the Wind From the West," 8-24, *TE* notes that even "authoritarian democrats like Malaysia's Dr Mahathir and Singapore's Lee Kuan Yew to the less autocratic leaders of Japan and Taiwan" are following Beijing's example in putting economic reform ahead of political liberalization. "If the Soviet Union becomes truly absorbed into the western camp, this could become the new division between East and West." The political economy of Asia is explored even more comprehensively in the survey, "Where Tigers Breed," 11-16.

TE focused on the perceived shortcomings of Japan all year, and in "The Rot in Japan," 7-13, it argues that "If Japan really was cleaning up its financial mess, a stock market crash would follow as night follows day." "Can Tokyo Repent?" 8-3, calls on the Japanese to both better regulate their financial system and open it up to more competition, labeling the current Japanese securities market as a "big but smelly oddity." *TE* suggests political reform following the downfall of Prime Minister Toshiki Kaifu in "Japan's Lost Leader," 10-12, arguing that Japan must begin getting its political house in order so that it can measure up to its international responsibilities. "To take them wisely, Japan needs a modern system of representative government — not the introspective and corrupt cabal who have humbled Mr Kaifu."

Subcontinent coverage continues to be one of *TE*'s strong suits. The mini-survey "The Reincarnation of Caste," 6-8, thoroughly reviews the prevalence of the caste system in India today and its impact on politics, government, and life in general. "Death Among the Blossoms," 5-25, is an exceptionally well-written report on Rajiv Gandhi's assassination and India's political crisis. Noting that Gandhi's killers are still unknown, *TE* writes that "It is clear, though, what killed him: the current of political violence that runs from separatist terrorism to the small-time brutality of local hatreds," and that the "Indians' disillusion with the state is compounded by the failure of successive governments to deliver economic growth." A survey on India, "Caged," 5-4, was described by *New Yorker* contributor Ved Mehta in "Letter From New Delhi," 8-19, as being "a comprehensive and searching treatment of India's economic problems," which was "perhaps the most widely read and discussed" article published on that subject all year, and that while many Indians agreed with *TE*'s central prescription of abandoning Nehru-style socialism, it "cannot be adopted, because the whole democratic political apparatus is oiled by short-term considerations. . ."

TE was once again a valuable source on British political developments. In one of the best reporting efforts we saw by *TE* all year, "Was It, or Was It Not, a Plot?" 3-9, a mini-survey on the downfall of Margaret Thatcher, *TE* reports that while Mrs. Thatcher is now telling friends she was brought down by a "constitutional coup" the truth is that "Mrs Thatcher's fall may have involved disloyalty, but not conspiracy. It was a tragi-comedy that lurched through unlikely crises to an unexpected denouement: a drama in a tiny political world ruled by hubris, coincidence and blunder."

TE has labeled itself as being "unashamedly Americanophile," which is not to say that it is sentimental towards the U.S. Quite the opposite. When post-war euphoria was at its zenith in early March, *TE,* in "On Top of the World?" 3-9, made the deflationary point that "To defeat a country with the national product of Portugal took 75% of America's tactical aircraft and 40% of its tanks. Some unipolar gunboat." *TE* was consistently on President Bush's case all year in editorial leaders and the "America Survey." Its Washington correspondent, in "A Nation of Rock-Solid Realism and Clear-Eyed Idealism," 2-2, draws on history to comment that while George Bush may be on the verge of a great victory, the president should remember that "after leading Britain to a glorious victory in 1945, Churchill and the Conservatives were soundly beaten in the election — because British voters thought Labour could offer them more at home."

All year *TE* found President Bush wanting on domestic policy, its columnist "Lexington," in "George Bush's Domestic Laments," 6-22. writing that on the domestic front, "Prepare your ears for a year's worth of whine." In "Racism's Back," 11-16, *TE* contends that Bush's condemnation of David Duke "would carry more conviction had Mr Bush not won his election to the presidency in 1988 on the back of television advertisements attacking his opponent for supposed leniency towards a murderer." During the autumn, as the president's popularity plummeted with the weak recovery, *TE,* in "President Panic," 11-30, argued that such personality traits as "frenetic insecurity, his stubborn networking, his faith in action and distrust of words are most effective," may serve Bush well in times of crisis, but that in the current economic downswing, Bush would be well-advised to sit tight and wait it out. "It is a storm to be endured. There is virtually nothing he can do to boost the economy in the next few months. He should say so, and concentrate instead on a domestic agenda — health and education reform — that will win him plaudits after the recovery arrives."

We continue to be impressed by *TE*'s coverage of other domestic ills inflicting the U.S., *TE* obviously impressed by the country's past efforts at assimilating various ethnic groups into something approaching a multicultural whole, and seeing the American experience as an example an increasingly shrinking world can learn from. Of course, this means that *TE* is alert to the slightest sign that the U.S. may be backtracking from this ideal. In "My Country Tis of Thee," 5-11, *TE* warns that the U.S. should try to retain its image as a melting pot, and avoid becoming a mosaic, as the advocates of affirmative action and opponents of making English the official language are proposing. In the accompanying mini-survey "Yes, They'll Fit In Too," 5-11, on recent immigrants to U.S. shores, *TE* notes that "They possess the qualities that enabled most of the earlier arrivals to take on the American character, to become Americans. They too will acquire the American flavour, while adding a few new spices of their own. Without them, life in the United States would be poorer and duller for everyone."

181

TE's coverage of domestic America was highlighted by an examination of the plight of black Americans in the 3-30 issue. In the leader, "America's Wasted Blacks," 3-30, *TE,* employing the perspective that comes with distance, cut through the ideological shibboleths and psychological hang-ups which pass for domestic consideration of the problem, to argue that America should "forget such racially minded solutions [affirmative action, reparations, black separatism] altogether. If America were to attack the reasons for the underclass's existence, the beneficiaries would be disproportionately black." This editorial was followed by a mini-survey, "A World Apart," in which *TE* pulls no punches. "The slums in America's great cities are shameful. They are a damning indictment of the richest country in the world. The problems that fester in them are not peripheral: they constitute America's main domestic challenge today."

TE also published a survey on the domestic U.S., "The Old Country," 10-6, by Michael Elliott, which we nominated for 10 Best consideration for General Reporting. Elliott provides a breathtaking look at current trends and developments, such as the internationalization of the U.S. economy, the denationalization of the U.S. government, and the rise of so-called multiculturalism. He is so good on the specifics that we can even put up with his thesis, with which we do not necessarily agree, that the prosperity and world role the country enjoyed during the Cold War were "aberrant" in world history, much as it fits in with *TE*'s editorial policy overall.

That policy advocates a multilateral world with international economics viewed through an IMF-G7 prism. In "Aid and Enterprise," 5-25, *TE* opposes the Bush administration's idea that the International Finance Corporation, an arm of the World Bank, should lend less to governments and more to private businesses, *TE* arguing that the loans are necessary to build the infrastructure in developing countries, while promoting better economic policies. "Above all, though, the Bank should be harsher on bad economic policy — even when (America, please note) this annoys governments which the Bank's rich-country shareholders would prefer to be friends with." Commenting on post-election India in "Rajiv's Heirs," 6-22, *TE* notes that "In one sense the management of the economy is about to pass into safe hands: those of the IMF," who, *TE* predicts, will insist on reforms that will bring down the country's deficit, tariffs, and quotas.

In "The World Order Changeth," 6-22, *TE* attempts to place a conceptual framework on the new international environment by contending that the world terrain is now dominated by one peak, the G7 nations, who espouse democracy and the free market economy. In the new world order, *TE* sees the G7 nations promoting such economic values as free trade through such international economic organizations as GATT, the World Bank, the IMF, and U.N. economic agencies, while coping with political crises through clubs of nations, such as the EC and the U.N. *TE* tried to steer clear of illusions, however, in the mini-survey "To the Victors, the Spoils — and the Headaches," 9-28, looking over the state of the new world order as it attempts to cope with such problems as the transition of socialist economies to market ones, trade difficulties, the new nature of sovereignty, and the enforcement of international law. "The democracies cannot go charging around like so many Galahads, looking for maidens to rescue."

The major international financial scandals of 1991 were seen by *TE* as evidence that more regulation was needed. Commenting on the BCCI mess in "Behind Closed Doors," 7-13, *TE* argues that "The first lesson of BCCI is that regulators should intervene early in the affairs of a mismanaged bank," and "The second main lesson of BCCI concerns international, especially European, regulation. Every bank needs a strong lead regulator, capable of following its worldwide operations, even into the secret-banking havens exploited by BCCI." In "Lessons from Maxwell," 12-14, *TE* calls for a tightening of Britain's pensions law and libel law in the wake of the Maxwell Communications debacle, while noting that it is "naive" to "assume that an [English] SEC would have prevented the Maxwell affair; after all, America is not famous for its lack of scandals."

The "Business" and "Finance" sections continue to offer comprehensive coverage of those two domains, and our readers usually find themselves gleaning valuable information, although they note that, unlike the other sections, "Business" and "Finance" articles tend to be more geared toward a specialized audience. They also note that *TE* is better at providing condensed information on such topics as free trade and world stock markets than it is at commentary, citing as an example *TE*'s report on Soviet debt, "What Is To Be Done?" 8-24, our readers pointing out that *TE* has taken leave of the reality of the disintegration of central Soviet control. "Business" and "Finance" section reports often reflect the editorial outlook outlined elsewhere in *TE,* and in "Under the Volcano," 9-7, for instance, *TE* uses a 61-year-old Japanese restaurant owner who lost up to $1.8 billion in the Tokyo stock market to dramatize the "lava" erupting from the country's financial scandals. We've also received complaints about the small type size *TE* uses for its economic charts and graphs, one reader comparing them to business cards of optometrists who use the smallest type available.

TE traditionally closes with a section devoted to "Books and Art," and it is a tribute to the *TE* editors that its literate tone is in keeping with the fine writing throughout the magazine, the section not seeming to have been stapled in our edition by mistake. In "Out of America's Web," 3-23, we find a critical review of Robert Reich's latest book, *The Work of Nations: Preparing Ourselves for 21st Century Capitalism,* with *TE* contending that Reich's prescriptions of levying higher taxes on "rich brainworkers" to finance greater government programs and economic planning would "...(a) create a brain drain from America and transfer most corporate headquarters outside it; (b) direct more of American spending through the cost-unconscious bureaucratic elephantiasis which has produced Soviet steelworks in Omsk." The notion of supply-side incentives has crept into *TE*'s columns at a glacial pace, however. It's basic analytical framework remains stolidly demand-side.

Editor: Rupert Pennant-Rea

Address: 25 St. James Street
              London SW1A 1HG
              United Kingdom
              (In the U.S.) (212) 541-5730

Circulation: 1990 — 200,000 North America; 425,000 Worldwide
              1991 — 213,109 North America; 475,535 Worldwide

Far Eastern Economic Review

Kipling's famous white tombstone may have warned of the fate of foolish Westerners who try to hustle the East, but *Far Eastern Economic Review* has little to fear in this regard. Each week the *Review,* a wholly-owned subsidiary of Dow Jones and Company, Inc., provides a gold seam of data and information on the political economy of the region, packaged in punchy reports and analytics that often match the rhythm of life in this corner of the world.

Editor Philip Bowring oversees a network of journalists and intelligence gatherers that blankets the region, even with a bureau in Hanoi. In addition, the *Review* draws on correspondents in other cities that impact on the Asian scene, including Washington, London, Moscow, and Vancouver. While the *Review*'s coverage is devoted to Asia, which extends from Vladivostok to Islamabad, the magazine is global in outlook, the editors well aware that in the world economy no region is an island.

The *Review* publishes no regular editorials, which is not to say that the *Review* has no editorial outlook. Its reports often mirror the concerns and hopes of the region, especially the threats to economic development and political stability.

The war in the Persian Gulf was seen as a threat to both, the *Review* on its 1-24 cover asking what the war was being fought for, and on its 3-7 cover labeling the war "lousy." Regional editor Charles Smith, in "Loyalties Under Fire," 1-24, provides a masterful summation of the "bemused" attitude Asian countries are taking toward the conflict, noting that they "tend to view the Gulf as a regional problem which is of little direct concern to them rather than one demanding global involvement," while noting the adverse impact this attitude can have on relations with Washington. Following the cessation of hostilities, Smith, in "The Gulf," 3-7, voiced new fears for the region, observing that "By pressing ahead with a ground war after the launching of a Soviet peace initiative, and even after Iraq's withdrawal announcement, the US may have alienated supporters as well as critics in the region." In "Pax Americana," 3-7, then-Jakarta bureau chief Michael Vatikiotis, Islamabad bureau chief Salamat Ali and New Delhi bureau chief Hamish McDonald document why "The prospect of a Pax Americana looming in the wake of the Gulf War is the obvious cause for concern for several major Asian countries."

The *Review*'s coverage of Operation Desert Storm was distinguished by its ground-level reports from Asian countries, especially ones with sizeable Muslim populations, on popular opposition to the war. In "Division of the Spoils," 3-7, Bowring, international finance editor Anthony Rowley and London correspondent James Bartholomew expertly examine the expected benefits of lowered oil prices on the region. On a more prosaic level, there was the lesson drawn by the Tianjin factory manager who was quoted in "Trying to Keep," 1-31, as telling his staff: "Saddam is very brave to face the US in this way. . .Imagine what we could do in our factory if we had this pure will to risk everything."

Of course, one key Asian element of the war story was Japan's handling of the crisis, and this was covered thoroughly in the *Review,* Washington bureau chief Susumu Awanohara once again excelling at conveying the official U.S. perceptions on the perceived policy failures of this key Asian ally, in such reports as "Early Casualties," 1-24, and "Ties Frayed by Resentment," 2-14. Japan's struggle to redefine its role on the new global stage was authoritatively covered by the *Review* throughout the year, the magazine keen to both the broad outlines and subtle nuances of this story, sensitive to the regional impact of Japanese power while not afraid to offer criticism when warranted.

The *Review* focused on "Japan and the World," in its 6-20 issue. In the introduction, Charles Smith writes that "What [Japan] needs is a world view which will enable it to stop pretending it is a medium-sized client state with an outsize economy." The need for reform was the theme running throughout the "Focus," Rowley, in "Affluence with Influence," 6-20, warning that "without political reforms and inspired leadership, there is a real risk that Japan could revert to isolationism, or at least resort to championing a form of Asian regionalism less demanding than the challenges of internationalism." In "A Strong Case for Reform," 6-20, Tokyo correspondent Louise do Rosario is able to provide a fresh look at an-oft-told tale, the growing stagnation of the LDP and the resulting hindrance on Japan's aspirations to world leadership.

An underreported story, the Japanese foreign ministry and its role in Japan's difficulties in relating to the outside world, is the focus of the 7-18 cover story. In "Carrying the Can," and "Missing Links," Tokyo bureau chief Robert Delfs is sharp on the institutional weaknesses of the Japanese foreign minister, weaknesses exacerbated by Japanese politics and Japanese bureaucracy. The institutional weaknesses of the Japanese Ministry of Finance is viewed as being behind the recent scandals roiling the Japanese financial system in the cover story "Ministry of Myopia," 9-12, Rowley dryly writing that the MOF "appears to have outrun its competence in certain areas." While Rowley writes that the current crisis could result in financial sector administrative reform, including the creation of an independent regulatory body along the lines of the S.E.C. in the U.S., he is not optimistic that such change will come about.

In "Kinder Co-Prosperity," 10-3, K. Das adroitly uses the visit of the emperor and empress of Japan to Malaysia to examine the lingering ghosts from the war years. Susumu Awanohara stepped out from the pack of writers on deteriorating U.S.-Japanese relations as the 50th anniversary of the attack on Pearl Harbor approached in the cover story "And the Winner is. . ." 12-5. Awanohara deftly moving beyond the belligerent posturing by extremists on both sides to capture the diverging attitudes by U.S. elites and the U.S. public on Japan: "One hypothesis is that the US public is more honest about American frailties than the elite."

The *Review* also offered thorough coverage on the other major international story of the year, events in the Soviet Union, the *Review* particularly strong on Soviet Central Asia coverage. In the cover story "Holding the Line," 6-27, then-Beijing bureau chief Tai Ming Cheung produces a remarkable piece of military intelligence reportage, scoring the first-ever interview given by Col. Gen. Viktor Novozhilov, commander of the Far East Military District. The article expertly conveys the reasons behind Asia's growing nervousness over Soviet military deployment in the region. While the Soviet army is demobilizing 120,000 troops in the region under a plan announced by Mikhail Gorbachev in December 1988, the Soviet Union is steadily improving its equipment, and this qualitative upgrading has regional capitals worried, including Tokyo, a topic addressed at length in the accompanying article, "Old Apprehensions," 6-27. We received the same high level of reporting on the economic designs of Moscow in the region in "On the Brink," and "Permafrost Is Melting," 8-15, both by Seoul correspondent Mark Clifford. Clifford is sharp and clear on how Moscow's optimism on using the Soviet Far East as an *entrepot* for foreign capital, technology and skills "has outstripped reality."

The failed coup and subsequent collapse of Soviet communism was, like all major events, examined primarily through an Asian prism. In "Bitter Medicine," 9-9, Cheung, Lincoln Kaye and Taipei bureau chief Julian Baum examine the fall-out in the last remaining communist giant in full detail, offering insight we did not see elsewhere on the impact recent developments will have on Chinese policy toward Taiwan. In "Big Brother Boris," 9-5, Moscow correspondent Sophie Quinn-Judge is alert on early signs of Central Asian unhappiness over expressions of "Russian chauvinism," accompanying the ascension of Boris Yeltsin. As Soviet dissolution heated up, Quinn-Judge penned a valuable profile of Kazakhstan President Nursultan Nazarbayev, "The Coming Man," 10-3, noting that with his peasant background he is no "sheltered intellectual," having seen "his father chop down his apple trees when the government decided to tax them." "The Coming Man," nicely complements "Parting of the Ways," 10-3, on the political and economic dynamics developing in the region as the center falls apart.

The major regional geopolitical story in 1991 was on the Korean peninsula, and the *Review* did not disappoint, consistently keeping readers ahead of the curve on developments both North and South, as well as interstate relations. The *Review* once again was an invaluable listening post on the North, and that shrouded nation's efforts at implementing an ideology of *Juche,* or self-reliance, while improving ties with the outside world. In "Birth of a Legend," 2-21, Aidan Foster-Carter penetrates behind the curtains obscuring "Dear Leader" Kim Jong Il, a remarkable piece of political intelligence. In "Sagging With a Swagger," 5-30, Seoul bureau chief Shim Jae Hoon is comprehensive on how North Korea is facing up to "its greatest crisis since the Korean War of 1950-53."

The *Review* was also on top of North Korea's nuclear weapons program, striking a careful balance of concern and alarm, smartly placing the story in the larger context of political developments on the Korean peninsula. In "Playing From Strength," 5-9, the *Review* alertly notes that while tensions may be rising over the nuclear issue, "they may represent an overture to the removal of land-based nuclear weapons from the peninsula." Susumu Awanohara is thorough on concerns by Washington over linkage with its nuclear weapons in the South in "Bomb Disposal," 8-22. As tension heightened toward the end of the year, the resourceful Peter Hayes provided firsthand denials from Pyongyang in "Kim's Elusive Bomb," 11-7, reporting what "senior officials in the government claimed . . .was a detailed account of the country's nuclear program." Hayes was unable to get to Yongbyon, site of the disputed nuclear complex, but he was able to provide a valuable view "from the other side of the hill," outlining legitimate North Korean security concerns given the turbulent history of the Korean peninsula.

South Korean coverage was also superb. In the 10 Best nominee cover story "South Korea's New World Order," 5-9, Philip Bowring and Seoul bureau staffers Shim Jae Hoon and Mark Clifford score an interview with President Roh Tae Woo, who provides a window into Seoul's unification policy: "We don't want abrupt changes creating social and political instability in the North. What we want is a sort of gradual change so that both South and North can develop together in peace and restore our common national identity." Shim Jae Hoon provides an important look at the growing depolitization of the South Korean army in "Coup Worries Fade," 3-14. As student unrest broke out late in the spring, the *Review* had a focus on South Korea, "Beyond the Teargas," 5-30, a series of articles thoroughly examining the political and economic factors behind the country's move toward "centrist moderation" in the past four years. The expected economic consequences of reunification for both sides is expertly examined by Shim Jae Hoon in "The Inevitable Burden," 8-22, Hoon reporting that most policymakers in Seoul now want to avoid an East German-style collapse in the North. The *Review*'s Korean coverage fully prepared readers for the diplomatic breakthrough in December.

The *Review* also kept an eagle eye on Hong Kong, its coverage increasingly concerned by Chinese efforts to assert control six years ahead of schedule. Hong Kong was the subject of the only editorial we saw in the *Review* this year, "Peking's Revenge," 7-18, which condemns the British government's handling of the dispute with Beijing over the construction of a new airport for Hong Kong, the *Review* stating that "by doing a direct deal with Peking, London has castrated the present colonial government in Hongkong and the future SAR government." In the cover story "Turning Up the Heat," 2-14, Bowring and Hong Kong bureau chief Emily Lau write that "while London speaks eloquently of principles and justice in the Gulf, its attitude towards Hongkong is characterised by an opportunism which makes a mockery of the promises in the Sino-British Joint Declaration." As 1997 approaches, the *Review* will continue to be an important source for this key story.

Once again the *Review* provided a number of cover stories on Asian business trends and regional businessmen. In the 10 Best nominee and highly readable, "Merchant Mandarin," 2-7, Jonathan Friedland is comprehensive on the reasons behind the huge success of commodities and property tycoon Robert Kuok, Friedland outlining how Kuok was able to amass and hold onto his fortune through brilliant business tactics and shrewd networking in both financial and political circles. Jakarta correspondent Adam Schwarz, in the cover story "Empire of the Son," 3-14, deftly reports on the changing of the generational guard at the Salim Group, "Indonesia's (and the world's) largest Chinese-owned conglomerate."

The potential impact of the North American Free Trade Agreement was explored in depth by Susumu Awanohara in the cover story "Enter the Latin Dragon," 7-11, while the regional fall-out from the BCCI scandal is handled superbly by Jonathan Friedland in the cover story "Rest in Pieces," 9-26, Friedland dryly noting that "the perception of BCCI as a Third World enterprise that First World regulators capriciously penalised is open to challenge." In the cover story "Golden Triangles," 1-3, the *Review* features excellent economic reportage on efforts to forge smaller economic growth "triangles" between nations with Asean, the *Review* illustrating why "small plans are much more likely to succeed than big ones." We have complimented the *Review* in the past for its coverage of the arrival of satellite TV to Asia and that exemplary coverage continued in 1991, the year Asians were glued to round-the-clock coverage of events in the Persian Gulf and the Soviet Union. In the cover story "News From Nowhere," 11-28, Margaret Scott thoroughly examines the social, political, and commercial ramifications already being fought over by governments and entrepreneurs, Scott reporting that many Asian officials are uneasy at the prospect of the U.S.-owned CNN being the main source of news for Asians.

The *Review* continues to provide remarkable intelligence on day-in, day-out developments on individual countries in the region. Among the correspondents particularly impressive this year were Manila bureau chief John McBeth, New Delhi bureau chief Hamish McDonald, and Seoul bureau chief Shim Jae Hoon, all three more than up to the task of covering the momentous developments that occurred on their beat this year, from the closure of Clark Air Field to the assassination of Rajiv Gandhi. We also want to single out Hanoi bureau chief Murray Hiebert, and not just because he is the only Hanoi-based correspondent we regularly see. Such reports as "Defeated by Victory," 6-13, on the Vietnamese army's efforts to cope with that country's own "peace dividend," and "Market Test," 8-1, on the gradual return of ethnic Chinese into the waters of entrepreneurship, are textbook examples of fine foreign reporting. Also worth a mention is editorial cartoonist Morgan Chua. Usually four or five drawings by Chua grace the *Review*'s pages each week, along with the occasional cover. Like talented editorial cartoonists everywhere, Chua is able to aim at both the brain and the gut, his caricatures of Asian leaders and power brokers and their foibles both complement the *Review*'s straight reports and carry the stories forward.

Margaret Scott replaced Lincoln Kaye as "Arts & Society" editor this year, the section continuing to offer literate, thoughtful reports and articles on the nexus of culture and geopolitics, the highlight this year being a series on political cartoonists in the region. The book reviews, under books editor Don Cohn, are also usually worth a look. "Arts & Society," placed in the middle of the magazine, provides a fine segue between the political-economic reportage in the first half of the book and the "Business Affairs" section which comprises the back half. Managing editor Ron Richardson, who did so much to broaden the coverage offered in "Business Affairs," left the *Review* in late 1990, but there hasn't been any slackening in either the quality or quantity of data and analysis under business editor Nigel Hollaway, such regular features as "Economic Monitor," "Invisible Hand," "Shroff," and "Research and Innovation," adding to the breadth of the *Review*'s coverage of week-to-week business and financial developments in the region.

No review of the *Review* would be complete without mention of the weekly's two regular columns, "The 5th Column," and "Traveler's Tales." "5th Column," is written by outside contributors, typically academics, businessmen, activists, or retired government officials, usually arguing for reform in one sphere or another. As in any forum of this sort, the quality can vary, but overall "5th Column," offers valuable insight at the thinking being done on the cusp of Asian societies. In "Dramatic Reversal," 3-14, for example, Bui Tin, deputy editor of *Nhan Dan,* the daily newspaper of the Vietnamese Communist Party, writes on the need for new thinking on the part of Hanoi as Vietnam's problems deepen: "The leadership certainly cannot remain deaf to the aspirations and demands of a whole people. . ." Three months before she was awarded the Nobel Peace Prize, Burmese opposition leader Aung San Suu Kyi produced "Freedom From Fear," 7-18, an eloquent testimony to the moral necessity of dissidence in totalitarian societies: "It is the cumulative effect of. . .sustained effort and steady endurance which will change a nation where reason and conscience are warped by fear into one where legal rules exist to promote man's desire for harmony and justice while restraining the less desirable, destructive traits in his nature."

Contributing editor Derek Davies handles "Traveler's Tales," which usually features amusing examples of "found humor," discovered by Davies or by readers, consisting of billboards, menus, and print advertisements inadvertently mentioning bodily functions or containing mangled English phrasing. It is a sort of bar room version of those little space fillers one finds in *The New Yorker.* Davies's forays into commentary are less successful, his views belonging to the English school of anti-Americanism, post-Empire class.

This was especially pronounced in his commentary on the Gulf War, and in his 1-24 column he writes "It is as if most of the nation have transformed themselves into miniaturised John Waynes." He is contemptuous of the media coverage of the conflict in the 2-21 column, which he finds melodramatic, blaming it on military censorship. "An air raid siren in Saudi Arabia or Israel is treated like the Final Trump and the explosion of a Scud missile like Armageddon." Writing on the aftermath of the war, 5-30, he is equally contemptuous of what he perceives to be U.S. hypocrisy, claiming that the country's many shortcomings "would be more bearable if the US cut out the bullshit and declared itself to be in pursuit of its ends by means of cynical Realpolitik. . ." Like most anti-Americans of his stripe, Davies's real complaint about the U.S. is that it is not 19th century Great Britain.

Finally, we must mention the *Review*'s superb coverage of Asian immigrants in the U.S., proof that no angle of the Asian story is ignored by the weekly. Particularly outstanding this year was Susumu Awanohara's report on Korean Americans, "All in the Family," 3-14. The story is hooked around the 14-month boycott by African-Americans of a Korean grocery in Brooklyn, New York, Awanohara bringing a degree of sensitivity and understanding to this incendiary topic that was sorely lacking in stateside publications.

Editor:	Philip Bowring
Address:	GPO Box 160
	Hong Kong
Circulation:	1990 — 73,221
	1991 — 71,441

Forbes

"Our ideology, if there is one," said editor-in-chief Malcolm S. "Steve" Forbes, Jr. in a May interview with *Reason* magazine, is "let business be done by consenting adults." In other words, *Forbes* is not a business magazine that will appeal to the feeble-hearted who crave coddling from pro-subsidy, protectionist hand-holders in Congress; *Forbes* is for the strong-willed whose passion is the lively, rough and tumble realities of business in a capitalist society. This free-market creed guides the reportage and analysis of the magazine that advertises itself as the "Capitalist Tool."

With the death of Malcolm Sr. last year, it is Malcolm Jr. who is now keeper of the free-market flame. At his right hand is 70-year-old editor James W. Michaels, the magazine's unwavering anchorman of editorial quality for the past 30 years. The unsettling departure of Assistant Managing Editors Edwin A. Finn and Steve Lawrence in November, 1990 had led to speculation that Michaels would retire sooner rather than later. But for now at least, Michaels remains at the helm, allowing Steve Forbes more time to deliberate the critical question of Michaels' successor. As for the positions vacated by Finn and Lawrence, Stewart Pinkerton has been added to the ranks.

Other significant changes at *Forbes* were stylistic rather than editorial. The 2-18 issue premiered a redesign, the magazine's first complete makeover since 1987. Although we were pleased with some of the subtle alterations, such as a new layout allowing for longer stories, we were thrown by the jumble of pictures and headlines that dominated the redesigned cover. Apparently, we were not the only readers jarred by this new packaging; the magazine returned to its traditional, uncluttered full-page cover art in the following issue.

On the editorial side, *Forbes*' cover stories continue to be muscular and jarring, a tradition at the magazine. But occasionally we find that the reporters get carried away, packing showy verbal punches when a more contemplative approach might have served readers better. Take for instance, Laura Jereski and Jason Zweig's "Step Right Up, Folks," cover 3-4. This harangue on recapitalization tools such as "pay-in-kind bonds, interest deferrals and principal protectors" labels them all as mere "quack cures." Although the authors do raise a number of credible points about the pitfalls of "paper interest," their rampant flippancy and ambiguous data left us wondering if they'd furnished us with only one side of the story.

Jereski and Zweig's cover story was only one of several disturbing reports on leverage, junk bonds and recapitalization that seemed to clash with the magazine's "Let business be done by consenting adults" editorial mission. Even as junk bonds were hitting record highs, the journalists at *Forbes* were curiously warning against them. Instead of cool-headed investment advice we were served up hot-headed hyperbole based more on hunches than fact. Matthew Schifrin, who wrote last year's fiery "Pay Up. . .Or Else," 8-6-90, constructed an equally intense

"Sellers Beware," 1-21, in which he warns "naive," "ordinary investors" to steer clear of junk bonds because they aren't supervised as closely as stocks — good advice for the "naive," but we weren't sure of the point, since the vast majority of junk bond players are highly-sophisticated institutional investors who already understand the "mine fields" that surround these sharply discounted securities.

By far the most unsettling piece of this genre was "We're Doing Just Fine," 3-18, a slug-fest written by Phyllis Berman and Roula Khalaf. The victim? Former Drexel Burnham investment banker Leon Black, whose major crime, it seems, was to have successfully emerged from the break-up of Drexel with the job of managing $1 billion for the French government-controlled bank, Credit Lyonnais. The funds will allow Black to buy into failed or failing companies, as well as purchase discounted junk bonds. "Exxon would be unlikely to put Captain Joseph Hazelwood in charge of cleaning up the Alaskan oil spill," the authors wisecracked. "But Wall Street is different." Granted, Black is controversial, but the pot shots at his character and family prompted one reader to ask in a 4-15 letter to the editor: ". . .how many years should [Leon Black] serve for dressing carelessly and having a wife who snaps at people?"

On other topics, *Forbes* cover stories were less strident, more instructive. Contributing Editor Susan Lee, who returned to the magazine in 1990 after a three year absence, kicked off 1991 with a 10 Best nomination, "Are We Building Ourselves New Berlin Walls?" cover 1-7. In this thought-provoking essay on international trade, Lee masterfully delineates the crossroads at which the world's trading partners stand: a rejuvenation of GATT or a slide into regionalism which Lee warns could "degenerate into a severe spate of protectionism." James Cook constructs a vigorous expose of how public-sector unions are seeking to expand their power in "Collision Course," cover 5-13. Through careful analysis of union leaders' statements, he comes to the persuasive and unsettling conclusion that the unions are not only after higher wages but also control of their job descriptions with no interference from taxpayers. He cautions that unless politicians take action, the result will be similar to England's experience under the Labour government. Peter Huber's "Junk Science in the Courtroom," cover 7-8, an excerpt from his new book *Galileo's Revenge: Junk Science in the Courtroom* goes after bogus "scientific" testimony which is increasingly distorting the U.S. legal process and costing consumers and businesses billions of dollars. "The most fantastic verdict recorded so far was worthy of a tabloid: With the backing of 'expert' testimony from a doctor and police department officials, a soothsayer who decided she had lost her psychic powers following a CAT scan persuaded a Philadelphia jury to award her $1 million. The trial judge threw out that verdict. But scientific frauds of similar character, if lesser audacity, are attempted almost daily in our courts, and many succeed." Then there's Gretchen Morgenson's excellent "The Trend Is Not Their Friend," cover 9-16, which expertly delineates consumers' slow but sure move toward lower priced supermarket house labels, eating away at brand name profits. With plenty of credible evidence, Morgenson predicts that the shift will cause an industry-wide consolidation. And the "Forbes 400 Richest People in America," cover 10-21, was especially revealing this year, prefaced by George Gilder's outstanding essay, "The Slippery Slope of Wealth," 10-21, which only shows how this year's Forbes 400 mirrors a stagnating economy where wealth remains in the same old hands, but captures the essence of economic dynamism: "The central drama of economics is not the struggle between rich and poor. . .but the struggle between the past and the future, between the capitalist drive to invest in new ventures and the socialist impulse to preserve existing jobs, businesses and concentrations of wealth." And Leslie Spencer shatters the myth of Greenpeace in a muscular "The Not So Peaceful World of Greenpeace," with Jan Bollwerk and Richard C. Morais 11-11, exposing the popular and well-financed organization's disturbing dark side which may be reformed with the departure of David McTaggart who has led Greenpeace since 1980.

Business profiles remain a *Forbes* forte, and this year's offerings were as crisp, probing and informative as ever. The magazine's correspondents are skilled at giving the total picture, weaving into their profiles information and observations that give us a sense of how individual businesses and industries are affected by and contribute to the international economy as a whole.

Gretchen Morgenson's "Barbie Does Budapest," 1-7, which explains how Mattel has kept Barbie popular in children's playrooms for 31 years, examines how, after "a stunning 95% penetration with the fashion doll among U.S. girls age 3 to 11," Mattel is hoping to popularize Barbie in Europe and the Far East. Another topnotch profile by Morgenson was "Is Efficiency Enough?" 3-18, which lauds Colgate Chairman Reuben Mark for his transformation of the company, but cautions: "This is an efficient company, to be sure, but efficiency is only part of the game; growth is the other part. With 13 years to go to retirement, Mark has time to put some growth into the company. Unless he does, investors may soon be wondering if Colgate is really worth 16 times earnings." Steve Weiner turns a critical eye on 3M's inability to come up with new products in the magnetic media business in "A Hard Way to Make a Buck," 4-29. Ferreting out the facts, he discovers that it wasn't R&D that was asleep, but management. "A Flying Lexus," 8-5, is a remarkable gem from Howard Banks who offers the chin-scratch possibility of an airborne Toyota. Why not? The capital is there, the technology too. Even liability costs favor a new entrant. On the auto industry, Jerry Flint takes an in-depth look at how U.S. automakers are getting battle-ready in Europe in "Will the (New) Maginot Line Hold?" 7-8. Flint observes that in warring for European market share, the Japanese "seem to be following. . .the same pattern they used in their successful invasion of the U.S." Flint's "We Do What Mexicans Do," 9-2, was also sharp, discerning that even though U.S. automakers are having troubles at home, they're quickly gaining profits in Mexico, expanding market share and saving money on car production. "With its hardworking people and low wages, Mexico is becoming a key piece in Detroit's entire effort to become profitable again." And a clear-eyed, investment-minded Marcia Berss tells us how CEO Dwayne Andreas and Archer Daniels Midland smooth out the notorious cycles of the commodity business in "Plowing Washington for Profit," 9-16: "Andreas has made an art form out of plowing Washington for markets, tax breaks and subsidies. He says: 'We don't fight it. We work with the government.' Government intervention may make poor public policy, but ADM shareholders must love it. ADM's stock was in the top 8% performers over the last five years."

In the "Computer/Communications" and "Science & Technology," departments of *Forbes* we find such forward-looking pieces as George Gilder's "What Spectrum Shortage?" 5-27, on the infinite supply of radio spectrum, or David Churbuck's "Watch Out, Citicorp," 9-16, a fascinating account of why congressional haggling over bank reform may be of secondary importance to the technological revolution that is making the old banking system obsolete. And there's Kathleen Wiegner's crisp sketch of Trimble Navigation, which is using satellite geometry to open up new markets in surveying and vehicle tracking in "Down to Earth," 10-28. But we must admit, that although these two relatively new sections get stronger each year, they're still outdone by other business magazines, especially *Business Week*. On the other hand, *Forbes* has some of the strongest coverage of marketing topics. In addition to the excellent reports that appear on the cover and throughout the magazine, Joshua Levine's "Marketing" section carries such colorful and offbeat stories as Cecily Patterson's "From Woodstock to Wall Street," 11-11, on how Birkenstock's Margot Fraser successfully sells her "bathtub-shaped" orthopedic sandals to the pinstripe crowd.

To complement all of these business profiles, the "Law and Issues" department keeps a close eye on the economic and political environment in which consumers, entrepreneurs, businesses and industries function. In 1991, the section ably chronicled how the rising tax burden was undermining the economy. Janet Novack's "Tax Politics as Usual," 5-27, expertly examines how an administration tinkering with the tax code to encourage young workers to save could actually deprive older people, "who have resolutely saved for their retirement," of the ability to use lump-sum distribution of IRAs to buy retirement homes or businesses. Equally strong was her "Hidden Persuaders," 9-16, a perceptive look into the new market-oriented think tanks that are popping up at the financially troubled statehouse level and challenging old vested interests. William Tucker also frequently contributes to this section. His "Unpopularity Tax," 6-24, demonstrates just how desperate state governments' search for new tax revenue has become in order to support their huge spending habits: "In November 1990 Wisconsin began trying to collect sales tax on drinks served on airplanes that were flying over the state. The gambit failed only when the Wisconsin Court of Appeals overturned the practice." In the same vein his "A Leak in Medicaid," 7-8, shows how eighteen cash-strapped states have constructed complex plans to legally pad the Medicaid bills they send to Washington for reimbursement, costing the Treasury at least $2.5 billion this year. One source notes that the scam, "may change the very nature of the whole federal-state partnership." Richard Phalon follows up on James Cook's "Collision Course," cover 5-13, with an excellent analysis of how a bloated public sector supported by some of the highest taxes in the nation is worsening NYC's budget woes in "Argentinization of New York City," 11-11.

Forbes overseas is a mixed bag. In the Pacific, we appreciate bureau manager Andrew Tanzer's emphasis on the region's grass-roots entrepreneurial endeavors. His "War of the Sales Robots," 1-7, shows us why Japan's high-tech vending machines ". . .can move as much product as a medium size convenience store," and teaches us more about this dynamic new niche industry in one page than most writers could tell us in three. And he seems so comfortable discussing the specifics of the Japanese computer market in "How Apple Stormed Japan," 5-27, that we almost forget he's talking about a foreign country. He ferrets out dozens of reasons — from design to distribution — for Apple Computer Inc.'s dazzling turnaround in Japan: "In many ways the Mac — which lets users point to pictures instead of typing arcane computer commands — is the ideal machine for handling 'kanji,' the thousands of characters that the Japanese adapted from Chinese, because it offers a graphical interface for a graphical language." Also in the Pacific bureau, Gale Eisenstodt and Hiroko Katayama construct an excellent analysis of how Japan's tax laws are making the Japanese real estate market look weaker than it really is in "What Goes Up. . ." 3-18: "The government has yet to address most of the reasons behind high land prices. Tax laws, for example, still encourage farming in urban centers. With little tax to pay on undeveloped land as long as it is held — but huge capital gains taxes to pay if it is sold — Japanese tax policy is a major obstacle to more efficient land use. Bending to the wishes of big companies, last December the government failed to change tax laws that encourage land hoarding and hinder supply." One development that is bound to enhance *Forbes'* already solid coverage of this region is the printing of a new sister magazine which debuted in October. *Zibenjia,* which is published in Hong Kong, serves the Chinese-speaking market with translated adaptations of articles from *Forbes* as well as original reports of special interest to this new audience.

In Europe, bureau manager John Marcom Jr. and correspondent Peter Fuhrman do an admirable job of covering the political and economic turf of that important region. While Marcom bangs out perceptive European business profiles, Fuhrman more often probes broader issues, offering such enlightening inquiries as "Aidez-Moi," 4-15, in which he tells us to stop worrying about the EC's generous aid to farmers, and look instead at Europe's mushrooming industrial subsidies which "have grown so large and prevalent that the 12 European Community national governments now dole out more money in corporate aid than they take in from corporate taxation." He runs us through numerous meaty examples of blatant and "hidden" industrial subsidies which are "at least six times greater, as a percentage of national income, than U.S. handouts to industry." And before the big Soviet breakup, Fuhrman considers the Baltic republics' chances for freedom in "Is It Mere Wishing?" 8-19, and gives a quick snapshot of some enterprising Baltic thinkers who plan to use practical economic ploys to outwit any Kremlin efforts to stop their march toward independence.

Aside from Marcom and Fuhrman's occasional jaunts into Eastern Europe and the Soviet Union, coverage of that region is mainly left to Vladimir Kvint, a Distinguished Lecturer at Fordham University and Babson College. Although the editors boast that his "Russia as Cinderella," 2-19-90, made Kvint "perhaps the first writer to predict that the Soviet Union would come unglued," an observation we think many would dispute we don't get the impression that he has a full grasp of the Soviet Union's political economy. In his disappointing post-coup essay, "Siberia: A Warm Place for Investors," 9-16, he wonders why anyone should worry about the break upof the Soviet Union. "This fission is a wonderful development. Breaking the vast empire into more manageable pieces, grouped on economic rather than on political lines, presents tremendous opportunities for foreign business." A nice idea, but not once does Kvint recognize the key to this economic and political stability that provides so much potential — a convertible currency. It is the absence of this key element that causes so much uneasiness. Steve Forbes pointed out the importance of a sturdy ruble a few issues later in his 10-21 "Fact and Comment" column, which suggested to avoid a starving Russia the ruble should be backed with gold.

As for the columnists at *Forbes,* the biggest news this year is the addition of Thomas Sowell, a black economist and senior fellow at the Hoover Institution. Through his column, "Observations," he brings an intelligent and provocative new perspective to the magazine. His "The High Cost of Identity," 8-5, cites civil strife in Yugoslavia as a starting point in decrying political "multicultural" movements. And commenting on the circus-like confirmation hearings of Judge Clarence Thomas, Sowell decries the degradation of the confirmation process in "Integrity Is the Issue," 10-28: "It has taken centuries of struggle by giants to establish the ideal of 'a government of laws and not of men.' Today, pygmies are trying to reduce it all to a question of a judge's 'views' on some 'issues,' whether he will be a 'champion' of this or that group, or of this or that cause. . .They promote a dangerous misconception about the role of the courts and the rule of law. Where a judge 'stands' on 'issues' is far less important than where he stands on judging."

All in all, 1991 was a strong year for *Forbes.* Amid economic recession, the correspondents and editors of the "Capitalist Tool" continued to champion free-market creativity.

Editor-in-Chief:	Malcolm S. Forbes, Jr.
Editor:	James W. Michaels
Address:	60 Fifth Avenue New York, NY 10011 (212) 620-2200
Circulation:	1990 — 735,000 1991 — 735,000

Foreign Affairs

We anxiously waited to see which direction *Foreign Affairs* would recommend for U.S. foreign policy elites as they tried to forge a new world order out of the ashes of the Cold War and the Gulf crisis. Would there be an equivalent of the "Mr. X." article of 1947 that would serve as the blueprint for policy for the next 40 or so years? The answer was no, which is not to say that *FA* had a quiet year.

"We need to start selectively disengaging abroad to save resources and seize the unparalleled opportunity to put our house in order. We should avoid new entanglements in the Middle East, withdraw the bulk of our armed forces from overseas and cut back drastically on foreign aid." This statement is not a nearly-forgotten plank from the 1972 Democratic presidential campaign that mysteriously surfaced onto our screen but a direct quote from "Downgrade Foreign Policy," 5-20, an op-ed published by *FA* editor William G. Hyland in *The New York Times.* In an essay that had an almost surreal touch, like a *Wall Street Journal* editorial calling on workers everywhere to seize the means of production, one of the highest mandarins of America's foreign policy establishment argued: "What is desperately required is a psychological turn inward."

Even in our day and age where virtually nothing can be taken for granted, "Downgrade Foreign Policy" can have a certain shock value. Hyland, we have been assured, has not turned isolationist, but is deadly serious in his efforts to alert the country to the necessity to focus on the country's domestic well-being, which he sees as being in its worst shape since the Great Depression. Unfortunately, he falls back on President Harry Truman's post-war model for dealing with the Cold War as an analogy to address the problem, as he calls for Washington to forge a new domestic doctrine, "supported with real money, just as the Marshall Plan was."

Too often this stale, statist thinking permeated the analytical frameworks with which *FA* and its contributors addressed major policy challenges this year, including the ability of the U.S. to compete in world markets and the collapse of the Soviet Union, *FA* weighing in more and more on the debate over the perceived decline and role of the U.S. in the "New World Order," such as it is.

For example, Jeffrey E. Garten, reviewing Robert B. Reich's *The Work of Nations: Preparing Ourselves for 21st Century Capitalism,* and Robert Kuttner's *The End of Laissez Faire: National Purpose and the Global Economy After the Cold War* in "Rethinking Foreign Economic Policy," Summer, is critical of some points raised by Reich in his vision of economic integration and Kuttner's concept of economic nationalism, but is supportive overall of their effort to jump-start a national debate on this subject. "If they do not cause America to think hard about where it is headed in the coming decades, it is unlikely that anything in writing can or will."

Robert D. Hormats drew on the ideas advanced by both Reich and Kuttner, along with Hyland among other influences, in "The Roots of American Power," Summer. Hormats warns: "The danger for the United States at the end of this century is not imperial overstretch but domestic underperformance — a failure to collectively mobilize America's considerable advantages and resources to meet the multiplicity of internal social, political and economic challenges of the 1990s and the attendant consequences of such a failure for America's global role." Hormats argues unimaginatively that the roots of American power are its savings and investment, roots which he feels were either damaged or ignored during the 1980s. His emphasis on improving the quality of the U.S. workforce echoes Robert Reich, while his call for the U.S. to regain its economic competitiveness and retain its superpower status is reminiscent of Robert Kuttner's call for the U.S. to "organize" its economic policy to compete in the new economic world order. "The Roots of American Power," was nominated for 10 Best consideration by the editors.

Not surprisingly, it was also in the pages of *FA* that Harvard faculty members Graham Allison and Robert Blackwell fully outlined their concept of a "Grand Bargain" between the West and the Soviet Union in "America's Stake in the Soviet Future," Summer. Allison and Blackwell sketch out four possible scenarios for the immediate Soviet future, finding bad news for the West in virtually all of them as the Soviet leadership struggles to deal with "four systemic crises," those of "authority, union, the economy and political power." Arguing that, because of its continuing nuclear arsenal and large conventional forces, the U.S. has "notable political-military and diplomatic interests at stake in the future expression of Soviet external policies," and that "there is a middle ground between empty, even feckless, lectures from afar and excuses from the same distance for Gorbachev's every undemocratic action," the authors call on the West to offer the Soviets a deal. ". . .in an effort to forestall Soviet futures that would most deeply threaten Western interests and global stability, a coalition of Western governments led by the United States should immediately design and offer to the Soviet Union. . .a bargain of Marshall Plan proportions. The terms: substantial financial assistance to Soviet reforms *conditional* upon continuing political pluralization and a coherent economic program for moving rapidly to a market economy."

"America's Stake in the Soviet Future," is arguably a watershed article in many ways, given the impact the "Grand Bargain" concept had on debate going on within foreign policy circles at the time, but the importance attached to government-to-government relations and the

Marshall Plan reference illustrate the failure to produce a major conceptual breakthrough. Allison and Blackwell are essentially arguing that the management of revolutionary changes should be left in the hands of officials and bureaucrats, who have the background, experience, and, one suspects, the necessary *savior faire,* to handle these matters.

To be fair, *FA* did present the other side of the argument as well. In "The Soviet Union Adrift," America and the World, nominated by *FA* editors for 10 Best consideration, Richard Pipes offers a breathtaking survey of the prospects for reform in the Soviet Union, preparing us fully for events which transpired later in the year. Drawing on Soviet academic writings and surveys, Pipes expertly paints a portrait of a society where the governing center formerly provided by the Communist Party, is falling apart while the would-be replacement — state institutions — are failing to take hold, resulting in chaos, anarchy, and growing conflicts within the Party between conservative and democratic elements and between the central government and the governments of the 15 constituent republics. Pipes writes that "the regional decentralization now underway is only partly driven by nationalist ideas; it is motivated in large measure by the inability of the center to provide proper economic and political leadership," and dismisses Western aid as a spur to aid Soviet reform efforts since ". . .its foreign debts have quadrupled from 1985 to 1989, to 85.8 billion rubles, without producing any improvements in the country's political or economic condition."

The pages of *FA* were filed in 1991 with experts eager to share their informed opinions on the "New World Order" and the U.S. role in it. If none produced any real breakthroughs at least readers got a good sense of the debate taking place within foreign policy circles. The "America and the World" issue was particularly strong in this regard. Charles Krauthammer, in "The Unipolar Moment," concretely lays out the unipolar argument. In "The Bush Foreign Policy," Michael Mandelbaum is prescient on the weaknesses of President Bush's low-key leadership style, but falls back on the soggy contention that current U.S. economic policy, with its high budget and trade deficits, is disastrous for emerging free market economies around the world by driving up the cost of capital abroad and leading to protectionist measures at home, and wonders if George Bush is the right man to bring about the necessary changes. "Apart from his personal inclinations, Bush's presidency rests on a coalition of forces and interests that offer no political basis for economic policies in support of the international trends favored by the United States."

William Pfaff adopts an existential approach in "Redefining World Power," America and the World, arguing that in the new multipolar international environment the U.S. is one power among several with strengths and weaknesses and that "The great lesson of how the Cold War ended may be stated in these words: being is superior to doing." Pfaff presages Hyland's op-ed, calling on the U.S. to shift its concentration to its domestic ills. "The foreign relations of the nation rightly dominated its attention during the half-century now ending. To make that its continuing priority risks becoming an attempt to prolong artificially what Americans have thought, with reason, their heroic passage on the modern stage, but in doing so to fail the true tests the United States now confronts. The national challenge is within."

FA continues to be a forum for former high-ranking officials. Former national security adviser Zbigniew Brzezinski, in "Selective Global Commitment," Fall, contends that the immediate post-Cold War international environment will be one in which Western policymaking will be dominated by "functional pragmatism as well as transnational institution-building." Translated, this means ideology is out, economic well-being and regional trading blocks are in. Despite the title, though, Brzezinski calls for little in terms of real cutbacks from U.S. commitments abroad, offering instead a vision of a relatively benign world order. In a similar vein, former Joint Chiefs of Staff Chairman Admiral William J. Crowe and Alan D. Romberg, in "Rethinking Security in the Pacific," Spring, view U.S. geopolitical concerns in Asia and how to address them in an era of shrinking defense budgets. The article "grew out of discussions at a Council on Foreign Relations study group," and reads like consensus summaries which reflect all points of view, effectively challenging none.

Admiral Stansfield Turner, the former CIA director, takes up the cause for the U.S. intelligence community to become more involved in conducting economic espionage in "Intelligence for a New World Order," Fall, a notion we still find dubious. McGeorge Bundy, national security adviser during the Kennedy and Johnson administrations, offers a much stronger argument on the necessity for strict enforcement of nuclear non-proliferation, while his companion as Defense Secretary during those turbulent years, Robert S. McNamara, teaming up with Carl Kaysen and George W. Rathjens, continues his crusade for total nuclear disarmament in "Nuclear Weapons After the Cold War," Fall. While President Bush would pick up on some of their suggestions, including the removal of all tactical nuclear weapons from the European theatre, their argument that "It is in America's deepest interest, even in the short run, to continue on the path of delegitimizing war and the unilateral use of military force in relations among states, and to lead the way to worldwide acceptance of this view," seems as elusive as ever.

Much of *FA*'s attention in 1991 was devoted to the Gulf War and its ramifications. In "The Road to War," America and the World, 1990/91, the editors offer a brief summary of the crisis in the Persian Gulf, from Iraq's invasion of Kuwait to the first day of hostilities, pointedly noting that "George Bush did not blunder into war," but its contributions tended to be better when focused on one aspect of the conflict than on comprehensive analytics.

Fouad Ajami, in "The Summer of Arab Discontent," Winter, places the Iraqi invasion of Kuwait in the context of Arab world politics and the historical differences between the gulf states and the Arab states of the north, writing that before oil ". . .the lands of the north had the rivers, the agriculture, the advanced cities, while those in the gulf peninsula relied on locusts for their protein. All this is part of a vanished past now, as the 'have-nots' rail against the oil states," thought-provoking but not profound. In "The New Arabia," Summer, former State Department Arabist James E. Akins recycles a lot of conventional wisdom about the region, predicting that the Gulf states will continue to dominate with their money, the Palestinians will continue to suffer, and the U.S. will continue their dependence on foreign oil, playing right into the hands of Saudi Arabia, whom Akins unaccountably views as "the Arab Sparta, the Arab Israel. It will train and arm its own army; it will buy the world's most sophisticated weaponry; it will keep the Americans on hand to give support when needed."

Peter W. Rodman is better in "Middle East Diplomacy After the Gulf War," Spring, a sober reflection on the difficulties that Washington, despite its increased standing in the region, will face as it tries to grapple with the Arab-Israeli conflict. While he writes that Washington will be well advised to avoid any large-scale peace conferences in the months ahead, his focus on the necessity for incremental improvements in state-to-state relations, based on "concrete indications of 'new thinking' " from all parties on such issues as the Palestinians, captured much of the dynamics of the Bush administration's post-war diplomatic tactics.

The quarterly did provide several valuable essays on individual states in the region. In "Jordan and the Gulf Crisis," Winter, Stanley Reed, the Middle East expert for *Business Week,* presents a brief for King Hussein and his policy during the Gulf crisis, placing the Hussein pro-Iraq tilt in economic and domestic political context and positioning him as an important figure to both sides in Middle East negotiations in the past and possibly in the future. Bruce R. Kuniholm, in "Turkey and the West," Spring, expertly positions that country's new geopolitical role. Daniel Pipes, asking "Is Damascus Ready for Peace?" Fall, provides a timely, clear-eyed assessment of Hafez al-Assad, "the virtuoso politician of the Middle East," from whom political survival equals physical survival.

The contributions on Israel were penned by players on the current Israeli political scene. In "Israel After the War," Spring, Ze'ev Schiff, Defense Editor of the Tel Aviv daily, *Ha'aretz,* surveys the strategical and existentialist questions raised by the Gulf War and specifically the Iraqi missile attacks on Israel, writing presciently that "The debate in Israel today is not just about military questions per se but about the future character of Israeli society in the absence of peace," and calling for a compromise solution with the Palestinians and Arab states. Likud politician Ze'ev B. Begin, in "The Likud Vision for Israel at Peace," Fall, draws on the Bible to stake Israel's claim to the occupied territories and Jerusalem; U.N. resolutions 242 and 338 to call on the Arab states to negotiate with Israel, and the Camp David accords to sketch out a framework for any possible deal for Palestinian autonomy. The resulting essay is a good picture of Israeli hard-right bluster: "It is inconceivable that the mayor of [an American town called Shiloh] could decree it illegal for a Jewish family to live there, just because they are Jews and some Americans living there might be, as they say today, 'sensitive;' " and legitimate concerns: "Should Israel believe untested assumptions about Middle Eastern leaders, or should it hold them to certain standards?" as the Shamir government heads, uneasily, toward a peace conference.

There were also a number of essays devoted to ancillary subjects related to the Gulf War, several of which were particularly noteworthy. Michael J. Glennon, former legal counsel to the Senate Foreign Relations committee, writes with an authentic, insider's feel on how the three branches of our national government really operate, "The Gulf War and the Constitution," Spring. In "Moscow and the Gulf War," Summer, Graham E. Fuller, a former vice chairman of the National Intelligence Council at the CIA, knowledgeably charts the twists and turns of Moscow's handling of the Gulf crisis, from the initial invasion last August to the end of Operation Desert Storm, documenting how Gorbachev was under pressure from both the right, especially the military, and the left, pro-democracy forces. William J. Perry, Undersecretary of Defense for Research and Development during the Carter administration, provides one of the best wrap-ups on the performance of high-tech military equipment in the Gulf War that we saw anywhere, "Desert Storm and Deterrence," Fall, although he shies away from drawing any long-range deterrent strategy out of Desert Storm, other than the warning: "No one should be deluded into believing that the military capability that can easily defeat an army with 4,000 tanks in a desert is going to be the decisive factor in a jungle or urban guerrilla war."

In the above mentioned "The Road to War," *FA* editors also note that "1990 was indeed a 'defining moment,' but the shape of the post-Cold War order was far more uncertain at the end of year than it had seemed at the beginning." An attempt to provide some defining shape to that "order" was the theme of "Toward the Post-Cold War World," Spring, nomiated by *FA* editors for 10 Best consideration. In this adaptation from the forthcoming *American Defense Annual: 1991-1992*, John Lewis Gaddis, the Distinguished Professor of History and Director of the Contemporary History Institute at Ohio University, authoritatively outlines a post-Cold War international environment where the U.S. tries to maintain a balance between the forces of integration and fragmentation. "We need to maintain a healthy skepticism about integration: There is no reason to turn it into some kind of sacred cow. But we also need to balance that skepticism with a keen sense of how unhealthy fragmentationalist forces can be if allowed free rein."

FA contributors examined the implications of fragmentation and integration throughout the year. Hanns W. Maull, in "Germany and Japan: The New Civilian Powers," Winter, argues that rather than posing any threat to the international system in general and the U.S. in particular, Japan and unified Germany are harbingers of a new age of international actors enmeshed in webs of economic interdependency. "New Civilian Powers" seems a paradigm, if an unintentional one, of the whole debate of centralization versus decentralization, Maull contending that this system will make national governments both more and less important, arguing at one point, for example, that because of its nature economic power will not be manipulated by national governments — "the implications of interfering with interdependence may be unpredictable and very costly for all concerned," while later writing that "interdependence will imply intense conflicts over the distribution of its costs and benefits — and continue heavily to involve national governments."

Theodore H. Moran, in "International Economics and National Security," Winter, provides a quick survey of current international economic problems, offering policy prescriptions that tend to split the difference between competing schools of thought, such as this passage on Japan:

"American policy, therefore, faces the task of preventing the political process from tilting too far in either direction, toward Japan-bashing at one extreme or toward toleration of economic imbalances at the other." V.P. Gagnon, Jr., in "Yugoslavia: Prospects for Stability," Summer, offers a detailed case study of the dangers of fragmentation.

While *FA* likes to maintain variety in its contributors, several are perennials, including George F. Kennan, whose contribution this year, "Communism in Russian History," Winter, provided a somber curtain-raiser to events in the Soviet Union. Kennan wrote dispassionately, yet chillingly, on the "calamity of epochal dimensions" imposed on the Soviet people by the October 1917 Revolution, and its implications as the country tries to move into the post-communist age. Kennan's warning on the dangers of the Soviet territory splintering apart resounded throughout 1991.

The editors at *FA* are paying more attention to such global issues as the population explosion and the environment, publishing this year "Population Change and National Security," Summer, by Nicholas Eberstadt. Eberstadt, a Visiting Fellow at the Harvard University Center for Population Studies and a Visiting Scholar at the American Enterprise Institute, shatters several myths about population growth, including its perceived connection to poverty and environmental decline, and looks ahead to the near future where, if present trends continue, the majority of the world's population will be living in what is known now as the undeveloped world. "Imagine a world, indeed, very much like the United Nations today, but with rhetoric in the General Assembly informing policy on a global scale, directing actions affecting the lives of millions of people on a daily basis."

We hope that the editors bring this kind of fresh, original thinking to other issues, including GATT, the European Community, the World Bank and the IMF, in the near future, challenging the myths surrounding these institutions.

Editor:	William G. Hyland
Address:	58 East 68th Street
	New York, NY 10021
	(212) 734-0400
Circulation:	1990 — 115,000
	1991 — 117,626

Foreign Policy

Other journals may be vehicles for the voice of the U.S. foreign policy establishment, but *Foreign Policy* sees its role as providing a forum for fresh, ground-breaking perspectives on the events foreign policymakers are talking about now, while positioning readers for the developments foreign policy experts will be talking about five to ten years down the road. Naturally, this calls for discrimination and foresight, and through the years editor Charles William Maynes and *FP*'s editorial staff have exhibited a discerning eye and remarkable prescience; separating thinking-on-the-margin from marginal thinking and the hysterics from the historical. Of course, not every grape is vintage and not every piece that appears in *FP* improves with age, but more often than not, whether we finish an *FP* article feeling either illuminated or outraged, we know that at least we have been engaged in the on-going foreign policy debate.

FP does not see itself as favoring any one particular school of thought, which is not to say that Maynes is not outspoken on the major events of the day. In 1991 the major event was the Persian Gulf War, and in a provocative essay written on the day the war began, "Dateline Washington: A Necessary War?" Spring, he answers his own question in the negative. Anticipating the worst (but covering himself, such as writing "Even if the casualties are light, because war is always a gamble, historians will have to ask whether the gamble was prudent"), he studies the main reasons advanced for going to war with Iraq and dismisses each one, arguing for example, that it was the world's military response, not Iraq's initial invasion, that is endangering world oil supplies. At the end Maynes zeroes in on the support the war is receiving from Jewish interests in the U.S., and argues that ". . .the crisis in the Middle East has moved beyond a point where the United States can continue any longer to pay greater attention to the domestic sensitivities of others than to its own interests."

Not surprisingly (especially, we suspect, to Maynes), the article touched off a firestorm of criticism from prominent Israeli supporters, including AIPAC and *New Republic* Editor-in-Chief and Chairman Martin Peretz. Maynes replied to his critics in his response to a reader's letter in the Summer issue, denying that he was impugning the patriotism of Jewish-Americans by noting how few of them are in America's volunteer armed forces and arguing that they were failing to note that he had also called on Washington to use its new leverage to move the Arab states toward acceptance of Israel. Maynes went on to discuss the growing trend to "delegitimate public discussion of sensitive topics" in the U.S., citing such examples as the plight of African American families and the "politically correct" movement on the nation's campuses. "Will honest discussion of Middle East issues also be ruled out of bounds?" Evidently not while Maynes has anything to say about it.

The Middle East and the attendant issues raised by the Gulf War were examined thoroughly in the pages of *FP* during the year, the editors and contributors tackling such delicate issues as Arab democracy, Israeli human rights violations, and the U.S.-Israeli relationship head-on. Tom Farer, in "Israel's Unlawful Occupation," Spring, draws a parallel between Iraq's occupation of Kuwait and Israel's hold on the occupied territories, writing that "While there is no causal connection between them, Iraq's and Israel's actions are certainly parallel in the limited but important sense that each involves the violation of similar legal duties," and goes into detail on Israel's violations of the Fourth Geneva Convention, like a prosecutor presenting a case before a jury. Perhaps the case can be made, but we feel some perspective could have helped — like the human rights records of the rest of the Middle Eastern coalition against Iraq.

In the forward-looking 10 Best nominee "Reforming Israel — Before It's Too Late," Winter, Leon T. Hadar, a former New York correspondent for the *Jerusalem Post,* argues that "Instead of accommodating itself to the changes in the international and regional environment,. . .Shamir's Israel is beginning to occupy a position comparable to that of Fidel Castro's Cuba," and calls on the U.S. to begin using its influence on the Israeli electorate to begin bringing about changes in that country's economic and foreign policies instead of settling for "business as usual." Former Carter administration domestic adviser Stuart E. Eizenstat, in the timely and important "Loving Israel — Warts and All," Winter, examines the "evolving attitudes" of Jewish Americans from the days when they had "images of ever wise and just Israeli prime ministers and of Israel generals who combined Napoleon's strategic genius, General George Patton's determination, and Audie Murphy's personal courage," to the present, when "American Jews are moving from a one-dimensional, idealized vision of Israel to a more realistic view in which Israel is loved, warts and all." Our appreciation of the Hadar and Eizenstat articles increased as the year progressed.

Of course, the Arabs came under scrutiny in *FP* as well. In the 10 Best nominee "The Need for Arab Democracy," Summer, Muhammad Muslih and Richard Augustus Norton contend that "Saddam Hussein is a radical example of Arab malaise," a malaise arising out of the lack of democracy in the Arab world and what they view as the maldistribution of wealth and population. They call on the U.S. to sponsor Conference on Security and Cooperation in Europe-styled negotiations in the region to deal with such issues, or "baskets," such as human rights and the environment, and we thought that while it's possible negotiations with Israel might help bring about democracy and social justice in the Arab states, somehow it seems doubtful. After all, peace with Israel did little for the lot of the average Egyptian. In a similar vein, Ahmad Chalabi, in "Iraq: The Past as Prologue?" Summer, draws on the "liberal and democratic" constitutional monarchy of King Feisal I and recent declarations by contemporary opposition groups to argue that "Democracy. . .is possible in Iraq," but argues simultaneously that the ethnic diversity of Iraqi society will both serve as a protector of democratic government and be less of a factor once the dictatorship is gone, underscoring the difficulties that democracy will face in a fractured country such as Iraq. *FP* also provided an important piece on another of the major players in the region, the Palestinians, in Marin Indyk's "Peace Without the PLO," Summer, Indyk establishing the newly-aligned constellation of power in the Middle East which opened the way for the peace talks in Madrid in the fall.

The above three essays were placed in a conceptual framework by former CIA official Graham E. Fuller in "Respecting Regional Realities," Summer. Fuller warns that a restoration of the pre-war status quo in the Middle East will represent a failure of U.S. policy, and calls for the establishment of a Palestinian state tied to a negotiated resolution of the Arab-Israeli conflict, along with the introduction of democracy into the Arab world, which he views as essential for ending the "paranoid" way the Arabs currently view themselves and the world.

We also appreciated "Dateline: Washington: Victory and Delusion," Summer, by Martin Walker. As post-war euphoria was reaching its zenith, the Washington bureau chief of *The Guardian* whips the confetti away from his eyes long enough to contend that the Gulf crisis was a disastrous distraction from America's domestic ills and the growing crisis in the Soviet Union. He also punctures the growing myth that Operation Desert Storm was virtually risk-and-error-free, zeroing in on such military shortcomings as the fact that allied aircraft flew less than two sorties a day during the air war, when, except for an occasional Scud, allied air crews were operating under peacetime conditions: "Had NATO air forces managed only two sorties per aircraft per day in a European war, the commissars would be in 10 Downing Street by now."

Those commissars Walker mentioned also played a large role on the world stage once again this year, and *FP* played a key role in placing headline events on such developments as the nationalism issue and Gorbachev's deteriorating political position in proper prospective. Martha Brill Olcott, in "The Soviet (Dis)Union," Spring, concisely argues how Gorbachev's carrot-and-stick approach to the rise of nationalism, the carrot being economic reform, the stick being military crackdown, has been a complete failure because of Gorbachev's insistence on preserving the Union at any cost. We also receive a critical look at Gorbachev's tenure in office in Dimitri Simes's "Gorbachev's Time of Troubles," Spring, Simes documenting how Gorbachev has brought himself to this critical passage in Soviet history where the country lays uneasily poised between chaos and crackdown because of his "own acknowledged failure to understand how fundamental were the deficiencies of the system he wanted to improve, and where the logic of his reforms would lead." As for the U.S., Simes calls on policymakers to appreciate the stake the U.S. has in a peaceful resolution and accept that the Soviet Union as it now exists has no future, while realizing that there is little Washington can do to shape the outcome: "Events in the Soviet Union have their own dynamics that rarely correspond to American preferences."

FP has always made an effort to search for what it feels are authentic voices of key non-U.S. players in world developments which significantly impact on the U.S., and it was in this tradition that associate editor Thomas Omestad traveled to Moscow during the spring to solicit a package of essays from participants in the on-going debate over that country's future. The result was two essays from both sides of the growing Soviet divide which held up relatively well after the events in late August.

From the right, Viktor Alksnis, the so-called "black colonel" and a founder of the *Soyuz* faction in the Soviet parliament, wrote on the dangers to democracy by the rush to independence by republics attempting to short-circuit the established proceeding for secession in "Suffering From Self-Determination," Fall. While Alksnis did not participate directly in the coup attempt, his essay enabled us to understand why it was the imminent signing of the new republic treaty that proved to be the spark that lit the fuse. From the left, Artyom Borovik, former foreign editor of *Ogonyok* magazine and current editor in chief of *Sovershenno Secretno,* argued in "Waiting for Democracy," Fall, that democracy was impossible in Russia until the union dissolves and the generation of leaders that came of age under Stalin has passed from the scene: "The fundamental contradictions in the policies of Gorbachev himself reflect the same contradictions in the minds of his generation."

Even as the Soviet Union was dissolving *FP* was already looking to the problems ahead, including the fundamental question of how to manage the post-Cold War world. The editors were evidently concerned that the end of the U.S.-Soviet rivalry may make the world safe not for democracy but for future conflicts, and debated the possible outlines of the new world order throughout the year. Former Defense Department official Earl C. Ravenal, in "The Case for Adjustment," Winter, a 10 Best nominee, sees both the United States and the Soviet Union as exhausted superpowers and predicts that the international arena in the years ahead will see a system of "general unalignment" of nations and a policy of nonintervention by the United States and other nations. "The shape of the entire system — as well as the conduct of the individual members — is moving beyond the determinative reach of either the United States or the Soviet Union. The age of the superpowers is passing." However, former U.S. diplomat Marshall Brement in "U.S.-U.S.S.R.: Possibilities in Partnership," Fall, advances the idea of Washington and Moscow working together, in a "comprehensive structure of superpower cooperation," in such vital areas as banning the spread of high tech weaponry to the third world, peacekeeping missions (he sketches out how such a joint mission could be a key element of a Middle East peace accord) and humanitarian efforts. It is an attractive notion, the "eagle and the bear teaming up to stop the thief of Baghdad," in the words of John le Carre, but Brement glosses over how the rest of the world might react to such an arrangement, although we can already picture both the Chinese and the French having a terminal case of the vapors.

As the unipolarists and multipolarists continued to battle it out in the nation's op-ed pages and think tanks, Ted Galen Carpenter, in "The New World Disorder," Fall, zeroed in on what he saw as the "essence" of President Bush's increasingly fuzzy vision of a "new world order," the idea of America as an enforcer of international law and protector of national sovereignty. "Washington would become either the social worker or the policeman of the planet — or, in a worse case scenario, it would seek to play both roles." Carpenter argues persuasively that while America cannot withdraw from the world, neither can it allow its policy agenda to exceed its resources, an argument that echoes Walter Lippmann's criticism of President Harry Truman's policy of containment. "Instead of embarking on quixotic crusades for global stability or global democracy, the United States should use the end of the Cold War as an opportunity to adopt a less interventionist role." The essay is weakened only by making virtually no mention of international economics.

FP understands that the role of the U.S. in the world will be a key domestic political issue, and in the 10 Best nominee "Bush's Foreign Policy: Masterly and Inaction," Fall, Terry L. Deibel, a professor of national strategy at the National War College, delivers a dissenting opinion to the prevailing conventional wisdom that whatever his domestic failings, the President deserves high marks for his handling of foreign policy. While Deibel gives Bush high marks for restoring day-to-day competency in American foreign policy while de-emphasizing ideology, he contends that "in broad policy toward Eastern Europe, the Soviet Union, and China, in crafting a genuinely new world order, and — perhaps most important — in facing the pervasive domestic weaknesses that hamper U.S. national security strategy, Bush has failed to provide the kind of leadership these revolutionary times require." Deibel ties Bush's perceived lack of strategic vision to his lack of convictions, and while his criticism is informed, it is also all over the ideological map, Deibel finding much in the Nixon, Carter, and Reagan presidencies to both compliment and condemn. As to the U.S. role in the new world order, Deibel offers little more than a call for more aid to the former Soviet bloc and lowered deficits at home: "The Bush administration offers foreign policy without strategy, management without leadership, a kind of competent drift." Perhaps, but the administration's critics fail to offer a viable alternative here.

The rest of the world was not totally ignored in the pages of *FP* this year, with many of the articles trying to fit regional issues into the post-Cold War environment. This was especially true in its contributions on Europe. In the 10 Best nominee "The Case for Leadership," Winter, Stanley Hoffmann warns that unless European security structures such as the EC and the CSCE are strengthened, the future of Europe could be decided by Berlin and Moscow. These fears were echoed somewhat in "Keeping America in Europe," Summer, by Jenonne Walker, a sharp critique of U.S. policy toward Europe, which Walker, a senior associate at the Carnegie Endowment, regards as being outdated with its insistence on using NATO as its forum for European involvement. Walker argues that the U.S. risks being marginalized as the threat of a Soviet invasion dissipates and European concerns turn to such matters as economic integration and nationality disputes, concerns that will be handled through continent-wide structures such as the EC and the CSCE.

Relations between Moscow and Berlin were the focus of "U.S.S.R.-Germany: A Link Restored," Fall, by W.R. Smyser, the best look we saw all year, anywhere, on the geopolitical ramifications of the new German-Soviet relationship. Smyser, a former counselor for political affairs at the U.S. embassy in Bonn, observes that in many ways German-Russian relations have returned to the state they were in during the late 19th century and the time of the Reinsurance Treaty, which means that Germany, a NATO member, will be in the position of respecting Moscow's interests and preserving Soviet stability while still relying on Washington for security. Smyser believes Washington, Bonn, and Moscow can pull this off, with some deft diplomacy: "All three countries have to cooperate to make the work of each effective." Smyser does not need to be remind us of what happens when German-Russian relations become ineffective.

The Third World was not slighted in the pages of *FP* during the year either. Among the stand-out efforts were Tina Rosenberg's "Beyond Elections," Fall, a 10 Best nominee that stepped beyond the usual cliches of debate over Latin American policy to argue that elections alone are not the only, or the most reliable, indicator of democracy in Latin American countries. Rosenberg connects the development of Latin American countries to their colonial past, and draws on the writing of de Tocqueville to contrast those societies where people are "*inhabitants*," and governing institutions have little legitimacy, and societies where people are "*citizens*," with a stake in the preservation of the social order. Andrew Mack, in the timely "North Korea and the Bomb," Summer, examines North Korea's nuclear weapons program and its implications for the peninsula, sounding an early alarm on what, by the end of the year, was brewing into a potentially serious international crisis. In the 10 Best nominee "Dateline China: The People's Malaise," Winter, by Judy Polumbaum we learn why the post-Deng environment looks hazy to outsiders — it is because nobody in China has any clear idea either.

FP also continues to search out issues that may seem tangential to traditional foreign policy concerns, but which do have an impact on the formulation and implementation of U.S. foreign policy or which affect the societies U.S. foreign policy is designed to deal with. Environment is one example, and in "A 'No Regrets' Environmental Policy," Summer, C. Boyden Gray, counsel to the president, and David B. Rivken, associate general counsel or the Department of Energy, energetically defend the administration's much-maligned international environmental policy, arguing that it is both necessary and more productive to balance environmental concerns with economic development, social stability, and national sovereignty. We learn how environmental resources have been, and will continue to be, sources of conflict in the Middle East, in M.A. Adelman's "Oil Fallacies," Spring and Joyce R. Starr's "Water Wars," Spring, both pieces adding to our understanding of how commodities can lead to conflict.

Culture and its impact was another concern. U.S. State Department official Michael Vlahos, in the 10 Best nominee "Culture and Foreign Policy," Spring, provides an exercise in foreign policy as anthropology, arguing that the future international environment will be shaped not by globalism or tribal nationalism but by "cultural area villages" transcending national boundaries and that the U.S. will have to drop the illusion, created and sustained during the cold war, that the rest of the world wants to become just like us: "On the contrary, if America continues to despoil its ideals in the stubborn pursuit of the conceit once called 'being a superpower,' the world will begin to spurn such ideas."

However, William S. Lind, in "Defending Western Culture," Fall, vigorously argues that conservatives searching for a post-Cold War agenda can find one in defending "Western culture" which he equates with "Judeo-Christian values" and man's attempts to control his environment. While Lind sees a U.S. increasingly besieged by such outside forces as Latin American drugs, militant Islam, resurgent Hinduism, and an increasingly powerful China, he writes that "America's strategic aim should be to connect itself to as many other cooperative power centers as possible, in supportive fashion, while isolating its enemies." Lind makes a thought-provoking case, but he himself writes that the West has put itself through three "civil wars" in less than a century and one still has the feeling that, even with the collapse of communism, the West will continue to be its own worst enemy, and that if it falls, it will not be due to Shining Path or the 12th Inman but by its own hand.

International economics continues to be one area where *FP* falls short, offering few essays dealing directly with the subject and its contributors rarely addressing it in their work on a variety of topics, many of which impact on or are influenced by the international economic scene. The editors seem to recognize that economic insitutions such as GATT, the G-7, and the European Economic Community will assume greater importance as mechanisms for managing the new international system. We hope that *FP* will bring the same degree of sophisticated skepticism to the debate over these institutions as it has to other major developments on the international scene. *FP*'s reluctance to comment on or explore the relentless failures of these institutions in the past has been one of the publication's major shortcomings.

Editor: Charles William Maynes

Address: 2400 N Street, NW
                Washington, DC 20037
                (202) 862-7940

Circulation: 1990 — 27,724
                1991 — 27,500

Fortune

We've noticed a subtle but favorable shift in editorial priorities at *Fortune,* a new interest in pertinent political and economic issues. We still hear stories of editorial intervention from Time Warner's corporate headquarters, and the publication is still dominated by CEO polls that gather too many blue chippers who say too little. Its economic forecasts tell us next to nothing about what's moving the economy, and germane policy analyses are noticeably more frequent. The decision to open a bureau in Moscow is perhaps the most striking indication that *Fortune* is attempting a turnaround. But while the publication has made strides, it still has miles to go before it can return to its esteemed position as the flagship business periodical that once commanded the attention of the nation's decision-makers.

There are also heartening signs that editor Marshall Loeb, who has been accused of handling *Fortune* more like a profit center than a sacred trust, is now focusing on the publication's traditional editorial mission. Reacting decisively to the outbreak of war, the editors made an impressive decision to replace the scheduled annual cover, "America's Most Admired Corporations," traditionally one of the top three sellers of the year, with a three-article special report that went to press on the third day of fighting.

The editors are also giving more space, if not more thought, to important economic issues. In addition to numerous lengthy articles on the state of the economy, *Fortune* has added "Economic Intelligence," a new column of ideas, analysis, and commentary that follows the "Fortune Forecast." While we appreciate the magazine's increased attention to this subject, it is quite obvious that the writers and editors observe the economy from a Fortune 500 standpoint, offering scant analysis of entrepreneurial capitalism. Indeed, it is the GMs, GEs and IBMs of this world that most often capture coveted spots on the cover of *Fortune,* and it is probably no coincidence that most of the publication's advertisers come from the upper echelon of business. But as this year's Fortune 500 cover story, "Who May Thrive Now," 4-22, by Terence P. Pare, makes clear, the 1980s, which created new competition for the nation's giants by providing capital to a long dormant entrepreneurial sector, changed the very nature of the Fortune 500: "In general, the 1980s proved a far more tumultuous decade than the 1970s. In 1980, roughly three-quarters of the companies that had been on the 500 ten years earlier still remained on the list. But by 1990, nearly half those on the 500 in 1980 had fallen off."

It is with this new reality that *Fortune* must come to terms. Michael Dell, pictured on the cover of the magazine's "America's 100 Fastest Growing Companies," 10-7, by Alan Deutschman, started Dell Computer in 1984 from his University of Texas dorm with $1,000 savings. "By beating IBM and Compaq on service and price, Dell Computer has shot to $679 million in sales, a sure bet to make its debut on the next Fortune 500. Dell, 26, will be the youngest entrepreneur ever to join this exclusive club. . ." With access to capital no longer hindering intellectual potential, it takes a few years rather than a few decades to reach the ranks of the Fortune 500. But instead of rejoicing in this new dynamic, some voices at the publication seem to be on the defensive, somewhat hostile to the forces shaking up their "exclusive club." Typical of this mentality was "The Deal Decade: Verdict on the '80s," 8-26, by Edmund Faltermayer of the *Fortune* board of editors. With little more than anecdotal evidence to back up his arguments, Faltermayer is highly critical of highly-leveraged buyouts, recapitalizations, takeovers, junk bonds, and other financial tools popular in the '80s. By viewing the fact that "more than a third of the Fortune 500 industrials were swallowed up by other concerns or went private" as a purely negative development, and characterizing debt as inherently bad, Faltermayer fails to see that some of these same financial tools provided capital to thousands of entrepreneurial non-investment grade companies that created millions of new jobs, thousands of new products, and a more competitive U.S. business environment. By the end of the article, his "verdict" looks hollow indeed. Oddly, contributing editor Anne B. Fisher sent out a very different message four months earlier in "Don't Be Afraid of the Big Bad Debt," 4-22. In contrast to Faltermayer's characterization of corporate debt, Fisher provided a credible, well-documented argument that "Corporate debt isn't as onerous as you might suppose." "The debt Cassandras wail that leverage hurts American companies' ability to keep up with global competitors. Because debt service is consuming so much of their cash flow, the argument runs, U.S. corporations can't spend as much on research and development as their rivals overseas and are hard put to scare up the capital for global expansion. Both worries are legitimate, but there is surprisingly little evidence to sustain either." Her conclusion: " 'Both in the U.S. and globally, the competitive battle won't be won on the basis of who is more highly leveraged,' [Stephen Roach] says, 'but rather who is more productive. And debt can be a tool for productivity.' " While Faltermayer's message certainly gets much more play on the pages of *Fortune,* Fisher's contrary perspective exposes the forces of change at the magazine. The type of editorial inconsistency displayed in these two articles is rare at the publication, and reveals that perhaps a debate about the new realities of what it takes to make the Fortune 500 is taking place. Of course, with lending and venture capitalism constricted during this recession, Pare's observation in "Who May Thrive Now," cover 4-22, that the 1990s should be rewarding for a host of Fortune 500 companies with "a sharp focus, *deep pockets,* and the wit to exploit their intellectual capital" could foretell a return to the earlier days of the Fortune 500, when giants didn't need to dance and entrepreneurs had no access to the "exclusive club."

The magazine's Washington bureau is also struggling for its identity. Lee Smith and Robert Norton attempt to tackle significant news stories emanating from the nation's capital, but Ann Reilly Dowd continues to weigh down the bureau's credibility with her lollipop profiles of the administration. While Lee Smith crystallized the major themes of the war in his forward-looking "What Comes Next," cover 2-11, Dowd contributes little more than trivia with "How Bush Decided," — a comment from George Bush's brother, who Dowd refers to as "William 'Bucky' Bush," and a note that the president "even went to bed on January 16 at his regular 11 p.m."

If the rest of this piece had wowed us with insights maybe we could have swallowed the rest, but this was nothing more than a re-hash jazzed up with trivia. Her follow-up, "Winning the Peace: What's Next for Bush," cover 3-25, is a little better, at least touching on the pertinent issues — the U.S. role in Middle East peace, the frailty of the U.S. economy, the 1992 elections — but there's virtually no scrutiny. She notes that "Bush and his team seem untroubled by the prospect of a string of domestic stalemates. Aides feel they already have a fine list of legislative accomplishments on which to run. . ." The fact that voters might not tolerate a passive approach to the recession or other policy issues is a non-issue for Dowd. Even as the Beltway debate over the recession was at a zenith, Dowd carelessly dismisses any chance that fiscal policy would do any good over the next twelve months — "That's already baked into the cake," her only contribution to the debate in "How George Bush Could Lose," 11-18.

Meanwhile, Smith and Norton try with mixed results to get beyond the fluff. Smith weighed in with several strong pieces, his best, "A Cure for What Ails Medical Care," 7-1, offers the "shrewd-consumer model" as a cure for the nation's growing health insurance problem. Based on free-market principles and the perceptive observation that consumers make the most practical decisions about their own money, and thus create a more competitive environment for health-care providers, Smith's plan asserts that the individual, not his or her company or the government, should be responsible for the purchase of health insurance. Also worth noting was Smith's "How the Average American Gets By," cover 10-21, an inspiring anecdotal look at Middle America's financial dreams and frustrations, and "Trial Lawyers Face a New Charge," 8-26, which examines the difficulty of reversing the hemorrhaging costs of product-liability suits.

Rob Norton provided a mixed portfolio this year. His "Alan Greenspan's Strategy Now," 4-8, was one of the more insightful analyses of Greenspan's leadership of the Federal Reserve that we'd seen in the business weeklies, giving us a good feel for the man and the policymaker. And he gets part of the equation right in "Should You Worry About the Deficit," 10-7, noting that the government should cut spending and not raise taxes, but missing the bigger picture that deficits don't take as big a chunk out of the GNP if the economy is growing. "Far more troubling than the deficit's level is its trend. After peaking in 1983 at 6.3% of GNP and hovering around the $200 billion mark through 1986, the deficit actually fell during the late 1980s, both in dollar terms and, more sharply, as a percent of GNP. . .This year, the net deficit will be up to $222 billion, or 4% of GNP." This is good reporting on the numbers but where's the analysis of why the situation turned sour so quickly. Similarly, he gives us plenty of data to chew on in "What Ought To Be Done About Taxes," 3-25, but loses credibility with vague, unsubstantiated statements about the effects certain tax cuts would have on the economy. His "Lessons From the Recession," 11-18, reveals a complete lack of understanding of the dynamics of the recession.

Profiles of Fortune 500 companies remain a mainstay at the magazine, and we must admit, when correspondents set out to dissect a company's strengths and weaknesses, their profiles rival the best at any business publication. For example, successfully reining in most of the "heavy-handed commentary" we criticized last year, Carol Loomis did a magnificent job of dissecting the problems leading to IBM's earnings dive in "Can John Akers Save IBM?" 7-15, a 10 Best selection. Supported by a cache of revealing details, she is critical where appropriate and appreciative where proper. This professionally-handled piece is a model of business journalism. "Indeed, the biggest indictment of Akers's management would seem to be that he has failed to fix IBM's marketing problems. He came from the world of sales. Surely he should have managed to whip it into shape. He is still trying. Under way is yet one more revamping of U.S. marketing. . ." Technology companies are ably covered by associate editor Brenton R. Schlender from San Francisco, his "How Fujitsu Will Tackle the Giants," 7-1, the best we'd seen on this anonymous computer colossus. Intelligent and perceptive, Schlender portrays the people and strategies behind Fujitsu and its U.S. investments, such as Amdahl. On the other hand, his "The Future of the PC," cover 8-26, marks the tenth anniversary of the personal computer with a re-heated overview of what's to come and an accompanying photo opportunity for Microsoft's Bill Gates and Next's Steven Jobs in "Jobs and Gates Together," a bust of an interview, as neither one has anything to say. Peter Nulty weighs in with a fitfully interesting "The New Look of Photography," cover 7-1, a primer on new photo technologies that is too gee-whiz on the gizmos and too promotional of Kodak.

Bill Saporito remains a stellar analyst of the ups-and-downs of a retail industry struggling through a recession, but he was too hyped up in "Melting Point in the Plastic War," 5-20, exaggerating competition in the business which he says "vibrates with testy lawsuits, back-stabbing business practices...as exciting as a shark feeding frenzy." On the auto industry, veteran Alex Taylor, III weighed in with such newsmaking stories as "The Odd Eclipse of a Star CEO," 2-11, which speculates on the reasons former Ford CEO Don Peterson departed the company, and delves into the question of where Ford is going, and how fast, under new CEO, Harold Poling. Taylor was at his best for "BMW and Mercedes Make Their Move," 8-12, an excellent exploration of Mercedes and BMW's strategic plans as they release their latest models in the lucrative U.S. market where they must compete with a growing number of Japanese competitors. Other polished efforts in this genre were Thomas A. Stewart's "GE Keeps Those Ideas Coming," cover 8-12, a look at how the man who wrote the book on management, CEO Jack Welch, is rewriting it, and "America's Most Successful Merchant," cover 9-23, by senior editor John Huey, a savvy profile of Wal-Mart's Sam Walton.

When the correspondents move away from analyzing specific companies, and try to make broad generalizations about management trends, they sometimes stumble. Thomas Stewart's "Brainpower," 6-3, is a low-wattage cover story on the role of intellectual capital as "corporate America's most valuable asset and...its sharpest competitive weapon." There's a little too much reliance on aphoristic-style insights, simplified to the point that they have little impact, or resonance; the subject great, but Stewart's treatment almost pedestrian. While Brian Dumaine's "The Bureaucracy Busters," cover 6-17, tackles the interesting topic of how too much bureaucracy can hinder the creative process, his conclusions too general to be really useful to top managers. Similarly, *Fortune*'s special issue, "The New American Century," spring/summer 1991, was an enterprising project that simply took on too many broad topics to cover any of them satisfactorily. One of the worst of the year was Kenneth Labich's "Can Your Career Hurt Your Kids?" cover 5-20, a hand-wringing bit of tripe that sounds like a rejected script from "Thirtysomething." One exception to this rule was Brian Dumaine's "Closing the Innovation Gap," cover 12-2. Not only does Dumaine and his sources make some striking points about the U.S.'s "dearth of managers who know how to drive the creative process," but he perceptively recognizes the role of interest rates and taxation in the innovation process: "High real rates force managers to avoid gambles that might be worthwhile if the stakes were lower and to bypass projects that don't promise a fast payback — projects that other nations, with lower real rates, will tackle. Perhaps worse, a capital gains tax higher than in virtually any other developed country slashes the rewards of successful innovation. An adventurous startup that doubled in value over the past decade would provide its investors with a return, after inflation and the capital gains tax, of just over 1% annually. Under those rules, why bother?"

The most worrisome undercurrent for *Fortune*'s writers continues to be the threat of editorial interference from the executive offices of parent company Time Warner Inc. One glaring intervention surfaced on the pages of *The Wall Street Journal* in an article by Laura Landro entitled, "Writer Quits Fortune, Citing Meddling by Time Warner," 6-26. The report asserted that Graef S. Crystal, an expert on executive compensation who has prepared the magazine's list of highest paid executives for the past four years, informed editors he would not prepare another survey, citing editorial interference. "In the most recent survey, in Fortune's June 17 issue, [Time Warner chairman and CEO] Mr. [Steven J.] Ross topped the list of highest-paid executives with 1990 compensation that Mr. Crystal valued at $39 million, almost double the next-highest-paid chief executive on the list...[Crystal] originally calculated the value of the options Mr. Ross had been granted at more than $100 million. After consulting with Fortune editors, Mr. Crystal said that to get the survey published, he agreed to break all large stock-option grants in the survey into thirds, resulting in the $35.8 million valuation for Mr. Ross's options." These are the types of charges that continue to weigh on *Fortune*'s credibility.

On the foreign front, the big-wigs at Time Warner were on hand for the opening of its bureau in Moscow. With typical *Fortune*-esque fanfare, Time Warner editor-in-chief Jason McManus, *Fortune* managing editor Marshall Loeb, and international editor Donald Holt flew over for an official opening celebration for 125 guests. Soviet president Mikhail Gorbachev unexpectedly chose the visit to grant the magazine's long-standing request for an exclusive interview; *Fortune* editors proudly noted that it was his first ever with a U.S. business magazine. But what could have been a journalistic coup for the infant bureau turned out to be little more than a public relations coup for Gorbachev and *Fortune*.

Executive Editor Allan T. Demaree plugged the interview by recounting some of Gorbachev's praise for *Fortune* in "Editor's Desk," 12-31-90: " 'I welcome the leaders of such a powerful, world-renowned, and authoritative publication as *Fortune*,' [Gorbachev] said. 'I read articles from your magazine.' Loeb and McManus thought they would have 15 minutes, but the Soviet leader clearly wanted to deliver a message and gave them 45. '*Fortune*,' he said, 'has to make profound analyses, get to the root of things, see what is happening and how it will develop.' " And deliver a message was just what Gorbachev did in "What Gorbachev Wants From Business," 12-31-90; *Fortune*'s profound analysis, however, was conspicuously missing in what turned out to be more of a speech by the Soviet president than an interview with him. The new bureau chief, Paul Hofheinz, seemed to play virtually no role in the interview, but that's just as well for his credibility. The piece read like a press release from *Izvestia*.

Fortunately, the big guns went home a few days later, leaving a very competent Hofheinz to go about the neglected task of scrutinizing the situation in the U.S.S.R. His first major piece, "The Soviet Winter of Discontent," 1-28, provides a striking portrayal of the unraveling of Soviet society amid economic decline. But Hofheinz is noticeably vague about the flawed economic strategies causing the deterioration. He penned his best work following the failed coup d'etat, "Let's Do Business," 9-23, an impressive assessment of the problems and promise that lie ahead for the Soviet political economy. Hofheinz deftly touches upon on all the cogent issues: the need to stabilize the Soviet currency, political and economic cooperation between the republics, etc. We do, however, wish he had more closely scrutinized the problems with Grigori Yavlinski's austerity plan. Hofheinz seems to have a strong grasp of Soviet culture and politics, and if he continues to hone his understanding of the Soviet economy, this potent writer could become an influential voice from Moscow.

Under the expert direction of Carla Rapoport, *Fortune*'s Tokyo bureau has long been a yardstick for other business magazine bureaus in Japan. Her ambitious probe of the shifting relationship between the U.S. and Japan, "The Big Split: Japan Vs. the U.S." cover 5-6, was laudable political-economic reportage, although we were surprised that she overlooked the significant advantage afforded Japanese investors by that country's low capital gains tax rate on equities, an incentive not available to American investors. Otherwise, Rapoport deftly depicts Japan's increasingly polemical rhetoric toward the U.S.: "Don't blame us, say more and more Japanese. Most revealing is a report titled *Japan, the U.S., and Global Responsibilities* [which]. . .states that the U.S. must abandon its preoccupation with the bilateral trade imbalance: 'The U.S. should stop regarding each new tack in its efforts to resolve the trade imbalance as a panacea.' Looking at the matter coldly, the Japanese are right. While Americans earnestly push for a level playing field, the Japanese know that such a field doesn't exist." Susan Moffat, who left the magazine midyear, supported Rapoport in Tokyo with such impressive reports as "Picking Japan's Research Brains," 3-25. Rapoport was reassigned to the London bureau in the fall, leaving the Tokyo post unfilled. With Paris correspondent Shawn Tully stateside since December 1990, and no new assignments yet made to that European city, Rapoport will have her hands full as *Fortune*'s only correspondent in Western Europe.

As for the difficult task of getting someone to fill Rapoport's shoes in Tokyo, Hong Kong correspondent Ford S. Worthy has expanded his coverage for the time being to encompass Japan, producing the best work we've seen from him in a long time. His "Asia: Can the Koreas Get Together?" 2-11, is a sweeping analysis of the powerful economic and political forces impregnating the post-Cold War Koreas with the notion of change, and perhaps ultimately reunification. Rich in history, Worthy's essay examines how changing superpower relations are rewriting the future of the Koreas: "Before perestroika, Kim Il-sung could bank on a bailout by Moscow. But the shift from barter trade to hard currency may prove a body blow. More than half of North Korea's foreign trade is with the Soviet Union, including nearly half of oil imports. The North may be able to switch some purchases from the Soviets to China, its second-largest trading partner and still a loyal ally. Kim has asked Beijing for more aid, but because of its own economic struggles, China is hardly in a position to become North Korea's major benefactor." Other topnotch pieces by Worthy include "Japan's Smart Secret Weapon," 8-12, an insightful look into the "fundamentally different" and seemingly "imprecise and loosely joined" way the Japanese forecast, monitor and interpret costs. "Like its famed quality philosophy, Japan's cost-management system stands Western practice on its head. For example, American companies developing a new product typically design it first and then calculate the cost. If it's too high, the product goes back to the drawing board — or the company settles for a smaller profit. The Japanese start with a target cost based on the price the market is most likely to accept. Then they direct designers and engineers to meet that target." It's known as "target costing" and it sounds simple, but Worthy makes clear that the impact on profitability is profound. Also stellar was his "The Pacific Rim: Keys to Japanese Success in Asia," 10-7, a smart look at why Japan fares so much better in Asia than the U.S.". . .what distinguishes the Japanese approach is an emphasis on flexibility, information gathering, and personal relationships. Squishy as they seem, these concepts are as central to Japan's selling successes in Asia as are its quality products." But Worthy doesn't leave this as a nebulous concept, providing a bundle of credible examples to back up his assertion.

There are small heartening signs of change at *Fortune,* but indications are that these new ideas will blossom slowly. For the time being the publication continues to struggle to find its identity under the management of a much-changed parent company, and in a much-changed business environment where "exclusive clubs" are no longer so exclusive. Its "top-down" perspective on the workings of capitalism remains, we think, its most serious deficiency.

Editor: Marshall Loeb

Address: Time Warner, Inc.
Time-Life Building
Rockefeller Center
New York, NY 10020-1393
(212) 586-1212

Circulation: 1990 — 672,042 National
1991 — 681,850 National

FW

In 1902 a 25-year-old named Louis Guenther founded a publication which he intended to be "a forthright and honest journal, which would discuss the pitfalls and merits of various securities." In the 90 years since that precise editorial mission was laid out, *FW* has greatly expanded its scope — at times adding rich new dimensions to its coverage; at other times straying too far, losing sight of its original purpose. Just last year, we raised yellow flags about the magazine's growing tendency to wander off in too many unrelated directions. This year, *FW* celebrates its 90th anniversary with a new mix at the top of its masthead, including a new deputy editor, John F. Berry. The changes have re-focused and re-energized the publication. Gone are the ambiguous, sometimes contradictory, social policy pieces that we questioned last year; back in the spotlight are the financial and investment reports that were Guenther's trademark.

FW cover stories were decidedly more focused on business and industry profiles, with occasional forays into peripheral management issues, such as R&D, benchmarking and labor. But we found none of the vague and preachy social policy covers like "How Doctors Have Ruined Health Care," cover 1-9-90, or "Betting the Country," cover 2-20-90, that we were critical of last year. Alexandra Biesada sheds fresh light on an old technique that has quickly become a popular buzzword in corporate headquarters across the nation in "Benchmarking," cover 9-17, a worthwhile look at the hows and whys of studying and emulating the methods used by a company that excels in a particular activity. "Listening to Labor," cover 9-3, a special report by chief correspondent Dan Cordtz, was one of the better Labor Day analyses we saw, providing a unique perspective on how worker involvement programs are empowering employees and supplementing, rather than undermining, labor union representation. Cordtz's other special report, "Corporate R&D," cover 10-1, constructs a credible case to support his thesis that "Perhaps it is not inept R&D that lies at the heart of the U.S.'s competitive decline, but rather inept R&D management." Indeed, we saw great improvement in Cordtz's reporting this year. The former television correspondent made a distinctive break with the 30-second-sound-bite style we criticized last year, and provided rich, informative examinations of pertinent issues. Unfortunately, he didn't write much until the latter half of the year, spending most of the first half preparing *FW*'s 90th commemorative anniversary issue, "American Business: The Golden Century," 6-25.

On banking, Robert Wrubel's "The Empire Strikes Back," cover 1-22, gives us the low-down on the Bank of America's return to prominence. He credits the bank's turnaround under former CEO Thomas Clausen, but notes that ". . .the real factor. . .was luck. . .[W]hen interstate banking fever struck California commercial banks in the late Eighties, BofA was too hamstrung to make any of the high-premium, high-dilution acquisitions that such competitors as First Interstate are only now paying the price for." Now BofA is picking through the ruins of the industry and pays blue plate special prices for sick banks and thrifts: "It's a nice deal all around. BofA gets to grow fast and cheap." Senior writer Wrubel, one of the strongest correspondents on the *FW* masthead, was on leave for most of the year, writing a book about Northrop, but returned late in the fall with "GM Finally Fights Back," cover 11-26, a fascinating exploration of General Motors that takes us down in the trenches to discover that, despite a dismal financial year, GM is now beginning to see positive long-term results from its major corporate restructuring in the 80s. Jack Willoughby's probe of Citicorp's "tubocharger of growth" in "Too Big to Fail," cover 8-20, is savvy reporting on the institution's double leverage which constitutes "a staggering 146% of the company's fully consolidated net worth — which means for every $1 of equity reported to shareholders, there's an additional 46 cents in debt working as equity in the subsidies."

On real estate, Adrienne Linsenmeyer brushes aside the political ball and chain that weighs down the Resolution Trust Corp.'s sales of assets in "Priming the Dump," cover 3-19, and provides a number of straightforward business suggestions to reverse the stagnation of S&L assets. Robert McGough has been producing outstanding work on the airline industry all year. His "Changing Course," cover 7-23, is a very vivid visit with Bob Crandall, the CEO of American Airlines who is about to redirect his company for a second time in a decade. McGough focuses on Crandall's "combative" style of management, not a new topic, but captures it with such flare and amazing detail that we discover new aspects of Crandall's management personality, as well as his opinions on the economics of the industry: ". . .he argues that, at least in the airline industry, there is actually more competition nowadays than under regulation. In 1978, American Airlines held a monopoly on 30% of its routes and shared duopoly on 35%. Today, it has at least three competitors on every route — although some of those competitors are weak indeed. 'If we went back to regulation, we would be returning to a circumstance where creativity and imagination and entrepreneurial vigor isn't valued,' says Crandall. 'You do that to any business, you destroy it.' "

The business of sports is gaining noticeably more attention at *FW,* but the correspondents are still finding their footing on the subject, the quality of the reporting still variable. The one sports cover story, "How Much America's Pro Teams Are Worth," 7-9, by Anthony Baldo with Alexandra Biesada, Holt Hackney, Michael K. Ozanian and Stephen Taub, was an enterprising attempt to strip professional sports franchises of their cloak of secrecy, and provide a ballpark estimate of their financial worth. We're not sure if this new focus on sports will be embraced by *FW*'s conservative investment audience, but we were impressed by this particular endeavor.

The magazine continued its traditional CEO of the year cover in 1991, honoring Cap Cities/ABC's Daniel Burke in "Cap Cities/ABC Hangs Tough," 4-2, by Anthony Baldo. On the international front, *FW* also paid tribute to "Europe's CEO of the Year: Lord Hanson of Hanson Plc," and "Asia's CEO of the Year: Joichi Aoi of Toshiba," cover 10-15. To be sure that the two CEOs received equal billing, *FW* put Hanson on half of the covers and Joichi Aoi on the other half. This was a little hokey for our tastes, but the profiles found inside more than made up for this public relations ploy. Sharon Reier expertly handled the Hanson profile, giving us an excellent feel for his commitment to the shareholder and to entrepreneurial capitalism in its purest form. Richard Meyer's profile of Joichi Aoi, on the other hand, focused primarily on the CEO's very personal management style. We were glad to see that there was less hype surrounding the CEO of the year coverage this year, and meatier reporting. We described last year's cover on GE's Jack Welch as "an exclusively positive, almost cult-like piece." This year, there was more depth, and noticeably less fluff.

Also on the topic of CEOs, *FW* replaced last year's trendy "Wall Street's 100 Highest Paid," 7-10-90 with a much more insightful "Compensation 500," cover 10-29, by compensation expert Graef S. Crystal who became a contributor to the magazine this year following a fallout with his former employer *Fortune,* which he had accused of manipulating his compensation calculations in order to make it look like Time Warner Inc.'s chairman Steven Ross was compensated in the $30 million range rather than the $90 million range. What makes *FW*'s "Compensation 500" unique is that it is much more than the useless list of CEO compensation figures found elsewhere. Instead, it is a potent and revealing examination of what these top CEOs *should* be paid, and actually recommends specific dollar amounts for pay raises or cuts based on Crystal's complex quantitative analysis.

We also appreciate *FW*'s unique survey of the nation's cities and states. At first glance, such topics don't seem to blend in with the magazine's investment focus, but in fact readers who follow the municipal bond markets will find the information in these reports quite useful. Katherine Barrett and Richard Greene present an ambitious study of everything from the economic relationship between city and state to privatization of public services to suburban annexation and taxation in their special report, "American Cities," cover 2-19. Dan Cordtz's contribution, "Managing New York," stands out as one of the best in this eight-article survey, revealing how the Big Apple's burgeoning bureaucracy has made the city sluggish through waste and unconstructive policies: "Some 330,000 people work for the city, more than for any private company in the state of New York. Over the past decade that number has risen by 50,000, while the population growth (according to the Census Bureau) has been stagnant. The trend is especially striking in the school system, where employment has rocketed by 40% since 1980, although the number of pupils remains the same." On a broader scope, *FW*'s second annual probe of the financial status of the 50 states, "The State of the States," cover 5-28, also by Barrett and Greene, took on special significance this year with the multi-billion dollar shortfalls haunting state legislators and governors. Although it is difficult to judge the accuracy of *FW*'s rankings, we took a look at New Jersey, where *MediaGuide* is published, and found this prescient comment six months before the November elections: "Political Notes: Governor Florio's bull-in-China-shop tax changes not dissimilar to ongoing efforts in other states. . .Conventional wisdom says Republicans may take both houses in November."

One area that still needs a lot of work is *FW*'s coverage from the capital. We have not been impressed in recent years with D.C. bureau chief James L. Srodes' direction, or should we say lack of direction, for the bureau. The work produced by Srodes and D.C. correspondent Lauren Chambliss is inconsistent in quality, and does not usually complement the magazine's financial reportage with pertinent economic policy analysis. For instance, we weren't sure how Chambliss's criticism of Congress's charade of campaign contribution reform, "Big Pack Attack," 4-16, fit into *FW*'s mission, especially since Chambliss concludes the piece by blatantly advocating taxpayer financing of campaigns as the best way to create a level playing field by eliminating PAC money: "What can be done? Probably the answer would be public financing — that is, taxpayers' money — to pay for all campaigns. . .That would put an end to the money-grubbing by politicians and special interests." She is much more judicious in "Hang 'Em High," 7-9, a muscular examination of the "worrisome powers" of the U.S. Sentencing Commission which plans to extend its dubious rules to cover the sentencing of corporate defendants effective November 1: ". . .the commission has the awesome power to virtually eliminate judges' personal discretion in handing out sentences to individuals convicted of federal crimes." But once again the pertinence for *FW*'s audience is vague. Much more relevant was her "Capital Gains R.I.P.?" 1-22, a succinct summary of how the administration fumbled the ball on a capital gains tax cut, and the dim prospects for a cut in 1991. There's nothing especially fresh here, but Chambliss makes clear that behind-the-scenes support is growing even though the Bush team seems inclined to "switch rather than fight." Now there's an issue of importance to investors. Chambliss went on leave in September and will be returning in mid-1992. That leaves Srodes as *FW*'s lone voice from the capital. If he flushes out hard-to-find details as he did on the top-to-bottom restructuring of commercial banks and financial markets in "Forced to Reform," 1-8, the bureau will fare just fine, but if he leaves as much unexamined as he did in "Rude Awakening," 9-17, a mere skim of the Treasury auction reform movement embracing Washington, then we'll be searching out his byline less and less. Surely the editors of such a well-informed financial magazine are cognizant of the fact that the investment climate is directly affected by the policies that swirl out of Washington. Why the magazine's Washington bureau remains so undirected is a puzzle to us.

One of the most promising decisions made by *FW* editors this year was to move talented Southeast bureau reporter Sharon Reier overseas to Amsterdam where she has filed consistently superb reports since January. Shunning the broad economic and political themes that permeate coverage of Europe, Reier has opted instead to pen in-depth profiles of individual European enterprises, expertly weaving in the political and economic policies influencing each company. We find her reporting technique extremely insightful and useful. For instance, Reier's "Gas Goliath," 1-22, skillfully ties in the regulatory and financial pressures shaping British Gas's controversial bid to become a global player.

Tokyo correspondent Richard Meyer is also getting more play this year, although his work remains average. Such pieces as his contribution to the 3-5 cover, "Split Image," asserts that half of Japan is vigorously pursuing globalization, while the other half is only feigning it. This is an interesting theme, but Meyer devotes only two paragraphs to what could have been the basis for the entire article: "The main barrier to true globalization is the Japanese equity structure. Stock is cross held and very little finds its way into public hands, so companies are dominated by Japanese institutions." He's better in "Inside the World's Most Powerful Bank," cover 4-30, a surprisingly candid conversation with Yoh Kurosawa, president of the Industrial Bank of Japan. But as with many of his profiles and reports, the emphasis is more on management philosophy than finance, more on peripheral details than decisive facts. In the case of this report, Meyer leaves the financial analysis until the second half of the piece. One thing that Meyer should be applauded for is his even-handed coverage of Japanese business. All too often Tokyo correspondents practice bashing rather than reporting on Japan, an exercise Meyer does not engage in.

On the whole, *FW* editors stand out as some of the best in the business at focusing their international and domestic correspondents on a single theme. Even though *FW* has fewer correspondents than some of the bigger business weeklies like *Business Week,* the editorial coordination necessary to fully capitalize on its network of journalists is still commendable.

Indeed, *FW*'s editorial mission has become increasingly international. The magazine's "Global Reports" get sharper each year. This year's outstanding "International Issue," 3-5, focused on trade and finance, a subject bound to please *FW*'s sophisticated investment audience. Stephen Kindel kicks off this 11-article cover story with "The New Corridors of Power," 3-5, a brilliant assessment of the unstoppable forces of international trade. In another perceptive contribution, "Super Bank," cover 3-5, Kindel teams up with Amy Barrett to examine the Bank for International Settlements' "steadily growing role in supervising international banking practices." The authors advise that whether the international community agrees with BIS policies or not, it should heed this super bank's growing sphere of influence. Sharon Reier weighs in with "Dutch Takeover Treats?" 3-5, a stellar examination of some of the crucial battles that are being fought as the EC struggles toward integration, in this case, the dilemma of the Dutch companies which have built in airtight "technical barriers" to deter takeovers: "Critics believe that such airtight defenses are what keep price/earnings ratios low on the Amsterdam Stock Exchange. And there are institutional investors who protest that the power managers have comes at the expense of the shareholders." On the other hand, Reier notes, German EC commissioner Martin Bangemann has originated a proposal to encourage European takeovers to meet competition from Japan and the U.S. "Under the Bangemann proposal, Holland's armory of 'technical barriers' would be abolished. 'But,' objects Sib Bergsm, executive vice president of finance for Akzo, the major Dutch chemical and pharmaceutical company, 'the Bangemann proposals only limit technical barriers and do nothing to attack structural barriers. In the Netherlands, we would be left with hardly any defenses, and France and Germany would be inaccessible. They want a level playing field, but it is becoming more unlevel than before.' "

"Empires of the Sky," cover 5-14, a 10 Best nomination, was another stellar global report, and the most forward-looking assessment of the shaken airline industry we'd seen all year. Packed with authoritative quotes and creative ideas from industry insiders around the world, this outstanding nine-article exploration whisks us through all the fascinating dimensions of the industry's emerging global order — from the effects of deregulation to the practical consideration of global liberalization to the possibility of multinational airlines to how to get Swiss flambe on a Swiss Air flight leaving Islamabad.

The magazine's 11-12 global report on real estate, however, was not as cohesive as the others. While the report carried some interesting snapshots of real estate markets around the world, it was noticeably oriented toward the U.S., and wasn't as cognizant of the interdependence of global markets. For instance, the lead article in this nine-piece report, "Real Estate," by Adrienne Linsenmeyer, points to the removal of restrictions by the Garn-St. Germain Act in 1982 as the start of the U.S.'s real estate problems. But, only a few paragraphs earlier she says, "Today, the real estate crisis is as real in Japan, the U.K. and Sweden as it is in the U.S." These foreign markets don't fall under the jurisdiction of U.S. legislators, but Linsenmeyer never ponders what might have been the common problem that drove these countries down a similar path. Linsenmeyer's "Go East Young Developer," is the best of the bunch, giving us a crisp sketch of real estate development in space-starved Berlin where "the banks are willing but the bureaucracy is not."

Although not a cover story, the magazine's global report on the media, "The Enemy Within," 4-16, spearheaded by senior editor Anthony Baldo was quite good. As with sports, *FW* has turned a spotlight on the media industry, regularly carrying reports on specific media companies and trends. We were especially appreciative of Ellen Benoit's contribution to this nine-article report, "The C-Word," cover 4-16. Amid talk of reregulating the cable industry, Benoit gives a smart, contrarian perspective on how competition is working in several markets and, if encouraged nationwide, would prove much more effective.

As for *the* international story of the year, the war in the Gulf, *FW* was swept up in the wave of apprehension that overtook the media in the weeks before the 1-15 deadline. Stephen Kindel wandered beyond his original theme, the impact of war on the U.S. economy, to forecast the worst in "Imperial Overstretch?" 12-25-90: ". . .history tells us that with a few notable exceptions, wars are always long, drawn-out affairs. American military history is filled with miscalculations. . ." "Speaking Out" columnist Kermit Lansner followed up in the same issue with an equally pessimistic "Countdown to War?" in which he underestimated public support for Bush's stance on the conflict: "Where we stand now is that the original arguments for our involvement in the Gulf have lost their power — if not their validity. . .if the President cannot muster the support of the American people, the country will be in for a messy and tumultuous time."

Like *Forbes, FW* is not editorially designed for breaking news and thus didn't carry a cover story on the outbreak of war like *BusinessWeek* and *Fortune.* The magazine did, however, produce a handful of pieces related to the crisis. One of the best, Adrienne Linsenmeyer's "Saddam Hussein's U.S. Oil Man," cover 1-8, appeared just before war ensued. Linsenmeyer reports that oil man Oscar Wyatt had been negotiating a sale of 50% of his Coastal Corp's oil refining market with the Iraqi government before it invaded Kuwait. She implies that, despite the trade embargo of Iraq, Wyatt's December 1990 trip to Baghdad was probably more than just humanitarian, as had been reported. Although the evidence is mostly circumstantial and the tone occasionally over-accusatory, the link was certainly worth exploring. *The Wall Street Journal* expanded on the Wyatt story in a 3-11 front-page article. Just weeks before the dramatic Allied victory, though, Washington bureau chief James Srodes penned a one-dimensional "The Affordable War?" 2-19, which seemed terribly out of touch with the stock market's confident estimation that news from the Gulf indicated a short, affordable war.

Even after 90 years of publication, *FW* remains capable of change, constantly adapting to a shifting investment climate. We have seen dramatic improvement in the publication over the last year, and feel confident that this dynamic business biweekly will continue building on its strengths and working diligently to overcome its weaknesses.

Editor: Geoffrey Smith

Address: 1328 Broadway, 3rd Floor
                 New York, NY 10001
                 (212) 594-5030

Circulation: 1990 — 500,000
                 1991 — 500,000

Harper's

For more than 140 years, *Harper's* has gathered and imparted ponderings and ruminations from a cross-section of American thought. The quirky and the mainstream, the humorous and the sobering, frivolity and profundity, somehow fit together between the pages of *Harper's,* gratifying the publication's eclectic, but loyal, audience. While the work that appears in the "Readings" section of the magazine is reprinted from other publications, there are several original essays in each issue.

We find it increasingly difficult to read through "Notebook," the editorial offering of editor Lewis Lapham. We've simply tired of that form of sound and fury that he attempts to pass off as serious thought and criticism, but is merely self-centered pretentiousness and haughty weariness. Lapham substitutes polished, fiery invective for critical analysis, and we learn nothing new from his efforts. That is certainly the case with "A Pardoner's Tale," 1-91, in which he uses the occasion of a discourse on Ronald Reagan's *An American Life* to prattle and ooze cosmic flatulence: "The book doesn't bear reading. . .If we accept the Reagan autobiography as anything other than an insult and a mockery, we commit a kind of suicide. History embodies the triumph of memory over a spirit of corruption, and if we deny the truth of our existence, we lose the right to our own names."

Another glaring example of his snobbish perspective was "Justice Horatio Alger," 9-91, on the nomination of Judge Clarence Thomas to the Supreme Court: "If Judge Thomas didn't espouse Justice [Thurgood] Marshall's liberal views (if, in fact, he was a doctrinaire conservative best known for his liege man's service to the mean-spirited bias that Marshall detested), well, then, too bad, and so much the worse for the adherents of the hated L word. Let the civil rights people bitch and moan and whine; let the National Association for the Advancement of Colored People worry about finding its way out of the maze of conflicted feelings." Lapham seems utterly unaware that, in the guise of care and concern, he has conveyed a glaring bias that *all* black people and organizations must subscribe to the "L word," and that "conflicted feelings" are somehow an affront to a people that Lapham considers of one mind and ideology. We doubt that he would invoke such generalizations if he were discussing a political organization not dominated by blacks.

Lapham also produced a major essay last year outside of his editorial column, "Democracy in America," 12-90, and the responses to it in the Letters to the Editor pages 2-91 give us a bead on *Harper's* readership and audience. We found revealing this agitated letter from a Chicago reader:

> Democracy in America? It's only the folks with the money and/or the guns who ever use the word 'democracy' and think that they mean it. It's a justification to them. Go ahead. Try to take them up on it. The meaning of it. The MEANING of it. See just how quickly the money and the guns come a-pounding at that flimsy little door.
> As I write this, the sun has barely come up. There's a police siren blaring through my open window. Someone less than honorable (i.e., poor) wanted something he could not buy. Same sad story. . .

We do still find fine writing n the monthly. "Passing Views," 1-91, by Edward Hoagland, was a delightfully relaxing yet stimulating ride on a transcontinental train, looking for America. Anton Shammas, of course, may always be depended upon for his similarly well-written observations on the land of the free from the perspective of a Palestinian. We get a fine taste of his particularities in "Amerka, Amerka," 2-91: "Maybe I will never cease to look East for my images and metaphors, no matter how deep I have travelled into the American way of life." James Traub's "A Counter-Reality Grows in Harlem," 8-91, was a jarring look at the "reductio ad absurdum" found when the radio dial is tuned to "The Gary Byrd Show."

Washington Editor Christopher Hitchens' "Capital Letter" was an especially delicious examination of *realpolitik* in the Gulf, in which he revealed a game gone tilt with "Why We Are Stuck in the Sand," 1-91. U.S. policy has simply assured that future wars will now be necessary, he concludes. Interestingly, Hitchens looked up some of Saddam Hussein's former friends in the West and discovered that they are in the forefront of today's "Obliterate Iraq" claque. Also provocative was his "Unelected, Unlawful, Unchecked," 10-91, in which he studied how the CIA subverts the U.S. government at home.

On the bicentennial of the passage of the Bill of Rights, *Harper's* "Forum" feature, "Who Owes What to Whom?" 2-91, focused on whether the expansive talk of individual rights has undermined our notions of obligations and community. Nicely addressed by the participants was the question of whether we need instead a Bill of Duties. In the 5-91 "Forum," *Harper's* posed the question, "What is the New World Order and, in terms of realpolitik, whose is it?" The resulting "Defining the New World Order," 5-91, provided rich and diverse perspectives from Owen Harries, editor of *The National Interest,* Ian Buruma, foreign editor of *The Spectator* in London, and Richard Barnet, co-founder of the Institute for Policy Studies. Another "Forum" feature, "Does the White House Want a Domestic Policy?" 7-91, gathers together Jack Hitt, Richard N. Bond, William Janklow, Jack Kemp and Kevin Phillips for a discussion of the administration's domestic policy tactics. Several of the themes raised by the participants resounded in domestic policy pieces throughout the rest of the year, but what this "Forum" crystallized best was the outward disdain Jack Kemp and Kevin Phillips hold for each other. Typical of their bickering was this exchange:

> Kemp: "Kevin, you needn't fear that anyone believes you are in the business of giving sincere advice."

> Phillips: "I'll give you some sincere advice if you decide to run for president again, Jack. Don't do it!"

Christopher Hitchens's follow-up piece, "The Loyally Complicit," 7-91, was equally hard-hitting with the verbiage, but was much more thought-provoking in its analysis of why Democrats have been reduced to wallowing in centrism and bipartisanship.

Harper's best cover feature had to have been, "She Wants Her TV! He Wants His Book!" 3-91, pairing, in a (mostly) polite conversation over dinner about our image culture, Camille Paglia and Neil Postman. Prof. Postman describes as dangerous "the discontinuity of emotion that television promotes, its unnatural evocation, every five minutes, of different and incompatible emotions." But Paglia retorts that as "there is no sense to reality," then "television is actually closer to reality than anything in books. The madness of TV is the madness of human life." When Postman raises concern, that TV commercials are now the most powerful source of socialization, draining deep religious and cultural symbols of their profundity, secularizing and debasing them, Paglia responds that there's nothing to worry about: "popular culture is an eruption of paganism — which is also a sacred style...it's not that the sacred has been lost or is being trivialized...We've returned to the age of polytheism. It's a rebirth of the pagan gods." Postman is overwhelmed by Paglia, and in fact is driven to drinking more wine and puffing more cigarettes. "So idolatry has triumphed," he observes, and down the road Paglia piques exasperation with one more of many provocative remarks: "I think Jesus was a brilliant Jewish stand-up comedian, a phenomenal improvisor. His parables are great one-liners."

The magazine's "Essay" feature is always worth perusing, providing characteristically fresh perspectives from a wide range of thinkers. In April, Walter Russell Mead, the author of *Mortal Splendor: The American Empire in Transition,* joined *Harper's* as a contributing editor, and will be writing several times a year on international relations and political economy. His first essay, "Dark Continent," cover 4-91, takes us on "a grand, grim tour of the New Europe" where ancient and dangerous strains of nationalism bubble beneath the surface. Especially outstanding was Louis Menand's "What Are Universities For?" cover 12-91, a sweeping essay in which Menand asserts that the real crisis on university campuses is not how much T.S. Eliot versus Alice Walker students are reading, but the purpose of a university, its very identity in modern society. The "insistence, on the part of academics and nonacademics alike, on making higher education the site for political and social disputes of all types, and on regarding the improvement of social relations and the mediation of political differences as one of higher education's proper functions, has produced ridiculous distortions. Thus we have a debate, for example, in which the economic rights of women are argued about in terms of reading lists for introductory literature courses — as though devoting fewer class hours to male authors might be counted a blow against discrimination in the workplace." Reflective and fresh, and a perfect example of the best of what passes through the clearinghouse of ideas known as *Harper's*.

Publisher:	John R. MacArthur
Editor:	Lewis Lapham
Executive Editor:	Michael Pollan
Managing Editor:	Ellen Rosenbush
Address:	666 Broadway New York, NY 10012 (212) 614-6508

Circulation: 1990 — 201,754
                1991 — 203,180

Harvard Business Review

Although it was an impressive year on the editorial front for *HBR*, 1991 at the venerable magazine will probably be remembered for the internal strife that spilled over into the daily press. Fortunately, despite the reported cloakroom politics and infighting, the bimonthly journal carried first-rate articles for the harried operating manager as well as for the academician and management consultant.

The turbulence surfaced in a *New York Times* piece by Allison Leigh Cowan titled "Management Citadel Rocked by Unruliness," 9-26. Cowan reported that senior staffers were chafing under the reign of editor Rosabeth Moss Kanter, whose management style was described as imperious and arrogant. Although none of those involved would be quoted, the *Times* piece reported that in April editorial director Alan M. Webber and managing editor Nan Stone petitioned Harvard Business School dean John H. McArthur to have Kanter relieved of her day-to-day duties. The article also said that two associate editors, William Taylor and Bernard Avishai, had left the publication after clashing with Kanter. Cowan observes: ". . .there is a tale worthy of a business case study in how such a well-respected management journal got to be the Beirut of the business press, and, in particular, how [Kanter] a noted expert in motivating employees and on misuse of power in the workplace could have left herself open to political snipers."

One of the criticisms found in the *Times* piece however, perplexed us, that is ". . .the review has been so starved for copy that its staff has been doing what was once unthinkable: It has been calling lesser-known authors and dropping hints that their submissions might be welcome." From our view, the masthead continues to be filled with top experts like Robert B. Reich, Peter F. Drucker, and George Gilder. In fact, we think *HBR* places too much emphasis on big-name bylines. Reich's "Who Is Them?" 3/4-91, which coincides perfectly with the release of his new book *The Work of Nations: Preparing Ourselves for 21st-Century Capitalism,* was not worth the time. And although we usually appreciate a Peter Drucker piece, his "Reckoning With the Pension Fund Revolution," 3/4-91, was perhaps his six zillionth piece on the subject, and surprisingly redundant for a pace-setting publication like *HBR*. Only George Gilder's superb "Into the Telecosm," 3/4-91, a breathtaking reconnaissance of the breakthroughs that will come from the domain of reality governed by the action of electromagnetic waves, is distinguished.

As for the *Times* report, it's difficult to evaluate how much of this to-do was legitimate and how much was standard office politics. In terms of what *HBR* published, however, 1991 was a quality performance, starting with a 10 Best nomination, "The Computerless Computer Company," 7/8-91, by consultants Andrew S. Rappaport and Shmuel Halevi. The piece argued that, by the year 2000, the most successful companies will buy computers rather than build them, and predicted dire consequences for old-line manufacturers. George Gilder hailed the issue as "the most important HBR published in the last decade. . .Rappaport and Halevi have fathomed the essence of an economic era."

Another troubled industry that came under the *HBR* spotlight was banking. The 5/6-91 issue led with "A Blueprint for Financial Reconstruction," an article by McKinsey & Co.'s Lowell L. Bryan drawn from his book *Bankrupt* which was surely the focus of many congressional discussions of how to reform the banking and financial services sectors. The same issue included a lively, funny and provocative piece by computer entrepreneur Safi U. Qureshey, "How I Learned to Live With Wall Street," 5/6-91, that should be required reading for start-up managements contemplating a public offering. The piece, which appeared in the "First Person" column is a perfect example of why we like this new department so much.

The broad spectrum of service industries was examined in a superb 9/10-91 issue, with a particularly fine piece by Stephen S. Roach, "Services under Siege — the Restructuring Imperative," that demonstrated how feeble productivity gains have been in the U.S. service sector. And a welcome skeptical contrarian viewpoint on the recycling boom by Harvard Business School Prof. George C. Lodge and Assistant Prof. Jeffrey F. Rayport, "Knee-Deep and Rising," showed how well-intentioned environmentalism can be a marketplace fiasco.

As for *HBR* departments, "Four Corners" is designed to engage an international audience by exploring "business insights that cross borders." But in 1991, the section did anything but that. Typical of the section were such articles as professor Arpad von Lazar's quaint but unenlightening "Work and Unity: Germany the Morning After," 3/4-91, or the picturesque "China's Grasp and Hong Kong's Golden Eggs," 5/6-91, by journalist Kevin Rafferty. Both were pleasant, descriptive cultural essays, but offered virtually no decisive or fresh business insights to engage busy international managers. The concept of "Four Corners" has immense potential, but the choice of articles will have to be much more selective to make this department effective.

The "HBR Case Study" is much more useful, offering hands-on advice from top managers on a variety of difficult but common business dilemmas such as "The Case of the Downsizing Decision," 3/4-91, by Alan S. Train; "The Case of the Environmental Impasse," 5/6-91, by Alissa J. Stern; and "The Case of Unequal Opportunity," 7/8-91, by Mary C. Gentile. "In Question" taps perspectives from business and academia to explore questions of business's role in society. One outstanding examination was "Is American Business Working for the Poor?" 9/10-91, by Mary Jo Bane and David T. Ellwood, the piece offers a startling graph entitled "How Work Can Penalize the Poor," and offers enterprising, no-nonsense ideas on how to increase the economic value of work. And finally, in the "Debate" section of the magazine "readers and authors face off over *HBR*'s last issue." We appreciate this section because it often adds another dimension to our understanding of topics already discussed in the publication and provides continuity between issues.

In addition, the magazine continues to devote many pages to letters to the editor — by far the most expansive letters section of any business periodical. This makes the back of each issue rather like a computerized "bulletin board" for ideas, responses and debate. The list of signatures at the bottom of the letters often reads like a who's who of the corporate world and business academia. In fact, the letters section is often the first part of the magazine we turn to after a skim of the table of contents.

On the negative side, *HBR* still has a tendency to let its ego get in the way of its coverage. The global survey commissioned by Kanter, "Transcending Business Boundaries: 12,000 World Managers View Change," 5/6-91, which reportedly was so formidable a challenge for the publication's staff that the magazine came out late, resulted in pages of tedious, unremarkable reading. And Kanter's two pages of "From the Editor" that begin each issue can be safely skipped. Although the magazine commendably devotes many pages to an interview format with notables, the Q&As are too frequently of the softball, "Oh tell me, great man" variety, and need to be sharpened with more critical questioning. A perfect example was editorial director Webber's "Crime and Management: An Interview with New York City Police Commissioner Lee P. Brown," in which Webber doesn't challenge Brown's admiration of Sweden's "full employment" policies even as Swedish voters were preparing to vote out the government for such costly socialist policies. One exception to this was William Taylor's sharp interview with ABB Asea Brown Boveri's Percy Barnevik "The Logic of Global Business," 3/4-91, which gives a lucid explanation of how a "multidomestic organization" arranges itself and strategizes to maintain the flexibility necessary to succeed in a global economy made up of many unique nations.

Taken as a whole, it was a good for year for *HBR*. Here's hoping that during 1992 the publication can make more news in its own pages and less in the business press about their internal conflicts.

Editor:	Rosabeth Moss Kanter
Address:	Soldiers Field Boston, MA 02163 (617) 495-6182
Circulation:	1990 — 205,700 1991 — 212,000

Human Events

The tried and true conservative counterweight to the liberal and leftist press, *Human Events* remains the editorial conscience and spiritual guide to traditional conservative movement. A reliable barometer of the conservative philosophy, *HE*'s writers and editorialists are consistently challenging the ideological purity of those in power, particularly in the White House.

HE was one of the first publications to wonder about the invincibility of the President. The editorialists also questioned early the utility to the conservative cause of John Sununu, who many within the movement at one time thought to be an asset. The lead editorial "Will Sununu Sink Conservative Hopes for Bush Policy Changes?" 12-15-90, points out the then-Chief of Staff's hostility to conservative lawmakers such as Rep. Newt Gingrich, "and, as is now well known, Sununu rudely treats even Bush supporters who dare, not to challenge, but just question the wisdom of the White House. Yet Sununu, many insist, is crucial to getting the President to agree to a conservative agenda for 1991 and 1992, since nobody trusts Dick Darman to carry water for conservatives, no matter what he 'agrees to' in his bargaining sessions with Gingrich, Weber and others." The writer predicts that there will be a conservative contender to run against Bush in the primaries: "For a variety of reasons, including apprehension over the Administration's Gulf policies and grave disappointment with the White House's performance during the recent budget battle, conservatives are increasingly talking up a possible challenge to George Bush in 1992." The editorialist picks former Delaware Gov. Pierre (Pete) DuPont as the frontrunner for the race. A few months later, a hopeful Jeffrey Hart asked "Will Gordon Humphrey Challenge George Bush?" 2-9, in New Hampshire, probably the best training ground for conservative candidates. The discontent within the movement that was evident in *HE*'s pages early this year surely helped lead conservative Pat Buchanan to declare his candidacy in mid-December.

This is the adversarial course *HE* stayed throughout the year, questioning the administration's ideological commitment to the conservative cause by challenging the ideological purity of its policies in order to shift the tenor of debate. *HE* is never anti-administration, necessarily, or anti-Bush, or even anti-Democrat, but steadfastly, unalterably pro-conservative. Often the criticisms are framed in terms of the people around Bush, rather than the President himself, and thusly *HE* is able to argue reasonably without sounding or seeming disrespectful. In "Conservatives Troubled by Bush's Education Program," 5-11, the editorialist questions the feasibility of Bush's ideas on education. There is, though, a hardline rebuttal to Irving Kristol's *Wall Street Journal* op-ed, "The Conservatives Find a Leader," 6-3. In "George Bush Is *Not* The Conservatives' Leader," 6-22, which the editors at *HE* nominated for consideration in our 10 Best section, the editorialist soundly rebukes Kristol and any conservative who would buy the idea, particularly when it comes to taxes: "The President, as we've noted before, did not just slightly 'bend' off his no-tax pledge when he signed off on that budget deal; he shattered it beyond recognition. . .the legislation actually *raised* marginal tax rates — which Bush also pledged he wouldn't raise — and then, amazingly, virtually ruled out *future* tax cuts, including the President's own capital gains tax cut, which he had repeatedly stressed was essential for restoring this country's economic health! Conservatives are supposed to be satisfied with this record, to believe that the man who presided over this disaster is our leader? Give us a break." Other items on taxation were equally virulent and prescient; as early as the State of the Union address, *HE* was questioning the President's commitment to the domestic agenda, and recommending HUD

Sec. Jack Kemp as "the point man for his [Bush's] growth-oriented domestic agenda," in "Bush's 'State of Union' Gets Mixed Reviews," 2-9. M. Stanton Evans savages Richard Darman in "Budget Debacle Means Darman Should Resign," 8-3: "While being touted as a near-genius by the Washington press corps, Budget Director Richard Darman has been presiding over one of the most shocking disasters in the history of U.S. economic policy." The editorialists are particularly disdainful of Bush's sudden wake-up call in "President in Danger of Kicking Away Economic Issues," 11-2, taking aim as much at his staff as the commander in chief: "Treasury Secretary Nicholas Brady has been arguing that the economy is better than many are saying, and that the country is likely to grow out of the recession. If it ain't really broke, don't fix it, is Brady's theory." *HE* does not mince words. At the same time, the editorialists are supportive of Bush in his battle with Israel, "Bush Is Right to Take on Shamir," 9-28: ". . .Shamir and Sharon appear not to know the real meaning of the word 'thanks.' Their attitude toward the U.S. has been 'give us your money, send us your sons to protect us, subsidize our highly socialist system, and then buzz off. Meanwhile, we're going to continue expanding on the West Bank.' President Bush is saying that he's not going to accept these absurd demands, and he's right."

What's rather refreshing about *HE* is that there is rarely a conventional feel to *HE*'s polemics, the editors instead thinking through their arguments and bringing them to a logical conclusion. The sole example of a knee-jerk perspective that we found, "Conservative Movement Should Take Well-Deserved Bow," 9-7, contained the standard arguments on how all the credit for the fall of communism should be laid at the doorstep of the conservatives. But this was an aberration. We see particularly the creativity and purity of *HE*'s conservative beliefs with the weekly's coverage of the Persian Gulf War. Initially anti-war, and credibly, conservatively so, *HE* came full circle — logically — to support the President by the time the decision to fire had been made, debating the steps throughout the process with "Bush Backers Concerned About 'Land War' Talk," 12-22-90; "Bush Close to Triumph in War Against Saddam," 1-26; "Nation Should Take Heart in Early Gulf Successes," 2-2; and "Hail to the Chief!" 3-9: "Conservatives have never had a big crush on George Bush. But the overwhelming majority of them, along with the nation at large, were lustily singing the President's praises last week over the rout of Saddam Hussein and the liberation of Kuwait. . .For the moment — and it is a heckuva moment — Bush has become the Mother of All World Statesmen." But throughout, *HE* remained cautious, with "Bush Should Rule Our Land War in Gulf Crisis," 1-23, "Baghdad Journalists Endanger Persian Gulf Operation," 2-23, and "Bush Should Stick With Air War Against Saddam," 3-2. Where so many had been urging a full-speed-ahead approach, *HE* examined policies and strategies with a discerning eye, ready to pounce on flawed ideas.

HE was extremely supportive of the Clarence Thomas nomination, as one would expect from a conservative Washington weekly. What was different, and rather refreshing, about *HE*'s support was that it was taken from a purely political perspective, viewing the event in particular from the angle of the Democratic attempts to torpedo the nomination. The lead editorials "Liberals Prepare Fierce Battle Over Thomas Nomination," 7-13; "Liberals Seem Stymied by Thomas Nomination," 7-20; "Thomas Should Triumph in the Lion's Den," 9-14; "Democrats Viciously Twist Thomas' Legal Philosophy," 9-21; "The Borking of Judge Thomas," 10-19; and "Thomas Finally Confirmed," 10-26, all dissect in some aspect the strategems of the Democrats, additionally examining the implications for the failures of the party leaders: "The losers were Democratic lawmakers, who riled their black supporters by opposing Thomas, most of the Democrats on the Senate Judiciary panel and the professional 'feminists' who were unrelenting in their efforts to destroy the nominee," 10-26. These editorials were extremely useful from that perspective.

HE was also persistent in covering the development of the "October surprise" conspiracy theory. This was material *HE*'s editors were especially proud of, having nominated much of it for consideration for our 10 Best section. As early as the 5-25 issue, Herbert Romerstein was casting doubt on the validity of Gary Sick's version of events, "The Sick Tale of a 1980 Reagan-Iran Hostage Deal," taking apart Sick's case point by point, in a manner that was later repeated by both *The New Republic* and *Newsweek* magazines. The political implications of any potential investigation are discussed in "No Probe Needed of Reagan-Bush Campaign," 5-25, with the editorialist concerned about the political power of such an investigation: ". . .before any investigation is concluded, the Bush Administration will be reeling from the wealth of irresponsible accusations and innuendo that will be 'uncovered' and lovingly fed to a hungry media." So thorough was this treatment, according to editors at *HE,* that the authors of the *TNR* article, Steven Emerson and Jesse Furman, turned to *HE* as a source of information before publishing their fine expose, we find in " 'October Surprise' Proves Dud, But Demos Won't Let It Die," 11-23, a rare editorial where *HE* gave itself an obvious pat on the back.

While there are rarely any staff bylines that appear in the magazine, the list of bylined contributors is long and impressive. Warren Brookes, Reed Irvine, Cliff Kincaid, Joseph Farah, Jeffrey Hart, John Chamberlain, Donald Lambro and Cal Thomas, among others, have all appeared in *HE*'s pages. There is even the occasional moderate, such as James J. Kilpatrick, "What Politics of Race and Sex Are Doing to Campuses," 5-11, in which Kilpo reviews Dinesh D'Souza's *Illiberal Education*: "Let this much be conceded to the racists who are promoting remedial racism at American colleges and universities: Our institutions have indeed been remiss in teaching cultures other than Western culture. No other concessions need be made. . .The book is restrained, temperate and devastating."

There's certainly no 'kinder, gentler' perspective maintained at *Human Events.* In an era of mushy conciliation, except on the part of the far-left press which steadfastly clings to socialism, we find this combative attitude refreshing and necessary to the development of a worthy debate over policy and polemic. It is for this reason that we continue reading — and enjoying — this trim weekly tabloid.

Editor:	Thomas S. Winter
Address:	422 First Street, SE Washington, DC 20003 (202) 546-0856
Circulation:	1990 — 28,000 1991 — 24,000

Insight

It was a turbulent year for *Insight,* this up-and-coming newsweekly losing editor-in-chief Arnaud de Borchgrave, having three different individuals in the key deputy managing editor slot and undergoing not one, but two major editorial makeovers. It is a tribute to managing editor Kirk E. Oberfeld and his staff that *Insight* remains editorially sound, able to deliver the goods on the major international stories of the day, while continuing to scoop other publications on stories related to domestic and social issues, a recommended "second read" for news consumers after getting the day's headline events in their newspaper or on TV.

De Borchgrave departed in May, and while he had been titular head of *Insight* since its inception in 1985, he had very little to do with the day-to-day running of the magazine, that responsibility largely falling to the deputy managing editor. Tod Lindberg occupied the post at the start of the year. He departed in May, and his replacement was John Podhoretz, who was returning to *Insight* after a tour of duty at the magazine's sister publication, *The Washington Times.* At the same time, *Insight* underwent its first major editorial re-design of 1991, radically revamping its format beginning with the 5-6 issue, altering both the graphics and the editorial content. Gone were the weekly "Briefings" on Congress, government, foreign news, business, taxes, new technology, health, and the law, which were labor intensive and cut into valuable editorial time. Gone was "The Last Word" at the back of each issue. Gone, also, was any semblance of hard news in the second half of the book.

The new *Insight* opened with "Hall of Shame," which the editors evidently saw as the "mutation" of the briefings sections, and was part of an overall concept of concentrating all short material up front. The "Hall of Shame" features such wings as "Your Tax Dollars at Play," which pokes fun at perceived government abuse of taxpayers' dollars, and "Stop the Pressies," deals with the media, the 5-6 edition criticized the decision by NBC and *The New York Times* to publicize the name of the alleged victim in the Palm Beach scandal. "Blue Smoke and Mirrors," was aimed at various political and social activists, while "School for Scandal" covers colleges and universities. "Hall of Shame" quickly acquired an intent following, many of the items being submitted by readers who had tried to interest their local press in the story first. Like many features that are meant to be calculatedly outrageous, "Hall of Shame," can walk a thin line at times, and in "Your Tax Dollars at Play," 7-8, *Insight* crossed over, running a feature on Senator Edward Kennedy's unpaid parking tickets in Arlington County, VA., "Park it Carefully, Teddy." The item reports that: "The tickets for Kennedy's 1989 Crown Victoria had mounted since September. No word on whether there were women, live or dead, in the car with him." The reference was condemned by readers, and in the 8-5 "Dialog," the editor apologized "if we caused any offense to those concerned with the memory of Mary Jo Kopechne, who was in a car with Sen. Kennedy in July 1969 on the bridge at Chappaquiddick."

The second half of the book was renamed "Cultural Gulch," and featured TV, movie, and book reviews along with articles on show business and cultural topics. The premier stories in the 5-6 issue included a report on an acting school for cats, "The Catsing Couch," and a profile of Wayne Newton, "He Isn't Just Las Vegas Anymore." *Insight* introduced its new look as being "a feistier, visually livelier magazine for the '90s," and that it is putting "a higher premium on telling important stories you'll find nowhere else. We're redeploying our resources to permit us to dig deeper to expose political corruption, hidden agendas and behind-closed-doors deals."

We were disturbed, though, by the paucity of hard news in the 5-6 issue, a feeling shared by *Insight* readers, who made their feelings known in letters to the editor. Oberfeld finally stepped in, with "New Insight on Insight," 7-8, defending the increased culture coverage and the dropping of the health and business sections. "We are not an entertainment magazine. But both high and popular culture are being used more than ever to send political messages about which the public is unaware. We make you aware in such ways as rating the political biases as well as the sex and violence content of the films."

The heavy emphasis was largely due to the influence of Podhoretz, who moonlighted as movie reviewer. As time went on, however, the "Cultural Gulch" label was quietly dropped, and the soft news features slowly thinned out, until a greater balance was created between hard and soft news. Late in the year Podhoretz left, and Richard Starr assumed the mantle of deputy managing editor. *Insight* also underwent its second metamorphosis in 1991. The magazine now runs three or so stories up front, followed by a dozen or so columns written by *Washington Times* regulars such as Richard Grenier, Wesley Pruden and Paul Craig Roberts, under the section heading "Fair Comment." The back of the book now consists of "Reader Comment," "Hall of Shame," and "The Last Word."

The media graveyard is full of magazines that were forced to publicly reinvent themselves, but as we said earlier, for the most part the diminution in *Insight*'s editorial size was not matched by a decline in net quality. *Insight* sees its mission as probing on the key margins of events, and it fulfilled that mission in 1991, turning up original angles on such heavily covered subjects as the Persian Gulf War and original stories on social and cultural issues of the day.

Insight's war coverage was devoted not to headline developments but to comprehensive treatment of important war-related topics that were often shunted off to side-bar status in other newsweeklies. "The Fever Chart on War," 1-28, examines public opinion about the crisis in depth in several stories, including Daniel Wattenberg's "Media Mask View of the Gulf." "The New Face of News," 2-18, provides as fine a look as we saw anywhere on media coverage of the conflict, with particular emphasis on CNN, including "A Little Network Plays Giant Role in Gulf Coverage," by Eric Felten, and "CNN at the Front Line of News," by Jonas Bernstein. Felten, in "War's Price Tag May Fall," 2-25, cuts through the statistics and political posturing to determine the true cost of the war to the U.S., *Insight* coming up with a figure of $50 billion that turned out to be close to the mark. Susan Sternthal, in "Past Glories Shape Destinies of Arabs," 3-4, and Stephen Goode, in "The Call to Jihad Proves a Strategic Call Indeed," 3-4, offer textbook studies of the Arab world. In "A General's Cunning Quashed Saddam," 3-18, Richard Mackenzie scores an exclusive interview with Desert Storm commander Gen. H. Norman Schwarzkopf, who discusses his "Hail Mary" strategy which won the ground war in a matter of days.

We questioned some of *Insight*'s war coverage, however. In an "Editors' note" accompanying an article by Susan Katz Keating on POWs, "Issue of POWs and War Crimes Is an Old One," 2-11, *Insight* stated that it has "chosen not to publish photographs of captured U.S. servicemen, in the belief that publication serves the propaganda interests of Iraq rather than any legitimate journalistic purpose." A noble gesture, to be sure, and one which won *Insight* the thanks of servicemen and their families everywhere, but by taking such a stand, *Insight* seemed to be identifying itself with official conduct of the war, and we believe news publications should maintain at least the appearance of being independent from any government endeavor.

Insight also provided solid coverage on the fallout from the death of communism. The editors feel that *Insight* has been out in front of the competition on the Soviet story the past few years, and while other newsweeklies can also make a credible claim in that regard, *Insight* did provide a number of important and fascinating cover stories on such diverse but related topics tied to the collapse of communism.

Jonas Bernstein, in "Stalking the Past of a Police State," 1-21, vividly captures the moral and political issues raised by the East Germany's secret police past, and in "How to Loot a Nation," 7-8, he is comprehensive on the Sandinista expropriation of government goods and property. His report on the failed Soviet coup, "A More Perfect Disunion," 9-9, is thorough on the nationalist questions poised by the collapse of the Soviet center. In "Patriot Games," 9-2, which appeared the week of the coup attempt, David Brock thoroughly updates us on the political and technological status of Ronald Reagan's Strategic Defense Initiative, while positioning this key national security story for the immediate future. The U.S. navy is afforded the same treatment from Philip Gold in "Anchors Away," 10-7. Henrik Bering-Jensen provides one of the best reports we saw anywhere on the beleaguered Polish economy in "Poles Apart in New Era," 9-23.

Insight featured few cover stories related to U.S. politics in 1991, the editors apparently feeling few political stories warranted cover treatment. There were plenty of cover stories on American society and culture, those subjects being *Insight*'s specialty, the editors selecting an eclectic mix of topics a step or two removed from the daily hurly-burly while still being relevant to readers. They by-and-large succeeded in this regard, with one or two notable exceptions. We generally found these stories to be much more tightly edited this year, without sacrificing length or breadth of coverage, and often increasing the story's impact.

The editors search out cover stories that can be deliberately provocative, such as "Ronald and the Reagan Bashers," 7-22, in which Daniel Wattenberg provides a timely, if unapologetic, defense of the Reagan administration in the face of recent attacks, especially Haynes Johnson's *Sleepwalking Through History* and Lou Cannon's *Role of a Lifetime*. The article features an "exclusive interview" with the former President, but instead of seeing Reagan answering specific questions on such topics as his $2 million speaking engagement in Japan or the renewed questions about the 1980 campaign, the reader is treated instead to the standard Reagan generalities, such as on the federal deficit: "When I hear a congressman talking about 'my deficits' — well, the president can't spend a penny. The Congress is all that can spend money."

Much more successful is Eric Felten's report on "The Times Beach Fiasco," 8-12, an appropriately skeptical story on governmental backtracking on the hazards of dioxin, coming nearly ten years after the EPA ordered the evacuation of Times Beach, MO, where the roads were contaminated with dioxin. Noting that besides being embarrassing for the government, Felten writes, "the politics involve a constituency far more powerful than Missouri homeowners: Vietnam veterans who claim they were put at risk of cancer when exposed to the dioxin-laden defoliant known as Agent Orange between 1962 and 1970."

Stephen Goode, one of the finest writers on *Insight*'s staff, often drew the cover stories on America's growing cultural divide, and produced original, thought-provoking reports on this topic. He provides a fresh look at the heavily-covered "politically-correct" movement on the nation's campuses in "All Opinions Welcome — Except the Wrong Ones," 4-22, a profile of Donald Kagan, dean of undergraduates at Yale and a staunch defender of traditional academic freedom. In the delightful "Mozart Mania," 9-30, he fully captures the various faces of the composer vying for public acceptance, from the party animal of *Amadeus* to dignified adult to the politically correct operas presented by Peter Sellars: "Clearly, the composer comes bursting out of every box he's forced to occupy." His contribution to the controversy swirling around the 500th anniversary of the would-be discovery of the New World, "Debunking Columbus," 10-21, cuts through the revisionist efforts on both sides to find that: "The image of Columbus that becomes ever more clear is a religious mystic half at home in Europe's medieval past."

Helle Bering-Jensen's cover story on "The Neotrads," 10-14, while well written in a mock-anthropology tone, was late, appearing months after *Time* ran a cover on the same topic. The editors thought that her cover story exposing several questionable practices in the publishing industry, "Ghosts in the Attic," 8-19, got buried by the Soviet coup attempt. While "Ghosts" is certainly prodigious in its research, Bering-Jensen tracking down and speaking to several professional ghostwriters, we felt the story lacked the impact of *The New Republic*'s earlier cover story on U.S. publishing. In the revealing "Pay Up or Else," 5-20, Eric Felten exhaustively documents how broadcasters are being forced to pay off pressure groups and law firms who challenge their license renewals or station sales, and the editors felt that this story had the potential to be its most controversial cover story of the year.

That honor went instead to Patrick Boyle's expose of alleged sexual abuse in the Boy Scouts, "The Scouts' Badge of Dishonor," 6-17. We could understand the problems many readers had with this story, sharing them ourselves. The reporting here reeks of innuendo — "Camping trips — in many people's eyes the essence of Scouting — are the most popular places for Scout leaders to have sexual relations with boys," and voyeurism — Boyle drawing on court testimony to take readers inside the tents where sexual abuse allegedly occurred. Indeed, the bulk of the article is devoted to the graphic details of two case histories, and the sidebar stories deal with such topics as Boy Scout founder Lord Robert Baden-Powell's alleged repressed pedophilia, including excerpts from his diary. The article is followed by a four-page list of "416 [Molester] Cases from 1971 to 1990," drawn from "court records, personnel records from the Boy Scouts and news reports."

The editors found that the readers who sent in mail on the piece were evenly split — half wondering how *Insight* could possibly print such a story about such a sacred institution as the Boy Scouts, the other half confessing that they had undergone a similar incident in their past. This story was not up to the usual high standards we normally associate with *Insight*. We also wonder why, if the editors felt it important enough to merit cover treatment, they did not assign it to somebody like Helle Bering-Jensen, who could have gotten to the bottom of things without resorting to tabloid-style writing.

It was the inside sections that suffered most from *Insight*'s redesigning efforts this year. Health and Business were especially hard hit, like characters in a struggling Broadway musical who see their parts greatly reduced until they are virtually written out of the script, although we were impressed by what we saw of Carolyn Lochhead's work on the U.S. economy and New York City. Cultural coverage under Podhoretz was never dull. He assumed the role of movie critic, rating the sex, violence, and political quotients of movies on such scales as "ice to hot" and "slap to gore," while auditioning for the John Simon mantle of criticism, writing in his review of *Robin*

Hood: Prince of Thieves, "This Robin Needs a Rescuer," 6-24, that: "It is certainly true that the beautiful but butch Mary Elizabeth Mastrantonio whose romance with Costner can best be described as frosty — doesn't seem in the least maidenly."

Just as impressive, in their own way, were the book reviews, the editors drawing on reviews that had run in the *Washington Times,* and the profiles, the editors seeking original spins on celebrities from the world of politics or the arts or, increasingly, celebrities who straddle both worlds. In "Kevin Costner Dances with the GOP," 8-5, Daniel Wattenberg imaginatively "outs" Kevin Costner, documenting that the star of such politically correct movies as "Dances With Wolves" and "JFK" is actually a closet Republican. Mark Lawrence Ragan, in "Stand By for ... This Quirky Newsman," 8-5, pens a three-dimensional profile of radio newsman Paul Harvey, Ragan illuminating on how Harvey, with his corn ball commentary, five-alarm speaking style, and liberal outlook on such issues as Vietnam and abortion has managed to become an institution for Middle America. "Harvey in person is nearly indistinguishable from Harvey on the radio: a Norman Rockwellish figure who spins folksy stories depicting the wit and homespun wisdom of ordinary Americans." In "Most-Listened-to-Talk Show Host Rings a Bell With Conservatives," 8-19, Wattenberg captures right-wing radio host Rush Limbaugh in all his irreverent glory. This section of the book is gone now, along with Podhoretz.

So, the question remains, whither *Insight*? The magazine has lost more than a third of its staff, including such heavyweights as Christopher Elias, Philip Gold, Carolyn Lochhead, Richard Mackenzie and Bill Whalen. Announcing on "restructuring and 'reallocation of resources' " in April, *Washington Times* Corp. senior vice president Ronald S. Godwin noted that "It's raining on newspapers and magazines all over the country." In November, *The Washington Times* began including the magazine as a supplement to its newly-inaugurated Sunday edition, and rumblings have reached the *MediaGuide* that several other editors around the country have expressed interest in running it in their Sunday newspapers as well. If *Insight*'s future lays in that direction, then so be it, but we will miss this original alternative to *Time, Newsweek,* and *U.S.News & World Report.*

Managing Editor: Kirk E. Oberfeld

Deputy Managing Editor: Richard Starr

Address: 3600 New York Ave., NE
                          Washington, DC 20002
                          (202) 636-8800

Circulation: 1990 — 460,997
                          1991 — 439,687

In These Times

We remain impressed in our second year of reviewing the trim socialist tabloid out of Chicago. Published by the Institute for Public Affairs, *In These Times* marked its fifteenth anniversary, 11-6/12, celebrating with a centerfold of excerpted editorials from their history which remain startlingly fresh and current. An editorial dated 2-9-77 on the Soviet Union, for example, perceptively pinpoints the drift of the U.S.S.R. and Eastern Europe from the socialist ideal that *ITT* espouses: "[T]he lack of political freedom in the Soviet Union and in Eastern Europe is a matter of genuine concern for socialists everywhere, both because it violates the basic principles of socialism and because what happens in the world's first socialist country and in its European sphere of influence tends to define what people everywhere. . .perceive socialism to be. It is important to understand why the Soviets and Eastern European governments are the way they are; and it is equally important to do whatever can be done to democratize them." Fifteen years later, in "The Second Revolution," 9-4/10, the editorialist assesses Gorbachev's tenure, finding his flaws to be that "he moved too slowly, thereby losing popular credibility as an advocate of fundamental change. And he remained convinced that a substantial core of party leaders shared his commitment to genuine democratization — in other words, that the party was a viable vehicle for the realization of his goal." Both are characteristic of *ITT*. *ITT* is a publication which firmly and unapologetically pushes for the constant refining of the socialist framework, rather than defending it, as many other journals of the left are apt to do.

On *ITT*'s fifteenth birthday, it's apparent that the tabloid is continuing to establish itself on the national level. James Weinstein, editor of this handsome tabloid, pops up on the "MacNeil/Lehrer NewsHour" from time to time. Washington correspondent John Judis moonlights on the pages of *The Wall Street Journal* and *The New Republic; TNR* is where we first read Judis. Judis was joined this year in the Washington bureau by John Canham-Clyne, who performed rather well in his first year at *ITT*. We're impressed by the perceptivity of Salim Muwakkil, whose observations on racial issues are consistently startling and smart. Labor and business correspondent David Moberg eruditely assesses his subjects with a socialist bent. It is unfortunate, though, that three weeks before *ITT*'s birthday, editor Weinstein had to use the centerfold of the magazine to make an urgent fundraising appeal, stating baldly that "our ability to publish a high-quality newsweekly and to maintain our national presence is in danger." While *ITT* had been conducting a fundraising drive throughout the course of the year, none of the small appeals near the table of contents has the impact of Weinstein's letter. "Because we have always operated hand to mouth, downturns like this bring us to the brink of disaster. . .we owe our freelance writers and photographers some $100,000. Many will no longer write for us and others are angry. We owe a wide range of suppliers tens of thousands of dollars more, which means that promotional operations are threatened. And our paychecks are beginning to bounce like spilled ping pong balls." We hope sincerely that this does not mean the eventual end of the weekly, as *ITT* is one of the most reliable sources of intelligent perspectives from the left.

The main strength of *In These Times* can be found in the smart dispatches of its staff correspondents. Whether we agree with their perspective or not, we're generally made to reconsider our own ideas in the course of reading their dispatches. John B. Judis seemed to slack off a bit this year, his cerebral discourses not up to the work of years past. One of his best efforts came later in the year. "American Evangelism," 10-9/15, is an intriguing delineation of America's future role as falling between evangelizing democracy or realistically prioritizing the domestic: the challenge "will be to discover a foreign policy that transcends both evangelism and narrow realism — a policy that satisfies Americans' democratic ideals, but that is also firmly and openly grounded on the country's economic and social needs." David Moberg argued cogently against a fast track for free trade between Mexico and the U.S., offering alternatives rather than ideological polemics. In "Free Trade No Cure for U.S.-Mexico Ills," 4-17/23, he urges more democratic debate over the terms of a free trade agreement, making some good points about the advantages of a slow and thorough examination of the issue. And in "U.S., Mexico Agreement Should Stress Development," 6-12/25, Moberg offers some fine tuning on fast track and the free trade agreement. John Canham-Clyne makes a strong case in asserting that the real reason for GOP opposition to the Dellums and Bonior appointments to the House Permanent Select Committee on Intelligence was their votes for the Boxer Amendment to restrict the use of covert operations, "Desperately Seeking an Intelligent Community," 2-20/26. And we get forthright, resilient criticism from Salim Muwakkil in "Race, Class & Candor," 5-22/28, a appraisal of the left-liberal orthodoxy for having "stifled debate on racial issues." Muwakkil is not throwing in the towel to conservative thinking, but instead declaring the necessity for the left to eschew "political correctness" and seek new approaches — "even if they are called 'new paradigms.' " The left deserves the beating and defeat it is taking in America's cultural war, he advises, reminding us that "whenever some wayward lefty dared to suggest that African-Americans actually bore some responsibility for the decay corroding their communities, he or she would promptly be chastised for failing to understand economic subtleties. By refusing to face certain realities of the time, the left missed the boat."

The foreign correspondents are less rigorous, but still worth reading. From Upper Silesia, Poland, Paul Hockenos provides a very satisfying account of what ethnic Germans in Poland are thinking now that the communist state has collapsed and Germany has reunited, "German Right Finds Fertile Soil in the 'Eastern Regions,' " 3-20/26. Hockenos reports that many ethnic Germans in Poland assumed that somehow Silesia would be reunited with Germany, but now facing the reality they are attracted to the League of German Expellees which has helped them win municipal elections and refuses to put to rest the notion of a Silesian reunification. But European editor Diana Johnstone is sometimes not up to the standards of *ITT*. In "Under the Big Lie," 2-6/12, she strains credibility on motives for the Gulf War, but this is "reporting" to the converted: "This is not a war for noble causes. . .not even altogether a war for oil. No, this is a war between two near-bankrupt countries. . .both poured their resources into preparation for war. Both are caught with huge debts and one big asset: a modern war machine. So both, rather than be trapped with the debts, have preferred to go for broke with the assets." Even as commentary, this is simplistic, ideological ranting, mere assertion without any attempt to produce a drop of evidence.

The freelance material provided by *ITT* is consistently strong, Weinstein and managing editor Sheryl Larson selecting only the best material. Jerold M. Starr urges reinvestment in Vietnam as well as updating the scene, in "Vietnam Looks to Improve Its Economic Standing," 3-27/4-2; Starr sees no incongruity in having a market economy and a socialist system, evincing the flexibility in reporting and ideology for which we so value *ITT*. In "Hollywood's Mega-Monster Horror Hits and Misses," 3-20/26, Miles Harvey examines the gynophobia in Hollywood, via "Fatal Attraction," "Misery," and "Eve of Destruction"; much of this has been said before, but Harvey makes it fresh with the addition of "Misery" and "Eve of Destruction." Bob Bernstein is surprisingly astute on the tax problems facing the states, and the problems with the solutions, such as increasing the state sales tax in "Taxing Problems," 7-17/23. Unfortunately, Bernstein proposes no alternatives, and although he notes that the "ideal situation is to have a balanced tax structure that doesn't rely too heavily on any one of the state's major revenue sources," he never addresses the issues of spending cuts, which would eliminate or alleviate some of the taxing problems he discusses. "In Person" editor Joel Bleifuss expands Gary Sick's "October surprise" theory in "Truth: The Last Hostage," 4-17/23; this was one of the best representations of the theory we saw in the leftist press, as we get reporting instead of polemics. Bruce Mirken provides a solid overview of the progress made on AIDS, as well as the flaws in the system, "Burning Out on AIDS 10 Years After the Fall," 5-29/6-11, but Mirken's complaint that there is no ACT-UP in Africa seems like complaining about the lack of caviar while starving in Ethiopia. Similarly, Mitchell Hartman gently reminds us that the battle is still joined on AIDS in "A Loss of Optimism in the Time of AIDS," 6/26-7/9, making a persuasive case that this issue is no longer high on the list of priorities of the government, as "the Bush administration decided at the last minute to cancel about three-quarters of the U.S. public health service delegation to the conference on budgetary grounds." Kevin Kelly's series on the airline industry, "Plane Monopoly: Flying New Order Skies," 4-24/30, "The Airline Industry's Haves and Have-Nots," 5-1/7, and "Lawmakers Hold Their Breath as Airline Industry Tailspins," 5-15/21, together comprise a smart dissertation of the coming of a global industry that includes American strategies and a case for government re-regulation.

The columns and departments are superlative as well. *ITT* excerpts Mark Twain's "War Prayer" for the backpage of 2-13/19, a pointed and poignant exercise. "In Person" 2/27-3/19 by Michael Ervin details the life and times of "Antonio Martinez: Treater of Torture," and director of Chicago's Marjorie Kovler Center for the Treatment of Survivors of Torture, as well as anything we see in *TN*'s Aryah Neier's "Watching Rights" column. A three-dimensional profile of Mike Farrell, B.J. Hunnicutt of "M*A*S*H*," is done by Wim Roefs in the "In Person" column, 5-15/20, "Mike Farrell: Square-Inch Subversive," detailing his very left politics, which he works on at the grass roots level. The "In Person" on Mary Lucey, "Mary Lucey: Rage Uncaged," by Carol Tice 5-29/6-11, is appropriately timed to the tenth anniversary of the first cases of AIDS. Lucey is HIV-positive and is an advocate for women in prison with

AIDS, and, as Lucey is a former inmate herself, this carries much weight, and Tice makes the most of her electrically-charged personality and anger. Daniel Lazare's review of "New Jack City," on the backpage "It Don't Mean Jack," 4-17/23, is as much an overview of social conditions as the film; we usually discount this type of review, where film mysteriously becomes documentary, without that being the filmmaker's intent, but this is done quite well, and the disinformation in the film seems well documented. Will Nixon takes the easy way out in "A Free Speech From the Wild, Man," 4-3/9, a "Life in the U.S." selection. He begins marvelously, giving us an inside look at the folks who carouse and sleep in the infamous Times Square theaters, noting trenchantly "The porn world of Times Square came as quite a shock to the uninitiated — me — and I've never been tempted to go back. All of the grand arguments about pornography, from violence to freedom of speech to the degradation of women, looked awfully abstract and irrelevant from the seats of the Big Apple Theatre and the Cameo Cinema. The crowd was the real story here, not the rabbit-work up on the screen. But the moralizers always prefer to stick to the celluloid; it saves them the trouble of real people, real problems." Then, instead of examining the "real people, real problems," Nixon goes ballistic on Rev. Douglas Wildmon and his American Family Association and *AFA Journal* and its many targets.

The editorials are equally strong and compelling. "Billions for War, Not a Cent for the Warriors," 2/27-3/19, is a strong argument for fair benefits for veterans of the Persian Gulf War. Although the editorialist is a bit rabid on Bush: "What could more clearly reveal the true priorities of the Bush administration? War is the health of the state and the benefactor of the military contractors and other powerful financial and industrial interests. Working people and the poor get all the praise, but just so long as they do not actually benefit — except at the expense of their peers — from their service," he does make his case that yellow ribbons look nice, but the real challenge for the government now is proper compensation. "Veterans of this war deserve the most generous benefits and the widest possible range of opportunities from their government. And the cost should be paid right along with the war's other 'incremental' costs. No fair-minded person could think otherwise." And, typical of *ITT*'s pushing to expand the boundaries of socialism, the pair of editorials, "The Making of a Truly New American Left," 6-12/25, and "The Left Needs to Reorder Its Priorities," 6-26/7-9, urge the definitional reorganizing of the left and the leftist ideology ("In large part, the left's problems stem from its own self-definition," 6-12/25) in much the same way *The Washington Monthly* has done in past years. There's too little detail here on what the new left would do, but the editorialist certainly draws the lines between right and left clearly in the first, though the priorities are jumbled in the second. In the "Dialogue" column of 8-7/20, Steve Lilienthal writes a solid critique of an editorial of 5-15. The title says it all: "In Criticizing the DLC *ITT* Resorts to Stale Ideas." Editor James Weinstein responds in kind, "Nibbling at the Edges Can't Create a Second Party." It is indicative of *ITT*'s openness to dialogue and ideas that the editors are willing to print this kind of point-counterpoint. It's exactly this which makes up the stuff of debate, and keeps the magazine fresh.

Now that *In These Times* has further established itself as the premier journal of the left with its creative and fresh approaches to socialism, the other publications that are left-of-center seem to have been shaken out of their respective stupors. That weekly bastion of Marxism, *The Nation,* is beginning to look for proletarian and populist alternatives to Marxism, without necessarily renouncing their long-held beliefs. "Minority Report" columnist Christopher Hitchens advocates a pause to assess "common interests," stating quite frankly that "By any knowable definition, which must include the socialist one, the Soviet system was the perfect failure. In the lives of its own citizens and subjects, and in its contact with any real movement outside its own borders, it killed everything it touched," 10-7. Hitchens even asks "what possible reason can there be for nostalgia at the closure of this abysmal system?" *Mother Jones* editor Douglas Foster redefined the mission of his bimonthly in the 11/12-91 issue, promising a plethora of "tough questions [that] *Mother Jones* will investigate in the coming years. Posing them, and beginning to provide some answers, will require, of course, stripping away the thick layers of secrecy imposed on subjects that deserve open, full, sharp, and democratic debate. Our job is to provoke such debate."

The best way to describe *ITT* is found in the tabloid itself, immediately under the masthead: "*In These Times* believes that to guarantee our life, liberty and the pursuit of happiness, Americans must take greater control over our nation's basic economic and foreign policy decisions. We believe in a socialism that fulfills rather than subverts the promise of American democracy, where social needs and rationality, not corporate profits and greed, are the operative principles. Our pages are open to a wide range of views, socialist and nonsocialist, liberal and conservative. Except for editorial statements appearing on the editorial page, opinions expressed in columns and in feature or news stories are those of the authors and are not necessarily those of the editors. We welcome comments and opinion pieces from our readers." With *The Nation, Mother Jones* back in the fray, and *The Progressive* entering it, *ITT* will have to work hard to maintain its preeminent status. The next few years should be an exciting time for the socialist ideology as these publications toil to recast it in a workable mode. We look forward to the dialectic.

Editor: James Weinstein

Managing Editor: Sheryl Larson

Address: 2040 N. Milwaukee Avenue
                    Chicago, IL 60647
                    (312) 772-0100

Circulation: 1990 — 42,000
                    1991 — 28,000

Mother Jones

Celebrating its 15th anniversary in 1991, *Mother Jones* seems to be finally losing the left-wing *People* magazine feel it acquired over the last few years. *MJ* is featuring more hard news on the cover and in its pages of late, an encouraging sign that it is getting back to the hell-raising that was Mary "Mother" Jones's and the magazine's trademark. The magazine is still somewhat in a transitional period, editor Douglas Foster and company adjusting to the move from a monthly to bimonthly and various staff changes, but we see signs of a revitalized *Mother Jones,* one that's ready to challenge the status quo. While the bimonthly schedule may keep the magazine from being on the cutting edge of *news,* it will not keep *MJ* from asking pertinent questions on the cutting edge of *policymaking.*

Douglas Foster refreshingly redefined the mission of *Mother Jones* in an anniversary "Editor's Note," 11/12-91, trying to inspire and reflect a "spirit of restlessness and insurgency with a combination of investigative scoops, political commentary and cultural coverage. Through politically thin times, which the magazine's founders could not have predicted, we've delivered this melange with a measure of humor, too, in an effort to avoid becoming what one editor here calls 'The Magazine for Cranky People,' by Cranky People." Despite Foster's appraisal of setbacks for the different causes that *MJ* has espoused at various times, such as gay rights and the anti-war movements, Foster and the magazine, seem ready to take on the world. Introducing the cover story by former *Washington Post* investigative reporter Scott Armstrong, Foster categorizes the goal of *Mother Jones* thusly: "These are the kinds of tough questions *Mother Jones* will investigate in the coming years. Posing them, and beginning to provide some answers, will require, of course, stripping away the thick layers of secrecy imposed on subjects that deserve open, full, sharp, and democratic debate. Our job is to provoke such debate." Now that's hell-raising.

The most impressive cover of the year for *MJ* was Scott Armstrong's "The Eye of the Storm," 11/12-91. An investigative report of alleged ties between the Carter, Reagan and Bush administrations to the Saudi royal family which facilitated execution of Operations Desert Shield and Storm, Armstrong draws a convincing scenario in which the U.S. and Saudi Arabia quietly cut a series of deals in order to establish a U.S. military presence in the region, beginning as early as Carter's presidency. Although too much of this is understandably based on anonymous sources to be ultimately convincing, the picture of events that he paints is quite plausible, making a strong argument that much of the superstructure for Desert Storm had to be in place long before Iraq invaded Kuwait, simply from a logistical angle. More importantly, "the continuing reluctance of the Saudi royal family to reveal its agreements with the United States has led to what one former Pentagon official calls the 'myth of virgin intervention,' and obscures the long-term implications of the NATO-sized military network now in place in Saudi Arabia." Armstrong also notes that should factions within the Saudi royal family that are anti-U.S. come into power, this base structure could be used against U.S. allies in the region, or in ways contrary to U.S. interests, underscoring additional dangers to Middle East peace.

Most of the remaining covers addressed political questions. David Beers, in "PC? B.S." 9/10-91, offers good reporting on the supposed race riot at SUNY-Binghamton, debunking the ominous tone of other reports, but his efforts are undercut by a final, highly personal blast at conservatives, which, rather than convincing us of the illusory nature of political correctness fermented and promoted by conservative paranoia, leaves us knowing only that Beers doesn't like George Will, Midge Decter, or Dinesh D'Souza, known when he was editor of *The Dartmouth Review* as "Distort D'Newza," according to Beers. In the same cover treatment on political correctness and race on campus, black professor Troy Duster of Berkeley provides an interesting perspective in "They're Taking Over!" 9/10-91; Duster, however, doesn't ask the question that if blacks and whites are segregated on campus via black-only, white-only fraternities, then where's the diversity? In "Just Say Whoa!" 7/8-91, David Beers effectively juxtaposes the harm-reduction programs in Europe and Bush's War on Drugs, a superb examination that is ultimately short-circuited by the strange conclusion about the use of police dogs in L.A., with Beers openly comparing the LAPD to the Gestapo. The looks at the drug programs in Liverpool and Amsterdam are smartly executed; he never judges either his subjects or the subject matter in this clear-eyed view. The "We Hate Kids" cover, 5/6-91, covers quite a few bases: Marian Wright Edelman offers "Kids First," a compendium of why kids don't come first and what can and should be done; in a *MJ* forum, Rep. George Miller (D-Calif.), Margaret Brodkin, Roberta Achtenberg, Reggie Daniels, Arlyce Currie, Michael Wald, and Joseph Marshall bat around different ideas and perspectives on the possibilities of a child-care grass-roots movement, although we find no consensus in "Clout"; in "Rock-a-bye Nino," Anne Nelson gives us an idea of the emotional maternal conflicts over finding a caretaker, or nanny, in this case several of whom are Hispanic, and an anonymous Salvadoran offers the flip side with "Nanny: Confessions of an 'Illegal' Caregiver." There's a report card for George Bush, with the facts, his promises and his actions, "What's He Got Against Kids?" There's also a startling photo essay, focusing on runaways and throwaways, "Street." Finally, this cover treatment is rounded out from a child-to-adult transitional perspective: Paula Fomby's "Why I'm Glad I Grew Up in a Gay Family"; Michael Hornsby's "We're Saving Black Lives in My Boy's Club" (the aforementioned Reggie Daniels from "Clout" one of them); and Emelyn Cruz Lat's "Emancipated." It's a serious treatment of a serious topic, finished up with a list of organizations "Kid's Aid: Where You Can Turn." After all the *People* magazine covers, this is quite invigorating, and impressive.

Two cover treatments early in the year were throwbacks to the *Mother Jones-People* era, which now hopefully has come to an end. While these solid covers satisfy, they are not a steady diet, and we're happy to see that *Mother Jones* doesn't plan on making them one. Stephen Talbot serves up director Oliver Stone in "60s Something," 3/4-91, an insightful profile and political assessment of Stone and his work, in which Talbot nails him for his inaccuracies: "I don't want writers or filmmakers to sanctify or sanitize the sixties. I prefer my history quirky and my heroes human. But I do want 'cinematic historians' like Stone to get it right." Talbot, a filmmaker himself, pegs Stone well: "Stone is clearly filled with all the passions of the sixties, and treats them seriously, but his films are ultimately about *him;* his disillusionment, his war, his rage, his redemption through art." *Los Angeles Times* reporter Ronald Brownstein's book is trimly excerpted for "Hollywood Hardball," 1/2-91; we get enough of a sense of Brownstein's appraisal of the Hollywood-Washington connection that we don't need to run out and buy the book.

Mother Jones' features are beginning to impress us more as well. Beating out *New York* and other weekly magazines, Lotte Marcus tells us of the "Therapy Junkies," 3/4-91, blaming much of the source for those addicted to therapy on the booming anti-stress market. "It's important to recognize that, whatever concealed catch-22s are found entrapping Julia in her repetitive lockstep of prayer, purge, rage and fatigue, she has also become a chronic cultural casualty: a victim of the profitable growth and entrepreneurial triumph of that burgeoning flotilla of well-stocked, appealingly 'karmic,' cash-or-credit-card magic shows flooding the country." While her anecdotes compel, her assertion that this "seems a direct consequence of the Reagan era, when the whole cult of wellness worship really took off" doesn't convince, as she doesn't tell us how it happened. We cheer for Dee Rivers Stimson as she fights to help rebuild Beehive, South Carolina, after the devastation of Hurricane Hugo, "Beehive & Me," 1/2-91. She makes us feel: "Each [destroyed] dwelling had been more than a house; it had been a repository of cross-generational history, a place where a great-grandmother's bed continued as marriage bed, birth bed, death bed, a place where families still gathered after church on Sundays to cook, to eat, to watch children play, to hear elders in porch rockers reminisce, a place where each room had its particular texture and comfort." Managing editor Peggy Orenstein takes a very funny look at virtual reality, via a convention, in "Get a Cyberlife," 5/6-91: "By now I was hungry, so I strolled over to the virtual eating exhibit that a group of local art students had set up. I didn't know what to expect — perhaps it could make me feel virtually full. Perhaps no calories would be involved. There was a reservation book graced with a real red rose outside the closed-off room. I wrote my name down. There was a ten-to fifteen-minute wait for a table. Just like real life, I thought. I wondered where I could get a virtual Stoli while I waited." A Russian-American journalist, Vladimir Klimenko profiles the new right in the Soviet Union, "The Coup Next Time," 11/12-91, giving us the lowdown on more of the men who would be king, Vladimir Zhirinovsky, Sergei Kurginyan and Col. Victor Alksnis. And Michael DiLeo vividly describes Lompoc inmate Dannie M. Martin and his brief career in journalism as a writer for the *San Francisco Chronicle* in which Martin detailed life inside the prison walls, "Writer with Convictions," 1/2-91.

Mother Jones still offers profiles and examinations of people on the left, most notably of the long strange trip of the life of Malcolm X to the movie screen, the latest attempt being made currently by Spike Lee. But despite the worthiness of the topic, Anne Thompson's treatment in "Malcolm, Let's Do Lunch," 7/8-91, never quite takes off in discussing to whom Malcolm's legacy and life truly belong, Thompson relating instead the revolving doors of directors, writers and cast members in the film, and incidentals such as Malcolm's daughters forming their own rap group. Let's hope this gossipy profile is the last of its kind that *Mother Jones* offers.

The "Departments" sections offered particular punch this year, from the freelancers to the columnists. Daniel Ellsberg, who released the Pentagon Papers, turns up with "Not Again!" 1/2-91, on the potential for disaster in the Persian Gulf, arguing rather eloquently against offensive troop movement of any kind and for Congress keeping its war powers. In "Inside the Home," 3/4-91, Jill Frawley is violently disturbing on conditions inside the nursing home, made more cogent in her being a former staffer: "The silence is ominous in the evening. Nothing to do; no place to go. The residents sit and wait for death. The staff is ground down in despair and hopelessness." We get a bird's-eye view of affirmative action from a Nigerian in New York, "Can I Quota You?" by Dele Olojede 7/8-91, valuable from his perspective as he goes from being negative to positive as he moves from being the victim to the beneficiary, revealing as such: "Affirmative action has its sad side effects. I believe that many whites, including some of my coworkers, harbor the thought that I was employed by a major American newspaper mainly because I am black. Sometimes I'm suspicious that when an editor commends my work, perchance he or she really means that, for a black man, I'm doing quite well. This doubt dogs my every step, turning me into a target where once I held the arrow." Jim Coffman examines the growing religious diversity as young women in Algeria choose the *hijah* to express new freedom in Islam, "Choosing the Veil," 11/12-91, as much a psychological as sociological profile of changing mores in the country, done well as a snapshot.

The columnists are growing stronger as well. Barbara Ehrenreich has been succeeded by the "Impolitic" column and columnist Molly Ivins, who also appears in *The Progressive.* Roger Wilkins "Uncommon Ground" impresses with his tough perspectives on racial issues. Both are rated for the first time in this edition of *MediaGuide.* MJ lost "1619 East Crowley" columnist Lynda Barry to Broadway, of all places, her characters from the column now featured in a Barry production. She finally finds her own voice, rather than hiding behind her character Edna's, in "War," 3/4-91, an intensely personal and powerful examination of how Barry reacted to the Persian Gulf War, and how World War II affected her mother, who is from the Philippines. "Like her, I developed a hatred for the Fourth of July, when the sound of firecrackers and Piccolo Petes transformed my mother into a terrified eight-year-old who locked herself in the bathroom to hide from the bombs. And like many children of parents who survived the war, I lived with her involuntary envy of my peaceful childhood. I lived with the guilt of having it. Her unbelievable shouts of 'If I had known my life was going to turn out like this, I would've let the Japanese kill me!' were echoed in the homes of Jewish kids I knew, whose parents shouted things like, 'I didn't survive the camps for this!' In our homes the war never ended." She convinces that "war becomes a part of our DNA," ending with a well-aimed broadside at Bush for "purposefully" bringing it into American culture when "other options remain." Ralph Nader finishes up his year of columns no more strongly than he started, a disappointing portfolio. In "Rip-off, Inc." 5/6-91, Nader doesn't go far enough, restricting his discussion of corporativism to those corporate takeovers of taxpayer assets, but what about corporativism in the abstract?

With strong columns, more politicized topics, and investigative reports and reporters, Foster and his staff should find it fairly easy to "provoke debate" and raise a little hell. We look forward to both in this newly-energized *Mother Jones.*

Editor:	Douglas Foster
Address:	1663 Mission Street, 2nd Floor San Francisco, CA 94103 (415) 558-8881
Circulation:	1990 — 160,000 1991 — 110,000

The Nation

One of the last remaining bastions of communism appears to be falling, or at least is beginning to crumble. In his "Minority Report" column, 10-7, Christopher Hitchens blasts the communist system embodied in the Soviet Union: "By any knowable definition, which must include the socialist one, the Soviet system was the perfect failure. In the lives of its own citizens and subjects, and in its contact with any real movement outside its own borders, it killed everything it touched." Hitchens adds "what possible reason can there be for nostalgia at the closure of this abysmal system?" In a calculated blast at the hardliners and fellow *TN* columnist Alexander Cockburn, who in his "Beat the Devil" columns had been bemoaning the failure of the Soviet coup and castigating the plotters for their lack of strategy, [see "Beat the Devil," 9-9, for example], Hitchens finishes up this ground-breaking column by advocating moving on from communism to a refined socialism that must evolve over time. "[A]nd once various kinds of false consciousness, of which Stalinism and Brezhnevism were signal examples, have been heaved over the side, it will remain relevant to suggest that the world's workers, by hand and by brain, might be wise to, well, reflect on common interests."

A few short years ago, *The Nation* would not even consider running such heresy, so steeped in Marxist dogma were the writers and editors. In the past, the creativity and enthusiasm at the weekly has ebbed and flowed directly parallel to the fortunes of the leftist movement. Founded in 1865, the ideas in *TN* gained currency under the stewardship of Paul E. More, who headed the magazine in the first quarter of the century. As the socialist movement grew during the '30s and '40s, and receded during the post-war years, so did the circulation and influence of *TN*. We have frequently observed that the writers and editors at *TN* have clearly felt that ". . .the history of the world is still the history of the struggle between 'Them' and 'Us' " (*The 1989 MediaGuide*). Thankfully, the cast and crew of *TN* seem to be moving out of the Cold War mode, readying the magazine for new issues in socialism, to fight new battles in the redefinition of its philosophy.

Though the Hitchens "Minority Report" surprised us with its vehement stand on the death of Soviet communism, this theme of redefinition could be found in *The Nation*'s pages throughout the course of the year. *TN* devoted the greater portion of the 4-22 issue to input in redefining perspectives from the left, in four articles edited by Marcus Raskin and the late A. W. Singham. Raskin's "The Road to Reconstruction" is muddled on the problems with Soviet socialism, but at least he realizes they are there, speaking of the "deformation" of ideals and the need for "empathy" in a socialistic society, but this rather good discussion descends into a diatribe on the Persian Gulf War, tangential at best and suffering from a jerky, abrupt transition. Mary Kaldor, in "Taking the Democratic Way," outlines the origins of the new concepts of "civil society [which] suggests an entirely new form of politics appropriate to confront both the repression and bureaucracy of the single-party state and the electoral machinery of modern Western parties." She meanders, though, and we're left wondering precisely where she stands on the suggestions she's made. In "A Matter of Principle," Aryeh Neier examines the left vs. right reaction to the issues of human rights over the past decade, concluding there's room for improvement on both sides, an exercise neatly tied together. Finally, Gar Alperovitz offers "Socialism Based In Community," a simplistic evaluation of the capitalist system as compared to the socialist. Overall, this tells us little about how exactly these four would redefine issues on the left, as too often the authors are busy picking apart the failings of the right to carefully examine the changes on the left. But perhaps it's best to categorize the failures on both side before building a consensus with what remains.

The features that lead us into *The Nation* are more inviting. There is less of a tendency towards knee-jerk polemics; rather, many of the essays are thoughtful and thought-provoking, particularly some of those on the front page. The best example of this is the 10 Best nomination for General Reporting, "The Media Goes Wilding in Palm Beach," 6-24, by Katha Politt. Politt sharply decimates the case for naming the victims point by point, until we are thoroughly and irreversibly convinced, using the Palm Beach-Smith case as a starting point. Former *Washington Post* reporter Morton Mintz offers two informative pictures: "Seldes Hangs Up His Typewriter," 3-11, a fun interview with George Seldes at age 100; and "Marketing Tobacco to Children," 5-6, a well-written compendium of the evidence, moderately persuasive that the tobacco companies are evil for marketing to kids. Following an earlier article in *In These Times,* David Corn gives us a good legislative profile of "Wellstone — Senator From the Left?" 4-1, the freshman from Minnesota, encapsulating both the Senator and the left very well: "By pushing out the leftward boundaries, Wellstone can ease the task of his more moderate colleagues and help produce tangible victories." Surprisingly, Corn and Amy Lowrey, an intern given her own byline in the best *Washington Monthly* fashion, do not object completely to the dropping of trade barriers in "Fast Track to Unemployment," 6-3: "With the emergence of a global economy, trade barriers have indeed become harder to maintain and justify. But the response should not be a policy of anything goes." Rather they attempt to make a case for a shifting of priorities within the fast track: "A socially conscientious pact would include measures to protect the environment, wage levels and working conditions. It would also include retraining provisions, enhance consumer safety and take on the knotty issue of Mexico's $95 billion debt, the real obstacle to that nation's development." Hmm. Andrew Kopkind provides a lively mix of commentary, reflections and solid Q&A by Kopkind with Rep. Bernie Sanders (I-Vt), the U.S. House's first self-proclaimed socialist in ages, in "Bernie Sanders Does D.C." 6-3, doing a fine job with background and in soliciting from Sanders a clear picture of his political perspectives and agenda. Going against *TN*'s anti-war positioning is Erika Munk's "The New Face of Techno-war," 5-6, in which Munk reports that the destruction of Baghdad was limited, seeing it with her own eyes. And Camilo Jose Vergara offers a sorrowful look at homeless shelters scattered throughout the boroughs, "New York's New Ghettos," 6-17. All in all, a rather impressive portfolio.

This is not to say *The Nation* turned in anything near a flawless performance. There is still plenty of silly stuff coated with pseudo-intellectualism. Lloyd DeMause presents "The Gulf War as Mental Disorder," 3-11, an application of the techniques and methods of psychology in Post-traumatic Stress Disorder to the nation's consciousness in events leading up to the Gulf War, a thoroughly bizarre assessment: "Although people have become familiar with the notion that the homicidal and suicidal acts of individuals might stem from underlying mental disorders, it is less common to consider the possibility that the homicidal and suicidal acts of entire nations — wars — might also stem from temporary mental disorders. Nevertheless, there is historical evidence for the thesis that the current gulf war is a shared emotional disorder, with diagnostic symptoms, psychodynamics and childhood origins very similar to the disorders that occur in individuals. An understanding of this disorder is particularly crucial in appreciating the emotions connected with any peace overtures." Andrew Kopkind's "The Rising of the Wretched," 5-6, is simply awful in the continuing series of "Rethinking the Left." While Kopkind gets the problem right — "The right was allowed to set the terms of the fifteen-months' debate about the failure of socialism. The left must capture the debate about socialism's future" — his framing of the question is terrible. He tells us that it is *capitalism* that has failed and that it wasn't socialism in Central Europe — it was "whatever-it-was": "The great debate about the nature of the world order began with the breaching of the Berlin wall in November 1989. It ended barely fifteen months later with the invasion and the destruction of Iraq. If the promise of a kind of socialism died in the wreckage of Central Europe, the greater promise of a capitalist order with peace, prosperity and opportunity for all perished in the carnage of the Persian Gulf war. For if the short space between those two historic bookends demonstrates anything, it is that capitalism is logically prevented by its own fatal flaws from delivering the goods, and that socialism still stands a chance. History is alive and kicking." Good grief.

The foreign correspondence is intellectually rather slack. George Black, the de facto foreign editor, left late in the year to write a book examining the Chinese pro-democracy movement. David Singer is most valuable in that he frequently provides views and perspectives from European countries only covered regularly in the *Financial Times,* though he is sometimes unsophisticated. In "Gorbachev — Two Steps Backward?" 2-18, Singer finds it difficult to tell us what the battle among the factions in the U.S.S.R. is all about, but he makes a credible attempt to state what it is not about. Without whitewashing Gorbachev, he debunks the so-called "democrats" now grouped around Boris Yeltsin; advocates of a Polish-style policy that bring a dramatic fall in living standards and a sharp rise in unemployment are hardly "democrats." The lead editorial "Gorbymania, Gorbyphobia," 4-8, is smart on viewing Gorbachev as the only real way to move the country in the right direction. In "Shining Path Is Gaining in Peru," 4-29, Robin Kirk looks inside the guerrilla movement and what President Fujimori is doing to combat them, but she never mentions the ideology of the Shining Path, which is decidedly Marxist. And Sara Miles gives us the "Lessons of El Salvador," 5-27, a poetic exploration of what "forward" movement means in the "very small country on the periphery of a world turned upside down."

The columns and the editorials vary in quality from week to week and author to author, but are generally acceptable. The lead editorial "Remember the Home Front," 2-18, on the State of the Union address, hits home on the shortcomings of the speech. "The United States is spending $133 billion for its armed forces to defend Western Europe — nearly $20 billion of which goes toward its military presence in Norway alone. But it would, of course, be unthinkable to repatriate some of that money to alleviate suffering at home — unemployment, AIDS, urban blight, the neglect of children, insufficient health care. Instead President Bush summons the nation to a 'great struggle' for 'decency and humanity' 'halfway around the world.' In the struggle for those values at home he is AWOL." The lead editorial "What's in the *Daily News*?" 4-1, lauds the purchase of the New York City newspaper by *socialist* "media baron," Robert Maxwell, but the linking of the terms socialist and media baron sounds a tad incongruous to us. "Minority Report" columnist Christopher Hitchens is best when he rises above his own stream-of-consciousness and presents his evaluations logically, as he did in his 10-7 repudiation of communism. Aryeh Neier continues to watchdog human rights and human rights abuses the world over in the "Watching Rights" column. He's more effective than, say, Abe Rosenthal of *The New York Times,* as Neier maintains a world view that is based on fundamental human rights, rather than dogma. Elizabeth Pochoda inaugurated a "Reading Around" column, 4-8, but her efforts so far are not yet up to the information on magazines and critiques of news coverage that we see in New York's *Village Voice.* David Corn keeps us up-to-date on the "Beltway Bandits," dissecting some of the intricate relationships involved in the BCCI scandal, 11-25. And Calvin Trillin regularly gets in his licks with his quirky poetry. In "Eureka!" 3-11, we're told: "The drug trade will stop./The hungry will feast./And peace will break out/Throughout the Mideast./The homeless will get/The homes of their dreams,/While Japanese ride/In Cutlass Supremes. . .It all can be done,/The White House maintains:/We just cut the tax/On Capital Gains."

The remaining columnist is the "Beat the Devil" scribe, Alexander Cockburn. Our once favorite Marxist seemed positively unhinged in the pages of *TN* this year. The 4-8 issue carries two long letters in protest of Cockburn's "Beat the Devil," 2-4, which castigated Amnesty International for reporting certain data — 312 babies pulled from Kuwaiti incubators by the Iraqis — because it was "politically convenient." Cockburn further critiques Amnesty's overall performance on Nicaragua and Panama. One letter comes from Winston Nagan and John G. Healey from Amnesty International, the other from fellow *Nation* columnist Aryeh Neier, who turns the tables on Alex quite effectively as executive director of Human Rights Watch by calling Cockburn's own estimate that "more than 1,000 and possibly as many as 2,500" civilians killed in Panama into question: ". . .another division of our organization, Americas Watch, was able to verify the killing of only some 300 civilians in Panama. . .we see no basis for the estimates offered by Cockburn. Could it be that Cockburn offers such high estimates because, with his politics, he finds it 'politically convenient'?" Cockburn's response runs a full two pages, in half the type size of the original column, making it an estimated 2.5 times as long. His pomposity — "None of this [bias] should be discomfiting, so long as it is borne in mind that human rights organizations have biases (e.g., against definitions of human rights that might have too 'political' a content) and inhibitions (e.g., against being consigned to the editorial dustbin as being 'radical' or 'anti-West')" — makes this tough to stomach. We get more of Cockburn's ruminations in "Beat the Devil," 7-29/8-5, this time on nationalism and forced emigration, from Nazi Germany to the present situation in Yugoslavia. "It's enough to make one yearn for the Austro-Hungarian Empire, which did impose upon large portions of Middle Europe some kind of transnational respect for minorities, as did the Communists in the postwar period now concluded." Almost completely disconnected from logical thought in many of his columns, Cockburn is fast becoming unpalatable.

One of our favorite features is *TN*'s book review section. Always tart and saucy, literary editor Elsa Dixon never runs a dull review. There's never any doubt as to where the reviewer stands, and frequently we're left chuckling at the sharp wit of the freelancers and impressed at the broader themes tackled in the reviews. Pagan Kennedy's review of Bret Easton Ellis' *American Psycho,* "Generation Gaffe," 4-1, less a review of the book (". . .we should note that simply to give *American Psycho* yet another bad review here would be to beat a dead horse — or, more in the spirit, to gouge its eyes out, nail its legs to the floor and crack the bones, then compare its eviscerated guts to the kiwi souffle at the Odeon.") than of the literary atmosphere and literati who spawned the author. "Yet few reviewers have bothered to quote from the less sensational parts of the book, to show Ellis at his weakest, when he isn't using corpses or fashion to dress up his prose. Here's a moment from the end of the book, when Bateman supposedly comes to understand himself: 'I saw a desert landscape that was unending, resembling some sort of crater, so devoid of reason and life and spirit that the mind could not grasp it on any sort of conscious level and if you came close the mind would reel backward. And backward runs the mind as reel such sentences.' By lauding Bret Easton Ellis for *Less Than Zero*, the literary establishment provided the jolt of electricity that brought a Frankenstein monster of a book to life. And just as in the horror flicks, the mob, armed with pitchforks and torches, is chasing down the beast — and its presumed alter ego, Ellis — rather than its true creator." *The Nation* also devotes an issue to the spring, 6-10, and fall, 11-18, books, reviewing the hottest items of the publishing seasons. In a review of Bob Woodward's *The Commanders,* "Why We Fought," 6-10, Jon Wiener hits Woodward right between the eyes for his clairvoyant ability to probe the minds of all the Persian Gulf commanders save the president, the ultimate commander, a terrific critique. Andrew Kopkind reviews *Cures: A Gay Man's Odyssey* by Martin Duberman, "In Straight America," 6-10, Kopkind courageously "outing" himself within the review, adding additional depth and power to his perspective. *New York* magazine's John Leonard is positively acidic on Norman Mailer's *Harlot's Ghost,* "The Trouble With Harry," 11-18: "When his battery's charged, Mailer windmills from one paragraph to the next — baroque, anal, Talmudic, olfactory, portentous, loopy, coy, Egyptian; down and dirty in the cancer, the aspirin or the plastic; shooting moons on sheer vapor; blitzed by paranoia and retreating for a screen pass, as if bitten in the pineal gland by a deranged Swinburne, with metaphors so meaning-moistened that they stick to our tumps, with 'intellections' (as he once put it) slapped on 'like adhesive plasters.' When he chooses to, he also speaks in tongues." One of the magazine's strengths, the "Books & the Arts" section is second to a select few, a list perhaps only comprised of *New York* and *The New Republic.*

With *The Nation* at least opening its ideological framework for revision and improvement, there will be exciting years of competition ahead in the left-of-center press. Finally, the long-time contender has joined the fray with the younger upstarts who help to define the course of the left: *In These Times, The Progressive* and *Mother Jones.* We look forward to seeing where the years take *The Nation,* and the causes it espouses.

Editor:	Victor Navasky
Address:	72 Fifth Avenue
	New York, NY 10011
	(212) 242-8400
Circulation:	1990 — 91,614
	1991 — 97,135

The National Interest

The National Interest continues to offer some of the most challenging theses regarding the post-Cold War era, at times advancing provocative new conceptions regarding the shifting relationship of forces globally. Editor Owen Harries sets the tone, being particularly keen on the enormous change in the *tempo* of world affairs, emphasizing in "Of Unstable Disposition," Winter 1990-91, how very stable actually, and even monotonous, was the Age of the Cold War. During that period, "Not only was there no world war, but there was no serious danger of one." Moreover, and here Harries parts company with some prominent conservatives and neoconservatives, "stability is a — arguably *the* —conservative value, and it is precisely in such circumstances as these, when sweeping changes seem entirely, unconditionally, and self-evidently welcome, that the conservative stress on the importance of continuity, gradualism, predictability, and order — and on the danger of large, convulsive, open-ended changes — assumes relevance."

Drawing an initial conclusion from the Iraq crisis, Harries advances the view that the U.S. should aim for not consistency, but discrimination. "If an instance of regional imperialism has only regional consequences, there is no need for the United States to involve itself. . .It is only when the actions of a would-be regional hegemonist have consequences that threaten global order and stability — yes, stability — that the United States, as the only true global power, should intervene." Harries's essay, which rejected the fixed universalist vs. neo-isolationist framework of the debate, propounded excellent political-economy and was nominated by us as one of 1991's 10-Best commentaries.

Harries was again especially astute and thought provoking in "Drift and Mastery — Bush Style," Spring 1991, an assessment of how sound the President's strategic judgements have been. "First, [with regard to the collapse of communism], masterly [sic] inactivity, then [with regard to Iraq] masterful engagement." Harries is less approving of the latter, noting among other insights, the irony of how the very magnitude of U.S. response to the invasion of Kuwait ensures that it cannot be a convincing precedent for the New World Order.

Wall Street Journal "Potomac Watch" columnist Paul A. Gigot provided a concise near-comprehensive critique of U.S. policy blunders leading up to war with Iraq in "Iraq: An American Screw-Up," Winter 1990-91, which *TNI* editors nominated for 10 Best consideration. We'd seen bits and pieces of this story here and there, but Gigot put it all nicely together for us. "America and Israel — How Bad Is It?" was the other main feature in the same issue. A symposium around the view of Steven L. Spiegel that the end of the Cold War signals the end of Israel's role as a strategic asset for the U.S., the feature was an especially rich presentation of critical comments on the thesis.

Daniel Pipes, director of the Foreign Policy Research Institute, delivered pungent criticism of the conceptual shortcomings of U.S. longrange policy for the Middle East with "What Kind of Peace?" Spring 1991. Stability again was an underlying theme in this look at the larger questions of policy in the wake of Kuwait's liberation. Pipes concluded that the U.S. will find it exceedingly difficult to translate military victory over Iraq into a lasting political success.

A critique of mainline Protestant leadership's witness against the war with Iraq, "The Churches and the War," Spring 1991 by Harvard's Center for Science and International Affairs fellow Robert P. Beschel and Duke University professor of political science Peter D. Feaver, pithily sums up the irrelevance of their effort: "Anti-Americanism is not a useful paradigm for U.S. policymakers who turn to the church for moral guidance." The effort by James Bowman to provide a related look at the U.S. Catholic Bishops' attitude toward the war stumbles with an unacceptable assessment — the bishops, he asserts, were speaking less as representatives of the church universal than as a kind of "rather provincial American universalist." What then of the Pope, who also opposed the war?

Contributing editor Robert W. Tucker, in the somber "Quarterly" essay "Justice and the War," Fall, eloquently questions the justness of Desert Storm by examining the war on the question of *proportionality,* that is, the relationship between the values preserved by using force and the values sacrificed by using force. To Tucker, this comes down to the damage inflicted on the civilian population of Iraq. He pungently observes that while precision weapons may give the illusion that noncombatants are safer than ever before, war is still driven by strategy, and the U.S. strategy during Desert Storm was to draw up the broadest possible military objectives while keeping U.S. casualties to an absolute minimum. As a result, much of Iraq's civilian infrastructure was targeted. "The melancholy conclusion to which these considerations lead is not that the manner in which the war was waged made it an unjust war. . .but that its conduct resulted in deplorable consequences which cannot be simply shrugged off as the unfortunate though inevitable by-product of war." "Justice and the War" was one of the few essays we read in *TNI* that stayed with us long after we had read it.

The other major international story of 1991, the collapse of the Soviet Union, did not receive quite as much attention as the Middle East. While we saw some material that was forwardlooking and engaging, much of the analysis came up short. Too often, it seemed, the contributors were too quick to seize on momentary zigzagging to the right as evidence that the Soviet clock was being turned back to 1985, by "ruthless, cunning, and determined hardliners" who, despite 75 years of evidence to the contrary, were still viewed as being able to control events with the precision of Swiss watchmakers and the steely resolve of grave diggers during a plague.

Bruce D. Porter, Bradley Senior Research Associate of the Olin Institute for Strategic Studies, Harvard University, in "The Coming Resurgence of Russia," Spring, looks ahead to the immediate future, and predicts that a coup attempt is unlikely as is a "left-wing coup" by impatient reformers led by Boris Yeltsin, because neither action would have the support of the military. "Though events could yet force Moscow to yield autonomy or independence to certain republics, the odds seem to favor its retaining most of the present federation." The essay was nominated for 10 Best consideration by *TNI* editors. In "Crackdown," Spring, John B. Dunlop, a senior fellow at the Hoover Institution on War, Revolution and Peace draws on the events in the Baltics in January to warn that "We appear to be witnessing the beginning of an ambitious rolling coup, which threatens to spread from the Baltic to the remaining twelve Soviet republics." While Porter provides some good details on the tactics of the eventual coup leaders in the first half of 1991, he warns that "The crackdown, carried through with ruthlessness, cunning, and determination, could well succeed; and if it did, the consequences would be long lasting."

In "The Secret History of Perestroika," Spring, Yale student Frederick Kagan advances the thesis that the current generation of Soviet reformers can trace their roots back to Otto Wille Kuusinen, "Lenin's man in Finland during the October Revolution," who created a small cadre of proteges, led by Yuri Andropov, who in turn advanced the careers of like-minded party careerists such as Mikhail Gorbachev. As fascinating as this thesis is, the essay is never able to overcome one serious flaw, the performance in office by men like Kuusinen and Andropov. By the end even Kagan is conceding that these party *apparatchiks* were, for the most part, "uninhibited opportunists," without a clear vision for Soviet society or a unifying, underlining principle which they would not break or even bend. Kagan concludes that Gorbachev's failings are not so much personal as symptomatic of the character flaws of the "intra-party reform group" which produced him, but Kagan never addresses the other reformers — and revolutionaries — the party also produced, such as Eduard Shevardnadze and Boris Yeltsin.

Writing after the failed Soviet coup attempt in "The Hour of the Demagogue," Fall, Stephen Sestanovich, director of Soviet and East European studies at the Center for Strategic and International Studies, masterfully draws on Russian history and recent experiences in Eastern Europe to document the indispensable role the "liberal demagogue" can play in tapping "popular hatreds, resentments, and grievances in the mundane work of creating and fortifying a pluralist constitutional order," as former Communist societies make the transition from totalitarianism to democracy. Nominated by *TNI* editors for 10 best consideration, "Hour of the Demagogue," was the best essay on the former Soviet Union we read in *TNI* all year, Sestanovich enabling us to understand why the forces of democracy, as personified by Boris Yeltsin, were able to prevail over both the forces of "moderate reformism" and the unreconstructed right.

Of course, the collapse of the Soviet Union and the end of the Cold War raised a host of new questions for the U.S., questions explored at length with varying degrees of success. In "The Shape of the New World Order," Summer, nominated by the editors for 10 Best consideration, James Kurth, a professor of political science at Swarthmore College, straightforwardly contends that the "next stage of history" will be dominated by "states practicing the social market and organized capitalism," and examines at length one of the states, *Mitteleuropa,* placing its capital in Berlin. "The order of *Mitteleuropa*," he artfully contends, "will depend on the German charioteer's prowess and skill," but the charioteer does not seem to be off to a very promising start. In "Cheap Excuses," Summer, Alan Sked, a senior lecturer in international history at the London School of Economics, draws on Germany's recent behavior during the Gulf crisis to argue stridently that Bonn has, in recent months, "proved provincial in the extreme, placing narrow, national interests before those of Europe and the free world." Sked is as nasty as he can be to the Germans here, stopping short only of calling them "Fritz."

In a "Postscript," *TNI* informs us that when Sked's article was originally published in London in February, the British Foreign Office received an official protest by the German Embassy, and that Whitehall described the article as "unhelpful and extremely ungenerously expressed," but that "Germany's legal experts" had concurred with Sked that Germany's constitution did allow it to take part in efforts to enforce U.N. sanctions and resolutions, Sked having quoted a constitutional clause enabling Germany to "enter a system of mutual collective security." While Sked may have won a debating point here, one wonders what worries English commentators like Sked, a pacifist, non-aggressive Germany or a Germany ready to sound the muster at the first whiff of an international crisis.

Perhaps both. The real fear of the English over European unity and the end of NATO seems to be the end of a U.S. presence in Europe, the U.S. having served as a protector against both the Bear and a resurgent Germany. Sked admits as much, writing in "Cheap Excuses," that "the free world will simply not remain free for very long if the American eagle is obliged to mate with a teutonic, double-headed European ostrich." Boris Johnson, EC correspondent for the London *Daily Telegraph,* writes in "French Chiefs," Fall, that "When the federalists speak of the need to 'lock' or 'bind' Germany in, what they mean is 'keep Germany locked in' to a bureaucratic apparatus of their own devising." Johnson goes on to decry the lack of British effectiveness in protecting its own interests in the emerging European "superstate."

Interesting as these viewpoints are, they are, of course, *British* viewpoints, and only one British viewpoint at that. While *TNI* may be philosophically opposed to European political and monetary unity, believing, as many U.S. and English conservatives do, that 1992 should be for the most part free trade only, British interests may not always coincide with U.S. interests. It may be in London's interest for the U.S. to keep several divisions in the heart of Europe, for instance, but is it necessarily in the U.S. interest to do so? These are not questions likely to be addressed by English commentators, for obvious reasons. Much as we appreciate receiving foreign perspectives on international issues, we hope that as 1992 approaches *TNI* addresses the challenges of European unity and future security arrangements on the continent from the non-sentimental perspective of what is best for U.S. interests, such as it already does with other international questions of the day.

The other major state "practicing the social market and organized capitalism," referred to by Kurth, is, of course, Japan, and its emerging role in the world was addressed in the Fall issue, readers receiving two ostensibly diametrically opposing viewpoints. In "The Headquarters Nation," Leon Hollerman, a professor at the Claremont Graduate School, contends that while Japan may soon dominate the world economy, it will do so not out of any long-planned conspiracy, but simply because of its policy of harnessing its public and private sectors to meet national political and economic interests. Karel van Wolferen answers right back, in "No Brakes, No Compass," Fall, that "The Japanese economic juggernaut has no brakes," and that much like Gertrude Stein's Oakland, when it comes to Japan's national interest, there is no there there, simply political, bureaucratic, and industrial elites who confuse the country's national interest "with the prosperity and perpetuation of their own organizations." Van Wolferen is contemptuous here of "self-censorship" by Japanologists in the U.S., arguing that "Complacency, once merely unattractive, is now dangerous," and that his analysis, along with that of Hollerman's, "should not be dismissed as 'Japan bashing' or be met with accusations of ignorance, racism, or other unworthy motives." Of course not, which is not to say that the arguments are not without flaws. All industrial nations try to integrate their public and private interests to some extent — what's good for General Motors, after all, is good for America — and what to one observer may be a dangerous case of "lack of accountability," may simply be proof once again of the axiom that all politics are local to another. One gets the feeling that the Japanese are moving ahead, not because they cheated on the way the international "game" is played, but because they played better than anyone else, for whatever reason, and that if the U.S. is losing control of its destiny, then the place to look is in Washington, not Tokyo.

On a more philosophical plane, the Summer issue featured two essays on "Democracy," "The Next South Africa," by Francis Fukuyama, and "Religion and the Third Wave," by Samuel Huntington. In "The Next South Africa," which was nominated for 10 Best consideration by *TNI* editors, Fukuyama, the author of the forthcoming *The End of History and the Last Man,* attempts to draw a connection between Afrikaner prosperity and political reform as a case study in a "common internal pattern of socioeconomic development" connecting "liberalizing revolutions" currently taking place around the globe, in countries as diverse as the Soviet Union and Brazil. Some of our readers still find Fukuyama a little too Hegelian for their taste. In an "Exchange," in the Fall issue, *New Republic* senior editor Jacob Weisberg argued that Fukuyama's analysis "does a better job of explaining why apartheid was ultimately doomed than why it tumbled when it did," and that while "there is a strong correlation between socioeconomic advance and democratic development around the globe," the linkage "falls short as a causal explanation." In his reply, Fukuyama writes that "As I feared," he has been misunderstood as an economic determinist, and he believes there is a linkage between industrialization and democratization, "politics and ideology must intervene."

Noted political scientist Samuel P. Huntington, in "Religion and the Third Wave," Summer, sensitively yet unsentimentally examines correlations between religion and the level of economic development and democracy in society, finding that "The logo of the first fifteen years of the third wave could well have been a crucifix superimposed on a dollar sign," and wondering what might lay ahead for East Asian dominant-party states combining Western procedures and Confucian values when they encounter economic downturn or stagnation.

Besides academics and policymakers, *TNI* attracts working journalists as well, who usually expound further in depth on themes raised in their columns, usually with mixed results. *New Republic* senior editor Fred Barnes, in "Winners and Losers," Summer, produces no surprises — other than the observation that "there was more coverage of this war than of any in history" — and we must confess to having problems with articles like this, which reduce a life-and-death enterprise like war to a political scorecard. Another *New Republic* senior editor, Morton Kondracke, produced a primer on "Mexico and the Politics of Free Trade," Fall, and while there was little new here for readers familiar with the subject, a general audience encountering the topic for the first time was able to get something out of it. *Washington Times* columnist Richard Grenier, in "Hollywood's Foreign Policy," Summer, has fun in skewering the current generation of American directors, actors, and screenwriters for apparently being out of touch with the American mainstream when it comes to foreign policy and U.S. intervention abroad. While some of his barbs hit home, we have to take exception to his veneration of such Hollywood "heroes" as John Wayne and Sylvester Stallone, who sat out the major conflicts of their generations. And Grenier at times seems to favor the dubious principle that patriotism equals blind support for the foreign policy of whatever president happens to be occupying the Oval Office at the moment, although we know that is not his intent.

We continue to enjoy *TNI*'s book reviews, the contributors often able to add fresh perspectives to books that have already been heavily reviewed elsewhere. Columnist Robert D. Novak, reviewing Bob Woodward's book on the Pentagon, *The Commanders,* pointedly observes that by failing to gain access to the commander-in-chief, Woodward has tried "to write *Hamlet* without the Prince." In "The Ultimate Resume," Summer, Fareed Zakaria, a Macarthur fellow at the Center for International Affairs, Harvard, uses his review of Godfrey Hodgson's biography of Henry Stimson, *The Colonel,* to outline the role Stimson played in marrying the principles of traditional "American Realism" with modern U.S. diplomacy. While we may disagree with Zakaria with the essential benign nature of *pax Americana* —Desert Storm did not usher democracy into Kuwait — he makes his case well. This is true, also, of Michael Lind's critique of Daniel Patrick Moynihan's *On the Law of Nations,* "Moynihan's Law," Winter 1990/91. Lind, assistant to the director of the Center for the Study of Foreign Affairs, U.S. Department of State, argues for a middle course between the surrendering of national sovereignty, as he sees liberals like Moynihan calling for, and the total repudiation of international law, which some conservatives are calling for. He presents the traditional conservative argument well, but never discusses the fact that it is this cynical attitude toward international law — using it when it suits our interests, ignoring or breaking it when a president feels it necessary — which weakens international law more in the long run than an openly hostile attitude toward it would.

We remain impressed by *TNI,* publisher Irving Kristol and editor Owen Harries having created a forum for conservative intellectual thought on U.S. foreign policy. Areas of improvement still remain, however. Foreign economic policy considerations remain a weakness, and there was little on the Third World in 1991, *TNI* concentrating on such heavily-covered big accounts as the Middle East, the former Soviet Union, and Europe. In addition, we found some of *TNI*'s entries to be thinner in substance this year, often recycling ideas we had already come across elsewhere, a shortcoming made even more pronounced by the presence of such heavyweights as Huntington and Fukuyama. Of course, neither *Foreign Affairs* nor *Foreign Policy* are models of consistent excellence, though we still feel that the material in *TNI* could be more substantial. *TNI* continues to be challenging and provocative in a field where pomposity and tendentiousness are more often the norm, but there remains room for intellectual heft in its pages.

Publisher: Irving Kristol

Editor: Owen Harries

Address: 1112 16th Street, NW
Suite 540
Washington, DC 20036
(202) 467-4884

Circulation: 1990 — 5,024
1991 — 4,000

National Journal

The Capitol Hill publication for up-and-coming politicos, staff aides and lobbyists, *National Journal* regularly provides an insider look at the ways Washington works, or doesn't work, as the case may be. *NJ* doesn't deal so much with policy, or policy prescriptives, as with how policy is made, detailing the players, the mechanics, and all the sometimes mind-numbing facts and figures that enter into a government policy decision. Few facets are overlooked. With such a perspective, *NJ* rarely makes it outside the Beltway, and, when it does, probably has a readership limited to ex-Beltway residents, and aspiring Beltway types. No matter; for that tiny, particular constituency, *National Journal* continues to be required reading.

Not a news magazine as such, *National Journal* still garners important angles on the movers and shakers in the nation's capital. One such profile, of Senate Majority Leader George Mitchell, is a 10 Best selection in Political Reporting, "The Judge's Trials," by Richard E. Cohen 7-13. This sturdy composite of the political fortunes of Mitchell is one of the first to question his waning influence in politics; parts of this selection are based on Cohen's *Washington at Work: Back Rooms and Clean Air,* published in December. Another angle on a political event is explored by Julie Kosterlitz in "Health Care: The Issue for 1992?" 11-16, a 10 Best nominee in which she blasts the conventional assessment that health care will be *the* deciding factor in the '92 presidential race, via the Thornburgh-Wofford race in Pennsylvania. These articles are typical of the work of *NJ* as its selections are consistently centered around the function of government and politics, sometimes examining the minutiae, sometimes dealing with broader themes. While this focus is not necessarily of interest to the general reader, or even to the policymakers themselves, as *National Journal* can be obtuse in its meticulous reporting of particulars, *NJ* is read loyally by staff aides and those with business in Washington, if not by those in Congress and the White House itself.

National Journal weathered losing not one, but two of its managing editors this year without any noticeable decline in quality. Richard Corrigan died of a heart attack January 3, first stricken in the *NJ* newsroom. His obituary in *The Washington Post* sung his (and *National Journal's*) praises appropriately: "A gifted writer, Mr. Corrigan occasionally published stories on the lighter side of the day's issues, and these broadened the tone of a magazine that is esteemed first of all for the care and thoroughness of its reporting." With *NJ* since its founding, Corrigan was succeeded by columnist Dick Kirschten. Charles S. Clark left later in the year, and was replaced by Bill Hogan. With all the turnover, some of it rather dramatic, *NJ* continued to vigorously report Washington doings.

Among them, the staff correspondents at *National Journal* cover most conceivable aspects of government. From Capitol Hill to the White House, the budget to the U.S.'s role in the international arena, all are dissected and laid bare in *NJ*. The political sections in *NJ* are probably the most informative for staff aides and lobbyists, if only for the names and faces of the policy players that can be passed along to superiors to help grease the wheels of policymaking. Analytics, generally, are not *NJ's* strong suit, although several of their correspondents are honing their abilities to a noticeably sharp edge. Richard E. Cohen, in addition to his 10 Best selection, examines how, as congressional committee influence weakens, aides are acquiring new roles and influence — and the complaint is that they're assertive, arrogant and lusting after power, "People of Influence," 6-15, quoting Sen. Trent Lott (R-Miss): "I think we have too much staff, too many around here. . .sometimes staff members think they are the Senators." The report was a hotly discussed item in the Beltway. This issue, dedicated to "The Hill People," also provided a listing of senior staff that is actually paid more than the congressmen whom they serve, an item that was picked up and disseminated by the national press. Dick Kirschten, before ascending to the position of managing editor, details the infighting and fractiousness at the Leadership Council on Civil Rights in "Not Black-and-White," 3-2. While this trim examination of the forgotten minority, the Hispanics, is of some interest, we get little sense of the organization's political importance or clout. Chief political correspondent James Barnes had an off year, penning rather pedestrian articles such as "Liberal Democrats Feeling Their Oats," 1-5, a laundry list of how the Democrats are holding seminars and discussion groups to redefine their platform, and "Still Missing Reagan," 3-2, typical on the conservatives and CPAC. "White House Notebook" columnist Burt Solomon always gives us the lowdown on the White House staff, as in "Halfway Through Bush's Term It's Turnover Time for Staff," 2-16, an otherwise low caliber exercise, considering the mid-term shift in emphasis to re-election. Similarly, information useful only to insiders and up-and-comers is found in "For Bush's Staff, Discretion Is the Better Part of Power," 8-3, on press and public relations at the White House, and "Bush Evokes All the Right Feelings Without Rolling in the Flag," 10-12, on Bush's public appearances as everyman at Disney World, the Grand Ole Opry and so on. While *NJ's* stock in trade is this kind of insider perspective, we'd appreciate a deeper appraisal of the workings of government on the national level.

National Journal also covers various peripheral topics connected to the smooth functioning of the Beltway. Regulation, lobbying, education and demographics are among the subjects that are examined in their relationship to governance. Margaret E. Kriz in "Boosting Nuclear," 2-23, is very intelligent on the pros and cons of nuclear energy, and the external factors which have led the Bush administration to begin to push for industry expansion: "The war has focused the public's attention on one of America's most pressing energy problems: its rising dependence on foreign oil. [president of the American Nuclear Energy Council Edward M.] Davis says that nuclear power is the solution to that dependence and to the nation's other major energy problem, the declining surplus of electrical generating capacity. Electric cars can replace today's gasoline-powered fleets, he argues, and nuclear energy can fuel transportation and supply the nation's growing electricity demands. The industry also touts nuclear power as the solution to global warming. Unlike coal and other fossil fuels, nuclear fuel does not emit gases that are thought to increase the earth's temperature." Health care correspondent Julie Kosterlitz works to bring us the politics of health care, would-be policymakers and shapers of health care as a national issue. She blows Sen. Edward Kennedy's cover in "Agenda Setting. . .Again," 1-19, by reviewing his past empty promises on health care as he once again tries to set the agenda with rhetoric on reform, scoring many points, one of which is summarized by Dukakis' campaign adviser, Robert Berenson, who said that health care reform "is complicated, and not easily reducible to election kinds of rhetoric." Law correspondent John W. Moore adeptly categorizes the shift at the margin of the war on drugs from the casual to hard-core user, "Rethinking Drugs," 2-2. In keeping with *NJ*'s credo of providing appraisals of key players in and out of government, Moore relates how the S&L bailout has become a bonanza for lawyers, "First, Pay the Lawyers," 4-27, as regulators seek to sort out the disaster. Similarly, in "Dead in the Water?" 5-18, Carol Matlack gives us a bird's-eye view of how, after five years of breathtaking expansion, Hill & Knowlton Inc.'s Washington office seems to be running out of steam; she gets off to a good start in her discussion of whether or not the marriage of P.R. and government relations ever really worked, but Matlack quickly descends into a list of who's gone where and why. And in "Connected Couples," 7-2, Matlack never really addresses the ethical issues so current when the spouse of a member of Congress is a lobbyist; her Rolodex-like listing of who's married to whom, and what each lobbies for, will be useful to those who want to get inside, however.

Finance and economics are covered in this same manner, with *NJ* providing the names and faces of policymakers rather than in-depth discussions of policy itself. In "Capital Gains Heresy," 3-9, Lawrence J. Haas gets the political wrangling over the issue, as the Democrats begin to discuss how "a cut that's targeted at gains on investments in new (small) businesses might look less like a tax giveaway." As befits *NJ,* this was the best job we saw of assembling the details on the proposals circulating among the Democrats who, ". . .if they were to support a targeted cut, could portray themselves as pro-growth, thus easing some of the public's anxiety about how they'd manage the economy." From the same issue the editors at *NJ* submitted Paul Starobin's "Bypassing Banks," cover 3-9, for consideration for our 10 Best section. A discussion of the changing roles of banks with the advent of various kinds of alternative financial institutions and how changing investment and borrowing patterns are robbing banks of much of their traditional business, Starobin compiles different opinion as to what the future of the banking industry should be, intriguing, but ultimately inconclusive. Also nominated by *NJ*'s editors for 10 Best consideration is Jonathan Rauch's expose of how taxpayers are taking much of the risk for business failures, in the form of government financial guarantees, "You Lose, We All Pay," 4-6, a solid look at the dangers. Rauch also provided the data outlining the case that Bush is one of the most regulatory presidents since Carter, "The Regulatory President," 11-30, importantly noting how massive social regulation is helping to stifle the growth of small business. International trade correspondent Bruce Stokes is organized and detailed on the international markets and how interdependent they are, and the potential need for international regulation in "As the World Trades," 8-17. Stokes does not advocate, but quickly builds his case in the light of Japanese securities scandals and other international quirks. Kirk Victor provides clear, sharp views of the relationship between government and the communications industry, " 'FIN-SYN' Battling and Billing Goes On," 4-13, on how the FCC's decision to relax its 1970 financial and syndication rules — "fin-syn" to insiders — left both producers and networks fuming, prompting a ferocious lobbying fight, and with "Disconnections," 5-11, a profile of the five FCC regulators who rule on cutting edge communications issues, such as "finsyn," and how they are miscommunicating.

National Journal does not stint on the foreign policy arena. David Morrison, their resident foreign policy maven, appeared in sources from *Government Executive* to *In These Times,* in addition to *NJ*. With "Getting Ready for the Next Battleground," 3-23, Morrison examines U.S.

combat readiness in the wake of the victory in the Gulf and the beginning of military budget cuts, quoting senior military officers who doubt it could happen as quickly. Rochelle Stanfield moved to the demographics and immigration beat, covering intragovernmental affairs, while former foreign policy reporter Christopher Madison returned to his old beat from covering the Congress. Madison quickly moved up to speed with such dispatches as "Cambodia Divisions," 5-4, an examination of how the Hobson's choice situation in Cambodia has again split U.S. policymakers over whether to continue to aid resistance groups aligned with the Khmer Rouge. He offers very good examples of the sparks that have been flying between Reps. Solarz and Atkins, along with helpful background on Cambodia itself. Stanfield also adjusted quickly to her new territory, providing adequate work both before and after the move. Her discussion of the disarray in the Soviet Union, "The Other War Zone," 2-2, has depth, noting the point made by Madeleine Albright of the Center for National Policy — Gorbachev never pretended to be a democrat and has never consented to dismantling the communist system, but Americans ignored those shortcomings because of the dramatic reforms he *did* lead. And in "School Business," 7-27, Stanfield outlines the different approaches business would take to reforming schools, a thorough, though overlong, reading: "The problem for much of American industry is that its strategic weapon for the economic battles of the future is being trained by a public school system operating on a Korean war-era intellectual level."

National Journal made attempts this year to do feature stories with broader themes. In addition to "The Hill People," 6-15, *NJ* offered a special report outlining predictions for "America in the '90s," 9-28. This ambitious project looks at the family, "Strains in the Family," by Rochelle Stanfield; demographics, "Rule Suburbia," by William Schneider; business, "The Cutting Edge," by Paul Starobin; "Work Force Workfare," by Kirk Victor; the changes for the U.S. in the post-Cold War world, "Gunbelt Diplomacy," by David Morrison; and Congress, "Inevitable Change," by Richard E. Cohen. Nominated by *NJ*'s editors for our 10 Best section, this exhaustive effort brings together a terrific amount of information, but, despite all the facts and figures cited, there's little here that actually tells us where the country might be going — except to the malls.

The columns at *National Journal* are mired in the mundane. William Schneider, who so impressed us with his political acumen in *The Atlantic* several years ago, seems downright depressed by the lack of direction in the Democratic party; he gets all the correct detail, but only infrequently puts things in context. He's completely conventional in "Suddenly, The Quayle Factor Revives," 5-11, as Bush's irregular heartbeat forced the country to consider Dan Quayle as president, Schneider asserting that this gives the Democrats an opening for 1992; when people vote for Bush, they might actually be voting for Quayle. Schneider relies heavily on polls to make his points. Jack Germond and Jules Witcover can be fresher, as with "Yeutter Will Be a Team Player at RNC," 1-12, a smart evaluation of the possibilities of Clayton Yeutter in the RNC top spot, pegging him as a potentially key player in Bush's reelection campaign. As "State of the States" columnist, Neal Peirce is frequently superficial, apparently never leaving his District of Columbia office for these state political profiles. In "Lessons From a Political Pariah," 3-6, he is unconvincing on the tactics of New Jersey Governor Jim Florio, who has one of the lowest approval ratings in history because of his ramming a $2.8 billion tax package through the Legislature last year — much of the money being pumped into "disastrously under-financed inner city schools." Peirce never looks at the damage the package has continued to cause the N.J. economy, as small businesses fold and large businesses cut back where they can or move out altogether.

National Journal, with its hefty subscription price, has to make every word worthwhile to those in government to maintain its base. *NJ* generally manages to provide insider views for insider people, more so for those who aspire to the heights of power in Washington rather than those who have attained it. With its listings of key people on the issues of the day, replete with assessments of where and how they fit into government, *NJ* is not the selection for the casual reader. *National Journal* is the trade magazine for aspiring politicos.

Publisher:	John Fox Sullivan
Editor:	Richard S. Frank
Address:	1730 M Street, NW
	Washington, DC 20036
	(202) 857-1400
Circulation:	1990 — 6,014
	1991 — 6,000

National Review

The Wick Allison era at *National Review* came to an abrupt end in 1991, the publisher departing in mid-October after having teamed up with Brit John O'Sullivan to retool *NR,* both financially and editorially. Besides becoming more intellectually vibrant, *NR,* under Allison's direction, began branching out into such endeavors as a book division responsible for a highly popular college guide; a "NR Town Hall" computer network, and the National Review Institute. Bidding farewell to Allison in a memo to *NR* staff and readers in the 11-18 issue, *NR* founder William F. Buckley, Jr. noted that under Allison's tenure *NR* circulation grew by 45 percent, and advertising revenue was up by 27 percent. "Get this: Of the forty weekly and fortnightly magazines published in the U.S., *NR* is the only one to show a growth in page sales in 1991."

Appropriately enough, Allison's replacement, Ed Capano, is a *NR* lifer who rose through the ranks during his thirty years on the production side of the magazine, and who became associate publisher in 1983. While it is still early in his tenure, it appears that he will compliment editor O'Sullivan as he makes *NR* a forum for such diverse voices as Daniel Patrick Moynihan and William J. Bennett, who signed on this year as a senior editor. As drug czar, Bennett fashioned himself as a general engaged in a war, and he fits right in at *NR* where ideas have been drafted, trained, equipped, and then ordered into battle against Hollywood liberals, Washington Democrats, moderate Republicans, unreconstructed Marxists, multiculturalists, government regulators, and all who march under their banners. The result is an exciting publication which can now go the distance with any heavyweight out there in the political publication division.

We found *NR* to be a fascinating barometer of mainstream conservative feelings toward President George Bush. Editorializing on the President's domestic policy and the economy in "Strait of the Union," 2-25, *NR* prophetically warns that without a capital-gains tax cut, the coming economic recovery may be as weak as the recession that preceded it: "Capital-gains-tax relief is an idea whose economic time has come. It deserves a better fate than the fact-finding commission which the President has recommended for it." Marking the first anniversary of an editorial expressing deep dissatisfaction with Bush, *NR,* in "New Best Friend," 8-12, praises the President for his handling of the Gulf crisis and his apparent turn to the right on such issues as civil rights and abortion. "Conservatives. . .owe George Bush their plaudits for his behavior this year — notwithstanding our raspberries past and, all too probably, to come."

It didn't take long for the raspberries to reappear. In "Darmageddon — The Sequel," 8-26, *NR* castigates the Bush administration for not taking the same "minimalist approach" to governing that Ronald Reagan did, so that budget deficits today do not perform the same "fiscal function" that they did during the Reagan years, when the fear of higher deficits helped restrain spending. "Had Mr. Bush followed through on his campaign pledge — a flexible spending freeze, lower capital gains taxes, and, above all, *no new taxes* —the deficit 'problem' would be a manageable one gradually disappearing into history. The recession might never have happened; it would certainly have been less severe. Such are the rewards of bipartisanship."

By the end of the year, *NR* seemed to be essentially writing off the Bush presidency, stating in "Fortune Favors the Brave," 12-16, that "Unless President Bush makes a major, explicit, and convincing turn to the right. . .we can no longer support his Administration. And such a transmogrification seems at present unlikely." Significantly, *NR* examined seriously the pros and cons of a presidential campaign by columnist Patrick Buchanan, noting that "On many issues — taxes, spending, quotas, crime — Mr. Buchanan speaks for all conservative," while holding out the hope that a "happy warrior" will emerge to take up the conservative cause. "Fortune Favors the Brave," perhaps the most important editorial in *NR*'s recent history, indicates that 1992 is likely to be a turbulent year on the U.S. political scene.

On other domestic issues, *NR* continues to be unapologetically right, take it or leave it. Commenting on the LAPD-Rodney King incident, "Thugs with Badges," 4-1, *NR* notes that "law and order can't be maintained by crime," but that "It's no extenuation of these thugs' behavior to ask, however, whether it may be best understood less as purely gratuitous violence than as a sort of cynical vigilantism, stemming from the collapse of effective prosecution." Applauding the Supreme Court decision banning the mentioning of abortion in federally-funded health clinics, "Right of Subsidy," 6-24, *NR* states that "No private body can dictate the terms on which it accepts federal funds. If Planned Parenthood cannot subscribe to these not-very-stringent conditions, it should be removed from the public dole, and if that requires a presidential veto of legislation passed by an abortion-happy Congress, so be it."

NR championed Clarence Thomas and his nomination to the Supreme Court, drawing a favorable contrast between Thomas and the justice he was replacing, Thurgood Marshall, "The Image of Justice," 7-29. "This contrast is important and sends a welcome message to the part of the black community that is disaffected from its 'leaders.' The message is: you have a right to your own opinions." Commenting on the Clarence Thomas-Anita Hill imbroglio, "Senatorial Harassment," 11-4, *NR* contends: "Whether you believe Miss Hill depended mostly on whether you subscribed to (or were cowed by) the feminist mythology according to which even the most innocuous-seeming male is a rapist at heart and a presumptive harasser."

Domestic coverage in *NR* continues to be anchored by Washington bureau chief William McGurn, whose reports usually lead off the "On the Scene" section. At times McGurn produces reports which complement the main editorial — on 12-16, for example, he follows up "Fortune Favors the Brave," with "The Bush That Stole Christmas," writing critically on the "The Gang of Three" — OMB Director Richard Darman, then-Chief of Staff John Sununu, and Treasury Secretary Nick Brady — for standing in the way of a pro-growth package. "Indeed, the Gang of Three sound like Soviet commissars talking about meeting their November widget quotas while their citizens are waiting on bread lines." Other times McGurn writes on a subject that, while not in the headlines, is of interest to anyone concerned with the political scene, as in "The Democrats 'Lee Atwater,'" 7-29, telling us all about "James Carville, a down-and-dirty Louisiana born lawyer turned Democrat consultant." His cover story on Republican congressional leaders Bob Michel and Bob Dole, "The Two Bobs," 12-2, echoed Allison's past criticism of the Republican congressional establishment and its disinclination to upset the status quo.

NR also draws on a deep well of regular conservative writers — having Terry Eastland, for instance, report in full on the backroom efforts to sink the Thomas nomination, "Advice and Descent," 11-4. And it was in the pages of *NR* that White House aide James Pinkerton sketched out the principles behind the much-heralded "new paradigms" in "New Paradigms, Old Principles," 1-28. Ben C. Toledano, reporting on David Duke's gubernatorial campaign, "The Lull Within the Lull," 10-21, labels Duke a "press-made person," but writes: "Even George Bush, on a good day, would have difficulty finding fault with his platform. . .The problem is not with the proposals but with the proponent." Warren Brookes's cover story on Richard Darman, "Dead Wrong Again," 10-7, lacks the columnist's usual crisp touch and fails to move the story forward, Brookes merely summarizing conservative criticism of the budget director and the agreement he helped create in 1990.

Of course, much of *NR*'s attention in 1991 was devoted to the nternational scene, and the editors are justifiably proud of the coverage they provided on the Gulf War and the collapse of communism in the Soviet Union with their limited resources. *NR* supported the war, in a manner that was refreshingly free of jingoism. In "Cry Havoc," 1-28, *NR* writes that Iraq must be made to withdraw from Kuwait, pay reparations, and agree to international supervision of a reduction of its military might. "If war is indeed required to achieve these aims, President Bush should not shirk from waging it." As the smart bombs began to fall *NR,* in "The New Face of War," 2-25, notes: ". . .we must recognize that despite the precision of our weapons we are dealing out death and destruction on a vast scale. Unavoidably, this means the inadvertent punishment of civilians: if we knock out power stations and burn up refineries and gasoline stocks, if we destroy Iraq's transportation system and the warehouses that hold food for Saddam's armies, civilians will suffer, too. This should not cause us to stay our hand, but it is a sobering thought." *NR* was critical of the President's subsequent decision not to march all the way to Baghdad, however, writing in "No Desert Quagmire," 5-13, that "In short, unwarranted fear of a 'quagmire' has driven us into a small swamp."

War coverage encompassed all angles. Armchair generals could enjoy Alistair Horne's "Of Men and Missiles," 2-25, in which the veteran correspondent outlines the conflict, drawing on such diverse sources as a briefing with General Schwarzkopf in December 1990 and historical analogies, including South America's War of the Triple Alliance, in 1864. Eliot A. Cohen, in "After the Dust Settles," 2-11, calls the air-war strategy "the proper one" in order to win both the war and the peace afterward, when, Cohen argues, it will be important that Saddam not be shown as a victor by having inflicted heavy casualties on the coalition. As the war entered the ground combat phase, retired colonel Trevor N. Dupuy, in "The Way of the War," 3-18, informs readers what to expect next, unfortunately the war was over before the issue appeared, but subsequent events proved Dupuy right about one thing: "Until a new Iraqi government is established and makes peace with the allies, there could be unrest, violence, and anti-coalition activity for some time, particularly in outlying regions to the north and west." Dupuy subsequently offered a superb wrap-up, "How the War Was Won," 4-1.

War coverage in *NR* was not limited to conceptual pieces. *USA Today* correspondent Donald Kirk, the only American print journalist in Baghdad the night of January 16th, wrote about his experiences in "Middle-East War Diary," 2-25, and contributed "From the *Souk,*" 3-18, a revealing, street-level report from Amman on Palestinian reaction to the Gulf War. *NR* continued to print dispatches from Kirk throughout the year, on post-war developments in the region and, in the autumn, his reports from Vietnam. Throughout the war and the immediate aftermath, *NR* drew on journalists on the ground both in the Gulf and in other important locales, such as Moscow, to provide comprehensive coverage.

In his first effort for *NR,* "Rebirth of a Nation," 3-18, senior editor Bennett wrote on the growing perception that the successful Gulf War is enabling the country to put the Vietnam syndrome behind it, picking up on such pop cultural clues as a recent "Saturday Night Live" sketch poking fun at the media coverage of the war. "When *Saturday Night Live,* the counter-culture comedy show par excellence, prefers the military to the media, a major cultural shift is taking place." We also found in *NR* the finest article on the anti-war movement we saw anywhere, David Horowitz' "Coalition Against the U.S." 2-25.

The historic events in the would-be Soviet Union were also covered in depth in *NR.* Not surprisingly, *NR* was skeptical up until the end. Commenting on the crackdown in the Baltics and Gorbachev's efforts to reinstate central planning, "On the Moscow Homefront," 3-18, *NR* states: "With his popularity at an all-time low, Gorbachev has little to gain from the free choice of Soviet citizens. He needs the repressive possibilities of the Soviet system. Recent events do no more than confirm that he has come to that realization." *NR* rejected the thinking behind the idea of a "Grand Bargain," offering aid to the Soviet Union in exchange for promises to reform, "No Bargain," 6-24: "The very fact that the Soviet authorities, with the richest natural resources in the world, are looking to the West to give them massive aid while hesitating, so far, to initiate serious structural change is all the proof one needs that they have their priorities wrong. Western aid to the present Soviet system will only make genuine change slower and more painful."

The collapse of communism in August was a personal triumph of sorts for the magazine and the values it has been espousing for 36 years, a fact Buckley noted in a special column, "We Won," 9-23. Let history show that *NR* was gracious in victory, finding a kind word to say about Gorbachev: "This Soviet pluralism, we should concede, was the legacy of Mikhail Gorbachev," Boris Yeltsin, "[he] deserves a bouquet," and the Russian people. "Russians, it turns out, as like people everywhere, capable of choosing good as well as ill." Lest anyone worry, however, *NR* is still not dropping its guard, noting that Marxism was borne of "nineteenth-century utopian impulses," which live on in such contemporary forms as "ecological fascism, health fascism, forbidden-speech codes, radical feminism, reverse racism, multiculturalism, and so on," advanced by alliances of "minorities and outsiders such as gays, feminists and the discontented of every stripe."

NR's coup coverage rivaled its Gulf War coverage in its breadth. The news of Gorbachev's overthrow broke just as the 9-9 issue was going to press, but *NR* was able to squeeze in a last minute interview with noted Sovietologist Robert Conquest, who clearly outlines the issues and personalities involved, noting that "[The coup leaders] might (or one of them might) simply lose their nerve: they are playing with fire, and they know it."

The 9-23 issue was devoted to the coup and its aftermath, *NR* noting that "Lenin would never have believed this. And Walter Duranty wouldn't have reported it." Highlights included roving correspondent Radek Sikorski's report from Vilnius, "Strings Attached," and Robert Conquest's essay "Reflections on the Revolution," which offers thoughtful criticism on the desire by international leaders to preserve some sort of strong center. Charles Fairbanks, in "Getting It Wrong?" offers revealing documentation on how Sovietologists have been consistently wrong on developments over the years, this essay appearing before a similar effort by Peter Reddaway in *The New York Review of Books*, "The End of the Empire," 11-7. *NR* even ran an excerpt from Aleksandr Solzhenitsyn's *Rebuilding Russia: Reflections and Tentative Proposals*, "Our Own Democracy," 9-23, in which the Nobel laureate insisted that democracy could grow in Russia, if it had local roots and people willing to defend it.

Other noteworthy cover stories include editor John O'Sullivan's successful attempt to deal with what he views as an inherent contradiction in "Reaganomics" and "Thatcherism," the efforts to ensure economic competition, which is inherently destabilizing, with an ideology based on conservative values, in "Is the Heroic Age of Conservatism Over?" 1-28. *NR* expertly dealt with the issue of academic freedom in our universities under the current campus political climate by printing an adaptation of a speech delivered by University of Chicago sociology professor James S. Coleman upon receiving the 1990 Sidney Hook Award from the National Association of Scholars, "A Quiet Threat to Academic Freedom," 3-18. In the best cover story we saw on domestic issues in *NR* all year, the 10 Best nominated "The Siege of Yonkers," 5-13, Lorrin Anderson memorably documents the racial tension resulting from Federal Judge Leonard B. Sand's attempts at desegregating housing in the city of Yonkers, N.Y., Anderson expertly noting that by focusing in on race, Sand missed out on the key question of class in housing patterns. It is this type of clear-eyed reporting that advances conservative arguments further than a hundred boilerplate editorials condemning "social engineering."

NR continues to offer special sections devoted to a wide-ranging discussion of major issues of the day, the editors more often than not avoiding an overlapping of opinions, presenting instead thought-provoking essays that examine current debates from all angles. A two-part symposium on the Middle East, "Can America Bring Peace?" 8-26 and 10-7, featured such contributors as J.B. Kelly, Yitzhak Rabin, and Ralph de Toledano, and captured fully the great divide separating Arab from Israeli as the Madrid peace conference approached. A special supplement on a papal encyclical to mark the centenary of *Rerum Novarum*, "The Pope, Liberty, and Capitalism," 6-24, drew on such writers as Milton Friedman, Michael Novak, and Robert A. Sirico, many of whom found a vindication, if qualified, for the market system and a rejection of collectivism. As is often the case where the spiritual meets the secular, the emphasis comes down on the secular. Kenneth Minogue, professor of politics at the London School of

Economics, for example, labels the pope the "Chief Executive Officer of the greatest multinational corporation in history," "[S]pecializing in moral and theological products, it dominates its market the way IBM dominates computers. . ."

As usual, *NR* also devoted a number of covers to cultural and social issues, and in 1991 we came away disappointed more often than not. In "Are There Episcopalians in Foxholes?" 7-29, senior editor Richard Brookhiser provides an entertaining read on the decline of the Episcopalian Church as it moves further from tradition, although the analytic line is a bit weak. Critic-at-large Joseph Sobran's cover story on Madonna, "Single Sex and the Girl," 8-12, is well written, but fails to offer any original criticism on this cultural and marketing phenomenon: "It isn't just that she's hopelessly banal whenever she tries to share an insight. It's that she has reached that pitch of egomania at which celebrity supposes itself oracular." *New Criterion* publisher and *Commentary* music critic Samuel Lipman asks "Can We Save Culture?" 8-26, issuing a clarion call for conservatives to retake control of American culture — "the realm of meaning and value" from liberals, although we feel that anyone who takes to the arts out of doctrine, instead of artistic sensibility, is bound to fail.

The editors continue to tinker with the regular departments, making changes here and there, increasingly making the book livelier to read. "The Protracted Conflict" column was renamed "World in Conflict," though not surprisingly, the pessimism and skepticism toward international actors remains. In "An Attack of Pactitis," 8-12, Brian Crozier condemns the rush by Western European nations to sign treaties with the Soviet Union and the great value placed by diplomats on retaining current borders. "By trying so hard to preserve 'stability' and the status quo, the foreign policy experts and their bosses, our elected leaders, are getting in the way of a *status quo post* that might have prospects for real stability — one in which the United States and the European democracies would look to their own interests instead of their enemy."

"Books, Arts & Manners," continues to feature the incomparable John Simon as movie critic. We are told that some people subscribe to *NR* just to read Simon and we believe it. *NR* now has a theatre critic as well, Eva Resnikova, who also critiques dance for *The New Criterion*. There is still no regular TV critic, however, as evidently no talented writer is willing to spend the hours necessary in front of the tube. Literary editor Brad Miner departed late in the year to return to the publishing industry, and we share O'Sullivan's sadness in seeing Miner depart. During his two and a half years at *NR,* Miner had enlivened the book reviews, striking an artful balance between major works of fiction and non-fiction and *NR*'s self-imposed imperative of paying notice to virtually every conservative book. And his inside knowledge of the publishing industry made "Random Notes" must reading for anyone interested in books, professionally or personally.

NR now features "The Gimlet Eye," and "The Misanthrope's Corner," on its back page instead of "Off the Record." We believe the decision is a positive one, and as much as we found "Off the Record" to be informative, we thought it was the wrong note on which to close a magazine devoted to reflective thought and witty writing. Longtime "Gimlet Eye" writer D. Keith Mano has departed, however, following the sale of his new novel, *Topless,* to Hollywoodland. Mano has been replaced by Scripps Howard News Service editorial writer Andrew Ferguson. He starts off on a strong note, in "Mossback Meets Guns 'n' Roses," 10-21, where he dutifully tries to relate to the new Guns 'n' Roses album, *Use Your Illusion II,* and finds that he can't. "As the fogey within me asserts itself, I worry that I will struggle vainly against it and wind up like one of those potbellied guys you see waddling through America's college towns, dressed in colored T-shirts and bell-bottoms and sporting handlebar mustaches, the guys who refuse to get the message, which is this: the popular culture has passed them by, as it must all of us."

Publisher:	Wick Allison
Editor:	John O'Sullivan

Address: 150 East 35th Street
               New York, NY 10016
               (212) 679-7330

Circulation: 1990 — 150,000
               1991 — 150,000

New Perspectives Quarterly

This handsome quarterly brings together perspectives and opinion from respected intellectuals, political activists, noted authors and major thinkers on one topic per issue. *New Perspectives Quarterly,* a scant six years young, has emerged as one of the most intellectually attractive and stimulating magazines in a long time. Never stuffy or pompous, *NPQ* explores and engages the issues of the day without being prosaic or esoteric.

One of *NPQ*'s strengths is that the editors are able to pull together diverse intellectual opinion without making their treatments seem either haphazard or disjointed. Instead of viewing topics through a more traditional left vs. right, liberal vs. conservative prism, *NPQ* garners opinion from all along the ideological spectrum. Though the editors are decidedly liberal, as we see in the introductions to each issue, there's never any hint that the editors are framing an issue. Rather, the scholarly folk whose names appear in *NPQ*'s pages are permitted to retain their own voices. The thought-provoking essays take us into the minds of such esteemed thinkers as Yelena Bonner, Hans Kung and Gish Jen on topics such as the rising tide of nationalism, the changing international order, and racism. These perspectives are rarely found in other places, and never in such readable form.

In addition, *NPQ* is meticulously focused. Each issue is devoted to a singular subject with broad implications for the world. As such, a world view is employed; the axis is never American, but global. Foreign perspectives are not only welcome, but sought, and are necessary to maintain *NPQ*'s tart vitality. *NPQ* does not limit itself in any way, most importantly, intellectually or ideologically. Where there are ideas, *NPQ* will ferret them out and present them at their unique roundtable for our consideration.

Editor Nathan Gardels and senior editor Marilyn Berlin Snell share the duties and privileges of introducing each issue with a column outlining the themes of the featured topic, perceptively linking each article. In "Opening the Cactus Curtain," Winter, Gardels and Snell lead into the issue of exploring the changes in Mexico the free-trade agreement will bring, with contributions from intellectuals, authors and politicians from President Carlos Salinas de Gortari to Mexican journalist Carlos Monsivais. Gardels and Snell provide here a broad overview of the changes discussed in the interviews, essays and conversations to follow, only half tongue-in-cheek on the downside of the opening of a North American trade zone: "By making the forbidden link with the *Yanquis,* Salinas has invited in their meddlesome civil society. For, along with development dollars will come democratic norms. Along with toothpaste and tourists will come Jimmy Carter's fair-election observers, public-opinion polling by the *Los Angeles Times,* human rights scrutiny by America's Watch, analysis and debate by *NPQ.*" Aware of their own role in spurring such analysis and debate, Gardels and Snell are tough in conducting their interviews and molding conversations into essays, conscious of the importance of preserving the original sense of the conversation and carefully walking the line between editing and editorializing.

Just as importantly, *NPQ* retains a sturdy sense of history. Rather than providing quick snapshots, an instant history of a world event, by nature *NPQ* provides more pensive appraisals with its offerings of didactic views and philosophies. The treatment of the issue of nationalism, "The New Babel," Fall, begins with an important interview with political philosopher Sir Isaiah Berlin, "Return of the Volksgeist." Berlin traces the phenomenon of nationalism back through the modern age, taking us on an impressive tour of history in which we find that "in our modern age, nationalism is not resurgent; it never died. Neither did racism. They are the most powerful movements in the world today, cutting across many social systems." This interview is followed by essays and coversations from Carlos Fuentes, Yelena Bonner, Alexander Solzhenitsyn, Price Sadruddin Aga Khan and Pico Iyer. Even Disney CEO Michael Eisner is consulted in "It's a Small World After All," where he uses Voltaire as a defense for the popularity of U.S. culture abroad: " 'If they go to see one of my plays,' Voltaire wrote, 'it is probably a good play. If they don't go, it is probably not a very good play.' The same is true for American entertainment in general."

A similar sense of history runs throughout all the issues of *NPQ*. A grouping of selections on "The Last Modern Century," Spring, assesses the future by examining the past for clues. Rather than trumpeting the "end of history," we find a cogent examination of the "fate of the religious imagination at the turn of the millenium and ask whether ethnic and religious revivals will make this the last modern century." As Nathan Gardels notes in his introduction, "The great question at the turn of the century was whether, in a new age of science and technology, religion and traditional culture could survive. The question for the next century is whether we can survivie the technological age in their absence. . .As the last modern century comes to a close, the recovery of the sacred and the soil needn't lead to a restoration of the past. If leavened but not desecrated by the experience of modernity, it will lead to the conservation of the future." A critical assessment of race, "RACEism Will Always Be With Us," Summer, rather depresses us with its realism. From Jesse Jackson to Jack Kemp to Nicholas Lemann to Arthur Schlesinger Jr., diverse views are presented and discussed. All see different root causes and solutions to the particular problem of race and the racial barriers that separate, some more convincing than others, but all intriguing and intelligent. We're always required to reassess our own position on an issue after *NPQ* is finished with it.

This one-time newsletter of the Institute for National Strategy has emerged as a journal of preeminent thought since merging with the Center for the Study of Democratic Institutions. A trim little quarterly teeming with insight and information, *New Perspectives Quarterly* is quickly becoming a must read for us.

Publisher:	Stanley K. Sheinbaum
Editor:	Nathan Gardels
Managing Editor:	Marilyn Berlin Snell
Address:	10951 W. Pico Blvd., 2nd Floor Los Angeles, CA 90064 (213) 474-0011
Circulation:	1990 — 10,000 1991 — 10,000

The New Republic

The New Republic continues to be the blue chip franchise of U.S. political commentary, attracting the cream of the crop of writers and policymakers, its editorial style more often than not providing undergrad wit and post-grad wisdom that both illuminates contemporary events and puts them in perspective. Unlike many other publications in this field, who often approach issues with so much solemnity one can almost hear organ music in the background, *TNR* champions academic freedom, an interventionist government and an assertive foreign policy with enough high-level energy to light up northwest Washington for a year. Even when one disagrees with *TNR*'s outlook, or feels that the magazine has gone over the top, one cannot divert one's attention. Reading *TNR* can be like watching the class straight-A student placing a cherry-bomb in a desk when the teacher's back is turned.

Things might even get more unpredictable now that Andrew Sullivan has taken over the reins as editor, replacing Hendrik Hertzberg, who remains as a senior editor. The 28-year old Sullivan comes from Britain, bringing several prefixes with him, including "Tory," and "gay," outing himself on the latter in a "Washington Diarist" column, "Sleeping With the Enemy," 9-9. "Sleeping With the Enemy," appearing a month after "Pride and Prejudice," 8-5, in which senior editor Morton Kondracke confessed to being a "prude," left senior editor Jacob Weisberg wondering in another "Washington Diarist" column, "Miata Culpa," 10-14, if the "confessional mode" was going to become increasingly popular at *TNR*. Perhaps. The same week "Miata Culpa" appeared, *TNR* published "Kindest Cut," in which *Washington Monthly* contributing editor Scott Shuger gives a detailed account of his vasectomy, which he labels "the most personally and socially responsible thing I've done in a long time." Uh oh.

Sullivan's early months were marked by several substantive cover stories, to be sure, including an 11-page effort debunking the "October Surprise" controversy still surrounding the 1980 Reagan-Bush campaign, "The Conspiracy That Wasn't," 11-18. Steven Emerson and Jesse Furman exhaustively undermine the credibility of key witnesses being advanced by such proponents of the arms-for-delayed-hostages-release theory as former NSC staffer Gary Sick. "The Conspiracy That Wasn't," is a hopeful sign that the kind of journalism that encapsulated the "weekly blend of passionate engagement, skeptical argument and original reporting reinforced by a strong sense of value," which won *TNR* a 1990 National Magazine Award for general excellence for magazines under 100,000 circulation under Hertzberg's editorial hand, will continue under Sullivan.

Hertzberg's last year was marked by extensive coverage of the major international and national issues of the day. Since the initial invasion of Kuwait last August, *TNR* had taken a hawkish stance toward Iraq, and this stance continued throughout Operation Desert Storm. In January, as Congress debated between continuing with the sanctions or giving the President backing to go to war on January 15th, *TNR* published "The Stakes in the Gulf," 1-7/1-14, by Stephen J. Solarz. Solarz, a Democratic congressman from New York who began his political career as campaign manager for one of the first anti-Vietnam war candidates in the country, laid out the strategic and moral case for the use of force in the Gulf.

After the war began, *TNR* continued to attempt to assuage liberals who hung a yellow ribbon on the front porch while harboring secret doubts and guilt. In "No Vietnam," 2-18, Paul Starr, a co-editor of *The American Prospect* and a teacher at Princeton, presents the liberal brief for supporting a war against Iraq, including a ground war to liberate Kuwait, in a manner that almost suggested a Vietnam Protester Anonymous meeting.

About the only *TNR* opposition to war, or questioning of it, appeared on the front and back pages, in the "TRB" column and the "Diarist" page. Senior editor Michael Kinsley was in South Africa when the war began, but returned home and immediately began expressing eloquent opposition to the war, in such columns as "Dink Stover at War," 2-18, and "Dead Iraqis," 3-18. The moral issues raised by the war were also the topic of senior editor Robert Wright's "Nantucket Diarist" column, "No Man Is an Island," 2-18, in which Wright contends that despite Bush's protestations about a new world order, "when push came to shove, he was moved by something deeper and older than thought."

The troubling moral issues raised by war were also examined in the finest article we saw on Operation Desert Storm in the pages of *TNR* or anywhere else, C.D.B. Bryan's cover-story profile of the commander of U.S. forces in the Gulf, General H. Norman Schwarzkopf, "Operation Desert Norm," 3-11. Bryan, who first met Schwarzkopf in 1971, when he was researching his now-famous book on U.S. soldiers mistakenly killed by their own forces in Vietnam, *Friendly Fire,* drew on his relationship with Schwarzkopf to draw a three-dimensional portrait of "The Bear."

TNR's war coverage was distinguished by its reports from the Middle East by freelance writer Michael Kelly, who became *TNR*'s special correspondent in the Gulf region. A full entry for Kelly can be found in the "Foreign Correspondents" section of *MediaGuide*.

As the war wound down, *TNR* applauded President Bush's performance (while noting he still has an "execrable domestic record") in "The End of the End," 3-18, while sounding a somber note on Iraqi casualties in "The Dead," 3-25. However, latent sympathy for Iraq and support for the President's Iraq policy quickly dissipated, *TNR* quick off the mark in criticizing the President's handling of post-war developments. In "Rest in Pieces," 4-8, *TNR* argues that "The dismemberment of Iraq by its long-suppressed populace, and with our acquiescence, would be a gain for all the peoples of the region," while in "Dances With Wolf," editorial 4-22, *TNR* states that "Our betrayal [of the Kurds] is a human tragedy and an ethical disaster." In "Staying There," 7-29, *TNR* calls on the President to use any means necessary to remove Saddam Hussein from power: "Until the butcher of Baghdad is gone or buried, the Gulf war cannot be won, despite all of Mr. Bush's triumphalist rhetoric."

TNR's writings on the Arab world often exhibited hardline attitudes expressed in purple prose. Editor-in-Chief and Chairman Martin Peretz, in "Worst Enemy," 3-25, writes that "The butchery inflicted on Kuwait was precisely what [the Arabs] expected. Indeed, it was what so excited those who took to the streets in support of Iraq in various Arab capitals. In this part of the world governments and movements are not a guard against bestiality, but its provocateur. Indeed, a war that does not take frenzied revenge for grievances real and imagined is hardly deemed a war at all." In "Unpromised Lands," 6-3, he draws on the writings of Hannah Arendt to argue that without the national rights that come with belonging to the group in power, people such as the Kurds are without protection for human rights as well. As to the other famous stateless group in the Middle East: "To compare the claims to nationhood of the Kurds and the Palestinian Arabs makes for some interesting ironies in the politics of the Middle East. The passion for a distinctive Palestinian state among the Arabs, unlike that among Kurds for a Kurdish state, is derived less from that people's intrinsic history than from their intimate encounter with the Jews." Writing on the Madrid peace conference in "The Gain in Spain," 11-25, *TNR* observes that "On the way to autonomy... Palestinian narrative will never acknowledge the luck of the draw: that of all potential enemies, they, the Palestinians, had drawn the Israelis."

TNR devoted two issues to the collapse of communism in the Soviet Union, 9-9 and 9-16/23, and uncharacteristically the contributors, who ranged from Tatyana Tolstaya to Walter Laqueur, failed to move the story forward, instead echoing what we were reading and seeing elsewhere on such subjects as Boris Yeltsin and the dangers of nationalism. Long critical of basing U.S. policy on Gorbachev's good intentions, in "The August Revolution," 9-16/23, *TNR* states that "As this magazine has long predicted, the disintegration of the Union was inevitable, and the assertion of nationalism is likely, in places, to be savage," and comes out in support of Sen. Bill Bradley's plan, outlined in *The Washington Post,* 8-29, to establish "along with the European Community and Japan, a Marshall Plan-style office in Moscow that would provide aid...and technical assistance to cooperating republics that establish market economies, agree to trade freely with one another, and reduce defense spending."

This kind of musty approach to policy is usually evident in *TNR*'s approach to domestic economic issues as well. While a staunch defender of free trade, in "Rio Grande Illusions," 5-27, *TNR* endorses the fast-track approach to a trade agreement with Mexico, with editorials like "The Slump Hump," 11-18, which intones: "Fundamentally, America's problem is not that the economy isn't growing now, but that for the last twenty years our rates of savings, investment, and productivity growth have all trailed those of our major competitors. The task facing the U.S. government is to remove this encumbrance, not to concoct gimmicks to make 1992 safe for incumbent politicians."

The Year 1992 was frequently on the mind of *TNR,* with sharp-tipped articles seemingly intended to deflate the balloons of Democratic presidential hopefuls. Morton Kondracke kicked off the year with "Bill Folds," 1-28, comparing New Jersey Bill Bradley to "a fading jump shooter." Writing on Senator Sam Nunn's performance during the Gulf crisis in "The Mystique of Sam Nunn," 3-4, Sidney Blumenthal contends that Nunn has been exposed as being "decidedly mortal." Mario Cuomo received a whole issue, and in "Broken Record," 5-6, Kondracke asserts that "a close examination of Cuomo's eight-year record as governor indicates that New York's current woes are the result not just of the recession and Reagan-era cutbacks, but also of chronic bad management. And Mario Cuomo shares much of the blame." In "Tsnooze," 8-12, Jon Keller documents why "Among those who have watched [Paul] Tsongas's rise from young county-politics reformer to a one-term Senate career cut short in 1982 by cancer. . .it's not uncommon to find skepticism about the gaps between Tsongas's rhetoric and his record."

Perhaps the last word on all of this was provided by *TNR* in "The Wimps Factor," 9-2, where the magazine bemoans the lack of Democrats willing to put themselves and their careers on the line by challenging George Bush in 1992. "It is not that the non-candidates lack vision. Indeed, their collective vision has emerged out of their various acts of studied reticence. In this vision, all of them see themselves as president, having gotten to the Oval Office by an easy, relatively unobstructed path. They will have triumphed by a politics without struggle, leaving their images — their permanent records — unblemished. Animating this vision, however, is not so much prudence or shrewdness as narcissism."

Which is not to say that *TNR* will be endorsing George Bush for re-election. *TNR* was on the President's case all year. In "Don't Look Down," 4-15, Blumenthal is prescient on how "the high optimism that Bush has generated can curdle into disillusion. Resting on his laurels is the form his hubris would take." Senior editor Fred Barnes, who turned in another year of yeoman service on the "White House Watch," vividly captures the void at the center of domestic policy inside the administration in "The Slump Thing," 11-4. "The Slump Thing" was matched with "The Drifter," 11-4, Blumenthal's gleeful political obituary for the President. Savage as Blumenthal can be at times, however, *TNR* also instituted a regular "Notebook" feature, the "Bushism of the Week," which, if nothing else, demonstrates that the President can be his own worst enemy. The "Bushism" for the week of 11-25, for example, was promoted as Bush's "heart-felt, sincere, from-the-gut opposition to fellow Republican David Duke": "I want to be positioned in that I could not possibly support David Duke because of the racism and because of the. . .bigotry and all of that."

David Duke was, of course, one of the more extreme manifestations of a year which saw growing racial and cultural tension in the U.S. While many commentators treated these issues warily, like they were downed power lines in a murky pool of water, *TNR* jumped right in, head first, then gleefully analyzed the intensity of the sparks.

In the editorial "The Derisory Tower," 2-18, *TNR* labels the efforts to install multiculturalism in academic curriculums as being "one of the most destructive and demeaning orthodoxies of our time," and goes on to devote an entire issue to the subject, highlighted by Irving Howe's spirited defense of the concept of making distinctions of value and the idea that Western culture is worthy of study, "The Value of the Canon." Marxist scholar Eugene D. Genovese, in "Heresy Yes — Sensitivity, No," 4-15, demonstrates acute intellectual integrity and sounds the tocsin against the new dark ages stalking universities. In counterbalance, Kinsley, in one of his best "TRB" efforts all year, "P.C. B.S." 5-20, writes that "After wading through much of the anecdotage of PC hysteria, my own conclusion is that very little of it supports the charge that anyone's right of free expression is being stifled, let alone that there is a reign of terror on campus."

TNR was thorough and outspoken on racial relations in the U.S. as well. The unrest in Washington was the subject of two fine cover stories in June, "Over the Rainbow," 6-10, by Charles Lane, and "Latin Mass," 6-10, by Peter Skerry and Michael Hartman, informed reports on the growing friction in urban areas brought by on Hispanic immigration. *TNR*'s 10-14 cover effort on the violence in New York's Crown Heights district, "Invisible Man," by David Evanier, and "Crown of Thorns," by Jonathan Rieder, uncompromisingly and unapologetically zero in on anti-Semitism in the black community and the rising tribalism in U.S. society, as evidenced in New York City in the 1990s. In *TNR*'s best effort all year on race relations, "How Do They Do It?" 8-5, Charles Moskos examines how one institution, the U.S. Army, has managed to become a racial success story without falling back on such policies as affirmative action or quotas. "So what can be transferred? Maybe a broad lesson: race relations can best be transformed by an unambiguous commitment to non-discrimination coupled with uncompromising standards of performance."

Race was one of the key elements in the most explosive domestic story of the year, the nomination of Clarence Thomas to the Supreme Court, a controversy on which *TNR* spoke with a wide variety of voices. When Supreme Court Justice Thurgood Marshall retired and President Bush announced Thomas as his replacement, *TNR* treated the story with cynical levity in the 7-29 "Notebook," drawing an analogy between Jesse Helms's campaign ad in the autumn of 1990 addressing white fears over racial quotas and the White House's stated preference of placing either an African American or a Hispanic on Marshall's seat. "No one seriously believes Mr. Bush when he says he thinks Mr. Thomas is the most qualified person for the job of Supreme Court justice." *TNR* also took Virginia Governor Wilder to task for casting a slur on Thomas's impartiality because of his Roman Catholic background.

One week later, in "It's OK to Ask," 8-5, Michael Kinsley defended Wilder's question, if not his wording of it, drawing on the criticism Mario Cuomo has received because of his policy of not allowing his religious beliefs to drive policy: ". . .you cannot denounce Cuomo for illogic and then complain that any special curiosity about a Catholic's views on abortion amounts to an unconstitutional 'religious test' for abortion." Kinsley's real point here is that it is perfectly acceptable for the U.S. Senate, in the course of providing its advice and consent on judicial appointments, to ask nominees questions about their judicial philosophy and how it would affect their vote on specific issues, including "the leading controversial controversy of the past two decades," *Roe v. Wade,* arguing that "Anyone with no opinion on it isn't qualified to sit on the Supreme Court."

Kinsley remained consistent on this point until the end, arguing in "Liars and Boobs," 10-21, that Thomas's insistence that he had never seriously thought to "the most controversial constitutional ruling of our day," made him out to be either a perjurer or a phenomenon worthy of mention in the *Guinness Book of World Records*: "If Clarence Thomas has no opinion about *Roe v. Wade,* he is just about alone in the world."

While other commentators would pick up on Thomas's testimony and erroneously argue that Thomas was claiming to have never *discussed Roe v. Wade* (he admitted to listening to discussions on the subject while never expressing an opinion himself), Kinsley seemed to be virtually alone in questioning the credibility, and professional stature, of a attorney who spent much of his professional life in a highly conservative administration who appeared to be claiming to have had never given enough *thought* to the abortion issue to have formulated an opinion on it. In addition to his opposition to Thomas, the integrity of the entire judiciary confirmation process was a concern of Kinsley's throughout the hearings, the co-host of "Crossfire" seeing the Thomas nomination as the inevitable end product of a cynical system which had passed on Anthony Kennedy and David Souter, writing in "Liars and Boobs" that "there is nothing wrong with the confirmation process that a few more rejections wouldn't cure."

Kinsley diverged from the editorial page, in opposing Thomas up until the end. In "The Thomas Nomination," 10-7, *TNR* comments that "Our worry about Judge Thomas is not so much that he has too many firm principles, but that he appears to have too few," but votes thumbs-up on the nomination anyway. "Mr. Thomas is no less qualified than Justice Kennedy, who was rushed through the confirmation hearings with nothing like the inspection accorded to Mr. Thomas."

Of course, *TNR* did not know it at the time, but the senatorial inspection of Clarence Thomas was just beginning. Commenting on the Anita Hill-Clarence Thomas confrontation in "Mr. Thomas Goes A-Courting," 10-28, *TNR* states that "the controversy itself will perform its usual magic, by tainting the nominee, even if he is acquitted. It is a fittingly farcical end to a farcical process," while in "Conservatism Betrayed," 11-4, *TNR* takes the position that by deciding to focus on his race, Thomas undermined the conservative agenda he was sent out to defend. "Mr. Thomas's 'lynching' remark during the last days of the hearings was perhaps the logical end to this strategy. But it was also the end of his conservative strategy." Hendrik Hertzberg, in "What a Whopper," 11-4, contends that by going along with the White House strategy of painting Anita Hill as engaging in an elaborate conspiracy to derail the nomination, Thomas "has forfeited his honor and besmirched his country."

TNR managed to engender controversy of its own in several cover stories during 1991. Jacob Weisberg's report on the ills of the U.S. publishing industry, "Rough Trade," 6-17, appeared when the ABA Convention was opening in New York, and drew heated response from the industry. Readers got a taste of it in "Publish and Perish," 7-15/22, five pages of correspondence on "Rough Trade," from such writers, editors, and agents, many of whom rose to the defense of Simon & Schuster editor Alice Mayhew. For our part, we noticed that while Weisberg was hard on book editors for allowing factual errors to slip by in the rush to the marketplace he committed one of his own, crediting *Time* for having first divulged the "sordid contents" of Bret Easton Ellis's graphic novel *American Psycho,* when actually it had been *Spy* which performed this particular public service.

The other explosive cover, which may have led to as much controversy behind the scenes at *TNR* as it did to the participants, was "The Power of Myth," 8-19/26, Andrew Ferguson's deconstruction of Bill Moyers. Ferguson argues that the man familiar to PBS viewers as an opponent of governmental abuses of power and supporter of such pop gurus as Joseph Campbell and Robert Bly is a hypocrite, his hands dirtied by his experiences as a top aide to President Lyndon Johnson and his ability to reap financial gain while working for public television, at one point calling Moyers's arrangements to get around the funding rules as "money-laundering."

Moyers, apparently tapping the iron man within, chose to respond by taking out a two-page ad in *TNR,* "An Open Letter to the Editor From Bill Moyers," 10-7, labeling Ferguson's article as being "McCarthyite" and "abominably inaccurate," and concluding that "If [Ferguson] were a gentleman, I would challenge him to a duel. If he were a journalist, I would challenge him to appear with me before any panel of impartial editors in the country. As he is neither, I will rest my case on your readers' sense of fairness." In his reply, Ferguson states that "Stripped of the artful irrelevancies that Mr. Moyers offers in mitigation, most of what is written there simply confirms what I wrote in my article." Exchanges like this one are what dialectics, *TNR* style, are all about.

TNR continues to be justifiably proud of its back section, "Books & the Arts." While the apparently immortal Stanley Kauffman continues as film critic, Robert Brustein brings bite as theater critic, his role as a theater professional affording him firsthand observations on the multicultural battles being waged on both sides of the curtain. The book reviews continue to impress, *TNR* more often than not matching up the right book with the right reviewer. There is, though, the occasional misfire. *New York Times* White House correspondent Maureen Dowd's review of Kitty Kelley's *Nancy Reagan: The Unauthorized Biography,* "Ol' Blue Lips," 5-13, goes over the top, Dowd apparently using up an eight-year backlog of anti-Reagan quips and observations. Much more effective are efforts like "Operation Desert Shill," 9-30, Gregg Easterbrook's devastating critique of General H. Norman Schwarzkopf. "There is shame. . .in refusing to discuss the deaths caused, while being all too happy, for a price, to natter on about anything else."

Editor-in-Chief: Martin Peretz

Editor: Andrew Sullivan

Senior Editor: Hendrik Hertzberg

Address: 1220 19th Street, NW
                  Washington, DC 20036
                  (202) 331-7494

Circulation: 1990 — 100,000
                  1991 — 100,000

Newsweek

Katharine Graham's brainchild is the only tried and true *news*weekly left intact at the close of an extraordinarily bad year for the genre. *Time* has begun the process of turning itself into a cultural and essay magazine after several years of experimenting with essays in the guise of news items. *U.S.News & World Report* sticks steadfastly to its credo of presenting only "News You Can Use," although we do find a respectable amount of hard news remaining in its pages. *Insight* is well on its way to becoming the Sunday Magazine of *The Washington Times;* although still distributed to subscribers, it is part and parcel now of the *Times*'s Sunday edition and, like *Time,* has undergone massive staff and editorial cuts. What was once a crowded market, with each publication jockeying for position, has now been left almost exclusively to *Newsweek*.

Fortunately, the editors seem to have arrested *Newsweek*'s slide into becoming a *People's Home Journal,* which we worried last year might be the ultimate fate of the weekly. The silly "Special Editions" that kept appearing in our mailbox, outlining and defining our quality of life or what our quality of life should be, have been recast to some degree. The "Special Editions" are becoming just that. Although "How Kids Grow," Summer, seemed more appropriate as a supplement to *Parenting* than to *Newsweek,* we did like "When Worlds Collide," Fall/Winter, which, instead of approaching Columbus's anniversary of the discovery of the new world from a strictly politically correct perspective, examined the changes wrought overall in a balanced, thoughtful manner.

We'd also complained last year about the growing dearth of hard news items featured on the cover of *Newsweek*. This trend, too, has been reversed. There is a lesser number of soft news features appearing on the cover, soft news defined here as anything not relating directly to politics, international affairs, the economy, or a singular news event, such as, say, the anniversary of Pearl Harbor. There were only 22 covers devoted to soft news this year — almost a direct reversal from the ratio of soft to hard news covers last year, when we saw 29 soft news covers, and only 23 covers examining hard news items. Now we see a marked changed even in the soft news coverage. Rather than getting a regular diet of covers such as the frivolous "Poison Pen: The Boom in Trash Biography," 4-22, or the goofy "What Do Men Really Want?" 6-24, *Newsweek*'s soft news covers more often featured such interesting and educational topics as science, "Heavens!" 6-3, and "How Dinosaurs Lived," 10-28; health and nutrition, "Fed Up!" 5-27, "Lead and Your Kids," 7-15, and "Halcion," 8-19; race, "The New Politics of Race," 5-6, and "Tackling Taboos," 6-10; political correctness, "Thought Police," 12-24-90; and AIDS, "Doctors with AIDS," 7-1, " 'Even Me' — Magic Johnson," 11-18, and "Safe Sex," 12-9. Those covers which addressed hard news topics tackled tough issues, both domestic and global: the Kurds, " 'Why Won't He Help Us?' " 4-15; recession, "Riding Out the Recession," 1-14; and "What Recovery? The Bite on the Middle Class," 11-4, and the presidential election campaign, "No Bull," 10-14. More than ever before, we want to open *Newsweek,* and we're invited in by the seriousness of the cover selections.

Some of this improvement is probably due to realignments in the top levels of management. Editor Maynard Parker took over day-to-day editorial responsibility from Editor-in-Chief Richard M. Smith when he acquired the duties and title of president. Parker has worked hard to keep *Newsweek* moving along at a smart pace, obtaining exclusive first-serial rights to both Gen. H. Norman Schwarzkopf's autobiography, projected publication in Spring 1992, and Boris Yeltsin's personal account of the Soviet coup attempt, projected publication in Fall 1992. Two columns, "Behind the Lines," by Jonathan Alter, and a "Straight Talk" interview with the presidential candidates, were inaugurated this autumn to begin to assess the field for 1992. Parker also added several contributing editors. One, Col. David Hackworth (ret.), had already been appearing throughout the Persian Gulf War as a special correspondent; we welcome his addition, as we were impressed by some of his reconnaissance during the war. Frank Deford, former editor-in-chief of *The National,* came aboard late in the year, in time to pen a rather moving argument for this 50-year mark to be the last remembrance of Pearl Harbor, "Maybe We Should Forget It," 11-25, including a note of how the incident was burned into our national consciousness: "Pearl Harbor was the first example of national cluster emotion. As that phenomenon, it lives not as a historic event but as personal recollection, not much different from a first kiss or a high-school graduation." Lorene Carey, author of *Black Ice,* was added to the masthead as well; we get a sense of her book and her experiences in "A Children's Crusade," 11-4, an overview of her feelings at being a black who went through an all-white prep school. At the same time, few people were dropped from the masthead, although there was the customary movement in and among the bureaus. It's encouraging that, at a time when the other newsweeklies are retrenching by downsizing, *Newsweek* is expanding modestly and cautiously, with those at the helm prudently planning for the magazine's future.

What's even more promising are the special projects *Newsweek* has been turning out. These long, thoughtful essays are well researched and well written, always examining topics worth exploring. A wordy, but worthwhile, exploration of the life and times of Clarence Thomas is featured on the cover, 9-16. "Supreme Mystery," by David Kaplan et al., is an in-depth examination of Thomas's life, although not of his judicial philosophy. It is noted in the introduction that it took the team two months to put this together, and it's quite possible, judging from the wealth of information and fresh quotes they offer. They do not ignore the central paradox of Thomas either: "Precisely because he was black, he was given position and place. Yet because he was black, he was denied the recognition he deserved." A sound debunking of the October surprise conspiracy theory is offered after months of investigative work by a team of *Newsweek* reporters, "The Making of a Myth," cover 11-11. The groundwork had been laid the previous week with John Barry's "One Man, Many Tales," 11-4, in which Barry and a group of reporters dissected the claims of Ari Ben-Menashe, allegedly a key player in the October surprise. Barry led the team of "The Making of a Myth" as well. An exhaustive effort, the *Newsweek* expose coincided with a similar treatment by *The New Republic.* Although *TNR's* article, written by Steven Emerson and Jesse Furman, was quite good, *Newsweek's* team went out and got interviews with Ben-Menashe and Jamshid Hashemi, where Emerson and Furman only employed secondary sources to detail the doings of those two in their pivotal roles in expanding the reach of the theory. Justifiably excited about these in-depth exercises, *Newsweek's* editors nominated "Supreme Mystery," 9-16, "One Man, Many Tales," 11-14, and "The Making of a Myth," 11-11, for 10 Best consideration.

Newsweek's coverage of the Persian Gulf War was respectable, the magazine more than keeping pace as far as the newsweeklies were concerned. There were many examples of solid reportorial effort, particularly in defining the weapons and strategies of the Persian Gulf commanders. A special report which *Newsweek's* editors nominated for our 10 Best section, "The Path to War," cover 1-21, is an exceptional overview of strategies and possibilities that reflected the concern of policymakers and commanders alike, without seeming biased or intractable. This issue contains our first real look at Col. Hackworth, who was an anchor for the weekly's war coverage. In "We'll Win, But. . ." Hackworth applies his expertise in combat to devise potential strategems and outcomes, but it's his lead that stays with us: "Never has such force been assembled on so small a battlefield. If war comes to the Persian Gulf, more than 1 million soldiers will clash across a front no larger than Massachusetts." The articles of the cover "Hard Days Ahead," 2-4, on Operation Desert Storm, include some inside information on the war's early hours: "The weak point in Iraq's early-warning net was discovered on its southern border, where there was a gap in radar coverage. As Stealth aircraft and cruise missiles made the first attacks, U.S. commandos were helicoptered into Iraq through the gap. They widened it by blowing up two early-warning radar stations. This created a radar-free corridor for attack planes, some of which fanned out to destroy the air-defense control center and radars in Iraq's southern sector. The radars were all pointed south, and the warplanes swung around to the north to attack them." Beginning with the 2-4 issue, *Newsweek* featured special pullouts (maps of war zones, 2-4; a pullout poster with weaponry and the generals, 2-18); *Time* would follow their lead, 2-25, with a special pullout battle map and key weapons. Russell Watson et al. postulate on "Four Ways the War Could End," 2-18, the scenarios fairly conventional, but acceptable newsweekly fare. Henry Kissinger turns up for "A Scenario for the Endgame," 2-25, with sensible and rather astute advice: "It is crucial for the prospects of a creative postwar policy that Saddam cannot claim any success. Saving his face mortgages the peace." But he offers no outline for the "creative postwar policy," he suggests. Also worthy of note is Ken Adelman's "Star Wars in the Desert," 2-4, an outline of how the weapons developed during the Reagan years are now winning the war against Iraq. John Barry and Evan Thomas provide a quick and pensive examination of where the military might want to go with its hardware in "War's New Science," 2-18. Complementing this is Gregg Easterbrook's " 'High Tech' Isn't Everything," 2-18, one of the first articles to question the rosy reports of technological success and applying this success to policy: "Now that an ideal-circumstances application of air power and electronic superiority has harmed but hardly routed little Iraq, perhaps the idea that gizmos can conquer all will finally be relegated to the Tom Clancy little boy's fantasy world where it belongs. Let us have no delusions that advances in smart weapons can make any nation invincible — or that any degree of technology can alter the underlying ghastliness of war."

The on-the-scene reports were lively and credible. Tony Clifton offered a first-person account "on the Kuwaiti border" of the first skirmishes of the ground war with "Going into Battle With the Tiger Brigade," 3-4. Christopher Dickey reports from Amman on Saddam Hussein's strategy for a prolonged war, "Rope-a-Dope in Baghdad," 2-4, in which we also get a "Lifestyles of the Rich and Famous" view of his underground bunker: "It boasts such luxuries as a sauna and fourposter bed with a red silk canopy; such precautions as walls built to withstand atomic blasts — there are even toilets tested for radiation." Dickey is rather disappointing in "The Blunderer from Baghdad," 2-25, though, taking the conventional and widely-touted view that, although Saddam Hussein understands his own country, he hasn't a clue about the big, wide world around him. Col. David Hackworth meshes information and strategic expertise in "Keep the Pressure Up," 2-25, as he evaluates the latest incidents in the war theater and Saddam Hussein's offer to pull out.

A special issue, "Victory!" 3-11, wraps up the major events and relevant players in the Persian Gulf War, the overviews quite serviceable: "After the Storm," 3-11, by Russell Watson et al.; "The Rewards of Leadership," by Ann McDaniel and Evan Thomas with Howard Fineman, on Bush's windfall; "A Soldier of Conscience," by Tom Mathews with C.S. Manegold and Thomas DeFrank, on Gen. H. Norman Schwarzkopf; "Kuwait: Rape of a Nation," by Steven Strasser et al.; the details of "A Textbook Victory," by John Barry and Evan Thomas; "Move Forward and Shoot the Things," by Tony Clifton, a recounting of his experiences with the Tiger Brigade 3-67 "Hounds of Hell" battalion; "Anatomy of a Cakewalk," by Ray Wilkinson, an overview of the march into Kuwait; and Col. David Hackworth's "Lessons of a Lucky War," placing events in a strategic context. Editor of *Newsweek International,* Kenneth Auchincloss offers a bird's-eye view of what the international community thinks of the U.S. and its position after the Gulf War, "America's Giant Step," 3-11, an erudite, balanced examination. Like many other publications and television programs, *Newsweek* salutes the fallen, "The Heroes Remembered," 3-11, with photographs and short anecdotes. The weekly also lists the "Non-Battle Deaths" and makes no bones about the fact that this is an incomplete list: "Many of the war dead are remembered on the following pages. The low casualty count came as a relief to many Americans who had fearfully anticipated a chemical attack or a long, grinding ground war. But a seasoned warrior took little comfort. 'I would tell you that casualties of that order of magnitude [are] almost miraculous,' said Gen. H. Norman Schwarzkopf last week. '[But] it will never be miraculous for the families of those people.' " Tom Mathews offers the well-researched special report, "The Secret History of the War," cover 3-18, a tidy roundup of the war from the intelligence and strategic points of view that was nominated by *Newsweek*'s editors for 10 Best consideration.

Unlike the other newsweeklies, *Newsweek*'s coverage of the war and its effects continued to be thorough and in-depth long after hostilities had ceased. While the follow-ups *Newsweek* provided were not always as impressive as the dispatches from the war itself, the follow-through was further evidence of the magazine's desire to present itself as a serious purveyor of news. Christopher Dickey gives a response to the question, "Could the Rebels Really Rule?" 4-15, seeing no end to the vicious divisions which will fracture whatever coalition or compromise may come out of the uprisings in Iraq. His "A Nation in the Valley of the Three Frontiers," 5-6, is an equally sorrowful appraisal of the Kurdish situation, lacking the sensationalism of many similar stories, but also some of the edge. Rod Nordland evokes the pain of repatriation in "Going Half the Way Home," 5-13, his writing further emphasizing the plight of the Kurds; his "A Kinder, Gentler Quagmire," 5-27, is vivid and detailed from Iraqi Kurdistan, with hints of more hardships to come; and in "Saddam's Secret War," 6-10, Nordland travels through Kurdistan to find remnants of villages destroyed by Hussein prior to the Gulf War, the tragic anecdotes moving us by hinting at Saddam's brutality, without manipulating our emotions. Tony Clifton supplements the Kurdish coverage with "Burying the Babies," 4-22, utterly editorial in his conclusion that the West really must do something, anything to help these Kurdish refugees, but we're hard-pressed to dislike the piece. First he makes us feel, and then he makes us culpable: "It seems to me that if a coalition of Western and Arab nations could form itself a few months ago to free the people of Kuwait, and if they could spend billions of dollars and risk thousands of lives to achieve that aim, then in all conscience they have to work out how to do it again for a people far more helpless than the Kuwaitis ever were." The Colin Powell cover, 5-13, is less a profile of the four-star general than a poorly disguised advertisement for Bob Woodward's new book *The Commanders*. Much of Evan Thomas's lead article, "The Reluctant Warrior," is based on Woodward's research, and then is followed by pertinent excerpts from *The Commanders,* as if we hadn't had enough of them already. Pentagon correspondent Douglas Waller gave us salient detail on the special forces deployed in Desert Storm, "Secret Warriors," cover 6-17, this selection nominated by the editors at *Newsweek* for our 10 Best section. Col. David Hackworth effectively examines "The Lessons of the Gulf War," 6-24, while still being quite readable: "One thing above all must be remembered. Desert Storm was the mother of all military anomalies. It was a war unto itself, not a model for the future. Just one example: will the United States ever face again an adversary who will give us six months to build up our strength?" A cover treatment of women in combat, "Should Women Fight to Kill?" 8-5, provides a smart debate on the question: Barbara Kantrowitz explores "The Right to Fight," with Eleanor Clift and John Barry; Hackworth then offers a sterling examination of the question of women in combat, "War and the Second Sex"; and finally, Army captain Carol Barkalow argues that "Women Have What It Takes," an impressive, rounded treatment.

The foreign correspondence the remainder of the year was also quite respectable, as well executed as we've seen in many a year in *Newsweek*. The issues covering the attempted coup in the Soviet Union highlight this. An entire edition devoted to "The Second Russian Revolution," 9-3, is led off by international editions editor Kenneth Auchincloss with "Falling Idols," a cogent examination of what may take the place of the communist system. Tom Morgenthau, with Fred Coleman and Carroll Bogert, catalogue the shifting players in "Now Comes the Witch Hunt." Rod Nordland predicts that the failed coup may cut the Baltic states loose sooner than we think, "Fast Track to Freedom," Tom Mathews et al. detail the actual events of the coup, "The People vs. the Plotters." Rounding this out, along with the various foreign dispatches edited in New York, is former Prime Minister Margaret Thatcher, who urges that the West take the initiative in "We Must Not Falter Now." The "Crackup" cover 9-9, appropriately takes up nearly half the magazine and is given "Special Report" status with stories covering various angles of events (and repercussions of events) in the Soviet Union, an impressive effort in size and scope. Russell Watson et al. lead off with "End of an Empire," in which the disintegrating union is examined, and different scenarios, some more plausible than others, are explored. In "The Coup Maker's Secrets," by Tom Mathews et al. appears to have an inside track on the coup, through "documents" obtained by *Newsweek,* along with other nebulous but evidently reliable sources, but as so few sources are cited specifically, we do have a hard time judging the veracity of some of this. Andrew Nagorski examines the "Questions of Loyalty," in which we find that the backlash against those involved in the coup and those accused of being involved is quite severe. Douglas Waller, in "A Nuclear Nightmare?" and Charles Lane with Waller and Ann McDaniel in "How the West Can Win the New World Order," trimly explore the security risks and possibilities for a real and lasting peace. "Democracy Deferred" by Tom Post with Melinda Liu, Kari Huus, Marcus Mabry and Rebecca McKinnon, is a fine examination of how events in the Soviet Union have impacted on Beijing, until the last lines, which, unfortunately, set our teeth on edge: "Last week the State Department expressed strong concern about the fate of Chen [Zemin] and Wang [Juntao], tried as 'counterrevolutionaries' last February and sentenced to 13 years each. Their cause has given fresh impetus to congressional bills for a Radio Free China, backed by a dozen lawmakers and exiled Chinese dissidents. Perhaps significantly, George Bush — Beijing's staunchest apologist in Washington — hasn't yet said no to the project." Beijing's apologist? Peter Katel tells of how "One Man Is an Island," noting the hard line that Fidel Castro continues to take in the face of increasingly difficult odds of success. But the biggest coup is *Newsweek*'s excerpting of Eduard Shevardnadze's *The Future Belongs to Freedom,* here entitled "The Tragedy of Gorbachev"; we only get two pages, but the perspective is valuable: "As a man and as his former comrade in arms, I agonized through the 72-hour nightmare of Gorbachev's confinement in the comfortable palace jail of Foros. He was a prisoner of the junta. But when he returned and spoke at the press conference, I saw that he was still a prisoner — of his own nature, his conceptions, and his way of thinking and acting. And now I am convinced that none other than Gorbachev himself had been spoon-feeding the junta with his indecisiveness, his inclination to back and fill, his fellow-traveling, his poor judgement of people, his indifference toward his true comrades, his distrust of the democratic forces and his disbelief in the bulwark whose name is the people."

"Soviet Crackup" coverage continues in the 9-16 edition, with a series of six articles on further events and repercussions. "And Now What?" by Russell Watson et al. chronicles the growing economic crisis, late, but better late than never. Michael Meyer's "Kaliningrad: The Old Guard Hangs On," relates the state of affairs in the Baltic city, strategically important because it is the Baltic fleet's home, along with "several tank divisions and a massive air-defense force. Nearly half a million troops and their families are based in Kaliningrad, along with a sizeable nuclear arsenal." In "An Unpardonable Amnesty," Jonathan Alter and Michael Meyer offer a clear snapshot on pardons for Lithuania's Nazis, who may be guilty of "heinous" crimes but are being rehabilitated because of frame-ups and slipshod work by the KGB. Howard Fineman serves up what is by now the conventional wisdom in "Bush: The Churchill Scenario," in which he postulates that Bush could lose the peace, as Churchill did, but he doesn't get around to telling us how until the last column. Tom Morgenthau with John Barry, Douglas Waller and Eleanor Clift examine "A Moment for Dreams," smartly assessing if the true end of the Cold War will bring, finally, the much-vaunted "peace dividend." "But downsizing the U.S. military will be no simple matter — and abolishing the CIA, in the view of many policymakers, could be a drastic mistake. Even assuming the Soviet military is no longer a global threat, the United States will almost certainly retain a leadership role in assuring world stability. That means maintaining a combination of military forces that can be deployed to deter — and if necessary, win — regional conflicts almost anywhere in the world. It also means maintaining enough intelligence 'assets' to identify threats to regional security — threats like Saddam Hussein." To round this out, Peter McGrath pens "Articles of Disunion" in which he draws historical parallels to the formation of the U.S. in the late 18th century to current feelings in the Soviet Union. The series rounds out with Russell Watson et al. and "Sorry About That, Comrade," 9-23, a solid overview of the Soviet Union's cessation of aid to Cuba and Afghanistan; there's even a quick appraisal of the potential for U.S. aid going to the Soviets at the close, but we don't get a sense here of the urgency of the situation. We do wish, though, that *Newsweek* would come to rely more directly on the journalists abroad, rather than just harnessing their talents to sidebar treatments. This 1991 coup was the third covered in Russia by Moscow bureau chief Fred Coleman, but frequently writers in New York and Washington are seen rewriting work from the foreign arena. While we recognize this is only in keeping with the fine Henry Luce-*Time* tradition, the practice of multiple bylines has become unwieldy at all the magazines, and we think it may be time for *Newsweek* to go directly to the source.

The Washington bureau, under the command of Evan Thomas, still has a few wrinkles in its reporting to iron out. Decidedly cynical, the folks in the bureau, particularly star reporters Thomas, Howard Fineman and Eleanor Clift, don't hide their jaded feelings about Beltway matters, and we find ourselves having to discount their snideness in order to cull information from their dispatches. This problem became so acute that Vice President Dan Quayle refused to be interviewed by the Washington team during the flap over Bush's heart arrythmia, although he was available to nearly every other major media organ in the country at that time. Thomas noted in "The Quayle Handicap," 5-20, that "Quayle spokesman David Beckwith said the magazine was being punished for unfair coverage of the vice president." While "punished" and "unfair" seem a bit strong, we can understand the apprehension of anyone dealing with the bureau on the record. At least the bureau does not maintain its cynicism along partisan lines; what the reporters are scornful of seems to be government and the process of governance in general, which sometimes replaces serious, thoughtful analysis with sarcasm and specious argumentation in the process. In "This Time, Being Outside Is In," 8-9, Fineman and Clift attempt to connect the candidacies of Sen. Bob Kerrey and former Gov. Jerry Brown with very tenuous links: both have "eyes that reveal their inner journeys, both are admirers of Mother Teresa." We get David A. Kaplan's solid analysis in "Good for the Left, Now Good for the Right," with Bob Cohn 7-8, on a sixth Supreme Court vote for "conservatives" looming with the resignation of Thurgood Marshall, but this is a bit overcooked on the hardline theme: "The American system has forever boasted it is 'a government of laws and not of men.' Trouble is, that's not true. In the ideological pitch and roll represented by the Supreme Court's journey from Earl Warren to William Rehnquist, there is a kind of poetic justice: he who lives by judicial activism dies by judicial activism. The symmetry seems in the nature of things, the balance quite right. Pity the constitution."

The best work out of the Washington bureau came with skepticism as a side dish, not as a main course. Howard Fineman presents "The No Bull Campaign," cover 10-14, an outline of rules and issues for a real campaign that the editors at *Newsweek* nominated for our 10 Best section, but which is the pinnacle of cynicism in spots: "Politicians are well aware of the dirty little secret behind all the popular demands for straight talk: Americans say they want truth, but they don't like what they hear when they get it. Real truth telling, as opposed to mere style, usually loses more votes than it gains. Few voters really want to face the choices and sacrifices that deeply honest leadership would demand." Boo! Evan Thomas's "There Is Always Something," 10-21, is quite strong and perceptive, although he takes his cue from Suzanne Garment's book *Scandal,* more an indictment of the press than of the government: "Human nature has always been weak, and among the grasping, even weaker. What's new is watching it revealed every day on C-SPAN. . .If anything, reporters, who for all their zeal can be lazy, are better at ferreting out human lapses than more serious institutional failings. Hence, the press pounced on the womanizing John Tower, Bush's choice to be secretary of defense, but largely ignored the S&L fiasco until it was $500 billion too late." In another strong effort, Howard Fineman gives us a solid reading on the growing influence of the Democratic Leadership Council with "Duel of the Democrats," 4-8, that's without his usual sarcasm. We see much promise in the talents at the bureau, but this tendency to be arrogantly sardonic must be stamped out.

The business coverage, which has tended towards fluff in the past, still leans toward the unusual and the effervescent. Two covers this year proved *Newsweek*'s intention to cover broader issues, however. "Riding Out the Recession," 1-14, included an examination of the current downward economic trend, "Riding Out the Storm," by Annetta Miller et al., and a discussion of how to manage in tough times, "A Guide to Surviving the Long Siege Ahead," by resident economic advice columnist Jane Bryant Quinn. This is followed up with "What Recovery? Bite on the Middle Class," a compilation of articles on angles from the political, "That Sinking Feeling," by Larry Reibstein et al. and "The Cuomo Dilemma," by Howard Fineman; to the human, "Living on the Edge," by Marc Levinson, "Middle Class Blessings," by Rich Thomas and "How to Make It Through '92," by Jane Bryant Quinn. These sensible treatments inform in the best newsweekly tradition, giving us a utilitarian sense of the larger picture. But these were exceptions. More typical was "Pity the Wall Street Wives," by Annetta Miller with Nina Darnton and Bruce Shenitz 9-23, a gossipy and frivolous exercise examining what the Wall Street Wives, such as Carolyn Roehm and Ivana Trump, are doing now.

The columns at *Newsweek,* both on the back page and within the magazine, are among the strongest in the business. Meg Greenfield and George Will share back-page duties, giving the magazine a one-two knockout punch to round it out. Jane Bryant Quinn and Robert J. Samuelson split the economic column chores. Quinn had a very good year, relatively speaking, whereas Samuelson, for the first time in our memory, was utterly abysmal.

There are many quirky features in *Newsweek* that draw us in. We always peruse the quotes and cartoons in "Periscope," and, like many armchair quarterbacks, we never miss a "Conventional Wisdom Watch." On a more serious note, the "My Turn" column always offers excellent op-eds, from folks you might not see on *The New York Times*'s pages on subjects not applicable to *The Wall Street Journal.* "Don't Write Off Thomas," by anthropologist and Lincoln University president Niara Sudarkasa, 8-19, would grace the pages of many an op-ed section with its strong arguments for keeping Thomas in mind. Although she is not in full agreement with Thomas, not being a conservative, she advocates giving him a full and just hearing: "As African-Americans, we have always fought for access to America's institutions of power and influence. We demanded representation regardless of who was sitting at the table. When we raised our clenched fists in the cry for 'black power,' I don't think we meant power for black liberals only. Thomas should not be barred from serving on the Supreme Court because he does not speak for the liberal black leadership of what we think is the majority of black people. The fact that he speaks for many blacks, including a growing number of black leaders, should carry some weight." Long before the tragic drama of Magic Johnson unfolded, *Newsweek* presented "There Is No Safe Sex," by Robert C. Noble, a professor of Medicine at the U. of KY College of Medicine, authoritatively debunking the same-sex myth: "Abstinence and sexual intercourse with one mutually faithful uninfected partner are the only totally effective prevention strategies." Mikhail Alexseev, member of the U.S.S.R. Assn. of Journalists and a visiting NATO scholar at the U. of WA-Seattle, offers "No Cream for Fat Cats," 6-17, an argument for no welfare for the Soviet Union, citing its rich resources and its dependency on government to start with. Alexseev convinces us that any help from the U.S. in the form now being discussed via, the Harvard group, would be fatal.

We think there is still a big market niche for a *news*weekly to fill. This is borne out by *Newsweek*'s circulation figures, an all-time record high since its inception in 1933. The U.S. circulation climbed to a whopping 3,420,167 in the first half of this year; newsstand sales jumped 25 percent over this period when compared to the preceding year. And *Newsweek* is expanding abroad as well, adding a Korean-language edition to the already successful Japanese-language edition which debuted in 1986. *Newsweek* is the only U.S. weekly newsmagazine publishing foreign-language editions. It now seems that *Newsweek* will be the likely successor to *Time* as the preeminent newsweekly on the planet.

Editor:	Richard M. Smith
Address:	444 Madison Avenue
	New York, NY 10022
	(212) 350-4000
Circulation:	1990 — 3,227,522
	1991 — 3,100,000

New York

New York offers the best — and occasionally the worst — of the Big Apple to New York area residents, week by week, in every area imaginable. Broadway premieres, society profiles, ethnic troubles throughout the boroughs, beat cops and traffic cops, all find their place in the magazine. As the financial capital of the nation, the city's atmosphere and fiscal stability are vital to the smooth operation of the world economy, and we appreciate *NY*'s view from that perspective. But what we like best about *NY* is simply that it is as enjoyable as it is informative, and is one of the more sought-after publications when our mail arrives. The weekly is fun because its staff, writers and editors relish living and working in the five boroughs of New York City, for all the drawbacks. Although we prefer suburbia, we envy them their infectious enthusiasm and obvious affection for the city.

The style and feel of *New York* stays consistent from year to year due to the steady stewardship of Edward Kosner, editor and president of the weekly. *NY* was acquired in June by K-111 Holdings, a partnership owned by Kohlberg, Kravis, Roberts & Company, from Rupert Murdoch's News Corporation as part of a group magazine purchase. The division that runs *NY,* K-111 Magazines, is run by the former head of Macmillan, Harry A. McQuillen, who just came aboard in October. *NY* had also gotten a new publisher at the close of 1990, Janice Grossman. In spite of all the managerial changes, however, the editorial personnel remains enamored with the city and excited about its prospects.

The staff journalists at *New York* are its backbone, unlike any other city magazines that rely on outsiders. Evident at *NY* is the consistently high quality of its reporting and reporters, particularly on the city's body politic. Journalist Michael Kramer, now with *Time* magazine, turned in his most memorable performance during his tenure at *NY.* The current political reporter, Joe Klein, ranks among the best in the business, his sharp examinations of race relations, Big Apple politics and "The National Interest," quite competitive and frequently surpassing the perspectives found in more prestigious journals. As such, Klein's editors nominated a plethora of his material for consideration for 10 Best citations. Three stand out, and are indicative of his considerable talents as a reporter and analyst. In his 10 Best selection for Political Reporting, "Ask Not? Don't Ask?" 6-3, Klein is merciless in assessing a life of liberalism without virtue, illustrated in "the Kennedy slide": "[Ted] Kennedy took the family tropisms past several key boundaries. He divorced; he broke the law — and, most important, he allowed liberalism's essential message to slip from sacrifice for the common good to *entitlement,* from 'Ask not what your country can do for you. . .' to 'You deserve a break today.' " Klein astutely examines the stalemate between City Hall and Albany, "The Real Deficit: Leadership," cover 7-22, measuring the costs in the city's suffering in the interim. He offers a perceptive view of events in Crown Heights, Brooklyn, after an Hasidic Jew ran down a black child following a traffic accident, in "Deadly Metaphors," 9-9; sharp on racial matters, Klein remains cool when events bring tempers to their boiling points. In his sterling examination of the Anita Hill-Clarence Thomas hearings, "Tabloid Government," 10-28, he cuts to the heart of the Hill-Thomas controversy as "goverment by Geraldo." Klein smartly takes apart the entire proceeding piece-by-piece and brings it to conclusion, predicting in this smart assessment both "left and right will have some surprises in store" in Thomas' career as an associate justice.

The other columnists at *New York* intrigue us and often stimulate our thinking. Christopher Byron, "The Bottom Line" columnist who came to *NY* from *Forbes* a few years back, added considerably to our knowledge about the BCCI scandal, digging up tidbits of information that others missed. This body of work ("The Big Muddy," 6-24; "What Price Vigilance?" 7-22; "Inside a Pirate Bank," 8-5; "Cable TV's BCCI Connection," 8-19; "A Noriega Laundry?" 8-26; "Adham the Untouchable," 10-7; "Spooky Stuff," 10-28; and "Bush and BCCI," 11-11) was nominated for 10 Best consideration by his editors. "On Madison Avenue" columnist Bernice Kanner displays a light, deft touch that brings her dispatches to life. She flows through a history of boycotts via PR and ad campaigns with ease and grace in "Forcing the Issues," 2-11, putting the trend toward boycotting into perspective: "Boycotts are often more successful against a company's image than against its bottom line, says [*National Boycott News* editor Todd] Putnam. Boycotts used to take between five and ten years to get results, but now they take about two. That's because they're better organized and get more media attention: Corporations recognize the damage potential much earlier." Media columnist Edwin Diamond tackles issues in journalism that, while centered on examples in the New York press, often address broader themes. In "Horror Story," 8-12, Diamond indicts the N.Y. coverage recycled by the national press in the rape of the 3-year-old girl by her uncle in a park bordering the FDR drive: "The Associated Press, Reuters, CNN and *USA Today* started spreading the news. 'It fit the stereotype,' says Paul Leavitt, national-wire editor of *USA Today.* 'You know: This couldn't happen in Flat Grass, Iowa. Only in New York.' " Then the story began to fall apart. Twenty subhumanoid New Yorkers did not stand by, gawking, while a child was raped. Rather, the motorists who were close enough to see what was happening did something decent and even brave — they chased the suspect, called 911, flagged a patrol car. But the record has yet to be corrected by many news organizations that carried accounts of the initial horror show. It is the old images of journalism that have been reaffirmed: reporters too dependent on sources, editors rushing into print or on the air, everyone stealing from one another. Only in the press!" We salute Diamond for doing his small part, fully documented, in clearing up the mess, indicting even the "Metro" section of *The New York Times* which recycled some of the *Daily News*' accounts.

The remainder of the staff of contributing editors impresses as well. Jeanie Kasindorf semi-profiles David Hampton, the con artist who inspired John Guare's "Six Degrees of Separation," in "Six Degrees of Impersonation," 3-25, a very strange profile for a very strange man; she makes the most of Hampton's quirks and we read to the end. John Taylor's cover, "Don't Blame Me!" 6-3, is superbly pointed at the hypocrisy of the "new culture of victimization," from Rose Cippolone — who sued three cigarette companies after developing lung cancer because she smoked a pack and a half a day for 40 years and the warning labels weren't strong enough to stop her — to Marion Barry, whose drug bust was everyone's fault but his own. This cover was submitted for 10 Best consideration by *NY*'s editors, along with Taylor's examination of the PC movement, "Are You Politically Correct?" cover 1-21. This insightful look at political correctness came early, and, surprisingly, stayed fresh, even with all the ink spilled on this subject. We always peruse Eric Pooley's material, his hard-hitting dispatches giving us the grittier side of the city. In "Reality 101," 10-21, Pooley gives us a bit of reality in detailing the training program for Assistant District Attorneys in Queens in which the ADAs are treated to close-up views of the jobs of the people they will rely on to make their cases — from the medical examiner to the beat cop, they get a taste of it all. Pooley's lead with two ADAs pulling guns on a man with a gun threatening to kill somebody is "Reality 101" for the reader too, downright harrowing to read until we find the situation is a training exercise.

New York's features often offer a flavorful assortment of topics concerning actually *living* in the city. It's a singular magazine that can go from an article on race relations or national politics to Marilyn Bethany's "Flea Market Fever," 4-8, a listing of the world's most famous and profitable for collectors and interior designers. Bethany turns up again on the cover with "Surviving the City in Style," 10-7, a photo opportunity for the more glamorous apartments in the city, in which Bethany and the magazine offer a nice selection of lifestyles, and rooms, about which to fantasize. *NY* lists a selection of clubs for different sports hobbies in "New Jock City," 4-15, a quintessential *NY* feature. *NY* runs its traditional weekend-getaway inn feature on the cover, "All-American Weekends," by Michael W. Robbins 4-22, *NY* offering the best, and only the best, even outside New York. Bargain hunters will relish "Read This Magazine and Save a Fortune," cover 5-6, an "Ultimate Insider's Guide to Sales and Bargains" which takes us through the contradictory idea of the New York bargain, replete with hints about where to go for everything from shoes to wines to summer homes. Also typical of *NY*'s taste for finding bargains in a town that is notoriously known for overpricing, we find "Cheap Sleep," by Vincent Frontero 6-3, advice on bargaining down room costs, as well as recommending some inexpensive hotels. Bernice Kanner gives us a delightful look at what it's like to be a traffic cop, joining Unit

111A, the Dept. of Transportation's "answer to the Green Berets," for "Hot Tickets," 7-15; a good sport, Kanner spends much of the assignment directing traffic and writing tickets. Janice Hopkins Tanne offers an exhaustive guide to health care in the city, in which we find specialists, general practitioners, and hospitals ranked, "The Best Doctors in New York," 11-11, "The Best Hospitals in New York," 11-18, and "How to Be a Savvy Consumer," 11-25, a refreshing compendium after media reports of cases of negligence and malpractice in the city. We get a real sense of the sleazy character of Wall Street's Dennis Levine, through his book *Insider,* cover 9-16, but this excerpt tells us nothing about Milken or Boesky, and in fact, skims over the fact that Levine turned them both in — Boesky rightfully, as Levine had direct evidence of Boesky's complicity — to cut his own sentence. In "Dead Ends," 11-11, Robert Bent takes us on a delicious tour of New York graves, of all things, as we visit the final resting places of, among others, Joan Crawford, Lou Gehrig, Louis Armstrong, Herman Melville, and Mae West. Everyone's fantasy of moving to a desert island is brought down to earth by Denise Melinsky, in "Living the Fantasy," 9-9, as she relates her experience of moving from New York to Fiji and back again. And in "The Mick Hits 60," 9-30, Ross Wetzsteon is evocative and bittersweet without being maudlin on the quintessential Yankee Mickey Mantle, on the occasion of his 60th birthday.

The reviewers in the back of the weekly are the bluntest and most forthright in the business. Between them, John Leonard, David Denby, Gael Greene, Kay Larson, John Simon, Tobi Tobias and Rhoda Koenig provide us with the best of what to do and where to go during our leisure time. John Leonard takes no prisoners in his examination of PBS's "Frontline: The Election Held Hostage," reviewed at the close of a collection of programs, "One Half of One Man's War," 4-22: "[It] is a better-late-than-never backward look at persistent rumors that in 1980 the Reagan campaign people cut a deal with the Ayatollah Khomeini. . .*Frontline,* by reporter Robert Parry's own admission, fails to find a smoking gun. But it does detail a lot of suspicious circumstantial evidence, and it's hard to think of a more plausible explanation for the subsequent Iranscam bizarrerie, though Walter Goodman will try when he hates this program in the *Times.*" Using quotes from the book to back up her assessment, Rhonda Koenig is equally frank in her review of Harold Brodkey's *The Runaway Soul*: "Adolescent plodding and vulgarity set the tone of this long-heralded (or threatened) novel rather than the soaring poetics Brodkey's hero repeatedly aspires to and fails to grasp." John Simon, in "Upbeat, Downbeat," 10-21, a duo of reviews of "On Borrowed Time," George C. Scott's most recent Circle in the Square venture, and "Babylon Gardens," by Timothy Mason, wastes no words in praising Scott's performance while putting qualifiers on his staging, and simply excoriates Mason's effort as "a highly pretentious and profoundly sophomoric play, which tries to parlay a schematic jadedness into an allegorical overview of America, unearned either by its melodramatic attitudinizing or by its witless attempts at humor." Oh.

One of the most refreshing things about *New York* magazine is that the editors and staff do find so many things worthwhile about the city, even while calling for improvement. The weekly provides as vivid and complete a picture of New York City life as we are likely to find anywhere. Kosner must take care, however, that this meticulously balanced brainchild of his, and former editor Clay Felker's, does not become jaded. We hardly want to open *NY* of 9-2, so disgusted are we by the cover, "Confessions of a Young WASP," by Lang Phipps, who is pictured rather seriously in loafers (no socks, of course), white pants, tie, blue dress shirt and navy blazer complete with pocket handkerchief, looking up from his book, *Tribal Feeling* by Michael Astor, while lounging in a white wicker chair at the beach — the Hamptons, no doubt. In this wasted exercise, Phipps tells us of WASPS and how they assimilate (they don't), WASPs and sex ("lousy"), a profile of perpetual snobbery: ". . .a childhood of programming in tribal life, with its strict conventions of style, its protocol, left me momentarily unprepared when I entered the Meadow Club two summers ago and came face to face with the Hollywood actor James Woods. 'What's *he* doing here?' I thought reflexively, aghast, feeling like sanctuary had been penetrated by an interloper. In an instant, I remembered that one of the club members is tight with Oliver Stone, the film director and Woods's friend. Woods was obviously a guest of this member, staying the weekend at the club. A pretty cool thing actually, but for just a moment I was thrown: The contrast had been *too* much." This isn't universal to New York, and certainly isn't up to *New York*'s more down-to-earth approach to life in the city. But as with the Sherilyn Fenn pinup cover of last year, "Summer Pleasures," 7-2/9-90, this seems to have been an aberration. For the best of New York, and more, *New York* is a must, a superlative compendium and indispensable guide to the city's politics, economics and life in general.

Editor: Edward Kosner

Address: 755 Second Avenue
               New York, NY 10017
               (212) 880-0700

Circulation: 1990 — 437,412
               1991 — 437,000

The New Yorker

While it may not necessarily be the "best magazine in the world," there is no denying that *The New Yorker* occupies a unique niche in American magazines, each week presenting an eclectic mixture of commentary, fiction, reportage, and criticism. Readers may roll their eyes at the unsigned "Notes and Comment," which often seems to be much more Upper East Side trendier-than-thou, or wonder what could have been going through the editors's heads when they decided to commission a fifty-page article on some postage stamp sized country, but above all else, *TNY* aims to be a literary experience, and on that level it usually succeeds.

TNY was on the move in 1991 — literally. On February 22nd "with a great, long sigh," *TNY* vacated its home since 1935 for "fresh new offices" right across from its old address on West 43rd Street. Discussing the move in "Notes and Comment," 3-11, *TNY* notes that: "When Harold Ross started this magazine, in 1925, he planted it on West Forty-fifth Street; then it spent fifty-six years on the north side of Forty-third, and now we have made it across to the south. At this rate, in a thousand years we should be on Fourteenth."

Some would say that *TNY*'s glacial progression towards 14th Street matches its editorial outlook. True, *TNY* has yet to affect anything remotely smacking of a "downtown sensibility," save perhaps for the inclusion of an "Edge of Night Life" section to its "Night Life" listings of New York cabarets and clubs. But fans of the magazine would argue that at *TNY* tradition is everything. Indeed, it is no doubt a point of pride at the magazine that a reader entombed in the old offices at West 43rd Street, freed only now when discovered by sympathetic movers, would find a current edition reassuringly recognizable, in format if not content.

The linchpin of the format continues to be "Notes and Comment," those brief essays which open the magazine each week. They have evolved somewhat since 1926, when E.B. White wrote little vignettes of life in New York during the prohibition era, now generally opening with a serious piece commenting on a major story in the news, before offering "Notes" devoted to virtually any topic under the New York sun, penned by staffers and outside contributors such as John Updike, Garrison Keillor, and Richard Brookhiser.

TNY remains rigidly liberal in editorial outlook. Writing on the Gulf War in the 2-4 issue, it argues that "It was a colossal failure of politics that plunged us into this war. Now that the fighting has begun, all we can do is hope that it ends quickly — and remind us that when the astonishments of war are behind us we will almost certainly be back in the dark and uncertain thicket of Middle Eastern politics." A friend wrote in on 2-11 on how his anti-war sentiments were coming to feel "unreal" in the face of Saddam's behavior and the performance of the U.S. military, until he attended an anti-war demonstration in Washington. "But now, surrounded by well over a hundred thousand fellow-citizens who had been through something like the same experience and had been unable to suppress their doubts, I felt the life being knocked back into me."

"The Talk of the Town," 10-28, was devoted solely to the Clarence Thomas-Anita Hill hearings. In the opening, the magazine intones that ". . .if Hill was telling the truth it might well be that Thomas, who by all accounts gave her in her subsequent career every professional courtesy he could, felt that he had earned a reprieve from things he had, in a weak or uncalculating moment, once done to her. The anger he displayed before the committee would not have seemed so genuine, perhaps, if he had not, in some deep, Nixonian way justified his behavior to himself first." The section concludes with a letter from "a young man "raised in a family of ardent feminists who states that the hearings raised his own male consciousness to the difficulties women face in our society. "They had on tap a vein of anger that bewildered me. . .I owe them an apology. They had experienced things that I had not, and had tried to tell me truths that I had chosen not to hear."

"The Talk of the Town" does have its virtues, usually when *TNY* leaves politics aside and searches out the follies, foibles, and eccentricities of life in New York City in the last half of the 20th century, *TNY* observing it all in the bemused unexcitable tone of one affecting the blank-slate curiosity of a child and the knowing skepticism of an adult. The 7-15 "Notes and Comment" is typical, and after opening with a valedictory to outgoing Supreme Court Justice Thurgood Marshall — "With Justice Marshall's resignation, an important symbol of this country's achievements in civil rights has been lost and an influential voice in their favor stilled," *TNY* moves on to a quick profile of Martin Doyle, restaurant owner and book lover, who hunts throughout New England for free books to give away to customers who stop by "The Traveler," on Interstate 84 in Union, Connecticut. " 'Baked beans and mayonnaise and tartar sauce and books and whatever,' Mr. Doyle said. 'Lots of combinations.' " *TNY* then attends a press conference to announce the plans to merchandise a character from a TV show, "Family Matters," noting that "We wanted to know how we should feel about getting a press release saying 'Urkel-mania Takes the Country by Storm,' considering that until the press conference we had never heard of Steve Urkel."

The middle of the book continues to be devoted to lengthy profiles and non-fiction articles, and we noticed that the articles published this year were more often than not tied into developments in the news, giving them an additional relevancy. As the prospect of a major land battle fought with chemical weapons loomed in the Persian Gulf, Thomas Whiteside produced an outstanding two-part series on chemical warfare, "The Yellow-Rain Complex," 2-11 and 2-18. In a prodigious journalistic undertaking, Whiteside, in Part One, reexamines such controversies as the alleged use of those weapons in Laos during the 1970s, and in Part 2 the suspected 1979 explosion at a Soviet biological weapons plant resulting in an outbreak of anthrax in the Soviet city of Sverdlovsk. After offering documentation that the "yellow rain" phenomenon was really caused by bee excrement and the anthrax outbreak was caused by contaminated feed grain, Whiteside concludes that "What is clear is that in the postwar era each of the governments of the great powers was behaving permissively, at the very least, toward the creation of a runaway program of chemical weapons development."

Soviet coverage was also strong once again in *TNY*. In the superlative "The Politics of Neighborhood," 6-3, David K. Shipler artfully illustrates the political opportunities and administrative failings of *perestroika* at street level, proving once again that even in a society undergoing a revolution, all politics is local. In "The Coup," 11-4, Robert Cullen reports from Moscow on the events of last August as seen through the eyes of participants, both Yeltsin supporters, including a former Soviet helicopter pilot who helped coordinate the defense of the White House and a worker at Moscow Radio M, and opponents such as Lt. Col. Viktor Alksnis and Marshall Akhromeyev, who spoke to Cullen in June and dismissed any possibility the Soviet military would participate in a coup. A week later, in "After the Coup," 11-11, Shipler masterfully examines the forces behind the headlines of the day as the center falls and the leadership disappears into a void. "It is less dramatic to build the institutions, the structural checks and balances, and the political habits that could prevent people from having to go to the barricades again, and the failure to begin such a process of construction was troubling many of those with whom I spoke." In the fascinating "Opening Windows," 12-2, David Owen profiles U.S. entrepreneur Kenny Schaffer, who was able to translate a love of rock and roll and a talent for electrical engineering into a consulting business that was able to penetrate the Soviet business scene and set up "what is in effect an independent long-distance-telephone company inside the Soviet Union."

The non-fiction highlight of the year in *TNY* were the excerpts from Clark Clifford's memoirs, "Serving the President," with Richard Holbrook, 3-25, 4-1, 5-6, 5-13, 5-20. Despite the self-serving tone the excerpts take on at times, and the outside distraction of the BCCI scandal, the memoirs do offer a firsthand look at history being made at another time, when the U.S. faced monumental challenges on the international scene, and rose to meet them before becoming bogged down in the morass of Vietnam. "The Truman Doctrine, as it came to be called, took more than forty years to succeed, was often controversial and expensive, and was at times misapplied — most notably in Vietnam. But a major war with the Soviet Union was avoided during a dangerous half century, and by 1989 it was clear that the Cold War, as we knew it, was over. That was the direct, if long-delayed, result of the policies laid out in 1947 by President Truman and followed, despite all the political controversies at home, by every one of his successors. No President could wish for a greater legacy."

There were fewer political profiles than usual, the only one of note being Richard Brookhiser's "Dancing With the Girl That Brung Him," 10-28, a witty profile of Massachusetts State Senate President William Bulger. Brookhiser cuts through the south Boston Irish pol stereotype to document how Bulger's political philosophy, which combines the maxim "all politics is local" with the perspective of ancient history, has seen him through a turbulent career which has included the school busing riots of the mid-1970s, the Republican resurgence and subsequent austerity drive in the early 1990s, the enmity of the media, and being the brother of a suspected Boston mob boss.

TNY regulars had a very good year overall. The 1990 National Magazine Award for reporting went to *TNY* for a Connie Bruck article analyzing the merger of Time Inc. and Warner Communications, "The World of Business: Deal of the Year." In 1991 Bruck profiled former Wall Street trader John Mulheren, Jr. in the illuminating "No One Like Me," 3-11, detailing how this manic-depressive sufferer got caught in the undertow of the prosecutorial wave that swept across Wall Street in the late 1980s because of several dealings he had with Ivan Boesky. She was superb on both the "hardware" and "software" aspects of the MCA-Matsushita deal in "Leap of Faith," 9-9, observing that "While one may argue that in an increasingly global world national boundaries and identities will over time tend to blur, and that concern about Hollywood's being American-owned is chauvinistic and retrograde, it appears that the Japanese have approached their Hollywood acquisitions with a traditionally nationalistic mind-set."

We were impressed by Middle East correspondent Milton Viorst, "The House of Hashem," 1-7, satisfyingly thorough on how Jordan was being affected by the crisis in the Gulf, while "Report From Baghdad," 6-24, is detailed on the post-war geopolitical situation inside Iraq, Viorst adding material that humanizes this story as well. "After the Liberation," 9-30, is evocative on Kuwait and that country's efforts to rebuild, physically, politically, and psychologically, from the ashes of the Iraqi invasion, while "Report From Madrid," 12-9, is a revealing look at the backstage diplomacy at the Middle East peace conference.

There was some improvement in the "Letter From Washington" this year, Elizabeth Drew offering sharper analytics and reporting, especially on the Gulf War. In the 5-6 "Letter," she provides one of the best delineations we saw anywhere on the Bush administration's decision not to aid the Kurdish rebels, a decision, she writes, that was based partly on unproven geopolitical concerns about the need to preserve a stable Iraq and domestic political concerns about getting bogged down in a quagmire. "The President had largely stuck to his publicly stated goals — though the objective of smashing Iraq's military machine hadn't been so clear. Had he then expanded those goals to include something that was murky and could have been messy, a President's credibility the next time he tried to rally support for a limited military purpose would have been gone. *That's* where Vietnam comes in."

European correspondent Jane Kramer provides an excellent look at the various prisms through which Europe '92 is being viewed in her "Letter From Europe," 7-29. "Businessmen today say that '92 is really about money, and politicians say it is really about power, and ordinary people — people on the street — say it is really about 'anticipation,' but nearly everyone says it is also about the *volonte* of Jacques Delors to make 'Europe' happen." We were disappointed, however, by her "Letter From Berlin," 11-25, Kramer, who was early on the difficulties facing a reunited Germany in 1990, offers essentially a rehash here.

Diplomatic correspondent John Newhouse offers a fascinating report on the high-stakes diplomacy and hard bargaining which drove the U.S.-British negotiations over the reassignment of financially strapped T.W.A. and Pan Am's Heathrow routes to United and American Airlines in "Air Wars," 8-5. His survey of missed opportunities and miscalculations on both sides in the aftermath of the Iraqi invasion of Kuwait, "Misreadings," 1-18, breaks no new ground though. Newhouse's expertise on international diplomacy returned in "A Collective Nervous Breakdown," 9-2, where he is comprehensive on Europe's cynical efforts at forging new economic and security structures as the continent enters the post-Cold War age, Newhouse documenting that while each individual nation is paying lip-service to the cause of "European unity," each government is putting its own interests first, especially Washington, Bonn, and Paris.

We continue to enjoy the "Letters" postmarked from cities abroad, often the best-written articles in *TNY*. Amos Elon, in "Report From Jerusalem," 4-1, usefully debunks one myth about Palestinian reaction to the Iraqi Scud attacks on Israel. "For more than a month, I have been looking for anyone who saw with his own eyes the 'dancing on the rooftops.' I have found no one, and have come to suspect that this may be one of those famous myths of war which capture the imagination of a people because they confirm deeply ingrained prejudices in the political culture, like the widespread stories of rape and other atrocities in Belgium during the First World War." Elon also produces a chilling report on Austria's inability to come to terms with the ghosts of its past as it prepares for the emergence of a "new, Austria-centered *Mitteleuropa*" in "Report From Vienna," 5-13.

Ved Mehta, in the atmospheric "Letter From New Delhi," 8-19, conveys the ethnic, economic, and political tensions in India's current season of discontent. "In political and official circles here — and also among people generally — there is a sense of dread about the economic, political, and religious direction of the country which I don't remember encountering in any of my other visits over the past twenty-five years." We get an illuminating report on the wages of democracy in Argentina in Alma Guillermoprieto's "Letter From Buenos Aires," 7-15.

Analytical efforts, often published in the "Reflections," column, were uneven this year, the writers failing to offer conceptual breakthroughs to match the historical developments of our time. In "The Uses of Force," 4-29, Richard J. Barnet recycles his earlier assertions that economic strength, not military might, will be the measure of superpowers in the future, Desert Storm notwithstanding. "Japan has no marines ready to parachute into distant markets, no flotilla elbowing Matsushita's and Sony's way into the world's great shopping malls." Robert Heilbroner pokes fun at the inexact nature of the "science" of economics in "Economic Predictions," 7-8, amusing but ultimately pointless. Much more impressive is William Pfaff's "Islam and the West," 1-28, a scholarly essay expertly placing the current crisis in the historical perspective of the turbulent relationship between Islam and the Western world.

The back third of *TNY* continues to be devoted to criticism and lighter features. Regular "American Scene" contributor Calvin Trillin only appeared once this year, perhaps preoccupied by his new one-man stage production and the publication of his new book. However, "You Don't Ask, You Don't Get," 2-25, is vintage Trillin, a bemused report on the rags-to-riches-to-rags story of Frankie Lymon and the Teenagers and the battle over the royalty rights to their biggest hit, "Why Do Fools Fall in Love?" Roger Angell continues to be one of the best sportswriters in the business, the perfect Virgil to the American mythology of the national pastime. His account in "Ninety Feet," 12-9, of watching the ceremonies marking the last game ever played at Baltimore's Memorial Stadium on TV with tears in his eyes left a lump in our throat as well.

Paulene Kael retired after 14 years of influencing a whole generation of American film criticism, leaving "The Current Cinema," in the very capable hands of Terrence Rafferty. *TNY* still offers no TV criticism, but other forms of pop culture are not ignored, in "Illusions," 11-11, Elizabeth Wurtzel reflects on the phenomenal success of the politically incorrect hard rock band Guns 'N' Roses, Wurtzel writing that "this, in the end, is what the band's popularity is all about: in a world where — for fear of being called racist, sexist, or in some other way bigoted — civilized people feel hemmed in and scared to say how much they hate something, even when their reasons are perfectly legitimate, Guns 'N' Roses seem blissfully ignorant of such concerns."

The book review continues to offer literate essays on subjects as diverse as Theodore Dreiser and the Peloponnesian War. Book review highlights in 1991 included "Mars," 3-1, George Steiner's dissection of Donald Kagan's *History of the Peloponnesian War;* "The Last Emperor," 2-18, Louis Menand's study of the history of TV in America in a review of Sally Bedell Smith's biography of William Paley, *In All His Glory;* and "Illiberalisms," 5-20, Menand's quietly devastating critique of Dinesh D'Souza and his acclaimed book on current campus tension, *Illiberal Education.* Menand writes that while he shares D'Souza's concern about the encroachment of politics into college curriculums, he also zeroes in on flaws he finds in D'Souza's arguments and D'Souza's background, including his past involvement in some of the worst excesses of *The Dartmouth Review* and Princeton's *Prospect.* "It is not pleasant to see a man who did so much to poison the wells now turning up dressed as the water commissioner, and it will be apparent to most people who read "Illiberal Education" that the book's promise of balance is a false one." Occasionally a review misfires or descends into polemics, in "Reagan's Book," 12-24-90, Francis Fitzgerald turns in a formula Reagan-bashing review of the former President's autobiography.

Circulation at *TNY* dipped a bit in 1991, but remains near an all-time high, and ad pages are up, despite an industry trend in the opposite direction and the cancellation of some travel ads during the Gulf crisis. Who knows? Come the year 2991 Eustice A. Twilley may be looking out his office window at Washington Square Park.

Editor: Robert Gottlieb

Address: 25 West 43rd Street
                New York, NY 10036
                (212) 840-3800

Circulation: 1990 — 623,229
                1991 — 615,260

The New York Review of Books

In this rushed age of instantaneous news and prepackaged analysis, *The New York Review of Books* continues to be the thinking news consumer's delight, each issue of the fortnightly featuring thought-provoking essays on major international, national, cultural, and literary issues of the day. While some of the sclerosis we noted in recent years seems to be gone, *TNYRB* still fails to bring the intellectual vigor to economics that it does to other issues, often falling back on social democratic prescriptions that are unimaginatively presented.

The prototypical *TNYRB* economic contributor is Felix Rohatyn, who, in "The New Domestic Order?" 11-21, writes that "a little more than two hundred years after we achieved political independence, our financial independence has come to an end," and calls for greater cooperation between business and government and a massive investment in new technology and infrastructure, financed through public and private pension funds. "The failure of communism does not guarantee success at home. That success will require the highest level of political leadership that we have had in decades as well as understanding and sacrifice by the American people."

One month earlier, Robert Heilbroner decried the "self-crippling aversion to taxation" in the U.S. He draws on an essay by Louis Ferleger and Jay R. Mandle in the July-August issue of *Challenge* to contend that Americans pay the least amount of taxes as a percentage of GDP of all industrial nations, arguing that the U.S. should follow the lead of other nations by collecting more revenue through sales and value added taxes, not taxes on personal income. Michael M. Thomas, in "The Greatest American Shambles," 1-31, provides a look at the financial practices of the 1980s through an orthodox liberal prism. "The S&L crisis teaches the real cost of a politics that aggressively advocates, as Reaganism did and Bushism would like to do, that the true enemies of the people are the representatives that the people elect, in effect a dismissal of the idea of the 'common weal.' Offered to replace government is the concept of an entrepreneurial, market-based individualism which will get it right, but which in fact has absolutely no interest in the functions that government performs that no private person or private group can or will." In "A Tale of Three Cities," 3-28, Garry Wills reflects on poverty in America and the federal government's efforts to deal with it, centered around a review of Nicholas Lemann's book: *The Promised Land: The Great Black Migration and How it Changed America.* "Again, Republicans talking about empowerment say 'money is not the answer' to education and other problems (They never say that about missiles or capital formation programs.) What do we need more — peace and a trained citizenry at home, or a New World Order that sends up beautiful rockets from a rotting civic and industrial base?"

Not all domestic coverage, however, read like a 25th anniversary salute to the Great Society. Some of our readers thought that Joan Didion's dissection of what ails New York, "New York: Sentimental Journeys," 1-17, centered around the issues raised by the Central Park jogger case, was over-long and clumsily written in spots, but we agreed that she piqued the city's almost numb conscience, and, unlike many New York critics, did not mistake the symptoms for the underlying disease. John Gregory Dunne provided the best essay we saw anywhere on the alleged LAPD brutality case in "Law & Disorder in Los Angeles," Parts 1 & 2, 10-10, and 10-24, a superb mixture of reporting and analysis. With the precision of a diamond cutter Dunne expertly sets the incident in context of both Gates's controversial career and the changing demographics of the City of Angels. "The City today is like the Balkans, rich with blood feuds that outsiders can scarcely understand."

Not surprisingly for a publication that prides itself on being the literary equivalent of what "a good, small liberal arts college should be," *TNYRB* devoted attention to the ongoing debate over "multiculturalism," strongly defending academic freedom. C. Vann Woodward, in "Freedom & the Universities," 7-18, pens a favorable review of Dinesh D'Souza's *Illiberal Education: The Politics of Race and Sex on Campus,* which Woodward describes as being "probably the most extensive critical study yet made of an academic convulsion that has been treated evasively or disingenuously by its administrators and with much more strident polemics by its activists." Indeed, Woodward barely touches on the book, writing instead on how academic freedom and academic standards are coming under increased attack by minority students and professors who view "their culture as determined by their race." Woodward's essay resulted in one of the liveliest "Letters" department all year, " 'Illiberal Education': An Exchange," 9-26.

Ronald Dworkin provided superior efforts on the U.S. judiciary in 1991. Reviewing Charles Fried's *Order and Law: Arguing the Reagan Revolution — A Firsthand Account,* in "The Reagan Revolution and the Supreme Court," 7-18, he is appreciative of Fried's attempt to provide an intellectual framework to conservative judicial philosophy which does not rely on "original content," arguing instead that "judges enforcing the Constitution must interpret that document constructively, by trying to identify general principles of political morality that provide the best justification for the document not clause by clause but as a whole, conceived as a fundamental structure for just government."

The nexus of personal and political morality was the centerpiece of "Justice for Clarence Thomas," 11-7, Dworkin expertly zeroing in on what he perceives to be the real failing of the Senate Judiciary Committee, its inability to pick up on an interpretive school of thought on natural law which holds that "abstract or vague or otherwise unclear laws, including the abstract claims of the constitution, should be interpreted, so far as their language permits, to conform to the objective moral rights the natural law doctrine assumes people to have." Had they picked up on this, Dworkin argues, Democrats could have stripped away conservative claims of the judicial "neutrality" the judges are presumed to have, and to which Clarence Thomas laid claim. "[Thomas] would have opened himself up to exactly the discussion of his substantial views of moral principle he was so anxious to avoid, presumably because he knew how unpopular his would be with the senators and their constituents."

TNYRB was once again an important source on developments in the Soviet Union and Eastern Europe. In "Native Son," 2-14, *Washington Post* correspondent David Remnick examines Aleksandr Solzhenitsyn's " 'modest contribution' to the current debate," his essay "How Shall We Organize Russia?" which appeared in *Komsomolskaya Pravda,* 9-18-90, and *Literaturnaya Gazeta,* 9-19-90, in which the exiled Nobel winner called for the dissolution of the Soviet Union. Remnick brilliantly plays Solzhenitsyn's ideas and the current Soviet political landscape off one another. A different Soviet Nobel Prize winning writer was the subject of John Bayley's "Pasternak's Great Fairy Tale," 3-7, a reprint of the introduction to the recently issued trade paperback edition of Boris Pasternak's classic novel *Doctor Zhivago.* Bayley writes eloquently on "Pasternak's vision of Russia under the Soviet regime as like a land bewitched by an evil enchanter, an enchanter whose agents may nonetheless exercise a power of arbitrary preservation, as well as of destruction," and we realize that he could have just as easily have been writing about life in the Soviet Union today, as the Government lurches more violently between repression and reform.

That lurching was at the heart of *TNYRB*'s Soviet coverage all year. Jeri Laber, Executive Director of the U.S. Helsinki Watch Committee, contends in "The Baltic Revolt," 3-28, that "A careful study of available information indicates that the violence in Lithuania and Latvia in January was in fact the result of a failed coup, an unsuccessful Soviet attempt to overthrow the pro-independence governments of the Baltic republics and establish direct presidential rule by Mr. Gorbachev." In "Russia After Perestroika," 6-27, Abraham Brumberg foresees greater democracy, greater weakening of the communist structure, and the greater irrelevancy of Mikhail Gorbachev. "He is not likely to resign, as urged upon him by the miners and some radical intellectuals. Nor is his popularity rating about to improve more than marginally. Rather, the revolution that he unleashed and for several years marked with his powerful impulses and visions will find new channels and new leaders as elections take place nationally and in the republics."

The shadowy relationship between Gorbachev and the hardliners was a key theme running through *TNYRB*'s Soviet coverage all year. Martin Malia offers a multidimensional study of the failed coup and the events leading up to it in "The August Revolution," 9-26, placing a lot of the blame on Mikhail Gorbachev and his rollercoaster relationship with the Soviet right, noting that his swing back to the left after a winter of retrenchment infuriated the conservatives he himself had put into office and created the impression that no one was in charge at the center. "With their own careers at stake, all that these people were fighting for was the preservation of the Party, state 'property,' and the Union — which Gorbachev himself had been trying to preserve in his more sophisticated manner." However, Peter Reddaway takes exception to Malia's contention that the events of last August removed the "ambiguities" surrounding Russia the past two years in the fascinating "The End of the Empire," 11-7. "The current political order is highly confused; it is not yet pregnant with a new order."

There were fewer contributions from Timothy Garton Ash in 1991, but in "Poland After Solidarity," 6-13, he provides an exceptional report on Solidarity, from its inspirational origins to its present position as a fallen idol, wracked with internal dissent and political infighting. Not surprisingly, Walesa strides over events, issues, and personalities like a colossus, and Ash finds himself placing Walesa as "a Polish Thatcherite," noting the irony of "A Thatcherite Poland, then, as the final outcome of Solidarity?" Late in the year, Ash joined with Michael Mertes and Dominiqu Moisi to issue a strong appeal to the EC: "Let the East Europeans In!" 10-24.

TNYRB was keen on the critical issue of nationalism awakened by the events in the ex-Soviet Union and Europe. Conor Cruise O'Brien, in "Nationalists and Democrats," 8-15, draws on Ireland's move toward democracy following its successful rebellion against Great Britain to argue that the rising tide of ethnic nationalism will not necessarily smother the nascent democracies in newly liberated Eastern Europe. "I think that case history, despite its many disquieting aspects, does carry at its core a somewhat reassuring message for the new democracies of Eastern Europe. Democracy in a nearly emerging state can, after all, cope with nationalism, given a bit of luck." In the sparkling "Two Concepts of Nationalism: An Interview with Isaiah Berlin," 11-21, Nathan Gardels and the old fox examine the evolution of nationalism in Europe since the Middle Ages, tossing in such diverse references as Johann Gottfried Herder and MTV as Berlin offers a compelling case for pluralism in the face of inclusive nationalism on one side and globalization impulses on the other. "We can't turn history back. Yet I do not wish to abandon the belief that a world which is a reasonably peaceful coat of many colors, each portion of which develops its own distinct cultural identity and is tolerant of others, is not a utopian dream."

TNYRB continued to be strong on the remaining communist superstate. Roderick MacFarquhar ties the collapse of the Soviet Communist Party to a predicted collapse of the Chinese Communist Party in "The Anatomy of Collapse," 9-26, arguing that in both cases, the leaders at the time fatally undermined the "totalitarian triangle" of charismatic leader, Party bureaucracy, and Marxist-Leninist doctrine. "Totalitarian systems can withstand pressure from social forces; they tend to fall apart when their leaders, out of a desire for radical change ignited by some external challenge, take actions that help to destroy the system." In "The Myth of Mao's China," 5-30, Jonathan Mirsky takes an uncompromising look at the issues raised by *China Misperceived: American Illusions and Chinese Reality,* Steven W. Mosher's payback to the professional community of China watchers, who Mosher believes caved in to official Chinese pressure in 1983 and acquiesced in his dismissal from Stanford University after he published a series of articles in a Taiwanese newspaper about China's horrific policy of forced birth control. "The book is severe in its criticism and sometimes painfully accurate; it can be vulgar, unfair, and evasive, and it is also sometimes wrong." Later in the year Mirsky produced a superb essay on Vietnam at peace and at war, "Reconsidering Vietnam," 10-10.

The biweekly offered thorough coverage of the Gulf War, much of it critical in tone of the Bush administration's decision to shift from a policy of containing Saddam Hussein to forcibly ejecting Iraqi troops from Kuwait. Michael Massing, in "The Way to War," 3-28, argues half-convincingly that the administration's response to the invasion of Kuwait became driven by logistics, overheated rhetoric, and decision-making by a handful of advisors, none of whom were Middle East experts, resulting in a policy that favored war over sanctions and a diplomatic solution. *Time* correspondent Scott MacLeod, reporting from Amman with "In the Wake of 'Desert Storm,' " 3-7, sounds a dire warning about the consequences of the Gulf War, apparently basing his observations on what he was seeing in the shadow of the Amman mosques, writing that "militancy and extremism will pose increasingly serious threats to moderation." In "Kuwait: The Last Forty-Eight Hours," Executive Director of Middle East Watch Andrew Whitley documents the "carnage" inflicted by allied bombers on Iraqi troops retreating from Kuwait City in the last days of the war, commenting that "on one ground — launching indiscriminate attacks likely to cause civilian deaths, by destroying identifiable vehicles carrying the sick and wounded — the allies could be charged with war crimes, at least for one terrible night's work." The intensive allied bombing of Iraq was criticized in "Iraq and Its Future," 4-11, by Iraqi exile Samir al-Khalil, who asks "Does an entire country have to be crippled to enforce a principle?"

Theodore Draper, examining the erosion of Constitutional restrictions on executive war-making abilities in "Presidential Wars," 9-26, provides some excellent historical background before going off on a tangent, attacking Charles Krauthammer's model of the U.S. as the undisputed leader of a unipolar world and George Bush's concept of a new world order — "His slogan represents some kind of imperial ambition, if without an imperial vision;" so instead of getting a look at the deeper institutional forces involved we get just one more attack on the Gulf War as an exercise in American *machismo*. In one of the better *TNYRB* essays on the war, *Financial Times* editor and columnist Edward Mortimer, in "Iraq: The Road Not Taken," 5-16, offers a clear-eyed assessment of Washington's decision to end the war with Iraq when it did, a decision Mortimer agrees with, and Washington's handling of the post-war policy toward Iraq, a policy Mortimer disagrees with, arguing that the U.S. should have intervened on the side of the rebels while making the right diplomatic moves. Massing journeyed to Iraq in the spring, and in "Can Saddam Survive?" 8-15, he delivers a valuable firsthand report on the growing defiance of Saddam and growing anti-Americanism as the sanctions continue.

Other major concerns on the international scene were covered as well, of course. In "The Pax Axis," 4-25, and "Against the Japanese Grain," 12-5, Ian Buruma writes thoughtfully on how the shortcomings of Japanese democracy hinder that nation's assumption of the superpower mantle, contrasting the Japanese unfavorably with the Germans. James Fallows, addressing the increasingly-asked question, "Is Japan the Enemy?" 5-30, argues that the diverging interests between the two countries, fueled by the end of the Cold War, Japan's drive for self-sufficiency, and the perception of American decline, is likely to create greater friction between Tokyo and Washington in the decade ahead. Fallows draws on Japanese corporate strategy in Thailand to examine the potential ramifications of free trade in Mexico in "The Romance With Mexico," 11-7, concluding that if U.S. workers are to benefit then guidance will be needed from Washington, "developing the educational system and providing the investment incentives that will support an economy with high wages and high technology." However, we later learned that Fallows may have committed many factual errors in a *Rolling Stone* article he wrote on the Japanese higher education system, and we discounted his work accordingly.

There were several important essays on human rights in *TNYRB* in 1991 as well. David J. Rothman and Aryeh Neier, in "India's Awful Prisons," 5-16, document the human rights abuses and rampant corruption in India's criminal justice system. In the haunting "On Gaza Beach," 7-18, Israeli journalist Ari Shavit writes unstintingly about his experiences as a guard in a prison camp for Palestinians: "In Gaza our General Security Services. . .amount to a Secret Police, our internment facilities are cleanly run Gulags." "On Gaza Beach" is less an essay on Israeli-Palestinian issues than a mediation on evil and the wounds the Arab-Israeli conflict is inflicting on the Israeli conscience. "It is not, at this hour, a matter of territories in exchange for peace. It is a matter of territories in exchange for our humanity."

Much of *TNYRB*'s Israeli coverage was characterized by informed criticism of the Likud government. Avishai Margalit, in "Israel's Great White Hope," 6-27, authoritatively examines the impact of Soviet Jewish immigrants on Israeli society, politics, and the larger Middle Eastern equation, noting that "the Israeli right wing will be faced with a difficult decision if the United States would provide support for the immigration only if Israel were to give up territory as part of an agreement with the Arabs." This theme was developed further by Arthur Hertzberg, former president of the American Jewish Congress, in "Showdown," 10-24, Hertzberg contemptuous of the Shamir government's efforts to play on the emotional guilt of Jewish Americans to drag them into its dispute with Washington over the expansion of settlements in the occupied territory. "There is a pathetic aspect to these contradictory attitudes, and to the way the Shamir government has been using them for its own purpose."

The Third World was not ignored, either. Few journalists are keener observers of the developing world (or the developed world, for that matter) than V.S. Naipaul, and in "The Shadow of the Guru," 12-20-90, readers get a different version of material in Naipaul's new book *India: A Million Mutinies Now*. Naipaul examines the rise of Sikh extremism in India, writing that "The establishing of a Sikh identity was a recurring Sikh need. Religion was the basis of this identity; religion provided the emotional charge. But that also meant that the Sikh cause had been entrusted to people who were not representative of the Sikh achievement, were a generation or so behind." Equally impressive is "A Handful of Dust: Return to Guiana," 4-11, in which Naipaul journeys back to the South American nation of Guiana, to see how the nationalist-Marxist leader Cheddi Jagan is doing now that history has passed him by, and finds that like the protagonist of the Waugh novel, Jagan is living a life of "social extinction."

In *TNYRB*'s best effort on the Third World, Kenneth Maxwell, in "The Tragedy of the Amazon," 3-7, and "The Mystery of Chico Mendes," 3-28, looks beyond the "ecology martyr" image of Mendes being created by liberal writers, activists, and Hollywood to place Mendes in the context of his revolutionary ideology and Brazil's murky world of commerce, development, lawlessness and politics. "In fact," Maxwell writes in the 3-28 piece, "the ecological and social crisis in Brazil was caused by some of the same factors that led to the ecological disasters in the Soviet Union and Eastern Europe: failed overcentralized planning, rigidly organized management, private greed and special privileges, corrupt and ineffective justice at the grass roots, as well as permeating, callous disregard by the rich for the poor."

It was in the pages of *TNYRB* last year that Senator Daniel Patrick Moynihan called for the abolition of the CIA, and this year, in "The Nuclear Threat: A Proposal," 6-27, former defense secretary Robert S. McNamara teams with physicists Hans A. Bethe and Kurt Gottfried to call on the U.S. and the Soviet Union to make "a very deep and swift cut in US and Soviet nuclear forces," down "from their present total of approximately 50,000 warheads to something on the order of two thousand." The authors are prescient on the two greatest threats of nuclear war in the post-Cold War age, the instability in the Soviet Union and the potential rise of Third World nuclear powers. The authors gloss over some key points (such as verification of tactical nuclear weapon disarmament and the role of other current nuclear powers, such as China) but this essay is designed to provoke thought and debate, and it certainly succeeds in that regard.

Co-Editors:	Robert B. Silvers and Barbara Epstein
Address:	250 West 57th Street, Room 1321 New York, NY 10107 (212) 757-8070
Circulation:	1990 — 130,000 1991 — 120,000

Policy Review

This fine, slim quarterly of the neoconservative Heritage Foundation continues to bring in new viewpoints and perspectives to the cause, pushing at and stretching the boundaries of conventional conservatism. Although editor Adam Meyerson often turns to well-known conservatives, such as Fred Barnes in "The Politics of Less," Winter, to serve up prescriptives, there's a surprising willingness on Meyerson's part to veer from established conservative thinkers. *Policy Review,* true to its name, goes to the policymakers to assess the direction of the conservative thinking, incorporating the views of Republican firebrand Rep. Newt Gingrich (R-Ga.) to Democratic Gov. L. Douglas Wilder of Virginia.

The goal of the Heritage Foundation, as *PR* publisher Edwin Feulner puts it, "is not to join the Washington establishment. It is to create a new establishment that will supplant the old," "Building the New Establishment," Fall; Feulner also observes that ". . .our greatest institutional achievement has been to build Heritage as a permanent Washington presence here to stay for the long term. My overriding managerial objective has been to make sure that Heritage is a permanent part of the Washington policy-making apparatus." Heritage, according to Feulner, is a part of the process while challenging the philosophy. Meyerson works hand-in-hand with those goals with his selection of material and interview subjects for *PR,* though, he has tried hard to steer the magazine clear of becoming a *Policy Review of the Heritage Foundation.* It is only this year for the first time that *PR* has devoted an issue to the work of the Heritage Foundation, Fall, and Meyerson carefully notes in his introduction that ". . .*Policy Review* was deliberately set up not to be a house organ, but rather an independent magazine dedicated to advancing conservative ideas and talent. Unlike our sister publications, the *Brookings Review* and the *American Enterprise,* we do not carry the name of our institution, and it is not unusual for *Policy Review* to publish arguments at odds with arguments made in other Heritage publications."

One of the strengths of *PR* are the interviews, usually conducted by Adam Meyerson. Rightly or wrongly, Meyerson lets his subjects run on at times, so we get a real sense of what they think and where they stand. A Meyerson interview with Republican Gov. Tommy Thompson of Wisconsin gives us a close-up view of his tax-slashing, business-friendly policies that have helped to avoid the budget crises so many other states are facing, "Land of Milk and Money," Spring. We also get a look at Thompson's pilot welfare programs that have contributed to a reduction of the welfare rolls, and hear his advice to the President: ". . .based on our experience, I would strongly recommend cutting capital gains taxes at the national level. Keeping down taxes on capital gains encourages entrepreneurs to take risks. It gives them the incentive to invest, to expand their operations, and in the process put more people to work. A cut in these taxes is not a break for the rich. It's an inducement for growth and ingenuity." Rep. Newt Gingrich also gets tough on the President early, "Miracle Whip," Winter, seeing re-election difficulties due to the budget agreement: "In retrospect, Bush shouldn't have gone to the [budget] summit at all. . .Giving up the tax pledge was a terrible error, because it struck at the core of people's respect for politicians. Bush had built up a rapport with the American people, who thought he was someone who would do what he promised. They trusted him. Losing that trust was a more serious consequence of Bush's raising taxes than any damage done to the economy." Gov. L. Douglas Wilder of Virginia is interviewed in the same issue, seeing trouble ahead for Bush, "Low-Tax Liberal," Winter. While not a conservative in the strict sense of the word, Meyerson fleshes out Wilder's fiscal conservative side, which Wilder then relates to the mammoth waste in evidence on the national government level. Meyerson interviews Sen. Phil Gramm (R-Tex.) in "Summitting with the Enemy," Spring, letting him get away with all sorts of nonsense: ". . .in reality, voting against the [budget] summit agreement was indirectly a vote for fewer spending control measures, higher taxes and more destructive taxes in terms of wealth and job creation." Although one editor's note does correct Gramm's mistake on spending as a percentage of GNP, this is one instance where Meyerson should have followed up on some of Gramm's goofy assertions, rather than letting him loose. But for the most part, Meyerson's technique works well.

While we still find some conservative boilerplate in *PR,* there's more now that piques our interest. "The Great American Tax Debate," Spring, brings together notable conservatives to "discuss the when, where, why, how much and whether of cutting federal taxes," offering some intriguing ideas, with a memorable line from Grover Norquist: "Mae West's observation about sex is true of tax cuts: All tax cuts are good tax cuts." Katherine Kersten provides a rather intriguing examination of conservative feminist ideas, "What Do Women Want?" Spring, a 10 Best nominee from *PR*'s editors, drawing an interesting distinction between conservative and traditional feminism: "Like other feminists, the conservative feminist sees the promotion of justice and equality as a primary goal of public policy. Yet she understands these principles quite differently than do most contemporary feminists. Specifically, the conservative feminist tends to see *individuals* as having rights to justice and equality, while other feminists tend to see *groups* as having such rights." Clarence Thomas's much-publicized 1987 speech before the Heritage Foundation is reprinted in its entirety, a valuable exercise in looking at the isolation of the black conservative, "No Room at the Inn," Fall, differentiating between ideas and labels: "The dual labels of black Republicans and black conservatives drew rave reviews. Unfortunately, the raving was at us, not for us. . .our ideas themselves received very positive reactions, especially among the average working-class and middle-class black American who had no vested or proprietary interest in the social policies that had dominated the political scene for the past 20 years. . .The ideas were okay. Republicans and conservatives, especially black ones, were not." In a selection nominated by *PR*'s editors for our 10 Best section, Associate publisher Burton Yale Pines brings out the parallels between Bush and William Howard Taft, whose Roosevelt supporters turned on him for betraying the legacy of Teddy Roosevelt, his predecessor in office, "Bull Moose Revolt," Winter, an intriguing perspective that noted the conservative tide turning against Bush early in the year. The White House's James K. Pinkerton juxtaposes the lessons of policymaking in Desert Storm effectively onto domestic policy in "General Schwarzkopf's New Paradigm," Summer, drawing the line in no uncertain terms: "Losing policies didn't work better as they got older in South Vietnam, and they won't work over time in the South Bronx." And "If we can impose accountability on the Pentagon, why can't we extend it to the domestic bureaucracies as well?" Pinkerton, though, never quite tells us how to get there.

It is only infrequently that *PR* enlarges its mandate of "advancing conservative ideas and talent" to strictly social issues. In A 10 Best nomination from *PR*'s editors, William R. Mattox, Jr., bemoans the lack of time and attention children get from today's parents, "The Parent Trap," Winter, but we're not sure his simplistic solutions, such as "marriage bonuses," will help solve the problem. As with so many conservative essays on "Unplanned Parenthood," Summer, Frederika Mathewes-Green concentrates on the morality of abortion, rather than the question of birth control. Rita McWilliams's dissertation in *The Washington Monthly* was much more cogent on the subject, "Why Aren't Pro-lifers and Pro-choicers Pro-contraception?" 7/8-91. Occasionally, *PR* will tackle a social issue, but the clear bent is governmental, practical and ideological.

There is still, unfortunately, a good helping of boilerplate to be had at *PR*. Robert Kaufman gives us the very standard Bush-as-Churchill view, "The Line in the Sand," Spring. In "Russian Roulette," Summer, Charles Fairbanks, Jr. still sees the Soviet Union as a strategic threat, one that is compounded by internal disarray and logistical restructuring: "Control over many conventional weapons has so broken down that one can buy an armored personnel carrier in the Soviet Union today for the cost of a 1982 Toyota in America." While central control and communism were *les betes noires* of the conservatives, it seems that the lack of a central command structure is even more frightening; while this is a worthwhile effort, we have to work quite hard to glean Fairbank's pearls of wisdom buried within. Along the same line of thinking, there's little new in Adam Meyerson's "Why Communism Failed," Fall. While it's accurate enough for Meyerson to note, and note quite eloquently, that "Communism was a universal failure because it was misunderstood and, worse, was contemptuous of human nature," soon we find that Meyerson is again pidgeonholing his appraisal with the Soviet Union as the Godless communist oppressor: "Nor was there any place for love or friendship or community in Communism. Marx saw the family simply as an instrument of exploitation, rather than the building block of a loving and caring society. And while the destruction of the family was never really put into practice in most Communist regimes, their goal was to destroy virtually every other institution between the individual and the state. The positive attraction of Communism came mainly from its vision of universal human brotherhood. But even this vision was impoverished and dessicated. The Judeo-Christian religious tradition and Anglo-American political tradition offer much richer visions of human brotherhood, combining universality with a respect for the individual, the family, the private voluntary organization, and the local community. There was, of course, no room for God in the Communist vision."

Despite the occasional backsliding into conservative conventionality, *PR* continues to gain momentum in becoming a new voice in the conservative movement. In the Spring issue, a ringing discourse by Sen. Malcolm Wallop for Senate members to stand by "The Courage of Our Convictions," is subtitled "A Call to Arms for Senate Conservatives." *Policy Review* is gradually becoming the call to arms for all conservatives.

Editor: Adam Meyerson

Executive Editor: Thomas Atwood

Address: 214 Massachusetts Avenue, NE
                Washington, DC 20002
                (202) 546-4400

Circulation: 1990 — 14,000
                1991 — 14,000

The Progressive

We've been watching the course of *The Progressive* for several years now, trying to ascertain where this trim monthly fits in the constellation of publications helping to define the direction of the American left. With the collapse of communism and the peripheral damage to socialism, the contributions of *The Progressive* have become more important as the left struggles to restructure its framework. Founded in 1909 by Robert M. LaFollette, Sr., *The Progressive* maintains an accute relevance in this post-Cold War era as an organ that forthrightly expresses indignation when the national conscience seems to bend before the assertion of an American triumphalism and the entrenched, sterile wealth of the Establishment.

TP's strength is surely its editorial page, and it is here that the heart of the publication is best revealed. It began the year with a particularly forceful indictment of the U.S. march to war with Iraq, "The Propaganda War," 1-91. "There is no reason whatsoever for the United States to shed blood in the Persian Gulf," the editorial asserted, proceeding to systematically take apart and debunk the alarums being spread regarding Iraq's capability for use of nuclear weapons. "Vestigial Congress," 2-91, was sharp and to the point on the performance of Congress in the Persian Gulf crisis: "the national legislature has become a purely vestigial organ — one that no longer serves any useful purpose." Resolute in its opposition to the Gulf War, *TP*'s editorials were consistently hard-hitting. "We hear it described as 'the war no one wanted,' " it began in its cover-page editorial "The War Some Wanted," 3-91. "Nonsense. Some wanted it, pressed for it, undermined every effort to avert it, ultimately started it, and are waging it now." With a few stray thoughts, the editors pose some excellent questions in "America Triumphant," 4-91: "What happened to the formidable Iraqi threat" that was used to justify the massive military response by the U.S.? "When will the liberation of Kuwait [from its undemocratic binds] begin?" And "How will we now achieve 'stability' in the Middle East?"

An especially insightful editorial, "Soviet Rumblings," 2-91, borrowed an astute conception from the Italian Marxist Antonio Gramsci to put into sharp perspective the crisis in the U.S.S.R.: "The old is dying and the new cannot be born. In the interregnum, a great variety of morbid symptoms appear." The editorial was critical of Soviet efforts to join the IMF and World bank: "those U.S.-dominated institutions. . .insist on imposing the most regressive social policies on member countries — the elimination of subsidies on such basic items as food and gas, and the devaluation of the currency. Such an economic regime will impose austere hardship on an already besieged Soviet people." The editorialist carefully constructs a case that the U.S. Supreme Court is "Public Enemy Number One," 8-91, citing rulings which have given the police greater powers of search and seizure, clearly a dangerous trend. And the editorialist urges Bush to bolder action on arms control in "Bombs Away," 11-91: ". . .there is an even larger and more urgent goal: The renunciation of military force as an instrument of national policy. Here, too, the current world situation provides a historic opportunity to take genuinely bold strides, not propaganda pirouettes."

But the true credo of *The Progressive* can best be found in "Surprised? Not Really," 6-91. The editors are tough on the press coverage, or lack thereof, of the Iran-contra affair and the "October surprise" conspiracy theory, citing the few journalists who followed the story and continue to do so. "Was the evidence revealed in 1987 ironclad? No. But it was certainly strong enough to warrant further investigation. Did all those major newspapers that are always competing for the Pulitzer Prize put their highly touted investigative reporting teams on the story? No. Did the television networks? No. . .The President and his men don't think they have to answer questions posed by the likes of *In These Times* and *The Nation,* and the small publications of the Left don't have the resources to send reporters all over the world chasing down leads. Stories that warrant investigation and mass exposure start out in such publications all the time, though. Far too often for the health of society, that's where they stay." It is exactly for this reason that we value *The Progressive* —their consistently intelligent challenge to the establishment.

Its first cover story this year, though, "The General in Charge," 1-91 by managing editor Linda Rocawich, came nowhere near the level of the editorial effort. Rocawich attempted to produce a profile of Gen. H. Norman Schwarzkopf that might fit a preconceived mold, portraying him as "someone who often said he would make general before he was forty and didn't care what it took to do it." But she really has no evidence to back up the spin she tries to give the profile, asserting at one point that a couple of men who served under him in Vietnam said that "enlisted men referred to him, behind his back, as the Bloody Butcher." She tries to keep alive an insupportable assertion that perhaps Schwarzkopf was responsible for the deaths of U.S. servicemen by friendly fire in Vietnam more than once, and that perhaps he was also culpable for similar deaths in Grenada where he was deputy commander of the U.S. invasion of 1983. A better effort on the war, "Just the Good News, Please," by Debbie Nathan 2-91, is a very effective critique of the Pentagon's preference for "Hi-Mom" coverage of the U.S. troops in the Gulf, and we read here one of the better initial accounts of the restrictions being put on the media's coverage of this crisis. (Along with ten other publications and news organizations, as well as several writers, *TP* filed a federal lawsuit on January 10, challenging as unconstitutional the severe restrictions imposed by the Pentagon for press coverage of the war in the Persian Gulf.) Once the war was underway, *TP* presented as its cover feature "Voices of Reason," 3-91, an assembly of several opponents to war with Iraq who offered their insights as to why the conflict in the Gulf had turned into a global crisis. In an interview with Karl Bremmer in the same issue, Sen. Paul Wellstone (D-Minn.) joins the critics, advising that out of the U.S. action "I see a new world disorder, a primitive world linked to violence." Michael T. Klare, who often pens reports on military issues for *The Nation,* makes a spirited case for the charge that the war against Iraq was a "war of annihilation," in which the destruction of Iraq was an end in itself. In "One, Two, Many Iraqs," 4-91, Klare asserts that "this was a throwback to a more primitive era, when the dominant empires and kingdoms attempted to preserve their paramount status by killing off all the men and boys in conquered territories so as to avert armed revolts in the future." The same issue also contained an interview with Ramsey Clark by Claudia Dreifus, in which the former U.S. Attorney General asserts that the civilian casualty toll in Iraq from coalition bombing runs has been far heavier than reported in the U.S.: "The idea that there's pinpoint precision is ridiculous, a great falsehood."

Most of the remainder of *The Progressive* is devoted to social issues and commentary. Peggy Simpson looks at the turning back of the clock in Eastern Europe regarding women's rights with "No Liberation for Women," 2-91: "The women of Eastern Europe are at a critical point. It's not just their jobs that are in jeopardy; it's the view society as a whole has of their role. . .Women's problems have been put aside after every revolution. . ." Morton Mintz, formerly of *The Washington Post,* exposes the grotesque practice of shipping and selling American-made cigarettes abroad, "Tobacco Roads," 5-91, a selection nominated by *TP*'s editors for 10 Best consideration. Mintz details how American trade policies are facilitating tobacco product sales outside the U.S., as well as the massive human cost — according to a World Health Organization report, if current smoking patterns persist, 500 million people now living, 70 percent outside the U.S., will be killed by tobacco-related diseases. The July issue is devoted to the war on drugs, or lack of one, "What War on Drugs?" a collection of articles challenging U.S. policy, particularly in the foreign arena of the global drug trade, "The CIA Connection" by Alfred McCoy, and "Troops, Not Talks in Bolivia," by Jo Ann Kawell. This cover treatment only stretches credibility when Eric Sterling argues that the existence of the war on drugs is "Trashing the Bill of Rights," taking us through the first 10 Amendments of the

Constitution and outlining how the drug war is violating each. We're taken on horrific but important tour of the prison system by Heather Rhoads, "The New Death Row," 9-91, an expose of how the prison system handles inmates who are HIV-positive. One of the stories left untouched by the mainstream press, this impressive article was nominated by *TP*'s editors for 10 Best consideration. Almost coinciding with a *New York Times* series on mental hospitals and children, "Kids in the Cuckoo's Nest," by Holly Metz 12-91, is told from the child's point of view, rather than focusing on the industry itself. In this eye-opening perspective, Metz outlines the legal rights of children, as well as how and why the process of hospitalization varies from state to state; this overview was also nominated by the editors at *TP* for our 10 Best section. Immediately following Metz's article, is another child-centered article, Ed Griffin-Nolan's "Dealing Glue to Third World Children," 12-91, the story of how in Honduras, H.B. Fuller, an American company that is "the largest seller of industrial adhesives in Latin America," is involved in the debate over mustard oil as an additive, which would prevent the glue-sniffing prevalent among Third-World kids. Where else could we find such a story?

Bernard Nossiter appears with some frequency, commenting primarily on economic policy. In "A Welcome Slump," 1-91, he declares that "Curing the slump is not hard. The first and swiftest policy requires a large increase in the supply of money. . .matched by fiscal exuberance, a program to *increase* the deficit by 1 or 2% of national output — somewhere in the range of $50 to $100 billion. The main thing is to get the money and credit to provide people with income to spend on consumer goods, which in turn generates more jobs and more disposable income," a point of view one may still hear advocated among some layers within the Democratic party. He strikes a more insightful note in "Sand Dollars," 4-91, an assessment of who nets what from the war: "Thanks to a campaign brilliantly waged by the Air Force, otherwise reflective people have been persuaded that future wars must be fought at the edge of technological fantasy."

There's still a lot of wasted space in *TP*. June Jordan's column every other month heads the list in this category, her ravings detracting from any claim *TP* might put forward for serious political commentary or discourse. We read in "The Big Time Coward," 4-91, for example, why it was that President Bush wouldn't go along with what she described as a Soviet-Iraqi proposal for withdrawal from Kuwait: "Saddam Hussein is not a white man. He and his Arab peoples must be destroyed." The editors also showed terribly poor judgement in running "The Sexual Connection," 4-91, by John Gottlieb. One of Gottlieb's friends is sexually aroused by a videotape of a B-52 bomber: "Look at that B-52. It's like a large flying dick with wings! Doesn't that give you a hard-on?" It at least gave Gottlieb a burst of "creative insight" — "I got to thinking. Was there a connection between sex and the Gulf War?" Well, "there was much talk of the 'big sixteen inch guns' on the battleship *Missouri.* I noticed that the Pentagon's 'bomb's-eye-view' videotapes had an almost sexual quality. A long, flying projectile climactically made contact with a target — a munitions depot with a huge set of barn doors down the middle — and exploded. Even those of us who were against the war felt a tinge of exhilaration and excitement." Hey, even women, he advised, weren't immune to the sexual imagery and exhilaration of high-tech warfare. "For God's sake!" a female colleague told him, "Watching those videotapes gives *me* a hard-on!" Good grief. *Mother Jones* columnist Molly Ivins appears regularly, her "Small Favors" the last word in the magazine. She begins "Trends Aplenty," 1-91, with a crude, tasteless joke, but quickly recovers with her homespun brand of witty insouciance: ". . .mostly it [1990] was the Year the People Got Mad. That their anger didn't seem to lurch off in any particular direction doesn't detract from the phenomenon. It's what we always do in time of crisis in America — saddle up, mount horse, and take off in 360 different directions." She produces a serious critical observation regarding banking reform in "Season of Drear," 2-91: "And the reason deregulation. . .will save the banks is that what we need is bigger banks. So we can be competitive with the Japanese, you see. Friends, this is horsepucky. . .Wait until you see a banking industry with seven majors. Seems to me that it's a simple concept — the concentration of wealth is a Bad Idea."

We get a sense of the clientele to which *The Progressive* appeals by a look at the letters to the editor that appear in the monthly. An especially provocative symposium last year, "Where to From Here?" 11-90, resulted in a revealing array of points of view expressed in the letters that appeared 1-91. They reflect the issues with which *TP* readers are grappling in trying to redefine the tasks and perspectives of the American left after the collapse of communism. From a Massachusetts reader we learn that "major progressive changes will occur only when a full-scale depression results. . ." An Arizona reader, though, asks "When, oh when, oh when will the straight Left start dealing with its own homophobia?" A reader from Berkeley, Cal., advises that "We must first take power under the old system, and the battle requires the largest coalition possible." From San Francisco, another reader urges "Drop the socialist rhetoric. . .It is simply a tactical necessity." "Democracy is more neutral, comfortable, and non-threatening," suggests a reader from Washington, and it "removes the bias barriers." From Oregon, "Politics need not equal compromise," we read. "The time is ripe for the Left to organize and form a third party." Succinctly put, from Fallbrook, Cal., we read what may best sum up the state of the left at the moment: "Sadly, many of us are as confused as ever." Under the editorship of Erwin Knoll since 1973, *The Progressive* has worked long and hard to alleviate that confusion, and will undoubtedly continue to provoke and prod the Left to action.

Editor: Erwin Knoll

Managing Editor: Linda Rocawich

Address: 409 E. Main Street
Madison, WI 53703
(608) 257-4626

Circulation: 1990 — 35,000
1991 — 35,000

Reader's Digest

The homey, Norman Rockwell-ish pleasures of this nearly pocket-sized magazine were extolled in the trendiest format possible, in an episode this fall of Fox TV's "The Simpsons." Satirized as "Reading Digest," *Reader's Digest* surely could not help but be pleased with the plug on one of the most popular television programs in the country.

The strength of *Reader's Digest* remains its selection of topical items covering the world at large and the U.S. in particular, its articles and essays usually infected with the can-do spirit of the monthly, and which offer reasonable, common sense solutions that often seem logical and effective, but never simplistic. Read literally the world over, with a worldwide circulation of more than 28 million, and translated into 16 languages, *Reader's Digest* premiered its Russian language edition in July; the experimental edition is available on newsstands in the major cities of the Soviet Union — Moscow, Leningrad, Kiev and Kharkov — with an initial circulation expected at 50,000, with a goal of 100,000 circulation in two years. *Reader's Digest* will even offer subscriptions to the Soviets.

While most of the material that appears in *RD* has appeared elsewhere, there are quite a few items that are written for *RD* by some of the most prominent journalists in the country, Rowland Evans, Robert Novak and Fred Barnes among them. The staff journalists at *RD*, including Rachel Flick, Ralph Kinney Bennett and Robert James Bidinotto, are all good writers with adequate reporting skills. But for all the talent evident in the magazine, *RD* offered little this year that surprised us. In past years, there has always been at least one dispatch that has had far-reaching implications, as with Bidinotto's "Getting Away With Murder," 7-88, the story of Willie Horton told in horrifyingly personal terms, and Bidinotto's "What Is the Truth About Global Warming?" 2-90, an important update in the debate over the existence of the greenhouse effect. This year there was no such dispatch, either from the contributors or from the staff.

This is not to say *RD* did not consistently offer original items of interest over the course of the year. Evans & Novak suggest term limits are "The Best Way to Clean Up Congress," 3-91, but the dynamic duo uses few new arguments. Evans & Novak also provide a light profile of the president of the Russian Republic, "Is Boris Yeltsin for Real?" 7-91, useful for those who haven't gotten a good look at the famous Russian leader as yet. Fred Barnes reveals the "Dirty Secrets Behind the Budget Mess," 2-91, but most of this is old news. More interesting is Barnes's profile of Antonin Scalia, "Top Gun on the High Court," 7-91, and while we don't come away with a sense of the associate justice, Barnes's broad strokes provide an outline of his personality and judicial approach. John Barron's "Breaking the IRA's American Connection," 3-91, is less a spy story than a morality play. In "The Rape of Kuwait: Why War Came to the Gulf," 4-91, Ralph Kinney Bennett and Rachel Flick simply retail the rumors about the Iraqi invasion, including the memorable "babies thrown out of incubators" story which was later called into question by witnesses and authorities. Bennett tells us only of "The Vision Behind the Patriot," 5-91, replete with personal details on Donald Banks and Floyd Wimberly, but there is little on the Patriot's actual evolution in technological or financial terms. *RD* is also preoccupied with law and order, plaintively reminding us of the need to get tough in the war on crime by offering "Why Free Criminals to Kill?" 6-91, a police widow's poignant lament by Maura Mills Irby, and Robert James Bidinotto's wrenching "Freed to Rape Again," 10-91, in which the examples are as awful as you'll find in any police logbook. Both were suggested as 10 Best nominations by *RD*'s editors.

RD often serves an important function in disseminating information to a massive audience. Many readers, we're sure, didn't necessarily know the details of how European and U.S. companies helped to subsidize the war build up of Saddam Hussein and Iraq, information provided by Rachel Flick in "How We Appeased a Tyrant" 1-91, a timely and topical exercise that was nominated by *RD*'s editors for 10 Best consideration. In "Myths About the Homeless," 6-91, Robert James Bidinotto explodes some of the accepted assumptions. Although we've seen this before, the information he provides is worth repeating as these misconceptions are so prevalent in our culture; he even offers some common sense solutions: "establish mandatory supervised care for the mentally incapacitated"; enforcement of the vagrancy laws, and enactment where necessary; and "help those in need to help themselves." Submitted for 10 Best consideration by *RD*'s editors, Rachel Flick's "Does Affirmative Action Really Work?" 8-91, provides anecdotal material on the policy, compelling enough, but there's no real answer to her question. An exclusive by David Satter that was submitted by *RD*'s editors for our 10 Best section, "What Young Russians Really Think," 3-91, reports the results of a *RD*/Institute of Sociology at the Soviet Academy of Sciences and while this interests, there's no mechanism for change provided, which belittles the numbers somewhat. Malcolm S. Forbes, Jr. called this an "astonishing poll" in his "Fact & Comment," *Forbes* 4-1. With "China's Daring Underground of Faith," 8-91, and "Rape of the Golden Land," 12-91, Fergus Bordewich provides vivid and sad examinations of repression in China and Burma respectively; both were suggested by *RD*'s editors as appropriate 10 Best selections. Also nominated for 10 Best consideration was John Barron's "KAL 007: The Hidden Story," 11-91, an informative compilation of the tale of the doomed airliner allegedly shot down by the Soviets. But while all these items are topical and timely, there was nothing that *startled* with new fact or illumination.

The condensed material intrigues and often disseminates important information. *Time*'s controversial expose of the Church of Scientology appears 10-91, "Scientology: A Dangerous Cult Goes Mainstream," by Richard Behar. The Church of Scientology filed suit in Switzerland to try and block publication of the article in Europe, an indication of the wide readership of *RD*. A former *Sports Illustrated* writer, now with *The Miami Herald,* John Underwood, vividly links cause and effect between 2 Live Crew and teen problems, "How Nasty Do We Wanna Be?": "Civilizations do not give out, they give in. They come apart not in a flash but by the inch. In a society where anything goes, everything, eventually, will. We will write funny columns about attempts to keep that disintegration from happening. We can ridicule the 'do-gooders' and the 'morals police' who seek to save us from our own worst instincts. But in the end, the joke may well be on us." We find Donald Dale Jackson's "Who Killed Sue Snow?" 2-91, to be eerily prescient; this recounting of the only product-tampering case that was solved tells the tale of Stella Nickell, who murdered Ms. Snow and her husband Bruce with cyanide-laced Extra Strength Excedrin capsules to collect on her husband's insurance policy. Ms. Snow simply bought the wrong bottle in the drugstore. The issue was out several weeks before two people in Washington state died from taking cyanide-tainted Sudafed capsules in mid-February; a third victim survived. A charming offering from venerable comedian George Burns, "My Friend Jack Benny," 2-91, delights us. Reprinted from *Fortune,* we find Erik Calonius's "Is This Airplane Safe?" 6-91, with fully documented complaints about FAA inspection procedures, as well as boondoggles by the airlines, useful for those who fly. In "100 Dreams," 5-91, Carolyn Males details the story of the Trickle Up Program, a nonprofit organization that has become an important part of the economic transformations moving through the developing world. TUP fights global poverty with $100 grants, and we were immediately skeptical, but Males details just how effective the effort has been, since 1979 the program has helped "over 130,000 of the world's neediest people in 90 countries win small, life-saving victories over poverty," an *RD* story that's worth clipping and mailing to your Congressman. Importantly, *RD* chooses to reprint from the *Congressional Record,* 6-91, the words of congressmen both pro-and anti-Desert Storm, from the debates in early January about the use of force. Given the prevalence of C-SPAN, and other networks which aired much of this live, it's unlikely that some folks didn't hear or see at least part of it, but it's certainly eye-opening to see this in print, a powerful reminder both of the way our government works and of the war debate itself.

The book and "special" sections are generally interesting, although the excerpts and articles are mostly biographical in nature rather than political. An exception is the condensation of *Eichmann in My Hands,* "I Captured Adolf Eichmann," 2-91, by Peter Z. Malkin and Harry Stein, in which the pair offers an inside look at the Mossad, riveting and compelling on its most famous success. The lessons taught by the men who captured Eichmann " 'Once we're certain,' Meir said, 'why don't we just kill the bastard on the spot?' Uzi nodded. 'We all share that feeling, I'm sure.' Meir shook his head bitterly. 'What chance did he give those people?' he demanded. 'I *saw* them, the ones that survived. What kind of consideration did he show them?' For a long moment, no one made any response. 'Let's never forget,' said Uzi finally, 'that's part of the difference between him and us.' " seem to have been long forgotten on the West Bank. More typical is the "Special Section" story of aerialist Angel Wallenda and her fight against cancer, "An Angel on High," 3-91' Henry Hurt movimg us with this sterling picture of her past, her personality and her unquenchable spirit. *RD*'s editors were obviously impressed, nominating this memorable portrait of a memorable woman for our 10 Best section.

The remainder of *Reader's Digest* is comprised of self-help, feel-good material that is generally useful, although not necessarily newsworthy. The 3-91 issue is typical: "When to Keep Your Mouth Shut," by Jean Parvin; "Why Our Hair Turns Gray," by Lowell Ponte; "How Lucky People Get That Way," by Ralph Kinney Bennett; "Beware of Health Hype," by Robert L. Taylor, M.D.; "Madeline Cartwright Brings Hope to Class," by Richard Louv; "Sex Secrets About Men Women Should Know," by Barbara De Angelis. These selections alternately charm, inform, advise, and uplift from month to month, and are worth skimming.

It is precisely the homey, warm quality of *Reader's Digest* that we find particularly evident in its self-help material that constitutes a large part of *RD*'s appeal, both to Homer Simpson and the world at large. One of the most poignant "Letters to the Editor" we've seen appears in the 8-91 issue from Cpl. Scott Raub of the U.S. Marine Corps. Stationed in Saudi Arabia, a driver got five copies of *RD* and handed them to him. "As soon as I opened it, the monotony of desert life — biting fleas, ready-to-eat meals, sand in almost everything — seemed to disappear. It was like a letter from home." Now apparently stateside, Cpl. Raub finishes by noting, "I still wonder how those Saudis got hold of a current Reader's Digest. I guess I'll never know. But one thing's for sure: they gave this homesick soldier an eloquent reminder of what he was fighting for." An irrepressibly American magazine, *RD* will surely be inspiring readers all over the world for years to come.

Editor:	Kenneth Y. Tomlinson
Address:	Pleasantville, NY 10570
	(914) 238-8585
Circulation:	1990 — 16,296,919
	1991 — 16,250,000

Reason

The monthly for "Free Minds & Free Markets" continues to broaden its base of readers without losing its decidedly libertarian bent. Now proudly boasting a circulation higher than *Commentary, The Washington Monthly, The Progressive* and *The American Spectator,* Los Angeles-based *Reason* offers impressively practicable solutions to complex problems, never losing sight of its intractably libertarian perspective.

Founded in 1968 by Robert Poole, Jr., now *Reason*'s publisher, this trim magazine is one of the few publications to spawn a foundation, rather than the more commonplace course of the foundation giving birth to the magazine. Unlike, say, *Policy Review,* the relationship between *Reason* and the Reason Foundation is symbiotic, one working off the other in research and writing to further libertarian ideas and solutions to government policy quandaries. *Reason* is simply not a typical house organ as so many of the other foundation publications are. Rather than merely trumpeting the ideological line of the think tank, or responding to the views of its supporters, the magazine fashions original libertarian prescriptions and views often using the raw-data research and resources of the Reason Foundation. The best example of this is "Talking Trash," cover 8/9-91, by editor Virginia Postrel and Lynn Scarlett, director of research for the Reason Foundation. In this article, nominated for our 10 Best section by *Reason*'s editors, the pair argues recycling and garbage disposal is more complicated than one would imagine, responding to the current thinking that getting back to the basics is the best course, by making comparisons filled with minute details. "For instance, in Mexico City, most consumers squeeze fresh oranges to make orange juice. The peels are then thrown away. Americans, by contrast, tend to buy packaged frozen concentrate. As a result, the typical Mexican household tosses out 10.5 ounces of orange peel each week; the typical American household throws out 2 ounces of cardboard or aluminum. Meanwhile, back at the orange juice factory, the peels are collected and sold to make animal feed and other products. If all the orange juice drinkers in New York City individually tossed away their orange peels, one day's haul would weigh as much as two ocean liners."

One of the primary reasons for the appeal of *Reason* is the fervor of belief in libertarian solutions. The staff at *Reason* truly believe that there are few government and societal ills that the combination of a "free mind and a free market" can't cure. Where in some publications this kind of ideological inflexibilty would be stifling, the editors and writers at *Reason* continue to devise creative positions, rather than cookie-cutter polemics. We attribute much of this success to Poole, the original guiding light of the magazine who took it from a nearly unillustrated polemical magazine to an attractive monthly addressing world issues, and to his young editor, Virginia Postrel. Barely past the dark side of 30, Postrel is surely at the beginnings of an illustrious career, her monthly columns clever and often offering intriguing perspectives that we don't see elsewhere. In "Fuelishness," 5-91, Postrel provides a strenuous argument against a national energy policy, which we need no more than a "shampoo policy or a socket-wrench policy." And she smartly applies the libertarian perspective to the Clarence Thomas-Anita Hill harassment hearings, postulating on the dangers of the loss of free speech and of imposing one's view on another person in "Poetic Injustice," 12-91, seeing how the feminists have shot themselves in the foot: "Feminists like to claim that 'sexual harassment is not about sex — it's about power.' The truth is a bit more complicated. First, sexual harassment *is* very clearly about sex. Lots of bosses harass their employees in non-sexual ways. . .And if sexual harassment is about power, the power works both ways. . .The furor over sexual harassment teaches men that women are simultaneously extremely fragile and extremely dangerous. Any little thing can set us off. And once we're offended, we can ruin your life. The wise man will, therefore, never be alone with a female colleague, least of all behind a closed door. That means no manager-to-manager discussions of personnel or budgets, no confidences, and no confidence. It means the workplace becomes once again a boys' club, where the real work is done by men and women are there just for decoration."

Reason also actively attempts to spur debate to spice up its pages. Postrel hosted a foreign policy symposium, held in Washington in December 1990, with *Reason* publishing the transcript in "In for the Cold War," 3-91. The first in a series of discussions, this is notable for Postrel's ability to hold her own against such heavyweights as Ted Galen Carpenter, director of foreign policy studies at Cato, Benjamin Frankel, editor of *Security Studies,* columnist Charles Krauthammer, Joshua Muravchik, a resident scholar at AEI and author of *Exporting Democracy,* and Daniel Pipes, director of the Foreign Policy Research Institute and author of five books on the Middle East. This thoughtful discussion is useful for insight into at least the minds of these gentlemen. But, more importantly, the selection closes with the notation: "In our June issue, REASON will run a special Letters section on post-Cold War foreign policy. We invite letters to the editor that extend the discussion, propose alternatives, or take issue with viewpoints expressed in this roundtable." In June, the letters run over five pages, from such readers as Tom Bethell, John M. Hood of the John Locke Foundation, and Juliana Geran Pilon of the National Forum Foundation in Washington. We would have liked to have seen some kind of response to the response, however; it would be most interesting to follow an active debate in *Reason* over the future role of the U.S. at home and abroad.

The features in *Reason* are generally well conceived and well executed, with the monthly format permitting authors to focus on broader themes that are occasionally interconnected. For example, the June issue is devoted to television. We get wide ranging selections of the state of television, from former *Washington Times* writer Rick Marin's amusing, though scattershot, examination of " 'TeeVee Intellectuals,' eggheads writing about television the way they once did about Melville," in "PopCultCrit," to Thomas Donlan's "The Sharper Image," an excerpting of the *Barron's* writer's new book on HDTV and technology, *Supertech.* John Hood's "Flick and Choose," is probably the best of the grouping, providing further intriguing perspectives on the Gulf War and television coverage, seeing this as the first "remote-control war." Hood makes the case well for an intelligent news consumer choosing the best war coverage from among the plethora of sources available between the networks and cable. The remaining three articles deal effectively with micro-television issues. In "Pain and Cable," Thomas W. Hazlett retells the story of Carl and Clinton Galloway, who went to the Los Angeles City Council with an idea about building a cable system in South L.A., had their idea stolen and then were shaken down, but we need to already be familiar with the case to get full appreciation here. Charles Oliver sees stormy weather ahead for PBS in "Beyond Big Bird," putting forth the idea that they must further diversify because so much of their current programming is covered now by cable stations like A&E and Discovery. And we get a bird's-eye view from ABC consumer affairs reporter John Stossel in "Who's the Boss," 6-91, wondering why he isn't censored more often, given the fact that the networks frequently depend on his targets for advertising revenue. But there's little of a forward nature here; while this gives us a clear picture of what's happening today, we don't discover what's in store for the future.

Similarly, the July issue is devoted to the Soviet Union. Unfortunately, we have the same complaint. While the examinations of current trends and players has distinct value, there's no postulating about the future, much less which courses of action might be best for the Soviets to undertake in order to have a future as a nation. Paul Craig Roberts offers the assessment that "thus, the Soviet Union is being privatized as a result, in large part, of governmental paralysis. Our own interventionists will find the result distasteful, but it is not an outcome that should surprise or distress libertarians," in "Privileged Privatization," in which Roberts describes what is, in effect, a Soviet fire sale in which the communists will get the pick of the litter. In a nomination by *Reason*'s editors for our 10 Best section, Cathy Young questions the ability of the Soviets to become capitalists after generations of communist rule and centuries of Czarist tyranny, "Searching the Soviet Soul," but the key insight here is her linking of the mental logjam to confidence in the government: "Nor can they ever be certain they'll get to keep the fruit of their labors." Phaedra Walker provides an interesting snapshot of "An Island of Capitalism?" where we learn of Valentin Fyodorov's efforts to improve the standard of living on the island of Sakhalin by implementing many of the free-market initiatives floating around the U.S.S.R., using Western businesses and systems as a model. Adam Garfinkle of the Foreign Policy Research Institute gives advice on "Coping With Collapse," outlining the desperation of the Soviet situation and the lack of a U.S. response. He does, though, note the outside chance of a coup attempt: "A second possibility, probably the least likely, is that the Soviet Union will in time — maybe after a failed attempt at Communist restoration — develop an attenuated authoritarian order, if not a liberal democracy, and a more or less market economy." The Heritage Foundation's Leon Aron provides an eye-crossing examination of "Yeltsin's Chess Game," his divisions of the regimes confusing: "Had it not been for Yeltsin, Gorbachev-2 [the 'reactionary Communist regime'] would have most likely have opted for a salami technology of repression — cutting democracy slice by slice, quietly arresting, firing, closing down newspapers, and canceling television programs." Huh? To round this out, William D. Eggers, also from the Heritage Foundation, adequately outlines the players with mini-biographies in "The New Opposition." These skimpy profiles, though, don't satisfy on this important facet of the development of a new Soviet Union. Still, this ambitious undertaking shows a new seriousness on the part of *Reason* magazine to become a key player in the policy arena.

The vast majority of issues, though, are comprised of unrelated topics, as with most policy journals. There's rarely a feeling of discontinuity to *Reason,* though, as all the articles are bound together with the common thread of libertarianism. All turn on an axis of "Free Minds & Free Markets." In "Closing the Net," cover 1-91, Greg Costikyan relates how new laws are closing in on the vast network of Bulletin Board Services and computer hackers; while Costikyan makes good points here about the nature of these seizures, he's unconvincing when he argues that those under suspicion of computer crime should retain their computers. Typically libertarian, Walter Olson's "No Secrets," cover 2-91, on the law's invasion of one's privacy, is too thickly penned on depositions and questionnaires. Jacob Sullum takes a tour of ALCOR's labs, which specialize in freezing the terminally or chronically ill in the hopes of reviving them when a treatment for their ailment is found, in "Cold Comfort," cover 4-91. Sullum and *Reason* see the struggling cryonics movement as a fight for the individual's right to dispose of one's remains in whatever way one desires.

It's apparent that *Reason* perceives part of its role as safeguarding against government interference in day-to-day living. Jacob Sullum argues strongly against a jail term for Michael Milken in "Milking Milken," 2-91, arguing government overkill: "Milken acted wrongly in breaking the rules of the exchange. Whether or not the federal regulations are valid exercises of government power, Milken had agreed to abide by them. Violating reporting requirements was therefore a breach of contract. Such breaches, however, are properly handled as civil matters. Milken had already been banned from trading, and he had agreed to pay $600 million in fines and restitution. Why send him to jail?" Randy Fitzgerald presents the Kafkaesque story of Alex and Kay Council, in "Taxes and Death," 3-91, whose battles with an IRS mistake and harassment drove Alex to suicide in order to provide for his wife. Rick Henderson makes his case that the government guidelines for defining a wetland are too loose in "The Swamp Thing," 4-91, but this is thick in terminology such as "hydrology," making this tough to slog through. He's more readable in "Is California 40 Percent Wetlands?" 4-3, a followup on the op-ed pages of *The New York Times*. And using broader brushstrokes, Steven Hayward is extremely perceptive in "The Children of Abraham," 5-91, a 10 Best nomination that is less about the ideological heirs to Lincoln, than the meaning of the Civil War as a turning point, and how the direction of the country has been removed from the founding fathers intentions: "James Madison, in the famous *Federalist 10,* wrote that the first duty of a government founded on equal rights and individual liberty is to safeguard the *unequal results* such a regime will inevitably produce. Humans are not equal in natural attributes such as strength and intelligence, but they are equal in the decisive political respect that they be *governed* without their consent and that their rights are inviolable by government, no matter how large the majority that wishes to violate their rights."

And, or course, *Reason* does not hesitate to address politics. John Hood provides a startlingly good appraisal of the political savvy of Doug Wilder, "Wilder & Wilder," 3-91, concluding his many policy faces — conservative, moderate, liberal — make him "a winning combination." "Capitalist Tool," 5-91, is a great interview with Malcolm S. Forbes, Jr., by Virginia Postrel & Charles Oliver, especially keen on Forbes's idea of how we could have sunk Iraq without firing a shot — send in the IMF. In "Giving 'Til It Hurts," 10-91, Barry Chamish traces the course of money privately donated to Israel to its destination, eye-opening on the waste. Daniel Mitchells skewers Dick Darman in "Still a Raw Deal," 10-91: "Because of the threat of future tax increases, a favorable reinterpreation of the 1990 agreement will have catastrophic consequences. Fortunately, for every clever quote Darman can provide in defense of the agreement, there are dozens of facts demonstrating last year's deal continues to be a monumental mistake. By every criterion important to economic growth and budgetary responsibility, Darman's budget moved fiscal policy in the wrong direction." And, in a 10 Best nomination from *Reason*'s editors, Loren E. Lomasky effectively critiques Bush's response to the Soviet coup attempt, "Coups and Constitutions," 11-91: "Some coups threaten liberty and others — such as the one that toppled Romania's Ceausescu — advance it. Let us hope that we have a president cognizant of that difference, and let us hope further that he someday comes to speak as forthrightly in defense of liberty as he does of an arid constitutionalism."

Reason is quickly becoming a major force in the area of political journals with such efforts cited here. Only *National Review, The New Republic* and *The Nation* have higher circulations. Given the venerable history of these three publications, *Reason*'s ascent is that much more impressive. Of course, *Reason* still has a long, long way to go before reaching the prominence in circulation of these magazines, but it is apparent that the ideas in *Reason* continue to gain notice and respect. Not too bad for a 23-year-old monthly from Lotusland.

Editor:	Virginia I. Postrel
Address:	3415 S. Sepulveda Blvd., Suite 400 Los Angeles, CA 90034 (310) 391-2245
Circulation:	1990 — 40,000 1991 — 40,000

The Spectator

Though considered by some to be the in-house organ of the British political class, we continue to find *The Spectator* a satisfying source on international developments and English society. Editor Dominic Lawson draws on a wide range of staffers and contributors to present a coherent world view from the perspective of unreconstructed conservatives in the classical sense. One gets the feeling *Spectator* contributors, whether they consider themselves unreconstructed Thatcherites or disciples of Neil Kinnock, all trace the decline of Western civilization to the day Cornwallis surrendered at Yorktown. Like all well-written, well-edited publications, the

Spectator has much to offer those who like to be informed while savoring the power of the printed word, with the added fillip of intellectual snob appeal which comes attached to British publications these days. It should be noted that the weekly is an acquired taste, its blend of journalistic brashness and literary irreverence perhaps oft-putting to readers raised on a steady diet of U.S. publications, at least those that aim at the lowest common denominator.

In 1990 the *Spectator* made headlines with Lawson's interview with then-U.K. Sec. of State for Industry Nicholas Ridley, whose crank-up-the-RAF-and-fight-the-Huns-in-the-air-and-on-the-sea approach toward European unity first drove him and subsequently his boss, British Prime Minister Margaret Thatcher, out of office. The *Spectator* produced no such bombshells this year, perhaps because the luckless Ridley has now become a verb in British political circles, as in "The *Spec*' won't Ridley me," or perhaps because Ridley-styled outbursts are now out of fashion in the John Major era. Tellingly, the *Spectator,* which runs a regular cartoon series called "The Suits," which pokes corrosive fun at cookie-cutter corporate executives and their ilk, now features "The Suit," starring PM Major. In a typical "Suit," a group of Major look-alikes, cluster around a sign reading "John Major Appreciation Society," observing that they don't know "if he's shown up yet."

The *Spectator*'s views toward his predecessor shine through in "Margaret Thatcher: The Silent Years," 2-16, by political editor Noel Malcolm, who offers unqualified praise for Thatcher and her policies, "To have been forced out of the premiership at a time when her energy was unflagging, her vision undimmed and her oratory unsurpassed. . ." while portraying Thatcher as struggling valiantly with undeserved exile to the political equivalent of Elba. Malcolm was later named a joint winner of this year's T.E. Utley Memorial Prize for political writers under the age of 35 (he shared the prize with Andrew Gimson, a former deputy editor of *The* Spectator).

European unity, the issue at the heart of the Ridley interview, continued to be a major concern of the *Spectator* in 1991, the magazine warning in "A Timely Insult," 10-26, that: "We cannot blame [European Commissioners] for exercising rights which we ourselves have given them. What we can do, and must do before Maastricht, is think twice about giving them any more." In "The English Sunday," 12-7, the *Spectator* contends that "the Englishman's liberties are at stake," over recent German-backed efforts to end Sunday trading. The *Spectator* alertly drew on the example of the EEC's handling of the Yugoslavian crisis to bolster its arguments about the inability of the EEC to provide for the security concerns of Western Europe, in "Clear as Mud," 8-10, the *Spectator* contending that "The process of common foreign policy-making tends to induce mutual paralysis," while in "Bleeding to Death," 11-23, the *Spectator* condemns the EEC's policy of "exemplary even-handedness" toward Serbia and the independent-minded Slovenia and Croatia. "No position, surely, could be more even-handed than placing one's hands under one's bottom and sitting on them." Following the failed Soviet coup attempt the *Spectator,* in "Cry Freedom," 8-24, states that "The evidence suggests that an attempt to forge a common foreign policy would probably be so lacking in essential decency as to endanger the peoples of the Soviet Union and the West." And in "Options for Trouble," 11-16, the *Spectator* cites the Persian Gulf crisis as evidence that Francois Mitterrand's idea of leaving Europe's defense in the hands of Europeans as being "moonshine."

At the heart of the *Spectator*'s animus toward European unity seems to be the fact that unity has a human face, and it is the face of a Frenchman, Jacques Delors. In "The French Empire of Europe," 6-8, Boris Johnson, EEC correspondent for the *Daily Telegraph,* writes darkly that Delors is at the head of a "pink tide" of forty-something French Socialists, many educated at the Ecole Nationale d'Administration, intent on using European economic unity as a Trojan horse in which to restore French monetary sovereignty. It "The Making of a President," 12-7, Johnson documents how Delors, "homo foederalis," has successfully turned the unelected post of EEC commissioner into the equivalency of a head of state, partly through a personal mixture of "brilliance and lust for power," partly through the institutional desire for the smaller EEC states to erode the powers of the larger states. In the only slightly tongue-in-cheek "A Maastricht

Phrasebook," 11-23, under the heading "Delors, Jacques," Charles Moore describes the office of "The President of Europe," as one that "does not officially exist," but whose holder "has more power than the Holy Roman Emperor. He is French, by the way."

Moore also identifies the European Commission as the "body which runs the EEC," noting that "Normally, a commission is a body which carries out the wishes of others. This one has dispensed with that encumbrance: it devises the laws itself," and the "Franco-German axis," as "A slang phrase, meaning the way Europe is run." The other member of this "axis," Germany, is discussed in John Laughland's "The Thousand-Year Reich," 6-22. Laughland, a Lecturer in Politics at the Sorbonne, claims to be making no moral judgments as he outlines how contemporary German designs for European unity are a continuation of policies begun by the Nazis. "It is impossible to say whether there is a secret agenda behind the plans of Economic and Monetary Union, but it is strange that the Bundestag has determined that the 'independent' European Central Bank should be in Frankfurt."

The *Spectator* continues to be nothing if not realistic toward Mikhail Gorbachev and the Soviet Union, generally finding little use for either. In "No Excuses," 1-19, the *Spectator* condemns both the crackdown in Vilnius and the efforts of Western governments to maintain good relations with "reformist" communist leaders such as Gorbachev, no matter what their actions. "There is an unfortunate pattern here: the same arguments are being used to exonerate Mr Gorbachev as were harnessed in the defence of Deng Xiaoping in China." The *Spectator* persistently argues that economic reform will only come about through self-determination and democracy, not massive aid programs to a government which obstructs both, in "The Price of Gorbachev," 6-1, the *Spectator* contending that "Every time [Gorbachev] presents himself, in increasingly Messianic tones, as the only solution, we need to pinch ourselves to remember that he is just part of the problem," while in "Money They Don't Need," 8-31, the *Spectator* warns that "Splendid as the events of the last week have been, this is no time for sentimental or profligate generosity." Commenting on the failed coup attempt in "Cry Freedom," 8-24, the *Spectator* states that now "The West must give its backing to Mr Yeltsin unequivocally."

Steve Handelman, Moscow bureau chief for the *Toronto Star,* continues to anchor the *Spectator*'s Soviet coverage, and we continue to be impressed by his work. He produces an early and engaging portrait of Kazakhstan's president Nursultan Nazarbayev in "The Third Man," 4-27, whom Handelman alertly pegs as being the peacemaker between Gorbachev and Yeltsin before hitting the mark on the future of the Soviet state: "[Nazarbayev] raised shivers in Moscow a few months ago when he floated the idea of an alliance between Kazakhstan, Russia, Ukraine and Byelorussia." In "Some Chicken, Some Kiev," 8-3, he expertly sets the stage for that key republic's eventual secession, noting that "If Ukraine is not yet independent in fact, it is already independent in spirit." His cover story on the potential role of the Red Army and the weapons at its disposal as both the Cold War and the Soviet Union come to an end, "Oh What a Lovely Thaw!" 11-9, is thorough on all aspects of the country's "16th republic." BBC foreign editor and *Spectator* contributor John Simpson penned two impressionistic reports on the failed coup attempt, "Defending the Faith," 8-24, and "Hammering Away at the Old Order," 8-31.

Not all the *Spectator*'s Soviet coverage was up to the standards of Handelman and Simpson. In "No Aid at All," 9-7, Peter Bauer and Anthony Daniels provide a pointed diatribe on the folly of subsidizing the Soviet Union, taken in context of helping any country financially, claiming that subsidies, "like certain drugs, . . . are habit forming." A valid argument, but too one sided in its condemnation of help. Foreign editor Ian Buruma stumbles through a report on Soviet Jews emigrating to Israel in "Another Exodus," 1-5, never fully examining the consequences or drawing any conclusions from his interviews. Mark Urban fails to develop a firm grasp on the future of the KGB in "Business as Usual for the KGB. . ." 9-28, arguing that the Bear's spy service will remain entirely as is.

The *Spectator* supported the war to drive Iraqi forces out of Kuwait. In "Labouring in Vain," 1-12, the editors condemn Labour Party waffling over the use of force to drive Saddam out of Kuwait, writing that the British opposition party is being "driven by confusion and spinelessness" and that "it seems [party leader Neil] Kinnock may be steering his party to the precipice of appeasement. . ." In "Finishing the Job," 3-2, the *Spectator* states that "It is clear that Saddam ought to be thoroughly discredited," but cautions that his actual overthrow should be left to the Iraqi people themselves.

To be sure, not all its coverage took on a sun-over-the-yardarm-fire-the-cannons-at-will approach to the conflict. The magazine's war coverage was highlighted by John Simpson's refreshingly candid on-the-spot reporting from Baghdad, which is discussed in full in the *MediaGuide*'s Foreign Correspondent section. Simpson's dispatches were one example where the *Spectator*'s style of personalizing international events actually paid off. In "No Need to Retaliate," 2-16, James Buchan accurately pins down why Israel won't retaliate against Iraq despite the Scud launchings, and just as accurately labels Saddam a "schmuck!" *Daily Telegraph* Defence Editor John Keegan, in "The Instrument of Catastrophe," 1-12, is right on the money on how the Iraqi military would be wiped out, getting it down to the army surrendering in droves. Australian journalist Murray Sayle's cover story on the ambivalent feelings raised by the Gulf War in Japan, "Unconditional Surrender II," 2-9, is as fine a treatment of this subject as we saw anywhere.

Less useful was Ian Buruma's cover story on the role of religion in the Gulf War, "What Are We Fighting For?" 2-2, the points he raises tangential to the events in the Middle East. In "America Goes for Broke," 2-23, Nicholas von Hoffman spends the entire article lambasting the U.S. for its over-extension in areas of war and monetary policy, evoking nostalgia for the Hamiltonian Bank of the United States. Theodore Dalrymple produces a surprisingly lackluster report on support for Saddam in India in "Crazy for Saddam," 2-23. And we were disappointed by Edward Mortimer's examination of resurgent Islamic fundamentalism, "After Saddam, What Next?" 1-26, the *Financial Times* columnist raising good points but not leaving himself enough room to explore them.

The *Spectator*'s post-war Middle East coverage was distinguished by its reports on the ill-fated Kurdish uprising, the Palestinians, and Western hostages being held in the region. In "Murder By Helicopter in Kurdistan," 4-13, Charles Glass does not suppress his anguish and outrage at the world's abandonment of the Kurdish people, and his eyewitness accounts are a damning indictment of amoral international power politics. John Simpson produced eloquent criticisms of the Western world's cynical abandonment of the Kurds in such reports as "The Writing on the Wall," 4-27, "Settling Sadda," 6-15, and "Surviving in the Ruins," 8-10. *Spectator* reader Roger Cooper, in "The Inside Story," 4-13, provides a firsthand account of how he was able to survive five years behind bars after being pulled off a Teheran street and accused of being a spy. It seems the secret to survival in such circumstances is to keep the mind occupied as much as possible, Cooper surviving by working out mathematical equations in his head. In "Hopeless In Gaza," 5-4, Ian Buruma produces his best effort of the year, an intelligent assessment of the situation on the Gaza strip, and how nothing is really being accomplished by any of the forces involved.

Other foreign coverage in the *Spectator* in 1991 focused on Europe and the United States, the reports often hit-and-miss efforts, usually written in caustic tones. In "The Secret Police State," 7-27, Caroline Sinclair provides several examples of the strangeness of Swiss life. The article might have had more impact if we hadn't already read John le Carre's take on Switzerland, "The Unbearable Peace," in *Granta* No. 35. We received two superficial reports on the difficulties of German unity this year, "And Never the Twain Shall Meet?" 6-29, by Anne McElvoy, and "A Ghost in Wolf's Clothing," 9-28, by Mark Almond. "The Pontiff's Polish Problem," 6-8, Anne Applebaum's report on the decline of the Catholic Church's prestige in Poland, is too narrowly focused. Anti-clericalism was also a theme of "Here's to Whom Mrs. Robinson?" 1-5, Geoffrey Wheatcroft's terribly cynical view of modern Ireland: "It is moving away from the clericalism which made it, by repute, the last priest-ridden theocracy in Europe."

The U.S. took it on the chin in such articles as "The Idiot Village," 9-28, Michael Lewis's facile look at the emptiness of Aspen, Colorado. *Daily Telegraph* Washington correspondent Stephen Robinson, in "Very Like a Quayle," 5-11, seems more sure of Quayle's abilities than many U.S. commentators, but argues that the press makes or breaks Vice Presidents anyway. Robinson's cover story proclaiming that President Bush is overrated as an international leader, "Partial Vision, Selective Morality," 10-5, is late, echoing what we had already been hearing and reading elsewhere for several months.

Of course, the *Spectator* continues to be a singular source for English society and culture, once again covering such concerns of the British upper class as agriculture, wayward British youth, and the Catholic Church. In the cover story "Animal Rights and Wrongs," 6-29, Andrew Kenny takes a roundabout way to tell us he is against animal rights and animal rights activists. Ross Clark provides a slightly tongue-in-cheek look at bovine artificial insemination in "Shotgun Marriages," 9-28. We receive an in-depth look at the growing problem of disposing of dead animal livestock in "Unquiet Graves," 9-7, by Simon Courtauld. Theodore Dalrymple, in "Nasty, British and Short," 9-28, zeroes in on the malaise afflicting the youth of England: "They are unemployed and often profoundly unemployable: they are intolerant of any external restraint on their behavior, and cannot fix their minds upon anything for more than a few moments. What job could one give them?"

Dominic Crossley-Holland, in "Getting Past the Devil's Advocate," 2-2, takes a bemused look at the record number of saints and blesseds named by Pope John Paul II: "It helps to be in holy orders, or to live in a Latin country, or to die young." William Cash adopts a conversational tone, more appropriate to a pub talk than a moral discussion, on the Catholic Church's rulings on birth control in "Thermometers and What-Not," 9-7. Our readers thought that Damien Thompson's all-out attack on Opus Dei, "Beating a Path to Sainthood," 9-28, bordered on yellow journalism. Thompson hammers home the severity and the supposed strangeness of this sect by dissecting the life of its leader Josemaria Escriva de Balaguer, who is up for sainthood, without indicating why normal business people would want to be part of it.

Two *Spectator* cover stories that merit special mention include "Goofy Capitalists," 10-26, Michael Lewis's hilarious account of the IMF gathering in Bangkok, Lewis documenting why, just as war has become too important to be left to the generals, international finance has become too important to be left to the bankers. On a different plane, Amanda Craig, in "Poor Woman, Poor Potential Human," 1-5, provides a harrowing account of an abortion. Her straightforward reporting style, with no punches pulled, no editorializing, shows what a grim procedure abortion is, regardless of one's ethical, moral or political beliefs. "A dismembered arm half the size of a finger takes two of three attempts to pull out."

The regular contributors, such brand-name writers as John Mortimer, Auberon Waugh, and Taki Theodoracopulos, continue to soldier on, attempting to cope with a world they never made, often in as politically incorrect a manner as possible. Waugh, in "Time to Take Up a Position Against All Groups Everywhere," 9-28, takes offense to special interests groups representing gays and lesbians, who, in their efforts to suppress all opposition to their causes, smother intelligent discussion. "I do not think I am a homophobe, although I strongly believe that we should all look askance at any single-issue pressure group which does not represent our own special interest. It is one thing to resist the persecution of homosexuals, another to load them with privileges, one thing to give them a hearing, another to silence the opposition or suppress any information." The highlight of the year from Taki was "The Hard Cell," 2-9, an insightful, if rough, recounting of his time spent in prison on a cocaine possession charge. "Personally, the ugliness of prison is such that I didn't think of sex at all. Being surrounded by misfits does for the libido what Saddam Hussein has done for marine life down south."

The back of the book continues to feature fine state-of-the-art reviews and criticism, the standouts including book reviewers Anita Brookner and James Buchan, media columnist Paul Johnson, and pop music critic Marcus Berkman. As an additional service to its readers, on 7-27 the *Spectator* inaugurated a new feature, "Your Problems Solved," in which "Mary" responds to reader inquiries on common, everyday social dilemmas, such as the one posed by a reader: "How can one best humiliate someone at a drinks party?" "Mary" advises the reader to place a large plastic barrel of "something really addictive and messy," next to the person in question. "It will only be a matter of ten minutes or so before even the most strongminded person will begin to make a repulsive spectacle of himself."

Editor:	Dominic Lawson
Address:	56 Dougherty Street London WC1N 2LL England 011-01-405-1706
Circulation:	1990 — 39,100 1991 — 39,379

Time

Time is dead — or close to it. *Time,* that once grand vision of Henry Luce, is certainly no longer *Time* as we know it. After several years of internal debate over the eventual character of the newsweekly, Time Warner Inc. head Jason McManus and *Time* editor Henry Muller announced the birth of a new *Time,* the redesign to take place over the next year. This *Time* would shift coverage away from breaking news events to more essays and cultural coverage.

When we first began *MediaGuide* seven years ago, Henry Anatole Grunwald was at the helm. *Time*'s focus was news, churning out the pithy summaries of the week's events that made Luce's brainchild so popular. We noted our relish in guessing the annual "Man of the Year" selection, a favorite pastime, finishing up our review in *The 1986 MediaGuide* by noting "*Time* is still clearly the best of the newsweeklies, packaged to give the once-a-week reader enough of what's going on in the world to get through almost any cocktail party." The following year we celebrated *Time*'s perception of "its responsibility to its readers as a comprehensive presentation of the week's news, so much so that it felt it necessary to almost apologize for the 6-16 issue 'American Best.'. . .Where *Newsweek* is no longer taken seriously as a newsmagazine by the public policy elite, *Time* has regained some of the influence it had in its heyday," *The 1987 MediaGuide.* When Grunwald retired at year's end and the new team of McManus and Muller took the reins, we continued to praise *Time*'s utility in rounding up the week's events in *The 1988 MediaGuide,* and were excited about the infusion of "new blood" at the top, which we hoped would produce a deeper commitment to reporting.

The first year under McManus and Muller was a steady-as-she-goes diet of news and information, until plans for the new format were unveiled in the 10-17-88 issue. In *The 1989 MediaGuide* we heralded Muller's apparent reaffirmation of Luce's philosophy, writing that "In a world saturated with information — from radio, television, newspapers, specialized magazines — TIME's responsbility more than ever is to deliver understanding beyond the sound bites and headlines: incisive reporting, thoughtful analysis, distinguished writing, compelling photography." Adds the editor, "That's why we have introduced some new voices in TIME, along with a broader spectrum of points of view." We did not realize at that moment that this meant a complete repudiation of objectivity, with reporters and correspondents free to use the pages of *Time* to advance whatever causes, opinions, or political agenda they please. Ever since, *Time* has been a terminal case.

As McManus and Miller have now declared officially, *Time* will no longer be a *news*weekly. This is really not much of a surprise; the magazine has long been moving away from its niche as a serious purveyor of news. No *news* magazine could have offered such covers: this year, *Time* gave us the real Nancy Reagan in "Is She That Bad?" 4-22, telling us "what's true — and what's not" in the Kitty Kelley book; a travelogue of "Orlando," 5-27, home of Disney and MGM; a profoundly vapid essay on the nature of "Evil," by Lance Morrow 6-10; the implications for relations between the sexes in a movie, "Thelma and Louise," 6-24; a pointless collection of opinion on personal responsibility in "Busybodies and Crybabies," 8-12, a topic treated much more intelligently in both *New York* and *The Economist;* and a "Special Issue" valentine to "California: The Endangered Dream," 11-18, in which Henry Muller notes in the managing editor's column: "This special issue on California fulfills a long-standing ambition of mine: to explain this amazing state to a national and international audience that knows it better for its cliches than for its complexity." Oh.

Most distressing about this latest re-format is that the weekly is due to lose a substantial number of reporters and writers, dealing a mortal blow to the heart of the newsweekly. Bureaus will be closed, and the ones that will remain open are scheduled for cuts. The Washington bureau will take a 6-person cut in a 23-person office, more than a quarter of its staff. Already the magazine is losing talented people who have been offered severance packages. Former deputy Washington bureau chief Laurence I. Barrett has left, as has veteran congressional correspondent Hays Gorey and diplomatic correspondent Christopher Ogden — Barrett and Ogden continuing to write for *Time* temporarily under contract. But once news is removed completely from *Time,* we are hard pressed to define what remains.

We're also left wondering what niche a weekly cultural magazine would occupy, particularly given the talent now at the magazine. There is already a *People* (published by Time Warner, no less), and under a weekly deadline schedule it would be extremely difficult to produce rigorous cultural commentary in the same vein as the competition that now exists, at the monthly *Chronicles,* for example. We examined a back issue of *Time* specifically for its cultural coverage at random and we are not encouraged. The 5-13 "Dance" feature, "The Dawn of the Martins Era," by Martha Duffy, on the Peter Martins' restaging of the ballet, "The Sleeping Beauty," is a mish-mash and feels extremely edited. Robert Hughes stays well within politically correct boundaries in the "Art" section, in "How the West Was Spun," 5-13, a wishy-washy review of American Frontier paintings at the National Museum of American Art: "Religious and national myths are made, not born; their depiction in art involves much staging, construction and editing, under the eye of cultural agreement. Whatever the crucifixion of a Jew on a knoll 2,000 years ago looked like, it wasn't Tintoretto. And the American West of the 19th century was rarely what American artists set out to make it seem." But is art truth, and is it supposed to be? Hughes prefers to rip into the artists and the "foundation myth" they created, and we believed. Paul Gray doesn't review Milan Kundera's *Immortality* in the "Books" section, "A Plunge into Fancies," 5-13; he dances around the plot, instead submerging us into the psyches of characters we know nothing about. But the depths of silliness are reached in "A Happy Birthday for the Kids of Kane," 5-13, as Richard Corliss is so strident it's hard to imagine this article got a go from the editors. He's just plain overblown in putting four cult movies on a level with Orson Welles' "Citizen Kane," as "they come close to the spirit and intent of that eternally young masterpiece. They treat film technique as a living language; they taunt, dazzle, delight." Maybe so, but Corliss' pompous hyperventilations here convince us he ought to stay away from the technique and stick to film: "Poison," a trio of short stories dealing with repressed "sexual longing," celebrates the "pristine virtuosity of [director Jean] Hayes' craft"; "Paris Is Burning," the story of Harlem drag balls, is a "thrilling documentary"; "Water and Power," a 57-minute documentary is "gorgeous and zippy. . .an intoxicant without the hangover"; and "Begotten," is a "nightmare classic. . .filmed in speckled chiaroscuro so that each image is a seductive mystery, a Rorschach test for the adventurous eye." We can appreciate the creative camera angle and unusual perspective as much as the next cinema aficionado, but, although this *sounds* good, it doesn't *say* very much. No, the future doesn't look bright.

It wasn't all bad news for the newsweekly, however. There were several instances, some heralded on the cover, where good reporting won out over the "voice" mentality. The most consistent example was with the team of Jonathan Beaty and S. C. Gwynne and their work on BCCI; the duo offered two exceptional examples of reporting for a newsweekly. A 10 Best nomination from their editors, "The World's Sleaziest Bank," cover 7-29, was the first to have "pieced together a portrait of a clandestine division of the bank called the 'black network,' which functions as a global intelligence operation and a Mafia-like enforcement squad." The pair does a tremendous job of reconnaissance, incorporating for the first time evidence of terrorist connections and describing in detail typical operations of the "black network," the original purpose of which "was to pay bribes, intimidate authorities and quash investigations. But according to a former operative, sometime in the early 1980s, the black network began running its own drugs, weapons and currency deals." Allegations of a cover-up at the Justice Department are also outlined and discussed. They follow this particular aspect up with "Too Many Questions," 11-11, detailing the Edward Rogers-BCCI link to the Bush administration, adding more salient information to the now-burgeoning story.

Former *Forbes* writer Richard Behar provides an exhaustively informative expose of the cult of Scientology, "The Thriving Cult of Greed and Power," cover 5-6; this strong indictment of L. Ron Hubbard's "church" was also nominated for 10 Best consideration by *Time*'s editors. We're somewhat disturbed by the pit-bull feel of this, though, almost as though Behar went into the story knowing he'd be doing an expose, rather than a straight dispatch. Although less than sharp on the economics and annoyingly tuned into what Bush is thinking in places, the treatment of George Bush's split personality problems, "A Tale of Two Bushes," "Men of the Year" cover 1-7, by George J. Church, Dan Goodgame and Michael Duffy, effectively defines the lion-hearted international Bush and the disinterested, tentative, domestic Bush. Sylvester Monroe interviews author Shelby Steele on Clarence Thomas in the "Interview" section, "Nothing Is Ever Simply Black and White," 8-12, a superb defense of the Supreme Court nominee. Despite the PC value of Eugene Linden's "Lost Tribes, Lost Knowledge," 9-23, on how ancient customs can be decimated by contact with the outside world and by progress in remote areas such as Papua, New Guinea, we found it quite interesting and refreshing to find major changes in attitudes towards tribal customs. Philip Elmer-DeWitt offers an amazingly readable and informative review of new treatments in "Curing Infertility," cover 9-30. But much of the year was not wheat, but chaff.

Despite snappy graphics and snazzy themes, many covers did not pack the promised punch. After Bush's heart arrythmia, a quartet of stories outline why Dan Quayle should get the boot and who should replace him, "Five Who Could Be Vice President," 5-20, leaves no doubt how *Time* feels about the current Veep, *Time* missing the point that if the combo ain't broke, don't fix it. Interestingly, the recommendations of Dick Cheney, Nancy Kassenbaum, Colin Powell, Carroll Campbell and Pete Wilson come unbylined. A timely, sensitive exercise by Nancy Gibbs, "Date Rape," 6-3, a discussion of the issues involved, is undercut by the strange, insensitive photography: the cover subject, Katie Koestner, looks like a pouty vamp out of *Vogue* on the cover, then is pictured on the inside pages as a fresh-faced college student posed spread-eagled on the ground while she studies. Rather than a discussion of the ethics involved in the Marissa-Anissa Ayala case, in which parents had a child to provide transplantable bone marrow for a daughter with cancer, we get Lance Morrow's wild evaluations in "When One Body Can Save Another," 6-17: "The surgeons bent over the grail: a 14 month-old girl named Marissa Ayala. . .In 20 minutes they removed about a cup of the viscous red liquid — the stuff of resurrection . . .A brave surreal gamble. . .It called up brutal images — baby farming, cannibalizing for spare parts. Many saw in the story the near edge of a dangerous slippery slope at the bottom of which they glimpsed an abyss, and maybe the shadow of Dr. Mengele at work." Yuk. And that's just the first page. *Time*'s late, following *Newsweek*'s cover lead of six weeks or so earlier with "Misleading Labels," 7-15, a trio of articles in which Christine Gorman examines the labeling controversy, Anastasia Toufexis checks out the pyramid proposal and Dick Thompson offers a reasonbly enlightening profile of David Kessler, head of the FDA. The cover on Jodie Foster, "A Screen Gem Turns Director," by Richard Corliss 10-14, recycles a similar cover treatment by *The New York Times Magazine,* timed to coincide with the release of "Little Man Tate," Foster's first effort at directing. Claudia Wallis doesn't seem serious in exploring the different kinds of alternative medicines, in which she even lumps chiropractic care with crystal healing, "Why New Age Medicine Is Catching On," cover 11-14, the overall tone not skeptical, but snide, portraying some of these folks as outright charlatans, "Or perhaps you'll find yourself in a herbalist's lair. . ." and so on.

The Washington bureau trudges onward, despite the cuts in staff. Margaret Carlson, now deputy bureau chief, is probably the best reporter in the bureau, when she's not expounding in her dispatches. Senior writer Walter Shapiro offered a fine dissertation on Bush's "America 2000" plan and Lamar Alexander's plans for the Department of Education in "Tough Choice," cover 9-16; he only gets editorial in the end, calling for a state to run a real free choice school system and let the chips fall where they may. The most howling example of editorialism from the bureau came during the Thomas-Hill sexual harassment hearings. Nancy Gibbs, Jill Smolowe, Richard Lacayo, Michael Kramer, Margaret Carlson and Jack E. White each give their opinion on "Sex, Lies & Politics," cover 10-21, in seven articles attempting to hash through the Hill-Thomas mess. We find the definitive line coming in "A Question of Character" by Richard Lacayo, where *Time*'s stand is revealed in his inherent assumption that Thomas is at fault: "The bedeviling paradox that emerged last week was this: How could Thomas have been one man to the world and another to Hill?" Well, uh?

Time's coverage of the Persian Gulf War was adequate, done mostly by veteran correspondent George J. Church in fine Lucian tradition, credible roundups and overviews of the action. Lisa Beyer made some acceptable contributions as well. Bruce Nelan and Strobe Talbott handled the military and strategic points reasonably well from Washington. The magazine did have a few surprises in store, however. We get an exclusive "The Inside Story of Moscow's Quest for a Deal," 3-4, by Yevgeni Primakov, Gorbachev's personal advisor who took part in the Aziz meetings, and finishes up with "My Final Visit with Saddam Hussein," 3-11, about an insider an account as we get as to the final Soviet peace initiative, although he winds up doing some Monday-morning quarterbacking: "In Gorbachev's view the differences between the formula to which Iraq had agreed and the proposals from a number of other countries were not so great that they could not be worked out in the Security Council in one or two days. Certainly these differences were not so substantial that they justified a further escalation of the war. The Soviet U.N. representative was instructed to request an emergency session of the Security Council. However, as dawn broke on Feb. 24, the ground offensive of the multinational coalition began." *Time* followed *Newsweek*'s lead on follow-the-action Special Pullout maps. Although *Time* had been using fancy inside-the-magazine graphics, after *Newsweek*'s 2-4 map of war zones and 2-18 poster with the weaponry used and the generals in charge, *Time* started doing the posters, 2-25, combining *Newsweek*'s two with a special pullout battle map and key weapons. But *Time*'s "War of Images," 2-25, seemed to politicize the immense suffering of the Iraqi people, the pictorial compendium surely inflaming anti-war sentiment with its closeup of a little boy's ghastly wounds to his legs, crudely sutured, for example. The disclaimer that *Time* is only trying to "put the human impact of the war into focus" does not help to balance this, as it's the sometimes gory photographs we take with us, despite the qualifiers: "But they [the photos] cannot tell the whole story. They do not show Saddam's destruction of Kuwait, where no photographers can go. And they do not show the large areas of Baghdad. . .that have remained untouched throughout the carefully targeted air campaign." In this case, it is apparent that the weekly substituted photos for the comprehensive articles that were badly needed for objectivity's sake. *Time* later put together a Desert Storm computer disc that's advertised in the 4-22 "From the Publisher" column: "The disc can be 'played,' with the help of an attachment costing $400 to $900 dollars, on most personal computers."

The other major foreign story this year was, of course, events in the Soviet Union. In true newsweekly fashion, much of the time the magazine did not rely directly on their Moscow correspondent, John Kohan, but instead used writers from New York to make an assessment based often on Kohan's reporting. The prolific George Church was usually the roving correspondent of choice, as with "Anatomy of a Coup," 9-2, and "Into the Void," 9-9. Kohan struts his stuff in "A Chastened Character in Search of a Role," 9-9, an insightful examination of Gorbachev, post-coup, predicting Gorbachev will remain in power, and that it's simply the luster that's been removed. Kohan notes succinctly the division between Gorbachev and Yeltsin, saying the Russian president is "the stuff of grand legends, not sound policies," particularly during the coup, preferring instead Gorbachev's "cautious" leadership style. But he thinks that the alliance helps to balance the country. Michael Meyer perceives the importance of "Kaliningrad: The Old Guard Hangs On," 9-16, the home of the Baltic fleet and "several tank divisions and a massive air-defense force. Nearly half a million troops and their families are based in Kaliningrad, along with a sizeable nuclear arsenal," where the communists retain a measure of power. Meyer notes also that "social unrest is growing, and not all anger is directed at the communists," but at the transferral of Soviet troops from Germany and Eastern Europe to the region and at substandard living conditions.

Due to the many changes at *Time,* the "Business" section no longer appears with weekly regularity. John Greenwald, when he appears, provides barely adequate anecdotal, if economically unsophisticated, coverage. He's a two-handed reporter talking two-handed economics in "A Slump That Won't Go Away," 10-14, blaming the current recession on the spending binge of the '80s and the deficit, which here, was caused by the spending binge of the '80s. He then encourages us to buy more to solve the problem of the current recession, which was caused by too much deficit spending to start with: "fickle buying habits have left executives scratching their heads. 'There is this very erratic pattern,' notes Harold Poling, chairman of Ford, whose restyled Ford Taurus and Mercury Sable models have been slow to roll off new-car lots. 'Dealers will have a positive week, then one when nothing happens. It looks like a long, drawn-out and weak time ahead.' " An earlier article by Janice Castro, "The Buyers Are Back," cover 3-18, is overly optimistic on the upswing in the real estate market; several good weeks do not an upswing make. And, as with most, she attributes it to the "Desert Storm surge" and lower interest rates, never looking for the root causes. *Time*'s writers are better when dealing with straight business news stories. In "Small Wonders," 2-11, Richard Behar uses Jeff Katzenberg's memo at Disney on cost-cutting as a prism through which to look at the rest of the studios, some of which are cutting costs, some of which are not, including a goodly smattering of costs and quotes. Andrew Tobias is repellent in his noxious "Money Angles" column, a near-parody of economic commentary. In "Amount Due? Zero, Thanks!" 6-17, he advises us to pay bills in advance to save a few cents — on stamps.

The essays vary in quality from author to author, from sub-par to sterling. Hugh Sidey continues to offer down-home Washington wisdom, his "The Presidency" column made all the more valuable by his thirty-odd years of presidential coverage. The "America Abroad" columnist, Strobe Talbott spent much of the year recycling conventional insights, overtaken, apparently, by the speed of change in the world. We had high expectations for Michael Kramer and "The Political Interest," which he has not yet met. In "Nobody Does Nothing Better Than Shamir," 9-30, Kramer bases most of this on a conversation he had several years ago with Yitzhak Shamir, in which Shamir told him he does not believe in trading land for peace. But Kramer doesn't update this directly from Shamir, telling us that other people *know* that he still thinks this, despite "his willingness to attend the peace conference." And then there is the perfectly awful Lance Morrow, who seems destined for superstardom in the New Time Order, he's so frequently awarded cover assignments such as the aforementioned "Evil," 6-10, and "When One Body Can Save Another," 6-17. We dread what comes under his byline. His "Nation" essay as lead news item, "The Trouble With Teddy," 4-29, is the sanctification of Ted Kennedy, after the Palm Beach scandal broke. On his drinking: "Those who watch Kennedy at work on Capitol Hill observe a stamina, energy, attention to detail and intellectual alertness that contradict the image of Kennedy as a feckless drinker. An alcoholic, especially at the age of 59 after years of habitual drinking, often finds it difficult to keep up with his work, or to keep a job at all." On his "extremely rich, varied, complex" personal life: "On a day when the weather is mild, he sometimes takes his 100-year-old mother Rose for an outing in her wheelchair along the streets of Hyannis Port." And finally on his love life: his dates "range in age from the mid-30s to 42 to a bit over 50. All are women of brains and professional stature, not bimbos." Morrow never offers a shred of supporting data for any of his assertions.

We have long decried the change in tone in the newsweekly that's taken place over the last few years, as the reporters and editors were freed to include "voice" in their dispatches, no matter the subject. While "voice" adds flavor to commentary, it is an inadequate substitute for reporting. Despite quite a number of impressive projects this year, the magazine generally remains a moribund cacophony of screeching that adds little of news value to the mix. Now the new leadership team of Jason McManus and Henry Muller are planning to remove the *news* content from the magazine in favor of more culture and opinion, putting their stableful of promising reporters to pasture. Goodbye, *Time.* It was nice to know you.

Editor-in-Chief:	Jason McManus
Editor:	Henry Muller
Address:	Time Warner, Inc.
	Time-Life Building
	Rockefeller Center
	New York, NY 10020-1393
	(212) 586-1212
Circulation:	1990 — 4,295,000
	1991 — 4,249,000

U.S.News & World Report

Real estate tycoon Mortimer B. Zuckerman's efforts at *U.S.News & World Report* seem to be finally paying off, the newsweekly now consistently delivering substantive coverage of major developments both at home and abroad, with a corresponding rise in newsstand sales that have enabled the magazine to weather the depression afflicting the news industry. Indeed, for the first time in *USNWR*'s history, the magazine has overtaken *Newsweek* in ad pages, and will finish in second place among the big three of newsweeklies.

Zuckerman attributes the magazine's success to his decision to increase "service journalism," or, as he told a *New York Times* reporter, "stories that affect the everyday lives of our readers." While we were a bit concerned over the direction this seemed to be leading toward — *USNWR* featuring cover stories ranking the "Best" of everything from hospitals to U.S. politics, or featuring subjects more suitable for *National Geographic* —the magazine's coverage of major news stories remains as strong as ever, and it is time to give credit where credit is due. Although the beakers seemed at times about ready to blow up in his face after six years of laboratory work, Zuckerman has apparently concocted a new formula to enable a newsweekly to justify its existence in the TV age.

To be sure, *USNWR* continues to deliver the goods on hard news, as demonstrated during the Gulf War. The crisis predominated in the pages of *USNWR* during the first quarter of the year, and was the only subject to make the cover from early January through the end of March. The coverage was not comprehensive, in that it did not record every missile fired and every diplomatic initiative that went nowhere; the days when the newsweeklies could compete with TV in that regard are over, the victory having been as decisive as the liberation of Kuwait. But *USNWR,* through extensive pieces examining strategy, tactics, and breaking events, along with on-the-spot reporting from the Middle East and Washington, expanded our understanding of the events playing out on our TV screens.

One highlight of *USNWR*'s war coverage was commentary by Gen. Michael Dugan, the former Air Force Chief of Staff who was dismissed in the autumn of 1990 for telling two reporters the allied plans for an all-out air campaign against Iraq should war arrive. In "The Air War," 2-11, he offers an insider's feel of the air war, from the target selection process to the hardware and ordinance involved to such crucial decisions as the one made by Gen. H. Norman

Schwarzkopf that the military would have one single, integrated air campaign under one commander. "As a result, for the first time, all U.S. air forces are acting under a single operations plan and following a single air tasking order."

In a cover story on the coming ground war, "Preparing the Ground," 2-4, Stephen Budiansky with Bruce B. Auster and Peter Cary, present an overview of U.S. strategy which reports that: "When the allies finally do move on the ground, they will be counting on high technology to offset Iraq's advantage in numbers. Plans call for flanking Iraqi positions in Kuwait to the west while simultaneously punching through at weak points and perhaps launching an amphibious landing to the east and helicopter-borne assaults to the rear." Except for the amphibious landing, which was a piece of deliberate disinformation put out by the military, *USNWR* was right on the money. After the war was over, editor-at-large David Gergen, in "Why America Hates the Press," 3-11, wrote that "This magazine, for example, learned nearly two weeks in advance where allied ground forces would strike and that amphibious operations were a fake, but it withheld disclosure. Several other news organizations made similar decisions."

Unfortunately, because of its earlier press run than *Time* and *Newsweek, USNWR* missed the start of the ground war in its 3-4 issue, the cover story, "The Gulf War's Final Curtain," deals mostly with the last-minute diplomatic maneuvering between Washington, Moscow and Baghdad, the news overrun by events before the magazine even hit the stands. To its credit, however, *USNWR* did report that "The battle plan for Desert Storm remains secret, but military officials say one option is a lightning-fast attack north all the way to the Euphrates River, trapping the Republican Guard behind fast-moving American mechanized forces and the heavily armed VII Corps to the south, and cutting off the vital city of Basra from Baghdad. Marine amphibious forces off the Kuwaiti coast could cause even further confusion by attacking from the east, or even just by bluffing."

Some of *USNWR* coverage of the war made news itself. "The Bear," 2-11, a highly favorable profile of Gen. Schwarzkopf — "a general who knows soldiers and loves them, who knows war and hates it" — includes an interview in which the General, when asked his reading of Saddam Hussein, replies in part: "I would also tell you that we have several reports that Saddam is a very distraught man, that he has three doctors treating him with tranquilizers, which may say something about his mental states." The allusion to the use of tranquilizers was picked up by other news organizations and widely reported. Another *USNWR* interview which caused a bit of a stir was one with Vice President Dan Quayle featured in "The Real Target?" 2-18, in which Quayle indicated his support of targeting Saddam Hussein personally.

The magazine's on-the-ground coverage was uneven. Much of it was along the lines of Peter Cary and Mike Tharp's effort "The Boys Next Door," 2-18, a report from Saudi Arabia on the soldiers at the front lines, which was overloaded with quotes and adjectives. "They are young, tough and smart — confident, well-trained professionals, using the best weapons ever made. . . They are also lonely, dirty, weary, brave, fearful and utterly sick of being here. To a man and woman, they want to leave the desert and return to what they know and love."

USNWR received a 1990 National Magazine Award for Feature Writing for a special report, "Vietnam Story," by senior writer Joseph L. Galloway. Covering a contemporary war in 1991, Galloway's concentration on the U.S. Army 24th Infantry Division paid off when that outfit was selected to sweep into northern Iraq to envelop the Iraqi Republic Guards. Unfortunately, his account of that crucial mission, "The Point of the Spear," 3-11, was crammed to the bursting point with facts and figures. Too many sentences read like this: "With some 290 Abrams tanks, 270 Bradley Fighting Vehicles, 72 155-mm howitzers, nine multiple-launch rocket systems, 18 Apache attack helicopters and 6,000 wheeled vehicles, the 24th had sliced through more than 200 miles of the rugged rock fields and deep desert dunes of Iraq in less than 36 hours, and after a day and a half it was 36 hours ahead of schedule."

Having presciently identified Saddam as "The World's Most Dangerous Man," way back in June 1990, *USNWR* continued to keep an eye on his regime after the war faded. In the chilling cover story "Saddam's Secret Bomb," 11-25, a team of reporters, led by Stephen J. Hedges and Peter Cary, documents how Iraq was able to build its nuclear weapons program through the help of Western companies and how the threat, while diminished, still remains. It reprints a warning delivered by one Iraqi physicist to U.N. inspectors: "You can bomb our buildings. You can destroy our technology. But you cannot take it out of our heads. We now have the capability."

USNWR also continued to deliver exceptional coverage of developments in the Soviet Union, as the economic and political disintegration it began predicting as long ago as 11-20-89 enveloped the country. In the 4-8 issue, *USNWR* published the findings of a public opinion poll taken in the Soviet Union during March, and in the numbers was the Soviet story for 1991, with Boris Yeltsin coming in at 70 percent for Soviet president, Mikhail Gorbachev at 14 percent, and with 73 percent saying "no" to supporting the government headed by Prime Minister Valentin Pavlov. Eighty-one percent expressed dissatisfaction with living conditions in the U.S.S.R., and 41 percent said "no" when asked if economic reform could succeed in the framework of the existing union. Twenty-nine percent said "yes"; 31 percent didn't know.

The magazine published a special issue, 9-2, in response to the coup attempt in the Soviet Union. With the editors nominating the issue for 10 Best consideration. Among the highlights: an interview with former foreign minister Eduard Shevardnadze, who tells *USNWR* that "The main point here is that Mikhail Gorbachev has made this most serious mistake. It was *he* who has made the main mistake by forming such a team for himself." The Russian-speaking Douglas Stanglin, who, with his wife Victoria Pope, having replaced Jeff Trimble in the Moscow bureau, was quick-off-the-mark in seeing trouble for Boris Yeltsin in "Fanfare for the Common Man," observing that "even his admirers worry that his brilliance at the barricades will fade once he returns to the tedious work of governing." In "Bush's Brand New Phone Pal," Kenneth T. Walsh is superb on President Bush's handling of the crisis.

Soviet coverage late in the year included "Harvest of Pain," 10-7, Stanglin's comprehensive report on the agricultural crisis; "Three Days That Shook the World," 11-18, by Jeff Trimble and Peter Vassiliev, which expertly places the events during the three days of the coup attempt in the context of the gross miscalculations made by the coup leaders; and "There Is No Way We Can Turn Back," 12-2, an interview with Gorbachev conducted by Zuckerman and Stanglin. Twice during the interview the beleaguered first and last President of the Soviet Union warns of a "catastrophe" if the Union should break apart. When asked if he has learned not to trust economists, a bemused Gorbachev replies: "We cannot do without economists, and we cannot do without the experience of the world economies. The recent experience of Mexico, the experience of Brazil — I think all of that is unique."

Overall foreign coverage in *USNWR* continues to be evenly acceptable, the magazine's regulars reviewed in full in the Foreign Correspondent section of the *MediaGuide*. "Worldgram," still provides concise intelligence briefings on developments overseas, and this year *USNWR* began a new feature, "America's New Rivals," commentary and reports on Germany and Japan. *USNWR* augments its overseas coverage with the use of stringers, including such superstars as Christopher Bobinski of the *Financial Times* and contributing editors Josef Joffe, Timothy Garton Ash, and James Fallows. In the cover story, "The Mind of Japan," 12-2, Fallows contends that "The war against America was the dark side of what is, in the eyes of Japan's leaders, a legitimate and continuing struggle: the attempt to raise the nation's standing in the world and above all to free it from outside, Western control."

The magazine's domestic political coverage remains respectable, with its fair share of scoops. Along with the *Washington Post*, *USNWR* broke the story about then-White House Chief of Staff John Sununu's use of military aircraft, Kenneth T. Walsh, Stephen J. Hedges and Bruce B. Auster reporting in "John Sununu's Flight Plans," 4-29, observing: "Most telling is how many administration figures are anxious to see Sununu get his comeuppance. His tough management of the Bush administration has earned him a good many enemies who think he's due for trouble." In the follow-up, "The Flights of Air Sununu," 5-6, Walsh, Hedges and others offer more detail on Sununu's use of official aircraft for personal trips, and in "Sununu's Final Days Among the Jet Set," 5-13, *USNWR* discloses that "[White House Counsel Boyden] Gray considered recommending that the chief of staff be denied the use of government planes. Sununu objected strenuously. . .Gray also is expected to recommend that the chief of staff get official approval for each trip in the future." Walsh, in "Sununu Through?" 7-8, reports that "*U.S. News* has learned that in New York two weeks ago, Sununu mentioned a critical column by *New York Times* columnist William Safire and asked a prominent Jewish Republican, 'Do you think that critical column could've come about because I'm Lebanese, and he doesn't like my position on Israel?' "

USNWR provided thorough coverage of the other major Beltway story of the year, the Clarence Thomas nomination to the Supreme Court, although not always in the no-frills, straightforward manner we expect from *USNWR*. In "The Crowning Thomas Affair," Steven V. Roberts, Jeannye Thornton and Ted Gest chart Thomas's personal and political odyssey from his youth in the poverty-stricken, segregated south to his career as a professional black conservative in Ronald Reagan's Washington. What makes this story stand out is its emphasis on bargain-basement pop psychology we normally associate with other publications. At one point, *USNWR* writes "If Thomas is afraid of losing the confirmation, he also worries about winning it," and "Perhaps [if he's confirmed] the furies driving him will abate. Perhaps then, having been judged as fully worthy, the new justice will be able to judge others less harshly." The only real item of news value here, and only because of subsequent developments, was the disclosure that while at Yale, Thomas "was at the dining hall when it opened for breakfast at 7, sometimes regaling other early risers with hilarious descriptions of the X-rated movies he liked to watch for relaxation." Gloria Borger, Walsh, Thornton and Gest provide good details on the events leading up to the hearings, including Hill's "political naivete" in hoping that her charges would force Thomas to withdraw without her having to go public.

Walsh, Borger, Roberts and Gest are reviewed in full in the Social/Political Reporters section of the *MediaGuide,* but we want to single out Walsh here for special mention, as he has a superb pipeline into the workings of the Bush White House and an astute read into the President's psyche. A cover story on President Bush's evolving view toward Gorbachev, "The True Believer," 7-1, includes an interview with the President, who tells Walsh that "I've been convinced all along that he's committed to reform." An interview with the President is also a highlight of "Commander in Chief," 12-31-90/1-7-91, a revealing profile detailing his convictions as the U.N. deadline with Iraq approaches, Walsh removing any lingering doubt we may have had about Bush's ability to pull the trigger. Of course, a reporter at that level can be at the mercy of his sources. Covering the administration's response to the upheaval in the Soviet Union in "A New World," 9-9, with Dorian Friedman in Washington, Walsh reports from Kennebunkport that while some outside experts are calling on Washington to propose deep cuts in nuclear arms beyond the START treaty "such thinking strikes Bush as naive and premature. His immediate goal, according to senior aides, is minimalist: simply to encourage Gorbachev, Yeltsin and other Soviet leaders to keep the nuclear weapons in a few reliable hands."

The analytical efforts are anchored by Editor at Large David Gergen, still one of the sharpest Beltway observers around, able to bring the authority of an inside player into his commentary, and "Tomorrow" columnist Michael Barone, who is not afraid to give readers a dose of political science along with his handicapping efforts.

USNWR received a 10 Best selection for General Reporting from *MediaGuide* last year for its cover story on the explosion on the U.S.S. Iowa and subsequent Navy investigation. The newsweekly offered several cover stories on the national security beat this year, none as good as the Iowa story. In "The New Spy Wars," 6-3, Brian Duffy with Jim Impoco report on the CIA's efforts to find a new role for itself now that the Cold War, its reason for being, has ended. The story is unremarkable, except for a brief side-bar interview with Deputy Director Richard

Kerr. Kerr, who first sounded a warning last summer that Saddam Hussein would invade Kuwait, tells Duffy that one "dramatic" shock that could come up is in North Korea. "Missions Implausible," 10-14, by Stephen Budiansky with Bruce B. Auster, is comprehensive on the difficulties the Pentagon is facing in positioning itself in the New World Order, but we had already read the basic thrust of the story elsewhere.

Business and financial coverage in *USNWR* ranges from straightforward to self-help, with varying degrees of quality, our readers noting that overall, even at its best, *USNWR* seemed to be operating on a principle of not overestimating the sophistication of its readership. In "The Best Mutual Funds for 1991," 2-11, by Jack Egan, we noted that despite the large space devoted to charts of mutual funds, none of the top performers on the charts were listed among the recommended funds. Our readers gave mixed reviews to the magazine's "Money Guide," 7-15, giving high grades for concise writing and presentation, but questioning some of the advice being given and wondering if the underlying theme, encouraging readers to invest now, was really appropriate for a news magazine. In Jack Egan's opening article "News You Can Use," one reader was reminded of a boilerroom come-on for the stock and bond market, and questioned the financial future of eight of the top ten stocks listed in the accompanying "50 Top Small Stocks." However, we found Leonard Wiener's "1991 Tax Guide," 3-18, helpful, Weiner not repeating the instructions on the federal forms themselves, but pointing out examples and rulings on matters easily skipped by most taxpayers.

Economics and business coverage in *USNWR* in 1991 was spotty at best, the magazine particularly coming up short on macroeconomics. In "Heavy Lifting," 5-6, Robert Black, Don L. Boroughs, Sara Collins and Kenneth Sheets argue that, because of the heavy debt in the consumer, corporate, and government sectors, the current recession is not a normal one where falling interest rates will motivate buying and spending as a recovery mechanism. Several weeks later, however, in "Bush's Leap of Faith," 7-1, Eva Pomice, Robert F. Black, Don L. Boroughs and Sara Collins contend that the Federal Reserve caused the recession and the Fed is the only entity that can help end it through the lowering of interest rates. "Living With Less Inflation," 10-7, by David Hage with Don L. Burroughs, Robert F. Black and Sara Collins, is unconvincing on the dangers of disinflation, such as when discussing the effect of the stagnant real-estate market on a typical couple: "a drop in their home's value would hinder their ability to trade up. . . and generally sap their sense of affluence."

"Economic Outlook" columnist Sylvia Nasar departed late in 1990, moving to *The New York Times.* The editors elected to replace her with two economists, MIT economics professor Paul R. Krugman and Claremont Economics Institute chairman John Rutledge, apparently leaving it to the readers to sort out the differences in their tea-leaf readings. In "Why the World Won't Run Out of Capital," 4-15, for example, Krugman contends that the alarm over a global capital shortage is basically in Wall Street and that the world's money supply is relatively normal. One week later, in "Don't Expect a Lasting Recovery After the Recession," 4-22, Rutledge predicts that a growing worldwide capital shortage will push U.S. interest rates higher later in the year. They fell.

We were again impressed by the opening section, "Outlook," assistant managing editor Donald Baer offering a weekly compendium of news, statistics, information-bytes and analysis, Baer always making his selections with the reader — the non-Beltway reader — clearly in mind, giving "Outlook" additional value for the general reader. "Washington Whispers," remains a veritable goldmine of intelligence nuggets on national and international movers-and-shakers. In one of the most remarked-upon "Whispers," of 1991, "Literally Correct," 4-29, *USNWR* discloses that Vice President Dan Quayle, worried that his staff of lawyers and PhDs "may be losing touch with the common people," has ordered them to start reading *People* to "put them in touch with the feelings of 'real people' who live 'in the real world.' " John Leo, "On Society" columnist, continues to be a must-read, although he has a tendency to be overwrought on occasion. In perhaps the most controversial column he penned all year, "Toxic Feminism on the Big Screen," 6-10, he writes that the nominally feminist movie, "Thelma and Louise," has "an explicit fascist theme." Mortimer B. Zuckerman and David Gergen remain as backpage columnists, their work for the year, along with Leo's, is reviewed in full in the Commentators section of the *MediaGuide.*

In last year's *MediaGuide,* we expressed concern over the growing prominence that features and "News You Can Use" were receiving at *USNWR.* While our concerns have been allayed somewhat by *USNWR*'s Middle East and Soviet coverage this year, we still feel the magazine goes overboard at times in its efforts to choose the "Best This, That, and the Other Thing." We are told that these issues are big hits, especially the "Best Colleges and Universities" issue, and *Time* and *Newsweek* are now picking up on the idea. We are also told that efforts such as the magazine's cover story on "America Before Columbus," 7-8, goes over well in schools. As we said at the beginning, perhaps Zuckerman has finally discovered the way for newsweeklies to survive in the CNN age. Perhaps. Still, as we look over the "Big Three" of *USNWR, Time,* and *Newsweek,* we are occasionally reminded of a joke that supposedly made the rounds of the *New York Times* newsroom when that publication was experimenting with new features in an attempt to increase circulation back in the late 1970s: "There's a new section starting next week. It's called 'News.' "

Editor-in-Chief:	Mortimer Zuckerman
Co-Editors:	Merrill McLoughlin and Michael Ruby
Address:	2400 N Street, NW Washington, DC 20037-1196 (202) 995-2000
Circulation:	1990 — 2,511,000 1991 — 2,311,000

Utne Reader

We continue to enjoy "the best of the alternative press" that we find offered in the *Utne* Reader's pages. Canvassing an enormous amount of material to assemble each issue and consistently selecting topics that pique their interest, and ours, founder and editor Eric Utne and his staff give the trim bimonthly a familial, user-friendly feel. They clearly write for themselves as much as their audience, and encourage active interaction between the editorial staff and the readers, and among the readers themselves, as with the "Salon" cover, 3/4-91, by forming *Utne Reader* networks. Utne credibly describes the *Reader*'s thematic makeup in the 11/12-91 "Editor's Note" column: "*Utne Reader* is neither a political magazine nor a lifestyle magazine. We're a *cultural* magazine. Our beat isn't high culture, as in the New York arts scene, or the pop culture of *People* magazine. We're more interested in the emerging culture." Utne and the staff of the *Utne Reader* are quick to discern the concerns of the general population, particularly in the cover treatments which celebrate life and the experience of life.

Utne Reader draws its material from an incredibly broad spectrum of sources, adding value to their perspectives. More intriguingly, the editorial team isn't hemmed in by any ideological boundary; any idea that intrigues them can be found in the pages of the quirky, eclectic *Reader,* a far wider range of thinking than found along a conventional left/right line. "At *Utne Reader,*" writes Utne, 11/12-91, "we're convinced that the left/right axis no longer describes the political territory. . .In our view it is more accurate and more interesting to describe the range as a constellation rather than an axis." This is *Utne Reader*'s principal utility: its ability to cull information from diverse materials to mold lush, thought-provoking articles and sections.

The cover selections this year addressed such universal topics as spirituality, "Does the Spirit Move You?" 1/2-91; conversation, "Salons," 3/4-91; masculinity, "Men," 5/6-91; work v. leisure, "For Love or Money," 7/8-91; death and the afterlife, "Facing Death," 9/10-91; and political life, "Why Americans Hate Politics," 11/12-91. In terms of cultural mores and philosophical questions, it doesn't get much more basic than this. Still, the treatments are not facile, but sophisticated and surprisingly cohesive. The first issue of 1991 is a lively compendium which stresses the movement toward spirituality without limiting the discussion to the boundaries of organized religion. The inspiration, according to the "Editor's Note" column, comes from Utne's 8-1/2 year-old son Sammy, who asked "Dad, if we had a religion, what would it be?" But while the journey is personal, the *Reader,* as always, takes care not to step on anyone's toes, offering alternatives rather than solutions. The cover begins with an excerpt of Garry Wills's *Under God* entitled "Religion: A Constant in American Politics," an exploration of the inextricable intertwining of religion and politics, despite the separation of Church and State: "Neither Jefferson nor Madison thought that separation of church and state would lessen the impact of religion on our nation. Quite the opposite. Churches freed from the compromises of establishment would have greater moral force, they argued — and in this they proved prophets." Other offerings outline relationships between "Spirituality and Therapy: Toward a Partnership," by Katy Butler, *Family Therapy Networker,* ask "Do Kids Need Religion?" by Anthony Brandt, *Parenting,* take us on an odyssey of "Rediscovering Judaism," and "A Living Faith" both by Abe Opincar, *San Diego Reader.* Sidebars round this out with alternate views: "An Atheist Speaks Her Mind," by Leah Fritz, *Ms.;* "On Worshipping All Life," an interview with Steve Darden, a Native American, and "Spirituality of the Arts," an interview with choreographer and performer Maria Cheng, both excerpted from *The Search for Meaning* by Phillip Berman. The *Utne Reader* provides the natural follow-up a few months hence with "Facing Death," 9/10-91. We get an excerpt from Stephen Levine's *Who Dies?,* "Conscious Dying," and from Stephanie Ericsson's *Companion Through the Darkness,* "The Agony of Grief," intriguing perspectives on the processes of death and dying. "Rituals" outlines the way different cultures view death culled from various indigenous newsletters and newspapers, and from *The Elmwood Newsletter,* Chellis Glendinning sensitively probes "The Politics of Death." These expansive, intelligent cover treatments are typical of the others, in both size, topic and scope.

The remainder of the year the cover was devoted to the physical pursuit of living rather than the spiritual or corporeal. "For Love or Money," cover 7/8-91, follows up on the *Time* magazine cover "The Simple Life," 4-8. As a more comprehensive treatment, the *Reader* goes well beyond compiling anecdotes on how Americans feel about work and the work environment. We get "Remaking a Living," by Brad Edmondson in a special to the *Utne Reader,* in which he chronicles the "*desire* to change," rather than actual movement to *Time*'s 'simple life;' from the *Fairfield County Advocate,* Jennifer Kaylin tells her own story of "Downward Mobility," a personal look at 'life in the slow lane;' Barbara Brandt of the Shorter Work-Time Group of Boston makes a call for "Less Is More: A Call for Shorter Working Hours;" and the *LA Weekly*'s Michael Ventura's bitter portrait of the workplace, "Someone Is Stealing Your Life," so strong a perspective that the editors ran it with a qualifier noting mixed staff reaction to printing it, and asking for reader feedback for later publication. The selections featured in "Men," 5/6-91, range from downright silly to rather provocative. "A Time for Men to Pull Together," by Andrew Kimbrell, gets mushy on the "legacy of loss" men have faced, as the "demands of the industrial era have forced men off the land, out of the family and community, and into the factory and office." Barbara Ehrenreich's "Angry Young Men," *New York Woman,* is notable for its frightening portrait of male anger and frustration resulting in death for two teen-age girls on Long Island; but what do we do? "Men as Success Objects," by Warren Farrell, *Family Therapy Networker,* tells us what we've always suspected, that men are doubly judged as handsome and successful, whereas women are only categorized according to appearance. Larry Leitch's "Do You Know Who Your Friends Are?" examines the bonds of male friendship. Rounding out the section, Scott Russell Sanders dissects "The Men We Carry in Our Minds," *Milkweed Chronicle,* a remembrance of things past, at least Sanders's past. Grass-roots politics are celebrated in the "Why Americans Hate Politics" cover, 11/12-91. E. J. Dionne Jr.'s new book of the same name is excerpted, outlining and defining the problems with an apparently apathetic electorate. Ellen Ryan in "Growing Politics in the Backyards of America," David Morris in "You Can Fight City Hall," and John Resenbrink in "Protest Too Much," outline the possibilities for grass-roots politics for the 1990s. The section closes with an excerpt from *The New Republic,* "How to Beat Bush in '92," a mostly conventional assessment from *TNR*'s favorite academics and columnists. The "Salons" cover, 3/4-91, advises us "how to revive the endangered art of conversation and start a revolution in your living room." While interesting reading, we suspect this is less about the Algonquin Round Table and conducting a modern-day equivalent, than a subtle plug for a new electronic *Utne Reader* Online Salon. An intriguing idea, "Salons" doesn't seem to fit as well as other selections they've had.

Featured items also interest. We get a bird's-eye view of what it's like to be lucid and in a nursing home, "The Story of a Nursing Home Refugee," 1/2-91, by Katharine M. Butterworth, *Whole Earth Review,* one of the few articles we've ever seen that comes from the patient's point of view. While she doesn't get into policy, Butterworth suggests alternate solutions for elder care need to be made available. It's so often assumed that people who go into 'homes' will never be able to resume a normal life, and while that may be true for many, it is by no means the rule of thumb that some take it to be: after two separate stays in two care facilities, Butterworth lives alone at age 91. Helen Cordes offers a compendium for "Re-examining Abortion," 3/4-91, that really reexamines the issue for a change, rather than just gathering a selection of the traditional pro-choice or pro-life perspectives. This introduces several additional articles that we'd not have seen without the *Reader*: "The Global Politics of Abortion" by Jodi Jacobson, *Worldwatch Paper 97;* "Men & Abortion," by Laurie Eastman, *Friends Journal;* "The Seamless Web Philosophy," 15 women's views, and a response, "Holes in the Seamless Web," by Max Dashu, both from *Sojourner;* and "Reproductive Ethics," Jean Bethke Elshtain, *The Progressive.* It's an impressive panorama of opinion on the subject and we come away informed. Again, *Utne Reader* follows up with a related topic, adoption, in "A Child at Any Cost?" 11/12-91, again assembling a smorgasbord of data from divergent sources and varying angles; from the parent's view to the adopted child in an interracial family, an extremely introspective exercise which makes us reflect upon the issue rather than the politics involved. A collection of "Black Voices," 9/10-91, is equally pensive, bringing together the views of black citizens on the crisis in the black community, particularly on the underclass.

We peruse the various departments and columns attentively, as we always find something of value. The "Gleanings" column, 1/2-91, was terrific — offering alternative views such as "True Crime Stories," by Essex Hemphill, Pacific News Service, as to why he fears black men as a black man more than say, the Ku Klux Klan or AIDS, and "Anti-Gentilism Among Jews," from Michael Lerner at *Tikkun.* Always intelligent, this section cuts against the grain and offers new views on various and wide-ranging debates. In the "In Brief" section, Laurie Ouellette probes the relationship between feminism and size discrimination, "As Fat as They Wanna Be," 3/4-91, describing several journals penned specifically with full-figured women in mind. Ouellette celebrates the "honesty and spontaneity" of the new generations of magazines of the underground in the "Mixed Media" section, 11/12-91, and her enthusiasm is infectious. Jay Walljasper's "Zeitgeist" column rounds out the magazine well, with the executive editor addressing the issues of the day. In "O Canada: A Closer Look at the Neighbors," 3/4-91, Walljasper frets about the Free Trade Agreement limiting Canada's sovereignty, making it by proxy the "51st state," informative for those who aren't familiar with Canada and Canadian politics; Walljasper presents a quintessential Canadian view, whether he knows it or not.

We are truly astounded by the constantly fresh insights Utne and his staff bring to the *Utne Reader.* How do they find such interesting material issue after issue? The bimonthly operates with a tiny staff, and the amount of the reading the staff must do each month has to be staggering. It's clear, however, that it's a labor of love, and that this former newsletter will continue to grow and prosper for some time to come.

Publisher/Editor: Eric Utne

Executive Editor: Jay Walljasper

Address: 1624 Harmon Place
Minneapolis, MN 55403
(612) 338-5040

Circulation: 1990 — 225,000
1991 — 240,029

The Washington Monthly

Fast approaching the standard retirement age of 65, Charles Peters showed signs of wear and tear at the end of last year after twenty-plus years of producing the *Monthly*. He described his frustration, "Tilting at Windmills," 10-90: ". . .I find myself becoming twitchier with each passing year. The problem is that the older you get, the more things you've seen go wrong. The more aware you are of the possible disaster inherent in any course you choose to take — other than staying in bed — the more apprehensive you become." He was rumored midyear to be considering offers for *The Washington Monthly* from two groups of potential buyers, but with his steady vision of the *Monthly* as a public service tool, we can't picture him selling to a large consortium that would turn the middle-aged *Monthly* into a new version of *The New Yorker* or another version of *The Washingtonian*.

Peters could not have been encouraged by the stinging criticism hurled at him by Jack Shafer of the Washington *City Paper*. "I'll admit that a tenderfoot can benefit from reading the magazine, but for no more than two years," Shafer writes in the "News Bites" column, 2-22. "Why two years? Because that's the standard tour of duty for the Brilliant Young Editors who serve under Neoliberal Chief Charles Peters. Peters uses the same two-year learning curve to instruct each new batch of BYEs in the fundamentals of the gospel. Inevitably, they end up rewriting stories that were done to perfection years ago by the likes of James Fallows, Taylor Branch, Nick Lemann and Gregg Easterbrook. The subjects are as predictable as they are worn: the argument for national service; means-testing of entitlements; the justification for higher gasoline taxes; tax strategies to soak the rich; the case for workfare; the case for cheap military weapons that work; and efficiency in government and other goo-goo panaceas, not to mention the universality of the lessons Peters learned while working for the Peace Corps. Readers could save themselves a bundle over the subscription price by buying a year's worth of used back issues and divining the gospel from them." We disagree. For all the "recycling" that Shafer sees, we still find fresh insight and see the dogged determination to reform the government and both political parties. This perseverance is part and parcel of *The Washington Monthly*, which has done an impressive job watchdogging the government over the past two decades.

Perhaps it is Peters' perception that the end of history is not yet on us that convinces us of the pressing need for publications such as the *Monthly*. "As the Cold War continues to wind down, what should replace communism as our number one enemy? Tribalism is my candidate. It lies behind everything from Arab terrorism to Japanese protectionism," Peters wrote, 1-90. As history spins inexorably onward, so does government, and the necessity for publications to keep an eye on the functioning of government remains urgent. We don't expect the *Monthly* will lose its utility any time soon, if ever.

Katharine Boo, James Bennet and Chris J. Georges are the current 'Brilliant Young Editors' under Peters's tutelage. Boo came on board to succeed Scott Shuger who departed earlier in the year to freelance. Bennet is due to graduate at the end of '91 from the Peters boot camp where an editor works 60 hours a week or more, and is paid only a $10,000 yearly salary. Georges got the job as Bennet's heir apparent, making it onto the masthead for the 11-91 issue. This quick, high rate of turnover makes for a *Washington Monthly* diverse in quality from year to year, but keeps the material and perspectives largely fresh.

Unfortunately, Bennet just didn't seem to have the same panache as either his predecessor Shuger, or Shuger's predecessor, *New York Times* reporter Jason De Parle. Amid the whining about how the White House press corps lets the president get away with murder, Bennet offers a wealth of information on how journalists perceive themselves and their jobs, "The Flack Pack," 11-91; Peters nominated this particular effort for 10 Best consideration. Peters also nominated Katharine Boo's "What Mother Teresa Could Learn in a Leather Bar," 6-91, convincing us that private organizations can better care for AIDS victims than the bureaucracy, but Boo limits her discussion mainly to gay men, where the epidemic has taken on intravenous drug users and women and children, who are almost nonentities here. Overall, however, Boo shows more flair. In "Vanity Fare," 9-91, she shows real insight on the problems with general interest magazines and their focus on celebrity: ". . .under the heading 'Personalities' in a 1971 *Esquire,* there's simply Dean Acheson's memoir of Harry S. Truman. That sort of editing wasn't premised on giving readers purely what they clamored for. It was about offering them something they didn't know — yet — they should care about. With the right writer and enough vigor, they would care. And that — not deft prose, not acid analysis — was the real power of the general interest magazine." Georges, the new kid on the block, has yet to appear in the pages.

One of the other strengths of the *Monthly* is the high quality of the material that is gleaned from outside sources. Departing editor Scott Shuger offers "The Stealth Bomber Story You Haven't Heard," 1/2-91, in which he outlines the boondoggle over the B-2, raising cogent points about the efficiency of the funding and testing of the plane, also nominated by Peters for 10 Best consideration. Former *Washington Post* reporter Morton Mintz constructs a compelling indictment of the insurance industry, "The Dangers Insurance Companies Hide," 1/2-91, particularly Aetna, which insured A.H. Robins, the maker of the Dalkon Shield. Peter Gray gives us a firsthand look at driving around in a Chrysler that runs on compressed natural gas rather than gasoline, "Kicking the Oil Habit," 3-91, including some creative suggestions as to policy alternatives for energy efficiency. John Gill Freeman takes much of his data from other sources, in "Bookshelves of the Vanities," 6-91, to explain how the New York Public Library, with all its endowments, allows its branches in the boroughs to close because of a 1901 agreement with Andrew Carnegie stipulating that the city maintain the branches. Submitted by Peters for the 10 Best section, "Why Are Droves of Unqualified, Unprepared Kids Getting Into Our Top Colleges?" by John Larew 6-91, makes a good case for eliminating the nearly automatic admittance of alumni into the best schools, but we don't find out if Larew, class of '91 and former editorial chair of *The Harvard Crimson,* was affected in any way by the Harvard admissions policy. In "Why Aren't Pro-lifers and Pro-choicers Pro-contraception?" 7/8-91, former *Washington Times* correspondent Rita McWilliams makes a good case that both a pro and anti abortion stand is counterproductive, summing the situation up plainly in her lead, describing the scene in front of a D.C. abortion clinic: "Threading her way between. . .two factions this chilly Saturday morning is a lone woman — make that girl — wearing sweat pants, a hair ribbon, and braces. Both camps on the sidewalk claim they care deeply for this young woman. The anti-abortion 'counselors' say they want to prevent her from committing an act that will plague her the rest of her life. Members of the 'clinic defense force' say they are protecting her fundamental right not to carry an unwanted child. But both sides have already failed this woman. In this age of scientific technology, an era in which birth control should be cheap, effective, and widely used, she shouldn't be here in the first place." Tina Rosenberg follows this up with a complete examination of the history and success of Profamilia, the family planning project in very Catholic Colombia, "Winning the Trojan War," 7/8-91. And we think of Betsy Dance's "Why American Roads All Go to Pot," 11-91, each time we get on the highway; her contrast of U.S. to European highways is quite striking in outlining the U.S.'s use of shoddy materials, a short-range view that does not take into account either cost-benefit analysis or estimate the road's life, an absence of warranties from the builders at the heart of the problem.

In selecting additional material for the *Monthly,* Peters often chooses authors with personal experience who know whereof they speak. A former public servant, Lois Forer argues against the "depersonalization" of government and politics in "Patron Saints," 7/8-91; although we're not sure bringing back party machines is precisely the correct answer, it might be a start, an interesting premise made more compelling by her experience. Maxim Kniazkov's "Hack in the USSR," 6-91, is eye opening on the Orwellian workings of the Soviet press, via Kniazkov's years with TASS. Peter Kornbluh, Malcolm Byrne, and Tom Blanton — senior analyst, director of analysis, and deputy director, respectively — of the National Security Archives, dissect Oliver North's statement after his charges were dismissed that he is "totally exonerated," in "Ollie Oops," 11-91. They don't tell us anything we don't already know, but it's useful in citing North's Iran-contra hearing testimony. And in "Too at Home Abroad," 9-91, a foreign service officer, using the pseudonym Harry Crosby, scores quite a few points on the shortcomings of the foreign service, such as the folks at the embassies abroad being unable to do anything outside their homes or their jobs except take a taxi because they can't speak the language of the country to which they're assigned.

There are, however, the occasional misfires. Elizabeth Lesly is flawed on taxing the Church in "Pennies From Heaven," 4-1, as she seems to have set her sights mainly on the Catholic Church. There's no mention of Temple-taxing, for example, and her snide tone undercuts her argument; she asks us to "set aside your perfectly reasonable anti-anticlerical bias for a moment, you'll discover that to favor taxing churches you don't have to be a nun-basher avenging the times Sister Mary whipped chalk at you in the fourth grade." Ugh. Beth Austin's "Pretty Worthless," cover 5-91, is a silly review of the worthless moral content of today's films, an exercise conducted more constructively last year in *The New York Times*' Sunday "Arts & Leisure" section. Naturally, Hollywood's golden years are personified by "Mr. Smith Goes to Washington," "To Kill a Mockingbird," and "On the Waterfront," but at the time those movies were produced, studios were turning out hundreds of movies a year rather than dozens, most of them less than notable by Austin's standards — "Curly Top," "An American in Paris," and so on — thanks to relatively inexpensive production costs. To top it off, Austin ignores the quality of film today, although she does mention films that "confuse the rule," such as "Dances with Wolves," "Glory," etc., dismissing them summarily.

The remainder of the *Monthly*'s pages are devoted to books, mostly volumes political in nature. Michael Lewis, author of *Liar's Poker,* does a terrific book review of *Conduct Unbecoming: The Rise and Ruin of Finley, Kumble* by Steven J. Kumble and Kevin J. Lahart, "Lawyer's Poker," 1/2-91. Lewis skewers the national law firm and its enormous fees, writing in the same madcap, pointed style as *Liar's Poker.* Appropriately enough, *WM* is the first to excerpt alumnus Nicholas Lemann's book *The Promised Land,* giving us the scoop on Pat Moynihan in "Slumlord," 5-91. Similarly, we get a taste of *Newsweek* Washington bureau chief and former *Monthly* editor Evan Thomas's book, *The Man to See: Edward Bennett Williams — Legendary Trial Lawyer, Ultimate Insider* in "Inherit the Mint," 10-91. In this excerpt, we are guided through the case of John Connolly's bribery trial, in which Williams defended the Texan, offering a vivid sense of how lawyers manipulate the jury and the witnesses to win, rather than in pursuing justice. *The Washington Post*'s Marjorie Williams reviews Suzanne Garment's *Scandal: The Culture of Mistrust in American Politics* and Larry J. Sabato's *Feeding Frenzy: How Attack Journalism Has Transformed American Politics,* in "Is It Any of Your Business?" cover 9-91. Garment comes off better, offering a more sophisticated appraisal, and Williams makes the cogent point that both writers are flawed in the evaluations of journalism's 'golden age,' or even that there was one. But after raising the question of where to draw the line in print, we're disappointed in what we find in Susan Threadgill's "Who's Who," 10-91. This titillating item that would seem to overstep the bounds: "As practically everyone knows by now (see for example the *National Journal* of July 13), **Robert Zoellick** and **Margaret Tutwiler** are **James Baker**'s two closest aides...The *American Spectator*'s **David Brock** recently provided a delicious detail indicating how special their relationship is. 'I assume,' Brock says, attempting to distinguish between the roles of Zoellick and Tutwiler, 'that Zoellick does not receive a fresh rose on his pillow every night while on the road with the secretary.' Who's Who's own Deep Throat adds another detail from the 1988 presidential campaign. When Tutwiler and Baker were traveling with the president, they occupied adjoining rooms — except when Mrs. Baker was accompanying her husband. . ." This seems beneath the standards of *The Washington Monthly.*

Charlie Peters remains rather depressed by the governmental and liberal failures to do anything to reform themselves, in spite of *The Washington Monthly*'s decades of advice. In "Tilting at Windmills," 11-91, Peters seems downright sad: "It is a sad fact that in *The Washington Monthly*'s long struggle against the overlawyering of America, our fellow liberals have seldom been at our side. I suspect the reason is that many of them are lawyers and are thus not likely to be among the profession's more zealous critics. Unfortunately, the legal profession has not been the only case where liberal identification with a group has made professional criticism of the profession — even at its worst tendencies — much too rare. In the seventies, liberals failed to question the labor unions' aggressive pursuit of wage increases without regard to productivity increases, a pursuit that contributed mightily to the decline of American competitiveness. The groups liberals are still reluctant to criticize are teachers and civil servants. In this sense, liberals have become enablers, encouraging the professions to resist needed reform." This is all the more reason for Peters and *The Washington Monthly* to continue fighting. Peters and co-author James Bennet give us the definitive phrasing of the mission of *WM* in "America: A Repair Guide," 7/8-91: "Since our second issue in 1969, which featured an article on 'How the Pentagon Can Save $9 Billion,' the *Monthly* has tried to break the journalistic mode by not just carping but coming up with solutions to the problems plaguing society's most important institutions — indeed, even reformulating and repeating those solutions when they go ignored." Fortunately, *WM* has largely avoided "carping," and, in a day and age when many major media outlets flit from story to story, it's refreshing to have a publication dedicated to change and offering practical and practicable solutions.

Editor:	Charles Peters
Address:	1611 Connecticut Avenue, NW
	Washington, DC 20009
	(202) 462-0128
Circulation:	1990 — 30,000
	1991 — 33,000

THE RATING GUIDE

We have further refined the ratings for this seventh edition of the *MediaGuide,* toughening the standards for inclusion and evaluation. We have virtually eliminated the (-) rating, except in cases where the correspondent has fallen from a star or above, unlikely as that may be. Anyone ranked below a full star in a previous edition has been deleted, unless his work has shown improvement. We consider all journalists reviewed to be at the top of the profession, the big leagues of print journalism. Inclusion in the *MediaGuide,* regardless of the stars received, is an indication of the journalist's prominence, of his or her position above the ordinary and routine.

All ratings are based on work written in 1991, but in order to review a full year's work, we include material from December 15, 1990 through December 15, 1991, due to the constraints of production deadlines, our newsyear. Quantity means very little; it's quality we seek. We cite at least three pieces in each write-up; we read and evaluate countless more. The reader may notice that journalists with the same rating may have accompanying positive or negative remarks within the entry, but this invariably indicates that one has moved up to that rating, the other down. Dozens of journalists have been dropped from the 1991 edition; some have become editors, some changed professions or retired, some because we saw no need to continue commenting negatively on their work. We find the system to be biased toward the center. It's harder to lose ground at the very top because we tend to read most of the output there for the rewards of doing so. It's also harder for those at the bottom to move up, especially if the trend is downward, as we tend to pass over them and miss potentially good material. As with many things, past reputations have a ripple effect.

The standard for reporters are the three basic criteria for the wire services: fairness, accuracy, and balance (objectivity); plus three additional measures which elevate the material toward excellence: depth of reporting, writing skills and consistency. For commentators, the basic criteria are content reliability and a minimum level of interesting material presented on a regular basis; plus three more: depth of insight and information, presentation (persuasive ability), and consistency. In order to give a single rating rather than address each point individually, we merge the ratings during a series of discussions, reviews and edits.

($1/2$ ★) Failing the secondary criteria on one or more counts.

(★) Good. Reporters: professional. Commentators: worth trying.

(★ $1/2$) Good/very good. Very good inconsistently.

(★ ★) Very good. In reporters, above average reporting and writing, average analytical skills. In commentators, generally interesting content and presentation.

(★ ★ $1/2$) Very good/excellent. Above average in consistency.

(★ ★ ★) Excellent. In reporters, superior reporting and writing, above average in analytical skills. In commentators, superior content and presentation, frequent important information and insight. ·

(★ ★ ★ $1/2$) Excellent/exceptional. Approaching the very best.

(★ ★ ★ ★) Exceptional. In reporters, loftily objective, pacesetters for the profession in reporting and writing, penetrating analytical skills, always worth reading. In commentators, pacesetters for the profession in journalistic integrity and independence, must reading for insights and information, a consistently well-defined point of view.

THE HIGHEST RATED JOURNALISTS OF 1991

Brookes, Warren T.	*The Detroit News*	Financial Dispatch	★ ★ ★ ★
Crovitz, L. Gordon	*The Wall Street Journal*	Commentary	★ ★ ★ ★
Dempsey, Judy	*Financial Times*	Foreign Dispatch	★ ★ ★ ★
Evans & Novak	*Chicago Sun-Times*	Commentary	★ ★ ★ ★
Keller, Bill	*The New York Times*	Foreign Dispatch	★ ★ ★ ★
Klein, Joe	*New York*	Domestic Reports	★ ★ ★ ★
Morrocco, John D.	*Aviation Week & Space Technology*	National Security	★ ★ ★ ★
Safire, William	*The New York Times*	Commentary	★ ★ ★ ★
Tanner, James	*The Wall Street Journal*	Financial Dispatch	★ ★ ★ ★
Truell, Peter	*The Wall Street Journal*	Financial Dispatch	★ ★ ★ ★
Bacon, Kenneth H.	*The Wall Street Journal*	Financial Dispatch	★ ★ ★ ½
Brittan, Samuel	*Financial Times*	Financial Dispatch	★ ★ ★ ½
Cullison, A. E.	*The Journal of Commerce*	Foreign Dispatch	★ ★ ★ ½
Fineman, Mark B.	*Los Angeles Times*	Foreign Dispatch	★ ★ ★ ½
Gigot, Paul	*The Wall Street Journal*	Commentary	★ ★ ★ ½
Harden, Blaine	*The Washington Post*	Foreign Dispatch	★ ★ ★ ½
Krauthammer, Charles	Washington Post Writers Group	Commentary	★ ★ ★ ½
Mahar, Maggie	*Barron's*	Financial Dispatch	★ ★ ★ ½
Marsh, David	*Financial Times*	Foreign Dispatch	★ ★ ★ ½
Mortimer, Edward	*Financial Times*	Commentary	★ ★ ★ ½
Nash, Nathaniel C.	*The New York Times*	Foreign Dispatch	★ ★ ★ ½
Raspberry, William	*The Washington Post*	Commentary	★ ★ ★ ½
Sanger, David E.	*The New York Times*	Foreign Dispatch	★ ★ ★ ½
Waldmeir, Patti	*Financial Times*	Foreign Dispatch	★ ★ ★ ½
Williams, Carol J.	*Los Angeles Times*	Foreign Dispatch	★ ★ ★ ½
Williams, Juan	*The Washington Post*	Domestic Reports	★ ★ ★ ½
Angier, Natalie	*The New York Times*	Science Reports	★ ★ ★
Apple, R. W., Jr.	*The New York Times*	Domestic Reports	★ ★ ★
Bangsberg, P.T.	*The Journal of Commerce*	Foreign Dispatch	★ ★ ★
Barber, Lionel	*Financial Times*	Domestic Reports	★ ★ ★
Barnes, Fred	*The New Republic*	Commentary	★ ★ ★
Blumenthal, Sidney	*The New Republic*	Commentary	★ ★ ★
Buchan, David	*Financial Times*	Foreign Dispatch	★ ★ ★
Buchanan, Patrick	Tribune Media Services	Commentary	★ ★ ★
Byrne, John A.	*BusinessWeek*	Financial Dispatch	★ ★ ★
Carey, John	*BusinessWeek*	Financial Dispatch	★ ★ ★

Carley, William M.	*The Wall Street Journal*	Financial Dispatch	★ ★ ★
Cook, James	*Forbes*	Financial Dispatch	★ ★ ★
Covault, Craig	*Aviation Week & Space Technology*	National Security	★ ★ ★
Darlin, Damon	*The Wall Street Journal*	Foreign Dispatch	★ ★ ★
Davidson, Ian	*Financial Times*	Foreign Dispatch	★ ★ ★
Diehl, Jackson	*The Washington Post*	Foreign Dispatch	★ ★ ★
Dionne, E. J., Jr.	*The Washington Post*	Domestic Reports	★ ★ ★
Dobrzynski, Judith H.	*BusinessWeek*	Financial Dispatch	★ ★ ★
Donohoe, Catherine	*The Washington Times*	Domestic Reports	★ ★ ★
Drogin, Bob	*Los Angeles Times*	Foreign Dispatch	★ ★ ★
Easterbrook, Gregg	*Newsweek*	Domestic Reports	★ ★ ★
Fields, Suzanne	*The Washington Times*	Commentary	★ ★ ★
Fleming, Thomas	*Chronicles*	Commentary	★ ★ ★
Forsyth, Randall W.	*Barron's*	Financial Dispatch	★ ★ ★
Fraser, Damien	*Financial Times*	Foreign Dispatch	★ ★ ★
Freedman, Alix M.	*The Wall Street Journal*	Financial Dispatch	★ ★ ★
Friedman, Thomas L.	*The New York Times*	National Security	★ ★ ★
Goodman, Walter	*The New York Times*	Domestic Reports	★ ★ ★
Grenier, Richard	*The Washington Times*	Commentary	★ ★ ★
Gupta, Udayan	*The Wall Street Journal*	Financial Dispatch	★ ★ ★
Harwood, Richard	*The Washington Post*	Commentary	★ ★ ★
Hoagland, Jim	*The Washington Post*	Commentary	★ ★ ★
Ibrahim, Youssef M.	*The New York Times*	Foreign Dispatch	★ ★ ★
Ingersoll, Bruce	*The Wall Street Journal*	Financial Dispatch	★ ★ ★
Kelly, Michael	*The New Republic*	Foreign Dispatch	★ ★ ★
Kinsley, Michael	*The New Republic*	Commentary	★ ★ ★
Kristof, Nicholas D.	*The New York Times*	Foreign Dispatch	★ ★ ★
Kurtz, Howard	*The Washington Post*	Domestic Reports	★ ★ ★
Lamb, Christina	*Financial Times*	Foreign Dispatch	★ ★ ★
Leo, John	*U.S.News & World Report*	Commentary	★ ★ ★
Lewis, Paul	*The New York Times*	National Security	★ ★ ★
Liscio, John	*Barron's*	Financial Dispatch	★ ★ ★
Lowenstein, Roger	*The Wall Street Journal*	Financial Dispatch	★ ★ ★
Mallet, Victor	*Financial Times*	Foreign Dispatch	★ ★ ★
Massing, Michael	*Columbia Journalism Review*	Domestic Reports	★ ★ ★
Mathews, Jay	*The Washington Post*	Domestic Reports	★ ★ ★
Mauthener, Robert	*Financial Times*	National Security	★ ★ ★
Miller, Judith	*The New York Times*	Foreign Dispatch	★ ★ ★
Morrison, David	*National Journal*	National Security	★ ★ ★
Norman, Peter	*Financial Times*	Financial Dispatch	★ ★ ★
Norris, Floyd	*The New York Times*	Financial Dispatch	★ ★ ★
O'Brian, Bridget	*The Wall Street Journal*	Financial Dispatch	★ ★ ★
Opall, Barbara	*Defense News*	National Security	★ ★ ★
Ozanne, Julian	*Financial Times*	Foreign Dispatch	★ ★ ★

Pear, Robert	*The New York Times*	Domestic Reports	★ ★ ★
Peel, Quentin	*Financial Times*	Foreign Dispatch	★ ★ ★
Pollack, Andrew	*The New York Times*	Financial Dispatch	★ ★ ★
Polsky, Debra	*Defense News*	National Security	★ ★ ★
Postrel, Virginia	*Reason*	Commentary	★ ★ ★
Randal, Jonathan C.	*The Washington Post*	Foreign Dispatch	★ ★ ★
Reier, Sharon	*FW*	Foreign Dispatch	★ ★ ★
Reinhold, Robert	*The New York Times*	Domestic Reports	★ ★ ★
Remnick, David	*The Washington Post*	Forgein Dispatch	★ ★ ★
Roberts, Paul Craig	*The Washington Times*	Commentary	★ ★ ★
Salwen, Kevin G.	*The Wall Street Journal*	Financial Dispatch	★ ★ ★
Sawyer, Kathy	*The Washington Post*	National Security	★ ★ ★
Schlesigner, Jacob	*The Wall Street Journal*	Foreign Dispatch	★ ★ ★
Schmemann, Serge	*The New York Times*	Foreign Dispatch	★ ★ ★
Schrage, Michael	*Los Angeles Times*	Finanical Dispatch	★ ★ ★
Seib, Gerald	*The Wall Street Journal*	National Security	★ ★ ★
Seligman, Daniel	*Fortune*	Commentary	★ ★ ★
Shales, Tom	*The Washington Post*	Domestic Reports	★ ★ ★
Sikorski, Radek	*National Review*	Foreign Dispatch	★ ★ ★
Silverberg, David	*Defense News*	National Security	★ ★ ★
Sowell, Thomas	Scripps-Howard News Service	Commentary	★ ★ ★
Thomas, Paulette	*The Wall Street Journal*	Financial Dispatch	★ ★ ★
Tyler, Patrick E.	*The New York Times*	National Security	★ ★ ★
White, David	*Financial Times*	Naitonal Security	★ ★ ★
Williams, Daniel	*Los Angeles Times*	Foreign Dispatch	★ ★ ★
Zachary, G. Pascal	*The Wall Street Journal*	Financial Dispatch	★ ★ ★

JOURNALISTS

COMMENTATORS

Adelman, Kenneth. Tribune Media Services. (★ ★)
We've come to value the perceptive appraisals of defense and security issues from the former director of the Arms Control and Disarmament Agency. Although less effective out of his realm of expertise, it's apparent Adelman is becoming more comfortable with the work requirements of the pundit's mantle. Adelman rightfully lauds Dr. King Jordan, the deaf president of Gallaudet University, in "Putting Ability in Focus," *The Washington Times* 1-25, but Jordan sounds too good to be true in this one-dimensional profile. Smartly, Adelman is one of the first to give the credit to Ronald Reagan and his procurement and development programs with "Star Wars in the Desert," *Newsweek* 2-4. And he ably distills the anti-war views of a "Clergy Out of Touch," *WT* 3-4, over the Gulf War: "Nothing Iraq did in Kuwait — nothing militarily, none of its brutality, no burnings, no torture — merited a moral mention." In "How to Limit Everybody's Missiles," *The New York Times* 4-7, he calls for the expansion of the U.S.-Soviet INF Treaty "into a multilateral treaty that bans Scud-type missiles," arguing that it is "ludicrous that Iraq and North Korea can legally have Scud missiles while we and the Soviets cannot," and contending that verification can easily be done through a ban on missile flight tests. Adelman makes an effective case with "Served Best by Intuition?" *WT* 5-22, that " 'gut-feeling' or 'instinct' may be a better guide to good choice than. . .factors set down in words, analyzed and weighed," illustrating the point with sharp examples. He offers timely, astute commentary in "What's Getting in Gates' Way?" *WT* 7-10, on the fortunes of the nominee for CIA director, in which Adelman underscores two factors about Robert Gates that give context to the flurry of charges against him and the delay in his hearings: "He is less risk-averse and more strongly identified with presidential leadership. . .and. . .he is too much a master of the Executive Branch and too little intimidated by congressional titans." Adelman ponders the implications of "America's New Supremacy," *WT* 9-8, but concludes there will be few repercussions, a too-rosy scenario.

Ajami, Fouad. *U.S.News & World Report.* (★ ★)
Contributing editor. We saw less of Ajami in print as his duties as a consultant for CBS News increased exponentially with the start of hostilities in the Gulf. He's preferred in print, as he has the space to flesh out the bare bones of his broad conceptualizations. In "Innocents Abroad," 12-31-90/1-7-91, Ajami makes a persuasive case that no matter the outcome of the Iraq crisis, the U.S. is in the Middle East to stay. He raises some interesting points with "Into the Dangerous Twilight," 3-11, as he places the Gulf War in historical context, but he's long-winded at times. With "The Summer of Arab Discontent," *Foreign Affairs* Winter 1990/91, Ajami places the invasion of Kuwait in the context of Arab world politics and cogently observes the historical differences between the gulf states and the Arab states to the north. In "The Gods Must Be Angry," 6-24, Ajami, reporting on Kuwait's postwar security concerns, notes with irony that "Kuwait has been betrayed by the very gods it once sought to propitiate," such as Saddam Hussein and Arab nationalism. He offers a detached look at the rising tide of nationalism in central Europe, in "Tribal Fantasies in Europe," 7-8, noting the inherent contradiction of tribalism in the face of the formation of the unified EC trading bloc. His "The End of Arab Nationalism," *The New Republic* cover 8-12, on the rise and fall of Arab nationalism in the

postwar Middle East is part biography, part scholarly tract: "The kind of world men and women bumped into when they stepped out of the abstract texts of nationalism — the world of daily experience — was nowhere to be found in the works of the Arab nationalist historiography." We wish Ajami had drawn a sharper connection between the personal and the political, however. He ponders the role of the UN in "Where the Warrior Comes to Rest," 10-7, on how the historic developments in the world are affecting the institution: "The question which will now be asked is whether the United Nations will serve as a cover for American power, merely do our bidding and reflect our expectations." He precisely details the difficulties faced in America's efforts to jump-start the Middle East peace process in "The Stubborn Neighborhood," 11-4, a sober effort to end a year of tumultuous change in the region.

Baker, Russell. *The New York Times.* (★ ★ ½)
"Observer" columnist. Part of Baker's appeal is that he can be angry without being caustic or bitter, tempering his outrages with gentle humor. When not completely frivolous, he's quite effective. Uncharacteristically disoriented on the Pentagon, the press, and blurbs on book jackets in "Soft Soap Does the Trick," 1-29, he has nothing to tie this together. He is very funny on the downsizing of detergents from the filler-packed jumbo size to the streamlined concentrate, "Jumbo Was a Humbug," 2-5. In "We Rose Above Reality," 3-12, Baker offers a charming lesson in romance: "Strange as it now seems, 'romance' didn't even promise carnal gratification, which has been the main subject of the Top Forty ever since America became rich, fat and sporty. A fine romance his was, Fred Astaire sang ironically: it didn't even involve kisses." He is rapier sharp with "So Happy Down South," 4-16, as media attention turns from the Kurds to the alleged Palm Beach rape and the Nancy Reagan-Kitty Kelley bio. Smart on the Veep in "Making President Quayle," 5-7, Baker perceptively discovers why the press is so acrimonious: "He was so utterly average, in fact, that the press promptly turned him into a big joke, there being nothing the average American is quicker to laugh at than his own frailties, once they are disguised to look like somebody else's." Baker hits the bull's-eye again with "Scipio, to Hannibal," 6-25, a 10 Best selection for Commentary on what's wrong with multiculturalism: "As now taught, history is neither multicultural nor unicultural; it is nocultural. At a time when any teaching of it would be a step forward, we ought to be able to agree that while either the multicultural or unicultural stuff would be splendid, in the meantime we could use some anycultural history." By this time, we are not only nodding along, but quietly cheering. He offers cogent, amusing reasons as to why Bush shouldn't seek a second term in "Not Half Likely," 8-13. Baker effectively lampoons modern mores and manners by giving such classics as *Moby Dick* and *Anna Karenina* soap opera trimmings in "Life in Soapland," 9-24. And "Suggest and Destroy," 10-15, is strong on Anita Hill and Clarence Thomas, as Baker avoids taking a side, but focuses on the hearings, pointing out as a lawyer herself, Hill must have known what was coming.

Barnes, Fred. *The New Republic.* (★ ★ ★)
"White House Watch" columnist. With the rigors of '92 just around the corner, Barnes seemed to be pacing himself this year. While he is still essential reading, we found fewer unusual angles, fewer of the singular insights that we have appreciated as his trademark. In "Bush's Great Escape," *The American Spectator* 1-91, Barnes surveys the '90 elections and is one of the first to find voters sending Bush a message for '92 on domestic issues such as taxes and quotas. Gushy on the early stages of the Gulf War, "Finest Hour," 2-11, Barnes makes the hackneyed comparison of Bush to Churchill. He is original in noting here, though, that if things go badly, Bush's situation will be similar to Nixon's in '69, when Nixon decided against a rapid pullout from Vietnam despite mounting casualties and political unrest at home: "But Nixon was certain that abrupt retreat was wrong, just as Bush is sure that anything short of driving Saddam out of Kuwait is unsatisfactory." We've heard about "Dirty Secrets Behind the Budget Mess," *Reader's Digest* 2-91, ad infinitum; Barnes incorporates no new information. He recycles conventional wisdom that Saddam Hussein underestimated Bush in "The Unwimp," 3-18. He is harsh, but persuasive in "The Old Bush," 4-22, as the President goes "fuzzy" and indecisive yet again. In "Quayle Alert," 5-27, Barnes cogently assesses the Veep at the height of media

hysteria, including a rundown of Quayle's considerable influence on policy. He fleshes out the background of how "Bush has become the most forceful administration lobbyist on the civil rights bill," in "Uncivil War," 6-24, noting Bush's alternative and the Democratic bill aren't very different. His "Weirdo Alert," 8-5, a detailed examination of the Thomas nomination, contains little we haven't seen elsewhere. Barnes sounds like an old gossip in "All the President's Perks," cover 9-2, on how White House perks have proliferated since the Nixon administration, dropping several references to John Sununu. Barnes examines the politics, again, of the Civil Rights Act, "Off to the Races," *TAS* 10-91. He rounds out the year strongly with "The Slump Thing," cover 11-4, as he takes us inside the administration to capture the void at the center of domestic and economic policy. This discussion of the battle between the entrepreneurs, led by Jack Kemp, and corporativists John Sununu and Richard Darman, intensifying as the election year approaches with the economy still sluggish, was probably the best effort we saw from Barnes this year.

Barone, Michael. *U.S.News & World Report.* (★ ★ ½)
Senior editor. This former *Washington Post* editorial writer never broke stride in the transitions from columnist to reporter back to columnist again, always bringing effective, trenchant perspectives to issues of the day. When we read his column, we often wish he had more space to make his views known. Barone views the Persian Gulf War through a historical prism in "This Time, They're Heroes," 3-18, on the way Americans fight their wars and the effect it has on American society. He perceptively notes the pressure on minority districts in "Republican Jujitsu Against Liberals," 4-22, as the GOP presses voters to unseat several of the strongest Democratic backers of civil rights. In "To Be Young and Republican," 5-6, Barone points out the theory of political cycles may be in trouble because for the last decade, younger voters have turned Republican, finding the best explanation for that in the new book by William Strauss and Neil Howe, *Generations*: "These young Americans are looking not for redistribution or liberation but for order — a predictable, rational framework in which they can work to achieve their goals." He pungently examines the implications of moderate Democrats dropping from the '92 race and liberal Democrats preparing to enter in "Once Again, Democrats Swing Left," 7-1, and assesses the odds: "Some think that a populist appeal, with calls for economic redistribution and trade protectionism, can produce a majority. But there is precious little evidence for that in election results over the nearly two decades in which the income distribution has been growing less egalitarian." Barone draws an intriguing parallel in "Assessing the Clinton Factor," 8-12, musing on the possibility of a run by Arkansas Gov. Bill Clinton: "just as [Barry] Goldwater's victory, irrelevant for November, shaped future politics by expanding the Republican base among white Southerners and Northern ethnics, so a Clinton nomination, even if he loses, might expand the Democratic base among Southerners and young voters who are now heavily Republican." He argues that the Democrats can't rely on a sagging economy or minor scandals to defeat George Bush in "Happy Days Aren't Here Again," 10-7, as "most voters don't switch parties unless things go dreadfully wrong and unless the party in power fails to provide the first thing citizens demand from democratic government: the order and stability that give people room to lead their personal lives." But we already know that.

Barry, Dave. *The Miami Herald,* Tribune Media Services. (★ ½)
"Wit's End" columnist for *The Washington Post Magazine,* Barry is one reason to at least open it on Sunday morning. His irreverent columns careen wildly from subject to subject, like a ballistic missile run amok; sometimes he even manages to hit his targets. He misses the mark with "Why Not the Funniest," 1-6, as he declares his candidacy for president, announcing, among other improvements, that domestic agencies in his administration would be replaced by "the Department of Louise." Barry uproariously blows apart the fad of selling used jeans in "Cowboy Jockeys," 2-24: ". . .used cowboy jeans are selling briskly at $50 a pair in San Francisco and $65 a pair in New York. The ones with the holes are considered the most desirable. . .Here are two quotes about this trend. . .FROM THE OWNER OF A NEW YORK CITY STORE THAT SELLS THE JEANS: 'It gives a bit of romance.' FROM AN ACTUAL TEXAS

COWBOY: 'It sounds pretty stupid.' " Scattershot with "Mad Science," 3-10, he tepidly lists the weird things scientists do, such as reviving fleas after freezing them to minus 321 degrees. Southpaws will enjoy his adventures with right-handed implements from school desks to chain saws, "Dog Bless Lefties," 6-30, while agreeing with his debunking of the theory that lefties are another species. Vintage machine-gun Barry in "Body Heat," 7-7, he wickedly mulls the consequences of the baby boomers growing older, positing that when 50 million women experience menopause and hot flashes in 2010, the polar ice caps will melt. Barry deftly explains the general inability of men to make commitments in "Mr. Commitment," 8-25: "Guys are born with a fundamental, genetically transmitted mental condition known to psychologists as: The Fear That If You Get Married, Some Single Guy, Somewhere, Will Be Having More Fun Than You." His "Grass Menagerie," 10-20, is goofy but certainly atmospheric on the Arcola Broom Corn Festival, an event which celebrates the Illinois town's broom corn production, Barry poking fun at both himself and apple-pie America.

Beichman, Arnold. *The Washington Times.* (★)
Beichman once seemed to be forever frozen in Cold War rhetoric. We see some signs that he may be thawing out and examining events through a different prism, as with "How the Soviet Melon Bounces," 10-20, drawing on personal experience in the Soviet Union to dissect the food distribution system, or lack thereof. Similarly, "Forebears of New-but-Old Orthodoxy," 3-27, is fresh and one of the strongest essays we've read from Beichman, on political correctness on campus: "It is the era of McCarthyism of the left: Accusation becomes indictment becomes evidence becomes damnation." But much of the year he spent trooping Cold War colors. He warns that Boris Yeltsin may end up a Soviet Thomas Becket, in "Birthday Wish and Warning," 1-31; while this isn't exactly news, Beichman pulls this together well. In the pedestrian "Watching from the Sidelines," 2-13, he toots America's horn as Japan, Germany, China and the Soviet Union sit on the sidelines during the Persian Gulf War. He reminds us that the possibilities for other Chernobyl incidents still exist in the U.S.S.R., "Untold Chernobyl Fallout," 4-25, but Beichman only relies on the word of Univ. of Alberta professor David Marples, with a broader perspective needed. In "Power in Kremlin Shadows," 5-7, Beichman sees the KGB's hand in everything, but proves little. Similarly, in "No Lack of Funds for Fronts," 6-11, he darkly asserts that Gorbachev's begging the West for help is a partial result of a propaganda campaign supported by hard currency, part of the U.S.S.R.'s "active measures" program. In "Socialism's Residual Vapors," 7-3, Beichman sets up a Marxist straw man, Ishmael, to interview, but this device falls short. Beichman proffers a list of those who fought communism in the West, days after the Old Guard of the Soviet Union gave its last hurrahs in "Roster for the West," 9-2, but it seems somehow inappropriate to scramble for credit so soon.

Bethell, Tom. *The American Spectator.* (★ ½)
"Capitol Ideas" columnist. Bethell's restrained columns too often rely on established, inside-the-Beltway interpretations, offering little original conservative thinking. He is at his freshest outside D.C.'s city limits, as he then exercises his considerable talents as a reporter. Bethell's tempered, thoughtful account of his participation in a Stanford anti-war teach-in is the best we've seen from him in a long time, "Stanford, Angela, and Me," 3-91; he pokes fun at campus radicalism while sharing the radicals' anti-war sympathies. But he coasts too frequently. Bethell gives us no new insight in "Politics Misconstrued," 1-91, a conservative critique contending that "Bush seems to think that politics entails negotiating with known quantities in a private room rather than reaching out to an unknown, wider audience," and that this has brought him to ruin. In "Patriotism Doesn't Mean Mindlessness," *Los Angeles Times* 2-5, he begins and finishes quite credibly on the Persian Gulf War, but in the center he rambles about Gorbachev and the Soviet threat, typically conservative. "So, What Exactly Did We Win?" *LAT* 3-11, is conventional and annoyingly pontifical on the war, and how we "enjoyed" it. Bethell does a good job in getting a handle on SDI technology and making it understandable, "Star-Wars Wars," 4-91, but it sounds as though he hasn't been out of the laboratory in ages. Thoughtful with "Original Sin in the Promised Land," 6-91, Bethell praises the reporting and writing of Nicholas Lemann in

The Promised Land, using all the standard arguments to critique Lemann's traditional liberal big-government approach to the problem of poverty. In "Good as Gould," 8-91, Bethell doesn't conclusively establish his claims that evolutionists reformulate their theory to fit the fashionable liberal beliefs of the times. Bethell celebrates homosexuals who renounce the lifestyle and return to Christianity, in "Exodus," 10-91, but his blind acceptance of the theory that homosexuals are made, not born, seems simplistic; he even argues homosexuality can be "spread by proselytizers." He meanders in "The Center Folds," 11-91, attempting to draw a parallel between the decentralization of power in Moscow and the conservative dream of decentralization of government in Washington. Bethell then lapses into taking potshots at old targets.

Black, George. *The Nation.* (★ ★)
Foreign editor of *The Nation,* we see Black on the op-ed pages of the *Los Angeles Times* where he plies his trade with intellectual vigor, although he sometimes displays a distracting cynicism on U.S. policy abroad. Black chastises the media for demanding hard data rather than broadening the inquiry into the questions of morality during the Gulf War, scoring effective points with "Rolodex Army Wages a Nintendo War," 1-27. In "Just How Far Is Bush Prepared to Go in War?" 2-17, Black tries to make the case that the possibility of the use of nuclear weapons in the Gulf exists, but so much hangs on dubious research, such as polls, that he lacks credibility. Rabidly misanthropic in "Forget Ideals; Just Give Us a Punching Bag," 3-3, he emphasizes how quickly any pretense of "defending democracy" was dropped from the Gulf War, sharply critiquing what he perceives as the content of Bush's New World Order — "America kicks butt." In the superlative "Why Bush Wants Hussein Kept in Power," 3-17, Black acknowledges he was wrong on the variables of U.S. casualties and sanctions, but he comes back with trenchant exposition of where he and other critics of the Gulf War were not off the mark: "all the talk of 'just wars' and 'new world orders' cloaked less savory forms of self-interest. . .The Iraqi opposition groups understand quite well that the lives of thousands of their followers have been sacrificed on the altar of *Realpolitik.*" Cuba might be the next target of "those disgruntled conservatives," Black warns in "Are Jingoists Savoring Next Morsel?" 4-22, but he isn't persuasive. He highlights the dichotomy well between "Rich and Poor, Under the Volcano," 6-24, a compelling juxtaposition of the poor Filipinos who died and the Americans at Clark and Subic bases nearby who escaped the eruption of Mt. Pinatubo. In "Why Bring Dirty Old Ways to New World?" 9-16, Black begins by drawing a strong parallel between the CIA and the KGB and how they might fit into a post-Cold War world, but descends into a standard discussion of Gates and Iran-contra allegations. He effectively links 17th-century white settlers in Connecticut to the Canadian Hydro-Quebec project, as both took resources from the Indians, "Indian Lands, White Man's Real Estate," 10-13; although Black takes a while to get to his point, it is worth the effort.

Blumenthal, Sidney. *The New Republic.* (★ ★ ★)
Senior editor. Always offbeat and influential, Blumenthal's columns offer the same spice that permeated the "Style" pages of *The Washington Post.* His views of the political scene are sharply defined, with well-chosen topics, although he can tend toward the acerbic, as with "Bull Mouse," 1-7/1-14, a pungent examination of Bush's emulation of Teddy Roosevelt. More restrained with "The Mystique of Sam Nunn," 3-4, he places Nunn firmly in the tradition of Southern politicians Carl Vinson and Richard Russell, noting that Nunn drew on Russell's early doubts about Vietnam for his Gulf policy. Blumenthal examines thoroughly Bush's tendency to define himself through the Persian Gulf War, while refusing to address domestic concerns in "Don't Look Down," 4-15. He grasps the importance of Mario in "Cuomo Vadis?" 5-6: "It is a parochial — but electorally significant — truth that Cuomo *is* the angry middle-class homeowner to whom the Republicans have pitched their appeal since the days of Richard Nixon." He drips acid in "Claiborne Pell's Twilight Zone," 6-10, a marvelously savage profile of Pell, trouncing him for allowing the Foreign Relations Committee's dwindling influence and for his interest in the "spectral." Equally barbed in "The Genius," 7-29, Blumenthal sets his sights on John Sununu, insightfully identifying his tragic flaw as the "overheated desire" to be a member of the WASP

establishment, a la Sherman Adams and George Bush. He looks over the paper trail left by April Glaspie, "April's Bluff," 8-5, noting discrepancies between her now-famous cable to Washington following her meeting with Saddam Hussein and her subsequent testimony before the Senate Foreign Relations Committee, concluding that "the cable suggests that Glaspie willfully misled the Senate — and that the administration let her brazen distortions stand for their own reasons." But Blumenthal can't uncover those reasons. In "The Half-President," 9-30, he is at his best, comparing Bush to a French president who mingles with other heads of state, leaving the domestic " 'housekeeping' to a premier. But there is no U.S. premier." Blumenthal wraps up the year with "The Drifter," cover 11-4, a political obituary for Bush, with the stagnating economy and the rise of the social right merely more nails in the coffin. Much of this argument has been made before, but this is as complete a package on the topic as we have seen. Good job, Sidney!

Broder, David. *The Washington Post.* (★ ★ ½)

We continue to follow faithfully the work of the long-standing dean of the political press corps. There's no one better at handicapping the national elections, once they get going, but during the off years, when Broder sits inside the Beltway, he too often lacks the insight we've admired. In "How to Fix Congress — Advice From the Alumni," 1-6, Broder surveys former congressional leaders who recommend financing reforms, but he doesn't inquire why the gentlemen failed to act on reform while in office. He offers an unusual perspective with "Who's the Fairest of Them All," 2-13, pegging Dick Darman and Barney Frank as two of the best minds in Washington, despite their antithetical budget outlooks. In "Think Again, Democrats," 3-6, Broder makes an effective call to Democratic leaders in Congress to put their opposition to U.S. force overseas behind them so they can present a credible alternative to Bush's New World Order and "rejoin the national debate." He sees the potential for political realignment in "Bush Could Take the Hill, Too. . ." 4-7, a smart perspective citing Quayle's view that the '92 model should be the 1980 Reagan campaign. But with "Bogus Campaign Finance Reforms," 6-2, it takes us two readings to discern that Broder is fretting that congressional Democrats are passing yet another law to narrow competition. Broder further reveals his limitations in "Is Rockefeller Ready?" 7-21, where we learn only that Jay Rockefeller is toying with a balanced budget amendment, and that "The publicity burst has caused him to advance his presidential time table from 1996 to 1992." He ponders the lingering effect of "Reaganomics — Political Magic for Republicans," 8-11, thoughtful on the 10th anniversary of the Reagan tax reform: "However mixed the economic results, Reaganomics has been a political ten-strike for the Republicans." In "Who Needs Conventions?" 9-4, Broder convincingly sees the waning influence of the party conventions as limiting the democratic process, as the candidate is chosen long before. "Cuomo: Just a Mirage?" 10-23, is very astute on the shortcomings of Mario, with Broder predicting early that Cuomo will not solve the problems of the Democrats, even if he should run. A disappointing year.

Buchanan, Patrick. Tribune Media Services. (★ ★ ★)

Now officially a presidential candidate, Buchanan's fiery rhetoric leaves little surviving its path, from politicians to fellow columnists. From his *Washington Times* "Commentary" slot, he follows a scorched-earth policy with passionate, persuasive volleys that are undeniably effective. In "Who Keeps the Peace?" 1-14, Buchanan is convincing, arguing the aftermath of a Gulf War could be worse than the current situation. Still dovish with "Raising the Gulf Stakes?" 2-20, he warns against ground war, with a superlative summation: "Where we saw a desert despot making a conventional land grab, Mr. Bush saw a Hitler seizing the Sudetenland. As with Capt. Ahab in his pursuit of Moby Dick, conviction has given Mr. Bush an iron resolve that is remarkable in a man his enemies used to call a 'wimp.' " In "Collision Course?" 3-13, Buchanan prompts more sadness than anger about the sources of hatred between Israelis and Palestinians, the list of grievances for both casting a forlorn shadow over the region. With gusto, Buchanan revises the Hollywood revisionists of the fifties saying the Hollywood Ten got what they deserved, and less, in "A '50 Lens Out of Focus," 4-12. "Crackup of the Conservatives," 5-1, is hyperactive, even for Buchanan, as he castigates the neo-cons: "Like the fleas who conclude they are steering the dog, the neo-con's relationship to the movement has always been parasitical." In "How the

Driving Game Is Played," 6-24, he is politically insightful on why "there's blood in the water" regarding John Sununu, putting the blame on an unfed press coupled with Sununu's chronic "pressbaiting." Buchanan addresses the accusation that Churchill withheld news of the impending Japanese attack in order to guarantee U.S. entry into WWII, in "Advance Warning of Pearl Harbor?" 8-14, this troubling column softened only by John Toland, who says the facts are correct but the conclusions incorrect and that Churchill surely would have warned FDR. His neo-isolationist bent is evident in "Now That Red Is Dead, Come Home, America," *The Washington Post* 9-8, as Buchanan aligns himself with William Hyland and Scotty Reston. Despite the dichotomy, there's no denying he has the courage of his convictions, as always. Buchanan lines up squarely for Thomas in "An Objective Secured. . ." *WT* 10-21, surprisingly celebrating the process in the Clarence Thomas-Anita Hill fiasco, as only conflict can bring us to democratic consensus.

Buchwald, Art. Los Angeles Times Syndicate. (★)
Buchwald continues on his merry way, fabricating witty dialogue on current events in his attempts to tickle our fancy. He always brings a smile, but rarely the belly laugh that's clearly his goal. We're not sure we've got the point in "Retirement Game Lacks the Players," *Los Angeles Times* 1-22, as Buchwald strikes up a conversation between himself and a retiree, as all their free time weighs on the minds of retirees until they go mad with boredom. "Strategies for Fighting That Wimp Image," *LAT* 3-12, is fluffy stuff on how politicians against the war might combat the "wimp" factor. Buchwald hilariously goes shopping for a used S&L in "Kicking Tires at the Used S & L Lot," *The Washington Post* 4-11, discovering the government has hired used car salesmen to sell the S&Ls off at "Crazy Sam's Savings and Loan Lot" in Rockville: " 'We have some unbelievable buys on 1987 and 1989 savings and loans. Here's a sporty little thrift model. It's hardly been used because the owner is doing 10 years in San Quentin. You can open it up for business tomorrow morning.' " Silly on John Sununu's travel troubles, "Special Restrictions May Apply in Less Friendly Skies," *LAT* 5-14, Buchwald describes what Sununu might have to go through at the ticket counter when flying commercial. Pointed with "Willie or Won't He?" *WP* 6-13, he envisions GOP operatives visiting the Maryland Penitentiary and trying to convince a reluctant Willie Horton to run again in 1992: " 'Willie, you're facing one 85-year sentence and two life sentences. It isn't going to hurt you to be part of the '92 election. We can't promise, but we wouldn't be surprised if another seat opens up on the Supreme Court.' "

Buckley, William F., Jr. *National Review,* Universal Press Syndicate. (★ ½)
The conservatives' conservative, Buckley's essays can tend to the esoteric and serpentine, thickly conceived and executed. Buckley is impenetrable in "Year of the Protectionists," *The Washington Post* 1-2, densely arguing against agricultural subsidies. "Some Things Are Better Left Unsaid," *Los Angeles Times* 2-3, is more clearly written but flawed on Section 211 of Executive Order 12333, which prohibits the assassination of heads of foreign states by U.S. government employees. Buckley seems to be saying here that it's okay if America does it, but not if we get caught. He gives a good rundown in "Vietnam and Desert Storm," *National Review* 2-25, of the differences between the two to blast the hypothesis that by using military force the U.S. is "courting" yet another Vietnam: "To compare the two is the equivalent of comparing the Grand Canyon and Niagara Falls. They are both military engagements, as the two sites are great natural phenomena. Beyond that, they are — as night, to day." Buckley softpedals the obtuse language in "Get Saddam Hussein," *NR* 5-27, drawing on scholarly discussions of the Nuremberg trials to argue that the international community *does* have the right to go after Hussein. "The Quayle Bit," *NR* 6-10, is a lively defense of Quayle: "The entire press corps is playing Kitty Kelley to Dan Quayle." He defends the White House decision to keep John Sununu more prosaically, "In Re Sununu," *NR* 7-29, through which we yawned. Surprisingly, Buckley is only able to give two cheers for "Democracy — A Cure-All?" 8-12, finding it inefficient and expressing an almost nostalgic attraction to such strongmen as Franco and Pinochet. He celebrates the end of communism in "We Won," 9-23, a special "Notes & Asides"

column on *NR*'s historic commitment to total victory over Communism, even in the face of setbacks and missed opportunities. Apparently shocked by the "60 Minutes" segment on the availability of handguns to kids, Buckley argues trenchantly for handgun restriction, in "Guns and Children," *NR* 10-21, putting things in rare point-blank style: "progress isn't being made when children can buy a gun for one hundred dollars."

Chapman, Stephen. *Chicago Tribune,* Creators Syndicate. (★ ½)
Chapman's libertarian perspectives are gaining in sophistication and effectiveness, although he is infrequently original or cerebral. Chapman argues that the new federal budget is anything but austere, "Austerity Nowhere on the Bill of Fare," *The Washington Times* 2-15: "In Mr. Bush's first two years, outlays rose in every category of federal action — agriculture, education, the environment, transportation, you name it," additionally noting Bush has not vetoed a spending bill nor has he ended any federal programs, no matter how superfluous. He argues that the Poles should only have to give back 40 percent of the debt accumulated during the communist era, a la post-war Germany, "Collectors at Poland's Door," *WT* 3-14, an interesting idea, phrased poorly. In "Liberty Up in Smoke?" *WT* 4-1, Chapman defends smokers and tobacco companies, taking the libertarian stance that smokers know the dangers and have a right to smoke as tobacco companies have a right to supply the cigarettes. "Credit Report: Friend or Foe?" *WT* 6-10, is solid on how credit reports may actually facilitate lending, rather than restrict it: "These reports have proliferated because they allow lending transactions between enormous numbers of people who have never met or done business with one another." In "To Help the Jobless Without Added Cost," *WT* 8-6, Chapman gets out the message of Univ. of Chicago economist Robert Topel, who argues that unemployment benefits would be better apportioned if they were extended past six months, but only after a waiting period of one month (the current waiting period is one week). Chapman doesn't give us enough financial detail, but the common sense aspect of this appeals to us, as someone out of work for six months is almost surely to be in more desperate straits than someone unemployed a week. He chides the Univ. of Alabama for putting a muzzle on a professor because of his religion, "Clash of Faith and Academia," *WT* 9-17, trenchantly asserting "the fact that (Professor) Bishop expresses admiration for Jesus Christ rather than Bear Bryant doesn't bring him into conflict with the U.S. Constitution."

Charen, Mona. Creators Syndicate. (★ ★ ½)
Getting stronger after a few years of trial-and-error punditry, Charen culls possibilities and solutions creatively out of the mire of national and international policy, moving beyond the conventionality we'd noted last year. With "Fog of Mideast Fantasy," *The Washington Times* 1-29, she sees the potential early for a peaceful Palestinian settlement, smartly arguing the problem must be clearly viewed before it can be solved. In "Dangerous Liaisons With Despots," *WT* 2-12, Charen takes *The New York Times* report that Baker betrayed agents in Syria's terrorist network, and blasts Bush for allowing Syria and Hafez al-Assad into the coalition, but she omits too much detail to keep our undivided attention. She is insightful on the Presbyterian committee report on sex, "Sexing Up Their Faith?" *WT* 4-25: "The churches make a fatal error when they assume that in order to staunch the hemorrhaging of members. . .they must sex up their message. . .Why do we need Presbyterian advice on 'Christian sexuality' when we've already got the Playboy philosopher?" She postulates importantly in a semi-defense of Ted Kennedy, "Liberal, Sexist or Both," *WT* 6-20, that "Liberalism has been a bad bargain for women. With indispensable aid from feminists, liberals tossed away the old traditions of chivalry and respect. They promised equality instead. The equality is still pending — the respect may be gone forever." She expands on this theme after the Anita Hill-Clarence Thomas debacle in "Harvesting What Was Seeded," 10-20, but Charen never quite gets to the heart of her thesis of how the feminists helped to create the problem of sexual harassment. In "When Roe Goes," *WT* 7-3, Charen is perceptive on turning over abortion to the states, rather than leaving it to the Supreme Court, welcoming the debate: "It won't be the stale old 'baby killers' vs. 'religious fanatics' slugfest, but rather a more subtle examination of the kind of abortion laws we can live with as a nation." In "On Judging the Judge," *WT* 9-8, she questions the timing, not the accuracy, of conservative ads attacking three liberal senators on the Senate Judiciary Committee. Conservatives should let the left throw the first punch, says she.

Chase, Alston. *The Washington Times.* (★ ½)
Chase's reporting and interpretive skills seem superficial and facile next to the erudite polish of Warren Brookes, particularly as he appears to have lost his anchor on environmental issues this year. In "Bagged and Bundled for 1991: Vanishing Species," 1-1, Chase is simplistic and goofy on the hope that the New Year would bring a resurgence of the Golden Rule. He meanders in "Eco-Terrorism of Bygone Battles," 2-4, less about the ecological implications of the oil spilling into the Gulf than the hellishness of war in general. We find adequate reporting in "Spinning a Big Green Marble," 3-28, on the changing face of the environmental movement, as the green wave goes global. Similarly, in "Reward for Park Misdeeds," 4-16, Chase reports on the National Park Service boondoggle over its budget allocation for the National Natural Landmarks program, asking Congress for a tenfold increase, but Chase offers no solution except for the obvious: "NPS must first clean house, and be more honest with both public and Congress." He draws a strong parallel between the political misconceptions of the Germanys, from fascist to communist, to the charting of "our course through upcoming environmental debates," and we are intrigued, "Deadly Power of Bad Ideas," 6-11. Chase is scathing on Ted Turner and his decision to house bison rather than cattle on his Montana ranch, distractingly so, in "Bovine Scatology From Tender Ted," 8-13. Chase argues convincingly rather that it is man who has mismanaged the animals and the land, advising trenchantly that environmentalists ought to address the water problems in the west, but he can't overcome the nasty lead. And in "Putting the Mind Before the Land," 9-30, Chase's central argument that we must educate people to treat the land with respect is sound enough, but his organization is poor. An off year.

Cockburn, Alexander. *The Nation, In These Times.* (★)
A terrible year for one of our favorite polemicists of yore, Cockburn's refusal to reassess his own perspectives in the wake of the complete implosion of the communist ideology has rendered his "Beat the Devil" columns in *The Nation* and "Ashes & Diamonds" columns in *In These Times* sterile and nearly inarticulate. In his final column for *The Wall Street Journal,* "In Parting: Disasters I Feared Are Coming Horribly True," 1-17, Cockburn loses all sense of decorum as he berates the idea of a Gulf War and the opinions expressed on the *WSJ*'s pages. He is savagely illogical on Eduard Shevardnadze, "Ashes & Diamonds," 1-16/22, acrimonious without building a strong case, calling Shevardnadze "a compliant equerry" to James Baker, among other things. With "The Press and the 'Just War,' " *TN* 2-18, Cockburn pompously informs us there is no just war. In "Bush & P.C. — A Conspiracy So Immense. . ." *TN* 5-27, he rants about the new McCarthyism. Cockburn begins calmly in "Solidarity Against the Law in America," *ITT* 6/26-7/9, a discussion of the bill to make it illegal for companies to hire permanent replacements, but he begins to whine about the media coverage of labor, turning apoplectic: "News teams *were* covering a miners' strike that year — in the Soviet Union. Moral: if you want to win a strike, get backing from members of Congress and plenty of sympathetic play in the press, best do it in Eastern Europe or the Soviet Union, where the price of freedom isn't going to come out of an American capitalist's pocket." We get yet more of Cockburn's ruminations in "Beat the Devil," 7-29/8-5, on nationalism and forced emigration in Yugoslavia: "It's enough to make one yearn for the Austro-Hungarian Empire, which did impose upon large portions of Middle Europe some kind of transnational respect for minorities, as did the Communists in the postwar period now concluded." In "Beat the Devil," 9-9, Cockburn reviles the incompetence of the coup planners, decrying their lack of strategy and bringing in the Salomon T-bill scandal to show what kind of world Yeltsin 'aspires' to, plainly unhappy at the failure of communism to reassert itself. Cockburn's understated tone serves him well in "Ashes & Diamonds," 10/16-22, surprisingly muted on Clarence Thomas, Anita Hill, and the nomination. He finally scores some points on the laxity of the Senate Judiciary Committee. C'mon Alex, get it together.

Cohen, Richard. *The Washington Post.* (★ ★)
Cohen no longer subjects his readers to constant personal odysseys of self-examination and discovery, returning more frequently to the political realm, where he seems refreshingly original after several so-so years. Just back from Baghdad, he admits his natural dovish tendency, in

"Faces of Baghdad," 1-18, but comes to a surprising conclusion on Hussein's brutality: "Maybe there is no such thing as a good war, but this one, given Saddam's nature, comes close." He offers a forceful, critical assessment in "Israel: The Bitter Fruit of Occupation," 2-8, on Shamir's decision to welcome into the ruling coalition a political party that calls for the transfer of Arabs out of the West Bank. Cohen is forthright in his critical appraisal of the Brady Bill in "Handgun Madness," 4-3: "The main cause of the handgun problem, the unequivocal right of most Americans to buy a pistol, would not be changed by this bill." He makes a good point amid all the chaff in "Surveying Rape," 5-19: "Rape, including date rape, is both a serious problem and a serious issue. . .But if rape is defined so broadly that huge numbers of men and women find themselves portrayed as rapists or rape victims, the truly awful nature of the crime will be vitiated and no one will benefit." In "More Important Than Race," 8-6, Cohen discusses the NAACP decision not to support Thomas, his review of affirmative action taking a different twist: "The NAACP, unlike the Urban League, was able to look past Thomas's race and concentrate instead on other qualities — in this case, ideology. For that decision, in historical terms as tough as they come, it ought to be congratulated. But the organization should apply the same principal to affirmative action: to judge a person not by his or her race, but by other factors — especially economic need." Cohen asserts persuasively in "A New Kremlin Role," 9-3, that the Kremlin could still play a vital role in forestalling the potential ethnic violence that could erupt as resources become scarce. He still incorporates the sensitive male into his columns, however. Cohen meanders through a discourse on "Life After Death," 7-7, admitting he doesn't want to die. And he gets up close and personal in "Cry for Silence," 10-20, arguing we should only cry when we feel like it. Manufactured emotions are never healthy, but he doesn't express himself very well here.

Crovitz, L. Gordon. *The Wall Street Journal.* (★ ★ ★ ★)
"Rule of Law" columnist. Crovitz's elegant discourses on legal matters involving finance and business are brilliantly conceived and outstandingly argued. There's no one quite like him in American journalism. He projects provocative implications well beyond the issues at hand with an intellectual vigor unique to the *Journal*'s languishing page. "Coming to America: The End of Contracts," 1-9, is an eloquent discussion of the peril of Judge Schneider "invalidating" Paramount's contract with Art Buchwald: "If we are going to let judges rewrite contracts as they see fit, no supposedly legally binding agreement will give any assurance to either side that their bargain means anything." The subsequent reversals of Wall Street sentences make Crovitz's appraisal in "Milken Prosecution: The Rise and Fall of Allegations," 2-27, even more impressive: "Claims that Mr. Milken somehow defrauded investors are a disappearing act worthy of a three-ring circus. The disproportionality of $318,082 is the hardest evidence yet that U.S. v. Milken had more to do with a political and selective prosecution of the 'junk bond, takeover king' than any alleged crime the symbol committed." He follows up later with "Even a Junk Lawsuit Can Separate Villains From Phantoms," 5-29, a brilliant dismantling of the government case against junk bonds. Crovitz systematically dissects the California ruling that threatens the Political Reform Act of 1990, "Lawmakers Sue for Their Jobs — Another Reason for Term Limits," 6-19, his precise logic making the ruling ridiculous. "Lawyers Seek Senators as Advocates Against Quayle Reforms," 9-18, is a marvelous examination of how contingency lawyers are financing liberal Democratic campaigns to prevent reform advanced by the Veep. "Congress May Regret Trying to Bork Justice Thomas," 10-16, is Crovitz at his best, a 10 Best selection for Commentary: "The ghost of King Henry VIII must have had a chuckle watching the latest use of the anti-legal process he invented to skewer political opponents, the Bill of Attainder. The Senate Judiciary Committe effectively issued a Bill of Attainder against Clarence Thomas by charging him with a crime while denying him any criminal procedure to disprove the claim. The Constitution prohibits legislators from using this ploy to brand a political opponent a criminal, but what's a constitutional right to the senators who were desperate to block Justice Clarence Thomas?"

Eastland, Terry. *The American Spectator.* (★ ★)
"Presswatch" columnist. His evaluations of the press in *TAS* are generally acceptable, written from a conservative and critical view. His freelance op-eds are more satisfying, more provocative. "The Sunday Soaps," 1-91, is an adequate review of the Sunday talk shows. Eastland argues more effectively that the press missed the big story of the Gulf War, that of the enlargement of presidential powers under the skillful hands of Bush, "The Power Executive," 5-91, an interesting premise, although the argument displays a weak grasp of the Constitution and traditional conservative skepticism toward executive power. In "Title VII Upended," *The Washington Times* 6-5, a very competent treatment, he tells us of how pro-quota laws are being made via agency and judicial rulings, making the valid point that despite "the President's vow last year to sign a civil rights bill but not a quota bill. . .his own bill. . .is a quota bill." Perceptive with "Bush and the Politics of Race," *The New York Times* 7-3, on the Clarence Thomas nomination, Eastland observes that with Thomas, Bush has found a judge likely to be difficult to oppose while avoiding the appearance of creating a racial quota on the Court. He criticizes NBC News president Michael Gartner and his printing the name of the alleged victim in the Palm Beach scandal, forcefully dissecting Gartner's reasoning in "Against Her Will," 7-91. In "Commander Woodward," 8-91, Eastland does an effective job of cutting through some of the hype surrounding Bob Woodward's book *The Commanders* in *The Washington Post* and *Newsweek,* passing along secondhand information that the book was 80 percent accurate, but we're not likely to ever know which 80 percent. He provides cogent analysis of the media coverage of Thurgood Marshall's resignation and Clarence Thomas' nomination in "Thomas Linked to Marshall," cover 10-91, adroitly listing the stories the press has overlooked or ignored, particularly that of ideological diversity within the black community.

Evans, Rowland & Novak, Robert. *Chicago Sun-Times,* Creators Syndicate. (★ ★ ★ ★)
The dynamic duo has weathered all manner of events in the political arena, and, now that communism has had its final death knell, it can be safely said the pair has seen and covered everything of public policy importance in the past quarter-century or so. Their experience and powers of interpretation make them invaluable political observers. This trait is particularly evident in the acute "Judicial Armageddon," *The Washington Post* 7-1, a 10 Best selection for Commentary. The pair is cautionary on the potential for a protracted ground war, painstakingly citing different materiel canceled which might have been of use, "Intimations of a Long War," *WP* 1-25. Smart in "Democrats and The Mexico Trap," *WP* 4-15, the pair adroitly asserts that the Democrats run the serious risk of alienating Mexican-American voters as the party opposes the free-trade agreement due to its marriage to U.S. labor: "To assume that Mexican Americans are as disconnected from their mother country as African Americans are from their ancestral lands could be a disastrous political miscalculation." "Operation Money Storm," *WP* 5-13, is important, as the team confirms the jawboning carried out by Nick Brady on two Fed governors to bend their vote in favor of easing. They challenge the conventional assessment that recovery is on the way, "What Recovery?" *WP* 5-31, highlighting the serious capital shortage problem caused by regulatory excesses: "it is a rule of thumb now that an entrepreneur must come up with a half million dollars in cold cash to borrow a million." It's in "Sununu Bashed," *WP* 6-24, that we learn Sununu thinks he is a victim of a media vendetta, aided and abetted by a coalition of forces who are opposed to his right-wing views and, he believes, "because he is a second-generation Lebanese-American who is not fully supportive of Israel's demands on the United States." The pair is the first to sense the ominous implications of "Gorbachev's Waning Powers," *WP* 8-2, citing a pro-Russian, anti-Gorbachev letter from the hard-line *Sovietskaya Rossiya* and signed by Deputy Defense Minister Valentin Varennikov and Deputy Interior Minister Boris Gromov, among others: "Their cry came dramatically close to suggesting assassination or a military takeover." And in "Low-Growth George," *WP* 10-7, the pair spare no one in calling to account the White House for the slow growth of the economy, identifying the villainous triumverate of Darman, Brady and Sununu, who now stand in the way of even a "modest" growth package offered by Sen. Phil Gramm (R-Tex.) and Rep. Newt Gingrich (R-Ga.).

Fields, Suzanne. *The Washington Times,* Los Angeles Times Syndicate. (★ ★ ★)
A staunch, unyielding conservative, Fields pushes against the flaws of liberal social policy until it gives. In "Trying to Save Teens From Themselves," 1-3, she makes a very effective argument that quick-fix solutions aren't the answer, but provides no alternatives to the stopgap measures she derides. With "Faces Absent from the Crowd," 3-21, Fields states unequivocally and persuasively that a culture of character is desperately needed against the epidemic of violent deaths rooted in the breakdown of the traditional family: "Middle-class sophisticates smugly mock the nuclear family with a father who knows best and a mother who is home after school, but it's precisely the absence of this nuclear family and its moral certitudes, handed down generation to generation, that has bred a generation of young people who have no respect for any experience beyond their own streets, and often not much for that." In "Taking a Leap of Umbilical Fantasy," 5-21, Fields persuades that, despite equal rights myths and the parental leave package, it is more important for mothers to stay with children than fathers. She draws her own precise line in the sand with "The Drums of Equality," 6-4, opposing allowing women in combat. Later, in "Hasty Gender Surrender?" 9-23, Fields misses a golden opportunity to point out the contradiction of feminists wanting women to be able to serve in combat but not wanting mommies shipped off to war. Fields sensibly advocates a time period for evaluating second thoughts in this standard report. In "Are the Cub Scouts Ready for Margo?" 7-2, she proffers a lyrical argument against courts litigating the Scouts as the first female sues to join: "One of the pleasures of growing up is the unabashed pleasure a child can take in the company of children of the same sex. . ..(Today we call it 'bonding,' but we used to call it friendship.) Must the courts make such things difficult, if not impossible?" Instead of running a victory column for Clarence Thomas, Fields submits the column she would have run if he'd been defeated, "But What If?" 10-21, cogently and correctly identifying the implications of his loss: The new morality that defeated him "is driven by the secular concerns of feminism and what is 'politically correct,' the rigid public orthodoxy that decrees that only one way of looking at things is tolerated in the interests of achieving 'justice for all.' "

Fleming, Thomas. *Chronicles.* (★ ★ ★)
Editor. Fleming's fertile mind and elegant prose carry us through his complicated, challenging dissertations on political and social issues. His writing has been honed to a finer edge than in earlier years. In the delightful "Divorce — Italian Style," 1-91, a 10 Best nomination, Fleming discovers that the local spirit of the old Italian republics is still alive, a rich picture of Italy rarely viewed outside the country. Fleming is a regular combatant in the battles within the conservative movement, delivering bare-knuckled blows to the neo-cons in "The New Fusionism," 5-91: "We don't need to reform the nation; we need to take it back from the occupying army of government officials and managers and interest groups that treat the citizenry like a conquered army." He combines the populism of radical Jeffersonianism with the aristocratic distaste for equality of John Randolph, in "America Through the Looking Glass," 6-91, acute in his perception of the battle between corporativism and populism as the central policy focus for the rest of the century. Fleming forthrightly maintains that "The Big Lie of modern American life is that the assimilation process worked. It didn't," in a spirited and thought-provoking "The Broken Promise of Ellis Island," 7-91, using his sharp polemical skills to debunk the myth of the Melting Pot. We came away from "Science Fictions," 8-91, with a new insight on dystopian literature, which we dislike because it seemed to simply purvey Malthusianism. Fleming forces us to consider it from another angle: "In a society poisoning itself on dishonesty," these kinds of "fiction and films may be the only means we have of considering the social and moral diseases that we are inflicting upon ourselves. They are inherently anarchic and prepare the mind for rebellion against an oppressive system." And with "America, From Republic to Ant Farm," 10-91, he provides intellectual discourse of how population growth has contributed to the rise of the state, and how unlimited growth has not only its drawbacks, but a "labyrinth" of dangers, to which he provides some radical solutions, including a cessation of aid, both international and domestic — welfare — to allow population growth to expand more in proportion to available resources.

Francis, Samuel. *The Washington Times, Chronicles.* (★ ★)
National and cultural affairs columnist for the *Times* and "Principalities & Powers" columnist for *Chronicles*. One of the many journalists matriculated from a government post, he quickly established himself as a force. He can be, however, rhetorically excessive where he would be better served by finesse. Francis correctly perceives the fundamental social and political conflict as "between elite and non-elite," "Principalities & Powers," 1-91, building a case for the formulation of a new polemic, but he sounds a bit too much an ideologue. "Traditional American conservative defensive strategy is no longer practicable," Francis announces in his "P&P," 3-91, but he sounds more like a revolutionary than a polemicist, and we turn the page. More focused in a bitter, fiery "Beautiful Losers," *Chronicles* 5-91, he scathingly assesses the failure of conservatism: "Not only has the American right lost on such fundamental issues as the fusion of state and economy, the size and scope of government, the globalist course of American foreign policy, the transformation of the *Constitution* into a meaningless document that serves the special interests of whatever faction can grab it for awhile, and the replacement of what is generally called 'traditional morality' by a dominant ethic of constant gratification, but also the mainstream of those who today are pleased to call themselves conservatives has come to accept the premises and often the full-blown agenda of the left." Too sectarian in "Better to Turn Out the Lights," *WT* 6-7, he suggests that the conservatives' flutter over the nomination of Carol Iannone to the National Humanities Council is perhaps misplaced, but he does not convince. He develops an effective defense of sovereignty in "Found in G-7's Fine Print," *WT* 7-23, cogently warning against the G-7's enlarging U.N. power: "if we can intervene in the internal affairs of other nations. . .why can't others intervene in our affairs when they claim we fail to live up to the standards they demand?" He incisively takes up the issue of the battles over classical Republicanism in his compelling "P&P" columns, 8-91, 9-91, declaring "the American Republic is defunct," proceeding to define the principal issues in American politics today.

Gaffney, Frank. Freelance. (★ ★)
The director of the Center for Security Policy and former Reaganaut identifies with clarity the subtle shifts in policy and direction that might otherwise go unobserved. In a sharp appraisal of Reagan's 'Peace Through Strength' policy, Gaffney provides a delightfully wry lead to "Credit Where Credit Is Due," *The Washington Times* 1-29, noting that "so feverish have become the recent paternity claims and counterclaims by former government officials over who deserves credit for the technological wizardry exhibited in Operation Desert Storm's opening hours that nothing short of genetic testing seems likely to resolve the matter." With "Will U.S. Unilaterally Disarm?" *WT* 3-4, he sounds a Cassandra-like warning that, with budget reductions and arms control pacts, the U.S. is now engaging in unilateral disarmament, but assembles serious supporting evidence. He focused in "Trying to Put Moscow on the Dole," *WT* 5-7, identifying the pernicious content of the "insidious resolution" by Sen. Robert Dole (R-Kan.), recommending the President approve Moscow's request for more agricultural credits, but we lose interest as he outlines a laundry list of proposed conditions. Gaffney catches the minute, important shift on Star Wars with "A Tilt That Could Kill SDI?" *WT* 7-1, warning that without the kind of commitment to SDI that the B-2 had from the President, the U.S. remains vulnerable. He develops a credible critique of the strategic disadvantages of the Strategic Arms Reduction Treaty, "START Treatment for the Symptom," *WT* 7-22, but gets into sticky grounds in proposing mixing systemic approaches to arms control centered on "facilitating the rapid and wholesale transformation of the Soviet Union along democratic and free market lines." As ever, Gaffney forces serious reflection on U.S. geo-strategic defense policy. In "With Friends Like These. . ." *WT* 8-19, he is clearly on the side of the Israelis in this discussion of Bush's handling of the Middle East peace process, ignoring the complex Palestinian issue. But we cannot discount his cogent points about the dangers of Bush's suggesting moral equivalency between the hostages in Lebanon and "Israel's detention of terrorists captured while conducting — or organizing — attacks on the Jewish state."

Gelb, Leslie H. *The New York Times.* (½ ★)
Formerly a heavyweight national security correspondent, more recently deputy editor of the *Times*' editorial page, Gelb has had a wretched time adjusting to the intellectual rigors of an on-deadline, twice-weekly column. Replacing Flora Lewis as "Foreign Affairs" columnist almost seems to be more than he can handle, so clearly is he stretching his trite proposals. He'll do better when he replaces wordy punditry with old-fashioned hard work. One of his better pieces came early. In "A Final Pause," 1-13, Gelb reconceptualizes the Israeli situation with a powerful proposal: seize the initiative and announce an Israeli-Palestinian peace plan that would allow Israel to shape the negotiations and we sit up and take notice. But such columns were few. He joins the cacophony of columnists calling for a domestic agenda, "Mission Possible," 4-21, rhetorically compelling if not original: "What gave us strength in the gulf was our national resolve and passion, the very ingredients needed now to find the money and the ideas to save ourselves." Gelb has only feeble support for "Oil Fact and Follies," 5-19, postulating that the U.S.S.R. may be running out of oil, spelling trouble for the U.S. as an oil importer, but he ignores the global energy potential available to take up Soviet slack. In "The Old Trickster," 6-5, Gelb is content to take potshots at Richard Nixon's syntax, rather than appraising his thinking: "The Old Trickster also worries that Mikhail Gorbachev's recent swing toward reform 'has been uncritically accepted as irreversible. . .' Notice the suave use of the passive to obscure whom he's talking about." The depths are reached with "Why the Political Mess?" 7-3, a rather muddled compendium debating the role of the media in politics and the response of the people, advocating Bill Moyers for president and bringing back the system of government by elites. His sketchy analysis of Bush's arms control initiative in "Mr. Bush's Conversion," 9-29, puts this in the obvious context of Capitol Hill politics. Gelb comes as close as he can to accusing Clarence Thomas of perjury in the awful "Untruths. . ." 10-27, a post-hearing and post-confirmation swipe at the associate justice for testifying "he had never discussed Roe v. Wade and abortion."

Gergen, David. *U.S.News & World Report.* (★ ★)
The former White House communications director always offers, like fellow alumnus Pat Buchanan, an insider's perspective on Washington happenings. Although not as forceful as Buchanan, Gergen brings a spirited point of view to his columns, and sometimes is successful in persuading us to alter our thinking. A celebration of the new-found respect for the military, "America's New Heroes," 2-11, is organized well, but Gergen gives us no surprises. He shows thought where others have been overwrought, "Why America Hates the Press," 3-11: "The gulf war should make [the press] re-examine its biases: The press needs to expunge Vietnam from its soul as much as the nation does. It should not become a cheerleader for the military, but neither should it reflexively oppose every use of force. Each case deserves to be reported on its merits." We get a lively defense of the Mexico free-trade pact in "Don't Say No to Mexico," 4-29, Gergen envisioning a "grand economic union" reaching from the Yukon to the Yucatan and warning Democrats about their opposition to the agreement before they end up "once again. . .on the wrong side of history." Gergen buttresses his call for a government shift to the domestic agenda in "A New American Order," 6-17, by noting that now even the top thinkers of the foreign policy establishment, such as William Hyland, are saying the same thing. In a spirited defense of the Supreme Court nominee, "The Brief on Clarence Thomas," 7-15, Gergen cuts through stale arguments that all blacks are victims or that the underclass will be with us always, viewing Thomas as an important new voice: "Now comes Clarence Thomas insisting that if both races shape up, blacks can still make it on their own. He should know." In two dispatches from the jury box, "America's Legal Mess," 8-19, and "Ruling on Quayle v. Lawyers," co-written by Ted Gest 8/26-9/2, he argues persuasively in the first that the explosion of lawyers and lawsuits are having a drag effect on the economy and follows up with a loud cheer for the Vice President's ideas on reforming the system. Gergen, clearly outraged by the Thomas-Hill hearings, "How to Improve the Process," 10-28, calls forcefully for a streamlining of the confirmation process: "If the nation is to restore a measure of civility and common purpose in meeting its domestic crisis, it must find ways to end the relentless, ugly assaults upon the character of its public figures."

Germond, Jack & Witcover, Jules. *National Journal.* (★ ★)
Very much a part of the Beltway establishment, the venerable pair continue to be reliable in appraising the barometer of political winds from a Washington perspective, but frequently they lack the subtle edge that would increase the accuracy and detail of their forecasts. They're delightfully smart in evaluating the potential of Clayton Yeutter in the top spot, "Yeutter Will Be a Team Player at RNC," 1-12. "1992 Politics Held Hostage to War," 2-2, is perceptive in seeing the Democrats as a split party, particularly when it comes to '92. The pair postulates in the middle of Bush's sky-high poll ratings, that "it is even possible that some less clear situation will develop — an arguably successful conclusion to the war but a messy aftermath in the Middle East and the economy at home that would alter the list of voters' priorities." In the 10 Best selection for Commentary, "Tsongas Enters Democratic Vacuum," 3-23, they wax over Tsongas as the champion of a fresh, new course, but note his "central idea is not new — that the United States must adopt an industrial policy similar to those in Japan and Germany if it hopes to compete with them and ultimately to generate the resources to deal with pressing domestic needs." Months later, this was as good an assessment as we'd seen of Tsongas. There's too much guessing in "A New Political Calendar for 1992?" 5-18, the team disorganized in examining which states will have primaries when and why. In "Race: It's Hard to Change the Subject," 6-8, they rehash much of the old Willie Horton material as the duo reasserts that Bush is planning to run on "what he likes to call 'values,'" apparently feeling that race divisions shouldn't be a subject, despite the prevalence of the subject in the news apart from politics. There's solid reporting evident in "Bradley Is Out Front on Civil Rights," 7-20, a good dispatch on N.J. Sen. Bill Bradley's attack of Bush's civil rights record. The duo reviews what is common knowledge on Capitol Hill in "Bush Resisting Domestic Policy Debate," 8-31, on the politics of the President's reluctance to fight the Democrats on domestic policy in '92, the team sensibly betting the deciding factor will be the performance of the economy as the election nears. And "The GOP's Stake in Louisiana Election," 10-26, is a conventional Beltway appraisal of the Louisiana gubernatorial run-off between former governor Edwin Edwards and state senator David Duke.

Geyer, Georgie Anne. Universal Press Syndicate. (★ ★)
Geyer offers unique views of the world via her vast experience in international globe-trotting. There is almost always a new angle in her dispatches, although she stretches in places to maintain her originality. In "Bagged and Bundled for 1991: Unfulfilled Dreams," *The Washington Times* 1-1, Geyer compares 1989 and 1990 as antithetical points in this intriguing exercise: "In 1989, just about everybody in the world showed us what they could do; in 1990, they showed us what they could not do." She examines the moral and spiritual vacuum in the U.S. that hampers domestic policy, "Without Domestic Roots," *WT* 2-11, well defined but ordinary. In "Journalism on the Fly," *WT* 3-6, she effectively dissects, without denouncing, the press by telling us why they were the only Americans to lose the war, as the new breed of foreign correspondent has "gone on endlessly and fruitlessly on themes that never had any geopolitical reality." Geyer vigorously takes the press to task again in "Pit Bull Pressies and Tai," *WT* 9-8, calling the coverage of the alleged rendezvous between Tai Collins and Sen. Charles Robb (D-Va.) an example of "junkyard dog journalism." She chillingly perceives the Bay of Pigs as a dividing line, "Back to the Bay of Pigs," *WT* 4-10, starkly reminding large nations of the dangers of intervention. But in "Grand Riddle With No Answer?" *WT* 6-10, Geyer takes too long to say that we shouldn't give Gorbachev money for reforms that aren't even "on the drawing board," reasonable, but unoriginal. She sees India in broader terms, "A Tragic Saga Not Just About India," *WT* 5-27, as the ethnic, religious and regional conflicts in India are replayed in other nations. And Geyer insightfully discerns the "Ominous Pattern of India's Chaos," *WT* 10-24, as the fanatics there are not poverty-stricken rebels, but middle-class intellectuals, making the argument which history supports, that the country is ripe for revolution: "But the movements of change this time are not against a tyranny and not even particularly for an ideology. Far from the old protests against political oppression, these are protests, ironically, against the inner — and thus far more bedeviling and dangerous — upheavals of prosperity."

Gigot, Paul. *The Wall Street Journal.* (★ ★ ★ ½)
"Potomac Watch" columnist. Gigot, a former Reagan Treasury official, is devastating in his appraisals of the flaws and foibles of the Bush administration. He was particularly savage, exceedingly sharp on the weakness of domestic policymaking at the White House. His Friday column hits three times in four, enough to make it among the best read in Washington. Gigot discloses that dissenting views on Iraq policy were locked out in "A Great American Screw-Up," *The National Interest* Winter, a sharp critique of U.S. foreign policy for Iraq during the '80s. In "The Bush-Team's One Man Economic Policy," 2-15, he lambastes the administration for its lethargic approach to the domestic economy: "The Bush administration issued an economic report this week running to 411 pages. But its essence can be distilled into four words: Let Alan do it. That's Alan as in Greenspan, chairman of the Federal Reserve and the Volga Boatman of the U.S. economy." In "Economic Growth: The Once and Future Issue," 5-3, Gigot is savvy enough to sniff out key shifts, briskly identifying Washington's policy stupor and casting a look at forces that might break the log jam. Gigot applauds the end of "The Domestic Doormat Era," citing Bush's tougher stands on domestic issues, "In White House, It's No More Mr. Nice Guy," 6-7, also seeing the shortcomings, particularly on the growth agenda: "On domestic issues, Mr. Bush is playing tougher, but he's still playing mostly defense." Gigot takes Fed Governor Wayne Angell at his word on supporting the move to ease in "Hard-Money Man Versus Soft-Money Town," 8-9. While it's an intelligent analysis of the Fed's inner workings, Gigot needs to be more discerning in both his questions and evaluation, as he asserts that the markets heralded the move, and they did initially, but the day that this piece went to press, the long bond took a hit and the stock market slid 12 points. He rails delectably against the Washington "smear machine" in "Scandal Machine May, at Last, Have Gone Too Far," 10-11, deliciously skewering the press and citing Maureen Dowd of *The New York Times* for asserting "if more senators were women they would somehow reach different conclusions about unproved accusations; the burden of evidence doesn't matter. She even adopted the novel technique of quoting a female reporter who had in turn questioned a male senator who had judged Mr. Thomas more credible than Ms. Hill. 'It was a gender and generational problem' opined this reporter-turned-expert on male psychology. Then on Thursday, Ms. Dowd somehow discovered that the 'Capitol is covered in mud.' Ms. Dowd is like the arsonist who reports her own fire to the police."

Goodman, Ellen. *The Boston Globe,* Washington Post Writers Group. (★ ½)
Goodman slides back into the mire of post-feminist illogic rather than liberalism as often as not, her subjects at times downright odd. She takes a cue from the far left with "The Politics of Norplant," *The Washington Post* 2-19, warning against "women control," using as an example the judge who stipulated implantation as part of a female child abuser's sentence, ultimately unconvincing. Goodman wrings her hands in "What Lessons From Easy Victory," *WP* 3-2, worrying the U.S. might learn the 'wrong' lessons from the Gulf War. Still soggier on "Schwarzkopf: Post-Rambo Role Model," *WP* 3-16, Goodman tries to pass off the General as the proto-male of the '90s: "There is the sense of a man whose authority is hard-won through internal struggles not just through stars and stripes. In the search for a new model of male leadership, he seems like the real thing." She opines in arguing that criticism of Sen. Kennedy may not be "fair," "Talk of Ted," *WP* 5-18: "there's an edge of ageism and even Puritanism. . .in the gossip and groans." More cogent with "Women, Rape and Privacy," *WP* 4-20, on the publication of the alleged victim's name in the Palm Beach rape scandal, she contends that society has not yet reached the point where a woman can feel no shame in calling herself a rape victim. Along the same line, "One Freedom Not Yet Won Is the Freedom From Fear," *Los Angeles Times* 8-2, is a surprisingly muted, rather perceptive essay on the real issue facing the women's movement today, and it's not equality: "The right to walk down a street, across a campus, into a fraternity house, resonates strongly among women — especially young women — as any civil right. Indeed, it may define, in the most literal terms, the progress of the women's 'movement.' " She makes a nice, homey comparison between Mother's and Father's Day in "His Day Is Feeling a Lot Like Hers," *LAT* 6-14. "Thomas's Nomination: The Irony," *WP* 7-6, is strictly conventional on the irony of having Clarence Thomas succeed Thurgood Marshall. She

throws in the towel on "The Thomas Nomination: Ho, Hum," *WP* 9-14, arguing calmly that the confirmation of Clarence Thomas will make little difference in a court already dominated by conservatives.

Greenberg, Paul. Freelance Syndicate. (★ ★ ½)
Greenberg has adopted a more rigorous posture in *The Washington Times* "Commentary" pages. The editorial page editor of the *Pine Bluff* (AK) *Commercial* now sounds as much like the sharp-edged William Safire as the folksy Russell Baker, to whom we've compared him previously. Greenberg handles both the picaresque and the political, particularly civil rights, with new confidence. He evokes the "Spirit of an Age," *WT* 2-4, a wonderful tribute to the late Red Grange, the "galloping ghost" of the 1920s in which Greenberg asserts that to see Grange on film is "to sense the adulation, and liberation of another time, and to remember uncaptured grace." He sharply calls *Scientific American* to account in "When Science Calls in the Inquisitors," *WT* 3-18, as the journal rejects the work of a writer who espouses creationist, not evolutionist, views. Greenberg could have reviewed the scientific background of Forrest Mims to strengthen his case, however. He offers rigorous, sound commentary on how far the issues raised in the proposed Civil Rights Act of 1991 are from "civil rights" in "Whatever Happened to Civil Rights?" *WT* 4-18. These issues are not ones "that rally a great people; they are the stuff of special-interest politics and legal maneuvers. This is not the core of a great movement; it is the detritus of moral cause that has become one more lobby." Greenberg expands this theme in an effective eulogy for the civil rights movement that has lost the moral high ground in its struggle for power, "Rights in Repose," *WT* 6-26. He furnishes a ringing indictment of liberalism and Thurgood Marshall, among the best of many similar screeds we saw from the right, "Promise Postponed," 7-3: "The sickness of American liberalism is mirrored in Thurgood Marshall's jurisprudence. . .It offers various preferences based on race or sex in the name of equality; it confuses favoritism with justice; and it pushes intellectual intolerance in the name of reason. . .It has become illiberal." His "Notes on a Vanishing Nation," *WT* 9-3, random, though interesting, thoughts on the disintegration of the Soviet Union seems uncharacteristically slung together, however. And in "Clearest Message of the Inquiry," *WT* 10-17, Greenberg makes a strong case that the Senate Judiciary's handling of Anita Hill's allegations would be funny if the whole situation hadn't been so serious. "As the French say, it was worse than a crime; it was a blunder."

Greenfield, Meg. *Newsweek, The Washington Post.* (★ ★ ½)
Greenfield's tightly-packed columns in *Newsweek* are serious and erudite, and we often have to work harder than we do with the backpages of the competing newsweeklies to get her complete message. It's usually worthwhile, though, as the editorial page editor of *The Washington Post* always provides some angular payoff. She cautions against the "single-bad-man" theory in "The One Man Enemy," 2-4: ". . .by now we should have learned that no matter how much terror bolsters their rule, these enemies of ours are not just loners; they represent at least an element of their own population and the problem does not necessarily disappear or die with them." In "Palm Beach Runaround," 4-29, she offers the thesis that if one-tenth the energy expended in the Palm Beach fiasco had been dedicated to the allegation, we'd know if a rape had been committed or not. She shows insight in examining the debilitating consequences of the tendency to take the short view of history, "Buy — And Read With Care," 6-10: "We produce our so-called history before we have even quite lived it, let alone tried to assemble and understand it. . .This habit of seeing history in terms of months rather than years or decades or centuries is what accounts for our continual surprise at the things that cause wars, rebellions and general grief elsewhere in the world." Intensive personal reflections pull us through an otherwise routine "The Fellowship of Patriotism," 7-8, on the American experience, set against dubious straw men of "right-wing fantasies" and "PC conscience keepers" who threaten it. Greenfield smartly addresses the problems with "The Dropout Democrats," 9-16, putting it as succinctly as we've seen: "Programs become obsolete. The values they were meant to promote do not. Programs can and must be junked when their time comes, and new ones must be put in their place. The values

that animated them will only be junked by cynics and opportunists or politicians too dumb to see that they need to be given new life, new programmatic form in a changed world." Greenfield winds up the year searching, again, for the honest man with "In Search of the Truth," 10-28, a strong argument for pursuing Anita Hill's case of sexual harassment, in which her cogent points about the mishandling of the process ring true.

Grenier, Richard. *The Washington Times.* (★ ★ ★)
Guarding against revisionism on the American cultural scene, Grenier gleefully skewers those who would try to rewrite history, particularly through the medium of film. We wish he would turn his hand to the world at large more frequently, though, as his dispatches on international events of yesteryear are unmatched. Grenier eats John Le Carre alive in "Politically Correct Perfidy," 2-9, for his turgid prose, dull plots, lifeless characters and views of "moral equivalence" between the U.S. and U.S.S.R., highlighting a particularly silly scene from Le Carre's latest where a daughter of a British spy has become a prostitute to somehow protest capitalism: "The average American would find this ludicrous. But your university-educated, book-reading public is slurping it up. So all enlightened politically correct people who want to enlist their daughters as prostitutes to protest American interference in the Persian Gulf can sign up here." Merrily ruthless on Kevin Costner's distortion of history in "Dances with Wolves," "Indian Love Call," *Commentary* 3-91, he treats us to an account of Indian life and practices during the "Dances" period, a 10 Best selection for Commentary. Grenier is ditzy with "Hellfire's Blazing Revival," 4-30, goofy on "Defending Your Life" and Hollywood author Julia Phillips, but his madcap style makes it work. Funny on the historical inconsistencies of Costner's "Robin Hood," "What Robin Hood Learned in Vietnam," 6-10, he never makes his case for a pro-Arab Robin Hood, despite his citation of Morgan Freeman's Moor character. Grenier delectably skewers the Soviet coup, liberals and the American media in "All That Left, Right Stuff," 8-30, the kind of exercise at which he excels: "In Moscow, dozens of Russian intellectuals have apologized to me for the ignorant confusion of 'left' and 'right' in Soviet usage. . .But these Moscow intellectuals needn't have apologized, because the American press, with only the rarest exception, has swallowed the Soviet confusion whole. There can only be one reason: For many American journalists, operating at an advanced stage of historical illiteracy, 'left' and 'liberal' can only be good, 'right' and 'conservative' can only be bad." In "Price of Division," 10-19, he is one of the few commentators who puts the Thomas-Hill fiasco in a global context, giving us the view from Europe and the Soviet Union in this smart perspective that's made all the more valuable by its originality after the reams of ink spilled on commentary on this subject.

Hentoff, Nat. *The Village Voice, The Washington Post.* (★ ★ ½)
"Sweet Land of Liberty" columnist. Hentoff stands squarely on the U.S. Constitution as the base for his themes, usually avoiding thick legal language and welcoming intelligent debate over issues which help to "secure the blessings of liberty for ourselves and our posterity" in his *Washington Post* column. He's particularly tough on the political correctness movement. Hentoff smartly indicts Vartan Gregorian in "Newspeak from a University President," *WP* 2-26, reviewing the Brown case of expelling a drunken student for racist, homophobic and antisemitic remarks: "An independent-minded president would have tried to determine how to straighten this student out. A PC president, horrified by the offensive drunken language, wants to keep the campus tidy and civil." He fashions his discussion of religious freedom well in "Playground Bible Bust," *WP* 4-2, a study of a fifth-grader in Oklahoma who regularly discussed the Bible with several playmates during recess — until the school authorities made her stop. In "Torture by Nunchaku in Los Angeles," *WP* 6-29, Hentoff exposes the case of Deborah Grumbine, who was peacefully sitting and praying in protest in front of an abortion clinic when the LAPD used the "potentially lethal Okinawan martial arts weapon" on her; she subsequently miscarried her own baby. Hentoff easily recognizes and reveals the truth of "Heresy Hunt: The Character Assassination of Carol Iannone," *WP* 7-8, blowing the whistle on precisely that operation as it is being conducted by opponents of National Endowment for the Humanities advisory council member nominee Iannone: "Her qualifications do not really matter to her accusers. Iannone is under siege because

her opponents do not like her views." In "Whitewashing Political Correctness," *WP* 9-21, he sees the political correctness movement for what it is, a clear-eyed perspective: "To be sure, PC is not a force on every campus, but it continues to create self-censorship among both students and faculty members at many colleges." Hentoff comes close to making his case in "The Trouble With Hate Crime Laws," *WP* 10-14, in a structured defense of first amendment freedoms now being restricted by hate crime statutes "for the greater good of social civility," but he's not specific enough as to how he would accommodate the first amendment and civility.

Hitchens, Christopher. *The Nation, Harper's.* (★ ½)
The "Minority Report" columnist of *The Nation* and Washington editor of *Harper's,* Hitchens spins out left-of-center perspectives with a British polish. His fervent interpretations of the landscape are sometimes distorted by his ardor, though, as he persists in his habit of substituting passion for polemics. His discussion of the controversy over Bret Easton Ellis' *American Psycho,* "Minority Report," 1/7-14, is inherently flawed as Hitchens savages NOW for the boycott and Simon & Schuster for refusing to publish it, as they published a book even more heinous to Hitchens — Reagan's *An American Life.* He loses his grip in "Minority Report," 2-25, choosing to make sport of all who invoke Churchill's name, rather than effectively debunking the Bush-Churchill analogy: "Senator John Tower, alleged to be awash in Wild Turkey before his confirmation hearings, had his defenders argue that Churchill was none the worse for a quart or two of cognac." Hitchens offers a smart "Minority Report," 3-25, on the Persian Gulf and Iraq's offer to comply with U.N. Resolution 660 via the Soviet Union, repulsed by the descriptions of the "turkey shoot." He makes a strong argument for the "October surprise" via Robert Parry and the "Frontline" documentary, "Minority Report," 4-22, but he never mentions that Parry himself admits there is no smoking gun. In "Minority Report," 7-1, Hitchens unconvincingly links Bush's failure to remember where precisely he was the "October surprise" weekend of October 19-20, 1980, to his denial of remembering the infamous "voodoo economics" line, which is preserved for posterity in the television archives. He tries to tie up loose ends of the "October surprise," "Minority Report," 7-29/8-5, citing an ABC-TV/*Financial Times* report of 6-20 that the Israelis were involved, but there's not enough information here to persuade. His "Minority Report," 10-7, surprises from Hitchens, as he advocates moving on from communism and socialism to . . . what? He doesn't quite know yet, as he suggests leaving it to the "world's workers," but it's obvious he's on his way: "By any knowable definition, which must include the socialist one, the Soviet system was the perfect failure. In the lives of its own citizens and subjects, and in its contact with any real movement outside its own borders, it killed everything it touched."

Hoagland, Jim. *The Washington Post.* (★ ★ ★)
Back in Washington after four years in Paris, Hoagland continues to impress us with his new maturity that brings clarity and insight to his columns, leaving behind the smugness we'd seen in previous years. He received a 1991 Pulitzer for his "searching and prescient" columns on the growing crises in the Persian Gulf and the Soviet Union. In "The Message Behind a New Kind of War: Why There Will Be No Pause in the Campaign to Destroy Saddam Hussein," 1-20, Hoagland deftly examines the strategy of destroying Hussein's military capabilities, rather than going into Kuwait. Speculating on Hussein's strategy in "Saddam's Grisly Plan," 2-5, he received wide play with the assertion that Hussein "may rely on a mountain of Iraqi dead. . .to shatter Western resolve and turn America and European opinion against the war." Shrewd on "The Practical Gorbachev," 3-26, he makes the same point former Foreign Secretary Eduard Shevardnadze would make when asked if Gorbachev has changed from reformer to repressor: "It is not Gorbachev who has changed so much as the circumstances in which he operates. To expect more — or less — of him is to misunderstand the nature of, and possibilities for, change in the Soviet Union today." In "Sanctions to Topple Saddam," 5-20, he correctly assesses the import of signals indicating the Bush administration is determined to use economic sanctions to force Hussein out: "As long as Saddam is in charge, skillfully mixing images of defiance for local consumption and reasonableness for gullible foreigners, he is a threat to Iraq, to regional

security and ultimately to George Bush's place in history." We get a superlative report from Czechoslovakia in "In Eastern Europe, Fearing the Fall," 6-13, as Hoagland examines how the region fears the ramifications of the growing chaos in the Soviet Union, and how the Czechoslovakian idea of having the West subsidize Soviet trade is a bad idea. We get nothing really thought-provoking until the close of "Another Round in a Long Struggle," 8-22, Hoagland's ruminations on the failed Soviet coup: "Gorbachev and Yeltsin must now face the danger that if there is a next time, the coup leaders will shoot first and make announcements later." He blames Yeltsin's bad first impresssion and the President's political prudence for the administration's backing away from its post-coup support for the Russian President in "Tilting Against Yeltsin," 9-5, a rather standard assessment.

Ivins, Molly. *Mother Jones, The Progressive.* (★ ★)
Columnist for the *Dallas Morning News,* Ivins designs coherent, convincing arguments despite her sometimes nasty streak, which is most evident when she pokes fun at her Texas home base. Her prescription of higher taxes for the rich seems facile in "Deep Voodoo," *MJ* 1/2-91, although her description of the problem inherent in the tax code is memorable: "In 1988, Michael Milken made $500 million. Same year, the Teacher of the Year made $36,000. That's a nice piece of change; you can put dinner on the table with that. If Milken were a hundred times more socially useful than the Teacher of the Year, he would have made $3.6 million. Ten thousand times, $360 million. But he made more than that — he made $500 million. That made him worth fourteen thousand times the Teacher of the Year. And it put them both in the same tax bracket." Ivins shies away from the economics and offers an enjoyable look at the inanity of it all in "IRS Is Us," *MJ* 3/4-91. "War, Texas Style," *MJ* 5/6-91, is rather hard on the Longhorn State, portraying the state as jingoistic and, well, stupid. Equally disdainful in "Plot to Overthrow the West," *TP* 6-91, she sets up as a straw man a fellow columnist from the *Dallas Morning News* who doesn't like affirmative action or political correctness and rebuts his (or her) arguments by saying "We live in a culture in which people drive around with bumper stickers on their pickups that say things like, DO A GOOD DEED TODAY — BEAT THE HELL OUT OF SOMEONE YOU LOVE and IF YOU LOVE SOMETHING, SET IT FREE — IF IT DOESN'T COME BACK, HUNT IT DOWN AND KILL IT. The words 'nigger' and 'spic' are still in common usage everywhere, including the state legislature. The biggest problem at the University of Texas is drunken fraternity hazing. And these folks are worried about creeping political correctitude?" Ivins is drolly biting in "Magic Moments," *MJ* 7/8-91, on the silliness of campaigning early and how much Ivins misses it, and after reading this and remembering the foot-in-mouth incidents she recounts, we do too. She comically dissects Bush's mannerisms and speaking style in "The Thing Thang," *MJ* 11/12-91, a persuasive bit of satire in which Bush really becomes "Mr. Rogers doing John Wayne": "Margaret Thatcher may have had her limitations, but at least she never referred to trouble as 'deep doo-doo.' "

Judis, John B. *In These Times.* (★ ★)
Washington correspondent. Judis succeeded Marxist Alex Cockburn on the opinion page of *The Wall Street Journal,* evidence of his growing clout as a political observer. Like Cockburn, he appears in a multitude of venues, generally trenchant and unsparing, but we saw signs of an intellectual slackness that suggests he's not sure of his footing. In "Bill Folds," *The New Republic* 1-28, Judis provides a cutting assessment of Sen. Bill Bradley (D-N.J.) after his near-defeat in the '90 race, making the case that Bradley's caution makes him unsuitable as a presidential candidate. "Reflections on the New Conservative Paradigm," *ITT* 12/26-1/15, is very smart on what the new paradigm debate may entail, in terms of philosophy and policy. He needs greater support for "Time for an American Industrial Policy," *WSJ* 2-14, uncharacteristically flimsy on subsidies for certain industries. He shows off in a rhetorical discourse, "Telling Left from Right in These Times," *ITT* 4-17/23, an interesting but esoteric exercise on the political use of the terms 'left' and 'right' that he rehashes in "Looking Left and Right: The Evolution of Political Direction," *ITT* 6-12/25. Judis is perceptive on Democratic problems in "Can the Dems Produce a Candidate to Challenge Bush in 1992 Election?" *ITT*

5-1/7, a valuable dissection of potential candidates and Bush's vulnerabilities. In "Lacking a Cold War, the CIA Engineers a New Field of Study," *ITT* 7-10/23, Judis exposes the CIA's Japan-bashing, via the Rochester Institute of Technology, which the CIA is using as a base for Japan studies: "If the CIA and RIT can portray Japan as a threat comparable to the Soviet Union, then they can justify spending for economic rather than military intelligence." In "Why Bush Voucher Plan Would Be a Poor Choice," *ITT* 9-18/24, Judis smartly addresses the flaws of Bush's America 2000, asserting bluntly "the real crisis in education may be in the White House rather than in Maine or the other states." And "American Evangelism," 10-9/15, is an intriguing delineation of America's future role as falling between evangelizing democracy or realistically prioritizing the domestic: the challenge "will be to discover a foreign policy that transcends both evangelism and narrow realism — a policy that satisfies Americans' democratic ideals, but that is also firmly and openly grounded on the country's economic and social needs."

Kilpatrick, James J. Universal Press Syndicate. (★★)
Celebrating his 40th year in commentary, Kilpo has evolved into a genuine graybeard, somehow reviving himself from creeping pomposity, his armchair observations more forceful and incisive than we have seen from him in years. He potently comes down against presidential term limits in "Repeal the 22nd Amendment," *The Washington Post* 1-8, quoting Truman: "The result of the Amendment has been twofold: it has undermined necessary presidential power to conduct the great public business assigned to that office, while simultaneously denying the people their most hallowed democratic right of having whomever they desire hold their offices for as long as the people desire." Kilpatrick reports the real scandal at the National Endowment for the Arts is not the controversy over the nature of the art, but the fact that artists on the panels give grants to each other, forming an elite circuit money flow, "NEA: Nobody Here but Us Artists," *WP* 3-25. "Sony Is a Meanie," *WP* 4-27, is mere griping about Sony suing a restauranteur for using the name "Sony" in naming the eatery, and Peabody Coal Co. violating mine safety laws to illustrate bad management; the frivolous and the venal don't mix well here. In "At the Court of Rehnquist: Royal Petulance," *WP* 5-4, Kilpatrick slams the Supreme Court for a recent ruling designed to deter the filing of "frivolous" or "malicious" cases by indigents. He makes an effective case in "One for the Indians Too," *WP* 7-23, on renaming the Custer National Monument — the only monument named for an officer — the Little Bighorn Battlefield National Monument. Kilpo is amusing but pointed with "Away With Autodialers," *WP* 8-6, in this taut case recommending laws against computer-generated phone calls and autodialers. Equally tough, Kilpatrick comes out in support for the Danforth compromise on civil rights, with reservations, which he outlines in "Civil Rights: Pass the Danforth Bill," 8-13. He spares few with his newfound combativeness, here taking Bush head on: "the president's stated reason for opposing Danforth's key bill may best be described, in a kindly word, as baloney."

Kinsley, Michael. *The New Republic.* (★★★)
Kinsley, an incandescent intellectual liberal, challenges ideas on both the left and right, forcing their advocates to use muscular logic to answer his arguments. He is less effective of late, however, as he has somehow become a champion for Beltway ideas and the Beltway mentality, an increasingly awkward position. Unwilling to give Bush a free ride in a well-constructed "Dink Stover at War," 2-18, Kinsley convincingly asserts Bush's pre-Kuwait invasion policies towards Iraq "undermine any pretense that the war we're now engaged in results from the president's admirably simple Sunday school morality." Sober in "Dead Iraqis," 3-18, he probingly examines American unwillingness to face up to the harsh realities of the Gulf War. In a spirited defense of the free trade agreement with Mexico, "Holy Guacamole!" 4-1, Kinsley shrewdly compares arguments protectionists are making now to those made about free trade with Europe after World War II: "It's not the 1940s anymore. . .must we really shy away from competition with *Mexico??* Pathetic, if so." But for much of the remainder of the year, he was in a Beltway self-defense posture. He sets his sights squarely on DNC headquarters in "Mr. Fix-it," 4-22, coming down hard on Clark Clifford for BCCI and on chairman Ron Brown for his business and lobbying dealings. Kinsley effectively links GOP race relations and quotas in "Hortonism, and

the Making of a Quota Issue," 6-7, cogently observing that the GOP and Democratic bills are not all that far apart. Long before the Clarence Thomas confirmation hearings became a sideshow, Kinsley defensively asserts that "It's OK to Ask," 8-5: the senators on the Judiciary Committee "have the right and duty to make substantive judgments about a future justice's philosophy and to vote against him if they disagree — or if he won't reveal it in reasonable detail." He expands this theme in the 10 Best selection for Commentary, "Liar or Boob?" 10-21. Kinsley rails against the hypocrisy of Thomas' defenders in "Desert Storm," 11-11, "as Thomas supporters weave their exculpatory scenarios — even in print — they seem remarkably indifferent to the fact that they are indicting their own man for perjury." Kinsley reveals his true devotion to the Beltway in "It's Your Fault," 10-28, asserting that as flawed as the federal government is, the real fault lies outside the Beltway, not within it. "Real respect for democracy takes it for granted that government is by the people when it performs badly, just as when it performs well."

Kirkpatrick, Jeane. Los Angeles Times Syndicate. (★)
Weakened by the lack of a sturdy post-Cold War foundation, the former U.N. ambassador seems stuck in the same old groove. Kirkpatrick rarely incorporates new perspectives, instead relying on static assumptions inappropriate in a dynamic world. In "Brotherhood Is Drowning in Bloodshed," *Los Angeles Times* 1-27, she says little more than Arabs have always conducted politics by violence and until that changes there cannot be peace in the region. In "First, Peace With Israel," *The Washington Post* 3-26, Kirkpatrick makes the obvious recommendation that the Arab states should first make peace with Israel before the U.S. sells them arms. She argues unconvincingly both that Castro is on his last legs and that he is a direct military threat to the Southern U.S., "The Fantasies of Fidel," *WP* 4-1, sounding almost paranoid. In "America's Mysterious Policy. . ." *WP* 6-3, Kirkpatrick raises a lot of questions about the administration's post-war policy in the Middle East, but makes no attempt to answer them. "The Priority of Freedom," *WP* 7-8, is replete with one-dimensional abstractions on the issue of Yugoslavia, offering aphorisms instead of analysis. A discourse on Saddam Hussein's untrusworthiness, "Bargaining in Bad Faith," *WP* 9-30, adds nothing to our knowledge: "Saddam and his regime will do what they must as long as they are *forced* to. . .Iraq's intention to produce nuclear weapons has been clear since at least 1981." Kirkpatrick pleads the case of Earnest Sands, suspected of murdering his wife in Saudi Arabia, after the Embassy did not take up his cause as a U.S. citizen in a muddled "American Citizen — Islamic Justice," *WP* 10-28: ". . .the issue here is not his guilt or innocence. It is the failure of U.S. officials to ensure that Sands receives basic legal protections." Her one shining moment came in the uncompromising "Two Murders in Managua," *WP* 2-25, strongly written and reported on the absence of law and order there, due to the tolerance of political violence and the power-sharing between the Chamorro government and the Sandinistas: "democracy requires the rule of law, and rule of law requires police and courts that are above politics, not part of it. Sandinista control of these institutions is contributing to disorder. Surely, it is time for Chamorro to reconsider this form of power-sharing."

Kondracke, Morton. *The New Republic.* (★ ★ ½)
Senior editor. Kondracke's intuitive appraisals of events in the Middle East were once again satisfying and knowledgeable this year, the foreign arena being his forte. His domestic commentary seemed less surefooted, but still eminently worth reading as this leading neoconservative wrestles with ideological cross-currents. In "Listening to King Fahd," *The Washington Times* 1-15, Kondracke offers an excellent analysis of the potential repercussions of having American troops on Saudi soil, particularly as a result of cultural tension, speculating as to possible post-war scenarios. He looks beyond the headlines in "The Fine Print," 2-25, a valuable overview of Bush's plans for a "new world order," cautioning, "George Bush obviously wants to build a New World Order the way the Truman and Eisenhower administrations did after World War II, but he's got to watch out that the country doesn't turn isolationist and treat his dreams as it did Woodrow Wilson's after World War I." He detects the fallout in "Party

Pooper," 3-25, a overview of the Democrats' Gulf War posturing, correctly identifying the party's split on domestic policy as between two camps: Walter Mondale-interest groups-big government and Gary Hart-new ideas-decentralization. In "Broken Record," 5-6, Kondracke offers a smartly critical appraisal of Cuomo's gubernatorial record: "a close examination of Cuomo's eight-year record as governor indicates that New York's current woes are the result not just of the recession and Reagan-era cutbacks, but also of chronic bad management. And Mario Cuomo shares much of the blame." Kondracke gives the once over to the U.S.-Israeli dispute over expanding settlements in the occupied territories for Soviet immigrants in "Unsettling," 7-29, adding little new. Taking a cue from John Judis, Kondracke offers "Senator Lazarus," 9-2, an appraisal in which, like Judis, Kondracke finds that despite Bill Bradley's challenging Bush on various issues, his cautious nature is still holding him back from making a White House run. He begins to gear up for '92, bringing us a sharp assessment of "Slick Willy," 10-21, better known as Bill Clinton, and his presidential bid based on "postliberalism," a postmodern form of ideology borrowing from the left and right to win the center. "Clinton's message has every sign of being the right one; and his oratory suggests the messenger may be the right one too."

Kramer, Michael. *Time.* (½ ★)
"The Political Interest" column all but disappeared for much of the year, as Kramer attempted to capture the defining moment in the Persian Gulf War. He added nothing to either the vivid pictures coming from the Gulf or the policy debate in Washington, and too frequently substituted rumor and innuendo for old-fashioned solid reporting. Semi-thoughtful on Saddam Hussein and the events leading up to final confrontation on the Saudi-Kuwait border in "The Moment of Truth," 1-21, Kramer at least captures the mood, noting how discouraging events have proven after the end of the Cold War. He has no cohesive theme to tie together "Arabs and the Aftermath," 3-4, a confused collage of Middle East politics. Completely immersed in melodramatic *Time*speak in "Chaos and Revenge," 3-18, Kramer offers his impressions of life in Kuwait City, stringing together unconfirmed anecdotes of atrocities such as gang rapes, killings of children, and so on. He also is quoted in "From the Publisher" of the same issue, somewhat immodestly, as "We journalists are considered liberators as much as the troops are" in response to Kuwaiti enthusiasm for the Americans, documenting *Time*'s search for truth. In "Gates: The Buck Doesn't Stop Here," 4-1, Kramer skewers the L.A.P.D. head for his involvement (or lack thereof) in the police brutality charge brought against his men, citing that "Leadership will either be a constant inspiration or instant depression." In a ragtag update on Kuwait, filed from the capital city, "Kuwait: Back to the Past," 8-5, Kramer doesn't say much that hasn't already been documented in other places in a more timely fashion; a good reminder, but little more. In "Nobody Does Nothing Better Than Shamir," 9-30, he bases most of this on a conversation he had several years ago with Yitzhak Shamir, in which Shamir told him he does not believe in trading land for peace, but the author doesn't talk to Shamir again to update this conversation, telling us instead that other people *know* that he thinks this way still, despite "his willingness to attend the peace conference." And in "Shame on Them All," 10-21, he rambles on the Thomas confirmation, moving uneasily to term limitation. He also quotes the White House, "off the record," saying that the Thomas nomination itself was motivated by racial politics.

Krauthammer, Charles. Washington Post Writers Group. (★ ★ ★ ½)
Consistently provocative, Krauthammer bests his opposition with elegantly constructed arguments and savagely eloquent prose. He was especially trenchant on Gulf War issues and fallout. Krauthammer describes how Hussein can 'lose' a military engagement with the West and still emerge politically victorious, ". . .And Why Saddam Fights," *The Washington Post* 1-17. Unrelenting, he defends the air war in "A Cause for Sorrow, but Not Guilt," *Los Angeles Times* 2-15: "[Iraq] indiscriminately attacks Israeli civilians, boasts that it will turn Tel Aviv into a 'crematorium' — then complains of attacks on its civilians. It scorns a dozen U.N. resolutions demanding that it withdraw from Kuwait — then complains that the allied war effort

has gone beyond the U.N. mandate for getting it out of Kuwait." Krauthammer sharply appraises the Soviet gambit for Gulf peace in "Cold War II," *WP* 2-21, but he leaves no room for the possibility that Moscow might have a legitimate concern that the coalition is overstepping its U.N. mandate. In the 10 Best selection for Commentary, "Must America Slay All the Dragons?" *Time* 3-4, he soundly debunks the "false everywhere-nowhere dichotomy [that] is the moral pillar of American isolationism." Tough in "Tiananmen II" *WP* 4-5, Krauthammer convincingly links the Kurdish situation to the Tiananmen Square massacre. He forthrightly defends the Vice President in "Dan Quayle's Bum Rap," *WP* 5-10, underscoring Quayle's accomplishments and strengths. He takes things to the absurd on political correctness, hilarious and savage with "The Crudest Sort of Meanness," *LAT* 6-2. "Clarence Thomas and the Liberal Orthodoxy," *WP* 7-12, is a splendid assessment of the impact Thomas' nomination will have on the legitimization of black conservatism: "Thomas is a living threat. His confirmation would repeal the current official recognition of the civil rights establishment as the sole legitimate representative of black people in America." He turns "Why Arms Control Is Obsolete," *Time* 8-5, into an interesting but obvious defense for SDI, arguing effectively that the real danger is from the intent to use arms, and that the real problem now is proliferation, using Iraq as a most timely example.

Kristol, Irving. *The Wall Street Journal.* (★ ★ ½)
The "Godfather" of neo-conservatism, founder and publisher of both *The Public Interest* and *The National Interest,* Kristol is best known for his essays in *The Wall Street Journal.* He remains as cosmic and intellectually audacious at 71 as he was as a CCNY socialist, but his cranky insensitivity to races and cultures other than his own mars his work this year. He's sometimes so far ahead of the curve that material remains fresh months later, as in "The G.O.P. Message: A State of Disunion," *The New York Times* 1-27. Kristol addresses a serious concern among conservatives: the absence of any sense of mission in the administration, a 10 Best selection for Commentary which foreshadowed Bush's political difficulties over domestic policy later in the year. In his "After the War, What?" 2-22, he is brutal in denouncing the New World Order: "It is all a fantasy. To begin with, there is not going to be a New World Order, just the old world disorder in new configurations." But he tramples over the Arab cause, ridiculing Arab history as "one of relative stagnation and political impotence," with almost no contribution to civilization. In "The Conservatives Find a Leader," 6-3, Kristol sagely observes the doings at a *National Review* conference, concluding that conservatives have permitted Bush to win their loyalty, even though they disagree with much of his domestic agenda. But presciently he notes: "If the economy continues to stagnate, or begins to deteriorate, his popularity will erode and his leadership will be called into question." Kristol is again brutal in "The Tragedy of Multiculturalism," 7-31, raging that multiculturalism is the fault of blacks and the social problems in the ghettos. There may be a germ of truth, but Kristol, who uses a subtle scalpel whenever critiquing the foibles of Jews, whacks away with an ax: "Though the educational establishment would rather die that admit it, multiculturalism is a desperate — and surely self-defeating — strategy for coping with the educational deficiencies, and associated social pathologies, of young blacks." In a clever defense of the Reagan years, Kristol muses on his own relative prosperity in "The 1980s — Looking Beyond Reagan," 9-11, noting his fellow academics do not "see any connection between their increased prosperity and the 'decade of greed' they are quick to denounce. After all, that increase did not result from the vulgar pursuit of money on their part — only from other people's vulgar pursuit of money." As for scandal: "A decade of prosperity and high growth always produces speculative excesses (Just look at scandal-ridden Japan!)" Just calm down, Godfather.

Lambro, Donald. *The Washington Times.* (★ ½)
Chief political correspondent. Like David Broder at the *Post,* Lambro wears the hat of both reporter and pundit. His work now shows a new maturity and sophistication, particularly when he addresses economic issues, which indicates he is growing comfortable with both roles. Effective with "Hunted by Trade Fears," 4-1, he praises the proposed free trade agreement

between U.S. and Mexico, arguing persuasively that it will benefit both nations. He offers more intricate analysis than we found in other accounts of "Economic Anxiety Within the GOP," 5-6, on the concern of some within the Administration that some tax incentives are necessary to lift the economy out of recession, assembling a fully detailed picture. In "Turning to Private Services," 6-3, Lambro details the libertarian perspectives of Reason Foundation project Privatization Watch, which was also covered in *Reason.* Although not original, he does a credible summarization job, bringing the debate over the privatization of public services such as garbage collection to a broader audience than *Reason* magazine might otherwise reach. "Economic Distress in Wake of Higher Taxes," 10-24, is a smart, ringing call for tax relief at the federal level, citing both recent state and federal tax increases that have left voters poorer and angrier, and the economy in the dumps, and in addition, have not solved the problem of deficits, either federal or state. "When will they ever learn? Raising taxes does not reduce the deficit, it suppresses economic growth, which is the wellspring of government funding." Despite its "Commentary" placement, he offers less interpretation than reporting in "Payroll Tax Cut Gaining," 2-7, a news item of who's on which side in the payroll tax debate that's worthwhile from that standpoint, but we don't find out what Lambro thinks. In "Reaching for the Donkey's Reins," 1-21, Lambro perceptively discerns the growing schisms in the Democratic party over direction and ideology. But subsequent assessments of the Democrat's troubles, such as "Adrift in a Dismal Political Swamp," 3-19, "A Party at War With Itself," 7-1, and "History Playing Cruel Tricks on Democrats," 9-3, offered little new.

Leo, John. *U.S.News & World Report.* (★ ★ ★)
"On Society" columnist. Leo is determinedly detached on social and cultural issues, offering cool, keen assessments. Where others play on emotion, Leo uses logic, frequently persuading us that his perspectives are the correct ones. In "Community and Personal Duty," 1-28, Leo smartly appraises how the emphasis on individual rights can undercut the concept of community. He rebuts with detachment the thinking of those "Protesting a Complex War," 2-4, reaching back to the writings of I.F. Stone during the Vietnam years to put peace protesters, then and now, in perspective: "[This war] is not a referendum on the Reagan years and not a theater for personal alienation, not an open invitation to resume the extraordinary social chaos of the Vietnam era as if that were a normal side effect of all wars, good and bad, legal and illegal." Leo forcefully outlines the hate campaign militant gay organizations have carried out on the Church, in "The Gay Tide of Catholic-Bashing," 4-1, savage on the failure of his fellow journalists to recognize it as such: "Famous newspapers and commentators who scour language for the faintest hint of insensitivity to gays, blacks and women show little interest in this foot-stomping bigotry toward Catholics." In "California's Racial Arithmetic," 6-24, he informs on the very live issue of quotas that exist, providing a graphic example of quota-mania with a U.S. Forest Service task force report on Work Force Diversity, which puts the "proper quota" for the disabled at "5.9 percent." Leo gets his hands on a copy of New York's report on multicultural social science programs in "Multicultural Follies," 7-8, and hacks through the "grisly prose" to find a multicultural smoking gun — a recommendation for public schools to "teach each racial and ethnic group its own private tribal truths." Leo points out the dangers of "Harassment's Murkey Edges," 10-21, intelligently pondering the subjectivity of such charges, and as the issue becomes defined in law, increasing the likelihood of "an era in which a lot of males, guilty and innocent, are likely to be tainted by unsubstantiated charges." But in "Score One for Operation Rescue," 8-26/9-2, Leo continues to straddle the fence on abortion, coming out in support of the Operation Rescue protesters in Wichita while refusing to call for abortion to be banned outright.

Lerner, Max. *New York Post,* Los Angeles Times Syndicate. (★ ★ ½)
Lerner's several generations of experience make his perceptions of the world at large invaluable. Having seen so much in one lifetime, he has become increasingly more philosophical in his "journalism of ideas," perceptively viewing events in a long-term context. In "The West Against the West?" *The Washington Times* 1-14, Lerner catalogues how the West, particularly Europe,

helped arm Iraq, warning perceptively that those countries could also be the first to make concessions. His firsthand view of much of the 20th century's history is handy in "Franklin Dwight Bush," *WT* 2-7, an examination of Bush as fusion of Eisenhower and Roosevelt in continuing to structure the world order with the U.S. as last superpower, most lately evident in the Gulf War. Lerner uses Kitty Kelley to launch into an examination of historians, "High Noon of an Era," *WT* 4-11, making a cogent point along the way on politics, personality, and one's place in history: "Unless a president has lived an expressive life — however flawed because human — he will find that the necessary intuitive connection with the American people themselves is beyond his grasp." He remains similarly unimpressed with Bob Woodward's latest effort, *The Commanders,* in "Leaky Method," *WT* 5-9, arguing vigorously there is no reason to trust Woodward's "Trust me" journalism based on leaks: "Why make an exception for him when we have made it for no past historians? We don't exempt them from the rules of evidence that have stood the test for millennia." He smartly answers Gregg Easterbrook's *New Republic* discourse recommending the limitation of Supreme Court terms, "Limit Court Terms?" *WT* 8-19. While acknowledging and listing the advantages of term limitations, Lerner still admits he's not convinced, insightfully pointing out that great legal minds need time to mature and that the real problem is the fact that the presidents who appoint them have been of the same party for all but four of the last twenty-three years, thus creating a 'packed' court. Lerner defends Israel on its reluctance to trade land for peace in "Coming to the Mideast Table," 10-27: "Only Israel is being pressured to surrender territory that it fought successfully to win and that it needs critically for its defense and survival." It's ultimately unconvincing, but probably only because Lerner takes the defensive, rather than the offensive, and letting the history he knows so well speak for itself.

Lewis, Anthony. *The New York Times.* (★ ★ ½)
"Abroad at Home" columnist. Lewis offered more important polemics this year, but our one-time favorite leftist still has a long way to go before matching his stellar performances of years past. His columns show more originality of thought, but don't have the belligerent, intractable logic of earlier days when Lewis was a must-read. Lewis argues strongly in "A Dark Trumpet," 1-25, that because of the dynamics of the Middle East, "now that we are in [the war], to pull back would be far worse than pressing the war to the quickest possible end." In "The Old Order," 2-4, Lewis sees clearly the detention of Palestinian moderate Sari Nusseibeh as a purely political act, sending a message to Palestinians that Israel will never negotiate for withdrawal of occupation forces from Gaza and the West Bank. We see flashes of the old Lewis in this fiery discourse: "President Bush should understand that his ideas on a new world order will not come easily to the Middle East, where so many prefer the old order." He soberly reminds us in "What We Have Wrought," 3-29, of the destruction visited on Iraq by the allied bombing and subsequent turmoil. Lewis offers a passionate echo of an *Economist* article on blacks in "Confidence and Will," 4-1, calling upon Bush to spend his political capital in a real war on poverty, but Lewis offers no real advice. He literately addresses the question of televising executions, " 'Their Brutal Myth,' " 5-20, drawing on Charles Dickens and, more impressively, his firsthand experience witnessing an execution to argue against the idea. "Mr. Justice Marshall," 7-1, is the requisite tribute to Marshall, without the mushy sentimentality. Lewis intuitively catches the contradiction inherent in Gorbachev's professed continued belief in communism, even after the coup attempt in "Triumph and Decline," 8-23: "The tumult of these days leaves us, then, with an ironic possibility. At the moment of his triumph, history may be leaving Mikhail Gorbachev behind." His argument, however heartfelt, is flawed in "Time of the Assassins," 10-14, as he suggests that the Senate Judiciary Committee not castigate Anita Hill for not filing a complaint during 1982-83. But, if, as Lewis notes, the Supreme Court did not make verbal harassment a crime until 1986, the retroactive nature of charging Thomas for an alleged act that wasn't a crime at the time seems more to not only justify the tough questioning of Hill, but necessitate it.

Lindberg, Tod. *Insight.* (★)
Lindberg lost his spot as "The Last Word" columnist temporarily due to a reformat of the weekly; the column later resumed as a result of reader protests. Although much of his material is rather rote, we still see intermittent flashes of promise in his more intuitive columns. In "Playing with a New Rule Book," 12-24-90/1-7-91, Lindberg offers a cursory summary of what George Bush faces that contains nothing new. With "A Lift for Bush's Other Face," 2-18, he smartly urges that the President spend his political capital accumulated in the potential success of the Gulf War on domestic issues, relatively early and perceptive on the subject. Lindberg hits hard with "Bush Brushes Gorbachev Aside," 3-11, celebrating the irrelevancy of the Soviet Union in the final days of the Gulf War, a typical conservative perspective. "Naysayers' Scramble for Defense," 4-1, is rather nasty and puerile on how the Democrats and others against the Gulf War will run for cover on this subject: "The 'We'll never know if sanctions would have worked' ditch," and so on. In "Why Let Principles Foul Up a Promising Political Strategy?" 6-3, he reflectively argues that the GOP's current strategy of ensuring more minority congressional districts in the hope this will create more Republican seats elsewhere clashes with the party's principled stand on equal opportunity and a race-blind society. And in "That's the Real George Bush We're Finally Getting to See," 7-1, Lindberg's argument that the President deserves the benefit of the doubt on his zig-zags on domestic policy strikes a new high for gullibility: " 'Trust me' is the message. And of course not everyone who delivers such a message is selling a car or a miracle elixir. Some people deserve to be trusted." He shows considerable thought in "Wave Maker, Not a Surf Bum," 9-23, as he responds to Pat Buchanan's latest call for a return to isolationism: "His doctrine of 'America First' — an aggressive nationalism that does not suffer fools gladly — is in essence a doctrine of 'America only.' "

Matthews, Christopher. *San Francisco Examiner,* King Features Syndicate. (★ ½)
Washington bureau chief for the *Examiner,* Matthews' spirited prose offsets his modest analytic skills. He strengthened late in the year as possibilities opened for the Democratic presidential contenders. Matthews argues mutely and ineffectively that Saddam Hussein is no Hitler and the Middle East no Munich, "Mirage of Munich Orchestrated by Hawks?" *The Washington Times* 1-15. He loses his grasp on his analogy in a silly "The Daddy and Mommy Parties," *Los Angeles Times* 2-10, dividing Republicans and Democrats along the lines of fathers and mothers respectively in 1950s sitcoms: "Daddy brings home the bacon; mommy makes sure everybody gets a decent slice. Daddy can be partial; mommy battles for justice. Daddy can be tough; mommy is compassionate. He worries about the GNP. She worries about the kids' feelings and lunch money." He draws clearer lines in ". . .Amid Partition Politics," *WT* 4-12, claiming the GOP has conceded domestic policy to Democrats, while Dems have conceded foreign policy to the GOP, a situation not to a voter's advantage: "Instead of getting two options in the foreign, economic and social policy areas, he gets one. . .The fact is, both parties have traded territory for peace." Matthews is standard, "Midnight Rider. . .Lopsided Odds," *WT* 5-3, if optimistic, on presidential candidate Paul Tsongas, telling us he's an intelligent man who is sounding an economic alarm for the Democrats and the nation. In "And Pragmatism," *WT* 6-3, he takes the moral high ground on doing business with China, but whines while doing so, calling some of Bush's arguments "pathetic": "Listening to President Bush defend his China policy at Yale last week was like opening a set of Chinese boxes. Open one and find another. Get past one Bush argument for business-as-usual with Beijing and be faced with another one." Matthews scores some points on the appeal of Jerry Brown as a presidential candidate in "Turning on the Crowd," *WT* 9-6, but he isn't quite convincing here, perhaps because he's only exploring the possibility himself. But he intrigues with an effective "To Borrow a Strategy from JFK?" *WT* 7-29, making the comparison that Mario Cuomo in 1991 is sounding a great deal like John Kennedy in 1960, as they stress the same economic themes.

McCarthy, Colman. Washington Post Writers Group. (½ ★)
McCarthy is so violently pacifist that his thinking on the Gulf War and its aftermath tended towards the hysteric. Thus, he was completely ineffective for much of the year, many of his

columns serving neither truth nor history. So repulsed were readers in letters that *The Washington Post* finally moved his weekday column to the backpage of the comics section. McCarthy is unusually restrained but naive in "Wise Men, or Suicidal Fools," *WP* 1-20, arguing that Bush and Saddam should have settled their differences through "peaceful conflict management" techniques. He bashes the clergy, in particular the Catholics, in a rambling "Asking God to Bless War Is Blasphemy," *Los Angeles Times* 2-5, falsely portraying priests as jumping on the Gulf War bandwagon with no thought or meditation. Determinedly inaccurate in "The Cowards' Air War," *WP* 2-17, he brutally links Baghdad with Dresden: "Relentless aerial bombardment — lately about as surgical as operating on a cornea with machetes — is a systematic destroying of Iraq's electricity, water and sewage facilities." (One *Post* reader called this column "offal," 2-22.) He is completely rabid on "Schwarzkopf's Price for Glory," *WP* 6-30, irrationally describing Stormin' Norman as "a hustler who has large lusts for money." McCarthy repulses with "Disposable Pets," 10-5, on the overpopulation, sterilization and euthanasia of domestic pets, in which we must swallow hard just to get past the lead: "Do consenting adult animals have constitutional rights to copulate?" He's only palatable when he tones down his characteristic shrillness. In ". . . And the Insults," 7-6, McCarthy rises adequately to the defense of Clarence Thomas against charges that he "thinks white," pointing out the inherent silliness of the proposition: "Sooner or later — no, sooner or sooner — the illogic would carry the argument over the line to ridiculousness: If there are blacks who think white, then are there whites who think black?" Similarly, "Mandated Altruism," 9-14, is well-reasoned on a proposed Maryland law mandating 75 hours of public service from high school seniors. He doesn't address the law's constitutionality but questions whether mandated kindness is kindness at all: "What good is community service if it's not from the heart?"

McGrory, Mary. *The Washington Post.* (★ ★ ½)

Mother Mary put away the acid, convinced for the moment that the pen is mightier than the needle. She articulates and addresses her concerns credibly, only infrequently turning scathingly sulfuric. In "George Bush, Come Home." 1-8, McGrory makes a disjointed but rather effective list of her anxieties about impending war: "As the count down for war begins, the president is in another world. He is reliving World War II (Saddam Hussein is Hitler) and refighting Vietnam." McGrory makes a few clever observations in her ruminations on "Bush's Winning Ways of War," 2-21, but ultimately this seems more like sour grapes than anything else. She draws a muscular parallel between the King incident and the Gulf War's "turkey shoot" in "Video Violence in L.A.," 3-12, seeing the two as indications of America's penchant for violence. She gleefully points out in "Top Gun or Loose Cannon?" 4-2, on the Schwarzkopf-Frost interview in which the General insisted he wanted to go all the way to Baghdad, that "we have insisted on kidding ourselves that he [Schwarzkopf] is really a humanitarian who just happens to be in a line of work that involves causing large numbers of people to be killed or wounded." McGrory soberly probes the charges that the 1980 Reagan-Bush campaign swung a deal with Iran over the hostages and the apparent reluctance of Democratic leaders in Congress to investigate in "Reluctance on Hostage Probe," 5-21, but draws no solid conclusions. "Vive La Difference!" 6-23, is a valentine to French Prime Minister Edith Cresson and her outspokenness, which McGrory sees as a refreshing antidote to the hypocrisy prevalent in U.S. politics. Along the same lines, in "Hill's Counsel for the Senate," 10-8, McGrory provides a sturdy defense of Anita Hill and an equally sturdy indictment of the Senate, prior to their delaying the first scheduled vote for confirmation to hear her story: "They cannot ignore her. Women will remember that the Senate didn't think she was worth 24 hours of their time." "Right On, Better Angels," 7-26, is a stirring defense of Sens. George Mitchell and John Danforth for their respective views of the MFT treaty for China and the Civil Rights Bill. At her finest, McGrory baits Mario Cuomo, venting her fury at the man who has the best message in years, "A Messenger Who Won't Deliver," 8-13: "Peerless at the podium, petulant in the pit. That's Mario Cuomo, the heavyweight Democrat who refuses to challenge George Bush."

Meyer, Cord. News America Syndicate. (★)
Like fellow Cold Warrior Jeane Kirkpatrick, Meyer is still searching for a solid post-Cold War framework within which to craft his prescriptions for a new world order. In the interim, he offers more reportage than appraisal, respectable enough as reporting goes, but definitely unexciting commentary. In "Walesa's Daunting Challenge," *The Washington Times* 1-11, Meyer is economically naive on international debt reduction for Poland and what bright skies it may bring. He catalogues the players well enough in "On the Brink of Yugoslav Disunity," *WT* 2-22, a solid delineation of the factions in Yugoslavia that threaten to blow the country apart, but this is less opinion than news analysis, and not very analytical at that. "Peace Now's Jump Start," *WT* 3-8, is a mildly interesting report on the recent "Peace Now" meeting, but Meyer doesn't take the time or space to evaluate the information he presents. In "Castro Puffing on Last Cigar," *WT* 4-26, Meyer actually thinks Castro has given up smoking, linking Fidel's non-smoking to his mounting worries and concerns on his less-than-idyllic island. He hems and haws over China's most-favored-nation status in "Should China's MFN Go Away?" *WT* 5-10: "We must keep the pressure on the Beijing gerontocracy to free the last of the Tiananmen demonstrators and to grant more freedom, but we don't need an MFN cancellation to drive the lesson home." While he offers alternatives and makes a good case for the implementation of some kind of carrot-and-stick mechanism in U.S. dealings with China, he needs better organization to improve his argument. Meyer is rather sharp in "To Steady Angola's Course," *WT* 6-21, a solid evaluation of prospects for peace and democracy in Angola. He takes the opposing side of conventional wisdom, taking a critical look at the new KGB and making an adequate argument for keeping the CIA, not trimming it down, in "Revising Clandestine Priorities," *WT* 9-13.

Mortimer, Edward. *Financial Times.* (★ ★ ★ ½)
"Foreign Affairs" columnist. Perceptive and thought-provoking, Mortimer is able to cull unique insights on the geopolitical scene. He excels at geo-strategic reconnaissance, and was particularly impressive and important in a year of tumultuous change. He is superlative in dissecting the rhetoric and actions of the Bush presidency in the post-Cold War era with the 10 Best selection for Commentary "Reality v Rhetoric in New World Order," 12-28-90: "What we see is not a genuine coming together of world powers to act in concert, but rather an assertion of American leadership which most of the rest of the world feels obliged to go along with." Mortimer assumes a durability for Saddam Hussein's reign, advancing a plausible argument in favor of a negotiated settlement between him and the allied Gulf forces in "Peace Poses Even Harder Questions," 2-5. He returns to the same theme — whither post-War Iraq? — with "The Iraqis Deserve Better," 3-6, cautioning the West from succumbing to the temptation to foster another strongman in Baghdad. Mortimer is righteously indignant over the failure of the Western coalition to ensure that the civil war in Iraq was fought on more equal terms in "The World Fails the Kurds Again," 4-3, his indignation well supported by information indicating the many options for allied policies that could have provided Iraqis with the opportunity to overthrow the Baghdad regime. He offers a clear-eyed assessment of the decision to end the war in "Iraq: The Road Not Taken," *The New York Review of Books* 5-16, along with a dissection of post-war policy. He ruffles many feathers with his handling of the question of Turkey's relationship to the future European Union in "Problem Awaiting a Solution," 5-8, properly critical of Western Europe's foot-dragging, castigating Turkey for its shortcomings on economic, political, and human rights policies while still scoring an emphatic point for admission. Mortimer had once proposed merging the G-7 with NATO, letting NATO function as its military arm; he adds another dimension to the new world order in "The Summit of the North," 7-17, rich with insight. He perceptively outlines the possibilities for geopolitics in the framework of a hardline Soviet government in power during the coup, "Back Towards the Old World Order," 8-20, shifting gears quickly and effectively.

Novak, Michael. *Forbes.* (★ ★)
"The Larger Context" columnist. One of the unusual pairings between publication and columnist, Novak administered less theology and more rhetoric of late, with mixed success. But

he generally steers clear of the business topics covered in the magazine, sticking instead to its basic free-market ideology. He reveals the media's, particularly television news', penchant for big government in "They Love Big Government," 1-21, supporting his argument with trenchant, and sometimes outrageous examples of TV journalists, one of his better efforts for the year. In "Iraqi Lessons," 2-18, Novak effectively captures the euphoria following the first successful week of war against Iraq, inspiring but not unique. He ponders the new world order in "Pax Americana," 4-29, closing with a pleasing blend of philosophy and modern day global politics: "The new world order, then, is a world in which international pressures are now building to increase the number of three-sided social systems. These are systems based upon republican (democratic) forms of polity, on free economies and on cultures that protect freedom of conscience, information and ideas." He is soggy and a bit condescending in "Europe's Coming Decline," 7-8, as Novak resigns himself to European unity, offering one discerning bit of wisdom that the EC '92 is really a "race between the statists and the free marketeers, with the former at this stage edging slowly ahead." He pens a timely wake-up call for parents who may still think that their children are getting a balanced university education, "Back to School," 9-2, wisely concluding: "Is it healthy for democracy when its cultural leaders have a view of reality far out of accord with that of the leaders of its economic and political systems? Diversity of viewpoint is extremely valuable in a democracy — but not when its components are kept hermetically sealed from one another in isolated enclaves." He finally addresses economic policy in "Socialism's Last Stand," 10-28, urging Bush to look past the dubious goals of the egalitarians: "Why doesn't Bush return to the economic successes of Reagan? Why doesn't he stop the poverty-increasing 'kinder and gentler' stuff, and finish the job on socialism? Cut the capital gains and other taxes. Restore incentives. Attack the parts of the welfare state that destroy family life. Get this country moving again."

Page, Clarence. *Chicago Tribune,* Tribune Media Services. (★ ★)
The 1989 Pulitzer recipient continues to trenchantly cut to the heart on black issues, both in print and during his guest appearances on "MacNeil/Lehrer NewsHour," but he doesn't often offer prescriptions to his diagnoses. Page offers no cohesive way out in "How Not to Fight Poverty," *The Washington Times* 1-2, although he has the right solution: "Birth control won't end poverty. Work will. The best way to reduce the ranks of the poor is to help get them educated, trained and employed especially when the new jobs of the 1990s are crying out for skilled labor. With money of their own, who knows? They might even have fewer children." He blames the public for not demanding more freedom of the press in the Persian Gulf War, but isn't quite persuasive, "No Mercy for Messengers?" *WT* 2-11. In "Brutality and Cycles of Fear," *WT* 3-19, Page examines the LA police case, noting that although black urban areas have high crime rates, "poor blacks, the primary victims of black crime, have not rallied forcefully for tougher law enforcement, it is largely because past crackdowns have resulted too often in crackdowns on innocent black people's heads." He offers a solid, persuasive defense of Georgetown in "Student's Charges Flunk Fairness Test," *WT* 4-26, on its fight with a student who exposed the fact that blacks score lower on law school admissions tests than whites. In "Swimming Away from the Mainstream?" *WT* 5-31, Page is concerned about what seems to be a self-imposition of segregation on African-Americans and other minorities, using a mock commencement speech to address the new tribalism which "has worked its way down into high schools." His emphatic message: "As minorities, we must be concerned with the preservation of our culture and identity, but we also must learn how to understand and get along with members of other groups if we are to swim successfully in the mainstream." Page gets personal in a thoughtful assessment of the PC phenomenon in the nation's newsroom, "PC Debate Reaches Into the Newsroom," *WT* 9-13, noting editors have to walk a politically fine line, having to "be mindful of their diverse audience's diverse concerns yet courageous enough not to back away from controversy when they think they're right." But he is surprisingly lukewarm in a tribute to Thurgood Marshall, "Legacy of Conscience," *WT* 7-2, a strictly rote appraisal of the man and his life.

Peirce, Neal R. *National Journal.* (★)

"State of the States" columnist. Peirce's state by state examinations are too frequently superficial, giving us less research than necessary to form a truly convincing, constructive appraisal. We get a good mini-profile of the prospective N.C. speaker of the house, Daniel T. Blue, using Blue's success as a black legislator as a springboard to look at minority politicians nationwide, "Minorities Slowly Gain State Offices," 1-5. Peirce is all over the map in blaming the defense budget for urban blight, "Neglecting Cities, Paying for War," 2-2, failing to seriously focus on the problems in state and local government which contribute to the decay. He needs to take a closer look at the damage N.J. Governor Jim Florio has done to the economy of his state before reviewing "Lessons From a Political Pariah," 3-6, in which Peirce basically states that while Florio's tactics may be harsh, they are noble: "Maybe winning isn't everything. Maybe an occasional governor who is content to be a one-termer, trading in his popularity to achieve a basic change, serves his state better than political survivors." He dissects the term limit debate fairly well in "California Grapples with Term Limits," 4-13. He is snide in "Continuing Education for Judges?" 6-22, examining the question of judges untrained in environmental issues confronted with environmental lawsuits: "Is there a realistic chance that thousands of judges in the 50 states will rise to the level of knowledge and sophistication that tough environmental cases pose? It's easy to be pessimistic. Fortunately, many highly competent people are appointed to judgeships." Half-baked in "Cutting Government Down to Size," 7-6, he examines the proposals of Florida Gov. Lawton Chiles and his Lt. Gov. Buddy MacKay, a powderpuff overview with Peirce asking no tough questions of either gentleman. Peirce comes out in favor of Japanese philanthropy where they have plants in the U.S. in "Japanese Largess: Good Money After Bad?" 9-28, arguing speciously that with the "incestuous" intermingling of U.S. and Japanese society, "open dialogue and frank criticism are essential. . .philanthropy may be a good place to start." He points out that film isn't real life when it comes to the inner cities, "A Moving Picture of Urban America," 10-26, but it sounds as though he never left the screening room to pen this: what are the differences he sees between the city-based films such as "Jungle Fever" and reality?

Postrel, Virginia. *Reason.* (★ ★ ★)

Postrel's pensive examinations of current issues stay true to the libertarian posture of the monthly. A fine writer, her arguments continue to be superbly constructed, although they are not always brought to a distinct conclusion. She only has half the solution in "Blind Trust," 1-91, on vaguely worded laws, the parameters of which must be set by the courts, concluding that "it would be great if courts started to throw out vague laws" but never concretely suggesting voters throw out vague lawmakers. She uses history and logic in "What's Fair in War?" 2-91, an exceptionally good examination of the "fairness" issue in the volunteer army. Postrel is thoughtful with "Historical Certainties," 3-91, an intelligent and credible evaluation of the situation before the Gulf War. In "Cybernetic War," 4-91, she draws original lines between cybernetics from other kinds of warfare: "*Cybernetic* suggests high technology, and much has been made recently of high-tech weaponry and of high-tech journalism. But modern warfare has always been distinguished by its use of technology, from repeating rifles to tanks to atomic bombs. And technology has always driven warfare, and vice versa, from the stirrup onward. What really distinguishes cybernetic warfare is that it substitutes machines for manpower, capital for labor, brains for brawn." She makes an erudite libertarian argument against a national energy policy, which we need no more than "shampoo or socket-wrench policy," in "Fuelishness," 5-91. Postrel is uncharacteristically confusing on the state of feminism, "Why Women Can't Commit," 6-91, covering too much. She is out of sorts in "Bad Choice," 7-91, listing and amplifying all the bad things and dangers about school choice, offering no alternative. She pulls together "Policy Relapse," 8/9-91, serving up the idea that everything old is new again, particularly health care: "Suddenly, it's 1971 again. We have snapped back to that period of political adolescence when any problem — no matter how complicated — seemed solvable if only Congress would pass a law." Postrel and Lynn Scarlett try to do too much in "Talking Trash," cover 8/9-91, everything you ever wanted to know about solid waste disposal, informative but rather overwhelming in scope.

Pruden, Wesley. *The Washington Times.* (★ ★ ½)
Editor-in-Chief. Fiercely defensive of his own daily, Pruden has always been at his best when pulling the wings off his competitors, particularly those at the paper across town. We appreciate his sulfuric subjectivity, although he's not for weak stomachs or faint hearts, as he can be nasty. He is funny on Congress and the lame-duck resolutions praising the President and the troops, "Our Brave Boys on Capitol Hill," 1-18, but he goes over the line with Tom Harkin, who "once posed as a combat pilot in Vietnam until everyone found out that he was just there as a tourist." Pruden savagely attacks *Washington Post* columnists Colman McCarthy and Mary McGrory, both of whom, he thinks, have been ranting and raving about the Gulf War, "There's No Mercy in the Gas War," 2-20: "Mr. McCarthy attacked Colin Powell and characterized the Americans in Saudi Arabia as cowards because they're using their best weapons used on themselves. This strikes the manly Mr. McCarthy as not quite cricket." He takes us through an amusing romp on the Kitty Kelley book — "Mrs. Reagan had affairs with several men before she married the Gipper, which will no doubt shock le tout Washington, where virginity is highly prized, but no one will be surprised in Peoria, where they think that's what Hollywood is all about" — in "This Just In from the Upstairs Maid," 4-8, although he does take a cheap shot at Ted Kennedy, the "Zipper Disease. . .poster child." Pruden trenchantly underscores the fact that the *Washington Post* appears to be waging a purely partisan Get-Sununu campaign, "The First Slice Is Out of Sununu," 6-24: "The capital graveyards are full of Republicans who lie beneath headstones inscribed: 'Here lies a fool, who thought amiable reason would appease *The Post.*' " In "A Judge's Threat to a Coward Town," 7-24, Pruden loads up and blasts away at critics of Clarence Thomas, in typical Pruden style, leaving little in his wake. His subsequent defense of Thomas, "The Judge Meets the Dating Game," 10-7, is unyieldingly tough on the Senate for the entire Hill-Thomas debacle, but contains lines which are sure to offend female readers, feminist or not, with its offensive phallic imagery and just plain disrespect: ". . .it's true that often a woman would marry a telephone pole if she could get a pair of pants on it. . ." More palatable, he bids a gleeful hail and farewell to *Pravda,* the Soviet house organ that was a casualty of the failed Soviet coup, "Posting Farewell to Poor Pravda," 9-15.

Quindlen, Anna. *The New York Times.* (★)
"Public & Private" columnist. Mostly mush. In a *New Republic* review of *Object Lessons,* Karen Lehrman acknowledges that while Quindlen consistently humanizes political issues, "she self-consciously refuses to discuss the issues, abstract and political, at stake in the debate, and assumes that bringing her sensibility to bear on the thoughts and feelings of the central character is enough," "She the People," *TNR* 6-10. We concur in this assessment. Quindlen vents her spleen on the N.Y. Giants' pro-life video in "Offensive Play," 1-24, her specious argument for celebrities taking stands on political issues not extending to pro-choicers. Quindlen indulges the worst kind of ethnic stereotypes regarding the Irish in "Erin Go Brawl," 3-14, hypocritical on the St. Patrick's Day parade and gay marchers. She relies on heartrending anecdotes on a Jersey City pre-school program, "Preventive Medicine," 4-25, offering little hard information how this might be applied elsewhere. She is insightful and funny on how talk shows do not portray "The Human Condition," 5-2: "The Human Condition is not your condition. Your condition is mortgage payments, lost dry cleaning, fleas on the cat and 10 pounds overweight. The Human Condition is sex change candidates whose families have taken them to court to bar their surgery, sisters who have been married to the same man and people who have their stomach stapled." Although she makes some cogent points about reporting, and proving, sexual harassment, "Listen to Us," 10-9, she sounds dopey in this weak defense of Anita Hill, talking about the "hole in the consciousness of the [Senate Judiciary] committee that empathy, however welcome, could not entirely fill" due to the lack of female representation. But it's her illogical diatribe on the Persian Gulf parade, "Instant Replay, Confettied," 6-9, that is unintentionally revealing. As she aligns herself with the pacifists: We "who thought that this war was wrong and have had that conviction reinforced by its aftermath, the carnage in Iraq and the closing of the American mind to anything but our own supremacy. But we only mumbled our objections, then and now, because we feared being caught by the patriotically correct." Someone fearful of voicing an opinion logically, clearly and forcefully simply shouldn't be on the op-ed page of the *Times.* Send her back to "Life in the 30s."

Raspberry, William. *The Washington Post.* (★ ★ ★ ½)
Raspberry's clear, crisp grasp of incendiary racial issues make his thoughtful, precise evaluations all the more important. His perspectives on civil rights were particularly distinctive as the battle took shape; we've come to rely on his smart but cool-headed appraisals that never mince words. In "Support, Not Protest," 1-23, Raspberry perceptively notes in a visit to anti-war protesters in Lafayette Park that they are "not at all clear that their continuing protest offers no policy alternative that makes sense." He is one of the first to argue for racial objectivity in the civil rights struggle, "Service, Rewards, Fairness," 2-11: "Base benefit on color alone and fairness goes out the window. Base them on objective circumstances — poverty. . .and you disarm the opponents, even if blacks remain the disapportionate beneficiaries." He sounds a similar theme with a ringing indictment of the new civil rights bill, a 10 Best selection for Commentary, "Race-Based Advantage Is a Detour," *Los Angeles Times* 3-17, pinpointing the critical problem: "The black consensus is that white resistance to the agenda of the civil-rights leadership is nothing more than latter-day racism, a new mean-spiritedness that is 180 degrees away from the attitude that helped to produce civil-rights legislation. . .We still say we want to be judged by the 'content of our character,' but our agenda is based on the color of our skin." Raspberry frets realistically that the D.C. Mt. Pleasant riots may be a harbinger of things to come, "Grim Reruns of the '60s," 5-8, as the same problems exist. He sturdily defends Clarence Thomas, "Some Wrongs Can't Be Righted," *LAT* 7-3, evidence of Raspberry's unimpeachable integrity, as he calls to account the hysterical rhetoric coming from the anti-Thomas lobby. Thomas, he advises, is not saying there is no government role in correcting the racism's evils, but that he "parts company with the civil rights establishment on the question of group remedies." Raspberry sounds a cautionary note amidst the hurrahs for the fall of communism in the thought-provoking "Their Failure Doesn't Make Us a Success," 9-4, linking the Soviet and European nationalist troubles to our own, warning "What is more likely — what, in fact, seems already underway — is an increase in disputes, claims and counterclaims across ethnic, geographical, gender, political and economic lines. What is happening in Europe could happen here."

Roberts, Paul Craig. *The Washington Times.* (★ ★ ★)
An economist by trade, Roberts continues to improve his presentations in dissecting economic issues. He is not quite as strong on the social front, except where it bears on budgetary matters. He is prescient in his examination of Ted Kennedy's attempts to move health bills through Congress, "Throwing Sand in Economic Gears," 12-21-90, incisively revealing the shortcomings of Canada's national health service. Roberts sharply details how to save billions in bailout costs, "Rescuing Real Estate Will Save Banks and the Economy, Too," 2-18: "A reduction in the capital-gains tax rate, a shorter capital-recovery period, and the elimination of the 'passive investor' rules would breathe life back into real estate values, save many financial institutions from failure, and save the government — or taxpayers — billions of dollars in bailout costs." He deftly pegs the '91 Civil Rights Act as a quota bill, "Playing Quota Games," 3-7, with the relevant facts and figures backing him up. In "Bush's Teflon Deficits," *The Wall Street Journal* 5-6, Roberts superbly highlights the fact that all the hysteria over deficits under Reagan, who resisted tax hikes as a response, is muted now under Bush who has deployed the tax hikes, making a forceful case that the hysteria was primarily hype so as to provide a suitable environment for a tax hike push. He solidly argues against a Soviet bailout, "Bearhug Bailout," 6-6: "The Soviet Union lacks the institutions to make effective use of Western aid. If it had the institutions, it would not need the aid. If it gets the aid in advance of the institutions, they will be bureaucratized and stillborn." His strictly social commentary is less than effective, however. In "Roe Dragging Anchor?" 9-4, his cogent points on abortion and the court's basis for abortion as medicine rather than law are obscured by his dire predictions of lawlessness should the Supreme Court continue to decide cases outside the Constitution, foreseeing "armed conflict" during the confirmation process. And in "Massacre Message Misread," 10-21, Roberts uses the Texas massacre by a lone gunman to call for looser gun laws, a perverse appraisal: looser gun laws mean "Someone among the 100 to 120 people inside the restaurant would have been armed, and the gunman would have been dropped long before he killed 23 people." "Wyatt" Roberts does not assess the utility of the average handgun easily carried in one's purse or pocket against a semiautomatic assault pistol.

Rosenfeld, Stephen S. *The Washington Post.* (★ ½)
Rosenfeld's rather obvious characterizations do little to advance the foreign policy debates raging within the Beltway, as he returns to his habit of stylishly recycling the conventional wisdom. He straddles the fence on U.S.-Soviet relations in "Rite of Russia," 1-18: "The Bush people caught up to this standard just in time to witness Soviet reforms start going into reverse. It is a cautionary lesson to those who would project any movement in Soviet Politics, in any direction, out to the end. Better to hedge a bit and see how events go." Rosenfeld is thoughtful on differences and similarities between the Vietnam protesters and the anti-war movement, "Protest and the President," 2-1, but this is only one of many we saw. He offers nothing really new in "Military Doctrine Today," 3-22, pointing out that the military's successful air-land battle doctrine in the Gulf was the marriage of time-proven military strategy with modern equipment and logistics, praising, as did so many others, the Pentagon for having learned valuable lessons from Vietnam. Rosenfeld deconstructs the administration policy of avoiding the "Lebanonization" of Iraq, "Worse Than Being Lebanonized," 4-26, mildly thought-provoking as he observes the obvious: "Lebanonization. . .isn't the worst thing that could happen. The worst is communal and even physical annihilation. Americans are unaccustomed to addressing such desperate contingencies in their own lives. Many others in the world, however, are not so fortunate." Rosenfeld overreacts in "Gulf Giddiness," 5-31, to a statement by Colin Powell in a Don Oberdorfer story that he hasn't "the foggiest" idea if America's position of world preeminence will lead to greater or lesser military involvement overseas, concluding that intervention isn't all its cracked up to be. In "Heroism and Realism," 6-28, he offers a middle ground course for the Yugoslav republics, "limited sovereignty or, better, self-limited sovereignty," but, despite the interesting premise, it doesn't seem quite realistic. Rosenfeld offers only obvious "preliminary and unsolicited guidelines for those upholding an ethnic cause," in "Tips for New States," 7-5, such as violence is a bad idea.

Rosenthal, A. M. *The New York Times.* (★ ½)
"On My Mind" columnist. Rosenthal received the Human Rights in Media Award from the International League for Human Rights this year, deservedly so as he persists in his lonely quest for justice for prisoners of conscience around the planet, using his column as a podium. As in days past, however, his cogent points can be undercut by the frantic, hyperventilating tone sometimes permeating his prose. He is restrained and forceful in "Support the President," 1-11, a call for Congress to back the President as war looms. "The Soviet-Iraq Axis," 2-19, is mere heavy breathing, using "axis" to extend a Nazi metaphor to Moscow, with no information to support his "axis." In "Forgotten Friends," 3-5, Rosenthal reminds us — again — of the students in Beijing and folks fighting for freedom who have kept up their fight while we were busy with Iraq, but his whiny manner grates. He makes a surprisingly powerful invocation to action on the Iraqi rebels, whom he links here to the Jews during WWII, "The Jews of Iraq," 4-5, reprising this theme in "America at the Vistula," 4-9, a strong and bitter linking of the Kurds and Iraqis to the victims of Naziism, this time the Poles and the rebels of the Warsaw ghetto, tough on Bush and his decision to let well enough alone, thus "protecting his political margin." He is marvelously understated in "Saddam Hussein's Pistol," 5-10, on Hussein and his omnipresent danger to peace, warning against getting back into the political bed with the dictator: "He will go on shooting his pistol into the air, preening before the Arab world, showing plainly that he remains a gun pointed at the world. For the U.S., as long as he lives and rules, Saddam Hussein will be the true, deadly quagmire." Rosenthal is just plain nasty in "Mistakes of the War," 7-12, his venom obscuring otherwise persuasive arguments that were made more relevant as Hussein's nuclear capability and intentions come to light. During the coup attempt, he sounds the obvious warning that the administration should hedge its bets in the Soviet Union, "The Last Act," 8-20, by dealing with other politicians besides Gorbachev, should Gorbachev be "politically resuscitated." And "An Autobiography," 9-17, seems a knee-jerk effort on President Bush's decision to hold back on loan guarantees for Israel: "The chapter confirms that in international affairs, foreign nations and peoples trust this Administration at their own risk."

Royko, Mike. *Chicago Tribune,* Tribune Media Services. (★ ★ ½)
Royko's riotous humor took on a sharper edge, the columnist honing his wit to a fine knifepoint with which he mercilessly dissects the flaws and foibles of his subjects. In "Without a Place to Flop," *The Washington Times* 1-1, Royko is uncharacteristically bitter on how "do-gooders" do more harm than good via the homeless, and how "reforms" got them there. He is funny on the lumberjack fashion ads, "Lacking Only the Rugged Bouquet," *WT* 2-13, which are even appearing in the pages of *The New York Times*: "There was a picture of a handsome male model, dressed as if ready to go out and stalk a grizzly, although he might have trouble finding one on Manhattan's Upper East Side. (Someone should have told him that grizzly hunters do not pose with hand on hip.)" Royko has no pity for Ivana Trump as she turns down a ten-million-dollar settlement from The Donald, "No Fury Like This Buyout," *WT* 3-27, moderately diverting. He is sympathetic to Lisa Olson in her encounter with the New England Patriots and subsequent lawsuit, "Her Suit Barely Fits the Issue," *WT* 5-1, falling back on his original solution of having Olson carry a large pair of pruning shears in her purse. Royko lambastes the legislators for their ill-advised enactment of a special 10% tax on luxury items, "Congress Misses the Boat on Taxes," *WT* 6-4, smart commentary on how "Congress came up with a tax that loses money, has wiped out thousands of jobs and deprives the Treasury of millions in income tax dollars. Not to mention the misery that comes with being tossed out of work or losing a business." Rostenkowski's defense of the luxury tax provides Royko with more fodder in "Rosty's Taxing Thoughts," *WT* 6-20, dealing the tax, Congress and Rostenkowski a fatal blow. Royko not only examines the career of Jerry Brown, but examines how and why the moniker "Governor Moonbeam" has stuck to them both, "Retrieving the Glow," *WT* 9-6. Royko anointed Brown 'Governor Moonbeam,' and later renounced it, only to have it appear inevitably in news stories, usually followed by 'due to his unorthodox lifestyle and political leadership.' As Royko notes, Brown's lifestyle and leadership had nothing to do with it: "he got that nickname because a guy in Chicago was stringing some words together one evening to earn a day's pay and tossed in what he thought was an amusing phrase."

Rusher, William A. Newspaper Enterprise Association. (★)
"The Conservative Advocate" columnist. There's little that appears under Rusher's byline that surprises, particularly as this armchair advocate has taken to culling so much from the daily press, rather than pursuing his own leads. He speculates on the degree of the leftward shift of the "post-conservative" era, "Post-Conservative GOP Gravity Test?" *The Washington Times* 1-16, concluding obviously that prominent Republicans are more moderate than in the Reagan years. He muses on the difficulties of electing a president from one party and a Congress from the other, "Chronic Splitting Political Headache," *WT* 2-19, standard on this impasse: "My friends, we are asking for chaos — and since this is a democracy, we will probably get it." Rusher is conventional in praise of Bush's Persian Gulf policy, particularly his slamming the door on Gorbachev's peace proposal, "America's Role Proclaimed Anew," *WT* 3-1. He sounds like theologian Cal Thomas in "Casting Out the Demons," *WT* 4-12, surprisingly effective in discussing evil in the wake of the "20/20" segment on exorcism: ". . .If you believe, like I do, that there is an independent force for evil around in the world, actively hostile to God and bent upon the destruction of His handiwork, mankind, then there is nothing implausible about the concept of "possession," or a belief in the validity of exorcism." He is robustly cynical with "Rearranging the Deadly Probabilities," *WT* 6-7, an offbeat column in which Rusher wryly asks why bother to stop smoking, eat nutritional foods and jog constantly to save a few years since you'll live those few years when you're too old to care. "The Logic of Choosing Cuomo," *WT* 8-30, is a perfectly conventional assessment of Mario Cuomo and what his pluses and minuses are as presidential candidate that could have been written four years ago, so little do we find out what Cuomo is thinking now. In "Tracing a Travesty to Its Roots," 10-17, Rusher rouses himself a bit, at least giving us strong opinion and vigorous language when assigning blame for the Thomas-Hill fiasco. The criminals he indicts however are all the standard ones: Biden, the unknown staffer who leaked the FBI report, America for electing these Senators and Hill herself.

Safire, William. *The New York Times.* (★ ★ ★ ★)
"Essay" columnist. The consummate *Times*man relishes the provocative these days, Safire inciting controversy with bombshell reporting and incendiary analysis. He has made a spectator sport of dissecting Bush administration policy and personnel, zeroing in on the hapless chief of staff, his work on this subject meriting a 10 Best selection for Commentary. The Bush administration was deeply shaken by "In Deep Sununu," 6-20, in which Safire sent the signal that conservatives are viewing the connection of the chief of staff to their agenda as a serious liability: "John Sununu should be dumped because he lacks a Presidential aide's most essential attribute: political judgement." When Sununu shot back through *The Wall Street Journal* and Evans & Novak, Safire returns fire with "Sununu Blames the Jews," 6-27. Safire, as usual, has the last word: "Thus does John Sununu depart, creating a supernova of bigoted resentment to make himself a household name at his President's expense. Spiro Agnew is alive and well and working near the Oval Office." Continuing the barrage, Safire reveals possible links between "B.C.C.I. and Sununu," 10-28, via the connection between Ed Rogers, Sununu's "right-hand man, political protege and personal press agent," and Sheik Kamal Adham, the former chief of Saudi intelligence accused of being the BCCI's front man, and the $25,000-a-month fee being paid to Rogers for "legal expertise as well as 'duties that could border on political.' " He's trenchant on policy as well. In "Gorby's Black Berets," 1-14, while recognizing that there is not a military option for stopping Soviet aggression against Lithuania, Safire nonetheless makes an effective case "that does not mean the world is helpless," and spells out several serious "distinctives" that the West can send to Mikhail Gorbachev. Safire is powerful with an indictment of the Bush administration for its failure to help the Kurds, "Follow the Kurds to Save Iraq," 3-28: "To this inglorious end, we are ready to turn our face away from the wholesale slaughter of innocents and to abandon the last best hope of the beginning of freedom in Iraq." He is equally merciless in a follow-up, featuring biting commentary that was surely read with agony at the White House, "Bush's Bay of Pigs," 4-4, calling Bush's Kurdish policy "dishonorable." And on the Soviet coup, Safire urges Bush to overcome his fear and go all out to encourage the dissolution of the communist party and Soviet Union, "After the Fall," 8-29, correctly assessing the potential: "With the Soviet monolith broken up and a commonwealth established to negotiate arms reductions, the world will be a far safer place."

Samuelson, Robert J. *Newsweek,* Washington Post Writers Group. (½ ★)
Samuelson, who only three short years ago we heralded as "fresh" and as a "serious *student* of the world political economy," appears to have packed it in as a serious student of anything. His appraisals of even the most trivial issues are facile and superficial. In "Saddam Is No Profit Maximizer," 1-21, Samuelson correctly but obviously identifies the central problem of the Gulf crisis as overall stability in the region. A condescending opening sets the tone for "A Slow Fix for the Banks," 2-18, a simple evaluation: "You're forgiven if you skipped the Bush administration's plan to overhaul the banking system last week. Let's face it: bank reform is deadly dull and hugely complex. But pay attention anyway. It matters." Samuelson calls for a "stiff" energy tax, from 20 to 30%, "Tinkering With Energy," 3-4, never examining the fiscal repercussions. He is off the mark with "The Joys of Mowing," 4-29: "In an era when almost everything is beyond our control, our lawns are not. We are a better country for our lawns, and we need more — not less — grass." "The Numbskull Factor," *The Washington Post* 6-26, is pretentious filler, in response to a survey request by a management consultant. In "The Chilling of America," 6-10, Samuelson calls for the refitting of air conditioners to conform to new CFC regulations, if we have to use them at all, and he'd rather we wouldn't, as sweat "builds character." With "Slow-Motion Solutions," 7-1, Samuelson tries to tell us how to make government work more efficiently, but his solutions would create more backlog. We get the bright side of recession in "A Shakeout in Services," 8-5: "What no one says (but everyone recognizes) is that recessions are a grim sort of industrial policy," concluding a "messy recovery" may be coming: "What are the odds of this? No one knows." And while Samuelson outlines the problems of the Soviets candidly and with some sophistication, "Now, Let's Aid the Soviets," 10-14, his solutions of throwing money at those problems is simplistic. He tells us the Soviets

need a viable currency, but not how to get there; he tells us that farm policies should be altered by removing price controls in the republics, but doesn't examine the implications. A disappointing portfolio.

Schneider, William. *National Journal.* Los Angeles Times Syndicate. (★ ★)
Schneider's surveys of the political landscape contain all the correct detail, but still lack context too frequently to give us a sense of the overall picture, leaving it to us to compile different dispatches and add them up. In "Public Backs Gulf War as Last Option," 1-12, Schneider uses poll after poll to indicate public support for U.S. military force against Iraq as a last resort, trimly articulating the Democrats' dilemma over the war. Nasty in "Finger-Pointers, Naysayers May Rue Being Right This Time," *Los Angeles Times* 1-27, he sees the war in purely GOP political-gain terms: "You can see 1992 campaign ads now. Saddam Hussein will become Willie Horton. 'Remember Jan. 12, 1991? That's when the Democrats in Congress voted to let Saddam Hussein out on furlough. They wanted to give him another chance to rape and pillage a small, defenseless country.' " He reasserts this in "If Politics Were Waged Like War," *LAT* 3-10, a stronger argument against politicization of the war. Schneider echoes current sentiment forcefully and credibly in "Bush Insists It's World War II, Anti-War Activists See Vietnam," *LAT* 2-10: "Saddam Hussein knows he cannot win a military victory. So he is pursuing a political strategy. His objective is to break U.S. political resolve." There's evidence of Schneider's wit and political acuity in "Feuding Democrats," *LAT* 5-19, a good appraisal of splits in the Democratic party and possible '92 candidates. We see flashes of the crafty, insightful Schneider in "Playing Games With the Court," *LAT* 7-7, a perceptive appreciation of the administration's strategy for navigating the treacherous waters surrounding Clarence Thomas, somewhat grudgingly rendered: "The nomination has the potential of dividing rank-and-file blacks. And it could fracture the alliance between civil-rights and women's rights groups." Schneider offers a solid assessment of the politics of the Hill-Thomas fiasco, "Thomas Vote Is a New Weapon for GOP," 10-26, concluding "the Thomas episode gives the Republicans a powerful piece of ammunition to use against Congress. The President won a war. The Democrats in Congress can't even manage a hearing." But in "Rule Suburbia," 9-28, he intriguingly offers the assessment that the suburban population explosion has contributed significantly to presidential politics, as most folks in the suburbs vote Repbulican, and most in the cities vote Democratic, but he doesn't explore what about each party appeals to each region.

Seligman, Daniel. *Fortune.* (★ ★ ★)
"Keeping Up" columnist. Seligman, oscillating in and out of semi-retirement at *Fortune,* never fails to impress us with his wit and verve. His lively appraisals are packed with information, including a healthy bit of pith and punch for good measure. It's clear he relishes writing "Keeping Up," and his enthusiasm is contagious. Seligman lists his "Groans Aplenty," 1-28: "The discovery in Nexis late last month, of 147 references to the 'decade of greed,' a phrase that got wings with the Milken sentence and by year-end was being worked in by op-edsters looking for the deeper meaning of the Trump divorce." He praises "60 Minutes" for its 12-30-90 segment on acid rain, 2-11, which left Seligman "persuaded that the acid rain scare was based more on ideology than on empirical data — that, in fact, the data then available showed acid rain to be a relatively minor problem on which it would be absurd to spend billions of tax dollars." His sharp dissection of Fred Trump's unusually-structured loan to son Donald is right on the money, 3-11: "The loan took a most original form: Fred Trump, age 85, arranged for his lawyer to visit the Castle, march up to a high-stakes blackjack table, and buy some $3 million worth of $5,000 chips. Instead of then playing blackjack, as any normal sentient being might do, the lawyer placed them in a satchel and presumably lugged them back to Fred, who now had his collateral. ...[because] 'Chips are always redeemable,' states the mighty Casino Control Commission." He takes a savvy shot at Clark Clifford and his memoir, 5-6, ironically recalling the Truman White House poker game with rules which Seligman notes "could only have been devised by liberal democrats." He devises an effective critique of Labor Secretary Lynn Martin's "glass-ceiling" initiative which seeks to create more high-level corporate jobs for women and

minorities just as Bush is speaking out against quotas, 9-9. Also included is a tribute to the PC's tenth anniversary, in which Mr. 'Keeping Up' takes on a animated trip through PC history, from the early days to today's complex PC world filled with viruses, anti-virus software, and 800 help lines. Seligman is surprisingly frivolous, 11-4, dabbling in "producerism," the Justice Dept.'s challenging the VMI decision, and finally the *1991 Journal of Psychohistory.* But being frivolous, it lacks his usual punch.

Shields, Mark. *The Washington Post.* (★ ★ ½)
Shields puts a fresh spin on accepted beliefs with his sincerely populist sentiments, directly challenging the Washington politicos who would so blithely shut out the world beyond the Beltway. In "Beware the Quicksand," 1-16, Shields strongly defends House Democrats representing blue-collar districts voting against the war, arguing that their constituents see "a national leadership exactly like that during Vietnam, a leadership which boldly asks some 450,000 Americans to make the ultimate sacrifice of life itself and then cowardly cringes rather than dare ask the rest of us to pay even another buck in taxes or to limit our mindless gas guzzling." Shields postulates as to "Why Democrats May Be the Big Winners," 3-9, going against the prevailing wind, arguing that the renewed respect of the federal government created by the Gulf War along with Bush's lack of any hardcore political support are an opportunity: "Because of circumstances largely beyond their control, the Democrats face a confident and optimistic electorate prepared to seriously consider bold public leadership." With "Tehran Hostages: The Story That Won't Go Away," 5-11, Shields makes a reasonable and logical call for investigating the "October surprise" allegations, while admitting that the Democratic "silver bullet" for Bush is undoubtedly a pipe dream. "Democrats: The Party's Almost Over," 6-10, is an engaging effort by Shields to wake up the Democrats to the dangerous demographic discrepancy between the two major parties: "As the typical Republican moves from a room of his own to an apartment of his own to a home of his own, the ardent Democrat moves from his own home to the retirement home to the nursing home and, yes, to the funeral home." In "No Need for Mud in Campaign '92," 8-13, an examination of the first post-Cold War presidential race, Shields perceptively sees a historic opportunity to fully debate the future of the country — if the politicians don't blow it with negative campaigning. Reminding us of the voters in "Finally Fed Up in Massachusetts," 9-20, Shields travels to the heart of Kennedy Country and discovers that their "tolerance. . .has been stretched to the breaking point," by the Palm Beach fiasco and his performance during the Thomas confirmation hearings which effectively "destroyed any last illusions that Kennedy still has the stature and the moral power to deliver for the causes he believes in."

Sidey, Hugh. *Time.* (★ ★)
"The Presidency" columnist. Sidey measures Presidential events and personalities with a calculating eye, the surface of his evocative columns realistic while still vivid and atmospheric. He offers sober impressions of Washington as the U.S. teeters on the brink of war, "The Cold Hand of War," 1-21, tough and dignified. Sidey is surprisingly strong and grimly proud of the President's handling of the business of war, "Waiting for the Bugle Call," 2-25, making no bones about the political landmines along the way, such as the possibility of high coalition casualties, should the ground war begin and continue for any length of time. He is practical but not quite cynical on Bush's popularity, "Of Force, Fame and Fishing," 3-11: "But the hazards of such an exalted position in the world are obvious. . .The tributes to Bush last week in the U.S. Congress will endure about as long as it takes to say 'pork barrel.' The instantaneous maneuvering of the diplomatic corps for Bush's favor was heard at dozens of dinner tables through the week." Sidey doesn't examine why a group of historians gave Ford and Carter higher marks for their tenures than Ronald Reagan, much less why Reagan remained uncredited for the economic expansion, "What Links These Six?" 4-15, leaving us unsatisfied. In "The Greatest Eclipse," 6-3, Sidey effectively ties veteran Democrat Clark Clifford's disgrace on BCCI with the eclipse of the Democratic Party. He is tough in "Why Bush Has Trouble Firing Sununu," 7-8, calling for the axing of the Chief of Staff, putting it quite plainly: "A similar [to

the Regan dismissal] boot in the behind is now in order for Bush's chief of staff, John Sununu. His abuse of public facilities and trust and George Bush's presidency is just wrong. His apologies and contrition are shams. Sununu has shot himself in both feet and some other parts, has diminished a talented and devoted White House staff, and has insulted the intelligence of Bush and now the country." Sidey then recalls other cabinet firings in his memory. He offers an overview of presidential dealings with communist dictators of the Soviet Union and how they sometimes were hoodwinked, "Rebuilding a Moral Framework," 9-9. Sidey seems to feel these days are over, and we are relieved.

Sobran, Joseph. *National Review,* Universal Press Syndicate. (★ ★ ½)
His muscular arguments and sometimes startling appraisals are loyally, although not blindly, free market, bordering on libertarianism. Sobran's intellectual discussions remain accessible to all, however, and are always worthwhile. In ". . .and Odd Lights," *The Washington Times* 1-17, he strongly contrasts the differences between Lithuania and Kuwait, devastating the popular moral equivalency: "Lithuania is nearly the opposite of Kuwait. It's the victim of imperialism, whereas Kuwait owes its very existence to Western imperialism. Lithuania remains religiously, linguistically and ethnically distinct from its conqueror. Kuwait is an international fiction, a pseudo-nation." Rather plaintive on the cosmic thinking of the government, he advises conservatives to "get cranky" as too much of what government does smacks of central planning, "Not a Member of the Cosmics," *WT* 2-12: "Having been a citizen of the Great Society, I understand I'm about to become a member of the New World Order. Gosh. It's certainly been a full life." Sobran intrigues on Noam Chomsky, "Hard-to-Place Phenomenon," *WT* 3-27, surprisingly respectful of Chomsky's intellect and integrity, although it's plain Sobran doesn't agree with much of Chomsky's philosophy. He calmly dissects Kitty Kelley in "Stature of the Target," *WT* 4-11: "She has made a splash and a bundle. Congratulations. Enjoy it. But spare us the yammer of the Need to Enlighten the General Public." In "LA Lawmen," *The Wanderer* 3-21, Sobran chides some conservatives for their fixed "right-wing" attitudes regarding Rodney King and the issue of police brutality. His essay "Single Sex and the Girl," *National Review* cover 8-12, on cultural and marketing phenomenon Madonna, is well written, but in the end he fails to come up with any original insights. Sobran sings the praises of Libertarians and their presidential candidate, "Against the Force Nexus," *WT* 9-6. Libertarians, he notes, want a minimal government performing the essential functions of protecting citizens against force and fraud, seeing the promise of their candidate in their credo: ". . .force and fraud are actually the two chief tactics of government as we alas know it — fraudulent promises kept by extracting money from citizens by force." A-ha.

Sowell, Thomas. Scripps-Howard News Service. (★ ★ ★)
Sowell poetically articulates the conservative side in debates over social policy. A Hoover Institute fellow of depth and precision, Sowell's dissertations generally persuade and often move us. He is not impressed with media protests over the Persian Gulf pool restrictions, "Sound Bite Journalism," *The Washington Times* 1-5, giving full credit to the courage of the press, but castigating the whiners: "The First Amendment does not require the government to supply the media with information. . .[and the public] is not clamoring for incidental details that will jeopardize American lives." Sowell trenchantly ravages the government tendency to simply throw money at social problems through social programs, "Throwing Money and Intercepting It," *WT* 2-19, as bureaucracy eats up the budgets anyway: "Part of the money gets intercepted by bureaucrats, consultants, social workers, academic researchers and others who gather round these programs like flies around honey." He responds to the cliche "if we can win a war in the Persian Gulf, why can't we. . .?" in "Postwar Politicking," *WT* 3-13, logically asserting that just because government can do one doesn't mean it can, or should, do the other: "There is no law that says there must be an expert who can fix everything that goes wrong in human life. But as long as we think there is, there will always be someone to step forward to claim the titles and take our money." He is chilling on how ideas can have disastrous effects, "Cruelty of the Abstract," *WT* 4-30, focusing on a toddler taken from white parents because she's a minority.

Sowell philosophically examines the need for mutual influence, of the good sort, naturally, in "Influence Amid the Wages of Freedom," *WT* 7-4: "If we ever reach the point where no one else influences our behavior, then we will not have achieved freedom, but barbarism." In "The High Cost of Identity," *Forbes* 8-5, Sowell uses civil strife in Yugoslavia as a starting point to decry the "multicultural" movement, noting the dangers of the divisiveness: "What has enabled the U.S. to escape the fate of such strife-torn multiethnic societies as Yugoslavia or Sri Lanka is that the people of this country still think of themselves as Americans." He correctly perceives the importance of continuing the battle to clear Clarence Thomas' name, "Awaiting the Thud of Another Shoe," *WT* 10-20, predicting Hill's story will unravel further, and warning "Sexual polarization is a luxury we cannot afford, in a country where the family is eroding already."

Summers, Col. H. G., Jr. (Harry). Los Angeles Times Syndicate. (★ ★ ½)
Summers' paternal presence on NBC News during the Persian Gulf War was curiously comforting, as were his frequent, well-versed and knowledgeable columns on military strategy. He provides a professional's tactical appraisal of current strategy in the Persian Gulf War in which he outlines the options but, importantly, reveals no plans, "Allied Forces to Target Iraq 'Center of Gravity,' " *Los Angeles Times* 1-22. In "Limiting Collateral Damage," *The Washington Times* 2-12, Summers reverts to the history of "collateral damage" to make his case: ". . .even the best attempts cannot absolutely guarantee no civilian deaths or no destruction of civilian property. . .one thing is certain: With the tens of thousands of air sorties flown so far, and the tens of thousands of bombs dropped, if allied aircraft were indeed carpet-bombing Baghdad, Baghdad would be no more." On the eve of the ground war, in "Strategic Offensive Outline," *WT* 2-20, Summers reviews the play to date against the problems the U.S. military faced in Korea and Vietnam, when we were on the "strategic defensive" because of political fears of drawing in the U.S.S.R. In "Military Leadership for Tomorrow," *WT* 4-25, he makes an effective argument that the new army chief of staff is a man for the new, conventional warfare age. He then makes the case that it indeed *is* a new age of conventional warfare in "How to Be the World's Policeman," *The New York Times Magazine* 5-19. Summers offers a marvelous perspective on the Persian Gulf War in "Too Early to Write War's Last Chapter," *WT* 6-6: " 'What were the results of the French Revolution?' someone once reportedly asked Chinese Foreign Minister Chou En-lai. 'It's too soon to tell,' was his reply. Critics of the Persian Gulf War have no such perspective. Instead of Chou En-lai's 180 years, they can't manage to wait 180 days to render their verdicts." He truly makes "A Better Case for the B-2 Bomber," *WT* 8-22, a learned, readable argument for funding for the plane, which, like its B-1 brother, a "barely flyable disaster," everybody loves to hate. Summers celebrates the fact that the Joint Chiefs are finally in control of strategic policies, rather than think-tankers, citing historical examples of civilian-made military disasters, such as the concept of limited warfare, to make his point, "Strategies for the Future," *WT* 10-17.

Talbott, Strobe. *Time.* (★)
"America Abroad" columnist. The year's events seemed to overtake Talbott; it was all he could do to recycle the conventional wisdom, though he did so with style and flair. The opening lines of Charles Dickens' *A Tale of Two Cities* are quite apropos in "Best of Times, Worst of Times," 1-7, but Talbott concentrates primarily on the tribalism in Eastern Europe and the Soviet Union, missing the real tribal conflict in the Middle East — the one that's about to explode. He muddles through a discourse of Saddam Hussein's strength in "The Villain's Advantage," 2-11, which is apparently that he doesn't play nicely: "The U.S. and its partners are trying to limit casualties in their ranks and among civilians in Iraq, while Saddam boasts of his willingness to lose tens of thousands of his own troops in a single engagement, and deliberately targets cities." In "God and Man in the Gulf," 3-18, Talbott repeats the popular misconception that Islam is the problem in instituting democracy in the Gulf, that "things are the way they are because God says so," showing a lack of understanding of Middle East culture, as well as a lack of appreciation for changes in Kuwait, where some are starting to think about a redefinition of rights. He laments in "The Old Magic Is Gone," 4-29, that Mikhail Gorbachev is losing support at home which

undercuts his ability abroad, an obvious appraisal. Talbott seems contrary in "Growls in the Garden," 6-10, in which he simultaneously supports the policy of backing Baltic claims for independence while saying Georgian independence is an internal Soviet problem, because the Baltics have offered rights to minorities, but Georgia has not. Talbott's stronger with "The Delicate Balancing Act," 7-29, making a persuasive case, citing other columnists, that George Bush's much vaunted foreign policy skills may someday go to waste if he doesn't get going domestically. In "Goodfellas," 8-5, an op-ed masquerading as news piece, he is insightful in dissecting the players on the world stage. Talbott offers an instant history lesson in "Prelude to a Putsch," 9-2, an attempt to discover the underlying causes of the coup by examining the histories of the participants and the events leading up to it, interesting but premature. Talbott frets over the possibility that the now-recognized Baltics will keep their nuclear weapons, "Heading Off a Chain Reaction," 10-21, but it seems a leap from the Baltics using this as a bargaining chip to their becoming nuclear powers.

Thomas, Cal. Los Angeles Times Syndicate. (★ ★)
Thomas continually avoids proselytizing, even as he preaches. He is refreshingly frank about his own beliefs, sharply seeing world and national events through a prism of personal Christianity, but because Thomas doesn't necessarily evangelize, we never feel intimidated. He interests with speculations about Armageddon, intriguing from his born-again perspective, "Wave of Prophecy," *The Washington Times* 1-17. Thomas is extremely perceptive with "The Press, Gulf and Gaps Between," *WT* 2-11, on what the people want and what journalists do: "Most of the public does not share Sam Donaldson's view that the press 'reports what we find and see to the best of our ability.' They are put off by Mr. Donaldson's next line: 'If people don't like it, I'm sorry, but they really need to know what's happening.' They would, indeed, like to know what's happening. They just don't want the editorial spin put on it. Just give them the facts. And get them right. Most people are smart enough to draw their own conclusions." The closest he gets to evangelizing is in "The Modern Church Grows Irrelevant," *Los Angeles Times* 3-8, a compelling argument that the Church must return to basic theology in order to help assist the world's ills, occasioned by the ever-changing face of mainstream religion. Thomas is stirring in his defense of the Reagans after the publication of Kitty Kelley's book, "Aim of the Game," *WT* 4-11, stinging on the author: "Will her gains ill-gotten from besmirching someone's reputation go to the homeless and the drug addicts she says the Reagans ignored? The homeless and addicted had better not count on it." Thomas is surprisingly lax in "Have Faith in Converts From Communism," *LAT* 6-24, in this non-starter interview with Sergei Krasavchenko, chair of Boris Yeltsin's Committee on Economic Reform and Ownership, via a Heritage Foundation conference. He misses also the bull's-eye on Clarence Thomas, "Shape of the Battle Ahead," *WT* 7-2, seeing only the specific arguments over the reinterpretation of the Constitution and the construction of a conservative Court. Thomas decisively attacks the study on homosexuality, "Blaming the Brain," *WT* 9-5, citing other scientific studies that suggest homosexuality is not preordained biologically. "Politics, not science or (heaven forbid!) theological inquiry, become paramount in this unrelenting quest to validate and vindicate what had been widely considered, before politics intruded, aberrant behavior."

Tyrrell, R. Emmett, Jr. *The American Spectator,* King Features Syndicate. (★)
Editor-in-Chief. Tyrrell seems positively uninspired, his balloon deflated by the end of the Cold War, which lives on in Tyrrell's work, as it does in the work of so many Cold Warriors. He has surprisingly little to say, despite the new frontiers confronting conservatives. He uses revelations from recently published memoirs by Khrushchev and a former KGB official to contend that the conservatives were right about Algier Hiss and the Rosenbergs, "You Must Remember Hiss," 1-91, but he is plainly milking the subject. Tyrrell is refreshingly pragmatic in offering unsolicited advice in "A Memo to George Bush," 2-91, smartly urging him to match the "old wing" of the Republican party, whose members "get things done" with the "Thatcher Wing" whose members "have the passion, the energy, the numbers, and the ideas that made the Republican party the power that it was in your first year and a half." Drab in giving an award

for "The Worst Book of the Year," 3-91, to Kevin Phillips' *The Politics of Rich and Poor,* Tyrrell has nothing new to say on this tired subject. Stronger with "PC People," 5-91, he rhetorically assaults the "politically correct" movement supposedly sweeping the nation's campuses, blaming it all on "1960s radicals." He bores us with a subdued "Operation Hamill-Lewis," 6-91, a treatment of an obvious target: liberal politicians and commentators such as Pete Hamill and Anthony Lewis who opposed the war and who are now calling for the U.S. to rescue the Kurds and Shiites. In "The Borking of Carol Iannone," 7-91, Tyrrell tries to defend Carol Iannone by noting that the right has plenty of "second-rate minds" guarding what they perceive to be intellectual orthodoxy, but this kind of defense only serves to poison all who touch it. He is simplistic in "Company Man," 10-91, a half-baked defense of the performance of the CIA over the past decade, in particular, the role played by beleaguered nominee Robert Gates, who "served brilliantly" under Casey. Tyrrell observes insightfully in "Ghoulish Hungary," 11-91, that many Eastern Europeans continue to emulate the American political and economic models and American conservatism, despite their often physical resemblence to American protesters from the 1960s: "Some even wear sandals, but all would shock the Western left-wingers, not to mention America's liberals."

Wattenberg, Ben. Newspaper Enterprise Association. (★ ½)
This neocon Democrat remains solidly reliable, but Wattenberg must learn to pare down his appraisals and hone them to a finer edge. As it is, he frequently tries to cover too much. Wattenberg castigates Democrats infected with the "Vietnam virus," which paralyzes foreign affairs capability, "Avoiding the Miscues. . .and the Virus," *The Washington Times* 1-16, via the Gulf War vote. In "A Tale of Two Deserts," *WT* 2-13, he effectively links the situation of booming Las Vegas and exploding Persian Gulf, the difference between having economic and political freedom, an original twist which pinpoints the reason why the resource-rich desert is failing and the resource-poor is succeeding: "Markets are more important than minerals. Markets spur the imagination, which allows people to create wealth, not just use it up." Wattenberg muses on the melting pot, "Mixing It Up in the U.S.A." *WT* 3-20, standard but uplifting: "Remember this: Immigrants do not come to change America, they come to share in the American dream. . .There is mystical quality to it. It is fitting, and it is no accident that the leader of the world should be populated by people from everywhere, descended from everyone." Wattenberg's facile with "Mixing Fortunes," *WT* 5-1, telling Congress to do nothing about the Civil Rights Bill because it's a bad idea and because the Supreme Court was right on affirmative action. He makes the case for more critical reporting, more scrutiny of press releases and official figures in "Reading Beyond the Media Hype Lines," *WT* 5-22, charging the media is doing a less-than-adequate job in interpreting figures which results in sloppy stories about crime, housing, hunger, etc. to get into print and into broadcasts. "Yeltsingrad Bound," *WT* 6-19, is superfluous on renaming the streets and squares and towns of the Soviet Union after Yeltsin's defeat of the communists. In "Cause and Effect," *WT* 7-3, Wattenberg swings back and forth on the metronome theory of politics, using the political theories of Kevin Phillips and E. J. Dionne, Jr., as the two furthermost points on the arc, a dizzying exercise that only concludes both parties must reform. He makes some unrealistic suggestions ("Free China") in "Using Clout Wisely," *WT* 9-4, although his idea of a U.S.-Soviet trading bloc, once they get on their feet, intrigues.

Weisberg, Jacob. *The New Republic.* (★ ★ ½)
Weisberg dropped a bomb on the publishing industry, "Rough Justice," 6-17, making his mark in his first year in a senior position at the magazine. His critical appraisals of national politics follow in the tradition of *TNR;* after seeing such promise, we expect with seasoning Weisberg will become a force on the staff. In "Shadow Boxing," 1-14, Weisberg delivers an assessment of Jesse Jackson as he moves to the periphery of the Democratic party as D.C.'s "shadow senator," detailing a shift in Jackson's political fortunes since that decision, but noting that "the issue of statehood will conflate with the issue of Jesse." He takes a critical look at the anti-war movement and its far-left sponsors, "Means of Dissent," 2-25, based on firsthand observations

at several D.C. rallies, noting that while the protesters have learned a few lessons from the Vietnam era, "They remain emotionally and intellectually stuck in a '60s rut." We get the inside scoop in "Family Feud," 5-20, on the escalating tensions between the Democratic Leadership Counsel, the Democratic National Committee, and the Coalition for Democratic Values. In "This Is Your Death," 7-1, a gruesome, effective cover on capital punishment, Weisberg draws on medical experts and others to give us a graphic sense of an execution, predicting televising executions may not lead to prohibition. He takes a bemused look at the battles between the "neocons" and "paleocons" in right-wing columns, think tanks and foundations, "Hunter Gatherers," 9-2: "The paleocons believe the neocons have 'hijacked' the movement by gaining a financial stranglehold over its institutions. Beneath the high-minded debate, there's a battle for hard cash." But it's his critical look at American publishing that we remember. Timed to coincide with the American Bookseller Association convention, with "Rough Justice," 6-17, Weisberg contends that editors are less concerned with manuscript quality than with making the biggest deal or signing the hottest writer, resulting in books that are sloppily edited, filled with factual and grammatical errors, and are overlong and underedited, naming names such as Simon & Schuster editor Alice Mayhew, who brought us *Nancy Reagan* and *The Commanders*.

Wicker, Tom. *The New York Times.* (★ ★ ½)
"In the Nation" columnist. Although Wicker can be stuffy and conventional in his appraisals, there's lately a refreshing erudition in his prose that is becoming more and more prevalent. Wicker offers a good evaluation of the potentially divisive nature of aims which could support a protracted war, in "The Key to Unity," 1-30, one of which, the removal of Saddam Hussein, could splinter the coalition, a standard assessment, quite well stated. In "What's the Real Goal?" 2-20, he stops viewing the Persian Gulf conflict through a Vietnam lens and addresses the growing discrepancy between the coalition's original objectives and Washington's apparent aims: "If the goal becomes the complete subjugation of Iraq and the destruction of its Government, the new world order is going to look all too much like plain old power politics — perhaps even as a sort of Pax Americana in the Middle East." Wicker picks up on the recent Air Force admission that 70% of the bombs dropped on Iraq missed their target in "An Unknown Casualty," 3-20, restrained yet forceful on military censorship. Wicker neatly draws the lines between the flaps over John Sununu's trips, Robert Clarke's stock trades, and Chuck Robb's general indiscretions in "What's Improper?" 5-1, concluding that the appearance of impropriety is as important as its actuality as far as the public is concerned, an obvious but elegantly penned close. Although he endorses Robert Reich's call for heavier taxation of the rich, Wicker raises several key points on taxes in "A Time for Action," 5-29, perceptively noting that the real barrier to recovery is last fall's "disastrous" budget agreement. He's fired up with "Investing in America," 8-18, saying the government should damn the deficit, "a vastly overrated threat, and *invest,* for a change in the American people." An elegant critique of the Democrats never despairs, "A Tale of Two Faces," 8-11, defining the party's old and new faces: "By November 1992, however, it's not too far fetched to suggest that the face of invincibility may look more like a map of economic decline." Wicker even manages some praise for Bush, where it's due, in "Courage and Vision," 10-3, on the nuclear arms reduction initiative that "took courage, as well as the vision that George Bush is often accused of lacking. He could hardly have chosen a subject of greater importance for his demonstration of both."

Wilkins, Roger. *Mother Jones.* (★ ★ ½)
"Uncommon Ground" columnist Wilkins was awarded a 10-Best citation for Commentary last year for his incisive argument that "White Racism Is Still the Problem," *The Washington Post* 12-5-90. Though he has not again hit this pinnacle, his work is a sobering, poetic reminder that the Bush administration still does not have a base for an effective social policy. He hits unconvincingly at the foundation of democracy in "Frank Talk," 1/2-91, pegging Rep. Barney Frank (D-Mass.) as the "best breed of Democrat," who thinks "There's too much Constitution worship in this country. It is a good document, but separation of powers is a bad idea. Divided government doesn't work." Amidst a groundswell of Persian Gulf hurrahs, Wilkins offers a

sterling discourse reminding us that we are still "Losing the War on the Home Front," *Los Angeles Times* 3-4: "we need to have the courage and the staying power to look homeward. Where is the greatness if our generation is the one that liberated Kuwait City and lost New York?" Wilkins makes a sturdy defense of his repetition of the race theme, "Bush's Quota Con," 3/4-91, drawing a unique parallel to Willie Horton, who, says Bush, "wasn't designed to stir up fears about a black rapist, but rather was an instrument for discussing good prison management. The deniers are anxious to believe him. The alcoholic says, I can control my drinking. The racist says, there's nothing wrong with us — it's those people who are defective. In both cases, the denier is impatient and sometimes even angry at whoever calls attention to that which is being denied." In "Cheating the Future," 5/6-91, Wilkins makes the case that the Harlem child at risk is as important as any, more so as he is the one on the margin. He incisively pinpoints the problem with politics, although he limits his discussion to the GOP in "Dirty Secrets," 7/8-91: "They plumb our souls with polls and focus groups. And then *they follow us.*" Wilkins defends multiculturalism, without sounding the ideologue, sensitively using his own experience at U. of Michigan as a guide, "A Modern Story," 9/10-91: "I received no instruction of any kind that suggested that anybody black, Negro, or colored had contributed to anything of value to its country. . . .white kids were at least as severely damaged. They were learning the same lessons about the capacities and human worth of people of color."

Will, George. *Newsweek,* Washington Post Writers Group. (★ ★)
Will has an extremely long reach, via national print and national television, but his grueling deadline schedule is whittling him down bit by bit to where it is becoming a chore to read him. His prose is dense, a case of too much work for too little news and substance. In "War's Long Echoes," *The Washington Post* 1-18, Will notes that the Persian Gulf War's "longest reverberation" may be from Arab participation in the coalition, punishing another Arab state. Will is all over the map in "After the Dust Settles," 2-25, leaving the central point to the end: "The fact that a messy peace may leave the Middle East at least as messy as it was last Aug. 1 does not discredit Desert Storm. Neither does the fact that some rich nations have, in effect, rented America's military. But it could become tiresome." He makes his points well in "A Land Fit for Heroes?" 3-11, but he gets progressively pompous, winding up positively windy: "This is a perishable moment, and a propitious moment to say: As we welcome home the heroes from their sacrifices, let us make some symmetrical sacrifices to make this a land fit for heroes. The business of America is not business. Neither is it war. The business of America is justice, and securing the blessings of liberty." He bemusedly returns to the canine in "Mario Cuomo: Passionately Out of Style," *WP* 4-11: "Mario Cuomo, who has always had both the mournful countenance of a basset hound and the serrating edge of a Doberman, is feeling frisky but not friendly." Will takes things to the absurd on PC, "Curdled Politics on Campus," 5-6, but his conclusion that the first business of higher education is higher education, not political indoctrination, is admirably penned. In "President Odysseus," 8-12, Will resorts yet once again to canine sentiment in describing Bush as "Gorbachev's poodle," his salient points on Bush's domestic policies lost in the nastiness. He clearly relates the theories of Harvard Law Professor Mary Ann Glendon, who's just published *Rights Talk* argues there is an ever-expanding "menu of rights," so much so that the individual wins and society loses, "Too Much of a Good Thing?" 9-23.

Williams, Walter. Creators Syndicate. (★ ★)
"A Minority View" columnist. One of the many economists turning their hands and heads to social policy, Williams brings us back to earth with tight, prudent insights when the other pundits have thrown caution (and common sense) to the wind. As a black conservative, he truly is "A Minority View," though the tide is turning. He makes suggestions for a few more politically correct euphemisms in "All the Vogue on Campus," *The Washington Times* 1-14, savagely funny: "Whites ought to be called 'pre-black,' short people 'pre-tall'. . .dumb students who buy into all this, 'pre-smart' and administrators who let them get away with it, 'pre-brains.'" Williams is vivid in "Updating Cuba's Revolution," *WT* 2-15, as Fidel Castro goes backwards

in asking his comrades to sell jewelry to give to the government to pawn, among other things. Williams oversimplifies somewhat in an explanation for congressional fudging over corporate tax increases, "Tax Chicanery to Delude Taxpayers," *WT* 3-19: businesses don't pay taxes, people do, in one way or another. He celebrates the bicentennial of the Bill of Rights with almost a lament for the more moderate interpretations of the second, fifth and ninth amendments, "Celebration. . .or a Requiem," *WT* 4-9: "The Second Amendment is not a deer-hunting or duck hunting amendment. It affords us some protection against wanna-be tyrants." Williams makes a solid argument in favor of immigration, as people are an invaluable resource, "Most Likely Destination," *WT* 5-24. In "Rarely in the Fine Print," *WT* 6-7, Williams claims the media picture of black America is simply not accurate, cataloguing a number of new black publications challenging the entrenched "civil rights establishment." He whittles away at the idea of Afrocentrism, in "When Bias Gets in the Way," 7-16, pointing out that accomplishment and achievement must come first, then followed by self-esteem: "Making extraordinary personal sacrifices of time and effort to excel academically, start a business, master an instrument or a sport is a more reliable road to success than a million recitations of 'I am somebody' and Afrocentrism." Williams forcefully plugs the libertarian argument likening government redistributionism to outright theft in "Clinging to the Taxpayers' Leases," *WT* 9-2: "In other words, stealing is stealing, whether done privately or collectively."

Yoder, Edwin. Washington Post Writers Group. (★★)
Yoder was a surprising voice of reason in commentary this year. Where others seemed shrill, Yoder showed restraint, and made his point with clear-eyed logic. Yoder rationally discusses the war debate in " 'Unconditional Surrender' — An Extravagant Demand," *The Washington Post* 1-26, arguing that we should "limit ourselves to the job at hand, and leave jihads — holy wars — to the Arabs." He descends into a conventional argument about Dresden in "Hussein Has His Own 'Smart Weapon': TV," *Los Angeles Times* 2-15, after a forceful opening on the bunker bombing: "Yet as the swift and somewhat bored allied defensive reaction suggests, this is the kind of accident whose effects we cannot ignore, whoever is at fault. Hussein has chosen the battleground of mass psychology. He knows that Western opinion is wedded to dimly recalled civilities, including the basic rule against the needless and deliberate killing of civilians." In "Church-State Separation: A Flawed Test," *WP* 3-23, a dissection of the Lemon v. Kurtzman test over church v. state, Yoder sagely counsels more flexibility than is now allowed, convincing us the Lemon test is "sordidly mechanical." He incisively points out that at its heart the Sununu travel controversy is over the dichotomy between the chief of staff's carefully crafted public image of a frugal public servant and the jetsetting reality, "Puritan in Babylon," *WP* 4-25: "In short, the high style is entirely defensible for a man as important as John Sununu. But those who live it should have the grace to speak more cautiously of our impending fiscal ruin, or else travel, as would better suit their declared philosophy of government, by horse and buggy." He takes on the Supreme Court in "The Radical Agenda of a Triumphant Chief Justice," *WP* 6-30, a lengthy critique of William Rehnquist, keeping his tone respectful as he postulates Rehnquist wishes to reapportion the court *a la* Earl Warren. Yoder updates the battle of the sexes, "His Words and Hers. . ." 10-10, insightfully viewing not only sexual harassment but the Thomas-Hill hearings as further evidence that men and women don't always communicate in the same way. Men and women are "as someone once pictured England and America: 'two peoples divided by a common language.' "

Zuckerman, Mortimer. *U.S.News & World Report.* (★)
Editor-in-Chief. Zuckerman's bombast continues to be unimpressive, his logic often trite and his assessments unimaginative. He rarely brings us closer to understanding the issues of the day he attempts to dissect. Zuckerman adds little to the list of "Hussein's Many Miscalculations," 1-28, telling us the U.S. is in a war we didn't want with a man we "do not understand." He throws everything but the kitchen sink into "The Public Outsmarts TV," 2-25, obscuring his central point — "the fears of many that TV and the media would overwhelm American public opinion have proved groundless. Americans are not dummies and can make judgments fully independent

of the media," — with the clutter. He goes easy in "Let's Close the Arms Bazaar," 3-18, offering up some smart policy prescriptions for the post-war Middle East, including regional security agreements based on economic and humanitarian elements, a lower level of military balance, and a ban on the transfer of equipment and know-how of nuclear, biological and chemical weapons to the region. In "A $13 Billion Misunderstanding," 6-3, a mish-mash on U.S.-Japanese relations, he sophomorically lectures both on how to get along with each other, urging Japan to "*volunteer* to help finance the United Nations peacekeeping force in Northern Iraq and even participate in it; and it could make an official commitment to invest in U.S. Treasury bonds during negotiations to put trade on a fair footing." Zuckerman wants to dump Gorbachev and the central government in "The Center Should Not Hold," 7-1, simplistic in his assumptions: "The choices for the West are between the Soviet people and the Communist Party. There is no moral compromise here. To support the central government, with its bloody past, its failed present and its ambiguous future, would be a moral and political catastrophe — placing the United States in the pillory of history." "Remember! Remember!" 8-12, is a typical one-note effort from Zuckerman on the Middle East as the parties move toward a peace conference: "Revenge and hatred, not resolution, are elements in the Arab approach. Fear, rather than hope, dominates the Jewish mind." He's more thoughtful with "Black and White in America," 10-28, rather perceptive on the effect of the Clarence Thomas hearings. He argues here that "America must nurture programs based on need rather than on race," as current programs are not supported by a population that is no longer guilt ridden.

FINANCIAL REPORTERS & COLUMNISTS

Abelson, Alan. *Barron's.* (★ ½)
Editor. With his extensive Wall Street network and decades of experience in market analysis, Abelson can still send a stock for a ride, but his evaluations of the broader forces moving the markets seem less potent each year. More and more, we find that he favors caustic commentary over cogent analysis. On 1-7 he kicks off the year with a disorganized harangue against what he considers "voodoo economics" — lots of sarcasm but very little substance. In the midst of the air war, Abelson wastes his 2-4 column pondering if Saddam Hussein has a sense of humor in light of his death threat against Italian opera director Gian-Carlo del Monaco. The second half of the column is so skewed toward easy money that it has limited value. After a little too much ranting and raving in his 2-11 column about the backwardness of the administration's proposed banking reform, Abelson makes a few cogent observations: "The inevitable result will be that scads of small banks will shrivel up and blow away, and the industry will consist solely of large institutions in big cities with good airports." We welcomed the thoughtful and timely appraisals on the war, 2-18, in which he relies on Maggie Mahar and "her knowledgeable sources on the Persian Gulf" to assess Saddam Hussein's dubious peace proposal. On 3-25, he reveals "melancholy reservations on the odds for a quick emergence from recession," but his reasoning on this worrisome subject is conventional. Bankruptcy is the topic of his 5-27 column: ". . .today, there's no shame at all in being bankrupt. Quite the contrary: It's the creditors who can go hang. And that's true for nations as well as individuals." After a crisp few paragraphs, he is back to superficial subject-hopping, and then on to some worthwhile investment advice on airlines. On 7-15, Abelson dabbles but never delves into a host of timely subjects — the Japanese stock market scandal, BCCI, American banking standards, Soviet plate passing, etc. — but we walk away with only useless snatches of important stories. In his 8-5 column, Abelson tells us to expect a blitzkrieg on the Fed from a worried George Bush who is slowly becoming aware of the anemic state of the alleged recovery. But Abelson, himself, engages in a little Fed bashing, calling its stance "paralytic."

Andrews, Edmund L. *The New York Times.* (★ ★ ½)
"Patents" columnist. Despite his official beat, Andrews penned his most impressive work this year on the politics shaping the dynamic telecommunications industry. He enthusiastically lays out an important vote facing the FCC which could "inject new competition" into the cellular phone industry in "Threat to Cellular Phone Services," 2-13. The lobbying efforts of a worried cellular phone industry are carefully weaved into this balanced report. " 'Baby Bells' Wait; Hope Judge Relents," 3-10, is a lucid examination on Federal District Court Judge Harold H. Greene's powerful and controversial influence over the telecommunications industry: The Bell companies, the FCC, Justice and others "argue that he has greatly overreached his authority. They contend that rather than deciding only narrow antitrust issues, Judge Greene has transformed himself into a one-man regulatory agency, usurping the authority of both Congress and the F.C.C." Investigating a bit further he discovers that Greene's outbursts aren't always reflected in his decisions: ". . .the angry rhetoric can be misleading. Judge Greene has approved the vast majority of the Bell's more than 100 waiver requests." Offering one of the most detailed perspectives on the FCC's decision to allow networks to acquire full resale rights to shows, Andrews' "Rule on TV Reruns Revamped by F.C.C.," 4-10, perceptively characterizes the debate this way: "The rerun vote, which comes after a nasty and expensive lobbying effort, pleased neither the networks, which wanted complete freedom, nor Hollywood producers and studios, which wanted to keep restrictions in place." In his Sunday business lead, "Pursuing Al Sikes' Grand Agenda," 6-2, the chairman of the FCC's ambitious plans to overhaul communications policy are crisply profiled. However, Paul Farhi at *The Washington Post,* constructed an even more far-reaching portrait of Sikes. His "Speculation in New TV Field Raises Fears," 9-2, is a useful alert for amateur investors wooed by misleading sales pitches on the purchase of government licenses for wireless cable.

Ansberry, Clare. *The Wall Street Journal.* (★ ★)
Pittsburgh. Ansberry has proven herself a nimble and competent reporter, but it's clear that she is at her best when given space to lavish readers with her vivid, descriptive style. Her "U.S. Exports Turn Into Ports in a Storm," 1-17, offers nothing exceptional on the "bread and butter" role exports have assumed for recession-battered manufacturers. On the other hand, her extensive history of USX Corp., "Family Faces Changes as USX Edges Out of the Steel Business," 2-22, is a beautifully written feature. As USX moves away from steel to energy, Ansberry takes us on an anecdotal tour of an era when steel and USX were synonymous: "Softball-size balls of hot coke spilled over open blast furnaces; white-hot sheets of steel twisted up into the air like taffy when the flowing metal hit a snag." Her "Men of Steel See No End to Leaden Prices," 3-19, is a punchy piece on supply and demand's impact on the steel industry. As USX pursues its future with Marathon Oil, Ansberry explores the company's identity crisis in "Corry Is Moving to Energize USX's Image," 4-8: ". . .convincing the world that energy is USX's mainstay is like arguing that the Queen Mary is a spaceship." She is complete in detailing how USX's Charles A. Corry plans to change this image problem. In "Nucor Steel's Sheen Is Marred by Deaths of Workers at Plants," 5-10, she constructs a compelling page-one story of life-threatening safety problems at Nucor. But with only circumstantial evidence, she proposes shaky links between the company's higher than average death rate and its financial success. Her clear-eyed look at exports, "U.S. Manufacturers' Export Prospects Get Darker as Prices Fall, Dollar Rises," 6-20, eschews gloomy generalizations and puts the latest numbers into proper perspective. And "After All This Time, Female Fans Swoon When Frankie Sings," 9-24, is a hysterical A-hed on how singer Frankie Yankovic makes female senior citizens giddy.

Armbruster, William. *The Journal of Commerce.* (★ ★)
Foreign trade and shipping. The workman-like Armbruster seems more probing this year, enriching his characteristically solid reports with useful interpretations. "Rubbermaid Plans to Put Bounce in Foreign Sales," 2-14, is sharp on the company's plans to go global, but we'd have liked more detail on the executive assigned to spearhead the expansion. With "Box Trade Picture Dim; '92 Should Be Better," 2-19, he crafts an interesting picture of this industry's unique, double-edged view of U.S. trade flows: "Imported goods shipped in oceanborne containers are headed for a steep nose-dive. . .The growth in exports. . .will not be high enough to offset the anticipated 6.4% plunge in imports carried in containerships, resulting in an overall 2.1% drop in volume. . .." His front-page analysis, "Japan, German Gulf War Records May Dampen Ties," 3-1, was rich in quotes, but Armbruster failed to adequately scrutinize his sources' comments. On the other hand, he covered all of the bases in "Subsidy Debate Resumes," 3-11, a multidimensional look at the agricultural subsidy debate stalling GATT negotiations. His deft characterization of the impact a 10-pound bag of rice can have on U.S.-Japan relations in "Rice Incident May Hurt Japan Trade," 3-20, zeroes in on the broader tensions behind the scuffle. He is balanced in assessing U.S. wariness toward a Japanese proposal for joint research in developing a sixth-generation computer in "US Computer Makers View Japanese Proposal Warily," 4-2. The sidebar, "US Must Share Technology-Imbalance Blame," 4-2, takes the U.S. to task for its contribution to the imbalance of technology flows, warning that America's "not-invented-here" syndrome often leads companies to ignore valuable overseas research. In "Executives Say AID Becomes User-Friendly," 7-2, Armbruster skillfully characterizes the positive change at the Agency for International Development which is now taking much more interest in business, trade and capital projects. He offers a quick but vivid snapshot of the competition between the trucking and railroad industry in their quest for a share of the lucrative intermodal business with the containership industry, "Big Rig Victory Would Have Ravaged Rail Intermodal Business, Snow Says," 9-25.

Auerbach, Stuart. *The Washington Post.* (★ ★)
International trade. Finding his footing on yet another new beat, the quality of Auerbach's work remains inconsistent, but he shows flashes of potential, especially on the U.S.-Mexico free trade negotiations. In his generic update on GATT, "U.S. Sees Ray of Hope on GATT," 1-30, he sees

possibilities in Carla Hills' announcement to seek more time to reinvigorate the collapsed talks. He is much better in "1.5 Billion in U.S. Sales to Iraq," 3-11, a breathless account based on leaked records that disclose the administration was selling high-tech goods to Iraq right up until the eve of its invasion of Kuwait. His richly detailed "U.S. Relied on Foreign-made Parts Weapons," 3-25, is keen on the strategies and politics of last minute global procurement of essential electronic parts for U.S. troops in combat in the Persian Gulf. Although we see hints of a press release in "Traveling Salesmen for U.S. Exports: Commerce Team Visits Cities," 4-3, Auerbach provides a useful look at Commerce's increasingly global outlook. In one of his best pieces, "Splitting Protectionist Seams," 5-12, Auerbach make sense out of the "crazy-quilt politics" and unusual splintering effect the U.S.-Mexico free trade debate has had on traditionally protectionist lobbies like the textile industry: "a growing number of U.S. manufacturers of clothing, fabric and fiber are supporting. . .a North American free-trade zone. . .as a way to make their companies more competitive in world markets and allow them to increase U.S. employment by creating more skilled jobs here and shipping the lower-paying jobs to Mexico." He is highly perceptive in "A Hot Prospect for U.S. Investment Cools Fast," *Weekly* 7/15-21, assessing why U.S. businesses are less enthusiastic about investing in a Soviet Union that is extremely moody and unpredictable in its embrace of free market and foreign investment policies. His "U.S., Japan to Study Auto Sales; Reviews Set on Trade Deficit of Cars, Parts," 9-18, is too one-sided from the U.S. viewpoint on trade with Japan.

Bacon, Kenneth H. *The Wall Street Journal.* (★ ★ ★ ½)
Banking. Transferring from health and education, Bacon evinces a surprisingly powerful grasp of the complexities of banking. He views each legislative adjustment with one eye on the future, an intelligent approach during the industry's chaotic restructuring. Bacon has quickly emerged as one of the finest on this beat. His "Big Banks Would Get Vastly Broader Powers Under Treasury's Plan," 1-6, masterfully surveys the debates likely to emerge as the historic banking reform proposal moves through Congress. Joined by Ron Suskind for "U.S. Recession Claims Bank of New England as First Big Victim," leder 1-7, we're offered a far-reaching look at the implications of this government seizure. He is way out in front with "Treasury's Plan to Overhaul Banking Could Diminish Fed's Regulatory Role," 2-8, questioning whether Treasury's restructuring plan will encourage banks to seek national charters from the Comptroller of Currency to escape tighter Federal Reserve monitoring. In "Banking-Reform Proposals Are Already Rattling the System and Making the Credit Crunch Worse," 4-16, he studies the proposals' negative effects on small-town banks. Warns one quoted banker: "A cutback in insurance. . .coupled with the too-big-to-fail doctrine, is a formula for people leaving the reduced-insurance banks and going to the banks declared 'never to fail.' " With clear analysis and precise reporting Bacon puts the day's news into a broader context in "Administration Suffers Setback on Bank Laws," 5-15, recounting the administration's narrow failure to push through its proposals to scale back deposit insurance. His brief but important "Fed Agrees on a Compromise to Limit Long-Term Lending to Troubled Banks," 6-27, expertly recounts the Fed's agreement to limit long-term lending to sick banks through its discount window. His "Panel Approves Bill to Reform Banking Laws," 7-1, is a typically solid dissection of Treasury Secretary Nicholas Brady's debate with the bill's opponents who contend that continued deposit insurance could lead to future taxpayer bailouts. Astute on House Banking's efforts to limit extensions of emergency credit to critically ill banks in "Faster Bank Closings Will Cut FDIC Losses," 9-23, he characterizes how the move will change attitudes in bank boardrooms. His "Cracking Down: The New Banking Law Toughens Regulation, Some Say Too Much," 11-29, was the best work we saw on the banking legislation as it finally emerged from Congress. He receives a 10 Best in Business/Financial Reporting for this outstanding effort.

Banks, Howard. *Forbes.* (★ ★)
Washington bureau manager. Celebrating 10 years with *Forbes* in 1992, Banks pleasantly surprised us with more forward-looking assessments on the aerospace industry this year. His previous work experience in aerospace, combined with a stint as Industrial Editor at *The*

Economist, allows him to intelligently evaluate both the corporate and technological aspects of this gigantic industry. He is instructive in "Lessons From the Gulf War," 2-18, an insightful essay on U.S. defense capabilities against ballistic missiles. While cheering U.S. "Patriot missiles knocking the bad guys' Scuds out of the sky," he ponders the "sobering side to this success" and warns of the Patriot's limitations: "We need a ground-based system that would be able to take out short-to-medium-range ballistic missiles. . .at a much higher altitude than can the Patriot." Disregarding the obvious pitfalls of doing business in a politically shaky U.S.S.R., Banks remains surprisingly upbeat on possible Soviet-U.S. airplane manufacturing ventures in "Is That a Tupolev on Boeing's Horizon?" 3-18: ". . .putting Western engines and equipment on Soviet wings transforms their performance, according to computer simulations." Through quotes and examples, Banks effectively distills the cautious attitude of Boeing's top management in "Running Ahead, But Running Scared," 5-13. Despite a record year, the company is running as though its life depended on it. Well aware of the fickle nature of this industry, Banks points out the realism behind this approach: "Companies that fail to run scared often end up out of the running." In "A Flying Lexus," 8-5, he asks us to consider an airborne Toyota Motor Corp. which is thinking of making a small light aircraft. Banks makes a persuasive case for the effort taking off successfully. His "Full Thrust," 9-16, is a snappy depiction of the exhilaration and collective sigh of relief that can be heard at General Electric's jet engine division following news that it won a highly competitive contract from British Airways.

Barmash, Isadore. *The New York Times.* (★★)

Retail. After 26 years of service, Barmash has reportedly taken the *Times* up on its early retirement offer, departing in August. In his last year, he shined on the comings and goings of retail's glittery personalities, but was increasingly formulaic in his treatment of nuts and bolts stories about the industry's financial woes. Nevertheless, Barmash leaves big shoes to fill at the *Times.* His "Big Change Is Expected for Sears," 1-28, is a reliable but bland update on the woeful state of affairs at Sears and the sweeping changes being considered to turn the company around. He is light on pertinent business numbers in "Even the Affluent Aren't Buying," 2-23, but still assembles a nice sampling of perspectives on the current recession from the eyes of battered retailers. Keeping in mind the perils of brand extensions in his well-constructed "Oxxford to Diversify After 77 Years," 3-9, Barmash examines the suitmaker's reasons for moving into shirts, ties and colognes. He is less enterprising in "Federated Will Offer a Reorganization Plan," 4-27, a dry but serviceable report for investors curious about Federated's plans to seek permission to offer cash and notes to its unsecured creditors. An opinion on the deal from the affected creditors would have completed the report. "In Retail, It's Perilous at the Top," 5-17, is the type of retail trends piece that Barmash does so well. Using chairman Frank Doroff's hasty departure from Bonwit Teller as an example, Barmash effectively profiles an entire industry in upheaval: "The long list of resignations and dismissals reflects the pressure in the executive offices brought on by weak sales, ill-fated takeover attempts and strategic blunders. Some bosses were fall guys for costly mistakes. Others were victims of consolidations. But many others, especially those trained as merchants, found themselves ill-equipped to grapple with the swirl of financial, operational, strategic and merchandising problems that now confront retail chains." Packed with examples, his "Talking Deals: Opportune Times For Big Barterers," 6-20, tells us why bartering is back in vogue: "American companies are hardly sneezing at product-for-services exchanges at a time of erratic sales and lean profits." In "Retailers Hunt, but Few Heads Fit," 7-29, he explains why retailing's top recruiters are having such a tough time finding fits.

Barrett, William P. *Forbes.* (★★)

Southwest bureau manager. While we enjoy Barrett's colorful renditions of offbeat tales, we feel he is concentrated too much on the eccentric, denying us his creative insights on more pertinent business issues in his region. We'd like to see him return to the range and balance he achieved in his portfolio last year. He plays the sleuth in "Father of His Country," 1-7, foraging for facts about the mysterious Dominion of Melchizedek which turns out to be a non-existent country created by scam artist Branch Vinedresser who "sold scores. . .of meaningless charters for banks, insurance companies and other corporations." Barrett queries, "What's the point of all this creativity? If Vinedresser can create securities that other people believe have value, he can trade them for other securities that really might have value." This is great investigative journalism, although Barrett could have found a more apropos conclusion than the frivolous editorial jab at junk bonds he uses: "Americans bought hundreds of billions in junk bonds. Why not junk countries." His "I Work Hard," 3-18, is a curious little human-interest story about the child of a prominent fugitive trying to make good. A little luck here, an angel there, and the kid's brains add up to about $2 million, legitimately! Certainly an interesting set of circumstances, but we missed the punchline. For "A Blank Check It Was Not," 4-29, he lands an exclusive interview with Citicorp's new big shareholder, Alwaleed Bin Talal Bin Abdulaziz Al Saud. Barrett furnishes us with clever insights into the man who, at age 36, stands to exert control over Citicorp's shaky finances and management. He is especially keen in observing the differing perspectives of the two parties: Citicorp's chairman John Reed says he is glad to have "stumbled" upon Alwaleed; Alwaleed says, "Citicorp may have stumbled upon me, but I didn't stumble upon Citicorp." Hmmm. In "The Widow Martinez," 6-10, Barrett expertly dissects the bizarre and cozy deal struck by lawyers of Circle K Corp. and the lawyers of a woman whose husband was murdered at a Circle K convenience store. He is also adroit in "Sucker Play?" 8-5, a hard-hitting but well-documented critique of dealmaker Charles Hurwitz's handling of the Kaiser Aluminum offering.

Bartlett, Sarah. *The New York Times.* (★ ★ ½)
Back from authoring a book on KKR, the inquisitive Bartlett penned precise examinations of the Big Apple's budgetary problems. In "For Banks, Suitors May Be Few," 2-9, Bartlett asks the million dollar question: "What if the Treasury Department threw a party and nobody came?" She warns ". . .when it comes to luring in more capital by allowing commercial and industrial companies to own banks, the administration may be sorely disappointed. . ." Her "A Straight Arrow's Inexplicable Fall," 3-24, is the story of fund manager Patricia Ostrander of Fidelity Investments who is being sued by Fidelity for alleged ethics violations: "Among other things, the suit contends that she allowed the New America High Income Fund to be used as Mr. [Michael] Milken's dumping ground for particularly unattractive securities." But we wonder why Bartlett didn't question these allegations more thoroughly. As she reports, the fund didn't start until February 1988; surely she realizes that Milken had been effectively driven from Wall Street long before. "The City Strains to Hit a Financial Target That May Be Too Small," 5-5, is quintessential Bartlett, crisp and vigorous. Questioning if the $100 million deficit-ceiling that was legally mandated in 1975 is an unrealistic target in 1991, she asks us to "Imagine a huge 747 trying to land on a dirt strip that ends abruptly after 200 feet and you will have some idea of the financial exercise the Dinkins Administration is currently engaged in." As the Big Apple's traditional tax base falls, she questions the city's role in social services in "New York's Government: Is It Too Big?" 5-10. This eye-opening comparison of services across the nation puts NYC's burden into context. Her "New York's City Workers: Freeloaders or Scapegoats?" 6-2, is perceptive on the debate between labor and the city: "The question is whether both sides are going to continue debating the merits of givebacks and deferrals, or whether they will eventually discuss a more fundamental issue: how the city and its work force can deliver services more efficiently." She draws a colorful and informative sketch of the maze of bureacracy faced each day by NYC's expediters in "A New York Trade Thrives on Red Tape," 9-13.

Bennett, Amanda. *The Wall Street Journal.* (★ ½)
New York, management. Bennett hasn't improved much during her years on this beat. Even when taking on substantial topics, she handles them superficially, which was especially bothersome in a tough economic year riddled with difficult decisions for management. Her "Fear of Gulf War Disrupts Businesses," 1-11, was pretty light stuff, especially for its prominent placement on the front page of the "Marketplace" section. To make this newsworthy, Bennett should have ferreted out more specific examples of major projects that have been halted or put on hold due to the January 15 deadline in the Persian Gulf. She is more informative in

"Workplace: Middle-Aged Managers Find Willingness to Adapt Aids Rebound From Layoffs," 2-8, an engaging look at how laid off executives aged 50+ are creatively turning their age and experience into attributes during their job searches. Her "Wave of Mergers Hits Consulting Firms," 2-20, is a tepid review of consulting mergers as she is about a year behind the curve on this topic and is light on the dynamics of the consulting industry. In "Executive Pay: Hard Times Trim CEO Pay Raises," 4-7, she pens a broad sweep of executive compensation and touches lightly on the debate between shareholders and CEOs over pay and stock options. Amid the plethora of articles written on executive pay this year, Bennett's was not a standout. In her well-researched "Management: Downsizing Doesn't Necessarily Bring an Upswing in Corporate Profitability," 6-6, Bennett examines the worth of layoffs during recessions and discovers that in some cases they may be unproductive. Also quite good in "Paying Workers to Meet Goals Spreads, but Gauging Performance Proves Tough," 9-10, she examines more closely than usual the success and failure of pay-for-performance efforts at various companies.

Berg, Eric N. *The New York Times.* (★★)
Chicago. A competent generalist, Berg is reliably solid on the facts and frugal with the words. His coverage of the wrangling at financially-troubled Sears has been especially perceptive. In "Heileman Chapter 11, but Upbeat," 1-25, he gives us a complete picture of the reasons the G. Heileman Brewing Company filed Chapter 11 and is solid on the positive and negative implications of the move. He adeptly handles the speculation surrounding Groupe Schneider's proposal to acquire the Square D company in "French Company Makes Bid of $1.8 Billion for Square D," 2-20. With little information available, Berg gives investment readers a useful characterization of talks between the two companies. As the *Times*' man on the shake up at Sears, Roebuck & Company, Berg provided well-rounded sketches of unfolding events. His "Embattled Sears Plans to Shrink Board's Size," 3-14, perceptively depicts the company's move to shrink its board of directors to block dissident shareholder Robert A.G. Monks' attempt to win a seat: "Although Sears portrayed the move as an effort to give outside directors a greater voice in the troubled retailer's affairs, one result is that it makes it more difficult for a dissident shareholder to win election to the board this year." Similarly, "Dissident Sears Holder Fails to Win Board Seat," 5-10, was an excellent analysis of the aftermath of Monks' failed bid. Berg captures the essence of the investor's criticism of Sears: "One of [Monks'] principal charges against the company has been that the Sears board has been managers' rubber stamp, allowing the same executives to run the company despite years of decline." His downbeat report, "An American Icon Wrestles With a Troubled Future," 5-12, provides extensive detail, but there's not enough from management on what it's doing to remedy the decline. In "Financial Plight of a Top Insurer Could Shake Faith in the Industry," 7-15, Berg competently delineates the ripple effect likely to be caused by the seizure of one of the most conservative and respected insurance companies in the country, Mutual Benefit Life. Following the downfall of several insurance companies, he spots an embarrassment for credit agencies in "Insurers' Rates Are on the Spot for Inaccuracy," 8-4: "Mutual Benefit, for example, enjoyed A.M. Best's top rating of A+ until July 3, six days before it was taken over. Moody's had Mutual Benefit listed as an A company, and so did S&P."

Bernstein, Aaron. *Business Week.* (★★)
Labor editor. Following a beat that seems to invite bias from many reporters, Bernstein maintains a refreshingly balanced perspective on the characteristically contentious debates between labor and management. In "Letting Teachers Call the Shots," with Patrick Howington, 1-28, Bernstein is upbeat on an innovative incentive-pay system being undertaken in Kentucky that is keyed to how well schools' students perform. With his finger on the pulse of management/labor relations at AT&T, his "Bad Connection at AT&T," 4-22, gives us a detailed picture of mounting tensions: ". . .with more layoffs on the horizon, the days are gone when AT&T stood hand and hand with labor." "Quality Is Becoming Job One in the Office, Too," 4-29, gives a solid sense of where our generation of workers stands as compared to past generations, and includes a detailed survey of today's creative office-quality programs. His

illuminating survey of four northern states in "Family Leave May Not Be that Big a Hardship for Business," 6-3, reveals that most employers are offering maternity leave without a federal law. In "The Teamsters and the Mob: It May Really Be Over," 6-17, Bernstein updates us on the organization with a smooth summary of the government's cleanup efforts since its 1989 RICO suit. He lauds some of the new election rules, but suggests the feds may be going too far in charging non-mob Teamster officials with petty crimes. His forward-looking "Joe Sixpack's Grip on Corporate America," 7-15, assesses the growing dollar amounts of worker-owned stock and elaborates on the pros and cons for both companies and employees. He pens a judicious and sophisticated opinion on the murky debate over the legality of replacement workers in "You Can't Bargain With a Striker Whose Job Is No More," commentary 8-5. Crystallizing the double talk surrounding the issue, he observes: "In short, you can't fire strikers, but you don't have to hire them back. That contradictory position. . .is the sole basis for the Supreme Court's stance on whether replacement workers conflict with the right to strike. . ..[A]n honest look at permanent replacements leads to one view: take away strikers' jobs, and you take away their right to strike."

Bernstein, Harry. *Los Angeles Times.* (★)
Labor. Still a mouthpiece for the pro-labor lobby, Bernstein nonetheless has toned down the vitriol aimed at his ideological adversaries and comes up with some useful analysis this year. In "Ruling May Curb Harassment," 2-5, Bernstein unsuccessfully tries to play the legal expert by oversimplifying a "remarkable" court that said "judges and juries should look at sexual harassment charges from a 'reasonable woman's' point of view instead of the traditional, male-biased 'reasonable man's' perspective." He is better in "Let's Enforce Immigration Laws," 3-19, constructing a solid case for enforcement of the 1986 Federal Immigration Reform and Control Act. He zeroes in on Washington's policy vacuum in "Now Let Bush Defeat Recession," 3-12: "Rising unemployment is still a serious problem that the Administration offers no proposal to alleviate, other than to euphorically wait for an unplanned, unpredictable free-market economy to create more decent jobs." True, but with his own feet squarely planted in the government spending camp, Bernstein is unable to come up with any creative solutions of his own. In "AFL-CIO Should Shun Soviet Battle," 4-9, a level-headed Bernstein advises the AFL-CIO to urge its Soviet counterpart, the miners' union, to drop its demand for Gorbachev's resignation: "A more productive approach. . .would create a coalition of U.S. coal industry management and union leaders to offer their advice on mining technology and labor-management relations." Bernstein reprimands rebel UAW members at Douglas Aircraft in "Democracy Goes Amok at Douglas," 4-30, accusing them of crossing the line between "healthy democratic debate and destructive internecine warfare." He clearly demonstrates how these dissidents can undermine well-constructed labor-management agreements. His timely assessment of labor's growing financial muscle, "Forays Into Finance Benefit Workers," 6-25, asserts that the more than $1 trillion in workers' pension fund reserves will empower beleaguered unions. Bernstein warns, however, that increasingly there will be power struggles for control of these massive funds as in California where governor Pete Wilson has proposed to take control of CalPERS, the $62.4-billion California Public Employees' Retirement System. He gives an insider's touch to "Teamsters' Election: Honest but Tainted," 10-1, but is clear-eyed on the Teamsters' progress against corruption as well as in areas that still need work.

Berry, John M. *The Washington Post.* (★ ★)
Now covering domestic rather than international economics, Berry penned some adequate work on the banking sector, although he was seemingly unable to explain the forces jarring that industry. On the other hand, his coverage of the Federal Reserve was consistently original and highly-perceptive. His unprovocative "U.S. Banking Industry Facing Sweeping Changes in '91," 1-2, was merely a broad skim of the challenges facing the U.S. banking industry. He was better in "FDIC Chief Blasts New Bank Plan," 2-8, a brief report packed with strong, authoritative quotes on the proposal to overhaul the banking system. There is nothing in Berry's "A Quick, if Modest, Lift for the Economy," 3-3, to set it apart from the pile of so-so press reports assessing

the possibility of an economic recovery. His "Did Greenspan Face Fed Revolt?" 4-18, though, is a richly-detailed, well-sourced and very enlightening investigation of news reports that the authority of Federal Reserve Chairman Alan Greenspan was being challenged by the regional Federal Reserve banks: " 'I think the whole thing is a tempest in a teapot,' said Robert Black, president of the Richmond Federal Reserve Bank, and supposedly one of the inflation 'hawks' worried that the Fed has been cutting rates too much." His enterprising survey, "Is America Overbanked?" 4-21, impressed with a sturdy grasp of the stats. Berry sees the consolidation ahead as a beneficial weeding out, but we'd have liked more questioning of the long-term reverberations of this trend throughout the entrepreneurial borrowing sector and the economy as a whole. He is purely a numbers cruncher in "Fed Reduces Rates to Boost Economy," 5-1, competently reporting on this technical economic adjustment, but giving no clues about the move's broader significance. He is more discerning in "Undiminished Inflation Fears Keep Interest Rates Sluggish," 5-24, noting the dubious impact of the widening gap between long-and short-term rates, but he is still weak on the pressures bringing this to bear. His "Sinking the Think-Tank Mentality," *Weekly* 7/8-14, is a respectable scrutiny of criticism that the Fed is too cautious because it is comprised of like-minded, inflation hawks. He briefs us on a big name trade conference in "Economists Say Blocs May Block Free Trade; Regional Accords Seen as Troubling," 9-4, but there's nothing new here on the debate over free trade blocs versus free global trade.

Berss, Marcia. *Forbes.* (★ ★ ½)
Chicago, senior editor. With plenty of experience in both the world of journalism and business, Berss is able to construct knowledgeable and well-written business profiles with the feel of a company insider. Although not her best work, "Real Testing Times," 1-21, is nonetheless an interesting profile of Kathleen Hempel's rise from secretary to CFO of papermaker Fort Howard Corp. But with Hempel charged with bringing the company through tough times, Berss could have foregone some of the personal details and included more on Hempel's plans for the company. In "Nothing Is in the Bag," 3-4, Berss incisively explains why Morton International is the leader in the expanding airbag market despite rival TRW's bigger size and budget. In "If at First You Don't Succeed. . ." 4-1, she is skeptical of the Carlyle Group's ability to stage a turnaround, observing that even the company's good Washington connections can't undo the bad deals and uninformed decisions made in the past. In "End of an Era," 4-29, Berss reports that the fourth and fifth generation owners of America's largest privately-held company, Cargill Inc., are preparing for an ESOP, and family members are both pleased and worried. She vividly depicts the gnashing of teeth that has resulted from the bitter decision between cash and control. She is sharp and fair-minded in "The Bad Boy of Advertising," 7-8, an able profile of Martin Sorrell, chief executive of the debt-laden ad company WPP Group. Keenly observing why his "hardheaded, unsentimental thinking" has skyrocketed him to the top, she observes: "It's not calculated to endear him to the general public, but it certainly equips him well not only to negotiate the vicissitudes of all that debt but to adapt to a fast-changing advertising business as well." Her excellent "Plowing Washington for Profit," 9-16, explains how and why Dwayne Andreas, CEO of Archer Daniels Midland, smooths out the notorious cycles of the commodity business: "Andreas has made an art form out of plowing Washington for markets, tax breaks and subsidies. . .Government intervention may make poor public policy, but ADM shareholders must love it. ADM's stock was in the top 8% performers over the last five years."

Bleiberg, Robert M. *Barron's.* (★ ★)
After 45 years with the Dow Jones weekly, Bleiberg announced his retirement in 1991. He did less writing than usual in his final year, no doubt handing his page over to aspiring editors instead. We will miss his rich, instructive analyses buttressed by his sturdy grasp of history. A reliable watchdog of regulatory overreach, he pens "Regulators' Lynch Mob," 2-4, which applauds Jonathan Eisenberg, a Washington lawyer who wrote a daring, bylined article criticizing a legal decision by the powerful Stanley Sporkin, former head of the Enforcement Division of the SEC: " 'Assigning Judge Stanley Sporkin in the Lincoln Savings & Loan case,'

caustically wrote Mr. Eisenberg, 'was a bit like assigning Eliot Ness to preside over the trial of Al Capone.' " In "Free James Sherwin!" 3-25, he urges us to remember his 1989 comments on the trials of James T. Sherwin, former vice president of GAF Corp., who is charged with stock manipulation and securities fraud. As the courts consider proceeding with a fourth trial against Sherwin, Bleiberg returns to this brilliant dissection of the government's shaky case to drive home his message: "Four trials on dubious evidence are several too many. By any standard, the threat of quadruple jeopardy is cruel and unusual punishment. Free James Sherwin!" His polemic on TV news, "Turned Off, Tuned Out," 5-20, is perhaps a bit heavy-handed, especially since it doesn't discuss the numerous deceits of other news media, but Bleiberg does make some convincing points about "mounting public distrust" of TV news and he backs up his charges with plenty of examples. Following the assassination of Rajiv Gandhi, Bleiberg comes down hard on India in "Socialist Dinosaur," 6-10: ". . .the country, still under the baneful influence of the British Fabians, stubbornly persists in embracing the full panoply of socialist public policy. . .Not surprisingly, even in a good year, foreign investment rarely exceeds $100 million, while the beggar's bowl is constantly held out to the International Monetary Fund, World Bank and other footless global lenders." This is muscular armchair reporting on the political economy of a government which has "doomed two generations to grinding poverty." In "Socialists, Get Lost," 10-14, he makes a very convincing case for privatization, a process which he confirms with facts and figures is working well all over the globe, and should be taken more seriously by the U.S. federal government.

Boyd, John. *The Journal of Commerce.* (★ ★)
Domestic economy. There's little on the subject of domestic transportation that goes unnoticed by this skilled beat reporter. An excellent fact-gatherer, Boyd serves up plentifully-detailed reports on this vital, but oft neglected, underpinning of the U.S. economy. In "SP Sets Up St. Louis Barge Link to Haul Coal From Rockies," 2-11, he briskly relates Southern Pacific Transportation Co.'s activation of a barge connection at St. Louis for its Rocky Mountain coal trains, "a development that would put such SP-carried coal within reach of a much larger part of the nation." Examining how an abundant wheat harvest turned into a shortage in "What Happened to Wheat Crop?" 3-11, Boyd observes: "As the amber waves became amber mounds at home, and without the big outlet overseas, wheat's price plunged." He discerningly concludes that lower prices made wheat competitive with corn, and farmers snapped it up as feed, thus the shortage. Providing a unique item on how U.S. companies are gearing up for North American free trade in "Mexican Carpets Roll Into Canada By Rail," 3-15, Boyd reports on an extension of the largest U.S.-Mexico stack train service to Canada: ". . .this new transport system. . .links all three potential partners of a North American free trade agreement in a low-cost, high-speed freight service that uses time-savings clearance techniques." He brings enthusiasm and fresh news in "Upper Stretch of Ouachita Poised for Barges," 5-14, reporting on a new barge route opening in the upper Ouachita River: "Besides altering the freight equations in lower Arkansas, using that part of the Ouachita could bolster a navigation project now stalled by environmental concerns and funding from Louisiana." In "Dubai Trade Show Proves a Big Hit for US Exporters," 6-4, Boyd captures the excitement following the overwhelming success of the Dubai, UAE trade show which has U.S. businessmen wearing "ear-to-ear smiles." The event " '. . .capitalized brilliantly on the strong good will toward the United States and highlighted Dubai as a regional trading center of great consequence,' said U.S. Commerce Undersecretary J. Michael Farren." He is straightforward on Southern Pacific's financial woes and its search for a partner in "Southern Pacific Considering Truck Link Similar to Quantum," 10-24.

Bradsher, Keith. *The New York Times.* (★ ½)
Trade. The switch from the telecommunications beat early in the year clearly placed Bradsher in unfamiliar territory just as important trade issues were unfolding. Consequently, his reports usually only skimmed the issues, lacking the insights we craved. In one of his last telecommunications pieces, "A Weak Outlook for Phone Giants," 1-10, Bradsher displayed a

strong grasp of the forces that shape business cycles in the nation's long-distance phone companies. With intellectual property rights an increasingly hot trade topic, we appreciated his thoroughness in "Panel Asks Bush to Cite 3 Nations," 4-26, which reports on the trade implications of a recommendation from the Economic Policy Council to officially cite China, India and Thailand for tolerating violations of American copyrights and patents. Bradsher touches upon all the pertinent political and economic angles of the issue. In "U.S. Ready to Penalize Japan Over Endangered Sea Turtles," 5-17, he grasps the reason why the Bush administration has chosen to make sea turtles a trade issue with Japan — "It wins friends in the environmental movement, costs no money, shows toughness on trade and cannot be labeled protectionist because the United States does not have a tortoise-shell industry" — but he doesn't expand on the broader tensions that were hinted at by his sources. Bradsher gets lost with canned rhetoric that holds little water in "U.S. Trade Deficit Dropped in March to an 8-Year Low," 5-18. He'd do better to eschew the theoretical jibberish of "deficit" journalism and ponder the real-world impact of the balance of trade on capital flows. Without pointing fingers, he insightfully examines the differences between two U.S.-Japan agreements in "The Big Contrasts in 2 Japan Pacts," 6-6: "The semiconductor talks ended with an agreement nearly two months before the deadline, and with little acrimony. The final deal relied heavily on private companies, with a minimum of direct government oversight. The construction negotiations, by contrast, ended a month after the deadline and after the United States trade representative published in the Federal Register a request for public comments on how best to ban Japanese companies from American public works projects." He pens an eye-opener on the actual dollars involved in U.S. aid to Israel with "U.S. Aid to Israel: $77 Billion Since '67," 9-23: "$16,500 for each Israeli citizen."

Brittan, Samuel. *Financial Times.* (★ ★ ★ ½)
The U.K.'s recession was at the center of economic commentary in that country. Brittan splendidly performed the rigorous task of assessing what policies were feeding the problem and especially which policy prescriptions would exacerbate it. In "The Anatomy of UK Recession," 12-20-90, he surveyed policies that could help a self-corrective process, and gave solid analysis of the pernicious consequences of an ill-timed sterling depreciation and monetary stimulation. Emphatic in "How Lower Inflation Will Bring Recovery," 1-7, he asserted that the U.K.'s prolonged recession is not a consequence of Germany's monetary policy or British interest or exchange-rate policies. He again defended a strong D-Mark in "A Shortage Postponed," 1-10, challenging the idea of a world shortage of capital. However, he failed to consider U.S. fiscal policies in his assessment of short-term forces making for world recession. He displayed a similar oversight in "France Now Holds the Key," 2-4, but his main point — that French determination to stick to its D-Mark parity will deprive the British of "a softish option" — was substantial. He discerned an important economic moral from the critiques of economic policy made by British monetarists — the danger that international regulators are "taking over monetary policy by default with dire results" — in "Panic-Mongers on the Rampage," 2-14. Throughout the year, he rigorously scrutinized the use of interest rate cuts and sterling depreciation, and in "Saving Monetarism From Monetarists," 4-4, a 10 Best nomination, he demolished the economic prognostications of the "Liverpool Six" monetarists who were "pandering to the belief that governments, rather than markets, determine output and employment." Another 10 Best nominee, "Capitalist Re-Entry: A Tale of Two States," 5-30, eschews conventional assessments of what ails united Germany. He points out instead that "the anti-competitive features of the German economy. . .which were until recently an affordable luxury have become a grave handicap." We were persuaded by his criticism that Western economic summits are "an irrelevant farce" in "Time to Put an End to the Summit Farce," 7-15: "A way has to be reinvented by which the handful of leaders who really matter. . .can talk to each other quietly." And in "From the UK Polls to Performance," 9-19, he advises those that peer at growth tables "that it would be good to get away from gazing at rates of change and look instead at the actual levels of output that ultimately determine living standards."

Brookes, Warren T. *The Detroit News,* Creators Syndicate. (★ ★ ★ ★)
His incisive perspectives are recommended reading for policy buffs looking for fresh viewpoints on everything from the budget to environmental legislation. You don't necessarily have to agree with Brookes to appreciate his intelligent, well-researched opinions; he always adds something new to the debate. Brookes blasts the accuracy of the U.S. Census report on household wealth in "Skewed Census Wealth Data?" *The Washington Times* 2-4, and as usual, makes his point convincingly. He pooh-poohs theories of U.S. industrial decline in "Whatever Happened to Deindustrialization?" *WT* 2-14, showing that manufacturing productivity grew in the '80s at three times the rate of the '70s. His "Second Front Against Spenders," *WT* 3-11, is a splendid analysis of how some governors are effectively cutting spending and slashing bureaucracy in their states. He urges Bush to follow this lead on the federal level. In "Will EPA Turn the Curve Red?" *WT* 3-19, he constructs a devastating account of the threat to the auto industry posed by the EPA's new emission standards which he says will eventually cost consumers $9 billion a year while ". . .buying a 40-percent reduction in only 3 percent of all car emissions." His "The Newest Odd Couple; Bush Being Carterized," *WT* 4-24, was the best short summation we saw on the Moynihan-Social Security debate with Brookes going back to 1937 to quote GOP Sen. Arthur Vandenberg on why SS should not be on a pay-as-you-go system: ". . .the Roosevelt Treasury was trying to keep payroll tax rates higher than needed." And in "Green Book of White Lies," *WT* 5-7, he recounts the three kinds of untruths — lies, more lies, and statistics — and uncovers serious distortions of data by the CBO in its reports, Brookes even getting an admission of that fact from its director. "Quayle's Sharper Edge," *WT* 5-15, is an eye-opening examination of the VP's effectiveness in heading the Council of Competitiveness that has liberals fuming. Although environmentalists condemn pesticides, Brookes notes in "Weeds in Organic Furrows," *WT* 7-22, that chemicals have allowed the world to increase food production to the point that nowadays government mismanagement, not food shortages, causes famines. He is muscular with a cover story on the economic foibles that led Richard Darman to underestimate the budget deficit by $319 billion in "Dead Wrong Again," *National Review* 10-7. He died in late December; he will be missed.

Bulkeley, William M. *The Wall Street Journal.* (★ ★)
Boston. When he wants to, Bulkeley is more than capable of dazzling us with definitive evaluations of the computer industry. But all too often, we get only half-baked reports that underemploy his estimable talents. His "It Needn't Always Cost a Bundle to Get Consumers to Notice Unfamiliar Brands," 2-14, is a snappy marketing piece in which he showcases creative ways companies promote their names without spending a wad. Joined by G. Pascal Zachary for "Microsoft's Windows Opens a Big Lead," 3-8, we're offered a revealing critique of Microsoft's popular Windows software, but we'd have liked more comments from Microsoft sources and proponents of the software. In "Data General's Stock Rises From Ashes," 4-26, Bulkeley precisely discerns how cost controls have boosted Data General profit margins while other computer stocks languish. Contributing to a special on technology basics, Bulkeley pens an instructive, engaging and layman-friendly primer on why software is so complicated in "Technology, Economics and Ego Conspire to Make Software Difficult to Use," 5-20. His "Battered Computer Stocks Could Fall Further," 6-21, is a respectable gathering of perspectives on the future of specific computer stocks, but the quotes he includes on the direction of the overall industry are mostly generic. On the other hand, he pens a highly perceptive analysis of the changing nature of the computer industry in "Computers Become a Kind of Commodity, To Dismay of Makers," leder 9-5, crisply characterizing the constant restructuring necessary to deal with the commodity pricing that now dominates a market used to much higher profit margins: "[W]ith the companies constantly leapfrogging each other with machines that run the same software, the industry is condemned to ceaseless innovation, price cutting and product cycles that are nasty, brutish and short. The ever-more-rapid pace of innovation is demonstrated by Sun Microsystems Inc., which has spurred many of the changes. Sun introduced eight generations of computers in its 9 1/2-year existence. In the old days, product cycles took three to five years, and companies had plenty of time to recoup research and development costs."

Burgess, John. *The Washington Post.* (★)

Computers and telecommunications. We slogged through another mediocre year with Burgess. Evincing less and less enthusiasm and curiosity, he offers little beyond the basics, and his bland style increasingly resembles wire copy. With little evidence, he stretches for a war-related angle in "Sudden Surge in Telephone Calls Could Overload the Nation's System," 1-12, and comes up with a slightly alarmist report that if war breaks out "some telecommunications experts worry that a sudden surge in phone calling by ordinary Americans trading the news could overload the nation's phone system and cause a temporary breakdown." In "Bush Administration Includes China in List of Trade-Restriction Offenders," 3-30, he reliably spews out the necessary facts on the U.S. citation of China as a growing "protectionist offender." But there's no apparent theme or analysis to glue this list of facts together. "Arms Export Loan Plan Draws Fire in Congress," 5-3, is serviceable coverage of Rep. David Obey's (D-Wis.) opposition to giving "one dime" to the U.S. Export-Import Bank if the Bush administration wins congressional authorization to use up to $1 billion of the bank's loans to finance arms exports. The possibility of an emerging Asian trade block has been widely covered by the business press, but Burgess's "In Asia, If It Looks Like a Trade Bloc. . ." 6-2, is succinct and includes enough detail to make this piece worth the time it takes to read. In one of his best articles of the year, "Computer Companies Engage in Price War," 6-3, Burgess gives us a clear sense of the increasing competition in the computer industry created by "Clone" manufacturers who offer computers of equal quality at rock-bottom prices. This is putting immense pressure on traditional industry leaders like IBM who are used to getting premium prices for their products. Of course, Burgess could have tied in the international reach of these clone computer makers to give us a handle on their appeal overseas where IBM has had strong sales until this year. Very brief in "Comsat's Goldstein Is U.S. Intelsat Candidate," 9-21, he reports that Irving Goldstein has been named the official U.S. candidate to head the communications consortium Intelsat.

Byrne, John A. *Business Week.* (★ ★ ★)

Senior writer. One of the most colorful writers on the *BW* masthead, Byrne spent much of the year scrutinizing the mind-set of the nation's executives who are under intense pressure to perform in these tough economic times. Illustrating his flare with a business feature in "Why Headhunters Are Hunting Each Other," 1-14, Byrne lights up a "brouhaha" brewing in the financially-strapped executive search industry whose companies are increasingly stealing each others top personnel: ". . .the only way to grow may be to hire good people from competitors if they can bring their business with them." His sobering "CEO Disease," with William C. Symonds and Julia Flynn Siler, 4-1, carefully reveals how egotism can breed corporate disaster: "Much of the damage done by an afflicted CEO is insidious, striking at the heart of the corporation's ability to compete: employee morale." "Salaries at the Top Finally Stop Defying Gravity," with Kathleen Kerwin, 4-15, is only a so-so summary of CEOs whose pay has declined during the recession. He is much better in "The Flap Over Executive Pay," 5-6, a broader and more balanced analysis of the CEO pay scorecard. In a recessionary economy, with profits down, Byrne asks some tough and germane questions: "How can Chrysler, awash in red ink and fighting for survival, afford to give Lee Iacocca $4.8 million?" The article also elucidates the role of stock options as compensation. Taking his annual look at the state of U.S. business education in "Wharton Rewrites the Book on B-Schools," 5-13, Byrne reviews the curriculum changes being instituted by the U. of Pennsylvania's Wharton Business School. Instead of the traditional, hardcore, nuts-n-bolts MBA program that made Wharton famous, the school has begun a more holistic program which it hopes will train leaders for the 21st century with a more humanistic, futuristic curriculum. Although this sounds innovative, we'd have liked more probing into the specific advantages of this approach. His review of *The New Individualist: The Generation After the Organization Man,* "Is the Company Man Really a Goner?" 8-26, is a sprightly and balanced evaluation of "a great idea" that "sorely needed an aggressive editor. . .[and]. . .at times descends into sociobabble."

Byron, Christopher. *New York.* (★ ★)
"The Bottom Line" columnist. Byron's perspectives on financial and economic issues are worth perusing, but we've noticed that many of his macro-economic analyses are hamstrung by a Keynesian demand model. In "The Omen," 2-25, he compiles multiple opinions on the meaning of the DJIA surge, but like most of the press corps he was unable to come up with any conclusive insights. Following up on his "There Goes the Neighborhood," 1-15-90, with "In the Dumps," 3-18, Byron catalogs recent events surrounding NYC's illegal dump site scandal in a solid interim report and winds up calling for an investigation of the state bureaucracy. In "The Kindest Cut," 4-8, Byron makes his case for a tax cut: ". . .unless significant amounts of cash are put back in people's pockets quickly, the economy may wind up emerging from the current recession like a drunk trying to stand up in the gutter: Halfway through brushing himself off, he could be falling down all over again." He evinces characteristic skepticism in "High Spy," 5-13, an intriguing look at Jules Kroll and Kroll Associates, who did a "60 Minutes" investigation of Saddam Hussein, although much of his information had already been revealed in Byron's "Bottom Line" column, "The Iraq Connection," 2-11. Both reports emanated from a publicly distributed paper from the Simon Wiesenthal Center. Despite Byron's best efforts, the enigmatic Kroll remains a mystery at the end of the piece. Byron's atmospheric comparison of '61 and '91, "Where Have You Gone, Roger Maris?" 6-10, bogs down a bit with its heavy reliance on statistics to compare the two, but we appreciated the effort to construct this unique comparison. His "Slip-Sliding Away," 9-16, is an I-told-you-so, reflecting back on his 4-8 column, "The Kindest Cut," in which he warned that "predictions of a sustained recovery wouldn't pan out and that without an immediate tax cut to offset the recessionary drag of Washington's disastrous budget accord a year ago, growth in consumer spending simply wouldn't happen." But in "Cut and Run," 11-4, he misses the point that all tax cuts are not created equal, and misleads with this assertion: "Unfortunately, to spur growth, a tax cut must by definition add to the deficit; otherwise, as [political scientist Norman] Ornstein observes, 'it won't stimulate anything.' "

Carey, John. *Business Week.* (★ ★ ★)
Washington. We're very impressed with Carey's effective fusion of his real-world scientific experience and obvious acumen in the area of industrial and scientific policy. *BW* seems to be capitalizing on his specialized talents by assigning him to stories that showcase these complementary strengths. His book review of Dennis Overbye's *Lonely Hearts of the Cosmos: The Scientific Quest for the Secret of the Universe,* "It All Started With the Big Bang, Didn't It?" 2-25, provides so much detail on the book that we feel we've already read it. . .well, almost. Keeping in mind that his readers are laymen, Carey clarifies a complex scientific debate like a pro in "Cutting the Red Tape on AIDS Drugs," with Maria Shao, 2-25. This is top-notch reporting on a new and controversial procedure that could greatly shorten the FDA approval process for AIDS drugs. In place of clinical trials, FDA is considering a faster, but unproven, tack: ". . .researchers are proposing to test a drug's effect by measuring so-called surrogate markers — key biochemical changes the drug produces in the body." Like your favorite science professor in "It's All in the Magnets," 5-6, Carey breaks down the complexities of the Superconducting Supercollider (SSC) into comprehendible terms: "It all depends on the magnets. Because they operate in series, like old-fashioned Christmas-tree lights, one bad one could shut the SSC down." His "It's Going to Get Harder to Zap Those Pests," 6-17, is an astute examination of the formidable challenges Congress faces in trying to regulate pesticides. In this very instructive report, Carey meticulously scrutinizes the numerous considerations of this contentious debate — politics, health, environment, and economics. In one of his best pieces, "Will Uncle Sam Be Dragged Kicking and Screaming Into the Lab?" 7-15, he expertly dissects the great ideological debate over the value of having a U.S. industrial policy: "The larger question is whether 'critical technologies' programs. . .can slow the industrial slide. It may well be that tax policies, environmental regulation, health care costs, the value of the dollar, and industry's own resolve will determine U.S. competitiveness. . ." He is sharp on congressional moves to give the FDA a new set of regulatory teeth in "The FDA May Soon Be Able to Back Up Its Snarl," 10-28.

Carley, William M. *The Wall Street Journal.* (★ ★ ★)

An outstanding writer, a veteran of the old school, Carley's winning style makes us forget that we're ingesting oodles of pertinent facts. Reminiscent of his excellent coverage of air safety in years past, he penned a strong "Page One" investigation of airline pilot screening in "How a Marginal Pilot Landed at a Big Airline and Made a Fatal Error," 1-9, a scary and well-researched tale that raises enough questions about the soundness of the screening process to spark a policy debate. In his suspenseful "How Iraq Attempted to Kill a Dissident in the United States," 2-27, Carley sweeps us through the web of details surrounding an eerie failed plot by an Iraqi diplomat out to assassinate Sargon Dadesho, an Assyrian living in the U.S. who actively champions the cause of this minority in Arab-dominated Iraq. In a world where the most important wars are increasingly being fought on economic battlefields, Carley's "Corporate Targets: As Cold War Fades, Some Nations' Spies Seek Industrial Secrets," 6-17, offers a shocking and revealing look at the world of international industrial espionage: "Last year, a French magazine reported that French employees of IBM and Texas Instruments Inc. handed over company documents to French intelligence agents, who in turn passed them on to a French computer maker." Following up on his 1-9 leder, Carley pens a pithy "Transportation Safety Board Urges FAA to Review Pilot Examiner Program," 6-13, recapping the National Transportation Safety Board's efforts to goad the FAA into reviewing and possibly revamping its pilot examiner program to increase safety. As corporate intelligence becomes ever more important in the marketplace, his "The Sting: How the FBI Snared Two Scientists Selling Drug Company Secrets," leder 9-5, tells an intriguing and eye-opening tale of increasingly complex efforts by the FBI and corporations to crack down on those who pirate company secrets for their own profit.

Carroll, Paul B. *The Wall Street Journal.* (★ ★)

We've come to rely on Carroll as one of the best chroniclers of IBM, but in this crucial year of challenges for Big Blue he proved himself perhaps too intimate with his subject, unable to assess IBM's flaws impartially. On other topics such as "Computer-Ordering Method Helps Newcomer Blossom," 1-22, Carroll is still reliable. Here, he surveys the rapid growth of an interesting entrepreneurial endeavor which allows customers to use computers to order flowers for worldwide delivery through FTD member florist shops. Back on IBM in "IBM Earnings Shock Raises New Concerns on Economic Rebound," leder 3-20, he constructs a terribly lopsided assessment of what ails Big Blue. From this account we get the impression that all its troubles stem solely from external forces. Only in the last paragraph does Carroll even hint that IBM might be at least partially culpable for its own decline. "IBM Bends its Rules to Make a Laptop," 4-15, was another piece that raised flags. Carroll's report is laced with exclamations only PR could love: "IBM finally did it, announcing a technically elegant machine that fills the remaining hole in its product line." He seems to want to help IBM repair its tattered image: "...to get the product right IBM had to shake up its organization and take some risks. The process says a lot about how IBM is trying to remake its culture." Carroll redeems himself with a rich "Reprogramming Itself, IBM Now Wants to Become a Big Supplier of Little Parts," 5-15, a landmark piece that captures the company's strategic shift into the parts-supply business. In "Akers to IBM Employees: Wake Up!" 5-29, we find chairman John Akers even more critical of Big Blue than Carroll: "Although IBM may publicly blame its problems on a slow economy, Mr. Akers is saying the real problem goes far deeper. He is telling IBM managers that IBM has been steadily losing market share to competitors...He is complaining that the quality of IBM products is inadequate." In light of this report, we question why Carroll initially failed to scrutinize IBM's line that the economy was behind its woes. He is up close and personal on the woeful environment at IBM in "Computers Indicate Mood at Big Blue Is Practically Indigo," 8-7, giving an inside look at a short-lived network where employees conveyed their gloominess to each other.

Chambliss, Lauren. *FW.* (★ ½)

Washington. Chambliss went on leave in September and will be returning to *FW* mid-1992. As we noted last year, the caliber of her reporting is erratic. She fares well with straightforward topics but seems overwhelmed by difficult or complex issues. She also displays an irksome tendency to champion certain positions in her reports. Her "Capital Gains R.I.P.?" 1-22, is a succinct summary of how the administration fumbled the ball on a capital gains tax cut, and the dim prospects for a cut in 1991. There's nothing especially fresh here, but Chambliss makes clear that support is growing even though the Bush team seems inclined to "switch rather than fight." She pens a worthwhile piece for curious taxpayers in "Electrotax," 2-19, a practical pro and con assessment of the IRS's new computer filing system. In "Is Gold Dead?" 3-19, she takes an over-simplified look at why the old adage "when calamity strikes, gold prices soar" hasn't been the case lately. Her hard-hitting "Big Pack Attack," 4-16, criticizes both parties in Congress for their charade with regard to reforming campaign contributions from PACs. But, she blatantly advocates taxpayer financing of campaigns as the best way to create a level playing field by eliminating PAC money: "What can be done? Probably the answer would be public financing — that is, taxpayers' money — to pay for all campaigns. . .That would put an end to the money-grubbing by politicians and special interests." Campaign financing is an important issue that deserves a multidimensional discussion, not advocacy. She is much more judicious in "Hang 'Em High," 7-9, a muscular examination of the "worrisome powers" of the U.S. Sentencing Commission which plans to extend its dubious rules to cover the sentencing of corporate defendants, effective November 1: ". . .the commission has the awesome power to virtually eliminate judges' personal discretion in handing out sentences to individuals convicted of federal crimes."

Charlier, Marj. *The Wall Street Journal.* (★ ★ ½)

Denver. A truly versatile journalist, Charlier's smart style and inquisitive reporting always make for an interesting and educational read. In "Brewers Shake Off a 3-Year Hangover," 1-15, she serves up a hearty mug of information on the latest trends in the beer brewing industry. In "Big Brewers Will Be Among Wallflowers At the 1991 'Spring Break' Beach Parties," 3-13, Charlier tells us why Spring Break may no longer be synonymous with drunken, rowdy teens. Beer brewers are under pressure to tone down their advertising to that crowd: ". . .instead of plastering Coors banners all over the sites of volleyball tournaments on the beach, the Adolph Coors Co. distributor will supply simple point-of-sale table cards and posters for bars and liquor stores." Demonstrating she can handle hard financial news with the same ease as a feature, Charlier constructs an info-packed "Occidental Petroleum Encounters Trouble Getting Price it Wants For 51% Stake in IBP," 3-26. In this assessment of IBP, the big meat packer that the late Occidental Petroleum chairman Armand Hammer often called "a jewel" in his corporate empire, Charlier speculates on why a 51% stake in the company which has been on the block since January isn't selling: "so far, gem collectors have been scarce and now analysts are wondering. . ." Her "Gold Explorer Strikes it Rich by Sticking to its Specialty," 4-22, is a rich profile of Crown Resources Inc., a unique gold exploration company that benefits by sticking to its specialty of finding gold, letting the big companies extract the ore: "While the average finding cost for gold in the U.S. is about $130 an ounce, Crown spent about $5 an ounce to locate the 1.2 million ounces it owns." She alerts us to a marketing technique that is definitely on the move in "Restaurants Mobilize to Pursue Customers," 6-10, a great piece about mobile merchandising. With restaurants on wheels becoming more and more popular among franchisers, Charlier tells us who is getting involved and why, providing plenty of worthwhile information for casual readers as well as investors who follow the industry. Her "They'll Prove It's Never Too Late to Take a Walk on the Wild Side," 9-12, is an enjoyable little ditty on "a bunch of great old broads" who want to save the wilderness.

Cohen, Laurie P. *The Wall Street Journal.* (★ ★)

Having wrapped up her sometimes controversial coverage of the Wall Street insider trading cases and moved on to financially-oriented topics, Cohen is exhibiting the traits of a more careful, thorough reporter. In "Some Bondholders Believe Bally Is Gambling Against Bankruptcy Via Debt Buy-Back Card," 3-1, she raises pertinent questions about the circumstances surrounding the mysterious buy up of bonds issued by Bally Manufacturing, which had been missing debt payments. She doesn't try to palm her information off as fact, but rather throws several possibilities on the table for investors to ponder before buying or selling. She takes a no-nonsense look at what small individual investors need to watch for when trading junk bonds in her "Let the Small Investor Beware These Junk Bond Prices," 3-18, and cautions that reliable information is especially hard to come by in over-the-counter trading. Her "Want Your Biotech Stock to Soar? Be Sure It Has a Bullish Analyst," 4-24, follows the roller coaster ride of Immunex Corp.'s stock in order to exemplify the profound impact bullish or bearish securities analysts can have on biotechnology stocks. Says one quoted source, " 'Unlike General Electric, these stocks often have no earnings, revenues, dividends or even products on the market. Investors don't understand the science, so analyst sponsorship is critical.' " She cautiously ferrets out the facts in her competent investigation of two volatile biotech stocks, "Amgen Shares Tumble as Genetics Institute Reportedly Hires Top Lawyer in Patent Rift," 6-7. With the two companies in a patent dispute, Cohen attributes the price moves to rumors that Harvard constitutional law professor Laurence Tribe may have been hired by Genetics Institute to take its patent battle with Amgen to the Supreme Court. Her "Stiff Civil, Criminal Penalties Are Likely for Salomon," 9-23, is a balanced examination of what lies ahead for Salomon and those employees implicated in the Treasury auction scandal.

Cohen, Roger. *The New York Times.* (★ ★ ½)
Publishing. After more than a year at his new post, Cohen is providing valuable vignettes and personal bios of the major players in publishing. But word is that he'll soon be off to an entirely different assignment as the economic correspondent in Paris. In the meantime this active reporter has co-authored a biography of Schwarzkopf that apparently made his mission as an objective publishing reporter more challenging. In "Seeking Stars, Hollywood Is Spending Freely on Books," 2-9, Cohen accurately presents the Hollywood publishing house connection and tells how some books are commanding six digit figures to be turned into movies, even before they're published. He succinctly covered the biggest brouhaha in the industry this year in "Reagan Biography: In Quest of What?" 4-10, correctly pegging Kitty Kelley's craft as being a fusion of journalism, biography, and scandal writing. He piles on the pliable information in his pithy "When a Best Seller Is at Stake, Publishers Can Lose Control," 5-12, observing that for publishing "the imagined Golden Age is hard to find," and "Commerce and culture have always lived in uneasy concubinage in publishing." In "Profits — Dick Snyder's Ugly Word," 6-30, Cohen delivers an overly glowing bio of Simon & Schuster chief Dick Snyder, complete with an appraisal of the company. Cohen glazed over a possible conflict of interest in "Big Gamble on Schwarzkopf," 7-15, reporting on Gen. Schwarzkopf's autobiography contract with Bantam Books just after completing his own version of Schwarzkopf's life for Farrar, Straus & Giroux. He was also criticized in print by the *Village Voice* for writing an overly optimistic article on Harold Evans and Random House, while having been under contract at Random House to help write an autobiography of Fiat chairman Giovanni Agnelli. His "A Las Vegas for the Orlando Crowd," 10-2, is a spiffy little marketing piece, but Cohen is a little starry-eyed on the prospects for another financially successful casino in Las Vegas, where casino overcapacity could stifle profits.

Commins, Kevin. *The Journal of Commerce.* (★ ★)
Chicago. Serviceable on numerous subjects, Commins has a crisp, clean reporting style and dependable eye for detail. Chronicling the toll that stiff competition and a bad economy are taking on the St. Lawrence Seaway in his "Seaway's Future Unsure as Cargoes Dip," 2-1, Commins tells us how maritime executives are urging cost cutting to combat this cyclical decline. Contributing a rather useless piece to *JC*'s special report on "Futures & Options," his "See a Tweezer Bottom? Analysts Say Beware," 3-13, meanders through a bunch of gobbledygook on trendy technical approaches to market assessment — absolutely nothing of substance here. At

the end of the piece, Commins also neatly slips in a plug for *JC*'s parent company, Knight-Ridder, without mentioning the relationship — careful! He is better in "Irresistible Returns Lure Investors," 3-13, giving us a useful look at the oodles of money pouring into the hands of successful commodity trading advisers: "Since 1985, the amount of money invested in public commodity funds has grown from $258 million to over $2.9 billion, according to Managed Accounts Reports." Commins proves well-versed in the specifics of barge and rail transport in "Soviet Deal Would Help Barges, Rails," 6-3, a valuable discussion of the impact that the issuance of agricultural credit guarantees would have on American grain carriers hard hit by the recession: ". . .railroads have an advantage over barge lines in that they move a substantial amount of grain domestically. Indeed, despite the drop in loadings, grain rates and hopper car leasing rates have remained firm. Barge lines, in contrast, are captive to the vicissitudes of the grain export market. When exports decline, barge rates invariably fall." He keeps it short and sweet in "Chicago Merc to Help Panama Form Exchange," 6-27, a punchy, unique little piece on the Chicago Mercantile Exchange's broad strategy to market its exchange management expertise to countries trying to develop financial and commodity markets. Keeping us abreast of the latest grain transport trends with "High Barge Rates Boost Railroads' Grain Business," 9-30, he reports that railroads are currently winning over customers from other types of transportation with attractive rates.

Cook, James. *Forbes.* (★ ★ ★)
Executive editor. Even as he celebrates his fifteenth anniversary with *Forbes,* Cook continues to cultivate fresh, provocative material and to hone his spirited, probing style. He always gets high marks for accuracy. He pens an engaging and informative profile of The National Geographic Society's ongoing popularity and prosperity in "The World Is Our Theme," 1-21. Amid enjoyable and telling details about the "benevolent but firm grip" of the Grosvenor family which has run the Society since 1899, Cook weaves in important business numbers, and the fact that "Other magazine publishers and rival cartographers. . .have frequently protested that the Geographic's tax-free status confers on it an unfair competitive advantage." In his succinct and insightful "Camel In the Tent," 3-18, Cook surveys competition-enhancing trends in the electric utilities industry spurred by independent producers. With a keen understanding of what inspires such trends he observes, "For an independent producer, a penny saved is a penny earned. For a regulated utility, a penny earned. . .risks being returned to the consumers in lower rates." He constructs a vigorous expose of how public-sector unions are seeking to expand their power in "Collision Course," 5-13, a 10 Best selection for Business/Financial Reporting. Through careful analysis of union leaders' statements, he comes to the persuasive and unsettling conclusion that the unions are not only after higher wages but also control of their job descriptions with no interference from taxpayers. He cautions that unless politicians take action the result will be similar to England's experience under the Labour government. In "There's Plenty on the Plate," 7-8, Cook directs his analysis toward his investment-minded audience to pen a sharp portrait of SCEcorp, the parent of Southern California Edison Co. whose dynamic chairman has championed alternative energies. Zeroing in on the successes of the company's four-year-old non-utility subsidiary, Mission Group, Cook notes, "SCEcorp's earnings growth has been sluggish for several years now, and Mission offers a prime opportunity to get them growing briskly again." He offers a brisk assessment of the lifestyle attributes that are increasingly drawing big business to small-town America in "Exodus," 9-16.

Cowan, Alison Leigh. *The New York Times.* (★ ★ ½)
Accounting. Showing marked improvement, Cowan is producing more authoritative, well-sourced and highly-educational reports, although she sometimes gets a bit heavy-handed with Eighties bashing. She is sharp in "When the Bank Can't Back the Bond," 1-20. Noting the plight of Tierney bondholders following the takeover of the Bank of New England, Cowan competently dissects the hazards of standby letters of credit. Again gearing her work toward bondholders in "Chairman's Role in Rexene Feuds," 2-4, she constructs a solid case study. Here she casts a wary eye on the dubious role of William J. Gilliam, "a brash young deal maker in the 1980s" who

helped with the company's buyout and stock offering, and now has effective control of the troubled company. However, we'd have appreciated more quotes to back up the report. Her "Belzberg Is Turning Reins Over to Nephew," 3-4, is a straightforward account of the passing of the reins at First City Financial Corporation from 62-year-old Samuel Belzberg to his 40-year-old nephew Brent S. Belzberg. Although peppered with unnecessary jabs at the Eighties, "Bottom Fishing With R.D. Smith," 3-29, is nonetheless a very well-constructed and balanced analysis of the pros and cons of investing with R.D. Smith & Co. which "is profiting from other people's misery by trading the stock and debt of the troubled companies, both for itself and its customers." Cowan quotes investors who say they appreciate the company's "savvy research" but are wary of conflicts of interest that could arise as the company places its own money in the same establishments as its investors. She is extremely perceptive in "Gaping Loophole For Petrie Stores," 5-13, an instructive lesson for shareholders. Here, Petrie's shareholders invested in Toys 'R' Us when it was trading for pennies and now must realize amazing, *taxable,* financial gains. She outlines a tax loophole that shareholders say management is in no hurry to try because, unlike shareholders, they have no intention of selling. Her "A Game Maker's Winning Moves," 7-4, is an engaging look at the creative marketing strategies of small game makers on absurdly low budgets. She pens a heartfelt report on Willie Nelson's desperate attempts to pay off his taxes in "Willie Nelson Hopes for a Hit; So Does the I.R.S." 9-2.

Crossen, Cynthia. *The Wall Street Journal.* (★ ★ ½)
New York. Crossen delights again this year as she colorfully covers a wide range of topics with equal ease. She holds a mirror of the times up to businesses who believe themselves to be recession-proof in "Who's Afraid of the Big Bad Slump?" 1-28. Crossen picks out numerous interesting companies and examples; "A toy-store owner told *The Washington Post* that the $500 six-foot Paddington Bear was 'almost recession-proof' because it's bought by 'guilty fathers in high-income families with broken marriages.' " Her "A Scud in Tel Aviv Is a Powerful Image for Jewish Charity," 2-26, is a comprehensive, informative piece on the United Jewish Appeal-Federation which raises more than "American Cancer Society, CARE and the March of Dimes combined." She samples the publishing beat with "Martha Stewart Living: Fantasies for $3," 3-28. This piece examines a ladies' magazine that stresses the joys of being a housewife. Never condescending nor demeaning to a seemingly '50s idea, she provides insightful and informative material. Her nostalgia-tinged "Gone Are the Days When Tom Swift Was a Serious Nerd," 4-16, seemed appropriate on the front page for elder businessmen reminiscing on the books of their youth. Crossen also assesses the times, focusing on the need to replace the old Tom Swift for a updated boy's action hero. She must have been scraping the bottom of the bowl for topic ideas for "Creative Expression Is in Full Flush at Kohler Factory," 5-22, yet still files an interesting, if at times funny, piece on the Kohler toilet and bathtub factory, and the idea of having artists alongside factory workers. Her "I Want Stock, Sister; Golf Clubs, Brother; And Hair, Hair, Hair," 9-16, is an engaging A-hed on "forecasters of the baby boom" who "use a combination of statistics, studies, interviews, history and gut instinct" to try to pin down the tastes of this huge group of consumers.

Crudele, John. *New York Post.* (★ ½)
Syndicated columnist. We read this active reporter's work in the *Los Angeles Times* and *The Washington Post.* He was even reportedly on his way to television with FNN before the buyout by CNBC. But we fear he is more concerned with quantity than quality as his reports often lack depth. His "Markets: If You Don't Know What to Do With $50,000," *LAT* 1-6, is a bland piece of investment advice in which Crudele predicts "that stock prices will go lower in the next few months. . ." Then in "Six Reasons to Stay Out of the Market," *WP,* 1-13, penned just before the war began, he warned: "Put that telephone down before you call your broker, here are a half-dozen perfectly legitimate reasons why you should not buy stocks right now." Ouch. In "Why Big Blue's No Big Deal," *WP* 4-21, he ponders whether the market can do well while IBM is doing so lousy. But his reasoning that it can because the market "isn't reacting to outside events like the economy" seemed wobbly to us. Playing the contrarian in "The Flip Side of Falling

Rates," *WP* 5-12, Crudele takes a worthwhile look at the negative side of lower interest rates. Then, with the government's 30-year bond hitting 8.47%, he asks the right question in "Rising Interest Rates Worry the Markets; Investor Switch to Bonds Is Feared," *WP* 6-16: "At what level do rising interest rates start drawing investors away from the stock market?" But his follow-through is wishy washy. In "Over-the-Counter Issues Spur Investors' Debate," *WP* 7-14, Crudele superficially hems and haws over whether the Nasdaq will skyrocket or dive; then wanders into a superfluous discussion of how the Japanese manipulate small stocks. In the end, he doesn't come close to answering his own question. He is better in "The Trendless Summer," *WP* 9-1, observing that it's hard to make stock predictions based on summer trends. "But this year, predicting the stock market is even more difficult. . .because stocks did virtually nothing. . .On June 2. . .the Dow Jones industrial average closed at a record 3035.33. Months have gone by since then — the Soviet Union is in chaos, Salomon Brothers Inc. is a mess and the nation's economy seems to be slipping again — and the Dow is still within a few points of where it was on June 2." Eye-opening, but he never explores how Washington's policy void is weighing on the markets.

Cushman, John H., Jr. *The New York Times.* (★ ★)
Washington. Cushman's dance card was filled with an assortment of assignments this year — from reporting on domestic transportation in the familiar world of Washington to covering the chaotic post-war situation in Kuwait. He handled the range of these responsibilities durably, producing competent factual reports. Stateside for "Foreign Airlines Can Raise Stake in U.S. Carriers," 1-24, Cushman chronicles the subtle but important administration shift toward the globalization of U.S. airlines. He rightly observes the limited impact of this move, noting that foreign airlines will still be unable to effect control if they invest in U.S. carriers. For the amount of information imparted in "Military Experts See a Death Toll of 25,000 to 50,000 Iraqi Troops," 3-1, Cushman should have kept it much shorter. Besides, we're not sure that "guesstimating" the body count without any reliable sources of information is a worthwhile journalistic exercise. His "Road Officials Say Little Is Done to Cut Pileups in Fog," 4-27, is an interesting report on a subject not often discussed: "Even though hundreds of people die every year in [fog related] crashes, almost nowhere in the country are highways equipped to help drivers." He rounds out the piece by exploring some safety options being bounced around at a meeting of the National Transportation Safety Board. In "2 Sides Are Sharply Divided on Transportation Bill," 5-22, Cushman effectively overviews the various special interests and political camps debating the Transportation Bill: "As competing interests vie for the money, sharp divisions have arisen: between metropolitan centers and agricultural regions, between advocates of better highways and those who favor mass transit, between states whose residents pay more in gasoline taxes than they receive in Federal aid and those in the reverse situation." Surveying the post-war consumer market in Kuwait City, Cushman's colorfully-written "Now, Kuwaiti Battle Is in the Consumer Market," 6-4, reveals that opportunities abound for creative marketeers. He offers a competent, measured report on the latest theories on what caused a fatal jetliner crash in Colorado in March in "Rudder May Have Caused Jet Crash Fatal to 25," 8-21.

Day, Kathleen. *The Washington Post.* (★ ★)
Day has a sturdy grasp of government's ever-shifting grip on the marketplace. Be it loosening with deregulation or tightening with new activism, Day keeps her eyes on a number of agencies and keenly ferrets out the motivation behind their latest move. In "Disenchanted With Deregulation," 1-11, she studies the ill-timed arrival of banking legislation. After all the industry's lobbying done in hopes of broadening the types of business it can engage in, Day tells us "deregulation of the financial markets may prove to be a nonevent. Few will want — or have the financial wherewithal — to plunge into other's shaky business, many observers say." In "A New Activism on Antitrust Policy," 1-13, Day expertly discerns the broader implications of the FTC's "most aggressive antitrust inquiries in a decade," the investigation of pricing practices in the infant formula industry: "Whether anything comes from this particular investigation, legal scholars and politicians agree, the FTC's willingness to undertake it at all signals a new activism

on anti-trust matters, possibly even a desire to break legal ground. . ." But Day fails to examine the possibility of FTC overreach. She stretches a non-story too far in "The Trials of a Traveling Regulator," 3-6, reporting on John Dingell's (D-Mich.) questioning of SEC chairman Richard Breeden's travel schedule. Following through on her 1990 coverage of Donald Trump's financial woes in "Trump, Banks Near Deal on Dismantling Empire," 4-26, she gives a straightforward account of his latest financial posturing. In light of the Bridgeport, Conn. decision to file for bankruptcy, Day pens "Bridgeport's Big Test," 6-19, in which she talks with lawyers, politicians and municipal bondholders who wonder if this is the start of a trend. She enriches this solid report with a useful history lesson on Chapter 9. In "Gutfreund Silent at July Meeting," 8-29, she relies solely on anonymous sources. But she seems to be on to something as these sources recount that while meeting with Treasury Undersecretary Robert Glauber in July, Salomon Chairman John Gutfreund didn't mention that a Salomon trader had concealed the purchase of Treasury Securities in February even though he'd been aware of this fact since April. Upon learning of the violation four weeks later, her sources say Glauber and others were "particularly incensed."

Dentzer, Susan. *U.S.News & World Report.* (★ ½)
Senior writer, business and economics. While she is a competent fact-gatherer skilled in the language of "economese," Dentzer's analyses continue to be typically conventional and generic. Her "As the Banks Crumble," 1-21, is a formulaic rundown of the problems facing U.S. banks and the proposed reforms, with a melodramatic warning near the end: "Just as the 1970s and '80s exposed global overcapacity in steel and auto making, the '90s seem likely to prompt a bloody shakedown among large financial-services firms worldwide." She pens a serviceable analysis, "Bank Reform," 2-18, on the administration's proposed bank reforms and the opposition it faces over such provisions as allowing banks to sell insurance state-by-state. "For all the carping, many bankers think the Bush plan could go a long way toward curing much of what ails the troubled industry." In "Tallying the Cost of War," 3-11, Dentzer overviews the cost of Operation Desert Storm, noting that "Like the conflict itself, the tally contained a number of surprises." But her evaluation is vague and pertinent numbers are few, variables numerous. Even by the end of the article, we still have no clear picture. She passes along the findings of a new Council on Competitiveness report in "Staying Ahead in High Tech," 4-1, which calls for less emphasis on "Big Science" projects and more public-private sector cooperation. "In the aftermath of the gulf victory, the council's report could help spur a public-private coalition to head off an even higher-tech defeat." Her thought-provoking "Downward Mobility/Blue-Collar Workers Watch the American Dream Fade Away," *The San Francisco Chronicle* 5-19, assesses the wage squeeze on America's working class and argues that the manufacturing sector has no future, with neither traditional government spending nor targeted tax cuts reviving it. "But today, with growth in the labor force slowing. . .the challenge isn't so much to generate more jobs — but rather smarter workers in more innovative industries that then can channel the fruits of success back to employees." Her survey of the massive economic problems confronting the Soviet republics, "Economy In Crisis," 9-9, is out of the apocalyptic school with Dentzer foreseeing millions starving to death this winter. She is thoughtful in "The Graying of Japan," 9-30, assessing the societal, economical and political implications of the aging of the Japanese population.

Deutsch, Claudia H. *The New York Times.* (★ ★ ½)
Sunday "Business." We enjoy ever higher-quality, more full-bodied business profiles from Deutsch each year. Her "Managing" column, now in its second year, is maturing nicely and she is gradually procuring more space from her editors for other energetic Sunday stories. In "Executives, Take Your Risks," 1-27, Deutsch chronicles the transformation in corporate America, reporting that in these hard times companies are offering stock-related incentives in lieu of salary or cash bonuses. She is keen on the gray areas of this type of incentive, weaving in numerous definitive quotes. Says one source, "They finally realize that stock programs that are all upside and no downside do not assure that executives will act in the interest of all

shareholders." Her engaging "Goya Braces for a Challenge From the Food Giants," 2-24, springboards from a profile of the nation's largest privately-held Hispanic company into an everything-you-want-to-know examination of the Hispanic food market. With a knack for assessing companies with an objective eye, Deutsch pens "A Catalogue House at Center Stage," 3-3, a comprehensive history of Horn & Hardart, the restaurant chain "that added the word Automat to the language," but is now moving on to the catalogue business. After taking us through all the company's bumpy years as restauranteurs, Deutsch sketches H & H's prospects for continued solid growth in the competitive catalogue business. Her two-part series on child care begins with "More Care for the Corporate Kids," 6-9, a quick look at unique daycare options offered by companies. The second piece, "The Learning Curve in Day Care," 6-16, is better, examining in depth the growing trend in which schools are "spurning custodial care in favor of 'educare,' the term coined by educators for day care with an educational component." Increasingly, she tells us, corporations are under pressure from employees and educators to restrict educational grants and subsidies to "programs that stimulate children, rather than just supervise them." In "Getting Through Recession on Real Estate's Pricey Side," 8-18, she explains why conservative residential real estate developers Bob and Bruce Toll "have made it through three recessions without a stain of red ink." The key, they say, is "incremental growth."

Deveny, Kathleen. *The Wall Street Journal.* (★ ★ ½)
Smart and savvy on numerous topics, Deveny is a luminous writer and a dogged fact-finder. We're especially impressed this year with her marketing profiles which are dependably insightful and engaging. Mid-cold season, she pens an instructive "Copycat Cold Medicines Proliferate," 2-1, reporting on marketing strategies bound to give consumers a headache: "[M]any marketers simply churn out slightly varied combinations of commonplace ingredients. Other companies. . .hawk identical products under different names — a practice that is perfectly legal." Her "Perelman's Vaunted Marketing Skills Produce Only Mixed Results at Revlon," 3-4, is a revealing look at Revlon's ups and downs since Ronald O. Perelman acquired the cosmetic company six years ago. Deveny sees past the Perelman glitz and, by focusing on the stats, market share, etc., crystallizes the company's weak areas: "Although [Perelman] built up the company's department store business through acquisitions, Revlon's share of the prestige market — 25% in the 1970s — had dwindled to 10% by 1988." In "Seeking Sunnier Sales, Lotion Makers Play on Fears," 5-24, she tells us that "More than ever, marketers of sunscreens are pitching their products as balms for a dangerous world." Uncharacteristically, she meanders a bit, focusing more on the dangers of sunning than on companies' attempts to market to "ageing baby boomers' fears of developing skin cancer." But she is quickly back on track with pertinent numbers and observations on this major shift in consumer behavior. Expanding on an important trade publication article in "U.S. to Wine Makers: It's Time to Get the Lead Out," 6-6, Deveny concisely reports that wine makers may face impending regulations concerning the level of lead in their products. Her best piece of the year, "As Lauder's Scent Battles Calvin Klein's, Cosmetics Whiz Finds Herself on the Spot," 6-27, takes us to the frontlines of the marketing battle between Calvin Klein's Escape perfume and Estec Lauder's SpellBound. Deveny sounds like an insider as she profiles the people shaping the two companies' marketing strategies and gives us a solid feel for an ever more competitive fragrance market hit hard by the recession. She is lively and informative on frenzied marketing efforts for the latest toothbrush technology in "Toothbrush Makers Hope to Clean Up With Array of 'New, Improved' Products," 10-22.

Dobrzynski, Judith H. *Business Week.* (★ ★ ★)
Senior writer. Constantly sharpening her multifarious talents, Dobrzynski expertly handles topics as diverse as the business of fine arts and shareholder activism. Her "There's Still Life in the Old LBO," 1-21, is a meaty update on new activity at established LBO firms. Dobrzynski really knows her way around these complex issues and unlike so many assessing the aftermath of the 1980s, she admirably remains a clear-headed and dispassionate observer. Her commentary, "Should You Sue Your Investment Banker for Lousy Advice?" 2-18, analyzes the underpinnings of numerous cases in which investment bankers are being taken to court for their

role in advising companies that ultimately took on too much debt. While sympathetic to their plight, she sensibly reminds us: "The fact that investment bankers are mercenary. . .does not necessarily imply that they are legally culpable. . .[U]nless they specifically forced an action, it's hard to see how under U.S. law, bankers can be blamed for poor corporate decisions. Directors may not abdicate responsibility, and they have no business voting for options they don't understand." Penning another commentary on the arts business, "A Tax Break for Art's Sake Is No Luxury," 4-1, is a brilliant dissection of the devastating impact the 1986 tax reforms have had on precious art donations. By explicitly showing how a one-year tax "window" is dramatically reversing that trend, she argues for a restoration of these breaks despite Congress's aversion. Her "Who Says You Can't Make Money in the Theatre?" 6-3, is an able, but narrow, description of the investment end of three successful partners' productions. She is clear and informative in "Is Pete Wilson Trying to Mute a Shareholder Activist?" 7-1, showing how California's budget crisis is giving Gov. Wilson reason to try not only to get more funds out of CalPERS, but also to get control of its board. Her "Cutting Loose From Shareholder Activists," 7-8, is a reflective analysis of shareholder activism during the '91 proxy season. Despite gains, she notes the constraining effect that state's legislative removal of the threat of hostile tender offers has had on activism. For "Time Warner," 7-22, she receives a 10 Best, along with Mark Landler, for outstanding coverage of one of the biggest shareholder stories of the year, the contraversial Time Warner rights offering.

Donlan, Thomas G. *Barron's.* (★ ★ ½)
With the departure of Robert Bleiberg, Donlan assumes the position of editorial page editor, and faces the the estimable challenge of filling the shoes of a long-time cornerstone at *Barron's.* Well aware that an article with a Donlan byline means extensive information and analysis, we look forward to watching the page develop under his stewardship. His pre-Gulf War "Delayed Payment," 1-7, is a surprisingly compact compilation of facts on the "hidden costs" of Desert Shield "which have yet to have a major impact on federal spending." He sees a big spending battle looming on Capitol Hill after the crisis reaches a peaceful solution or war is declared. In "Vigilant Watchdog," 3-25, he effectively interviews Marianne K. Smythe, the SEC's director of the Division of Investment Management, who is in charge of fund regulation. Donlan's pointed questions force Smythe to clarify how far she sees the hand of the SEC reaching into the regulation of mutual funds. He is highly informative in "Rattling Their Playpens," 5-20, a sweeping, multi-dimensional overview of the important decisions that rest in the hands of Congress and Judge Harold Greene — the power to allow the Baby Bells to participate in other businesses: "The Baby Bells are fighting as if the course of regulation will determine their future business success. Indeed, it may. . .By the end of the Nineties, local telephone companies will probably face competition from cable television and a new generation of radio telephones. If they are not to be reduced to managing the network for service providers, they will have to be able to offer customers more services and products themselves." His "The Sharper Image," *Reason* 6/91, is an extremely in-depth study of the bumpy regulatory battle that lies ahead for HDTV — with free-marketers on the one side and industrial policy types on the other. He comes down hard on the "sheer deception" of pension fund benefit insurance in "Keep the Faith," editorial 7-1, asserting that the Pension Benefit Guarantee Corp., the FDIC of pensions, is underfunded. His advice: "The U.S. needs to freeze existing employer pension plans, bail out the ailing ones before they grow unmanageable, and terminate the tax-deductibility of employer-sponsored savings. Then give blanket tax exemption to individual retirement savings plans." Looking beyond McDonnell Douglas's current prosperity in "Riding for a Fall?" 10-21, he challenges Wall Street's blue skies scenario, finding clouds on the company's horizon in its loss of commercial airplane market share to Boeing and Airbus Industrie, and even deeper troubles on the defense side of its business.

Duke, Paul, Jr. *The Wall Street Journal.* (★ ★ ½)
Economics. Duke's admirable work last year was recognized with a promotion, but he departed the paper in the fall for parts unknown. He is a conscientious, reflective reporter with clear

potential, and we look forward to seeing his byline surface elsewhere. He avoids alarmist phrases in "U.S. Industrial Production Fell Further in December," 1-27, a straightforward news account handled thoroughly. He includes a useful selection of quotes and competently puts the latest gloomy statistics into proper context. In "Squeezed Suburbs: Boomtown Budgets Suddenly Are Pinched as Tax Takes Dwindle," leder 4-3, Duke's descriptive, detailed writing takes us 40 miles northwest of D.C. and plants us smack in the middle of the Loudoun County's wrenching budget crisis. An attractive boomtown in the '80s when tax rates were low but revenues high, Loudoun now has more people and a dwindling budget. Duke doesn't delve too far into the broad economic forces shaping the situation, but he expertly crystallizes the tough choices cash-strapped local policymakers will have to make in the near future. Just as Americans rush to file their tax returns Duke files "IRS Excels at Tracking the Average Earner, But Not the Wealthy," 4-15, a balanced critique of the IRS's lopsided record of collecting unpaid taxes — average and lower-income filers increasingly get nailed while corporations and wealthy individuals' failure to pay increasingly goes undetected. "The IRS says it can explain the disparity. Individuals earning over $100,000 and big corporations, the agency says, tend to have complex tax matters that require the personal attention of agents, and there simply aren't enough agents to go around." In "Taxing Business: Will Computers Lead the Chase?" 6-10, Congress and the IRS are arguing over whether the IRS should operate a computerized system to check if corporations are reporting all of their income just as it already does for individuals. Duke is balanced, pointing out the hefty amount of unpaid taxes that the system could track down, but also careful to point out the numerous drawbacks. He takes a rich, interesting look into the growing frustrations of unemployed inner-city teens in "Urban Teen-Agers, Who Often Live Isolated from the World of Work, Shun the Job Market," 8-14.

Eichenwald, Kurt. *The New York Times.* (★ ★ ½)
Wall Street. A shrewd observer with a knack for clarifying the convoluted legal, ethical and financial questions that confront Wall Street. His professional work on the crisis at Salomon Brothers was characteristic of his careful, balanced reporting. "Wall Street on a War Footing," 1-9, is a useful piece on how the markets prepared to handle volume surges brought on by war jitters. He is impeccably balanced in "What Constitutes an 'Exchange'?" 2-8, an expert handling of the complex legal debate over what makes up a securities exchange in the age of technology. In "Private Placement Off to a Slow Start," 3-14, he is clear-eyed on the much "ballyhooed" Rule 144a as it approaches its first anniversary, and finds those with initially high expectations are dissatisfied. Taking us to a high-tech battleground in "Wall Street's Cutbacks Sidestep Fat Budgets for High-Tech Trading," 4-7, he reveals that cash-strapped investment firms are forging ahead with "a virtual arms race for technology," and in the process revolutionizing competition. He tries to get a handle on KKR's new buying binge in "Kohlberg, Kravis Rouses Itself," 4-29: "The deals are vastly different from the firm's well-worn leveraged buyout formula...in the 90s, it is turning to 'build-ups,' in which it enlarges existing companies by acquiring assets." Assessing AT&T's takeover of NCR, he predicts less competition in the latest stage of the hostile-takeover era in "Blue-Chip Phase for Hostile Deals," 5-8, observing that the shortage of capital for small companies "has meant that only the best of the blue chips have access to the capital needed for a large buyout." He gives us the lowdown on Shearson's recent deals to restructure its finances in "Shearson Gives Itself a Face Lift," 6-5, speculating that this will keep them out of the equity markets, good news for shareholders. On the Salomon crisis, his "S.E.C. Widens Inquiry in Treasuries Scandal," 8-20, "New Troubles for Salomon: Suits Grow; Clients Defect," 8-22, and "Salomon Cuts Off Former Managers," 9-6, were typical of his judicious handling of this scandal: As a reporter he gathered the full spectrum of reactions, but as a writer and chronicler, he admirably avoided inserting his own value judgments.

Fabrikant, Geraldine. *The New York Times.* (★)
Media. Though anchored with well-researched facts and figures, Fabrikant's articles rarely rise above the ordinary as she focuses her sights on the movie industry. She doesn't paint as rosy a picture as the *NYT*'s Edwin McDowell does of the deal in which General Cinema Corporation

bought the beleaguered Harcourt Brace Jovanovich publishing house in "Harcourt Deal Raises Questions," 1-31. The piece is loaded with figures but lacks form. A scorecard is needed to tell the players in "A Tremor From Paramount as No. 2 Official Is Named," 3-19. We learn that Stanley Jaffe is going to be president and CEO at Paramount Communication Inc. but not much else in regard to the "tremor" of the title. One easily digestible article was "Big Stakes at Small Film Company," 4-2, in which she highlights James Robinson, president of Morgan Creek Productions, an independent film company. But we learn little about his movie industry niche, or how his and other small independents survive among the giants. Her "Murdoch Gets a Generous Price," 4-27, is a generally confusing article on K-III Holdings' buy up of some magazines. She contradicts herself saying that the advertising dollar is drying up yet "projections in the financial documents. . .assumes that advertising revenue will grow to $41 million, from $36 million in 1990." Another report on the film industry "M-G-M-Pathe Is Surprise: A Low Cut-Cost Hit," 6-3, provides some interesting reading as she examines the failing MGM-Pathe studios, but loses steam when she closes by merely listing pending movie releases. She is complete in "Forstmann Little and Whittle End Talks," 10-12, gathering plenty of speculation as to why talks between these two giants broke off.

Farhi, Paul. *The Washington Post.* (★ ★ ½)
Farhi is becoming an important player on the business pages of the *Post.* We're not sure why his beat remains marketing, advertising and media, as his most elucidating work has been on policymaking at the FCC. His enthusiasm shows through in "Interactive TV Moves a Step Closer With FCC Proposal," 1-11, a report on a proposed radio-based system that "would provide both broadcast and cable viewers an expanded range of services, such as on-screen TV guides, shop-at-home catalogues, access to automatic-teller accounts and the latest news from a wire service without requiring special cables or use of a telephone or personal computer." In "Shrinking the Food Dollar," 2-4, Farhi scrutinizes "downsizing," the dubious term used when the net weight of a product has been reduced while its price and outer package remain practically unchanged: "Downsizing isn't new nor is it illegal. But some consumer groups and government agencies see the practice as deceptive and on the increase." Rounding out a Time-Warner announcement with quotes and insights in "Advanced Fiber-Optic Cable TV Link Planned," 3-7, Farhi reports that the nation's second-largest cable-television company says "it will link thousands of its cable TV subscribers in the New York City area with a new fiber-optic transmission network that dramatically expands the amount — and nature — of the programming and services its cable systems carry." Farhi receives a 10 Best award in Business/Financial Reporting for "Waves of the Future," 5-5, the best profile we've seen of chairman Alfred C. Sikes, "a low-tech kind of guy" with a "high-tech vision of the future." In weighing Sikes chances to "remap much of the communications landscape," Farhi explores the chairman's relationship with Congress, well-funded lobbyists and fellow FCC members. He notes that skeptics defer to "an independent-minded group that stunned him recently by voting against his effort to repeal rules that keep ABC, CBS and NBC from selling programs on the TV rerun market." Outstanding work. Providing an anecdote of the tough times for news gathering organizations, Farhi compactly reports that United Press International has laid off dozens of employees and is in deep financial trouble in "UPI Lays Off 70 Workers as Cutbacks Take Effect," 9-18.

Feder, Barnaby J. *The New York Times.* (★ ★ ½)
New York. Defying our characterization of him last year, Feder brought color and enthusiasm to a wide range of business topics, and still managed to incorporate the plethora of facts he is so skilled at uncovering. His "Profits, and Problems, for Recycler," 1-8, is a stellar exploration of the business and economic considerations inherent in the plastic recycling industry. Feder unearths many uncommon points about the business as he smoothly sweeps us through this easy, readable piece. He describes the wonders and practical savings of "remote-diagnosis" in "Repairing Machinery From Afar," 1-30, a fascinating cost/benefit look at the process of solving a wide variety of customer problems from service centers hundreds of miles away. In "The

Insurer's Role in Waste Cleanup," 2-7, he sheds light on the legal bog of hazardous waste litigation as insurers and policyholders bicker over murky legal areas. Writing with the investor in mind in "McKesson: No. 1 but a Doze on Wall Street," 3-17, he dazzles with an insightful dissection of the strengths and weaknesses of this drug distribution company that processes up to 5,000 orders per hour. In another gem, "Failure Group Thrives on Disaster," 3-15, he colorfully profiles a Wall Street favorite, Failure Group Inc., "the nation's largest consulting firm devoted to analysis of accidents and disasters." He gives us a sense of how technological trends may affect future profits in "Defending a Superconducting Niche," 5-4, a decisive exploration of the value of Intermagnetics General Corporation, a leading independent supplier of products based on superconductivity. In "The Test Track Is King of the Road No More," 5-26, he tells why stationary testing equipment is saving automakers time and money. His outstanding Sunday business leader, "In the Clutches of the Superfund Mess," 6-16, is a superb examination of the broad and dubious reach of Superfund: "Long delays, regiments of lawyers, blizzards of documents, a widespread sense of being unfairly singled out to shoulder others' responsibilities — this is life in the clutches of. . .Superfund." Feder tells us that the mess has led critics to declare "that some form of Government-operated no-fault system, financed by industry, is needed instead." The nation's second-largest waste disposal company is showing disappointing results, and in "Browning-Ferris Unnerves Wall St." 9-5, Feder tells us the company's problems may be deeper than Wall Street thinks.

Ferguson, Tim W. *The Wall Street Journal.* (★ ½)

"Business World" columnist. Settling into his second year in this position, Ferguson had more hits than misses in his choice of topics. His execution, however, still gives the impression that he is scratching his head mid-column, disturbing the flow of information and leaving us flustered. "Good for the Walkers," *Barron's* 1-7, is a credible and enlightening opinion on the destructive nature of the 13-year-old Community Reinvestment Act. On the other hand, his "If Only Our Tomahawks Could Take Out Our Torpor," 1-22, is a monotone thumbsucker that wastes our time scratching its head over whether the U.S. economy is strong enough to withstand war with Iraq. As a big push for expanded unemployment payments hits Washington, he reflects on creative alternatives in "Jobless Relief Costs Curbed, but Incentives Still Need Work," 3-19, and throws out the idea of tax-deductible individual accounts. He is strong on California's political economy in "Bond Market Stays Sunny for California; Will Holders Get Burned?" 4-9, pondering if the state can keep its AAA credit rating in light of its budget crisis. In "Elite's Earnings Are Exposed and Taxed. . .and It's a Scandal?" 5-14, Ferguson serves up some interesting kernels of info on how the tax code contributed to the inequality of U.S. incomes throughout the '80s. But he wanders so much that he loses our attention mid-column. One of Ferguson's better offerings, "Casual-Wear Chief Opposes Hemming In China Trade," 5-28, is an enlightening talk with the chairman of Bugle Boy Industries, William Mow, a native of China who came to the U.S. in 1949. This is a valuable "dollars and cents" perspective from a U.S. businessman who understands international trade and the value of money to a Chinese laborer with little energy for the international human rights debates. A good start on the credit collapse of recent years and its drag on the economy drifts into murky prose in "U.S. Isn't Borrowing a Page From Its Last Recovery," 8-20: "The colorful critics of junk raised muck that the high-yield highbrows cannot afford to ignore."

Flanigan, James. *Los Angeles Times.* (★ ★)

Business columnist. Our criticism of Flanigan's work as too basic for sophisticated readers doesn't hold water this year. Although not as consistent as we'd like, he is struggling to assess more advanced topics this year. In "Signposts Will Mark Economy's Direction," 1-6, he offered rare level-headed perspective: "In a worrisome time for the world economy, wait for evidence and be wary of forecasts." His unique analysis of the shrinking trade deficit, "Exports Are Up, but We're 'Winning Ugly,' " 2-17, made us think twice about the positive press we'd read on the subject: "Even though a low dollar helps U.S. industry in world markets, you're poorer in many ways. Obviously, your dollar buys less in foreign goods. . .Traditionally, American workers had more to buy with their wages than workers in any other country. . .thanks to imports bought at the expense of the U.S. trade deficit." Just before the seizure of First Executive, Flanigan tells investors not to worry in "Storm in Insurance Industry Has Passed," 3-27. Although he recognizes the warning signs, he asserts that California will not let policyholders get hurt, and in the bigger picture he sees the trend as a free market purging in which "the flawed merchandise has been washed out of the markets." Flanigan lays out some convincing anecdotes about the changing U.S.-Japan relationship in "Confronting Japan in the Post-Postwar Era," 5-5: "It's a complex situation, not to be understood by criticizing Japan or praising it." But ignoring other possible tacks, Flanigan promotes "a policy to back U.S. technology," or an industrial policy, to bolster the U.S. economic position. Flanigan spent the summer on special assignment to cover the Middle East where he did an exceptional job of assessing the region's economic future in the aftermath of the Persian Gulf War. We appreciated: "Saudi Deals Pave Way for Oil Price Stability," 6-9; "Ghost of Syria Past Is Scariest Threat to Syria's Future," 6-23; "Change Could Turn Mideast Into an Economic Superstar," 6-30; "Israel's Economic Future Hinges on Top Resource: People," 7-7; and "Eventually, Iraq Will Be One Hot Business Prospect," 7-28. In "Hallmark's Line on Cable's Future," 9-25, he tells us that the fact that the long-term thinkers at Hallmark Card invested in Cencom Cable Associates "says a lot about prospects for cable and about the future of marketing personal products."

Flint, Jerry. *Forbes.* (★ ★)
Senior editor. While still clearly one of the most practiced chroniclers of the auto industry, Flint left us with unanswered questions at the finish of several of his reports. He is unquestionably knowledgeable, but we fear his expertise may cause him to skim over issues that need to be examined for readers unfamiliar with the territory. He is too general in "Somewhere East of Suez," 12-24-90, drawing us in with news that General Motors plans to build a market from scratch in the burgeoning Asian-Pacific car market which could rival Europe by the end of the century. But beyond the splattering of numbers on GM's current position in the global market, we get little on the company's plans to achieve its targeted market share in Asia. He is also somewhat ambiguous in "Diggin' In," 3-18, speculating on U.S. automakers' chances of holding their own against the Japanese. He emphasizes that the Japanese are "introducing models that compete more against each other and European sedans than against Detroit-made iron," but doesn't make clear what prompted the switch, guessing only that the falling dollar played a role. He is much better with "Roots," 4-29, a very sharp look at the impressive growth at the Buick division of GM. He attributes the shift to general manager Ed Mertz's understanding of the mature Buick consumer who prefers the "muscular grace" of an earlier era to chasing the latest fad. Flint is also careful to note how troubles at GM may come into play: "While Buick is gaining market share. . .(it) might be cannibalizing Oldsmobile rather than beating the outside competition." His in-depth "Will the (New) Maginot Line Hold?" 7-8, is a very instructive examination of how U.S. automakers are getting battle-ready in Europe where the Japanese "seem to be following. . .the same pattern they used in their successful invasion of the U.S." Flint's analysis is instructive and is supported by plenty of specifics on how various U.S. automakers plan to combat the Japanese on European turf. In " 'We Do What Mexicans Do,' " 9-2, he explains that U.S. automakers may be having trouble stateside, but they're quickly gaining profits in Mexico, where they are gaining market share and saving money on car production. "With its hardworking people and low wages, Mexico is becoming a key piece in Detroit's entire effort to become profitable again."

Forsyth, Randall W. *Barron's.* (★ ★ ★)
His "Current Yield" column appears in *Barron's* "Capital Markets" section which is billed as "A compendium of timely news, analysis and opinion." With intelligence and extensive research, Forsyth fills the bill and then some. He packs in juicy fiscal and monetary tidbits that policy junkies thrive on in "Bonds Ease as Reality Sinks In," 1-28: "[S]ince reserve requirements were reduced, the [FOMC] has been having trouble estimating banks' demands for excess reserves."

His "Peace Is at Hand," 2-18, is a tidy and perceptive wrap up of the markets' precise response to Saddam Hussein's suspect proposal to withdraw from Kuwait. He shows his acumen in "Fed Eases — but How Much?" 4-15, discerning that despite news of a Fed easing, "it was arguable that the old target remained in place." With a useful mix of expert opinions and pertinent statistics in "Columbia Gas Pains; Feeling Her OATS," 6-24, Forsyth talks of the role Greenspan and Congress, Columbia Gas and bankruptcy, and the persistent recession, all played in pushing bond prices lower. He offered the most exceptional insights we'd seen on the Fed's troubles with M2 targets in "Global Rate Tug-of-War," 7-29. Deferring to the Bank Credit Analyst's Interest Rate Forecast which points out that " 'The Fed has noted that the large spread between savings rates and borrowing cost makes it attractive for consumers to finance their expenditures by running down M2 balances rather than taking out new loans.'. . .But the drop in the interest rates hasn't pushed down M2's velocity, which is the rate of turnover of the money stock, the Interest Rate Forecast further observes. 'The impact of banking consolidation on financial flows is largely responsible for the decline in velocity, and that suggests that velocity may have suffered a permanent upward shift and could move higher. Therefore, the Fed should be tolerant of money growth in the lower part of its target range as long as disintermediation from the banking system continues.' " Two key points define his pithy column, "Deficit's Too Small For Salomon," 8-12: First, with the deficit growing by leaps and bounds, he ponders pertinently — can the Treasury afford to go it alone without Salomon Brothers which admitted to overbidding at a number of auctions? Second, he observes the twentieth anniversary of the year Nixon took the U.S. off the gold standard by highlighting today's soaring deficit.

Freedman, Alix M. *The Wall Street Journal.* (★ ★ ★)
Food and beverage. Expanding the realm of beat coverage, Freedman not only voyages through the daily ins and outs of this multi-million dollar industry with ease, but she skillfully delves into its murky impact on society. Her outstanding three-part series on food habits in the inner city, which included "Amid Ghetto Hunger, Many More Suffer Eating Wrong Food," leder 12-18-90, "Fast-Food Chains Play Central Role in Diet of the Inner-City Poor," leder 12-19-90, and "An Inner-City Shopper Seeking Healthy Food Finds Offerings Scant," leder 12-20-90, was a sensitive handling of a delicate subject. With tact, plenty of facts and frank but compassionate observations, Freedman wove an intricate narrative of destructive eating habits brought on by life in the inner city. Her inquisitive "Campbell Chief Cooks Up Winning Menu," 2-15, surveys how Campbell is faring under new CEO, David W. Johnson: "Wall Street is convinced that the perennial laggard is poised to be the food industry's next highflier." But Freedman isn't starry-eyed and throws out plenty of tough questions. In "New Smoke Signals at Philip Morris?" 3-26, she puts her finger squarely on the tobacco maker's quandary: "Now also the nation's largest food company, should Philip Morris throw its weight behind a business that grows faster and boasts a more wholesome reputation, but which isn't nearly as profitable?" She was late with "Rumor Turns Fantasy Into Bad Dream," 5-10, the tale of an affordable and popular NYC soft drink whose sales were decimated after a smear campaign claimed it would sterilize black men. She offers plausible speculation as to who might be behind this malicious plot. Her outstanding marketing analysis, "Winston Hopes 'Fresh' Pack Will End Years of Stale Marketing, Prop Up Sales," 6-25, reads like a case study. Winston hopes its new "FlavorSeal" will win marketshare, but skeptical sources say, "This is a brand-maintenance idea, but it isn't a brand-building idea." We found more insights in "Potent, New Heileman Malt Is Brewing Fierce Industry and Social Criticism," 6-17, a quick, easy piece on the pitfalls of marketing a high-alcohol malt liquor to minorities. Her follow-up "Malt Advertising that Touts Firepower Comes Under Attack by U.S. Officials," 7-1, is equally intelligent. In "Western Union Plans Network to Cash Checks," 8-23, we're offered a perceptive inquiry into Western Union's move into the check-cashing business which will put it in direct competition with present check cashers that also serve as Western Union money-wiring agents.

Freudenheim, Milt. *The New York Times.* (★ ★)
"Business and Health" columnist. Showing noticeable improvement, this competent journalist is writing fresher, more analytical material. His "Accountability In Health Care," 2-19, is an adequate overview of new tests to measure the effectiveness of the health care system. But we didn't understand why he neglected a thorough look at the test itself, though he found space to list the test participants. He is much more thorough in "Removing the Warehouse from Cost-Conscious Hospitals," 3-3, an enthusiastic profile of medical supplier Baxter International's "stockless inventory" system which Freudenheim expertly explains from top to bottom. His important and early discussion of emerging health care legislation, "Reshaping Laws on Insurance," 3-5, is a bit arduous, but still gives a useful sense of the proposals being deliberated. A dry execution obscures an important topic in "Effect of Decision by Supreme Court," 4-30, a discussion of a recent Supreme Court ruling upholding regulations that may make it easier for unions to organize hospital workers. His "Drug Makers Face Pressure to Restrain Price Increases," 5-7, is balanced on the debate over federal laws that require drug producers to discount prescription drugs to Medicaid. Frank and practical in "Medicaid Payment Ordered for Drug for Schizophrenia," 5-25, he pens a clear-eyed cost assessment of state Medicaid programs' new financial responsibility for clozapine, "an expensive drug that could help tens of thousands of psychotic patients." He keeps it short and sweet in "Computers Say: Take 2 Aspirins," 6-25, a straightforward account of a pilot computer health care program that diagnoses patients based on at-home questionnaires. In "F.D.A. Gets Tough on Drugs Offered for Unapproved Uses," 6-29, he judiciously handles the sticky debate over the promotion of treatments that lack FDA approval. He notes concern over unanticipated side effects, but also considers that "doctors and drug makers say they are keeping patients alive with treatments that the F.D.A. might take years to approve." In a special report, "Health on a Budget: One City Embraces H.M.O.s, Offering a View of the Future," 9-2, he scouts the horizon for future options in healthcare, and finds the use of HMOs in Minneapolis a window to the future.

Freudmann, Aviva. *The Journal of Commerce.* (★ ★ ½)
An ace on the ever-shifting regulatory environment to which the insurance industry must adjust, Freudmann spearheads some of the best work on this oft-neglected reporting niche. Her "Industry Group Plans to Offer Compromise Antitrust Proposal," 2-26, is a proficient synopsis of efforts to pacify consumer groups bent on repealing the McCarran-Ferguson Act which protects the industry from collusion allegations. In "Insurers Clash Over Antitrust Stand," 3-18, she discerningly assesses tensions ensuing from an industry position paper which asserted "life insurers do not need most of the existing antitrust exemptions they have under the McCarran-Ferguson Act." She clarifies the gist of a draft proposal in "Dingell's Trial Balloon Points to Federal Regulatory Role," 3-25, contending that John Dingell (D-Mich.) "has in mind a substantial federal role in regulating insurers' financial practices." In "Is Government Regulation Necessary?" 3-26, she fully examines the debate over "proposed federal roles in setting and enforcing nationwide solvency standards." Showcasing her acumen in "Life Insurers Group Does About-Face, Opposes Changes in Antitrust Immunity," 5-31, she crisply explains The American Council of Life Insurance's decision to oppose the Brooks bill by fending off changes in the antitrust exemption rather than advancing alternative legislation. As the bank reform bill emerges from subcommittee, she tallies the score in "Insurers Emerge Relatively Unscathed in First Round on Banking Reform Bill," 6-11, a lucid breakdown of insurance-related issues: "The subcommittee removed federal deposit insurance coverage for individual participants in certain pension plans that invest in bank insurance contracts, or BICs. The vote was a clear win for insurance companies that sell a competing financial instrument..." Her "Investors Demand Reforms at Lloyd's," 6-24, is complete on the ire of individual investors hit hard by Lloyd's recent losses. Still doggedly tracking the bank bill, she pens a richly-detailed, "Insurers, Agents Unhappy With Banking Bill," 7-1: "Bullets that life insurers and agents had dodged in...subcommittee in early June found their mark last week when the full committee acted." Her "Banks Lose Momentum on Insurance Powers," 8-6, is a useful analysis that captures the confusing path that's being carved for bank reform because of substantial differences between the two House committees working on the bill.

Fuerbringer, Jonathan. *The New York Times.* (★ ½)
New York, currency markets. Although he usually takes on timely, attention-grabbing topics, his rigid neo-Keynesian follow-through is often too fragmentary and orthodox. He rarely illuminates the ebb-and-flow political and economic forces contouring the currency markets. Overtly in the Bush camp on worldwide interest rates in "The Bundesbank as Bogyman," 2-3, Fuerbringer criticizes the German central bank's move to push up its key short-term rates just as the U.S. is lowering rates and calling for reduced international rates. He devotes virtually no space to evaluating the suitability or impact of this U.S. pressure. His "What Is Driving Rallies in Europe?" 3-11, is a cursory overview of global stock market rallies. Fuerbringer cites numerous technical factors and throws in some generic analysis such as: "One reason for the rally seems quite clear: There are institutions and investors with cash who initially missed the upturn in stocks and now want in." He is better in "The Dollar and Overseas Stocks," 4-14, constructing a useful examination of how the dollar's rally may affect overseas stocks. He gives several plausible reasons to expect an unexpected reaction from overseas stocks. Also good in "Divining Europe's Muddled Signs," 5-19, Fuerbringer blends Poehl's announcement that he will resign from the Bundesbank with recent economic news. It's a competent assessment of Europe's attempts to shape compatible monetary policies that take into account such European variations as Germany's high interest rates, anti-inflation stance and weak currency, and Spain's strong currency and rising inflation. He piqued our attention and held our interest in "Why Swiss Bank Shunned Gold," 6-2: "Swiss Bank portfolios are based on the dollar, and the bank wants to avoid the risk of a rising dollar, which can eat sharply into capital gains when the dollars are invested in non-United States markets, as was the case in the first quarter of the year." His "A Profitable Niche in Today's Grim World of Banking," 8-4, is a humdrum report on the profitability of foreign-exchange operations at banks that fails to ask why Union Bank of Switzerland jumped to No. 5 from No. 17 in customer preference. "Soviet Gold News Has Little Impact," 10-29, is a very mediocre assessment of why Soviet economist Yavlinsky's shockingly low estimate of the Soviet gold supplies didn't send the price of gold through the ceiling. Fuerbringer overlooks the fact that many gold watchers questioned Yavlinsky's estimates, and fails to recognize gold's role as a monetary indicator that is moved more often by currency rates than the relatively stable supply of gold.

Gleckman, Howard. *Business Week.* (★ ½)
Washington. With a solid network of contacts in government policymaking circles, Gleckman fills his well-sourced reports with sturdy facts. Beyond the particulars, however, this year he did not deliver any of the provocative angles we've seen from him in the past. In his commentary, "Surprise! A Few Budget Ideas Worth Fighting For," 2-18, Gleckman reprimands the administration for its lackadaisical approach to domestic economic policymaking. Although his take-from-the-rich-give-to-the-poor framework has its limitations, his call for a "serious airing" of numerous proposals is valid. His logic in "The Pay-As-You-Go Budget: Dead at Five Months?" commentary 3-25, reminds us of a shaky scientific theory which forwards a causal linkage before weighing the variables. Gleckman blames a growing budget deficit on the loopholes in Darman's pay-as-you-go budget rule, but never considers the possibility that heavy taxes, a recession, and a fiscal policy void could be contributing to the government's deficit woes by wiping out tax revenues. His "Playing Pin the Tax Policy on the Donkey," 5-20, is informative but not novel on the array of economic proposals being kicked around by the Democratic party as it tries to formulate a coherent policy: "The confusion isn't entirely bad. The good news is that Democrats are snapping out of their fiscal-policy funk and trying to develop a tax plank for the 1992 campaign. The bad news is that their initial forays have GOP strategists looking forward to a new assault on those 'tax-and-spend' Democrats. It's enough to do a President's heart good." The topic of Gleckman's "Washington's Misleading Maps of the Economy," with John Carey 6-3, was discussed elsewhere but not as broadly. He warns that the disturbing inaccuracy of government statistics, "takes its toll" on policy decisions. He not only points out how underfunded government statistics agencies are, but makes clear that the calculation of statistics must be redesigned to keep up with a technological and ever-changing global economy. His very enlightening but tardy commentary, "How the Budget Deal Has Choked Off America's Choices," 9-16, reveals just how constrictive the 1990 budget deal is to the economy.

Greenwald, John. *Time.* (★)

Senior writer. If you're in a hurry and need the facts straight up, Greenwald's not bad, but if you're looking for cogent economic evaluations, he is usually well behind the curve. In "Fallen Emperors of the Air," 1-7, he tells us the woeful stories of TWA and Pan Am, but instead of analyzing what went wrong, he waxes nostalgic over their illustrious histories. His "Rebuilding a Ravaged Nation," 3-11, is a sketchy outline of what must be done to restore Kuwait and who will be helping out with the task of rebuilding. The sidebar notes that the Japanese are absent from the bidding, as they were from the coalition. Although much of his "Did Saddam Skim Billions?" 4-8, was based on a "60 Minutes" report, Greenwald delivers a good, clear recap of Saddam's finagling. In "Whose Company Is This?" 5-6, Greenwald tries to assert that shareholders are playing a more active role in running companies, using ITT as an example. But we wanted more examples to be persuaded that this was the widespread phenomenon he believes it to be. He serves up "economese" in "Crawling Out of the Slump," 6-17, a typical two-handed economic summary of the anemic recovery. His lightweight assessment of the banking sector's mergers and acquisition binge, "The Large Economy Size," 7-15, tells us almost nothing about this consolidation's impact on the economy or what Congress can do to facilitate lending so the economy doesn't stagnate as mergers are occurring. Relying heavily on the observations of Robert Reich in "Permanent Pink Slips," 9-9, Greenwald pens a dubious evaluation of the nation's unemployment woes. Very conventional in "A Slump That Won't Go Away," 10-14, he falls back on a little '80s bashing in this two dimensional assessment of the economy.

Grover, Ronald. *BusinessWeek.* (★ ★)

Los Angeles bureau manager. As he did last year, Grover excelled at sketching vivid portraits of Hollywood media and entertainment crowd. But his economic and business pieces, although better than in the past, still seemed strained, as though he wished he were doing something different. In "People: Stanley Gold Is Still Giving Chase," 2-25, Grover piques our curiosity with his compact profile of dealmaker Stanley Gold who hasn't been able to pull off a deal in months: ". . .Gold, 49, and his team of three dealmakers are on the prowl again. They have spent the past few months sifting through mountains of documents and have narrowed their takeover search, they say, to three candidates. . .An announcement could come in March, Gold hints." His "Can Guber and Peters Live Up to Their Hype — and Their Spending?" 3-25, is a tasty tidbit on two freespending movie producers. Like a snack, it is neither terribly filling nor substantial, yet does provide a small bit of flavor on these two enigmatic figures in the business. Grover serves up a delicious slice of Hollywood in "MGM Is Becoming a Little Shop of Financial Horrors," 4-15, recounting how small-time moviemaker Roger Corman filed a petition in an L.A. federal bankruptcy court to put movie giant MGM-Pathe into bankruptcy. His "NBC Is No Longer a Feather in GE's Cap," 6-3, is a well-rounded review of NBC's recent shaky performance and the current and possible options of its parent company, General Electric. The engrossing article "Not All of Robin Hood's Derring-Do Will Be on the Screen," 6-10, tells the tale of Morgan Creek Productions, founded only three years ago, which made the big-budget blockbuster *Robin Hood* possible. Good insights into movie cost and profit factors. The plethora of figures in "High Noon at Tucson Electric," 8-5, encourage little interest in this story of mismanaged diversification at the faltering Tucson Electric. This is dry reporting that only a Tucson Electric shareholder could appreciate.

Gubernick, Lisa. *Forbes.* (★ ★)

Senior Editor. Although she tends to get a little chit-chatty, Gubernick's interesting blend of razzle-dazzle Hollywood hype and business acumen nicely augment *Forbes'* commitment to covering the entertainment field as a major U.S. industry. Her "Jane Fonda's Bank," 3-4, is an entertaining and cautionary tale of two investment managers involved with celebrities and Hollywood's top talent agency, Creative Artists. Artists, such as Jane Fonda, worry their financial dealings will be leaked back to their agency prompting this moral from Gubernick: "Show biz and the banking biz just might not mix well." In "Making History Pay," 5-13, Gubernick accurately and ominously assesses why bank companies hire Bruce Weindruch's

History Factory to do archival and historical searches: the end of a century prompts companies as well as individuals to take stock in their history as a way of easing the transition into a new millennium. The title of her "Jack Kennedy Slept Here," 4-29, is an instant indication of the lightweight content of this piece on Santa Barbara, California. Gubernick's shopping-list style of writing here merely recounts expensive restaurants and hotels in this seemingly ritzy and superficial town. In "Italian Soap Opera," 7-22, she gives us just that, a soap opera, involving a feud that pits Contessa Agusta and her ex-husband Count Corrado Agusta against each other for a billion dollar estate. Gubernick throws in lots of figures so it seems more at home in *Forbes,* but a soap is still a soap. Amusement park investors will surely be cheered by her " 'Terror with a Smile,' " 9-2, a concise and informative look at the profitability of Sandusky, Ohio's Cedar Fair amusement park, which is much smaller than Disney, but dollar for dollar is much more profitable.

Gupta, Udayan. *The Wall Street Journal.* (★ ★ ★)
Venture capital and small business. Gupta's "Enterprise" reports are always worth checking out for the fresh information and new angles this dedicated pro uncovers. He is clearly one of the keenest evaluators of the entrepreneurial sector. We sunk our teeth into his "States Take Different Paths to Spur Small Businesses," 1-9, a discerning look at the growing commitment to small business development in Colorado and Iowa. His contribution to *WSJ*'s five-part "New Alliances" series, "How Big Companies Are Joining Forces With Little Ones for Mutual Advantages," 2-25, is a top-notch exploration of the why's and how's of this promising entrepreneurial trend. His other contribution to the series, "Sony Adopts Strategy to Broaden Ties With Small Firms," 2-28, is also outstanding, divulging that Sony and others are quietly forging unique and successful cooperative ventures with small high-technology companies: "Unlike IBM and other big high-tech companies, Sony doesn't want an equity stake in a collaborator," but using small companies "to sell its rewritable optical-disk drive — in combination with its own sales to Hewlett-Packard Co. - -Sony commands approximately a 58% share of the burgeoning optical-drive business. . ." It's unusual, but Gupta misses the boat in "Kevin Kinsella Seeks to Raise $50 Million Capital Pool," 5-20, a profile of venture capitalist Kinsella who is combing for money to invest in entrepreneurial companies without much luck. Gupta wonders why Kinsella is having trouble because the result of investing in a company early can bring "spectacular" capital gains. Had Gupta explored the high taxation of capital gains, he might have been able to put his finger on the problems. In "Small Firms Turn to Composite Bonds," 5-23, he clues us into yet another important financing trend — the use of composite industrial bonds to "raise money for groups of companies that are too small to go it alone." His perceptive "New Fund to Increase Capital for Minority Ventures," 6-3, takes an in-depth look at efforts to reverse the decline of private capital for minority venture funds. "Looking South," 9-20, is a semi-useful skim of investment prospects in South America, but it could have delved deeper.

Haas, Lawrence J. *National Journal.* (★ ★)
Budget and taxes. Better on the politics of policymaking this year, Haas penned constructive assessments of government strategies on various political and economic issues. Unfortunately, he rarely embraces the spectrum of an issue, leaving us searching for more details elsewhere. Introducing some startling statistics in "Stalled Rescues," 1-19, Haas effectively argues for the expansion of federal programs for the poor. He asserts that even though many high-profile programs enjoy broad bipartisan support, they reach fewer than half of those eligible, but he could have been more creative on funding possibilities for such programs. He illustrates the bog of Washington's bureaucracy in "Programs that Never Say Die," 3-2, explaining why old or failing programs rarely get cut. He lists three programs which have been nominated to go, but could have expanded the list to give us an idea of just how pervasive this problem might be. He tells us there's more talk about capgains among Democrats than Republicans in Washington these days in his perceptive "Capital Gains Heresy," 3-20, an adept explanation of the Democratic camp's motivation for mulling the idea over: "a cut that's targeted at gains on

investments in new (small) businesses might look less like a tax giveaway." His "Panetta's '92 Budget," 4-13, is a rather muddled assessment of House Budget Committee chairman Leon Panetta's budget resolution which demonstrates the restraints of modern budget-making. After declaring that Panetta's cost-cutting plan is similar to Bush's, Haas goes on to stress their significant differences. In "More Bang for the $," 4-20, he provides a satisfactory assessment of why proposals to set performance standards for government programs are gaining momentum. But he fails to fully develop a key issue — whether the federal government is too big to measure itself systematically. He tells us public officials around the nation are watching to see how the largest state resolves its fiscal problems in "Spreading the Pain," 6-22, but his execution of this theme is unfocused. And in "Creative Financing," 7-20, we learn how states have found new ways to finance their share of the fed-state medicaid program, which in turn draws more money from Washington. Strong on the economic problems confounding the men in D.C. in "Deficit Doldrums," 9-7, he perceptively points to last year's budget deal as the crux of the problem. In "Fear of Filing," 10-5, he is overlong and arcane on the overlong and arcane forms poor working people must fill out to receive the earned-income tax credit.

Hamilton, Martha A. *The Washington Post.* (★ ½)
Transportation. Hamilton capably serves up the facts, but in this time of upheaval in the airline industry we need someone to put the scramble of ever-changing data into context. Since she doesn't consistently do this, we usually turn to others first. Her "Pan Am Files for Bankruptcy," 1-9, illustrates both her proficiency at fact-gathering and her failure to look beyond the day's events to tell us the broader meaning of this event. She is better in "New Continental Chief Navigates to New Image," 1-15, informing us of the different styles of Continental's previous CEO, Frank Lorenzo, and new CEO Hollis Harris: ". . .if Lorenzo may be remembered as an empire builder, than Harris's contribution may well be as a morale builder." But, she is light on the profit numbers that will be a critical measure of Harris's success as Continental tries to emerge from bankruptcy. The best we saw from Hamilton this year was "U.S., Canada Seek to Forge 'Open Skies' Pact," 3-8, a well-rounded exploration of the future links between U.S. and Canadian air: "In the background of the U.S.-Canadian talks are the changes anticipated in the European Community next year that are expected to begin consolidating what has been several markets into one large market whose carriers also will compete in the United States and the Pacific. The changing airline industry landscape in Western Europe may make it harder for U.S. carriers to compete there." Trying her hand at environmental issues with "Forest's Fate Splits Environmentalists," 5-15, she gives a balanced presentation of the brouhaha between oil companies forging ahead with oil development in the Amazon basin in eastern Ecuador and environmental groups trying to stop them. In "Turning Cans Into Cold Cash," 7-2, she gives us an intriguing story on "reverse vending machines" that "instead of dispensing junk. . .take it back," accepting aluminum cans, glass or plastic in exchange for supermarket coupons or cash vouchers. Hamilton gives us plenty of details on the product, the "cadillac" of which is manufactured by Environmental Products Corp., and on the pros and cons of using the machines. She is detailed on the historic retooling taking place in dozens of industries to accommodate an international agreement to phase out the production of ozone-depleting CFCs in "The Costly Race to Replace CFCs," 9-29.

Harris, Kathryn. *Forbes.* (★ ½)
West Coast, entertainment industry. We weren't as impressed with Harris this year, as she too often gives us snapshots, when we'd prefer richer, more detailed portraits of this multi-million dollar industry. In "Mind Over Rock Videos," 1-21, Harris opens her shutter on the Cable Discovery Channel and its success in the era of vapid TV programming. But the report is neither an in-depth study on the reason for success of Chairman John Hendricks nor a straight entrepreneurial angle — a little of both blurs its purpose. She fares much better in "Mr. Lonelyhearts," 2-4, a quick, sharp sketch of Paramount Communication Inc. and its chairman, Martin Davis who's not yet willing to be bought out by Japanese interests like other major entertainment companies. Harris draws on insightful information and we come away with a

larger picture of this side of the industry. She is abrupt in "Feeding Frenzy," 4-1, a gruff piece on Hollywood talent agents whose deals make the Mafia look like a charity organization. The article gave us a feel for their practices and a few examples, but this was little more than a skeleton investigation. Her "Making Money on Rotten Ratings," 5-27, is not so much about the lilliputian Fox Television network, as it is on the leviathan nature of the three major networks. But the article is too short to give us a true grasp of why fourth-placed Fox is making money while third-place CBS is losing it hand over fist. Also wanting was her "Seduced by Charlottesville," 7-8, which reads like a visitor's brochure to this Virginia town, rather than a report on it. On the other hand, her profile of Rupert Murdoch's debt-laden News Corp., " 'A Big Dose of Realism,' " 9-2, is very thorough: "Rupert Murdoch. . .is doing what doesn't come naturally to him. From being an eager buyer of media in properties in a seller's market, his News Corp. has been forced to become a seller in a buyer's market."

Hayes, Thomas C. *The New York Times.* (★ ★)
Dallas. Although Hayes handles many topics efficiently, he handles none expertly. He is usually complete and balanced, but typically shies from the complexities of an issue. His "Thoughts After Layoffs: Making Do and Moving," 1-9, is a well-rounded report on the aftermath of defense industry layoffs in Texas following the Pentagon's cancellation of the A-12 attack aircraft. Hayes neatly ties in personal quotes and perspectives on how the Fort Worth-Dallas area will deal with the 3,000+ newly unemployed. But on a more intricate subject, "A Lean, High-Tech Industry Poised for Postwar Growth," 2-10, Hayes delivers an unsophisticated analysis of the prospects for future growth in the oil industry. He is much more insightful in "Lockheed Fends Off Simmons," 3-19, explaining that Harold C. Simmons' failure to win three seats on Lockheed's board "demonstrated how big companies have gained a stronger hand in turning back corporate raiders." His "Global Oil Giants Expected to Surge," 4-19, is a cursory examination of the future of oil stocks. Hayes doesn't provide the unique or valuable investment insights readers of the "Market Place" column are looking for. Despite his conspicuous pro-natural gas bias in "Bottom-Fishing in the Gas Patch," 5-19, Hayes produces a great Sunday business lead on a dynamic company trying to initiate change in this lackluster industry. In addition to giving us a strong sense of Enron Corp.'s unique vision, he effectively weaves in the promise and perils of the entire natural gas industry. The secrets behind Wal-Mart's success is a hackneyed subject, but even so Hayes manages to flesh out fresh information on the company's amazing supplier network in "Behind Wal-Mart's Surge, a Web of Suppliers," 7-1. In "Zeroing In on Oil Far Below the Sea," 8-7, he is there with all the exciting details on seismic analysis, the latest technology in the search for oil.

Henriques, Diana B. *The New York Times.* (★ ★ ½)
"Business Day." Wowing us with an impressive year of consistently enterprising topics and crisp perspectives, Henriques jumps a full star in this year's *MediaGuide.* Her well-researched "Fidelity's Secret Agent Man," 1-27, looks at Kelso Management Company, a little-known side of Fidelity's sprawling financial empire, "one that plays hardball under the firm hand of Kelso's intense and aggressive president, Dorsey R. Gardner." A charming lead draws us into "A Money Manager's Soap Opera," 2-17, a stylish piece on how corporate pension funds are attracted to money managers who promise to outperform the market. Clear and instructive on the promise and perils of biotechnology stocks in "Disguising the Risks of Research," 2-3, she also keeps the investor in mind in "Tracking Environmental Risk," 4-28, a cutting-edge exploration of the dawning field of environmental record-keeping and databases. Henriques' "Students in a Class on Investments Say the Lessons Meant Big Losses," 5-26, tackles the complexities of an important case in Florida in which students are filing suit against their broker for using the classroom to peddle his high-risk investments. She is uncharacteristically sophomoric in her review of the confusion jolting the markets in "For This Quiz, The Answer Is More Confusion," 6-16. Back in form for "Ignore Foreign Stocks at Your Own Peril," 7-7, she offers a smart, fresh perspective on where to look overseas for high rates of return and low levels of risk: "it may actually be riskier to stay at home." She receives a 10 Best nomination for "Piercing Wall Street's

'Lucite Ceiling,' " 8-11, a powerful and revealing profile of M.R. Beal & Company, one of the fastest-growing minority-owned investment banking firms on Wall Street. Eschewing conventional handouts Beal notes that blacks have "had social and political advantages. . .Now we need the economic advantage." Her "Ambitions for Soviet Deals Are Suddenly Placed on Ice," 8-20, is a brisk mid-coup overview of the wait and see approach among private investors in the Soviet Union.

Herman, Tom. *The Wall Street Journal.* (★ ★)
"Your Money Matters" columnist. His topics more inventive, his advice more instructive and his sources more diverse, Herman's work underwent a renaissance of sorts this year. In "Money Supply Regains Status as Indicator," 2-4, he thoroughly examines an important shift at the Federal Reserve where the money-supply figures are being revived as an important economic barometer. He gives us a solid sense of the history of this indicator which had lost import for many years. We questioned his objectivity in "Not All Discount Brokers Offer the Same Bargains," 3-6, a muddled comparison of discounters to full-priced brokers that winds up with Merrill Lynch and Shearson Lehman patiently explaining that discount brokers don't provide the valuable research that the big houses offer. Hmmm. Herman serves up just what the title promises in "A Primer for Fund Investors at Tax Time," 3-15. The opening line says it all: "For mutual fund investors, tax time can be a nightmare." Herman eases their confusion with straight talk and plenty of facts. He is on target with "Still-Weak Economy Leads Many to Predict Lower Interest Rates," 4-29, a clear assessment of inflation expectations and bond yields. However, some consideration of the impact further easing might have on yields would have been fitting since the Fed did ease the next day. Focusing on financial fundamentals in "These Bonds Offer Safe Route in the Municipal Market," 6-3, Herman instructively examines the particulars of "pre-funded" municipal bonds. He is thought-provoking in "Bonds Lure Optimists On Inflation," 6-17, gathering sophisticated observations from the contrarians who advise clients to put their money in bonds despite Wall Street's fear that economic growth equals inflation: "Good news for the economy doesn't have to be bad news for inflation or bonds, the bond bulls say. Money-supply growth has remained moderate, which many analysts say indicates lower inflation. And the price of gold, often viewed as a barometer of inflation pressures, has traded in a narrow range for many months." Echoing the old buy on the cannons theme in his "Despite Treasury's Scandal, the McFaddens Say Now Is the Time to Buy Discount Corp.," 8-28, he gathers contrarian opinions that say despite investigations into possible collusion in the government bond market, it's time to buy stock in Discount Corp, a "primary dealer." But his supporting evidence isn't very convincing.

Hershey, Robert D., Jr. *The New York Times.* (★ ★)
The Times' "indicator" man, Hershey is charged with assessing each and every statistical blip out of Washington. It's a thankless job, but Hershey seems to go along with the *Times'* indicator fixation. We'd like to see him step back more often and question the value of this exercise, as he did in his impressive "How Accurately Does the Government Measure the Pinch of Inflation?" 4-7, which examines the accuracy of the closely watched Consumer Price Index: "One of the biggest criticisms of the consumer index comes from Albert Sindlinger, the veteran researcher. . .By his calculations, an appropriately constructed index would show that, primarily because of taxes, consumer prices over the last year climbed more than twice as fast as the 5.3 percent posted by the Government's rate." Number crunching in "New Data Suggests Nation's Recession Could Be Slowing," 2-16, he sketches a vague and useless overview of new industrial output figures. His "Economy Index Up, Spurring Optimism on Recession's End," 3-30, is also a dull compilation of generic observations that gives us virtually no sense of the broader forces steering the economy. He gets all the facts right in "Bank Loans Still Tight but Less So," 5-17, but offers scant analysis of the deeper message behind Federal Reserve Chairman Greenspan's important testimony. We were all ears for Hershey's engaging economic ponderings in "Advice to Patriots: Save, Don't Spend," 5-22, but although he throws out numerous worthwhile issues, he doesn't develop any of them thoroughly. He weaves interesting historical insights into

"Economic Index Posts 3d Advance in a Sign Recession May End Soon," 6-1, an upbeat report on the upward movement of the composite index of leading indicators. But despite the rich detail, this is still a micro-reading of the economy that has very limited use for sophisticated readers, and may mislead average readers. He is decidedly more pessimistic in "Reading Revisited: Recovery Sags," 9-19, offering yet another anecdote of the recession, Reading, Pa. which exemplifies the staying power of this economic downturn.

Horovitz, Bruce. *Los Angeles Times.* (★ ★)
Marketing. Horovitz's skills sharpened considerably this year as he took on numerous marketing and advertising debacles with vigor and insight, giving the *Times* bite in its marketing coverage. Though the direction of the subject matter in "Some Companies Find They Get More Mileage When Ads Are Rejected," 2-5, is a bit obvious, this short, decisively-written report zeroes in on hard facts, explores ethical questions, and queries a varied supply of sources, resulting in an sharp, informative article. In "The Pratfalls in Promotions," 4-28, he pens a long but entertaining piece on advertising and promotional gimmick wars, giving Horovitz an opportunity to display his estimable knowledge in the field. His interesting trend piece, "L.A. Agencies Are in Need of a New Image," 5-19, on the L.A. advertising market and its fall from prominence, is kept lively throughout, making it enjoyable even for those who don't regularly follow the ad agency business. Two articles on 6-25, "Cigarette Ad Ploys Spark More Protest," and "Brewer Faces Boycott Over Marketing of Potent Malt Liquor," are short enlightening examinations of powerful companies seemingly overstepping their legal advertising bounds. The former examines the Philip Morris and R.J. Reynolds tobacco companies' attempt to skirt the law with misleading advertisements. Horovitz covers most of the bases in this report, save for any opinion from the Federal Trade Commission. The latter piece puts Horovitz on the ground level of what could be a long fight between G. Heileman Brewing Co., who targeted its high-alcohol malt liquor to minorities and government agencies and consumer groups. He covers the numerous aspects of the topic well and launches a worthwhile discussion of other infringements on government advertising restrictions. In "Volvo Makes Smash Return," 9-20, we learn that Volvo is returning to network advertising after having been fined $150,000 by the FTC for a misleading TV spot. Horovitz tells us the company is going to extraordinary lengths to make certain that everything is on the up-and-up this time around, ". . .with consumers increasingly skeptical about the believability of most advertising, such point-by-point documentation may soon become the rule rather than the exception."

Ingersoll, Bruce. *The Wall Street Journal.* (★ ★ ★)
Washington, agriculture and food issues. Doggedly keeping watch over the government's distribution of subsidies, Ingersoll received two awards from the 1991 Aviation/Space Writers Association writing awards program. The quality of his work this year is once again award winning. Foregoing his regular beat to cover war-related issues early in the year, his "Patriot Missile's Success Against Iraq's Scuds Knocks Star Wars Prospects Into Higher Orbit," 1-29, is an informative piece on the positive prospects for SDI after the war in the Gulf. Ingersoll gives us a balanced view for the internal debate and a solid sense of the growing number of Beltway types who have been won over by the success of smart weapons in the war. However, we'd have appreciated a list of companies whose fortunes are most tied to SDI's future. He is riveting in "Payments by U.S. Exporters to Iraq Are Probed as Lawmakers Unravel a Tangled Business Link," 2-15, in which he divulges how U.S. exporters may have indirectly financed Iraq's defense build-up by giving into Iraq's demand for payoffs or payment of Iraqi business debts. His "FDA Finds Bunk in Bottled-Water Claims," 4-10, is a revealing report that turns the spotlight on misleading bottled water claims: "Artesia Waters, for example, doesn't mention that its water, a favorite at the Bush White House, is heavily processed and comes from the same underground source that San Antonio taps for its municipal water supply. And 31% of the brands surveyed. . .were found to be tainted with bacteria." He lands a 10 Best nomination for his compelling investigation of legal abuses of government subsidies in "Federal Subsidies Flow to Rural Phone Firms that Have Lots of Cash," leder 5-23. This is the type of careful, yet

provocative, in-depth journalism that launches policy debates in Washington. He shows off a sturdy grasp of his subject matter in "FDA Proposes Relabeling Most Packaged Food," 6-24, a clear assessment of the intricate balance of interests that must be accommodated in the labeling or relabeling of food products. Fearing that an upcoming "60 Minutes" report will assail MSG, the food industry has launched a major PR defensive Ingersoll tells us in "Food Industry Awaits With Queasy Stomach a *60 Minutes Show*," leder 10-17, a telling look at the power of the press to bring about hysteria as "60 Minutes" did with its Alar scare last year.

Ingrassia, Paul. *The Wall Street Journal.* (★ ★ ½)
Detroit. An able chronicler of the arduous and constant shifting of gears at the Big Three, Ingrassia assembled solid, insightful reports and analyses, but with less profundity than in years past. Joined by Joseph White for "Deft Steering: GM's New Boss Runs Into Many Problems — But Little Opposition," leder 2-8, Ingrassia wastes too much time lavishing praise on GM's new chairman Robert C. Stempel for being the kind of bite-the-bullet leader who takes his lumps along with the rest of the team. Yet, except for Stempel's cost-cutting efforts through layoffs and the elimination of bonuses, there's barely anything on his plans to turn the troubled automaker around. Joined by Clay Chandler for "Shifting Gears: Just as U.S. Firms Try Japanese Management, Honda Is Centralizing," 4-11, we're offered a strong assessment of the unique course Honda Motor Co.'s new president Nobuhiko Kawamoto is plotting for the company. "A couple of years ago, when Chrysler Corp. looked for another car company that it wanted to emulate, it chose Honda...But now that Detroit is trying to pattern itself after Honda, the Japanese company itself is charting a new course that, ironically, emphasizes more individual responsibility for decisions. It's a move certain to befuddle America's management gurus." He writes a light and engaging feature on why Detroit is finally recognizing the benefits of working with the Japanese in "Japanese Firms Come to Detroit, and City Is Glad to Have Them," leder 5-7. He highlights the numerous advantages the growing Japanese community has brought to the city, especially desperately needed jobs: "Michigan has nearly 300 Japanese companies, a sixfold increase in eight years." Flabbergasted by the Big Three's attempts to charge Japanese automakers with dumping minivans in the U.S. because the Japanese charge a lower wholesale price to dealers in Japan, Ingrassia gives us "More Self-Destructive Protectionism From Detroit," op-ed 6-7, a persuasive and hard-hitting critique of this latest senseless move by Detroit: "It's hard to say whether the charge is outrageous or just silly, but it's clearly self-destructive. Japanese competition actually is rejuvenating the U.S. auto industry in ways that not even Big Three executives expected a few years back." His "Ratings of Ford's First Nationwide Cut by Moody's," 9-27, is a compact look at the troubled First Nationwide whose parent company, financially troubled Ford Motor, has had to infuse huge amounts of capital into the thrift.

Ivey, Mark. *Business Week.* (★ ★)
Houston bureau manager. Ivey continues to slide away from his three-star rating in the 1990 *MediaGuide*. Although he serviceably tracks the big stories in his region, he rarely musters up the original material or full-toned analysis we praised him for in years past. His "A Booby Prize for Panhandle?" 1-28, is a fact-filled overview of post-acquisition Panhandle Eastern Corp., a debt-laden natural gas pipeline company that's losing major amounts of cash to tumbling prices. Ivey tells us that the new CEO has a strong record, but as one source put it: "They need someone who can walk on water." In "Continental: Writing the Book on Chapter 11," co-written by Michael Oneal 3-18, we get a knowledgeable but surprisingly upbeat report on Continental's fight to emerge from bankruptcy: "Continental Chief Executive Hollis L. Harris is using the Bankruptcy Code masterfully." His "Big Oil May Have Hit a Gusher — in the Soviet Union," with Rosemarie Boyle, Rose Brady, and Peter Galuszka 5-20, is a short but proficient overview of the differing approaches of two Western oil companies to developing deals in the U.S.S.R. Inspired by two big strikes, Ivey pens "The CAT Scans of the Oil Patch," with Richard A. Melcher 6-10, a readable technology piece on computer-aided exploration, which since the late '80s has slashed finding costs for oil and natural gas. He is late but thorough with "Will This

Bubble Ever Burst?" 7-15, a multi-faceted exploration of the crash in natural gas prices, which examines the differing attitudes of big and small producers toward the glut. Confirming that he was initially too enthusiastic about Continental's restructuring in his 3-18 article, Ivey writes "The Mess at Continental: 'We Had to Change Course,' " 8-5, in which he tells us that Harris has lost much control and airline veteran Robert R. Ferguson, III, now has "a mandate from the board to make changes as he sees fit. Continental executives. . .say that Ferguson is preparing a restructuring program that could include layoffs, big asset sales, and even some departures from certain markets." This clear-headed study of what went wrong and why, makes up for Ivey's initial miss.

Jenkins, Holman, Jr. *Insight.* (★ ★ ½)
A knowledgeable and probing analyst, Jenkins is capable of lucid assessments on a wide range of unique subjects. But his coverage of the Persian Gulf War was a bit disappointing, lacking the potency we'd come to expect from him. In "The Mood of U.S. Consumers Is More Bearish than Ever," 12-24-90/1-7-91, he constructs an interesting contrast of consumers' pessimistic mood and economic statistics which suggest things are not as bad as they seem. His cover on the Persian Gulf War, "When Skies Clear After Desert Storm, What's Next?" 2-4, is mainly a survey of armchair experts predicting possible scenarios for the post-war Middle East. Among the observations is one truly preposterous passage contrasting Iraq's "futile" Scud attacks on Israel and the allied bombing of Baghdad: "Though infinitely more effective, allied bombing was so precise that most residents could have felt safe going about their business as usual." As the war winds down he pens a serviceable "For Allies, No Calm Following the Storm," 3-11. But he makes a cavalier reference to the bomb-shelter tragedy: "The bombing. . .may have been another message aimed at testing the loyalty of Saddam's lieutenants. The families of leading Baathists were said to have been sheltering inside." He is better in "Trying to Determine Who Owns the Store," 4-1, a knowledgeable survey of the political and economic challenges facing the newly restored government of Kuwait. Jenkins observes that one of the biggest questions is who owns the country's wealth, the royal family or the people: "For the moment, the battle does not have the makings of a revolution. Indeed, both sides have good reason for wanting to see it settled quickly and quietly." In "The Great Debate: Who Was Behind the Ruble Follies," 6-17, he takes an in-depth look at the frenzied rumors and ruble trading late last year which resulted in former Soviet Prime Minister Valentin S. Pavlov claiming there was a Western conspiracy to sink the Soviet economy. Jenkins traces the frenzy to shadowy American financier Leo Emil Wanta and to the Soviets themselves. His attempt to be witty in "Children's Crusade," 7-22, ends up snippy on West Virginia Governor Jay Rockefeller and his National Commission on Children: "Tip O'Neill once said the Republican Party existed to provide employment to the 'idiot sons of millionaires.' He might have added that the Democrats are more selective. They take the smart ones and make them presidential contenders." In "On the Cutting Edge of the Diamond Trade," 8-12, we find a colorful article on diamond merchant Maurice Tempelsman and his involvement in the intrigue of African politics.

Johnson, Robert. *The Wall Street Journal.* (★ ★ ½)
Chicago. Johnson's reports are always imaginative and engaging, so we're glad to see that this stylish writer is striking a better balance between form and substance this year. With the war in full swing, Johnson takes us to command central at a major armored vehicle maker in "FMC Moves to Keep Clients Like the Army Supplied During the War," leder 2-11. This highly-readable report is packed with lively depictions and solid analysis: "One FMC military liaison already in Saudi Arabia, Thomas Hutson, recently. . .cut through the bureaucracy to get a new door delivered within 24 hours. Such service to customers could be crucial to FMC. . .a strong performance against Saddam Hussein's army is essential to keep Congressional critics quiet and more orders coming in." In "The CEO Vanishes, Leaving a Company Besieged, Perplexed," 3-15, Johnson vividly characterizes the financial and personal uncertainty gripping the financially-troubled Y&A Group, an engineering company in Missouri, which is now desperately trying to cope with the mysterious disappearance of its CEO, Malcolm Cheek. He

is incisive in "Tenneco Turnaround Is Bogging Down," 4-29, expertly dissecting the reasons why Tenneco isn't performing up to investors expectations. Taking a fun and frivolous jaunt into the world of power golfing, he pens "Forget the Polyester; Blasters' Tourney Is Golf for Real Men," 5-14, where the point is distance not accuracy. In "Lone Star Mammal of Lone Star State Is a Little, Wild Cat," a-head 6-10, he recounts the loony tale of why Texans have spent $65 million in state and federal funds to save the ocelot even though "Biologists say. . .they aren't sure whether there were ever that many ocelots in Texas." A delicious anecdote for those who believe some banner environmental causes are just plain frivolous. He breezes us through his brisk overview of the difficulties of marketing natural gas, "Glut and a Poor Image Dash the Grand Hopes Held for Natural Gas," 8-2, noting that price swings, delivery problems, and consumer wariness have eroded the industry's credibility.

Johnston, Oswald. *Los Angeles Times.* (★)
Washington. He still has a long way to go, but Johnston improved somewhat this year. His reports remain very formulaic, rarely probing, but a few of his pieces indicate that he is capable of more. His "Iraqis Put Warplanes at Ancient Temple, U.S. Says," 2-14, is a competent handling of news that Saddam Hussein parked two warplanes near the ruins of an ancient temple in the historic city of Ur. Johnston flavors the piece with rich descriptions of the historic significance of this precious archeological treasure. He adheres to formula in "National Jobless Rate Rises to 6.5%," 3-9, reporting on the latest dismal job stats and the Federal Reserves' response to ease. But there's nothing to set this apart from the wire reports. In "Bulk of Americans Living Longer but Blacks Are Not," 4-9, it appears that Johnston is merely regurgitating the facts of a press conference. Doing scant additional fact-gathering, he leaves several important statistics out, saying that "No specific rate was given." On the economy Johnston does little more than follow the bumps and blips, as in "Latest U.S. Reports Suggest Recession May Be Nearing End," 6-14. Like most of his reports on the economy, this doesn't look beyond the numbers. His "World Bank Economist Takes a Different Tack," 5-7, is a somewhat unbalanced profile of Michael Dukakis' former chief economic adviser Lawrence H. Summers, who is now chief economist at the World Bank. Johnston tells us that it was believed Summers would slow the bank's push toward free-market economic policies, but he is now unabashedly urging Third World economies to pursue the market-oriented policies. But too much play is given to what has changed in Summers' outlook, and too little to what has not. He is somewhat original in "Behind April's Expanded Trade Deficit Is a Sign of an Economy on the Mend," 6-20, eschewing conventional wisdom on the expanded trade deficit. He is sharper than usual for "Quebec Offered Role as 'Distinct Society,' " 9-25, authoritatively exploring Canada's new constitutional reform package which "is designed to strengthen the Meech Lake 'distinct society' offer to Quebec by also emphasizing that provincial governments such as Quebec have primary authoritiy over cultural affairs, education and broadcasting — key issues in Francophone Quebec."

Jones, Alex. *The New York Times.* (★ ½)
Press. Somewhat distracted this year, Jones and his wife (and co-author) Susan E. Tifft of *Time* magazine spent part of the year writing and then defending their controversial book, *The Patriarch: The Rise and Fall of the Bingham Dynasty.* His sixth year on the beat, this Pulitzer Prize winner was well-primed to assess the major NYC newspaper story of the year; the labor disputes and eventual sale of the *Daily News.* He was uncharacteristically lackluster in "The Battle to Come," 3-13. This was merely a perfunctory rehash of how the *News*'s demise would affect other hometown papers. We expected more detail and insights from Jones on this principal story. He is back on track with "How the Strike at the News Took on a Life of Its Own," 3-17, vividly highlighting the problems the *News* and its union had before the arrival of Robert Maxwell: "And so with Mr. Maxwell's satin-swathed derringer at their heads rather than the Tribune Company's .45, the unions made the deal." His delightful, "To Papers, Funnies Are No Joke," 4-8, traces the development of comics and their impact on readership and sales of daily newspapers: "editors are rethinking all aspects of their papers to make them more appealing as

a matter of long-term strategic necessity, and the funnies can be a potent tool." The piece includes an interesting revelation by Jones that the *Times* itself reconsiders its "abstinence" from time to time. He is disorganized and choppy in "Change at Top of Publisher's Group," 5-7, making for difficult reading, with Jones giving us only minimal insights into Cathleen Black as she becomes chief executive of the American Newspaper Publishers Association. On the other hand, he showcases his insider knowledge of the press in "The National Sports Daily Closes with Today's Issue," 6-31, chronicling the swift demise of the paper. Jones covers all the bases — management, distribution, advertising, and the editorial staff — in this complete and readable piece. He offers some striking facts on a shrinking newspaper industry in "At Many Papers Competition Is At Best an Illusion," 9-22: "in a significant number of cities. . .what seem to be two separate newspapers are actually products of the same reporting staff, with minimal differences in news content. . .There are 63 communities with two or more daily newspapers, compared with 172 in 1980. . ."

Kanner, Bernice. *New York.* (★ ★ ½)
"On Madison Avenue" columnist. Kanner is sprightly and savvy on the inner workings of advertising, and for those who follow this industry closely, her columns are recommended reading. Her "Forcing the Issues," 2-11, chronicles the histories of boycotts through PR and ad campaigns: "Boycotts are often more successful against a company's image than against its bottom line, says [*National Boycott News* editor Todd] Putnam. Boycotts used to take between five and ten years to get results, but now they take about two. That's because they're better organized and get more media attention: Corporations recognize the damage potential much earlier." Her "Scents of Accomplishment," 3-18, is a tidy recounting of the marketing challenges and successes of Chanel's and Burberry's new perfumes for men and women, respectively. In her neat and readable "Plymouth Rocks," 4-22, she tells us how the "bad boy" of the ad world, Ed McCabe, is out to redesign Plymouth's quiet image as a peddler of sleep, leisure and business attire. Their new ad reads: "Who you sleep with is none of our business." She is lively and informative on the test market towns of America in "Ordinary People," 6-3, with a light touch that makes this piece fly. Her "Hot Tickets," 7-15, is a delightful feature on traffic cops, with Kanner joining Unit 111A, the Dept. of Transportation's "answer to the Green Berets." She is one heck of a good sport here, directing traffic, writing tickets and whatnot. Kanner points out the growing number of ads that resemble one another in "Double Takes," 9-9, but she doesn't give us an idea of where this trend is taking the industry. Better in "Tune in Tomorrow," 10-28, where she takes us right to the Madison Avenue storyboards for a fun and smart look at serial advertising.

Kilborn, Peter T. *The New York Times.* (★ ★ ½)
Washington, "Workplace" beat. Kilborn is striking a better balance between style and substance this year. Composing handsome labor features from downtown NYC to the coal mines of Kentucky, he was more apt to blend in the necessary statistics and economic analysis. "The Daily News Strike Tests the Will of Weakened Labor," 1-27, is a multidimensional assessment of why the strike at the *Daily News* "has become an important trial for an American labor movement that has been losing ground for decades." He fully develops his observation that the strike has focused attention on the controversial use of permanent replacement workers. His richly-detailed and beautifully constructed "Scraping By, Illegally, Mining Kentucky Coal," 3-3, reads like a chapter from a wonderful novel. But ever so subtly Kilborn weaves in the requisite statistics, facts and perspectives on "wildcatting," or illegal mining. With another report from the area, "Out of Kentucky Soil, Into Their Hearts," 3-15, he tells the story of one woman's valiant struggle to open a clinic for victims of black lung disease. In "Convenience Store Jobs: High Risks Alone at Night," 4-7, he takes us beyond the headlines following an indictment in a 7-Eleven store murder to inform us that more clerks get killed than any other occupation except taxi drivers. Trying to play social psychiatrist in "How a Work Force Responds When Equal Rights Is a Goal," 5-12, Kilborn is heavy on the generalizations on how members of the workplace struggle with affirmative action. Conceding that there are no statistics to prove his

thesis, Kilborn stretches news of a few job discrimination suits into a lengthy "U.S. Workers Say Japanese Keep Them Out of Top Jobs," 6-3. His sobering "For Forlorn Millions, the Recession Goes On," 7-28, looks anecdotally at the long arm of recession as it batters unemployed workers across the country. Also somber was his " 'Crunch Issue' at Nursing Homes: Aides' Pay," 9-5, a revealing look at the demanding work of minimum wage nursing home aides, "in many cases, the wages are too low to lift the aides above the poverty line and off welfare."

Kleinfield, N. R. *The New York Times.* (★ ★ ½)
Sunday "Business." "Sonny" Kleinfield's relaxed, sonorous style is perfectly suited for leisurely, in-depth Sunday reading. He takes a perky look at why "convention center fever is raging" in "The Latest Municipal Malady: Convention Center Fever," 2-24, an engaging examination of the bottom line pressures confronting convention centers, and the reasons that enthusiasts believe the number and size of conventions will continue to expand. His Sunday business lead "Random House's Glitzy New Imprint," 3-17, is a shameless puff for the tiny publishing branch of Random House, Turtle Bay Books, run by Joni Evans. His "He Had Money, Women, an S&L, Now Don Dixon Has Jail," 3-17, is an easy read about a high-flying thrift owner. You know the story, call girls for the board of directors, a $40,000 painting for the Pope, etc. But there's not much here beyond the lurid high spots. In his best of the year, Kleinfield expertly explores the burgeoning scanner data industry in "Targeting the Grocery Shopper," 5-26. He skillfully delineates the latest and most promising phase of this industry-altering marketing tactic — targeted electronic marketing. Supermarket chains now have such things as Shoppers Clubs that provide discounts to entice customers to carry special mag-striped member cards. "The scanners allow supermarkets to monitor what sells and what does not. But who is buying has been missing. The mag-striped cards attach a name to the purchases, permitting a supermarket to begin building a data base on each customer." His "In Search of a Good Borrower," 5-19, candidly profiles Sterling Bancorp's ultra-conservative ways which haven't always paid off, but are earning respect as other banks swallow huge losses on their high-risk portfolios. And his "Short Order Cook," was an absolutely delicious behind the scenes tale of an industrious New Yorker who serves up lunch orders at the speed of light. Slightly melodramatic in "Gang in Bias Attack: As Tough as Image?" 10-24, he chronicles the lives of a group of NYC hoodlums, the "Kings Highway Boys." "There is a democratic undercurrent to its members' suspected capers. They have beaten blacks. They have beaten whites. They have beaten Jews. They once beat somebody because he was fat."

Knight, Jerry. *The Washington Post.* (★ ½)
Washington business columnist. Although Knight is a competent, intelligent reporter, he rarely breaks new ground on the important issues he covers. His "Regulators Rescue New England Banks," 1-7, was a standard wrap up of the latest bank seizures in the northeast with all the requisite facts, but nothing fresh. On the other hand, we get a good feel for the differing schools of thought on federally-insured deposits in his perceptive "Regulators: Keep Option on Deposits," 1-10. He is superficial again in "Treasury to Relax Bank Rules," 2-21, filed from the "New England banking summit" where the region's governors are meeting with administration reps to discuss tactics for dealing with bank failures. The Treasury's "loan splitting" idea is mentioned, but only hastily. In one of his most probing pieces this year, "A Rising Revolt on Deposit Reform," 3-17, Knight gathers observations from a wide range of critics of deposit reform, from "a Main Street coalition" that fears taxpayers will have to pay more bills to Treasury Secretary Nicholas Brady, who contends that "Using FDIC-insured deposits, bankers can make what FDIC Chairman L. William Seidman calls 'heads-I-win, tails-the government-loses' bets." In "House Bank Panel to Ask Clifford, Altman to Testify," 4-12, he solidly recounts news that these two prominent Washington lawyers will be questioned regarding their role in BCCI's secret takeover of First American Bank. But Knight does no digging here. With junk bonds the government's favorite scapegoat for thrift failures, Knight's "RTC Finds Some S&Ls Lost Big in Bond Markets," 5-9, was an eye-opening look at major S&L losses caused by investing in the "safest of investments," U.S. Government bonds. He is thoughtful in "Bush and

Dingell Following in Their Fathers' Footsteps," 6-25. Noting that John Dingell, Sr. supported Glass-Steagall and Prescott Bush opposed the Bank Holding Company Act, Knight nicely develops an interesting deja vu: "Following in their fathers' footsteps, George Bush and John Dingell today are headed for a confrontation on those same issues." His eye-opening briefer on the condition of D.C. banks, "Bank Losses Here Worst in Nation; Seidman: One-Fifth of Real Estate Loans Are Overdue," 9-11, reports that banks in the nation's capital "are in worse shape than those in any other part of the country," according to FDIC chairman Seidman's estimates.

Kuttner, Robert. *The New Republic,* Washington Post Writer's Group. (★ ★ ½)
Economics, commentary. An inquisitive and creative thinker, Kuttner is an important liberal voice. E.J. Dionne, Jr. of *The Washington Post* even considers him a new Democratic "guru." Even those who don't agree with his elastic Keynesian economics, should acknowledge he adds something unique to the debate. We regularly turn to his monthly column in *Business Week.* In "U.S. Is 'Last Superpower,' to Its Detriment," *Los Angeles Times* 1-25, he fails to make the case for his vision of the Persian Gulf War as the extension of the military industrial complex, saying that we have "foolishly launched a second era of militarized Pax Americana. As we watch the devastating effects of this war, we will continue to do so on Japanese televisions." Developing an odd new angle in "Postwar Economics," *New York Times Business World* 3-24, he argues the end of the Cold War *almost* freed the U.S. from the burdens of Pax Americana, but the Gulf War added new burdens. He promotes a "plainly socialistic health system" in "Health Care: Why Corporate America Is Paralyzed," *BW* 4-8, but instead of delving into the bottom line savings he believes this system could produce, he goes on too long about big businesses' inability "to put aside their ideological qualms." He takes a bull-headed, all-or-nothing stance in "A Vote for Free Trade with Mexico Is a Vote Against Free Trade," *BW* 5-6: "At minimum the Administration needs to decide whether it wants to be a regional colonial power or the architect of a universal system of universal trade." Kuttner loves paradoxes and in "Why Business Needs a Stronger and Wiser — Uncle Sam," *BW* 6-3, he finds one: "The American contempt for government, paradoxically, is harming American free enterprise." He makes an interesting, somewhat convincing case for reining in "our deep libertarian streak" and finding a way "to use government as an instrument of common purpose." In "A Second Opinion on the Democrats' Health Plan," *BW* 7-1, he takes a more critical look at "play-or-pay" health care, and instead "a 'single payer' system, supported by tax revenues, in which everyone would be insured." Kuttner writes from an ideal world where enormous taxes can be levied without a negative economic impact. He is surprisingly short sighted on immigration issues in "Illegal Immigration: Would a National ID Card Help?" *BW* 8-26, advising the use of a national ID card to slow the tide of illegal workers, but failing to explore how creating economic opportunities in the home countries of these foreign workers would have a much more lasting and far-reaching impact on the problem.

Labaton, Stephen. *The New York Times.* (★ ★)
Washington, banking. With big shoes to fill following Nathaniel Nash's departure for South America, Labaton kept a watchful eye on those charged with cleaning up and redirecting the decimated S&L industry and the shaky banking sector. Although not yet fully seasoned on this beat, he is becoming an increasingly important source of information and analysis. His "U.S. Is Taking Over Northeast Bank to Head Off a Run," 1-7, is competent deadline reporting that neatly ties in the important issues surrounding the seizure of the Bank of New England. But his initial report on the Treasury's proposed banking reform, "Administration Presents its Plan for Broad Overhaul of Banking," 2-6, failed to consider the plan's dim chance of passing unchanged. He played catch-up the next day with "Much of the Banking Overhaul Plan Is in Doubt," 2-7. He is heavy on details but light on analysis in "Wall Street's Ambitious Top Cop," *NYT's Business World* 3-24, yet another profile of SEC chairman Richard C. Breeden's power grasps. Rehashing the RTC's ongoing problems in "U.S. Will Enhance Deals for Buyers of S&L Holdings," 5-16, he is poorly organized, not describing the RTC's new incentive marketing plan until the sixth paragraph. His "Are Banks Going Down the Same Path as S&Ls?" 6-16, was

insightful, but still only a poor reproduction of William Greider's piece in the 6-13 *Rolling Stone*. For those following the RTC closely, Labaton's "Seidman Will Seek $80 Billion," 6-19, was a critical look at where Seidman and the administration stand on sensitive RTC issues. He is also solid in "Third Banking-Overhaul Bill Is Near," 7-12, proficiently assessing yet another banking plan, a Senate Banking Committee offering that differs substantially from the administration and House versions. He paints a rich and sweeping study of the changing disposition of the American people toward banking legislation in "Regulatory Overhaul Advancing," 9-9, which encompasses a wide spectrum of cogent perspectives: " 'In the 1930s, we assumed that decentralization was the way to prevent mischief, and there was a basic mistrust of bigness. . .fueled by a period of populist upheaval,' said Robert B. Reich. . .'Now the world has changed fundamentally, through advances in technology and the globalization of the marketplace. As a result, the concerns of the 1930's are not on anyone's mind.' " He lands an important story that *The Wall Street Journal* carried from the wires in "Panel in Bid to Revamp S.&L. Bailout Funding," 10-3, reporting on a narrowly approved amendment sponsored by Rep. Kennedy 2d (D-Mass.) that would require the government to either raise taxes or cut other federal programs to continue the rescue effort.

Laderman, Jeffrey M. *Business Week.* (★)
Associate editor. Laderman continues to spew out gobbledygook on the markets, rarely launching a tenable study of the political or economic forces steering them. In a year riddled with important economic questions, his oversimplifications were even more glaring than usual. His cover story on the surge of the DJIA since January 16, "Has the Market Gone Bonkers?" with Suzanne Woolley and Michael J. Mandel 2-25, is mediocre at best. With no theme, no theory, Laderman places his bets on the Federal Reserve: "The rally seems real. The stock market always looks forward, and this time it likes what it sees: a Federal Reserve embarked on a campaign of cheap money to revive the ailing economy." He is optimistic in "Why the Bulls Are Betting on Greener Pastures," 3-18, a brief overview of what lies ahead for the stock market. His analysis is neat and straightforward, but offers little for sophisticated readers to chew on. In "A Fast and Furious First Quarter," 4-15, he packs in interesting tidbits on the mutual fund players who fared spectacularly well and just okay in the "ballistic" first quarter stock surge. There's enough here to warrant interest from financial readers with their eye out for the latest leader on the investment score sheet. His "KKR, on a Winning Streak, Gets Bopped by a Book," 5-20, looks closely at the charges of shady financial practices raised against KKR in Sarah Bartlett's new book, *The Money Machine*. He ponders the impact these accusations might have on KKR investors, then concludes that KKR has made so much money for its clients that few will make a stink. He is reasonably interesting but not particularly enlightening in "They Love Stocks that Are All Beaten Up," 7-15, an overview of beaten-down stocks such as IBM whose high dividend yield attracts "value" investors. His "Ashes to Ashes, Funds to Funds," 9-30, takes a rather bland look at the growing number of small, poorly performing mutual funds being merged into peppier portfolios.

Landro, Laura. *The Wall Street Journal.* (★ ★)
Entertainment and media news editor. We observed more consistently serious business reporting from Landro this year, as she made an effort to enrich her reports with important details on the financial side of this financially-troubled industry. Her sharp and well-researched "Orion Pictures Needs Big Capital Infusion to Survive," 2-11, fully explores Orion's theatrical interests, management, acquisitions, debt and mergers, providing plenty of documentation that even the entertainment industry isn't recession-proof. She files another detailed article on the business aspects of the entertainment industry in "Despite a Robust Basic Business, Picture Is Flawed for Cable TV," 3-21, a comprehensive overview of cable operations, regulations and pricing: "The paradox of cable is that the basic business is wonderful, but everything else has taken a turn for the worse." This piece held plenty of solid information for investors, even if it was a bit dry. "Tartikoff Will Try to Polish Paramount's Image," 5-2, served up more filler than fact as Landro throws names around in this long-winded piece. In "Studios Set Spate of Summer

Releases," 5-8, it took us until the middle of the article to realize this was little more than a listing of summer movies, Landro giving us very generic information as to why studios are releasing various movies at different times. Her "Time Warner Learns SEC Plans Review of Proposed $3 Billion Rights Offering," 6-13, seemed arid and confusing on Time Warner's "rights offering." She provided little in-depth analysis of what the offering entailed, or its implications for Time Warner investors. She is much better in "After Stock Debacle, Some Ask: Will Hubris Undo Time Warner?" co-written by Randall Smith 7-19, a 10 Best nomination, which gave us excellent depth and definition on the workings of Time Warner under Steven J. Ross. The professional presentation of the material allowed readers to judge Ross's flamboyant spending style without pushing an "excess" theme to excess. Her "Hallmark Unit to Acquire Cencom Stake in Transaction Valued at $1 Billion," 9-20, isn't quite as farsighted as James Flanigan's piece that appeared a few days later in the *Los Angeles Times,* but she offers plenty on the technical and financial aspects of the Hallmark-Cencom cable deal that will take Hallmark "from virtually no presence in the cable industry into the ranks of the top 20 cable operators."

Lawrence, Richard. *The Journal of Commerce.* (★ ★)
"Trade Scene" columnist. Although the overall quality of his work continues to fluctuate, *JC*'s point man on international trade for over 20 years is venturing more often into turbid subjects, and interjecting more creative thinking into his appraisals. His commentary "Two Nations on the Brink," 1-30, creatively compares the political economy of the Soviet Union and Brazil, knocking both Soviet president Gorbachev for floundering on economic reform and Brazil's president, Fernando Collar de Mello, for his "Draconian economic stabilization program." "Mr. Gorbachev's economic move last week — a confiscation of large-denomination ruble notes to pare the country's monetary base and thereby curb inflation — seemed almost a Kremlin version of Mr. Collor de Mello's assets freeze." Yes. In "Long Live US Protectionism," 2-27, he introduces us to Bill Gill, the "consultant, author, lecturer and unabashed protectionist" who wrote *Trade Wars Against America,* a "history of U.S. trade and monetary policy" which Lawrence tells us is "an inch-thick tome that shreds myths, offers a mix of curious — sometimes startling — facts and is chock full of provocative historical interpretations." Interesting enough theme, but Lawrence doesn't seem to try to place in context any of Mr. Gill's debatable assertions. He serves up an observant "Japanese Firm Resorts to US Dumping Law," 4-19, on the twisted tale of how the U.S. arm of Japanese-owned Brother Industries has brought anti-dumping charges against the U.S.-based Smith Corona Corp. which imports portable electric and automatic typewriters from its plant in Singapore. His analysis is simplistic in "Trade Balance Outlook Improves," 5-20, characterizing the shrinking trade deficit as positive even if the numbers are fallout from a recessionary economy. His "World Bank Reform, US-Style," 6-19, is an important behind-the-scenes look at the imbroglio resulting from the Treasury's campaign to make the World Bank more supportive of private enterprise through closer coordination with its affiliate, the International Finance Corp. He is more balanced than usual on the trade deficit in "US Trade Deficit Climbed in July to 6-Month High of $5.9 Billion," 9-20, citing sources who do not see the latest numbers as a big problem.

Lazzareschi, Carla. *Los Angeles Times.* (★ ½)
High tech. Lazzareschi delivered several solid business features this year, but on the major high tech stories she typically reacted with the pack — spewing out the details of press conferences and news releases, but rarely hazarding original angles. "In High-Tech Marriages, Little Bliss," *The Washington Post* 12-30-90, she carefully examines the downside of AT&T's move on NCR Corp., noting that high-tech mergers don't typically work out as planned, but fails to explore AT&T's reasons for forging ahead with the takeover. Building upon a timely war angle in "War Speeds Shift to New Phone Technology," 1-24, she shows how restricted travel plans are bolstering teleconferencing and global satellite communications. Her most in-depth pieces of the year, "Smart Way to Unclog Roadways," 3-30, was a far-reaching canvass of future "smart cars" that will contain navigation and communication devices to steer drivers clear of heavy traffic. But Lazzareschi is careful to balance her excitement with pragmatic concerns. As a professor

at an environmental think tank put it: " 'These systems are sexy and they attract a lot of money. . .[but] the smart car is technology that doesn't address the fundamental societal problems of traffic congestion and driving patterns.' " She gives sound coverage of IBM's weak financial showing in "IBM Will Cut 10,000 Workers to Reduce Costs," 3-29, but there's nothing especially fresh here. Following the $7.4 billion merger of AT&T and NCR, she was once again noticeably pessimistic about the union in "Will This Marriage Succeed?" 5-7: "If there is a chance — and there is no unanimity on that point — analysts say it will only be if AT&T keeps its hands off NCR and allows the computer company's managers to operate autonomously far outside the sometimes stifling bureaucracy of the century-old telephone company." She weighs in poorly on the woes at IBM with "Chairman Faces Immense Task in Reshaping IBM," 6-2, a parochial assessment of the company's problems and chairman John F. Akers failure to fix them. Lazzareschi keeps it superficial and unenlightening, scanning the major themes we saw explored much more fully elsewhere. On the other hand, her "Unisys Plans to Spin Off its Defense Operation," 10-1, is a well-researched little piece on computer maker Unisys's plans to issue 20 million shares of common stock in its defense unit, Paramax. While most believe defense cuts make it a rough time for such a move, one of Lazzareschi's well-informed sources makes the valid point that "if you're buying fewer ships and airplanes, electronics have to become more sophisticated to protect what you have."

Lelyveld, Michael S. *The Journal of Commerce.* (★ ★ ½)
Boston, senior correspondent. Our question: How does Lelyveld uncover such unique intelligence on the Soviet Union from Boston? An outstanding reporter and astute analyst, his dispatches on the Soviets have quickly become required reading. One thing that concerns us, though, is his heavy reliance on anonymous sources. In "Soviet Tax-Dodging Hurts Investors," 1-28, he discerns why the Soviet government has become increasingly wary that Western joint ventures are being used as tax dodges. His important scoop on World Bank and IMF meetings with dissident Soviet republics, "World Bank, IMF Met with Rebel Soviet Republics," 2-4, is Lelyveld the sleuth at his best, even though the report is based entirely on anonymous sources. Following his equally eye-opening follow-up, "Banks' Meetings with Republics Send a Signal to Gorbachev," 2-6, a letter-to-the-editor on 2-8 from the Chief of Information and Public Affairs at the World Bank denied Lelyveld's reports, but *JC* stood firmly by his version of story. His op-ed on Soviet Prime Minister Valentin Pavlov's accusation that Western banks tried to oust President Mikhail S. Gorbachev by amassing rubles, "Plots, Paranoia and the Ruble," 2-15, clears up some of the misconceptions surrounding Pavlov's controversial statement. Lelyveld concedes that it is troubling that the "Soviets have taken a vicious swing to the right," but notes that even more troubling is "the possibility that there may be some basis for Mr. Pavlov's paranoia." In "Soviet Unity Moves Raise Hopes for Economic Reform," 4-26, he gathers perspectives on the agreement between the Soviet central government and nine Soviet republics on a union treaty and the "unexpected unity" of Gorbachev and Yeltsin. He pulls the anonymous source maneuver once too often in "Soviet Deal May Snag US Credits," 5-15, a potentially important report about an alleged deal that "will transfer all Soviet natural resources, including oil and natural gas, to republics that sign a union treaty." His "New Soviet Regime's Economic Orders Spell Disaster, Western Experts Say," 8-20, provides insights into the disastrous implications of the Soviet State Emergency Committee's economic orders following the coup against Gorbachev.

Levin, Doron P. *The New York Times.* (★ ★ ½)
Detroit. Capable and workmanlike, Levin is solid on the inner-workings of the Big Three as he covers the automakers' woes from a marketing/management perspective. His "Chrysler's Heirs Are More Apparent," 1-15, is a tightly-written report on Robert A. Lutz's appointment to president of Chrysler, a sure sign he is a leading candidate to succeed Lee A. Iacocca. Levin gives us a good sense of the other candidates and how Lutz mirrors and differs from Iacocca: "Mr. Lutz. . .like Mr. Iacocca, is charismatic, outspoken. . .But Mr. Lutz differs from Mr. Iacocca in one important respect: He believes Chrysler should proceed without help from a larger auto

maker." He is snappy in "A Pace Car Made (Quickly) in U.S.," 2-26, a colorful piece on how patriotism and protest prompted Chrysler to shift gears and replace a Japanese two-seater as its pace car for the Indianapolis 500 with a new made-in-America model called the "Dodge Viper." His "Saturn: An Outpost of Change in G.M.'s Steadfast Universe," 3-17, foresees the promise the GM Saturn plant's new collaborative management style holds for the company and the American auto industry as a whole. With compelling statistics, Levin constructs a useful marketing study in "Detroit Strives to Reclaim Lost Generation of Buyers," 4-9. He indicates that Detroit has a lot of work to do if it wants to woo young, independent buyers: "altering the perceptions of young buyers. . .who are not familiar with domestic models and never grew up with them. . .is proving to be a daunting problem." In "Almost New Is Good Enough, Much to Detroit's Annoyance," 5-28, he skims the big bargains to be found as rental cars are sold back to dealers to the tune of low mileage and sizeable discounts for the consumers. His rich depiction of the end of an era in Detroit, "With Debt on the Menu, A Monument Is Closed," 6-21, details the closing of the London Chop House, which was once host to "Motor City's powerful and celebrated." In "An Auto Glut That Won't Go Away," 7-28, he discerns that the auto industry is swimming in overcapacity: ". . .the arithmatic of overcapacity is simply too nasty to allow every model — and every plant — to survive." His punchy report on Honda's new 1992 Civic VX, "A Fuel-Efficient Grab for Power," 9-20, reports that the five-seater's expected fuel-efficiency rating of 55 mpg is spurring a U.S. mileage debate, and fears in Detroit that the Civic VX "may become a powerful weapon in the hands of those who favor stiffer auto fuel-efficiency standards."

Lewis, Peter. *The New York Times.* (★ ★ ½)

"The Executive Computer" columnist. In an era in which technology changes at the speed of light, Lewis is a vital source of consistently high-quality information on the latest offerings of the computer software and hardware industry. In "The Latest Excel Leapfrogs its Spreadsheet Rivals," 1-20, he instructively compares the new Microsoft Excel 3.0 to other personal computer spreadsheets and briefly details its unique features. With the insights of an industry insider he pens "Operating Systems for PC's Grow More Confusing," 3-3, an excellent discussion of the diverging approach Microsoft and IBM are now taking in the design of operating systems. He conveys the reassuring results of a study by the National Institute for Occupational Safety and Health on the effects of emissions from video display terminals on pregnant women in "Trying to Assess the Potential Hazards of Video Terminals," 4-21, and alerts us to misleading marketing claims from companies that sell screens to block electrical fields. His insights in "For Macintosh Users, a Very Long Wait Is Over," 5-19, are also valuable, offering a practical look at Apple's upgrade of its Macintosh operating system, System 7.0. Lewis not only addresses the technical aspects of the change but gives us an idea how this new system is likely to play in the competitive marketplace of computers. His "A Sleek and Powerful Portable From A.T.& T.," 6-2, is a lucid explanation of AT&T's new Safari portable which he believes offers powerful communications and networking tools as well as other attractive features. His "What's in I.B.M.'s and Apple's gunsights? Microsoft," 7-14, is a top-notch examination of the implications of the IBM-Apple alliance and the industry-wide scramble to team up for competitive advantage. In "The Brave New World of I.B.M. and Apple," 10-13, he points out that it is software, not hardware that directs a consumer's purchase of a new computer. Therefore, IBM and Apple's alliance to create a new computing environment in which a Power PC could run virtually any software would change the name of the computer sales game and wrest control of the industry away from Microsoft, which now dominates software.

Light, Larry. *Business Week.* (★ ★ ½)

Corporate finance editor. Well versed on many financial topics, Light transcends the latest business press corps craze to assess his financial subject matter in the same way that a successful investor looks at his portfolio — logically not emotionally. His fact filled, "Invasion of the Bottom-Fishers," with Robert D. Hof 1-21, thoroughly overviews the creative financial deals being struck by some of the nation's "Reichmann wannabe[s]" who are scarfing up deeply discounted properties hoping to ride out the recession and cash in big when the real estate market recovers. Light is vastly underemployed for "If You Can't Find a Buyer, Find a Tenant," 2-25, a gathering of simple suggestions on how to rent if you can't sell your home. In "Real Estate's Loss Is Martin Taplin's Gain," co-written by Iren Recio 3-18, the authors neatly show us the ropes of the lucrative workout business which is thriving as a result of the real estate collapse. Along the way, we're introduced to Martin W. Talpin, a successful workout specialist who pulled off the sale of debt-ridden Heritage USA. He pens a crisp portrait of Ronald O. Perelman's prize acquisition, Revlon, in "Why Perelman Faces Life Without Makeup," with Monica Roman 4-1, a worthwhile report packed with speculation that Perelman's heavy debt will cause him to sell off at least some of the Revlon empire. Light lines up all the possible buyers and gives us a concise, elucidating look at their reasons for considering a purchase of all or parts of the company. In his savvy "The Complex Art of the Chapter 11 Deal," 5-27, he uses numerous examples to alert investors to the pitfalls of taking over a company that has filed for bankruptcy. Light's well-constructed commentary, "Letting the Air Out of Insurers' Overblown Assets," 7-8, showcases his financial acumen. He argues that insurance companies should mark their assets to market "say, once a quarter — and send the results to policyholders, who would have a better idea of what they've bought." His "The Edifice Complex: Two Concrete Studies," 10-7, is an engaging, well thought-out review of Tom Sachtman's *Skyscraper Dreams: The Great Real Estate Dynasties of New York* and Douglas Frantz's *From the Ground Up: The Business of Building in the Age of Money.*

Lipman, Joanne. *The Wall Street Journal.* (★ ★ ½)
"Advertising" columnist. Though she occasionally bogs down in the finer details, Lipman has an indisputably solid grasp of her subject matter which makes for intelligent, perceptive reports. Although her " 'Upfront' Study Finds Weakness for Networks," 4-2, was really just another bad economy story, Lipman brings fresh, alert reporting and style to the theme. In "FCC Refuses to Delay Ruling on TV Reruns," 4-9, we get a solid, well-informed account on the "fin/syn" proposal dealing with the property of syndicated shows. Her pithy thumbnail sketch of Rupert Murdoch, "Murdoch May Have to Sell More Assets," 4-27, packed in the pertinent financial information: "merging Murdoch's Sky TV with its rival British Satellite Broadcasting, is losing about $10.3 million a week." She is brisk and to the point in "Ads on TV: Out of Sight, Out of Mind?" 5-14, a cohesive look at why magazine advertising campaigns are more memorable than TV ones, and cost less. This meaty report is chock-full of interesting quotes. In her engaging "Eddie Lampert Makes the Right Connections and Makes Millions," 6-27, Lipman sketches an extensive profile of Wall Street hotshot Edward S. Lampert, Yale '84, who at 28 is already finding that persistence and talent pay off. . .by the millions. In "ABC to Relax Longstanding Guidelines for Ad Content," 9-5, she reports that ABC, bowing to pressure from advertisers, is loosening its standards for competitive claims and doctor endorsements in ads. But she doesn't really explore the implications of this shift for consumers.

Lippman, Thomas W. *The Washington Post.* (★ ★ ½)
Lippman has carved out a unique and important niche covering energy issues as they swirl through Capitol Hill. Faithfully postured with one ear to the ground, he has proven himself keen at detecting policy pockets bubbling beneath the Beltway. Evincing a strong grasp of the themes of the energy policy debate, Lippman pens "Energy Legislation Proliferates on Hill," 2-8, a careful and balanced characterization of the various camps in the energy policy debate - -the administration's free-market philosophy and the big new initiatives of the Democrats. In "Energy's 'Mountain Building Up,' " 2-12, he clarifies Energy Secretary James D. Watkins' statements about the mounting costs of waste cleanup and the construction of the Superconducting Super Collider which he says are shortchanging other projects. Zeroing in on what could be one of the biggest lobby fights this year, Lippman's "Opening Up the Halls of Power," 3-10, fully examines the debate over whether "unregulated, profit-oriented corporations should be encouraged to enter the electricity marketplace by excluding them from tight federal restrictions." Offering strong analysis, he concludes that "In the short run, this is a complicated,

intramural political fight. . .Over the next decade, however, the outcome will help determine who owns the facilities that produce electricity, what fuels they use, where the power plants will be located and how much the power will cost." He reads between the lines in a very intelligent summary of the conservation debate, "Energy's Action Plan Appears Mired in Debate," 3-7, reporting that the Dept. of Energy had generally supported conservation initiatives, "but department officials have been silent since the Dec. 21 meeting, prompting reports that conservation options have been scrapped at White House insistence." In his reconnaissance of the R&D going into alternatives to gasoline-fueled cars, "Gasoline-Fueled Cars May Be Running Out of Time," 7-6, Lippman speaks authoritatively and provides layers of data to support his assertions. His "Filling It to the Billion-Barrel Rim," 8-5, is a top-notch discussion of the debate over the Energy Dept.'s Strategic Petroleum Reserve which pits the administration and oil companies, which want to boost the reserves, against congressional Democrats who don't want to pay for the plan.

Liscio, John. *Barron's.* (★ ★ ★)
Commodities editor. Often impertinent, Liscio carefully scrutinizes all the economic facts and figures germane to the commodities markets. Where Jonathan Fuerbringer of the *NYT* watches currencies and commodities with one eye, Liscio uses both. As a result, some of the freshest reports available in the press appear under his byline. His "The Truth Is a Lie," 1-21, vividly clarifies the impact the week's astonishing events had on commodities. First the apprehension as fighting broke out in the Middle East, then news from the Pentagon that the war was going "very, very well" — gold for March delivery plummeted $30.10 in one day and "Silver and platinum also headed lower, but their losses were limited by the thinking that a quick end to the war in the Persian Gulf would revive the economy and thus create demand for what are basically industrial metals." In "Demand-Side Economics," 2-4, he is too quick to pooh-pooh the Fed's citation of "evidence of abating inflationary pressures" and its reason for lowering the discount rate. Yet, in the same column he stumbles through an explanation of why gold has dropped throughout the crisis. He is much better in "Brigitte Bardot, Freddie Krueger and Gold," 4-15, designating himself as one of the few not to believe that gold is on the verge of skyrocketing: "Gold bugs are more than twice as dense and 100 times as ornery as silver investors. . .No matter how many times they get buried in the market, they keep coming back, like Freddie Krueger." To drive home the point, he talks with Merrill Lynch metals analyst Ted Arnold who counsels, "The gold market is still called the gold market. But it has totally changed and will not return to its former self." His premise is persuasive in "No Base Forming in Metals," 5-20, but he is not as discerning on the reasons behind sluggish prices, as usual, relying too heavily on a conventional source. He is more creative in "Everything But the Facts," 7-22, convincing us that linerboard is "an extremely reliable economic barometer," then clearing up news reports that the Soviet Union has just 374 tons of gold reserves, saying the gold market barely reacted because this isn't news at all. His analysis is terrific in "Trading Points," 8-5, uncovering why the government's GNP numbers for the 2nd quarter are malarkey because they are based on dubious assumptions that create a mirage of slight growth, when in fact more realistic deductions would probably have indicated negative growth.

Lochhead, Carolyn. *Insight.* (★ ★ ½)
New York. A knowledgeable reporter and lucid writer, Lochhead views the nation's problems through a populist conservative lens. She was laid off with others in September due to tough times at the publication, but has signed on at the D.C. bureau of the *San Francisco Chronicle*. Her "Luxury Tax Gives Builders of Yachts a Sinking Feeling," 2-11, assesses the damage the luxury tax increase has had on the yacht industry. She throws around a lot of statistics in "How Tax Increases, Runaway Spending Fuel Budget Deficit," 2-25, but bases her argument on overgeneralizations like "Because taxes rise as incomes rise, a mere freeze in government spending would rapidly erase the deficit." She is much more in-depth in "Skiing Safety Bill Creates a Storm," 3-11, chronicling how the parents of a young New Jersey girl killed while skiing have spearheaded a proposed bill in the N.J. state legislature to mandate safety measures

on ski slopes. She presents both sides of the story, but seems weighted against the bill: "In essence, the bill addresses a freak accident with sweeping legislation that would affect all New Jersey skiers and ski areas." In " 'Return' of Native Americans Challenges Racial Definition," 4-22, she questions recent census findings in which more respondents are identifying themselves as American Indian, leading Lochhead to conclude that many of the respondents may be hoping to qualify "for special benefits under affirmative action programs." With a barrage of statistics and findings for her cover story on infant mortality, "Cradle to Grave," 5-6, she credibly argues that the problem isn't as severe as some suggest and that illegitimacy, not poverty, is really the crux of this problem. Her other cover story, "Fruit Fight," 7-29, fully examines how the cartel which controls the California fruit industry is coming under increased attack from would-be independent growers. Portraying NYC as the Freddy Krueger of cities in her terrific "Big Apple Takes Bite From Its Own Future," 9-16, a 10 Best nomination, she conjures up images of businesses and private citizens under siege from muggers, municipal bureaucrats, and unions. "Many observers now seem to agree that structural reform of the way city government operates is desperately needed."

Lohr, Steve. *The New York Times.* (★ ★ ½)
Impressively bounding onto the pages of "Business Day" this year, after several years in London, Lohr dazzled us with dependable high-quality explorations and profiles in the turbulent banking sector. His Sunday business piece, "Banking's Real Estate Miseries," 1-13, opens with an arresting lead and continues with a thorough follow-through on the foundations of the bank crisis: "Imagine every office building in Manhattan empty, a commercial ghost town. Now double it. That's how much vacant office space — 500 million square feet — there is in the United States today. Behind much of that empty office space stands the nation's banking system." His contribution to the *NYT*'s front-page series, "Banks Under Stress," "One Bank's Experience of Failure: U.S. Presence Soothes the Fearful," 2-18, was uncharacteristically routine, reporting on Bank of New England's failure and how quickly panic ends when the FDIC steps in. On the other hand, he masterfully handles "Site for Toxic-Waste Cave Stirs Texas Political Fight," 5-6, an excellent report on a major policy question now unfolding — toxic-waste disposal. Lohr gives us a substantial overview of the issue while taking us through the specifics of the situation in Texas. He has an appropriately wide scope for "Recasting the Big Banks," 7-17, an impressive news analysis of the basis for the merger of Chemical Bank and Manufacturers Hanover which reflectively weighs the perception by some that a wave of major bank mergers can provide a panacea for the ailing banking sector. Taking us to the "tax and regulatory haven" of the Cayman Islands, "Offshore Banking's Umbrella Shields More Than B.C.C.I.," 8-11, he explains why it was apparently a popular place for the "financial shenanigans" connected with the "litany of alleged transgressions" of BCCI. At the same time, he constructs a thoughtful and balanced anecdote of the lax regulation of international banking. And although there's nothing really new in "At the End of a Twisted Trail, Piggy Bank for a Favored Few," 8-12, Lohr is able to make clear to the lay reader how BCCI was able to beat the system for so long.

Loomis, Carol J. *Fortune.* (★ ★ ½)
Board of editors. The dean of distaff business writers in the U.S., Loomis remains ever curious about the comings and goings of corporate America. Always knowledgeable and robust in her features, she successfully reined in most of the "heavy-handed commentary" we criticized last year. This year she focused her inquisitive mind and estimable skills on evaluating rather than bashing the U.S.'s most powerful companies. The result was some profoundly insightful business journalism. In "Citicorp's World of Troubles," 1-14, she turns a critical eye on the financially-troubled bank, warning that although Citicorp may be too big to fail, it "is not too big to flounder." Uncharacteristically, she gushes with praise in "State Farm Is Off the Charts," 4-8, calling the successful insurer "the Fort Knox of the insurance business" and "the industry's most successful corporation — indeed, one of the nation's great businesses." But, to be fair, she does present plenty of evidence to back up her admiration. She slips back into her prosecutorial mode

and tells only one side of the story in "What Fred Carr's Fall Means to You," 5-6, slamming Carr with flippant remarks about his downfall which she says occurred "when the world soured suddenly for his pal Michael Milken." On the other hand, she does a magnificent job of dissecting the problems leading to IBM's earnings dive in her 10 Best selection for Business/Financial Reporting, "Can John Akers Save IBM?" 7-15. Supported by a cache of revealing details, she is critical where appropriate and appreciative where proper. This professionally-handled piece is a model of business journalism. "Indeed, the biggest indictment of Akers's management would seem to be that he has failed to fix IBM's marketing problems. He came from the world of sales. Surely he should have managed to whip it into shape. He is still trying. Under way is yet one more revamping of U.S. marketing. . ." Following-up on her 1-14 piece, she comes down hard on Citicorp in "How Does Reed Hang on at Citi?" 11-18, one of the toughest indictments we've seen yet of the banks woes. In her scathingly funny blast at securities industry cold call sales pitches, "Have You Been Cold-Called?" 12-16, she draws out brokers who comment candidly, "Basically it's a white-collar sweat shop."

Lowenstein, Roger. *The Wall Street Journal.* (★ ★ ★)
New York, "Heard on the Street" columnist. Lowenstein is a vital source of uncommon information for stock market players. This year, though, he occasionally revealed a worrisome tendency to play the closet technician. Preoccupied with raw data, he sometimes ignored other equally potent forces shaping the value of stocks. We thought his "Citicorp Travels Around World Seeking Capital," 1-29, should have been P. 1 as he carefully reports that the nation's biggest banking company needs $4-5 billion in capital and is finding it a tough sell on $1.5 billion of convertible preferred. Playing the contrarian on bank stocks in "One Tiny Bank's Story Tells Why Stocks of Big Ones Face Tough Turnaround. . ." 1-17, he shows how even well-run banks like Cullen/Frost Bankers of Texas are surviving, not prospering. He poses a crucial question for those weighing a move back into bank stocks: "How many modern bankers would proclaim, as [Tom Frost, the chairman of Cullen/Frost] does, that the confidence of depositors matters more than that of shareholders?" We found plenty of meaty financial thoughts to chew on in "Rebuilding Kuwait: Rates Facing Pressure," 2-28. He takes a useful look at the tide-swimmers in the defense industry in "As Street Rallies Around the Defense Stocks, Analyst Shoots Down Long-Term Prospects," 3-28. Once again, the closet technician in "Investors in Bank Stocks, Flush From Rally, Confront Unpleasant Fact of Earnings Season," 4-10, he comes up with much less sophisticated analysis than we're used to. But he is solid on the complexities of the junk market in his upbeat "Banana 'Junk': Investors Doubt They'll Slip Up," 5-24, showing why Chiquita's new issue resembles the more conservative junk issues of the early 1980s. We found more technical mumbo jumbo in "Goldman Study of Stocks' Rise in '80s Poses a Big Riddle," 6-6, a quirky report on Barrie Wigmore's "X" factor, the intangible factor which Wigmore says boosted 38% of the S&P during the 1980s. This was a rare opportunity to seriously examine what shaped the 1980's stock surge, but instead, Lowenstein lets Wigmore expand on foolish ideas such as "This 'X' factor. . .may be attributable to changing social attitudes, such as a willingness to assume more risk." His colorful opening for "Tenneco Is in Dividend Pickle Analyst Says, Not Relishing Mustard on His Computer," 7-31, in which an analyst will eat his computer if Tenneco doesn't cut its dividend this quarter leads into a valuable bull-and-bear case study of Tenneco. Rather than advancing unsolid conclusions in "Real Estate Slump Takes Heavy Toll on Trizec, but Some Blame Subsidiary for Much of Its Ills," 9-23, he asks the experts all the pertinent questions about the health of Trizec, one of the largest publicly traded real estate concerns in North America, and produces an extremely useful analysis.

Maggs, John. *The Journal of Commerce.* (★ ★)
International Economics. As Keith Rockwell's replacement, Maggs was handed a respectable pair of shoes to fill, but he has quickly proven himself more than capable, confidently picking up the trade beat with sharp, concise reports. He fully updates us on tensions at the stalled GATT negotiations in "French Back EC Farm Reform; New Plan Seen Months Away," 1-16, and skillfully summarizes a satisfying interview with the undersecretary for economic affairs on

GATT negotiations, Richard McCormack, in "Slow Pace of Uruguay Round Could Further Protectionism," 2-20. In "GATT Breakthrough a Political Plus," 2-25, he discerns that an agreement "pledging 'specific binding commitments' to negotiate reductions in each of the three types of farm trade protection," will positively impact the U.S. fast-track vote. With the press focusing on Japan's non-role in the Gulf, Maggs reveals other divisive issues in "Bush Says US-Japan Trade Friction Remains a Major Divisive Issue," 3-25: "President Bush told a senior Japanese official that congressional frustration with Japan has more to do with its restrictive trade policies than with its role in the Persian Gulf war." He lands two important interviews with Mexican President Carlos Salinas de Gortari, "Mexico Aims to Break Unions' Hold on Port," 5-28, and "Salinas Says Free Trade May Be Key to Solving Some of Mexico's Problems," 5-29. The second is the most far-reaching, making crystal-clear Salinas's pro-growth aspirations and ambitions for the free-trade agreement. He is up to par on the administration's latest blink on renewal of China's trade status in "Hills Studies Plan Linking China MFN to Membership in GATT for Taiwan," 6-17. In "Gephardt Is Wary of Bush Strategy in Mexico Talks," 8-6, he walks us through House Majority Leader Richard Gephardt's concerns about Mexican free trade, giving a solid feel for the Democrat's position following fast track approval. He clarifies the uproar over Canada's termination of its agreement with the U.S. on softwood lumber trade in "Canada Breaks Pact With US on Lumber Tax," 9-4: "Canada claims that increases in 'stumpage fees' and other charges by provincial governments have reduced the amount of federal tax collections by 90% and only 5% of Canadian lumber exports are still covered by the pact."

Mahar, Maggie. *Barron's.* (★ ★ ★ ½)
Remarkably well-informed on a wide array of subjects, Mahar files yet another striking portfolio of brisk and discerning reports. Her riveting investigation of the Pan Am 103 bombing, "Unwitting Accomplices?" 12-17-90, brings to light startling new evidence that CIA bargaining for the hostages may have protected a drug route used to bomb the flight. In "What Price War?" 1-21, she compiles extensive raw cost estimates for the Gulf War, but with so many variables this early, we fail to see the point. In one of the most discerning analyses of the post-war oil scene, "Crude Prophecy," 2-25, she expertly weighs the political and economic considerations likely to shape the oil producers' decisions: "Overlooked by the cheap-oil crowd on Wall Street is that the Saudis lack the production capacity to keep pumping oil at expanded war-time levels." "Taken for a Ride?" 4-15, is the absorbing tale of how Mitsubishi bought the all-American, family-owned Value Rent-A-Car, and got tangled up in a messy and costly legal battle. Typically ahead of the margin, Mahar provides a great service with "An Upward Turn South of the Border," 5-13, giving an upbeat and savvy outlook on the turning of the corner in Latin America. On the BCCI scandal, her thorough and probing "Unnatural Reserve," 5-20, quoted Sidney Bailey, commissioner of financial institutions of Virginia, who many years ago tried to deny an application by Arab investors who wanted to acquire Financial General Bankshares of Washington which later became First American Bankshares, Inc.: "What's needed is not more law. There were laws. They just weren't observed. The law did require the Fed's approval of this acquisition. And they granted it — over my objections." Although she could have trimmed down her lengthy profile of Disney, "No Mickey Mouse Company," 6-24, she makes a convincing argument to Wall Street that Disney still has long-term growth prospects overseas. Post Soviet coup, she offers outstanding insights into the volatile Soviet political economy in "Death of an Empire," 9-16, filing a candid and jolting three-hour interview with Soviet economist Vladimir Popov who believes hyperinflation and nationalism are leading the country toward another coup.

Markoff, John. *The New York Times.* (★ ★ ½)
Computers. A vivid, well-apprised writer, Markoff ferrets out unique topics and issues from the outer bounds of the computing world, with a special flare for supercomputers. He wows us with "A Fresh Eye on the Environment," 1-31, a fascinating look at how the world's fastest supercomputers are being used as environmental tools because they "can accurately simulate the complex chemical interactions in the atmosphere." His state of the art "An Aging Dancer Fights to Keep Up," 2-10, takes a compelling look at the magnitude of the race to develop the next

generation of computers. Markoff observes that the ever-increasing competition has Silicon Valley "obsessed. . .with checking its pulse." Fascinating with "Using Computer Engineering to Mimic the Movement of a Bow," 2-17, he details attempts to create computer-based technologies with "the ability to capture musical information far more subtle than the sound of a tone." He chronicles rough times at Big Blue in "I.B.M. Faces a Harsher World in 90's," 3-21, substantially analyzing what ails the computer giant: "I.B.M. . .finds itself surrounded by hundreds of smaller, quicker rivals. Unable to stand up to I.B.M.'s firepower, these companies seek to change the rules of engagement to a new way of computing known as open systems. . .The shift to open systems challenges the heart of I.B.M.'s business. . ." For the unveiling of Convex Computer Corp.'s first supercomputer, Markoff pens " 'Micros' Vs. Supercomputers," 5-6, a well-informed look at why the big supercomputing boys are "worried by 'killer micros' — compact, extremely fast work stations that sell for less than $100,000," and may cause an industry shakeout. Updating us on the hottest computer story of the year in "I.B.M.'s Chief Criticizes Staff Again," 6-19, he fails to step back for the long view on Big Blues's mounting problems. He takes an engaging look at a group of programmers' utopian dream gone wrong in "Locking the Doors in the Electronic Global Village," 7-28. The dwindling quantity of phone numbers is the subject of "As Telephones Multiply, Dialing Will Take Longer," 8-18, an informative survey of how various possible solutions would affect phone users.

McCarthy, Michael J. *The Wall Street Journal.* (★ ★ ½)
Marketing. While McCarthy spent most of last year focused on coverage of Coca-Cola, this year he broadened his horizons with an engaging potpourri of topics crafted into well-rounded articles. He started out the year a little slow with "TV Coverage Heightens Stress of War by Keeping Viewers in Constant Touch," 1-24, a pseudo-psychoanalysis that goes on too long about people who get addicted to Gulf War news. And his "Frito-Lay Bets Big With Multigrain Chips," 2-28, reads like an embellished press release with only a small reference to the Center for Science in the Public Interest's observation that Frito-Lay's "healthful" Sun Chip products "are a fairly fatty food." He's much better in "Marketers Zero In on Their Customers," 3-18, showcasing his uncanny antenna for trends and giving us an insightful look at the next wave in sales — store-specific marketing. McCarthy's marketing expertise also shines through in "Keeping Careful Score of Sports Tie-Ins," 4-24, a sharp, in-depth piece which focuses on the swell of company sponsorship of sports: "Since 1986, the number of companies sponsoring events has doubled. . ." His "Pressure Grows at Coke as Ads Go Flat," 8-2, is a zippy little piece on how Coca-Cola's advertising has lost momentum while Pepsi has been creating memorable television spots like the one with Ray Charles crooning, "You've Got the Right One Baby, Uh-huh" — currently the most popular ad in the nation, according to one survey. He is savvy on the reasons behind PepsiCo Inc.'s price-cutter Taco Bell's latest move to discount breakfast items in "Taco Bell Plans Bargain Menu for Breakfast," 10-22: "Attacking the breakfast market is also part of a broader strategy of protecting Taco Bell's core business, Mr. [John] Martin [president of Taco Bell] says. Some competitors, to subsidize discounts on lunch and dinner items, such as hamburgers, have charged higher prices on breakfast items, he says."

McCartney, Robert. *The Washington Post.* (★ ½)
New York. Now two years on the beat, McCartney is starting to find his footing on Wall Street. With increasing confidence and an expanding network of sources, we saw bursts of potential, but he is still not as consistently discerning as we'd like. Following the seizure of Greater Providence Deposit Corp., he captures the flavor of politics and finance in Rhode Island in "Early Warnings of Trouble in Rhode Island," 1-6. His sweeping overview of the bull market, "Confidence Signals Rally May Continue," 3-3, is well-sourced and touches on most of the forces boosting the markets momentum, although he failed to explore how the tax environment may come into play. We get a little of this and a little of that in "Turning a Private Eye on Saddam Hussein," 3-26, a superficial profile of Wall Street private detective Jules Kroll, hired by the Kuwaitis to track down Saddam's money trail. In a lucid "Overseas Profits Are Ailing," 4-6, he adeptly handles the complex effect the dollar's strength and slower overseas sales are having

on U.S.-based multinationals' profits. He is on to an important trend in "The Rush to Stock Up on Capital," 5-16, noting the fast pace at which companies are issuing new stock. But he only hints at the reasons why, limiting the richness of his analysis. He judiciously profiles chairman John Reed in "Citicorp's 'Whiz Kid' Comes to a Sadder, Wiser Age," *Weekly* 6/24-30, sturdily assessing Reed and Citicorp's past mistakes and crucial retrenchment plans, but failing to examine possible growth strategies in a drastically changed banking environment. In "The Might of the Living Buyout Victims," *Weekly* 8/26-9/1, he tracks investors hard hit by LBO-generated bankruptcies who are hitting back in courts, and winning favorable settlements. But perhaps the most important question, who should be culpable for the decisions that led to the ill-suited LBOs — CEOs, boards of directors or investment bankers — is left unexplored.

McDowell, Edwin. *The New York Times.* (★ ★ ½)
More "heads-up" coverage of the high speed publishing industry from the talented McDowell, who keeps us abreast of publishing's swift mergers, fascinating personalities and unique quirks. He competently catalogues the facts in "Harcourt Accepts Bid From General Cinema," 1-25, noting that Harcourt Brace Jovanovich is willingly being swallowed up by the Hollywood giant because few jobs will be lost in the move. But he bypasses powerful pressures coming to bear in a beleaguered publishing industry. His front page "A Spy Novel's Boosters, It Seems, Aren't," 4-13, reconstructs the unsettling tale of how an author allegedly fabricated endorsements from John Le Carre and Joseph Wambaugh in order to sign an expensive book contract. McDowell has done his legwork, but reaches no conclusions on the alleged hoax. His "British Publisher Enters the U.S. Foregoing Its Past Noms de Plume," 5-6, is a substantial primer on London publishing company Dorling Kindersly Ltd.'s efforts to penetrate the U.S. market. Showcasing his publishing acumen, he takes on a dynamic ride through the heart of the industry in "Searching for Gems in the Slush Pile," 6-17, a great story about day-to-day business with all the accuracy and pizzazz we expect from McDowell. He takes a quick look at the dull impact the sinking of a Greek cruise ship off South Africa has had on the cruise industry in "Impact on Cruise Industry of Liner's Sinking Is Small," 8-7, reporting that travel agents hope the disaster, which is under investigation, was an accident and not an act of terrorism which traditionally causes mass cancellations. His "New Vistas for Tourism's Mr. Italy," 10-29, is an enjoyable visit with Mario Perillo whose Perillo Tours has organized excursions to Italy for decades, but has also diversified to keep up with current traveling trends.

McGough, Robert. *FW.* (★ ★ ½)
Senior editor. This dynamic, well-rounded reporter has wowed us all year with his highly-perceptive reporting, laudable interview skills, and graceful, articulate writing-style. His most outstanding work is on the airline industry. In "Don't Count Chickens," 1-8, he homes in early on the "excruciating tension" developing between the British Government and competing U.S. airlines over United Airlines' deal to buy Pan Am's routes to London's Heathrow Airport. After showing why British negotiators are "Caught between a rock and a hard place," McGough bounces through all the maybes of a deal that will impact the shaky U.S. airline industry. He characterizes "LBO funds turned equity recappers" as a devilish pursuit in "Faust in the Boardroom," 3-5, scrutinizing the recapitalizations being orchestrated by "former LBO-meisters" who have become "born-again value investors." His 10-Best selection for Business/Financial Reporting, "Empires of the Sky," cover 5-14, was one of the best airline pieces of the year. This multidimensional exploration of the international airline industry's new order covers everything from domestic deregulation, to global liberalization, to protectionism, to overcrowded airports, to how to get flambe on a Swiss Air flight leaving Islamabad. Packed with authoritative quotes. He also impresses with "Yankee Clipper," 6-11, a rich profile of CEO James F. Orr, III, and UNUM, "his trendsetting $9.8 billion-in-assets Portland, Me.-based insurance company" which is becoming one of the most profitable in the insurance industry through "demutualization." In "Changing Course," cover 7-23, he takes us on a very vivid visit with Bob Crandall, CEO of American Airlines, who is about to redirect his company for a second time in a decade. McGough focuses on Crandall's "combative" style of management, not a new

topic, but he does it with such an amazing eye for detail that we discover new aspects of Crandall the manager. His "The Texas Cannonball," 8-6, was another sparkling and well-constructed business profile, this time of Bill Agee, CEO of the construction firm Morrison Knudsen, which is attempting to raise money to build a Texas version of France's superfast TGV trains.

McNamee, Mike. *Business Week.* (★ ★ ½)
Washington. Covering the Federal Reserve in a critical year, McNamee compressed a wide range of facts into crisp, compact studies and typically struck an impressive balance of political and economic analysis. Far from his best work, "The New Face of Recession," with Karen Pennar 12-24-90, was generally accurate on the basics, but very narrow minded on the origins of the recession, which is blamed squarely on the Fed without consideration of other potent forces. He's better in "The Fed May Be Seeing Things," 2-4, skeptical of Chairman Greenspan's "leaning against the winds of pessimism" on the economy, and on target with analysis of why a relaxed monetary policy isn't stimulating the economy. His "Rescue the FDIC — The Tackle Bank Reform," commentary 2-18, is a well thought out critique of the Treasury's bank overhaul proposal. McNamee faults the authors of the plan for fixating on the horizon and missing craters at their feet. His "The Treasury Is Whipping Up a Potion for the Banks," 3-4, is a thorough examination of a proposed package of regulatory and accounting changes designed to get banks to step up their lending. He makes a nice call in advance of the G-7 meeting with "Nick Brady's Lonesome Call: Lower Interest Rates," with Blanca Riemer and John Templeman 5-6: "As the world's most powerful economic club, the G-7 ought to be wrestling with such serious concerns as the big capital crunch. But Brady's solution — print more money — matches neither the world economy's current needs nor its long-term demand for capital. The G-7 communique will have to find a polite way to tell him so." Joined by Catherine Yang for "Reform, or a Crackdown on Banking," 7-15, he intelligently assesses the emerging banking bill, noting that "buried in the measure are harsh proposals that would. . .impose stiff constraints on banking regulators and crack down, probably too soon, on banks that fall on hard times." The Bank of America is offered as one successful institution that might not be around if tougher regulations had been in place at the time of its crisis in the mid-'80s. "Just When Bank Reform Seemed Almost in the Bag," 9-9, is an incisive review of why momentum for banking reform is slowing: "some banking lobbyists think that the legislation now taking shape may be worse than the status quo. Says one reform advocate: 'Kill it before it multiplies.' "

Mitchell, Constance. *The Wall Street Journal.* (★ ★ ½)
New York, credit markets. With bond investors barraged with perplexing economic signals this year, Mitchell shied from outright speculation, and opted instead to shower her readers with a wide variety of opinions on expected yields. But we'd still like to see her dig deeper into the political and economic forces moving the credit markets. In "Bond Firms Seek Tougher War Clauses," 1-15, she does a fine job of clarifying the reasons for a request by underwriters to "cancel the sale of corporate or municipal bonds if hostilities here or abroad jolt the financial markets." Capturing the confusion enveloping the bond markets in "Bond Prices Seen Falling In Recovery," 3-11, she observes that, for the most part, big bond investors are ignoring bearish economic news and positioning themselves for a more inflationary environment. She alerts bond investors to a potentially market jarring move in "U.S. Considers Call of Treasuries to Cut Its Costs," 4-10, and strikes gold with a pithy " 'Real' Bond Yields Are at Lowest Level in a Decade," 5-28, gathering perceptive speculation on the direction of bond yields. Her "Companies Rush to Sell New Bonds," 6-24, is a clear, competent analysis of the "frenzied pace of new corporate bond issuance." And once again pondering to buy or not to buy in "What's the Yield-Curve Bond Message?" 6-3, she gathers a nice balance of observations on the meaning of the difference between the yields of long-and short-term bonds which are hitting the steepest curve since October 1985, but she never gets to the heart of the issue. In "Bonds Tied to Stocks Top Others," 7-1, she observes that the outstanding performance of junk bonds in the first two quarters of 1991 is "challenging some long-held theories about how bonds should perform in a recession." But her analysis of why is shallow. She falls back on that old two-dimensional thinking that growth always means inflation in "Long Rally in Bonds Rewards Investors But Can It Go On?" leder 10-22.

Moberg, David. *In These Times.* (★ ★ ½)
Senior editor. Like the magazine he works for, Moberg makes no attempt to be objective, but the viewpoints from his leftist landscape are consistently fresh and provocative. He impresses with "Working Without a Net," 1-23/29, rationally assessing the dearth of unemployment coverage available. Although he relies heavily on U. of Chicago's Rashid Khalidi in "Mideast Management When the War Is Over," 1-30/2-5, he pulls together scholar's thinking well, and persuades that goals are lacking for post-Saddam Iraq. His best work of the year, "Can Public Rescue the Infrastructure in a Tale of Three Deficits?" 2-13/19, is a nearly supply-side analysis of the third deficit of public investment in the infrastructure. He even mentions the "increasingly important 'human capital' of skills and knowledge" before binding himself up in the econometric models of David Alan Aschauer and Alicia Munnell. While he scores many political points in "Vietnam Syndrome Only in Remission," 3-20/26, he falls victim to the perception of the U.S. as war machine. He takes the standard labor line of losing jobs to cheap Mexican wages in "Free Trade No Cure for U.S.-Mexico Ills," 4-17/23, but manages to construct a sturdy argument for slow and thorough deliberation of the issues. His three-part study of education begins with "Choice No Easy Remedy for American School Ills," 5-15/21, a sensitive, probing piece on the issue of choice, based in large part on the work of John Chubb and Terry Moe of Brookings and the case for free-market schooling. The second piece, "For Better Education, It's a Choice Combination," 5-22/28, presents the downside of choice, but offers no real alternatives. And finally in "Chicago School Reform Battles the Bureaucracy," 5-29/6-11, he tells Chicago's success stories, but fails to explain how to tailor these ideas for other cities. Eruditely assessing the Senate Democrats' bill in "A Canadian Remedy for Health-Care Ills in the U.S.," 6-26/7-9, he observes: "While the bill would expand protection for the uninsured, it would do little to hold down costs and could worsen health coverage for some currently insured workers." But his praise of the Canadian system comes too quick and overlooks the problems it would face in the U.S. In "Teamsters Dabble in Democracy," 7-10/23, he is atmospheric on the Teamsters for a Democratic Union meeting in Disney World, giving a birds-eye view of the changes embracing the unions. But his look into the problems of chlorine and related chemicals, "Chlorine Compounds: Unsafe for Any Need?" 8-7/20, is too thickly written to be truly informative.

Mongelluzzo, Bill. *The Journal of Commerce.* (★ ★)
West coast editor. Succeeding Mark Magnier as West coast editor, Mongelluzzo brings more than a decade of experience in the area of shipping to his coverage of this booming center of trade. He is sharp in "New Rules on Customs Units at Least Six Months Away," 2-19, a compact briefer on "the somewhat controversial selection process" for centralized examination sites, privately operated warehouses designated by U.S. Customs for the inspection of cargo. In "Hanjin Swings Into Pendulum Service," 3-11, he skillfully explains the pros and cons of Hanjin Shipping Co.'s effective vessel utilization through a pendulum that uses Asia as its fulcrum to carry cargo westbound from North America, eastbound to Europe and then back again. He is one dimensional on the textile industry's opposition to fast track in "Textile Makers See 'Fast Track' Vulnerable to Weak Economy," 4-19, failing to explore the split developing in this traditionally protectionist coalition, a story being followed closely by others. More discerning in "US Textile Makers Plan Mexico 'Fast-Track' Fight," 4-16, he foregoes the ideological hooey and zeros in on more pragmatic union voices. Part of a special report on electronic data interchange (EDI), Mongelluzzo's excellent "E. Europe Anxious to Get Online," 6-18, reports on the crucial scramble there to develop automated customs services and brokerage industries. He throws out a few new details in "US-Mexico Free-Trade Agreement Seen Benefiting Maquiladora Industry," 6-25, but there's nothing especially fresh on the bigger free trade picture here. Tracking the disclosure that a Long Beach harbor commissioner had business dealings with port tenants, Mongelluzzo expertly examines conflict-of-interest regulations in "Port Probe Highlights Conflict-Code Debate," 7-10. He spreads hopeful news for the battered natural gas industry in "Clean Air Rules Cut Calif. Utilities' Oil Use," 7-16, reporting that environmental concerns have led the Los Angeles Department of Water and Power to announce the signing of long-term contracts that will "virtually take it out of the spot market for residual fuel oil." In his crisp, front-page report, "Ship Lines Sharpen Focus," 9-16, he reveals how ocean carriers are riding out the rough times through strategic marketing.

Morgenson, Gretchen. *Forbes.* (★ ★ ½)

Senior writer. Freed from the hardcore financial stories she covered last year, Morgenson is now showcasing her luminous writing style and intelligence, discerning the vigor and vulnerabilities of American companies and industries competing in the global marketplace. With Mattel's Barbie still very popular and profitable at the ripe old age of 31, Morgenson asks in "Barbie Does Budapest," 1-7, how does Mattel do it? "She comes in a wide range of prices, so that almost everyone can afford a Barbie. . .[and]. . .As the popular vision of what a girl should be changes, so does Barbie." With Mattel achieving "a stunning 95% penetration with the fashion doll among U.S. girls age 3 to 11," the company is planning to take Barbie global. Her "Is Efficiency Enough?" 3-18, is a perfectly well-rounded business profile of Colgate Chairman Reuben Mark who has been lauded for his transformation of Colgate from "sleepy and inefficient to lean and very profitable." Morgenson's thorough examination of the company's strengths and weaknesses reveals that Mark does not place much credence in growth, especially domestic growth: "This is an efficient company, to be sure, but efficiency is only part of the game; growth is the other part. With 13 years to go until retirement, Mark has time to put some growth into the company. Unless he does, investors may soon be wondering if Colgate is really worth 16 times earnings." In "The Doctors and the Dealmakers," 4-15, she takes a probing look at doctors who have a piece of the profits in businesses they refer their patients to. With flare, she whisks us through a detailed " 'Where Can I Buy Some?' " 6-24, giving us all the whys and hows on Maybelline's latest line for dark colored skin, an untapped market which made the company an outstanding $15 million in one year. She expertly delineates a trend that will affect everyone from grocery shoppers to consumer goods packagers and their shareholders in "The Trend Is Not Their Friend," cover 9-16: slowly but surely lower priced supermarket house brands are eating away at brand name profits, indicating consolidation lies ahead. "It will not take a stampede of shoppers away from name brands to house brands to cause a crimp in profit growth. . .Even a modest shift to house brands, threatening all-important volume, will cause the makers of branded goods to moderate their price increases."

Mufson, Steven. *The Washington Post.* (★ ★)

Economics. Refreshingly, Mufson doesn't play the ideological games that taint much press coverage of the economy. His work is defined by balance, although we'd like to see him sink his teeth into meatier economic assessments. In "South Africa 1990," America and the World 1990/91, he takes a multidimensional look into the past, present and future of this troubled country. He presciently predicts one of the biggest deficits in history in "$50 Billion Added to Deficit Forecast," 1-8, but his reasoning why is murky. Formulaic in "Sweeping Bank-Reform Plan Unveiled," 2-6, he throws together the requisite quotes on the proposal's future in Congress, but doesn't dig beneath the surface. Much better in "Getting Ready For a World of Difference," 3-8, he pens a full-bodied profile of Lewis Thompson Preston, Bush's nominee for president of the World Bank. In "Are Some Banks Really Too Big to Fail?" 3-24, he ponders responses to this contentious question, meticulously balancing arguments from all sides of the issue. He is brief, perceptive and balanced on the administration's not so subtle push for lower global interest rates in "U.S. at Odds With Other Powers on Rates," 4-26. And, as far as it goes, "IMF Shift to Eastern Europe Stirs Discontent in Third World," 4-28, is strong on the IMF's changing priorities. But we wonder why he didn't investigate the free-market policies being embraced by a growing number of Third World countries. In "G-7, IMF Depend on the World Bank," 5-1, Mufson reports that veteran G-7 watchers say the lack of solid news indicates a serious tiff may have occurred. His "The Democrats' Economic Heretic," 5-19, vividly profiles Robert Shapiro of the Progressive Policy Institute, a man "turning Democratic policies inside out to fashion an alternative economic platform." He strikes a fine balance of perspectives on the "Grand Bargain" plan in "From Harvard, an Agenda for Soviets," 6-14, an in-depth look at the authors of this controversial plan. His update on the budget director, "Dick Darman: Missing, But Still Very Much in Action," *Weekly* 7-15/21, reports that despite jokes that the director of OMB is MIA, Darman is quietly working on budget policy and his future. He is clear and complete on the shifting U.S.-Philippine political relationship in "Philippines Renegotiates $5 Billion in Debt With Banks," 9-4.

Murray, Alan. *The Wall Street Journal.* (★)
Washington, chief economics reporter. Murray is undoubtedly a brilliant political observer, but his tendency to use news reports to sell his own economic blueprint is an egregious abuse of his journalistic responsibility. In "Money Supply Pushed Fed to Lower Interest Rates," 1-10, Murray alerts that the Fed is keeping a close eye on M2. But he is basic and inconclusive in "One War Casualty — The U.S. Economy — Could Improve Soon," leder 2-27. In April, Murray made a mountain out of a mole hill, exaggerating dissension at the Fed. Between the lines, we read an agenda for easier money. "Dispute Flares Up at Fed Over Greenspan's Authority," 4-4, stuck basically to the facts, but "Democracy Comes to the Central Bank, Curbing Chief's Power," leder 4-5, was hyperbolic, declaring that a new assertiveness among the district governors damaged the economy in October '90: "Instead of combating the recession, the Fed's lack of action exacerbated it." He sees more discord in "Reserve Presidents Attack Plan to Allow FDIC to Borrow $25 Billion From Fed," 4-9. But he rescinds slightly in "Fed Fight Could Work to Delay Cut in Rates," 4-15, conceding that "The recent flare-up between the presidents and Mr. Greenspan concerned procedure, not policy." He irresponsibly exaggerates in "Global Recession: Too Close for Comfort," 4-29, yet another blatant call to print money. Better but late in "Obstacles to Recovery: States' Fiscal Squeeze," 6-17, Murray recognizes that collectively the increase in taxes at the state and city level will equal last year's federal tax hike, straining budgets and hindering the recovery. The usual Murray bias toward Keynesian austerity shines throughout "Last Year's Budget Pact Gains New Admirers For Curbing Spending in Economic Downturn," 7-3. But we're impressed that he gets Rep. Newt Gingrich who fought the budget package in '90 to say: "I've told them at the White House, I think they deserve more credit than I thought last year." In honor of Greenspan's reappointment, Murray chides the Fed chairman for his tight monetary policy in "Greenspan's Retention Emboldens Fed Hawks to Keep Money Tight," leder 7-11. He chooses a great topic for "Fed Banks' Presidents Hold Private Positions But Major Public Role," leder 8-1, on the inner workings of the Fed. Unfortunately, he turns this into another harangue against anti-inflation hawks. In "West, Doing a Partial About-Face, Wants Soviets to Retain Some Central Control of the Economy," 9-12, he takes a perceptive, well-sourced look at the U.S.'s contradictory messages to the Soviets. He views the tax cut proposals swirling around Washington as "snake oil" in "Tax Cuts the Answer? What's the Question?" 10-28, a muddled evaluation that asks all the wrong questions, and refuses to query why the deficit has ballooned since the 1990 budget deal went into effect.

Nasar, Sylvia. *The New York Times.* (★ ★)
Switching from *U.S.News & World Report,* Nasar quickly landed many of the premier economic stories at "Business Day." We've seen steadily more discerning reports throughout the year, and look for major political/economic analyses from her as she settles into the position. But she must still work harder to break away from her economic preconceptions. Her contribution to "Banks Under Stress," "The Risks and the Benefits of Letting Sick Banks Die," 2-20, was one of the most useful in the series, carefully and thoroughly exploring both sides of the banking debate. Although her historical analysis is a bit loose in "An Exception to the Rule of War: Inflation Threat Is Receding," 3-10, never mentioning the gold standard or greenback era, Nasar does presents a useful P. 1 exercise, tying a low inflation threat to tight monetary policy over the past four years. We're led to believe that "Boom in Manufactured Exports Provides Hope for U.S. Economy," 4-21, will be a sweeping overview of U.S. competitiveness in the global marketplace, but Nasar only goes halfway, failing to fully examine the impact a roller-coaster dollar is having on strategic planning. Her "Deflating the Post-Gulf Balloon," 5-29, is a quick, sobering assessment of flagging consumer confidence which had skyrocketed after the war, but is settling into a realistic range now that the not-so-optimistic facts are hitting their pocketbooks again. Nasar misses a rare opportunity to examine monetary policy in "The New Intellectuals at the Fed," 6-9, giving us neat, handy profiles of the Fed's most influential players, but failing to explore their responses to crucial policy questions. Much better in "For Fed, a New Set of Tea Leaves," 7-5, she alerts us to a new indicator being watched by Fed Governor David W. Mullins, which "uses the prices of Treasury bond options to measure investor uncertainty. . ." We'd have

liked more specific examples in her P. 1 "Third World Embracing Reforms to Encourage Economic Growth," 7-8, nonetheless, this is an uplifting overview of the pragmatism sweeping the Third World. Her "The Fed's Worry Over Money," 8-9, was the first solid explanation of M-2 as a useless monetary indicator we'd seen, but in "Rate-Cut Tonic: Good, Not Great," 9-18, she oversimplified easing's effect on the economy.

Nomani, Asra Q. *The Wall Street Journal.* (★ ★ ½)
Airlines. A fine, intelligent reporter, Nomani sees beyond the turmoil of the industry's restructuring and captures the excitement of an overhaul bound to streamline airlines for a new era of global competition. Her "Pan Am Seeks Chapter 11 Shield, Gets UAL-Backed Cash Infusion," 1-9, is a tightly-written report that hits all the bases, keeping us thoroughly informed of Pan Am's financial woes. Joined by Laurie McGinley for "United, American Cleared for Landing at London's Heathrow as New Era Dawns," 3-12, she sketches a competent review of the far-reaching implications of a U.S.-Britain air landing rights agreement that is expected to usher in a new era of trans-Atlantic air service. In her hard hitting but well-documented profile of TWA under Carl Icahn, "Trying to Save TWA, Carl Icahn Is Facing Intractable Problems," leder 4-29, she gives credit where credit is due and criticism where criticism is due, and there's more criticism than credit: "It is questionable whether Mr. Icahn can keep TWA alive much longer." She deftly handles some highly complex financial material in "TWA Proposed to Buy Back All of Its Debt," 5-16, regarding TWA's proposal to purchase its $1.2 billion in outstanding debt for cash. Following up on the story that landed her a 10-Best last year, Nomani's "NWA, TWA Agree to Alter Pricing Actions," 6-21, reports that the two airlines have "agreed to alter certain controversial pricing practices in what may be a precursor of broader changes within the industry." But she points out the proposed settlement "still leaves several controversial pricing practices untouched." She showcases her expert grasp of the subject matter in "Airlines of the World Scramble for Routes in Industry Shakeout," co-written by Laurie McGinley, leder 7-23, a superbly detailed piece on airlines' dramatic battle for global market share: "Just one route can significantly affect the bottom line: Within a month of start-up in January, United's Chicago-Tokyo service became its most profitable, with annual revenue projected at $225.5 million." In "Plaskett Is Attracting Flak for His Piloting of Pan Am," 8-12, she delivers a muscular, but balanced, critique of Pan Am Corp.'s Thomas Plaskett reportedly "haughty" handling of talks with possible suitors. As usual, Nomani includes plenty of detail and a wide-array of quotes.

Norman, Peter. *Financial Times.* (★ ★ ★)
Economics. Astute on the political and ideological battles shaping global economic policy, Norman enriches our understanding of these complex issues. He sharply poses the various dire consequences for the global economy presented by the G-7's "doing it my way" policy on currency markets, warning in "G-7 Sing the Sinatra Doctrine," 12-31-90, that "the main industrial nations have all but abandoned the goal of currency stability. . ." He identifies the origins of Britain's recession a bit too narrowly in "Hard Year for All, Painful for Many," 1-22, focusing singularly on monetary policy, to the exclusion of critical fiscal activities regarding taxation. Norman reveals the fluid, uncertain background against which decisions regarding Britain's recession will be made in "Caution in the Face of Challenge," 2-18, outlining Chancellor of the Exchequer Norman Lamont's limited options. He delves into the impact of Lamont's specific tax changes which were "creditable fiscal reforms that should improve the working of the economy," but focuses on financial disciplines influencing the government's choice of economic policies in "Hard Path to Virtue," 3-23. Norman provided a very informative perspective on the European Bank for Reconstruction and Development and its role in helping Eastern and Central European countries move toward market economies with his interview with EBRD president Jacques Attali in "Visionary with a Global Goal," 4-15. In "High Ideals and Small Deeds of Cold War Victors," 5-2, he smartly surveys the beginnings of a new world economic order, finding "a remarkable consensus over the principles by which the world economy should be managed," but still clear-eyed about the many policy disagreements among the world's leading industrial powers. In a sober "Economics Notebook" preview of the G-7

Summit, "London Summit Headlines Mask Main Agenda," 7-8, he is pessimistic on the G-7 commitment to push for a successful conclusion of the Uruguay Round trade talks. Should, or could, the Bank of England have assumed greater responsibility for the operations of BCCI's U.K. operations? Norman astutely addressed the question in "Regulatory Opportunities Were Missed in UK," 8-10, providing a multidimensional and insightful assessment. And his "First Fruits of Age of Austerity," 9-16, is an important interview with Norman Lamont who broadly hints of economic growth reforms being planned.

Norris, Floyd. *The New York Times.* (★ ★ ★)
"Market Place" columnist. Still a reliable, offbeat financial writer whose Sunday column is a must read for its frequent insights. His "Listening For a Scary Word: Depression," 1-13, is a timely, intrepid column on the potential for a more serious economic decline than the consensus anticipates. In "Evaluating Rally of Small Stocks," 2-11, he marvels at Nasdaq's second-best performance in its 30-year history, but omits any examination of the coincidence of its rise and how it may be related to shifts in monetary or tax policy. He constructs a very complex but worthwhile comparison of the changes in stock dividend payouts and the S&P 500 in "On Dividends, Bad News Grows," 3-6. Overviewing economic developments in England, the U.S. and Germany in "Attacking a Scourge of Civilization," 3-24, he gives crisp pictures, but doesn't tie them together as he should. He is uncharacteristically shallow in "At Last, Dow Closes Above 3,000," 4-18, attributing the Dow's landmark close to the most conventional indicators, failing to relate political news that's surely a part of the puzzle. With the money supply falling despite Fed easing, he asks the right questions in "The Fed Eased, But Where's the Money," 5-12: "maybe in a few weeks the Fed will revise away the recent drop. But if that does not happen, new questions will be raised about whether monetary policy is enough to get the economy moving again." He thoughtfully laments the NYSE's attempts to regain global market share by relaxing disclosure rules during certain sessions in "Loss Leaders and Secrecy at the Big Board," 5-26: "The risk is that eventually there will no longer be a central information source that has accurate information on market prices." He also makes a convincing case for maintaining disclosure in "The S.E.C. and the Death of Disclosure," 6-9. For those following Salomon's infractions, Norris' lucid "Shadow on the Market," 8-18, is a useful primer on how Treasury auctions work, and his "Tidying Up After the Mess at Salomon," 8-18, sums up the situation in a nutshell: "It will help [Salomon] that there is no danger Wall Street will soon run out of government bonds to trade."

Nulty, Peter. *Fortune.* (★ ½)
Board of editors. We saw slight improvement in Nulty's work this year. He spends less time confirming what's in the dailies but still fails to utilize his knowledge and contacts to their fullest extent. The result is credible, but not cutting-edge, reporting. He takes us to the Arctic National Wildlife Refuge in "It's Time to Drill Alaska's Refuge," cover 1-28, to show us why oil exploration won't upset Alaska's unique environment. Clearly siding with the pro-drilling camp, he nonetheless makes a credible argument for Congress to look beyond the political noise surrounding the Exxon Valdez oil spill, and pragmatically assess the positive aspects of drilling in Alaska. He is basically on target in his speculation on future oil prices in "The Fate of Oil," 2-11, foreseeing a Saudi-directed OPEC emerging from the war and stabilizing prices by the end of the year. His "The National Business Hall of Fame," 3-11, is a little hokey, but overall this is an engaging people piece about the businessmen who "have changed the world around them for the better." We get another respectable assessment of oil prices from him in "Fiery Wells Won't Ignite Oil Prices," cover 3-25. Based on the political and economic needs of the Gulf region following the war, Nulty estimates that in the coming months the moderate Saudis will press for prices in the $20-$25 range. Going beyond prices to look at the industry as a whole, his "Oil's Prospects: A Better Decade," 4-22, is a good reference piece with helpful charts, but still there's nothing definitive about his analysis. Fitfully interesting in "The New Look of Photography," cover 7-1, he pens a primer on new photo technologies, but is too gee-whiz on the gizmos and too promotional of Kodak. His complete and compact profile of Hokey Electronics' comeback from low profits, "Cashing in on Security," 10-7, covers all the requisite business bases and then some.

O'Brian, Bridget. *The Wall Street Journal.* (★ ★ ★)
Airlines. A competent profit and loss reporter, O'Brian reliably kept us abreast of the financial side of the industry's tumultuous restructuring. Her "American Airlines Faces Labor Impasse," 1-30, is a very balanced, well-sourced report on American's increasingly "acrimonious" talks with the union representing its pilots. In an increasingly global marketplace, American pulled out the stops to win the battle for TWA's valuable London routes, but O'Brian deftly characterizes the intensity of the battle in "AMR Is Fighting Many Foes as It Seeks to Finish Buying TWA London Routes," 4-2. Targeting investment readers in "Financial Worries Force America West to Cut Back," 4-29, she scrutinizes the books and assesses if troubled America West, famed for its aggressive expansion, will be able to return to profitability. She delivers a contrarian " 'Chapter 11' Airlines, Struggling to Survive, May Depress Prices, Profits at Strong Carriers," 7-9, showing how in the short run, healthy carriers probably won't benefit from all the bankruptcies: "The problem is that the healthy carriers. . .are competing with a startlingly large crop of Chapter 11 dwellers. . .Nearly a third of the airline industry's capacity is in the hands of carriers that are operating with court protection from creditors. . .That's enough clout to sway the industry on matters such as fares and promotions." With Delta airlines winning approval to purchase parts of Pan Am, she offers a multidimensional "Delta, Despite Victory in Pan Am Bid, Faces Some Big Challenges," leder 8-13, and ponders if the "methodical, Southern-based" airline now catapulted from third place to first is "ready for the rough-and-tumble that goes with first place in a deregulated airline industry?" She discerns a "major strategic shift" at American in "AMR, in a Sharp Reversal, Curbs Outlays, Jet Options," 9-12, expertly examining the retrenchment which involves cutting $500 million out of its five-year budget: "consumers may pay more for domestic airline tickets, as carriers shift from adding new seats to trying to get as much profit as possible from the seats they already fly."

Ott, James. *Aviation Week & Space Technology.* (★ ★)
Senior transport editor. Ott is providing consistently strong and thoughtful analysis on where the tumult in the airline industry might lead, especially at the Department of Transportation. In his excellent "Pan Am Filing a Sign of Consolidation, Not an Indication of Competition's End," 1-14, he argues that "Despite this consolidation and outcries to the contrary, competition in the U.S. should remain at about the same level, with a half-dozen carriers dividing the market." He expands on this theme further in "Skinner Backs Global View, Foreign Stakes for Airlines," 2-4, a commentary on Transportation Secretary Samuel K. Skinner's decision to support foreign investment in U.S. airlines: "Skinner recognized that the trend among world airlines toward globalization, partnerships and multinational ownership is restructuring the international airline business and setting up a new environment." His "Lawmakers Warned of Looming Capital Crisis for U.S. Airlines," 2-11, is complete on Skinner's congressional testimony which showed that "financially beleaguered U.S. airlines are nearing a capital crisis that will prevent even viable carriers from replacing and rehabilitating the aging commercial transport fleet." In "Air Cargo Deregulation to Split European and U.S. Airlines," 4-8, he argues extensively that "a multilateral agreement to deregulate air cargo will be the next step in a move to liberalize the world's airline industry, a development sure to divide U.S. and European airlines." He takes the Transportation secretary to task for his stance on labor relations and contract bargaining in "Skinner Stance on Labor Costs Provokes Criticism, Dismay," 5-20. His basic bread-and-butter reporting is just that, in such standard but nondescript articles as "Lauda Crash Probers Focus On Midair Thrust Reversal," 6-10; "Core U.S. Airlines Battling Hard to Survive International Competition," 6-17; and "Northwest Settles Price-Fixing Suit With Trust Fund, Discount Coupons," 6-24 tells most of its story in the headline. His "Mild Transatlantic Traffic Rise Seen as Competition Toughens," 10-14, a surprisingly strong market analysis of projected North Atlantic air traffic and its economic implications for major airlines, results in a survival of the fittest outlook: "The North Atlantic market is undergoing a huge transformation. . .The financial and marketing strengths of the Big Three [American, United and Delta], plus their cost efficiencies compared to European carriers, are throwing a scare into the Assn. of European Airlines."

Paltrow, Scot J. *Los Angeles Times.* (★ ½)
New York. Kind of a disappointing, grab-bag year for Paltrow, who dabbled superficially in numerous topics, but sunk his teeth into none of them. We hope to see him rebound soon. His best work of the year, an ambitious survey of the deterioration of city programs, "Cries for Help Go Unheeded," 2-4, is heavy on descriptive anecdotes and finger-pointing but light on solutions. Still, this was a valuable piece of analysis. We get nothing more than newswire coverage in "Ball Resigns as Chairman, CEO of Pru-Bache," 2-14, a mediocre report on George Ball's resignation from the struggling Wall Street brokerage. Paltrow could have done more with this. We found better detail on the U.S.-British aviation accord in "British Airways Loses Its Smooth Ride to London," 3-12, but Paltrow fails to articulate its broader implications or discuss the bubbling tensions that characterized the negotiations. He treads carefully in "SEC Says Executive Who Gave Analysts Data Broke the Law," 3-20, a professional examination of the SEC's "unusual use of insider trading laws" to file charges against the former chairman of Ultrasystems Inc., Phillip Stevens. Stevens' lawyer said "there is 'no recorded precedent' for a case against a corporate executive for passing information on to analysts." He gives a quick snapshot of Drexel Burnham Lambert's settlement with the IRS in "Drexel Settles $5.3-Billion Tax Case With IRS," 6-21, but the only quote in the report is taken from Reuters. He is much more in-depth in "Companies See No Rush Back to South Africa," 7-11, reporting that despite the relaxation of sanctions against South Africa, many states and cities still have laws in place "that prohibit government agencies from investing in or buying products from companies with interests in South Africa." Weighing in on Wall Street's latest financial scandals with "Many Large Clients Say They'll Stand By Embattled Salomon," 8-20, and "2 at Shearson Are Suspended," 9-6, he remains professionally objective and balanced in his coverage.

Passell, Peter. *The New York Times.* (★ ★)
"Economic Scene" columnist. A prolific writer, Passell is excellent on micro-economic issues, but follows the Peter Principle when tackling macro, as in "Does the Government Have the Stuff to End a Recession?" 2-11, a skewed telling of the government's management of the economy since 1962, and "For the Economy, the Gulf War Has Little Impact — So Far," 2-3, in which he feebly explains wartime economics via a model that sees war as inflationary. Passell also talks out of both sides of his mouth, calling for smaller deficits and higher taxes to increase the nation's savings rate as in "Mr. Macawber Was Right," 4-3, yet recommending expensive programs to solve the nation's problems as in "Pink Slips, Budget Blues," 3-13. On the other hand, he advocates free-market solutions for the environment in such stories as "Washington Offers Mountains of Debt to Save Forests," 1-22, which supports "debt for nature" swaps; "Greenhouse Gamblers," 6-19, a thorough examination of a possible market for greenhouse gas "offsets"; "More Green for Less Gold," 5-8, an examination of "Project 88" which makes the case "for market-based incentives as a cheaper, less intrusive alternative to traditional pollution regulation"; "A New Commodity to Be Traded: Government Permits for Pollution," 7-17, and "The 'No Regrets' Greenhouse Fix," 4-24, a look at "emissions-reducing initiatives that would pay for themselves in greater economic efficiency." Passell also devoted much creative energy to pondering the Soviet Union's economic crisis. In "Even Stalin Did It Better," 1-30, he too gently criticizes the Soviet confiscation of 50-and 100-ruble notes. But he intelligently compares and contrasts Gorbachev to General Pinochet of Chile in "Perestroika With Tears," 2-20. We also appreciated: "Gorbachev's Plan Could Shock More Than Just Prices" 4-7; "Putting a Price on the Soviet 'Grand Bargain,' " 7-8, following the start of the coup; "Economy Viewed as Achilles' Heel of New Regime," 8-21, which characterizes the coup leaders as "economic primitives"; and "Currency Muddle: Less Is More," 9-11, a perceptive post-coup piece on a "trading ruble." His analysis of social issues is a mixed bag, but he raises important questions. His critical assessment of NYC's 43-year-old rent control law in "Perestroika for Renters," 1-2, notes compellingly that "almost all the windfall goes to the affluent." In "Chronic Poverty, Black and White," 3-6, he points to a new study that shows there are plenty of poor white people too: "The good news here is that racism alone cannot explain the existence of America's underclass." He's narrow-minded in "The Truths About Welfare," 7-24, asserting that more tax

money is the only way to "give welfare recipients the skills and motivation to fight their way into the middle class." And in "Blacks' Setbacks by Association," 8-28, he can't seem to discern what keeps black men as a group from earning as much as whites. Could it be access to capital? His analysis of the reasons for the economic downturn and the anemic recovery, "Various Culprits for Ailing Recovery," 10-28, is equally shallow and unenlightening.

Pereira, Joseph. *The Wall Street Journal.* (★ ★)
Vivid, interesting and instructive are the adjectives that define this colorful journalist who has a flair for marketing stories and A-heds. He visits the American International Toy Fair for "As Toy Makers Unwrap New Products, They Hope Video Games Are Peaking," 2-11, and cautions that amid the dazzle of new toys, the conference will have a conservative tone and "will offer few clues to whether the industry can break out after four years of flat sales." "Given today's market clutter, name recognition is almost priceless," so Pereira shows how the little guys can creatively compete with the big money boys without investing the millions they sink into promotions in "Name of the Game: Brand Awareness," 2-14. He sketches an inspiring portrait of a runner training for the Boston Marathon in "He Paints Still Lifes but John Kelley, 83, Is Still on the Move," 3-26: "Mr. Kelley is to be the oldest competitor in the race this year — as he has been for 15 years." In "Nintendo Is Counting On New Super Game to Rescue U.S. Sales," leder 5-10, he tells us that "After zapping America's kids into a video-game frenzy five years ago, Nintendo Co.'s games are losing their zip." Pereira includes lots of detail as he speculates on the success of Nintendo's upcoming release of a new, more powerful and colorful game system. He investigates another weakening trend in "Are Ninja Turtles Headed for Ooze Whence They Came?" 5-22, pondering for investors who thought Ninja Turtles were impervious to decline, that "The Turtles could go the way of Cabbage Patch Kids." He gives convincing statistical information even Ninja loyalists will want to consider. His punchy piece on the Boston Sports Boxing Club, "Float Like a Butterfly Sting Like. . .Well. . .Like a Butterfly Too," 7-23, stylishly notes "there's no smoking, little swearing, and a sign posted on a bulletin board proclaiming 'No Sweaty Clothes Overnight.' No dank dark gymnasium, it caters to white-collar pugilists. . ." We loved "With Yogis' Help, a Baseball Player Looks for the Zone," 9-19, a really fun look at baseball player Brent Mayne's attempts to improve his catching through a ". . .Ayurveda, a Hindu system of medicine and well-being developed by yogis who never heard of Berra."

Platt, Gordon. *The Journal of Commerce.* (★)
Financial editor. With multinational corporations the norm rather than the exception these days, currency is a beat that cries out for a reporter skilled in political economy. Unfortunately, Platt is not actively involved enough in his columns to show us if he is up to this type of sophisticated analysis. In the early days of war, he gathers a corps of trading analysts to throw out generic quotes on the direction of the dollar for "Traders Expect Dollar to Continue Falling," 1-22, but they are way off the mark. Once again in "Traders Say Dollar Will Drop to New Lows After Rate Cut," 2-4, he simply chats with a few conventionally-minded traders and puts down their rather short-sighted opinions. He finally recognizes that the rally was indeed long-term and based on fundamentals in "Traders Predict Dollar Will Continue to Rally," 4-29, but even here Platt is a bystander. His "Dollar May Not Sustain Sharp Rise as Doubts Persist About Economy," 5-20, carries a number of perspectives which indicate that the business press corps may be alone in its euphoria over the "improving" trade deficit numbers. He quotes currency trader Jeff Birnbaum who says "the narrowing in the U.S. trade deficit to $4.047 billion in March. . .was largely the result of a decline in imports, which reflects weakness in the U.S. economy." Yes. He offers a sound assessment of why money managers think European investments will outshine U.S. investments for the rest of the year in "Money Managers Shift Funds From US, Japan to Europe," lead 6-14. He actually picks up some definitive observations for "Dollar to Maintain Strength, But No Sharp Gains Seen," 7-8, quoting Alan Shealy, manager of foreign exchange operations at Union Bank of Switzerland, as saying that "the 'real damaging factor for the Deutsche mark is the specter of a withholding tax' on interest income, even though

such a tax might not come into effect for some time." And in "Traders Expect Dollar to Fall Further Despite Favorable Economic Outlook," 7-22, he makes a number of useful observations about the G-7's role in keeping the dollar down. It is worth perusing his "Financing Trade," 8-21, a useful compilation of facts from around the world. Today's top items deal with currency fluctuations following the Soviet coup.

Pollack, Andrew. *The New York Times.* (★ ★ ★)
San Francisco. An exemplery technology reporter, Pollack is back on beam after a soft 1990, consistently providing an interesting and practical blend of business and technology issues in his well-rounded pieces. Although he does a lot of speculative hedging in "Semiconductor Outlook Is Mixed," 1-8, he neatly brings together a useful sampling of perspectives and facts for investors. In "War Spurs Navigation by Satellite," 2-6, he takes an electrifying look at the Navstar Global Positioning System, "an unsung hero of the American effort in the Persian Gulf war" and a new technology that could change navigation as we know it. He eschews the belief that military technology is superior to commercial technology with "In U.S. Technology, a Gap Between Arms and VCR's," 3-4: "Unencumbered by the burdensome military procurement regulations...makers of commercial products often rush ahead...Indeed, the Pentagon is buying more commercial products to save time and money. In a sense, therefore...A healthy commercial industry is considered necessary for the military." He asks all the right questions in "Medical Technology 'Arms Race' Adds Billions to the Nation's Bills," 4-29, a top-notch debate of the medical and economic issues involved in ever more popular high-priced, high-tech medical procedures. He does too much cheerleading in "Moving Fast to Protect Ozone Layer," 5-15, gushing over electronics companies that are phasing out chlorofluorocarbons and finding environmentally safe cleansers. And he is too optimistic about the outcome of IBM's meetings with Apple Computer in "Technology Links Will Be Discussed by Apple and I.B.M." 6-10. More clear-eyed in "A Quirky Loner Goes Mainstream," 7-14, following news of an "unthinkable partnership" with IBM, he takes us into the heart of the independent-minded Apple Computer Inc. "In search of new muscle and respect, Apple seems to be blasting off in contradictory directions, but the aims are clear: increase market share and survive in an industry going through the early stages of what is expected to be a massive consolidation." He briskly defines the strengths and weaknesses of the latest banking mega-merger in "BankAmerica in $4 Billion Deal to Acquire Rival Security Pacific," 8-13, and in "Keeping Up With the Joneses' PC," 9-13, he shows how personal computers are becoming replacement products, changing how computers are sold.

Power, William. *The Wall Street Journal.* (★ ★)
Securities industry. Power, a strong reporter who hasn't worked up to potential in recent years, spends his time uncovering important little Wall Street trends and stories that others don't bother looking into. Handling a mundane topic engagingly in "Brokerage Firms Boost Investor Fees," 1-9, he crisply explains how brokerage firms are dealing with tighter budgets, and surveys the pros and cons of boosting fees. He is uncharacteristically featurish in "Keeping Up With Down-Home Joneses," 2-12, profiling the brokerage Edward D. Jones & Co., "an oddity to most of Wall Street" because it has no offices in the Big Apple, its focus is on small towns and it's expanding. In "Commodity Exchanges Unmask FBI 'Traders,' " 3-27, he develops a big story with a richly detailed account of how the FBI tried to plant undercover agents at New York's major commodity exchanges. "The incidents show the depth of mistrust between the FBI — which exchange officials say never notified them about any undercover investigation — and the futures industry." He efficiently handles the complexities surrounding one of the largest settlements of a limited-partnership lawsuit in "Brokerage Firm Offers to Settle Investor Suit," 4-3, effectively weaving in observations about its implications. With many journalists sanctimoniously gawking over the Japanese brokerage scandal, Power's "Reimbursing Stock Losses? It Happens Here," 6-27, was refreshing indeed: "Just yesterday, the [NYSE] announced that it disciplined four brokers...for improperly 'sharing in losses' of customer accounts..." He examines why dissatisfaction with the quality of Wall Street research is at an all time high in

"Wall Street Research Faulted By Big Institutional Investors," 7-31. And in the highly aggressive world of info gathering, Power's "Street Fight: Bear Stearns vs. D.F. King," 8-22, serves as a germane anecdote describing how a D.F. King employee allegedly impersonated a Bear Stearns employee in order to collect confidential information. His "Salomon's Big Loss Could Well Become Goldman Sachs's Gain," leder 9-19, is a fair-minded assessment of how the Salomon scandal could benefit Salomon's "fierce rival" Goldman, Sachs & Co. Power is careful to point out that Goldman is also vulnerable, and could be drawn into this or other scandals.

Prowse, Michael. *Financial Times.* (★ ★ ½)
Prowse replaced Anthony Harris as *FT*'s man in Washington, and like his predecessor displays a saucy insouciance in his criticisms of Washington's alleged provinciality. His political-social-cultural observations are delightfully piquant, but his economic analyses are a bit too formulaic and hidebound at times. He places heavy emphasis on U.S. monetary policy, often at the unfortunate expense of important fiscal factors, as in "A Bear Hug From Greenspan," 1-21, on Fed targeting and money-supply decline. Similarly in "US Monetary Growth Moves to Top of the Fed's Agenda," 2-1, he perceives a policy shift at the central bank on monetary aggregates and develops a competent assessment of what it might portend, but never works in any perspective on the non-monetarist criterion of Fed officers such as Gov. Wayne Angell. In "Absorbed with Itself, in Spite of the War," 2-11, he lambastes Treasury Secretary Brady for making global economic stability worse "by saying he would like to see still lower US interest rates." Looking at the recession-mired U.S. economy in "Chinks of Hope Amid the Gloom," 3-22, Prowse unevenly reviews the evidence cited by optimists that the downturn will soon bottom out. Staying within a traditional business cycle model, he is ambiguous on the efficacy or liability of "faster monetary growth" and gives no attention whatsoever to key fiscal considerations, going so far as to project a dramatic economic snap-back. Prowse scolds the U.S. for its "thoroughly unhealthy" relationship with Japan in "Japan Deserves a Little Respect," 5-7, but reduces the lessons to be absorbed to a Keynesianesque impression that in Japan "the state plays a large, if often subtle role in influencing the distribution of resources," with no insight on the country's tax rate and monetary policies. "Sneaker Syndrome and Other Quirks," 7-29 is a typically wry observation on the strange behavioral traits of Americans, like women in $500 suits wearing white sneakers. He delves into how the U.S. distributes funding and what factors have influenced national priorities in "Scales Out of Balance," 8-13, and pens an insightful assessment of the educational challenge posed by the dearth of vocational training in the U.S. in "At the Bottom of the Class," 8-16. Examining poverty in America in "Buddy, Can You Still Spare a Dime?" 10-5/6, he takes a stab at the social conscience, insisting that the problem is getting worse while liberals and conservatives talk past each other in "ideological wars."

Quinn, Jane Bryant. *Newsweek.* (★ ★)
Personal investment columnist. As she has for well over a decade, self-help Jane serves up common-sense, bread-and-butter advice for Mom and Pop investors interested in steadily increasing the value of their investments with the minimum of risk. We find it easier to swallow as she sticks to this specialty, rarely pontificating on national economic policy as she has in the past. She is solid but simple in "The Boom of Cannons," 2-25, playing off the old adage "Buy on the cannons, sell on the trumpets," and gathering advice from accredited market watchers. But news that "in the market, the bulls have the floor and the war is already history" comes well into the rally. She offers practical advice for members of the reserves in "When Duty Has a Price," 3-11, forwarding practical financial planning tips to fit their special circumstances. She is bleak on pension/annuity plans following the collapse of Executive Life Insurance Co. in "Is Your Pension Fund Safe?" 4-22, and suggests numerous ways to protect our investments from losses. Just in time for Derby Day, she pens "My Paycheck for a Horse," 5-6, telling us how much she likes the races, and predicting that racing is "slowly reinventing itself," despite news to the contrary. Her savvy "The Hard New Facts of Pay," 6-3, is rather astute on the relationship between wages and productivity to a sound economy: "There's a paradox in low pay: any

company may earn more by paying its employees less. But when all companies pay less, workers wind up with so little money that all American businesses decline. The road back begins with the belief that lower wages will not do." She touts the booms in Mexico, Chile and, to some extent Brazil in "For Money, Look South," 7-1: "between 1975 and 1990, Chile's market delivered a compound annual return of around 30 percent, compared with 26 per cent for Korea and 11 per cent for the United States. . .and Mexico's. . .stocks up 1,034 per cent in U.S. dollars." There's nothing particularly new here for sophisticated investors, but for Quinn's Mom and Pop audience this is probably exciting news. In "Golden Years, Gold Included," 9-9, she lays out the basics on how to retire and have enough money. Her excellent examination "How to Save for College," 10-21, is quintessential Quinn: "Paying for college is the Matterhorn of personal finance. No one who has stood in those chill winds ever forgets them."

Quint, Michael. *The New York Times.* (★ ★)
NYT's bank merger man showed steady improvement, starting off taking things at face value but becoming increasingly more probing as the year went on and banking-merger-mania moved into high gear. His numbers-heavy survey "Bad Loans Take Toll at Banks," 1-16, is solid on banks' hunkering down, but Quint doesn't explore plans to return to growth. He is sound but not inquisitive on the administration's attempts to encourage lending through proposed accounting changes in "Accounting Proposals for Banks," 2-11. More thorough in "Fidelity Is Recast for the Future," 3-20, he pens a well-rounded profile of First Fidelity Bancorporation under new chairman Anthony P. Terracciano "a 'genetically programmed worrier'. . .not given to bonhomie." Quint walks us through Terracciano's cost-cutting plans, revealing why he has inspired investor confidence in only a year. His "Interest on Deposits Falls, But Loan Rates Stay High," 4-19, looks at how banks are covering their losses by keeping borrowers' fees high and the amount they pay savers lower. But he never ponders if such survival techniques can actually lead to long-term profitability. He succinctly conveys, but doesn't analyze, the Fed chairman's dismal thoughts on the future of banking in "Greenspan Urges Changes by Bankers," 5-3: "Besides avoiding risky borrowers. . .[Greenspan] said banks should expect large corporations to continue to raise funds without using banks." Showing marked improvement mid year, he impressed with "Big Bank Merger to Join Chemical, Manufacturers," 7-16, a highly insightful appraisal of the broader implications of this merger in light of the industry's consolidation fever. Even more perceptive in "Banking's Ultimate Goal," 8-15, Quint expertly discerns that, so far, banking mergers have "done little to correct one of the American banking system's greatest weaknesses — the lack of geographic diversification that leaves banking companies vulnerable to regional economic downturns." He delves into the complex question, "Bigger Banks, But Better Banking?" 8-23, probing various studies which indicate that "As mergers cause banking power to be concentrated in fewer hands. . .depositors tend to get lower interest rates. . .And borrowers, particularly small businesses are charged higher rates. . ." He thoroughly examines a new trend in "Balances Without Any Checks," 9-11, on banking's move away from canceled checks to cost-saving computer-generated images.

Rachid, Rosalind. *The Journal of Commerce.* (★ ★ ½)
Trade editor. Now a full year in this important editorial position, Rachid is a fountain of singular information on unique trade issues from all over the world. We like her "Trade Talk" column best when she focuses on one substantial topic, rather than skimming over many. She tries to cover too many topics in her 1-8 column, doing none justice. She's more concentrated in her 3-19 column, issuing an important alert for exporters and importers who may be assessed a charge by the USDA's Animal & Plant Inspection Service if its unusually quick push for an inspection fee goes through. She constructs a compact compilation of strong quotes from free-trade advocates in "Opponents Endanger Mexico Pact Over Non-Trade Issues, Backers Say," 4-11: Says one source "In the United States, the trade agenda is being fragmented. You can't take countries at two different levels and equalize them overnight. Human rights, environment, narcotics interdiction, immigration, loss of jobs — these have nothing to do with the free trade agreement." Her 4-16 column was a nice follow-up on what will happen to companies that have

invested in Caribbean-based production ventures when the U.S.-Mexico free trade agreement goes through. Rachid raises concern that there may not be the commitment to hemisphere-wide prosperity, that there once seemed. She provides a useful and very specific outline of the battle lines being drawn by textile importers, 6-4, including maintaining China's MFN status, settling the North American free trade agreement, phasing out the MultiFibre Arrangement through GATT, and more. More details on Mexico's amazing economic progress, 7-2, with Rachid noting "South of the border, Mexico's attractiveness is soaring. Chile, Venezuela and Colombia leaped to negotiate trade agreements." Her 8-6 column is an outstanding dissection of U.S. vs. Israeli-based Sharnoa Ltd. which manufactures computerized machine tools with Taiwanese parts and exports them to the U.S. As Rachid clarifies, the U.S. has a free-trade agreement with Israel but applies quotas to Taiwan, so determining where the product originates from has broad ramifications. "Rules of origin, which determine the 'nationality' and therefore dutiability of a product, is probably the most important new measure of trade policy. . ."

Ramirez, Anthony. *The New York Times.* (★ ★ ½)
"Business Day." Ramirez maintains that dazzling style we've come to appreciate, but is also slowly developing the scrutiny necessary for more sensible, less cheerleading, profiles. In "Sterling Car a Test for Grace & Rothschild," 1-23, he lays out advertising firm Grace & Rothschild's latest challenge, selling an expensive British vehicle "that $100 million in advertising and three other agencies have failed to move." Say so long to jumbo and super he tells us in "Soap Sellers' New Credo: Less Powder, More Power," 2-1, and say hello to "ultra." Superconcentrated detergents are the latest marketing craze: "Not since 'The Adventures of Ozzie and Harriet' was one of America's favorite television shows has there been such a big change in detergent formulation and packaging." He throws cold water on Wall Street's euphoria over RJR's latest issue in "Slide in Tobacco Sales Hurting RJR Nabisco," 4-13, pointing out with plenty of persuasive evidence that the company "has fundamental problems in its tobacco business." As it turned out, though, RJR had fewer problems than Wall Street had assumed. "Keeping the Gobblers, Chasing the Nibblers," 5-19, is quintessential Ramirez, enthusiastically examining how snack food producers are attempting to maintain their appeal to those who "shovel corn chips straight from the bag into their mouths" while spreading their appeal to "paunchy young professionals" who "count their Ritz crackers as they reach for the bean dip." Uncharacteristically formulaic in "Staley Develops Starch Substitute for Fat," 6-12, he provides little more than the requisite facts on this new food technology, and lacks the usual Ramirez flare. He shows his business acumen in "Will MCI Always Play David?" 8-22, a balanced and complete assessment of the perception that MCI might have gotten as big as it is going to get. His "The Pizza Version of Dialing '911,' " 9-9, is lively and informative on a unique technological venture between Domino's and AT&T called Store Finder that could "revolutionize how consumers obtain. . .goods and services by telephone. . ."

Reilly, Patrick M. *The Wall Street Journal.* (★ ★ ½)
Magazine publishing. The fast and furious fluctuations of the magazine industry in the current recession provided plenty of news for Reilly to sink his teeth into. He handled his assignments with his usual sturdy and sweeping grasp. His "Publishers Turn Page on Hype, Taking Subdued Approach to Magazine Rollouts," 1-8, a sterling overview. By the end, we're up to date on the latest magazine launches at a number of publishing houses, and have a good feel for the mood of the magazine industry as it tentatively enters 1991. His "Egos, Culture Clash When French Firm Buys U.S. Magazine," 2-15, is absorbing reading on Peter Diamandis who was dismissed as chief of the American branch of the French magazine empire Hachette S.A. after supposed cultural differences. The piece has a very insider feel to it. The recession is causing personnel chaos in magazineland as Reilly tells us in "Magazines Do Fast Shuffle With Editors," 3-27, a straightforward look at the staff changes and relocations, but Reilly doesn't really get to the heart of the problem — too many magazines chasing too few dollars. His "Ads Aimed at Students May Miss Mark," 4-15, is drier than usual, explaining advertisers' half-hearted attempts to get collegiate consumers to buy. Reilly files a short epitaph, "*The National* Calls

It Quits After 18 Months," 6-13, on the folding of this short lived sports daily. Since the paper never really made a dent against the local dailies and cable shows, it's fitting that the tombstone is not too ornate. His "If You Put TV, CD and VCR Together, They Spell 'Home Theater' to Marketers," 10-23, takes a snappy look at the marketing of hybrid entertainment systems that combine audio and video product lines.

Richter, Paul. *Los Angeles Times.* (★ ½)
New York. The *LAT* had Richter juggling such a hodgepodge of subjects this year that he was only rarely able to showcase his journalistic attributes in the media and movie industry arena. He handled the jumble of stories competently, but was clearly underemployed in the task. He gives a very insider feel to "Time Warner Merger Still a Work In Progress," 1-6, pouring over all the editorial and financial aspects of this mega-entertainment company with a fine tooth comb. Post Baghdad bunker bombing, he tries to gage support for the war in "Support for War Seen Despite Baghdad Deaths," 2-15, but his conclusion is mere common sense. He keeps it tight and balanced in "The NEA Defends Funding of Controversial Film," 3-30, reporting that the beleaguered chairman of the National Endowment for the Arts, John E. Frohnmayer, "fervently endorsed the controversial NEA-funded film 'Poison.' " In "FDIC 'Not Broke,' Seidman Says," 4-29, he pens a factual but underdeveloped look at the FDIC chairman's rebuttal to rumors, calling claims that the FDIC fund is nearly insolvent bunk. His superb, non-ideological column one, "A 'Great Society' Survivor," 6-20, is a very readable examination of the strengths and weaknesses of Head Start, "America's most popular social welfare program." "Indeed, support has been so broad that there is relatively little public discussion of the shortcomings and frustrations of Head Start: Its long-term benefits have not been proved, the program's quality is not consistent from center to center, and efforts to extend its benefits into the school years only now are beginning to take hold." He judiciously handles a delicate legal issue emerging in the William Kennedy Smith rape trial in "Testimony on Defendants' Past Actions Stirs Disputes," 7-25, a thorough hashing out of whether to allow evidence about the defendants' past alleged sex crimes. Balanced in "Bush Endorses All-Male Schools for Urban Blacks," 9-10, Richter reports that Bush doesn't have a problem with all-male schools, but critics call his stance gender discrimination.

Risen, James. *Los Angeles Times.* (★ ½)
Economics, international trade. Risen, a competent reporter, profiled several key economic policymakers this year, which makes it all the more difficult to understand why he virtually never explored the direction of economic policy. It's as if his whole year was a missed opportunity. Following the collapse of a privately insured bank, Risen superficially explores the nation's financial safety net in "Rhode Island Crisis Raises Issues on Federal Regulation," 1-5. He is better in his fascinating profile of the shifting Bush-Greenspan relationship, "Crisis Brings Fed Chairman Closer to Bush," 2-3, conscientiously assessing the historical precedence for Greenspan's expanding role, without implying that the Fed is being politicized. In "Bonn to Pay — but White House Denies Gulf War Profits," 3-27, he nicely details the diplomacy of financing the war: the U.S. defending its cost estimates and Bonn reluctantly coughing up the cash. He misses the opportunity to examine the direction of monetary policy in "Interest Rates Reduced by Fed," 5-1, one of the few reports to note Fed Gov. Wayne Angell's lone dissent. But Risen doesn't question the logic of the Fed's move. His column one, "Greenspan: Supreme Survivor," 5-30, is in-depth on Greenspan the philosopher and jazz saxophonist, but Greenspan the Fed chairman is skimmed over, a sure sign that this "rare" interview was more PR for Greenspan than a journalistic coup for Risen. His profile of chief economic adviser Michael Boskin, "President's No. 1 Economist Adds Power to the Post," 6-9, is also just so-so, with plenty on how Boskin has brought authority back to the committee of economic advisers, but little on Boskin's vision for the economy. "So far, Boskin has not made his name in Washington for. . .analyzing the U.S. economy and recommending cures for the recession. . .Instead, Boskin's main role. . .is to act as the Administration's key liaison with Fed chief Greenspan. . ." Risen doesn't question this role which epitomizes the administration's dependence on monetary

policy. He sticks to the basics in "Greenspan Gets a Second Term as Fed Chairman," 7-11, failing to develop interesting ideas from Greenspan's critics and President Bush. His "Fed Cuts Discount Rate to 5%," 9-14, is more thorough on the latest easing.

Rosenbaum, David E. *The New York Times.* (★ ★)
Washington, chief economic correspondent. There's some irony in the fact that Rosenbaum received a Polk award for his coverage of the 1990 budget debate, yet this year he ignores fiscal economic policy almost completely, placing the health of the economy solely on the Fed's shoulders. Macro-economics clearly remains beyond his reach and he will be transferred to a new beat in 1992. An observation made in his 7-11 report sums up his narrow outlook: "The nation's largest budget deficit prevents the President or Congress from using tax and spending policies to influence the economy. . ." Hmmm. His important interview with the Fed chairman, "Greenspan Warns of a Deep Recession if War Lasts," 1-31, gives Greenspan room to make several important points on monetary policy and the credit crunch, as well as defend his stance last autumn when some accused him of responding too slowly to the economic downturn. Suspect paraphrasing dominated "For Greenspan, Problems Not Confronted Before," 2-22, in which he says Greenspan blames the economy's problems on "Reckless lending practices in the 1980s, much of it resulting from favorable tax treatment of real estate projects. . ." — an odd view from a man who favors a zero capital gains tax rate which would enhance real estate values. He takes a statistic-heavy look at the unemployment rate in "Unemployment Is at 4-Year High With Jump to 6.5% Last Month," 3-9, refraining from overreaction to the gloomy data. We found plenty of lucid observations in "Greenspan for I.R.A.'s, Lukewarmly," 5-17, and "Fed Feels Left Out," 7-2, a perceptive look at why Washington isn't paying much attention to this vital government agency. He provides basically sound interpretation in "Greenspan Named for New Term as Chairman of Federal Reserve," 7-11: The "renomination of Mr. Greenspan almost certainly means that the Bush Administration has decided that the recession is a short and mild one that the President can weather politically. Had the recession been long and deep. . .Mr. Greenspan would probably have been made the scapegoat. . ." His "Clifford Calls Himself a Dupe in Banks Case," 9-12, was a careful and instructive dissection of the mood at the congressional testimony of Clark Clifford and Robert Altman. Rosenbaum not only tells us which questions were asked and how Clifford responded, but he tells us which questions were not asked by sympathetic or uninformed committee members. He raised questions with his very lopsided "Talk About Tax Breaks Is. . .Just Talk," 10-22, identifying a bit too closely with Rep. Dan Rostenkowski's agenda to discount the posturing on taxes in Washington in order to push off tax legislation until next year.

Rosenblatt, Robert A. *Los Angeles Times.* (★ ★)
In a year of mounting crisis for the insurance and banking sector, Rosenblatt reliably kept us abreast of the political scrambling on the issues. He has an eye for strong quotes, so we're sure he's capable of the bigger analytical pieces he seems to shy from. Weaving in the broader issues at hand in the seizure of the Bank of New England in "U.S. Seizes Bank Group in 3rd-Biggest Collapse," 1-7, he thoughtfully comments on federally insured deposits and the "too-big-too-fail" doctrine. Similarly, both "Banks Will Offer $10-Billion Plan to Bolster FDIC," 2-11, and "FDIC Seeks OK to Borrow Up to $30 Billion," 3-1, were steady-handed reports on the swirl of efforts to bolster the FDIC fund. As *LAT*'s point man on California's insurance failures, Rosenblatt didn't break new ground, but he did flesh out the issues. While most writers swallowed accounts that First Executive failed because of junk bonds, Rosenblatt tells otherwise in "State Allegedly Knew Executive Life Was Insolvent in '83," 4-26: "The chairman of a Senate subcommittee investigating the collapse. . .said. . .that the company was technically insolvent long before its troubles with the falling junk bond market. . ." He summarizes the California Insurance Commissioner's "tough line" with American Express which has a 28% share of First Capital in "Garamendi Says First Capital Needs Cash Infusion to Survive," 5-8 and takes an anecdotal look at how the failure of Executive Life affects the average Joe in "Insurer's Failure Ensnares Thousands of Casualties," 5-17, a query of how companies will compensate employees.

New legal ground is being broken as Rosenblatt reports in "U.S. Challenges Pension Switching," 6-13: The Labor Department is suing "two California companies for allegedly improperly replacing employee pension plans with annuities sold by Executive Life Insurance Co. The suits. . . mark the first time the government has challenged employers' action in picking insurance companies. . ." Solid reporting, but where's the analysis of the legal implications of this case. He is balanced on the uproar over Rep. John Dingell's bulletin that Citicorp is "technically insolvent," in "Citicorp Denies Dingell's Charge of Insolvency," 8-1, gathering opinions from both sides of the fence.

Rothenberg, Randall. *The New York Times.* (★ ★ ½)
Departing the *Times* in September, Rothenberg put in a superb final year of deft coverage with the wit, intelligence and style necessary to characterize the subtle nuances of taste and fashion that govern the gigantic ad and media industry. We look forward to the books he plans to write and occasional freelance pieces for the *Times.* In "Sister Papers Become Direct Rivals in Philadelphia," 3-4, he spryly captures how sister publications, the *Philadelphia Inquirer* and the *Daily News,* despite common ownership, are getting ready to slug it out for readership. He smartly puts his finger on a new trend in "An Image Maker Quits Politics," 3-27. noting that top Democratic consulting firm Sawyer/Miller is quitting the political arena for the corporate world, the second prominent image maker in months to throw in the political towel. He fingers a broader truth in his well-done "The Joke's On Whittle for Losing Best Seller," 3-14, revealing the irony of Whittle Communications' rejection of David Halberstam's *The Next Century* which subsequently became a bestseller for William Morrow: "several publishing professionals said that Whittle may have performed a service to their industry, by showing, however inadvertently, that there is a market for serious, non-fiction books substantially shorter than the 60,000 to 100,000-word trade hard cover." He is at his reporting best in "Benetton's Magazine to Push Vision, Not Clothing," 4-15, a fast, smart read covering Benetton's latest marketing ploy: the start-up of a non-fashion magazine. He's slightly confusing in "New Daily Takes on Racing Form," 6-3, following the two-horse race between *Racing Times* and the *Daily Racing Form.* He starts off saying it will be a long time before the *Racing Times* will catch up, then goes on to praise the paper for the rest of the article. His well-written "Arts & Leisure" essay, "Art or Schlock: Is TV Suitable for Framing?" 8-25, looks into the artistic questions raised by the upcoming opening of The Museum of Television and Radio. "This new museum is one of the few public institutions created and endowed by an industry to exalt that industry's own wares." In his highly-engaging *Magazine* piece, "Seducing These Men," 10-20, he takes us into the executive suite to witness firsthand how Subaru chose a new ad agency to promote its car.

Rowen, Hobart. *The Washington Post.* (★ ★)
Economics columnist. Less vitriol this year and more balanced analysis from the *Post*'s intelligent economic columnist. But he too frequently views the domestic economy through a traditional business cycle lens, limiting the originality of his insights. He compiles an interesting collection of big name quotes and guesstimates on the economy for "A Near-Depression. . ." 1-10, but doesn't glue the observations together with the necessary deep-think analysis. A conventional Rowen takes over in "Budget Miscalculations," 2-7, illogically viewing the deficit as just a big, bad dangling number unrelated to the slumping GNP or other crucial areas of the economy. The pros and cons of "fast track" with Mexico is the subject of "Trade Fight at the Rio Grande," 2-21, with Rowen noting that *maquiladoras* were originally "dominated by U.S. companies. . .But now, Matsushita, Sony, Sanyo, Toshiba and Samsung are also there." He nails down what will make U.S. products competitive in "Wonder Bread Economy," 3-7: "If America is going to register new commercial successes. . .it must earn them the old-fashioned way. . .by being superior. It won't happen by legislative fiat handed down by a protectionist Congress. . ." In "Missing: An Economic Strategy," 4-18, he critiques the lack of economic focus in U.S. foreign policy, citing State Dept.'s Robert Zoellick's remarks that "economic policy is and must become an increasingly critical component of the United States foreign policy strategy." But we never get much detail on the content of such policy. A lively and insightful conversation is had

with HUD Secretary Kemp in "Kemp's Supply-Side Pitch," 5-30: "Disarmingly, he conceded. . .that some of his colleagues say that 'if you ask Kemp what to do about the weather, he'll recommend cutting capital gains taxes.' " He goes to town on France's new Prime Minister, Edith Cresson, calling her "a world-class protectionist who turns. . .to 'industrial policy' to solve economic problems" in "French Folly," *Weekly* 6/3-9. But on the U.S. economy, he lets the administration off the economic policy hook, resigning himself to the view that "The only potentially effective counter-cyclical game in town is the one playable by the Fed with its powerful monetary policy chip — lower interest rates" in a disappointing "Waiting for the Dust to Settle," *Weekly* 8/12-18. He is very tough on the top executives at Salomon Brothers in "Salomon Saga," 9-12, suggesting the firm may never recover from the Treasury auction scandal, and that it is in for "significant, visible punishment."

Rudnitsky, Howard. *Forbes.* (★ ½)

Senior editor. Gearing the bulk of his work toward the sophisticated investor, Rudnitsky ferrets out contrary information on a variety of industries and companies. But his accuracy record is mixed. With Americans declaring personal bankruptcy in ever-increasing numbers, Rudnitsky surveys how lenders are trying to identify those likely to default in "An Excess of Plastic," 2-4, but while he gives a crisp snapshot of the situation, he provides no in-depth analysis of what caused this pervasive problem or how to alleviate it. His dull account of the increasing pressures on profits in the pharmaceutical industry, "An Industry Top?" 4-15, didn't convince us that this dynamic and still lucrative industry was about to take a hit. He's livelier and more probing in "Drugs By Mail," 4-15, chronicling the success of entrepreneur Marty Wygod's Medco, a small mail order drug prescription business that Wygod transformed into a $1.3 billion company through aggressive expansion and advertising. For the average homeowner his "Realty Wars," 6-10, was a comforting reminder that even sophisticated investors like Toys 'R' Us chairman Charles Lazarus, Woody Allen, and George Lucus, can take a beating in real estate. He elucidates the bizarre tax consequence of the recent ill-fated real estate tax shelter in "Salt in the Wound," 6-24, noting that the "boomerang effect," the IRS's way of recouping tax money that was initially deferred by the investor, is forcing investors who lost on real estate tax shelters to pay taxes on phantom profits. In "Sir Jimmy's Golden Deal," 7-8, he gushes over the latest financial maneuvers of billionaire Sir James Goldsmith, applauding his move into gold mining from timber. But with gold prices slumping we wondered where his journalistic skepticism had flown. Joined by Richard Stern for "The Gaijins' Revenge," 8-5, we're offered a crisp snapshot of how U.S. and British brokerage houses plan to capitalize on the Japanese brokerage scandals. He pours cold water on investors who recently ran up gambling stocks in "Who's Got the Royal White Tigers?" 9-30, revealing that profit margins already stretched, and Las Vegas casinos are facing future overcapacity.

Salpukas, Agis. *The New York Times.* (★)

Transportation. Salpukas' comprehension of the dramatic events shaping the airline industry is surprisingly narrow for a veteran. Not the type to ferret out fresh facts or comments, he didn't wake up to the new global order until midyear. He replays Eastern's troubles since deregulation in "Eastern Airlines Is Shutting Down and Plans to Liquidate Its Assets," 1-19, but the estimates of the airline's total debt and value of assets are skimpy. Bearing good news for Eastern's unsecured creditors in "An Auction Is Planned for Eastern," 2-1, he skims how they may gain from an auction of its takeoff and landing slots. He is surprisingly uninspired by a historic breakthrough in international aviation in "Britain Lifts Ban on New Heathrow Service," 3-6, completely minimizing the importance of this major step toward global liberalization. Better when spoon-fed the significance of these unfolding events by Transportation Secretary Skinner in "Accord Is Reached by U.S. and Britain on Airline Service," 3-12, Salpukas is still little more than an onlooker. Slightly more enthusiastic on the Israeli national airline in "In Adversity, El Al Turns a Profit," 5-8, he discusses its survival tactics during the war and chief Rafi Harlev's hopes to go private, but Harlev's plans aren't fleshed out. His "Pan Am Is Selling Overseas Routes and its Shuttle," 7-12, is a mere wrap up of the latest requisite facts on Pan Am's long downward financial struggle, not nearly as rich as others we saw. Probably his freshest work of the year, "For Singapore Air, a New Direction," 7-11, details the airline's plans to fly from New York beginning in 1993: The airline hopes lower fares will help them change "some ingrained travel patterns to get travelers to consider going to East Asia by way of Europe." He finally starts to see the bigger picture in "2 Airlines' Search for Global Status," 8-22, a respectable look at the domestic scramble for international routes. He observes that with the biggest airlines rapidly expanding abroad, second tier carriers are searching for competitive alliances. But his "American Airlines Reins In Growth," 9-12, was more so-so coverage, merely outlining CEO Robert L. Crandall's capital spending cuts.

Salwen, Kevin G. *The Wall Street Journal.* (★ ★ ★)
Financial services, regulation and the SEC. One of the best on this beat, Salwen expertly dissects the power plays between the CFTC and the SEC, and this year provided intelligent coverage of the Salomon Brothers scandal. In "CFTC Asks Senate Panel for More Power While Faulting a Plan to Oversee Futures," 2-8, he masterfully nuances CFTC chairman Wendy Gramm's request for more authority to seek monetary penalties, and effectively captures the political wrangling over the issue in "Panel Approves Bill to Bolster CFTC Powers," 2-27. Balanced and educational "Lone Wolf at CFTC Bares Teeth," 3-27, he skillfully assesses the debate over insider trading in the commodities market where CFTC's Fowler West wants to see insider traders jailed even though current laws governing the commodities markets don't bar insider trading. Salwen makes clear that there are also reasons to maintain the status quo. Profiling "Washington's new power couple," Wendy Gramm, chairman of the CFTC, and Sen. Phil Gramm in "Senate Feels the Impact of Marriage as Gramms Push Through Markets Bill," 4-26, Salwen conscientiously explores the appropriateness of the two corroborating to push through legislation that has given the CFTC new muscle. He alerts shareholders of SEC attempts to make it more difficult to keep certain pay questions off the proxy ballots in "Executive Pay May Be Subject to New Scrutiny," 5-16, noting the shift "could sharply change the nature of management accountability to holders." Even in his brief "Breeden Calls SEC Supervision of Advisers Poor," 7-26, he ably enriches our understanding with important background details on SEC Chairman Breeden's critique of his agency's "completely inadequate" regulation of investment advisers. Much of Salwen's work on Salomon's misconduct at Treasury auctions was done with Laurie Cohen, but he did have several stand out single byline pieces, including "Buffett Gives Details to Inquiry by House," 9-5, which captures the essence of Warren Buffett's tell-all approach and lawmakers' warm and cuddly response to this trustworthy midwestern business leader, as well as lawmakers' suspicion toward federal regulators' handling of the situation. He was equally observant in "Big Board Examined Salomon in April. . ." 9-13.

Saporito, Bill. *Fortune.* (★ ★ ½)
Board of editors. Although consistently a top-notch analyst of the ups and downs of a retail industry struggling through a recession, Saporito's performance is erratic on other topics, sometimes dazzling, sometimes disappointing. His astute overview of the past, present and future of the nation's real estate market, "Real Estate's Low-Rise Future," 1-28, is a little heavy on the gloom and doom at first, but winds up with an impressive look at the restructuring of the industry for the Nineties: "The basis for lending, building, and leasing allows room only for well-capitalized developers. Because the number of projects will be so limited, these master builders will have to be more skillful at managing their ventures than previous generations were. You won't see too many structures heading skyward on speculation because the new model developer has to put up 20% to 30% of the equity on projects, as opposed to as little as nothing." His quick, one page report on a Swedish furniture and housewares seller taking America by storm, "Ikea's Got 'Em Lining Up," 3-11, nicely captures the key to the store's success: "The real alchemy of Ikea is the company's ability to shift a variety of cost burdens onto the consumer and actually get him to like it." "Is Wal-Mart Unstoppable?" 5-6, was another brisk recap of how the retailing powerhouse is faring in the recession. There's nothing here to surprise people who follow merchandising, although he calls attention to a rising star in Target stores. Although he is

usually excellent on the credit card industry, he is too hyped up in "Melting Point in the Plastic War," 5-20, exaggerating that competition in the business "vibrates with testy lawsuits, back-stabbing business practices. . .as exciting as a shark feeding frenzy." He also strikes out with "The Owners' New Game Is Managing," 7-1, repeating tired stuff on baseball salaries we've seen elsewhere. He composes a first-rate marketing piece with "Liquor Profits Runneth Over," 11-4, taking the wide swath of an industry and deftly showing us the dynamics of products, people and regulation.

Schmidt, Susan. *The Washington Post.* (★ ½)
With a nose for scoops, but not much of an eye for analysis, Schmidt's coverage of the FDIC and RTC consists mainly of revealing dispatches on the latest slip-ups, in this her first year on the beat. Once she settles in, we hope she'll spend more time exploring the complex mandates of these agencies. Her lopsided "RTC Set to Redo '88 Deals," 1-17, examines the RTC's intentions to restructure its '88 S&L deals from the RTC viewpoint, with little regard for the investors involved. Her follow-up, "Treasury to Cancel Tax Breaks in 1988-89 S&L Deals," 3-7, is equally shallow. Starting to get a feel for her beat in "Panel: 'Where Were the Lawyers During the S&L Crisis?' " 3-23, she thoroughly examines a murky legal area concerning a lawyer's duty to turn in an institution making fraudulent loans. She shakes things up for Comptroller of the Currency Robert C. Clarke in "Bank Regulator Actively Trading," 4-30, disclosing his actions. Careful to emphasize that Clarke has done nothing illegal, she observes that he may have broken an ethics tradition of putting investments in blind trusts. Indeed, the news inspired the FDIC to review the ethics regulations that apply to its board members, as reported in "FDIC Reviews Rules Affecting Board Ethics," 5-1, again a very judicious handling of a story that definitely ruffled feathers. And as the story wraps up, Schmidt is once again fair and thorough in "Probe of Comptroller: No Ethics Violations," 6-5, reporting that Comptroller Clarke's investment practices show no evidence of conflict of interest, but "may give rise to an appearance of a conflict." The review recommended Clarke put his holdings in a blind trust. Back to the S&Ls, she gets wind of a flap in Kansas where a regional RTC chief has purchased $26,000 in paintings and sculptures to adorn his office in "RTC Office Art Stirs a Storm in Kansas," 6-12, a piece full of juicy ironies. In "Developer's Loan Default Spurs Foreclosure," 8-22, she succinctly recounts the financial woes of the once successful developer Mohamed Hadid. Her competent briefer on Clarke's re-confirmation hearings at Senate Banking, "Committee Critical of Comptroller," 9-20, notes that he will undoubtedly face tough questioning from a highly critical Donald Riegle (D-Mich.).

Schrage, Michael. *Los Angeles Times.* (★ ★ ★)
This creative business columnist who also appears in *The Washington Post* wowed us this year with consistently provocative perspectives on cutting-edge topics. He's forward looking just before the January deadline in "War Would Provide Test of U.S. Reliance on High-Tech Weapons," *WP* 1-11, asserting that Iraq will be the testing ground for America's high-tech weapons arsenal, a sophisticated experiment that will raise many new questions for military commanders in the field. His thought provoking op-ed, "Manager's Journal: Beware the Innovation Protectionists," *The Wall Street Journal* 1-14, taps into the ideas in his recently published book, *Shared Minds: The New Technologies of Collaboration* to stimulate interest in a new, open-door approach to R&D. Taking us on a fascinating trip to Baghdad 2006 in "Will Baghdad Be the Tokyo of the Mideast?" 2-28, he pens a creative, deep think-piece rich in allegory, history and insights: ". . .beyond doubt, the turning point in the region's economic destiny occurred with the 1993 signing with Japan of the Abbasid Agreements [which] marked the first comprehensive effort to create a regional climate for growth." He takes an exciting look at how the convergence of science and technology could revolutionize drug development and health care in the U.S. in "Is the Pharmaceutical Industry on the Verge of a Cost-Cutting Revolution?" *WP* 3-22, a talk with Alejandro Zaffaroni of Affymax, "a technology-intensive drug discovery company that combines organic chemistry with the microminiaturization techniques of silicon chips as a low-cost, high-volume way to match ligands with receptors."

Panning the latest critical technology list, he gets right to the heart of the matter in his brilliant 10-Best nomination, "Meaningless Lists of 'Critical' Technologies," 5-9: "The problem here is that people are focusing on the technologies rather than on the economic, industrial, governmental and scientific processes that create them." Playing the contrarian in a well-thought-out "Culture Clashes May Ruin Apple-IBM Deal," 7-11, he puts into perspective the "weird expectations" surrounding the IBM-Apple partnership. His "Adding Up a Solution to Competitiveness," 9-12, offers a fresh and enlightening angle on this hot topic.

Schwadel, Francine. *The Wall Street Journal.* (★ ★)
Chicago. This careful and diligent retail reporter, once again covered her beat thoroughly, keeping us abreast of the latest triumph or failure in the retail shakeout that has gripped the industry. "Commonwealth Ed Nuclear Station Put on NRC List," 1-25, is a competent, quick and balanced news account on a controversial topic Schwadel doesn't normally cover, nuclear power. Back in more familiar territory with "Sears Fourth-Quarter Net Falls 37% After Big Charge," 2-12, she pens a clear account of the troubled retailer's complex financial restructuring. But she could have enriched the piece substantially with a more in-depth exploration of the tensions at the top of Sears' management. She really showcases her knowledge of the retailing beat in "Shop Talk: What's in Store for Retailers," 4-9, compiling a who's who of retailers and succinctly assessing which are best equipped to survive the latest "Shopping Shakeout." Apparently the victim of a page one rewrite in "Turning Conservative, Baby Boomers Reduce Their Frivolous Buying," leder 6-19, Schwadel opens with uncharacteristically trivial comments about the "shop-till-you-drop mentality of the 1980s..." But once we get into her actual reporting, we find some interesting observations about why the important baby boomers sector is tightening its belt, although she relies too heavily on anecdotal evidence without the requisite statistical back-up on this important consumer spending trend. Her "Laura Ashley Chooses New Chief From Beyond World of Fashion," 7-18, is a lively and illuminating profile of Jim Maxmin, the "fashion neophyte" named as the new CEO of the struggling apparel and home-furnishing company whose once popular country floral prints have lost appeal according to the "cognoscenti of the fashion industry." For those who remember Susan Faludi's diatribe against Nordstrom's management on "Page One" of the *Journal* last year, Schwadel's "Nordstrom Workers Reject Their Union in Voting at Five Seattle-Area Stores," 7-22, was a welcome confirmation that Schwadel's more evenhanded coverage of the Nordstrom management-union debate had been much more accurate than Faludi's blatantly biased attack on the company. "In Spiegel, Ebony Aim to Dress Black Women," 9-18, she takes a quick, crisp look at a new clothing catalogue targeted at black women, and spots a trend: "The venture underscores a movement by mainstream marketers to target minority groups. With growth slowing on their mature product lines, these companies are trying to draw new audiences."

Shapiro, Eben. *The New York Times.* (★ ★)
With more hard news coverage from this colorful profile writer, Shapiro showed his competence and versatility. But his important coverage of the NCR-AT&T merger, which serviceably kept us abreast of the complex negotiations but failed to discern the deal's far-reaching impact, revealed a need to hone his analytical skills if he expects to be truly definitive. His "New Life for Rechargeable Battery," 2-15, competently discusses the improvements in rechargeable batteries that are capturing a larger market share of battery consumers. Keeping a close eye on the tricky NCR and AT&T talks in "NCR Chief Is Said to Accept Likelihood of A.T.& T. Deal," 3-8, he effectively captures the shift toward compromise. And one of his best, "A.T.& T. Pledges Higher Bid if NCR Board Is Removed," 3-20, is an insight-packed piece for investors that includes numerous useful perspectives on a federal judge's nullification of NCR's new employee stock ownership plan. He details each step toward an agreement with a fair amount of nuance as in "Harmony in A.T.& T.-NCR Tune," 3-29, but after following this story so closely, we expected a stronger wrap-up than his "A.T.& T. Buying Computer Maker in Stock Deal Worth $7.4 Billion," 5-7, which misses the opportunity to fully examine the deal's broader implications for communications industries. Evincing a healthy skepticism in "Can Prodigy Be

All Things to 15 Million PC Owners?" 6-2, he chronicles the ups & downs of Prodigy's on-line system which is jointly operated by IBM & Sears. His crisp, eye-opening look at Sony's inner workings, "Will Intramural Squabbling Derail Debt Ridden Sony?" 8-11, documents the "Ill wind and jealous rivalries" that threaten to undermine the synergies between its mainstay electronics group and its less profitable but flashier movie and record groups. His quick ride through the risky world of investing in software companies and retailers that thrive on Nintendo, "Investors Playing Nintendo Need Agility to Win Profits," 9-18, offered nothing especially fresh to investors.

Shear, Jeff. Insight. (★ ★)
Consistently reliable but rarely cutting-edge, Shear delves slightly beyond the surface of an eclectic cluster of interesting topics. He takes a critical, but limited, look at the Office of the U.S. Trade Rep. and the revolving door relationship between government officials and private lobbyists in "U.S. Trade Feels Foreign Influence," 2-18. His better-late-than-never look at the Lavoro banking scandal, "Federal Charges May Show Saddam Dug Own Burial Plot," 3-11, has Shear reporting on how the Iraqis, apparently in cahoots with the bank's directors, used the Atlanta office to redirect loans ostensibly for grain and industrial goods imports to finance their military build-up instead. His interesting "America Fumbles for Handle on Foreign Investment Mess," 4-1, examines the little-known Committee on Foreign Investment in the U.S., an executive branch mechanism for reviewing foreign investment set up in 1973 in response to the Arab oil embargo and the flow of petrodollars into the U.S.: "As much as anything in Washington, the committee is an expression of prevailing economic policy." He is sharp-eyed in his profile of T. Boone Pickens, "Reversal of Fortune Pending," 5-20, finding the unrepentant corporate raider down, but not out, as he attempts to resuscitate the natural gas industry and contemplates a gubernatorial bid in Texas. "Pickens's style is public, and that has a way of turning business deals into campaigns." He is also strong in "Charting Success in Virgin Territory," 7-8, an incisive profile of British entrepreneur Richard Branson, owner of Virgin Airlines, whose risk-taking habits extend into his daredevilish private life. On the other hand his "The Chip Pact Is Back," 7-29, was a surprisingly poor effort. This article on U.S. efforts to penetrate the Japanese market for semiconductors is virtually unreadable. Better in "Silicon Valley Upstarts Chip Away at Giants of Microchip Market," 8-19, he pens a computerese update on the latest business dealings and high-tech breakthroughs in Silicon Valley. "While computer hardware — the chips and connectors — will continue their prodigious advances in power, software is about to undergo a quantum leap."

Silk, Leonard. *The New York Times.* (★)
"Economics Scene" columnist. On domestic economic policy, Silk was once again knee-jerk Keynesian, allying himself with the easy money crowd even when lower short-term interest rates were doing nothing for the economy. He periodically fared better on other topics, but overall the 73-year-old's work has become stale and lethargic. He surveys the reaction of the financial markets to the Persian Gulf crisis in "Mideast Standoff's Effect on Business," 1-11, but there's nothing decisive in his analysis to pull us through the uncertainty of the moment. His "The Argument Over the Banks," 2-8, is a fine, tight commentary on Treasury's bank reform plan with a nice collection of quotes from Henry Kaufman, Albert Hart and Gail Fosler on why it doesn't make sense to strengthen banks by letting them do new things. But he spurts out unconvincing jibberish on the economic and moral decline of the U.S. in "The 'New Order' Is a Tall Order for the U.S.," 3-17. He seems almost desperate in "Bonn's Contrasts with Washington," 5-17, relying on questionable logic to prove that the U.S.'s ineffective easy money policy is okay, as is Bonn's tight money policy: "The difference in German and American monetary policies may represent contrasting national cultures, with Germans giving their highest priority to avoiding inflation and Americans to avoiding depression." Mmmm. He interviews Treasury Secretary Brady in "U.S. Will Press Plan for Growth in London Talks," 7-5, offering a useful look into Brady's willingness to accept inflation as a "price" of growth. In a nutshell, his "At the Summit, a Chance to Set the Stage for Growth," 7-14, is a thinly-veiled

call for easier money: ". . .one of the biggest challenges for the United States will be to persuade the central banks of the Western world to. . .push down interest rates by injecting more money into the international system." In "Brady's Message on the Scandals," 8-23, he deftly reads between the lines of Brady's reaction to Salomon's misconduct at the Treasury auctions: "If you can't forecast the public debt, just be sure you can sell it to the world." Although he leaves several variables unexamined in "Encouraging Clue Points to Recovery," 9-6, he offers an interesting perspective on how the yield curve has been a reliable indicator of the start and finish of recessions.

Smith, Randall. *The Wall Street Journal* (★ ★ ½)
A sharp observer of Wall Street's movers and shakers, Smith offers crisp insights into the financial and investment strategies of some of America's most prestigious companies. His best work this year was on the botched Time Warner rights offering. His "Asset Shuffle Angers Holders of E-II Debt," 1-28, is a very well-documented and eye-opening tale of the financial antics of CEO Meshulam Riklis which have been bad news for E-II Holdings' bondholders. He pens a neat, but limited assessment of why so many stock market analysts were trampled by a wartime bull market they didn't see coming in "Stock Market Swing Shows How Wrong Professionals Can Be," leder 2-26, a good story idea, but his execution is too general. He lucidly examines the implications of Goldman Sachs' well-informed purchase of depressed Tonka bonds in "Goldman Bought Bonds of Tonka Knowing Mattel Had Mulled Bid," 3-8: "Goldman's investment in Tonka bonds shows the opportunities. . .available to major Wall Street firms as they seek to operate both as advisers and investors." In "Drexel's Dealmakers Resurface to Repackage Old Clients' Deals," 4-9, Smith repackages a story that has already appeared in *Forbes* —ex-Drexelites are restructuring the companies that took on too much debt in the '80s. He smoothly assesses NCR's controversial holdout against AT&T in "NCR's Holdout Boosted AT&T's Bid by 22%, Yet Opinion Is Split on Tactic," 5-7, questioning if the maneuver was worth the substantial time, money and risk. Joined by Laura Landro for "After Stock Debacle, Some Ask: Will Hubris Undo Time Warner?" leder 7-19, we're offered excellent depth and definition on the workings of Time Warner under Steven J. Ross. The professional presentation allows readers to judge Ross's flamboyant spending style without pushing an "excess" theme to excess. Smith's zippy sidebar, "How Salomon Muscled Aside Merrill to Be Lead Underwriter on Big Rights Offering," 7-19, is also enterprising on what went wrong on Time Warner's original stock offering. Two months later, Smith adds credibility to his assessment of Ross's free spending ways in "Time Warner, With All that Debt, Backs a Dealmaker," 9-18, disclosing that Time Warner bankrolls East West Capital Associates which is run by one of its directors, former Lorimar Chairman Merve Adelson: "Several people. . .say the East West arrangement was a reward for Mr. Adelson's agreement to endorse the [1989] Lorimar merger [with Time Warner] and relinquish any operating role at the company."

Solomon, Caleb. *The Wall Street Journal.* (★ ★)
Solomon's coverage of the oil industry's domestic shifts nicely complements James Tanner's international oil coverage. We're impressed with Solomon's attention to accuracy and style, and look forward to the in-depth assignments he is bound to land in the future. Perceptive in "Pump Prices Look Ready for Run Uphill, But Image-Wary Oil Firms May Curb Rise," 1-16, he notes the wartime dilemma oil companies face: "Major oil companies don't want to raise prices too high, too soon right now. They fear a widespread backlash because they will also be releasing fourth-quarter earnings in a few days that are expected to show huge profits." His creative and admiring look at the colorful personalities who want to go back to the Middle East despite the chaos, "Many Ex-Hostages Head Back to Gulf; Question Is, Why?" 3-6, characterizes these men as "modern-day cowboys, independent and laconic Gary Coopers." In "Independent Gas Stations Cry Foul Over Price Wars," 4-1, he reports that consumers may be happy with 90-cent-a-gallon gas, but independents say that the big boys are running them out of business by waging a crushing price war. Solomon notes that if the independents go under there may be less competition and higher prices in the long run. Without the benefit of clear-cut information,

Solomon's "A Coastal Purchase of Burlington Resources El Paso Gas Unit Seen Bullish for Both Firms," 6-10, is a well-thought out assessment of rumors that Coastal wants to buy El Paso Natural Gas. Joined by Robert Johnson for " 'Friendly Fire' Downs the Soaring Career of a Gung-Ho Colonel," leder 9-10, we're vividly told the touching personal tragedy of Lt. Col. Ralph Hayles who mistakenly shot at two U.S. armored vehicles during the Gulf War, killing two American soldiers. The authors' compassionate telling, inspired many touching letters from servicemen and civilians alike. His compact assessment of Wainoco Oil's plans to acquire an oil refinery in Wyoming, "Wainoco Sees Purchase Aiding Quarterly Net," 9-30, deftly observes: "For Wainoco, a small natural-gas...company...the refinery acquisition...represents a diversification away from weak natural gas prices."

Srodes, James L. *FW.* (★ ½)
For a Washington bureau chief, Srodes is sometimes surprisingly superficial or out of touch with the events emerging from the nation's capital. As for the overall quality of his reporting and analysis, all we can say is that it's consistently inconsistent. Early in the year, he flushes out some hard-to-find details on the top-to-bottom restructuring of the capital markets in "Forced to Reform," 1-8. Among the particulars shaping up, "assets in bank portfolios would be 'marked to market,' " and signs of a "generally more aggressive regulatory and supervisory mandate." His highly-stylized "The Spirit of the Fed at War," 2-5, ably explores the mid-war mood at the Federal Reserve. His observations are ill-timed and ill-informed in "The Affordable War?" 2-19. Trying to discredit "the affordable war" theory just weeks before the dramatic allied victory in the Gulf, he quotes sources that imply that the markets are spooked by the expected long-term cost of the war, an odd observation amid a record-breaking bull market. His " 'Tom Terrific' Saves Chase Manhattan," 4-2, is an interesting, but not especially probing, talk with Thomas G. Labrecque who walked into the CEO position at Chase mid-crisis, and managed to turn things around with a massive retrenchment. Srodes lets Labrecque gloss over plans to return the bank to real growth. He embarks on an engaging investment chat with Gavin Dobson of Murray Johnston, Glasgow, Scotland's largest independent investment management firm, in "Dollar Defense," 9-3, examining how investors can minimize foreign exchange risk by using the dollar to lock in foreign equity gains. Dobson makes numerous interesting observations, although we'd have liked a little more input from Srodes. He leaves too much unexamined in "Rude Awakening," 9-17, skimming the Treasury auction reform movement embracing Washington. There was more information in the dailies on this issue than from Srodes who has two weeks to put his articles together. Much better in "Changing Customs," 10-1, we're offered a solid, fresh report on the complexities Customs officials face in valuing import duties on products because these days duties are affected by multinational parts, shifting exchange rates and complex trade agreements.

Starobin, Paul. *National Journal.* (★ ★)
Economics, financial institutions. Having settled into his beat, Starobin evinced a stronger grasp of the issues and was able to give us more depth in his coverage of a banking industry in turmoil. Sharp on the changing investment and borrowing patterns that are robbing banks of much of their traditional business in "Bypassing Banks," 3-9, Starobin skillfully examines the alternatives. He concisely delineates why legislation to overhaul the banking system is "stuck in the mud" in "Banking Package Stalled," 3-23, providing key examples of the feuding surrounding not only this proposal but the debate over the S&L bailout funds as well. In "Sitting Ducks," 4-20, he tells us that Washington's top three banking regulators — Greenspan, Seidman and Clarke — are trying to hold together an antiquated financial system that is in distress. Whatever goes wrong, he observes, they are the sitting ducks just waiting to be blamed. "They're necks are collectively in a noose," said Bert Ely, a financial consultant. His "Out the Window," 6-22, is a useful and timely discussion of the Fed's controversial "assistance" to struggling banks through its discount window. While some contend that the recession is only "a blip on the screen," Starobin discusses the more profound structural problems ailing the country in "Nation of Spenders," 7-20. In "BCCI's Washington Web," 9-7, he competently dissects the BCCI

connections with Clifford, Altman, First American and Hill and Knowlton, among others. He gathers plenty of anecdotal evidence to try to debunk the myth that cities are dying in "The Cutting Edge," 9-28. He is much more in-depth in "Distressed Debtors," cover 10-12, solidly examining what goes on in bankruptcy court, from the few who abuse the system to those who use it to start fresh and honest.

Stern, Richard L. *Forbes.* (★ ★ ½)
Senior editor. We saw fewer single bylines from the exacting and determined Stern this year. Perhaps he is mentoring *Forbes*' less-experienced reporters who are bound to learn from his precise style and dogged-research which make for consistently hard-hitting reports. His refreshing and historically-rich contrarian perspective on why Pan Am was done in, "The End of an Empire," 2-4, tells us that Pan Am is not a fatality of deregulation, but of "management errors and U.S. government dithering." "How did the U.S. Government help bring down Pan Am? International aviation is, by definition, not a free market. Governments, even now, allow the airlines to collude on fares and service. Routes are negotiated between the countries at each end." He disappoints with "Small Caps Reawaken," 3-4, an uncharacteristically bland, cursory overview of Ralph Wanger's investment strategies which offers no particularly fresh information for small cap traders. On the other hand, he is savvy and solid on the increasing competition the NYSE faces from alternative trading networks in "A Dwindling Monopoly," 5-13, observing that the biggest savings alternative systems offer come from cutting out the NYSE specialists who make the market for each stock. Joined by Tatiana Pouschine for "Can Donald Pay His Hotel Bill?" 7-8, we're offered a revealing follow-up to last year's eye-opening expose in *Forbes* of Donald Trump's dwindling finances. Stern and Pouschine disclose an audited financial statement which reveals financial woes at the Plaza hotel: "The Plaza's audited statements show that Trump continues to run the hotel only at the merciful sufferance of its creditors; last year cash from operations fell short of covering interest expense by about $20 million." "The Gaijins' Revenge," co-written by Howard Rudnitsky 8-5, is a crisp tale of how U.S. and British brokerage houses plan to capitalize on the Japanese brokerage scandals by grabbing a bigger slice of that country's futures trading business. Joined by Laura Jereski for "More Victims?" 9-16, we find an expert examination of how far the ripples may have extended when Salomon fixed the Treasury note markets last spring. The authors even raise questions about the cross-market exchange of information that could have had an wide-ranging impact throughout the financial system.

Stevenson, Richard W. *The New York Times.* (★ ★)
Los Angeles. Although we appreciated Stevenson's coverage of Hollywood a year ago, it was his improved coverage of banking and financial issues that stood out in 1991. His "Old Ways Are Dead," 1-8, is a sound news analysis on Defense Secretary Richard Cheney's decision to cancel the A-12 program which according to one analyst will sound " 'the deathknell for fixed-price contracting.' " He's heavy on the fiscal quarter reports in "7 Oscars for 'Wolves' Lift a Troubled Studio," 3-27, failing to round out the story with the blood, romance and adventure details appropriate for a story about the downfall of a multi-million dollar movie studio. He is also so-so in "Taming Hollywood's Spending Monster," 4-14, a limited report on runaway production costs as studios chase the next *Batman*. Better in "Carolco Flexes Its Muscle Overseas," 6-26, he takes an interesting look at Carolco Pictures as it prepares to release *Terminator 2.* "More than most companies, including the major studios, Carolco has positioned itself to take advantage of the fast-growing demand for movies abroad." He relies on conventional wisdom in "Gray Skies for California Banks," 7-8, a standard wrap up of the slipping results at California's major banks. Investors will find his "Awaiting the Next Big Bank Merger," 8-15, useful for its speculation about an acquisition of First Interstate Bancorp by Wells Fargo & Co. While he is strong on the benefits of such a merger, he also points out First Interstate's loan troubles, and questions how the banks' different management styles might come into play. Following Allstate's announcement that it will stop doing business in New Jersey, Stevenson provides a very astute analysis of growing insurer and consumer frustration in

"Insurance Reform in a Deadlock," 9-23. He discerns the challenges facing alternatives like no-fault insurance: ". . .enacting new or tougher no-fault laws has been almost impossible politically in many states, largely because of the opposition of trial lawyers, who have lobbied hard against any legislation that would limit the right to sue."

Stokes, Bruce. *National Journal.* (★ ★)

International trade. Stokes dabbles in the various trade issues with relative ease, but when given the opportunity to really dissect their economics, as in his spring piece for *Foreign Affairs,* he resorts to knee-jerk explanations about the evils of the "twin deficits." As Soviet President Gorbachev puts economic liberalization on hold, Stokes pens an authoritative analysis of U.S. efforts to keep reform on track in "Help On Hold," 2-2: "U.S. aid. . .is a prisoner of relations between Moscow and the republics. . ." With Hollywood marketers of films and TV shows eyeing major profits in Europe, Stokes' "Tinseltown Trade War," 2-23, usefully examines how they've wheeled out their glittery guns in Washington to shake up the trade debate following the EC's placement of a cap on U.S. TV program sales. In "Why OPEC Now Faces a Holding Action," 3-23, he looks into the prediction of an energy crisis during the Persian Gulf War which became a non-event despite OPEC's move to cut petroleum production. "It was a stopgap action to head off a world oil glut and a dramatic fall in prices." He is joined by Michael C. Aho for "The Year the World Economy Turned," which appeared in the "America & the World" issue of *Foreign Affairs* 1990/91. The caliber of Aho and Stoke's analysis is best described by their own characterization of the American economy as it emerged from the 1980s, that is "basically strong, but with some profound weaknesses." "Basically strong" is their premise that "If the United States is to remain an economic leader in the world, it must adapt its leadership style to the increasingly interdependent nature of the global economy." The "profound weaknesses" occur because their discourse focuses on the stale assessment that America is now paying the price for the "twin deficits" of the 1980s. On the other hand, we found plenty of insights and detail in his well-substantiated, "Greens Talk Trade," 4-13, which chronicles the political haggling between the Bush administration and environmental groups over the proposed free-trade pact with Mexico. With the economic summit in London largely spent debating financial assistance to the Soviet Union, his "Some Bargain," 7-13, provided a nice balance of perspectives from proponents and opponents of this high stakes economic gamble. Also, nicely detailed was his "As the World Trades," 8-17, a perceptive overview of the interdependence of the world's markets, and the need for standardized international regulation. He is conventional and too general on American doubts about the EC's ability to act as a unit in a disappointing "Neglecting Brussels," 10-5.

Sullivan, Allanna. *The Wall Street Journal.* (★ ★ ½)

New York, oil industry. Impressing us with several exemplary company profiles as well as consistently accurate insights into the direction oil prices would move in a volatile year, Sullivan seems likely to become one of the best on this beat in the near future. Co-writing the biggest story of the year with veteran James Tanner — the outbreak of war in the Gulf — Sullivan showcases her expertise in "A Major Oil Glut Offers a Cushion to Global Markets," leder 1-17, a clear and calm analysis of the war's impact on oil supplies and prices that makes clear it is consumer psychology, not verifiable supply information, that will be the key to oil prices during the crisis: "Psychology is so important. . .that U.S. Energy Secretary James Watkins has set up a communications link with the Saudi government to head off rumors and misinformation that might rock the wartime oil market." On target with "Oil Prices May Bottom Out at $15 a Barrel," 3-1, she examines the "uncertainty premium" that will keep analysts guessing about the future price of oil. Assessing the damage to Kuwaiti oil fields in "Even After Fires Die, Kuwait's Oil Fields Will Never Be the Same," leder 4-26, she deftly observes: "Kuwait's oil fields are losing some of their providential fizz. . .Kuwait oil will never be as easy or as cheap to produce again." Sharp on the economic and political implications, she notes Kuwait will consequently become more reluctant to encourage lower oil prices. We thoroughly enjoyed her "Cheap Gasoline and Full Service? It Must Be Heaven," a-head 5-24, a colorful sketch of Rudy Massa's

Gasoline Heaven where service is fast, fuel is cheap and the customer is king. With Kuwait frantically trying to get its refineries back to profitable production levels, Sullivan pens "Kuwait Moves to Restart Oil Refineries," 6-10, effectively capturing the resolve that is driving the Kuwaitis forward. Her excellent example of what a company profile should be, "Star of Restructured Texaco Shines Again," 7-8, gives investment readers definitive details and meaningful analysis on the past, present and future of the company. She is equally well-rounded in "France's Elf Aims to Be a Global Giant," 9-19, ably examining how and why the French oil company Elf Aquitaine is aggressively expanding under its new CEO.

Tanner, James. *The Wall Street Journal.* (★ ★ ★ ★)
Oil industry. Well-seasoned in the politics and economics of petroleum, Tanner provided rich analysis of the shifting sands at OPEC caused by Desert Storm. Dean of petroleum writers, he can't get much better than he was this year. Joined by Allanna Sullivan for the biggest story of the year — the outbreak of war in the Gulf — we're offered a clear and calm analysis of the war's impact on oil prices and supplies in "A Major Oil Glut Offers a Cushion to Global Markets," leder 1-17. His thorough and knowledgeable assessment of what the end of the war will mean to OPEC, "War May Encourage Oil Price Moderation by Bolstering Saudis," leder 2-25, focuses on the leadership role that will be taken by the moderate, but drastically changed, Saudi Arabia, and how its enhanced role may affect oil prices. On daily oil price updates such as "OPEC Output of Crude Oil Appears to Fall," 4-29, Tanner ably captures the dynamic connection of past, present and future production. Once again in "Oil Consumers, Producers' Joint Efforts to Avoid Shocks Is Gaining Momentum," 5-20, he points out that politics is as important as production when it comes to pricing oil, in this case a French-Venezuelan proposal to create a dialogue between producers and consumers to bring about the stabilization of prices. Filing "OPEC Leaves Oil Quotas Unchanged," 6-5, from a conference in Vienna, Tanner pens a typically concise and well-rounded report with plenty of important statistics, production ceiling targets, and authoritative reactions to them. In Iran for "Iran Pumps New Life Into Giant Oil Sites," 7-3, we're offered a clear-eyed overview of this country's efforts to boost its worldwide market share. But we'd have liked more on the politics of what Tanner calls "a massive push to restore the oil industry to its pre-revolution status." Tanner's coverage of a key OPEC meeting in Geneva was filled with astute observations. Both "OPEC Ministers Generally Back Plan for $2-a-Barrel Rise with New Exports," 9-25, and "OPEC Ministers Agree to Meet Demand in Winter, Setting Slight Rise in Output," 9-26, admirably captured the themes of the price-target debates, while "Saudi Arabia's Role at OPEC Meeting Test Many Alliances Within the Group," 9-27, expertly characterized Saudi oil minister Hisham Nazer's post war hot seat during the especially contentious conference in which Libya, Iran and others sharply criticized the Saudis' stance on prices. From Caracas, his outstanding reconnaissance, "Venezuela Now Woos Oil Firms It Booted in '70s Nationalization," leder 10-2, analyzes the changing political and economic global environment that has caused Venezuelan President Carlos Andres Perez to shift from booting out foreign oil companies as he did during his first term as President in the mid-1970s to wooing them back.

Taylor, Alex, III. *Fortune.* (★ ★ ½)
Detroit. We criticized this veteran auto reporter last year for failing "to embrace the global forces coming to bear in today's auto marketplace." This year, Taylor showed us that he does indeed understand what it takes to run an automaker in a competitive global marketplace, although we were chilled by the protectionist undertones in some of his pieces. After we cut through the lengthy and gossipy speculation over whether former Ford CEO Don Peterson was forced out or left on his accord, Taylor's "The Odd Eclipse of a Star CEO," 2-11, delves into the more pertinent question of where Ford is going, and how fast, under new CEO Harold Poling: "Poling's major challenges are to limit interim losses and to make sure that the two dozen new Ford models that will get to the U.S. showrooms by 1995 hit their agreed-upon cost targets. Cost cutting is Poling's specialty." His "Can Iacocca Fix Chrysler — Again?" 4-8, was a tiresome read, as everybody and their brother has dissected the Iacocca era as this icon approaches

retirement and Chrysler approaches oblivion. On the other hand, "How Buick Is Bouncing Back," 5-6, is a nifty piece that goes against the trend on how GM's Buick division is still selling cars at a healthy rate. A welcome success story: "There's nothing fancy about how Buick does it." He pens a puzzler in "Do You Know Where Your Car Was Made?" 6-17, taking a good thing — U.S. automakers sourcing parts from around the world — and making it sound like a horrible problem. Taylor's report is very protectionist in tone: "bad news for U.S. workers and consumers alike." Shifting 180 degrees, we found Taylor at his best in "BMW and Mercedes Make Their Move," 8-12, an excellent exploration of Mercedes and BMW's strategic plans as they release their latest models in the lucrative U.S. market where they must compete with a growing number of Japanese competitors.

Thomas, Paulette. *The Wall Street Journal.* (★ ★ ★)
Washington. One of the Washington bureau's gem reporters, Thomas gave us another year of gripping, muscular and well-documented reports on the S&L debacle. She's clearly the most consistently discerning reporter on this complex issue. In "A Seat on House Banking Panel, Long Prized, Is Now Shunned as a Nasty Political Liability," 1-8, she takes a crucial look at the changes taking place in this crucial, crisis-ridden panel which is losing a number of members. Thomas skillfully alerts us to the long-term impact this turnover could have. We found more juicy details and penetrating insights in "Round Two of the S&L Bailout Is Developing Into a Partisan Fight to Deflect Public Outrage," 3-8: ". . .Son of Bailout, the Bush administration's request for another $78 billion to keep the effort going, shows signs of degenerating into a partisan mess, with each party trying to saddle the other with the public outrage over the S&L debacle." "Sale of Failed Thrifts' Assets Sometimes Leaves Regulators Advised by Parties With Most to Gain," 4-3, is quintessential Thomas, riveting and well documented on the conflict of interest many thrift consultants face in providing advice to the government. Also, on the cutting-edge with "Regulators Are Ousting Top Managers in an Effort to Curb Banking Failures," 5-14, Thomas alerts us to this latest regulatory overreach: "These removals aren't due to fraud. . .but occur in the gray area of assessing executive competence." In "Bush Administration Lets Out Seams on Its Projections for Thrift Bailout," 6-24, she skillfully exposes the budgetary shenanigans going on at OMB over the estimates for the S&L bailout. She provides an incisive discussion of the RTC's recent issue of securities backed by mortgages from busted thrifts in "Mortgage-Backed 'Ritzy Maes' Stroll Down the Street With RTC," 7-12, noting that the new breed of securities which lack an implicit government guarantee "also represent a rare instance where the RTC, through adroit packaging, can actually add value to an asset being sold. . ." Upbeat in "Resolution Trust Corp. Makes Some Headway in Selling S&L Assets," leder 10-3, she keenly assesses how the RTC has advanced on the learning curve, moving assets more quickly now that it knows how to package deals.

Thomas, Rich. *Newsweek.* (★ ★ ½)
Chief economic correspondent. Thomas is consistently the best economic writer at the newsweeklies. Although we didn't find enough exploration of the balance between fiscal and monetary policy in Thomas's work this year, we were impressed by his clear-eyed coverage of the Federal Reserve. Joined by Marc Levinson for "Is Bush's Team Up to It?" 2-18, we're offered a broad skim of the complex relationship between the members of the administration's economic team — Brady, Darman, Boskin and Greenspan. Analysis of their economic ideologies is also simplistic. Thomas is more effective in "What If There's No Rebound?" 4-1, pinpointing the axis for recovery as the Fed and Fed chairman Greenspan: "He may not have much time. His term expires in August. Bush, a personal friend, may tolerate the slump through the spring. But if recovery isn't visible by summer, even a Teflon-coated Bush might want a Fed chairman who isn't so sticky." Reminding us of the main mission at the Fed in "A Food Fight at the Fed," 4-22, he reassures us that differences between the chairman and the regional bank presidents that had *The New York Times* and *The Wall Street Journal* hyperventilating are "minute." "Few understand that. . .[the Federal Reserve Board's] main aim is to maintain price stability and the value of a dollar." Joined by John Schwartz for "The Message in the Market," 4-29, we're served

an elementary explanation of the DJIA hitting 3000. In "Do CEOs Make Too Much?" 5-6, he examines the case of ITT where poor performance was rewarded by the board of directors with double the compensation for chairman Rand Araskog. However, he doesn't mention the fact that ITT is recovering from a difficult restructuring until the last paragraph, giving us an unbalanced view of things until the end of the report. In "Japan: All in the Family," co-written by Bill Powell 6-10, we find the authors buying completely into the myth that interrelated Japanese business groups, *keiretsu,* are wholly bad as they supposedly act like informal trading blocks. There's an upside to this system that should have been examined too. "The Pay Police," co-written by Larry Reibstein 6-17, begins rather frivolously, but turns into a rather smartly-turned overview of the structure of pay scales and incentives, and whether they should be tied to performance. Joined by Evan Thomas for "Where Did All the Money Go?" 7-1, we're deluged with statistics regarding state budgetary problems, but there's not enough cohesive analysis to hold the piece together. On the Salomon Brothers story, his "Cleaning Up 'the Club,' " co-written by Joshua Hammer 9-16, provided a solid, albeit familiar, roundup of all the pertinent facts surrounding the Treasury auctions scandal.

Trachtenberg, Jeffrey A. *The Wall Street Journal.* (★ ★ ½)
New York, retail. An experienced hand on the retailing beat, Trachtenberg ably steered us through these dark days in the retailing industry with instructive examinations of all aspects of the business. Taking us to the showroom floor, the restaurant table and the car lot in "A Buyer's Market Has Shoppers Demanding and Getting Discounts," leder 2-8, we find an engaging, but only mildly informative, anecdotal look at the recession's downward pressure on prices. He proves he can view retailing from an investors viewpoint in "Avon Rings Bells on the Street, but Economy and Expected Proxy Fight May Mute Its Call," 3-4, a thorough, proficient assessment of Avon as its shares hit a ten-year high. He notes that despite a positive cash flow, "all isn't serene at Avon." With a vast shakeout under way in the retail apparel industry, his "The Credit Crunch Is Latest Harsh Blow for Small Retailers," leder 4-9, is a revealing, hands-on account of how the credit crunch is strangling small retailers: " 'I've seen a fair number of fundamentally sound retailers who couldn't get working capital for the upcoming year qualify after they filed for bankruptcy,' says [banker] Mrs. [Darla] Moore." He's numbers oriented in "Campeau Units Revise Plans to Reorganize," 7-2, scrutinizing the Federated and Allied divisions' revised plan to raise cash and pay off key creditor groups. In "Fighting the Tide, Owner Tries to Revive Big Department Store," leder 8-14, he does a fine job of assessing the possibilities and frustrations retailing wizard A. Alfred Taubman faces in his quest to resuscitate the Wanamaker store in downtown Philadelphia. His "Ikea Furniture Chain Pleases With Its Prices, Not With Its Service," leder 9-17, is even more perceptive than an earlier piece we praised in *Fortune,* with Trachtenberg not only capturing the store's appeal, but scrutinizing the little quirks that will have to be worked out if the Swedish retailer hopes to succeed in the American market after its splashy ad campaigns have lost impact.

Treece, James B. *Business Week.* (★ ★)
Detroit bureau manager. Especially sharp at profiling the strengths and weaknesses of the auto industry's various domestic and international players, Treece takes a holistic approach to his subject by covering marketing, manufacturing, price, quality, financing, etc. In the depths of the recession, his hard-hitting and info-packed "Detroit Could Use an Air Bag Itself," 1-14, deftly characterizes the gloom in Detroit where the auto industry is waiting for the restoration of consumer confidence. ". . .about the only prop holding up auto sales is rental fleets, and they're a mixed blessing. Fleets now account for nearly 10% of all new passenger-car sales in the U.S., up from 6% in 1985. . .But the recent surplus of such nearly-new cars threatens to undercut the manufacturers' new-car sales to dealers." After a series of rollout snafus and one recall, we're told that sales of GM's Saturn are picking up in "Are the Planets Lining Up at Last for Saturn?" 4-8, but Treece doesn't thoroughly explore Saturn's hopes to carve out a long-term competitive niche. He was also upbeat on Saturn in "Getting Mileage From a Recall," 5-27, a brief but informative analysis of the positive implications to Saturn's recent recall of 1,800 cars. His

intriguing report on the "environmentally friendly" Dodge Neon, "A Car for Planet Earth," 6-17, tells us that this winner of a gold medal in the annual Industrial Design Excellence Award program is recyclable. Reportedly Chrysler's new production car, the PC, looks quite a bit like the Neon. Joined by Karen Lowry Miller for "Subaru Pulls Into the Image Shop," 8-19, the authors skillfully chronicle the shake up at Subaru, showcasing their solid grasp of the international car industry.

Truell, Peter. *The Wall Street Journal.* (★ ★ ★ ★)

Washington. On the global economy, Truell is among the best at the dailies. He has also been consistently one of the most perceptive and dogged reporters following the BCCI story. His "GATT Talks Remain Crucial to Trade," 2-11, is an articulate case for not allowing North American free trade to supplant the stalled GATT talks which would ultimately benefit the U.S. much more. In "The Group of Seven Faces New Challenges," 4-8, he sums things up for the G-7 beautifully: "In short, the world badly needs economic leadership." While his "Bush Is Rebuffed by G-7 on Lower Rates," 4-29, is competent in every way, it lacks Truell's usual depth of analysis, leaving us with unanswered questions about the political fallout of the U.S.'s whine for lower interest rates. Joined by Philip Revzin for a slightly hyperbolic "U.S. vs. United Europe," leder 7-15, the authors quote a few confrontational voices, and zero in on specific areas of contention. But this narrow approach makes it seem that controversy dominates the relationship, rather than flavors aspects of it. Truell examines how the BCCI scandal is throwing the Fed's credibility into question in "The Fed, Already Under Fire, Must Deal With 2 International Banking Scandals," 4-8: " 'The scandals,' says one former top bank regulator, 'are ammunition for those who say the comptroller should get it all' when it comes to bank regulation." In "How a Saudi Helped BCCI Scandal Spread from Miami to Encino," leder 6-13, he intricately details the role of Ghaith Pharaon who played the "front man" for BCCI in its transactions with First American. He makes no judgement calls in "Revolving Door Between Fed and First American May Help Explain Failure to Detect BCCI's Role," 9-6, but simply lists link after link of Fed officials who have been involved in business or social transactions with First American. Joined by Jill Abramson for "Clifford and Altman Deny Awareness of BCCI Control," 9-12, we're offered a competent recounting of key testimony. But Truell is better in the sidebar, "Fed Wouldn't Take Evidence on BCCI to Avoid Giving It to Jury, Memo Says," 9-12, an important glimpse into an incident in which the Fed "refused to accept vital evidence in the BCCI affair so that it wouldn't have to turn it over to a grand jury in Manhattan. . .[T]he memo from late 1990 provides the starkest illustration yet of the rivalry that appeared to grip various law enforcement agencies pursuing BCCI — a competition that has only slowed efforts to prosecute the bank."

Tumulty, Karen. *Los Angeles Times.* (★ ★)

Washington. New to the trade beat this year, Tumulty has quickly proven able to manage the details of international trade and interest rate issues. We look forward to her developing a more sophisticated understanding of currency's role in these debates. In "The Balancing Act of Reparations: Punishing Iraq Without Ruining It," 2-25, she provides a lucid discussion of the struggle to strike a "difficult balance" that ensures those who suffered at the hands of Iraq receive reparations without bankrupting and further destabilizing this troubled country. Her pithy report on the dispute over global interest rates, "U.S., Allies Square Off Over Interest Rates," 4-26, and her followup, "U.S.'s Bid for Global Interest Rate Cuts Fails," 4-29, clarify the schism between the U.S. and its allies over where global interest rates should be. Japan and Germany "insist that if the United States wants to drive the cost of credit down, it should do so by other means, including cutting inflation at home and getting its budget deficit under control. 'We are not against lower rates, but they must be earned,' said Karl Otto Poehl, president of Germany's Bundesbank." She skillfully weaves in the positions of various political lobbying groups in "Mexican Trade Pact Lobbying Growing Pitched," 5-13, giving us a well-rounded overview of the immense lobbying effort surrounding "fast track" authority for free-trade negotiations with Mexico. Her objective, blow-by-blow account of the House vote in favor of fast track, "House OKs 'Fast-Track' Mexican Trade Talks," 5-24, carefully balances the various concerns in the controversial debate. Not to overlook the broader GATT negotiations, she pens an educational update with "Nothing Short of a Miracle needed at Trade Talks," 6-2, effectively characterizing the contentious mood of these crucial talks which, if successfully concluded, "would provide a badly needed $125-billion boost in [U.S.] growth in the first year" according to the administration. Her marvelous early front page profile of Clarence Thomas' background, "Court Path Started in Ashes," 7-7, a 10 Best selection in Political Reporting, has Tumulty scouring sources in Pin Point, Georgia, fleshing out material on Thomas' grandfather, and making connections to the writings of Thomas Sowell. But she's not as strong in " 'Enterprise Funds' Get Off to a Rocky Start," 7-10, Tumulty's contribution to *LAT*'s "Rebuilding the Bloc" series. This is rather a quick superficial skim of an important topic with Tumulty failing to examine the currency issues that are key to the enterprise fund's problems. Filing "Banker Gives Ruble 2 years to Catch On," 9-19, from Moscow, she pens a serviceable overview of the disruptive struggle over currency issues between the independence-minded republics.

Uchitelle, Louis. *The New York Times.* (★ ½)
New York. Although he is still very often out of focus, hampered by the two-dimensional belief that there is an inflation/growth trade-off built into the economy, the unpredictable Uchitelle hit more often than he struck out this year. In "Federal Reserve Acts Warily in Combating This Recession," 1-11, he embarks on a sweeping review of the mindset at the Fed, but fails to back up his vague statements that Chairman Greenspan catered to the majority view in October 1990. His contribution to the "Banks Under Stress" series, "Reforms in Banking Call for a Shrinking U.S. Role," 2-21, heralds the attributes of the "two window" (insured and uninsured) solution without fully exploring the downside. Not until the end of this lengthy report does he touch upon warnings from small banks about how the "too big to fail" doctrine will cause a migration of funds from small to large banks. He resigns himself to the concept of higher taxes in "States and Cities Are Pushing Hard for Higher Taxes," 3-25, even though he recognizes that "the booming 1980's generated so much revenue from existing taxes that budget surpluses were commonplace." If he'd explored his own observation more carefully, he might have come up with a growth alternative to taxation. He is clear-eyed in "The Interest Rate Battles," 5-2, a sturdy analysis of Brady's "quixotic" attempt to lower worldwide interest rates while "trying to argue simultaneously that the recession in the United States is about to end and is also in danger of getting worse." Onto something in "Recovery Expected to Be Weak," 5-23, he concludes that a vigorous recovery looks farfetched, and lands a great quote from OMB's Darman: " 'Below-par economic growth is likely to endure well into the 1992 election campaign, but studies by political scientists show that voters will not necessarily be alienated. . .It is the direction, not the magnitude, that counts,' he said." His "Pressure on Fed Without Letup," 7-16, is better than expected on continued pressure on the Fed to ease, but he is still hindered by his belief in an inflation/growth trade-off. He paints a credible picture of a U.S. population increasingly uneasy about the strength of the economy in "Optimism Is Disappearing for a Solid Recovery Soon," 8-11. And his "The Annual Game of Auto Pricing," 9-10, is an interesting pro and con look at why automakers are ignoring the law of supply and demand and raising prices in these tough times.

Verity, John. *BusinessWeek.* (★ ★ ½)
Information processing editor. Verity takes us on exhilarating trips to the outer fringes of computer technology where we are privy to an amazing future. But capable of more than mere razzle-dazzle, Verity carefully fuses business and technology issues, making his articles valuable to both techies and Wall Street types alike. We appreciated the interesting observations in "Computers Will See Lots of Downtime," 1-14, in which he explains flat computer sales aren't only a reflection of a bad economy, but also mirror consumer puzzlement over which strategic direction to take their computing operations. In "Why 'Systems Integration' Sounds Like Poetry to IBM," 4-8, he provides a very astute assessment of the new emphasis on service: ". . .as growth in hardware revenue and profit slows, computer makers are turning to services as the golden

egg." In retrospect, his sources' observations about IBM's inability to reorient quickly proved prescient. The fascinating world of "infographics" is the subject of "The War on Information Clutter," with Jessie Nathans 4-29, explaining this revolutionary approach which favors "lucidity as much as style." "Computer Confusion," with Robert D. Hof, Richard Brandt, Jonathan B. Levine and Gary McWilliams 6-10, is a highly perceptive reconnaissance into the world of computer standards which has become so jumbled that it's chilling an already flat market. Joined by Gary McWilliams for "Is It Time to Junk the Way You Use Computers?" 7-22, we're offered an amazing look at the computer industry's latest buzzword, re-engineering: "Instead of using computers and information systems to automate the way a business has always run, you first re-engineer the process, then apply computing power to the new system." In "Multimedia Computing: PCs that Do Everything But Walk the Dog," with Sunita Wadekar-Bhargava 8-12, he captures the excitement of multimedia computing where "a laser-disk encyclopedia might have voices, video and sound to accompany the usual text and drawings." Joined by Evan I. Schwartz for "Software Made Simple," 9-30, the authors explore the amazing potential of object-oriented programming. And he takes a quick, info-packed look at efforts to reuse old chunks of software in new products in "At HP These Days, Old Software Never Dies," 9-30.

Victor, Kirk. *National Journal.* (★ ★)
A perceptive political observer, Victor is quite good at laying out the battle lines that surround specific telecommunications debates at the Federal Communications Commission. He has also proven himself capable on other topics such as in "Branching Out to Social Issues," 2-2, proposing the interesting thesis that shifts in demographics will change patterns of organization, thus necessitating a labor union opinion on social issues such as abortion and the Persian Gulf War. His solid examination of the lobbying problems broadcasters face over rerun rights, "Video Warriors," 3-2, is a rich review of this long-running and heated debate. The FCC's decision to relax its 1970 financial and syndication rules is fully explored in " 'FIN-SYN' Battling and Billing Goes On," 4-13. Victor makes clear why both producers and networks were left fuming, prompting a ferocious lobbying fight. In his perceptive "Disconnections," 5-11, he tells us why many believe that the five FCC regulators who rule on cutting-edge communications issues, such as "finsyn," are communicating to one another through short-circuited wires. He observes that FCC chairman Sikes "is considered to be a Missouri mule," while regulators Barrett and Duggan are equated with loose cannons. Examining two viewpoints on the future of the workforce during the next 15 years in "Work Force Warfare," 9-28, he taps into various studies, but concludes too abruptly that workers have no culpability for the widening gap between the workers' skills and those skills required by the workplace.

Wald, Matthew L. *The New York Times.* (★ ★)
Energy. Branching out his energy coverage to a wider array of issues, we saw marked improvement in Wald's work this year with some of his best reporting on nuclear energy issues. In his fascinating "A Company Is Finding the Good in Pollution," 1-9, he explores "A radically different approach to air pollution — converting harmful combustion waste products into something useful. . ." Discussing the disarray OPEC will face post-Gulf War in "Assessing the Damage to OPEC," 2-11, Wald gathers plenty of cogent facts and data, but lacks the authority of other OPEC-watchers such as James Tanner at *The Wall Street Journal.* His report on the steep decline in Soviet oil production, "Oil Experts Gloomy on Soviets," 3-23, carries this zinger from Gorbachev's old ally Stanislav Shatalin: "If I was a banker I would not invest a single cent in the economy." In Kuwait to review the extent of the war damage, he pens a disconcerting "Surge of Water Due to Well Fires to Cut Future Kuwaiti Oil Output," 4-9, which vividly depicts the "irreversible damage" sustained to its oil fields. His "Due Up for License Renewal: The Future of Nuclear Power," 6-24, is a worthwhile alert for both opponents and proponents of nuclear energy. Wald explains that because the nuclear industry's future depends so heavily on the continuation of existing plants, the NRC's upcoming review of safety standards could determine the future of this energy source. In "When the E.P.A. Isn't Mean Enough About

Cleaner Air," 7-21, he asserts that local governments and private businesses are now often imposing stricter environmental guidelines on themselves than even the federal government. But his belief that this is some type of "regulatory masochism" fails to accurately weigh the free market forces encouraging this trend. "U.S. Agencies Use Negotiations to Pre-empt Lawsuits Over Rules," 9-23, is a solid primer on an important new effort to get industry and interest groups together to hash out problems at the negotiating table in order to create rules acceptable to both, a tactic which the government hopes will reduce lawsuits over regulatory issues.

Warsh, David. *The Boston Globe.* (★ ½)
Business columnist. While we must commend Warsh for his creative choice of subject matter, his meandering style often loses us midway through. Still, we always give his columns, which we read in *The Washington Post,* a once-over to see what this intelligent thinker is dabbling in. For "Borrowing From Biology to Explain the Economy," *WP* 1-1, he choose an interesting topic — various economists and authors who rely on biological analogies to explain economics. But there's no direction to the piece, leaving us lost. The same problem arises in "Charles Kindleberger: Premier Recession-Caller Is No Wall Street Guru," *WP* 1-16. By the time we find out why Kindleberger, an MIT professor and economic historian, is the "one analyst who, more than any other, called the turn" in the economy, Warsh has already lost us. He plays the apologist for Treasury Secretary Brady in "Like Schwarzkopf, Brady Is Leading Troops in a Great and Desperate Battle," *WP* 2-6. But instead of examining the criticism of Brady, Warsh suggests that Brady's critics all have "vendettas." We're able to glean some interesting information on the political economy of various regions of the post-war world in "Americans Leading, Europeans Maneuvering, Japanese Thriving," *WP* 3-6. His book review of Richard Preston's *American Steel,* "Inside the Melt Shop," *The New York Times Review of Books* 5-26, is surprisingly well-crafted, conceding that, despite his appreciation of the book, Preston's "formula for tracing the intricate relationship between a machine and the men who build their careers around it has. . .shortcomings." His "Some Peculiar Economic Strengths Make the U.S. More Competitive," *WP* 6-26, offered only meager insights with Warsh merely listing those countries which are deemed most competitive by a leading European business school, and failing to contemplate the reasons why. Comparing the financial system to a "well-ordered zoo" in "A Well-Ordered Financial Zoo Is About to Have Its Cages Removed," *WP* 8-7, Warsh contends that the reversal of the Glass-Steagall Act and the McFadden Act will lead to a more chaotic zoo with no cages to contain the animals. He shows a clear lack of faith in free markets here.

Wayne, Leslie. *The New York Times.* (★ ★)
Finance. Still prone to soft leads, Wayne nevertheless impressed us this year with more consistent scrutiny of her subject matter. Indeed, she did some very impressive investigative work on the RTC's shaky affordable housing program. The first half of her "Banker Not Dejected by Bailout," 1-17, is heavy on the reminiscences of the good old days with Lawrence K. Fish, chairman of the failed Bank of New England. The second half is better with Wayne getting down to more worthwhile details on Fish's approach to managing the bank out of disaster. She is smart and alert in "Bank Regulators: Too Much Zeal?" 3-7, pointing out an important emerging trend in which a series of federal court decisions held that regulators "overstepped their authority." Wayne offers a timely and keen primer on the dawning wave of initial public offerings in "Company Hunger, Investor Interest Means a Hotter New-Issues Market," 4-14. Her best work of the year was an excellent two-article front-page series called "Vanishing Homes" that was bound to have rattled some cages. Both "Few of the Working Poor Get Houses in S&L Rescue Plan," 6-26, and "Housing Earmarked for the Poor Is Enriching Big Investors Instead," 6-27, were extremely revealing and competent investigations into the RTC's affordable housing program which shows scant evidence of having actually put foreclosed houses into the hands of low income people, as it was intended to do. Her serviceable but limited overview of the junk bond rally, " 'Junk Bond' Funds Show Strength," 7-4, doesn't ferret out the economic forces driving this bull in a risky market. Wayne gives us a very good feel for the shifting mood surrounding the debate over the repeal of Glass-Steagall in "Bank Barrier Shuns

Attack," 9-18, an expert analysis filled with superb quotes. She notes that the initially vulnerable law is displaying remarkable staying power: "Much of the resilience reflects a combination of fears among many members of Congress over tinkering with existing regulations while attention is focused on scandals involving Salomon Brothers and the Bank of Credit and Commerce International."

Weiss, Gary. *Business Week.* (★ ★)
Markets and Investment editor. Despite the inconsistent quality of Weiss' financial analysis, we saw more potential this year and were especially impressed by his early investigation into the May 22 Treasury bond auction, well before the Salomon Brothers scandal became public. He aligns himself with the gloom-and-doom pundits at the worst of all possible times in "The Market's 'Victory Lap' Could Turn Into a Retreat," commentary 2-25, warning mid-war and mid-bull market that "The likelihood is strong that the conventional wisdom of a relatively painless triumph is dead wrong. And that would be quite a comeuppance for investors." Compact and optimistic in "Motorola Is Doing the Right Thing," 3-11, Weiss looks into the possible payoff for Motorola which invested heavily in R&D cellular communications equipment in the fourth-quarter of 1990, even as demand turned sour. In "After-Hours Trading: A Very Small Step by the Big Board," Commentary 6-3, we're offered a serviceable analysis of the new one hour of after-hours trading at the NYSE, with the reasonable conclusion that round-the-clock trading is inevitable to meet competition. He's also only so-so in reviewing high-tech-based charting used by proprietary traders, arbs, and small options traders in an unsophisticated "So Many New Games — But so Many New Players," 6-10. Well before Salomon admitted to wrongdoing at the May 22 auction, Weiss sensed something was amiss and launched an important investigation, "Did Somebody Squeeze Treasury Notes?" with Dean Foust 7-1, which charges that Salomon Brothers Inc. may have put on a "short squeeze." He is crisp, clear and concise on the downside of NYSE's after-hours trading system calling it "the egg [that] may never hatch" in "The Big Board's Big Yawn," 7-8. On one page, he provides a broad sample of reports and quotes from the Street and comparisons with operations of competitive exchanges. His "Those Juicy Utility Yields May Lead to a Nasty Shock," 9-16, is a useful primer on the pitfalls of utility stocks which are becoming ever more popular among investors in search of higher yields.

Wessel, David. *The Wall Street Journal.* (★)
Washington. On routine economic subjects, Wessel is usually clear and competent, but when he delves into broader, more complex, economic themes we find his analysis to be terribly muddled. His "Fighting the Slump: Constraints Abound," 1-14, a compilation of thoughts on the recession and how to combat it is replete with simplistic Keynesian undertones. We were initially impressed by his muscular critique of Treasury Secretary Brady in "Is Brady's Treasury Up to Doing its Job? Many People Doubt It," 1-31, but there ended up being several holes in the piece, which prompted Paul A. Volcker, the former Federal Reserve chairman, to write a letter saying that his comments had been taken out of context. He is two-dimensional in "Fairness Issue Won't Go Away," 3-4, failing to look for creative perspectives on the tax debate. His "A High-Stakes Battle for an Integrated Market," leder 4-22, is also rather stale on the status of the free-trade agreement with Mexico, offering little we hadn't read several times in recent months. Much better in "U.S. Statistics on '90 Capital Inflow Are Off to the Tune of $73 Billion," 5-24, where he thoroughly scrutinizes the government's statistical mill, even daring to criticize his own paper and others for passively accepting faulty statistics on capital inflows to the U.S., noting that the Commerce Dept.'s figures don't account for a missing $73 billion. Although the premise that this recovery will be anemic is solid, in "No Barnburner, This Recovery," 6-3, his economic logic is, as usual, sloppy. For instance, he notes that the *Journal* was fooled in 1982, when the strength of the rebound took them by surprise, but he doesn't mention the role of the Reagan tax cuts in that recovery. His analysis is clearer on more routine subjects as in "Unemployment During June Increased to 7%," 7-8. We found "Immigration: Important, Again," 7-15, to be an odd, wandering piece on the "anxiety over immigration." Wessel clearly has some preconceived

notions that he's trying to confirm, so when the facts don't support his thesis he simply ignores them, resulting in a very muddled appraisal. His "Consumers Hesitate to Spend, Impeding Economic Recovery," leder 9-27, is a rather ho-hum repeat of why consumers aren't spending fast enough to help pull the economy out of recession. Wessel has no understanding of supply dynamics.

White, Joseph B. *The Wall Street Journal.* (★ ½)
Detroit. A plain-speaking reporter, White is skilled at ferreting out the latest marketing trends in the auto industry. But he is still not as multi-dimensional in his evaluations as we'd like, leaving us to search for richer perspectives elsewhere. He ably wraps up the bad news for the automotive industry in 1990 in "Stumbling Auto Makers Face Tough '91," 1-7, and gives us a useful preview of the "treacherous road" ahead. Joined by Paul Ingrassia for "GM's New Boss Runs Into Many Problems — But Little Opposition," leder 2-8, we're offered an overly complimentary profile of GM's new chairman Robert C. Stempel for being the kind of bite-the-bullet leader who takes his lumps along with the rest of the team. Except for his cost cutting efforts through layoffs and the elimination of bonuses, however, the authors offer very little information on the practical plans Stempel has for the troubled company. Bringing us a sign of the economic times in "Shifting Strategy, Ford and GM Attempt to Slow Sales of Nearly New Rental Cars," 3-15, he takes a telling look at Ford's unique efforts to pull in the reins on the nearly new rental cars that are flooding the market and threatening new car sales. And he explores the auto industry's creative attempts to mass market leasing as a way to lure cash-strapped consumers back into the auto market in "Auto Makers Sing the Praises of Leasing," 4-10. We've read a lot about the problems with GM's Saturn, and White's version of the story, "GM Struggles to Get Saturn Car on Track After Rough Launch," leder 5-24, while fairly complete on the big issues, isn't the most perceptive or detailed of the bunch. He is a little lopsided on the reasons behind rising car prices in "Even Detroit Concedes Sticker Shock," 8-8, allowing complaining Detroiters to carry on about expensive federal regulation without rounding out the piece with other important factors contributing to escalating costs. While his "GM Sets Off on a Market-Slice Drive," 8-22, is replete with facts and figures on GM's eight new cars, it doesn't give us a feel for the likelihood for success or failure.

Wiegner, Kathleen K. *Forbes.* (★ ★ ½)
West Coast. Adept at making complex high-technology issues comprehensible, Wiegner keeps her sights on the investment reader's interests when profiling high-tech companies. Her "Buggy Whip Chips," 1-7, is a gem of a business profile on how a $6 million company, Lansdale Semiconductor, "thrives on the trailing edge of the chip industry" which is fueled by "the great disparity between commercial and military product life cycles...Lead times are so long for a new military system that by the time it is designed, approved by Congress and funded to begin production, the chip company whose parts were in the original design may be ready to move on to other things." Landsdale is there with the chips. Offering an unique perspective on computer technology in "Optical Illusions," 3-18, she points out that while being late with new technology can be fatal to a company, "less often noted is that being too early can also be deadly." She uses "E-beam" machines as an example of an exciting computer chip technology that is decades away from overtaking current production methods. She really hits her stride in "Nasty Surprise," 5-13, an extremely well-written and informative look at how Fox Software beat Ashton-Tate in court over proprietary database software. "Suddenly, the company that had tried to protect itself in court (Ashton-Tate) emerged more naked than ever." Her colorful snapshot of Logitech Inc. which currently accounts for 35% of the worldwide computer mouse market, "Swatch It," 6-10, keeps an eye on the mounting competition. "With everybody moving into its turf, how can Logitech possibly stay profitable? [President Pierluigi] Zappacosta has done it with what he calls the Swatch strategy: He keeps turning out different designs of mice in the same way that Swiss pop watchmaker Swatch keeps coming up with new, creative designs." In "Teamwork," 8-19, she composes the compact tale of the tempestuous but ultimately triumphant journey of "smallish" Pyramid Technology in its deal with giant AT&T.

Crisply sketching Trimble Navigation's potential in "Down to Earth," 10-28, she shows us how the company is using satellite geometry to open up new markets in surveying and vehicle tracking.

Yang, Dori Jones. *Business Week.* (★ ½)
Now settled into her position as the sole correspondent at the Seattle bureau which she started up in 1990, we expected incisive, discerning assessments of the political and economic mood in the Pacific Northwest from Yang this year. But we've been surprisingly disappointed by the lack of depth in her reports. Her examination of the "terrible," "dismal," "sobering," outlook for the forest-products industry this year, "Forest Products Go Up in Smoke," 1-14, is heavy on what's wrong, but noticeably light on what the industry is doing to combat the financially threatening slump. Her years as *BW*'s correspondent in Hong Kong show as she reviews Edward A. Gargan's new book, *China's Fate: A People's Turbulent Struggle with Reform and Repression 1980-1990,* in "Tiananmen Square: He Saw It Coming," 4-1. She gives Gargan credit for prescience we never observed when he was Beijing bureau chief for *The New York Times* from 1986 to 1988. Following up on her coverage last year of the radioactive nightmare at the Hanford Nuclear Reservation, she writes "Letter from Hanford: Slowly Reclaiming a Radioactive Wasteland," 4-22, a riveting tale of "waste, fraud, incompetence, technical blundering, and mismanagement," as one source put it. Her "Dialysis, Gently," 6-17, could have been an exciting article on a sleek, modern, computerized, user-friendly dialysis machine, but it gets a little bogged down in describing the design process. She is more well-rounded in "Will Boeing Build a Behemoth to Defend Its Turf?" 8-19, fully exploring the pluses and minuses Boeing faces as it tries to decide whether to take on its main competitor, Airbus, by building a superjumbo plane, larger than its huge 747-400.

Zachary, G. Pascal. *The Wall Street Journal.* (★ ★ ★)
San Francisco. Well connected and well informed about the comings and goings in Silicon Valley, Zachary consistently provides cutting-edge reports on strategic shifts in the ever-changing direction of the computer industry. Beyond knowing who's doing what and when, he is able to lay out the implications of each shift. Early on news that Microsoft plans to build its future operating software around Windows in "Microsoft Corp. to Scrap OS/2, Refine Windows," 1-28, Zachary keenly observes that the move will further strain the company's relations with longtime ally, IBM. He is hard-hitting, but fair-minded in his critique of Businessland's founder, David Norman, in "Businessland Founder Struggles to Pull Firm Out of a Deep Slide," leder 3-18. He asserts that Norman, a visionary entrepreneur, seems to have overextended and misstepped at the worst of economic times, plummeting profits. Expertly laying out the details of the biggest computer news of the year in "Slow Growth Spurs Shake-Up in PCs: Apple Surges, IBM Stumbles as Prices Slide," 4-19, he notes that ". . .for the first time in years, IBM has surrendered its unit-market share lead in PCs." Zachary was much more clear-eyed on IBM's faults than most reporters. Joined by Stephen Kreider Yoder for "PC Firms Are Roiled by Change as Clones Gain on Brand Names," leder 5-16, we are offered a seminal piece on fundamental changes in the PC industry. Chock-full of pertinent data and killer quotes from top corporate buyers, this piece is bound to be pored over in computer industry executive suites. On the other hand, we were sorely disappointed by "Bechtel, Hurt By Slide in Heavy Construction, Re-Engineers Itself," co-written by Susan Faludi 5-28. Promising much more than it delivers, we're served a weak rehash of reports we've seen elsewhere on changes at mighty Bechtel. In "Two Computing Leaders Have New Plans: Microsoft Intends to Boost Windows and Undercut IBM-Supported OS/2," 7-29, Zachary takes us to the latest battle in the war between Windows and OS/2, which he perceptively observes "has huge implications for the future of the $70 billion PC market. Already, the growing popularity of Windows has vastly changed the balance of power among software developers. . ." Taking a sharp snapshot of Apple's efforts to expand its horizons through diversification in "Apple Wants To Grow Far Beyond Its Core," 9-27, we learn that the company is exploring consumer electronics, entertainment and mobile communications.

FOREIGN CORRESPONDENTS

Asman, David. *The Wall Street Journal.* (★ ★ ½)
Editorial. As "Americas" columnist for *WSJ,* Asman tracks Latin America's transition to supply-side, pro-growth, market-oriented economies, passing out praise when progress is made, and no-holds-barred criticism when establishment elites attempt rear guard actions, usually backing up his verdict with reams of information. A typical effort from him is "A Break in the Dark Clouds That Hover Over Peru," 2-15, a progress report on the success of Peruvian economist Hernando de Soto in breaking down regulatory and social barriers preventing the underground economy from operating out in the open. In "El Salvador's Guerrillas: Brutal Relics of the God That Failed," 3-8, he is unsparingly critical of outsiders who continue to back the FMLN and its claim to a share of power, but seems to oversimplify the guerrilla movement by labeling it a "criminal problem." On a similar note, in the ideologically-fueled "Central America Moves Toward Capitalism," 3-25, he writes approvingly on how Nicaragua and El Salvador are shaking off policy prescriptions of state intervention, contending "all state planners from the outside" can "no longer use Central American countries as their ideological test tubes." He is comprehensive on the opposition that still remains to President Collor's efforts to reform the Brazilian economy in "Brazil Flinches From Reform," 6-21, indicting "the same groups that oppose competitive openings around the world," from contractors to unions to nationalist intellectuals. In "Argentina — The Next Mexico?" 7-17, he provides a sturdy analysis of the supply-side economic tack being charted by Argentina's Finance Minister, Domingo Cavallo. He doggedly follows the trail of BCCI corruption in Latin America, "one of the most heavily regulated areas of the world," in "BCCI's Latin Tentacles," 9-30, and contends that BCCI is symptomatic of a region where "problems of corruption and underdevelopment stem from gross over-regulation combined with the protection of an elite for whom the rules do not apply." He stumbles through a disappointingly murky look at Mexican political reform in "Mexican Voters Stage Revolt Against Their 'Beltway' Crowd," 11-8.

Baker, Stephen. *Business Week.* (★ ½)
Mexico City. Baker has been doing respectable work from Mexico this year, offering offbeat observations from Mexican officials, however, a tendency to present impressions rather than analysis keeps his work lagging at times. In the informative "Mexico: The Salad Bowl of North America?" with S. Lynne Walker 2-25, he reports that if the free-trade agreement goes through, the U.S. will be buying its produce from Mexico and selling grain, a process already underway. We receive a useful look at how a top official of the Institutional Revolutionary Party views the reform policies in "Salinas' Plan: First Feed the People, Then Talk Reform," 5-27. A quick overview of the major issues in Mexico's elections, "International Outlook: Salinas Needs a Landslide — And an Honest One," 7-15, is far from complete, merely forwarding some interesting impressions on the campaigns of the two biggest opposition parties, the conservative National Action Party (PAN) and the left-of-center Democratic Revolutionary Party (PRD). We get a smart update on the shift back to North America by U.S. manufacturers who are discovering Mexico's advantages over China and other Asian manufacturing sites in "Assembly Lines Start Migrating From Asia to Mexico," and Dinah Lee with Peter Coy 7-1, while in the best effort we saw from Baker all year, "International Business: The Friends of Carlos Salinas," 7-22, he offers rich analysis of President Salinas's attempts to walk the tightrope between Mexico's power elite, of which he is a member, and the unsettling but lucrative forces of free trade. In "Marketing: The American Dream Is Alive and Well — in Mexico," co-written by S. Lynne Walker 9-30, he objectively documents how U.S. marketers and retailers are crossing the border to take advantage of the growing purchasing power of the Mexican middle-class market, without losing sight of the Mexicans still at the bottom rung of society. He is straightforward in "As Argentina Strides Ahead Will Its Neighbors Follow?" 10-7, reporting on Argentina President Menem's decision to tie the austral to the dollar, which Menem calls the turning point in his successful battle against hyperinflation.

Bangsberg, P.T. *The Journal of Commerce.* (★ ★ ★)
Hong Kong. A veteran observer of this gateway to China's booming southeastern provinces, Bangsberg continues to remain alert to investment opportunities in the region and worldwide trade-related issues which impact southeast Asia, one of the best on this beat. He delivers a knowing look at corporate strategy in "Evergreen Group Goes Ashore With International Hotel Chain," 1-4, writing on the Taiwanese transport conglomerate's efforts to diversify by investing in hotels in Asia and Los Angeles that cater to the business traveler. We receive good intelligence on China's efforts to expand its shipbuilding capacities in "Jiangnan Yard Builds China's 1st LPG Tanker," 2-25, a subject with which Bangsberg clearly is familiar. His reports offer plenty of detail, as in "Hong Kong Traders Fight Protectionism," 3-19, reporting on how local importers are launching a multimillion dollar campaign targeted at protectionist efforts for its textile industry. He expertly tracked the Philippine effort to attract foreign investment, especially from the U.S., all year. In "US Businessmen Seek Opportunities in Philippines," 6-12, he reports on U.S. companies which may be interested "especially in the energy sector," following passage of a new investment code by the Philippine Congress. And in an important update "Philippines Scales Back Export, Investment Goals," 8-29, he smartly connects declining foreign trade and investment in the Philippines to a devaluation of the peso, and notes that many observers feel that the Philippine effort may be too late, believing "the new focus of Asian-origin investment will be Mexico and Latin America broadly." Writing on a recent decision by Orient Overseas Container Line in "OOCL Adds Baltimore, Switches Belgian Port," 9-19, he expertly places the move in the context of the growing use of Antwerp as a port of call for shippers into the region. In "China Hopes Visit by EC Delegation Pays Off in Trade," 10-24, he is sharp on Beijing's efforts to increase trade with Europe as its U.S. market becomes clouded with political tensions, noting that the old argument China used to have with Washington over its trade deficit is already cropping up in Brussels.

Barnard, Bruce. *The Journal of Commerce.* (★ ★ ½)
Brussels. Barnard continues to be a clear-eyed observer of both the EC's efforts to provide a united front to the world and the nuances of internal divisions as 1992 approaches. His reports provide capable analysis of the obstacles which still remain to European economic and political union, as in "Outside Events Overshadow EC Progress to Single Market," 2-5, in which he observes that there just isn't enough time to resolve everything before 1992. In the "Europe View" column, "EC Police Start Crackdown," 3-26, he applauds the zest with which the antitrust division of the EC is moving to break up monopolies, both private and state-owned. "The commission must keep its nerve as it confronts recalcitrant member states." Writing on a proposal of an EC external affairs minister to allow Poland, Czechoslovakia, and Hungary into the EC as "member states" in "EC to Weigh E. Europe Status," 4-22, he captures the great opposition that still remains to having Eastern European countries join the Community. He is keen on shifts in relations between Bonn-Paris and Paris-London, in "EC Leaders Seek to Avoid Clashes at Two-Day Luxembourg Summit," 6-28, as EC members position themselves for the stretch run to Maastrich. In "EC's White Knight Is . . . Japan?" 7-9, he usefully looks beyond the signs of panic over Japan's encroachment into Europe to see how individual nations benefit from the Japanese: "Japan Inc. may be anathema in Paris, but in Dublin it spells jobs and exports for a peripheral EC company desperate to attract foreign investment." His non-EC dispatches can fall short, as in "Belgian Shipping Line Confirms Hunt for Partner," 8-1, where he doesn't take us much past the headline. Analyzing Germany's shift on deep cuts for EC farm subsidies and what it portends for both the EC and the Uruguay Round in "German Concession on GATT May Not Resolve Subsidy Issue," 10-16, he moves this story forward, pointing out that while the French and Irish agricultural ministries "continue to play to the farm gallery," Dublin and Paris, along with Bonn, understand that their best long term economic interests lie in liberalizing international trade.

Battiata, Mary. *The Washington Post.* (★ ½)
Warsaw. A fine writer with an eye for the ironic detail, Battiata once again provided serviceable coverage of Eastern Europe's efforts to shake off the hangover left from communist rule. In the colorful, if two-dimensional, "Separatist Slovaks Becoming More Vocal in 'Family Feud' With Czechs," 3-19, she observes that while the Slovaks are maneuvering to win concessions for Slovakia when the new constitution is drafted, "support for some kind of separate status seems to be increasing," fueled by economic fears. She provides an enjoyable look at the growing market for luxury cars in Warsaw, of all places, in "Wheeling & Dealing in Warsaw," 4-29: "Because Polish law exempts the handicapped from paying state tax on cars, many customers claim to be buying for handicapped relatives." Reporting on a more serious topic in "Prague Celebrates New Spring as Soviets Depart," 6-25, she effectively conveys the euphoric mood as the last Soviet forces leave Czechoslovakia, while touching on the serious problems the Soviets are leaving behind — "from extensive ground water contamination to live ammunition discarded in neighborhood trash dumps." Her Yugoslavia coverage offered moderate insights on Serbs in Croatia, "Ethnically Mixed Croatia Fears Civil War," 7-6, providing an adequate picture on how the Serbs in Croatia are holding up during the fighting, while in the anecdotal "In Croatia, Time Heals No Ethnic Wounds," 7-14, we learn firsthand how the Croatia-Serbia conflict is pitting lifelong friends and neighbors against each other. Covering a landmark event in Poland's shift from socialism to capitalism in "Factory's Downfall Symbolizes Failure of Reforms in Poland," 8-5, she routinely ties the failure of the Ursus tractor factory to Warsaw's decision to abandon central planning, while failing to give state-owned factories any autonomy or a new management system. In the moving "Estonians Let Freedom Sing," 9-9, she writes on how a singing festival in Tallinn became a celebration of independence, capturing the indomitable spirits of the Estonians, while in "Romanian Disruption Long-Term," 10-1, she is detailed on the repercussions for Romania following violent protests in Bucharest by rampaging miners.

Bering-Jensen, Henrik. *Insight.* (★ ★)
It was an inconsistent year for Bering-Jensen, whose reports on Europe were at times well-researched and skillfully written, but at other times lacked the depth we've come to associate with him. He takes a sweepingly overpessimistic view of the Soviet crackdown in the Baltics in the overlong "A Timely Smoke Screen," 2-4, commenting that "The picture that emerges is one of a broad counterattack against the democratic movements — an attempt not simply to produce a local outcome but to reverse the entire reform movement." He produces a nicely-rounded report on the dissolution of the Warsaw Pact, "Long After the Split, Soviets Admit the Marriage Is Over," 3-11, providing insights from experts who say the Soviets may foment trouble in the region to use as "scare stories" for their own people. In "Unsure Union Itches With Rivalries," 4-8, we get a once-over-lightly of the centrifugal forces at work in Yugoslavia. He can still impress, as in "Tory vs. Tory," 5-27, a comprehensive report on the internecine warfare now breaking out in the British Conservative Party, and displays a solid grasp on the issues, personalities, and history involved. "One thing has been demonstrated conclusively in the past months: Thatcherism without Thatcher is impossible." In "France's Iron Lady," 7-22, he adroitly places the beliefs of new French Prime Minister Edith Cresson in the context of her political career, observing that "The past decade has demonstrated that Socialists can be in power in France only if they do not pursue Socialist policies. Now they only need to find someone brave enough to get this across to *La Dame de Fer*." He provides a useful summary of the Bush administration's preference for placing international stability over other more idealistic concerns such as human rights in "A Tilt From Freedom," 8-5, illustrating how American foreign policy has been tugged between the two over the years. In his finest effort of the year, "Poles Apart in New Era," 9-23, he writes knowingly on the economic difficulties Poland is facing as it makes the transition to a market economy: "The problem is that to have the welfare state most Poles seem to want, you first have to create the capital to build it."

Bernstein, Jonas. *Insight.* (★ ★)
Insight expects its reporters to be able to write on a wide range of topics and Bernstein is usually more than up to the task, turning in a number of articles on foreign and national security affairs that are both informative and analytical in content. In "Stalking the Past of a Police State," 1-21, he demonstrates a feel for spying trade craft, as well as the moral issues raised by espionage in this report on how Germany is trying to cope with revelations from East Germany's secret police past. We were disappointed in "CNN at the Front Line of News," 2-18, which seems too heavily weighed in favor of CNN's critics. He rebounds in "Arabian Nations' Borders Are Just Lines in the Sand," 3-4, transporting readers back to the end of the First World War, when the European powers carved up the spoils of the fallen Ottoman empire, and demonstrating how the modern Middle East is a product of its past. In "The Soviets' Head Start," 5-27, he takes a one-dimensional look at the questions surrounding the Soviet SS-18 Mod 5 missile and the threat it allegedly poses to the new START treaty, resurrecting the so-called "window of vulnerability" from ten years ago. His best effort of the year is "How to Loot a Nation," 7-8, a comprehensive cover story on the *La Pinata Democracia* phenomenon in Nicaragua — the Sandinista expropriation of over a billion dollars of government goods and property, with the apparent agreement of the Chamorro regime. "Their critics say the Sandinistas are now basically crooks, the Vito Corleones of Nicaragua." He also produced a fine report on corruption in another communist country undergoing reform, the Soviet Union, in the cover story "Crime," 8-26, expertly placing the street crime and bureaucratic corruption in the context of a society with one foot in communism, one foot in a free market: "The Soviet Union, summer 1991, might be summed up in a phrase: too many people chasing too few dollars. Not rubles, which are worthless — dollars." His post-coup efforts on the Soviet Union were fine, "A More Perfect Disunion," 9-9, covering all the angles of the nationalist questions posed by the collapse of communism, while in "Glasnost With a Vengeance," 11-11, we learn why many of the KGB's secrets may never be revealed.

Beyer, Lisa. *Time.* (★)
An associate editor for the newsweekly, Beyer helps anchor the Middle East coverage, producing concisely written articles that at times offer a bit of insight into the diplomacy of the region, but at other times fail to add to our knowledge or understanding of Middle Eastern developments. Her thumbnail sketch of one of the runners-up for 1990 Man of the Year honors, "Saddam," 1-7, offers little new on the Iraqi leader, but Beyer's florid language certainly paints him well enough. She downplays the risk of the use of chemical agents by Iraqi forces in "Coping With Chemicals," 2-25, but waits until the end of the piece to inform us that biological weapons are more dangerous, and their use more likely, leaving us wondering what the fuss was all about. Her overview of the post-war Middle East, "Now, Winning the Peace," 3-11, although written with some subtlety and nuance, offers little new. Her reports on the upheaval in post-war Iraq, "Seeds of Destruction," 3-18, and "Wanted: a Strong Leader for a Broken Land (Not You, Saddam)," 3-25, suffer from their secondhand nature. She's better in "Walking the Beat in Iraq," 5-13, a sharp, informative piece on the options of the U.N. in its role in Iraq after the war, in which she places the current crisis in the context of past U.N. peacekeeping efforts: "the peacekeepers may have to stay for years, just as they have remained in Cyprus since 1964 and in Lebanon since 1978." She provides a brief but informed view of where each country stands as Middle East peace efforts stall once again in "On the Bridge to Nowhere," 5-27, while "No Quick Fixes in Sight," 6-3, offers a familiar look at the failure of the U.S.-led coalition to bring any real sense of order to the post-war Middle East.

Blustein, Paul. *The Washington Post.* (★)
Tokyo. Blustein's coverage of Japan this year was above wire service quality but just barely, his reports on such key stories as U.S.-Japanese relations and the securities industry scandal rarely taking us beyond the headline. Covering the latest diplomatic flap between Washington and Tokyo in "No U.S.-Japan Trade Peace Seen," 1-23, he routinely passes along the belief of U.S. officials that "U.S.-Japan economic relations appear headed for an unusually stormy year." He

does turn in the substantial analytic on occasion, in the "Outlook" essay "In Japan, the Politics of Hesitation," 2-17, providing a multi-dimensional survey on Japan's response to the Gulf crisis, charting how "What has prevailed is a curious mixture of realpolitik — bordering on what could be called realeconomik — and moralism." He can also get his hooks into a story — in "Trustbusters Take On the Dango," 5-14, he is informative on how a bid rigging scheme for U.S. military bases is leading to a major crackdown on illegal cartels. But he handled a key story for the year — financial scandals in Japan — sketchily at best. In "2 Major Japanese Securities Firms Concede Favoritism to Big Clients," 6-22, he works in the fact that a former *yakuza* leader had ties to President Bush's brother Prescott; and in "Japanese Scandal Widens," 7-23, he unimaginatively likens the growing scandal to a "bloodletting." Setting the scene for the G-7 summit meeting in London in "Conflicting Concerns to Strain Coordination," 7-14, he overgeneralizes that "Not since the early 1980s have the world's leading industrial economies been more out of sync then they are on the eve of the 1991 summit." Writing briefly on Japan's rising trade surplus with the West in "Japan's Awkward Trade Surplus," 9-7, he displays a flash of perception, reporting that Tokyo is worried about the timing — the U.S. is heading into a presidential election and Europe is moving toward 1992. "Both developments provide juicy political opportunities for advocates of protectionist legislation."

Bobinski, Christopher. *Financial Times.* (★ ★)

Poland. In a particularly trying year for the new Poland, the dependable Bobinski kept us well-abreast of the shifting fortunes of that country's political economy, although short-changing us on tax policy. His data was always reliable, the details original and salient. He provided us early on with fresh information on features of Poland's economic perspectives as in "Private-Enterprise Poles Push Into New Market," 12-19-90, on the shift back to the vast Soviet market by Polish companies; "Bielecki Pledges Free Market Policies and Speedy Privatisation," 1-7, a review of the new prime minister's first policy speech of the year; and "Precarious Freedom," 2-4, an assessment of the daunting economic problems the country faces in 1991. With "Sudden Switch to Hard Currency Trade 'a Mistake,' " 4-5, he brings us up-to-date on the vexing mutual trade and mutual debt problems between the U.S.S.R. and Poland. He smartly examines the emerging post-communist political geography of Poland in "Shaping Up for the First Free, Multi-Party Elections," and Anthony Robinson 5-3: "Parliament is still dominated by deputies from the old communist establishment," he reported, going on to provide a rich reconnaissance of the complex political mutations and transformations taking place. Bobinski delivers a very competent preview of pressures on the Polish government on the eve of the special parliamentary economic debate in "Walesa's Old Comrades Lead Assault on Financial Stringency," 5-21, giving us all the dire details on the country's worsening economic situation, making the point that "the electorate is swinging toward despair." The political side of the story was ably handled, Bobinski staying on top of the volatile pressures created by economic problems in "Walesa Willing to Adopt Force to Prevent Anarchy in Poland," 6-13, and "Walesa Tries to Damp Down the Flames," 6-14. In addition to his *FT* duties, Bobinski is also a stringer for *U.S. News & World Report.* In "The Gathering Storms," *USNWR* 10-28, he ably portrays the widespread discontent in Poland as the parliamentary elections approach. Noting that the state has become more interventionist as the economy deteriorates, he writes that "Now economic decisions have become political ones."

Bogert, Carroll. *Newsweek.* (★ ★)

Moscow. Bogert continues to produce noteworthy sidebar stories to the on-going crisis in the Soviet Union, delivering the telltale anecdote or quote that capsulates momentous events and sets the stage for what lies ahead. Reporting from Riga on deteriorating relations between Soviet troops and Baltic civilians in "Day of the Black Berets," 1-14, she effectively charts the warning signals of an impending crackdown. " 'The mood among officers is terrible,' says Col. Yuri Podalnitsky of the Baltic command. 'Throw one match, and the whole thing will explode.' " She is succinct but thorough on potential repercussions of the referendum on national unity, in "Which Side Are You On?" 3-18: "In the end, the referendum of reformers is reducing complex choices to a loyalty test." She provides key details on communists being wrested from their posts in the Uralmash plant in Sverdlovsk, where the Bolsheviks shot the last czar in 1918, in "Throw the Communists Out," 5-6. She samples Soviet public opinion in "Gorbachev's Weak Lineup," 8-19, and finds that Gorbachev doesn't have an effective team put together, but fails to explain the reasons behind the ineffectiveness. In "No Work Is Getting Done," 10-21, she provides a serviceable overview of the current difficulties in the Soviet Union, giving us the sense of the loss of momentum after the coup overthrow. She pegs a lot of hope on Yeltsin in "Boris's Bet: Russian Roulette?" 11-11, as she deftly sketches the Russian leader's economic program and the uncertainties it represents. " 'The speed of predictable economic collapse is over,' legislator Valentin Fyodorov told the Congress. 'Now begins the period of unpredictable collapse.' "

Bohlen, Celestine. *The New York Times.* (★ ★)
Budapest. Bohlen is an imaginative writer with a feel for both the geopolitical and humanitarian problems created by the dissolution of the Soviet empire, her dispatches often nicely complementing the main news stories of the day from that region. In "Warsaw Pact Agrees to Dissolve Its Military Alliance by March 31," 2-26, she effortlessly works in the political revolution that spelled the end for this military alliance. We receive a useful look at the problems raised at a practical level as Eastern European countries draft programs to compensate the victims of communist rule in "Hungarians Debate How Far Back to Go to Right Old Wrongs," 4-15. In the literate "Week In Review" essay, "Where the Fires of Hatred Are Easily Stoked," 8-4, she places Eastern Europe's growing ethnic strife in a cultural and historical context, while in "Hungarians Open Hearts and Homes to Yugoslavs," 10-18, the human interest angle is played up over the geopolitical angles of the story. Her Soviet coup coverage offered riveting on-scene reporting. In "Moscow Fears It Awoke to a Nightmare," 8-20, she evokes the atmosphere in the Moscow streets during the initial hours of the coup, while "Bare-Fisted Russians Plot a Last Stand," 8-21, takes readers right into the Russian Parliament building, as Boris Yeltsin and his supporters prepare for the expected military assault. "Given the situation, the mood in the room was remarkably relaxed, even upbeat." She was able to capture the poignancy of Communist Party loyalists struggling to cope with a world turned upside-down without ever lapsing into sympathy. In such dispatches as "The Truth Is it Hurts to Be a Silenced Organ," 8-27, we learn how *Pravda*'s staff was "feeling the unaccustomed pangs of an injustice done," while in "Red Square Pageantry Gives Way to the Angry," 11-8, she conveys the mood in Red Square as a small demonstration is held to commemorate the anniversary of the October Revolution. "As they took out their frustrations on politicians and entrepreneurs, people in the crowd displayed a kind of curdled nostalgia for the era when order was maintained in the Soviet Union."

Borowiec, Andrew. *The Washington Times.* (★ ★)
While this veteran spent less time writing from overseas this year, his daily reports and analytical pieces rarely failed to pick up on key nuances of developments in Europe and the Middle East. He does a fine job of placing Iraq's military actions in a grander political strategy in "A Beaten Saddam Could Yet Emerge as Hero in Arab Eyes," 2-4. In a sharp report on the Damascus Pact, "8 Arab Nations Agree to Become Gulf Watchdogs," 3-7, he is prescient, writing that "The coalition members eventually hope for a 'new world order,' a concept still blurred by conflicting ideologies and often clashing political ambitions." In "Spark of Hope Rises for Hostages," 3-15, he expertly places the latest "cryptic statement" from Syria on the potential release of Western hostages in Lebanon in full geopolitical context. We get a crisp background report on Albania's first free vote since 1939 in "Albania's Unrest Hurts Chances of Democracy," 4-3, while in "Pope Finds Catholics Split During Visit to Homeland," 6-3, he is concise on the social and political issues dividing Polish Catholics which have been brought to the forefront during the Papal visit. His summary on the Eastern European reaction to the attempted Soviet coup, "Former Satellites Fearful," 8-20, documents how this crisis occurred at the time Moscow was pressuring former Warsaw Pact members to sign "friendship agreements" that would preclude their future membership in NATO, an angle we didn't see elsewhere. Writing on the latest

diplomatic efforts to end the Yugoslavian civil war in "Fighting Dims Peace Hopes in Yugoslavia," 9-19, he notes that peace plans envision an EC peacekeeping force, which would entail using the WEU, which in turn would have to coordinate its action with NATO and "So far, NATO has been loath to get involved." Ahead of the pack with "U.S. Treads Lightly in Iraq," 10-10, he discloses that Washington is pulling back from its initial contacts with Iraqi opposition groups because of weak intelligence on the ground and the leaderless, fragmentary nature of Iraqi opposition to Saddam. A strong portfolio for the year, lacking only the extra dimension provided by dispatches from the field.

Boudreaux, Richard. *Los Angeles Times.* (★ ★)
Managua. Boudreaux produced vivid portrayals of the changing political landscape in key countries in Central America, but he needs to expand his attention to the economic side of developments in the region, having given us insufficient detail on this picture. He produced straightforward coverage of the El Salvadoran elections that saw candidates close to the FMLN win seats in the National Assembly for the first time. In "Salvador Vote Looms as Genuine Contest," 3-11, he stresses the apparent legitimacy of the elections by citing widespread participation of peasants in guerrilla-held territories, and in "Rebels' Allies Charge Fraud in Salvador Vote Counting," 3-13, he disentangles the technical issues which marred the voting. Nicaragua was still Boudreaux's major beat, and in "Nicaragua Economy Worse After Chamorro's 1st Year," 4-15, he deftly uncovers the political causes behind the country's disastrous economic unraveling, writing that "Sandinista-led labor unrest and resistance to the exiles' attempts to reclaim confiscated property have scared off the productive investment that was expected en masse with the change of regimes." He covers the reawakening of the contra movement in "Unhappy Contras Rearm, Again Roam the Highlands," 5-20, telling the story of one former contra squad leader, discontented "with [his] treatment during Nicaragua's year of peace." He is bullish on the future of Latin America following a conference of regional leaders in "After the 'Lost Decade' a Strong Latin Spirit," 8-6, while in "Cuba to Follow Own Socialist Path Despite 'Tragedy' of Soviet Collapse," 8-30, he reports on Castro's ideological intransigence in the face of a changing world. And a lighter note, "Castro's Revolutionary Cry: Let Them Eat Ice Cream," 11-5, reports on how an ice cream parlor set up by Castro during the 1960s to compete with the imperialist Howard Johnson remains in operation today. In one of his few efforts on economic reform, "The Drive for Reform Leaves Some Behind," 10-22, he offers three case studies of Mexicans "at the downside of the modernization effort," but quotes one plant manager: "We can either put on the brakes, cut jobs and survive economically or we drown and everybody loses out."

Boulton, Leyla. *Financial Times.* (★ ★)
Moscow. Boulton distinguished herself with her post-coup coverage and her reports on the Baltics before the breakup of the Union. At times, though, she recycles familiar topics, adding little new. Her post-coup reports helped establish some sense of direction of economic perspectives in the swirling situation there, as with "Yakolev Fears Hijack of New Revolution," 8-27, an interview with *perestroika*'s "godfather" who worried about the rise of a *lumpen* mood and consciousness rapidly spreading; "Making the Soviet Union Fit to Do Business In," 8-27, an assessment of the qualifications of the team of *apparatchiks* appointed to rebuild economic and political confidence; and "A Team to Share the Spoils of Victory," 8-27, an interview with Arkady Volsky, head of a fledgling Soviet equivalent of an employer's confederation and member of the economic reform team. She was an especially worthwhile source of information on the volatile situation in the Baltic republics early in the year, in such dispatches as "Baltics Draft Evasion Reflects General Unease," 1-9; "Defending With Bare Hands," 1-11; "Lithuanians Set for Long Siege," 1-21; and "Lithuanians Weigh Prospects of a Bloodbath," 1-29, in which she avoids the conventional characterization of all Lithuanians as fervid supporters of independence regardless of cost. She was strong on the evolving relationship between the center and the republics following the August coup attempt. She is thorough on how political fall-out from Georgian President Zviad Gamsakhurdia's inept handling of the Soviet coup attempt handicaps

the republic's drive for independence in "Georgia's Independence Crusade Turns Into Farce," 9-1. In "Republics Find They Need Gorbachev After All," 10-16, she sketches some of the reasons behind Gorbachev's latest political resurrection. A deft use of quotes highlights "Sultan of Soviet Change," 10-21, a "Monday Profile" of Kazakhstan President Nursultan Nazarbayevli whose strong pro-union views have made him a favorite of Western leaders and businessmen: "All our difficulties come from poverty. The main problem for all of us, including Russia, is a parasitic mentality. People must learn to take care of themselves."

Boustany, Nora. *The Washington Post.* (★ ★)
Beirut. Back in the Levant after a brief return home last year, Boustany continues to be a reliable source on developments in the Arab world, she is better in tune with street-level culture than are many of her peers on this beat. Reporting on Arab world reaction to Iraq's defeat and Saddam's role in history in the authoritative "Saddam: The Hero That Crumpled," 2-28, she finds opinion running from disillusionment to conspiracy theorists to those who believe Saddam saved his forces to fight another day. Dispatched to liberated Kuwait, in "Three Allege Beatings, Torture by Kuwaiti Interrogators," 3-13, she provides a graphic account of Kuwaiti reprisals against suspected Iraqi collaborators. She captures the frustration American G.I.'s felt in watching Republican Guard forces attack the town of Samawah with tanks and helicopters in the 10 Best nominee "U.S. Troops Witness Iraqi Attack on Town in Horror, Frustration," 3-31: "There is little [an American infantry commander] can do to ease their pain. 'I tell them, the war was to free Kuwait, it was not to free Iraq. That's the way it is.' " In the summer she produced a voluminous report on the Gaza strip, "Gaza Diary," 8-4, 8-5, 8-6, giving us an unforgettable look at life on the ground for Palestinians in that particular piece of occupied territory. In "Forgotten in Gaza," 8-4, she writes that "A three-week stay in the dusty shantytowns of the Gaza strip is like a visit to a forgotten planet," and goes on to document how the Palestinian community "is literally tearing itself apart" under the grinding pressure of Israeli occupation, which has brought with it a depressed economy, internecine violence, and oppressive taxation. In "The Toll on Gaza's Women and Children," 8-5, she reports allegations that Palestinians are psychologically and physically tortured during interrogations in an Israeli prison, and "Israel is Loosening Its Hold on Gaza," 8-6, provides the historical background on Israel's occupation of the Gaza strip and a glimpse at Gaza's possible future: self-government. She draws an impressionistic portrait of Beirut as that city emerges from 16 years of civil war to a Syrian-imposed peace in "Now Normalcy Stalks Beirut's Streets," 10-10.

Branigin, William. *The Washington Post.* (★ ★)
Manila. Branigin was on the road for much of 1991, part of the *Post* press pool covering the Gulf War, but late in the year he filed respectable dispatches on diplomatic and economic developments in Southeast Asia. His Gulf War coverage was often evocative, although typical of the genre. In the well-organized "For 1st Cavalry Tankers, War Was a Letdown," 3-3, he is able to outline the "elaborate deception plan" which enabled the allies to outflank the Iraqis, while capturing the mood of the soldiers. Reporting from liberated Kuwait in "Kuwait's Treasures Vandalized," 3-6, he details why "In some ways, Kuwait today resembles a city descended upon by modern-day Visigoths." Covering the post-war refugee crisis he produces "Retracing Trail of Destruction in Iraq," 5-22, a brief but gripping report on the destruction of Kurdish villages two years ago by Iraqi forces out to eradicate the guerrilla movement, and which helped put the current plight of the Kurds in perspective. He provides a colorful update on the Aquino government's unsuccessful efforts to recover any of the large amount of the loot allegedly taken by the fleeing Marcoses in "Quest for Marcos's Millions Fills Dockets, Pockets but Not Manila Coffers," 4-17. In "Marcos, a Curse and a Comeback," 7-5, he's amusing yet serious on the shadow Imelda Marcos continues to cast over the Filipino political landscape. He is sketchy on support for extending the Subic Bay Naval Base treaty from the military and business sectors in "Philippine Military Weighs In on Controversy Over Future of U.S. Bases," 8-19. However, he is out in front on the Khmer Rouge's efforts to find new respectability by passing itself off as a party now dedicated to liberal democracy and free markets in "Cambodia's

Khmer Rouge Seeking New Political Legitimacy," 9-1, commenting: "Few observers believe, however, that the Khmer Rouge leopard has changed its spots." He journeys to the Vietnam-China border in "Vietnam, China Share Blurry Borders of Trade," 11-5, to chronicle firsthand the growing underground economic activity between these two historic enemies, his detailed report increasing our understanding of this important geopolitical development.

Brauchli, Marcus. *The Wall Street Journal.* (★ ★)
Tokyo. Before going on leave, Brauchli focused on the key critical issues of Japan's political economy — especially on the workings of the Bank of Japan — and produced many scattered insights. But he shortchanged us by omitting a coherent overview, giving us insufficient information of the intense debate within Japan over the questions of growth and inflation. Reporting that Japan's "rate of growth this year will fall by more than half," he does provide adequate background and context for the Bank of Japan Governor Yasushi Mieno's policy choices regarding interest rates in the wake of economic slowdown in "Bank of Japan Governor Faces Tough Choices as Economy Slows," 3-5. We get an informed report on the problem of Japanese bank capitalization in the wake of the fall in the Tokyo stock market, and its implications for Japanese banks' international lending in "Japan's Banks May Soon Resume Loans, But Go-Go Days are Gone," 3-18. However, the ominous lead for "Japanese Stocks' Surge Worries Some Analysts," 3-18 — "The Japanese stock market is reacquiring some of its pre-crash characteristics" — requires more reflection and effort to set the scare stories in context. He adds to the confusion with "Japan's Central Bank Takes a New Tack," 4-8, treating the 1990 stock market crash as a consequence of "misunderstanding" between the Bank of Japan and market analysts. He collects some interesting statistics on capital investment in Japan, but misses completely the importance of the country's zero-rate capital gains tax on equities in "Japan Slows But Firms Still Invest Heavily," 4-22. In "Tokyo Stocks Plunge 3.15% to 1991 Low," 7-9, he provides a number-crunching report on the sharp drop in the Tokyo market and ripple affects on other Asian and European exchanges, Brauchli attributing the drop to concerns over the burgeoning securities scandal. Reporting from Peshewar, Pakistan in "Long Before BCCI, There Was 'Hundi,' " 8-13, he produces a well-written feature on how a centuries-old method for transferring money has entered the age of telephones, fax machines, and governments worried about hard-currency earnings.

Brooke, James. *The New York Times.* (★ ½)
Rio de Janeiro. Still a disappointment to us after his impressive African tour some years back, Brooke seemed to be developing a solid grasp on the Brazilian political economy early in the year, but his work tailed off. He was especially meager on the reform plans of the new economics minister, Marcilio Moreira. He surveys President Fernando Collor's latest effort to tame Brazil's inflation in "Brazil Skeptical Over Price Freeze," 2-11, but fails to provide fresh analysis. He contends that Collor's accomplishments have been overshadowed by his inability to control inflation in the comprehensive "As Collor Completes First Year, Brazilians Write Off Their Highest Hopes," 3-14. Reporting on the lavish conditions of the incarceration of the head of the Medellin drug cartel, Pablo Escobar, in his home town in "Drug Baron's Prison Has Every Comfort: Even Mom and TV," 6-21, Brooke never gives a clear picture as to whether the Medellin cartel is kaput or just regrouping. He is better in "The Drug War the P.O.W.'s May Have Won," 6-23, examining the Colombian government's deal with Escobar from the official perspective: "For Colombians, Bogota's efforts to keep Mr. Escobar in the style to which he has become accustomed, even while calling it imprisonment, is just fine, as long as it means they won't feel his wrath." He follows up on this in "Gaviria's Gamble," *Magazine* 10-13, profiling Colombian President Cesar Gaviria Truzillo and his policy of negotiating with the two biggest threats to Colombian political and economic stability, the guerrillas and the drug traffickers, despite heavy criticism from Colombian conservatives and the U.S. government. Late in the year he went to the Soviet Union where he produced some of his best work, "As Centralized Rule Wanes, Ethnic Tension Rises Anew in Soviet Georgia," 10-2, riveting on the growing bloodshed between Georgians and Ossetians, which some fear may be a harbinger of the civil war to come,

while "Chernobyl Said to Affect Health of Thousands in a Soviet Region," 11-3, effectively conveys the disagreement within the U.S. and Soviet medical communities on reports of degraded health in Byelorussia, five years after the Chernobyl accident.

Brooks, Geraldine. *The Wall Street Journal.* (★ ½)
London, covering the Middle East. Brooks continues to suffer from inconsistency, her reports at times rich in historical insight and vivid detail, at other times too speculative to be of much use. An example of the latter, "Saddam Watch," and Tony Horwitz 1-16, draws on "Veteran Saddam-watchers" who track Saddam's demeanor by his physical appearance. In "Power Vacuum," and Peter Waldman 2-28, she recycles conventional wisdom on the desirability of leaving a post-war Iraq with its territory intact. An example of Brooks at her finest is "The Lost People: In Humiliating Defeat, Can the Palestinians Finally Find Peace?" 3-6, where she smartly traces the background of shifting attitudes among the Palestinians regarding resolution of the Israeli-Palestinian issue. Her reports on the failed Kurdish uprising and the lack of support they received from the U.S. were almost too painful to read, and "Iraqi Kurds Awaken From Long Nightmare," 3-26, catches the high water mark of the rebellion, while "As Rebellion Fails, Kurds, Once Again, Flee Cities in Sorrow," 4-3, is gripping on the refugee movement into Turkey. She continues to have a knack for light fare, such as "Staying Airborne Above a War Zone Is a Bumpy Business," 7-10, on Beirut-based carrier Middle East Airlines, and "The Metamorphosis: Women Warriors Join an Arab Army," 8-8, on an all-female cadet class in the United Arab Emirates. In her best effort of the year "Veiled Capitalists: The New Revolution in Iran Is Taking Place on an Economic Front," 9-16, she takes us into Tehran's booming stock exchange and dusty bazaar to discover firsthand how President Rafsanjani's economic reforms are being played out; Brooks discovering a potentially explosive situation as the rich begin to feel the benefits but the poor, for the most part, have not. "Fortunately for Mr. Rafsanjani, hardliners aren't unified in their opposition to him." She strikes just the right note in "Together, Say Arabs and Israelis, We Could Do Wonders," and Tony Horwitz 10-28, on the hopes and dreams of ordinary Arabs and Israelis as the Madrid peace talks get under way: "The desire for business opportunities is, in fact, a common thread in the fantasies of both Arabs and Israelis."

Bruce, James. *The Journal of Commerce.* (★ ½)
Sao Paulo. As President Collor continued his efforts to reform the Brazilian economy, Bruce concentrated on how those changes were being played out in the key sectors of trade and maritime transport, providing perspective along with the numbers. We need to hear more from Collor's critics in Bruce's reports, though, if only for the sake of balance. In "Brazil's Own 'Perestroika,' " 2-7, his comparison of Collor's reform program to *perestroika* rises above triteness by his discussion of the state-oriented model Raul Prebisch of the UN Economic Council for Latin America promoted for the region in the post-war years. We need to hear from the unions in "Brazilian Exporters Slam Steep Charges by Ports," 4-25, an otherwise informative report on planned legislation to ease the high costs of business for the Brazilian Exporters Association. He is straightforward on the resignation of Economic Minister Zelia Cardoso de Mello and the entire top economic team in "Brazil Names Moreira Economic Minister," 5-10, seeing the move as a step forward for the Collor government's efforts to reform the economy and renew relations with international creditors. He provides good details on efforts of U.S. and French companies to move into the Brazilian market of private industrial investments and installation of telephone lines and terminals following President Collor's decree ending Embratel's monopoly over data transmission services in "Brazil's Open Telecommunications Mart Attracts Investors," 7-23. In "Study: Tax Level Cripples Investment in Brazil," 8-2, he passes along the findings of a study done by the Brazilian subsidiary of Arthur Anderson & Co. that Brazil's competitiveness continues to be hampered by high tax rates, legal restraints and "well-intentioned but inconsequential" nationalism, providing no perspective from the nationalists. Bruce stayed on top of trade disputes between Sao Paulo and Washington, including telecommunications in "Brazil, US Leaders to Discuss Sensitive Technologies," 9-20, and pharmaceuticals in "Brazil Runs to Catch Up in Latin America Patent Race," 10-24, detailing how the issues are embroiled in the nationalist cause.

Buchan, David. *Financial Times.* (★ ★ ★)
Brussels. Buchan excels at taking the reader through the ins-and-outs of EC politics as the Community hammers together accords on political and economic union, making arcane policy disputes comprehensible while never oversimplifying or losing sight of the big picture. He provides a balanced if slightly overwrought assessment of how EC fortunes are weathering the strains provoked by the Gulf War in "A Gulf in Europe," 2-8. In the authoritative "Emu Train Stopped in Its Tracks," 4-8, he documents how the steady movement within the EC toward economic and monetary union has gotten bogged down in the quicksand of European political integration: "In contrast to the tidy absoluteness of the majority EMU plan for a single currency and bank, the political agenda started ragged, and has gotten messier." He displays a light touch in "Single Community Market in Gambling is a Long-Odds Bet," 4-22, writing on the obstacles standing in the way of a single Community market for sports wagering and lotteries: "What ultimately distinguishes gambling from other financial services such as banking or insurance is that many people think it ought not to expand." He imaginatively updates the mixed success of EC efforts to flatten physical, technical, and fiscal barriers to goods, services, trade, and movement of people as 1992 approaches in "Twelve Slip Into Unflagging Pace in Frontiers Marathon," 6-17. He does an excellent job of breaking down the EC-EFTA agreement in "Irony of EEA Sop That Spurred Flood to Join EC," 10-23, observing that while the agreement was originally conceived by Jacques Delors as a mechanism for getting around the question of expanding the EC, the EEA "has in fact spurred countries to join the Community club," so that they'll have more say in EC proceedings that will now affect them. He is equally sharp on how the Dutch Government has drawn up a draft treaty for economic and monetary union that tries to split the difference on divisive economic issues in "The Dutch Dare to Tackle Currency Question Head-On," 10-29: "In essence, the conundrum is how to give Britain a let-out, without creating a bolt-hole through which others might escape their Emu commitments." He capped off the year with the 10 Best selection, "A Heath Robinson Design for Europe," 12-12, a masterful analytic on the Maastricht summit.

Carnegy, Hugh. *Financial Times.* (★ ★ ½)
Jerusalem. Alert to signs of policy shifts and developments, Carnegy picked up early on how Israel's economic ties to the United States would be drawn into its on-going dispute with Washington over the settlement program. He is thorough on the issues raised by Iraq's Scud attacks on Israel and allied pressure for Israel not to retaliate in "Under Fire on Several Fronts," 1-19/20, drawing on "Informed observers" to report that a retaliatory strike had been ordered until James Baker persuaded Prime Minister Shamir to hold off. Profiling hardliners in the Likud cabinet in "Extremists Who Want More Jewish Settlements," 5-18/19, he falls back on cliche, commenting that one proposal for the occupied territories "sounds suspiciously like the classic apartheid of South Africa and its black homelands." In "The Chinks in Shamir's Armor," 6-20, he provides a clear description of the dilemma of unpalatable truths faced by the government of Yitzhak Shamir as a policy fight brews with Washington over the settlements. He reports from one of those settlements, Adam, as the Likud government attempts to create irrevocable "facts on the ground" in the eye-opening "Settlements Obstacle for Israel," 7-22: "The scale of construction is such that even if Mr. Shamir were to reverse his refusal to freeze new building, the backlog of unfinished work would keep the cement mixers turning for many months to come." He was sharp on the developing peace process, as with "Another Piece of the Peace Jigsaw Falls Into Place," 10-19/20, which reports on how the resumption of Israeli-Soviet ties can be expected to move the process along, and with "Israelis Agree to Attend Middle East Peace Talks," 10-21, which warns that "a hitch could yet develop over the so-far unpublished Palestinian list if Israel objects to any of the names." Profiling one of the key names left off that list, Faisal Husseini, in "Palestinian Calling the Tune From a Distance," 10-26/27, Carnegy deftly captures the essence of that man and his cause. In "Israel Conscious of Weak Card Among its Aces," 10-31, he expertly outlines the role the Israeli government's susceptibility to external economic pressure — and the willingness of the Bush administration to wield it — is playing in Madrid.

Chesnoff, Richard Z. *U.S.News & World Report.* (★ ½)
Senior correspondent for the Middle East, Chesnoff's war coverage was usually buried in multiple-bylined cover stories, but his side-bar efforts through the year helped increase our understanding of political trends within the region. In "Israel's Home-Front Woes," 1-14, he adequately updates us on Israel's internal headaches, including the drought-stricken water supply, the Palestinian uprising, and the lack of jobs and housing for the Soviet immigrants. He produces a brief but perceptive look at Jordan's King Hussein and his pro-Iraqi stance in "Can the King Walk the Tightrope?" 2-25, observing that the King's efforts to stay ahead of the crowd could backfire. Chesnoff's account of how he and photographer David Turnley drove through allied and Iraqi lines all the way to newly liberated Kuwait City "Behind the Lines," 3-11, is vivid if not quite as gripping as other accounts we read: "The long highway into Kuwait was a kind of Death Alley. At some spots, it was almost completely choked by burned-out tanks and vehicles, among them the squad cars used by Hussein's secret police. In one spot, a headless, limbless torso blocked the middle of the road." He provides a moving account of the airlift of Ethiopian Jews to Israel in "Exodus," *The New Republic* 6-17: "The sight of 15,000 black Jews being embraced by 4 million white and brown Israelis is an eloquent response to the United Nation's resolution that Zionism is racism." His grasp on the Palestinian story is exhibited in "The Biggest Losers of the Gulf War," 8-5, an informative update on moderate Palestinians trapped between extremists and hardliners within the Palestinian movement and the Israeli government. He fully captures the flavor of Jerusalem and the reasons it looms so large in any potential Middle East peace negotiations in "A Holy City's Holy Wars," 8-26/9-2: "The claims to Jerusalem are as varied as the multicolored coats of residents, pilgrims and would-be prophets that jam its giant gates and narrow souks." In the illuminating "The Sound of Taboos Breaking," 11-11, he takes us out into the corridors at the Madrid peace conference where "the greatest progress" in breaking the ice between the two sides may have been made.

Christian, Shirley. *The New York Times.* (★ ½)
San Salvador bureau chief. An adept political reporter, the former Buenos Aires bureau chief hasn't yet gotten her arms around the political economy of her new beat, her rating suffering as a result. Writing on the "growing chorus of opposition" to President Carlos Menem's plan to pardon those who participated in the government's war against leftists in the 1970s "In Echo of the 'Dirty War,' Argentines Fight Pardons," 12-28-90, she leaves us in the dark whether this growing chorus is actually a threat to Menem's rule. She comprehensively covers the ruckus raised by U.S. ambassador Terence Todman's allegation that official corruption is hindering the ability of U.S. firms to compete in Argentina in "Bluntly Put, Graft Is Rife: U.S. Envoy Speaks Out," 1-16. Her serviceable survey on the accomplishments and criticisms of the Chamorro regime one year into office, "Chamorro at Managua Helm: Beloved but Also Under Fire," 4-12, is highlighted by an interview with Mrs. Chamorro, who says that she hopes to spend more time on the economy. In "Sandinistas Seek New Role to Play," 4-28, she artfully captures the existentialist crisis of the Sandinista leadership as it adapts to life out of power in a post-Cold War world; in the follow-up "Sandinistas Shed a Bit of Their Past," 7-23, she reports that while the Sandinistas are dropping references to Marxist-Leninism, the leadership continues to resist any meaningful change. Later in the summer her attention shifted to El Salvador, taking readers on patrol with the Salvadoran army as it pushes into guerrilla territory near the Honduras border as the peace talks drag on in "With Peace on Everyone's Lips, Killing Goes On," 8-28, a competent piece of combat reporting. The "Week In Review" essay "Ideology Fades, Battle Lines Sharpen," 9-8, tills no new soil on post-Cold War conflict in the region. Analyzing the U.N.-sponsored peace accord between the Cristiani government and the FMLN in "The Salvador Accord: Conflict Is Far From Over," 9-27, she passes over the particulars of the agreement to deal with the hardline attitudes prevailing on both sides which may yet sink the accord: "Indeed, observers of the process said the two sides often spent more time negotiating with their own people than with the enemy."

Church, George J. *Time.* (★ ½)
A senior writer for the newsweekly, Church has a flair for incorporating analysis into his reports, but he can cross over the line into editorializing, as with his coverage of the Kurdish crisis. His war coverage was generally solid and often offered insightful overviews, such as his report on the battle of Khafji, "Combat in the Sand," 2-11, and "Saddam's Endgame," 2-25, on Saddam's peace feelers. His reporting on the lead-in to the ground war, "Marching to a Conclusion," 3-4, was much more somber than the coverage we saw in *Newsweek,* very thorough in its step-by-step accounting. He provides an acceptable day-by-day recap of the ground war in "The 100 Hours," 3-11. His coverage of the upheaval in post-war Iraq suffered from a preachy tone at times. In "Keeping Hands Off," 4-8, he lists the reasons why Bush doesn't want to be there but just touches on the problems the U.S. has experienced previously in implementing governments in other lands, while in "The Course of Conscience," 4-15, Church editorializes that "[Bush's] unconscionable silence reflected a recurring problem of his foreign policy." In his cover story "Death Every Day," 4-22, he sweepingly concludes that "thousands of Kurds. . .will die every day that foot-dragging, bureaucratic bumbling and political maneuvering delay desperately needed relief." His reports on the Soviet Union were uneven, "Who's That Man With the Tin Cup?" 6-3, all over the map on Moscow's desire to enter the G-7 club, while "Boris Looks Westward," 6-24, is incomplete on Russian Republic President Boris Yeltsin. However, "Crisis of Personality," 7-15, is a useful and informative article on the psychology of the Soviet Union as it moves toward a market economy. His review of the death throes of Soviet communism, "Anatomy of a Coup," 9-2, provides details on the events while managing to avoid coming out strongly for any particular faction. Updating us on the post-coup chaos in "Into the Void," 9-9, he fails to bring in the urgency of the economic situation. He produces an evenhanded breakdown of the path to Madrid in "Must We Talk? Now?" 10-21, giving us some sense of the complications and the sheer accomplishment of just getting all parties to the table.

Claiborne, William. *The Washington Post.* (★ ★)
Toronto. With a major recession and the on-going issue of Quebec separatism, it was a difficult year for the Mulroney government and the Canadian people, but Claiborne's Canadian contributions were, on the whole, light. His Middle Eastern coverage was marked by resourcefulness and imaginative use of detail. He can deliver on the Canadian political economy when given the chance, in "After Two Years Many Canadians Still Distrust Trade Pact With U.S." 1-5, he finds that the jury is still out, noting that "in numerous interviews, critics and proponents of the pact produced identical documents issued by the official statistics agency, Statistics Canada, to make their case." Assigned to the Middle East as war broke out, he provided memorable ground-level reporting from Tel Aviv on the day after the first Scud attack in "False Alarms Rattle Israelis Fearful of More Iraqi Scuds," 1-19. He is also effective in conveying the horrors of war in "Kuwaiti Doctors Charge Torture, Killings by Occupiers," 3-1, a graphic summary of atrocities committed by Iraqi occupying forces as witnessed by Kuwaiti medical officials. He gets to the bottom of one mystery, interviewing an obstetrician who tells him "the Iraqis did not steal any infant incubators, as they were alleged to have done early in the war." In the amusing "Sun-Baked at Midnight," 6-24, he reports on how the residents of the Arctic Circle, Yukon, deal with the seasonal period of sun 24 hours a day, including midnight golf tournaments and drinks with an amputated toe in them. However, with NAFTA approaching, we feel that Canada should be more than fodder for feature stories. He travels to Iran and documents evidence of Iran's growing emergence from the dark days of the Islamic Revolution in the atmospheric "Iran Gives Indications of Mellowing," 9-10, taking readers into the air conditioned tomb of the Ayatollah Khomeini where mourners picnic. In his best Canadian effort all year, "Hard Times Busting Canadian Farmers," 11-1, he draws a vivid portrait of farmers in western Canada struggling through some of the worst economic conditions since the Depression.

Clines, Francis X. *The New York Times.* (★ ★ ½)
Clines was promoted to Moscow bureau chief following Bill Keller's departure, and the immediate effect was a net decline in the quality and quantity of this talented reporter's work. However, his coup coverage was generally literate and on-target after an initial miscue. In "Ally Who Soured on Gorbachev Warns of a Stalinist-Style Coup," 8-17, he describes Aleksandr N. Yakolev's warning as a "melodramatic flourish," pointing out that he made the same prediction last January. His rushed report on Gorbachev's ouster for the late edition, "Gorbachev Is Ousted in an Apparent Coup by Soviet Armed Forces and Hard-Liners," 8-19, manages to get the breaking developments across, while "On the Streets, a Shrug at a Falling Star," 8-25, artfully captures the cynicism and resentment in the Moscow streets following Gorbachev's resignation as party secretary. In the 10 Best nominee, "Gorbachev Pleads, But Breakaway Areas Defy Him, Putting Fate of Union in Doubt," 8-27, he adroitly portrays both the historical implications and the human drama of the apparent breakup of the Soviet Union. He paints a vivid picture of Ukrainian leader Leonid M. Kravchuk in "Apparatchik to Nationalist: Ukrainian's Fancy Footwork," 8-30. His major misstep of the year came in "Gorbachev Pleads for $100 Billion in Aid From West," 5-23, stating that it was "the first time [Gorbachev] had cited a specific figure." He was forced to backtrack the next day in "A Correction: On Gorbachev Aid Plea for Billions," 5-24, reporting that "A full version of [Gorbachev's] remarks in a rambling answer during a joint conference with Prime Minister Giulio Andreotti of Italy makes it clear. . .he did not ask for specific amounts of aid." Analyzing the Gorbachev-Yeltsin proposal to dissolve the Congress of People's Deputies and return vast power to the republics in "A Gamble With Chaos," 9-3, he passes along the routine observation that the plan contains many unknowns. He borrows a page from Samuel Beckett in "Waiting for Capitalism in Ever Longer Lines," 11-8, writing on the ever-lengthening lines at state-run stores for a shrinking supply of consumer goods while street market entrepreneurs, "too new at this to realize the value of a sales pitch," struggle to eke out a living.

Cody, Edward. *The Washington Post.* (★ ½)
Managua. Cody's beat encompasses Central America and Mexico, and there is precious little that is new or fresh in his relatively conventional assessments of Mexico under President Carlos Salinas de Gortari. His non-Mexican coverage was markedly better; his account of Marine 1st Division's Task Force Ripper during the ground war, "Marines Say Iraqi Performance Fell Far Short of Expectations," 3-3, deftly shows how events on the ground tied in to overall strategy and planning. In "The Salinas Revolution: Attacking Mexican Attitudes," 5-17, Cody superficially places Salinas's economic policy in a political and social context, writing that the "shift in attitude has thrown open the economy and transformed the atmosphere — if not always the facts — in which Mexican businessmen and politicians make their decisions." Examining Salinas's efforts at political reform in "Will Ruling Party Ride Salinas's Reform Bus?" 5-18, he digs no deeper than to note that certain traditions live on: "Despite his call for a modern revolution, Salinas followed a long custom and reviewed an hours-long May Day parade replete with uniformed union activists carrying oversized plastic pipe wrenches on their shoulders as if marching off to defend the 1910 revolution." In "More Mexicans Crossing Border," 6-24, he finds that "hard economic realities" have frustrated U.S. efforts to stop the flood of illegal immigrants seeking higher-paying jobs, his reporting here is sharper than his analysis. He imaginatively covers a key angle of the BCCI story in "BCCI's Gulf Benefactor," 8-18, traveling to Abu Dhabi and documenting the relationship between tribal ruler Zayed Sultan Nahayan and BCCI founder Agha Hassan Abedi, including Abedi's attempt to have Abu Dhabi bail out the troubled bank in early 1990. In "Mexico Modernizes but 'El Toro' Died by Old Rules," 10-25, he oversimplifies the Mexican reform efforts, presenting the turbulent life and violent death of one local strongman as being symbolic of "Mexico's problems in stopping drug smuggling, human rights violations and police corruption in the countryside, despite Salinas' repeated orders for change issued in Mexico City."

Coll, Steve. *The Washington Post.* (★ ★ ½)

New Delhi. Displaying the resourcefulness that helped him win a Pulitzer as a financial journalist, Coll kept on top of events in this increasingly important and complex region. He is knowledgeable on growing Hindu-Moslem strife over "religious turf" in "Hindu-Moslem Battles Sweeping India's North," 1-2, tying Hindu militancy to resentment over the rising Moslem birthrate. Assigned to the Gulf War as it was winding down, in "After Victory, A Sense of Unease," 3-12, he captures the challenges to the status quo in Saudi society following the war. He covers an important angle on the Bangladesh disaster we didn't see elsewhere, skepticism on the part of international relief officials at the announced death toll of 139,000, in "Relief Officials Question Bangladesh Death Toll," 5-13. Coll's coverage of the assassination of Rajiv Gandhi was disappointing, "Blast Kills India's Ex-Premier Gandhi," 5-22, is thorough, but he curiously calls Gandhi "a symbol of national unity" and "a symbol of national stability," while in the accompanying "Political Dynasty Comes to End," 5-22, he writes that "In some ways, Gandhi was felled by a political culture that he, his family and his party helped create during the last decade — a culture of violence and expediency. . ." On the trail of the BCCI story, he travels to the fabled "sultry sliver of coral sand due south of Cuba," in "Do Cayman Islanders Keep Secrets? Don't Even Ask," 8-13, and produces a feature which does little to advance the story. Much more impressive is "BCCI's Abedi: A Courtier's Ruin," 9-1, a comprehensive effort to place the BCCI scandal in the context of founder Agha Hasan Abedi's background in the former Indian kingdom of Mahmudabad. In "S. Asian Reformers Face Tough Hurdles," 9-8, he shrewdly connects the economic reforms underway in both India and Pakistan. He is chilling but thorough on how the ambiguity surrounding Pakistan and India's tactical nuclear warfare doctrines could lead to "catastrophic miscalculations" in a future crisis in "South Asia Retains Its Nuclear Option," 9-30. His grasp of India's intellectual life is demonstrated with "India's Introspective Inquiry," 10-22.

Contreras, Joseph. *Newsweek.* (★)

Johannesburg. Contreras's South African coverage is too heavily centered around the ANC and its viewpoint on the historic developments there. While the ANC is a major player we would like to see more on Inkatha and the divisions within the white community. In "Outposts of Apartheid," 1-7, he does an adequate job in explaining how some townships are taking advantage of a loophole in the repeal of the Special Amenities Act to maintain racial segregation. The remedy, Contreras writes, may lie in the courts. However, in "Judgement Day for Winnie," 4-29, we learn more about Winnie Mandela in a perceptive character sketch, than the case itself. Still on the Mandelas, in "Portrait of a Marriage," 5-27, he conveys the shifting complexities of the Mandelas' relationship with each other, and South Africa, as Winnie Mandela is convicted of kidnapping, Contreras's skilled writing bringing us close to the family without losing information. In "Is It Time to Lift Sanctions?" with Jane Whitmore 7-1, he uses the simplistic device of school grades to answer the question, but it works fairly well, as the writers give us reasonably good background information on which to assess their evaluations. He provides a serviceable overview of the Government's secret funding of Inkatha while negotiating with the ANC in "The Color of Money," 8-5, while in "Pretoria: One Group, One Vote," 9-16, he echoes ANC criticism of the political reform package currently being proposed by the government. Still, "The mere fact that South Africa's power players are prepared to settle their differences on one person, one vote around a table is itself a welcome change."

Cowell, Alan. *The New York Times.* (★ ★)

Rome. Cowell's European coverage is much like his Middle East coverage, strong on politics, culture and security, weak on economics. He did rise to the occasion of covering the war and chaotic aftermath in Iraq. In the perceptive "2 Risky Gambles for Jordan's Ruler," 2-8, he observes that by aligning himself with Iraq, King Hussein is gambling that he can stay ahead of Jordanian public opinion without hurting his ties to the West and that he appeal to wider Arab support. We get useful intelligence on the view from Damascus of exiled Iraqi opposition leaders and regional diplomats on the collapse of the revolt in "Kurds Assert Few Outside Iraq Wanted

Them to Win," 4-11. He then traveled to Iraq, capturing stories and insights we didn't find elsewhere, such as "Facing Iran, an Army With Resolve and Day Care," 6-5, on an army of Iranian exiles backed by Iraq; "Baghdad Hopeful on Kurdish Pact But Insists on Control of Oil Center," 6-6, a report from war-damaged Kirkuk on the prospects of a Kurdish agreement with Baghdad, and "Omens Amid the Ruins: A Voyage Across Iraq's Tattered Southlands," 5-30, from southern Iraq, Cowell providing data in his dispatch to back up his observation that "while the failed uprising among Iraq's Shiite Muslim majority has left Mr. Hussein feared enough to enforce his writ, his brief moment of vulnerability has not been forgotten." He deals with a heavily-covered topic in "Italy's Painful Plight: Huddled Masses at Its Door," 9-18, and adds little new. However, he is sharp on the advances and setbacks for both sides in "Serbs and Croats: Seeing War in Different Prisms," 9-24. Analyzing the Pope's visit to Brazil in "Pope's Law: Less Politics," 10-16, he adequately conveys the Vatican's attempt to split the middle between social activism and the Brazilian ruling class while Catholics defect to Protestant sects. He vividly captures the tense, almost frigid, personal atmosphere which prevailed at the opening round of the Madrid peace talks in "In Contact at Last, but Never Eye to Eye," 10-31. If Cowell would turn his talents to Italy's political economy, as E.J. Dionne, Jr. did, he might rise to the top of the *NYT* foreign pack.

Cullison, A.E. *The Journal of Commerce.* (★ ★ ★ ½)
Tokyo. Cullison is a fine reporter, and we have particularly high regard for his "Asia Watch" columns, where he exhibits an exceptional talent for giving the Japanese perspective on international and domestic developments without ever losing his critical distance. In "Japan Will Stand Tall in '90s," 1-23, he provides an authoritative look at the decade ahead, foreseeing a Japan with much more democracy and higher living standards domestically while a major player internationally. Addressing the question of Korean unification in "Laying Korean Ghosts to Rest," 3-20, he observes that it is unlikely to happen until both Seoul and Pyongyang renounce their claim to be the sole legitimate government for the Korean peninsula. He takes an astute look at U.S.-Japanese relations in "Finding the Common Ground," 4-3, calling on both sides to lower the volume and work together to bring down the U.S. federal budget deficit and force the Japanese bureaucracy to accept the virtues of free trade: "From the look of things, little meaningful progress is being made in either sector — unless lip service is assigned some weight." He puts the reader in the shoes of the average small Japanese investor as news rolls in that the "Big Four" brokerage houses paid out $1 billion to compensate their biggest customers for market losses in "Japan's Brokerage Boondoggle," 7-24. He offers us the view from Tokyo on Washington's latest round of threats concerning the *keiretsu* in "Bashing Japan's Corporate Clans," 8-7, talking to one LDP-connected attorney who suggests Washington might find it more effective to employ its own, much stronger, anti-monopoly laws. He is forward-looking on the Japanese car industry's research push into electrical cars in "Japan Plans Car of the Future," 8-21, reporting that they are already targeting Los Angeles, because of its high concentration of vehicles and stringent anti-pollution laws: "The U.S. auto industry can't say it wasn't warned of Japan's intention to corner this market." In the thoughtful "Slowly, Japan Opens Its Eyes," 10-30, he reflects on how Japan is slowly coming to grips with its behavior during World War II, although some efforts at selective amnesia remain.

Dahlberg, John-Thor. *Los Angeles Times.* (★)
Moscow. Dahlberg has shown a talent for adequately sketching day-to-day developments in the Soviet Union, but we were severely disappointed by his coup coverage, which time and again missed out on key elements of the story, especially the role of the military. In "Soviet Right Tightens Its Grip," 8-20, he begins with the assertion that "Backed by fearsome military might, the chiefs of the Soviet army, KGB and police and fellow right-wingers on Monday sequestered Mikhail S. Gorbachev, clamped a state of emergency on Moscow and swiftly moved." His report, "Fighting Erupts at Barricades," 8-21, erroneously declares that fierce fighting had broken out at the barricades and that two Yeltsin supporters had been shot to death by soldiers. In "Soviet Coup Collapses," 8-22, the emphasis is on what the newly-freed Mikhail Gorbachev

intends to do, while the tone of "Death Throes for the Party?" 8-24, is exemplified by the question mark in the headline. Covering the crisis in the Baltics earlier in the year, in such pieces as "Alfreds Rubiks: Latvia's Agile Man in the Middle," 1-29, and "Lithuanians Vote Today on Independence Issue," 2-9, he captures the nuances in a fluid situation. He provides a good read on the pulse of the Ukraine as the nationwide referendum on the Union approaches, "Soviet Unity Vote Divides Ukrainians," 3-17, while in "Soviets Vote in Unity Showdown," 3-18, he portrays the referendum as "principally a ballot box showdown between Mikhail S. Gorbachev and his radical rival Boris N. Yeltsin." Writing on the effects of price reforms in " 'Sticker Shock' Jolts Soviets on Eve of Huge Price Boosts," 4-2, he reflects exclusively the consumer's point of view, to the exclusion of the policymaker's or the reformer's. In "Soviets Face a Dark, Chilly Winter of Power Shortages," 10-19, he displays a sense of history as he surveys the various factors — ethnic feuds, independence movements, environment activists — which have combined to leave the ex-Soviet Union with a damaged fuel grid and potential energy famine as it enters the winter: "Politicians. . .are keenly aware of the dire consequences, if large numbers of citizens, who already worry about potential famine, must live in cold and dark homes as well."

Darlin, Damon. *The Wall Street Journal.* (★ ★ ★)
Seoul. Following a notable stint in Tokyo, Darlin is handling the Korean beat with increasing confidence and competence, paying particular attention to shifts and new developments in the volatile issue of U.S.-ROK trade relations. In "South Korea to Lend Soviets $3 Billion Over Three Years," *Asian WSJ* 1-28, he presents a finely detailed overview of the loan. We learn that Korea is the hottest new market territory in Asia for U.S. fast-food companies in a colorfully written "Korean Appetite for Fast Food Keeps Growing, to the Delight of U.S. Concerns," *AWSJ* 2-18. He finds solid signs of progress in the efforts of Korea and U.S. to resolve trading issues that arise from "misunderstandings," in "Koreans Indicate A New Willingness to Open Up Trade," 3-1, observing that the ROK's "charm offensive. . .is having some effect." He smartly works in key background and context in "Korea Rejects Applications From Big 4 Securities Firms," *AWSJ* 3-25, insightful on the country's decision to block Japan's securities firms from entering the ROK market. Among several splendid reports on economic policy, two in particular stood out: "Korea's 30 Biggest Firms Told to Shrink," 4-30, and "South Korea's Roh Tells Conglomerates to Sell Idle Land or Face Lending Cutoff," 5-3; both pieces on the efforts by the government to take on the *chaebol,* which the broad consensus in Korea blames for the country's loss of industrial competitiveness. In the excellent report "South Korea's Semiconductor Makers Seek Transition to Sophisticated Chips," 7-29, he provides solid information on the shifts in strategic thinking among the country's semiconductor companies. He provides plenty of details, which we took with a grain of salt, on how economic imperatives may force the "hermit nation" to expand its links with the outside world in "North Korea's Economic Decline Is Likely to Force End to Isolation," 9-17. The article suffers from no mention of growing international concern over Pyongyang's nuclear weapons program. Writing on Kia Motors's efforts to establish an independent sales network in the U.S. in "Kia Motor to Sell Its Compact Cars in U.S. by 1993," 10-25, he dryly notes that "It is a plan fraught with obstacles: For one, Kia doesn't yet make the models it plans to sell in the U.S."

Darling, Juanita. *Los Angeles Times.* (★ ★)
Mexico City. Darling continues to impress us with her well-researched economic background reports, and she is branching out into Mexican politics and culture as well, quickly becoming the *LAT*'s key source on Mexican developments. If she could break through on Mexico's tax system and impediments to local investment, she would boost her rating considerably. In the well-aimed "North American Talks Concern Japan," 4-4, she reports on how Japan is angling for a key role in the North American Free Trade Agreement: "Already, the Mitsui Research Institute. . .is exploring ways that U.S.-Japanese trade deals could complement a North American free-trade agreement, perhaps eventually resulting in a four-nation Pacific economic coalition." She offers sharp analysis of Mexico's diplomatic stance in "Mexico Savors Role as Mediator of Central America Conflicts," 5-4, placing its role as a mediator in regional disputes

in the context of its evolving relationship with the U.S. In "Mexico Gears Up for a Lively Campaign," 5-18, she captures the flavor of the upcoming midterm elections, while in "Can the World's Hottest Market Keep Climbing?" 5-18, she deepens our understanding of the workings of the Mexican stock exchange. In "Mexico Has Become Prisoner of Its Own Prison System," 6-1, she attempts a fresh rendition of a tired theme and succeeds, conveying the crisis in the Mexican penal system. She challenges assumptions that the free-trade agreement will turn Mexico into "little more than a nation of low-paid workers" in "Mexican Industry Eager to Make Its Imprint on International Market," 7-9, a well-drawn portrait of Mexico's "Monterrey Group" of industrial interests, who "own major U.S. manufacturing companies, issue stocks and bonds on U.S. capital markets and use the money they raise to increase their exports, mainly to the United States." Following the free-trade story further in the comprehensive "Free Trade May Spur Import Appetite," 10-22, she reports on predictions by economists that "Mexican manufacturers will increasingly turn to imports to expand the lines of products they offer domestic customers."

Davidson, Ian. *Financial Times.* (★ ★ ★)
Paris. A superior analyst, Davidson is a master at providing broad pictures of French political culture, all the while keenly sensitive to the critical marginal detail. He develops the theme of European cohesion in the wake of the Gulf War with "The Worst of All Worlds," 2-11, which was a bit too condescending in its estimation of France's Gulf policy, and "The Gulf Concentrates Minds," 2-25, in which he unveils a subtext beneath the useless rhetoric of national politicians that indicated a growing cohesion in Western Europe on foreign policy. In "France's Man of the Moment," 5-7, he delivers an extremely sharp assessment of President Francois Mitterrand on his tenth anniversary in office. His political savvy is well-demonstrated with "The Final Parting of the Ways," 5-16, in which he deftly examines the implications of the change of prime ministers in France. Davidson nicely deflates the hyperbole over Edith Cresson with a knowledgeable flair and professional ease in "A Man-Eater With No Teeth," 5-20. He captures remarkably well the central dilemma of the French constitution, "which is poised ambiguously between a parliamentary system and a presidential regime," in "Problems at Half-Time," 6-17, an assessment of the problems faced by President Mitterrand as France's economic recession narrows the government's room to maneuver. Expertly surveying Mitterrand's autumn of discontent as criticism swells over his handling of the Soviet coup attempt and performance of Edith Cresson as Prime Minister in "Marathon Man Falters," 9-4, he observes that while Mitterrand has always been a brilliant long-term strategist, "since 1989 and the fall of the Berlin Wall, the world has moved too fast for him." In "Why There Will Be a Treaty," 10-21, he persuasively argues that despite last-minute hitches over security issues, political and economic union will arrive at Maastricht and British voters should not be led to believe otherwise: "Many years may pass before we see an integrated European army of 100,000; but the era of national independence, even for relatively large countries like Britain and France, has gone forever."

Davidson, Joe. *The Wall Street Journal.* (★)
Johannesburg. We appreciate Davidson's ability to deliver straightforward reports on South Africa, with no perceptible bias showing through. However, his coverage could benefit from detailed ground-level reporting to flesh out the national issues he writes about. And with all the country's problems given an intensified volatility by South Africa's economic problems, his meager reporting on this front is a serious shortcoming. Reporting on the opening of the Winnie Mandela trial in "Winnie Mandela Trial Proving Painful for Both Pretoria, ANC," 2-27, he adequately explains why the disappearance of one prosecution witness and the reluctance of two others to testify has raised questions both about the competence of the government and the ability of the ANC to guarantee an independent judiciary in a future, majority-ruled state. He strikes an appropriately ironic note in "Namibia, a Year After Independence, Still Faces Sanctions of U.S. Localities," and Timothy Noah 3-22, detailing how Namibia continues to be punished by local, county, and state governments in the U.S. through a combination of ignorance and apathy which "does not auger rapid reaction to the time when democracy becomes inevitable

in South Africa." In "Judge Sentences Winnie Mandela to 6 Years in Jail," 5-15, he helpfully provides the background on the case. We get a knowledgable scene-setter on the first legal ANC meeting in South Africa in 30 years in "ANC Focuses on Conflicts Within Its Own Ranks," 7-2, Davidson offering sharp details on the differences between the local and regional representatives and the National Executive Committee. In the solid "De Klerk Plan Lets Blacks Vote But Aids Whites," 9-5, he concisely summarizes de Klerk's new constitution and the ANC's criticisms of same. In the best report we saw from Davidson all year, "Democracy Is Growing in Africa, as Ferment in Zambia Illustrates," 10-31, he effectively presents the election in Zambia as a paradigm of the "second revolution" sweeping across Africa. We wish he could bring this level of reporting to his South African stories.

de Cordoba, Jose. *The Wall Street Journal.* (★)
Miami. Although a talented writer, de Cordoba has a glaring weakness, more at home with political developments or law-and-order stories than with economics, and we find ourselves turning to the *Financial Times* and *The Journal of Commerce* for these stories and details. He provides good detail on the threat to Colombia's petroleum industry presented by the guerrillas (*elenos*) who don't like the government policy of granting concessions to foreign companies in "Guerrillas' Oil Pipeline Bombings Cloud Colombia's Quest for Foreign Investment," 1-9. Profiling Lloyd S. Rubin, an American banker in Panama who seems to thrive by promising funding for would-be entrepreneurs and not delivering, in "Smooth Talker," 3-26, he competently assembles the complaints and carries the observation of the Panamanian ambassador to the U.S. that Panama's wide open business laws have sometimes led to abuse. His florid account of a Floridian private eye who got caught up in the intersection of BCCI and Peruvian politics, "Private Eye, in Odd BCCI Tale, Tells of Snooping on Ex-President of Peru," and Michael Allen 7-30, reads like something out of an Elmore Leonard novel. Delivering a vivid portrait of Cuba after the failed Soviet coup in "Failure of Soviet Coup Leaves Cuba Stalled, Fidel Castro Isolated," 8-27 he finds that little has changed except for additional concern over future trade relations with the Soviets. He delivers a substantial report on the two men running Nicaragua today, Antonio Lacayo, Violeta Chamorro's son-in-law, and Sandinista Armed Forces commander Humberto Ortega, in "Odd Couple: A Political Neophyte and an Ex-Sandinista Run Nicaragua Today," 9-12, moving the story forward by observing that this axis is apparently based on personal ambition, Lacayo wants to run for President on a ticket united with the Sandinistas, while Ortega is seen by some as "striving to win U.S. favor so he can become Washington's man in the region — another Somoza." A bemused report on the deteriorating quality of Cuban cigars, "Are Havana Cigars Now Going the Way of Cuba's Economy?" 10-14, focuses more on the international cigar trade than on the besieged Cuban economy.

Dempsey, Judy. *Financial Times.* (★ ★ ★ ★)
Eastern Europe. An outstanding journalist who appreciates political economy, Dempsey's reports consistently tie together many dimensions of East European developments in a comprehensible whole that illuminates and informs us on the volatile events unfolding in the region. She covers the difficult transition to a market economy in the authoritative reports "Communists Stumble on Road to Reform," 1-3, and "Time to Sort Out Who Owns What," 4-16. She focuses on one country in "Poland Suffers for a Lack of Solidarity," 9-3, attributing the current political crisis to President Lech Walesa's efforts to undermine the Communist-controlled *Sejm* while the economy deteriorates. She set the standard for coverage of the Yugoslavian crisis, winning 10 Best selections for her efforts. Covering the beginning in "In Yugoslavia, the Centre Cannot Hold," 3-18, she smartly zeroes in on the dangerous game Serbian leader Slobodan Milosevic and the military are playing, hoping to protect the Communist center without provoking a civil war, "a task which will demand that rationality triumphs over emotionalism." Profiling Croatian leader Franjo Tudjman in "Survivor Out to Settle an Old Score," 5-11/12, she shrewdly notes that just like his Serbian nemesis, this former general, having ridden the nationalist tiger to power, now faces risks if he tries to tame it or if

he lets it go. She captures the complexities of the crisis in the highly-readable "Balkan End-Game," 6-27, giving proper attention to the way in which the political crisis is now feeding off an expanding economic malaise. She expertly charted the deteriorating situation throughout the summer, in such reports as "Milosevic Seeks to Turn Vision Into a Reality," 7-8, and "The Awful Shape of Things to Come," 8-6, noting in the earlier report that "If anyone held any illusions that reining Slovenia in, or reaching a temporary compromise over the republic's external borders, would ensure peace, the future is likely to disabuse them of such notions." She was superb on the EC's efforts to arrange a diplomatic settlement, mirroring the EC's pessimism in "Between Words and War," 10-12/13 and "Last Hope for a Lasting Peace," 11-5.

Dickey, Christopher. *Newsweek.* (★)
Paris. Dickey focused on the Middle East this year, striking a somber tone in some of his reports, a distractingly cynical note in others. Covering the Gulf War from Amman, his report on Saddam's strategy for a prolonged war, "Rope-a-Dope in Baghdad," 2-4, suffers from a "Lifestyles of the Rich & Famous" description of the Iraqi ruler's underground bunker: "It boasts such luxuries as a sauna and fourposter bed with a red silk canopy; such precautions as walls built to withstand atomic blasts — there are even toilets tested for radiation." Evaluating Saddam and his mistakes in "The Blunderer from Baghdad," 2-25, he recycles the conventional view that, while Saddam understands his own country, he hasn't a clue about the world beyond Iraq's borders. In "Eyeballing the Nintendo Apocalypse," *Rolling Stone* 3-7, he offers an impressionistic report on how journalists are trying to cover "another fax war," with the Iran-Iraq war having been the first. Asking "Could the Rebels Really Rule?" 4-15, he finds that no, they couldn't, drawing on a blunt State Department official's characterization of the Kurds as "losers." He offers a saddened appraisal of the Kurdish situation in "A Nation in the Valley of the Three Frontiers," 5-6, a report which lacks the sensationalism of many similar stories, but also some of the edge. However, the edge is as sharp as a sword in "Objective in the Gulf: Making the World Safe for Hypocrisy," *RS* 7-11/7-25, a highly critical if overly cynical, analytic on the post-war fallout and U.S. proclamations of victory: "With Desert Storm, Washington took a plunge into a struggle that won't go away, and for a new order, not the old one. We'll have to face it: Winning won't come easy." Scoring an interview with King Hussein in "Trying to Catch Our Breath," 8-19, he observes that the Jordanian ruler "may be the main factor" in the proposed peace conference. As that peace conference approached he produced several useful guides to the treacherous world of Middle East diplomacy, "What if The Talks Aren't All Talk?" with Margaret Garrard Warner and Theodore Stanger 11-4, and "Have We Got a Deal For You," with Theodore Stanger 11-11.

Diehl, Jackson. *The Washington Post.* (★ ★ ★)
Jerusalem. Diehl provided exceptional coverage of the Gulf War and political developments in the occupied territories, consistently capturing the shifting sands of regional diplomacy. In "Palestinians Dodging Iraq's Missiles Cheer On Saddam," 1-21, he objectively evokes the support for Saddam on the West Bank. He turns in a superlative reporting job in "Shamir's Unexpected Restraint," 3-19, documenting how Prime Minister Yitzhak Shamir refrained from retaliation because he did not want to play into Saddam's hands. He updates the *intifada* in "Turf Battles Overshadow Uprising Against Israel," 6-9, providing important intelligence on the growing clashes between PLO members and the Islamic Resistance, while in "Gaza, West Bank Arabs Assert New Moderation," 6-20, he moves the story forward, reporting on how this increasing Arab vs. Arab violence has led to "the growing ascendancy in the Israeli-occupied territories of intellectuals and politicians who, more than at any other time in recent years, are willing to assert a new agenda of moderation against both internal militants and the Palestine Liberation Organization outside the country." Analyzing the movement toward a Middle East peace conference in "Talks Push Shamir, Assad to Reveal Motives," 7-29, and "Captives, Peace Talks Caught in Mideast Power Play," 8-17, he keenly observes that both the Israelis and the Syrians are more concerned with relations with Washington than with each other. Discussing the dispute over the loan guarantees in "U.S., Israel on Collision Course," 9-16, he perceptively

points out that "Behind the calculations of all sides is the fundamental question of whether U.S. political or economic leverage can wrest Israel away from the expansionist course its governments have pursued over the last 15 years." Covering the opening round of the Madrid talks in "Sides Talk Past Each Other, Play to U.S." 11-1, he strikes a cynical pose, contending that U.S. hopes of Arabs and Israelis beginning serious dialogue have evaporated as "the talk has been largely in English, steered toward television, and designed to convince the world — above all America — of claims that would be largely irrelevant to any real dialogue within the region."

Dobbs, Michael. *The Washington Post.* (★ ★)
Moscow. At times routine in his reports, at other times resourceful and original, Dobbs had a particularly uneven year. His coverage of the first day of the coup attempt, "Crowds Mass Against Tanks," 8-20, contains little on the coup leaders themselves or their possible motivations, save a reference to Yanayev as "a colorless apparatchik" and writing that "Despite assurances. . .that market-oriented reform will continue, it seems likely that the change of regime will result in a move back toward the discredited command economy." In the superficial " 'Yeltsin Magic' Turns the Tide," 8-22, he refers to the Russian leader as the "strapping Siberian" and manages to work in references to Yeltsin's "fondness for alcohol and a habit of getting into embarrassing scrapes." Better is "A View From the Provinces," 9-2, a revealing report from the garrison town of Ryazan on the political passivity of the bulk of the population: "If the conspirators had been better organized and better led, the outcome could have been very different." In the well-written "Why Soviets Won't Starve This Winter," 9-16, he documents how the Russian people plan to get by this winter through "an informal supply system that is considerably more efficient than the state's." Covering Gorbachev's last-minute diplomatic intervention in the Gulf War in "Gorbachev Likely to Reap Dividends From Initiative," 2-21, he offers little new. Observing the fifth anniversary of the Chernobyl disaster in "Chernobyl 1986: A Moment of Truth," 4-26, he memorably conveys the fallout, literally and figuratively, from the world's worst nuclear power plant accident, which "has left a swath of agricultural land the size of Holland permanently poisoned." In the 10 Best nominee, "In Moscow, Running Out of Socks," 6-22, he doggedly goes all the way up the Soviet economic system to report on why a Soviet consumer cannot find a pair of socks to buy on the Moscow street. Toward the end of the year, he produced a prodigious three-part series on "New Times, Old Conflicts," — "Nationalism Eclipsing Communism," 10-27; "Rising Nationalism Hurts East Europe's Economics," 10-28; and "Ethnic Strife Splintering Core of Russian Republic," 10-29, which contained some information which was new, and much that was recycled.

Drogin, Bob. *Los Angeles Times.* (★ ★ ★)
Manila. A prolific writer, Drogin this year found himself covering disasters, both natural and man-made, and he responded with reports marked by literary merit, sharpness of observation and sheer pathos. He deftly captures the ambivalent mood of U.S. soldiers in "U.S. Troops Convinced Ground War Is Coming," 2-23, while the graphic "On the Road: Bodies of Iraqi Soldiers Lie Beside the Booty They Tried to Take," 3-2, brings home the horrors of the carnage on the road leading from Kuwait City to Basra, "the graveyard of the Iraqi army." In "Mad Dash for a Share of Billions," 3-13, he provides a colorful report on the convergence of international businesspeople into the physical and political chaos of newly liberated Kuwait. On a more serious note, in "Amid Deprivation, Emir's Palace Is Gleaming Again," 3-19, he vividly contrasts "war-ravaged" Kuwait City with the "sumptuous restoration" of the emir's palace, supervised by the U.S. Army Corps of Engineers. He performs a similar feat in "Relief Aid Trickles Out to Desperate Cyclone Victims," 5-6, covering the Bangladesh relief effort from a plane dropping supplies to stricken areas while not neglecting the government's less than impressive effort to respond. Returning to the Philippines in time for the eruption of Mt. Pinatubo, in "Volcano Clouds Future of Strategic Clark Base," 6-24, he is informative on what the disaster portends for the U.S. military presence in the country. Better than most daily reporters at working a broad canvas, Drogin superbly covered other countries in the region as

well. In "Megalomania Takes a Toll Down Under," 8-6, he memorably conveys the economic ruins left in the wake of a political scandal in Western Australia, while in "Trouble in Paradise: Behind Fiji's Facade, Turmoil Brew," 9-24, he provides plenty of detail on racial tension between Indians and native Fijians which has led to political instability and a brain drain of professionals and white-collar workers: "So goes life in the languid lane."

Drozdiak, William. *The Washington Post.* (★ ½)
Paris. Drozdiak offered straightforward reports on the French geopolitical scene, the Gulf War, and the European Community which were illuminating at times, but he has yet to develop a strong grasp for European economics. In "N. Africans' War Stance Makes Europeans Uneasy," 1-29, he provides a broad but informative survey of how domestic political pressures have forced the governments of Morocco, Algeria and Tunisia to move closer to Iraq during the war. Traveling to Iraq in April, he provides one of the first reports from Karbala on the aftermath of the failed Shiite uprising in "South Iraq Devastated by Revolt," 4-30, memorable on the "catastrophic" conditions there. He interviews newly-named Deputy Prime Minister Tariq Aziz in "Iraq Termed Committed to Democracy," 5-8, with the former Iraqi foreign minister insisting that he warned Saddam not to go to war but that Saddam just wouldn't listen. Covering France's biggest domestic story in "France's First Woman Premier Is Named to Succeed Rocard," 5-16, he routinely observes that Edith Cresson's ascension to the French prime minister's office is "expected to enhance the party's standing with France's 20 million women voters, who make up a majority of the electorate." We receive a useful Parisian perspective on deteriorating U.S.-Franco relations in "U.S. Shows Arrogance to Allies, French Say," 6-12, reporting that "Senior French officials" including President Mitterrand, foresee a clash ahead over European unity. Analyzing Western Europe's evolving reaction to the Yugoslavian crisis in "Conflicts Surface in Europe Over Yugoslav Crisis," 7-5, and "Lack of an Armed Option Limits EC's Yugoslav Peace Initiative," 9-5, he goes no deeper than to note that even as Europe makes great economic and political strides it still has some lessons of history to learn. Writing on the evident prosperity of the Italian economy despite a $1 trillion deficit in "Italians Stay on a Spending Boom While Country Threatens to Go Bust," 11-6, he fails to draw any real distinction between the booming north and impoverished south.

Engelberg, Stephen. *The New York Times.* (★ ★)
Warsaw. A talented, sharp writer — almost a wordsmith — Engelberg is adept at handling the political and cultural dimensions of the evolving new Poland. He is still struggling with the economic side of the story, though. He provides an informative overview of Czech economic reforms in "Czech Conversion to a Free Market Brings the Expected Pain, and More," 1-4. We were disappointed by "First Sale of State Holdings a Disappointment in Poland," 1-14, as he ponders the question of how the process of privatization might be accelerated while avoiding sale of Government property at bargain prices, but doesn't go anywhere with it. We follow a day in the life of Lech Walesa in "Polish Leader Treads Tortuous Path," 5-31, with Engelberg adroitly documenting how Walesa "is confident his common touch will help him avoid becoming praised overseas but reviled at home, as has happened with President Mikhail S. Gorbachev of the Soviet Union." Reporting from Kedzierzyn Kozle, he succeeds in illustrating how one sprawling chemical plant typifies the problems state-owned enterprises present to the Polish government's plans to introduce a free market in "Factories With Amenities Hinder Poland's Stark Turn to Capitalism," 6-3. Analyzing a papal visit in "Which Way Poland?" 6-11, he notes that the pontiff's plea that Poles not exchange communism for Western European secularism raises issues which go right to the core of Poland's post-communist existence, but leaves us wondering which way Poland will turn — secular or Catholic. He profiles Slobodan Milosevic, "the face of a darker-post-communism paradigm," and how he has used the cause of Serbian nationalism to remain in power, in "Carving Out a Greater Serbia," *Magazine* 9-1, a remarkable piece. As the parliamentary elections approached, with "shock therapy" the central issue, he provides a timely update in "Poland's Cure Is Taking Effect, but Side Effects Hurt," 10-25, and analyzing the vote in "In Polish Vote, a Clear Slap at Reform," 10-29, he positions the returns as placing a brake on the program, but never develops the story beyond this point.

468

Erlanger, Steven. *The New York Times.* (★ ½)
Erlanger's final year in Southeast Asia was disappointing, his Philippine dispatches especially affecting a superficial tone. He could still deliver a substantial report or memorable feature on occasion, but more often than not he seemed bored with this beat, already looking ahead to his next assignment, which we heard would be Moscow. In "Successor to Aquino? For Now, 'Call Me Mr.' " 1-3, he pens a thin account of the unorthodox campaign to succeed President Aquino being waged by Filipino Defense Secretary Fidel V. Ramos, unclear on Ramos's political platform, while "An Old Friend of Marcos Tests Campaign Waters," 1-16, is late on the prospective presidential campaign of Eduardo Cojuangco, Jr., the estranged cousin of President Aquino and one of the closest associates of former President Ferdinand Marcos. He paints a murky picture of the Vietnamese economy in "Its Gains Dissipated, Vietnam Tries to Salvage Its Economy," 2-17, with such vague lines as "The tax system is both inefficient and corrupt." He does provide a timely interview with interim Prime Minister Anand Panyarachun in "Thailand Coup Casts Up a Most Reluctant Premier," 4-30, in which he draws out the Prime Minister's feelings about democracy and the military "When a country that has gone through decades, centuries, of a predominate military role in the ruling of a country, you can't just throw them out. They have face, too." In "No Haven From Agony for Cambodians," 5-2, he produces a multidimensional special report on the plight of Cambodian refugees, who have been "leading lives of stupefying boredom ever since in United Nations-supervised camps, beholden to whichever political faction happens to administer them and allowed no choice as to affiliation" since the Vietnamese invasion twelve years ago. In the 10 Best nominee "A Plague Awaits," *Magazine* 7-14, he provides a horrifying account of widespread AIDS in the heterosexual population of Thailand, via that country's sex industry. Writing on the awarding of the Nobel Peace Prize to Myanmar opposition leader Daw Aung San Suu Kyu in "The Power of the Peace Prize May Be Lost on Myanmar," 10-20, he is pessimistic on the chances this icon of Western culture will have on alleviating human rights abuses in Asia, and overgeneralizes on cultural differences between East and West.

Farah, Douglas. *The Washington Post.* (★ ½)
A Bogota-based stringer, Farah covered America's other war in 1991 directly from the front lines, with reports that helped us understand why the anti-drug battle did not go as well as the battle in the Gulf. We got little on other stories in the region, however. In the thought-provoking "Meanwhile, What About the Drug War?" 2-24, he writes that the Andean countries feel that Washington has "abandoned" them, and that Operation Desert Storm has created the bitter perception that when "the United States is truly serious about achieving its goals, it is both ready and able to provide its allies with the resources needed." In the chilling "Record Murder Wave Overwhelms Medellin," 3-10, we learn the reasons behind the escalation of violence in that city. His coverage of the deal between the Colombian Government and drug trafficker Pablo Escobar was generally sharper than similiar efforts elsewhere. In "Sweet Surrender in Colombia," 6-10, he travels to Escobar's hometown of Envigado to report firsthand on the relationship between Escobar and the community. However, in analyzing Colombia President Cesar Gaviria's decision to negotiate with the drug barons, "Colombia Turns to Courts as Anti-Drug War Founders," 6-21, he simply presents both sides of the argument, without moving the story forward. An eye-opening update on the Cali drug cartel, "Drug Traffickers in Colombia Face Power Struggles," 7-9, reveals that the traditional leaders are being challenged by a younger generation of traffickers "who are more violent, more ambitious and more reckless" than their elders. He provides plenty of data on how BCCI bought out an ailing Colombian bank in 1985, and, working with Manuel Noriega, operated a multimillion dollar money-laundering operation for drug dealers in "Colombia Traffickers Banked on BCCI," 8-8. "We don't want to know how those people got the money and really we cannot be responsible for the morals of our customers," one BCCI official is quoted as saying to an undercover agent. In the graphic "Reign of Terror on a 'River of Death,' " 9-29, he uncovers a new angle of horror in Colombia's ongoing drug-trafficking nightmare.

Farnsworth, Clyde H. *The New York Times.* (★ ★)
Toronto. Despite major stories here, Canada was often short-changed by a tight newshole at most U.S. publications, so we always look for Farnsworth's byline. He draws on his years of experience in covering global trade and is quickly gaining a firm grasp on the Canadian political economy. However, his analysis is incomplete in "New Tax to Aid Canada in Trade," 1-21, as he fails to thoroughly explore the downside of Canada's value-added tax which may initially boost tax revenues and give Canada a trading edge, but could also send Canadian consumers shopping in the U.S. where there is no such tax. He is thorough in "Kickback Scandal Is Rocking Canada," 7-25, reporting on how a businessman, who charged that a cabinet officer demanded a kickback for an office building project in 1986, has re-emerged to shake the Mulroney government following a recent judicial decision to continue the investigation: "The legal action, which sows further public distrust in the Government, comes at a time when the Prime Minister is near rock bottom in polls." He zeroes in on the "negative effects" of the free-trade pact in "Free-Trade Accord Is Enticing Canadian Companies to U.S." 8-9, including the flight of Canadian firms to the U.S., but observes that "others note that the southern migration of business has been accelerated by the severe Canadian recession and by 'shortsighted' Government regulatory and social policies." In the authoritative "Separatist Fervor Fades in Quebec," 9-10, he documents how economic factors are leading Quebec businesspeople and entrepreneurs to back away from supporting all-out separatism: "Without the pan-Canadian linkages, the Quebec entrepreneurs say, the continuing recovery from one of the deepest postwar recessions would be even slower." Farnsworth's stronger efforts before leaving for Canada include "Japan, The Trade Gap and America's 2 Minds," 4-4, where he deftly characterizes the divergent priorities of U.S. consumers and producers that make trade policy with Japan such a sticky issue, and "Trade Focus Has Changed," 5-28, an informative update on the shifting nature of trade negotiations away from tariffs to much less obvious forms of protectionism, such as direct and indirect subsidies.

Fineman, Mark B. *Los Angeles Times.* (★ ★ ★ ½)
New Delhi. No one provides sub-continent coverage that is more comprehensive than Fineman's, both in detail and emotional impact. Through his reports we are able to comprehend and share the passions at work in this volatile region. In the haunting "Refugees From Iraq Describe Hellish Scenes," 2-5, he places the reader in Basra, as that city endures round-the-clock bombing which blocks out the sun. Returning to India, he produced "Poverty and Harsh Critics Surround Calcutta's Island of Communism," 3-2, a 10 Best nominee on a historical anomaly, a democratically-elected communist municipal government. He continued to cover India's sectarian violence with the touch of an expert, illustrated in such reports as "Hindu Throng Demands Temple on Muslim Shrine Site," 4-5, and "Lynchings Over Caste Stir India," 4-12. Fineman's coverage of Rajiv Gandhi's assassination, while informative, seemed rushed. In "Gandhi Assassinated During Crucial, Violent India Election," 5-22, he is able to place Rajiv Gandhi's death in the context of "the most violent campaign in Indian history," but the writing lacks his usual fine touch. However, in the inspired "S. Asia Buries Gandhi But Not Democracy," 5-28, he uses the turnout of south Asian leaders to Gandhi's funeral as the hook for a survey of the rising democratic trend in the region. He is pertinent on the economic reforms being implemented by Prime Minister Rao in "India's New Economics May Be First Shot in a Revolution," 7-30. During the summer he covered the BCCI story from the Pakistani angle, with such forward-looking reports as "In Pakistan, BCCI's Failure Is Seen as a Washington Conspiracy," 8-6, and "Pakistan Offers Sanctuary to Key BCCI Figure," of 8-12, reporting in the latter dispatch that U.S.-Pakistani relations could suffer as a result of the scandal. He was ahead of the curve on the important story of Islamic fundamentalism in Soviet Central Asia as communism collapsed, "Iran Makes Trade Inroads in Soviet Asian Republics," 9-30, a 10 Best selection detailing Iran's attempts to fill the growing vacuum, while "Tide of Islam Stirs Forces in Soviet Asia," 11-5, warns that authorities and moderate clerics may not be able to hold the line much longer against Muslims set on carving out new states of their own.

Fisher, Marc. *The Washington Post.* (★ ★)

Bonn. An astute observer of the German political and cultural scene, Fisher gives added dimensions to his reports and analysis by incorporating telling quotes and vignettes. He offers a concise presentation of the opposition in the streets and editorial pages towards the Gulf War in "Germans Torn Between Pacifism, Solidarity With Allied Coalition," 1-21, while in "Germany's Outburst of Yankee-Bashing: What's Going On?" 1-27, he examines Germany's identity crisis brought on by Operation Desert Storm, his analysis well-written, if routine. "The recurrent metaphor for Germany is the sheltered child who must now face the real world." Covering Chancellor Kohl's spiraling political fortunes in "Kohl Battling Political Collapse," 3-20, he comments that "Kohl could have avoided a political storm by admitting what was obvious to most Germans — that reconstruction would take more time and money than expected," but fails to dig any deeper. Reconstruction is the subject of the "Germans in East Press Economic Complaints," 4-9, where he travels to Leipzig and finds east Germans expressing the need for patience, while "Germans Divided by 'Wall in the Head,' " 5-11, is a well-organized survey of the psychological gap between west and east Germany, Fisher tying the gap to economics. Analyzing Bonn's decision to support the self-determination of the Slovenians and Croats in "Yugoslav Violence Revives Fears of Germany," 7-7, he smartly connects the decision to internal German politics aimed at criticizing Foreign Minister Hans-Dietrich Genscher. In "On Trial for Death at Berlin Wall," 9-10, he artfully humanizes four young former East German border guards on trial without lapsing into sympathy, writing that they "appear frightened and pale, quick to weep on the witness stand." In "Germany's New Destiny," 9-18, he is straightforward on Germany's efforts to carve out a new role for itself in the contemporary international environment. Marking the first anniversary of reunification in "On German Birthday, Easterners Await Happy Returns," 9-29, he backs up his optimistic findings with data from the field.

Forman, Craig. *The Wall Street Journal.* (★ ½)

London. Forman continues to produce sturdy, if unspectacular, reports on the economics of major international stories, providing details along with his analysis. He gives a satisfactory assessment of the grave political-economic fallout of Palestinian refugees from Kuwait in "War or No, Refugees Will Rattle Mideast," 1-7, providing important data on the accelerating economic slide in the occupied territories. He is also good on the details of the scale of the systematic, comprehensive sabotage of the Kuwaiti oil fields carried out under Iraqi occupation in "Havoc in Kuwait Was Well-Orchestrated," 3-4, affording us "A vision of hell." He was a serviceable source on the Yugoslavian crisis early on, "House Divided," 3-13, conveying the mood of the splintering country well, providing a sharp backdrop for the impression that "people live in a sort of suspended animation, uncertain about the present and even more uncertain about the future," while "Yugoslavia's Economic Reforms Falter," 3-18, puts the country's nationalist-ethnic tensions into context of the economic crisis. Covering the downturn in the fortunes of Swiss financial giant CS Holding S.A. in "CS Holding Suffers Unprecedented Skid," 5-20, he aptly connects the development to the recent trend of Swiss banks to diversifying into investment banking. "No longer are Swiss banks the rock-solid islands of conservatism and stability of years past; expanding interests in investment banking and securities have made them more erratic investments." He imaginatively profiles Abdullah al-Gabandi, director of Kuwait's overseas investments, who must finance the reconstruction of Kuwait without digging too deeply into Kuwait's nest egg in "Kuwait Juggles Needs for Cash, Overseas Assets," 6-5. Writing on international efforts underway to provide food aid to post-coup Soviet Union as officials there warn ominously of a shortage in grain production in "Soviets Expect Severe Grain Shortage; Some Hopes Pinned on Western Imports," 8-29, he seems to take official Soviet agricultural statistics at face value.

Frankel, Glenn. *The Washington Post.* (★ ★)

London. While Frankel kept readers up-to-date on the political dimensions of John Major's troubled first year in office, he often missed opportunities to provide us with a deeper examination of the U.K.'s economic condition. Posted in Egypt during the Gulf War, he drew on his experience in the region for such reports as "Egypt's Alliance Role Finds Minimal Dissent," 2-18, a comprehensive look at how Egypt is holding firm in its war policy and what it hopes to gain, and the "Outlook" essay "The Mideast's Other War: The Conflict Over Values," 2-24, in which he expertly outlines the deep schisms the crisis has exposed in the Arab world. In the gossipy "The Iron Lady's Steel Resolve," 3-6, he divulges that an embittered Margaret Thatcher and her "loyalists" have come to "believe in something they now call the 'Treasury Plot,' " involving senior Tories who worked for Major. He artfully captures the shadow that the 1916 uprising still casts on Ireland today in "A Dublin Easter 75 Years On," 3-31. Dispatched to Turkey to cover a contemporary ill-fated uprising, he produces such harrowing reports as "An Uphill Fight to Keep Kurds From Graveyard," 4-24, and "In Dahuk, Suspicion Fills Empty Streets," 5-4. Surveying PM John Major's difficulties six months into office in "Major, Tories in Deep Political Trouble in Britain," 6-12, he lumps together such various factors as the failing British economy, a lackluster cabinet and a public uproar over dangerous dogs as the reasons behind a Labour lead in the polls and heavy sniping within the Conservative Party, the piece lacking the extra layer of understanding which marks his Middle East efforts. He provides a vivid report on the political battle zone and economic disaster area Liverpool has become in "Liverpool Struggles Against Despair," 7-5. In "Shamir's Difficult, Lonely Decision," 7-24, he perceptively documents Yitzhak Shamir's glacial movement toward peace negotiations with the Arabs. He provides a chilling report on the new, alienated generation of Protestant gunmen with "In Belfast, a New Breed of Protestant Killers Comes of Age," 10-27: "The gunmen have operated in ways that are strikingly violent even for a community accustomed to killing."

Fraser, Damien. *Financial Times.* (★ ★ ★)
Mexico City "superstringer." There is simply no one better than Fraser at covering the day-to-day developments in the Mexican political economy, especially the pending free-trade pact with the U.S. and its repercussions on Mexican politics and society. He sets the standard for Mexican coverage with such reports as "Free Trade No Brake on Mexican Car Sales," 3-12, fully documenting why the Mexican auto industry views the upcoming NAFTA treaty as a plus, not a liability. In the multidimensional "Mexicans Yearn for a Manana That Brings the American Dream," 3-20, he searches out all aspects of this subject, reporting that while the FTA has broad Mexican support, pockets of opposition still remain. He provides all the key details on the privatization of Telemex in "Mexico Succeeds in a Fair Exchange," 5-17. Fraser was keen to the sensitivities still present in U.S.-Mexican relations, covering the domestic fallout from a leaked memo on Mexican foreign policy written by U.S. Ambassador John Negroponte in "US Pact Unlikely to Dent Mexican Distrust," 5-23, observing that "Mexican antipathy to the US, while perhaps receding as the two economies integrate, has a long history and will not be changed by one trade agreement." He is authoritative on the likely impact of the FTA on Mexico in "Peril and Potential South of Rio Grande," 6-3. Covering the Mexican midterm election in "Opposition Proves No Match for Mexico's Rulers," 8-28, he ties the success of the "oldest ruling party in the world," to Salinas's economic policies, the PRI's efforts at modernization, and the divisions on the left, going more in depth than others on this topic. In "Poverty Scheme Boosts Salinas," 9-11, he fully examines the issues raised by the Salinas administration's much-ballyhooed public works program "Solidarity," cutting through the hype raised by both sides to argue that "Solidarity's political success has been critical to continued support for the president's liberal economic reforms." In "Reform at a Risky Pace," 9-27, he smartly draws on the Mexican model of reform to examine the program begun by Venezuelan President Carlos Andres Perez.

Freed, Kenneth. *Los Angeles Times.* (★ ½)
San Salvador. Freed can display an admirable degree of sophistication and panache in his dispatches, often able to work the economic element into his stories, but his El Salvador coverage still suffers from a detectable bias at times. In one of his better Salvadoran dispatches, "Autopsies

Back Murder Charges in El Salvador," 1-6, he alertly observes: "The FMLN's behavior since [3 U.S. servicemen died when their helicopter was shot down over FMLN territory] raises questions about the rebels similar to those raised about the Salvadoran army after its troops murdered six Jesuit priests in November, 1989." Sent to Cairo during the Gulf War, he offers a valuable look at the renewed distrust between exiled Kuwaiti opposition leaders and the Sabah regime in "Kuwaiti Reformers Hope to Forge Vast Changes From Tragedy of War," 2-27. In "Is Arafat the 'Big Loser' or a Phoenix Who'll Rise Again?" 3-5, he refuses to follow the herd and pronounce Arafat politically dead. Returning to Central America and the site of the last major U.S. military engagement, he produces "Panama's 3-Party Rule Turns Into 3-Ring Circus," 5-6, a colorful yet detailed report on the disintegration of the coalition government in Panama, and the threat it poses to the economy. He gives us a political obituary of ARENA leader Roberto D'Aubuisson before the man has died, in "Salvadoran Rightist Terminally Ill With Cancer," 7-20, his observations on the effects of D'Aubuisson's passing on the political scene may be accurate, but seem in poor taste. Covering the peace negotiations in such reports as "Once Again, Effort to End Salvadoran Civil War Stalls," 8-17, and "Salvador Ceasefire Called Unlikely," 8-26, he seems to place the Marxist rebels on the same moral footing as the government. In a follow-up story, "Cristiani's Private Pact With Rebels Stalls Truce Accord," 10-5, he provides good background details on how a secret agreement, between President Alfredo Cristiani and FMLN leaders on an "affirmative action" program for ex-guerrillas in the reformed national police force, may sink the ceasefire accord.

French, Howard W. *The New York Times.* (★ ½)
Caribbean, based in Miami. French continues to stay on top of trends and developments in the Caribbean, packing more details than we had seen in the past, strengthening his insights, although he is still weak on covering Caribbean economic policy. He provides a vivid report on the crushing of a coup attempt in Haiti, a little over a month before President-elect Rev. Jean-Bertrand Aristide's inauguration, in "Troops, Storming Palace, Capture Plotters and Free President," 1-8, and in "Haiti Puts Its Hopes to a Test, And Passes," 1-13, he presciently observes that "The struggle to create a social ethic capable of nourishing Haitian democracy has only begun." In "Uneasy Caribbean Islands Warm to Motherland," 4-2, he writes imaginatively on the latest political development in the Caribbean: a move away from demands for independence. In the sharp report, "Castro Reopens the Gate to Exodus," 5-19, he examines the political and diplomatic issues raised by the growing number of Cuban refugees coming to the U.S.. Updating us on President Aristide in "After 6 Months of Changes, Haiti Is Surprised by Its Leader's Moderation," 8-4, he provides an informative snapshot of Haitian society as Aristide jettisons much of his left-wing rhetoric and opens negotiations with the IMF. Addressing the ramifications for Cuba of the upheaval in the Soviet Union, in "Soviets' Disorder Is Felt by Cubans," 9-3, he delves no deeper than similar reports on this subject, while in the more comprehensive "With No Chicken in the Pot, Cubans' Faith in Castro's Revolution is Waning," 10-10, he fully documents how things are going from bad to worse for the Castro regime and the people living under it. His Haitian coverage was as strong at the end of the year as it was at the beginning, analyzing Aristide's overthrow in "Army Strikes Back," 10-2, and observing that "the 38-year-old leader has fallen victim to Haiti's oldest game, a power play by soldiers fearing they were being cut out of the picture." In "A City With Grit Keeps Aristide's Banner Flying," 11-6, he reports from the Haitian port town of Gonaives, cradle of Duvalier opposition in 1985, where the residents continue to support Aristide, although he fails to fully explain what this portends for Haiti's immediate future.

Fuhrman, Peter. *Forbes.* (★ ★)
European bureau. Fuhrman continues to provide revealing snapshots of European companies, regional economic developments, and governmental policies, usually leaving us understanding the reasons behind their future success or failure. In the revealing "Way Above the Fray," 2-18, we learn why Mercedes is confident about its sales strategy despite the slumping U.S. foreign car market, Fuhrman going straight to the source, Werner Niefer, the 62-year-old chairman of

Mercedes-Benz A.G.: "There will always be customers who can pay very high prices for the very best cars in the world." He artfully adapts an ironic tone while surveying the French arms industry in "It Couldn't Have Happened to a Nicer Guy," 3-4, pointing out the "poetic justice" occurring in the Persian Gulf War as France battles an Iraq armed with French weaponry. For those who view Saddam Hussein as a friend of the Arab, dispossessed Fuhrman offers "Robbin' Hood," 3-18, a pithy assessment of the economic destruction Saddam has wrought on his country over the last decade. In the eye-opening "Aidez-Moi," 4-15, we learn to stop worrying about the EC's generous aid to farmers, as Fuhrman tells us it pales next to industrial subsidies which "have grown so large and prevalent that the 12 European Community national governments now dole out more money in corporate aid than they take in from corporate taxation." On the matter of state subsidies, "You Think Pan Am's Got Problems?" 6-10, he reports on efforts of the Walesa government to privatize the national airline, LOT, within two years. This is the occasional Fuhrman piece that left us wanting more specifics, as he falls back on such general observations as that running LOT "is a daunting challenge but not an impossible task." Writing on the Baltics' quest for freedom in "Is It Mere Wishing?" 8-19, he concentrates on the Soviet military-industrial complex set up in the region, displaying his talent for packing a ton of information into a short piece. Exporters will be invigorated by "Welcome to the Dollar Block," 10-14, Fuhrman fully examining the reasons behind growing enthusiasm for U.S. currency and goods in Central European countries.

Gargan, Edward A. *The New York Times.* (★ ★ ½)
New Delhi. Gargan has improved since his Beijing days, now positioning his stories so readers know what they portend for the future, alerting readers to such key regional developments as the reform efforts of P.V. Narasimha Rao and the Islamic fundamentalist resurgence in Soviet Central Asia. He provides an amusing (except to the soldiers involved) footnote to the Gulf War in "Marine Reservists in Kuwait Steam at 115 [degrees] and Ask Why," 4-28. He pens a knowledgeable sketch of internal divisions within Kuwait as that country emerges from the ashes of Iraqi occupation in "Kuwait Deeply Split on Vision of a Post-Occupation Order," 5-19. In "India's New Premier Challenges the System, and the Reaction is Predictable," 8-6, he authoritatively outlines how Rao, initially seen as a caretaker premier, has "stunned" the Indian political establishment, both left and right, with his plans for economic reform. Afghanistan comes with the New Delhi beat, and in "In a Despairing Afghanistan, There Is Caviar for the Few," 9-24, he vividly captures street-level capitalism in Kabul as the war enters the post-Cold War era, and in "Despite Civil War, Kabul and Afghan Rebels Hold Their Fire in Some Areas," 10-13, he effortlessly takes the reader to a government defensive position on a ridge 90 miles southwest of the capital to document the growing truce agreements being worked out between army officers and the Mujahedeen: "Now we have protocol with them. We don't fire on them and they don't fire on us." Gargan supplied exemplary coverage of the repercussions of the collapse of the Soviet center in Soviet Central Asia, in "Some Changes in Soviet Asia, But the Style Is Still the Same," 9-18, capturing the drama of communist leaders clinging to power in the republic of Uzbekistan. In the superb "A Dream of One Central Asia Under Islam's Banner," 10-11, he reports from Tashkent on renewed hopes of forging a new state of Turkestan. He updates us on the guerrilla warfare being waged by various separatist factions in Kashmir in "Behind Its Mountain Walls, Kashmir Wages Vicious War," 10-28, capturing the human tragedy behind the fighting with non-maudlin sensitivity.

Golden, Tim. *The New York Times.* (★ ½)
Mexico City. Golden came to Mexico late in the year, impressing us with his engaging writing style and resourcefulness in going after stories in the Mexican oil industry and southern Mexico. He needs to tighten his grip on Mexican politics, however. Raising the curtain on the Mexican midterm election and expected PRI landslide in "Faltering Mexican Opposition Back on Defensive," 8-19, Golden seems to mirror the cynicism polls have reportedly found among the Mexican electorate, as he attributes the PRI's success to its vast advantages in resources, election irregularities, and splits within the two main opposition parties, as well as the economic

improvement during the past three years under Salinas. He follows up on this with "In Mexican Politics, The More It Reforms the More It's the Same," 8-25, hinting that the PRI is still up to some of its old tricks despite the evident popularity of its economic program, but he is unable to come up with any solid conclusions, merely commenting that reform may be arriving a lot sooner than PRI officials would like to think. He is informative on the effects *Salinastroika* is having, and not having, on Pemex in "Warily, Mexico Drops Oil Guard," 9-25. In "Mexican Trade Pact Advances," 10-28, he is clear on the issues still dividing Mexicans, Americans, and Canadians as they begin drafting the treaty for NAFTA, and how U.S. domestic politics may interfere. He is properly bemused by the upcoming cultural treatments of the arrival of Columbus and the attendant controversy in "Columbus Landed, er, Looted, uh — Rewrite!" 10-6: "So far, the basic theme seems to be that the Atlantic Ocean in 1492 was a route leading inexorably to the Global Village." In "The Power and the Glory, With a Singular Twist," 11-7, he reports from southern Mexico on an activist priest caught up in a land conflict between peasants and landowners, and while he provides good details on the case, he fails to enfold President Salinas's agricultural reform plans into the story, touching instead on the Government's efforts to improve relations with the Catholic Church.

Greenhouse, Steven. *The New York Times.* (★ ★)
Paris. Scheduled to transfer to Washington D.C., Greenhouse's European economic portfolio contains reporting and analysis that at times does not get beyond the shop-window and the official statistics, but other times delivers authoritatively on a particular company or economic trend. He promises to address all of Eastern Europe in "Year of Economic Tumult Looms for Eastern Europe," 12-31-90, but only offers standard analysis on what to expect for Poland, Czechoslovakia and Hungary in 1991. In his finest report all year, the 10 Best nominee "Playing Disney in the Parisian Fields," 2-17, he tells us everything we want to know about Europe's first Disneyland opening in '92, "a $4.4 billion extravaganza sprawling over 5,000 acres of former sugar beet fields 20 miles east of Paris," and why it is surefire, even though three theme parks have recently failed near the French capital. In "U.S. Lawyers Flock to Brussels," 5-13, he provides a colorful report on U.S. law firms drawn to Brussels by the approach of 1992. We were disappointed by "Report Critical of Drop in Savings," 6-10, where he uncritically advances the thesis of the Bank for International Settlements that budget deficits in the U.S. are the main reason for a decline in savings, an alleged capital shortage and near-record levels of high interest rates. He unsentimentally reports on how the Gulf War has lifted arms dealers' spirits in "Selling Planes That Won the War," 6-21, while "7 Offer Moscow Technical Help," 7-18, is a serviceable report on the economic details of the London Summit. He is thorough on the Japanese-EC agreement on car exports in "Issues Linger in Europe's Japan Auto Pact," 8-12, deftly sketching what each side came away with. Dispatched to the Soviet Union to report on the economic repercussions of the collapse of communism, he produced such informative groundlevel reports as "How Soviet Chaos Stifles an Enterprising Factory," 10-9, on a Soviet electronics factory where the manager "sometimes talks like a character caught in a tragicomedy of economic errors," and "Soviet Depression Batters the Cows and Chickens," 11-1, a firsthand report from a collective farm on the factors contributing to the shortage of supplies on Moscow shelves.

Gumbel, Peter. *The Wall Street Journal.* (★ ★)
Moscow, scheduled to transfer to Paris. Gumbel finds it difficult to produce any reports out of the U.S.S.R. that are not heavily wrapped in analytical projections. Consequently, we often have to peel his dispatches, sifting through them for the solid core of information. His coup coverage was uneven, "Gorbachev's Downfall Raises Political Specter for Soviet and West," with Gerald Seib 8-20, raises broad future questions at the beginning, but improves later on, leaving room for doubt on intentions of the ruling clique. In "True Market Reform May Now Be Possible in Soviet Economy," with Alan Murray 8-22, we find another pitch for western cash to cushion the drastic leap toward the free market. However, with "How Not to Mount a Coup," 8-29, he makes an important contribution to the Soviet coup story, drawing on Gorbachev loyalists who opposed the takeover from within the Kremlin to draw a picture of a conspiracy "fueled in large

part by fear and alcohol," hatched by desperate bureaucrats who were taken in by Kremlin warnings of an imminent uprising and false reports about Gorbachev's health, and who quickly developed "cold feet" as opposition mounted. Gumbel's Moscow competitors quickly picked up on this. He was on the trail of the hardliners all year, in "Resurgent Communists Push for Soviet Crackdown," 2-4, illuminating the road ahead with a quote from Boris Gidaspov, Leningrad party boss on "waiting for just the right moment" to reassert the hardline tone: "If I were the party and the KGB, I would keep silent, choose clandestine activity and wait for people to tire of democrats and call for an iron hand." In "Soviet Hard-Liners Try for a Comeback," 6-19, he warns of an alarming turn of events in which "Communist party stalwarts and leading representatives of the army, the KGB and government apparatchiks" launched a campaign against Gorbachev and the union treaty. In "Russian Leaders Are Torn Apart by Infighting," 10-7, he provides one of the better updates we saw on the post-coup government, vividly capturing the vacuum of power increasingly surrounding the Yeltsin regime.

Haberman, Clyde. *The New York Times.* (★ ★ ½)
Jerusalem. Haberman's final months as Rome bureau chief were mostly quiet ones, distinguished by his outstanding coverage of the Kurdish refugee crisis. Shifted to Jerusalem when Roger Cohen's assignment there conflicted with his plans to write a biography of General Schwarzkopf, Haberman provided increasingly sure-handed coverage of the developing peace process. Assigned to Cairo during the Gulf War, in the informative "Kuwaitis Plan Big Restoration Effort," 2-27, he reports on Kuwaiti plans to rebuild their country. Dispatched to the Iraqi-Turkish border following the failed Kurdish uprising, he produced haunting reports on the logistical difficulties and the human suffering in such reports as "U.S. Military Takes Over Relief for Kurdish Refugees in Iraq," 4-13, and "The Plight of the Kurds Worsens as Relief Efforts Still Fall Short," 4-16. In the stand-out "Kurds Endure Mud and Cold and Fear the Worst," 4-11, he evokes the scene at one camp where "Hollow-eyed women peer out from the tents, some with hacking coughs brought on by sleeping outdoors in subfreezing temperatures. Mud-crusted children look hungry and frightened — that curdling fear a child feels upon realizing his parents are just as scared." He briefly surveys Israeli opinion in the street following Prime Minister Shamir's decision to go to a Middle East peace conference and finds an ambivalent mood of cynical optimism in "Israelis Greet Shamir's Assent With Relief and Usual Doubts," 8-4, but fails to probe much beneath the surface. However, in "The U.S. and Israel Collide at a Crucial Time in the Mideast," 9-15, he expertly places Shamir's decision to push ahead and fight for the loan guarantee in the context of domestic Israeli politics. In the timely "For Jews on West Bank, The Motive Is Economics," 10-13, he reports that much of the Israeli settlement program in the occupied territories is fueled not by ideologues but by Russian immigrants and young couples seeking affordable housing. He provides an illuminating snapshot of Israeli concerns and insecurities as the peace conference looms in "Israel Approaches Peace Conference in a Grim Mood," 10-20: "Still, more than a few people here are ready to take John Lennon's admonition to heart and give peace a chance."

Harden, Blaine. *The Washington Post.* (★ ★ ★ ½)
Warsaw. The regional fighting and refugee crises in Europe must have evoked memories of his African years for Harden, and his output in 1991 surpassed his best efforts as Nairobi bureau chief. In the well-written "Poland: New Soviet Workplace," 2-4, he is out in front on how Soviets are coming across the border to sell goods or work for subsistence wages, taking advantage of the sliding value of the Soviet ruble against the stable and convertible Polish zloty. We share his outrage of Kurdish relief efforts being undermined by logistics, chaotic conditions, and the Turks in "Get Us Off This Mountain," 4-15. His coverage of Yugoslavia was particularly outstanding, just the right mix of sharp analytics and keen on-the-spot reporting. In "Yugoslav Republic Splits From Nation," 3-17, he captures the drama of Serbian President Slobodan Milosevic's declaration that Serbia no longer recognizes the authority of the federal presidency, while the "Outlook" essay "Myth and Memory in Yugoslavia: A House Divided Risks Civil War," 6-23, provides the historical and cultural context of the worsening conflict between Serbs

and Croats in Yugoslavia. "As Croats and Serbs struggle to explain the looming breakup of their country, an explanatory metaphor that leaps to mind is of ethnic nations — and their leaders — behaving like hormone-crazed adolescents." He supplies all the detail we were looking for in the superior "Yugoslav Regions Assert Independence," 6-26, while "Sudden Death on Highway E-70," 7-3, is an exceptional piece of reportage, bringing home the hellish experiences of Yugoslavian soldiers pinned down under fire in Slovenia. He writes authoritatively on the impact of the war on the Yugoslavian economy in "Yugoslavia's Civil War Balkanizes Economy," 8-29: "For all the economic disruption...Yugoslavia retains the appearance of consumer normality." He provides a fine wrap-up of the Polish parliamentary election in "Poles Split in Vote for Parliament," 10-28, characterizing the vote as a "sobering signal to post-Communist governments across Eastern Europe that capitalist reform must be tempered with compassion."

Havemann, Joel. *Los Angeles Times.* (★ ★)
Brussels. Havemann specializes in European economics and its repercussions for the U.S., and his reports can be useful for anyone thinking of venturing over to Europe on business or as a tourist. He displays his ability to work a large canvas in "Costs of Declining Dollar Rise," 1-16, writing on the unprecedented decline in the value of the dollar at a time of international crisis and its impact for both the U.S. economy in general and for Americans in Europe: "Now, when the world looks for financial security, it doesn't reflexively look to the United States." He glosses over the fact that Germany was outmaneuvered by Britain during the Gulf crisis, presenting instead the polite version of intra-European frictions in "Europeans Finding Diplomatic Unity an Elusive Goal," 2-5. He seems to be issuing a call to arms for the U.S. insurance industry to take advantage of liberalized European insurance regulations in "Europe's Insurance Barriers May Soon Be Tumbling Down," 3-26, while "U.S. Travelers, Exporters Feeling Effects of Dollar's New Strength," 3-28, deftly reconciles the rival views that the sudden rise in the dollar's value is a "speculative bubble," vs. the opinion that the dollar "remains sharply undervalued." Later in the spring he began delving into the EC's cautious relations with Eastern Europe. In the tightly-focused "Walesa Asks Economic Support but Western Europeans Resist," 4-4, he emphasizes "Western Europe's resistance to opening its markets to cheap imports from Poland and the other new democracies of Eastern Europe," while "East Europe: Is the West Giving It the Business?" 4-13, offers a broader analysis of the same topic. In "A Rocky Switch to Capitalism," 7-8, he provides a large panorama of the birth-pangs of capitalism in Eastern Europe, the gist of which is: "A free market, seen as the antidote to communism in Eastern Europe, is proving to be a bitter pill." In "Europeans Are Lining Up for Applications to Join the EC," 7-16, he features some useful insights into Europe's changing political dynamics. He effectively presents the case that sooner or later European farmers will lose their political clout in "Europe Strives for Plan to Suit Farmers, Trade Demands," 8-6.

Hedges, Chris. *The New York Times.* (★ ½)
Cairo. Hedges is a versatile reporter, equally at home covering a gangster's funeral or a Middle East uprising, but while he is skilled at conveying the human costs of the depressed economies in the Arab world, he offers little on how the situation might be alleviated. While getting his eye-opening story on price-gouging by Saudi merchants near the Kuwaiti border, "G.I.'s Bristle but Pay Nonetheless as Saudi Stores Double Their Prices on a Desert Road," 2-11, Hedges was detained by the U.S. Army for six hours and had his press credentials temporarily lifted. Hedges was also detained, this time for several days, by Iraqi Republican Guards while covering the post-war rebellion and wrote of his captivity in two reports, "In Growing Disarray, Iraqis Fight Iraqis," 3-10, and "A Reporter in Iraq's Hands: Amid the Fear, Parlor Games," 3-12. Some of our readers found the accounts gripping, others pompous. He provides a well-drawn portrait of Kuwait one year after the invasion in "A Year Later Kuwait Sinks Into Malaise," 8-2. In the heart-wrenching "Egypt's Desperate Trade: Body Parts for Sale," 9-23, he writes on how the Egyptian poor are being driven to sell their body organs in order to raise cash, but fails to touch on what might be done to reform an economy which produced such desperate straits. Similarly,

in "An Army of Angry Men, With Backs to the Wall," 10-8, he provides good details on a growing North African powder keg: unemployed young Algerians who are creating a vibrant underground economy, alienated from the corrupt system and increasingly allied with the Islamic fundamentalists out of self-interest, not religious conviction. But we get little sense of the regional economic picture as a whole. Ever resourceful, he travels to the Iraqi-Turkish border to break the important news that Saddam Hussein is evidently evening-up the score with Turgut Ozal in "Iraqis Are Arming the Rebel Kurds in Turkey's South," 10-20. Interviewing Egyptian leader Hosni Mubarak on the eve of the Madrid peace conference, "Mubarak Warns Israelis on East Jerusalem Issue," 10-30, he fails to press hard for any details, merely passing along the Egyptian leader's warning that there will be no regional peace unless the Israelis end their annexation of East Jerusalem.

Helm, Leslie. *Los Angeles Times.* (★ ★ ½)
Tokyo. We turn to Helm for insightful reports on Japanese economics and culture, and how one is affected by the other, Helm often able to provide a more subtle touch on these topics than others on this beat. In "Long Haul for Japan's Plaintiffs," 1-14, he provides a revealing case study on the inequities of the Japanese legal system. We get a nuanced comparison of the two economies' supercomputer industries in "Japan Speeding Ahead of the U.S. in Supercomputers," 3-11. He brings his keen understanding of Japanese corporate culture to "The Rule of Work in Japan," 3-17, a thought-provoking profile of Japan's *shinjinrui,* or new breed of worker. "Despite the hopes of many American business executives, the *shinjinrui* are not likely to slow down the Japanese industrial machine." In "Now Playing in the Pacific: A Clash of Titans," 5-21, Helms produces an authoritarian "Regional Outlook" report on America's waning influence in the Pacific and Japan's rise as a regional economic superpower: "It may be premature to say Japan is putting into place the Greater East Asia Co-Prosperity Sphere that it sought in World War II to guarantee itself natural resources and markets for its products. But many common elements are emerging." He is clear on why Japan decided to drop its interest rate in "Japan Had Economy — and Its Image — in Mind as It Cut Rate," 7-3. However, our readers felt he went a little overboard in his criticism of the Japanese financial establishment in "How Nomura Took Care of Its Best Customers," 7-8: "As a deepening securities scandal continues to rock Japan, investigators are unearthing details of a stock scam that offers a rare glimpse of the shady back alleys behind Japan's stock exchanges — how Japan's top brokerage houses appear to play the Tokyo stock market as if they were running a private casino with the odds heavily favoring the house." The superbly researched "Japan's Leg Up in the Log Business," 7-23, explains the economics behind Japan's efforts to corner the U.S. market for unprocessed timber at the expense of U.S. lumber mills.

Henry, Neil. *The Washington Post.* (★ ½)
Nairobi. Henry has a firm grasp on regional trends in sub-Saharan Africa and is able to illustrate how these trends affect individual countries. However, he can be weak on the internal economic policies being followed by sub-Saharan nations. Typical of his work on the move toward political reform is "African Quest: Democracy," 1-3, a knowledgeable report on the domestic and international pressures that lead to the African democracy movement. He fully captures the horrors of Somalia's civil war in "War Guts Somalia's Capital," 1-30. In "Farm-Takeover Plan Roils Zimbabwe," 2-20, he delivers a serviceable report on the opposition stirred up by the Mugabe regime's plan to nationalize farmland predominately owned by wealthy white farmers, while in the colorful "Democracy Not Watered Down in Arid Botswana," 3-21, he writes in depth on the decision by President Quett Masire to postpone indefinitely a major river dredging plan in the face of tremendous public opposition. We wish he would pen more reports of this sort. He provides some stirring case studies of rising human rights activism in black Africa in "Africans Testing Waters of Dissent," 5-19. In "Mengistu Leaves Ethiopia in Shambles," 5-22, he ties Mengistu's downfall to the winds of change sweeping the African continent brought on by the end of the Cold War and the rising demand for a better life, his observations above the routine, while "Persistent Rural Insurgency Ends Years of Harsh Military Rule," 5-29, deftly

examines the regional differences between the factions. In the wide-ranging "New Breed of African Patriots Emerges to Press for Democracy," 7-4, he reports on how a new generation of Western-educated African elites are now fighting for reforms, but there is a lot here that is recycled. He artfully packages Malawian President-for-Life Hastings Kamuzu Banda as a paradigm of the typical African strong-man ruler whose time may be running out in "Africa's 'Big Men' Outliving Welcome," 9-9, while in "Kaunda Graciously Bows to 'Verdict,'" 11-3, he pens an eloquent eulogy for Kenneth Kaunda's political career, but provides little on what to expect from the incoming regime of Frederick Chiluba, uncharacteristically failing to move the story forward.

Hiltzik, Michael A. *Los Angeles Times.* (★ ★)
Nairobi. A skilled writer with an impressive feel for sub-Saharan Africa, particularly Kenya, Hiltzik continues to be an important source for developments in this region, although some have noted a tendency to lay the continent's problems at the feet of the First World. In the prescient "War Will Hurt Aid Efforts in Africa," 1-31, he predicts that the large-scale pullback of U.S. diplomatic personnel will have a devastating impact on development efforts, and several months later, in "Africa Hit by 'Donor Fatigue,'" 3-8, he sounds the alarm over the shrinking amount of relief the continent is receiving from the developed world; important stories, but Hiltzik seems to leave the impression that Africa's fate is totally in the hands of outsiders. He is detailed and thorough on one of the biggest domestic Kenyan stories of the year in "Kenya Arrests Outspoken Law Magazine Editor," 3-3, and "Kenya Lawyer Builds Case Against Repression — His Own," 3-26. He advances the thought-provoking proposition that Africa's economic future may lie with the "tinsmiths, carpenters and itinerant vegetable hawkers" in the "informal sector" in "Making Money Under Africa's Fierce Sun," 4-30, and we would like to see more original thinking like this in his work. In "Ethiopia Capital Under Control of Rebel Army," 5-29, he skillfully weaves together the diplomatic news from London with the military developments in the streets of Addis Ababa, and expertly positions the famine crisis in "New Ethiopia Turns to Old Problem — Famine," 6-1. Following the collapse of communism in the Soviet Union, Hiltzik spent a month reporting from the Baltics, and in the comprehensive "Baltics Find Freedom Isn't Easy," 11-5, he memorably conveys the post-independence hangover, cautioning against any expectations of a quick transition to Jeffersonian democracy: "Issues of social structure and group rights have to be solved by leaders basking in ethnic and nationalist victory who may not always act in ways that Europeans and Americans find acceptable or even comprehensible."

Hockstader, Lee. *The Washington Post.* (★ ★)
San Salvador. A resourceful reporter often able to turn up stories we do not see elsewhere, Hockstader's Central American coverage exhibited more depth this year, and he scored a major scoop during the Gulf War, making it into Baghdad before the war ended. While his dispatches were subject to Iraqi censorship, they still provided invaluable insights into that country in the final days of the war and the first few days of the fragile peace. In "Iraqis in Devastated Capital Worry," 2-28, he finds that the Iraqis are determined to defend their homeland. He filed "Death, Defeat Come Home to Baghdad," 3-7, far from Iraqi censors in Amman, capturing the "dark mood" of the capital as soldiers begin returning home from the front and rumors of uprisings in the north and south begin to filter in. He updates us on Guatemalan refugees in southern Mexico, who fled their homeland ten years ago, and who are still afraid to return, in the moving "After Decade in Limbo, Guatemalans View Future With Dose of Skepticism," 5-8. Once again his Haitian coverage was strong. In the prescient "Haiti's Poverty Tempers View of President-Priest," 6-6, he reports that while President Jean-Bertrand Aristide seems to have eased his stance against the U.S., foreign capitalists and the military, he remains hostile toward wealthy Haitians, and some fear he is building a cult of personality. Cuba commanded much of Hockstader's attention late in the year, and in "Kremlin Turnabout Pulls Cuba Up Short," 8-27, he shrewdly notes that by preparing the Cuban people for this eventuality, Castro may have painted himself into an ideological corner: "Having used the full force of his fiery oratory to

reject any fundamental change, it is hard to imagine how he can adjust at this late date to the new Soviet order." He examines Cuba's "Crippled Icon" status in depth in "Zero Option: Socialism's Last Stand?" 9-12, and "Castro Turns His People's Love Into Fear," 9-13, reports that are data-rich but leave us uncertain where Cuba is headed. Expertly analyzing Washington's latest effort to restore President Aristide in "Will Embargo Bend Haitian Army?" 11-4, he concludes that the country lies poised on the edge of a civil war.

Holden, Ted. *Business Week.* (★ ★)
Tokyo. Back to covering the ins-and-outs of the Japanese business scene after spending 1990 stalking the big game in the Japanese stock market, Holden generally kept the writing tight and the information abundant in his reports, although at times we could detect a distracted tone in his work. In the disappointing "International Business: A Tsunami of Red Ink Sweeps Across Japan," 2-25, he attributes the unprecedented number of bankruptcies in Japan to higher interest rates, while failing to work in other factors, such as the present Japanese tax structure. He pens a punchy profile of Japanese retailer Isao Nakauchi, a self-made billionaire who is "shaking up Japan's protective distribution system" and "treating Japan to American-style discounting," in "A Retail Rebel Has the Establishment Quaking," 4-1. In "Finance: Tokyo's Giant Brokers Take a Nasty Tumble," 5-27, he provides a serviceable overview of Japan's lagging markets, an overview limited to the here and now, with only a cursory treatment of the reasons behind the plunge or what might turn things around for Kabuto-cho, Japan's Wall Street. In "International Business: A Big Bundle of Hot New Exports," with Neil Gross, Dirk Bennett, James Treece, Paul Magnusson and bureau reports 7-1, Holden *et al.* report that "After years of declining trade surpluses with the world, Japan is riding a new export wave." There are some interesting points raised here, but the piece loses points, as it contains typically skewed *BW* economic deductions about trade flows, which we can't really hold Holden responsible for. He provides a concise, well-rounded account of the latest saga in the Japanese stock scandal saga in "The Stock Scandal That Won't Go Away," 8-12, while in "International Business: Lower Sales, Slower Factories. . .Where?" 9-16, he offers a credible analysis of why the Japanese economy is in for some less than robust times in the coming years if interest rates remain high.

Holley, David. *Los Angeles Times.* (★ ★ ½)
Beijing. Holley continues to provide solid and imaginative coverage of a China slowly emerging from its Tiananmen Square deep-freeze in 1991, his reports on political and economic developments often featuring a valuable cultural dimension. He is ahead of the pack on how improving relations between Beijing and Hanoi is leading to increasing cross-border trade in "China, Vietnam Becoming Better Neighbors, a Decade After Border War," 3-10. He packs a lot of vital information on China's efforts to attract domestic and foreign investment in "Industrial Parks in China Trying to Lure High Tech," 3-26. In "Tibet Braces for Anniversary of Chinese Rule," 4-13, he presents a vivid picture of simmering tension in that troubled land. In the fascinating "How to Make It Big in Business: Coastal Chinese Point the Way," 5-21, he reports on the cultural and economic history of China's southern coastal region and its impact throughout southern Asia as "the new openness. . .allows the people of this region to restore links with their distant cousins in Hong Kong, Macao, Taiwan, Singapore and beyond." We get an eye-opening report on changing sexual mores in China in "A Sexual Revolution in China," 5-27. In the "Column One" report "On China's Hungry Plateaus," 6-24, he artfully depicts day-to-day life in China's poverty-stricken inner provinces as the communist government begins the largest relocation project since 1949: "For the Beijing government, which still stakes its legitimacy on its claim to represent the interests of peasants and workers, the continued existence of grinding poverty cannot be ignored." On a similar topic, "Rural Entrepreneurs: Chinese Success Story," 8-13, he imaginatively highlights a little known feature of Chinese capitalist reforms, "a new breed of rural entrepreneurs." He smartly notes that the Chinese political leadership retains "nagging doubts" about the reliability of both the military and the next generation of party leaders in " 'Stick to the Socialist Road' Beijing Warns in Terse Threat to Dissidents," 8-27. He is alert to the geopolitical implications of a spiritual resurgence in the region with "In Mongolia, a Reincarnation of Buddhism," 10-8.

Horwitz, Tony. *The Wall Street Journal.* (★ ½)
London, covering the Middle East. Author of *Baghdad Without a Map,* Horwitz continues to be a reliable cartographer of the Middle East political landscape, well aware that in this region true readings shift with the sands. We believe his feature work often tends to the lightweight, however. He artfully juxtaposes contradictory reactions and shifts in thinking engendered among the Saudi population by war with Iraq in "As Iraqi Missile Falls in Riyadh, Saudi Arabians Discover Patriotism and a Stiffened Will to Fight," 2-13. In the entertaining "Robert Brown Finds Riyadh Is No Place for a War Buff," 2-20, he covers the efforts of the *Soldier of Fortune* editor to cover Desert Storm only to be kept away from the combat along with the rest of the "barking dogs" and "dorks" of the press corps. He brings home the shocking extent of the devastation left behind by the Iraqis in "Inside Kuwait City: Once a 'Paradise,' Now It's 'Like Hell,' " 2-28, while "Tense Homecoming," and Craig Forman 3-8, is clear on the chaos and governmental paralysis in Kuwait as the emir remains in a "funk" and in exile. He is clearly amused by the Sultan of Oman's efforts to make his country a "blinding oasis of order in the region," through a beautification program that makes Lady Bird Johnson look like a strip miner in "Surface Appearances Matter Very Deeply to a Sultan of Clean," 4-23, but provides little information on Omani society. In his strongest effort of the year, "Saddam's Popularity Reaches Rock Bottom as Iraq's Woes Grow," 7-25, he makes his seventh visit to Iraq and discovers widespread discontent with Saddam's rule. Many journalists of the time did, but Horwitz was one of the few to tie Sunni dissidence to the depressed Iraqi economy — i.e., the inability of the regime to deliver the goods. "Besieged from without, and rotting from within, Saddam Hussein's regime has nowhere to go but down." In "A New Palestinian Leadership Emerges From Arafat's Shadow to Steal Spotlight," and Geraldine Brooks, 11-4, he astutely observes that Yasir Arafat is unlikely to assume the mantle of elder statesman easily. We won't even go into "Endangered Feces: Paleo-Scatologist Plumbs Old Privates," 9-9.

Housego, David. *Financial Times.* (★ ★ ½)
New Delhi. Housego continues to hold down this old empire fort, conveying the heat and dust of Indian politics while viewing the Indian economy through a neo-colonialist IMF-World Bank policy prism that no doubt goes down well back home in England. In the prescient "Indian PM Faces Uncertain Future," 2-7, he updates Chandra Shekhar's political fortunes three months into office, noting that despite his demonstrated skills, his political survival still depends on the whim of Rajiv Gandhi, who "has had the unnerving experience of watching Mr. Chandra Shekhar reap the benefits of an alliance he engineered while his own star has been waning." He is knowledgeable on how political infighting is undermining Shekhar's efforts at budgetary reform in "A Passage to Paralysis," 2-22. Writing on the downfall of the Shekhar Government in the literate "Bound by a Damaging Past," 3-8, he routinely comments that the pending election will take place against a background of instability, and that with its foreign exchange reserves depleted and its budget postponed, India "needs IMF help more than ever." Reporting on Rajiv Gandhi's assassination in "Security Measures Shunned on Election Trail," 5-22, he alertly zeroes in on how the political leader had "thrown all security precautions to the wind" in order to regain "the contact with crowds on which power and leadership thrives in India," with an expected corresponding boost for the Congress Party at the polls. Analyzing the grim aftermath in the overwrought "A Nation Stretched to Breaking Point," 5-23, he labels the assassination "the greatest challenge since independence," and urges that "If the edifice of India is to withstand the additional strains, a strong and stable government needs to emerge." Writing on the government which did emerge, "India May Be on Brink of Burying Its Policy Taboos," 6-27, he enthusiastically notes that sheer political exhaustion will "make it easier for the Congress government to push through unpopular cuts in expenditure and increases in taxation." In "Multinationals Bewildered by Indian Stance," 9-20, he provides good details on how foreign firms are still encountering obstacles to investing in India.

Ibrahim, Youssef M. *The New York Times.* (★ ★ ★)
Paris. Ibrahim drew on all his experience to assess the political and economic winds buffeting the Middle East this year, and produced authoritative analytics and probing reports that were often ahead of the curve. In the remarkably prescient "Israel Expecting Iraq Missile Strike If War Breaks Out," 1-1, he expertly sketches Iraq's expected attempt to draw Israel into the coming conflict — and Israel's determination to stay out. He deftly draws on many sources to lay out all the speculation surrounding the assassinations of two senior PLO officials, "Paper Points to Iraqi in P.L.O. Killings," 1-17, placing each source in perspective. In "The Kuwaitis Who Stayed Have Some Scores to Settle," 3-10, he waits until the end to address an important point bearing on Kuwaiti affairs, the emergence of a newly assertive Saudi Arabia: "Western-style democracy is not on its agenda, and it cannot be expected to look kindly on any agitation for democracy next door." After the war he turned his attention to the economic problems of states in the region, helping to fill a gap in *NYT* Mideast coverage. In "Egypt's Price for Aid: Dose of Economic Reform," 4-18, he sharply assesses Egypt's mounting economic problems, making clear that debt relief was but a drop in the bucket and that without an internal growth dynamic, the country faces serious destabilization. In the superb "Iran Gingerly Tries a Bit of Pragmatism," 6-9, he documents the costs of the on-going struggle between militants and liberals, noting that "the only judgment that appeared safe was that of a West European ambassador who said the regime has reached 'the limits of its contradictions.' " He produces a comprehensive report on Algeria and that country's turbulent transition to democratic and economic reform, "In Algeria, Hope for Democracy but Not Economy," 7-26. While he effectively conveys the plight of Palestinian refugees expelled from Kuwait, "For Refugees in Jordan, Misery Without End," 10-3, his material on Palestinian discontent with the PLO leadership in Tunis is familiar. He provides a revealing read on the mood of the rest of the Arab world to Syria's intransigence at the Madrid peace talks in "Syria's Tough Choices," 11-3.

Impoco, Jim. *U.S.News & World Report.* (★ ½)
Tokyo. Impoco can be counted on to produce slick but thin reports on Japanese business and finance and their impact on U.S.-Japanese relations, often appearing in the "Business" section. He examines the questions confronting Japan as it emerges from the Gulf crisis in "Japan's Lessons of the Gulf War," 4-8, offering the routine observation that "The world's two largest economies are so intertwined that America cannot flog Japan without hurting itself." In "Can the Global Economy Find a Safe Harbor?" 5-27, he competently places the recent up-and-down trends in the Japanese economy in a global and regional context, commenting that "Tokyo has been diversifying its trade away from North America and targeting new markets in Asia." We get an interesting battlefield report from the international trading war zone on how Motorola was able to crack the Japanese microchip market in "Fighting Japan on Its Home Turf," 6-24: "The main lesson is deceptively simple: Knocking down trade barriers and competing head-on with the Japanese on their own turf should be a top priority." Surveying the recent scandals roiling the Japanese financial community in "Pulling Strings in Japan's Market," 8-12, he really only skims the surface, writing that "the financial misdeeds are focusing attention on what many consider the real cause of the problem: an ambiguous regulatory system that is built around opaque laws and administered by officials who enjoy wide discretionary powers in interpreting them." Writing on the change in Japanese political leadership in "Japan Plays Musical Chairs," 10-21, he is content to recycle a lot of conventional wisdom: "until Japan can overcome its aversion to strong leadership, revamp its political system and tell the world how it intends to use its economic power, its external relations are likely to remain rocky." However, he is good on the nuances of Japanese attitudes in "Forgetting Pearl Harbor," 10-28. In "Behind Diplomatic Smiles," 11-11, he writes convincingly on how hopes in Tokyo and Washington that "a new economic partnership between the nations will replace what has become an obsolete military alliance," may founder on the domestic political repercussions of Japan's growing economic ascendancy.

James, Canute. *Financial Times.* (★ ★ ½)
Caribbean. James is the best daily source for economic data and trends on Caricom, and if we have any complaints about his work, it is that his writing style tends to be awfully dry at times, as parched as white sand. Reporting on the last-minute attempt to prevent Father Jean-Bertrand Aristide from taking power by Roger Lafontant, "Death Knell Sounds for Haiti's Far-Right," 1-8, James has a rare misfire, writing that the suppression of the coup attempt by the army suggests that the "country's ultra-conservatives. . .have played their last card." He strikes just the right note of irony in "Columbus Makes Waves in the Americas," 2-7, on the controversy touched off by the approaching quincentenary of Columbus's arrival in the Americas, reporting that while the Dominican Republic is marking the occasion by constructing a towering lighthouse on the other side of the island of Hispaniola, they have torn down a statue of the explorer and tossed it "into the sea from whence he came." He is informative on the latest roadblock to the Caribbean Economic Community's efforts to create economic integration in "Caricom Slow to Put Common Into Market," 4-25. His grasp of the inner workings of Caricom are demonstrated in "Fares Row Blocks Caribbean Air Pact," 5-23, and "Caribbean Textile Producers Searching for a Sympathetic Ear," 6-14. In the historically-informed "Grenada Sentences Highlight Hanging Debate," 7-30, he expertly surveys the on-going debate in the region over capital punishment, noting that while governments still see it as a deterrent, public opinion is running the other way. He covers all the angles of Cuba's efforts to formally join the Caribbean Economic Community in "Neighbours Rally to Cuba's Call," 10-17. In "Unrest on Island of Tranquillity," 11-5, he provides superb details on growing political opposition on Barbados to Prime Minister Erskine Sandiford's decision to install an austerity program to meet conditions for IMF assistance instead of devaluating the currency. "If Mr Sandiford's administration were forced into a currency devaluation, this could have a domino effect on neighbouring economies, and also put pressure on the strong Eastern Caribbean dollar."

Jameson, Sam. *Los Angeles Times.* (★ ★)
Tokyo. Jameson continues to provide rich insights into the unique government-business relationship in Japanese culture, but his Korean coverage lacks the sure-handed precision that characterizes his Japanese reports. He leaves little uncovered on differences within the Japanese political establishment over aiding the allies in "Iraq Assails Japan Over Its Gulf Aid," 1-25. In the illuminating "Germans Taking the Inside Track in Car Sales to Japan," 2-4, we learn that the Japanese domestic automobile market is being breached by foreign imports, with Germany leading the way. The regional economy was one of the big Asian stories in 1991, and in the authoritative "Asia, An Emerging Center of World Commerce," 2-17, he expertly documents how much of it is fueled by intra-Asian investments. His handle on government-business relations was demonstrated in "Japan Warns Its Firms to Go Easy on Kuwait Bids," 3-4, where he reports that the government, wary of having the Japanese look like "a thief in a fire," has passed the word to Japanese businesses not to go after reconstruction contracts. His Korean coverage was inconsistent. In "Roh's Ruling Party Wins Sweeping Victory in S. Korean Local Elections," 3-28, he finds underlying political strength for the Roh government, while in "S. Korean Protests Reveal Extent of Public Discontent With Roh's Rule," 5-19, he finds that strength weakening, as the general public is increasingly disenchanted by the economy and political unrest. We thought we could detect some anti-regime bias in his Korean coverage over the summer, in dispatches such as "Soldiers to Help Ease Labor Pinch in South Korea," 7-8, and "Some Points of Light in South Korea," 7-9. Profiling the incoming Japanese Prime Minister in the intriguing "Miyazawa May Give Japan New Sophistication," 10-12, he characterizes the LDP careerist as "one of the few remaining Japanese leaders who remembers the generous policies that the United States carried out toward a defeated enemy." Jameson, unlike other Tokyo correspondents, evidently finds no resentment by Miyazawa over U.S. treatment of Japan during the post-war years.

Jones, Tamara. *Los Angeles Times.* (★ ½)
Bonn. While Jones seems to be rapidly assimilating herself into German culture and reflecting it in her reports, readers looking for in-depth German economic coverage will have to turn elsewhere. She adequately covers the debate over the location of the capital for the new Germany in "Shift Capital From Bonn to Berlin, Kohl Urges," 4-24. She attempts to pass off the village of Moedlareuth, pop. 52, as a microcosm of the psychological failure of unification in "In a German Village, West Is Still on the 'Other Side,' " 6-17, but this is one more "mood" piece that fails to come off. In "Potential for Instability Feared in New Germany," with Tyler Marshall 6-18, she fares better, producing a more conscientious attempt to understand and analyze why "Instead of the euphoria the world witnessed in Berlin that November night when the wall fell, the atmosphere in united Germany is one of resentment, fear, disappointment and confusion." She provides serviceable analysis in "Berlin Reclaims Glory as Capital of Germany," 6-21. Our readers found "Walls for Women in Germany," 8-6, thought-provoking, while "Coming Home to Rest After 205 Years, 6 Stops," 8-13, is a knowledgeable review of the shadows of German history. She continues on this theme in the insightful "Frederick the Great at Peace — Not Germany," 8-18, demonstrating a commendable ability to work German history into her work. In the amusing "Guzzling Beer With a Conscience in Munich," 10-8, she engagingly reports on how the venerable tradition of *Oktoberfest* is entering the 1990s by forging "a new image — as the most environmentally friendly beer bash in the world." She needs to begin tackling substantive economic stories, though, to fully round out her portfolio.

Kamm, Henry. *The New York Times.* (★ ★ ½)
Budapest. The globetrotting Kamm once again excelled at penning on-the-spot reports and features that placed a human face on major headline events of the day, while avoiding the twin traps of maudlin sentimentality or excessive cynicism. We get an insightful look at recent Jewish-Albanian emigration to Israel in "Joyful Jews From 'Another Planet' Called Albania," 4-11. Soviet immigrants moving into the fabled Negev desert town of Dimona are the subject of the fascinating "Soviet Emigres Arrive and All Is Remembered," 5-10, Kamm not blind to the fact that Dimona is also rumored to be the sight of Israel's nuclear weapons program. In the timely "In Golan Heights, Doubts Plus a Bit of Confidence," 7-24, he reports from the Golan Heights town of Katzrin, as Israel moves toward negotiations with Syria, artfully contrasting the mood there today with memories of the violent resistance to the surrendering of the Sinai desert town of Yamit under the peace accord with Egypt in 1982. He provides an evocative report about a Slovene village at war in "At a Border Town, an Uneasy Calm," 7-8. He masterfully conveys the triumph of Estonian independence, "The Icons Topple," 8-24, writing on the removal of a large statue of Lenin in front of communist headquarters: "The gilt lettering on the pedestal remains. In Estonian and Russian, Lenin is quoted as proclaiming that 'Soviet power is the way to socialism.' Perhaps imprudently, Lenin concluded that 'it cannot be defeated.' " He chillingly portrays Latvians celebrating their new freedom while troops of the Soviet Interior Ministry remain hunkered down in "Traces of the Old Guard Linger in a New Latvia," 8-28, while "Estonia's Foreign Minister Finds the Champagne 'Sour' but the Faxes Sweet," 9-3, is a delightful feature on Estonian foreign minister Lennart Meri as his lifetime of working for Estonian independence finally pays off. Following up on a story broken by Stephen Kinzer in "Lithuania Halts the Reversal of War Crimes Convictions," 10-17, he adopts a straightforward tone, with the subsequent praise showered on the *NYT* by a Lithuanian supreme court justice not looking awkward or self-serving.

Kamm, Thomas. *The Wall Street Journal.* (★ ½)
Rio de Janeiro. Kamm was able to penetrate a little deeper into South American stories this year, unearthing critical details on regional economic reform and the Brazilian arms industry. His analytical efforts sputtered at times, however. In the straightforward "Menem Cabinet Shuffled After Currency Dives," 1-30, he reports that the resignations underline the continued political and economic instability in the country. We learn how the Gulf War is impacting negatively on Brazil's troubled arms industry in the solid "War Levels Brazil's Defense Firms, Which Thrived

on Iraq's Purchases," 2-5. He packs a lot of revealing detail and statistics into "Brazil's Effort to Curb Inflation Face Hurdle: A Lot of People Like It," 3-29, but wraps them around a silly theme that there is "a kind of inflation culture in Brazil," and includes not a word about tax policies as they affect production. In "Guns, Guards and Wire: What Firms Need Most in Terror-Infested Peru," 4-2, he provides snappy selections that effectively make the point about security and health concerns in that beleaguered country. He produces a serviceable roundup of the effects of the Autumn plan on the Argentine economy in "Argentine Inflation Fight Stirs New Hope," 5-9, but Nathaniel Nash of *NYT* covered this subject more thoroughly, and a week earlier. In "Bolivians Fear a U.S.-Led War on Drugs," 6-24, he sounds a sober warning about the growing militarization of the U.S. anti-drug effort. His report on the Menem Government's efforts to modernize and then privatize its national oil company, "South Americans Push Sales of State Assets in Swing to Capitalism," 7-9, works well as a case study in Latin America's efforts to make the transition to a market economy. In "Brazil's Swelling Wave of Emigration Reflects Gloom About Nation's Future," 10-1, we get an anecdotal report on Brazil's worsening brain drain, with the larger issues mostly glossed over, while "Brazil Sells Off Big Steelmaker to the Public," 10-25, is concise on the selling off of Brazil's national steelmaker. Kamm is coming into his own as a reporter, and if he could sharpen his analytic skills he would move up rapidly.

Keller, Bill. *The New York Times.* (★ ★ ★ ★)
Moscow. Keller departed as bureau chief in January, but helped anchor the *Times* coverage of the coup attempt in August and the subsequent historic changes in the Soviet Union with groundbreaking reports and analytics that captured crucial developments other reporters missed completely or only caught up with later. His original analysis of Gorbachev's removal, "Gorbachev and His Fateful Step," 8-20, tracks the growing vacuum of authority that accompanied Gorbachev's efforts to split the difference between "a new generation of popular leaders," increasingly impatient with the pace of reforms, and the "hardliners," or "custodians of stability," increasingly worried about Western influence. Keller provided valuable insight into the possible motivation of the coup leaders that we did not find elsewhere. In "Old Guard's Last Grasp," 8-22, he expertly runs down the mistakes the coup leaders made, going into greater detail in "Plotters Who Had Handcuffs but a Poor Sense of History," 8-25, an excellent special report on "A Coup Gone Awry." In the superb "Collapse of an Empire," 8-27, he authoritatively examines the strategic, political, and economic issues raised by the accelerating break up of the Soviet Union. He travels to the city of Kiln, fifty miles from Moscow, to give us a revealing perspective on the historical events taking place in "View From a City of Skeptics: A Coup? It Hardly Matters," 8-29, reporting that the people there have been reacting to the events since "Coup Monday" with studied indifference. " 'We've gotten used to it,' [Yuliya Gladyshev] said. 'They're always springing some surprise on the people — a price increase, a monetary reform. We all feel like laboratory rabbits.' " In the 10 Best selection, "From Resistance of the Few to Revolt of the Masses," 9-15, he masterfully deconstructs the mythology already growing up around the bungled August coup, providing the first stark, knowing perspective on what the coup was all about. Earlier in the year, in "Soviet Loyalists in Charge After Attack in Lithuania; 13 Killed; Crowds Defiant," 1-14, he provides a graphic report from Vilnius on the bloody crackdown.

Kelly, Michael. *The New Republic.* (★ ★ ★)
Special Middle East correspondent. Kelly covered the Gulf War and its aftermath with stark, graphic reports that etched indelible images on the mind while capturing the political forces at work in the region. In "Blitzed," 2-11, he vividly evokes the first days of the U.S. bombing of Baghdad and a harrowing trip to Jordan: "[Baghdad] has finally discovered the obvious: a contest between a Third World semi-power fighting World War II and a First World superpower fighting World War III is no contest at all." He examines King Hussein's ambitions in "Desert Rat," 2-18, and "Speech Defect," 3-4, making a better effort than most reporters to place the King's precarious balancing act in full geopolitical context. Reporting on the allied sweep into Kuwait in the darkly poetic "Kiss of Victory," 3-18, he notes that he never even saw an Iraqi

soldier with a weapon in his hand, while in "The Rape and Rescue of Kuwait City," 3-25, he writes unsparingly on the atrocities the Iraqis left behind: "The corpse in drawer 12 had been burned to death with some flammable liquid. The body was curled like a fetus, and what remained of the head was still barely recognizable as a skull, but a skull that seemed to have been slathered in a brown viscous material and then baked in a kiln." Just as uncompromising is his depiction of the devastation allied bombers leveled on Iraqi soldiers trying to flee Kuwait City, "Highway to Hell," 4-1. His cover story on post-war Kuwait, "Rolls-Royce Revolutionaries," 4-8, received attention because of his revelation that the U.S. Army Corps of Engineers was being rushed into the war-devastated country to work on the emir's Bayan Palace, but just as important was his firsthand observation on discontent with the royal family in the highest circles of Kuwaiti society. He takes readers into the Kurdish refugee camps in Iran, "The Other Hell," 5-13, providing important details on this underreported story, as he documents how the Iranian government bears much of the blame for the horrific conditions. In "Back to the Hills," 6-3, he scores another scoop, divulging that Baghdad's defeat of the Kurdish rebels was less than the massive victory depicted in the press, and that a "delicate balance of power" now exists.

Kempe, Frederick. *The Wall Street Journal.* (★ ★ ½)
Bonn. Kempe continues to provide his share of scoops, particularly on the security beat, but we noted a tendency in some of his dispatches to lack sharp focus, especially when he was covering the east German economic scene and the Soviet Union. In "East Europe Offers Investors Big Profits and Big Perils," 1-11, he provides a useful sketch of the prospects for market economies in various eastern European countries, concisely laying out advantages and disadvantages of each. He develops some sense of how Germans are viewing relations with the U.S. in "German's Support for U.S., After Time, Grows Resolute," 2-11, but the scope is limited. He artfully conveys the factual strife in a "Soviet Lebanon" in "Soviet Georgia Is Torn by Groups Competing in Independence Drive," 2-21. Kempe continues to be superb at presenting the ground-level perspective of economic trends, as in the insightful "New 'Miracle': Germans Avoid Slump With Unusual Tactic: Subsidizing the East," 6-11, where he illustrates how working class *ossies* are coping with being a key part of Germany's new method of avoiding a recession: "Swallow a smaller neighboring country and then subsidize it so it can buy your products." He is bemused by Ronald Lauder's efforts to carve out a role for himself as an "Eastern European entrepreneur" in the colorful "Money Man: Ronald Lauder Is a Mover and Shaker in the Old 'East Bloc,' " 7-18. He writes that the main east German concern following the Soviet coup attempt is the potential loss of the Soviet market in "Fading Menace: Eastern Germans Now See the Soviet Threat Only as an Economic One," 8-26, before retracing a lot of familiar ground on east German economics. In "Aspiring Nations: As Independence Nears, The Baltic States Face Raft of New Challenges," 9-3, he provides good detail on problems confronting newly-independent Estonia, but the report tends to wander. He draws on a secret document prepared by the German government to fully document how German companies aided Saddam's efforts to join the nuclear age in the eye-opening report: "Report Links Three German Companies to Iraq's Nuclear Weapons Program," 10-7.

Kinzer, Stephen. *The New York Times.* (★ ★ ½)
Bonn. While Kinzer hasn't regained the influence he had as Managua bureau chief during the 1980s, his German coverage is respectable and resourceful, once again excelling at capturing stories on the margin. His contribution to a three-part series on "Eastern Germany in Despair," "Unity Brings Many Traumas to What Was East Germany," 3-10, alertly zeroes in on the industrial town of Cottbus, where he finds that private businessmen are having a go of it, including former communist officials. "They seem to have transformed themselves from Marxist ideologues to capitalist entrepreneurs without any political, moral or financial problems." In "Berlin and Bonn, Partisans Square Off as Vote for Germany's Capital Nears," 6-17, he comprehensively surveys the arguments for and against moving the German capital out of Bonn and back to Berlin. Kinzer was especially adept at alerting readers to up-and-coming German

political figures. We get a useful profile of new German Social Democratic leader Bjorn Engholm, "Odds Look Good for Germany's Odd Challenger," 4-16, learning that he is a protege of the more moderate Helmut Schmidt, while in "A German Who Dares, in Parachutes and Politics," 7-12, he deftly presents German Economics Minister Jurgen Mollemann, a rising star in the Free Democratic Party, who has overcome an early image as being a shallow outsider in Bonn circles. "Mr. Mollemann is part of a new generation of German politicians that is starting to elbow the older generation aside." Assigned to Lithuania during the Soviet upheaval, he breaks an important story, "Lithuania Starts to Wipe Out Convictions for War Crimes," 9-5, superbly contrasting the news that exonerations are being handed out to "thousands" of Lithuanians convicted by Soviet courts as Nazi war criminals with the reaction of international Jewish groups. He provides an insightful report on growing consumer spending by east Germany, in "East Germans, Nurtured by Bonn, Take Heart and Begin to Prosper," 9-29, an antidote to the typical gloom-and-doom reports we are seeing on this subject. Writing on recent neo-Nazi activity, "Klan Seizes on Germany's Wave of Racist Violence," 11-3, he strikes just the right tone, ominous but not alarmist.

Kirk, Donald. Freelance. (★ ★ ½)
Kirk started 1991 covering the Gulf crisis from Iraq for *USA Today,* and throughout the year he contributed reports on the Middle East to *National Review.* Readers found themselves transported to the locales he was writing from and coming away with an increased understanding of the stories behind the headlines. In "Shadow of War Looming Larger," *USA Today* 1-10, he vividly captures the pulse of the Iraqi capital on the eve of war. The only American newspaper correspondent in Baghdad when the war began, Kirk was able to use the CNN phone, and in "On the Scene: Baghdad 'Eerie,'" *USA Today* 1-17, the newspaper reprinted his observations: "The streets were dark and calm and somewhat eerie and there were no signs of bomb damage in the center of the street where we drove." He offers some illuminating firsthand impressions on his recent stays in Baghdad, Amman, Damascus, and Andana, Turkey, "Middle-East War Diary," *NR* 2-25, and in "From the *Souk*," *NR* 3-18, he provides a revealing, street-level report from Amman on Palestinian reaction to the Gulf War, reporting that "nobody here wants to be in the losing camp with Iraq, not for all the Saddam posters in the world, not for Arafat, and certainly not for the non-Palestinian, King Hussein." He was equally adept at covering the troubled peace as well. In "The Kurds' Fragile Peace," *NR* 7-8, he effectively conveys Kurdish unease as the allies depart: "The real fear. . .is that the Iraqis will hold back — and then resume business as usual six months or a year from now when the suffering of the Kurds is strictly yesterday's news." In "Operation: Desert Mop-Up," *NR* 8-12, he reports from Saudi Arabia as the United States confronts growing opposition to maintaining a permanent presence in the region, expertly moving the story forward. "For U.S. negotiators, the extreme sensitivities of Washington's allies pose almost as much of a problem as does the duplicity of Saddam Hussein, still ferociously clinging to his power base in Baghdad." He penetrates the veil surrounding communist Vietnam somewhat in "The Old Guard," *NR* 9-23, offering informed insight on how Vietnam's hard-line leadership is viewing with alarm the disintegration of its patron and benefactor, if only for the example being set for its own population.

Kraft, Scott. *Los Angeles Times.* (★ ★ ½)
Johannesburg. Always reliable and objective, Kraft usually offers a sober perspective on all sides in the South African maelstrom, sometimes seasoned with a circumspect sensitivity on the moral shortcomings of the ANC. We sometimes get the feeling Kraft knows more than he is telling. He is strong on the dynamics of the Mandela-Buthelezi relationship in "S. Africa Summitry: Key Blacks Meet," 1-29. He fully captures the one-step-up, two-steps-back progress of South Africa in "2 South African Blacks Find Freedom and Fear Coexist," 2-15. His coverage of Winnie Mandela's trial offers a deft mixture of courtroom fare and political perspective: In "Mandela Case: Key Test for Her White Lawyer," 3-13, he effectively captures the drama and moral subtlety surrounding the defense's cross-examination of one of Mandela's alleged victims, while in "Winnie Mandela Denies Role in the 1988 Beating of 4 Behind Her Home," 4-17, he alertly

points out that her husband spent the day in Zimbabwe. In the anecdotal, yet insightful "Whites Eye the Exit in S. Africa," 5-29, he fully documents how intertribal violence is undermining the efforts of black leaders to convince whites to remain, commenting that "Most of those contemplating a getaway are the more liberal, wealthier and better-educated whites, many of the same people who pushed so hard for black equality." Surveying the economic prospects for post-civil war Angola in the comprehensive "Postwar Path Looks Relatively Smooth," 6-1, he finds that a devastated infrastructure and lack of skilled workers may hinder free-market reforms. Covering the South African reaction to President Bush's decision to lift sanctions, "S. Africa Hails Move as Big Step to Acceptance," 7-11, he usefully looks beyond the hype to observe that "Most South African economists viewed the action as of great symbolic — rather than practical — importance." He provides a valuable report on the growing split within the Afrikaner community between reformers and conservatives, "In South Africa, the Latest Fight Is White Against White," 10-8, a split that is growing more violent as the day of multiracial rule inexorably approaches.

Kristof, Nicholas D. *The New York Times.* (★ ★ ★)
Beijing. A 1990 Pulitzer winner, Kristof offered superlative coverage this year on the dynamics of the U.S.-Sino relationship, fully capturing the nuances of this complex story. He demonstrates a strong feel for the workings of Hong Kong in "Bank Looks Beyond Hong Kong," 1-7. Writing on the recent rise of drug usage among Chinese youth in "Heroin Spreads Among Young in China," 3-21, he takes a rather interesting look back at the communist's efforts to wipe out opium following the 1949 revolution: "The measures were ruthless, but superbly organized." In "Chinese Ties: Frosty to Icy," 5-2, he expertly surveys the irritants in U.S.-Sino relations. He persuasively makes the case that the terrible suffering and destruction in Bangladesh wasn't simply the consequences of "natural forces," "In Bangladesh's Storms, Poverty More Than Weather Is the Killer," 5-11, masterfully outlining the political-economic framework that prevented action on policies that could have averted the huge scale of death and devastation. As the battle over extending MFN status heated up he provided the varying perspectives from the Chinese sides in such multidimensional reports as "Despite Rights Issue, Chinese Hope United States Trade Status Stays," 5-15, and "Doing Beijing a 2nd Favor?" 7-21. In "Hard-Liners in China: Old, But by No Means Out," 6-4, and "Suicide of Jiang Qing, Mao's Widow, Is Reported," 6-5, he fully updates us on the status of conservatives two years after Tiananmen Square. Surveying China's gradual re-entry into the international diplomatic community in "For China, a Summer of Diplomatic Triumphs," 8-22, he alertly picks up that Washington seems to be backtracking on the dangers posed by the M-9 and M-11 missiles. Hard information is scanty in "Beijing's Shivering Spine," 9-5, an analysis of Chinese fears of ethnic uprisings. He provides a rare and insightful look inside the Chinese intelligence service in "For Chinese Spies, the Enemies Are Everywhere," 10-18. In "A Stalinists' Paradise in Korea Founders," 10-27, he straightforwardly passes on unconfirmed reports of growing economic deprivation and political dissent in the North, well aware that what is really occurring there is anybody's guess.

Lamb, Christina. *Financial Times.* (★ ★ ★)
Rio de Janeiro. A talented writer, Lamb has rapidly developed into one of the most reliable sources on economic data and analysis on the Brazilian scene, able to enfold information into important national and regional trends. In the imaginative "Rio Seeks to Redeem Reputation in World Commerce," 1-5/6, she writes on the efforts of Rio businessmen to restore the glory and influence the city had when it was the Brazilian capital. She provides a masterful sketch of the Collor regime's efforts to launch its second anti-inflation program in ten months in the face of a skeptical public and business community in "Thumbs Down to Collor 'Scud Plan,' " 2-6. "The success of this plan. . .hinges on the government's administrative and marketing abilities, something it has not proved strong on so far." Covering the resignation of Brazil's economic minister Zelia Cardoso, "From Conflict to Consensus," 5-10, she alertly observes that while Cardoso's replacement, Marcilio Marques Moreira, may be more politically astute and diplomatic in his dealings with the Sao Paulo business community, his credibility too will be

undermined if he fails to bring inflation under control. She stays on top of the Brazilian economy in such comprehensive efforts as "Brazil Seeks to Come in From the Cold," 9-4, and "Collor's Crusade Crumbles," 9-23, noting in the latter report that politicians and the press are comparing the situation to 1964, when the military last overthrew an elected president. She effectively contrasts the international efforts to eradicate the drug trade with the poverty-stricken region of Chapare, central Bolivia, in "Poverty Thwarts Drugs Fight in Bolivia," 7-18, while in "A Protectionist Virus in Brazil's Computer Plans," 7-23, she is sharp on Brazil's protectionist policy toward information technology, quick to point out the failings of new legislation designed to open the country to foreign competition. In "An Amazonian Klondike Loses its Lustre," 10-25, she pens a picaresque report on Brazil's wildcat miners who still dream of striking it rich in the Amazon rain forest despite environmental and economic trends which portend doom for their chosen profession.

Lawday, David. *U.S.News & World Report.* (★ ½)
Paris. Lawday can produce sharp, well-researched reports on individual European nations, but he tends to view continent-wide issues with the Euro-optimism that we normally associate with Jacques Delors. In "Europe Without Thatcher," 12-31-90/1-7-91, for example, he writes that: "By the mid-1990s, when common citizenship rules are in place, you will be able to ask an Italian or a Belgian for his or her nationality and the answer may be 'I'm a European' — spoken with the same assurance with which an Iowan says that he's an American." On the other hand, his coverage of the crisis in Yugoslavia could be overwrought, as in "Raised Flags, Rising Heat," 4-1, where a quote from Bismarck about "some damn silly thing in the Balkans" touching off a European war, sets the tone. In "A Different Kind of War," 5-6, his best report of the year, he effectively evokes a "dank field of spring corn in northern Iraq," where U.S. Marines who sat out the war on ships in the Mediterranean are now constructing tent cities for Kurdish refugees: "Creating this rough-and-ready twilight zone as a provisional Kurdish sanctuary lacks the glamour of liberating Kuwait, and these marines feel it." In the well-organized "A Litmus Test for Germany," 6-24, he reports on the Bonn vs. Berlin debate, effectively contrasting the arguments on both sides. He is informative on Turkish President Turgut Ozal's vision of his country as a political and economic dynamo for its neighbors to emulate, "Turkey Aims To Be a Middle East Japan," 7-29: "Turkey sees itself as a sprinter surrounded by economic cripples and democratic laggards and dreams of being 'the Japan of the Middle East.' " His report on the prospects for a diplomatic solution to the Yugoslav crisis, "Death and Decay in the Balkans," 9-16, is superficial, Lawday never digging deeper than writing "Yugoslavia's bloody turmoil, and Europe's inability to handle it, is a warning to the dissolving Soviet Union: When ethnic tensions explode into civil war, it is almost impossible to put out the fires."

Lehner, Urban C. *The Wall Street Journal.* (★ ½)
Tokyo. Lehner showed some slight improvement over last year, often rising above mediocrity in his Japanese coverage, but slipping when he covered the political economies of other southeast Asian nations. In "Japanese, Soviets May Seek Land Pact," 12-17-90, he provides a solid update within Japan on the Kurile islands issue. He pays appropriate attention to Japan's sensitive relations with the U.S. as Japan prepares for Gulf War rebuilding in "Japanese Consider Taking the Initiative on Middle East Reconstruction Plans," 3-5. In "Tokyo Relents Slightly on Islands Issue as Gorbachev's Japan Visit Approaches," *A WSJ* 4-1, he bases too much of his report on discussion within the Japanese press over the possibility of an arrangement for Japanese sovereignty of four of the Northern Territories now held by the U.S.S.R., in exchange for extending economic aid to the Soviet economy. He provides a lengthy anecdotal report on the booming Thai economy and its adverse impact on the Thai quality of life, "Boom Time: Thailand's Economy Surges, and Country Is Feeling the Strain," 6-12, while "Growth Costs Taiwan in Social Dislocations, As the Big Time Looms," 8-5, is disappointing on aspects of that country's economic policy. He is sharp on what the ascension of Kiichi Miyazawa portends for U.S.-Japanese relations, "With Miyazawa as Japan's Prime Minister, Nation May Strengthen Role in Global Issues," and Christopher J. Chipello 10-14: "Mr. Miyazawa is capable of the kind of long-distance relationship with the U.S. president that some European leaders have — and of occasionally telling Mr. Bush something he might not want to hear."

Lewis, Flora. *The New York Times.* (★ ★)
Senior columnist. Although officially retired, Lewis writes regularly from Paris on the international issues of the day, her columns having an increasingly harder edge. She is less willing to put up with official excuses for policies designed to preserve the *status quo.* In "The Next Soviet Challenge," 2-6, she foreshadows the "Grand Bargain" by calling on Western leaders to make it clear to Gorbachev that "he can count on Western aid only if he delivers on the promise of a free market and liberty to his people." She is contemptuous of rising anti-Americanism created by the Gulf War in the hardhitting "A Shabby French Sulk," 2-20, labeling European reaction to the crisis "disgusting." However, her defense of Washington ended when the war did, her analysis of U.S. post-war policy offering informed, if at times conventional, criticism. In "Here We Go Again — Arming the Mideast," 3-21, she comes out against Washington's intentions to resume an arms build-up in the Middle East to maintain "balance," while in "America Deserts the Rebels Cynically," 4-3, she takes the allies to task for failing to support the Iraqi rebels. She is more incisive in "Cut the Saudis Down to Size," 7-19, clearly delineating where Saudi policy conflicts with Washington: "Saudi concerns are different and must not obsess U.S. policy." She travels to Japan for a firsthand look at troubled U.S.-Japanese relations, "The Great Game of 'Gai-atsu,' " 5-1, smartly zeroing in on the growing recognition by some Japanese elites that the practice of dismissing outside criticism as "Japan-bashing" is being used by Tokyo to justify international inaction. "The subtlety of relying on '*gai-atsu*' is that it helps keep the existing political structure in place, blaming somebody outside for uncomfortable accommodations that are needed without having to examine Japan's internal power relations." In the thought-provoking "End Nuclear Tests? Yes. Now," 10-22, she issues a strong appeal for a nuclear test ban, drawing on the testimony of experts to argue that weapons labs now are glorified make-work schemes for scientists: "With the end of the cold war, that's just what they should be doing — turning to other work."

Lloyd, John. *Financial Times.* (★ ★)
Moscow. The indefatigable Lloyd covered the tumultuous Soviet scene with an intense sense of the salient factors on the margin, providing critical detail in his dispatches that we couldn't find elsewhere. Unfortunately, he sometimes displayed a partisanship in favor of one side against others on the many political and economic battles throughout the country this year. His post-coup analytic, "Power to the Soviet Peoples," 8-27, presents an insightful reconnaissance of the territory to be covered as "a splintered politics is emerging among the diverse constituents of the disintegrating empire." The sense of a frustrated stop-start, forward-backward, approach came through in "Financial Specialists Warn Gorbachev of Catastrophe," 4-4, on the alarm over plunging revenues from the republics, and "Soviet PM's Offer Steps Up Momentum Toward Compromise," 4-26, on Prime Minster Valentin Pavlov's offer to include representatives of other movements in his government. We learn from "Gorbachev in Secret G7 Offer," 5-17, and "Economist at Centre of Soviet Aid Plea," 5-17, that economist Grigory Yavlinsky had a pipeline to Lloyd, but we had to begin questioning if the source was controlling the outlet with Lloyd's paean on behalf of Yavlinsky and Co.'s plan for economic program, "A Cheap Package at That Price," 5-22. While "New Clothes for a Threadbare Union," 7-2, was an analytical piece so Lloyd had some latitude, though we found him a bit too uncritical of the Yavlinsky plan, giving us platitudes rather than content analysis. Still, his perceptions into the special situation of the Soviet Communist Party were sharp: it's a "vast organism of about 18m people, with vast assets and with its people running almost everything in the centre. Unlike the Communist parties of east/central Europe, it is the mother of all parties and has nobody else to blame, and nowhere else to go." He borrows a page from T.S. Eliot, while comprehensively analyzing Boris Yeltsin's plan to administer economic "shock treatment" in "Yeltsin's Bitter Pill," 10-29: "The constituent parts of what was the Soviet Union, now thrown back upon their own resources, are about to discover how painful it is to build nations from a political, economic and moral wasteland."

Long, William R. *Los Angeles Times.* (★ ½)
Buenos Aires. Long's beat encompasses much of South America, and while he is alert to developing stories, he seems to be spread thin at times, he is best when he can focus on a theme. He grapples with regional economics in "Brazil, Argentina Grapple With Inflation," 2-2, a serviceable survey of the "serious trouble" South America's two biggest economies are in. He attempts a lighthearted look at Brazilians trying to have a good time in Rio as the economy deteriorates, "What, Me Worry? Not in Rio," 1-7, but the contrast between the grim conditions and summertime-fun-in-the-sun is handled too awkwardly to be truly effective. Reporting on the Latin American reaction to the Paris Club's concessions to debt-laden Poland in the inspired "Poles' Debt Relief Plans Stir Envy Among Latins," 5-28, he finds that while some region officials would also like debt forgiveness, others are willing to work things out with the banks. Some of his best material of the year focused on how Chile is coping with terrorism — past and present. In "Terror Attacks Send Jitters Through Chile," 5-6, he sharply positions what the current unrest may portend for Chile's newfound political stability, while in "Hated Symbol of Chilean Repression Prospers," 6-23, he soberly outlines how the former head of Chile's secret police has evaded prosecution for the Orlando Letelier assassination and managed to become a prosperous businessman. His survey of the Argentine media, "Good News Is No News for the Argentine Press," 7-9, merely skims the surface of this fascinating topic, while "Moving Into the First World on the Buddy System," 7-1, is too glib and gossipy on Menem's friendship with Bush. Writing on regional political has-beens, "Latin America's Fallen Climb Back Onto Power Scene," 7-23, he advances the questionable thesis that a "motley crew" of former presidents are maneuvering to stage career comebacks. In one on his most substantial reporting jobs of the year, "Peru Guerrillas Take Aim at Lima," 10-13, he takes us into the slums of the Peruvian capital to document how Shining Path is extending its influence among the poor and downtrodden.

Magnier, Mark. *The Journal of Commerce.* (★ ½)
Southeast Asia. Magnier inaugurated a new *JOC* office in Singapore, signaling the paper's recognition of the growing economic importance of the region. As the former West Coast editor, Magnier was an inspired choice, but in his first year, we saw more number crunching, and less analysis than he had exhibited in his domestic coverage. Perhaps because he is still familiarizing himself with the terrain. He covers the basics on Singapore business activity in dispatches such as "Compact Satellite System Launched in Singapore," 2-22, and "Singmarine to Build Ship Able to Carry Sulfur, Oil Products," 3-27. He is straightforward on a Pacific Economic Cooperation Conference in Singapore where Asian self-sufficiency in financing trade was emphasized, "Asia Seen Relying Less on Outside Capital in '90s," 5-28: "Venture capital has become a popular tool for strong regional companies hoping to become Asian multinationals, during a time when global bank capital is drying up." He covers both sides of the debate over curbing union benefits and power in "Unions Quietly Weather Harsh Economic Storm," 7-19, giving readers a good sense of the stakes involved. He was on top of developing regional stories, "Australia, Malaysia Clash on Trade," 5-10, explaining deteriorating relations between Australia and Malaysia to their backing of separate trade bodies, — East Asia Economic Group by the Malaysians, the Asia-Pacific Economic Cooperation by Australia. "In a world that is in danger of breaking up into trading blocs, the disagreement has potential implications for the global trading order." "US Still Opposes Asian Trade Bloc," 7-24, is timely on Washington's opposition to an East Asia Economic Grouping. He provides a good run-down of the political instability investors in the region will face in the months ahead, "Southeast Asian Investment Climate Likely to Turn Riskier, Less Stable," 9-16, commenting that Mexico figures to be the main benefactor, as investments will be diverted there should an FTA kick in. In "Thai Landbridge Could Be Built in Several Stages," 10-24, he colorfully updates us on Thailand's efforts to construct a land bridge, to transport oil from the Middle East, to enable shippers to bypass the Straits of Malacca.

Mallet, Victor. *Financial Times.* (★ ★ ★)
Middle East, scheduled for transfer to Bangkok. Mallet stood out from the pack of Middle Eastern correspondents this year with war coverage that had just the right note of skepticism and authoritative reports on the post-war environment. He conveys the almost surreal air of "normalcy" that prevailed in Saudi Arabia even after the war began, in dispatches such as "Saudis Stay Cool on Holiday," 1-16, and "War Effort and Fear Disrupt Saudi Businesses," 1-23. In "Dash Into the Desert Serves Saddam's Political Purpose," 2-1, he artfully deconstructs the spin control efforts being taken by all sides on the battle for Khafji, while in "Saudis No Longer Made of Money," 2-15, he fully examines the financial pressures, both immediate and longterm, which have resulted in a Saudi budget deficit and the "obvious embarrassment" of having to borrow from international bankers. In "Triumphant Homecoming Through Deserted Forces," 2-27, a model of reporting economy, he captures the ease with which allied troops rolled into Kuwait. His coverage of post-war Kuwait was outstanding, and he was quick on the mark of the division between the regime and the merchant class in "The Pains of Liberation," 3-9/10, while "Post-War Depression," 7-8, documents why "Kuwait. . .has escaped from Iraq, but not from its own past." He could be late on a story, such as with "Iraqi Stability 'May Hinge on Kurd Problem,' " 4-18, and "Strong Views, Weak Wills Mark Arab Boycott," 5-15, but even then he would go much deeper into the subject than earlier reports. He seems to view Saddam Hussein's survival with a mixture of disgust and disbelief, "Uneasy Sits the Crown on Unrepentant Saddam," 8-1, an analytic that lacks Mallet's usual deft touch: "Mr Saddam can nourish the idea that squeezing Iraq too severely will create the kind of bitterness which allowed Nazi Germany to emerge from the aftermath of the First World War." He is sharp and clear on the concerns of Israeli settlers in the Golan Heights in "Living in a Hill Bunker Amid a War of Nerves," 9-24, focusing on the fact that unlike the West Bank, hard-headed security considerations, not religious sentiment, will decide the fate of the Heights: "If Israel is safer without the Golan, then the Golan will probably have to go."

Marcom, John, Jr. *Forbes.* (★ ★)
London. Marcom can be counted on to provide both punchy company profiles and well-researched, far-reaching analysis on European economic developments. He is evidently not afraid to ponder longterm trends. In "Bundesbank Uber Alles," 12-24-90, he covers all the angles of Britain's move to tie the pound to the deutschemark, providing far-reaching analysis on what it portends for both the continent and the entire world. He offers an astute appraisal of the forces that are pushing Spain's peseta to unprecedented levels, "Spain on $500 a Day," 3-18, the only weakness that he's murky on solutions, hinting that devaluation might have been a solution but that "old remedy. . .is out because Spain is part of the European Monetary System." In "Battle of Zaventem," 4-29, he is clear on how Brussels-based DHL Worldwide Express's streamlined express-delivery system has enabled it to successfully combat such formidable competitors as Federal Express. However, in another company profile, "Moment of Truth," 7-8, he fails to match his enthusiasm for Scandinavian Airlines Systems (SAS) and its president Jan Carlzon with a comparable dose of scrutiny. In the engaging "Personal Affairs: An Awkward Cocktail Party," 9-2, he offers a testimonial to a privately-owned language school in the south of France, where total immersion is the teaching method. He provides a quick but solid report on the $8 billion industry of tour exhibits in "The Exhibition Industry: A Well-Kept Secret," 9-30.

Marsh, David. *Financial Times.* (★ ★ ★ ½)
Eastern Europe editor. Marsh ended his tour of duty in Bonn on a high note, his coverage reflecting his deep understanding of both the German character and German economics. No other Bonn-based daily correspondent seems to pay as much detailed attention to the Bundesbank as Marsh did, keen to both its inner workings and its relations with the outside political world. Passing on the findings of a recent public opinion poll, "Today's Germans: Peaceable, Fearful — and Green," 1-4, he alertly comments that the results seem to bear out Chancellor Kohl's complaint that Germans are too "provincial," in their attitudes toward

Germany's new role on the world stage. In "Peace Gives Germany a Chance," 3-26, Marsh is prescient about the myriad economic problems facing Germany. He worked the Bundesbank beat almost as if he owned it, "Bickering Over the Bundesbank," 4-15, comprehensively adding up the problems facing Germany's central bank. Problems, he points out, with implications for all of Europe. He also wrote that "there seem no grounds" for President Karl Otto Poehl to resign. He follows up with an exclusive news-making interview with Poehl, "Germany 'Will Not Cut Rates,' " 4-25, and "Now May Be the Best Time to Jump," 5-15, authoritative on the various policy differences Poehl has with Kohl and the Bundesbank council, which may be motivating Poehl to consider resigning after all. In the lengthy "Brothers, But Strangers in Their Own Land," 6-1/2, he brings his inimitable touch to the economic and psychological strains being felt by east Germans, elevating this report above the genre. He bids farewell to Germany in "Illusion Makes Way for Reality," 8-28, a breathtaking analytical effort on how "the classic land of *Doppelwahreit* —the double-truth," is having to grapple, somewhat unsuccessfully, with the problems raised by unification and the end of the Cold War. In the clever "And Don't Forget to Bring Your Bat," 10-31, he reprints a "confidential inter-government memo" from Helmut Kohl to John Major which reveals that both leaders have "got [their] reasons" for not going too fast on European monetary and political union, despite their public pronouncements to the contrary.

Marshall, Tyler. *Los Angeles Times.* (★)
Berlin. Marshall has yet to get a firm mooring on developments in unified Germany, too often overworking such themes as psychological divisions between east and west, while current events receive sketchy treatment. In his analysis of Germany's angst-laden reaction to the war in the Gulf, "Among Germans, Angst Over Gulf War Is Pervasive," 1-25, he concentrates on the symptoms, not the cause. Addressing the same topic in "Germany — the No. 1 Political Casualty," 1-31, he seems to presume that nothing worse may happen to a nation than to become displeasing in the eyes of Washington. He strikes an alarmist tone in "East Meets West — and Resents It," 3-16, on the growing frustration and anger felt by east Germans as their economic condition worsens and their status with west Germans plummets: "A people who 16 months ago rose up and freed themselves have effectively been delivered into unity as second-class citizens, with only marginal influence and treated so separately that many of them wonder about the very word *unity*." Occasionally he could delve into a subject underreported by others. He fully examines the most critical class of post-unification litigation, property claims, with "In the Old Bloc, Who Owns What?" 4-9, while in the well-researched "Germany's Judicial Nightmare," 4-25, he writes on how the former East German legal system is being revamped while being "buried under an avalanche of litigation." He is superficial on Karl Otto Poehl's resignation in "Poehl Plans to Retire as Head of Bundesbank," 5-17. In the lively "New Wall Divides Germany," 6-16, he critically examines the cliched images of east and west Germans as passive drones and swashbuckling free marketeers, respectively. He seems to romanticize the Yugoslavian civil war in "Serbs and Croats Face Off Along Frontier of Hatred," 7-14. We get one more look at the "cultural and psychological divisions" still remaining in Germany in "30th Anniversary for Berlin Wall," 8-14. He travels to a scene of recent violence against third world immigrants in "A Dream Dies in Germany's Racist Hotbed," 10-5, and provides a routine assessment of Germany's racial problems: "Germany's troubled history is viewed by many as cause enough for alarm."

McGregor, James. *The Wall Street Journal.* (★ ★ ½)
Beijing. McGregor is more than up to the challenge of covering the Chinese political economy and all its massive detail, his reports consistently illuminating and engagingly written. In "Light Sentences for Tiananmen Protest Unlikely to Boost China's Image at Home," 1-7, he is insightful on the standing of communist leadership in China. He provides some fresh details in "Foreign Business Confidence in China Remains Hampered by Its Cash Shortage," 1-17, on how this is affecting new investment and projects. In the imaginatively-written "Chinese Readers Have to Dig Around for Gulf War News," 2-8, we see how the Gulf War is being covered, and not

covered, by the official Chinese media. Profiling Chinese Premier Li Peng, "Chinese Premier Tries to Reform His Image as a Petty Bureaucrat," 2-25, McGregor gives readers a good idea of what life is like in China under his stewardship. In "Finance Minister Paints Grim Picture of Deficit-Riddled Chinese Economy," *A WSJ* 4-1, he puts together a clear picture of China's financial deterioration, even though the government released only selected data, while in "Jobless Peasants Swarm Through China" 5-2, he provides a compelling portrait of a brewing problem in China as the economic slump provides no employment for a growing rural population looking for jobs in the cities. We appreciate the color he is able to work into his economic reports, "China's Entrepreneurs Are Thriving in Spite of Political Crackdown," 6-4, a rich picture of the booming city of Guangzhou, while "Hainan, China's Free-Market 'Model,' Degenerates Into a Sin City for Cadres," 7-23, vividly documents how the island of Hainan, intended by Beijing to be a competitor with Taiwan, developed instead into an economic and moral free-fire zone for Party elites, and we were left wondering if Hainan was a harbinger of Hong Kong post-1997. In "Success Stories in China Stay Untold as U.S. Firms Strive for Low Profiles," 11-7, he is detailed on successful U.S. firms in China who are growing increasingly concerned about China's MFN status as the election year approaches.

Melloan, George. *The Wall Street Journal.* (★ ★ ½)
"Global View" columnist and editorial page editor of *The Wall Street Journal/Europe.* We always read anything that appears under Melloan's byline, confident this sturdy veteran will draw our attention to new aspects and fresh dimensions around the day's major issues. In "A Different Kind of Living-Room War," 1-21, he draws a shrewd parallel between TV coverage of the Gulf War and the high-tech weaponry the war is being fought with which minimizes casualties: "Fighting in a global fishbowl has surely guided the development of military technology along new lines." He nicely zings the Soviets, Belgians and Germans, "Apply the 'Little Red Hen' Rule to the Gulf," 3-4, noting "Few countries wanted a part in the war; a lot want a say in the peace." He serves up a sober appreciation of Turkey's role in the region, "Ozal: The Peacemaker's Broad Agenda," 3-22, one of his best post-war efforts. We find a fine array of fresh data on the Bulgarian economy in "Eastern Europe's Plea: Please Don't Shut Us Out," 4-8. In the thought-provoking "What T. Boone's Slim Pickin's Say About Japan," 5-6, he sharply raises the possibility that corporativism may well be more a problem for Japan itself than for any of its competitors. He adds to the *WSJ*'s impressive coverage on BCCI, painstakingly drawing a drug-money connection between the bank, close associates of Argentine President Carlos Menem, and Syria's Baath party in the 10 Best nominee "Drugs — The Argentine Connection," 4-25. In "Welcome to the New Chicago, Congressman," 6-3, he pens a vivid report on Richard Gephardt's appearance in the internationalist lion's den at the 1991 World Trade Conference of the Chicago Council on Foreign Relations. He offers one of the better analyses we've seen of the Japanese securities scandal in "How Japan's Success Tripped the Successful," 7-1, offering rich insights into how Japan's economic growth and the inefficiency of its narrowly focused financial sector brought the matter to a head. He comes out against quick-fix solutions to the Soviet agricultural crisis, "Feed the Russians? It Could Be Easy," 9-16, delivering a solid case for privatization of Soviet farming. But, "Phone Technology Is Opening Up New Worlds," 10-14, contains no fresh insights.

Meyer, Michael. *Newsweek.* (★)
Bonn-Berlin. Meyer's reports keep readers abreast but rarely in front of developments in Germany and points east. He does usually avoid the tendency to pepper his dispatches with commentary, a common shortcoming of newsweekly reporters these days. He brings us up-to-date on the state of affairs in Albania in "Stalinism's Last Stand," 4-15. In "Germany Thinks Pink," and Karen Breslau 5-6, he provides a serviceable roundup of the reasons behind the end of the reunification honeymoon for German Chancellor Helmut Kohl. He competently covers a dispute between Czechoslovakia and the departing Soviet army over who will pay for damages incurred during the twenty-three year occupation in "Pullout of the 'Barbarians,'" 6-10. In "A Return to the Crypt," 8-12, he discounts signs of resurgent German nationalism as "political

theater," making a strong case that the fanfare over the re-internment of Frederick the Great is just that, merely fanfare: "There are few real signs of resurgent German nationalism. Many dismiss the upcoming festivities as 'Kohl's folly,' an embattled chancellor's effort to woo right-wing voters." But one reader wondered why, if it was unimportant, did Meyer write on it. In the informative "Kaliningrad: The Old Guard Hangs On," 9-16, he relates the state of affairs in the city, home port of the Baltic fleet along with elements of the Soviet military-industrial complex, raising the possibility of greater unrest as troops return from eastern Europe. He provides a good snapshot of the pardons being issued by Lithuania for people convicted of war crimes during the Soviet regime in "An Unpardonable Amnesty," and Jonathan Alter 9-16. He delivers a wrenching report on the Serbian siege of a culturally significant Croatian city in "Dubrovnik Has Become a Hell," 11-4. Meyer writes that "The city that foreign invaders never harmed risks being destroyed by its own people," but the Croats may not agree.

Miller, Judith. *The New York Times.* (★ ★ ★)
Middle East. Miller's years of experience in this part of the world is evident in her confident style, she often combines a reporter's insights with a scholar's understanding. Her coverage of the transformation of Saudi Arabia into a nation-state was exceptional, in such reports as "Saudi and Proud of It: A New Nationalism Hedged by Uneasiness," 1-13, and the *Magazine* cover story "The Struggle Within," 3-10, noting in the latter that the war has left King Fahd "in a strong position to confront the dangerous internal opponents of his system's own creation. The question is: Will he choose to do so?" She answers that question, to some extent, in "Storm Over, Saudis Revert to Routine," 5-8, reporting that the King has resumed his traditional role of balancing conservative religious forces against liberals. Her interview with Saudi commander Prince Khaled ibn Sultan, "Saudi General Sees No Need for Big American Presence," 4-29, in which the Prince said no decision had been reached on stockpiling U.S. arms in his country, was news in and of itself. In the detailed "Kuwait's Joy Tempered by Rift Over Absolutism," 2-28, she reports on the rift already developing between the royal family and opposition figures, hours after Kuwait's liberation. Her imaginative report from Teheran on the apparent waning of the Islamic revolutionary fervor, "Islamic Radicals Lose Their Tight Grip on Iran," 4-8, compares it to Soviet communism in its obsolescence. Ever resourceful, she traveled to Tunis for "Arafat Sees No Damage to P.L.O. in War Stand," 3-15, and found Arafat defending his leadership while calling on the U.S. to bring about a Middle East peace. She followed this up several months later with "Nowhere to Go," 7-21, a superb *Magazine* report on the plight of the Palestinians in Kuwait and the occupied territories, Miller conveying how leaders such as Arafat seem out of touch and more radical factions are gaining ground. In another *Magazine* report on another developing human tragedy, the influx of immigrants into an increasingly inhospitable Europe, "Strangers at the Gate," 9-15, she provides a fresh look at a heavily-covered subject.

Miller, Marjorie. *Los Angeles Times.* (★)
Mexico City. Miller's output was slight this year, and while Juanita Darling picked up some of the slack, surely Mexico is important enough to *LAT* readers to warrant greater coverage. What little we saw of Miller's work left us with the same underwhelming impression we had last year. In "Traditional Healers Preach Gospel of Health in Rural Mexico," 2-12, we get a look into the world of the traditional Mexican healer, interesting, but we wondered if the performance of the Mexican stock market, number one in the world, and bustling economy wasn't a bigger story at the time. She takes a critical look at the Cuban press in "Under Castro, Cuban Journalists Raise Issues — But Little Else," 3-19, arguing that, as evidenced by their Gulf War coverage, "Cuban journalists see themselves as government insiders. They are propagandists as well as loyal critics," but she fails to mention that some observers said the same thing about U.S. press coverage of the war. She provides a poignant piece on the tragedies of war in "El Salvador's Rebels Are Training Again," 4-16, as she evokes life in a Cuban rehabilitation camp for blind and amputated Salvadoran guerrillas. Her output picked up during the summer, and she finally seemed to be settling into the Mexican rhythm of things. In "Mexico Officials Minimize Cholera Epidemic's Import," 8-15, she is thorough on how Mexico is handling this health crisis. Covering

the midterm election, "Ruling Party in Mexico Heads for Election Victory," 8-19, and "Victor in Mexico Vote Resigns Amid Charges of Fraud," 8-30, her reporting and analysis seems thin, simply tying the PRI's support to the personal popularity of Salinas and "a vast public works program," in the former dispatch. In perhaps her best effort on *Salinastroika* during the year, "Talking Land Reform, Free Trade and Zapata," 10-22, she artfully profiles Margarito Montes Parra, leader of Popular Farmers and Workers General Union, who straddles the two worlds of traditional peasant ideology and the efforts to modernize Mexican agriculture.

Moffett, Matt. *The Wall Street Journal.* (★ ½)
Mexico City. A colorful writer, whose work we have admired in the past, Moffett's Mexican coverage lately has been characterized primarily by a distracting cynicism for the PRI and other governing institutions. If he could tone down his cynicism to a healthy skepticism, readers might get a more accurate picture of the costs and benefits of *Salinastroika.* In "Feeling the Chill," 1-14, he provides smart context on the economic slowdown on the Mexican side of the border, as troubles in U.S. economy threaten Mexico's fragile economic recovery. We get a sordid tale of child labor exploitation in Mexican factories in "Working Children," 4-8, Moffett taking us through the issue with a specific child's plight which, like so much of Mexico's troubles, he attributes to the debt crisis. "This generation has been robbed of its childhood by a decade of debt crisis." In "Mexicans, Weary of 10-Year Debt Crisis, Register Little Opposition to Trade Pact," 5-13, he attributes apparent widespread public support of the free-trade pact to a combination of government-muzzled dissent and a population so battered by the debt crisis that it will leap at any opportunity to improve its lot, no matter, Moffett hints, how little they may really understand it. Attempting to draw a parallel between *perestroika* and *Salinastroika* in "Mexico and Moscow: Two Reform Paths," 8-22, he contends that Salinas has succeeded where Gorbachev has not, by placing economic reform ahead of political reform, his assessment of the PRI oozing with cynicism: "It is undemocratic, paternalistic, often corrupt and heavy-handed. . .it is just right for a country of pragmatists for whom pork-barrel counts more than political theorizing." In an otherwise well-written feature story on midwifes just north of the border, "Border Midwives Bring Baby Boom to South Texas," 10-16, he describes one such *partera* as being "as brown and broad as an adobe wall."

Montalbano, William D. *Los Angeles Times.* (★ ★)
Rome. An energetic, well-informed reporter, Montalbano this year seemed to substitute an element of cynicism in place of analysis in his coverage of Italian politics. His war coverage from Turkey was strong on the domestic fall-out, such as the perceptive "Ignoring Foes, Turkish Leader Takes a Gamble," 1-20, where he examines Turkish President Turgut Ozal's heavily-criticized decision to allow the U.S. to bomb Iraq from NATO bases in Turkey, and "Turks Feeling Closer to Gulf Battlefields," 1-23, which evokes the wartime mood in Ankara. He was also ahead of the curve on the Kurdish story, "Turkey Eases Hard Line Against Kurds," 1-29, as he travels to Diyarbakir, Turkey's largest Kurd-dominated city, and illuminates the ancient enmity between the Turkish government and the Kurds. We've long been impressed by Montalbano's Vatican coverage, and "Pope Calls for Broad Mideast Peace," 3-5, is a finely balanced exercise in getting across to the U.S. public the news that neither the Pope nor the Iraqi Christian community think kindly of Desert Storm, without, however, giving offense either to the Pope or to U.S. sensitivities. In "It's Time for 'Crisis' — so Andreotti Quits," 3-30, however, he falls back on witticism to put the latest cabinet crisis in perspective: "All week, politicians of sober mien and myriad political coloration have been meeting over coffee to earnestly inquire of one another whether this is a good time to have a crisis. They decided it is." He imaginatively captures Italy's changing political climate in "Voters Are Forcing Reform of Nation's Political System," 6-15, writing that the Italian electorate has decided that the time has come to "match their economic Ferrari with a political system more roadworthy than their rusty Model T." He continues to provide sophisticated treatments of the Vatican's diplomacy, "Pope Speaks in Support of Croatia," 8-18, capturing the Vatican's balanced diplomatic attitude toward ancient European ethnic hatreds, and "Pope Fears the Loss of Hard-Won Church Gains in Soviet

Union," 8-21, in which he observes that "Gorbachev's ouster imperils a religious renaissance in the Soviet Union and at the same time critically undercuts the Pope's dream of a Europe united from the Urals to the Atlantic."

Murphy, Caryle. *The Washington Post.* (★ ★)
Cairo. Murphy received both the George Polk Award and Pulitzer Prize for Foreign Reporting in 1991 for her coverage of occupied Kuwait in 1990. She was back in Kuwait, covering the story of its liberation in 1991, but she failed to capture the drama we found in her previous work. In "Kuwait's Longest Day: 'Tomorrow' Finally Dawns," 2-28, she offers some fine details on the Kuwaiti capital, but the report is curiously lacking in impact. She provides a well-organized survey of Kuwaiti discontent with the Sabah family in " 'More Democracy' Urged in Emirate; Right to Vote Becoming Key Issue," 3-10, but much of the material seems recycled. In her best post-liberation report, "Diverse Groups Defied Iraqi Invaders," 4-7, she offers a stirring account of Kuwaiti resistance to Iraqi occupation. Incisively analyzing President Mubarak's abrupt decision to withdraw Egyptian troops from Saudi Arabia and Kuwait, "Egypt Signals Discontent With Gulf," 5-11, she includes a much remarked-upon quote from an Arab diplomat that the Saudis want "blue-eyed soldiers to protect them." She makes a game attempt to draw an assessment on the level of Iraqi civilian dead in "Iraqi Death Toll Remains Clouded," 6-23, but, with few statistics or little hard information, she only manages to offer "some revealing glimpses of the emotional events" there. She is better on the insistence of Iraqis that continued economic sanctions are hurting them more than Saddam Hussein, "Iraqis Say Sanctions Hit the Wrong People," 7-5, noting that the message is conveyed even when government officials are not around. In "Iraq's War Defeat, Civil Strife Causing Crisis in Baath Party," 7-16, she provides the best report we've seen anywhere on the fall-out within the Baath party following Iraq's defeat in Kuwait and the post-war revolts. Bemusedly surveying the current tide of Iraqi public opinion, such as it is, " 'Intermission' in Iraq: Fear, Loathing and $48 Beer. . ." 9-8, she finds a tough-talking society that views the world, as a whole, as a conspiracy. She effectively illustrates that the Arab people may be ahead of their leaders when it comes to peaceful co-existence with Israel in "Arab Voices Echo With Fear, Hope," 10-30.

Murphy, Kim. *Los Angeles Times.* (★ ★)
Cairo. Murphy scored several important scoops this year, and her coverage began to exhibit a broader scope, indicating that she may finally be developing that intangible "feel" for the region. In "Saudis Wonder: Why Not Talk With Iraq?" 1-11, she produces one of the few reports we saw that indicated less than unanimous support within Saudi Arabia on the "no negotiations" stance with Iraq. She resourcefully draws on Arab analysts for "Revisiting the Legacy of Nasser," 2-26, on Saddam's pretensions of following in Nasser's footsteps as leader of the Arab Nation, making clear that Saddam is no Nasser. Her coverage of post-war Kuwait was generally solid, although we noted she tended to equate a return to normalcy with a return to a yuppie lifestyle in such reports as "Getting Back to Living: Kuwaitis Shop, Dance, Rebuild," 4-23. In "Palestinians Tell of Abuse From Resentful Kuwaitis," 3-8, she provides one of the earliest accounts of Kuwaiti retaliation towards Palestinian nationals, while in "Conditions Go From Bad to Worse in Kuwait City," 3-12, she beats a comparable *NYT* feature by a day. In the imaginatively written "Kuwait on Long, Bumpy Journey Toward Stability," 3-24, she reports on Kuwait's efforts to get its economy going again, noting that "What had been one of the most sophisticated economies in the Middle East has been reduced to little more than barter." She covers a lot of ground in "Cracks in a 45-Year Boycott," 5-22, a feature on the history of the Arab economic boycott of Israel, an informative article that would have benefitted from tighter writing. She routinely addresses the problems that Muslim fundamentalist groups pose to fledgling democracies in "Can Democracy and Fundamentalism Coexist?" 7-7, seeming to find that the answer is generally no. In the 10 Best nominee "The Gulf: An Uncertain Peace," 7-30, she displays an analytic breadth not evident in her earlier work. She vividly captures both the Arab hopes and fears riding over Madrid in "Arab World Uneasy Over Which Way Talks Will Go," 10-28, while in "For the Palestinians, New Faces and a Measure of Legitimacy," 11-3, she is comprehensive on the political comeback the Palestinians have made.

Nash, Nathaniel C. *The New York Times.* (★ ★ ★ ½)
Buenos Aires. This former banking reporter with an eye for detail and nuance arrived in Buenos Aires early this year, and we saw an overnight improvement in the *NYT*'s coverage of the Argentine political economy, the paper finally competitive on this critical story. He was superb on Chile as well. In the colorful " 'Dirty War' General vs. the Enforcer," 2-14, he masterfully captures the surreal touches of a provincial election pitting a right-wing general against a popular singer. He is not content to write another standard cholera story in "Spread of Cholera Brings Frenzy and Improvisation to Model Lima Hospital," 2-17, hooking his report instead on a Lima hospital where a doctor sees no signs of panic. He produces a memorable essay on Chile's painful coming to terms with its recent past in "Chile: Most Want the Past to Sleep, A Few Still Live in Nightmares," 4-7. Nash provides an excellent report on the monetary policy and other reforms being initiated by the country's new economics minister in "Plan by New Argentine Economy Chief Raises Cautious Hope for Recovery," 4-28. His report on the history of Argentina's Condor II missile program, "Argentina's President Battles His Own Air Force on Missile," 5-13, is of intelligence-quality. In the insightful "Latin Nations Get a Firmer Grip on Their Destiny," 6-9, he observes that OAS leaders are advocating democracy while moving away from "embracing the ultra-free-market policies that had currency during the Reagan years." He produces a comprehensive report on how former Peruvian President Alan Garcia is successfully beating back charges that he looted the country during his term in office with the help of BCCI's branch in Panama, in "Bank Scandal Enmeshes Peru Ex-Leader," 7-25. Nash demonstrates his expertise at covering financial scandal in "B.C.C.I.'s Flashy Man in Argentina," 8-1, a picaresque report on Ghaith Pharaon, and his efforts to construct a luxury hotel and a plantation in Argentina. In "Argentina Stays Tuned to Peronism and Its Politics of Personality," 9-15, he knowingly outlines how Menem has adopted the flamboyant leadership style of the Perons, while instituting policies diametrically opposite to Peronism: "Many here even go so far as to say that Peronism is out, Menemism is in."

Neff, Robert. *Business Week.* (★ ½)
Tokyo. Neff continues to provide serviceable beat reporting, keeping his finger on important trends, missing the mark only when he goes overboard on the commentary. Reviewing Shintaro Ishihara's controversial new book, *The Japan that Can Say No: Why Japan Will Be First Among Equals,* in "The American-Basher," 1-21, Neff aims more commentary at Ishihara than at the merit of his work, the review lacking the depth to be of much use. In the succinct trend-spotter, "Industries: Japanese Investors Take a Fast Boat to China," with Lynne Curry 3-11, he informs us China is being targeted for major investment by Japanese blue chip firms, and then he tells us why. We felt he was unaccountably rough on the Japanese, "International Outlook: The Japan that Can Say, 'We're Sorry,' " with Amy Borrus 3-25, and rather than characterizing the post-Gulf War "self-examination" as an important national debate, he sees it as a "bout of national self-criticism [that] may jolt leaders out of their habitual inertia." Any genuine insight here is undermined. He provides a light but interesting look at how U.S. companies in Japan are learning to woo young, bright Japanese men and women away from aggressive recruiters at Japanese companies in "International Business: When in Japan, Recruit as the Japanese Do — Aggressively," 6-24. He is far too editorial in tone in "Japan's Small, Smoke-Filled Room," 8-26, a condescending look at the Japanese political system: ". . .the murky, manipulative world of LDP factions, the quintessence of back-room politics." He charts how North and South Korea, little by little, are forging economic ties, "International Outlook: Asia's Next Powerhouse: An All-But-Unified Korea?" co-written by Laxmi Nakarmi 10-14, compact, but nothing especially new here.

Neilan, Ed. *The Washington Times.* (★ ½)
Tokyo. An old hand in these parts, Neilan excels at capturing the role Japan plays on the world stage, but too often this year seems to be using a Cold War prism, and important Japanese domestic stories, such as the scandal in the financial market, are generally neglected. In "Japan Said to Mull Postwar Aid for Iraq," 2-18, he alertly hooks the story around the possibility that

Moscow is apparently drawing Japan into its diplomatic efforts to end the war, quoting one Western diplomat: "[Moscow] might even be seen as being generous with Japan's money." He provides an interesting footnote as the ground war gets underway, "Japanese Labels Plaster Iraq," 2-25, imaginatively conveying the mixed emotions Japanese businessmen are feeling as Iraq and Kuwait — two countries they have invested heavily in — get hammered. In "Tokyo Views Visit by Gorbachev in April as a Yawner," 3-11, he delivers a good read on the mood of the Japanese public and diplomatic expectations as the once-ballyhooed Gorbachev visit approaches. Analyzing the consequences of Shanghai Mayor Zhu Rongli's promotion to Vice Premier in "Zhu Could Tip Balance, Ties Toward U.S." 4-4, he resourcefully draws on diplomatic sources who see an advantage going to the reformers. He provides some good data on Japanese assessments of Soviet naval strength in the region in "Japan Says Soviets Keep Formidable Force in Pacific," 7-29, but fails to provide any larger geopolitical context. Writing perceptively on the still-raw wounds in U.S.-Japanese relations 50 years after Pearl Harbor, "Tokyo Hints U.S. Equally at Fault for WW II Start," 8-19, he notes recent statements that Washington and Tokyo both bear guilt for the war are symptomatic of a new Japanese attitude: "Many Japanese are convinced that Japan should go into the 21st century as a forceful political player, commensurate with its economic power." He reports from the Soviet Pacific rim, "Vladivostok Tires of Waiting for Moscow, Looks to Future," 9-23, on how officials there are eager to introduce a market economy to the port city and begin economic development, a quick sketch that still manages to pack a lot of information. In "Japan Bridges Language Barrier," 10-12, he explains why the incoming Prime Minister Kiichi Miyazawa's fluency in English is a double-edged sword.

Newman, Barry. *The Wall Street Journal.* (★)
London, covering Eastern Europe. Newman keeps abreast of important stories and developments in the region, especially Poland, but his reports consistently lack the familiarity with the subject matter that can only come by going beyond superficial impressionism to in-depth examination. In "Albanians Awake, Fitfully, From a Kind of National Coma," 3-11, we venture into Albania as that country reemerges from the communist time-warp and becomes reacquainted with political and religious freedom. A quick in-and-out look, there is little on the Albanian economy. He is a bit better on the economic aspects of the Bulgarian story, "Broken Crutch: These Days, Bulgaria Longs for Its Old Ties to the Soviet Union," 4-30, as that Eastern bloc loyalist struggles with the loss of its commercial ties to Moscow: "What Bulgaria wants most. . .is a new Big Brother." He provides the secular perspective on the Catholic Church's efforts to implement "constitutional 'cooperation' " between church and state in Poland, "Catholic Church's Role Is Issue in Poland," 5-31, but the report suffers from lack of nuance. "For economists and politicians working to set market forces free in Poland, [the pope's recent encyclical] doesn't sound like a benediction." In "Mammoths May Be Extinct, But They Save the Elephants," 7-16, he produces a well-done feature story on how mammoth tusks are filling the market demand for ivory now that elephants are a protected species. In the sobering "Troubling Omen: Poland's Shaky Switch to a Free Market Is a Warning for Soviets," 9-18, he uses the plight of the Polish bus company Autoban as a model of the economic dilemma Poland's democracy faces, leaving readers to ponder "what will the new leaders just east of here be thinking when their revolution is two years old?" In "Voters in Poland Give No One Party a Dominant Role," 10-28, he does little to connect the election results to the Poles' opinion on the struggling economy, only attributing the low turnout to pre-election polls suggesting confusion over the high number of parties and "apathy in a dismal economic climate."

Noble, Kenneth B. *The New York Times.* (★)
Abidjan. Noble can pen feature articles as well as anyone, but his efforts at serious stories frequently fall short, usually due to a faulty analytical model too often tied to IMF policy prescriptions. In "The Once-Mighty Cast Out: Liberia's Fallen Tribe," 1-8, he brings home a budding human tragedy in the wake of the overthrow of the Doe regime, the retribution the Gio and Mano tribes are extracting on the members of Doe's tribe, the Krahn. Noble's Angola

coverage was competent, as in "As Angola Turns to West, Cubans Are Resentful," 4-9, where he fully updates us on the waning influence of the Cubans, as Angola discards Marxist-Leninist ideology. Writing on the upcoming elections in the serviceable "Angola's New War," 6-10, he observes that "Although the Government's political offensive has had some success, judging by the crowds at its rallies last week, the overall effort seems to be mired in popular skepticism." He can't quite measure up to the task of delivering the major story in Ghana this year, that nation's failure as an IMF "showcase for free-market reform," in "Ghana, After Hard-Won Growth, Is Faltering," 6-24. He makes little effort to determine why the collapse of economic growth occurred, settling for the standard IMF line that "the problem is not with their prescriptions but with the failure of Ghana to follow through on its commitments." In his best feature of the year, "A Country Is Plucked Clean, and the Feathers Fly," 7-24, he imaginatively reports on a ponzi scheme in Zaire which fleeced many people of their life savings, and which is rocking the government of President Mobutu Sese Seko. In "Zaire Coalition Ends 26 Years of Dictatorship," 9-30, he efficiently covers both the growing chaos in Kinshasa and the turbulent history of the Mobutu regime. Covering the chaos touched off by a soldiers' revolt in the Zairian capital, "In Zaire, Mounting Panic Amid Economic Chaos," 11-4, he routinely notes that the 3000 percent inflation rate can be traced to the huge budget deficit "that developed after the government abandoned an economic recovery program devised by the International Monetary Fund in early 1990 and increased spending."

Ottaway, David B. *The Washington Post.* (★ ★)
Johannesburg. Ottaway came into his own during his second year in South Africa, consistently delivering reports and analytics that revealed the nuances of the evolving political scene. In "Reform Called Incomplete in South Africa," 2-11, he does a solid job of dissecting official pronouncements and intentions as he analyzes President F.W. de Klerk's proposal to repeal several basic apartheid laws. In the concise update "ANC Ponders Winnie Mandela's Fate," 3-10, he reports that "After its initial close association with her cause, the ANC is discreetly distancing itself from the trial, trying to move out of range of potential fallout." Dispatched to Riyadh as the war ended, he sharply portrays the growing willingness of the Gulf states to play hard ball with Jordan and Yasir Arafat in "Gulf States: 'No Forgiveness' for Iraq's Backers," 4-1, while the incisive "Saudi Liberals See Reforms Unlikely," 4-16, is pessimistic on the chance for reforms in Saudi Arabia now that the war has ended. Returning to South Africa he produced "ANC vs. Inkatha: Anatomy of a Slaughter," 5-2, an exceptional ground-level report on a bloody clash between ANC and Inkatha supporters at a worker's hostel in Dobsonville, showing us the human story behind the mind-numbing statistics. He expertly recounts the backstage superpower diplomacy which resulted in the Angolan peace accord in "Milestone in Superpower Cooperation," 6-1. In the comprehensive "ANC Leadership Shuffle Leads to Focused, Aggressive Agenda," 7-9, he covers both sides of the story, noting that while de Klerk now has an organization he can deal with, the ANC sees the negotiations as, "in its own words, the next 'terrain of struggle.' " He is authoritative in "De Klerk Put at Risk," 7-24, on the crisis de Klerk faces by the revelations that the government has been secretly funding the Inkatha Freedom Party. In the wrenching, "In South Africa's Townships, the Killings Continue," 10-25, he reports from one township outside of Johannesburg where "the 'national peace accord' remains a pious wish on paper, yet another victim of relentless factional feuding, government helplessness or indifference, and bureaucratic delays on all sides."

Ozanne, Julian. *Financial Times.* (★ ★ ★)
Nairobi. It was a year of major upheaval on the African continent, and the intrepid Ozanne, shot at, wounded, imprisoned, and expelled throughout the region, was there to chronicle it all. His reports lingered in the mind, long after the headlines had faded. He pens a non-sentimental obituary for the Barre government in "Death Throes Grip Somali's Bankrupt Regime," 1-3, noting that Barre is bequeathing his country "a blood-stained legacy that any future administration will find hard to overcome." He follows up with "Suffering and Betrayal in Mogadishu," 4-16, superbly conveying the growing despair and chaos in the Somalian capital

as the people feel the international community has abandoned them. One quote, "If we were in the Gulf it would be different but this is Africa. Nobody cares," could serve as an epitaph for the continent. His masterful report on man-made obstacles to relief efforts in the Horn of Africa, "Civil War and Nightmare Logistics Plague Valiant Relief Effort," 5-11/12, is calculated to enrage us, and it does: "Yet at the end of this tale of woe, the most remarkable thing is the fact that most of the aid eventually gets through." Covering the downfall of the Mengistu regime, "Rebel Victories Force Ethiopian President to Quit, Flee Country," 5-22, he discloses that the U.S. had worked through the Zimbabweans to arrange Mengistu's departure, a key detail we didn't see reported elsewhere. In "Mengistu's Flight Brings Opportunity for Rebuilding," 5-22, he writes knowingly on Mengistu's 14-year reign in Ethiopia and strikes an optimistic note at the end, his expertise adding considerable weight to a conclusion that would sound false if made by others. With the advent of autumn came a new crisis, "Mobutu's End Game," 9-5, and he solidly places the blame for the economic crisis in Africa's second largest country squarely on the shoulders of President Mobutu. The historically informed "Zaire Hovers on Brink of Disintegration," 9-30, concentrates on Western efforts to restore stability: "The events are all reminiscent of a slightly distant past in the former Belgian Congo which many people hoped were buried in the history books."

Parks, Michael. *Los Angeles Times.* (★ ★ ½)
Moscow. Parks once again was a meticulous observer of the political and economic weathervanes at the top of the Kremlin, gauging the slightest shift in wind direction as gale forces moved in. He was an alert chronicler of the evolving Gorbachev-Yeltsin relationship, in such topnotch reports as "Gorbachev Foils Ouster Bid, Gets Yeltsin Backing," 4-25, and "Confidence Vote Won by Angry Gorbachev," 4-26. In the post-coup analytic "There's a New Sheriff in Town — and His Name is Boris Yeltsin," 8-23, he dramatically captures how the balance of power has shifted to the Russian President and what it portends for the country. Overall, however, his coup coverage was disappointing, as in "Back to the Past — But How?" 8-20, where he proclaims victory for the coup literally hours before its collapse, while "Yeltsin Backers Willing to Put Lives on the Line," 8-21, uses many phrases to describe Yeltsin except Russian nationalist, the one Yeltsin himself uses. Parks's coverage the rest of the year was generally fine, and in "Coal Strike to Force Closures in Other Industries, Soviets Warn Miners," 3-25, he provides a well-researched update of the catastrophic state of the Soviet economy's production process. Surveying Moscow's hopes for a "Grand Bargain" with the West in "Gorbachev Ready to Hand West a Bill for Perestroika," 6-9, he pointedly observes that Soviet plans for reform remain vague and Soviet threats of what will happen if the aid doesn't come sound empty. Superbly analyzing the growing crisis of confidence two months after the coup attempt, "Another Soviet Coup Likely and — Some Say — Welcome," 10-21, he writes that commentators are speculating that the plotters this time would be second-echelon members of the military, KGB and party, who feel it necessary to "consolidate" the gains made by *perestroika* while restoring political and economic stability. In "Moscow Seeks New Prestige as Superpower of Peacemakers," 11-5, he is perceptive on how Moscow's involvement in the Madrid peace conference is motivated partly by its desire to carve out a new role for itself as an international mediator, and partly to keep a centralized grip on foreign policy before the republics start having foreign policies of their own.

Parmelee, Jennifer. *The Washington Post.* (★ ★)
Addis Ababa. Transferring from Rome, Parmelee covered the last days of Ethiopia's civil war, and its aftermath, in richly-detailed reports that often left the reader feeling both moved and fully informed on events in that beleaguered country. In "Ethiopian Reform May Be Too Little, Too Late," 3-24, she is comprehensive on the efforts of the Mengistu regime to move away from Marxist-Leninism as the rebels close in: "Political reform. . .has remained mired at the rhetorical stage, despite the symbolic removal of Marxist icons from public places." She alertly observes in "Ethiopia Asks U.S. Help to Get Rebels to Peace Table," 5-3, that "The TPLF's 'true colors' remain opaque." She provides a haunting dispatch from Harerge Province in Ethiopia, where the civil war is preventing relief from reaching starvation victims in "Ethiopians Face 'Point of

No Return,' " 5-16. Her report on Mengistu's fall from power, "Ethiopian President Flees Country; New Leader Said to Seek Cease-Fire," 5-22, is thorough, but saves the details of Mengistu's flight into exile until the end, with Parmelee writing that "There was no great public outpouring of joy or dancing in the streets over the departure of Mengistu, who was widely despised." In the colorful "Ethiopians Taking First Steps Toward Creating a Democracy," 7-1, she reports on the elections of "Peace and Stability Commissions" to rule at the local level until a transitional government is established at the national level, documenting how "Commission members are chosen, often by a seemingly incongruous mix of insider politics and boisterous public debate." She provides an informative sketch of the problems an exhausted Eritrea faces in "After 30 Years of War, Eritrea Is Rebuilding," 7-31. She scores an interview with transitional government leader Meles Venawi, "Democracy and Dispute in Ethiopia," 10-22, providing a solid snapshot of the political situation at the moment. In "Kuwaiti Emir Snuffs Out Last Iraqi-Lit Oil Fire," 11-7, she artfully captures the ceremony to mark the end of the oil field fires set by the retreating Iraqis, where a "huge pastry was flambeed by a simulated oil well fire in the middle," while also discussing the outstanding issues which still remain.

Peel, Quentin. *Financial Times.* (★ ★ ★)
Bonn. Writing as sharp as ever, Peel isn't yet displaying the singular insights into political economy here that he showed in his past reporting from Moscow, but he has quickly become our journalist of choice on the German scene due to the vast amount of information he packages in his reports. In "Two Sides of a Coin to German Monetary Union," 7-26, he straightforwardly passes on the findings of OECD on the first year of German economic unity. His coverage of the first anniversary of unification was well written, if conventional in outlook, "After Joy the Angst," 10-3, where he contends that while west Germany's wealth should pull the country through, "that is certainly part of the problem, as well as the solution." In "Racist Attacks Mar German Unity Anniversary," 10-4, he plays up the racist angle, though he admits it to be "isolated." Much of Peel's German coverage was informed by the economic findings forecasting ten percent recovery in the east German economy in 1992 but stressing "that this cannot be seen as the beginning of a sustained upswing," which he reported in depth in "German 'Wise Men' See No Rising Star in East," 10-22. He aims his dry wit at Kohl's aspirations to international statesmanship while Germany grapples with major domestic crises in "Autumn of Discontent," 10-24, stating that "Chancellor Kohl behaves ever more as a law unto himself." In the comprehensive "First Year Hangover," 10-28, he warns that while east Germany remains in danger of relying on permanent handouts from Bonn, Germany remains committed to Western European integration and is not interested in turning into the colossus of the east — for now. Peel explores this topic further in the excellent, "Uneasy Giant Astride Europe's Political Fault Line," 10-28. Impressive Soviet efforts, from earlier in the year, include "Soviet Union Through the Looking Glass," 2-18, an insightful profile of new Soviet Prime Minister Valentin Pavlov, whose "first actions suggest that he is. . .quite ready to act like a bull in a china shop," and his valedictory, "Mutiny Aboard the Ship of State," 4-12, in which he masterfully sums up the current Soviet impasse, noting that while the Soviet people desperately want change in their governing structures, "they want to do it without plunging into the economic unknown."

Perlez, Jane. *The New York Times.* (★ ★)
Nairobi. Perlez brought the fine writing and sharp reporting skills that have always been prominent in her feature work to her straight news stories this year. We were particularly impressed by her coverage of the aftermath of the Ethiopian civil war. She provides a Dickensian look at abandoned Kenyan children prostituting themselves on the mean streets of Nairobi in "Nairobi Street Children Play Games of Despair," 1-2. We receive a solid report on the challenge being presented to the Moi regime by Kenyan attorneys with "In Kenya, The Lawyers Lead the Call for Freedom," 3-10. In the memorable "2 Months After Ousting Despot, Somalia Faces Life as an Abandoned Pawn," 4-4, she evokes a country disintegrating in intertribal warfare. She produces a serviceable, if rushed, survey of Lieut. Col. Mengistu Haile Mariam's turbulent reign in "Ethiopian Ruled Ruthlessly, Killing Colleagues and Shedding Alliances," 5-22, while her

rounded profile of Tigre People's Liberation Front leader Meles Zenawi, "A Hard-Line Marxist Who Mellowed," 5-30, passes along Washington's estimation of the victorious rebel. She scores a scoop in "After 3-Decade War in Ethiopia, Eritrean Finds Victory Is Somber," 6-10, accompanying rebel chief Isaias Afwerki on his subdued homecoming to a war-impoverished land, while in "Pupil of G.I.'s Does Well, as a Rebel," 6-27, she fills us in on Eritrean guerrilla chief of staff Sephat Ephrem, enabling us to understand how the rebels were able to perservere and finally triumph. She artfully captures the chaotic demobilization of the largest army in black Africa, "Ethiopia Troops Left in Misery After Last War," 7-22, while in "Kenyans Do Some Soul-Searching After the Rape of 71 Schoolgirls," 7-29, she places the recent mass rape and killing of schoolgirls in cultural context, admirably staying in control of her material. In "Kenya's President Is Tightening His Grip," 10-6, she fully updates us on Moi's intention to maintain his authoritarian ways. She was one of the few reporters covering the change of government in Zambia who actually filled in the blanks on labor leader Frederick Chiluba and what to expect from his administration, "With Pride Now and Economic Pain Ahead, Zambia Swears In New Leader," 11-3.

Pletka, Danielle. *Insight.* (★ ½)
Pletka is able to produce well-researched reports that offer a wealth of information, though some tighter editing would enable her to get her points across more clearly and concisely. In "Like Sand, Democracy Slips Through Arab Peoples' Hands," 12-24-90/1-7-91, she offers a two-dimensional look at the general lack of democracy in the Arab world, with too many overgeneralizations such as "More inimical to democracy than the religious mania is enduring tribalism," and "Ironically, it may be Saddam who frightens the Arab world out of the 13th century." She searches out all the nuances of Iranian diplomacy during the Gulf War, "Iran May Win Big by Staying on the Sidelines," 2-4, while displaying a firm grasp on regional diplomacy, "An Arab Security Blanket," 4-1. Her cover story on apparent Saudi backtracking from commitments made during the Gulf War, "The Saudis in Retreat," 6-24, starts out like an indictment of Saudi duplicity, but by the end she unexpectedly switches gears and writes that the Saudis are coming around anyway: "Both sides are regrouping and there is still hope for progress, but at a more modest and stately pace, in keeping with Saudi tradition and domestic constraints." An in-depth report on the up-and-comers in Israel's Likud Party, "The Heirs Apparent: Likud's Princes," 7-15, is marred by lines like "With Meridor too nice, and Olmert too not nice, only Bibi and Benny are left to fight for the ermine robe." She is solid on Hafez al-Assad and the country he keeps squarely under his thumb in "Under the Iron Fist: Inside Assad's Syria," 8-5. She provides the best backgrounder we saw anywhere on the loan guarantees at the heart of the U.S.-Israeli dispute, "A $10 Billion Missing Link," 9-23, paying as much attention to OMB accounting practices as Jewish settlements.

Porter, Janet. *The Journal of Commerce.* (★ ★)
Chief European correspondent. Porter is a steady producer of data-filled reports and concise analysis on European ports, charter markets, and other subjects of direct interest to *JOC* readers. General readers, however, might find her material too tough to slog through. In "Some Ship Lines Decide to Divert From Suez Canal," 1-22, she is comprehensive on how the international shipping trade is coping with the Persian Gulf War. In the "Europe View" column, "Sweden's Role in a New Europe," 3-5, she is sharp and clear on how and why the Social Democratic Party is finally dropping its ostensible policy of neutrality and applying for membership in the EC: "For many Swedes, the whole question of neutrality has long been a farce." While she has all the reasons why the Norwegian shipping industry is opposing a tax reform plan, "Norway Shippers to Lobby Against Tax Proposals," 4-15, a quote from a government defender of the program would have added some balance. Her familiarity with the European shipping industry and its efforts to weather the stormy seas of international trade regulation is exhibited in such dispatches as "Hamburg-Sud Deal Likely to Simplify Conference Tariffs," 5-28, which she places in the context of upcoming expiration on the present pooling system agreed to by European and Latin American freight conferences, and "Tanker Owners Float Idea for US

Pollution Fund," 6-12, in which she reports that the Norwegian Shipowner's Association feels that U.S. pollution liability claims include unlimited liability provisions that are "dangerous and intolerable." In an otherwise thorough "Smooth Sailing for Carriers," 8-21, she seems to take industry predictions of a rosy future at face value. In "Trade Documents to Be Released From BCCI Branches in Britain," 7-29, she is concise yet comprehensive on the ramifications for the world's shipping industry in the closure of BCCI by the British Government: "The bank's closure has seriously disrupted international trade, with local ship agents unable to release cargoes without proof of payment or title to the goods." In "Major Merger Opens Door for Big Shake-up at Sea," 9-23, she is knowledgeable on Cunard Ellerman's corporate strategy.

Powell, Bill. *Newsweek.* (★)
Tokyo. While Powell has continued to tone down his "Asian challenge" (read: threat) views, his reports continue to lack any real subtlety, and he seems to be losing his detachment, apparently approaching burn-out on this increasingly complex beat. In "Japan's Bursting Bubble," 4-1, we fail to learn if the land-price bubble may or may not go bust, and the linkage to some of the world's highest real estate value is conventional and tenuous. He duly reports Lee Iacocca's pleas for restrictions on Japanese automobiles, "Detroit Pleads Its Case," with Rich Thomas and Frank Washington 4-8, but he is not optimistic about Detroit's chances to compete. In "Japan: All in the Family," and Rich Thomas 6-10, he seems to buy into the myths surrounding interrelated Japanese business groups, or *keiretsu.* He is early on the worries over the 50th anniversary of the bombing of Pearl Harbor, "A Date That Will Live in Anxiety," 7-1, though most Tokyo correspondents did not pick up on this until August with the anniversary of the Hiroshima and Nagasaki bombings, or later. It is a case of "Asian challenge" redux in "Sayonara, America," and Peter McKillop 8-19, on the Japanese spurt of investment in Southeast Asia, traditionally a U.S. economic and investment stronghold. He provides much sound and fury on the scandals taking shape in the Tokyo financial market, "Is the Game Rigged?" with Joshua Hammer and Joanna Stone 9-30, but with few details on what actually happened: "Guaranteeing returns is the financial equivalent of putting a virus in a software program: the system doesn't work the way it's supposed to, and ultimately it may crash."

Powers, Charles T. *Los Angeles Times.* (★ ★)
Warsaw. We wish Powers would appear more frequently, his reports and analytics often containing original insights on the continuing transformation of Poland we don't see elsewhere. In the lively "Soviets Flock West to Poland, Eager to Wheel and Deal," 4-13, he reports on the peculiar entrepreneurial allure that Warsaw presents "to hundreds of thousands of Soviets flocking to Poland to trade cheap Soviet goods for hard currency and Western electronics, packing adventure and tidy profits into every trip." We learn how the Polish leadership is dealing with the issue of anti-Semitism "head-on" in the well-written, "Poland's Leaders Tackle Festering Anti-Semitism," 4-23. He provides good details on the growing opposition to the Balcerowicz plan from the Center Alliance, "In Poland's Economic Path — Potholes," 5-17, writing that the center-right political grouping wants "to see the zloty devalued to help boost imports." In "A Much-Changed Poland Awaits Pope," 6-1, he fully outlines the changes in Poland since Pope John Paul II's last visit in 1987, sensitive to the causes behind the church's decline: "Its critics say the church has begun to meddle too much in the schools, the bedroom and politics, and has been acting as though it were calling in its markers for its years of serving as a refuge for the political opposition and a haven of freedom throughout the long years of totalitarian rule." He provides a knowledgeable analysis of the burden on Polish industry of its traditional dependence exclusively on Soviet markets in "Soviet Belt-Tightening Puts Squeeze on Polish Industry," 6-25. He excels at vignettes that picture life in the new Poland better than most, as in "Jerzy Urban Happily Offends Most Everyone," 7-9, where he captures the irony inherent in the story of a former communist spokesman who is now peddling pornography, while "Life in the Dorm at the School of Hard Knocks," 7-16, is a colorful slice-of-life as experienced by working-class Poles. He finds a humorous side to Poland's first multimillion dollar free market swindle in "3 Whiz Kids Take Poland's Bankers for a Costly Ride," 8-14.

Prokesch, Steven. *The New York Times.* (★ ★ ½)
London. One of the *NYT*'s swingmen for Europe, Prokesch can produce serviceable dispatches on day-to-day events, but he's at his best when covering economic topics, such as the European auto market or the British financial community. In the knowledgeable, if statistics-laden, "In Europe, Too, Auto Sales Sag," 4-2, he reports that despite optimism over European unification and hopes for the Eastern European market: "Competition, capacity expansions and mounting Japanese ambitions in Europe could prevent the Big Six automakers from enjoying the benefits of a growing market." He effectively sets the scene for the first major talks in 15 years between Catholic nationalists and Protestant unionists in "Ulster Talks Open on a Divisive Note," 5-1, deftly laying out the issues dividing the two sides and the differences within the two camps. He fully updates us on how Volvo is aiming for the upscale car market in the U.S., while entering into joint ventures in Europe, "Volvo Searching Hard for Relief," 6-12, despite bitter French opposition to Japanese expansion into western Europe. He is informative on the troubles of the world-famous insurance company, "Losses Cause Distress for Lloyd's of London," 6-27, as it struggles to deal with mounting losses stemming from a remarkable series of disasters in 1988. In "Seized Bank Was Used by Terrorists," 7-22, he passes along the disclosure in *The Sunday Times of London* that British intelligence had learned that international arms dealers and terrorists such as Abu Nidal had accounts at BCCI, but the article goes no deeper than the headline. He artfully captures the unhappiness of the Swedish electorate, "Discontent in Egalitarian Sweden Threatens Socialists in Vote Today," 9-15, documenting that the government is particularly unpopular among the young: "It's impossible to make any money. The Social Democrats want everybody to be poor together." In "Maxwell Family Sees No Financial Upheaval," 11-7, he supplies good details on the business fallout from Robert Maxwell's death, reporting that while Kevin Maxwell is offering assurances on Maxwell Communications debt structuring and divestiture plans, "investor jitters" are evident.

Protzman, Ferdinand. *The New York Times.* (★ ½)
Bonn. Protzman provides straightforward coverage of the German economic and business scene, at times digging deep into a topic, at other times just skimming the surface. His contribution to a three-part series on "Eastern Germany in Despair," "Privatization in Eastern Germany Is Mired in a Collapsing Economy," 3-12, is the best of the lot, Protzman comprehensive on the difficulties the German government agency overseeing privatization is encountering. He provides a colorful report on the only major corporation thus far to push into east Germany, "Coke's Splash in Eastern Germany," 5-3, writing that Coca-Cola is a dead certainty to put the two existing east German brands out of business, "for reasons all too evident. . .the drinks sometimes contain unwanted surprises, like coke-embalmed flies." In "Germany Rolls Out Its Fast Train," 5-30, he writes engagingly on the formal introduction of Germany's new high-speed train service, noting that German President Richard von Weizsacker's train was fifteen minutes late. He is superficial on the circumstances surrounding Karl Otto Poehl's resignation as president of the Bundesbank in "Poehl, as Expected, Says He Will Quit Bank Post," 5-17, accepting at face value Poehl's statement that "My departure is not a demonstrative act or a sign of resignation, but is part of my longer-term life plan." We wanted more on the tensions between Poehl and the Kohl Government over the economic costs of German unity. He does address those costs in "A Cost of German Unity," 6-12, a succinct analysis of Germany's first trade deficit which Protzman, marshaling his facts, ties to the costs of unification. In the comprehensive "Greetings from Fortress Germany," 8-18, he offers the most detailed and enlightening report we saw anywhere on the impressive headway Toys 'R' Us has made in overseas markets, covering "both the lure and cold realities of the German market." We get an illuminating snapshot of the ramifications of the failed Soviet coup attempt on a Red Army unit stationed in Potsdam in "Soviet Troops in Germany Say They're 'Still in the Same Army,' " 9-3. He revisits one east German family a year after reunification, "Introducing Capitalism, Hard Work and Bananas," 10-4, an anecdotal report that does little to advance our understanding of the on-going east German story.

Randal, Jonathan C. *The Washington Post.* (★ ★ ★)
Middle East. Although he only put in half a year, Randal's pacesetting coverage of the Kurdish uprising helped break that tragic story to the world, and we're including him for that reason. In "U.S. Use of Bases Poses Risk for Turkey," 1-21, he is thorough on the geostrategic and domestic political factors surrounding President Turgut Ozal's decision. His coverage of the Kurdish uprising, from promising start to tragic end, was state-of-the-art, Randal poetically conveying the roller coaster fortunes of the Kurds, while never losing his professional detachment. He is excellent on successful Kurdish tactics to break the spirit of the Iraqi army in "Kurdish Uprising Aided by Clandestine Army Contacts," 3-23, and "Kurds Seize Iraqi Base and Work to Demoralize Saddam's Army," 3-28. In the 10 Best selection, "Kurds' Spring of Hope Collapses Amid Feelings of Betrayal," 4-3, he covers the Kurdish retreat into the mountains following the crushing of their revolt, superbly outlining the fatal mistakes by their leaders. Reporting vividly from a Kurdish refugee camp in Iran, "Misery As Far as Eye Can See," 4-16, he observes that "Iranians here seemed genuinely astounded by the lack of international relief aid." Later in the spring, he journeyed to Baghdad and captured several key stories on the margin, "Iraq Caught in Sanctions Pickle," 5-14, disclosing that international relief agencies are beginning to question the West's policy of maintaining tight sanctions on oil-rich Iraq "in a world full of genuinely poverty-stricken nations," and "Iraqis' Morale Ebbs as Sanctions, Saddam Persist," 6-1, ably documenting how Saddam's "fading aura of untouchability" is being matched by a public mood of "resignation and apathy." Analyzing the success of the Islamic Salvation Front in destabilizing the government in the multidimensional "Algeria Finds No Peace After Gulf War's End," 6-9, he probes both the economic and societal causes behind the unrest, contending that "arguably more damaging to the government [than economic mismanagement] was its persistent inability to energize a society profoundly influenced by the West."

Reid, T.R. *The Washington Post.* (★ ★)
Tokyo. Reid demonstrates a perceptive grasp of contemporary Japanese political and cultural issues in his dispatches, although tight space often prevents him from exploring events in substantive detail. He offers a brief, but informative, survey of the Japanese media's view of the post-war role of both Japan and the U.S. in "Some Japanese Praise, Others Assail New U.S. Image," 3-13. His analysis of the Gorbachev-Kaifu summit, "Gorbachev, Kaifu Both Winners at Summit," 4-21, is elevated by his grasp of Japanese history. He is sharp on what the political resurrection of such Japanese LDP warhorses as Yasuhiro Nakasone, Noboru Takeshita, Michio Watanabe and Kiichi Miyazawa says about the current state of Japanese politics, "Old-Line Leaders Try Comebacks in Japan," 5-20: "The reemergence of the tainted leaders to positions of influence reflects the power vacuum afflicting all of Japan's major parties. The old names are coming back to the fore because nobody else has emerged — either in the LDP or the opposition parties — to take their place." In the refreshing "Japan-Basking: New Pacific Era?" 6-16, he cuts through the current anti-Japan hysteria in the U.S. to argue that "In almost every substantive area, U.S.-Japan relations right now are in excellent shape — considerably healthier, in fact, than America's relations with many other allies." Covering the annual observance of the end of World War II, "Japan Recalls WWII Surrender," 8-16, he probes beneath the surface to find that this year, more than ever before, the Japanese are concentrating on their responsibility for the conflict: "This new focus on Japan's decision to attack the United States is driven largely by the national worry about America's reaction to the Pearl Harbor anniversary this December." Reporting on Toshiki Kaifu's fall from political grace, "Japanese Ruling Party Dumps Kaifu as Premier," 10-5, he provides details on the immediate setbacks which led to his resignation, while striking a proper cynical tone on LDP power politics — "As Kaifu learned the hard way today, when the public and the political establishment clash in Japan, the latter generally prevails."

Reier, Sharon. *FW.* (★ ★ ★)
Europe, based in Amsterdam. We were impressed by how quickly Reier distinguished herself on this important beat, displaying a rare talent for taking a company profile and developing it into political-economic reportage. For instance, "Gas Goliath," 1-22, expertly ties in all the regulatory and financial pressures shaping British Gas's controversial bid to become a global player, while "A Switch in Time," 2-5, is superb on how L.M. Ericsson is riding out the waves of the cellular phone industry. In "Dutch Takeover Treats?" 3-5, her contribution to an 11-article international cover story which was nominated as a whole for our 10 Best section, she provides an outstanding examination of some of the crucial battles that are being fought as the EC struggles toward integration, from the perspective of Dutch companies which have built in airtight "technical barriers" to deter takeovers. She provides an intriguing footnote to the on-going Soviet story, "Gorby's Grocery Gridlock," 4-2, profiling Axel Johnson AB, Sweden's leading importer of fruit, vegetables and houseplants, who has turned down an offer from the mayor of Moscow to run the city's food distribution system. Reier's superior profile of Guinness, "Getting Scotch Off the Rocks," 8-6, was marred only by the accompanying art work. In "Europe's CEO of the Year: 'Anybody Can Do This,' " 10-15, she paints a vivid portrait of James Hanson, CEO of the highly successful Hanson Plc., that conveys Hanson's commitment to the shareholder and to entrepreneurial capitalism in its purest form: "Like many of the wheeler-dealers of the 1980s, Lord Hanson's concept is to unleash the entrepreneurial talents he believes lie untapped beneath the bureaucracy of top management."

Remnick, David. *The Washington Post.* (★ ★ ★)
In his final year in Moscow, Remnick's coverage had a Tolstoyan touch, as he vividly portrayed both leaders and common people caught up in the forces of history, trying to bend those forces to their own will. He is now Edward R. Murrow Fellow at the Council on Foreign Relations. In the remarkably prescient "For Gorbachev, It's Back to Facing Intractable Problems," 8-2, he predicts who would support a coup attempt, and why it would most likely fail. His coup-week coverage was nominated for our 10 Best category. He certainly captures the drama of the moment outside the Russian parliament building, "Crisis Jolts Masses Out of Passivity and Onto Moscow Streets," 8-21, while "Three Days of Drama, Terror Will Shape the Future," 8-22, accurately predicts Gorbachev's imminent decision to quit as party general secretary and the party all together. In "Embittered Old Guard," 8-28, he provides a valuable update on the status of the remaining hardliners, noting that they might try to "grab up power under the new structures of independent republics," a phenomenon he documents firsthand in "Critics Assail Soviet Georgia's Ruler," 9-18. He was strong all year on the pulse of both the conservatives and the reformers as their fortunes waxed and waned. A 10 Best selection, "The Hard-Liners' Bad Boy Challenges Gorbachev," 2-8, memorably profiles the "black colonel," Lt. Col. Viktor Alksnis, "the angriest public face of an angry movement," while "Leningrad Democrats' Dream Wakes to Communist Reality," 3-24, evokes the troubles Leningrad democrats are facing as they struggle to put reforms into effect. He also produced several outstanding mini-epics on the changes being wrought by *glasnost* and *perestroika,* including "Tremors From Underground," 4-14, on coal mine strikes, and "As Gulag Fades, Warden Is Proud of His Career," 4-28, on a career prison guard. His economic coverage focused on the new businesses and businessmen being created by the move toward a market economy, including the revealing "From Apparatchik to 'Konsooltant,' " 6-3, and the comprehensive three-part series on "Soviet Capitalism: The Wild East,": "Brash New Breed 'Building Empires, Not Evil Ones,' " 7-7; "A New Brand of Corruption," 7-8; and "Socialism on the Run in a Ward of Moscow," 7-9. He was an original.

Revzin, Philip. *The Wall Street Journal.* (★ ½)
Now editor of *The Wall Street Journal/Europe,* Revzin spent his final year as Paris bureau chief penning in-depth reports on European trade issues and informative profiles of EC wanna-bes. He is early and informative on the problems inherent in smoothing out economic differences between EC countries through the Regional Development Fund in "Price of Unity," 12-17-90.

In the delightful "French Bureaucrat Gets His Orders: Make Le Rock Roll," 12-26-90, we learn the French government is subsidizing rock-and-roll. He efficiently assembles the views of east European leaders on the question of aid in "East-West Ties Are Fraying at the Edges," 2-22, the theme of development in the East as a continent-wide concern coming through. Reporting from Turkey, he interviews President Turgut Ozal, "Morning After: Turkey Waits in Vain for the Big Payoff From Gulf War Stance," 4-17, providing vivid detail on that country's hangover from Desert Storm. In his best report of the year, "Hardy Weed: EC's Farm Subsidies That Imperil Trade Have Deep Roots," 5-17, he visits two French farms, one large, one small, to provide ground-level insight on the EC's dispute with the outside world over a free-trade agreement, finds that the farmers are prepared to defend their way of life to the end: "They complain that the U.S. is asking for immediate dismantling of a salvageable system rather than gradual reform and is ignoring European geography, history and economics in order to impose on it a flawed American system." We get an adequate sketch of growing trade friction between the U.S. and Europe in "Euro-Muscle: A New Era Is at Hand in Global Competition: U.S. vs. United Europe," and Peter Truell 7-15, with Truell and Revzin offering French Prime Minister Edith Cresson as the voice of the new, hardline continent. In the informative "Moroccan King Envisions Mideast Peace," 9-23, he finds King Hassan II encouraged by President Bush's peace initiative and optimistic on his plans to increase Morocco's economic ties to the developed world, even to the extent of joining the EC: "If we're gentlemen, well-raised, and pay our debts, why shouldn't we join the club?"

Riding, Alan. *The New York Times.* (★ ½)
Paris. Riding's beat seems to encompass European political and cultural trends, and when a topic interests him he can produce an engaging, informative report. He offers a comprehensive look at France's efforts to arrange a diplomatic solution to the Gulf crisis in "French Maneuvering: Taking the Lead for Europe," 1-6, while "Europeans Warn Soviet About Aid," 1-14, is objective on the initial EC response to the crackdown in Lithuania. In the fascinating "Vietnam Echo Stuns France: Case of Treachery?" 3-20, he writes on the ghosts stored up by a war crimes case during the French-Indochina war. He produces a serviceable report on the accord reached in Lisbon between UNITA and the Luanda regime in "Angola Agrees on a Cease-Fire With Guerrillas," 5-2. Analyzing the "radical changes" in NATO's military structure, "NATO: Still the Armorer for Europe," 5-30, he shrewdly observes that "The immediate effect of the reorganization is to isolate France, which has taken the lead in trying to promote a new defense capability for the European Community." He is bemused on the political apathy of Spanish youth in "Spanish Politics? The Generation Gap Is Yawning," 6-17, lightweight fare on the consternation this is causing the generation of '68. In "If the Old Party's Dying, There's Life in the Fair," 9-16, he provides an amusing report on the state of the French Communist Party as it holds its annual *Fete de L'Humanite,* noting that "under [Georges] Marchais, the party still seems trapped in the past." His effort on the French political "malaise," "An Era of Change Challenges France's Self-Confidence," 9-29, has an obligatory feel to it. In an otherwise straightforward report on the Cambodian peace accord, "3 Cambodian Factions Sign a U.N.-Enforced Peace Pact; Khmer Rouge Shares Rule," 10-24, he writes at one point: "Cambodia's legacy of suffering dates back to the American incursions of 1970, described at the time as an effort to attack Viet Cong sanctuaries and supply routes. It had the effect of dragging the small country into the larger Indochina war." William Shawcross, call your office.

Robinson, Eugene. *The Washington Post.* (★ ½)
Buenos Aires. South American stories had a tough time making it through the "news hole" this year, but what we saw from Robinson generally illuminated political and cultural events in that region. He is weak on economic policymaking in the region, however. He effectively captures the surrealistic nature of Peruvian President Alberto Fujimori appearing with a captured Shining Path videotape, "Peru's President Narrates Video of Rarely Seen Guerrilla Chief," 2-21. He thoroughly surveys the chaos prevalent in Peru today, "Peruvians Puzzle Over President," 3-23, finding that the enigmatic and highly unpopular Fujimori brought many of his difficulties on

himself through his abrupt policy reversals. In "Venezuela Alarmed by Presence of Colombian Drug Traffickers," 7-7, he is straightforward on the growing scandals which indicate that Venezuelan institutions are being penetrated by Colombian drug traffickers. He provides a serviceable overview of the allegations swirling around the Argentine first family, "Menem Tries to Fend Off Money-Laundering Scandal," 8-14. In the eye-opening "Proposed Military Aid to Peru Treads a Precarious Path," 8-18, he reports on the likely pitfalls of the "intertwining" of U.S. aid to fight drug traffickers with the Peruvian Government's on-going battle with Shining Path, " 'In the Upper Huallaga, you might be talking about the same person,' [one] diplomat said. 'One day he might be wearing his guerrilla hat, and the next day wearing his drug trafficker hat.' " Robinson produced several prodigious efforts on the potentially explosive issues of race and cultural history in the region. In the 10 Best nominated series, "Indians Still Reeling From Their 'Discovery'; Latin Nations Confront 'Reality of Race,' " 6-23, and "Stone Age Crumbling; Modern World Threatens Brazil's Indians," 6-24, he writes in-depth on the ever present conflict between indigenous American tribes in South America and the descendants of European colonialists, while in the authoritative "The Battle for the Soul of Latin America," 11-3, he examines the role Latin America's cultural heritage from Portuguese and Spanish colonialism has played in the region's political and economic development, or lack of development: "The issues involved are abstract, complex and often controversial."

Robinson, Linda. *U.S.News & World Report.* (★)
Latin America. Robinson provides generally balanced, if unspectacular, coverage of this troubled region, though she seems capable of the objective analysis which would add heft to her reports. Her look at the year ahead for Cuba, "Fidel Castro's Last Battle," 12-31-90/1-7-91, contains little new, although she mentions that the Cuban American National Foundation, "the powerful focus of anti-Castro opposition in the U.S.," has pledged that any post-Castro regime will honor all outstanding debts to Moscow. Her thoughtful review of Stephen Kinzer's *Blood of Brothers: Life and War in Nicaragua,* "The Sandinista Decade," *The New York Times Book Review,* 4-7, notes that while the book raises the question of whether or not the Sandinista regime might have been more moderate if not for the U.S.-sponsored war, "...Mr. Kinzer's own critique of what he calls the regime's 'colossal misjudgments' suggests that the Sandinistas' policies were not just tactical responses to outside aggression but reflections of their deep political convictions." Updating us on the Salvadoran civil war, "Light at the End of the Tunnel?" 5-6, she scores an interview with FMLN leader Joaquin Villalobos, who has readjusted his rhetoric to the new, post-Cold War age: "I don't believe in Marxism as a religion but as a tool of analysis. After 100 years, any ideology is bound to be superseded." Reporting from Cuba on Castro's efforts to cope with the cutback in trade with the former Eastern bloc in "Castro's New Revolution," 6-24, she writes that "Cuban officials have begun moving thousands of city dwellers to the countryside to boost food production," but fails to go into whether the movement is coercive or voluntary. In "Mexico's New Revolution," 7-8, she asserts that Mexican President Salinas "has calculated that economic reform and political liberalization done simultaneously would risk social disintegration — so he has deferred opening up Mexico's political system to genuine competition," an assertion she does not support. In "Nicaragua's $1 Billion Battle," 7-29, she is late on the Sandinista land-grab when they left office.

Rockwell, Keith M. *The Journal of Commerce.* (★ ★ ½)
London. Rockwell succeeded Janet Porter as chief of European bureaus, and the move seems to have re-inspired him. He is once again offering penetrating reports on Europe's move toward integration, his analytic framework firmly grounded on the bedrock principles of free trade and free markets. In the perceptive "Mr. Major's Quiet Confidence," 2-5, he writes on how new Prime Minister John Major is having a greater success pushing Margaret Thatcher's policies on the Gulf War and European monetary union than Thatcher herself did, which he attributes to Major's low-key, non-confrontational manner, observing that "while the prime minister may be very much a meat and potatoes kind of man, he is also the kind of leader Britain needs." He is good on the details on internal EC differences over farm subsidies in "EC Pressure to Slash

Farm Aid Intensifies," 3-27. He effectively contrasts the opening of the European Bank for Reconstruction and Development with the barriers the West still continues to place in front of trade with Eastern Europe, "Protectionism Seen Drain on E. Europe," 4-18: "Slightly embarrassed Western leaders concede that in restricting access for Eastern European agricultural, steel and textile products, Brussels, Washington and Tokyo have stymied the region's attempts at implementing market economies." In the hard hitting "Time for Delors to Take a Stand," 5-21, he calls on Jacques Delors to stand up to the French farmers and cut EC farm subsidies, thus ending an obstacle to monetary union, agricultural trade with Eastern Europe, and the Uruguay Round: "Mr. Delors is clearly a man with vision. But perhaps that vision is being clouded by thoughts of the French presidency and its Elysee Palace." He is sharp on shifts in the Bonn-Paris axis on Common Agricultural Policy in "EC Marriage of Convenience," 8-6, as Germany has a new interest in a successful completion of the Uruguay Round to help alleviate economic conditions in east Germany and Eastern Europe. In "EC Officials Vow to Shift Freight Onto Railroads," 11-1, he is brief, but thorough, on EC concerns over congestion and pollution.

Ryan, Leo. *The Journal of Commerce.* (★ ½)
Canada. Ryan has now spent a decade as the *JOC*'s Canadian bureau chief, and his work reflects his experience. He is able to see the trade implications in virtually every story, and often incorporates the developing North America free-trade zone in his reports. In "Seaway's Outlook Uncertain After Traffic Fell 3% in '90," 1-2, he offers a concise report on the second successive annual traffic decline on the St. Lawrence Seaway. The writing is sharp in "Ontario Car Insurers Fight Government Takeover Proposal," 3-18, on mounting opposition by both the insurance industry and policyholders to the "the new left-wing government's" plan to take over auto insurance in the province, though we would have liked to have heard the Government's side. In the straightforward "Officials Seek to Allay Concerns About N. American Free Trade Zone," 4-26, Ryan reports on an appearance by Mexico's top trade official at a conference in Montreal. He provides an efficient rundown of the current difficulties of the maritime insurance industry, "Dramatic Capacity Decline Predicted for World Marine Insurance Market," 5-28. He is informative on what Canadian negotiators are hoping to get as they enter trilateral talks with the U.S. and Mexico on a free-trade agreement, "Canada Wants Greater Access to US Contracts," 6-5. He exhibits a deft understanding of the Quebec separatist issue, "More Unity, Less Government," 7-5, and notes that the quarrelsome province wants to forge a new relationship with Canada at a time many Canadians want to reduce the size of government and reduce duplication of services by the federal and provincial governments: "The trouble is, Quebec and the rest of Canada are leagues apart on how much power should be transferred to the provinces." Thoughtfully studying the incendiary issue of including cultural, or entertainment industries, in a free-trade pact, "Canadian Culture Under Siege?" 8-8, he observes that even though many Canadian and American interests coincide on the issue, Canadian efforts to protect at all costs its "cultural sovereignty," which it equates with its way of life, could scuttle the talks: "Clearly, Canadians and Americans have different agendas on cultural issues and suffer from a lack of mutual understanding."

Sanger, David E. *The New York Times.* (★ ★ ★ ½)
Tokyo. Sanger excels in documenting the implementation of strategies drawn up by Japanese business and government officials, and is better than most reporters at making abstract economic issues come alive. He also provides outstanding coverage of key regional security issues, and was out in front on the developing story of North Korea's nuclear weapons program. He masterfully uses Toyota "as an example, if an extreme one, of the pace at which many Japanese manufacturers are investing in new plants, new products and new technology," during a time of economic slowdown, "As U.S. Car Makers Cut Back, Toyota Is Expanding Briskly," 1-1. In the compelling 10 Best selection, "A New Car for Malaysia, New Influence for Japan," 3-6, he provides a case study on how Japan "has gradually transformed itself into the single most important element in the region's economy" by taking over the development of a Malaysian

national car, the Proton Saga: "The Japanese strategy is to play an unobtrusive but commanding role, trying to stay as inconspicuous as possible in a country that it invaded just 50 years ago." In the chilling "Jittery Asia Has Visions of a Nuclear North Korea," 4-7, he notes that a nuclear-armed Pyongyang could touch off an arms race with South Korea. Examining all angles of Gorbachev's disappointing trip to Japan in the comprehensive "Gorbachev's New Failure," 4-22, he notes that "Mr. Gorbachev may also have run into trouble because he was asking the Japanese to break one of their ironclad rules of business: Never build a factory where you do not already have a market." About the only thing Sanger doesn't tell you about Sony's new mini-disk technology in the 10 Best nominee, "A CD Advance Starts a New Battle," 6-19, is when it will be on the market. In "Soichiro Honda, Auto Innovator, Is Dead at 84," 8-6, he provides a rounded obituary of the late carmaker. We learn that unlike Sony and Matsushita, Toshiba is interested in cable TV more than movies, in the revealing "Toshiba Rewrites a Hollywood Script," 10-9. We get a well-written preview of the new look in Japanese cars, "Taking in the Tokyo Auto Show," 10-24, while "Nuclear Activity by North Koreans Worries the U.S." 11-12, expertly summarizes the latest intelligence estimates.

Schlesinger, Jacob. *The Wall Street Journal.* (★ ★ ★)
Tokyo. This young reporter, who first caught our eye covering the Detroit auto beat, continues to offer a fine mix of fact-laden reporting and forward analysis in his dispatches on Japanese technology, holding his own on this increasingly competitive beat. In "Japan Energy Plan Spurs Public Fission," 1-30, he takes a bit longer than usual to put the issue into focus, but by the end we have a clear picture of the battle over Japan's energy future. He raises a powerful challenge to the conventional wisdom that Japan can only make computer boxes, and not develop the ideas that run them, "Japan Makes Strides in Software Design," 2-8, richly reporting how most of Japan's progress in software comes from the private sector. We get a valuable follow-up to the FSX flap, "Europe Seeks Japan's Aerospace Market, Threatening Long-Time U.S. Dominance," 2-15, Schlesinger commenting that this move may be a consequence of U.S. intransigence on sharing of key technologies. In "Sony Is First With CD Player That Records as Well as Plays," 5-16, he expertly places both the product and Sony's strategy in the context of "techno-politics," as well as techno-economics, observing that "the timing is right now, not only because Sony claims the technology is good enough, but because Sony admits that the consumer audio market is bad enough." In "Japanese Buyers Are Critical of New Foreign-Chip Accord," 6-6, he ably probes beyond the rhetoric on both sides over the semi-conductor issue to find that both U.S. and Japanese companies are trying to work things out. He provides a revealing report on a "classic bilateral battle of technological pride" in "Fujitsu, Texas Instruments Gird for Chip Patent Battle," 7-22, writing that while several Japanese firms have already settled with TI, they did so only to prevent further anti-Japanese "propaganda" and are rooting Fujitsu on. He is sharp on how the hype and hoopla surrounding HDTVs cannot disguise the fact that they are still far from being a feature in every home, "For HDTV in Japan, the Picture Is Clear: Consumers Won't Buy it Until Price Falls," 10-7. He expertly presents the product's difficulties as a case study of how "the vaunted Japanese long-range planning and government-industry cooperation are sometimes susceptible to market forces."

Schmemann, Serge. *The New York Times.* (★ ★ ★)
Moscow. Schmemann won a 1991 Pulitzer Prize for Foreign Reporting for his coverage of German reunification in 1990. In 1991, he covered a nation coming apart. At his best, which he often was, he produced comprehensive, literate efforts which made the historic events come alive. In "Gorbachev Back as Coup Fails, But Yeltsin Gains New Power," 8-22, he captures the drama of the moment while portending what lies ahead for the Soviet Union, and in the remarkable "Week In Review" essay, "Across East Europe to Moscow, the Trail of Freedom Reaches Tyranny's Epicenter," 8-25, he offers his personal impressions on the political upheaval over the past two years: "In all the anti-Communist uprisings, what triumphed ultimately was not an alternative system, as the Communists would have it, but a profoundly human resistance to manipulation." His analysis of the Soviet referendum on national unity, "Gorbachev's Vote:

Post-Perestroika Era," 3-20, has a rushed feel to it, but he notes that neither Gorbachev nor the hardliners around him can "fully escape, manipulate or roll back the processes he had set loose." Gorbachev's efforts at political survival would be Schmemann's main topic this year. In "100,000 Join Moscow Rally, Defying Ban by Gorbachev to Show Support for Rival," 3-29, he seamlessly ties together the mass protests in the street and the political maneuvering in the Russian Republic parliament, while in "Gorbachev: Back in Fold," 5-22, he incisively examines Gorbachev's recent move back toward the center after a winter of crisis. He offers a vivid portrait of life in the Russian hinterlands, "From Russia to Leningrad, Russia's Timeless Heartland," 6-17. In "Soviet 'Democrats' Now Wrestle Over the Spoils," 10-8, he produces an important update on the inability of Soviet democrats, a "motley coalition," to cope with the post-coup aftermath as their nominal leader, Boris Yeltsin, takes time out to ostensibly write a book about the coup. We get a lyrical report on the anniversary of the October Revolution in Moscow and the newly-rechristened city of St. Petersburg, "Pre-1917 Ghosts Haunt a Bolshevik Holiday," 11-7, Schmemann writing that the event was marked by the "deliberate humiliation" of the revolution's legacy.

Schmidt, William E. *The New York Times.* (★ ★)
London. Schmidt's beat seems to encompass Great Britain, Egypt, and spot coverage of developments in Europe. For many reporters this would result in them being spread too thin, but Schmidt seems able to handle whatever assignment the editors throw at him, capably capturing both the big picture and the revealing details. In the insightful "I.R.A. Bombs and Motives," 2-20, he sheds some light on the shadowy world of terrorism. He pens an eloquent metaphor on the old chancellery building in the U.S. embassy in Cairo, which is being torn down and replaced by a high-rise office building, "Where Envoys Waltzed, Now the Wrecker's Ball," 4-9. Covering Gorbachev's Nobel acceptance speech, "Gorbachev, In Oslo, Links World Peace to Perestroika," 6-6, he alertly observes that "Mr. Gorbachev did not explain how a failure of Western economic support for his reforms could doom the chances for world peace. He argued only that such aid would benefit all by enabling Moscow to make even more 'constructive and significant' contributions to the emerging new order." Both his talent for feature writing and his grasp of British politics are fully demonstrated in "The Tories Run a Black in Colonel Blimp Country," 6-10, a profile of Conservative Party candidate for Parliament John Taylor, Schmidt writing that "Mr. Taylor's candidacy is being watched as a kind of litmus test" of Prime Minister John Major's intentions to build a "classless society" in Great Britain and broaden the Conservative Party base. In the inspired "12 Years of Cold Peace on One of Israel's Borders," 8-4, he examines Israeli-Egyptian relations, noting what may portend for Israel and the other Arab states as they prepare for a peace conference. He provides a colorful report from Moscow on the success of Western preachers in "sweeping across the spiritual ruins of the Communist landscape," in "U.S. Evangelicals Winning Soviet Converts," 10-7. In "Robert Maxwell Is Found Dead in Atlantic Off Canary Islands," 11-6, he efficiently presents the first, sketchy details on the publisher's last hours and what his death portends for his financial empire.

Shenon, Philip. *The New York Times.* (★ ★)
Bangkok. Formerly a legal affairs correspondent for the *NYT* Washington bureau, we noticed in the past that Shenon's best work tended to come from spot assignments overseas, and the decision to make him a full-time foreign correspondent was a positive one. Assigned to Saudi Arabia during the war, his "G.I.'s Poised on the Edge of the Unknown," 2-24, deftly captures the fatalistic mood of the soldiers on the front line, hours before the start of the ground war. In the tightly-written, "A Hard-Faced Schwarzkopf Sets Terms at Desert Meeting," 3-4, he artfully places readers right inside the tent where Iraqi military commanders formerly surrendered. He paints a striking portrait of the growing schism in newly-liberated Kuwait, "A New Divide for Kuwaitis: Who Stayed and Who Fled," 3-12. Reporting from Ho Chi Minh City, on the seventh congress of the Vietnamese Communist Party, in the straightforward "Vietnam Party Vows to Maintain Absolute Power," 6-25, he finds that the party leaders have no intention of surrendering their monopoly on power even as economic reforms continue. In August, he

traveled to Karachi to get to the source of the BCCI story, and produced several well-written, highly informative reports. In the revealing "Pakistan Rallies Behind B.C.C.I." 8-5, he finds the bank is still open and still has its defenders, who "say the debacle is a result of a conspiracy by Western bankers who want to crush an enterprising third world rival," while in "B.C.C.I.'s Best, and Worst, Customers," 8-6, he is thorough on how the bank's dealings with three brothers who headed a shipping company may have led to the bank's downfall. His coverage of the U.S. bases issue touched on the political, economic, and cultural fronts, in "How Subic Bay Became a Rallying Cry for Philippine Nationalism," 9-15, and "For Americans and Filipinos, Basics of Life Are at Stake in Fate of Navy Base," 9-29. In the literate "Back to Somerset Maugham and Life's Seamy Side," 10-10, he reports on how Singapore is trying to recapture the tourist dollar by restoring "what remains of its past, both the dignity and the debauchery." He comprehensively summarizes the reaction of the Bangkok diplomatic community to the Cambodian peace accord in "Cause for Alarm," 10-24.

Sieff, Martin. *The Washington Times.* (★ ★ ½)
Sieff is able to draw on a nearly endless supply of government officials, think-tank specialists and overseas sources, along with his own formidable experience and knowledge, to give impressive weight to his analytic efforts. His work can be original and thought-provoking, though at times it just echoes the headline. In "Timing of Soviet Crackdown Linked to Gulf," 1-9, for example, he gets the point across that Gorbachev is using the distraction of the Gulf crisis to step up pressure on the Baltics, but never digs any deeper. A much better effort is "Soviets' Latin Policy Keeps U.S. Guessing," 3-5, a concise summary of the conflicting signals Moscow is giving off in Latin America, Sieff commenting that "U.S. attempts to check Soviet initiatives in Central America are not always appreciated by governments in the region." We've seen Gorbachev cast as Lear, now, in "Wherefore Art Thou, Mikhail?" 4-5, Sieff projects him into the role of Hamlet, but adds little new to our understanding of the developing Soviet story. However, "Soviet Army Raids Called Political Tool," 4-26, presents a plausible account of one dimension of the power struggles within the U.S.S.R. He was keen on the nuances of the apparent Sino-Soviet rapprochement, "Events Re-Link China, Soviets," 5-13, and "Sino-Soviet Goal Is Keeping Party Alive," 5-14. Analyzing the Soviet coup, "Other Shoe Finally Dropped," 8-20, he forcefully argues that the die was cast last fall, when the KGB and the military formed an alliance against further reforms. Sieff also draws a contrast between the hardline Marxist coup leaders and *Soyuz* leader Lt. Col. Viktor Alksnis, whom he labels "an economic pragmatist," but fails to fully develop this key point. In "Russia-Ukraine Pact Derails Treaty," 8-30, he does a fine job of capturing the rapidly shifting relations between the republics and what remains of the center. He provides a comprehensive survey of the massive problems confronting the Russian republic, "Russia's Needs Go Beyond Freedom," 9-3. In "Israel Underestimated Bush's Opposition to Settlements," 9-20, he superbly captures the "cognitive dissonance" on the part of the Shamir Government which led to the crisis over the settlements issue.

Sikorski, Radek. *National Review.* (★ ★ ★)
NR's "roving correspondent" based in Warsaw. A talented wordsmith, Sikorski covers Eastern Europe with a sophisticated eye, sensitive to the long-term political, economic, and ethnic nuances that have come with the collapse of communism. A Polish native who went into exile during the communist years, "A New Beginning?" 1-28, expertly examines the threat poised to Poland's nascent democracy by the presidential candidacy of Stanislaw Tyminski: "The lesson of Tyminski's success is not that people are stupid, though many are, but that most in the newly free East view democracy only as a means to an end." Addressing the heavy-handed manner in which the Soviets are going about their troop withdrawals from east Germany in the vivid "The Red Army Remains," 2-25, he observes that "Because of their arrogance and clumsiness, the Soviets have missed the chance to maintain friendly relations with post-Communist Poland." In "Irreconcilable Differences," 3-18, he cleverly draws a parallel between Serbian efforts to keep Yugoslavia together by force and the proposed integration of Western Europe: "Unless Europe learns from the Yugoslav experience, it will repeat it." He travels to the site of the coal miners'

strike in Donetsk, in the starkly evocative "Notes From Underground," 4-29, and finds that even the Russian miners are supporting Ukrainian independence: "Without PhDs in political science they have grasped what many Western experts have still not understood: that the Soviet Union is too riven with contradictions for any reforms to succeed." We receive a masterful update on the political situation in Poland in "The Last Communist," 6-24, as Sikorski profiles Mieczyslaw Rakowski, "the last hope of Polish socialism" two years ago who now wonders if he wasted his life: "Communists may now posture as honest men who gave up power when circumstances permitted, but let us not forget that they never intended to do so." Superbly reporting from Vilnius on the adverse economic impact of independence, "Strings Attached," 9-23, he graphically notes that Soviet colonialism can have an adverse impact as well: "It is worth sacrificing microwave ovens, refrigerators, and holidays on the Black Sea for the knowledge that no cells need to be spruced up for your return."

Simpson, John. *The Spectator.* (★ ★ ½)
Foreign Affairs editor for the BBC, Simpson also contributes regularly to *The Spectator,* offering literate reports sharing his experiences in covering the major international stories of the day and offering his informed opinions on overseas developments, particularly in the Middle East. Reporting from Baghdad at the start of the year, "Herbivores and Carnivores," 1-12, he artfully conveys the growing mood in the Iraqi capital: "This war will, more than most, be diplomacy by other and much nastier means," while in "Battle Stations," 1-19, he is refreshingly candid on how it feels to be a correspondent awaiting a major military attack, humanizing this aspect of war coverage: "It brings out the Sydney Carton in one, of course." Simpson subsequently injured his ribs when he hit a desk during a U.S air raid, but he was able to provide one vivid eyewitness account on the amazing accuracy of the air war, "A Different Kind of War," 1-26. Simpson's coverage made him a reluctant "war hero" back home, and in the heartfelt, "Worse Than Saddam," 2-9, he is unforgiving of the way the British press hounded his family and made him out to be a hypocrite because he came into possession of a Saddam badge while recovering in an Amman hospital: "The tabloids are like a medieval quintain: they hit you coming and going." He expertly tracked efforts to free the remaining Western hostages in Lebanon, "The Free Subscriber," 4-6, and "The Art of the Deal," 8-17. He returned to Iraq in the spring and quickly became an eloquent critic of the policy which allowed Saddam to remain in power, "The Writing on the Wall," 4-27; "Settling Saddam," 6-15; and "Surviving in the Ruins," 8-10, writing in the latter piece that "No one in the White House appears to have argued that a nation which engages in a successful war has a moral duty to oversee the peace." Simpson published a book on the Gulf conflict, *From the House of War.* His coverage of the Soviet coup attempt was both wry and impressionistic, "Defending the Faith," 8-24, and in "Hammering Away at the Old Order," 8-31, he sardonically noted how the "official classes" in Moscow are now clamoring to attest to their democratic beliefs.

Sterngold, James. *The New York Times.* (★ ★)
Tokyo. Sterngold's coverage of the upheaval in Japanese financial circles at times lacks the authoritative touch of his Wall Street days. In particular, he never digs deeper in his analysis than tying the troubles of the Japanese system to perceived excess in business practices and lack of regulation. In "EIE: A Japanese Symbol of Excess," 2-12, for example, he writes that a financially troubled company being taken over by the banks symbolizes the "excess that swept corporate Japan in the overheated 1980s — just as they swept Wall Street." He quotes the owner: "Politics and business have nothing to do with each other," a quote he would put to the test during the year. His study of the Japanese corporate practice of buying Western art, as if it were real estate, during the 1980s, "Some Big Japanese Art Purchasers Are Under Scrutiny for Scandal," 4-23, fails to delve into how Japan's tax laws invite this practice. He artfully takes us inside the "dim hallways of the rundown finance ministry building" in "A Japanese-Style 'Old Boy' Network," 6-7, to show how retired senior Finance Ministry officials oversaw changes in the law separating banking and security businesses: "Perhaps the surest sign of the power of these three old boys is the fact that they deny having any." In "Symbols Are Louder Than Action,"

6-25, he routinely traces the burgeoning scandal surrounding Japan's more powerful securities houses and the finance ministry to lack of regulatory oversight from the political branch of government. He returns to this point in "Japan's Scandal: No Laws to Break," 7-15, noting that the failure to file charges so far, reflects the hazy nature of the Japanese regulatory system. He interviews Tadao Chino, Tokyo's "top financial policy maker" in the revealing "Japan's New Finance Official Plots an Independent Course," 8-5, and reports that "In perhaps his most significant comment, Mr. Chino said Japan wanted to transform its substantial foreign aid into a magnet for private capital." Reporting on a Western aid package to be run through the IMF, "7 Rich Nations to Help Soviets Plan Economy," 10-14, he perceptively notes that "the terms sketched out were very similar to the doses of bitter medicine that the fund has meted out to countries such as Mexico and Brazil."

Sun, Lena H. *The Washington Post.* (★ ★ ½)
Beijing. We were impressed by Sun's resourceful coverage of the Chinese political economy, especially the private sector and how it is affected by political events. In the colorful, "From Shoes to Shampoo, China's Shoddy Goods Test Frustrated Consumers," 1-29, she reports on the cost to the economy of the low quality of Chinese merchandise. She provides an informative look at how Beijing is retaining diplomatic ties to former communist states in "China Opts to Maintain Ties to Eastern Europe," 2-18. With "In China, A Clamor for Space," 4-30, she takes us right inside the cramped living quarters of urban Chinese, perceptive on why housing reform is such an explosive issue. She fully captures the disorganized response of the Bangladesh government to that country's cyclone disaster in "Bangladesh's Army to Head Relief Effort," 5-6. In the wide-ranging "U.S.-Sino Ties Remain Tense as Key Issues Block Rapprochement," 5-25, she notes that ending MFN status would weaken U.S. ability to influence reformers while "strengthening the dominant hard-liners who could blame foreign pressure for China's economic problems rather than the country's own failing system." Thoroughly updating us on the struggle for democracy two years after Tiananmen Square, "Dissident Struggle Still Alive in China," 6-2, she observes that "China's predominantly hard-line leaders are finding it more difficult to maintain their iron grip on political control without choking off economic dynamism needed for the country's survival." She is straightforward in her analysis of Beijing's efforts to retain its MFN status while not appearing to cave in to U.S. pressure, "On MFN, Chinese Send Mixed Signals," 7-7, while "Mongols Brace for Hard Times," 7-24, provides welcomed hard data on that country's bleak economic prospects as winter approaches. In "Chinese Battening Hatches," 9-11, she efficiently draws on inside sources to report on the siege mentality being adopted by Beijing in the wake of the Soviet collapse, while "China's Leaders Reportedly Concur on Reviving Quest for Free Market," 11-5, provides good intelligence on the gradual movement back toward economic reform, Sun keen on political shifts within the party.

Symonds, William C. *BusinessWeek.* (★ ½)
Toronto. In his first year on the Canadian beat, Symonds produced concise, well-informed reports, alert to such key Canadian stories as the recession and Ontario Premier Bob Rae. In "International Business: Shufflin' Off to Buffalo," 4-8, he ably documents how Canadian businesses hard-hit by recession are either being "swallowed up" in mergers which "create a far more efficient industry — but one with fewer companies and workers" or "fleeing high labor costs and taxes" and moving in droves across the border to Buffalo, N.Y. He continued to draw on his expertise on the sports industry, "Take Me Out to the Cleaners," 5-6, comprehensive on how the SkyDome, despite drawing consistently high attendance, has "become a study in how high-profile projects can become an immense financial drain — and how taxpayers can get stuck with most of the tab," and in "Top of the News: Bottom of the Ninth, Denver Leading," 6-17, he alertly tags Denver and Miami as the winners in baseball's upcoming expansion. In "International Business: For Corporate Ontario, Bob Rae Is Public Enemy No. 1," 7-15, he offers cogent analysis and sharp reporting on why the socialist Rae has business "seeing red," and is the type of backgrounder on the Canadian political economy we would like to see more of from Symonds. He is keen on the potential of a new 3-D software design in "Pushing Design to Dizzying Speed," 10-21.

Tagliabue, John. *The New York Times.* (★ ½)
Berlin. Tagliabue's German coverage often had a perfunctory tone to it this year; he was somewhat better on Yugoslavia beginning in late June. He is concise and quick on the German reaction to the Soviet crackdown in Lithuania, "In Germany, a Feeling of Shock at Crackdown," 1-14. He covers a lot of familiar ground in "Young Germans Still Flocking From East to West," 3-11, the second-part of a three-part series, "Eastern Germany in Despair." In the anecdotal "What Divides Berlin Now?" *Magazine* 4-7, he reports on the economic, professional, and psychological difficulties East Berliners are having in the new, unified state, writing that "...Western arrogance encourages a festering sense of inferiority in the East, in which everything linked with the old East Germany is second-rate and undesirable," adding little new to this heavily-covered topic. He is better in "The New Hitler Youth Are Troubling Germany," 5-15, a chilling account of growing "frictions" between neo-Nazi youth gangs in the eastern Berlin district of Pfarrstrasse and leftists, Tagliabue touching on the social and economic conditions which bred this phenomenon. In the informative "For Eastern Europe, Security Means More Than Tanks and Guns," 6-23, he writes on the growing concern of Eastern European regimes that economic dislocation will breed political instability. His Yugoslavian coverage was generally solid, "Yugoslavia Fails to Oust Militias," 6-27, effectively capturing the rising war of nerves in that country following Croatia's and Slovenia's declarations of independence, and "A Postwar Idol Falls," 7-1, perceptive on the Yugoslavian Army's role in the current crisis. However, "Renewed Fighting Wounds Yugoslav Economy," 9-5, is routine, Tagliabue devoting as much space to the latest round of fighting as to economic details. In "Old Rivalries in Eastern Europe Pose Threat of Infection," 10-13, he recycles a lot of familiar material on Yugoslavia, but also captures several nuances in policy by European governments.

Tanzer, Andrew. *Forbes.* (★ ★ ½)
Pacific bureau. Tanzer continues to go the extra mile and dig for the extra nugget of insight for his reports, which are models of concise reporting. In "Marketing: War of the Sales Robots," 1-7, he provides a valuable marketing piece on Japan's high-tech vending machines which are selling soda like hot cakes: "...a well-placed machine can move as much product as a medium convenience store — some 10,000 cans a year." He provides important intelligence to petrochemical investors and those affected by the petrochemical market in "Steamroller," 3-4, where Tanzer is thorough on how Asian countries are building petrochemical complexes and cutting into one of the best export markets for the U.S. He is so obviously comfortable discussing the specifics of the Japanese computer market in "How Apple Stormed Japan," 5-27, that we almost forget he is talking about a foreign country. Tanzer gives new life to the subject of China's Guangdong Province, "The Mountains Are High, The Emperor Is Far Away," 8-5, through his vivid prose and dogged research. Crisp writing characterizes "Heroes in a Half Shell," 10-28, on the fickle nature of the toy industry, but Tanzer could have provided a little critical analysis of Playmates, the company he profiles here. In the forward looking, "The Asian Village," 11-11, he examines the protectionist and legal challenges that lie ahead for STAR-TV, the first pan-Asian TV network.

Tempest, Rone. *Los Angeles Times.* (★ ½)
Paris. Tempest is a veteran observer of the French and their foibles, his reports often bolstered by a underlying sly sense of humor. He still comes up short on the French economy, however. He is clear and precise on the reasons behind French Defense Minister Jean-Pierre Chevenement's resignation on the eve of war, "Anti-War Activist, Iraq Supporter Resigns as France's Defense Chief," 1-30. His deep understanding of the French political culture underlines "French Revive a Pastime: Fretting About U.S. 'Imperialism,' " 2-15, a perceptive look at the latest outbreak of anti-Americanism in France. Tempest toured Francophone Arab North Africa after the war ended and produced some savvy political intelligence in such dispatches as "PLO Slashes Spending to Cope With Funds Cutoff," 3-30; "Algeria's Populist Politics Matches Ramadan Prayers and Free Meals," 4-1; and "N. Africa's 'Saddamania': More Show Than Substance?" 4-14, imaginatively writing in the latter report that "Like one of the seasonal desert

sandstorms that rage across the Maghreb, the pro-Hussein movement was full of sound and fury but short-lived." Knowingly surveying the innuendo and debate ignited by Edith Cresson's appointment as Prime Minister in "Cresson Confronts Paris Gossip Mill, Double Standard," 5-17, he writes that "the episode highlights a conspicuous inequality in French politics: When it comes to male politicians, private relations and sexual activities are considered strictly off limits. However, as the Cresson appointment has shown, the rules for women are different." In the amusing "Column One" feature "Euro-TV Tunes In to Hollywood," 7-11, he thoroughly covers a subject of great interest, no doubt, to L.A.: the growing influx of U.S. TV producers and creative personnel to Europe as network television there prepares to enter the age of competitive markets.

Thurow, Roger. *The Wall Street Journal.* (★)
Vienna. Thurow picked one of the most turbulent years in the continent's post-war history to transfer from South Africa to Europe, and while his reports generally reflected his solid professionalism, it is clear he still needs time to get acclimated. He interviews the ANC leader in "For Nelson Mandela, Time Is an Enemy," 1-29, but is unable to pin him down on specifics. Instead we get generalities on such issues as the need for one-man, one-vote democracy and negotiations: "As a former lawyer, he prefers to work out South Africa's problems over a negotiating table." We learn that baseball has arrived in Romania in the entertaining "Imagine Romania, of All Places, Having a Shortage of Bats," 4-8, while "Yugoslav Secessions Underscore the Forces Tearing Nation Apart," 6-26, is extremely slow moving on the Yugoslavian crisis, some of our readers bailing out before the conclusion. In "Question: How Many Countries Can Fit Into the New Europe?" 8-28, he is wry on the trend by various European ethnic groups to carve out a nation for themselves, with Thurow studying their role model, the Grand Duchy of Luxembourg, which has "wielded its sovereignty cleverly enough to become one of the most prosperous specks of Europe." The horror of the Yugoslavian war in one Croatian village is effectively contrasted with the diplomatic efforts to end the fighting, "In Croatia, the Fighting Is Never Far Away," and Mark M. Nelson 9-17. In "Attacks on Dubrovnik Sparking Outrage," 10-28, he adequately explains how the Serbian siege of the strategically-marginal port city of Dubrovnik is angering the outer European community, which wants to protect the city's preserved Renaissance heritage. How about the people?

Tuohy, William. *Los Angeles Times.* (★)
London. We were disappointed by Tuohy's coverage this year, as he provided little on the margins of British politics and the European community, and his analytical edge was duller. In "British TV, Newspapers Call in the Country's Army of Military Experts," 2-5, he routinely reports on how, like the U.S. media, the British press is augmenting its coverage of the Gulf War with guest commentators. His attempts to position the U.S. in the new Europe seemed to be agenda-driven, "In Wake of Gulf Conflict, NATO Sees U.S. in a Continuing Lead Role," 3-11, as he echoes official concerns about "various plans to create a separate European defense entity, inside or outside the European community," while in " 'Good Shepherd' Gathers E. European States to the Fold," 3-19, he is laudatory on the Council of Europe, warning us not to confuse this older, larger organization with the EC. He is awkwardly topical in "British Police, Courts Under Fire," 4-5, writing that the "wrongful imprisonment of suspected members of the Irish Republican Army" has "cast a cloud over British law enforcement in a fashion not unlike what has happened to the Los Angeles Police Department." Assigned to the Kurdish crisis, his coverage was generally informative, if at times overwritten, "Hungry, Exhausted Kurds Cross Frontier Into Iran," 4-13: "Above the towering white peaks, the sky played tricks, changing from a cerulean blue to an angry dark grey, then loosing showerlets of snow." We learn little on the question of abdication of Elizabeth II in favor of Charles, Prince of Wales, in the gossipy "Is the Sun Setting on Elizabeth's Reign?" 5-14, Tuohy offering some pop psychology of Charles. He adequately captures the debate over the prosecution of suspected war criminals in England, "Britain Prepares to Prosecute Nazi War Criminal Suspects," 5-24, wisely steering clear of judgment. He is expansive on the rising political forces of the Labour Party in "Labor Comeback

Has British Tories on the Defensive," 6-7, and sentimental on the fading of the British military in "Budget Cuts Swallow Up Some Royal Regiments," 8-6. In his best reporting effort all year, "Are Nations Set to Dodge the Draft?" 8-13, he thoroughly summarizes how military manpower policies around the world are evolving.

Wagstyl, Stefan. *Financial Times.* (★ ★)
Japan. Wagstyl can amass a wealth of information in his detailed and data-rich reports on Japanese political economy, but his analytical efforts often do not push beyond conventional wisdom. He provides plenty of detail on Japan's economic downturn in "The Juggernaut Slows Down," 3-27, but offers little discrimination among the data presented. He zeroes in for an assessment of the country's financial institutions in "Battered But Largely Intact," 3-19, focusing on the key concern of a plunge in the property market, but never taking the extra step beyond the conventional "cheap money" explanation to account for its distortions of the stock market. But then, nobody in the Western press noted Japan's doubling to ten years the holding period on real estate to get a favorable capgains differential. Providing us with background on the eve of EC President Jacques Delors's trip to Japan in "Tokyo Strives for Harmony With Brussels," 5-21, he writes that "Japanese officials blame macro-economics for the rapid growth of the country's trade surplus with the EC, but Brussels will not be satisfied with macro-economic answers." He accurately predicts little likelihood that Delors and Kaifu would make much more than symbolic progress in the political field. Wagstyl's fine handle on Japanese industry's moral code and the culture of Nomura Securities was demonstrated in "Once-Invincible Nomura Wrestles With Crisis of Confidence," 7-23, which provides an uncluttered perspective on how the brokerage house was hoping to curtail criticism by dismissing its chairman. Covering Kaifu's downfall later in the year, he was incisive if cynical on the inner workings of the LDP, "Japan's Prime Minister to Stand Down," 10-5/6, noting that Kaifu was forced out despite his high ratings in the polls: "Polls, however, played little part in the counsels of the LDP." Writing on Kaifu's successor, Kiichi Miyazawa, "Big Boy Pursues Seat of Shame," 10/12-13, he moves the story forward by noting that Miyazawa may try to carve out a niche for himself but that "Being clever has not always helped Mr Miyazawa in the past and may not help him now."

Waldmeir, Patti. *Financial Times.* (★ ★ ★ ½)
South Africa. Waldmeir was the best of the Jo'burg hands in 1991, consistently producing dependable, objective reports that were full of fresh information, new angles, lucid insights, and solid detail. She provides a very thorough examination of the realities of the dismantling of apartheid laws with "Cracks in the House of Cards," 1-31, a comprehensive look at the double standards still operating. She does an excellent job of supplying a detailed picture of the country's dismal economic situation as somber background on the outlook for constitutional advances with "The Economics of Ending Apartheid," 3-12. She solidly engages on the micro level, "Always Charge More Than You Paid for It," 4-9, a great report on courses designed to teach business basics in South Africa's townships, where decades of apartheid have stifled both the skills and spirit of enterprise. The most satisfying effort to assess the likelihood of peaceful transition to multiracial democracy we saw on this beat was "In Search of a Coalition," 5-7: "On the face of it, there seems little evidence that South Africa's democratic culture is strong enough to support power sharing. . .But. . .it has become increasingly apparent that no single political party will be able to govern alone." She was especially keen in ferreting out the important shifts taking place within the African National Congress, realistic on their potential for reality, "ANC Treads Warily to Avoid Battle Over Who Holds the Tiller," 7-2, reporting on the efforts of the organization to come to grips with the task of transforming itself into a political party. "Man Who Knows How to Negotiate," 7-6, was the best profile we saw of Cyril Ramaphosa, trade-union leader and newly elected secretary-general of the ANC, and "Signs of Maturity in the ANC," 7-8, was an assessment of the maturing unity within the organization despite its serious political challenges. In the fascinating "Why Murder Ended in Mpumalanga," 9-18, she thoroughly covers the success of white industrialists in mediating a cessation of black factional

violence in one black "homeland" town, cautiously suggesting this example may be followed elsewhere: "doing business in the new South Africa increasingly means taking an active role in politics."

Walker, Tony. *Financial Times.* (★ ½)
Cairo. A tireless reporter always alert to the key detail, Walker nicely augments the *FT*'s Middle East coverage. His economic reporting, often merely retailing the IMF prescription for the region, could use some fresh thinking. His dry British wit is evident, "Baghdad Puts its Faith in a Defensive War — and God," 1-11, as he observes such signs of the impending conflict as Saddam's growing boast that God will protect Iraq: "While this has pleased Islamic militants, it is not clear that it has brought much joy to Iraqi military professionals who must be watching with apprehension the build-up of forces against Iraq." He does as good a job as anyone in summarizing the possible scenarios running through Saddam's mind in "Eleventh-hour Calculations Facing Saddam on the Brink of an Inferno," 1-15. In "Mood of Extremism Spreads in Jordan," 1-24, he smartly traces the increasing political activity to the reforms set in motion by King Hussein two years ago. His coverage of the Egyptian economy centered around its relations with the IMF, in such one-dimensional assessments as "Egypt's IMF Deal Seen as 'Make or Break,' " 4-11, where he asserts that "The question is whether the economic accord marks the beginning of a genuine effort to liberalise or whether it is simply another stop-gap measure designed to hold international creditors at bay while attracting additional aid." "Egypt's Liberalization Hopes Run Into Bureaucratic Sands," 10-18, he charts how the country is falling short in meeting the IMF-imposed plan for reducing the budget deficit and liberalizing the public sector. Updating the Jordanian economy, "Jordan on the Rebound After Gulf Conflict," 5-31, his information is thorough but his analytical framework falls short, as he writes that "Jordan is certain to be required to institute further austerity." He does a solid job of capturing the diplomatic atmospherics in the region in "Sphinx-Like Figure Seeks Calm Waters at Helm of Arab League," 5-16; "Mideast Set For Exercise in 'Constructive Ambiguity,' " 9-3; and "US Tries Again After 25 Years of Failed Peace Efforts," 10-30.

Wallace, Charles P. *Los Angeles Times.* (★ ★)
Bangkok. Wallace continues to provide utilitarian coverage of this key region, focusing on relevant topics such as business and trade trends, although his analytical edge seemed duller at times. His Gulf War coverage was uneven, with "Once Again, Basra Becomes Target as War Returns to the Strategic City." 1-28, an informative background report on the current military significance of the star-crossed city of Basra, while "Western TV News Spurs 'Information Revolution' Among Arabs," 2-3, was light on the Arab perspective of CNN. Returning to Southeast Asia and firmer ground, "Pollution Is Price of Asia Boom," 2-15, he solidly documents the environmental damage inflicted in the region during the 1980s, but comes dangerously close to editorializing, asking "With population pressures building, a major question is whether Asia will sacrifice its record-setting economic growth of the past and accept somewhat slower growth as the price of a cleaner environment." His coverage of the overthrow of Thai Prime Minister Chatichai Choonhavan was straightforward, "Thai Military Seizes Power in Bloodless Coup," 2-24, noting that the previous three years of stability had enabled Thailand to experience the fastest growth on the planet. He failed to follow up on the coup with the strong analysis we've come to expect from him, limiting himself to reporting on the rapidity with which the military government is being accepted, in reports like "Junta Frees Deposed Leader of Thailand," 3-10. He foresees little in the way of reform coming out of Vietnam in the serviceable, "New Blood, Same Policy Likely at Vietnamese Party Congress," 5-17. As talk grew of creating a regional trade bloc of some sort, "Southeast Asia Warms to Trade-Bloc Plan," 6-1, he authoritatively summarizes movement in that direction thus far, pointedly observing that while Japan is becoming the largest trading partner and investor in the region, it is "clearly nervous about signing on to any trade plan that might raise protectionist hackles on the other side of the Pacific." In the forward looking "Forging a New Far Eastern Alliance," 11-5, he is detailed on the efforts of the Soviet Far East to develop economically, and the obstacles in its way.

Walsh, Mary Williams. *Los Angeles Times.* (★ ½)
Toronto. Walsh kept readers on top of significant Canadian developments with reports that were balanced and rich in information, if at times lacking the extra insight that would give readers the underlying sense of the real-life passions in the Quebec separatist drive. She provides an encyclopedic survey of the potential impact of an independent Quebec in "The Issue of Quebec Separatism Is No Longer an 'If' for Canada," 1-8. She is comprehensive on the reasons behind the Canadian recession in "The Hard Times Are Even Harder North of Border," 2-24. In "Quebec Panel Calls for 1992 Sovereignty Vote," 3-28, she routinely reports that recent polls show that a majority in Quebec would vote to secede, and in the slightly more insightful "Forum Takes Canada's Heartbeat," 3-30, she gives the other side of the story, what the English-speaking Canadians are doing about it, noting sardonically that "jaded Canadians have predicted that, come July, the Citizens' Forum won't tell English-speaking Canadians anything they couldn't have found out by going to the neighborhood tavern." In her feature stories she tried to find sources of Canadian national identity, with varying degrees of success. In the effective "In Canada, Hockey Is a Game of Life," 3-7, she comments that ice hockey is "as tied up in the it-ness of Canada as soccer is to Brazil or the bullfight to Spain." However, we found "The Mounties: The Pride of Canada Lives Up to a Legend," 4-23, to be little more than literary filler, Walsh writing gratuitously that the reputation of the RCMP "is of some consolation in Canada, a country always in search of itself and rarely able to identify true emblems of Canadian-ness with much conviction." In the 10 Best nominee "Nature or Power for Quebec?" 5-24, she is meticulous on the James Bay power project and its political implications. She has plenty of material in "U.S. Prices Are Definitely Right for Canadian Shoppers," 6-18, on Canadian consumers crossing the border to beat the new 7% tax on retail transactions, but she stretches the story out, devaluing its impact. She finally delivers the substantial analytic on Quebec that we'd been waiting for, "What's In Store on the Other Side of Quebec?" 7-23.

Watanabe, Teresa. *Los Angeles Times.* (★ ★ ½)
Watanabe's forte is the business of culture. Her best work is on Japanese-American business relations, and she has a knack for helping us see beyond the stereotypes that pervade coverage of Japan. She tells a highly enjoyable tale of two entrepreneurs intent on bettering U.S.-Japan relations through an international exchange — "stomach to stomach" in "Exporting Fast Food," 1-7. Watanabe breaks down all the stereotypes here, proving that an entrepreneur is an entrepreneur the world over. Her "Philippine Gusher Hopes," 2-4, is a lengthy skim of oil prospects in the Philippines and explains in very general terms what an oil gusher could do for this island nation's economy. Better in "Food Fight About to Erupt in Japan," 3-25, she constructs an original and insightful perspective on how the opening of Japan's beef and citrus markets could backfire on the Americans: ". . .the lifting of quotas could erode the commanding U.S. market position, developed in part through intimate relationships with the Japanese who controlled the closed system." She really showcases her talents in "Japanese Media Try to Export Coverage," 5-6, a fascinating exploration of the Japanese media industry's efforts to export news in order to reshape American views of Japan and, of course, make money to boot. "NHK [Japan Broadcasting Corp.], which is funded by the public but whose directors are political appointees, has launched a number of new international projects. The most intriguing proposal is for a Global News Network to move beyond Japan news and challenge CNN in the realm of international news for international audiences." She explores the difficulties one Japanese real estate company has encountered in the U.S. as it struggles up the learning curve in a difficult market in "Japanese Landlord Struggles with U.S. Culture Shock," 8-11. She's critical, but fair-minded in assessing Shuwa Investments which has run into financial pressures and disillusioned employees, vendors and tenants. Talking with California's top trade official in Japan, Jim Vaugh, in "We Should Listen to Japanese, Trade Expert Says," 10-7, we learn how a little cultural sensitivity can provide valuable information for U.S. businessmen dealing with the Japanese.

Weisman, Steven R. *The New York Times.* (★ ½)
Tokyo. Weisman had an off-year, his reports all too often reflecting a bored familiarity with some subject matter. Occasionally, a three-dimensional grasp of Japanese society surfaces in his work. He covers a seldom-seen story, "Japan's Homeless: Seen Yet Ignored," 1-19, although the problem seems smaller than suggested, with 119 homeless counted in Yokohama, city of three million. Comparative numbers with the U.S. would have helped. Analyzing the political controversy over an aid package for the war against Iraq in "Test for Japan's Leader," 2-8, he adroitly presents telling vignettes of political hardball, Japanese style: "Suddenly irked over opposition taunts, a Liberal Democratic Party lawmaker declared that it was 'imprudence' for one colleague to level criticism, especially since he was on the take for 500,000 yen, or about $3,800, paid 'as many as 20 times a year' from the ruling party." He produces a serviceable obituary of Rajiv Gandhi in "Rajiv Gandhi: A Son Who Won, Lost and Tried a Comeback," 5-22, describing the slain politician as "the reluctant Gandhi," forced into politics by the death of his brother in 1980 and thrust into the Prime Ministership in 1984 following the assassination of his mother. He is unfocused in "Series of Scandals Have Japanese Debating if Country Has Grown Corrupt," 8-19, surveying Japanese attitudes towards that country's capitalists, and finding that while some, especially the young, are disillusioned, "there is a widespread belief in Japan that the excesses of the recent scandals are merely exaggerated forms of what had been standard business practices and that those should not be discredited just because of the recent problems." In the same vein, "Is Big Business Getting Too Cozy With the Mob?" 8-29, is routine on the Japanese mob, or *yakuza,* and its ambivalent relationship with Japanese society. His best effort of the year, the *Magazine* cover story, "Pearl Harbor in the Mind of Japan," 11-3, is breathtaking on the impact of the war on Japanese society today, the finest report we saw anywhere on this heavily-covered topic. Why can't he write like this all the time?

Whitney, Craig R. *The New York Times.* (★ ★ ½)
London. The upheaval in the Soviet Union received the lion's share of Whitney's attention this year, and he was alert to key political and economic developments there, including the deteriorating economy and growing dissatisfaction with Gorbachev on the left and right. Analyzing the fallout from Gorbachev's handling of the Lithuanian crisis, "Gorbachev's Limits," 1-18, he shrewdly notes that "The intelligentsia is not going to determine Mr. Gorbachev's fate. But the military, and the managers and bureaucrats of the military-industrial complex that employs most of those angry pro-Soviet workers in the Baltic states could." He provides a solid sense of the disillusionment in reformist ranks, "Gorbachev Draws Ex-Backers Rage," 1-19. His account of an IRA attack on the heart of the British government, "I.R.A. Attacks 10 Downing Street With Mortar Rounds, Hitting Yard," 2-8, contains the essential facts, but fails to capture the drama of this event. The colorful *Magazine* piece "The Empire Strikes Back," 3-10, artfully conveys the atmospherics of Great Britain at war, while touching on the serious issues raised by England's role in the Gulf. As debate grew in the West over whether to help bail out the Soviet economy, he was strong on Gorbachev's failings in that area, in such reports as "More Pleas by Soviets," 6-5, where he observes that as Gorbachev calls for Western assistance the economy is worse off than ever, and "Soviet Snail's Pace," 6-20. Commenting on Gorbachev's historical appearance at the G-7 summit in London, "Toward a Smaller World," 7-18, he smartly observes that "What [Gorbachev] was saying, in effect, is that if he does what they want him to do, his country's vast economic problems will become, to a certain extent, theirs as well." In "Though Jobless, a High-Level Apparatchik Sheds No Tears for His Party," 9-4, he puts a human face on the party apparatchiks where unemployed following the collapse of communism, deftly avoiding the twin traps of cynicism and sentimentality inherent in such a topic.

Williams, Carol J. *Los Angeles Times.* (★ ★ ★ ½)
Budapest. One of the finest writers on the *LAT* foreign staff, Williams delivers indispensable coverage of Eastern Europe, consistently producing exhaustively-researched reports which cover the political, economical, and ethnic angles of the Yugoslav crisis and the region's move toward

reform. She masterfully evokes the fears ethnic Serbians are feeling as the province of Croatia surges ahead toward independence, "Minority Serbs in Croatia Fear New Genocide," 3-12. She is excellent on how Milosevic has undermined the country's efforts at economic reform, worsening domestic tensions, in the 10 Best nominee "Economic, Political Unrest: Vicious Cycle in Yugoslavia," 3-25. In the superb "Europe's Humpty Dumpty," 5-11, she documents how the various nationalist movements in Yugoslavia are taking things to extremes. She is sharp and clear on the wrongheadedness of Western diplomatic efforts to ease the worsening crisis by concentrating their efforts on Prime Minister Ante Markovic, a politician with no real following, and by insisting on maintaining Yugoslavia as it currently exists, "In Yugoslavia, West Backs a Man With No Following," 6-23: "Stymied over how to budge nationalist leaders from inflexible positions, the envoys appear to have clung to a policy of wishful thinking." She provides a sensitive and thoughtful tribute to the legendary primate of Hungary, Cardinal Mindszenty in "Mindszenty's Last Wish Will Finally Be Fulfilled," 4-30, while in "Bulgaria's Lack of Reform Stunts Nation's Rebirth," 5-19, she is impressively thorough on how Bulgaria's efforts to salvage its devastated economy by attracting foreign investment are being undermined by political instability. In "The Price for Democracy May Be a Higher Mortgage," 7-16, she produces a superior report on the political problems behind Hungary's $21 billion foreign debt. With "The Serbs and Croats Square Off," 8-9, she provides a gem of analytical clarity, while "Balkans' Graveyard of Hatred," 8-17, is a chilling survey of the past from which the present passions draw their deadly power. With "Miners Out-of-Control Thug Squad," 10-5, she deftly profiles the political Frankenstein that Romanian leader Ion Iliescu has created.

Williams, Daniel. *Los Angeles Times.* (★ ★ ★)
Jerusalem. Williams is a dependable source for lucid reporting and expert analysis of Israeli politics and Mideast diplomacy, his forays into the psychology of the Israeli people usually offering more penetrating insight than most. In "Streets Quiet, Shops Shut as Baghdad Watches Clock," 1-16, he artfully conveys the mood of the Iraqi capital on the eve of the U.N. deadline: "In general, the mood among Baghdadis staying behind was one of resignation, as if they were forced spectators at a contest whose rules they don't understand." He attempts to bare the soul of a whole nation caught in the agonies of war, "Direct Hit on Psyche of Israel," 1-31, and misses the mark only by his failure to mention the Palestinians, who were under fire as well. In the perceptive "Israelis Fear Another Loss After Victory," 3-3, he provides historical context on Israel's post-Desert Storm security concerns. In "PLO Uses Inducements, Warnings in a Bidding War for Loyalty of Palestinians," 4-13, he ably outlines the subterranean battle for influence taking place between the PLO and Arab states "actively looking for PLO substitutes." He captures Secretary of State James Baker's "winking and nodding style of diplomacy" in a knowing report on the diplomacy of the region, "Under Baker's Plan, Israel, Arabs Get All — and Nothing," 4-16. In "Capitalism Sprouts at Kibbutzim," 6-22, he sensitively documents how Israel's communal farms are trying to cope with a changing world where socialist principles are out-of-step with harsh economic realities. He expertly tracks the decline of the Israeli left, an underreported story, "Liberalism on Defensive in Once-Receptive Israel," 7-8, and "A Leftist Picks Fights in the Name of Peace," 7-23. Providing an in-depth evaluation of the ambivalent Israeli mood on the eve of the peace talks, "Many Israelis Skeptical About Talks, Suspicious of U.S." 10-28, he finds that "The mistrust seems based on an uncomfortable tangle of defense fears and racial stereotyping." In "Syrian Terms Shamir Killer in Bitter Session," 11-2, he imaginatively captures the atmospherics of the third day of the talks where "The diplomatic niceties, loosely fitting at best. . .peeled off like old paint in the suddenly bright sun."

Williams, Nick B., Jr. *Los Angeles Times.* (★ ★)
Nicosia. Williams provided sturdy ground-level coverage of Middle East events, with a particular talent for searching out the unusual and the unattended, and his analytics grew stronger as the year progressed. In the informative "Syria Stalls Iraqi Bid to Widen War," 1-25, he documents how the Syrian government effectively manages the mood in the streets of Damascus against Saddam Hussein's appeal, while in "After Years in the Wings of Arab Politics,

Assad Steers Syrians Onto Center Stage," 3-10, he produces an authoritative report on Syria's ascension back into the forefront of Arab world politics. In the forward-looking "What Next, Assad? Will You End Up Like Saddam?" 3-26, he urges Washington to be cautious in banking on Assad as a pillar of regional stability. He was sharp on the post-war power realignments in the region, "Who's Hot, Who's Not in Saudi Political Circles," 4-1, though frivolous in mood, but is perceptive and accurate in sketching the new pecking order in Arab politics. In May, he traveled to Iraq, "Battered Iraqi Port Emerging From Rubble," 5-20, penning a vivid on-the-scene report from Basra, as that city slowly begins to shake off the effects of eleven years of war and rebellion: "The only growth industry in the city is replacement of the ubiquitous roadside portraits of Hussein, many of the originals having been shot up by rebels." We get much more on the Iraqi economy and what it portends for Saddam's regime in the informative "Hussein Down But Not Out as He Rebuilds Iraq Regime," 5-27, learning why "The only acknowledged time bomb is the economy." Smartly analyzing Saddam's credibility problems with the U.N. and Washington over his compliance with cease-fire resolutions, "Hussein Trusts No One — and the Feeling Is Mutual," 7-7, he observes that Saddam is just as duplicitous in his dealings with foreigners as he is with his own people, noting that the current negotiations with the Kurds "are a portrait of the presidential technique: bend before superior force, then snap back to fill any vacuum." His knowledge of the shadowy world of Lebanese politics and religion is displayed in "Snatched Sheik's Fate: A Mideast Flash Point," 10-15, a profile of Sheik Abdul Karim Obeid which debunks his image somewhat as a terrorist leader.

Worthy, Ford S. *Fortune.* (★ ★)
Hong Kong. Worthy showed marked improvement this year, turning in work much more substantial than previously, but the temporary addition of Japan to his duties may stretch him a bit thin. In "Asia: Can the Koreas Get Together?" 2-11, he offers a sweeping analysis of the powerful economic and political forces impregnating the post-Cold War Koreas with the notion of change, and perhaps ultimately reunification. He thoroughly and sensitively examines the cultural and economic reasons behind the inabilities of multinationals to locate strong local managers, "Asia: You Can't Grow If You Can't Manage," 6-3. "Making It in China," 6-17, he provides an eye-opening look at how the debate over most-favored-nation status for China has U.S. manufacturers with big operations there worried. With the possibility of tariffs jumping to 70%, "Wal-Mart, K-mart, Sears, and other mass-market retailers would have to scramble to locate suppliers outside of China." We find a perceptive examination of the "fundamentally different" and seemingly "imprecise and loosely joined" way the Japanese forecast, monitor and interpret costs, "Japan's Smart Secret Weapon," 8-12. "Like its famed quality philosophy, Japan's cost-management system stands Western practice on its head." In "Special Report: The Pacific Rim: Keys to Japanese Success in Asia," 10-7, he provides a smart look at why Japan fares so much better in Asia than the U.S. does, backing up his assertions with a bundle of credible examples. In the fascinating, "Special Report: The Pacific Rim: Tapping Asia's Brainpower," 10-7, he examines the educational development of Asia's work force, and how it is being tapped for more highly technical labor projects by Japan and the West: "The region's revolution — from stitcher of tennis shoes to builder of disk drives to implanter of genes — is hardly complete."

Wren, Christopher. *The New York Times.* (★)
Johannesburg. Wren continues to provide adequate coverage of South Africa, covering day-to-day developments with little flair, although his analytic efforts can be strong on occasion. In "As Apartheid Fades, Uprooted Try to Go Home," 1-4, he provides a moving account of the Barolong people visiting the graves of their ancestors in their former homeland. He adequately covers both the personal anguish Nelson Mandela is feeling and the political ramifications over the Winnie Mandela verdict, "A Verdict Against His Wife Brings New Grief for Mandela," 5-19: "The potential damage to [President F.W.] de Klerk's plans has convinced many South Africans that the trial was not politically motivated." In the straightforward report, "South Africa Scraps Law Defining People by Race," 6-18, he fails to capture the drama of the overturning of the

Population Registration Act of 1950, the last major pillar of the apartheid system in South Africa. Analyzing the first ANC national conference within South African borders in three decades, "South Africa: New Reality," 7-8, he overreaches, contending that "the congress progressed in just over five days from a self-described liberation movement to a more mature and focused political organization, displaying a pragmatism that augurs well for talks with the Government." In "De Klerk's Victory," 7-11, he addresses the government's recent diplomatic gains, flashing some insight: "By leading South Africa back into international acceptance after years of isolation for its racist policies, [President F.W.] de Klerk is fulfilling his promise to whites that the respectability gained will outweigh their loss of privilege over the black majority." Updating us on the South African Communist Party's efforts to cope with a changing world in "Communists Struggling to Adapt in South Africa," 8-30, he is thorough and detailed, reporting that the SACP is toning down its Marxist-Leninist orthodoxy and divorcing itself from the ANC. He produces a vivid report from Luanda on the prospects for reform against the backdrop of the political campaign, "Rebel Front Says It Can Fix War-Battered Angola," 10-6, the finest dispatch we saw from him all year.

WuDunn, Sheryl. *The New York Times.* (★ ★ ½)
Beijing. A 1990 Pulitzer Prize winner, WuDunn is an astute all-round reporter on China, although her *forte* is business stories, and she strongly complements the political-cultural coverage provided by her husband and *NYT* Beijing bureau chief Nicholas D. Kristof. In "War Astonishes Chinese and Stuns Their Military," 3-20, she ably documents the implications of the allied victory for future Chinese defense policy, which has emphasized sheer numbers, not high-tech weaponry. She is comprehensive on the politics and economics surrounding Occidental Petroleum's attempt to rid itself of its $250 million investment in the open-pit An Tai Bao coal mine in China's Shanxi Province, "Getting Out of China Harder Than Going In," 4-25, reporting that "Despite Chinese annoyance at Occidental and determination to bargain hard, they need to maintain the impression that Occidental was able to leave gracefully and that the mine is a success." She provides a deft portrait of the confluence of economics and politics characterizing the Chinese reform movement in "China Revives Its Test of Capitalism," 5-23, writing that "Shenzhen's leaders apparently want to merge their economy into Hong Kong's, but it is unclear how far the hard-liners in Beijing will go." We get a full rundown of China's "dirty tactics" in its efforts to keep out imports with "In the Trade Wars, China Has Learned Guerrilla Tactics," 6-9, but she fails to probe any deeper analytically than to contend that "while most Western countries say they would like China to abandon more of its Government control of the economy, they are finding that China is maintaining socialism while also learning some of the ways that exporters like Japan and Taiwan cause headaches for foreign industrial countries." Her talent for conveying the mood of the leadership in brief, yet informative, sketches is displayed in "Chinese Aides See Cooler Soviet Ties," 8-26, a report on Beijing's reaction to the failed Soviet coup attempt. She smartly notes that by attracting bids from around the world for its national program of reconstruction, Taiwan will ease its diplomatic isolation in "Taiwan Sets Plans to Rebuild Nation," 10-27.

NATIONAL SECURITY/DIPLOMATIC CORRESPONDENTS

Asker, James R. *Aviation Week & Space Technology.* (★ ★ ½)
Space technology editor. Asker remains one of the most reliable sources for information on developments in space exploration and ballistic missile defense. In his "Army Eris Interceptor Destroys Dummy Warhead in SDI Test," 2-4, he combines compactness with a wealth of critical information to produce a stunning picture of the prowess of one of SDI's most successful technologies, the Exoatmospheric Reentry-vehicle Interceptor Subsystem. In his fascinating "Nuclear Rockets Gain Support for Propelling Mars Mission," 3-18, he brings together the virtues of a first rate journalistic scoop with the excitement of the brewing political fight in the space science community to promote hitherto taboo nuclear propulsion for interplanetary travel: "The new emphasis on nuclear propulsion for manned space exploration is seen as a way to accelerate critical industrial technologies. Although not often articulated, that goal — advancing U.S. economic competitiveness — underlies much of the Bush Administration's interest in lunar and Mars missions." He points out in "Research, Development for SDI Major Source of New Technology," 4-8, that "at least 30% of all new aerospace industry technology has been a result of [SDI] programs. . .Much of SDI's cutting-edge space technology has resulted from the relatively simple goals of making spacecraft smaller, lighter, more durable, cheaper and easier to produce." He effectively brings out the salient political dimensions of the fiscal struggles over the besieged U.S. space program in his "Station Work to Proceed During Funding Debate," 6-3. His excellent "Space Station, Survival Fight Casts Shadow on Earth Observing System," 6-17, portrays graphically how one space program, the Space Station, is pitted against another, the Earth Observing System, as NASA attempts to accommodate congressional funding biases, while "U.S. Will Rely on European Backup While Fixing Next Weather Satellite," 9-30, points to the need for greater international scientific cooperation in the area of global weather studies by satellite. In "Congress, White House Weigh Overhaul of Landsat Program," 10-28, he sheds light on the difference in space program philosophies that divide the White House and Congress.

Baker, Caleb. *Defense News.* (★ ★)
Army issues. He is virtually the journalist of record on anything that has to do with contracts involving the U.S. Army. This year in particular he chronicled the Army's endeavors to adjust its yet unclear future mission to the avalanche of budget cuts and systems reviews. His Desert Storm coverage was marked by an overly cautious frame of mind which caused him to miss the target in some of his forecasts. His "Iraqi Fortification Will Test Allies," 1-14, contains one of the better descriptions of Iraqi fortifications and a solid overview of allied engineer units' training to surmount them. He misfires in "Allied War Planners May Underestimate Will of Iraqi Soldiers," 1-28, where he stresses that "senior U.S. commanders may be underestimating the will of the enemy to withstand the air attacks." Worse yet is his prediction of "Archaic Tactics, Slow Vehicles May Hinder Breach of Iraqi Lines," 2-4, which relies too uncritically on sources. Another misfiring is "Allied Concern Grows Over Friendly Fire, Chemical Weapons," 2-25, which predicts that an allied land attack, while expected to bring a decisive victory, "is certain to result in thousands of casualties." In "Boeing, Sikorsky Win LH Competition," 4-8, he offers a good technical discussion of the differences in design of the Light Helicopter that gave Boeing and Sikorsky the edge over the losing team of McDonnell Douglas and Bell. "Technical Glitches Stall Short-Range UAV Effort," 5-6, is a very good report on delays by two teams, one led by Israeli Aircraft Industries and one by McDonnell Douglas, in the unmanned aerial vehicle (UAV) program. The Army's budget and mission redefinition problems are portrayed very effectively in such articles as "Despite War, Army to Build No New Tanks," 2-18; "Cheney, Army Secretary Clash on M1 Upgrade," 7-22, an excellent analysis of the politics of the battle over whether to continue to upgrade and produce M1 tanks; and "Funding Shortages Curtail Plans at Special Forces Center," 8-26, which reports that "The Special Operations Research, Development and Acquisition Center" is languishing because of "sharp funding reductions and manpower cuts."

Bedard, Paul. *The Washington Times.* (★)
White House. He seems to have settled on the role of retailing the outlook (and minor leaks) of a certain narrow base of patrons/sources in the Bush Administration whose stale conservative outlook has not yet had a chance to digest and assimilate the rapidly transforming world map. In the "U.S. Worries Israel Will Hit Iraqis First," 1-11, he gives too much credence to citations of bold assertions claiming the Israelis "will launch a pre-emptive strike" and "Iraq won't attack Israel." In "Despite Soviet Plan, War is 'On Schedule,' " 2-19, he reflects U.S. skepticism toward a Soviet diplomatic solution to avert war with Iraq. His "U.S. to Preach Arab Democracy," 3-4, is a loose collection of topics left unrelated, ranging from democracy in the Middle East to Soviet arms control policy. His mention of an attempt by Washington to "forestall a Soviet-sponsored alternative of communism or socialism" is indeed strange. In "Bush Seeks Varied Views in Preparing," 7-29, he gives a limited profile of the administration's policy advisory system, in which certain outsiders are brought in to give briefings. His "Bush Offers Soviets Top Trade Status — Baltics, Cuba Still Concerns," 7-31, doesn't get much beyond official quotes, while "Hails Summit as End of 'Era of Mistrust,' " 7-31, gives the bare news from day one of the Moscow summit, Bush's offer of most-favored-nation status to help Moscow's economy, but avoids putting all this in any context. In "White House Waits, Stunned," 8-19, he emphasizes the shock and disbelief in the White House's reaction to the Soviet coup d'etat, and without a hint of a suspicion that the United States was planning to challenge the plotters, reports that "The White House, shocked by the replacement of Soviet President Mikhail Gorbachev, went on a Kremlin watch early today in a dash to determine why the Soviet leader was suddenly replaced." His "Bush May Take High Road, Put Quayle in the Trenches," 9-16 is a profile of upcoming Presidential election strategy as spoon-fed to Bedard by someone in Vice President Quayle's retinue, putting emphasis on "conservative hard-liners such as Vice President Dan Quayle and Chief of Staff John Sununu...want Mr. Bush to lash out at the Democrats," presumably over the objections of House Minority Whip Newt Gingrich.

Bond, David F. *Aviation Week & Space Technology.* (★ ★)
National affairs editor. His job was to follow, report and analyze the effects of a changed world strategic picture and a declining economy on the weapons acquisition process. He did it very well, providing accurate coverage of the ongoing defense budget reductions and some of their effects. His "Dark Clouds, Silver Linings Emerge From A-12 Cancellation," 1-14, identifies the new ground rules for rejecting new weapons programs and is unhappy with their implications: "If not knowing how much it will cost to keep a program going is grounds for cancellation, problems faced by other important weapons systems just became more serious." In the "Defense Dept. Seeks to End F-16 Production, F-14D Remanufacturing," 2-11, he calculates the exact cost to aircraft manufacturers of the defense budget cuts, and gives a fine sketch of U.S. air capability that will result, and in "Budget Squeeze, Reduced Threat Cut U.S. Strategic Program Upgrades," 3-18, he analyzes the risks of relying on the Soviets to honor treaties that shape future U.S. strategic defense postures. He notes that while the U.S. program under the new budget is now left "with fewer weapons systems, at a slower pace and in some cases less capability than planned," nevertheless, "the military-industrial momentum for strategic modernization in the Soviet Union has not slowed down...[as]...Soviet leaders know that strategic weapons have become virtually their only claim to superpower status." He gives very good analyses of the economically leaner/meaner weapons systems being adopted in "Cost, Supportability Key to Boeing Sikorsky LH Award," 4-15, and "Boeing Sikorsky LH Operating Cost Targets 40% Below Army's Estimate," 4-22. His "Navy Wavered on A-12 Weight, Contractors Charge in Lawsuit," 6-17, takes the side of contractors against the Navy with good justification, in the case of the A-12 attack aircraft cancellation. His excellent "Congress Seeks 1992 Formula for F-16, F-117A Procurement," 10-21, sheds light on congressional motivations behind the disagreements over whether to promote the General Dynamics F-16 or the Lockheed F-117A, noting that "the conflict between these two aircraft programs is one of the most contested issues in the authorization conference."

Broder, John M. *Los Angeles Times.* (★ ★)
Pentagon. His analyses, observations and comments about the Gulf War were keyed more to helping the general public understand military issues than to contribute to the then-prevailing emotional hype. In "Will It Be War or Peace in the Mideast?" 1-8, he provided an exceptional account of the scenario for how the war will be unleashed against Iraq, which held up well as actual war broke out. His "U.S. Military Favors Early Ground Attack to Deliver Knockout Punch," 2-10, was among the more readable and jargon-free analyses of military tactics in the Gulf War, and his "U.S. Military Finding Key Deficiencies Amid Victory," 3-3, was a sharp assessment of U.S. strengths and weaknesses in the war, noting in passing that "one of the cruel ironies of history is that nations tend to learn much less from military victories than from defeats." In "U.S. Counts Lessons of Gulf Crisis," 8-2, on the first anniversary of the Iraqi invasion of Kuwait, he records the thoughts of the men and women who fought in the war. In "Global Nuclear Threat Eased, Hardly Ended," 9-28, he provides an account of the reasoning which led President Bush to remove "all so-called tactical nuclear weapons — the portable, concealable and widely deployed weapons that were developed chiefly to offset the overwhelming Soviet advantage in conventional weapons and manpower." In "Fear and Loathing Vanish From Pentagon's Annual Appraisal of Soviet Power," 10-5, he and Melissa Healy give us a cheerful review of the "Pentagon's annual publication 'Soviet Military Power'. . .a mere shadow of its former self. . .[from which] gone are the menacing photographs of jackbooted Soviet troops parading in Red Square. . .the general tone of fear and loathing that pervaded earlier editions."

Brown, David A. *Aviation Week & Space Technology.* (★ ½)
Southwest bureau chief. Brown provides a reliable stream of bread-and-butter aerospace industry issues ranging from labor-management disputes, as in "Airline Blasts Pilots for Delays; Contract Talks Climate Sours," 1-7; to the effects of dwindling government contracts, "Contractors Gird for Financial Fight in Wake of A-12 Program Cancellation," 1-14; or the industry's market prospects as a result of the successes of the Gulf War, "Performance of Military Helicopters in Gulf May Boost U.S. Industry Competitiveness," 1-28, which points out that "Five months of intensive operations in the Saudi Arabian desert by U.S. military helicopters have largely vindicated the design criteria and operational requirements laid down more than a decade ago for the present generation of rotorcraft. This. . .is expected to give U.S. manufacturers a major selling point in future international competitions." He also focuses on the airline companies' struggle to survive in "American May Challenge Ruling on Transfer of Six London Routes," 4-29, while in "Continental Plans to Emerge From Chapter 11 Within a Year," 5-20, gives us a very good outline of Continental's reorganization plan, whose two central features are that it "will call for all of the current corporations and subsidiaries to be 'collapsed into one airline corporation'. . .[and]. . .most of the airline's secured creditors will receive equity for the debt owed to them." Southwest Airlines' relatively healthy situation is described in "Southwest's Success, Growth Ties to Maintaining Original Concept," 5-27, which highlights the prudence that distinguished this airline from the others: "Southwest, an airline which both analysts and company officials agree currently has the best balance sheet and highest credit rating of any U.S. carrier, sees itself as having achieved this position by adhering strictly to the basic formula devised when the carrier was organized. . .grow big by thinking small and [be] ready to tackle the future by keeping its eyes on the past." On more esoteric topics his contributions are well researched and useful, as in "Demands on Joint EW Center Increase as Funding Crunch Reduces Manpower," 10-21, reporting that the "Joint Electronic Warfare Center (JEWC). . .is experiencing a 20%/year increase in requests for help, but a 5%/year reduction in funding."

Covault, Craig. *Aviation Week & Space Technology.* (★ ★ ★)
Senior space technology editor. Covault gave us a most remarkable portfolio covering the Gulf War, with a special emphasis on this war's unusual satellite-based combat component. His "USAF Missile Warning Satellites Providing 90-sec. Scud Attack Alert," 1-21, and "Recon

Satellites Lead Allied Intelligence Effort," 2-4, together are an invaluable reference text on the conduct of space-based intelligence operations in modern war as defined by the unique Gulf War where "no military conflict has involved as much satellite reconnaissance imagery as that being provided to the allied forces by the USAF/CIA spacecraft." He gives, in his outstanding "Desert Storm Reinforces Military Space Directions," 4-8, what could be the best published professional verdict on the Gulf War: "The gulf war 'was the first space war. . .it was the first war of the space age,' Air Force Chief of Staff Merrill A. McPeak said." In "Complex SDI Shuttle Mission Images Aurora, Rocket Plumes," 5-6, and "Missile Surveillance Capability Advanced by Discovery's Tests," 5-13, he reports extensively on the experimental military work done aboard Shuttle Mission 39 of the orbiter Discovery and gives a breathtaking view of U.S. space combat capabilities with global strategic/political implications that are greater than the results of the Gulf War. His "Synthesis Group to Urge Rapid Lunar/Mars Pace, Support for Station Role," 6-3, is probably one of the best public previews of what will be included in the recommendations for the Moon/Mars mission. Of his remarkable series of articles assessing Soviet space capabilities after the fall (e.g., "Soviet Military Space Center Offered for Commercial Lease," 9-16, and "Controversial Soviet Space Platform Linked to Energia Booster Role," 10-21), the most outstanding was "Soviet Aerospace Shakeup Has Strategic Impact," 9-30, which notes that "The dismantling or reorganization of key Soviet space vehicle and ballistic missile assets is resulting in a loss of management control across critical sectors of Soviet aerospace," and proceeds to identify certain critical facts not found anywhere else. In "Hubble Returns Good Data But Future Is Clouded," 10-28, he summarizes the ill-fated status of the $2 billion space observatory: "The crippled Hubble Space Telescope. . .is clouded by its series of malfunctions and the ability of new ground-based telescopes to approach some of Hubble's capabilities."

de Briganti, Giovanni. *Defense News.* (★ ★ ½)
de Briganti is a thorough, comprehensive and reliable source of developments in the EC's defense industry sector, almost never missing a beat when it comes to picking up on shifts in strategic posture and their implications for industry. This year he pioneered in reporting on Europe's growing interest in anti-missile defenses. He contributed also to Desert Storm coverage with such items as "European Countries Boost Support to Desert Storm — Opposition Political Leaders Decry NATO Role in Gulf," 1-28, contrasting Germany's dovish attitude to Turkey's enthusiastic support. In "Allies Ponder Bolstered Air Defenses," 2-11, he gives a very good overview of the different efforts and interests of Germany, France, Italy and Spain in anti-tactical ballistic missile systems. He picks up the same theme in "U.S., France Discuss Joint ATBM Program," 9-2, a first-rate scoop leaking the fact that "France should cooperate with the United States to develop an antitactical ballistic missile (ATBM) system, according to a report submitted in early July to French Defense Minister Pierre Joxe." The glitches encountered in the effort to amalgamate East and West German military establishments are discussed in "Germans Seek Ammo Solution," 3-25, an excellent presentation of the monumental task of disposing of much of the equipment and ammunition from the former East German military, and in "German Soldiers Find East-West Assimilation Process Difficult," 9-30, he focused on the fact that "Western Bundeswehr officers are skeptical about the sincerity of their Eastern comrades' conversion to Western values after a lifetime of Communist indoctrination." Issues of European moves toward military integration are explored in "France to Urge Export Policy Coordination," 4-8. "France, U.K., Want Europe Satellite Network," 6-3, reports on a proposed European Military Satellite Communications (Eumilsatcom) network being pushed by Britain and France; "France, Britain to Probe Joint Development of Antiair Frigate," 7-8, on a French-British decision to conduct a study on whether to jointly develop a new frigate; and "Firms Stall RM-5 Development," 8-12, a very good analysis of a decision by Aerospatiale, Messerschmitt-Boelkow-Blohm (MBB), and Matra to reconsider development of an upgrade to the Roland surface-to-air missile.

Dornheim, Michael A. *Aviation Week & Space Technology.* (★ ★)
Engineering editor. A steadily improving writer, gifted with versatility, he covers diverse topics ranging from air traffic accidents to space exploration, air combat technologies and tactics, and engineered materials research. His "737-Metro Crash Raises Controller Workload Issues," 2-11, and "One Metro at L.A. Mistaken for Another, Controller Says," 2-18, were a fair and balanced presentation of the conflicting points of view of air controllers and pilots on the matter of a tragic air crash. In the "X-31 Flight Tests to Explore Combat Agility to 70 Deg. AOA," 3-11, he turns out a gripping piece of writing on the highly technical issue of the joint U.S.-German X-31 research aircraft program "examining how aerial combat is affected by the ability to point and turn rapidly at low speeds. . .as all-aspect weaponry meant that tail-chase tactics no longer had to dominate short-range combat. Instead, just pointing at the adversary is sufficient, and this is greatly helped by being able to maintain control well beyond the AOA (Angle of Attack) for maximum lift." In his "ATF Contract Competitors Abandon Thermoplastic Resin as Major Material," 4-15, he discusses how "conventional aluminum and titanium alloys. . .are losing their dominance rapidly as specialized engineered materials and nonmetallics gain wider acceptance." His "F-117A Pilots Conduct Precision Bombing in High Threat Environment," 4-22, is a superb analysis of the stealth fighters' role in the Gulf War, which "in the process permanently altered the practice of air power." His "Magellan Scientists Chart Ambitious Mission Plans Following First-Pass Success," 5-20, is a mine of information on the Magellan spacecraft and its versatile mapping/exploring capabilities. "Computerized Design System Allows Boeing to Skip Building 777 Mockup," 6-3, is an extensive profile of Boeing's new modeling computer system "the Dassault Systemes/IBM CATIA three-dimensional computerized modeling system. . .which gives all parties in the design process instant access to the same drawing, promoting concurrent engineering." In "Raytheon Carves New Paths As Key Programs Wind Down," 10-21, he describes a company's strategy of surviving dwindling defense spending. His "Production of First Global Venus Maps Signals Shift in Magellan Studies," 11-4, reports that "The Magellan program's study of Venus has shifted into a new, broader phase of synthesizing detailed results into a global view of the planet."

Fialka, John J. *The Wall Street Journal.* (★ ★ ½)
Pentagon. Although Fialka's rating remains the same, he is impressing us more and more. Apart from his excellent Gulf War coverage, he crafted some other gems replete with precise and valuable information. In "Fixed-Up Fighters: Old Warplanes Get Brand New Electronics, Live to Fight Again," 9-19, he gives us a profile of the burgeoning aircraft-upgrading industry explaining how "at a time when sticker shock has shrunk the overseas market for top-line U.S. fighters, the prospects for the upgrading industry are rosy." His knack for brief but lively conceptual insights is evident in "Allied Troops Concentrate on Iraq's Artillery and Mines as Ground War in the Gulf Looms," 2-11, and "Allies' Battle Plans Changed Fast and Often, Confusing Friends, and More Important, Foes," 3-11. Written in the war zone, they balance lively combat reporting and skilled military analysis, especially in naming the important doctrinal achievement of the Gulf War: "New U.S. ground-battle doctrines. . .call for field commanders to make quick, innovative decisions, depending on the flow of battle." His impressive description of the tank battle that broke Iraq's Republican Guard in "The Climactic Battle: Iraqis Are Stunned by Ferocious Assault," 3-1, is a favorite. He shows ability to distill the essential in "NATO Sets Three-Part Plan to Respond to Military Crises with Reduced Forces," 5-29, reporting that "the plan will remove most U.S. ground troops from the most war-ready fighting category and will be followed with further major changes in NATO's command structure and the way nuclear weapons are deployed in Europe." Sobriety and balance, despite the alarmist headline, are the dominant features in his "Crisis Fallout: Soviet Chaos Upends Strategies for Averting Nuclear Miscalculation," 8-30, which concludes that during the Moscow coup d'etat, "the Soviet apparatus for ordering a nuclear strike may have been immobilized for much of three days." Commendable balance and conspicuous regard for the detailed fact characterize his "Employee Charges United Technologies Bribed 2 Saudi Princes in Helicopter Sale," 10-7, which reports on a lawsuit charging that United Technologies, "evading U.S. arms exports regulations, bribed two Saudi princes to initiate a $6 billion deal to sell Blackhawk helicopters to Saudi Arabia."

Finnegan, Philip. *Defense News.* (★ ★)
In addition to his continuing focus on SDI and defense budget issues, Finnegan contributed numerous very useful analyses of the financial conditions of key defense/aerospace firms — a crucial concern in this year of tumbling budgets and unprecedented changes in defense requirements. Occasionally he displays an impish knack of buttressing his point of view with clever arrangements of news material. His "Industry Consolidation Reflects Shrinking Market," 1-28, is a basic report on declining markets, shortages of capital and the competition facing military training and simulation companies. In "Pentagon Cancels 13 Weapons," 2-14, he iterates reductions in the defense programs and observes that the defense budget begins the process of refocusing the U.S. military toward a smaller force capable of rapid deployment. Good examples of his studies of the financial status of defense companies are "Solid, Conservative Martin Marietta Finds Favor With Analysts," 6-3; "Grumman Prospects May Rest on Future of Navy F-14 Fighter," 8-26; and "Analysts Anticipate Turnaround at Boeing Defense Unit," 9-30. In "Arms Control Advocates Rap Senate SDI Plan," 7-22, he takes note of the argument that the Senate proposal to focus on the development of a limited ground-based SDI by 1996, will involve abrogating the 1972 anti-ballistic missile treaty, and he cleverly plays off two different types of SDI opponents against one another. In "U.S. Reviews Missile Plans," 8-12, he shows that developing nations may be able to design or buy countermeasures to defeat theater missile defenses, and in this manner he subliminally provides arguments against the Senate's call for premature deployment of a limited SDI. In "Coup May Revitalize Some U.S. Strategic Programs," co-authored by George Leopold 8-26, he makes a well-grounded argument that the failed Soviet coup "could boost the long-term fortunes of the Pentagon's most controversial strategic programs." His "Skeptics Pan Senate Missile Defense Plan," 9-30, leaves the reader a bit puzzled over Finnegan's apparent support of the argument against early SDI deployment on grounds that "haste in developing an antiballistic missile system for the United States is unjustifiable considering the limited threat to the United States by 1996."

Friedman, Thomas L. *The New York Times.* (★ ★ ★)
State Department. Friedman demonstrates a superior intimacy with complex issues of global diplomacy. He has splendid access to high-level sources, which, when combined with his lucid analysis and penchant for the telling detail, make him one of the best of the professionals on this beat. He worked the Gulf War with a sharp sense of its many dimensions, always alert for the subtle shifts or critical nuances of differences on coalition policy. He provided a sharp insight into the pressures for a Baker-Aziz meeting, "Compromise Is Seen," 1-3; adroitly examined the pressures an Iraq-U.S. meeting would put on both countries, "Hello Baghdad," 1-6; delivered an excellent account of where the coalition stood on the timing and necessity of force to dislodge Iraq from Kuwait, "Baker Says Anti-Iraq Allies, Except Syria, Agree on Force," 1-14; and provided several solid reports on the state of the U.S.-Israeli relationship, among them, "Barrage of Iraqi Missiles on Israel Complicates U.S. Strategy in Gulf," 1-18, and "Hard Times, Better Allies," 1-21. His "Baker Finds Doors Open, Minds Sealed," 3-17, was deft reporting on Secretary of State Baker's "victory lap" in the region, where Baker found little room for maneuver on "land for peace" initiatives. Friedman produced a well-organized and very balanced survey of opinion of U.S. foreign policy experts on the administration's decision not to aid the Kurdish rebels in Iraq, "Decision Not to Help Iraqi Rebels Puts U.S. in an Awkward Position," 4-4, in which he kept himself out of the story, skillfully playing the President's policies and the critics off one another. He combined lucid analysis with telling detail in "Whose Peace in Mideast?" 5-17, a witty, perceptive examination of the "culture clash" between American and Middle East players in the latest frustrating round of peace negotiations, concluding "And so it is with the peace process — Mr. Baker and Mr. Bush are looking at their watches and the Arabs and Israelis are looking at their calendars." "Arms Talks: A Warm-Up," 6-10, brought us swiftly up-to-date on the recent flurry on arms control activity, Friedman noting that the issue is rapidly becoming an anachronism as Washington-Moscow relations center increasingly on economics. He was brilliant with "Syria's Move Toward Peace Talks," 7-17, expertly uncovering and examining the subtle shifts in Syria's perspectives regarding negotiations with Israel, appreciating them as a consequence of the end of the Cold War.

Fulghum, David A. *Aviation Week & Space Technology.* (★ ★ ½)
Military editor. Fulghum made an important contribution to our understanding of how the Gulf War has changed military doctrine. From his debriefings of combat pilots in "Lack of Opposition Puzzles Pilots Who Flew First Missions," 1-21, to his report of how new types of equipment have shaped new tactics in "EF-111s Jammed Radars to Open Air War Against Iraq," 2-4, we get a picture of a U.S. military organization harmonizing innovations in hardware, tactics and doctrine with prudence and creativity. His best was "Desert Storm Highlights Need for Rapid Tactical Intelligence," 2-11, in which he anticipates the "big bomb damage assessment flap" within the intelligence community that was later to erupt in the public domain. He traces battlefield performance to earlier budget decisions, and spots the hardware and budget implications of the lessons learned in the battlefield. Typical is his refusal to follow the general euphoria about the Patriot missile, when he notes that "the Patriot is a point defense weapon, and. . .If the allied military targets had been spread out, there 'wouldn't be enough Patriots in the world to defend' them all." In "Allied Air Power, Forward Controllers Back Arabs to Make Their Drive Succeed," 4-22, he details "the innovative use of General Dynamics F-16s and Fairchild Republic A-10s in lieu of long-range ground reconnaissance patrols." His "Latin American Defense Exports Suffer in Wake of Gulf War," 6-17, is a study of the effect of the Gulf War on the economics of Third World arms manufacturers: "The poor showing during the Persian Gulf war of military equipment not built or supported by the U.S. and other leading industrial nations could harm a Latin American defense industry already battered by economic downturns. . .nations with money to spend on arms now have the examples of Israel in 1973 and Saudi Arabia in 1990 to show how maintaining U.S. friendship and buying U.S. made arms can result in rapid reinforcement and direct support." In "Third World Threat, Military Budget Squeeze Shape Early Concepts of Multirole Fighter," 10-21, he gives USAF the benefit of the doubt when he argues that "the threat of Soviet arms sales to Third World nations rather than the threat of Soviet armed forces" justifies the USAF's multirole fighter project.

Gellman, Barton. *The Washington Post.* (★ ★)
His most memorable contribution was the attempt to view Operation Desert Storm from a slightly less intoxicated perspective than was prevalent in the mainstream at the time. In "Schwarzkopf Sees No Evidence Iraqis Are Close to Collapse," co-authored with Rick Atkinson 1-31, he compares allied sorties to U.S. bombing missions over North Vietnam, observing that ". . .thousands were directed against North Vietnamese fortifications, factories and other targets generically similar to those in Kuwait and Iraq." His "U.S. Smart Bombs Missed 70% of Time," 3-16, was a much-quoted article in which Gellman divulged figures on the number of bombs dropped during Operation Desert Storm and their effectiveness: "[Air Force Gen. Merrill A.] McPeak's remarks, coupled with new details on the accuracy of unguided bombs from a senior Pentagon official, added up to this startling picture of the air war: of 88,500 tons of bombs dropped on Iraq and occupied Kuwait, 70 percent missed their targets," and that "laser-guided 'smart' weapons, so indispensable to the military and political strategies of the air war, accounted for only 6,520 of 88,500 tons of destructive force that U.S. planes dropped on Iraq and occupied Kuwait. McPeak said they hit their targets about 90 percent of the time." In "Allied War Struck Broadly in Iraq," 6-23, he reports that Iraq's ruined infrastructure and the painful consequences for ordinary Iraqis "contrasts with the administration's earlier portrayal of a campaign aimed solely at Iraq's armed forces and their lines of supply and command." We learn that there was a deliberate campaign to create hardship for the civilian population by aerial destruction of the country's infrastructure. His "Last Coalition Units Are Leaving Iraq: Ultimatums Issued to Protect Kurds," 7-13, is a concise explanation of what Washington's ultimatum to protect Iraqi Kurds entails, with emphasis on those Turkish reservations which killed the rescue effort, as Istanbul is "skittish about public pronouncements" regarding the presence of an allied force to defend Kurds in Iraq. His "U.S. Military Took Precautions — Officials Were Braced for Profound Changes in Strategic Pictures," 8-24, provided us with an excellent overview of the U.S. defense establishment's posture during the Moscow coup d'etat.

Gertz, Bill. *The Washington Times.* (★ ★ ½)
His remarkable access to key sources and his need to further develop his own critical judgement, qualities in Gertz that we noted in previous years, were the probable cause of the slight decline in his rating this year, as he occasionally reflected the rashness of the sources supplying his numerous "scoops." "Iraqi Defector Says Baghdad May Hit First," 1-7, is a somewhat cautious presentation of such a scoop, suggesting that Baghdad might launch a pre-emptive strike against the U.S.-led coalition. He tends to overemphasize, Cold War style, Soviet mischief in the Gulf War, as in his "Soviets Use War to Boost Spying," 1-21, focusing on Moscow's intelligence behavior after one week of war in the Gulf, including expanded use of satellites, trawlers, embassies, gleaned from Gertz's extensive contacts in the U.S. Defense intelligence community. Similarly, "Soviets Giving Aid to Iraqis, U.S. Says," 2-4, charges that "the Soviets appear to be playing a double game," in the words of Gertz's spook source. And finally, "Russian Voices Directing Iraqis," 2-13, claims that allied surveillance is picking up Russian voices on Iraqi military radio, directing a tank battalion, and claims as its source a leftist French newspaper. His "Saddam Close to Nuclear Weapon," 6-11, in quoting one official as saying "We didn't touch Saddam's nuclear weapons program. He's still in business," and detailing the disclosures by a senior Iraqi scientist and defector to U.S. intelligence sources on Saddam Hussein's plans to construct a nuclear bomb, forms the basis of a mid-summer mini-war-fever that later abated. Slow to adjust his traditional anti-Sovietism to the new realities, he chooses to emphasize themes such as "Soviets Still Making Chemical, Biological Arms," 3-6; "Soviets Building Replacement for Illegal Radar," 5-7, which muckrakes about the putative successor to the infamous, dismantled Krasnoyarsk radar; and "Soviet Lies Assessed by Senators, DOD," 6-28. We find exaggerated claims in numerous pieces, whose only justification is the reference to "intelligence sources," as for example in "Bush Calls for Mideast Arms Curbs: Iran Now Top Threat in Region," 5-30, where Iran is supposedly emerging "as the greatest threat to Middle East peace," and the irrelevant "U.S. Spy Satellite Contradicts Soviets on Chemical Weapons," 7-8. He must avoid becoming a puppet of his spook sources.

Gilmartin, Patricia A. *Aviation Week & Space Technology.* (★ ★ ½)
Congressional editor. Gilmartin's reporting contributes enormously to the public understanding of how both the political and the defense-industry establishments are attempting to respond to the new, uncertain security and funding environment. In "Bush Plan to Refocus SDI as Defense Against Limited Attack Renews Congressional Debate Over Program," 2-4, she reports that "Cheney was instructed to change the focus of the SDI program to provide global protection against limited strikes (GPALS) after a review of sweeping changes in the international political and security environment," and analyzes reactions to this shift of focus in industry and Congress. Her "Lower Defense Budgets Forcing Industry to Boost Productivity and Reduce Costs," 3-18, is a superb characterization of the defense industry's response to the new environment: "Companies seeking to flourish in an era of sharply reduced defense spending are taking bold steps to spur engineering improvements and productivity gains. . .The shift to highly integrated enterprises or paperless factories now taking shape in the U.S. defense industry could boost productivity 30-50% within five to ten years." In "Gulf War Rekindles U.S. Debate on Protecting Space System Data," 4-29, while reporting that "Senior U.S. military officials warn that advances in technology and cost reductions are making space systems with military utility accessible to a wider range of users including Third World countries," she smuggles a strategic piece of intelligence saying that "SDI Director Henry F. Cooper predicted that the Soviet Union will ultimately cooperate with the U.S. and 'move beyond' the 1972 Antiballistic Missile Treaty." While maintaining reliable Hill coverage, Gilmartin offers a fine analysis of policymakers' concerns over the eroding defense industrial base in "Maintaining Defense Base a Challenge for the '90s," 6-17, which emphasizes "concern about challenges to the defense industry base wrought by the decline in U.S. military spending." In "House Defeats Compromise Foreign Aid Bill With Limits on Mideast Arms Sales," 11-4, she predicts that Congress in the future will "retain language that seeks a temporary moratorium of U.S. arms sales to the Middle East."

Gold, Philip. *Insight.* (★ ½)

Gold's style on the whole remains somewhat detached and speculative, even though he has amply demonstrated that he can handle the concrete and the particular when he so chooses. In his "Who Serves, Who Doesn't," *The Washington Times* 1-25, he ineffectively attempts to answer the objections of "upper-middle class white liberals [who] have deplored the absence of the white upper-middle class" from the "composition of America's all-volunteer military," with a historical excursion into the ancient traditions of conscript armies. His numerous attempts to draw generalized conclusions from Desert Storm, though very well informed, do not carry the force of conviction: In "The Lessons of War Lie in Wait," 2-11, a survey of the logistics, weapons, and tactics behind Operation Desert Storm, he concludes that future wars will be "high-intensity campaigns fought against Third World foes with First and Second World weaponry," and in "After the Storm, Back to Quieter Military Perils," 3-25, he repeats that "the next U.S. involvement may well be against neither a colossus nor a guerrilla band but against some Third World power which may not even exist today, armed with God knows what." On the other hand, "Aerospace Firms Biting the Bullet," 2-11, is a concrete, richly-detailed argument that the private aerospace business will have to hold up the industry as defense outlays flag: "A successful transition could also establish a more stable prosperity, not so beholden to that most mercurial of customers, the Department of Defense." Similarly, "Putting a Run on Industry," 2-25, is an effective rundown on Pentagon procurement and production policies during the past decade, with Gold zeroing in on "selective industrial surge capability" which, he notes, is "Pentagonese for the ability to accelerate production of such critical items as can be surged," but which became in practice "As many as you can, as fast as you can." His "Semper Fi Is Under the Gun," 6-10, is an informative look at intra-service warfare as General Carl Mundy prepares to replace General Al Gray as Marine Corps Commandant, with Gold documenting why "some officers are beginning to worry that Mundy may reverse, or permit the reversal of, many of Gray's reforms."

Gordon, Michael R. *The New York Times.* (★ ★ ½)

He provided balanced, hard-nosed coverage and analysis of the Gulf War by avoiding the pitfalls of martial intoxication so much in vogue at the time. On the larger issues of national security and strategy that were raised in this unusual year, for the most part he steered clear of the temptation to speculate. His "Final Iraqi Preparations Indicate Hussein Wants War, Officials Say," 1-15, was a short but important 11th hour report on the latest Iraqi preparations such as tightening defensive positions in Kuwait and increasing aircraft training that have "persuaded a growing number of Administration policymakers that President Saddam Hussein is determined to go to war with the United States, apparently believing that he may be able to exact a high casualty toll in ground combat and secure an acceptable settlement over Kuwait." His "Iraq's Kuwait Defense: 3-Tier Plan That Collapsed," 2-26, was a well-written "Military Analysis" of the Iraqi defeat in Kuwait describing how Saddam and his generals planned their defense based on the successful strategy from their war with Iran, and how the allies overcame it with flanking movements, air power, and skilled combat engineers. "It is often said that generals prepare to fight the last war, and that is what Iraq's military leadership appears to have done in this case." His "Cheney Reports Gulf Accepting a U.S. Presence," 5-10, is a straightforward account of Defense Secretary Cheney's announcement, on his return from the Gulf, that the Arab states were agreeable to a long-term U.S. military presence there, with Gordon observing that the decision to keep some of the arrangements secret, "illustrates the continued ambivalence on the part of gulf nations about the new American military role in the area." "The Last Arms Accord?" 7-16, is a "News Analysis" of the START agreement and the politics, geopolitical and bureaucratic, surrounding the negotiations, noting that "because Moscow and Washington have found it so difficult to wrap up this accord, it is unclear whether they can muster the necessary enthusiasm for pressing ahead with more far-reaching accords." In his "Room for Differences," 10-7, he argues that the pieces of Gorbachev's and Bush's nuclear weapons reduction proposals don't quite fit together.

Goshko, John M. *The Washington Post.* (★)
State Department. For all his accumulated years of experience, Goshko managed to remain bland and singularly unstimulating in his coverage during this most remarkable year. He sees his role as that of the purveyor of the attributed quote and the reporter of what shall be deemed a diplomatic fact. Although this gives the veneer of objectivity, his articles often prompt the question: what did he leave out of his report? In "U.N. Chief Issues Plea as Peace Efforts Fail," 1-16, he recounts a version of Perez de Cuellar's peace initiative in Baghdad, basing it on a quotation of a quotation: "On the question of withdrawal, [Perez de Cuellar] stated that the Iraqi people today regarded Kuwait as Iraq's '19th province' and 'would not even whisper the word withdrawal, as war was looming and such an utterance would give a psychological advantage to Iraq's adversaries.' " In "Soviet Sparks Hopes at Last Minute," 2-24, he overreacts to the very same Soviet diplomatic comments that he wants us to ignore as "more positive than warranted." In "Across Eastern Europe, a Fear of Abandonment," 3-17, he uses the pretext of a "News Analysis" to posit that anxiety in Eastern European democracies was soothed "when President Bush launched the ground war against Iraq." His "Baker Presses Kuwait's Leadership," 4-23, is as perfunctory as can be about Secretary Baker's concerns and actions over an Amnesty International report charging Kuwait with human rights violations. His "Israel Supporters Reject U.N. as Mideast Mediator," 5-4, turns into an objective fact the Israeli argument that the U.N.'s inevitable alignment with the Arab interpretation of U.N. Resolution 242 has "canceled its chances of having an effect on the peace process." In "Ethnic Strife Replaces Cold War Rivalries," 7-14, he argues that in the coming era regional and ethnic upheavals will replace the ideological struggles of the past, using Yugoslavia as the pivotal example. His "For Soviets, a Time of Renewed Promise and Peril," 8-22, is a survey of U.S. expert opinion of Soviet prospects following the coup d'etat and it includes the unorthodox but intriguing view that "If the chaos continues. . .you'll have a coup led by younger generals frustrated by what they perceive as civilian politicians impeding progress."

Greenberger, Robert S. *The Wall Street Journal.* (★ ½)
International relations. He is conversant enough with the intricacies of international topics, but more drawn to the way these topics are seen through the lenses of professional Washington. In "Gulf War May Offer Some Opportunities for U.S. to Rebuild Its Ties With Tehran," 1-28, he notes that the prospects of warmer U.S.-Iranian ties would be an "immense psychological blow" to Saddam Hussein, but neglects other consequences of such warming. In "Middle East Deck Is Being Reshuffled as War Nears End; Questions Mount Concerning Arab-Western Relations; Palestinian Cause Is Hurt," 2-27, he ventures the opinion that the big question after the war is "how much animosity toward the West has been stirred among the Arab masses. . .who might be more drawn toward Islamic fundamentalism," and in "Baker Fails to Win Israeli Compromise on Conditions for Mideast Peace Parley," 5-16, he suggests that the U.S. "was laying the groundwork for placing blame for the failure to achieve progress on both Israel and Syria." In "Cuba's Troubles Look Worse Than Ever," 6-26, he gloats from afar over food shortages in Cuba, but he hasn't even been to Havana. However, his "Baker Meets With Shamir in Bid to Sell Peace Plan," 7-22, delivers top-rate coverage of the Middle East peace process, and "Syria's Assad, in Accepting Peace Talks, Shows That He Knows How to Play Cards," 7-29, supports the conclusion that Syria's Assad "almost surely will get more out of the effort than he will be called upon to give." His "Pressure Builds on U.S. and EC to Help Eastern Europe, But Obstacles Remain," 8-26, forecasts that "pressure is sure to grow in Europe and Washington to help accelerate the integration of [former East Bloc] nations into a united Europe." In "KGB Files May Fill Holes in History. But With What?" 9-11, he offers a nice "what if" speculation which cautions that "gleaning the truth from the Kremlin files may be like trying to construct a biography of a pathological liar by reading his mail." "Israeli Cabinet Backs Joining Mideast Talks," co-authored by Amy Dockser Marcus 10-21, challenges James Baker's insistence on winning attendance to a Mideast peace conference, which "usually meant avoiding specifics."

Healy, Melissa. *Los Angeles Times.* (★ ★)

Pentagon. A major part of her conscientious work this year was devoted to the Gulf War and its aftermath. Her strong suit is a lively, captivating style of writing, especially when applied to reporting on the more spectacular aspects of the war. The youthful lack of analytical depth is compensated with hard-working research habits. In "Radar Choreographed the Allies' Aerial Ballet," 1-18, she presents an imaginative and well-informed report about the elaborate allied network that was required to coordinate the air armada attacking Iraq. She captures, in "High-Tech Missile Hits Bull's-Eye," 1-22, the euphoric feeling generated by the Patriot missile's early success, and in "U.S. Forced to Defend Basic Targeting Goals," coauthored by Mark Fineman 2-14, she takes the controversial Baghdad bunker bombing incident to suggest that Bush's strategy of letting the generals do their jobs was a touch unhinged; this appears slanted from the outset. "Ethnic Rebellions May Help Keep Hussein in Power, Powell Warns," 3-23, is an excellent rendering of Colin Powell's argument that U.S. aid to rebellious Iraqi factions might help keep Saddam in power. In "U.S. Readies Plan to Raid Iraqi A-Sites," 6-28, she juxtaposes diplomatic and military sources to produce a very good analysis of the Bush administration's reaction to news that Iraq's nuclear program was more extensive than originally believed. Her "State Wins, Loses on Base Closing," 7-1, reporting on the Pentagon Defense Base Closure and Realignment Commission's recommendations for California, incorporates a great deal of data, with an analysis of how these closings are occurring in response to a reduced Soviet military threat. She raises the possibility of a war crimes trial against Saddam, in "Pentagon Details Abuse of American POWs in Iraq," 8-2, but supplies less than needed about the mechanisms and political implications of what to do about it. Her "U.S. Speeds Review of Nuclear-War Plan," 10-4, is a very clear and useful report about what goes into revising the U.S. nuclear target list, the Single Integrated Operational Plan, and predicts that "to keep pace with the Soviet transformation. . .the United States [could] go 'above and beyond' the nuclear-arms reductions that President Bush announced last week by making deep cuts in the U.S. nuclear arsenal."

Henderson, Breck W. *Aviation Week & Space Technology.* (★ ★ ½)

Military electronics editor. His reporting has supplied a rich picture of current and prospective uses of advanced electronics and satellite technologies in modern warfare. In "Aircraft-Style Avionics Add Punch to U.S. Army's Next-Generation Tank," 1-7, he portrays a future tank's turret looking like a jet fighter's cockpit: "The new tank will have an integrated command and control network, inertial navigation and fire control systems, and digital displays which would look familiar to the crew of a modern fighter." His "DAPRA Contract Boosts Integrated FOG/Global Positioning System," 1-14, is an education on gyroscope-based, satellite-dependent guidance devices, explaining the differences in gyroscopic techniques: "Spinning mass gyros are analogous to mechanical computers, RLGs (ring laser gyros) are the vacuum tubes while FOGs (fiber optic gyros) are the solid state edition." He explains, in "Ground Forces Rely on GPS to Navigate Desert Terrain," 2-11, how our Global Positioning Satellite system with cheap, mass-distributed GPS receivers tell a small unit or an isolated individual soldier the exact coordinates of his location. In "Marines, USAF to Replace Aging Air Control Facilities With Modular Units," 4-8, a report on the program of "replacing aging tactical air operations control facilities" used by the armed forces, he describes the capabilities of "the new modules [which] proved their worthiness in action in Operation Desert Storm." In "Market for Military Computers Growing in Time of Tight Budgets," 5-27, he reports on the market for military data processing which "is thriving in the wave of Operation Desert Storm, which confirmed the value of both computerized weapons and support systems. . .the $43 billion defense electronics industry continues to be the healthiest part of the defense sector." His "Military Turns to Laptop Computers to Raise Fighting Effectiveness," 6-3, is a report on the laptop's success in the military, and "DARPA Directs Development of Mine to Detect, Destroy Helicopters," 6-24, is a fascinating description of an anti-helicopter mine whose "design includes a charge to throw the warhead up in the direction of the target." "Hardened Luggage Containers Eyed to Counter Bomb Threat," 10-28, contains some potential good news in air travel anti-terror security.

Hitchens, Theresa. *Defense News.* (★ ★)
Brussels bureau chief. There was considerable upgrading in Hitchens's output this year concentrated, for the most part, on Western Europe's inchoate endeavors to redefine its security identity between the end of the Cold War and the collapse of communism in the Soviet Union. In "Havel Warns West Against Allowing East Europe Drift," 3-25, she deftly analyzes the broader issues of NATO and EC membership of former Warsaw Pact members on the occasion of Czech President Havel's plea to be accepted by the West as "our countries are dangerously sliding into a certain political, economic, and security vacuum." In "Post-Cold War NATO Plans to Key on Reserve Forces," 5-27, she draws the implications that result from the fact that "NATO's new post-Cold War strategy and conventional force posture will put greater emphasis on reserve forces." "NATO to Rewrite Nuclear Strategy," 6-3, previews the strategy overhaul simmering at NATO headquarters, including a shift from land forces to air, from nuclear weapons to conventional, and from pre-targeting to doctrinal flexibility. In her important "U.S.-European Joint Programs Sink to New Low," 6-24, she issues a timely warning that as a result of the fact that "cooperative programs between the United States and Europe have slid to their lowest point in years," the danger exists that "separate, adversarial [defense] markets" will develop. The effects of the communist collapse in Moscow are ably discussed in "NATO Rethinks Role After Soviet Breakup," 9-9, in which she notes that "the breakup of the Soviet Union threatens to unravel hard-won consensus among the 16 NATO countries about the future of the alliance, reviving old debates about its military strategy and political role." She is right to keep warning about the potential of a Europe - U.S. rift in "Army Proposal Divides NATO," co-authored by George Leopold 10-21, reporting that "the proposal to expand an existing Franco-German brigade could drive a wedge between pro-NATO Britain and European Community backers such as France. Implicit in the plan is a reduced role for the United States in the defense of Europe." The same concern colors her "Europe Sharpens WEU Teeth," 11-18, which is tainted by the inexcusably unprofessional blunder of misidentifying German Foreign Minister Hans Dietrich Genscher as the "German Defense Minister."

Hoffman, David. *The Washington Post.* (★ ½)
State Department. Depend on Hoffman to supply the standard State Department line — with an occasional critical remark on minor detail. He is imaginative in the small, when it comes to weaving human interest into issues of policy, but in this unusual year at least, his imagination did not assist in grasping the broader picture. In "U.S.-Iraq Talks Fail to Break Gulf Stalemate; Aziz Says War Would Bring Attack on Israel," 1-10, he sees the Baker-Aziz talks in Geneva through Baker's eyes, noting that "Iraq showed no signs of buckling to international demands that it relinquish Kuwait immediately and unconditionally," with no attempt to portray Iraq's argument. His "Baker Attracts Interested Buyers to Postwar Marketplace of Peace," 3-17, is a typical imaginative-in-the-small "News Analysis" of Secretary of State Baker's stroll through a *souk* in Old Damascus to assess the chances of his Mideast peace plan: "Baker. . .stopped short of asking the many browsers in the marketplace what price they would pay for peace." "Witness to a Scene From Hell," 4-21, is sentimentally critical toward the administration's indifference to the Kurds, appealing to banal feeling to substitute for policy analysis: "Even in a short time on that hillside, it was impossible not to feel overwhelmed by the scope of the emergency. The dust, the smoky ashes, the silent faces formed a biblical tableau." In "Political-Economic Shift Is Key to Soviet Rescue," 6-4, he one-dimensionally notes that "officials and analysts believe that far too much public attention has been focused on the issue of aid, when the real problem is getting Gorbachev and his country on the road to lasting reform." His "Baker Says Assad Agrees to Attend Peace Conference," 7-17, is singularly uncritical of Syria and sets up Israel to be blamed should the talks fail. His "Talks Announcement Is U.S.-Soviet Gambit to Draw All Sides In," 8-1, finally gets the point of Bush and Baker's strategy to bring off a Middle East peace conference: "With the active cooperation of the Soviet Union, they want to close off any doors that might be used to escape from the conference table, and they want to make it attractive for the holdouts to come in from the cold."

Holzer, Robert. *Defense News.* (★ ★)
Well informed, meticulous in his research, a clear writer who enjoys privileged sources of information, Holzer is the person to be consulted about developments in the naval service. His "Contractors Play Key Role in Gulf War Operations," 1-21, is an excellent examination of the reliance of the Armed Forces on civilian contractors to maintain their ever increasingly technically complex equipment. In "Advanced Simulation Cuts Weapon Development Costs," 2-11, he emphasizes the importance of advanced high fidelity simulation testing in the development of new weapons systems in the face of declining budgets: "we can almost get simulation to model 99% of the real world, the only thing you don't have is the grime, sweat, and blood of a battlefield." In "Navy Struggles to Find Funding for Ailing Aviation," 3-25, he argues that naval aviation's capabilities are being severely reduced and that the "Navy will have to decide whether they will shift funding away from ships and submarines to fund naval aviation." In "Navy Ponders ATF Avionics in New Hornets," co-authored with George Leopold 5-6, he examines the use of the integrated electronic warfare system (INEWS) on the F/A-18 Hornet fighter, as well as its application to other aircraft. In "Navy Explores Advanced Technology for Future Cruise Missiles," 6-3, he reports on Navy research to add sensors to cruise missiles that would make them more autonomous on the battlefield. "To Create New Simulation Office," 7-8, reports on the formation of the "Defense Modeling and Simulation Office" to coordinate the military's numerous simulation programs. "Navy Initiates Long Term Effort to Convert Satellite Links," co-written by Neil Munro 8-12, is a fascinating report on stealthy communications where "Low probability of detection radio networks disguise their radio signals as background static" — only friendly radios with computers that know the pattern can detect the signals. His "Navy Shifts Focus to Project Power," 9-2, is a compact report focusing on the increased competition between the Navy and Air Force for long-range attack missions, as he explains that the Navy has moved from an "isolate the Soviet Union" orientation to power projection, using aircraft carriers, while the Air Force is pushing the B-2 stealth bomber.

Hughes, David. *Aviation Week & Space Technology.* (★ ★)
Northeast bureau chief. During Desert Storm, he reported on the performance of key weapons systems under combat conditions. His best was "Patriot Antimissile Successes Show How Software Upgrades Help Meet New Threats," 1-28, explaining how high-tech wars are won or lost before the shooting begins: "The Patriot. . .demonstrates what can be done by modifying computer software to enable a system to deal with a new threat. . .The idea to modify Patriot emerged in the late 1970s and early 1980s when the Soviets began improving the accuracy of their Scud missiles." In "USAF Uses Sparrows and Sidewinders in Successful Attacks on Iraqi MiGs," 2-4, he repeats the same kind of coverage for the Sparrow and the Sidewinder. Ever the bread-and-butter reporter of the less glamorous but always necessary areas of the trade, "USAF Studies Retrofitting 707s Into AWACS as Boeing Considers Shutting Production Line," 4-1, he covers the issues involved in "converting used Boeing 707 airframes into Airborne Warning and Control System platforms as the manufacturer nears a decision on ending AWACS production by closing the 707 line." His "USAF Adapts Off-the-Shelf Computer Hardware, Software in New Systems," 6-3, and "Advanced USAF Mission Planning System Will Serve Fighters, Bombers and Transports," 6-10, are superb in describing the versatility and diversity of choice gained as "the U.S. Air Force is using more off-the-shelf computer technology for mission critical functions in command, control, communications and intelligence systems in an effort to create flexible systems with built-in expansion capability." In "Tracking Software Error Likely Reason Patriot Battery Failed to Engage Scud," 6-10, he identifies the reason for the Patriot's failure to engage the Scud that killed 28 soldiers in their barracks during the Gulf War: "A Patriot missile battery that operated for four days accumulated a 0.36-sec. error in a software-driven tracking function." In "Delco Resonator Gyro Key to New Inertial Systems," 9-30, he reports on an attempt to commercially use "gyro technology developed initially for ballistic missiles," and in "GE Missile Warning Systems Rely on Staring Arrays," 10-21, reports on groundbreaking work with "indium antimonide staring array sensors" in "developing missile approach warning systems."

Kamen, Al. *The Washington Post.* (★ ½)
Foreign affairs. During the second year of his assignment to this beat, Kamen's contribution has been modest just as his choice of interests has been modest. Apart from a certain passing involvement in the issue of refugees and immigrants, it seems to us that his weakness has been a certain reluctance to develop any abiding areas of interest and, thereby, expertise. Examples of arms-length, albeit well-written foreign coverage include "Amid Disinformation and Confusion, Wartime Truth Is Hard to Come By," 1-19, surveying wartime disinformation campaigns in the Gulf War; the speculative "El Salvador's Factions Say Civil War May Be Nearing Resolution," 4-7; and "Nicaraguan Leader Seeks New U.S. Aid," 4-16, covering Violeta Chamorro's visit to Washington "with outstretched arms looking for new U.S. financial aid." Much better, well researched and spirited were his numerous reports on his own investigations into the world of refugees and immigrants, both illegal and legal. In "A Dark Road From China to Chinatown," 6-17, he reports on "the dozens of ways tens of thousands of Chinese enter the United States illegally each year in what immigration officials say is an increasing and seemingly unstoppable flow." His "Immigration 'Sweepstakes': Odds Will Favor the Irish; Program Earmarks 40% of Available Visas," 7-28, reviews the expected effects of a new Immigration Act provision whereby "40,000 green cards. . .will be handed out each year for the next three years." He is lively, entertaining and informative in "A Rock Band to Seattle, a Guerrilla Band to Florida," 8-12, and "New Wave of Refugees Making Haven a Home; Jobs, Kin, Chance Guide Refugees," also 8-12; both chronicle the great variety of compassionate and imaginative ways by which Americans offer shelter to such diverse types of refugees as a "Bulgarian rock band in Seattle. . .CIA-trained Libyan guerillas [and]. . .Soviet Pentecostals seeking refuge in this country." In his critical "An Investment in American Citizenship; Immigration Program Invites Millionaires to Buy Their Way In," 9-29, he pours scorn on an immigration program to sell U.S. citizenships for $1 million a shot: "Lady Liberty may still beckon to the 'huddled masses yearning to breathe free,' but Uncle Sam now extends a special welcome to those who can pay cash."

Kandebo, Stanley W. *Aviation Week & Space Technology.* (★ ½)
Technical editor. Kandebo's best work was done in covering the deployment of the Tomahawk cruise missile in Desert Storm. "Tomahawk Missile Excels in First Wartime Use," 1-21, also included some sensitive facts about the war missed by all the other media, when it reported that "missiles from U.S. ships in the Mediterranean also may have been used to strike Iraq if Syria allowed the weapons to overfly its territory to reach potential targets. . .[and]. . .cruise missile-equipped ships and boats are provided with Tomahawk firing solutions prior to leaving port," suggesting that the decision to go to war had been taken long before the U.N. resolution, and the congressional vote. He strongly favored Grumman's F-14 fighter for the Navy and wrote why in "Grumman Naval Aircraft Design Concepts Evolving From Current F-14 Versions," 4-29; "Versatile and Flexible F-14 Offered as Best Choice When Pitted Against F/A-18," 4-29, and "Grumman Makes 11th-Hour Offer to Get F-14 Into Fiscal '92 Budget," 5-6. These are unadorned, data-packed, dry and crisp reports written to be enjoyed by engineers and to be feared by bureaucrats in whose hand it rests to make the selections among competing weapons systems. As he reports that "Defense Dept. decisions to terminate the Grumman F-14 program and procure an advanced version of the McDonnell Douglas F/A-18 base have polarized the debate," he goes on to warn that "the F-14 and its derivatives are the more versatile of the two aircraft families and therefore would be the best choice to provide the Navy with maximum flexibility in future aircraft procurement." "Osprey Flight Tests Suspended After Crash of No. 5 Aircraft," 6-17, is an uncomplimentary account of the crash of a V-22 Osprey test plane, emphasizing that "officials have not been able to identify any specific reason for the crash." "Pratt Defines Development Path for F100 Fighter Engine Family," 9-30, is a good technical report on the future of fighter engines. In "Bell Boeing, FAA Work to Resolve Final V-22 Certification Issues," 10-28, Kandebo predicts that "outstanding issues surrounding interim certification of the V-22 tilt-rotor could be resolved by mid-1992," his most charitable opinion about this aircraft.

Kempster, Norman. *Los Angeles Times.* (★)
National security. Although his writing gives the impression that his judgment is very good and that he relies on sophisticated analysis, he avoids exploiting either and uses heavily direct quotes and undigested facts, often presented in the way officials would like to see them presented. His "Baker-Aziz Crisis Talks Fail: Both Sides Charge Inflexibility; Israel Threatened," 1-10, like the meeting itself, is a drawn out and very average discussion of Baghdad's attempt to link a withdrawal from Kuwait with an Israeli promise to abandon the occupied territories. In "Hussein Unlikely to Hold Power for Long, Bush Says," 3-28, he correctly puts emphasis on the "seemingly contradictory objectives of ousting Hussein while preserving Iraq's unity," but avoids any analysis other than repetition of Bush's own prediction that Hussein will fall. He claims, in "Saudis Confirm It: Count Them Out," 4-22, that Saudi Arabia's decision to decline participation may have "delivered a possibly fatal blow" to Washington's "two-track" Middle East peace conference, but avoids explaining why. In "Mideast Foes Like Peace But Not the Price, Baker Finds," 5-17, he outlines the Syrian and Israeli stances toward the U.S.-proposed Middle East conference, and concludes that "there is a de facto peace already, and the benefits of formalizing are not overwhelming," and suggests that "the defeat of Saddam Hussein's belligerent regime may have eliminated one incentive for Israel, Syria, Saudi Arabia and others to make peace." His coverage of the Moscow coup d'etat was just average, its high point being "Bush Calls for Return of Gorbachev to Power," co-authored by James Gerstenzang 8-20, graced with rather eerie bits of detail that add to the tension. In "Yugoslavia Arms Embargo Unlikely to Cut Fighting," 9-28, he correctly points out that the U.N. arms embargo will "allow Serbia to obliterate Croatia," given that federal troops can keep fighting for months without buying more weapons from abroad. In "Bush Against Sending GIs to Haiti," 10-5, he quotes extensively Bush's pious pronouncements against "using United States forces in this hemisphere," and, incredibly, fails to address the inconsistency of this statement uttered by the victor in Panama.

Kolcum, Edward H. *Aviation Week & Space Technology.* (★ ★)
Senior editor. Unfazed by the year's spectacular developments, Kolcum maintained his routine, keeping his usual calendar of works in progress. In "FAA, MIT Complete First C-Band Radar Tests for Detecting Wind Shears," 1-7, he gives an account of the FAA's weather hazard research program "to locate and analyze weather hazards near airports" whose purpose is to have the "Terminal Doppler Weather Radar (TDWR) installation in U.S. airports [which] is scheduled to begin in two to three years." In "Launch Complex Being Rebuilt to Meet Target Date for Mars Observer," 2-4, he notes the progress to refurbish NASA's Titan Launch Complex 40 in order to facilitate the launching of the Mars Observer craft next year. Of greater general interest is his "Gulf War Reinforces Value of U.S. Stealth Technologies," 2-18, in which, early on in Desert Storm, he gives valuable preliminary insights into the lessons learned in using new weapons systems, basically vindicating the Pentagon's doctrinal assumptions about them: "New stealth and precision-guided weapons technologies are proving themselves in Desert Storm. . .[and] Desert Storm experiences will bring subtle planning modifications into focus, but will not result in a massive overhaul in doctrine." Kolcum is usually on top of activities and news at the Kennedy Space Center where he has filed numerous routine reports, such as the "GRO Mission Countdown to Set Standard for Future," 4-15, reporting that "the processing flow and terminal countdown for the Gamma Ray Observatory space shuttle mission could establish the standard procedure for future flight because milestones were on target in virtually every sequence," and the "Revised Kennedy Processing Facility Supports Scaled Down Space Station," 5-6, reporting that "the facility that will prepare space station components for launch has been scaled down in line with the smaller version of the station recently unveiled by NASA." His "Military Leaders Say GPS Success in Gulf Assures Tactical Role for Satellites," 5-13, is a fascinating report from the proceeding of the 28th Space Congress, assessing the space aspects of Desert Storm where "space has come of age in combat."

Krauss, Clifford. *The New York Times.* (★ ★)
State Department. He produced some of the best and most highly appreciated information on the civil war in Ethiopia. He also was one of the few sources on much-neglected Panama. With "Rebels Are Posing a Threat in Panama," 1-21, he updated us on the existence of rebel organizations of former Noriega troops which, while lacking sufficient "popular support to engage in a prolonged offensive. . .can cause enough damage to slow the private investment needed to rebuild the economy." In "Dependence and Sovereignty Pull at Panama's Equilibrium," 2-11, he stressed the tensions that exist over questions of local sovereignty vs. reliance on U.S. aid, noting the reassessment of the U.S. invasion as popular resentment over the government's failure to produce healthy economic policies mounts. Krauss's report on the plight of Chad-based dissident Libyan fighters, once supported and trained by the U.S., "Failed Anti-Qaddafi Effort Leaves U.S. Picking Up the Pieces," 3-12, filled in the background details of their history and added fresh information on the arrangements of their transfer to Zaire. He reported on the fundamental political realignments taking place there in "Ethiopia and 3 Rebel Groups Look Toward U.S.-Led Peace Talks," 5-14: "All the major Ethiopian forces say they are looking to Washington to mediate a solution even though they have all espoused Marxist ideology at one time or another." The military collapse of Mengistu's regime was chronicled in "Ethiopian Guerrillas Mount an Offensive as Peace Talks Near," 5-20; "Ethiopia's Dictator Flees," 5-22; "Ethiopians Rejoice at Fall of Rulers," 5-2; "Rebels in Ethiopia Seize a Vital Port, Sealing Takeover," 5-26; and "In Addis Ababa, a War Comes Home," 5-27. The immediate post-revolution perspectives were spelled out with "Rioters in Addis Ababa Vent Their Anger on Americans," 5-30; "Top Ethiopia Rebel Talks of Democracy," 6-2; "Ethiopians Have New Rulers But Famine's Specter Lingers," 6-14; and "New Policies, Old Slogans in Ethiopia," 6-29. His information was authoritative and provided, at the time, one of the best pictures of the complicated political situation facing the country. His "In Policy Shift, U.S. Pressures Haitian on Rights Abuses," 10-7, details how the Organization of American States is coming down hard on ousted Haiti President Father Jean-Bertrand Aristide, for his apparent condoning of vigilante violence including necklacing.

Lardner, George. *The Washington Post.* (★ ½)
Together with Walter Pincus, he continued to pursue the Iran-contra scandal and rejoiced in this year's minor successes of the Special Prosecutor, but he also managed to do some more useful reporting on the anti-terrorism beat, where he was sometimes on and sometimes off the mark. Off the mark is "Anti-Terrorism Drive Intensifies," 1-28, based on a fear-mongering quote of someone who makes a living as a "counter-terror expert." The rather frightening quote is supposed to put an entirely new spin on the issue: " 'We haven't seen the real tough stuff yet,' said Vincent Cannistrarro, former chief of counterterrorism operations at the CIA. Right now, he said, 'everybody and his brother is just taking advantage of the Persian Gulf to go out and do what they want to do anyway.' " In "U.S. Faulted on Antiterrorism Funding," 2-27, he complains about the startling lack of funding for anti-terrorism measures, such as devices to detect plastic explosives, and comes close to lobbying. In "French Link Libyans to Bombings," 6-27, he provides evidence that the Pan Am 103 bombing was done by the Libyans, seeking revenge for the 1986 U.S. air raid: "Attacks against U.S. and French targets were discussed and decided upon at a meeting at Libyan intelligence headquarters in Tripoli in September 1988." A cynic might wonder if this is part of an effort to absolve the main suspects in the Pan Am 103 bombing, the Iranians, Palestinians, and especially the Syrians in a effort to move along the Middle East Peace process. In "CIA Probed, Used BCCI, Official Says," 8-3, he reports not only that, but also, according to CIA Deputy Director Richard Kerr, the CIA at one time had accounts there, an interesting snapshot that raises as many questions as it answers. A number of Irangate articles co-authored with Walter Pincus were attempts to resuscitate the scandal after the guilty plea of former CIA official Alan D. Fiers and during the Robert Gates confirmation hearings. Most notable were the "Ending Silence, Insider Lifts CIA Veil," 9-20, and "Gates's Memory Gaps Contrast With Others' Iran-Contra Recall," 9-23, which display a good dose of nastiness and unwillingness to bury a bone that has been chewed dry.

Lenorovitz, Jeffrey M. *Aviation Week & Space Technology.* (★ ★)
European editor. Unimpressive reporting of allied contributions to the air war campaign was Lenorovitz's unenviable fate during Desert Storm. Reflecting the rigid official control of public information, his dispatches hardly deviated an inch from what military briefers doled out, but at least he filled us in on what French officials had to say, "France Uses C.160G Aircraft to Perform Elint, ESM Missions," 1-21, and "French Use Jaguar Fighter/Bombers to Strike Desert Storm Targets," 1-28. His European product development reports were far better. In "Aerospatiale/MBB Team Begins Flight Testing Tiger Attack Helicopter," 5-6, he reports on the "maiden flight of the...French/German Tiger attack helicopter being developed as an advanced combat system for air-to-ground and air-to-air missions." In "Rafale C01 Fighter Exceeds Mach 1 on Maiden Flight, Reaches 36,000 Ft.," 5-27, he reports that "Dassault Aviation plans a rapid opening of the basic operational envelope for its Rafale C01 preproduction fighter." His "Soviet Ejection Seat for Buran Shuttle Qualified for Deployment at Up to 4 Mach," 6-10, is the elaborate tale of a newly-developed Soviet ejection seat. By contrast, "Cocom Eases Restrictions on Export of High-Tech Equipment to Eastern Bloc," 6-10, is succinct, both brief and informative, and it gives us a clear idea of Cocom's new policy rationale. "Europeans Facing Major Hurdles In Implementing Long-Term Space Plan," 6-17, is a very good, comprehensive survey of Western Europe's space program as "The European Space Agency...is preparing a major restructuring of [its] long-term space plan as it faces the dual tasks of controlling growing costs and meeting technical challenges of the multibillion dollar program." "Europe's Largest Transport Begins Flight Test Program," 11-4, is a package of informed articles forming a major survey of the European "Airbus Industrie's program to evolve a family of large transports based on the A340/330 design," and providing admirably detailed data on the performance, specifications and market potential of this major European competitor.

Leopold, George. *Defense News.* (★ ★ ½)
Moving considerably beyond his earlier interests in electronic warfare issues, Leopold is rapidly becoming a formidable reporter on developments in the global arms control environment with secondary, albeit very focused, emphasis on the global implications of certain high-tech issues. Some of his strategic coverage anticipated the daily press by weeks or months, as evidenced by "Arms Controls Experts Eye Multinational Effort to Stabilize Gulf," 2-25, and "China Markets Missile to Middle East Buyers," 4-8, an excellent treatment of missile proliferation in the Mideast with a focus on the alarming prospects of China's M9 and M11 missile exports. In "U.S.-Japan Relation to Struggle, Report Warns," 8-12, he points out that "None of the U.S. major bilateral relationships have been rendered so vulnerable to domestic pressures by the end of the Cold War as the U.S. relationship with Japan." His "Cold War Leaves Legacy of Instability in Asia," 9-30, is a convincing argument about "growing instability...in Asia's Pacific rim" as a result of the end of the Cold War. His stimulating analysis, "Change in China: Military May Hold Reform Key," 10-28, suggests that a regionally fragmented and perhaps pro-reform Chinese army leadership will call the shots, whose "biggest concern related with economic and political reforms is modernization of its outdated conventional forces which have not kept pace with China's small but advanced nuclear arsenal." His solid technical coverage was typified by such items as his "Allied Radar Hunters, Jammers Cloud Skies for Desert Storm," 1-21, reporting how the allied electronic warfare systems " 'made the Iraqis blind and deaf'...[as] allied electronic jamming and radar-hunting aircraft overwhelmed Iraqi communications and air defenses," his "U.S., Japan to Tighten Supercomputer Access," 6-17, a brief but sharply focused report about how these two "leading manufacturers of high-performance computers have agreed to tighten export restrictions to prevent the spread of nuclear weapons and ballistic missiles," and his "Improved Sub Data Flow Stresses Stealth Capability," 6-24, an excellent discussion of the developing Submarine Operational Automation System aimed to "manage the information flow to future submarine commanders [that] will focus on keeping the submarine quiet and stealthy."

Lewis, Paul. *The New York Times.* (★ ★ ★)
United Nations. Lewis, a particularly lucid writer, provides steady, solid coverage on this beat, which was especially crucial this year. Thoroughly professional, he maintains a rigorous concern for accuracy, and is appreciated within the diplomatic community as a most trustworthy correspondent. He reported that Arab diplomats were suggesting Iraq might consider a pull-out from Kuwait in exchange for a conference on the Palestinian-Israeli problem in "Arabs Say Iraq Plans Offer Linking Pullout to Israel," 1-11. Although rebuked by Baghdad as "wishful thinking," the rumors had been circulating widely and his report helped move Iraq toward clarifying their stance. He touched all bases on the terms and timetable for an end to the Gulf War in a tightly-written "U.N. Votes Stern Conditions for Formerly Ending War," 4-4. Lewis included important detail on the council's hands-off attitude toward the Kurds, citing Soviet reticence as a major factor. An evocative writer, he produced an exquisite feature on the devastating inflation raging in Iraq, "When All That Glitters Must Be Sold (for Scraps)," 7-25. Desperate Iraqi citizens were selling off their gold to the "hard-faced men who make money out of war," he reported; "the price of gold is a barometer of people's fears. And right now that barometer is firmly stuck at stormy." Lewis's coverage of the issue of Iraq's nuclear capacity was highly professional. He carefully set out the U.S. case that Iraq was attempting to conceal equipment used for making nuclear explosives, citing the claim of one Iraqi defector that as much as 90 pounds of uranium has been enriched to weapons-grade level with "U.S. Photos to Argue Iraq Hides Nuclear Material," 6-27. He provided the central details on the skepticism over Iraq's claim that it has produced insufficient amounts of plutonium for nuclear weapons in "Iraq Now Admits a Secret Program to Enrich Uranium," 7-9. He maintained important detachment on the issue, reporting that U.N. inspectors seriously doubt Iraq has 90 pounds of enriched plutonium and their conclusion that the country is not hiding nuclear installations, "Iraq Atom Effort Ruined, Inspectors Say," 7-18.

Madison, Christopher. *National Journal.* (★ ★)
Foreign policy. Madison, as do many of his fellows at *NJ,* tends toward the verbose, and although he makes occasional good points, we can get lost in his prose. He's stopped dropping names, fortunately, in favor of more substantive information. In "Follow the Leader," 1-12, he stresses that Congress's overwhelming reticence on the Gulf has been surprising, considering its activism on foreign affairs in recent years: "the first impulse of many Members was to punt: to seek safety in a debate about their own role in foreign affairs instead of directly debating President Bush's Gulf Policy." In "Foley's Muted Call to Arms," 2-23, Madison says that House Speaker Foley is a "shrinking violet. . .who refuses to package his ideas in digestible provocative soundbites." Even so, his speech to the National Press Club may have defined a post-Persian Gulf domestic agenda more cogently than anyone else: a triumph overseas does not help the economic disaster at home. In "Scrambling Vicar," 4-20, he argues that Jim Baker didn't get his "proverbial miracle" during the Persian Gulf War. In mid-April he was off for the fourth time on a high risk diplomatic mission to the Middle East, where it is far from certain that his gamble would produce peace or restore his clout in the administration. Beyond Baker's possible presidential ambitions, his stature in the administration affects his standing among allies as well. He argues convincingly that Baker has to share the limelight now with Scowcroft and Cheney. In "Foreign Aid Follies," 6-1, he predicts that although the White House wants fewer strings attached to foreign aid, it isn't likely to get its way, as special interest groups are up in arms, and key members of Congress are reluctant to give up their cherished "earmarks." "Whatever Happened to Lebanon?" 7-20, reminds us that with all the focus elsewhere in the Middle East these days, Lebanon though forgotten, has seen dramatic changes. The fight between Muslim and Christian factions, which has gone on for 16 years, has stopped due to the May 22 Treaty of Brotherhood, Cooperation and Coordination between Lebanon and Syria, with U.S. approval that has aided in putting Lebanon in Syria's sphere of influence.

Mann, Jim. *Los Angeles Times.* (★ ★ ½)

National security, covering Asia. A number of his articles stood way above his average work because, although meant as routine analyses, they turned out to be thumbnail sketches of serious regional policy reviews. Among the best were "U.S. to Offer Incentives for Vietnam Ties," 4-9, a superlative explanation of why "The Bush Administration has decided to launch a major diplomatic initiative toward Vietnam, offering America's former wartime adversary a series of trade and economic benefits and new steps toward normalization of relations"; "5 Forces Shape Asia Policy," 5-21, a noteworthy "effort to determine Washington's approach to Asia [by] reckon[ing] with the complex and delicate interplay among various American constituencies"; and "U.S. Weighing Deal to End A-Arms in Korea," 6-9, identifying "the advancing North Korean nuclear weapons program [as] the most serious security problem the United States now confronts in Asia." In "A Moscow Shift Toward the West," 8-27, he advances the intriguing thesis that "the Soviet Union — or its Russian replacement — appears likely to identify increasingly with Western Europe and the United States. . .while, on a surprising number of issues, Asian countries have recently begun to band more closely together — often in opposition to Western Europe and the United States." On a more modest level but still very good are his more routine items such as "Costs of Gulf Operation? Administration Won't Say," 1-11, harping on one of the season's favorite topics, i.e., "The Bush Administration is going to extraordinary lengths to avoid telling Congress how high the costs of Operation Desert Shield will be." In the sharp "U.S. Urges Japan to Improve Ties, Trade With Israel," 3-23, he offers the observation that "The Administration's new effort to foster Japan's relations with Israel is intended to. . .open the way for Japan to ease the financial burden in the United States in providing economic help to Israel." In "U.S. Moves to Curb Suspect China Goods," 10-5, he speculates on the reasons and intended effects of the fact that "In a groundbreaking case, the U.S. Customs Service moved. . .to hold up shipments of certain Chinese goods that are suspected of being produced by convict labor or forced labor."

Mauthner, Robert. *Financial Times.* (★ ★ ★)

A mature, thoughtful and articulate student of history, Mauthner stood out in this year of historic landslides and shakeups. He provided a calm and critically thoughtful approach to the Gulf War when most others were vying for front place in the cheerleading section. He was similarly cautious from the outset about the succor to Gorbachev provided by western governments. In "History Takes Its Revenge," 1-15, he argues forcefully that Western, particularly Washington's, faith in Gorbachev-as-deliverer is dangerously misplaced. With "The Linkage That Cannot Be Avoided," 1-22, Mauthner refuses to join the general euphoria of U.S./U.K. public and official opinion, predicting that Saddam is likely to survive, also noting that "the liberation of Kuwait and the restoration of its rulers will not be enough to restore stability to the region." In "Unclear War Goals Cloud Peace Aims," 2-12, he cautions that the unstated war objective, which is "the overthrow of President Saddam Hussein and his regime, if peace and stability are to prevail in the region," will undermine any realistic regional security system. His "A Question of Confidence," 6-5, is a logically ruthless disparagement of the then-current vogue of grandiose Middle East disarmament schemes, showing that "the history of arms control is littered with the wrecks of agreements forged in a context where a perception of mutual national interests did not exist." In "Nuclear Age Is Not Over," 7-24, he undermines the arms control crowd's euphoria from the conclusion of START by noting that "If the risk of war has been lowered, it is not thanks to the Start agreement, but to the new international political climate," and observes that the real security problems of the '90s and beyond will be proliferation of weapons technology, combined with the intensification of ethnic strife and migration. His "The EC Found Wanting," 7-31, in commenting on the Yugoslav civil war, endorses the peacemaking intentions of Europe's diplomats in the Balkans, but exposes the flaw of their efforts: they don't agree on what kind of entity should emerge from Yugoslavia. "The EC's Moment of Truth," 8-7, is an intriguing examination of the merits of the views of the "deepeners," those who want a small, exclusive, united European Community, *sans* East Europeans and Turks.

McManus, Doyle. *Los Angeles Times.* (★ ★)
National security. His coverage was thoughtful and versatile, contributing some refreshing insights to the vast commentary on the historic developments in both the Middle East and in the East. In "To Hussein, Risks of Peace Could Be Worse Than War," 1-13, he resists the popular temptation to demonize Saddam Hussein and argues that "he may have decided that he is better off taking a chance on war than on the crushing public humiliation he would suffer if he were to give in to President Bush's demands. . .these are not irrational calculations." His "U.S. May Add Removal of Hussein to Its War Goals," 1-22, pivots on the historical axiom that war goals can and do change mid-battle, and that not only isn't this anything unusual, it's normal. In "8 Arab Allies Back Bush's Initiative for Mideast Peace," 3-11, he minces no words: "But the Arabs attempted to redefine Bush's policy in their own mold, declaring that the aim should be to 'end the Israeli occupation of the Arab territories and to ensure the national rights of the Palestinian people.' " His dignified recounting of recent history and delicate delineation of the negotiating process is refreshing, as most seem to think the Arabs a backward people; McManus, obviously, does not. In "American Ghosts in the Gulag," 7-29, recently declassified documents indicate that dozens of U.S. sailors and airmen could have been secretly captured by the Soviets during the Cold War and held in captivity for decades. In "Next Step — START Treaty Leaves Both Sides Thinking, What Now?" 7-30, he quotes Soviet commentator Sergei Karaganov, that further nuclear cuts are unlikely since "Nuclear weapons, sadly but truly, are the only thing that gives us superpower status." His "U.S. Dilemma: Wooing 2 Top Soviet Leaders," 8-24, is a worthwhile and even humorous attempt to fathom why "President Bush. . .is attempting a delicate and perhaps impossible shift: pledging his heart simultaneously to both Gorbachev and Boris N. Yeltsin." In "Bush Prevailing in Battle With Israeli Lobby," 9-30, he examines the particulars which would account for the fact that "to the shock of Israel and its allies in Washington, Bush is prevailing in his fight to delay U.S. guarantees for $10 billion in loans to help resettle Soviet Jewish immigrants in Israel."

Mecham, Michael. *Aviation Week & Space Technology.* (★ ★ ½)
Bonn bureau chief. He provided excellent insights into the future outlook of European military, aerospace and high-tech related strategic issues. His "Gulf War Rekindles European Interest in Developing Military Satellites," 4-8, is laden with political implications reporting that "Europe's renewal of interest in military space programs was prompted by the need to verify Soviet troop activity and weapons withdrawals from Eastern Europe. Recent experience with U.S. space systems during the gulf war demonstrated the need 'above all for information' in any future conflict." His "Security of Eastern Europe Shifts Strategy Issues for Western Powers," 5-13, reflects Europe's ambivalence toward NATO: "If anything, Europe's security concerns are more complex today than they were two years ago when two alliances — NATO and the old Warsaw Pact — squared off against each other." In "NATO's New Strategy Stresses Mobility for 'Crisis' Management," 6-3, and "European Political Debate Will Delay Planning for Improved Weapon Systems," 6-17, he sheds light on the intricacies of Western Europe's evolving new strategic doctrine and posture, noting that "it is not clear. . .in which direction national defense ministries wish to go. Politics is not making the picture any clearer. This is not merely a case of declining defense budgets, although that is a major ingredient. Rather it concerns the need for a consensus on just what defense structure — if any — Europe may create for itself as a balance to U.S. leadership in NATO." His "Signing NATO's New Strategy May Be the Easy Part of the Summit," 11-4, is an exceptional strategic analysis of NATO's political role today, which singles out the basic irony which is driving NATO's fortunes at present, namely, "Today, NATO's former Warsaw Pact adversaries want the Alliance to provide them with a security blanket against the ethnic and national rivalries that the old communist order suppressed. The summit will not provide them direct comfort."

Morrison, David. *National Journal.* (★ ★ ★)
Defense. Throughout the year he has given us a series of excellent, in-depth analytical studies of virtually all the major issues of arms policy: trade, control, procurement and future prospects.

He remains one of the indispensable reporters on defense/security issues. In "Getting Ready for the Next Battleground," 3-23, he examines how the U.S. is now, after the Gulf War, embarking on the largest reduction of forces since the end of the Vietnam War. In "Deep Sixing the A12," *Government Executive* 3-91, he lambastes the military bureaucratic system that rubberstamps major weapons programs, and warns that unless measures can be found to solve this cultural problem, the failures will occur again, as he describes the A12 saga as "a major program deep sixed, contractors penalized, and brass-hatted heads rolling. The events leading up to it are all too indicative of business as usual." His "Still Open for Business," 4-13, is an excellent, in-depth piece on the topical subject of mixed signals out of Washington on closing down the Middle East arms bazaar in the face of the Gulf War and Iraqi massive build-up, while the Bush administration continues to push for arms sales to allies: Saudis, Egypt, Israel, etc. Our attention is captured at the outset with the great lead, "Czech made T-72 tanks can now be had at the Crazy Eddie bargain price of $100,000 each," as he argues that "the administration. . .haven't met an arms sale they didn't like." In "No Easy Out," 5-11, Morrison gives us another in-depth, interesting coverage of a ticklish problem, the destruction of chemical weapons in accordance with existing treaties: "Everyone is uneasy about chemical weapons — Nobody wants them to exist, but nobody wants them destroyed in their backyard either." "Revamping the Atomic Archipelago," *GE* 6-91, surveys the DOE's nuclear facilities stretching across the U.S.: "Over the decades, since World War II, the Energy Department's huge nuclear weapons production complex has churned out more than 60,000 nuclear weapons, aimed mainly at intimidating the Soviet Union," and analyzes the DOE's efforts to reorganize and revamp them after decades of managerial neglect and disasters.

Morrocco, John D. *Aviation Week & Space Technology.* (★ ★ ★ ★)
Senior military editor. Morrocco excelled in providing valuable and well-organized information on the Gulf War. From the very outset he understood better than any other journalist exactly what it is that must be watched and studied during this particular war, and organized his magazine's coverage accordingly. In his brief, but excellent, "Air Strikes Spearhead Mideast War," 1-21, a 10 Best selection for General Reporting, he lays down that "In narrow terms, the world's military establishments will learn a great deal about the efficacy of contemporary tactics and leading edge technology — stealth, night attack and electronic warfare systems, 'smart' and standoff weapons, and immensely complex software." Most of the military coverage during and after the war was engaged in reporting, examining and clarifying exactly these topics of tactics, technology and their interplay. His "Allies Attack Iraqi Targets; Scuds Strike Israeli Cities," 1-21, is an excellent tactical analysis of the opening moves of Desert Storm's air combat component, with a clear presentation of the different combat roles distributed to the different technologies. On the whole, Morrocco's coverage of the war leaves little to be added by future professional evaluations. His post-war military analyses are more cautious that others, perhaps a deliberate effort to counter the general euphoria. "War Will Reshape Doctrine, But Lessons Are Limited," 4-22, is based on the premise that "air power provided the decisive element," and that "the conflict validated the U.S. military's Air-Land Battle doctrine," but cautions that "it will be difficult to draw any conclusions about close air support given the limited scope of the ground war," and that "the lessons not learned from the conflict may prove to be as important as those that were." "Naval Aviation Plan Sacrifices Some Capability to Avoid Further Cuts in Aircraft Carriers," 5-6, explains why the Navy turned down the superior Grumman F-14 fighter plane, passionately favored by *Aviation Week,* in favor of the inferior but cheaper McDonnell Douglas F/A-18: "sacrifice some capability in order to avoid further reductions in the number of aircraft carriers."

Mossberg, Walter S. *The Wall Street Journal.* (★ ½)
National security. A decline in analytical rigor pushed Mossberg's rating back to its 1989 level. Animated by an impulse to root for off-the-beaten-path opinion, he made a minor splash with "High-Tech, Low-Casualty Success in War So Far Owes Much to Jimmy Carter's Defense Planning," 1-22, claiming that "Some of the most successful U.S. weapons and military strategies

being used in the war with Iraq owe their existence to an unlikely source: the much-maligned defense policies of President Carter," to which he got ample rebuttal from ex-Secretary of Defense Caspar Weinberger in an interview in *Human Events,* 2-2. He had a counter-productive, critical stance on the Gulf War, in "After a Week of War, Iraq's Military Still Shows Plenty of Punch," co-authored by John Fialka 1-23, where he overrates Saddam by claiming that "The better he husbands his resources the more likely it is that Saddam Hussein can turn the war into the 'mother of battles' he repeatedly has promised." In "U.S. Supplies of High-Tech Weapons Could Be Depleted If War Drags On," 1-25, he overrates the downside when he spins the claim that "The military could run out of some of the high-tech weapons that have done well so far." Unwarranted skepticism also colors his "U.S. Aides Await Bomb Damage Report in Considering Early Ground Offensive," 2-4. He fared better on other topics, "Back to the Race: Mideast Arms Outlays Seem Unlikely to Face Any Tough New Curbs," 3-4, noting that "far more elusive will be success in preventing the warlike states of the Mideast, including Iraq itself, from building deadlier new arsenals in the future," and the well-argued "Even the Scaled-Down Military Machine Planned for '95 Would Leave the U.S. a Still-Potent Force," 3-14. His handling of the Robert Gates nomination typifies the kind of journalistic behavior we would like to see much less of. He joined the drumbeat that was calling for endless, acrimonious hearings. His uninformative "Gates's Nomination to Head CIA Revives Questions About Iran-Contra Scandal," 7-15, and "Nomination of Robert Gates to Top CIA Post Is Turning Into a High-Stakes Gamble for Bush," 7-16, practice the art of "insinuendo," in the words of late Mayor Daley's immortal witticism. The "U.S., a Freed Colony, Is Now Committed to Preserving Soviets' Colonial Empire," 8-12, vents unexamined discomfort about Bush's reluctance to promote chaos in the Soviet Union.

Munro, Neil. *Defense News.* (★ ★)
He is a thoroughly informed specialist on issues of command, control, communication and intelligence, who can be counted on to keep us perpetually updated on developments in this field. As a prolific writer, his output has its ups and downs and there is no doubt that if he had limited himself to publishing only his best pieces, his overall rating would have been higher. Cumulatively over the year, his greatest contribution was that he identified from the outset the powerful, growing trend toward intelligence centralization in the U.S. armed services. "DoD Proposal Downgrades Space, Strategic Defense Programs," 1-28, reports on the proposed plan to create a new unified Strategic Command by merging U.S. space command and NORAD with Air Force Strategic Air Command and command of the U.S. Navy's missile carrying submarines. His "Improved AWACs, Allied Air Control Reduce Aircraft Mishaps," 2-25, could drive one to distraction with its excessive use of "officials said" attributions. His "Remaining Services Await Air Force Nod on Radio Standard," 5-6, is a useful piece on the "Saturn" radio standard which dictates how the services' radios exchange information, while sidestepping enemy eavesdropping and jamming. He argues persuasively in "DIA Reshuffle Will Consolidate, Bolster Commands," 6-10, that the Pentagon's intelligence reorganization plan will result in "centraliz[ing] oversight and control of intelligence within the office of Duane Andrews, assistant secretary of command, control, communications and intelligence, and within the multiservice regional commands. . .rather than the services." He emphasizes further in "Role of CINCs Increases as Budget Forces Shift," 9-2, the drift away from the services: "As the service chiefs argue over the allocation of roles and missions needed to justify funding, the multiservice commanders in chief (CINCs) find themselves with significant influence over the internal debates." In "U.S. Army Eyes C2 System," 9-23, Munro gives a fascinating report on a proposed "Army-wide computerized network to link company commanders, individual vehicles and helicopters. . .[which] would constantly broadcast the locations of friendly and enemy units. . .help front-line troops view intelligence reports, and allow front-line units to quickly come to each other's aid."

Nelan, Bruce W. *Time.* (★)
The rating of Nelan's international security coverage declined in proportion to the fortunes of *Time* magazine's man of the decade, Mikhail Gorbachev, and reflected a pronounced inability to adjust intellectual habits and presumptions to the elusive new realities of the global canvass. In his "Kohl," 1-7, he skims on how Kohl did put Germany back together again, and is offensively presumptuous in advising Kohl on his next steps — "possibly new taxes." In "A Slippery Slope," 1-7, he unimaginatively sums up the plethora of problems Gorbachev faces internally. In "How Targets Are Chosen," 2-25, based on the bunker bombing which killed Iraqi civilians, he recounts how the U.S. is trying systematically to avoid this kind of thing — one of the few places we saw an attempt to evaluate the mechanism. But this was only an attempt. "Could Saddam Have Done Better?" 3-11, is fairly standard Monday-morning quarterbacking of what Hussein might have done differently in order to have won the war, or prevented it altogether, while still keeping his power, his army *and* Kuwait. He retails, in "Free at Last! Free at Last!" 3-11, new stories of Iraqi atrocities, contradicting himself in a justification for publishing these rumors: "Such tales strain credulity, both because they are so shocking and because every war produces stories of atrocities that are later called into question. But similar accounts were common in the liberated city, and there was no reason to doubt them." His "Helping Him Find His Way," 7-29, is an overview of the London G-7 summit, with potential aid to the Soviet Union appropriately highlighted, and seems to have as its sole purpose to patronize Gorbachev. His "What Are These Two Up To?" 8-5, is a pretentious rerun of that genre of journalism which goes under subheads such as "Inside Shamir's Mind" and "Inside Assad's Mind," which tend to set one ill at ease from the start. This, however, turns out to be less an "inside" view than an entirely adequate overview of the Middle East peace process over the years, spanning the past twenty or so, and concentrating on the past few, with potential events leading up to a peace conference.

Nordwall, Bruce D. *Aviation Week & Space Technology.* (★ ★)
Avionics editor. During the Gulf War he commented on military aviation in a manner timely, useful and not found elsewhere. In "U.S. Relies on Combination of Aircraft, Satellites, UAVs for Damage Assessment," 2-4, he gives important pieces of information needed to understand the controversy around damage assessment in Desert Storm when he reports that "The U.S. does not have a strong, dedicated reconnaissance force for bomb damage assessment (BDA) in Operation Desert Storm, but is using a variety of satellites, aircraft and unmanned aerial vehicles (UAVs) to determine how effectively selected targets have been hit." In "Radar, Targeting Infrared Give Navy, Marines Precision Weapons Capability," 2-4, a valuable study of Gulf War technology, he focuses on U.S. Navy and Marine aviation's "unprecedented capability to detect and guide precision weapons to targets." His "Electronic Warfare Played Greater Role in Desert Storm Than Any Conflict," 4-22, draws from "pilot comments about the value of electronic warfare that are starting to leak out," but cautions that "despite those exuberant flight crew comments, Desert Storm was not a worst-case test, since the Iraqis clearly did not get the most out of their weapons systems. The overwhelming allied force also makes it difficult to judge the EW contribution." He argues, in the sterling "Key Desert Storm Technologies Vital to Future Competitiveness," 6-3, that "In many respects Desert Storm was an electronic war, in which reliable communications were the foundation for success and microprocessors supported virtually all communications." In "Highly Integrated System, Versatile Radar Win Kudos for Joint-STARS' Gulf War Role," 6-24, he provides a concrete example of one high-tech system's contribution to altering the face of war: "Joint-Stars (Joint Surveillance Target Attack Radar System). . .gave air and ground commanders long-range intelligence and targeting data on enemy ground forces, analogous to the Air Force's airborne warning and control system." In "Electronics Companies Form Alliances to Counter Rising Costs," 6-17, he portrays how the private sector accommodates to new market conditions and how the Pentagon provides the context: "Technology trump cards to be played every 5-10 years. The challenge for the Defense Dept. is to establish a process that ensures orderly evolutionary improvements."

Oberdorfer, Don. *The Washington Post.* (★★)
State Department. Here is an expert whose reliable writing moves between the routine and the competent, rarely soaring to surprise us with excellence. He is tenuously speculative about the Gulf War in "Shifting Alliances Reflect Changing World," 1-20, musing that "a new kind of war in the homeland of the world's oldest civilization illustrated dramatically last week how swiftly the world is changing." In "Gorbachev's Internal Policies Pose Dilemma for Washington," 1-27, he profiles how the Bush administration "grapples with how to disapprove of Gorbachev's increasingly odious domestic policies without destroying the dramatically improved international relationship with Moscow that is vital to U.S. policies in the gulf and many other areas." His "Missed Signals in the Middle East," 3-17, is one more recap of events leading up to the Iraqi invasion of Kuwait, and "Strategy of Solo Superpower," 5-19, is a dry, competent report on the Bush administration's "focus on preparing for regional threats 'in whatever corner of the globe they may occur' and move away from the traditional emphasis on a possible Soviet attack in Europe." In "Japan: Searching for Its International Role," 6-17, he argues persuasively that "Japan is in the early stages of a great shift in thought and action about its role in the world. . .taking the form of greater independence from U.S. policies." He issues, in "Looking East: Is American Losing Its Clout in Asia?" 6-30, a warning not to be ignored: "U.S. relations with key Asian countries face serious challenges, with the future more uncertain than it has been since the fall of Saigon in 1975. . .Administration neglect baffles Pacific nations — and threatens U.S. interests." His "Shift to Domestic Concerns Urged," 7-19, is an excellently argued justification of the fact that "some of the country's leading diplomatic specialists are calling for the administration to shift emphasis from foreign to domestic concerns. . .lest the United States be mired in a long-term social and economic crisis that will undermine the basis for a strong U.S. foreign policy." In "Soviet 'Collapse' Shifts the Axis of Global Politics," 9-1, he surveys the results of " 'The collapse of the Soviet Union'. . .[that] has launched powerful shock waves that threaten what is left of communism in every part of the world, bringing radical changes from the global politics of the Cold War era."

Opall, Barbara. *Defense News.* (★★★)
Not only an excellent writer, but also a tough military thinker, Barbara Opall (formerly Amouyal) is a writer to heed, especially by readers who are interested in the state-of-the-art of air warfare. She outlines, in "Air Force to Restructure Tactical Forces," 1-14, the Air Force's proposed "restructuring. . .plan [which] calls for the service to operate in peacetime as it does in war with. . .composite wings [that] would include a variety of combat aircraft, along with tankers, electronic warfare, reconnaissance planes and possibly, air transports." Her "Allies Deliver a High-Tech Storm," 1-21, heavily relying on exclusive Air Force sources, reflects the service's authoritative first assessment of the air campaign against Iraq, and attributes "the unusual low rates of attrition at the outset of the war to the precision accuracy of the radar-evading, night-fighting F-117A stealth fighter, the navigation and targeting capabilities of the F-15E and F-111 fighter bombers and a well-coordinated campaign to suppress enemy air defenses." With "AF Planners Advocate Quick-Strike Doctrine," 4-8, she is at the forefront of doctrinal developments, reporting that "Future conflicts involving the U.S. military are likely to be offensive in nature, with U.S. forces using the first minutes of battle to dictate the terms and tempo of war to overwhelm enemy forces." She warns, in "U.S. High-Tech Fighters May Lose Sales War," 6-17, that U.S. high-tech arms manufacturing may be pricing itself out of the market: "U.S. development of increasingly expensive high-technology aircraft. . .may aid European aerospace manufacturers in the global battle for exports." In "U.S. Develops New Smaller, Sleeker Sidewinder Missile," 9-23, she describes the expected role of the improved Sidewinder which "has the potential to quadruple the internal payload of the F-22 Advanced Tactical Fighter while adding longer range, higher speed, increased maneuverability and stealth to the existing family of air-to-air missiles." In her fascinating "Futuristic Gadgets Pilot Supercockpit," 10-28, she explains the combat philosophy and technology behind the emerging "supercockpit, or windowless cockpit [which] essentially buries the pilot behind laser-protective panels, onto which sensor-fused data and imagery are presented."

Pasztor, Andy. *The Wall Street Journal.* (★ ★ ½)
Pentagon. He had bad luck in his brief live coverage on the Gulf War, where he filed the unfortunate "As Ground Skirmishes Start, the Army's Scouts and Observers Play a Crucial, Dangerous Role," 1-31, a misrepresentation of the role of "scouts and observers" in a high-tech battle environment. But he more than amply compensated with his superior politico-military analysis. He displayed lucidity in identifying the causes behind political changes in "White House Derails Proposed Saudi Arms Deal," 3-13, reporting that "The Bush Administration has derailed Saudi Arabia's proposed purchase of $15 billion of high-tech U.S. weapons. . .in the face of increasing congressional opposition. . .and until the White House hammers out a new policy for dealing with the general issue of arms sales in the Middle East." His sound judgment and careful research produced, "Pentagon Plans 20% Cut in Civilian Jobs by Mid-90s, Reduction in Services' Power," 4-26, arguing that Dick Cheney's "revised 'management reform' blueprint" for the Pentagon "highlight[s] the erosion of power of the various military services and their uniformed chiefs during an era of declining defense spending." In "Gulf War Win Isn't Furthering Arms Spending," 5-20, he dashes illusions as he predicts that "The Gulf War. . .will have surprisingly little impact on the defense authorization bill the House takes up today." In "Mismanagement, Budget Cuts, Doubts Over Role Have Navy Sailing Against the Wind in Congress," 6-4, he draws attention to the fact that "mismanagement, deep budget cuts and fundamental questions about the navy's role in the post Cold War world have created one of the fiercest political squalls for the service since the bleak days following Pearl Harbor." In "Federal Panel Approves Biggest Cuts in Military Bases in Almost 40 Years," 7-1, and "Weapons Plans Backed by Bush Clear the Senate," 8-5, he displays expert handling of the defense budget process. In "Slimming Down: Bush's Arms Initiative Stirs Talk in Congress of Slashing Defense," and Michel McQueen 9-30, he criticizes Bush's unilateral nuclear arms cut as politically risky, "one that could easily backfire." His "Soviet Response Surpasses U.S. Arms-Cut Plan," and Peter Gumbel 10-7, cuts to the quick: "the scope and timing of Mr. Gorbachev's comments also seem shrewdly calibrated to fuel demands inside the U.S. for deep defense spending cuts the White House wants to avoid."

Pincus, Walter. *The Washington Post.* (★)
Assigned to the national security beat, he spent most of his energy chewing, albeit with subdued ferocity, on his old Iran-contra scandal bone to the detriment of contributions that he might have made in other vital areas of national security. When Gates's candidacy for CIA Director was made known, he was one of the first to focus on the Iran-contra aspect in his "NSC Deputy Scrutinized for CIA Post," 5-13, suggesting — wrongly, as it turned out — that "nominating Robert M. Gates to head the Central Intelligence Agency would reopen questions about his role during the Iran-contra affair." With "Iranian Alleges Casey Link to 1980 Deal on Hostages," 6-21, he tries to inject some passion into the languishing investigation by lending credence to "An Iranian arms dealer. . .Jamshid Hashemi, [who] said that he and his late brother, Cyrus Hashemi, worked the alleged arrangement out with the late William J. Casey during two meetings in Madrid." Pincus felt he finally got his vindication with "Ex-CIA Aide Admits Iran-Contra Role," coauthored by George Lardner 7-10, nicely reporting on the guilty plea of CIA official Alan Fiers, neatly connecting Iran-contra and the Bush nomination of Robert Gates to head the CIA. Also, "Ending Silence, Insider Lifts CIA Veil," and George Lardner 9-20, is well rounded and neatly detailed, getting all the highlights, in the testimony of Alan D. Fiers. The bad pun referring to Woodward's book in this title irks us, but the item itself is quite serviceable. "Gates's Memory Gaps Contrast With Others' Iran-Contra Recall," with Lardner 9-23, is an otherwise reasonable, though sparsely detailed, history of CIA involvement in Iran-contra that's hindered by the nastiness in the opening paragraph: "Robert M. Gates, nominated by President Bush last May to be CIA director, has had all summer to refresh his recollections about the Iran-contra affair but says he still can't remember much." And then: "Gates's memory, which has been keen in matters other than the scandal, has emerged as one of the few stumbling blocks to his easy approval by the Senate intelligence committee, although he is still expected to receive the committee's endorsement."

Polsky, Debra. *Defense News.* (★ ★ ★)
With reduced output this year, Polsky limited herself to excellent, judicious reporting on a limited number of specialized issues, mostly centered on the cutting edge of high-tech military developments such as night vision combat technologies, simulator technologies, chip manufacturing and selective monitoring of the financial health of defense companies. Her "Life-Like Simulators Are Almost Reality for Researchers," 1-28, is an impressive report on the military uses of "virtual reality" computing, probing into "how sophisticated computers can be used to immerse troops in distant battles without sending them into a simulator." In "Air Force Eyes LANTIRN Upgrade," 2-25, and "Army to Evaluate Low-Cost, Lightweight Night Vision Systems," 3-4, she reports on expected future developments in the "complex night vision system being used by U.S. Air Force pilots," and on the Army's pondering the high-tech "designs for low-cost, lightweight night vision systems" that could provide "a helmet-mounted display to allow soldiers to shoot targets at night." In "Price of Defense Environmental Violations Escalates," 7-8, she gives an important update on the escalation in fines and threats of imprisonment facing the defense industry for violations of environmental protection: "Increasingly, these laws target senior corporate executives for prosecution." Polsky calls attention to a dangerous "incentive" for prosecution: "government agencies will be under great pressure to show that tax dollars are being well spent." In "DARPA Energizes Tube Research," 7-29, she highlights a surprising technological feature of Desert Storm: "The Persian Gulf War underscored the need to revitalize the U.S. high-frequency power tube industry. Powerful new weapon systems, the war showed, need more than computer chips." A three-article survey, 9-23, on advanced research into "the Defense Department's 10-year, $1 billion campaign to develop lightning-fast computer chips," consists of "Production Costs Prohibit MIMIC Chip Proliferation," which argues that "only when a strong commercial market develops can MIMIC (Microwave/Millimeter-wave Monolithic Integrated Circuits) chips become truly affordable," and of "Large MIMIC Market Fails to Bloom," and "Chip Miniaturization Is Sizable Challenge," two brief items that expand nicely on the information contained in their titles.

Proctor, Paul. *Aviation Week & Space Technology.* (★ ★ ½)
Hong Kong bureau chief. He has been providing a prodigious stream of vital Far Eastern coverage, ranging from reports on companies, transport markets, high-tech challenges and economic conditions. He is a hard working, solid researcher and rewarding to read. His articles are worth reading not only by aviation and aerospace audiences, but also by anyone interested in developing a firm grasp of Japanese and Pacific Rim economic trends. In "Budget Cuts to Slow Growth of Japan's Aerospace Industry," 2-11, he argues that "terminations of critical military aircraft and missile licensed-manufacturing programs could hurt the [Japanese aerospace] industry which is responding with plans 'to boost export sales by improving' product reliability and cutting costs." In his "War and Recession Slow Tokyo Air Show Attendance," 2-18, he stresses "Japanese ambitions to become a world aerospace manufacturing power." His "Japan's Airlines Anticipate Decade of Strong Growth," 5-13, is the lead article of a package of nine (written with help from Contributing Editor Eiichiro Sekigawa) on the future of Japanese airlines, and summarizes: "Japanese airlines are planning for strong traffic growth through the year 2000 despite airport and airways capacity shortfalls." His refined, solid grasp of Asian economics is reflected in "Strong Asian Economy Boosts Outlook for Airlines, Industry," 5-27, reporting that "Asian airlines will generally continue to be profitable into the mid-1990s as strong regional economies, tourism and foreign trade stoke demand." His "Growing Economies, New Airports Stoke Pacific Rim Transport Boom," 6-17, is an excellent strategic economic analysis of Far Eastern commercial aviation: "Strong traffic growth stoked by growing regional economies and the opening of new Asian airports will likely continue the Pacific Rim air transport boom into the next decade." In "China Southern Invests Heavily to Meet Booming Passenger and Freight Demand," 9-23, he gives an excellent corporate profile of the expanding China Southern Airlines, "hard-pressed by the burgeoning economy of the Pearl River Delta, which is forecast to experience some of the world's strongest growth through the end of the decade."

Sawyer, Kathy. *The Washington Post.* (★ ★ ★)

Sawyer possesses the gift of imparting not only good information respecting scientific and technological developments, but also an undiminished sense of enthusiasm and marvel, especially as she reports on space matters, even when she must highlight the misery that comes with budget slashing, corner cutting and bureaucratic sniping. In her "Bush Adopts Advice on NASA Budget," 2-13, she finds a silver lining in President Bush's "tilting away from the money devouring the space station project and toward a more balanced menu of science and technology development." In "DOE Launches Foray Into Space Exploration," 4-30, she provides a valuable insight into the politics of the space program which prompted the Department of Energy to seek its own space projects to rival NASA, probably in order "to prevent it from developing a monopoly on space exploration," and also "to broaden the base of the space program." Her "Shuttling Into Orbit to Explore How the Body Adjusts," 5-20, is an excellent report on the design of the life sciences experiment on board the shuttle: "By observing what happens in the weightlessness of space, the scientists who designed the SLS-1 experiments hope to unravel the mysteries of the mechanisms by which the body. . .adjusts to gravity's comings and goings." Her "In the Shadow of the Moon," 7-12, is a spectacular report on the total solar eclipse as observed from Hawaii. Her "Space Rescue for Hubble Weighed," 7-31, reviews the status of planned repairs for the crippled Hubble telescope, still an undertaking worth its cost as evidenced by "A Stellar Fountain of Youth; New Stars From Old, Hubble Data Indicate," 8-22, reporting that "the Hubble has produced new evidence that dying stars can rejuvenate themselves when they collide with and capture each other." Her strong belief that the expense of the space program is worthwhile because of its payoff in scientific advances is vindicated in "Space Radiation Confounds Astrophysicists; Violent Bursts of Gamma Rays Emanating From No Known Source," 9-24, where she reports that "An orbiting observatory has upset existing astronomical theory by detecting violent bursts of gamma rays in space that could not have been produced by any known object or phenomenon in the cosmos."

Scarborough, Rowan. *The Washington Times.* (★ ½)

His major focus during the year was the Gulf War and the military acquisition battles in Congress and this skewed focus inhibited his ability to address and think through the less settling issues of national security that emerged with the demise of the Soviet Union. "Bombing Targets Guards," 1-24, is one of his many good war dispatches from Dhahran hampered only by the limitations on reporting and inquiry imposed on correspondents by the Central Command. "Saddam's Dare: Start Ground War," 2-11, is similarly limited and exemplifies the print media's inferiority to satellite TV in this war. He makes an excellent prediction in "Allies Ready, Willing and Able to Finish Job," 2-12, about how the allied ground offensive will be conducted, which actually gives away in advance General Schwarzkopf's big secret: "A full fledged invasion west of Kuwait into Iraq will attempt to outflank the occupying army and avoid its stiff fortifications." He reports in "Lockheed Mission: 21st Century Air Superiority," 4-24, the Air Force's awarding to Lockheed of the $65 billion contract "to build the Advanced Tactical Fighter, a revolutionary dogfighting jet built for stealth, super speeds and daring aerobatics," but does not handle adequately the problem of congressional funding. His "Panel OKs Setting Up SDI," 7-18, gives too optimistic an interpretation to the Senate Armed Services Committee's vote to "deploy 100 ground-based interceptors on U.S. soil," ignoring the Committee's corollary commitment to not allow space-based defenses. He accurately portrays in "Funding for SDI Awaits Final Word After Ups, Downs," 8-19, the differences between House and Senate and correctly predicts that the Senate would prevail. In "Cheney Calms Senators on B-2," 9-17, he discusses two senators' concerns over whether the administration will continue to support the B-2 bomber or pull the plug and he makes well-organized, excellent use of background material. His "Timing of Bush Initiative Irks GOP Senators," 10-2, is tapped into the conservative network and provides insight into the failure of the administration to forewarn senators of the planned cancellation of the rail-garrison MX before they fought a bloody floor battle over it.

Schmitt, Eric. *The New York Times.* (★ ½)
Pentagon. A meticulous, reliable and clear writer, Schmitt could have been easily graded with two stars were it not for the fact that his otherwise commendable caution impeded him from pursuing more challenging vistas. Solid grasp of facts and reliable inference are evident in his "Navy Urges Cheney to Give Aircraft Producers Aid," 1-3, in which he points out that "If the Navy's [procurement] plan is approved, the agreement could be one of the largest corporate bailouts in recent years and would probably set a precedent for other military contractors seeking billions of dollars of relief." In "$13 Billion Weapons Sale to Saudis Will Be Delayed," 1-5, he cautiously reports that "seeking to avoid a divisive battle with Israel's supporters in Congress the Bush Administration is postponing the second part of a large arms sale to Saudi Arabia, valued at about $13 billion, until the crisis ends," but neglects to note the opportunity for a larger policy reformulation embedded in the administration's move. In the observant "For Arabs on Ground, Fiery Help From Skies," 2-27, he argues that "Coordinating command and control among the myriad allied forces whose troops speak many languages and employ different battlefield tactics has been a chief concern for American planners since the Persian Gulf crisis started in August." He reports in "Displaced Iraqis Streaming Into Allied-Held Zone," 3-22, that "Coalition troops, mainly the United States Army, control 15 to 20 percent of Iraq, and under the Geneva Convention are responsible for the welfare of civilians in the occupied area," and strives to show the strictly legal behavior of the occupiers. In "Tensions Bedeviled Allies All the Way to Kuwait," 3-24, he notes that "Cooperation dissolved at key points only to be quickly and quietly patched up by high-level compromises, battleground improvisation and a bit of good fortune." His "Army Is Blaming Patriot's Computer for Failure to Stop the Dhahran Scud," 5-20, gives rise to the lie from the Central Command that the Scud which killed 28 servicemen "had broken into pieces as it descended and was not identified as a threat by the Patriot radar system." In "Despite Euphoria on Arms Control, Deterrence Remains a Potent Force," 7-30, he warns cogently that "the hope that a new era in arms control will begin. . .may be misguided."

Sciolino, Elaine. *The New York Times.* (★ ★ ½)
Washington, covering foreign relations. Discreet and thoughtful, she has a gift for epigrammatic summations. Filed from the Iraqi capital, her "Baghdad Schoolchildren Are Made Ready for War," 1-8, is a graphic portrayal of President Bush's demonization in Iraqi grammar schools: "The lesson of the exercise at the 500-student elementary school. . .is clear, if crude: Our President is good, the American President is bad, and we want you to know it." Her impish "Voice of the Pentagon Delivers Press Curbs With a Deftness Honed on TV," 2-8, is a kinder, gentler revenge on Pentagon press spokesman Pete Williams who "for all his once-a-week haircut and his disarming one-liners, Mr. Williams was once a gawky kid — 'kind of a supercharged nerd with all his pens lined up in his pocket.' " In her "Hussein's Errors: Complex Impulses," 2-28, she portrays Saddam as a man who has lived by the sword: "the language he best understood was the use of force. . .and, if the Iran-Iraq war was a guide, Mr. Hussein was not particularly skilled in the art of negotiating." She downplays the chances of revolt against Saddam Hussein in "Iraqi Shiites Wait in the Wings for a Role to Play," 3-5, and attributes the insurgency in the south of Iraq to "chaos in the streets because of an absence of law and order; antipathy toward Iraq's President. . .and wishful thinking on the part of Shi'ite opponents." In "Iraq Is Left to the Mercy of Saddam Hussein," 4-7, she thrives on the ironies of post-war Iraq where "the coalition that had pushed the Iraqis out of Kuwait fears the disintegration of the Iraqi state, and its leaders believe that only a strong central Government in Baghdad can prevent such a breakup." Her "Is Iran's Urge to Prosper Overtaking Its Islamic Zeal?" 6-2, displays once again Sciolino's knack for the *mot juste* when she summarizes that "economics, not revolutionary fervor, is now the driving force behind Iran's domestic and foreign policy." In "Familiar Shadow Darkens the Deal on C.I.A. Post," 7-21, she notes that the CIA "is increasingly seen as part of an unwieldy, drifting, out-of-step and possibly even redundant espionage establishment that must be overhauled." She highlights in "Scrutiny for Spies," 9-7, "the tension between a spy's oath to keep secrets and the duty to tell the Government the truth,"

and she declines to join the chorus of media calumniators of Robert Gates in the "Nominee for C.I.A. Is Expected to Win Approval of Panel," 10-18, as she reviews the various senators' extraneous motivations for supporting or opposing the nominee.

Scott, William B. *Aviation Week & Space Technology.* (★★)
Senior engineering editor. Displaying a newly-developed ability to translate superb engineering expertise into thoughtful, enjoyable English, on the whole, Scott covered his area extensively with his customary competence. His "Electro-Optic Targeting Tools Bolster Bombing Accuracy of Allied Aircraft," 1-28, was basically an off-the-shelf item comprised of file descriptions of the main known targeting systems used by allied aircraft in Desert Storm. He does a bit of whistle-blowing in the "B-2 Bomber Production Undergoes Initial Shakeout," 3-25, reporting some sort of apparently serious labor trouble at the Northrop B-2 production program, where "difficult personnel issues must be confronted as the use of low observable (stealth) technology forces fundamental changes in the way military aircraft are built." In "Lockheed F-22 Design Balances Stealth, Agility and Speed," 4-29, he explains how different philosophical outlooks on the shape of future air combat influenced the Air Force's decision to select Lockheed's F-22 as the service's future advanced tactical fighter, over its competitor, McDonnell Douglas' F-23: "The F-22 design is based on the concept that a 21st-century air superiority fighter will have to be effective in both beyond-visual-range and close-in turning engagements. . .In contrast, the Northrop and McDonnell Douglas design team embraced a competing philosophy that close-in engagements would be less likely in the future." In "Hughes Testing Radar, IR Sensors to Aid Reduced-Visibility Landings," 5-6, he reports on the benefits that would accrue from efforts to develop "sophisticated sensors that could enable commercial aircraft to land at airports normally shut down by adverse weather conditions." He reveals in "Triangular Recon Aircraft May Be Supporting F-117A," 6-10, that "The U.S. Air Force is believed to be operating several highly classified triangular-shaped stealth aircraft with its Lockheed F-117A fighters, to provide real-time imagery," and includes intriguing operational details and an artist's sketch. His "Funding Issues to Dictate Future of Navy's Forces and Purchases," 9-23, is an insightful report on damage control attempted at "the U.S. Navy's air arm, reeling from cancellation of approximately $7.3 billion worth of aircraft programs."

Seib, Gerald. *The Wall Street Journal.* (★★★)
Consistently competent, Seib wrote some of the more insightful analyses of what is at stake for the United States in the year's dramatic developments in both the Middle East and the (former) Soviet Union. In "A New U.S.-Soviet Relationship May Be Forged Behind the Scenes at Next Week's Moscow Summit," 7-24, though analytically cautious at the time, he managed to identify precisely what was to become the great vulnerability in President Bush's Soviet policy: "the most delicate part of Mr. Bush's trip to the Soviet Union. . .will come. . .when he is scheduled to visit Kiev, the capital of the Ukraine, and give a speech, probably to the Ukrainian parliament." Seib also produced some of the more solid overviews of the complicated policy objectives faced by the U.S. in the war with Iraq. In "U.S. Dilemma: How to Hammer Iraq in a Battle Without Smashing It, Emboldening Iran, Syria," 12-26-90, he thoughtfully addressed the issue of regional stability and balances of power with which the administration was grappling, and in "Shots Not Yet Fired Are Heard Round the World as Gulf Crisis Starts to Reshape Global Alliances," 1-9, Seib, looking over the horizon, suggested a *quid pro quo* for U.S. action on the Palestinian question would be high on the post-war agenda. He capably assessed the policy terrain, thoroughly examining the various dimensions and options, producing solid analysis instead of murky speculation, as in "Peace Initiative," 2-22, a finely-tuned look at the Soviet peace initiative. He very capably provided the background details on how President Bush orchestrated the swift allied victory with "Into His Own," 3-1. In a very efficient report on various policy approaches to U.S. economic aid to the U.S.S.R., "Issue of Aid to Soviets Subjects Administration to Strong Political and Economic Crosswinds," 5-31, Seib professionally handled debate over grain credits as a microcosm of the broader debate over the issue, giving us a sharp sense of non-traditional alliances coming into being over the policy. In "Gorbachev's

Downfall Raises Political Specter for Soviet and West," 8-20, he raises broad questions on the future at top of piece: "Will the Soviet people once again knuckle under to a regime they fear and despise?"

Shifrin, Carole A. *Aviation Week & Space Technology.* (★ ½)
London bureau chief. Shifrin showed ability to monitor and analyze those peculiar economic processes that one finds only in Europe as the continent proceeds toward unification. She has also followed and reported on the recession hitting European airlines and has sounded the alarm on the competitive danger that the European Airbus will pose to U.S. commercial aircraft manufacturers. In "European Carriers Counter Traffic Lull With Reductions in Staff, Services," 2-18, she reports on the draconian survival measures of European airlines, where "Cost-saving measures include extensive layoffs and phased reduction of employee levels, further cutbacks in capacity, delays in aircraft deliveries and a general hunkering down for an indefinite period." In "Airbus Targets Pacific Rim as Key Growth Market," 2-11, she gives a quick profile of Airbus Industrie's global sales strategy, names its major Asian clients and warns: "Airbus statistics show it has achieved a 63% share of the Far East/Australasia market with its A300 and A310 aircraft, in competition with the Boeing 767-200/300." In "Eurofighter Partners Use Many Advanced Materials to Keep EFA's Weight Down," 4-15, she not only presents the technically interesting report on the "carbon fiber composites, glass-reinforced plastics and other advanced materials [used] to keep the [european] advanced fighter's weight down," but also gives an instructive picture of how "the United Kingdom, Germany, Italy and Spain. . .[engaged] in a collaborative program to develop and build a new-technology air defense fighter aircraft for their air forces." Her "Aerospace Market Bright Despite Problems of Gulf War, Recession," 6-17, reflects the upbeat spirit of the Paris Air Show in reporting that "the long term outlook for the commercial aerospace industry and air carriers remains bright despite recent problems caused by the Persian Gulf war and recession and the continuing challenges of congestion, aircraft financing, deregulation." She details in "Middle East Becomes Britain's Largest Defense Export Market," 11-4, how "the Middle East has surpassed both North America and Europe as Britain's largest defense export market."

Silverberg, David. *Defense News.* (★ ★ ★)
His skill, experience and versatility were applied to numerous issues with good results, but his main contribution was his painstaking monitoring and analysis of the effects on future U.S. arms sales of the Gulf War, a topic controversial, and still unresolved. In his "U.S. State Department Delays Phase Two of Saudi Arms Sale," 1-7, he analyzes why the decision to delay a $14 billion "second phase of a U.S. arms sale to Saudi Arabia. . .came as little surprise to defense industry." He portrays the tension between State Department and Pentagon in his "Baker: U.S. Must Curtail Post-War Gulf Arms Flow," 2-11, which highlights Baker's commitment that "arms control in the Middle East will be one of the major challenges addressed by the United States after the war," as it contrasts with the "Cheney: Conventional Mideast Arms Ban Not in U.S. Interest," 3-25, where Cheney argues that "a ban on conventional arms sales to the Middle East would not be in the interest of the United States or its allies." In "Gulf War Is No Panacea for Defense Firms," 2-18, he cautions that despite the spectacular success of many systems in the Gulf War, "export prospects are not so promising." In "Sales of Armored Vehicles Hinge on Gulf War Outcome," 2-25, he details the state of the world market for armored vehicles and explains how future sales will "depend on how well they perform on the battlefield against Iraq." Israel's pronounced distaste for the Patriot is accounted for in terms of interest in "funding of Israel's own antitactical ballistic missile (ATBM) interceptor, the Arrow," "Israeli Aversion to Patriot Grows," 4-8. The massive congressional opposition to the arms industry is chronicled in his detailed "Senators Target Mideast Arms Sales," 5-20, and "House Panel Kills Lending Plan," 6-3. In "Official: Firms May Profit From Mideast Sales Curb," 7-22, he describes the types of constraints that Congress prepares for the arms industry "in the effort to restrain arms sales, and a code of conduct that applies not only to the defense industry but other industries as well." In "Lawmakers Reject Proposal to Finance Military Exports," 9-30, he morbidly reports "the death of an initiative to provide U.S. defense exporters with $1 billion in U.S. government export financing."

Smith, Bruce A. *Aviation Week & Space Technology.* (★ ½)
Los Angeles bureau chief. The quality of his reporting is uneven and displays cyclical ups and downs, probably due to the types of issues he addresses. His sterling "Pentagon Weighs Key Reconnaissance Issues Highlighted by Gulf War," 4-22, in which he reports that "Some defense officials maintain too much dependence was placed on satellites for imagery during the conflict, while not enough priority has been given to improving tactical reconnaissance aircraft capabilities during the past decade" is one of the best, most balanced and instructive presentations of the hotly controversial issue of what happened with tactical intelligence during the Gulf War. But his "Douglas Forecasts Solid Long-Term Growth in Asia/Pacific Despite Economic Concerns," 2-11, is problematical — basically a pep talk on behalf of Douglas Aircraft management. In the exceptional "Some Military Space R&D Projects Nearing Operational Applications," 4-8, he highlights the ironical side benefit of budget cutting: "At the heart of this research is an intense effort to reduce costs of future space systems while at the same time improving reliability and performance. In the current austere budget environment, this work is considered vital because of its potential to squeeze more operational value per dollar spent on space based systems." In "Army to Award Development Contract for Improved TOW Missile Infrared Sight," 6-10, he has a very good description of an Army program to improve anti-tank weapons: "The primary purpose of the TOW sight improvement program (TSIP) is to provide better target detection and identification, but the system will also add such features as range-finding, automatic tracking and the engagement of multiple targets to the missile system." He introduces, in "Agreements With China a Key Part of Douglas' Cost-Reduction Effort," 6-17, the prospect of aerospace industry overseas sweat-shops as "Douglas Aircraft Co.'s growing business relationship with the People's Republic of China is a significant part of the company's objective to become a low-cost producer of commercial transports during the 1990s. . .developing working relations with Asia companies, which have considerably lower labor rates." In "First C-17 Flight Marks Key Program Milestone," 9-23, he drums up enthusiasm for another McDonnell Douglas product, the C-17 transport.

Smith, R. Jeffrey. *The Washington Post.* (★ ★)
The unceremonious end of the Cold War has cured Smith of the bias problems we criticized in past years and has thus improved his rating. Also, his coverage of the Gulf War maintained a high professional and technical standard. In "Iraqi Tactics Surprise U.S. Officials," 2-2, he gives a very good evaluation of Iraq's incursion into Khafji, though entirely based on allied official accounts. His "Picking Right Weapon for a Target Is Complex Decision," 2-6, is a serious attempt to cut through official silence and figure out the allies' "precise target selection procedures [which] remain shrouded from public view [and which are]. . .more art than science." In "U.S. Special Forces Carried Out Sabotage, Rescues Deep in Iraq," 3-4, he tells the tale of "dozens of small U.S. 'special forces' military units [that] conducted reconnaissance and rescue missions behind Iraqi lines." His "U.S. Developing Atom-Powered Rocket," 4-3, is a scoop about secret development of a nuclear reactor-powered rocket, code-named "Timberwolf." In "U.S. to Press China to Halt Missile Sales," 6-11, he reports that in pressuring Beijing, "The principal U.S. aim is to halt planned Chinese missile sales to Pakistan and Syria," and gives an excellent profile of China's missiles-for-export program. In "Comprehensive Arms Pact May Be Last of Its Kind," 7-18, he presciently foresees that "The two sides. . .may build on START with what one official characterized as 'strap-ons,' meaning amendments calling for deeper cuts." His "New Debate Erupts Over 'Star Wars,' " 7-28, is an excellent and precise account of the pros and cons of "the Senate Armed Services Committee's. . .unexpectedly endorsing the deployment within five years of a much more limited defense against enemy ballistic missiles." In "Treaty Won't Require Arms Destruction," 8-15, provides some fascinating details showing that at the end, the START talks "ended up much closer to Washington's position than Moscow's." He concludes, in "Gorbachev Ends Era of Strategic Equality; Arms Initiative Disregards Numerical Parity," 10-7, that "Gorbachev's announcement of a substantial unilateral cut in strategic weapons marks the close of a 20-year era" of obsession with numerical nuclear equality.

Strobel, Warren. *The Washington Times.* (★)
State Department. In a year that saw vast changes in security and diplomatic affairs across the whole globe, Strobel's choice of topics was narrowly fixed on the Middle East, which he treated with obsolescently fixed criteria, sticking to run-of-the-mill anti-Iraqi sentiments, and a naive notion of "America's Arab allies." His hallmark was plodding, basic reporting in a mindset that refused to be challenged by the intrinsically challenging events of the year. In "Could Bush Afford to Let Saddam Stay?" 2-19, he allows war euphoria to cloud his judgment into insisting that leaving Saddam Hussein in power "would be anathema to Washington's Arab allies," an assertion that remains patent nonsense. "Baker Begins Testing for Arab Israeli Peace Foundations," 3-18, gives the impression that it is Arabs that push for fast results: "Arab leaders warned Mr. Baker that the postwar mood in the region — the so-called window of opportunity to solve a decades-old Arab-Israeli dispute — may not stay open very long. . .Washington appears determined to act before the window slams shut." In "Iraq Softens Stand Against U.N. Police," 5-15, he displays immature judgment in asserting that "Iraq might agree to an international police presence in Kurdish areas." In "Assad May Soften Stance on Mideast Parley," 6-28, he captures much better the driving logic which is moving the Mideast players toward the negotiating table when he notes that "Syria is believed to be leaning toward acceptance of U.S. proposals for a Middle East peace conference. . .[in] a move [that]. . .could leave Israel isolated and appearing to be responsible for blocking the peace talks." His "Rebels Make Major Gains in Northern Afghanistan," 8-5, attempts to resuscitate an old conservative hobbyhorse, coverage of Afghanistan's civil war. His assertive conclusions lack solid evidence and though claims of recent rebel gains seem plausible, one hesitates to follow Strobel when he dishes out rebel strategy as described to him over the telephone by a rebel leader's brother in London. In "U.S. to Raise Aid to Soviets, Congress Told," 10-3, he presents uncritically Undersecretary of State Robert Zoellick's argument before a House Foreign Affairs subcommittee, defending the Bush approach to post-coup aid to Moscow.

Toth, Robert C. *Los Angeles Times.* (★ ½)
National security, usually focused on arms control issues. In this extraordinary year, Toth kept his head respectably above water, in the sense of keeping up with developments as they were breaking — but keeping up within the context of the old, crumbling framework, and without any serious attempt to probe what the nature of the new might be. Early in the year, in "U.S.-Soviet Nuclear Treaties Have Downside: High Verification Costs," 1-11, he touches on a theme that remains all too real even though it has been buried under the avalanche of subsequent developments: "Although the Cold War is essentially over, the United States is saddled with the verification standards of the Cold War days, when politicians insisted that no cheating goes undetected." He was highly speculative, working with too little substance in "Ex-Warsaw Pact Nations Evolve Into Neutral Buffer Zone," 4-19, where he argues that East European nations "have already become an essentially neutral buffer zone between the Soviet Union and the West." In "New Ties to the Old Country," 5-14, he probes the impact of the end of the Cold War on influential East European-Americans, such as Sen. Barbara Mikulski and former Minnesota Gov. Rudy Perpich, as "Americans of East European ancestry are rushing to re-establish ties with the land of their forefathers." His "The Scariest Word to Soviets? It May Be 'Privatization,'" 6-24, datelined Volgograd, contains vivid conversations with Soviets on economics. He attempts to fathom the depths of the Russian political psyche in "Desire for Strong Leader Clashes With Support for Democratic Reforms," 8-20, a commentary on the results of opinion polls in which he argues that "the slim support for democracy in the poll. . .contrasts with the historic inclination of Russians to demonstrate subservience to authority and to yearn for a strong leader in times of trouble." A similar attempt to fathom the Russian opinion polls, "Russians Like Gorbachev, Prefer Yeltsin, Poll Finds," 9-16, shows poor judgment in drawing the conclusion that "the numbers document a crucial balance of strength between the two leaders as they cooperate and vie with each other in the creation of a new government."

Tyler, Patrick E. *The New York Times.* (★ ★ ★)
Late last year, Tyler moved from *The Washington Post* to the *Times* where he had one of his best years ever. His coverage of the Gulf War was consistently superior — accurate, focused, perceptive, sensitive to detail and nuance, exceptionally competent. He adeptly handled the weaponry and tactics of combat with Iraq that allowed the U.S. to achieve surprise in "U.S. Says Early Air Attack Caught Iraq Off Guard," 1-18, including telling political details as well: an Iraqi diplomat disclosed that "Iraqi leadership did not believe the Soviet Union and China would countenance an allied attack without further consultations by the Security Council." He provided authoritative assessments of the effect of allied intensive bombing on Iraq's fighting strength in "Best Iraqi Troops Not Badly Hurt by Bombs, Pentagon Officials Say," 2-6, and with "The Battle for Kuwait," 2-25, delivered a succinct explanation of U.S. strategy for taking on and taking apart the Iraqi forces in that theater. With Iraq on the verge of chaos, Tyler deftly explored the U.S. administration's post-war policy in "Stirring the Iraqi Pot," 3-21, establishing that no one could answer the policy question whether, let alone when, the Iraqi army might act to remove Saddam Hussein. A superior "Punished But Hanging On," 4-7, reports Saddam still standing, despite all his miscalculations, with the likelihood that "once the Iraqi economy is moving forward again, Mr. Hussein and his cosmetically rearranged cabinet can be expected to try to whittle, chisel and needle their way around every obstacle that the cease-fire resolution has placed before them." In another Tyler scoop, "U.S. Officials Believe Iraq Will Take Years to Rebuild," 6-3, he established that while "Administration officials had criticized the United Nations report. . .for describing the damage to Iraq with terms like 'near apocalyptic'. . .in their detailed review of each sector of Iraq's economy, the United Nations and United States assessments are not dissimilar." A firsthand report from inside Iraq, "Disease Spirals in Iraq as Embargo Takes Its Toll," 6-24, was a sobering account of the burdens placed upon the general population and humanitarian organizations by the 11-month-old international embargo on trade with Iraq. Tyler made every effort to verify what he described on the horrible and worsening public health situation in the country.

Vartabedian, Ralph. *Los Angeles Times.* (★ ★ ½)
Specializing in defense, aerospace and high-tech issues, Vartabedian made numerous valuable contributions to the discussions assessing the effects of the Gulf War on defense budgets and of future weaponeering. We found his 10 Best selection for General Reporting, the "Losing Clout" three-part series, 3-6, 3-8, and 3-9, to be a superlative examination of just these topics. In addition, in "High-Tech Warfare — A New Era," co-written by Sara Fritz 1-18, he gives a highly technical report on the Tomahawk missile, with the remark that "If this new generation of weapons proves to be as effective as the Tomahawk, experts predicted, the war with Iraq would be a boon for the defense industry. . .but one day of fighting will not erase the costly failures that have affected big defense programs." His "U.S. Risking Its Hard Won Stealth Secrets in Gulf War," 2-6, is a great article on the risks a country takes in deploying its latest technology, with a good discussion of the current stealth technology and weaving in stories as far back as ancient Greece to make his point. In the brief "Management Reshuffled at Douglas Aircraft Unit," 4-30, he displays good sound judgment over the unending, often controversial management reorganization program at McDonnell Douglas by emphasizing the program's continuity. He attempts to focus public attention on possible irregularities by Northrop on a security-delicate issue in "B-2 Jamming Unit May Have Been Canceled," 6-27, suggesting that the Air Force may have "curtailed development of a controversial, multibillion-dollar electronic jamming system for the Northrop B-2 bomber." "Unmasking the Stealth Radar," 7-28, is an excellent report on the status and complexity of the B-1 bomber's stealth radar system, describing the enormous obstacles that must be overcome, cost overruns, and critics of the technology, which ends on an upbeat quote from a supervisor of the machine ship. "When we started, I didn't think we could do it — but they are coming out great." In "McDonnell's Future in Doubt, Auditor Says," 10-4, he takes a second, less complimentary look at McDonnell Douglas, when he reports that the Pentagon believes, though the company denies it, "that McDonnell Douglas, facing hundreds of millions of dollars in previously unknown losses, is so weak financially that it may be forced to cease operations."

Wartzman, Rick. *The Wall Street Journal.* (★ ★ ½)
He keeps a sharp eye on developments in the aerospace industry and its efforts to adjust to its new, difficult environment. Although his research is meticulous and his argumentation careful, his greatest asset is the excellent, vivid and engaging style of writing that he brings to an area of journalism which is replete with top experts and poor writers. He gives an excellent profile of the corporate leadership that Chairman Daniel Tellep exerts over Lockheed in "A Raider Stalks It, But Leaner Lockheed Has Begun to Take Off," 2-14, noting that "Committed to financial consistency, Mr. Tellep has continued Lockheed's transformation from an airplane manufacturer to a more diversified high-tech company. Much of the change has been executed in his own image: analytically, methodically, without fanfare." His "Dog Fight: Futures Are at Stake as Teams Vie to Build Advanced Fighter Jet," 4-19, written from Edwards Air Force base, is Wartzman's fascinating account of the aerospace industry's competition for the Advanced Tactical Fighter: "In a hangar here, separated only by a corrugated-metal wall, sit the world's greatest jet fighter and the second greatest. Soon, the Air Force will announce which is which." Exemplary also is his rendition of subcontractors' woes in the time of military budget cuts in "Navy's Warplane Suppliers Complain About Mixed Signals and Cloudy Agenda," 6-4, noting how, "As the Navy tries to grapple with sharp budget cuts and its new role in the post-Cold War world, its suppliers face the daunting task of planning their own uncertain futures." He portrays vividly the new "propensity for aircraft makers to cooperate while pursuing the few big prizes left in the shrinking U.S. military budget," "Aerospace Firms Joining Forces for Navy Plane," 7-17, in which he reports that "Grumman Corp. joined with Boeing Co. and Lockheed Corp. to prepare a bid for the multibillion-dollar [Navy next-generation attack plane] program, while McDonnell Douglas Corp. and LTV Corp. announced a team of their own." His "Defense Stocks Get Market Boost; Establishment Unfazed by Moves," 8-20, is a terrific collection of quotes from the defense establishment, taking the Soviet crisis in stride.

White, David. *Financial Times.* (★ ★ ★)
Defense. His customary excellence on which we commented in years past was perhaps the reason why White, unlike many of his colleagues, did not succumb to the temptation of superlative and extravagant exercises in this year of mind-boggling strategic changes. In his "Face-off in the Gulf: The Military Equation," 1-13, an analysis right before the decision was made to go to war against Iraq, he points out that "Needing to bring the conflict to as rapid a conclusion as possible, US and other forces would try to keep up a round-the-clock onslaught." In "NATO Members Pressed to Restrict Sales of Arms," 2-20, he highlights the more interesting feature of calls to restrict arms sales to the Third World when he focuses on "preliminary studies on ways of simultaneously lowering barriers on arms trade between NATO members and raising the barriers on what and where they export." In "Smaller, Faster, Cheaper," 6-1, he offers a stimulating commentary on NATO's restructuring which offers the impish remark that it seems odd "that NATO should have agreed on the reshaping of forces before approving its new strategy. . .[it] has decided what the structure will be before saying what it is for." His "When Johnny Marches Away," 6-26, is an excellent survey of the status of military conscription as an institution worldwide, arguing that "conscription itself may well be on the decline," and illustrating the nature of modern military establishments with the observation that "no conscripts were among western combat troops sent to fight against Iraq." "NATO Hopes Lie in Fewer Obstacles to Arms Control," 8-23, is remarkable for its caution about the military benefits of the Soviet coup d'etat's failure, noting that "the failure of the Soviet coup has raised hopes in NATO that recent difficulties in pursuing arms control with Moscow will now ease. But doubts remain about the prospect for further mandatory cuts in military strength." "A Sharp Shock to the System," 10-5/6, is a surprisingly optimistic view of how the exposing of Iraq's nuclear program gave the Non-Proliferation Treaty (NPT) a shock that "could well do it good," as he attributes the treaty's "remarkable success" on the fact that it is "dependent on a delicate political balance."

Wines, Michael. *The New York Times.* (★ ★ ½)
National security. His strong suit is his insightful expertise of (at least some) of the CIA's labyrinthine workings in this period of its institutional redefinition. Even so, he seems to us to be prudently reporting only a fraction of what he knows in this intriguing area — a necessary precondition if his sources are not to dry up on him. His "C.I.A. Sidelines Its Gulf Cassandra," 1-24, is a first-rate report on how the CIA bureaucracy deep-sixed Charles E. Allen, its star analyst, "a 32-year C.I.A. veteran with the ominous-sounding title of national intelligence officer for warning," who predicted the invasion of Kuwait down to the hour, but "his forecast was disregarded, and top White House and Pentagon officials were surprised at home when Iraq marched into Kuwait." In his "2 or 3 Agents Are Believed Killed After Rare U.S.-Syrian Contacts," 2-7, he disclosed that several undercover agents, possibly working for Mossad, who had penetrated a terrorist group were exposed late last year after the U.S. confronted Syria with detailed information on Syrian involvement in terrorist activity: "It has remained a tightly held secret, in part because at a politically difficult time it raises the question of whether Syria deliberately misused American diplomatic communications to assist a terrorist group." In "C.I.A. in Search of a Role," 5-9, a wide-ranging "News Analysis" on William Webster's retirement, Wines looks back at Webster's stewardship of the Agency and examines the Agency's role in a post-Cold War world where, some Agency officials want to get involved in law enforcement and economic espionage while others don't: "Whoever succeeds Mr. Webster must quickly resolve those differences and convince Congress that the agency and other espionage agencies have compelling missions to perform in the absence of a serious threat of global war." His "Sununu Used U.S. Guard Service on New York Trips, Records Show," 6-27, was the *Times*' first direct hit against Sununu, reporting that the White House Chief of Staff "has used workers who guard federal office buildings in New York to drive and escort him on business, political and personal errands in the New York and New Jersey area, according to Government official's documents."

Wright, Robin. *Los Angeles Times.* (★)
National security. Informed, well connected and a bit too opinionated, she relies on rhetorical flourish and panders to popular sentiment. Her "Israel Lacked U.S. Codes to Protect Its Jets," with Ronald J. Ostrow 1-22, is a darkly accusing speculation that "the withholding of the codes indicates that the Bush Administration may have used more than pleas and promises. . .to persuade the Israelis not to strike back and risk damaging the gulf coalition." In "Iran Plots While Neighbors Fight," 2-5, she sees devious Iranian plots where others would discover only smart politics on the part of Iranians. Her "War Plan on Track — But What About the Peace?" 2-10, is sharply critical of the lack of focus by the administration on post-Gulf War policy. In "Gulf Crisis Rewrites the Policy-Makers' Guidelines," 3-4, she displays premature euphoria with the claim that "the Gulf War — rather than offering a single set of clear-cut, consistent rules for the future, offers an array of precedents, guidelines and caution-flags for future policy-makers." But with "U.S. Could Be Entangled in a Mideast Web," 4-28, her euphoria abates: "Iraq's internal turmoil, hardening lines on the Arab-Israeli conflict and Kuwait's bitter political infighting — have deprived the United States of a quick getaway from the scene of war and a smooth transition to the canvas of a 'new world order.' " In "U.S. May Have Missed Chance to Oust Hussein," 5-3, she offers uncritical support for a silly Democratic criticism of Bush's handling of the Gulf War's conclusion. Her "If Hussein Goes, Is This the Heir?" with David Lauter 5-7, is worthless sovietology-style gossip applied on Iraq for the purpose of pandering to popular lust for Iraq-bashing. Her "The Battle to Build a New CIA," 5-28, is a verbose expansion on the theme that "the CIA and its sister agencies are expected to face demands for the biggest overhaul in mission, funding and structure since they were founded." Her "Pair Emerge as Key Suspects in Libyan Terror," 7-21, is too romanticized an account of presumed Libyan terror chiefs, and builds literary stereotypes rather than imparts hard information. In "Coup's Failure Is a Global Boost for People Power," 8-25, she projects preconceived notions on the Soviet situation: "Defying a millennia-old tradition of Russian passivity, the demand for empowerment emboldened not only Russian Federation President Boris N. Yeltsin but hundreds of thousands of Soviet citizens." Empowerment? Po Russkii?

SCIENCE/HEALTH/ENVIRONMENTAL REPORTERS

Abramson, Rudy. *Los Angeles Times.* (★)
Environmental issues. Abramson has the thankless job of detailing the government position, which he handles adequately, with little evidence as to how he feels on any particular subject. He maintains his professionalism, although sometimes it's clear he is straining. We get a satisfactory and informative profile of Secretary of the Interior Manuel Lujan in "A Species No Longer in Danger," 2-14, where he is noticeably making an effort in this regard: "And knowledgeable sources confirm informally that an alert park ranger once caught him about to scratch his initials blithely in some of the ancient Indian carvings in one of the treasured petroglyph areas outside Albuquerque." "Energy Dept. Agrees to Pollution Penalty," 5-11, has a press release feel, but we still come away informed on the EPA fine imposed on the DOE for failing to meet the timetable on an Ohio nuclear plant cleanup. Abramson walks a fine line between advocacy and reporting in "Nuclear Power Industry Shows Signs of Revival," 6-13, keeping this balanced by citing the pros and the cons. He offers some background on the wetlands issue with "Draft of Wetlands 'Bible' Released Amid Controversy," 7-11, but we're ultimately left wondering what all the fuss is about. The eventual follow-up, "Experts Assail Proposed Rules for Wetlands," 11-22, again retails the fracas, but doesn't tell us what the rules are. Abramson relates the contents of the National Research Council report which recommends an earthquake detection system for California similar to the one already in use in Japan, "Early Warning System Urged for Earthquakes," 8-28, in which we discover that "California already has in place the most extensive seismic networks in the country. . .but [they] both are based on 1960s-era technology and were designed primarily for mapping earthquake structures and locating small quakes rather than for providing early warnings." Another panel's recommendations are detailed in "Smaller NASA Scientific Satellites Urged," 9-14, but there's little here beyond the report itself. Abramson frets over the growing number of experts who call "Soviet-Built Nuclear Plants 'Accidents Waiting to Happen,' " 10-18, but he doesn't provide enough information to keep us awake over this particular aspect of the Soviet disintegration.

Altman, Lawrence K., M.D. *The New York Times.* (★ ★)
"Doctor's World" columnist. With his M.D., Altman offers a perspective unique to journalism by bridging the gap between medicine and the layman. As such, though, this "Science Times" veteran doesn't report so much as explain, and we're left wondering what Altman could have added by digging a bit deeper. Altman is highly technical in "U.S. Approves Test of Blood Substitute From Cattle," 2-25, an evaluation of the testing of cow hemoglobin, "hemopure," which would help eliminate a small percentage of AIDS cases, as human blood would no longer be used for accident victims or transfusions. His work on ethics, which impressed us last year, now seems tentative. He compels with the story of Dr. Timothy Quill and "Diane," in "A Doctor Agonized, But Provided Drugs to Help End a Life," 3-7, giving us enough detail to empathize with all involved. But when Altman follows up with a broader discussion, "More Physicians Broach Forbidden Subject of Euthanasia," 3-12; he never defines the term itself, leaving us confused about what constitutes euthanasia: a doctor administering a lethal dose of drugs or the right of a patient to refuse treatment? And in "A How To Book on Suicide Surges to Top of Best-Seller List in Week," 8-9, Altman makes no moral judgement, although he does seem to take the Hemlock Society view that the book is just going to open the debate; *Final Exit* by Derek Humphry certainly appears to have struck a chord, but Altman doesn't examine too closely which one. With "In Strange Twist, Bush Is Suffering from Same Gland Disease as Wife," 5-10, Altman clearly plays the physician rather than the journalist, maintaining this tone throughout. He fascinates with a readable discussion of the incidence of cluster diseases, "A White House Puzzle: Immunity Ailments," 5-28, as George, Barbara and Millie Bush all receive autoimmune disease diagnoses within 16 months. He avoids taking a side in "AIDS Tests Urged for Many

Doctors," 7-16, as the CDC offers guidelines which urge doctors to take the AIDS test as well as the test for Hepatitis B, "and those infected should stop the procedures unless they get permission from a panel of experts and inform their patients." We appreciate his singular perspective, but we'd like to see more reportage.

Angier, Natalie. *The New York Times.* (★ ★ ★)
Angier won a Pulitzer for Beat Reporting for her work in 1990. She may soon even be the talk of New York, as *NYT* self-congratulatory advertisements put it, her dispatches always highly informative and entertaining, in the best tradition of the "Science Times," and as we'd expect from someone who began her career at *Discovery.* Angier reveals what we've always suspected in listing all the problems women have with their feet from wearing high heels, "Many Women Buy Foot Trouble With Fashionable High Heels," 3-7, but she never asks why designers make them that way, although she talks to Carolyn Roehm, among others. She fascinates us with the eye-opening "Can You Like a Roach? You Might Be Surprised," 3-12, including different information on how they raise offspring and relate to each other, as well as to their problems and the new effectiveness of pesticides. "Molecular 'Hot Spot' Hints at a Cause of Liver Cancer," 4-4, is eminently readable on what is perhaps the first step to cancer, "a tiny region of a single gene where toxins that infiltrate the liver seem to hone in, sabotaging the gene and touching off cancerous growth." "Gene Causing Common Type of Retardation Is Discovered," 5-30, is densely written but still informative on the fragile X gene. Angier brings to life a dispatch on the sometime stillness of animals, "Busy as a Bee? Then Who's Doing the Work?" 7-30, a fun feature that tells us why: better digestion, maintaining vigilance, and so on. Similarly, we learn from the "Science Times" lead, "Pit Viper's Life: Bizarre, Gallant, and Venomous," 10-15, in which Angier provides marvelous detail on the habits and nature of the snake; we relish every word of this 10 Best selection for General Reporting, and we don't like snakes. She sensitively probes the debate over "The Biology of What It Means to Be Gay," 9-1, carefully giving both sides a full hearing and clarifying some of the points: "Dr. LeVay in no way claims to have discovered the — or even a — cause of male sexual preference, but merely suggests he has detected something worth further investigation."

Bishop, Jerry. *The Wall Street Journal.* (★ ★)
A *Journal* regular for over a quarter of a century, Bishop furthers our understanding of science and health with his perceptive grasp of a multitude of topics, handling mathematics and medicinal research with equal aplomb. His contributions to the "Lab Notes" column provide us with an engaging compilation of unique scientific facts, and his 1-15 offering is no exception, with a look at "huge and mysterious atmospheric pressure waves" that have been detected in the Midwest. His "Mathematicians Find New Key to Old Puzzle," 2-15, is an adequate discussion of the "traveling salesman" conundrum. Though he brings this classic problem that has defied mathematicians for centuries down to non-mathematical levels, he doesn't fully explore its possible applications. He gives us a straightforward report of a field test in "Tobacco Plants Become Assembly Lines for Scientists Producing New Chemicals," 5-14, but he probably overstates the likelihood of its success. Although mostly a balanced and complete article, he might have included the fact that tobacco is desirable for genetic research because of its primitiveness. In "Scientists Find Nature of Major Genetic Mental Defect," 5-24, Bishop details the preliminary reports on the discovery of the "fragile X syndrome" that is "responsible for a major type of mental retardation." He outlines the outcome of such defects but not the reasons why the "X" is so fragile in some inherited cases. Although he is clearly knowledgeable of his topic in " 'Cold Fusion' Researcher Asserts Dozens of Tests Can't Be 'Ignored,' " 7-3, he can't seem to wrangle free from the multitude of element names and procedures that are foreign to the lay person. He pens a quick-paced report on the current research being made in one of the most commonly inherited fatal diseases in "Cystic Fibrosis Research Yields Potential Gain," 8-22, an easy, readable piece that centers more on treatment than on a cure. Reporting on scientist Peter Koi in "Weary of Red Tape, A Scientist Abandons Medical Establishment," 10-21, he takes a sharp, multidimensional look at the intricacies of experimenting with a new procedure for muscular dystrophy without government help which Koi feels will burden the project with time-consuming reviews.

Booth, William. *The Washington Post.* (★ ★)
Florida. Booth seized the reins on a multitude of major science and health stories this year, displaying an ability to produce more precise analytic pieces than we've seen from him previously. We look forward to seeing his reporting from his new post in Florida. In the overly long "Science and the Art of Money," 2-17, he takes a fresh look at the scientists challenging the "central dogma" that science in this country is in critical condition due to lack of funding. "The problem may be too many scientists making too many demands on a system that is straining to be generous." Booth expertly tackles two researchers thesis that the continents were joined together five hundred million years ago in "America and Antarctica: Long-Separated Siblings?" 3-27. His "War Continues on Shores of Gulf," 4-8, is an informative update from Saudi Arabia on efforts to clean oil spills created during the war; we learn "early efforts to clean up the spill were plagued by limited funding and equipment and a slow-moving bureaucracy." In "Forgotten Troops Hold Hill 99 — and Vice Versa," 4-28, he effectively conveys the maddening plight of a thousand Marines stuck in the sands of Kuwait. His fascinating "Maya Tomb's Clues to New World Disorder," 5-26, recounts the discovery of an ancient Mayan tomb in the jungles of Guatemala. Contrasting the two schools of thought on population growth in "With Twice as Many People, Planet Could Expect Boom — or Doom," 6-10, he sketches out the general theories for both, but, the article is superficial in tone. Covering the exhumation of the late President Zachary Taylor in the brief but detail-laden "No Evidence of Poisoning in Taylor Case," 6-27, he artfully takes readers right into the crypt. His "Pinatubo Exerts Global Influence," 7-8, is a scintillating report on the worldwide environmental effects of the eruption of Mount Pinatubo: "it may decrease the average global temperatures enough that the global warming many scientists believe is occurring will be swamped by Pinatubo cooling." In a chilling report on the cholera pandemic in South America, "Cholera's Mysterious Journey North," 8-26, he acutely details the possible causes of the disease and its spread.

Broad, William J. *The New York Times.* (★ ★ ½)
Science. We're always hard-pressed to categorize Broad, his work too wide-ranging to pigeonhole easily. He neatly handles all the scientific and security issues that come his way with the enthusiasm and excitement of a cub reporter. Broad gives us a timely perspective on nuclear weapons security with "Guarding the Bomb: A Perfect Record, But Can It Last?" 1-29, focusing on the strengths and weaknesses of U.S. and Soviet safety measures. He reviews the new difficulties with the redesigned space station, "Cut-Down Station May Fall Short on Space Biology," 3-26, as funding cuts eliminate experiments, his disappointment that the station is "more of a political showpiece than a vital research tool" evident: "Gone are plans to study the stars, to observe the Earth, to fix satellites, to fuel rockets, and to serve as a staging area for manned expeditions into the solar system. Aside from biology studies, the only remaining science goal is to see if weightlessness can aid such materials science research as growing exceptionally pure crystals." In "Wanted: New Ways to Battle Flaming Wells," 4-9, Broad gets not only the new ideas, but also the battle over the methods of extinguishing oil well fires, capturing the situation in one sentence: "The desert sand near a burning well has often melted into glass." His 10 Best winner, "There's a 'Doomsday Rock,' But When Will It Strike?" 6-18, is delectably non-technical, but still informative on asteroids hitting the earth and on what kind of damage might ensue. Broad's expertise is appreciated in the timely "Pentagon Considering Reactors for Missiles," 8-20, as he details the DoD plan to modernize land-based missiles by switching from rockets that are chemically-fueled to those powered by nuclear reactors. And Broad is plainly excited by the possibilities in "Breakthrough in Nuclear Fusion Offers Hope for Power of Future," 11-11, a trimly readable evaluation of the development by European scientists.

Browne, Malcolm W. *The New York Times.* (★ ★ ½)
Science. While we continue to learn from Browne's dispatches, there's less information to glean, and we have to work harder to get at it, as he slips below the three-star mark for the first time in several years. He still is one of the best science reporters we see, however. As a veteran war correspondent, his *Magazine* cover "The Military vs. The Press," 3-3, promised to be insightful,

but we were disappointed with his perceptions of being a pool reporter in the Persian Gulf War. Browne has lots of gripes here, and airs them all, additionally blaming the disappearance of CBS correspondent Bob Simon and his crew on the pool restrictions: "I cannot help feeling that part of the responsibility lies in a system that goads people into taking unnecessary — or necessary — risks." Huh? His dispatches on the war's technical aspects were better. He tells us how the bombs find their marks in "Invention That Shaped the Gulf War: the Laser-Guided Bomb," 2-26, interesting and readable on this technical topic, but it's premature on Persian Gulf weaponry, which was judged imperfect when the smoke cleared. Browne captures the essence of the work of forensic anthropologist Clyde Collins Snow well, "Scientist Tells Silent Victims' Tales of Terror," 4-9, as Snow pieces together parts of these puzzles from bones to discern stories of massacres and the like. He intrigues us with an examination of the possibility of recreating lost species through an amplification of DNA which is then inserted into an embryo, "Scientists Study Ancient DNA for Glimpses of Past Worlds," 6-25, very readable and strongly written: "With luck and ingenuity, they say, geneticists might one day recover enough dinosaur DNA to create a beast that is reasonably close to the original." While Browne adequately conveys the disappointment of astronomers observing the eclipse in "Dust From Philippine Volcano May Obscure Eclipse in Hawaii," 7-10, he loses all the excitement of the event in the process, reducing even the spectacular sunsets caused by the dust cloud to mere scattered forms of light. "Chemists' New Toy Emerges as Superconductor," 9-3, is fairly late on "Buckyballs," geodesic molecular structures held together by the electronic bonds between carbon atoms, named after Buckminster Fuller. Browne takes us through this with ease and clarity, as always, but we don't find anything new or significant here.

Bylinsky, Gene. *Fortune.* (★ ★)
Bylinsky adroitly juggles diverse subjects such as biotech research, defense contracting and corporate espionage with time-tested acumen, although he tends to go too heavy on the gee-whiz tone that dominates the magazine's science and technology coverage. For instance, he gives a glowing report of Martin Marietta's defense systems in "Eyes to Fly and Fight at Night: Martin Marietta," 2-25, touting the company's Lantirn night vision system and its subcontracted Patriot missiles, but without scrutinizing the glitches that were reported elsewhere. His "The New Attack on Killer Diseases," 4-22, is overly optimistic on the advances made in molecular biology and gene therapy that combat various ailments as well as cancer. Still, he is able to sharply impart interesting facts: "They found that the dementia accompanying Alzheimer's occurred much more often in those with no formal education." In "Biotech Firms Tackle the Giants," 8-12, Bylinsky assesses the success of smaller biotech firms fairly well, contrasting them to the medical giants that specialize more in chemistry than biology: The "executives of big drug companies dismissed the biotech scientists as 'gene jockeys' whose technologies they could always buy....[T]he big companies left Grand Canyon-size chasms for biotech companies to explore." In "How Companies Spy on Employees," 11-4, he dryly examines how companies monitor their workers, saying it "improves service, productivity, and profits," but we hear very little from employes, who undoubtedly have some concerns about this practice. In his brief "Finally, A Good Aphrodisiac?" 10-21, he only skims the surface of the issues surrounding news that biochemists are manufacturing synthetic "pheromones" that act as an aphrodisiac.

Chase, Marilyn. *The Wall Street Journal.* (★ ★)
San Francisco. Her AIDS-related stories continue to enlighten *Journal* readers as she competently scrutinizes current research, eschewing the hype common to AIDS coverage. Her attention to detail remains helpful as she traverses the murky landscape of medical research. Chase puts together an impressive piece of original investigative reporting in "Did Syntex Withhold Data on Side Effects of a Promising Drug?" 1-8. Though bloated with overwrought chronology, the expose flies with its unveiling of Syntex's development of Enprostril, "a new ulcer drug that promised to relieve the misery of millions — and earn the company big profits." In "FDA's Peck Steps In at Crucial Time for AIDS Research," 2-11, Chase looks at the director of the Food and Drug Administration's Center of Drug Evaluation and Research, Carl Peck,

with very little derision noted from AIDS activists. The abundance of acronyms such as AZT, DDC, DDI, make it a bit hard to follow, and research is far from complete, but this is a helpful road sign indicating the way. Her "Clashing Priorities, A New Cancer Drug May Extend Lives — At Cost of Rare Trees," 4-9, is a comprehensive report on the fight between a new drug to combat ovarian cancer, and environmentalists who oppose destroying the trees from which the drug comes. Fraught with examples and details in this human interest story, it falls short by not describing how the yew tree alone produces a cure. The decidedly non-medical "Study of Baby Talk Is in Its Infancy; Grown-Ups Go Gaga," 5-20, is a light article on baby talk and what it means: "baby talk is a genetically coded behavior that humans evolved for communicating with their young." In "Cut in U.S. AIDS Delegation Is Deplored," 6-17, we never really feel the outrage following the government cut in the number of doctors allowed to attend the Seventh International Conference on AIDS. Her news flash from the AIDS front, "Popular AIDS Treatment Is Illicit Copy of Hoffmann-LaRoche's New Drug DDC," 7-16, describes how patients with AIDS are going underground to get DDC. Although she fails to document the drug's effectiveness, those following the AIDS story closely will appreciate the detail in this report. She reports in "Using PCR Gene Technology, Physicians Can Diagnose Elusive Diseases Earlier," 10-30, that a polymerase chain-reaction device that can amplify DNZ strands for disease research sounds promising. Chase gives a perfunctory report, hitting all the topics (diseases, competition and accuracy) squarely, but without much zest.

Cimons, Marlene. *Los Angeles Times.* (★)
A disappointing year for Cimons, who never got beyond press release material and data in her dispatches. We saw little of the inventiveness in her work that first caught our eye. Most of her work this year was merely adequate, as Cimons stuck to regaling us with the reports and studies of various agencies, with a lack of imaginative reporting in evidence. "1st-Class Postage Rising to 29 Cents," 1-23, is dutiful, detailed reporting of the Postal Service rate increase, with Cimons assembling assorted griping from various sources including Jeffrey L. Perlman, manager of legal and regulatory affairs for the U.S. Chamber of Commerce, who says the increase "defies understanding," when the times are tough and service is down. In "Minority Gain in Early Use of AZT Questioned," 2-15, she outlines studies that show minorities either don't get the drug, or that the drug isn't as effective in the early stages, whether they're misusing it or there's biological reason. But this is inconclusive at best; even the experts she paraphrases warn that "caution [is needed] in interpreting the data, saying that further studies are needed to determine whether the racial distinctions are valid and why they occurred." She uses her figures and quotes to their utmost potential in reviewing an NIH report, "Boost in AIDS Research Funding Urged," 3-8, telling us little new. Cimons is quick and to the point in providing the necessary information in "Nation's Syphilis Rate Worst Since 1949, Despite Drug Cure," 5-17, augmenting this with some data and quotes from doctors at the Center for Disease Control. She adequately outlines the memo, from National Institute of Health director Dr. Bernadine Healy, to the Center for Disease Control, "Don't Bar Doctors With HIV, NIH Says," 6-11, but there's little of depth here. "House Votes to End Ban on Fetal Tissue Research Funds," 7-26, is balanced on the continuing controversy over fetal tissue research, despite a successful House vote, with Cimons remaining admirably detached. Her "Federal AIDS Commission Attacks Bush Drug Policy," 8-7, an overview of the AIDS commission recommending more effective drug treatment programs, is balanced, but it sounds as though Cimons merely pulled all the clips together. Similarly with "Study Shows a Million Teen Suicide Attempts," 9-20, the story isn't fresh or new, as was frequently the case with her portfolio this year.

Elmer-DeWitt, Philip. *Time.* (★)
Associate editor. Despite the *Time* habit of disseminating opinion instead of information, Elmer-DeWitt still manages to impart a goodly amount of data in his dispatches on health and technology. He dissects the classic AirLand operation in the Persian Gulf War, "Fighting a Battle by the Book," 2-25, using past military operations to guess possible outcomes. Elmer-DeWitt is ultimately inconclusive in evaluating the question "How Badly Crippled Is Saddam?"

3-4, but he gives us a solid roundup of the estimates in the process. Although the green side of *Time* peeks out in his "Death of a River," 7-29, a dispatch on a toxic rail spill in California, in which we must wade through the slime with *Time* and heed the call for safer cars and transport, Elmer-DeWitt's particular treatment was more balanced than the comparable Keith Schneider report that appeared later in *The New York Times* [see Schneider, Keith]. His lead irritates us in "The Doctors Take On Bush," 8-5, as Elmer-DeWitt takes the word of three doctors as speaking for the entire medical profession on the Bush "gag rule," although he does go on to clarify the fact that there is a debate within the profession with American Medical Association data and American College of Ob-Gyns objections. Despite all the technical information on the merging of PC, CD and TV technologies that Elmer-DeWitt assembles in "The World on a Screen," 10-21, we don't quite find out what a multimedia screen does, or what we'll do with it. His best for the year is the cover story "Making Babies," 9-30, an expansive treatment of the different ways to circumvent the finality of infertility, from in vitro fertilization to more recent methods such as microinjection, which injects a single sperm into the unfertilized egg. Elmer-DeWitt's effort is very readable and worthwhile, although not in-depth, though he doesn't even get to the hazards until the last page.

Gladwell, Malcolm. *The Washington Post.* (★ ★)
AIDS and science. Gladwell captured the marrow of the major science stories of the year, giving us the administrative and analytical viewpoints without becoming mired in the nuts and bolts of procedural scientific studies. His efforts at lighter features, however, often had a distracted tone. He provides comprehensive coverage of a major scientific controversy, falsified data, in "Scientist Retracts Paper Amid Allegations of Fraud," 3-21, offering a frank discussion of how "science should best be policed." His report on the controversy over AIDS-infected doctors, "Doctors With HIV Fear Restrictions," 4-2, is effectively lowkey, Gladwell succinctly noting that "Whatever the calculation, however, the controversy turns more on public perceptions of the risk than on the risk itself." He provides an insightful analytical look at the recent FDA actions against Procter & Gamble's Citrus Hill "Fresh Choice" orange juice and Ragu "Fresh Italian" pasta sauce in "FDA Adopts Fresh Approach to Labeling," 5-6. In "Assessing Physicians: Secrecy Versus Disclosure," 5-27, we receive a balanced report on the growing call, fueled by health insurers and consumer advocates, for fuller disclosure of a doctor's professional record, Gladwell pointedly noting: "the statistics penalize those physicians who take on the sickest patients or attempt the most difficult operations." He pens an interesting "Science" report, "The Subtler Shades of Racism," 7-15, on several recent studies which measured "aversive racism" in self-professed white liberals, Gladwell assessing that "This is the racism of people who would vote for a black president but might unconsciously steer away from sitting next to a black person on the Metro." In "How Driving Under the Influence of Society Affects Traffic Deaths," 9-2, he explores the inexact science of predicting automotive accidents, an exercise which proves to be ultimately pointless.

Hilts, Philip J. *The New York Times.* (★ ½)
Health, Washington. Hilts focused less on the scientific aspect of health than the comings and goings and the personalities of the various players who make the policy and do the research. Although his dispatches are useful, there's often little of impact in them. In "New Chief Vows New Vitality at F.D.A." 2-27, Hilts tightly profiles both Dr. David Kessler and the agency, including a look forward. We get lost in the minute laboratory detail halfway through "Crucial Research Data in Report Biologist Signed Are Held Fake," 3-21, an outline of the case of Nobel laureate Dr. David Baltimore and co-author Dr. Thereza Imanishi-Kari, who are accused of altering data in the paper, which "described findings suggesting that transplanted genes could stimulate a recipient's immune system to produce certain antibodies." "How Charges of Lab Fraud Grew Into a Cause Celebre," 3-26, is improved, a good insider follow-up to the Baltimore-Kari flap. Hilts is smart in allowing Imanishi-Kari to defend herself in the interview " 'I Am Innocent,' Embattled Biologist Says," 6-4; she offers an interesting reason for not faking the data (she has lupus and this work, if faked, would retard research for a cure for the disease), although

there's no explanation for statements within the Baltimore paper that she now admits were false, but "inadvertent." The emotional caliber of the debate over the use of fetal tissue comes through in Hilts's description of the subcommittee testimony of Guy and Terri Walden, who allowed aborted fetal tissue to be implanted to their child in utero while being personally opposed to abortion, "Fetal Tissue Use: Personal Agony in Medical First," 4-16. In "Bush Enters Malpractice Debate With Plan to Limit Court Awards," 5-13, Hilts never talks to any doctors, but the lawyers he interviews are overwhelmingly negative on Bush's idea to limit awards and forcing state compliance by tying legislation to federal aid for hospitals, detailing the bills of related players such as Rep. Nancy Johnson (R-Conn.) and Sen. Orrin Hatch (R-Utah). Hilts goes no further than the recommendations of the National Commission on AIDS in "AIDS Panel Backs Efforts to Exchange Drug Users' Needles," 8-7, an unadorned dispatch. Similarly, in "California to Test Children for Lead Poisoning," 10-12, we get detail from the state agencies, but none from the doctors.

Holusha, John. *The New York Times.* (★ ★ ½)
Holusha covers the business aspects of the environment, a beat to which he is well-suited and for which he was well-trained by his undergraduate degree in chemical engineering and his years as the *Times*'s Detroit bureau chief, covering the environmental reregulation of the automobile industry. Holusha takes us through "The Tough Business of Recycling Newsprint," 1-6, step by step, this readable discussion leaving few questions on the process, though the environmental effects or costs are unanswered. He regales us with the success of 3M in revamping its plants to conform to EPA standards, "Hutchinson No Longer Holds Its Nose," 2-3, by overhauling entire processes instead of adding pollution controls at the end of a cycle: "At a time when companies big and small must pay closer attention to the toxins they release into America's air and water, the $13 billion company has melded its environmental strategy — now 15 years old — into all layers of management and production." Holusha brings us to the cutting edge of cleanup technology with "New Techniques to Turn an Oil Spill Into a Collectible," 4-21, including a breakdown of the pluses and minuses of each potential treatment for oil spills, and for which types of spills each technique might be used. He's on the cutting edge again, this time in the realm of durable goods, "Making Disposal Faster, by Design," 5-28, examining how desks and cars are being designed in prototype models, to be easily disassembled and recycled; this dispatch is made more timely by the ever-increasing restrictions on landfills, which he points out briefly. Holusha expands our knowledge of fiber optics with "Adding Lanes to Data Highways," 7-24, but here he's specific only as to the current research and plans for using the technology, and we'd like to know more about what might be in the works. He's uncharacteristically dry with "Keeping a Gadget-Mad Nation Charged Up — and Safe," 9-22, a discourse on rechargeable vs. single-use batteries, that we have difficulty finishing. Off his general business beat entirely, Holusha is completely arid and incomprehensible on finding the perfect combination of metals "that represent a new state of matter that was previously unavailable," in "Layer by Layer to the Perfect Blend of Metals," 12-1. Keep him on the business-eco beat!

Kolata, Gina. *The New York Times.* (★ ★ ½)
Science and medicine. On this beat, Kolata is the scientific counterweight to Lawrence Altman's diagnostics, her experience at *Science* magazine evident in her smart dispatches. We still miss her work on AIDS, though, as the paper has been without a good, regular AIDS reporter since moving Kolata off the story, due to ACT-UP protests last year. She's adjusted nicely to the broader range of territory she now covers, and we never feel shortchanged. Kolata never descends into techno-babble in "Alzheimer's Researchers Close in on Causes," 2-26, a readable, intriguing overview of the genetics of Alzheimer's and the possibility that the disease is inherited; she even examines potential future treatments which would arrest the death of brain cells. On a similar topic, "The Aging Brain: The Mind Is Resilient, It's the Body That Fails," 4-16, Kolata interests but is dense on how the brain ages, affected largely by the ravages of disease rather than simply age. She carefully examines the physical and ethical questions involved in Dr. Peter Law's

theory of injecting normal muscle cells into deterioriating ones in "First Effort to Treat Muscular Dystrophy," 5-2, and we come away enlightened. In "After Decade, Many Feel AIDS Battle Just Started," 6-3, we see Kolata's talent on this beat as she somehow manages to bring together the diametrically opposed viewpoints of AIDS activist Larry Kramer and Dr. Anthony Fauci, director of the National Institute of Allergy and Infectious Diseases, by quoting Dr. Donna Mildvan, a researcher: "With my head, I know that we have made major strides. I know that. But with my heart, I know we haven't begun yet." As usual, she does a great job in supplementing study information found in *The New England Journal of Medicine* indicating a real difference in the treatment of heart disease based on sex, by using quotes from both sides of the debate over the data and examining what is to be done for future treatment, "Studies Say Women Fail to Receive Equal Treatment for Heart Disease," 7-25. And in "Parents of Tiny Infants Find Care Choices Are Not Theirs," 9-30, we get an extensive, probing examination of the ethics for the care of extremely premature babies, those weighing only 750 grams, or less than 2 pounds, at birth. Kolata is at her finest here; she makes us *think*.

Kosterlitz, Julie. *National Journal.* (★ ★)
Health, welfare, pensions, environment and energy. Like most of her fellows at *NJ,* Kosterlitz views her beat through a Washington policy prism. We appreciate this perspective, but, because of the labyrinthine nature of health care and government, she sometimes seems overwhelmed, perhaps still not quite acclimated to her wide-ranging beat. Kosterlitz did pick up an important newsbeat on the Wofford-Thornburgh race, however. In the 10 Best nominee "Health Care: The Issue for 1992?" 11-16, when all of the Washington press corps was screaming about the need for national healthcare because of the Pennsylvania race, Kosterlitz went to the state and talked to the voters, and concluded that "Wofford's victory reflects a vote for overhaul but not necessarily a vote for a particular kind of reform...Health care was a concern of virtually everybody, but the deciding issue for none of them." She tries to cover too much in "Softening Resistance," 1-12, a thick, unwieldy outline of the possibilities of an all-payers plan in healthcare, where business and the government, and Medicaid and Medicare would form an alliance to set uniform standards for pricing. Kosterlitz details the problems with Title X of the Public Health Services Act in "Ambivalence and Family Planning," 2-23, as it continues to come under fire from conservatives and pro-life activists despite the fact that the program never paid for abortions, raising good questions in the process. "Unrisky Business," 4-6, is replete with information and insights on how the insurance industry and its critics agree that reform is needed to guarantee medical coverage for the employes of small businesses. She smoothly examines the background of the generic drug industry and the FDA in "Drug Therapy," 5-25, explaining the behind-the-scenes maneuvering by Congress over action, as Rep. John Dingell "estimates that 33-50% of the companies that make up the generic industry either have been convicted or are under investigation" for falsifying data or bribing FDA officials. She details the progress of the disabled rights movement, "Enablement," 8-31, carefully pointing out that progress must not mean entitlement. But Kosterlitz is clearly out of her league in "Educated Guesswork," 10-5, a facile treatment of government cost-benefit analysis.

Kriz, Margaret E. *National Journal.* (★)
Energy and communications. Kriz continues to accept her information at face value, asking questions only infrequently. Her work rarely rises above the mundane, although we do appreciate her cataloguing of various players on this beat. In "Boosting Nuclear," 2-23, she is reasonable on the pros and cons of nuclear energy, and the external factors which have led the Bush administration to begin to push for industry expansion, but relies too much on the industry itself: "The war has focused the public's attention on one of America's most pressing energy problems: its rising dependence on foreign oil. [American Nuclear Energy Council President Edward M.] Davis says that nuclear power is the solution to that dependence and to the nation's other major energy problem, the declining surplus of electrical generating capacity. Electric cars can replace today's gasoline-powered fleets, he argues, and nuclear energy can fuel transportation and supply the nation's growing electricity demands. The industry also touts

nuclear power as the solution to global warming. Unlike coal and other fossil fuels, nuclear fuel does not emit gases that are thought to increase the earth's temperature." Oh. Kriz retails the view of energy analysts who worry that short-term cheap oil is lulling the public into a false sense of security, after the soaring oil prices during the Persian Gulf War turned out to be a false alarm, "Joyriding on Oil," 3-16, without examining anything in depth. She handles "Power Struggle," 4-6, well, detailing the electric industry's sharp division over proposals that are intended to bring a measure of competition to electric power generation. Kriz details the Congressional interest in raising the corporate average fuel economy (CAFE) standards in "Disconnections," 5-11, but she never answers the questions of how much oil is expected to be saved by raising the standards, or whether the environmental benefits outweigh the costs. She offers a profile of the Yankee Rowe nuclear power plant and the Yankee Atomic Electric Co., "Nuclear Wind-Down," 8-31, broadening the scope to include an assessment of the nuclear industry. Kriz provides a look at "Clean Machines," 11-16, a light documentation of the race to mass produce electric cars, including the ways industries and government will fit into the picture.

Lancaster, John. *The Washington Post.* (★ ★)
Interior Dept. A resourceful veteran on this beat, Lancaster offered more substance on the continuing skirmishes between environmentalists and political interests this year, while generally holding his biases in check. He fully covers the nationalist sentiments being stoked by Interior Secretary Manuel Lujan over the MCA-Yosemite Park controversy in "Lujan Wants Japanese Firm Out of Yosemite," 1-1: "Everywhere I go, people are not happy with foreign ownership of these. . .resources." He provides a balanced report on the growing dispute between pro-and anti-growth factions in Taos, N.M., with "In Taos, Some Fear Tourism Means 'Aspenization,' " 1-30. He draws on "confidential government documents" to challenge the view that the Exxon Valdez oil spill "was a transitory event whose worst effects were cosmetic" in "Long-Term Damage Seen From Exxon Valdez Spill," 2-21, a thorough report which cautions that "much of the data are preliminary." In "The Green Guerrilla," 3-20, he produces an in-depth profile of Earth First! co-founder Dave Forman, who evolved from Goldwater campaign volunteer to environmental radical, but in the end Forman is as much of an enigma as he was at the beginning. Updating us on the Alaskan oil spill cleanup in "Weighing the Gain in Oil-Spill Cures," 4-22, Lancaster provides an interesting case study on how environmental decisions are driven by politics and public opinion as much as by science. In "Western Industries Fuel Grass-Roots Drive for 'Wise Use' of Resources," 5-16, he is sharp on how a new "Sagebrush Rebellion" in the American west is developing, fueled by business interests borrowing tactics from the environmental movement the "rebellion" opposes. We learn how park rangers today are overworked, underpaid, and under the gun — literally — in the eye-opening "Trouble in Paradise," 6-24, Lancaster reporting that many Yosemite rangers "now wear bullet-proof vests beneath their distinctive green and gray uniforms. . ..." In "The Environmentalist as Insider," *Magazine* 8-4, he deftly profiles National Wildlife Federation President Jay Hair, who personifies the line where pragmatic compromise and co-optation merge.

Rich, Spencer. *The Washington Post.* (★ ½)
Health and Human Services. The veteran Rich remains consistent in his coverage, as knowledgeable on the ins-and-outs of U.S. healthcare policy as any journalist working this beat. But he rarely produces the superlative, imaginative reporting we crave as healthcare becomes increasingly politicized. His animated "Who Needs Medicaid?" 1-6, traces Medicaid's evolution from a " 'welfare medicine' program" to a catastrophic healthcare program, with mushrooming costs. The number-crunching "Social Security and Fairness: Should Tax Rate Be Cut?" 2-18, is a balanced, if dry, study of the Moynihan Social Security plan and Rep. Dennis J. Hastert's proposal to allow Social Security recipients to earn outside income without a reduction in benefits. His "Clashing Group Interests Make Health Care Overhaul Unlikely Soon," 4-29, is a knowledgeable survey of the various Democratic and Republican proposals floating around Washington for a national healthcare program, with Rich noting that "The health care debate is more intractable than most because of the huge size of the health industry, the fact that every

American is affected, and the enormous expense involved." He files an interesting report on a growing trend — employers providing complete medical facilities in the workplace in "Employers Becoming Pharmacist, Physician," 6-3, detailing how the facilities have saved employes money, and, in some cases, their lives. We get a weak news analysis on beleaguered HHS Secretary Louis W. Sullivan in "Critics Say Sullivan Lets Conservatives Guide Policy," 7-28, Rich content to merely enumerate instances where Sullivan caved in to right-wing pressure on policy and personnel appointments.

Satchell, Michael. *U.S.News & World Report.* (★ ½)
Senior Editor. Satchell delivers slick, detailed examinations of current environmental issues, although his writing can become partisan at times. In "Power and the Glory," 1-21, he provides a balanced look at the growing dispute between conservationists who want to protect the Grand Canyon and those who favor "the economical, nonpolluting convenience of hydroelectricity," aptly noting that "here, as elsewhere, the green equation is not so black and white." Graphic details on the abject poverty and deteriorating environmental conditions in northern Mexico brought on by the *maquiladoras* charge "Poisoning the Border," 5-6; Satchell, more of an advocate than usual, contends that "The border region is paying a growing environmental price for allowing the Mexican-based firms to operate beyond the restraints of the U.S. Environmental Protection Agency and the Occupational Safety and Health Administration." He strikes an alarmist tone in "A Vicious 'Circle of Poison,' " 6-10, on the use of pesticides, prohibited in this country, on crops in the Third World, Satchell reporting that workers are infected, and contaminated food is exported back into the U.S. He pens a colorful, if slightly lopsided, profile of Jack Healey, director of Amnesty International in the U.S., in "Nemesis of Third World Thugs," 8-26/9-2, detailing how this former priest helped turn the human rights organization into a popular cause, but failing to mention the criticism Healey is receiving from some quarters. His report on the plight of the American bald eagle, under attack from sheep farmers, "America's Beleaguered Bird," 9-23, is brief and disturbing. He spices "Any Color But Green," 10-21, with good details on the rising influence of the "wise use" movement and its opposition to the traditional environmental movement: "The emotional tinder kindling 'wise use' in the west is frustration over the growing loss of control over land and livelihoods."

Schneider, Keith. *The New York Times.* (★)
Washington, agriculture and energy. After years of having to discount Schneider's bias, we find ourselves reading everything he writes with a healthy skepticism. He often peppers his dispatches with pertinent detail, so we remain steady readers. In "Using Taxes to Discourage Pollution," 2-27, Schneider discusses how Louisiana ties taxation of business property and capital expenditures to its environmental rating, a balanced appraisal with nice touches of data. He does a credible job in explaining how part of the Florida Everglades is being restored to a natural state after development, "Returning Part of the Everglades to Nature for $700 Million," 3-11, but we'd like to have seen more specific costs. In "Is Nuclear Winter Giving Way to Nuclear Spring," 5-12, his succinct lead tells us all we need to know: "With global warming, research on safer reactors and the need for more energy converging, advocates of nuclear power see signs that the industry is overcoming years of public criticism and doubt." Schneider could give us more on the "convergence" as environmentalists confront dilemmas on conflicting goals, however. He catalogues accurately, and with no visible slant, the hesitancy of developers to the government flip-flops on the wetlands, in "Developers Are Wary of Bush's New Wetlands Plans," 9-2. His "U.S. Pushing States to Curb Water Pollution," 10-7, is just the facts. We get the recent history of chemical plant explosions in "Petrochemical Disasters Raise Alarm in Industry," 6-19, but we also get Schneider's bias, as he reports that oil and chemical industry executives are undecided as to whether there are common links in the incidents, but covers at length several suggested common causes being proposed by industry labor unions, research groups and OSHA. He tells a very different story from Philip Elmer-DeWitt on the same rail spill in "California Spill Exposes Gaps in Rail Safety Rules," 7-27, yelling that these chemicals are extremely dangerous in concentrated form, but we get no sense of what kind of

concentrations were spilled. He breathlessly cheers in "Utilities to Take Steps to Cut Haze at Grand Canyon," 8-9, noting the importance of the story, "one of the angriest and most visible environmental struggles in the American West." A mixed bag.

Stipp, David. *The Wall Street Journal.* (★ ★)
Boston. Stipp proves uneven once again this year. When he does hit paydirt, his articles shine with fine-tuned writing; absorbing and informative. His front-page leder "Brains Turn to Sponge and Scientists Find Some Bizarre Clues," 1-7, is a bit heavy on the clever, anecdotal writing — a style uncharacteristic of Stipp. We sense the hand of a front-page ghost writer primarily for the article's noticeable lightness on scientific facts. Though an interesting read, "Life-Cycle Analysis Measures Greenness, But Results May Not Be Black and White," 2-28, is not terribly cutting-edge on the debate over what constitutes, and who judges, environmental soundness. His "Does That Computer Have Something on Its Mind?" 3-19, is an enjoyable article on the old question, "can computers think like a person?" The answer is still no, but the computers do alright in a narrow range of questioning, Stipp indicates. "Buckyballs Give Researchers Big Bounce," 4-2, is an absorbing report on a unique configuration of carbon atoms whose uses have yet to be wholly defined. The article remains engaging mostly because the applications still exist in the realm of science-fiction. In "Consumers Who Can't Sort It Out Turn Recyclable Refuse Into Just Plain Trash," 5-9, Stipp turns this user-friendly topic into a fine article, highlighting the difficulties recyclers are having keeping out impurities. In the decidedly unscientific nature of "Mutant Fruit Flies Give So Much. . ." 5-23, he fails even to mention that fruit flies are used in genetic research because one can run through several generations in a short time. His "Heroin Medication May Help Alcoholics Avoid Relapses," 7-8, is a lively, readable report on Naltrexone, a drug that "seems to help recovering alcoholics make it over the hump of the first three to six months after they quit." Stipp's well-written " 'Wind Farms' May Energize the Midwest," 9-6, on the feasiblity of wind-energy is almost too optimistic, skimming the problems of the initial stages in the 1970s.

Taylor, Ronald A. *The Washington Times.* (★)
Environment. One of the *WT*'s utility reporters, Taylor covers everything from nuclear weapons to politics, but his primary focus is on the environment. It's clear from his lack of focus that he is wearing down, as his dispatches were not as impressive as his first year with the paper; he doesn't ask enough questions. He provides a light overview of the effect of the war on the environment, "Environment Could Be Big Gulf War Loser," 1-18. With "Officials Finally Warm Up to Climate Talks," 2-5, a review of U.N.-sponsored negotiations over the worldwide treaty to prevent global warming, it sounds as if Taylor traveled the hotel lobby and talked to whoever he could find to pull this together. Taylor balances "EPA Trying Carrot-stick on Industry," 3-11, providing views of the EPA, companies and environmentalists, but there's little depth. He doesn't cover the other side of the debate until the closing paragraphs in "Ozone Is Thinning Faster Than Believed," 4-5, and by then the hype has us: "Unless the phase-out of ozone-depleting substances is accelerated, U.S. residents born before 2075 will face 11 million more skin cancers a year and 275,000 more cancer deaths each year, Mr. Reilly warned in a speech to the Rotary Club in St. Paul, Minn. That means 5,000 skin cancer deaths a year and a doubling of skin cancer cases in the United States between now and the year 2040, EPA officials said." Taylor supplies the congressional testimony of veteran oil-fire fighter Red Adair, "Adair Seethes at Kuwaiti Red Tape," 6-12, a good snapshot, but nothing more. He provides clear detail on Defense Secretary Dick Cheney taking the nuclear arsenal off 24-hour alert, "U.S. Takes Nukes Off 24-Hour Alert," 9-29, offering specifics on additional reductions. His reporting of the efforts to broaden the environmental movement to minorities is studied and careful until the close, "New Focus Urged on Environment," 10-26, in which we find an unsubstantiated assertion: "Privately, the key leaders of the major environmental groups acknowledge that their boards of directors resist diversification of the decision-making leadership of their movement."

Waldholz, Michael. *The Wall Street Journal.* (★ ★)
Medicine and drugs. Waldholz won the International Biomedical Journalism Prize for his articles on tumor suppressor genes and their role in cancer, but his articles throughout the year remained uneven as he tackled a handful of medical research stories. In "Sudafed Recall Shows Difficulty of Halting Tampering," 3-5, Waldholz dutifully reports on the recent episode in Seattle of over-the-counter drug tampering along with the attempts manufacturers are making to devise tamper-proof products. "Possible Tool to Spot Cancer in Colon Found," 3-15, is a cerebral report on progress made by Dr. Vogelstein in isolating "a gene, called p53, that when defective can kick a growing colon cancer tumor into a final stage of malignancy." Delving into "Drug Industry Still Has Room to Merge," 6-25, a cognizant profile of larger drug firms needing to merge just to stay afloat, he provides some worthwhile notes for patient and investor alike: "developing a truly different drug that will be approved for doctor use in the year 2000 will come to $400 million, up from $150 million that it cost for a drug approved in 1990." But, Waldholz does nothing to enliven "FDA Panel Says More Study Is Needed of Warner-Lambert's Alzheimer Drug," 7-16, a dull compilation of details on the need for more research to be done on THA, a treatment for Alzheimer's disease. The information is acute, but the pacing is languid. His "Scientists Make Breakthrough With Colon Cancer Gene," 8-9, is an engaging update on Dr. Vogelstein's research on colon cancer, whose plan "is to find out exactly how APC and other genes' proteins check cell growth and then figure out ways to mimic their action." His "Brain Explorers Use Chemical Messengers to Design New Drugs," 10-25, is a glowing report on the drug Imigran which effectively reduces the pain of migraines, but he could have scrutinized the potential downside of the drug more thoroughly.

Weisskopf, Michael. *The Washington Post.* (★ ½)
Environment. Weisskopf continues to shed light on the inner gears and crankshafts of the political and bureaucratic machinery that creates and implements the nation's environmental policy. He provides a comprehensive report from Coors country on the debate over the economic impact of efforts to fight global warming in "From Beer to Utility Bills, Global Warming Measures Carry a Price," 2-4. In a related story "Ozone Layer Over U.S. Thinning Swiftly," 4-5, he delivers a straightforward account, balancing both the scientific and political angles, of NASA findings that the ozone layer is thinning twice as fast as originally thought. In the alarming "EPA Falls Far Short in Enforcing Drinking Water Laws," 5-20, he resourcefully draws on interviews, federal documents, and congressional reports to document a "lax enforcement record," which "highlights what congressional critics describe as a larger breakdown of the nation's system for protecting the public from the health hazards of unsafe drinking water." The report, though, nearly drowns in statistics and bureaucratic legalese. He tirelessly combs through EPA records obtained under the Freedom of Information Act and numerous interviews in "Administrative Costs Drain 'Superfund,'" 6-19, to reveal how Superfund appropriations are being used to finance the administrative costs of private contractors. In "Wetlands Protection and the Struggle Over Environmental Policy," 8-8, he pens an in-depth report on the recent policy battle over redefining wetlands, illustrating how "even for a White House whose top officials routinely get involved in the smallest domestic policy spats, the resolution of this issue reached new heights of political intervention."

Wilford, John Noble. *The New York Times.* (★ ★)
Wilford divides his time primarily between the stars and archeological digs. He seems more accustomed to being brought down to earth now, and although his cosmic dispatches are still his best work, he is gradually matching pace now on both beats. He offers a marvelous profile of cosmologist Dr. Allan Sandage, Edwin Hubble's "professional heir," in "Sizing Up the Cosmos: An Astronomer's Quest," 3-12, an eminent discussion of how the universe continues to expand, with a great quote from Sandage on the limitations of his field: "Science cannot answer the deepest questions. As soon as you ask why is there something instead of nothing, you have gone beyond science." Wilford is equally accessible in "Telescope Is to Open New Window on Most Violent Events in Cosmos," 4-2, detailing how the magic of the universe is revealed as

scientists prepare to send a telescope into space which can read gamma rays, keys to the phenomena abundant in space, such as black holes and quasars. Wilford includes the new information on Mayan history to buttress a fascinating account of the discovery of the tomb of "Ruler 2," "Tomb of Warlike Maya King Found in Guatemala," 5-15. He further refines Mayan history in a erudite discussion of "What Doomed the Maya? Maybe Warfare Run Amok," 11-19. Wilford interests us with a report fron Ulan Bator on how resurgent Mongolian nationalism is translating into a revival of Buddhism and the rehabilitation of Genghis Khan, "Buddha and Genghis Khan Back in Mongolia," 7-22, noting that while the portraits of Lenin and Stalin have been painted over, "the image of Genghis Khan is everywhere, on banners at a trade fair and postcards and in souvenir shops. A vodka is named for him, and a local rock group sings his praises." In "Fitfully, the Rotation of the Earth Is Slowing," 8-9, despite the esoteric subject, Wilford makes us care about this by relating it to the weather and atmospheric forces, but he doesn't ask, as scientists say "that such measurements are now 10 to 20 times more accurate now than they were 10 years ago," if the measurements are so precise as to really indicate a slowing or an improvement in instrumentation.

Winslow, Ron. *The Wall Street Journal.* (★ ★)
Health care. More often than not, Winslow is keyed into the information he conveys in his reports, producing engagingly charged copy, but occasionally his articles are unfocused. In "Cost Control May Harm Dialysis Patients," 2-20, he highlights how the U.S. is shortchanging its kidney patients on Medicare by cutting down the hours needed on special machines due to budget restrictions. The question he never gets to, though, is whether dying patients, due to the restrictions, cost more to Medicare in the long run than patients on the kidney systems. In "A Competitive Battle to Sell Surgery Devices Is Spurring Innovations," 4-16, Winslow writes of U.S. Surgical Corp. which is taking on the giant Johnson & Johnson's Ethicon division for dominance in surgery. Winslow manages the facts well, juggling recent instrument developments with projected profits. In "Rising Supply of Doctors May Be Bad Medicine for Health Care," 5-8, he compares the current U.S. abundance of doctors to the Canadian model which, despite stringent price controls, is facing significantly higher total physician costs "in parallel with a rise in the number of doctors." His "FDA to Target Doctor's Role in Drug Industry," 7-18, is a lifeless article on the FDA crack-down on promotional abuses in the pharmaceutical industry. But, he doesn't directly explain how watchdog measures will reform a system geared toward promotional perks. "Use of Birth Control Pill Surges in U.S.," 8-20, is a good retelling of a survey done by Johnson & Johnson on birth control and the use of the pill in women over 44 years of age. Winslow fails to examine the possible conflict of interest inherent in the fact that J&J is the biggest maker of the pill. He again overlooks such a conflict in "Heart Bypass Death Rates Vary Widely," 8-14, a rather lopsided article on the reasons death rates due to open-heart surgery vary widely between different hospitals. "Both reports are from collaborative groups of doctors" who "found little or no evidence to suggest that the number of procedures performed at a hospital or by a surgeon, or the number of tests. . .or even a surgeon's skill clearly affected overall performance." In "New Study Shows Inpatient Treatment May Be Best Course for Problem Drinkers," 9-12, Winslow shares the data from a report on the best way to help alcoholics recover: AA, inpatient treatment, or a combination. But the graph breakdowns he provides are too thick to wade through, and fail to crystallize into a final diagnosis.

SOCIAL/POLITICAL REPORTERS

Abramson, Jill. *The Wall Street Journal.* (★ ½)
Washington, lobbying and campaign finance. Abramson displays a healthy skepticism that helps her to remain detached, with taut, professional dispatches. She seems less comfortable with analytics, however. In a leder co-written by David Rogers, "The Keating 535," 1-10, she and Rogers review the Keating 5 affair, carefully extending the theme to all of Congress, as changing tactics and rising campaign costs continue to exacerbate the problem. Abramson tightly scrutinizes the Keating 5 preliminary report from the Senate Ethics Committee, "Cranston Is Only 'Keating Five' Member Who Is Charged With Ethical Misconduct," 2-28, a worthwhile exercise with some peripheral input from committee members, but without a great deal of analytic effort. She seems uncharacteristically biased in "Alexander Haig, Others, Fly to Kuwait in Search of Reconstruction Benefits," 3-15, using cynical language such as "many of those on the excursion are hoping to exploit those ties [to the U.S.] for business," and so on. Abramson informs with "U.S.-Mexico Trade Pact Is Pitting Vast Armies of Capitol Hill Lobbyists Against Each Other," 4-25, on the campaign over "fast track authority," but she provides no sense of who might come out on top or what the fight is really about, only skimming the surface. She scoffs at the notion of the alcohol industry trying to curb alcohol abuse in the leder "Selling Moderation," 5-21, giving us a balanced dose of skepticism. Abramson clearly and fairly outlines the potential conflicts of interest of U.S. congressmen owing money to lobbyists and even relatives, using Sen. Mark Hatfield's situation as a case in point, "If You're a U.S. Lawmaker, the Important Thing Really Isn't What You Owe, It's Who You Owe," 6-26. Abramson walks a fine line in "Interest Groups Paid for 4,000 Trips by House Members During '89 and '90," 9-13, offering both sides of the story. Her "Thomas Drama Plays in a Congress Teeming With Sex and Harassment," 10-11, is a scattered listing of senators who have been caught in the act, Abramson taking too long to get to the discussion of sexual harassment.

Allen, Charlotte. *Insight.* (★ ★)
Law. Allen's command of her material is beyond question, but her style has gone dry, rarely coming close to the lively and articulate prose we first heralded several years ago. She remains eminently competent and consistently informative on legal issues, but seems lethargic, perhaps unexcited about her beat and could be due for a new assignment. Allen previews the major SCOTUS cases in "Top Court Poised to Tip the Scales," 12-24-90/1-7-91, including informed speculation as to the impact David Souter may have, but she clearly lacks enthusiasm here. She takes us through the ins and outs of surrogacy in "When Motherhood Is For Sale," *The Wall Street Journal* 1-8, a muted effort. Allen too narrowly explores "The Awarding Side of Lost Pleasure," 2-18, on "hedonic" testimony in lawsuits, arguing for quality of life cash, never examining the ramifications of allowing such testimony or the economics of such an allowance — will malpractice rates go up, for example? She considers logically the possibility of trying Saddam Hussein for war crimes in "It's War, But Is it a Crime?" 3-11, a brief but comprehensive look at the history of war crimes, and noting the relatively new belief that wars could be deterred by holding individual leaders responsible. In "The Bankruptcy Boom," 6-24, we get a colorful piece on the bankruptcy courts in Florida, Allen profiling characters on all sides who are straight out of an Elmore Leonard novel: "[Ronald J.] Harris shuffles through his files. Here is the man with the seven Visa cards and the four MasterCards. He owes $64,000. Here is the man who paid his house note for a year with Discover checks. Here is the couple who won the Massachusetts lottery but still managed to get behind on their Chapter 13 payments." She seems biased in "A Justice Comes in from the Cold," 7-14, allowing Thurgood Marshall little credit for his years on the Court. Allen gives us a serviceable profile of C. Boyden Gray in "Bush's Right-hand Eminence," 8-12, insightfully classifying him as "a throwback to an earlier era in which the country's Protestant aristocracy ruled the highest levels of government, just as it did the highest levels of business." Her cover story "The Neotrads," 10-14, gently pokes fun while probing the deeper sociological forces at work in the latest Baby Boomer craze, the "neotraditionalist."

Allen, Henry. *The Washington Post.* (★ ★)
"Style." The *Post*'s Allen also seems to have lost a step. He rarely impressed us this year as he once did routinely with his precise, vivid wordsmithing. Instead, his subjects sometimes seem trivial, his treatments facile. Though he remains a competent reporter, Allen's gift for evoking scenes from other times, other places, has eroded. Reporting from Saudi Arabia in "Images of the Last Real War," 1-3, he can't quite conjure up a vibrant vision: "The trumpet shall sound and the dead shall be raised, or, as it keeps happening, the raised shall be dead, notwithstanding the words in the Bibles you see a surprising number of here in their tan and brown camouflage covers. Is there a green and black edition for the jungle?" Allen seems fairer to the military than other reporters on the cultural differences between press and Pentagon in "The Gulf Between Media and Military," 2-21, but the essay is overlong and overwritten. In the atmospheric "Memories, Wrapped in Paper," 3-13, he reminisces about his days at the *New York Daily News* during the '60s, when, he writes, the reporters and editors were still writing for the New York of 1948: "In the past few years, with Reagan and Bush making it safe for Mr. and Mrs. Front Porch U.S.A. to feel proud of themselves again, I thought the News was looking better, it might come back. The problem was, it had no place to come back to. Its New York had vanished." Allen spends too much ink on the background of "The Development of Neal Potter," 4-30, not letting the Montgomery County executive come to life until the close when Allen permits Potter to speak for himself. His professed inability to understand *New Yorker* cartoons leads to an enigmatic "Subtle, Subtle . . ." 5-26, in which he is unsure if it's his fault or the magazine's. Allen amuses mildly with an examination of the state of the Post Office and its lines in "Wait a Minute, Mr. Postman," 6-15, but he never really gets going. He doesn't appeal with "Young Fogies; The City's Twentysomethings, Up Close and Impersonal," 8-16, a review of certain groups in D.C. who aren't yuppies, but who they actually are Allen never quite defines. Allen stirringly evokes memories of 1940 in "Terminal of Endearment," 9-13, a short dispatch on the reopening of the restored Greyhound terminal on 12th and New York NW in D.C.

Alter, Jonathan. *Newsweek.* (★ ½)
Senior writer. We appreciated Alter's focused, clear-eyed assessments of press coverage during the Persian Gulf War, as he always provided an innovative angle or perspective. But post-war, with fewer hot press issues to cover, Alter was less in evidence. He offers a logical but standard argument as to "Why 'Linkage' Doesn't Connect," 1-21, terming Saddam Hussein's attempt to draw in the Palestinian issue "fallacious." He debates the question "Does Bloody Footage Lose Wars?" 2-11, reasonably concluding that "it is the results of war, not the esthetics, that in the long run sway public opinion." In "The Propaganda War," with C.S. Manegold, Douglas Waller, Ann McDaniel, Karen Springen and bureau reports 2-25, Alter outlines various propaganda tools on both sides, valuably observing that the "object of most of Saddam's propaganda is not the United States, Israel or even his own people, but uncommitted Arabs." He begins slowly in "Clippings From the Media War," 3-11, a critique of Gulf War coverage, picking up midpoint with several smart observations. Alter indicates that Kitty Kelley wasn't as meticulous as she might have been on Nancy Reagan, in "Wretched Excess," with Andrew Murr, Linda Buckley, Karen Springen, Mark Miller, Eleanor Clift and Thomas DeFrank 4-22, but much of this we've heard before. In a sidebar to the rape cover, "The Great Media Food Chain," 4-29, Alter does a good job of detailing the convoluted journey of the alleged Palm Beach victim's name from a British tabloid to *The New York Times,* including a sturdy examination of ethics. His "All Grown Up," *Esquire* 5-91, is pedantic on the theme of "If New York was the Sodom of the Eighties, Washington was the Gomorrah." Alter provides a clear snapshot in "An Unpardonable Amnesty," with Michael Meyer 9-16, on the pardons for Lithuania's Nazis, who may be guilty of "heinous" crimes but are being rehabilitated because of slipshod work by the KGB. In "Voters to Press: Move Over," 10-14, he critiques punditry, the "evil twin" of the press, as television and print personalities concentrate on the interpretation and the process and emphatically not the content of politics and political campaigns.

Apple, R. W., Jr. *The New York Times.* (★ ★ ★)

Chief Washington correspondent. "Johnny" Apple continues to settle in as the preeminent pundit at the Washington bureau, this year *consistently* giving us clear-eyed appraisals of the geopolitical scene. Although he doesn't quite yet have a completely integrated global perspective, events have helped him to formulate a framework that will develop further with time. On the eve of Bush's deadline, "New Plan: Battle Has a Mind of Its Own," 1-13, Apple turns pessimistic by recounting past optimistic calculations, sounding an appropriately somber note. He skeptically gives us the details from the briefing on the Baghdad bunker bombing, "Allies Deny Error and Cite Reports," 2-14, bordering on the anti-military: "No responsible officer was willing even to entertain the possibility that a basic mistake had been made. None doubted, or at least none admitted to doubting, that the building that was hit had a command and control role." Apple fuses accounts of the first reports of fighting within Iraq, carefully noting potential outcomes in "Iraqi Clashes Said to Grow as Troops Join in Protests; First Allied Captives Freed," 3-5. In "Another Gulf War?" 3-10, Apple fearlessly probes the questions raised by Saddam Hussein's survival. He examines the shortfall of representation of Hispanics in "In Clashes, a Hispanic Agenda Enters," 5-9, an important story. Apple sees the ugly possibilities in "Baghdad Rejects U.N. Police Force to Protect Kurds," 5-10, appraising White House reaction to the U.N. announcement, which means U.S. troops will have to remain in northern Iraq longer than the administration anticipated. His expertise is handy in "Superpower Weapons Treaty First to Cut Strategic Bombs," 7-18, a solidly penned overview of the G-7 meeting, paving the way to a Moscow summit on disarmament. His work on the coup, though, was more summarization than analytic: "The Next Chapter," 8-22, and "The West Must Be Quick on Its Feet," 8-25, are serviceable on events in the Soviet Union, but have little of the piercing insight we've come to expect. Apple stays decidedly neutral in "Senate Confirms Thomas, 52-48, Ending Week of Bitter Battle," 10-16, in this dignified and nonpartisan recap of the Senate debate and debacle of Thomas, and the vote.

Applebome, Peter. *The New York Times.* (★ ★)

National correspondent. Relegated too often to surveys rather than the analytic pieces we'd so enjoyed last year on race and politics, Applebome seems stale or bored. He still shows signs of penetrating intellect when dealing with a topic of substance, though, as in "Although Urban Blight Worsens, Most People Don't Feel Its Impact," 1-28, a delicately written appraisal replete with examples of the missing link between problem and solution on the underclass. Applebome goes nowhere with a country-wide survey, "Carnage in Baghdad Erases Image of an Antiseptic War," 2-14, his general anecdotes developed into general conclusions. He obviously feels for the soldiers in "Guardsmen Return From War They Didn't Fight," 3-27, describing the grumpiness as the guardsmen of the 48th Infantry Brigade return home after spending the war in training. He perceives clearly the complexity in "Atlanta and the Olympics: The Games Have Already Begun," 4-7: ". . .the effort to stage the games will be played out over a Byzantine power grid, along numerous fault lines of race and class. Potential conflicts include not just interracial ones, but also intraracial ones — some low income blacks are suspicious of the alliance between black politicians and the city's business interests." Applebome walks a fine line in "Epilogue to Integration Fight at South's Public Universities," 5-29, plumbing the issues in desegregating black southern colleges. In "Mill Town Pensioners Pay for Wall Street Sins," 7-30, we get anger from the pensioners, but little detail on the Cannon Mills buyout and the reinvesting of pensions in Executive Life, Applebome merely carping about the avarice of Wall Street. He only examines the immediate issues in "Bakker Pleads for Reduction of Prison Term," 8-23, an adequate snapshot. His economic inexperience shows in "As Recession Slows Growth, A Region Takes Stock Anew," 9-10, an anecdotal examination of the changing economies of six southern states; Applebome gives us no sense of state tax structures or GNP, etc., concentrating instead on labor-related data, such as per-capita income. His patchy "In Hometowns, Outrage Over the Senate and Adamant Support for Thomas," 10-15, haphazardly pieces together anecdotes from Thomas' hometown, Pin Point, Georgia.

Archibald, George. *The Washington Times.* (★ ★)
National correspondent. Archibald's dogged persistence hasn't yet set off fireworks as it did two years ago with the Barney Frank bombshell. Perhaps this is because he is shuffled from story to story, although he follows the National Endowment for the Arts with some regularity. In "Sexual Performers Lucked Into List for New NEA Grants," 1-1, Archibald stays on the case of John Frohnmayer, Karen Finley and Holly Hughes by exposing new grants and paraphrasing those in the know: "An NEA official said John E. Frohnmayer, the chairman of the endowment, will announce a record number of new grants in hopes that the grants to Miss Finley and Miss Hughes will not attract enough attention to set off another uproar." Archibald reports that "Senate Panel Chairmen Boost Staff With Surplus," 2-22, as the Senate can now carry over "surplus" funds from earlier years to add staff, an important dispatch on how government money is being frittered away. He and Joyce Price play Siskel and Ebert in "NEA Film Flap Gets Brush-off," 4-3, getting as many reviews of the film "Poison" as reaction to a $25,000 NEA grant to the creator. He carefully describes how a "Vaccine Halts HIV Progress in Tests," 6-12, a cautious, well-organized follow-up on a privately developed and genetically engineered AIDS vaccine that may restore immunity for the HIV positive; results had been embargoed, but *WT* independently learned of the story through interviews with Army doctors and representatives of the company that first developed the vaccine. In "Schools' War on Drugs Pays Homage to Drag Queens," and Joyce Price 7-25, the pair gets solid information on allegations that a N.Y. program called Youth Enrichment Services has used federal funds to have gay social events, indicting as well the San Francisco public school system. Archibald explores how Clarence Thomas' testimony plays out before conservatives, via traditional tests such as school prayer, "Thomas Rattles, Soothes Faithful," 9-13. He professionally handles the attempt of Clarence Thomas to make the government subject to sexual harassment laws while at EEOC in "Judge Tried to Extend Bias Laws to Congress," 10-9. Archibald reports this little known fact dispassionately and sharply.

Ayres, B. Drummond. *The New York Times.* (★ ★)
Washington, Atlantic region correspondent. Ayres, an always reliable veteran, continues to offer reliably done features, setting the scene well and then permitting his subjects to speak for themselves. Using this technique, though, at times leaves his material thinner than it would be if he fleshed it out himself. Deftly merging background information and quotes, he probes anecdotal evidence in "Across the South, a Clash of Doubt and Fervor," 1-9, finding that support for war with Iraq "often seems to be qualified, hemmed in tightly by doubts and qualms and conditions. It may not be the kind of support likely to see President Bush through a long, difficult war." Ayres informs on the mechanism of the draft in "Despite Pentagon Denial of Plans, Many Are Looking Over Shoulder," 2-4, should it be reinstituted; thankfully, he makes it clear at the outset that this is only an outside possibility, and we read the remainder with a sense of relief. In "Honeymoon for Mayor Continues in the Capital," 3-26, Ayres doesn't sugarcoat the problems of Sharon Pratt Dixon or shortchange her detractors, but it's apparent here that he has been affected by her infectious "can-doism." He tries to make the issues involved in "Judge in Capital Orders Reporter to Identify Source," 4-23, universal, but with little success, as this messy case in which *Washington Post* reporter Linda Wheeler is told to reveal her source, as she's already done so to her husband and another individual. It's too specific in circumstances to be broadened into a discourse on source confidentiality. Ayres vividly recounts the court testimony of Timothy Evans, who was sentenced to six weeks in jail for selling marijuana to a narc at UVA, "Student Pleads Guilty in Virginia Raid," 7-9. He is equally evocative in "Factory Fire Leaves Pall Over 'All American City,' " 9-5, on Hamlet, North Carolina which lost 25 people in a chicken processing plant fire; we get a feel of the village, along with a sense of the tragedy. Ayres supplies nice details in "Yankee Strategist Plans Campaign to Put a Virginian in White House," 10-15, on this sharp political profile of Doug Wilder's right-hand man, Paul Goldman. We're not quite sure from the piece how essential Goldman is to Wilder's future, however.

Babcock, Charles R. *The Washington Post.* (★ ★ ½)
Investigations. Molded in the Woodward-Bernstein tradition, Babcock helped uncover the story of John Sununu's travel perks, nearly toppling the White House Chief of Staff. The remainder of his portfolio consisted of substantial dispatches in which he continued to offer original angles. He provides a clear snapshot of Griffin Bell's testimony before the Ethics Committee in "Bell Speaks on Ethics at Senate S&L Inquiry," 1-91. Babcock admirably handles "M-1 Tanks Quickly Demonstrate Superiority," 2-27, giving us a solid rundown of the M-1's capabilities. In the important dispatch, "Spending for 1990 Hill Races Fell," 2-25, he informs us that even though overall spending for congressional campaigns fell between the 1988 and 1990 races, the spending gap between incumbents and fresh contenders continues to grow. Babcock got the Sununu travel story early and stayed on it throughout the year. With the 10 Best selection for Political Reporting, "Sununu: Frequent Flier on Military Aircraft," 4-21, he and Ann Devroy drop the bomb on the Chief of Staff, providing all relevant figures. The pair reviews Sununu's response in "Sununu Deems Only 4 Plane Trips 'Personal,' " 4-24, but, while they discuss how much Sununu reimbursed the government for which flights, we don't find out how much the trips cost. Babcock and John Yang cull "Ski Industry Lobby Paid Expenses for Sununu, Wife in Aspen," 4-30, from several different sources, an adequate follow-up. He broadens the travel perks theme in "Congressional Leaders Also Fly Corporate Skies," 6-21, outlining which congressmen solicit the use of corporate planes for official business; Babcock gives everybody just enough rope here, and they hang themselves. Babcock pulls "Strauss: $6.5 Million in Income Over 18 Months," 7-12, together well, with detail on Robert Strauss's finances. "FBI Investigating BCCI's Lobbying Effort in Georgia," co-written by Jim McGee 8-4, is minutely detailed but clearly explained on the links between the lobbyists, BCCI and the scandal that followed. He follows the Sununu flap with "Lawmakers' Travel Slows — But Not Much," 9-13, a satisfying breakdown of who's going where, and who pays for it, the opening hooking us: "If Congress is captive to an 'inside the Beltway' mentality, as some critics charge, it's certainly not because lawmakers never get out of Washington."

Balz, Dan. *The Washington Post.* (★)
Politics. Balz seems to be caught in the ennui endemic within the Beltway, advancing neither policy debate nor fitting events into an analytic framework. He persists in probing superficially, not providing the depth of information or insight we expect. Balz never examines Democratic reaction to Clayton Yeutter's appointment in "Yeutter Chosen to Be Republican National Committee Chairman," 1-8, a reheated GOP press release. With "Protester Disrupts Service at Church Attended by Bush," 2-18, Balz is barely above wire-service quality. He relies on unnamed sources in "After Bombs and Tanks, a Carrot and Stick," 3-16, on the White House scrambling to craft a policy on Iraq, never going any deeper than "All of this suggests that the current phase of the gulf crisis is every bit as complex as the decision making that led up to the war." Balz offers a trim update with "War Sharpens '92 Spotlight on Sen. Gore," 4-22, but this is little more than Al Gore as Hamlet. Standard in "Republicans Look to '92 as Year of Opportunity," 4-28, he speaks to different state party chairs for their views, but his conclusions are strictly conventional. Balz plays up Tsongas' "challenge to the orthodoxy of his party," in a straightforward manner on his kick-off in "Democrat Tsongas Begins Campaign for Presidency," 5-1. He spends too much time repeating Bill Clinton's critique of the GOP in "Democrats' Perennial Rising Star Wants to Put New Face on Party," 6-25, devoting only three paragraphs to Clinton's philosophy, turning the remainder of this mushy appraisal into a light biography. An adequate appraisal of the Democrats, "Call It the Summer of Democrats' Discontent," 8-26, is undermined by Balz's failure to explain his remark: "only [Jerry] Brown has a national reputation, and it isn't good." In the sharp evaluation of the presidential field and the party, "Democratic Field Set to Grow," co-written by E. J. Dionne, Jr. 9-2, the duo credibly ponders the political issues, postulating that the relative obscurity of some of the candidates may be beneficial, as it allows them to take risks, thereby advancing policy debates.

Barber, Lionel. *Financial Times.* (★ ★ ★)
Washington. Barber flavors his dispatches with a distinctively British perspective, continuing to report Washington politics with the one-two punch the *Financial Times* delivers so well. Unlike many of his fellows in the Washington press corps, Barber actively tries to fit the U.S. into the world at large, and we value his view. In "How Washington Slid Away from Conciliation," 1-18, he puts a British spin in expanding on Paul Gigot's *National Interest* article: "The story of how the US slid into war with Iraq is a chronicle of miscalculations." Barber incisively dissects U.S. jitters about the Middle East peace plan offered by Moscow, "Ultimatum Reflects US Fears About Soviet Plan," 2-23/24, correctly pointing how costly delay is. He accurately contends that the recession has effectively torpedoed Big Green in the U.S., "The Un-Greening of America," 4-13/14, making it clear that the movement is far from dead, but is redefining as well as redesigning its message. Barber outlines the difficulties inherent in the Middle East peace process, "Triumph, Then Trouble," 6-15/16, including some new angles, such as the effect of Bush's "determination" to get U.S. troops out as soon as possible. In "A Mirror Image of the 1960s," 7-19, we appreciate Barber's efforts to present a multidimensional profile of Clarence Thomas, and although we don't learn anything new, we found it more attuned to the complexities of the man, with Barber avoiding the folly of trying to categorize him. "Bush Warns of Risks of Soviet Disintegration," 8-27, is solid but unanalytic on Bush's not sending financial aid until the danger of anarchy in the Soviet Union has been averted. With typical British directness in "Bush Prepares to Cover His Domestic Flank," 9-5, Barber focuses on how Bush will move to preserve his capital: "In short, the president intends to play safe. He has 21 successful vetoes of bills since he took office, so it is easy to see why he is tempted to continue on this tack — even if the nation's problems continue to proliferate." Barber is out of his realm when discussing macroeconomics in "Hand of Friendship for an Old Foe," 9-30, but his appraisal of the politics of aid for the Soviet Union and how and why Bush is dancing about the question is appreciated.

Barnes, James A. *National Journal.* (★ ½)
Chief political correspondent. A promising journalist who has flashes of brilliance, but like so many of his colleagues at *NJ,* Barnes still insists on obscuring his insights in thick prose. He usually fails to make his work either fresh or exciting. In "Liberal Democrats Feeling Their Oats," 1-5, Barnes lists the various devices Democrats are using to redefine their ideology, such as holding conferences, seminars, starting magazines, etc., but we'd like to know more about what they're *thinking.* His "Still Missing Reagan," 3-2, is a typical "the conservatives are rudderless without Ronald Reagan" exercise, backed up by a meeting of the Conservative PAC, with his appraisal of Bush on some conservative litmus tests at least credible, if not terribly creative. Barnes tells us of cutbacks on the campaign trail in "Four for the Money," 3-16, as congressional fund raisers fear the demand for campaign money will exceed the supply in '92. He shifts gears too quickly in "Where's the Beef?" 4-20, on the shortage of Democratic presidential contenders, providing important background and information on fund-raising, but flip-flopping from subject to subject. Barnes tries to make sense of the Voting Rights Act in "Minority Poker," 5-4, taking a fair and objective approach, but not quite clearing up things entirely on how the Democrats must balance satisfying their key black constituency and holding onto the maximum number of House seats after redistricting. In his standard but in-depth report on campaign reform in the mire, "Reform Roulette," 6-22, Barnes startles us with a frightening quote from a D.C. law office partner whose PAC apportions $100,000 each election: "It wouldn't bother us one way or the other. There will always be ways for people to raise and coordinate the flow of money." He relies only on conventional sources such as Howard University's Ronald Waters for "Minority Report," 7-20, detailing relations between the black minority and the White House and the news media, raising an interesting point: "they [blacks] now see the nation's news media, counted as allies during the civil rights era, as all-too-willing messengers of black pathologies." In "Aiming at the Middle," 8-10, Barnes takes far too long to prove to us that Bush is vulnerable on the economy, a repetitive exercise that's overlong and overplayed.

Barrett, Paul M. *The Wall Street Journal.* (★)
Washington, law enforcement and Justice Department. Barrett did little homework this year, as was apparent in his sometimes skimpy dispatches. Still content to be merely comfortable on this beat, we see scant evidence of expertise. In "U.S. Cracks Down on Marijuana Growers," 1-10, Barrett gets some detail on Drug Enforcement Agency plans, but few costs involved. He lets the naysayers have a field day with "Bob Martinez, Bush's Proposed New Drug Czar, Is Criticized as Lacking Some Key Qualifications," 2-25, and although he offers some perfunctory supporting evidence, Martinez comes out the worse for wear. Barrett paints a bleak, unrelenting picture of the projects in "Epidemic: Killing of 15-Year-Old Is Part of Escalation of Murder by Juveniles," 3-25, offering no socioeconomic evaluation in this surface examination. In "Business Complains FTC Goes Too Far, Pressing Its Cases After Losing in Courts," 4-15, Barrett takes Coca-Cola as a case in point as the Federal Trade Commission further pursues antitrust suits, resulting in what one lawyer calls "double jeopardy," but Barrett's narrow focus detracts. In his disorganized "U.S. Charges 8 Ivy League Universities and MIT With Fixing Financial Aid," 5-23, Barrett gives us all the details on the settlement well before we knew specifically what was being settled. He and Stephen Wermiel provide little new evidence of the political savvy of the Thomas nomination in "The Marshall Seat: Bush's Court Nominee, A Black Republican, Is a Deft Political Choice," 7-2, an otherwise acceptable roundup. In "Mystery Man: Judge Thomas, Billed as Conservative, May Prove Unpredictable," 7-19, Barrett and Stephen Wermiel appear to have merely read the ink on the story, pulling this together without seeming to make a single phone call or asking a question on their own. "Through the Cracks," 8-7, is convoluted on the capture of Patrick Waldrop in Costa Rica, who faces extradition on drug charges. In "Thomas to Help Decide High Court Case on Liability of Cigarette Manufacturers," 10-22, Barrett tries to guess which way the court will rule, providing solid background on the Cipollones' case, the legal intricacies, as well as the court's docket.

Barringer, Felicity. *The New York Times.* (★ ½)
Washington, general assignment. Barringer additionally drew some feature assignments this year, to varied degrees of success. She even was moved temporarily back to the Soviet Union, giving us her most satisfying glimpses of life during her posting in Moscow. Barringer imparts the feeling of community quite well in "New Industry for Outer Banks: Home for Retirees," 2-11, the story of small-town North Carolina in which residents are fighting development. She can't breathe life into "Census Shows Profound Change in Racial Makeup of the Nation," 3-11, a percentage breakdown of who's what according to the census. "U.S. Ill at Ease With All-Male V.M.I." 4-4, is less on the U.S. position than a point-counterpoint between cadets and school officials on keeping Virginia Military Academy all male. As an ineffective counterweight to the much-criticized profile of the alleged victim in the Smith case, Barringer offers "The Accused in the Palm Beach Case: Quiet, Different and Somewhat Aloof," with Michael Wines 5-11, a carefully structured profile of William Kennedy Smith; Barringer and Wines cite part of the essay he wrote for medical school and are calling him "Willy" halfway through, indicating an intimacy which discomfits. Barringer hems and haws in "Compassion and Pragmatism on Help for Moscow," 7-8, her informal survey of U.S. opinion on the possibility of a bailout for the Soviets leaving us confused. "Screening for Breast Cancer: Questions of Cost and Quality," 8-19, a broad-ranging survey of practices of women and the history and technology of mammography is eye-opening without sounding like a public service announcement. Barringer correctly pinpoints the problem in "Soviet Barter: The Haves and Have-Nots," 9-19, as the lack of a stable currency which has led to a primitive barter system leaving many without food; she paints a wrenching, vivid picture that we remember. Barringer brings together expert opinion on erotomania, as well as memory retention and perception as it pertains to the Judge Thomas Supreme Court nomination hearings in "Psychologists Try to Explain Reason for Opposing Views," 10-14. An interesting report, yet still undeveloped.

Bennet, James. *The Washington Monthly.* (★ ½)
Editor. Bennet shares editorial duties at *WM* with Katharine Boo, picking up where his predecessors Jason DeParle and Scott Shuger left off. Bennet, however, matches neither Shuger nor DeParle in polemics, offering cursory evaluations and unimaginative solutions. He ends the year poised to join *The New York Times* Washington bureau. In "The Senate's Lame Doves," 3-91, Bennet argues unconvincingly that the debate in the Senate over military action in the Persian Gulf was no debate at all. He asserts that no one tried to change anyone else's position, and that the Senate was trying to make speeches, not policy; we remain uninfluenced, having seen much of the emotional debate live and uninterrupted on C-SPAN. Bennet makes a semi-persuasive case that diplomatic crossed wires helped lead to the final decision to use military action in the Gulf, "Sand Trap," 4-91, but his conclusion that "the tragedy of the Kuwait crisis is that we don't know if air-tight sanctions, combined with good-faith diplomacy, would have peacefully enforced international law" seems facile in the light of the mishaps he lists, particularly when he recommends "good-faith diplomacy" in the Middle East. In "America: A Repair Guide," 7/8-91, Bennet and Editor-in-Chief Charles Peters provide at least a credible list of different things the federal government could do to improve things, from education to the capital gains tax; while most of this has been printed earlier in *WM,* some entries going as far back as the 1970s, it's good to have it handy in one catalogue. Bennet gives us the conclusion before outlining the examples in "Bloat People," 9-91, a compendium of the nightmarish situations within district government that will *not* be solved by Sharon Pratt Dixon's targeting of jobs, not individuals, that will culminate in layoffs of 1,200 to 2,000 people within a certain salary range, lacking organization. And we get more griping about the flawed quality of the White House press corps in "The Flack Pack," 11-91, Bennet's cogent points lost in his long list of examples where reporters should ask the President tough questions, and don't.

Bering-Jensen, Helle. *Insight.* (★ ★ ½)
Writer. Henrik's spouse as well as one of the weekly's preeminent culture scribes, Bering-Jensen continues to bring an effervescence to her features that we appreciate. "Scandal Wrinkles Dead Sea Scrolls," 2-18, is a lively, informative retelling of the story of the Dead Sea Scrolls scandal, Bering-Jensen hooking us with a memorable opening: "It has been called the philological scandal of the century. Not that philological scandals come around that often, of course." She sensitively examines the question of giving children extra psychological help in wartime in "How Do Children Cope with War?" 3-11. In "BBC Tests CNN's Grip on the Global Market," 4-15, she takes us through step-by-step plans for BBC's global proposition, with a little history of the BBC thrown in and a delightful description of the institution: "As a Marxist Ethiopian official once explained his preference for the BBC World Service over Radio Moscow: 'It is truth read by gentlemen.' " Bering-Jensen is uncharacteristically thick in "NEH," 5-20, on Carol Iannone and her nomination to head the National Endowment for the Humanities, and the fighting that followed. She profiles Joseph Brodsky, Soviet dissident and emigre, Nobel Prize winner, and now Poet Laureate of the U.S. in "From Russia with Poetry," 6-24, a wonderfully vivid and lively discourse. Also well written, "The Best-Kept Secret of American Foreign Policy," 7-15, profiles a fascinating gentleman, Leo Cherne, chairman of the International Rescue Committee: "Match the humanitarian passion of an Albert Einstein with the swashbuckling resourcefulness of an Indiana Jones, and you get somebody not unlike Cherne, a man equally capable of addressing a Senate hearing. . .or bargaining over life and death with guerrilla leaders." But Bering-Jensen seems merely to be gossiping in "Ghosts in the Attic," 8-19, on the practice of hiring ghostwriters for novels bearing the names of celebrities and deceased authors; Jacob Weisberg of *The New Republic* said more about the woes of the publishing industry in half the space. She profiles Norman Mailer as *Harlot's Ghost* hits the stands, sharply placing this CIA epic in contrast to the author's public life in "Patriarchs Don't Pummel," 10-28.

Berke, Richard L. *The New York Times.* (★ ★)
Washington, general assignment. Berke once again provides balanced meat-and-potato reports after several years on the Hill. His up-close lawn seating allowed him a generous view of the

fireworks that occurred, namely, the Keating 5 ethics rulings and the Judge Clarence Thomas nomination hearings. His "In S.&L. Case, 2 Dramatically Contrasting Views," 1-14, is a solid overview of the Keating 5. He balances the questionable ethics involved by contrasting the greedy "cynical" and sympathetic viewpoints. A follow-up report, "Ethics Unit Singles Out Cranston, Chides 4 Others in S.&L. Inquiry," 2-28, touching all the bases from the verdicts to the reactions to the ethics committee's findings on the Keating 5, shows his evident knowledge: "The committee's inquiry was particularly complex because the rules guiding lawmakers' intervention for contributors and constituents are murky at best and the case itself was marked by political concerns." In "Behind-the-Scenes Role for a 'Shadow Senator,'" 3-27, Jesse Jackson's vision of D.C. the state is reasonably presented, with Jackson noting incredulously, "five states with real senators have fewer people than Washington." Yet Berke does not cast sufficient light on this issue of representative frustration. His slight "Week in Review" piece, "A Revival: The Campaign Finance Show," 5-26, provided little new information or analysis of the Senate debate over campaign financing. The other major story Berke brought life to was the nomination of Clarence Thomas to the Supreme Court in "Panel Plans to Press Court Nominee," 7-3, a good account that waits till the last paragraph to mention the professional relationship Thomas had with the lone Republican involved with the hearings, the "point man" Orrin Hatch. In an acutely penned "Two Democrats on Senate Panel Say They Will Oppose Thomas," 9-27, Berke includes the potential for passage of the nomination in committee and in the Senate as well as his Democratic opposition. His dispassionate coverage of the Anita Hill-Clarence Thomas hearings in "Women Accusing Democrats of Betrayal," 10-17, shows balanced restraint on the women's movement's plans on targeting Democratic Senators who voted in favor of confirmation and who are up for reelection.

Birnbaum, Jeffrey H. *The Wall Street Journal.* (★ ½)
Congress. Birnbaum has, thankfully, ceased relying on Rep. Dan Rostenkowski (D-Ill.); his reporting seems fresher as he begins to plumb new information from new sources. He starts the year with "New Congress, Full of Sound and Fury Over Iraq, Fuels Bipartisan Outrage by Signifying Nothing," 1-4, with the question of the possibility of military intervention. Despite congressional waffling, Birnbaum does get a smattering of opinion from high-ranking congressmen. Another military intervention article, "Roemer, A Dove Turned Hawk, Typifies Democrats Seeking Cover on War Issue," 2-18, is an interesting exercise in which Birnbaum takes Rep. Tim Roemer as a spin control doctor for the Democrats who voted against the war. Birnbaum is slightly off-kilter in "Bush's Surging Across-the-Board Popularity May Translate Into Greater Clout in Congress," 3-5, in which he bets incorrectly that the President's political capital will carry over into domestic issues. The off-base "Bush's Use of Lobbyist in Nomination Leads to Anger and Envy," 7-18, connects Clarence Thomas with General Motors in that they "Both will have vital business in the court next term and both will have had the same lobbyist. . ." Birnbaum shrinks away from his original premise of the lobbyist Duberstein at the end, deflating his theory. Birnbaum's effective "Congressional Democrats Choose Tax Fairness, Health Care as Issues on Which to Make a Stand," 7-31, gives us considerable detail on Democratic infighting to get to a fighting position: "a signal that the Reagan-Bush years are going to be heavily challenged." In "Rep. Anthony and Lobbyist Wall, Good Friends and Capitol Pals, Are Business Bedfellows, Too," 8-9, he digs to reveal a one-third partnership in Porterco Inc. between them; yet, Birnbaum doesn't quite make the case that there's a conflict here. His fuzzy "Congressional Democrats Put Self-Help First, Boding Ill for Party's '92 Presidential Nominee," 9-27, blames the lack of cohesion in the Democratic party on divided government, and an inability to agree on tax policy. In "Rostenkowski Doubts Tax Bill by This Year," 10-22, Birnbaum seems unneedfully defensive of Rosty as he appropriately highlights the House Ways and Means Chairman's opposition to passage of any tax bills.

Borger, Gloria. *U.S.News & World Report.* (★ ½)
Assistant Managing Editor for Special Reports. As with last year's assessment, we find her best commentary saved for TV shows such as "Washington Week in Review." Her few single byline

pieces were rather lackluster, breaking little news ground. She successfully turns a limp lead into a strong article in "Keating Five Afterlife," 1-21. Picking up steam, she intelligently examines the ripples the scandal has caused, via congressional self-examination and potential for actual reform. Her "Digging Out From the Gulf War Rubble," 3-25, is a rather standard dispatch on Democratic plans to move their own agenda after the Persian Gulf War, an adequate overview that assesses all the conventional moves and players. Borger's slick "One Week" essay, "Passing the Buck With a Smile and a Shrug," 4-1, examines the growing trend of people in power avoiding accountability, in which she duly notes in regard to Los Angeles police chief Daryl Gates: "Ducking responsibility has become an accomplished American art form." In "Democrats' Donkey Fight," 5-13, she insightfully raises another problem with the Democratic party: "The internal Democratic Party power structure is imploding, or at least turning upside down," a firm discussion of the beleaguered party. Her "Shootout at the Oklahoma Corral," 6-3, is an interesting sidebar to the cover story on the CIA that neatly investigates the growing friction between Congressman Dave McCurdy, chairman of the House Intelligence Committee and Senator David Boren, Chairman of the Senate Intelligence Committee. Borger provides a serviceable profile of Nebraska Senator Bob Kerrey as he gears up for his presidential run in "Introducing 'Present Man,' " 10-7. She highlights his open ambivalence to the political process; "In a larger way, Kerrey brings to his politics the intellectual turmoil and conflicts of a generation."

Brownstein, Ronald. *Los Angeles Times.* (★ ★)
Brownstein continues to be hampered by his Los Angeles base, missing the rough-and-tumble nature of Washington politics that he captured when he was at *National Journal* a few years back. He's best now on race relations, not politics. His sterling review of "veteran liberal journalist" James Ridgeway's recent book on white American racism "Rebirth of a Nation," 1-27, rightly corrects Ridgeway who overstates the movement's impact as "the influx of far-right thinking into mainstream politics." The adequate but tiresome "Most Wary But Will Support a Ground War," 2-19, provides a curt summarization of polls which generally supports the president in the Gulf War ground effort. His "Partisan Struggle Waged Over Michigan Deficit," 3-9, is a sharp breakdown of the havoc the balanced budget requirement is wreaking in Michigan. He takes the state as a case in point, but we get little sense how other states are coping. An above-par report by Brownstein, "Former Sen. Tsongas Declares Candidacy for Presidency," 5-1, is evocative in ways that other accounts were not on Tsongas announcing the Democrat's "journey of purpose." We get a good personal and political profile as well. Another liberal, Tom Harkin, Sen. from Iowa is written up at a meeting of libs in L.A. in "Liberal Democrats Get Preview of Presidential Possibilities," 6-23, but we found it slightly dry, providing only the facts, with no analytical twist. Brownstein correctly recognizes that economics is the key to the '92 election in his deft "Divided Economic Vision Blurs Democratic Outlook," 7-3, not ground-breaking information, but pointedly well written and insightful. His interesting but longwinded "Beyond Quotas," *Magazine* 7-28, displays new thinking on what Brownstein calls "the synthesis school of race relations," and what it may do to current voting blocs, his perceptibility infusing the piece with character. Brownstein dredges up little we've not heard before on the pitfalls of redistricting in "Minority Quotas in Elections?" 8-28, yet his neat, readable style is indicative of the work we've seen in the past and reminds us of what Brownstein is capable of doing.

Calmes, Jackie. *The Wall Street Journal.* (★ ★)
Congress and taxes. Calmes has yet to develop the economic sophistication necessary for her station, but we are impressed by her political astuteness in her first year-and-a-half on the beat. Her rather engaging piece "Congress Gets Its First True Child of the 1960s, A Republican With Dim Memories of Watergate," 1-3, is a disarming profile of Jim Nussel (R-Ia.), who is being sworn in that day as the House's youngest member. In "Gains-Tax Cut Study Is Spurned by Top Democrats," 2-13, Calmes provides adequate reporting on the refusal by Dems to participate in a bipartisan panel. Her spectrum seems limited here though, as she doesn't shed much light on Democrats who may support the committee. Calmes fails to capture the entire

portrait of Newt Gingrich in "In an About-Face, Gingrich Becomes an Apostle of Grass-Roots Politics, Averting Clashes in GOP," 3-27; though he recognizes his narrow win in the 1990 elections, we get little sense of how or if he'll change. She recognizes the importance inherent in "Rostenkowski Urges Congress to Allow a Dozen Popular Tax Breaks to Lapse," 4-11, in which the Chairman of the House Ways and Means Committee says "I'm not going to be having any of this capital-gains stuff." The compelling "Democrats Revive Bid for Tax Breaks for Many at the Expense of the Wealthy," 5-7, is a no-nonsense, detailed report which gives us both the congressmen and proposals involved, but she makes no attempt at evaluating the politics, or the package. In the "better late than never" file, "Momentum Grows Against Luxury Tax as Critics Complain it Enriches No One," co-written with David Wessel 6-12, is an examination of the repercussions of one of the provisions of last year's budget bill. "Many House Democrats Seize Race for Chief Whip as Chance to Express Ire About Party's Direction," 7-9, reports who's for what between Rep. David Bonior and Rep. Steny Hoyer as House Whip. We really don't find out how this will affect the party at large, but it's plain she sees hope here. Calmes' "Budget Pact, Undermined by Global Upheavals, Could Come Under Full-Scale Attack by Spring," 9-18, is an intriguing report on the Democratic assaults on the 1990 Budget agreement; what's missing is discussion of capgains and the growth Republicans.

Canham-Clyne, John. *In These Times.* (★ ★)
Washington correspondent. Together Canham-Clyne and John Judis plumb Beltway politics from a decidedly socialist perspective. Canham-Clyne is slightly less polemical than Judis, but no less informative or intelligent. His "Where Have All the Lessons Gone?" 1-16/22, charts the history of U.S. duplicity in the region around Iraq that's more compelling in retrospect as he predicts that Bush is "leading our nation into a disaster of terrible political and human proportions, whose roots lie in Vietnam." Canham-Clyne's puffy piece on the protest movement, "The Peace Struggle at Home: A Force to Be Reckoned With," 2-6/12, examines its tactics but never its shortcomings or clout (or lack thereof). In the neatly-penned "Desperately Seeking an Intelligent Community," 2-20/26, he makes a strong case asserting that the real reason for GOP objections to the Dellums and Bonior appointments to the House Permanent Select Committee on Intelligence is that they voted for the Boxer Amendment to restrict the use of covert operations. Canham-Clyne provides a smart assessment on the exploratory nature of McGovern's campaign in "George McGovern Tests the Presidential Waters," 4-10/16, although he falls from his mark when he fails to take into account anybody who's actually running at this point, such as Doug Wilder or Paul Tsongas. He presents a reasonable critique of the Brady and Staggers Bills in "Gun-Control Bills Shoot Blanks at U.S. Violence," 5-22/28. Canham-Clyne suggests we address the root problems of gun-related crime here, such as poverty and unemployment, but, as with other topics, he designs no mechanism for doing so. His sharply-written overview, "Tom Harkin Tests Waters for Presidential Campaign," 6-25/7-9, assesses Harkin's political strategy, which "seems to lie in reclaiming the political language expropriated by the right during the last 12 years."

Cannon, Lou. *The Washington Post.* (★ ½)
Los Angeles. After finishing a book on Ronald Reagan, Cannon seems content to follow the former President into semi-retirement. Despite Cannon's long and impressive career with the *Post,* he still hasn't captured the nuance necessary for the LA beat. His "Southern California District Reduces Water Supplies 31%," 2-13, is a solid, tactful update on water rationing, not a pleasant prospect, but Cannon handles this major West Coast story with discretion and professional aplomb. A sobering update on the water crisis, "Storms Ease Drought Along California Coast," 3-27, details how the state plans to store water for a drier day. Cannon presents a good breakdown of the situation. The balanced "Gary Sick's Lingering Charges," 5-13, on the op-ed page, helps to poke holes in Sick's case about the "October surprise." Cannon's Reagan book adds weight to this appraisal, despite his self-confessed doubts about William Casey. In "Pete Wilson: Now Read His Lips," 5-22, Cannon succinctly reports on Wilson coping with the political firestorm set off by his budget proposal; he also avoids the

gossipy tone common to the genre as he discusses how Wilson leaves himself open to a possible 1996 national office run. His "California Raises Taxes on the Wealthy," 7-18, is an adequate, if conventional, snapshot of how the hike in income tax will supposedly help to close the budget gap. Unfortunately we never learn how this will effect business. Cannon manages some dignity as he delves into the Reagan soap opera in "Reagan Says Nancy Didn't 'Purge' Pals," 8-2. He discusses the dismissal of three trustees from the RR Presidential Foundation: Ed Meese, Martin Anderson and William Clark, and the legend of Nancy Reagan. In "Ron Reagan, Talking Tough," 8-12, Cannon sculpts an insightful profile of Ron Reagan as his new late-night talk show debuts. Being the current Reagan specialist, Cannon concludes; "Ron Reagan's politics may be different from his dad's, but he is his father's son." His "Firms Flee California's Conditions as Other States Beckon," 9-1, is close, but doesn't hit the mark as he links the flight of businesses to other states to the corporate tax structure of those jurisdictions, anecdotal but still worthwhile.

Carlson, Margaret. *Time.* (★ ½)
Deputy Washington bureau chief. Carlson moves into Laurence Barrett's post from her senior writer position, but has been careful to keep her byline intact, whereas Barrett's nearly vanished. She continues to tone down the editorializing, and is one of the freshest voices in a cacophony of opinion at the weekly. Her "So Who's Minding The Store?" 2-11, begins quite admirably as a review of Bush's State of the Union address, but she gradually succumbs to a critique: "The domestic side of the speech. . .sounded as if it had been cobbled together by a committee of tightfisted accountants." Another piece that comes up short is her "No Donkeys in This Horse Race," 3-25. Alas, it's not all her fault that at this juncture no Democrats had thrown their hats into the presidential ring. Her attempt to shape the unmalleable is admirable yet premature. Carlson files a perceptive discussion on the issue of naming rape victims in the media in "Should This Woman Be Named?" 4-29. In regards to the Smith case she states: "the New York *Times* included the woman's identity in a long profile so unflattering that it could serve as a brief for a defense lawyer trying to discredit her." As part of the "Thelma and Louise" cover story, "Is This What Feminism Is All About?" 6-24, Carlson realistically points out that the film is not feminist: "As a bulletin from the front in the battle of the sexes, *Thelma & Louise* sends the message that little ground has been won. For these two women, feminism never happened." Yet, we do not come away convinced. Carlson's fine sense of detail adds merit to "Marching to a Different Drummer," 7-15, a surprisingly good summation and profile of Clarence Thomas in which she avoids the editorializing the magazine is so well known for. "The Busybodies on the Bus," 8-12, explores what public figures are doing to tone down their private lives; she castigates the rest of the press for mucking about, while writing from her own glassed-in house. Carlson unfairly rages in "The Ultimate Men's Club," 10-21, calling the Senate a "dysfunctional family" among other things: "Senators don't interact with women as colleagues — they have only two — and most of the other women they come in contact with are subservient."

Ceol, Dawn Weyrich. *The Washington Times.* (★ ★)
Supreme Court. Ceol shows every sign of someday becoming a top-notch reporter on this beat after only a year on the job. She consistently balances and carefully reports her stories, bringing to them a trim fullness. Her "Court Allows Busing to End Once Goals Are Met," 1-16, is a nice roundup of the Supreme Court decision which is a "historic shift away from using racial statistics as a bottom line." The nicely balanced and logically structured "Judges Throw Out Bakker Sentence," 2-13, provides insight on the case, supplying quotes from Alan Dershowitz who handled the appeal; its only flaw is its simplistic rendering of some of the legal aspects of the case. Ceol memorably calls the latest term "a yawner" in "High Court Keeps a Low Profile," 3-11, attributing this to the general synchronicity between the high and lower courts, as well as the fact that liberals are "more reluctant" to turn to a conservative court. Her piece delving into the legality of allowing testimony on the murder victim's character, in "Thornburgh Backs 'Impact' Testimony," 4-25, delivers the details, but not the drama of the arguments before the Court over the issue of "impact" testimony. Both "Pro-Choice Side Angry at Souter," 5-24, and

"Court: Public Money Banned for Counseling," 5-24, are professionally handled pieces on the Supreme Court decision concerning public money used to fund abortion. Ceol balances these report to give us the straight details. Her report on the status of the Miranda decision under the Supreme Court in " 'Right to Remain Silent,' " 6-13, is a good roundup of views from the legal community that concludes the "Miranda has become such a routine of police work that it is as much a part of policing as a summons book and police car." Her review of the record of Judge Thomas for his juridical philosophy in "This Candidate Has Paper Trail," 7-2, is neither definitive nor does it provide new information, but is useful nonetheless. Her lack of a conclusion mars "Experts Disagree on Confirmation Hearings," 9-24, an intelligent discussion on the value of having judicial nominees testify before the Senate committee, even as they decline to discuss their opinions on future court matters. Ceol resigned after a *WT* editor reconstructed her account of Sunday's tesimony in the Hill-Thomas hearings for some editions without removing her byline. One of the most promising reporters at the *Times,* she'll be missed.

Clift, Eleanor. *Newsweek.* (★)
Washington. Clift began the year relatively strong, offering at least two-dimensional work, but during the spring we began to see more signs of the cynicism we've complained of earlier. It's particularly a problem when she's teamed with Howard Fineman, both in tone and topic. Her "Challengers on Ice," 1-7, is an early appraisal of Bush's popularity in '92 hinging on the outcome of the Gulf War. The obvious premise of the piece becomes unhinged when it suggests that Ronald Reagan's reelection was sealed by "footage of students kissing American soil after their rescue from Grenada." Clift's " 'The Hairdo With Anxiety,' " 4-15, is an adequate, two-dimensional look at Kitty Kelley's biography of Nancy Reagan, interesting in that it may spark debate about where to draw the line in a tell-all biography. The strangely structured "Desperately Seeking Southerners," 5-13, highlights two southern senators, Al Gore of Tennessee and Bill Clinton of Arkansas, as potential nominees in the Democratic race for '92, though she conspicuously skimps on Doug Wilder of Virginia who she contends is "easily the steeliest of the three." She sees dire happenings occurring as the GOP tries to reach out to young voters who are Republican and pro-choice in her satisfactory "The GOP's Civil War Over Abortion," 8-5. Her light "Middle-Class Maneuvers," co-written by Howard Fineman 8-12, is merely a perfunctory overview of what the Democrats may do to appeal to the middle class. Her "This Time, Being Outside Is In," co-written with Howard Fineman 9-9, loosely links the candidacies of Sen. Bob Kerrey and ex-Gov. Jerry Brown. The writers indicate that both have ". . .eyes that reveal their inner journeys, both are admirers of Mother Teresa." We found no gleanable information included. She cribs much of her piece on eligible political bachelors from a *Washington Post* story in "The Bachelor Candidates," co-written by Clara Bingham 9-23, becoming slightly sexist and cynical about the matter: "Without wives as props, candidates will find it harder to substitute symbolism for substance." Her personal venom comes through in "Taking the Low Road," 10-28, as she absolutely blasts Sen. Alan Simpson for his intense grilling of Anita Hill.

Clymer, Adam. *The New York Times.* (★ ½)
Chief congressional correspondent. A veteran political reporter, Clymer spent most of his career at the *Baltimore Sun.* After a bit of waffling, Clymer has settled nicely into his new seat of assembling an adequate, almost impressive portfolio his first year. His "Congress in Step," 1-14, is a perceptive analysis of the House and Senate votes on the Gulf resolutions. He succinctly notes that "the regional divisions were almost as sharp" as the partisan divisions. The solidly reported "Senators Fear Allies Will Renege on War Payments," 2-27, is an update on Appropriations Committee hearings. Unfortunately nothing new is learned, causing anything past the headline to be superfluous. Clymer documents the end of D.C. bipartisanship as Congress' rally-round-the flag cause disappeared in "Cease-Fire in the Capital Comes to a Bitter Close," 3-7, his adept coverage capturing the fight: "Each side was working hard to deflate the other party's most potent political issue." The Democrat's current dilemma is noted in "Jobless Issue Proves Puzzle to Democrats," 4-28. Here, Clymer comprehensively outlines Rep. Thomas

Downey's proposal to extend unemployment benefits by raising, or really redistributing, the federal tax. Clymer does the best he can to decipher the difference between numbers and quotas in "Jobs Bill Would Allow Numbers Yet Ban Quotas," 5-29, but legal aspects bog the piece down halfway through, needing better organization. Getting the word from the 7-9 *Washington Post,* Clymer reports in "White House Hints at Easing Prohibitions on Abortion Advice at Clinics," 7-10, that the administration is reviewing the rules upheld recently by the Supreme Court, little more than a reasonable roundup. The substantially detailed "Help for Jobless Is Voted by Edge in Senate Is Shaky," 10-2, reviews what may happen to this bill to increase the length of time unemployment benefits may be collected. Clymer delivers a bird's eye view of Congress in microcosm on this one bill. His editorialized "Senate's Futile Search for Safe Ground," 10-16, is hard on the Senate without really providing enough context to justify it, although the last few days of the Hill-Thomas hearings certainly go a long way in indicting the Senate.

Cohen, Richard E. *National Journal.* (★ ★ ½)
Congress. Cohen exploded onto the political scene this year, tougher and more analytic than we'd ever seen him. His sharply quilled "Lame-Duck Congress," 1-19, notes experts in both political parties are predicting that the 1992 elections will produce at least 100 new members — twice the size of any new class since 1982. The appraisal of *NJ*'s annual survey of congressional votes in "Partisan Patterns," co-written by William Schneider 1-19, concludes that bipartisanship reigns, but is little more than prose wording of survey results. Cohen's tactfully done "Easing Udall Out of Committee Power," 2-2, is a rather gentle recounting of the power play, as such, of the Interior Committee, as acting chairman Rep. George Morris (D-Calif.) takes over from Morris K. Udall (D-Ariz.) due to Udall's debilitating battle with Parkinson's disease. Cohen chooses the interesting and timely topic of the 1990 freshman Congress coming to power at a time of strong anti-incumbent sentiment, and fleshes it out in "The Freshman Threat," 4-13, wryly noting that success in defeating established incumbents has many veteran members looking over their shoulders. In "Campaign Finance Saga Still Plays On," 5-4, Cohen deliberates the arguments for and against new proposals to limit spending, restrict or eliminate PAC's and mandate public financing of campaigns. It's a little disjointed in the specifics of these new proposals. Cohen's hotly discussed item in the Beltway, "People of Influence," 6-15, dealt with congressional committee power weakening as aides are acquiring new roles and influence, Quoting Sen. Trent Lott: "sometimes staff members think they are the Senators." His "The Judge's Trials," 7-13, is a sturdy composite of the political fortunes of Senate Majority leader George Mitchell. In this 10 Best selection for Political Reporting, Cohen sharply concludes: "The glow has dimmed on Mitchell's initial aura of command over the Senate and influence within his party." Not playing favorites, Cohen examines how Speaker of the House Tom Foley is doing in creating and/or promoting an agenda for the Democrats in "Faulting Foley," 8-13. Despite the title, Cohen seems to feel that Foley is more of "a scapegoat for the party's broader difficulties in the House."

DeParle, Jason. *The New York Times.* (★ ½)
Washington. Dissecting the relationship between social policy and government was DeParle's forte at *The Washington Monthly,* but since moving to the *Times* he sometimes seems sterile and unexciting. We expect he may still be making the transition from monthly to daily. DeParle's "Suffering in the Cities Persists as U.S. Fights Other Battles," 1-27, is almost too thick with figures from polls on poverty to federal spending data, though we can still cull much that is valuable. His "Ideas to Help Poor Abound, But a Consensus Is Wanting," co-written by Peter Applebome 1-29, is a good but finally unsatisfying compilation of different solutions to the problem of the welfare state due to no concrete conclusions on DeParle's part. His review of the State of the Union in "Bush Blurs Home Goals," 2-3, falters after his promising lead: "Republican aides and analysts responded to the domestic side of [the speech] this week as though it were a Rorschach test, with each projecting different hopes and fears." DeParle reports in "A State's Fight to Save Babies Enters Round 2," 3-12, on more federal and state support for women who can't stop having children. DeParle duly recounts, but never questions, the logic

of policy that perpetuates the problem. In " 'Thousand Points' of a Cottage Industry," 5-29, DeParle pens a quasi-profile of C. Gregg Petersmeyer, who runs the "thousand points" program, a feature which seems more bombast than substance. He provides a balanced assessment of Jack Kemp's stalled fortunes due to budget cuts in "Kemp's Proposals on Poverty Given Sympathy, Not Action," 7-1, astutely noting the problem: "last fall's budget deal, which required that any expansion of domestic spending in one area be accompanied by cuts in another." We ponder on what happened to all of DeParle's training at the *Monthly* in "Using Books Instead of Brooms to Escape Welfare," 9-9. This loosely structured report on school programs to train welfare recipients, is more concerned with congressional opinion than the programs themselves. His "Amid Housing Crisis, a Bitter Feud Over Policy," 10-23, is a broad overview of the fights between HUD Secretary Jack Kemp and the House and Senate Appropriations Committee head. We get a sense of the labyrinthine bureaucracy involved, yet there is too little substantive, insightful detail.

Devroy, Ann. *The Washington Post.* (★ ★ ½)
White House. She and Charles Babcock broke the story that almost cost John Sununu his job and political career; her work the remainder of the year was almost as impressive, though she still needs a bit of seasoning on this beat before matching Dowd or Apple of *The New York Times.* Her colorful snapshot of Bush's moral mission in "Revealing Moral Struggle, Bush Spellbinds Audience," 1-26, goes a bit beyond the press conference, but not much more. She files a balanced report in "Intelligence Panel Members Said to 'Concern' Bush," 2-8. This keen assessment provides good sense as to why there is apprehension and deep concern over the Democrats' handling of the makeup and direction of the House Intelligence Committee. The laudable "Sununu: Frequent Flier on Military Aircraft," co-written by Charles Babcock 4-21, broke the story that almost toppled John Sununu, detailed and complete, tough, but not nasty. The pair gets the figures, and one can see from reading this with 20/20 hindsight why this 10 Best selection for Political Reporting was such a bombshell in D.C. Devroy's "President Proposed Mideast Arms Curb," 5-30, is a concrete breakdown of what would be halted, as well as a steadfast discussion of the president's news conference. Her use of too many unnamed sources blemishes the piece however. The pedantic issue of Judge Thomas trying hemp is discussed in "Thomas Tried Marijuana While a College Student," 7-11. She cites other officials who have, but never asks any hard questions nor draws strong conclusions. Her "Bush Sees Gorbachev Free to Expedite Reform," 8-23, relies on too many anonymous "senior officials" to focus perspective on reform in the Soviet Union. There's evidence of a bit more digging on her part in "U.S. Delays Recognizing the Baltics," 8-27. She displays more of an international flair, pulling together information to see how U.S. action stacks up against the world community, going beyond the afternoon Kennebunkport press conference. Her "Bush Ready to Use Force if Iraq Bars Inspections," co-written by John Lancaster 9-19, is a neat delineation of the U.S. equipment and personnel that are already in the Middle East, the pair's breakdown of the situation quite sharp.

Dewar, Helen. *The Washington Post.* (★ ★ ½)
Senate. In a year of tumultuous congressional politics, we appreciated Dewar's smart, taut appraisals of events in chambers. Her excellent grasp of the congressional climate is exposed in the detailed "Exoneration Urged for Senators as 'Keating Five' Hearings End," 1-17. She vividly recounts the closing remarks of the Senators, bringing us into the scene without losing her own objectivity. Little of the fire we saw in Dewar's earlier dispatches is evident, though in "Panel Finds Violations by Cranston," 2-28. All the information is present here, but the drama is curiously absent in this surprisingly bloodless retelling of the Ethics Committee results on the Keating Five. Her "Democrats' Domestic Issues Highlight Party Divisions," 4-18, is a perceptive report on the difficulties Democrats in Congress are having in fashioning a domestic agenda. She rightly observes, "they find the immediate agenda packed with issues that highlight their divisions more than their strengths." In "Compromise Gun Control Plan Backed," 5-30, Dewar clearly sees all the potential for George Mitchell's alternative which "significantly alters

the framework of the debate as the Senate prepares to consider gun curbs as part of an anticrime bill this summer." Her "Senate Votes to Expand Federal Death Penalty," 6-26, is a fairly standard, though well-structured, roundup on the omnibus crime bill and the fighting over it. The nicely-rounded "Stealthy Coup Raised Senate Pay," 7-19, probes Senate fears of voter backlash as a Senate pay raise is passed in the dark of the night, an intriguing examination of the inner workings of the Senate. Dewar's half-hearted attempt, "Bush Said to Reject Rights Plan," 8-2, simply recounts Bush rejecting Danforth's compromise proposal on civil rights and Danforth gives up, saying he'll submit the bill without the support of the administration. Dewar provides a quick glimpse of the Senate working on an issue in "Senate Passes Bill to Lift Abortion Counseling Ban," 9-13, but fails to flesh the story out.

Diamond, Edwin. *New York.* (★ ★)

"Media" columnist. When we needed an evaluation of the New York media this year, it was Diamond to whom we turned. The NYU professor was as incisive and informative as we've ever seen him. He's very tough on the alleged recycling of styles Mike McAlary uses in "Big Mac Attack," 1-7, who defected from the *Daily News* to the *Post.* Unfortunately Diamond never really answers his own question of "Who, then, appears in the *Post* —Mike McAlary, the hot new kid on the block, or Mike McMimic, young artist in a hurry?" In "The Koch Affair," 2-25, Diamond shines a light on ex-NYC Mayor Ed Koch's brief (13 mos.) tenure with WCBS "Sunday Edition." His eye on New York never blinks in this excellent recounting of Koch's "death by a thousand tiny TV cuts." Unblushingly using tabloid style print in "Bold Rush," 4-22, he makes his point. Usually this kind of technique falls flat yet Diamond crafts it quite well: "What a time for the tabloids, for the columnists who put names in boldface. Sex and larceny at the **Kennedy** compound. Sex and greed in the **Reagan** White House." His "The Times' 'Wild Streak,' " 5-13, unfortunately is not tough enough on the paper of record printing intensely personal information on the alleged Palm Beach rape victim. Diamond doesn't include all the information here. He meekly makes no judgment call as to the value of the form of packaged TV news such as "48 Hours" in "What's News," 7-22. His "Horror Story," 8-12, is a compelling indictment of the NY and national press coverage of the rape of a 3-year-old girl by her uncle, Diamond brilliantly documenting the problem: "reporters too dependent on sources, editors rushing into print or on the air, everyone stealing from one another. Only in the press!" Although his extremely verbose "Old Times, New Times," cover 9-30, does repeat some of his information from earlier *New York Times* diatribes, it's worth a read for the incidental nuggets he mines about when Pinch takes over from Punch. He gives us what's new at the *New York Observer* in "Spying on the Observer," 11-4, Diamond noting of Editor Graydon Carter, who came from *SPY* magazine, "Old editorial habits die hard. *Observer* readers. . .espied the familiar smarmy references to. . .unflattering physical characteristics."

Dionne, E. J., Jr. *The Washington Post.* (★ ★ ★)

Politics. His book published, Dionne is now free to concentrate on politics and gear up for next year's presidential campaign and election. As always, we get from Dionne concise, innovative evaluations of the national scene. He acutely plumbs the differences within the Democrat party over U.S. policy in the Persian Gulf crisis in "Gulf Crisis Rekindles Democrat's Old Debate but With New Focus," 1-2, with sufficient quotes from Democrats giving a sense of the internal divisions. Disappointingly little policy is discussed in "U.S. Politics and the Churchill Analogy," 2-4, with Dionne tritely consulting many congressmen and consultants on whether Bush will be reelected or tossed out of office, as Churchill was in 1945. The overlong "News Analysis" of the new national mood following the end of the war in "Kicking the 'Vietnam Syndrome,' " 3-4, is basically a survey of conventional liberal and conservative viewpoints, with Dionne never really getting beyond the obvious. His "Housing Secretary's Hard Job Gets Harder," 5-3, is a very good overview on what Jack Kemp's been doing at HUD, although Dionne doesn't draw him out on any potential vision of activity beyond the Cabinet or post-1992. The perceptive "News Analysis," "Democrats Get Chance to Turn Health-Care Anxiety Into '92 Votes," 7-1, correctly notes: "Many who watch the health issue believe that Republican skepticism and differences among Democrats will doom legislation until at least after the 1992 elections." His "Staying Awake Through '92," 8-4, is a valiant effort at assessing the soporific Democratic party and an excellent diagnosis of its malady, but Dionne falters in recommending specific remedies, none of which are for the stagnant economy. In "Democratic Field Set to Grow," co-written by Dan Balz 9-2, the duo provides a sharp evaluation of the presidential field and the party itself. They credibly probe the political issues involved, postulating that the relative obscurity of some of the candidates may be beneficial, allowing them to take risks.

Donohoe, Cathryn. *The Washington Times.* (★ ★ ★)
"Life!" writer. Donohoe is one of the primary reasons we turn to "life!" as her surveys are crisp and informative, her profiles lively and evocative. She began the year quite oddly with "Rearviews of War," 1-14, an informal and somewhat gimmicky survey of the opinions of Washington cabbies on the Middle East and the potential for war. We give a quick nod to originality. Her sprightly "More Than Doughnuts," 2-7, is a timely feature on the USO that's charming, delightful, and informative as well. In "Anti-Warrior," 2-20, she sharply profiles James Webb, a Vietnam hawk, now a Desert Shield dove, in this crisp, effectively detached portrait. Unfortunately, Donohoe spends too much time in "A New Route for Jim Lehrer," 3-27, on "The MacNeil/Lehrer NewsHour" host's passion for buses, and too little on the man himself. The *Post* "Style" profile of a few years back was more revealing. "A Promoter of Heroes," 4-24, shows she is one of the profession's more accomplished profilers, pulling us into reading a feature on a subject that we'd otherwise dismiss, Dominique Lapierre, the author who gives spiritual dimension to sufferings, from poverty to AIDS, and this is no exception. Another profile full of tough, taut images, "Mike Peck's Mythic Battle," 6-7, highlights an army colonel who charges that there is "a deliberate and high-level attempt to discredit evidence of living Americans in Indochina." Ultimately we end up knowing we never really have gotten inside the man. Her "Watcher No. 1," 7-2, is a splendid portrait of Yuri Orlov, "the man who dared the Soviet Union to live up to the human-rights guarantees to which it subscribed." Donohoe's powerfully evocative "Trap of a Too Loving Father," 8-12, encapsulates the life and times of author Shirley Abbott, Donohoe really capturing her essence here, via her writing, a speech and an interview. The unfulfilling "Ward Just: Writing Best From the Margin," 9-24, is a scattershot sketch on author Ward Just; Donohoe never really gets a bead on him in the article and it becomes grossly apparent.

Dowd, Maureen. *The New York Times.* (★ ★ ½)
White House. While Dowd continues to craft evocative and informative "mood" features, we saw less this year of the exceptional political reporting we saw from her in previous years. Dowd also had the misfortune of penning the oft-criticized P. 1 Kitty Kelley piece and was responsible for the shrill coverage of feminist reaction to sexual harassment charges leveled at Clarence Thomas by Anita Hill, allowing her own agenda to get in the way. The spotty "All that Glitters Is Not Real, Book on Nancy Reagan Says," 4-7, apparently revels in the gossipy details from Kitty Kelley's *Nancy Reagan: The Unauthorized Biography.* Dowd asserts that "in Ms. Kelley's scalding portrait, Mrs. Reagan comes across as an unfortunate combination of a free-spending Mary Todd Lincoln and a power-crazed Edith Wilson." Dowd does exceptionally well with "Washington Goes to War, Besieging the TV Set," 1-29, a "mood" piece on George Bush, "the calmest man in Washington." Her three-dimensional report captures precisely the salient features of the time. In the pert appraisal, "Stars of Bush War Council Audition for Lead of Next Presidential Battles," 2-11, Dowd gives us a useful look at the array of presidential potentials. Dowd's "Bush, Proclaiming Victory, Seeks Wider Mideast Peace; Hints at Pressure on Israel," 3-7, highlights Bush's address to the joint session of Congress and the nation, a sharp, decisive roundup both of the speech and of the situation, peppered with detail and insight. "In Warmup for '92, Bush Defends Quayle and the 1980 Campaign," 5-9, is a piece with a wry lead setting its caustic tone: "President Bush moved today to beat back speculation on a pair of nettlesome political problems that make his re-election campaign less than the coronation his advisers have anticipated." Her strong, perceptive appraisal of Bush's Supreme Court appointee,

"Conservative Black Judge, Clarence Thomas, Is Named to Marshall's Court Seat," 7-2, delivers a sharp portrait of the man. She makes some sound points in "The Senate and Sexism," 10-8, but as with her 5-20 dispatch, her feminist flag-waving doesn't further the cause any. Dowd's "Getting Nasty Early Helps G.O.P. Gain Edge on Thomas," 10-15, is clearly partisan as she ravages both sides of the Senate Judiciary Committee. The only ones who come out well are the feminists whom she quotes at length.

Easterbrook, Gregg. *Newsweek.* (★ ★ ★)
Contributing editor. Easterbrook is found more frequently on the pages of other journals, particularly the opinion pages of the *Los Angeles Times,* moving from the environment to politics to technology without missing a beat. Easterbrook comes up with Sununu's number long before the military jet controversy in "Out to Make Enemies? Copy Sherman Adams — John Sununu Does," *LAT* 1-6, predicting with uncanny accuracy that "In repeatedly treating others with disdain, Sununu may be setting himself up for an Adams-like fall." Easterbrook files a hilarious report on the basic shoddiness of airline travel in "Service Industry? Airlines Remain User-Unfriendly," *LAT* 2-3, this half-travelog, half-swipe at deregulation hammering home its point. His "Robowar," *The New Republic* 2-11, is a valuable study on how high-tech weaponry is reducing general destruction, as evidenced by the first week of bombing raids on Baghdad, Easterbrook doing a good job in making this complex subject accessible to the general reader, without oversimplifying. He states in " 'High Tech' Isn't Everything," 2-18: "Let us have no delusions that advances in smart weapons can make any nation invincible," in regards to the technology used in Iraq. Yet, he fails to cite performance records of equipment used in the Gulf, leaving his point slightly muted. His "When Appearance Is All: Sununu Pursues the Trappings of Power," *LAT* 6-30, is a distended view of Sununu and his travel problems, Easterbrook uncharacteristically unfocused in this article. He is back on track in "The Sincerest Flattery," 7-29, as Easterbrook was one of the fellows plagiarized in a recent, widely noted case, he admonishes the culprits in a slightly tongue-in-cheek fashion. He tackles the nettlesome question of ten-year terms for Supreme Court justices in "Geritol Justice," *TNR* 8-19/26, making a strong case for reform that would fulfill the vision the Founding Fathers had, that "government should be a living institution."

Eaton, William J. *Los Angeles Times.* (★)
Washington, Congress with an emphasis on the House. The former recipient of a Pulitzer for International Reporting, Eaton brings little of his years of experience to his dispatches, which are rarely more than the bare bones of a story. In the strangely lopsided "Congress Shifts From Euphoria to Anxiety and Frustration With War," co-written by Paul Houston 1-24, the duo talks to nine Democrats and one Republican on how they feel after a week of the air battle in the Persian Gulf, but with no thread holding this together, we are left unimpressed. Eaton has Clayton Yeutter saying the Democrats will have to run for cover come election time regarding the Persian Gulf War in "Yeutter's Attack on Democrats Stirs Up Political Firestorm," co-written by Jack Nelson 1-25, with Democratic reaction and Republican re-reaction, but not much else can be gleaned from this report. His "Bush Assailed Over Global Warming," 2-6, merely records Sen. George Mitchell's speech, with light background of the Clean Air Act, little more than a press release. Eaton meekly examines how Democrats can overcome Bush's popularity after the Persian Gulf War in "Democrats Groping for Image-Building Issues," 3-9, but aside from name dropping, he just strings quotes loosely together in search of a story. His "Some Lawmakers Promise to Overturn Court Ruling," 5-24, a congressional follow-up to the Supreme Court federal clinics ruling, is little more than a list of who's on which side and only moderately useful as such. Eaton quills a taut "White House Reviewing Policy on Abortion Counseling Restrictions," 7-10, that serves as a wrapup on the abortion gag rule, with the White House appearing a tad more flexible than in earlier reports. He files a lively report on the managing of the Supreme Court nominee by Ken Duberstein and the White House in "Coaches Drill Thomas for His Senate Face-Off," co-written by Paul Houston 8-18, though regrettably Eaton never addresses the implications of such management. His "Bush Vows Veto of Israeli Aid Bill," co-written by Douglas Jehl 9-13, is a quick but sharp dispatch as to Bush's withholding of aid, yet its brevity hampers its usefulness.

Edsall, Thomas B. *The Washington Post.* (★ ★)
Politics. Edsall spent most of this year on his latest book, written with his wife. Though still in retention of his political acumen, Edsall rarely rises above the inconsistency of his present work. Despite the amount of anti-GOP bias or spin, "Quotas: Tempting Issue for GOP in '92," 1-15, looks at the issue only on how it might be exploited by the GOP, with little on the legitimacy of grievances, although the range of quotes and perspectives still provides us with useful information. In microcosm, Edsall's "In Louisiana, Whites Often Feel Ignored," 3-12, is a study that shows that in Louisiana the Democratic party is viewed as the party of special interests — the wealthy, big business and minorities, but he doesn't try to enlarge this to the national level. His analytical skills come to prominence in ". . .If Democrats Make It Easy," 4-7, an objective "Outlook" essay focusing on the political difficulties of a Democratic party that finds itself identified in polls with special interest groups and viewed by many with cynicism and suspicion. Edsall provides a serviceable case study of GOP and minority plans to carve out more congressional districts for themselves in "Texas Redistricting: A Case Study of Democrats' Struggle," 5-21, rightly highlighting the threatened urban white Democratic congressmen. Another redistricting piece doesn't fare as well, "Redistricting Will Erode Mississippi's White Power Base," 6-27, rather narrow in scope, providing no broader truths than a simple shift of power, the implications strangely absent. Edsall files a weak "News Analysis" on the Clarence Thomas nomination, "Politics and the Thomas Choice: Building the GOP's Black Elite," 7-2, rather rushed in tone, compounded by little more than a grab bag of quotes from Democrats and dredged-up images of Willie Horton. Edsall highlights the squabbling Rainbow Coalition in "Jackson's Bid to Build Coalition Flounders," 8-15, missing the implications: how the failure of the coalition will affect either Jackson's presidential plans or just getting out the Democratic vote. He taps populist sentiment in an anecdotal examination of the programs and primary of Gov. Ray Mabus, "Anti-Tax Governor Tries to Tap Quirky Mississippi Populism," 9-16.

Egan, Timothy. *The New York Times.* (★ ★)
Western correspondent. Egan was more restrained in his stories this year, maintaining a steady detachment that vastly improved his reporting. He writes a richly and satisfyingly detailed article on new pilot programs for several small Indian nations which may eventually lead to the elimination of the Bureau of Indian Affairs in "Sovereign Once Again, Indian Tribes Experiment With Self-Government," 1-16. Egan neatly addresses surface issues on the first step to socialized medicine in "Oregon Shakes Up Pioneering Health Plan for the Poor," 2-22, yet he doesn't explore such factors as doctor's soaring rates due to insurance and lawsuits. He takes a moderately clear picture of the current economic scene in "Northwest's Fortunes, Once Grim, Thrive Despite National Recession," 3-14, though he misses the tax structure that enticed Boeing, Nike and Microsoft to set up shop there. Egan's green tint colors "Fight to Save Salmon Starts Fight Over Water," 4-1, less a look at hydropower and what can be done about this than about the mystique of the wild salmon. His "Image of 'Man' Behind the Badge Changes," 4-25, is an empirical and sufficient look at the police officer, but we already gleaned much of this from Andrew Malcolm's work last year. Egan's "Apple Growers Bruised and Bitter After Alar Scare," 7-9, is a mea culpa by the *Times* for what "they [apple growers] say was an orchestrated scare," a timely and well-wrought effort. We get a cursory examination of state-supported health care in "Hawaii Shows it Can Offer Health Insurance for All," 7-23, with numerous questions left unanswered here by Egan. In an otherwise limp "Gambling Raid Angers Mining Town," 8-20, Egan notes: "In an age when banking scandals have cost the nation's taxpayers billions of dollars, many residents say the Government has spent far too much time and money on [shutting down] video poker machines in a crippled mining town." His "Washington Voters Weigh if There Is a Right to Die," 10-14, outlines the Washington state Initiative 119, which would allow doctor-assisted suicide, Egan covering the ground adeptly, leaving only occasional holes such as fundamentalist church views regarding the issue.

Farney, Dennis. *The Wall Street Journal.* (★ ★ ½)
Kansas City, social trends and politics. Farney seems perfectly content in his heartland posting, having escaped the rigors of Washington after years of rough-and-tumble politics. His folksy, amiable features are always worth reading, if not always on the cutting edge of either social trends or politics. His probing and worthwhile "An Old Kansas Cow Town's Reflections on War Mirror the Attitudes and Anxieties of the Nation," 1-17, successfully, if not unintentionally, banishes the notion of the country bumpkin and the heartland not knowing or caring what goes on outside Abilene. Farney delivers an atmospheric feature on Ft. Leavenworth's Command and General Staff College in "School for Army Officers Struggles to Adapt Doctrine to a New World," 2-7, but vagueness hampers our understanding of how the information he gives us fits together. He delves into water rights in the Midwest in "With Missouri River Now Low, Emotions Run High in 10 States," 4-2, with Farney admirably handling the topic in an area that doesn't often receive serious treatment. "Gov. Finney of Kansas, Thwarted by Legislators, Is in Danger of Becoming an Irrelevant Populist," 5-1, lacks Farney's characteristic corn-pone color, but still brings us a sense of Joan Finney's problems with the legislature. He files a great report describing the efforts to conclude a wilderness agreement in "Idaho Wilderness Negotiations," 7-11, wryly noting the combustible mix of partisan interest groups: "Brain surgery is a good analogy for the intricate negotiation process unfolding now." His "Bayou Politics: Election in Louisiana Features Vital Issues But Quirky Candidates," 9-6, is a highly readable and entertaining article on the gubernatorial race in Louisiana, but he's strangely disorganized, flipping from one point to another. We get a competent profile of Sen. Bob Kerrey in "Candidate Kerrey's Strength, and His Weakness, Is That He Has Been Defined Outside of Politics," 10-24. Farney fails to examine his track record, or his stance on certain issues in this style-over-substance portrait of the hopeful Democratic Presidential candidate.

Fineman, Howard. *Newsweek.* (★ ½)
Washington. Back to the business of newsweekly reporting after dropping out of sight for a year, Fineman is as caustic and cynical as ever. While we continue to read him for the nuggets he mines, it's tough to get past his snideness. His flimsy "Saddam and Bush: The Words of War," co-written by Evan Thomas 1-21, compares the rhetoric of Hussein and Bush and how it affects diplomacy, adversely, an obvious topic treated in an obvious manner. "The President's 'Spin' Patrol," co-written by Ann McDaniel 2-11, snidely implies that putting the best possible face on all events related to the Persian Gulf War by the White House, Pentagon, *et al.,* is dishonest and a political public relations plot. His "Dream On, Democrats," 3-18, is little more than a list of potential '92 Democrat sacrificial lambs, strung together with Fineman's witticisms. The purely speculative "Schwarzkopf for President?" 4-1, finds Fineman raising the Stormin' Norman as President flag, well aware there is yet no wind to unfurl it. His incisive pen crafts "What's a Pair of Paradigms? The Newest Odd Couples," 5-13, into a good examination of the unlikely alliances between political animals. He's at his darkest in "The Democrat's Mr. Right," 7-22, Fineman grotesquely and snidely stating: "The Democrats' search for a 1992 nominee has a funereal air — and why not, considering that dead Whig Zachary Taylor gets more respect than most live Democrats." The ephemeral "Middle-Class Maneuvers," co-written by Eleanor Clift 8-12, is a shallow overview of what the Democrats may do to appeal to the middle class. In Fineman's attempt to connect the candidacies of Sen. Bob Kerrey and ex-Gov. Jerry Brown, "This Time, Being Outside Is In," co-written by Eleanor Clift 8-9, the links are tenuous at best: "[both have] eyes that reveal their inner journeys, both are admirers of Mother Teresa." Fineman's cover "The No Bull Campaign," 10-14, is terribly cynical as he indicates that Americans say they want the truth from politicians but are afraid to live with it, which works fine as an essay, but not as a news story. He examines the white male as a voting bloc in "Playing White Male Politics," 10-28, an unusual but logical premise that plays out well.

Fritz, Sara. *Los Angeles Times.* (★ ★ ½)
Washington, Congress with an emphasis on the Senate. Fritz shows a new eye for detail and insight that impresses. Her highly technical "Column One" article "High-Tech Warfare — A

New Era," co-written by Ralph Vartabedian 1-18, centers on the Tomahawk missile, and though occasionally obtuse in spots, the article does provide generous amounts of information, the topic seemingly far from Fritz's congressional expertise. She provides a detailed rundown in "Ethics Panel Says Cranston Broke Rules in Keating Ties," 2-2, her well-organized, structured piece detailing the Senate Ethics Committee censuring and his steadfast denial. Staying with the topic in "End of the Line," 3-1, she is able to recount the tale, integrate previous material, and avoid judgement on Sen. Alan Cranston's demise with equal aplomb. Fritz files a solid review of other cases coming before the ethics committee in "Ethics Cases Lost in Shadow of 'Keating Five,'" 6-23, detailing the less notable cases lost in the Keating 5 press flood. Her "Nomination of Thomas Seen as Deft Political Stroke," 7-3, straddles the fence in appraising his chances of actually making it to the bench. Yet, her pertinent information is welcome: "If they oppose Thomas, analysts say, liberals may open themselves to the charge that they are discriminating against a minority nominee simply because his views are not in line with their own." Her sharply drawn "CIA Issued Early Warning on BCCI, Document Shows," 8-1, quickly points out that Senator Kerry's documentation made "counter allegations" that Robert Gates and the CIA covered up the BCCI scandal. "Lobbyists' Role Cited in Failure to Probe BCCI," 8-2, presents the testimony of former U.S. Customs Commissioner William von Raab and former Senate investigator Jack Blum, where we get mounds of detail on von Raab but little on Blum. In "Stalemate Seen in Cranston Case," 9-23, she provides an adequate recounting of the intractability of the potential Senate trial of Alan Cranston over his involvement with Charles Keating, but the use of numerous anonymous sources mars the piece.

Garrett, Major. *The Washington Times.* (★ ½)
National desk. Garrett provides serviceable overviews of key Capitol Hill issues, but, like many of his colleagues at the *Times,* Garrett doesn't ask the tough questions that would give his dispatches more teeth. Garrett began the year with a vivid "Bush: I'll Go 'Extra Mile for Peace,'" 1-4, that dealt with the opening of the congressional session as the debate over the Gulf and the budget begins. Little of substance on the budget can be drawn from "Democrats: Bush Figures With His Fingers Crossed," 2-5, with Garrett surveying a few influential Democrats, but nothing of vital importance comes through. He provides an early statistical assessment of what the Gulf War will mean electorally for the GOP in "GOP Figures to Gain on Hill," 3-15, surely speculative as there's a year and a half between the end of the war and election day. Garrett files a crisp summary of Democratic worries that the GOP will be able to capitalize on redistricting in "California Redistricting Unnerves Lawmakers," 4-9, unnecessarily noting that a candidate must have "a winning message," no matter what the district. His "Tsongas Enters Race that Democrats Fear," 5-1, is notable alone for its pithy and possibly prophetic opening: "Paul Tsongas is one Greek who clearly doesn't believe in omens." In "House Votes to Lift Abortion 'Gag Rule,'" 6-27, he furnishes a good microscopic examination of this particular vote, appropriately indicating that the "lopsided" margin of 353-74 doesn't reflect the deep divisions of feeling that did not necessarily fall along partisan lines. Garrett is unwittingly prescient in "Bush Calls Thomas To Highest Court," 7-2, as he notes "In his initial replies to press. . .Judge Thomas followed the taciturn [Justice David] Souter example." He delivers a quick and rather obvious breakdown on the Thomas nomination in "Moderate Democrats Seen Backing Thomas," 9-16, hindsight showing us it was a hasty assessment, but some information was quite accurate at the time.

Gerstenzang, James. *Los Angeles Times.* (★ ½)
White House. Gerstenzang offered more evocative detail that brought life to some dispatches, particularly during the Persian Gulf War. His "Bush Strives to Stay Above the Fray," 1-24, is vividly charged with emotion as it tells of "a tall, solitary figure and his two dogs" who at night "could be seen walking the south grounds of the White House." Gerstenzang presents a straightforward account of Bush's press conference in "Air Campaign to Go On Awhile, Bush Says; Silent on Land War," 2-12, on target as to the focus of the briefing as well as to the mood. His two-dimensional "Allies and Iraqis Plan Talks Sunday on Cease-Fire, POWs," 3-2, is a solid

report that unfortunately does not look past immediate plans. Unlike so many other dispatches, in "U.S. Glum on Mideast Peace Pact," 4-30, Gerstenzang states clearly in his lead: "The White House said Monday that its intensified push of a breakthrough in the Middle East peace process has produced 'slim' results." The clarity of his prose allows him to objectively detail who has agreed to sit down and who has not. Both "Bush Advisors Say Sununu Can Survive Furor," 6-24, and "Sununu Pleads for Harmony, Source Says," 6-27, are fairly inconclusive reports on the expenditure flap and contain a plethora of anonymous quotes from senior staff. His "Removal Seen as Setback for U.S. Diplomacy," co-written by Norman Kempster 8-19, is clearly preliminary on the ouster of Gorbachev, with few insights but a little background. Gerstenzang's finely-tuned "Bush Calls for Return of Gorbachev to Power," co-written by Norman Kempster 8-20, adds tension to this solid dispatch with delightful details: when administration officials met in "a high-level strategy session" held in the Roosevelt Room, we're told that this particular room is windowless. He gives little more than a compilation of Bush's several frantic press conferences in "Bush Exults as Gorbachev Regains Power in Kremlin," co-written with Douglas Jehl 8-22, yet the florid language here gives us a sense of both the urgency of the earlier situation, the evident relief of Bush, and apparently the reporters as well.

Gerth, Jeff. *The New York Times.* (★ ½)
Washington investigations. The *Times*' top investigative reporter in D.C., Gerth is limited by his perspective and scope, a good cop on the beat, but no Sherlock Holmes. Assigned late to the B.C.C.I. scandal, the body of work he accumulated for the year simply doesn't fit together well. His "Big Cut in U.S. Deposits Hastened Fall of Freedom Bank in Harlem," 1-29, is an adequate retelling of the demise of the small minority-owned National Freedom Bank, but Gerth stops just short of the "why" however. In "Report Says Mercenaries Aided Colombian Cartels," 2-20, he needlessly writes on the Senate staff study and testimony before the Senate Permanent Subcommittee on Investigations. The lack of substantial digging by Gerth mars "Iraqi Agents and Fronts Listed by U.S." 4-2, merely giving us press briefing detail from John E. Robson, Deputy Secretary of the Treasury, followed by a list of companies involved as fronts. His "Audit Finds Losses in Mortgage Funds," 5-19, provides a sufficient review that pegs another fiscal Federal Housing Authority shortfall, as well as future losses as Reagan Administration mismanagement and briefly examines how the FHA fits into the current situation at HUD. Gerth delivers a rather weak expose of the Federal Deposit Insurance Corporation in "F.D.I.C. Wields Powers in Deals With Few Checks and Balances," 6-13, as the unanswered question remains: Will government regulation or intervention make the F.D.I.C. more efficient? Hot on the banking story, Gerth gives us a substantial review of how flaws in worldwide regulation of the banking system helped to create the problems with B.C.C.I. in "Scandal Reveals Holes in Rules for Foreign Banks," 7-7. His shutter opens again on B.C.C.I. in "Federal Reserve Fines a Saudi Linked to B.C.C.I." 9-18, and though the background is fairly clear, we don't get more than a peripheral sense of how the Fed fining Ghaith R. Pahraon $37 million fits into the banking boondoggle. There's so little specific detail on the wheeling-and-dealing, making his case ineffective, in "Questions Raised on Revision by U.S. in S&L Asset Deal," 10-7. The generalities of this issue dealing with Government-owned commercial real estate, put up a smoke screen, possibly cloaking the fire and the smoking gun.

Gest, Ted. *U.S.News & World Report.* (★)
Senior editor. Gest's lack of flair was notably apparent, covering fewer important judiciary stories than in previous years as he tended to skirt the periphery of his topics with balanced yet unimaginative reports. His "The Aging Bulldog of Civil Liberties," 2-18, is a light but effective profile of the American Civil Liberties Union as it gets its first new president in 15 years, Nadine Strossen. Gest records the shift in product liability cases, with most winners now being the corporate defendants, not the plantiffs, in "Why the Injured Lose Suits," 4-8, but he takes the conventional approach in pegging the shift to the "conservative turn in the judiciary." In "The New Meaning of Equality," 6-17, Gest presciently lists the "key battlegrounds" of feminism as sexual harassment, spouse abuse, pregnancy and drug abuse and divorce, in which feminism and

the feminist trend is contributing a change; a solid sidebar, but this could have been an article on its own. He files a curious article on Justice Thurgood Marshall and the Supreme Court, "Next Stage: Court Lite," 7-8, Gest contending that they have a minimal impact on our daily lives: "If anything, that is Rehnquist's driving philosophy: Define the Constitution narrowly and let legislators do the big things that affect people." He takes a seemingly pro-choice, anti-Thomas slant in "When Push Comes to Shove on States' Rights," 8-19, this "One Week" column not terribly balanced in its appraisal of the values of states' rights. In "Ruling on Quayle v. Lawyers," co-written by David Gergen 8-26/9-2, the duo cheers the Veep for once, as he proposes reforming the legal system, including nice detail of what Quayle actually said. The thought-provoking "What's Really Going On Here?" 10-14, argues that while the nation focuses on Clarence Thomas, the Democratic-controlled Senate has consistently voted for Reagan-Bush appointees to the federal bench who are generally conservative.

Goodman, Walter. *The New York Times.* (★ ★ ★)

Television. With much of television's Gulf War coverage coming under fire, we came to appreciate Goodman's perceptive veteran's eye. For serious, literate commentary on television news, it's Goodman to whom we turn. His "Gulf Tensions: TV's Cause and Effect," 1-10, is a cynical essay on network coverage of the Gulf crisis and the Pentagon's efforts to control news coverage. The mildly amusing "Broadcasters in the Gulf and What They Merit," 3-4, has Goodman adding his own candidates for the Gulfies Awards, inaugurated by Bill Safire with his criticisms of the TV reporters on the mark. From his "Critic's Notebook" file comes "TV Images that Sear and Prod," 4-11, with Goodman cleverly connecting the recent TV footage of apparent police brutality in Los Angeles and the plight of the Kurdish refugees, and noting that "here were bursts of reality that must jar even the least reflective." His sober, if slightly twisted, reflection on the pros and cons of showing live executions on TV in "Executions on TV: Defining the Issues," 5-30, has him supporting the idea, albeit after bedtime, arguing: "Such regulations or understandings are not unprecedented. But the thing about democracy is, you have to take some chances." The straight-forward "The Wheels of Justice, Live on Cable," 7-3, is an honest appraisal of the Courtroom Television Network, which offers live coverage of trials. His "Summit Images: A Drummer and a Sales Manager," 8-1, is a witty summary of TV coverage of the Moscow summit, with Goodman observing that despite Mikhail Gorbachev's best efforts to spin-control events, the realities of his collapsing authority came through loud and clear. "TV Leaps to Cover Soviet Coup," 8-20, is a literate review of the coverage with Goodman noting that the decision of the new Soviet leaders to subject themselves to a press conference "left the hope that too much had changed in the Soviet Union for even hardliners to go back quickly. . .to the bad old days." He correctly cuts with "Appropriating History to Serve Politics on TV," 10-7, on Bush's politically advantageous introduction to "The Heroes of Desert Storm," a docudrama which Goodman dismisses as "so fake that it made the commercials seem like slices of life," a sad but strong commentary on the presidency.

Greenhouse, Linda. *The New York Times.* (★ ★)

Supreme Court. Greenhouse dutifully reports doings on the docket with much more verve and pluck than we've seen in earlier years, making the most of her sometimes dry material. She supplies solid background in "Court to Review Case From Georgia on Desegregation," 2-20, while sharply assessing the Court's workload. Her "Judicial Restraint and Its Repercussion," 3-7, is smart on the Supreme Court's evolving attitude toward judicial restraint in regards to the conservative groups losing the fight to strike down Alabama's punitive damages law. Although laden with briefs to outline her story in "Supreme Court to Review Record on Bias in Mississippi Courts," 4-16, we find nothing past the 4th or 5th paragraph necessary to expand her point on continuing patterns of segregation. Greenhouse focuses on the abortion question rather than the free-speech issue, which she sees as being the crux of the matter and the biggest threat to *Roe v. Wade,* in "5 Justices Uphold U.S. Rule Curbing Abortion Advice," 5-24. Her pro-choice bias shows, but almost imperceptibly. She once again becomes ensnared in the abortion quagmire in "A Wild-Card Nominee," 7-2, instead of drafting a strict evaluation of Thomas's decision. Along with Neil Lewis, the *Times* offers a one-two punch on affirmative action and abortion, with the ultimate decision decidedly thumbs down. She insightfully and poetically contrasts Thomas to Souter with "In Trying to Clarify What He Is Not, Thomas Opens Question of What He Is," 9-13: "Justice Souter did not feel pressed to remake himself; rather his fluent testimony gave the impression that his entire adult life had been a natural preparation for that moment." She builds a strong case, albeit without direct quotes, in "High Court's Aloofness Pierced by Thomas Fight," 10-18, on how the Supreme Court felt about and was affected by the Clarence Thomas-Anita Hill hearings. In "Questions About Thomas, the Man, Obscured Clues About Thomas, the Jurist," 10-27, she indicates that the Anita Hill brouhaha clouded the hearings, arguing that Thomas is surprisingly uninformed on recent Court work, but she stretches her case too thin, almost accusing Thomas of lying.

Gross, Jane. *The New York Times.* (★ ★ ½)
San Francisco. Gross is consistently and effectively evocative in her features, sensitively sketching and then fleshing out her stories. Her "mood-of-the-public" piece on the eve of war, "The Vietnam Generation Surrenders Its Certainty," 1-15, rings true as it reports that many protesters, and soldiers, from the Vietnam era are finding the Gulf crisis is dredging up complex emotions. Gross's "New Challenge of Youth: Growing Up in Gay Home," 2-11, is a sensitively drawn P. 1 below-the-fold feature on children in gay households, how they handle things, how the gay couples handle things, all anecdotal evidence, but of interest nonetheless. Her "California Painfully Faces Grim Truths of Drought," 2-26, is an entertaining feature on the creative ways Californians are weathering the drought, such as painting the lawns green. In her slightly lopsided "California Readies for Political Brawl Over Both of Its Senate Seats in 1992," 3-4, she unduly focuses on the Democratic side, as the GOP "can ride the coattails of a President whose popularity has soared with the swift victory in the Persian Gulf." She gets the information as well as the pathos in the emotive "Grandparents Unite Amid Drug War," 4-14, culling a great quote from a grandfather on the children: "We hope that they will become little crack missionaries." Gross examines acquaintance rape in "Even the Victim Can Be Slow to Recognize Rape," 5-28, but doesn't define the term well. Anecdotes certainly illustrate her point, but a ratio of acquaintance rape to those raped by strangers would have been helpful. "Stanford Chief Quits Amid Furor on Use of Federal Money," 7-30, focuses on Donald Kennedy, who resigned after allegedly using some federal dollars to decorate his home, with Gross objectively concentrating more on his tenure than the scandals. She pens a vivid and atmospheric "A City's Determination to Rewrite History Puts Its Classrooms in Chaos," 9-18, a good but bleak update on Oakland's rejection of California texts, and subsequent infighting over the curriculum.

Hall, Carla. *The Washington Post.* (★ ★)
Los Angeles "Style." Hall has come in from the beach to provide entertaining, lively profiles and features that have little of the California dreaming we saw in her reporting when she first was transferred. She now fits seamlessly into the *Post*'s pages. Hall files a lively "Quiet on the Wartime Set," 1-26, that sharply details the notable absence of protest from Hollywood over the possibility of military action in the Persian Gulf. She submits another colorful Hollywood piece in "Tinseltown's Solid Citizens," 2-26, that provides interesting mini-profiles of three character actors. Her mildly amusing "Stoppard, Playwright in Waiting," 3-27, raises the author and director of his own play "Rosencrantz and Guildenstern Are Dead" to life in this conversation, but we sit down with a celebrity and leave, not really knowing him. Her moderately insightful "Demi Moore, Semi Star," 4-14, lacks any vital punch. Despite the fact that neither Turner nor Fonda will talk to her, Hall does quite a serviceable job in "Ted & Jane Inc." 5-13, as she talks to friends and press agents and digs up different empirical anecdotes. The riveting, though scattershot "The Crosby Curse," 7-8, a portrait of the four sons of Bing Crosby from his first marriage, is compelling in its sad futility of the ex-wives, and now two sons dead from suicide. Hall delivers a powerful emotional punch in her, "In Pursuit of a Miracle," 8-1, the tragic moving story tells of Lorenzo Odone, who at 13 is completely incapacitated by ALD, adrenoleukosystrophy. Her "Jim & Ted's Excellent Adventure," 9-1, is a bright, bouncy profile of producers/distributors Ted and Jim Pedas, who work out of Washington, D.C., and though we're still not clear on precisely what they do, Hall does have infectious enthusiasm for the pair.

Hallow, Ralph Z. *The Washington Times.* (★)
National politics. A wise-guy conservative, Hallow continues to show a talent for amassing details which he only infrequently fits into a broader context. He rarely plumbs the depths of anyone's mind, using a he-said, she-said approach. A sketchy "Turning Disease Into Political Cause: First AIDS, and Now Breast Cancer," 1-7, delves into the new politics of breast cancer via increased pressure for federal funding. He skims surface issues and splices it with quotes throughout, a patchwork job. He provides an adequate dispatch on the Conservative Political Action Conference which may or may not mount a candidate against Bush for '92 in "Conservatives Push a Challenge for Bush," 2-11. The frustrating "Gramm Raked as Tax-Cut Foe," 3-1, seems rather nasty in its opening, calling Sen. Phil Gramm the "onetime heartthrob of the conservative movement, [who] ran after his followers yesterday trying to explain his opposition to a tax-cut plan." Hallow's "Garn to Retire, Hurts GOP Bid to Lead Senate," 5-30, is limited in scope on the retirement of Utah's Jake Garn, seeing this only from the perspective of the GOP campaigns, and missing the importance of Garn's Senate career. His shallow "Strauss Fills Bill as 'Generalist,' " 6-5, begins snidely: "President Bush must really believe in quotas, or he wouldn't have named former Democratic National Chairman Robert Strauss as ambassador to Moscow yesterday," and is followed by a selection of opinions from conservatives over the appointment. Gramm is back in *WT*'s good graces in "Senators Have Tax Ploy," 7-30, as he explains his (and Rep. Newt Gingrich's) tax plan to increase personal exemptions over lunch, but there's little economic savvy on Hallow's part. Staying loosely on the story, Hallow files, "Bush Makes Tax Cut a Domestic Priority," 8-2, once again giving further play to the Gramm-Gingrich proposal, but he still shows no sign of actually reporting on the economics of this. In "Michel Threat: A GOP Surprise," 9-24, Hallow has Senate Minority Leader Bob Michel announcing that to counter threats of an "October surprise" investigation, the GOP may launch an investigation into Democratic links to the Sandinista government in Nicaragua. He doesn't provide sufficient information to make this anything more than cursory.

Harwood, Richard. *The Washington Post.* (★ ★ ★)
Ombudsman. Harwood, a longtime *Post* staffer, brings to his critiques almost thirty years of insider perspectives; it's no wonder that he's at his best when upbraiding his colleagues at the paper. He still hasn't quite got a firm grasp on some of the macro issues facing the media, however. He provides a moderately interesting history of his topic when asking the question: "What's in a Byline?" 1-6, nearly grasping the crux of its importance, but it ultimately eludes him. He delivers an interesting column contrasting media depiction of the current enemy with the caricatures that prevailed during the Second World War in "This Is Not 1945," 2-24. Harwood notes that in 1991 we are demonizing the enemy leader, not an entire race, possibly resulting in a less destructive conflict. His "Sometimes Compassion," 4-28, is savage on the inconsistency of the press in doling out compassion, or, as Harwood puts it, "hellfire," using the Palm Beach-Smith case as a launching point. He changes the pace in "From the Top II," 4-14, making it almost eulogistic in tone, with Harwood ruminating on how Katharine Graham and Benjamin Bradlee combined to make the *Post* a great newspaper. His amusing "Portraits of Mr. Gates," 5-19, displays the widely varying major newspaper profiles of CIA Director-nominee Robert Gates. He notes mischievously that "The reader of these newspapers, including the local KGB station chief, may come away from them somewhat puzzled as to the true nature of the Gates psyche." Harwood provides a probing investigation of the plagiarism question in "Media Bandits," 7-21, referring to the recent firing of *Post* reporter Laura Parker, and reveals that virtually every journalist "borrows" and "recycles." His wryly amusing article on pack journalism, "Stuck in a Pack," 8-11, notes that ". . .pack journalism is more than scandal. . .it tends to produce consistently unimaginative, conformist and exclusionary pictures of the world." The uninspiring "Miss America: What Does The Post Think?" 9-22, chronicles the changing views of the *Post* and the writers it sends to the Miss America pageant.

Hedges, Michael. *The Washington Times.* (★ ★)
Investigations. Hedges is beginning to develop a sharper eye for detail and a better hand at constructing a framework for his stories, more consistently incisive and to the point than we've ever seen him. In "Merry It Isn't, But GIs Take Heart," 12-25-90, he writes of Christmas for U.S. troops in eastern Saudi Arabia, where "many said they preferred to treat Dec. 25 as just another day. . ." a colorful, lively account with no indulgence or exploitation of anything maudlin. With the U.S. 1st Infantry Division in "Mines, Tank Traps Settled in Kuwait," 1-28, he provides a rounded picture of the army unit, a superior Gulf snapshot with quotes from executive officers with the 1st Engineers providing strategic perspective. Another Gulf piece, "Out Front: Unwitting Doctors Take Lead in Desert," 2-4, is only mildly interesting as doctors end up as the forward force of a combat infantry division, Hedges treating this serious matter with excessive levity. He delivers a standard dispatch on Kuwaiti soldiers turning on Iraqis and Palestinians within the borders, "Liberated Soldiers Not Turning the Other Cheek," 3-13, the sadness and tragedy of these events not livening the piece. The piercing "Foley Looks at October Surprise," co-written by Jerry Seper 5-1, one of the few dispatches on the "October surprise" which also incorporates the Inslaw allegations, is neatly and trimly told, going beyond mere update quality. He piques our interest in "Deep Throat ID'd as Haig," 5-21, on Haig feeding false information to Woodward to topple a president he saw as "too conciliatory to China and the Soviet Union as well as weak on the Vietnam War." He raises as many questions as he purports to answer. He files a solid and organized dispatch on the odds that Pablo Escobar will be able to continue running his cocaine empire from jail in "U.S. Agents Say Escobar May Keep Running Cartel," 6-21, Hedges allowing the DEA agents and spokesmen he quotes to stand on their own and make their cases. His "Thomases: Different Roads, Same Direction," co-written by Jerry Seper 7-16, a purposeful and informative profile of Clarence Thomas' wife, Virginia Lamp, is the first such profile we saw. But why did they need two reporters to handle it?

Hinds, Michael deCourcy. *The New York Times.* (★ ½)
Philadelphia. Hinds lacks economic sophistication and as a result the big story — the fiscal follies in Philadelphia — went largely unreported. His features, however, are tightly drawn and evocative. His encompassing update "$150 Million Loan Buys Philadelphia Some Time," 1-18, is a thick but complete report on the immediate transaction if not the crisis. The "3 Firefighters Die in Fire at Philadelphia Office Tower," 2-25, is city blotter reporting that's actually done quite neatly, rising above standard. Hinds provides a straightfaced "Starring in Tonight's Erotic Video: The Couple Down the Street," 3-22, handling the topic maturely, and amusingly adding: "Scientific opinion is divided." His "Cash-Strapped Cities Turn to Companies to Do What Government Once Did," 5-14, is an overview/survey of cities privatizing public services such as garbage collection, a reasonable appraisal, yet the unions are suspiciously mute. His vaguely unsatisfying report, "Bush's Aids Push Gun-Related Cases on Federal Courts," 5-17, deals with Operation Triggerlock which will, according to Hinds, burden the federal system, but we gain no information as to whether the state court system benefits. Hinds pens a delightful and amusing "Edinboro Journal" piece, "Making Purple Martins Feel at Home," 7-15, on James R. Hill, III, who's looking and building the perfect home for the purple martin, a bird that winters in Brazil but spends spring on the east coast. He provides a massive overview of which states are doing what to make ends meet financially in "States and Cities Fight Recession With New Taxes," 7-27, but he doesn't address the real business implications of increased taxes. In "Poor Teen-Agers Learn How to Get a Job Done," 8-9, Hinds provides a nice little feature on McDonald's corporation's Freedom Theater in Philadelphia, at which trainees build self-confidence and self-esteem, an interesting angle, but Hinds fails to bring the dimension necessary to invigorate the piece. His "Democrats Look to the Senate Race in Pennsylvania for Lessons and Hope," 10-23, is a colorful account on Harris Wofford catching up to Dick Thornburgh in the polls. Hinds gets a piece of the action here, outlining their plans of attack, but little on what either thinks or will do.

Holmes, Steven A. *The New York Times.* (★ ½)
Congress. Holmes keeps track of the varied civil rights issues facing both Congress and the U.S. at large. As in earlier years, he assembles salient facts, but we rarely get a sense of the deeper battles brewing over the rights of minorities and disabled, among other groups. In "End of Jobless Benefits Pushes Many Near Despair," 1-28, Holmes tells sad stories of families in Troy, Ohio, who are broke after jobless benefits are depleted, but he never splits the seams to examine why, countrywide, it's harder to find employment these days. He uses the remarks of Justice official John R. Dunne in "Rights Bill Seen as Aiding Quotas," 2-8, to gauge administration feeling on the civil rights and quota issue, the curtness of the article belieing the importance of the issue at hand. In "Once, Welfare Meant Someone Else, But Recession Brings Home Its Sting," 3-11, he tells stories of new working-class welfare applicants and recipients in Framingham, Mass., offering only meager statistics and no sense of how endemic the problem is. In "Adjusting of Test Scores Inflames Rights Debate," 5-17, he details Rep. Henry Hyde's (R-Ill.) proposal outlawing the practice of adjusting test scores to allow for race, with Holmes explaining the testing process thoroughly, but his assessment of the political aspect slanted. He delivers a balanced evaluation of a rather silly, pedantic issue in "U.S. Rules Will Let Employers Reject Disabled Over Safety Issues," 7-23, noting that these rules will permit employers to reject the disabled when the jobs they hold cause a direct threat to their health. Holmes's common sense easily deflates the absurd need for a ruling. A small, but important report, "N.A.A.C.P. Assails Members for Backing Thomas," 8-9, deals with a growing schism within the black group over self-help vs. handouts as the Compton, California branch endorses Thomas. Holmes should have expanded the implications of this report. His "When the Disabled Face Rejection from Churches That Nurtured Them," 9-30, an intriguing but not particularly well-done report on churches that reject the disabled by not putting in ramps, is never developed any further than these few, apparently isolated cases.

Houston, Paul. *Los Angeles Times.* (★ ½)
Congress. While Houston generally offers journeyman reports containing relevant information, he still comes up short on interpretation. He is rarely subtle in his evaluations, consistently serving up the obvious. The surprisingly one-sided "Congress Shifts From Euphoria to Anxiety and Frustration With War," co-written by William J. Eaton 1-24, has the duo talking to nine Democrats and one Republican on how they feel after a week of fighting in the air in the Persian Gulf, yet they don't include how each voted in light of their "anxiety." He does give us a balanced report in "Angry GOP Senators Press for Alexander Confirmation," 3-8, on the ugly portrayal of partisan politics as the Democrats, Kennedy in particular, allegedly hold up Lamar Alexander's confirmation as Secretary of Education. In "House Rejects Bush's Plan on B-2 Bomber, 'Star Wars,' " 5-22, a nice smattering of politics on the House side as they reject Bush's defense plan, pegging it as a difference of "priorities," Houston appropriately focuses on the opposition, though a little more balance would have been helpful. He details the latest Senate amendments to the omnibus crime bill in "Senate OKs Death Penalty in Case Where Gun Was Transported Across State Lines," 6-27, a well-focused snapshot providing a crystalline image of the foreground, but all else is slightly fuzzy. The generously detailed "Senate Passes B-2 Funding, 'Star Wars' Compromise," 8-2, reports on the defense vote in the Senate, yet Houston doesn't tell us where this might end up, as the House voted quite differently on these issues.

Ifill, Gwen. *The New York Times.* (★ ★)
Washington metropolitan news. Ifill moved from *The Washington Post* to the *Times* early in the year, one of several young Washington reporters to bolt either from their post or their paper. The change of newsroom has led to steady improvement in her reporting, which remains efficient and trimly accurate while taking on a new measure of crisp confidence. In "Most Governors Taking Steps to Cut Budgets," *WP* 1-3, Ifill takes a quick look at why so many are facing shortfalls, pinning it on federal cutbacks on welfare programs and the recession. Ifill's debut at the *Times,* "States, Following Bush Plan, Ask Congress to Consolidate U.S. Aid," 4-9, sufficiently outlines a plan on block grants for federal aid to states. In "Big New Round of Base

Closings to Be Proposed by Defense Chief," 4-11, she supplies nice detail on both the closings and proposed down-sizing, along with congressional infighting to preserve bases within one's own district. She reports in "Bill to Set a 7-Day Wait to Buy Handguns Hits Crucial Obstacle," 5-8, how the Staggers bill would "derail" the Brady bill. We would like to have seen more comparison between the two, and cost of each to taxpayers. Her solid dispatch, "Bush Says He Will Rely on Cheney in Deciding on Which Bases to Close," 7-2, gives us the latest rundown on base closings, Ifill getting good quotes from interested parties to fill this out further. She begins to come into her own in "Gephardt Makes It Official: He's No '92 Candidate," 7-18, a well-rounded piece on Gephardt and his decision not to run for president in the next election due to his duties as House Majority Leader, fleshing out the article by examining the other candidates. She seems a bit partisan in "Calls to Review Budget Pact Rise," 10-2, concentrating mostly on the Dems, giving us a sense of the process and the potential, but Ifill never fully articulates the economics of the budget agreement. In "Facing a Tide of Voter Anger, Politicians Look to Channel St." 11-3, she opens with exactly the right words: "America is in a sour mood," an excellent summary in advance of Election Day.

Innerst, Carol. *The Washington Times.* (★ ½)
Education. As always, Innerst stays abreast of key developments taking place within education. Unfortunately, she too frequently consults only the theoreticians and the administrators, and we don't often find out how these new ideas play out in practice. She furnishes an intriguing look at the changing position of military schools in the face of proposed military cutbacks and the Persian Gulf crisis in "Military Schools Under the Gun," 1-2, in which she stops just short of advocacy. Innerst reports on multiculturalism being kept in check at Boston University in "BU Reasserts Values of Western Culture," 2-5, augmented with a good selection of quotes. In "Study: Parents' Attention Gives Oriental Pupils Edge," 3-5, she provides an excellent account of a study by a University of Michigan professor on differences in approach and consequences of Asian and American parents regarding their children's academic lives that was both timely and sincere. Her " 'Education President' Slates New Tests, Revamped Schools," 4-14, solidly breaks down components of Bush's "America 2000: An Education Strategy," but its practicality in the classroom is never examined in regard to teachers or principals. She reports in "School Cuts Endanger Boston U. Experiment," 5-30, that Boston U. is frustrated by running the Chelsea, Massachusetts school district. We gleaned information here on the finances, but Innerst misses the issue of management — what were the details of the agreement? She takes on multiculturalism again in " 'Anti-European' Curriculum Hit," 6-20, a good preliminary discourse on the New York state history report that advocates a multicultural approach, but though early, we would like to have heard from the trenches. Her lightweight and fuzzy "Accrediting Body Disputes Alexander," 8-2, dealt with Sec. Lamar Alexander's refusal to approve Middle States Association of Colleges and Schools and the Commission on Higher Education because they are using their ability to accredit schools to arbitrate board positions. Innerst is clearly out of her league in "NOW Is the Right Time for the 'New Party,' " 9-16, reporting on the National Organization for Women taking steps to form its own party, and although this picture is fairly well defined, she concentrates on gender issues rather than politics.

Isikoff, Michael. *The Washington Post.* (★ ★)
Drugs, justice. Isikoff shows more depth and breadth in his reportage, moving beyond the press release mentality we noted last year. His anecdotal "In Dhahran, The Press in a Pressure Cooker," 1-23, dwells on the restriction placed on the press corps in the Gulf, with an interesting take on the soldiers enlivening the story. Isikoff's breakdown of survey results in "Study: White Students More Likely to Use Drugs," 2-25, doesn't hesitate to point out the flaws, but he never denigrates the value of the study in contradicting the widely-accepted notion that drugs are a black problem. His "Gun Pipeline: From Ohio to Streets of Philadelphia," 3-12, is the chilling well-told story of Ruben Floyd who purchased semiautomatics in Ohio, taking advantage of that state's lax gun laws, and resold the weapons, at high mark-ups, to Philadelphia street gangs. He files a solid report in "Brady Handgun Bill Sent to House Floor for Vote," 4-24, is a pointed

update on the fight over the Brady bill, as well as the Staggers proposal for a national hotline. Another frightening report from the law enforcement front, "Gun Dealers' 'Great Scam,' " 5-8, concludes virtually anyone can qualify for a federal gun dealer's license, taking advantage of the minimum requirements and lack of available records, chilling and absolutely convincing. His "Hard Time: The Mission at Marion," 5-28, is an evocative article on the fortress-like federal prison in Marion, Ill., where some of the nation's most notorious and most dangerous prisoners are kept. Isikoff writes: "To prison reformers and social critics, the trend is a throwback to the Dark Ages of penology." He casts doubt on the authenticity of the photo of three MIAs that surfaced recently in "U.S. Pilot Allegedly Shown Alive in Photo Is Dead, Vietnam Says," 7-19. Isikoff handles this rather grisly job professionally, coming to no firm conclusion but presenting all the evidence on each side with equal vigor. Reporting on the plea bargains in the Noriega case, he provides a good roundup and serviceable update in "Plea Bargains, Fees for Witnesses Against Noriega Questioned," 9-9.

Jehl, Douglas. *Los Angeles Times.* (★ ★)
White House. Jehl moved to Pennsylvania Avenue from the drug policy beat this year and now moves on to *The New York Times* D.C. bureau. He did not have the skepticism at the White House that he did on his previous beat, a matter of not yet having the right contacts, perhaps. Jehl provides a graphically up-close-and-personal look at a briefing prior to mission for soldiers in "1st Cavalry Gears Up for Perilous Scouting Foray Across Border," 1-23, three-dimensional even without quoting any dogfaces. A similar piece, "Turning Into a Lean, Mean Fighting Machine," 2-10, has a title belying the flabbiness evident; it's just about a battalion preparing for battle in Saudi Arabia, with no drama, no suspense. Although mainly anecdotal, "After Sunset, Rules of War Change Drastically," 2-23, does provide a valuable sense of being in the war zone, the vivid beginning setting the tone: "In 24 hours in the field governed mostly by nature there is light and then there is almost total blackness. . .Camps only next door fade to nothingness as dusk deepens. . ." Jehl's "Iraqi Commander's Diary Offers Glimpse of Desperation in the Bunkers," 3-6, is less reporting than recounting of a translation of an Iraqi diary found in the remains of a bunker in Kuwait, riveting to read, though we would have appreciated more. His lack of a sense of nuance mars "U.S. Suspends Cuban Visa Applications," 7-30, subsequent to Larry Rohter's piece in the *Times,* and a bit inferior, with Jehl merely recounting State Dept. maneuvering. He delivers solid workmanship in "Some in Agency Oppose Gates as CIA Chief," co-written by Michael Ross 8-2. The team conveys a good sense of allegations going from within the CIA to the Senate Intelligence Committee, with a nod to where in the Agency they might have originated. His "Bush Exults as Gorbachev Regains Power in Kremlin," co-written by James Gerstenzang 8-22, is little more than Bush's several frantic press conferences that day, but does properly exhibit the evident relief of Bush. Jehl pens a quick but sharp dispatch in "Bush Vows Veto of Israeli Aid Bill," co-written by William J. Eaton 9-13, but unfortunately this is little more than a news conference summation of Bush withholding aid.

Johnston, David. *The New York Times.* (★ ½)
Justice. Johnston keeps avoiding the analytic and although he provides adequate dispatches, he can be dry and uninviting in presenting his information. Johnston files a peripheral, unimaginative profile of John R. Dunne in "Justice Department's Civil Rights Chief Is Sitting on Sidelines of Main Battle," 1-10, where we get little sense of the politics around him, or of the man himself. His "Antidrug Nominee Is Assailed at Hearing," 2-27, is standard copy on Martinez' confirmation hearing for the post of drug czar, but at least Johnston gets some feedback from Washington insiders, notably Sen. Paul Simon, who opposes him. The overwrought "In Justice Dept. of the 90's, Focus Shifts From Rights," 3-26, writes of Dick Thornburgh's reign as Attorney General, though the title has little to do with the actual article. Johnston tackles Thornburgh again, giving us his testimony in front of Senate Judiciary Committee in "Bush, Pushing His Bill on Crime, Bends Again on Gun Control Law," 4-19. Pointedly reported, he includes thorough background and some evaluation of the reasons the administration had for retreating on the semi-automatic debate. His quasi-profile of John

Frohnmayer of the National Endowment for the Arts falls short in "Lightning Bolts From Left and Right Can't Resist Arts Endowment Chief," 5-3, more an appraisal of his performance that lacks specific detail. In the restrained, "Ex-C.I.A. Aide Says He Told Superiors of Iran Arms Deal," 7-10, he details the documented testimony of Alan D. Fiers, who is now cooperating with Lawrence Walsh, and Johnston keeps his jumping up and down in check. He takes a skeptical view of "at least five intelligence officials" facing new allegations in the Iran-contra affair in "Officials of C.I.A. Face New Scrutiny in Iran Arms Case," 8-7, probing, but we never really get a sense of what it is being the "subject of the inquiry." He reports in circles in "Elliott Abrams Admits His Guilt to 2 Counts in Contra Cover-Up," 10-8, repeating again and again that Abrams pled guilty and that it may or may not lead the Iran-contra investigation into the Reagan State Department.

Kenworthy, Tom. *The Washington Post.* (★ ½)
Capitol Hill. Kenworthy only intermittently offers an appropriate mix of background and context, as his habit of missing the larger picture while covering narrow topics is beginning to creep back into his work. In "Security Clampdown at the Capitol Called Most Stringent in Recent Times," 1-30, he supplies an adequate rundown of what extra measures Secret Service and U.S. Capitol Police were taking to protect the Capitol during the President's State of the Union Address. He lists a few reasons why Dems are so quiet, mainly "overwhelming public support" for Bush objectives in "Hill Democrats Mute Criticism of Bush Actions," 2-21. The absence of how queasy Democrats feel about their party-line vote in January opposing the use of force is conspicuous. His "From Capitol Hill, A Potshot at Saddam," 2-27, is a quick but otherwise overlooked item on Rep. Bob McEwen calling a press conference to introduce, again, a congressional resolution endorsing the assassination of Saddam Hussein, but it's too sketchy for a formal portrait. He files an interesting, "Progress Seen Against Hill Incumbents," 3-24, on the Coalition to End the Permanent Congress, getting out the relevant points: "Aggressively bipartisan. . .fed up citizens. . .special interests. . ." and so on. He provides some detail on the fight over defense in the '92 budget in "Senate Approves '92 Budget," 4-26, but the murkiness of the piece proved tough to wade through to reach the conclusion. His "Rostenkowski's Honoraria: $310,000," 6-15, is a satisfactory dissection of the shying away from honoraria: "In just three years, for example, the number of senators who chose not to accept speech fees for their personal use has more than doubled, from 19 to 40."

Klein, Joe. *New York.* (★ ★ ★ ★)
Politics. The quality of his interpretations still superlative, he remains the man to beat on the New York, and often the national, political scene as well. Klein pointedly takes on city hall in "Less Than Zero," 2-25, giving early warning of the disaster NYC is becoming, especially sharp on where Mayor Dinkins fell short — deficit financing, the structure of city government and the unions. In "President For Life," 3-11, he deftly moves from Bush to Vietnam to the Democrats disarray. Klein falters slightly in "Root-Canal Work," 4-8, a rudimentary study of NY state and city budgets that's not very useful. In the 10 Best selection for Political Reporting, "Ask Not? Don't Ask?" 6-3, he sharply pinpoints where Ted Kennedy, the Democrats and liberalism went wrong — "Kennedy took the family tropisms past several key boundaries. He divorced; he broke the law — and, most important, he allowed liberalism's essential message to slip from sacrifice for the common good to *entitlement*." One of the best political reports we've seen all year. In "The Real Deficit: Leadership," 7-22, he serves up a smart and astute assessment of the stalemate between Dinkins and Cuomo on the budget and how the city suffers in the interim, vintage Klein. He stumbles, but never falters in "Arkansas Traveler," 8-12, an intriguing profile of Bill Clinton, Governor of Arkansas, that's insightful on both his pluses and minuses, but not done with Klein's usual boldness, seeming rather tentative in places. The clever and on-target, "The Temptation of Mario," 9-16, takes a leaf from C. S. Lewis' book and brings Cuomo and Satan together for a little basketball and political needling from multiculturalism to the budget. Klein's "Beating Bush," 11-4, is a good, but not great, try at a Democratic White House scenario for 1992, but it fails by not addressing economic policy, simply acknowledging Dems

don't have a program. His 10 Best nomination, "Tabloid Government," 10-28, incisively cuts to the heart of the Hill-Thomas debacle as simply being "goverment by Geraldo." He smartly predicts both "left and right will have some surprises in store" in Thomas' judicial career as an associate justice.

Kowet, Don. *The Washington Times.* (★ ½)
Media. Kowet spent the first three months of the year tracking the flubs of the media during the Persian Gulf War in a special "Media Notes" columns, little more than a list of who did what on the air. He now seems misplaced in his perch, as his profiles of various and sundry media folk are much more insightful and complete than his media commentary. In "When Journalists Cross the Line," 1-4, Kowet rehashes much of the flap over the April 1990 pro-choice march in which, among others, Linda Greenhouse of *The New York Times* participated, and adds little to what we already know in this disappointing exercise. Kowet provides a nearly three-dimensional profile of Yue-Sai Kaan, host of "One World" — the most popular show in China in " 'One World' of Yue-Sai: Diverse Look for China TV," 5-27, giving us beneficial background and allowing her to speak for herself. His "Morton Kondracke's Middle Road to Success," *Insight* 6-10, is a superb profile of the *New Republic* senior editor and "McLaughlin Group" regular, Kowet giving us a full sense of the professional and personal Kondracke, and his "panoramic political vision that compels him to see all sides of every argument at once." His "Prime Time Watchers See Society Through a Distorted Screen," 7-1, is a breathless report on three researchers who have made the apparently astounding discovery that the producers of most primetime shows are to the left of the mainstream, with Kowet ominously warning us that their liberal views "have penetrated every aspect of American television." He quills a professionally detached profile of ABC's White House correspondent in "Brit Hume Does It Right," 7-9, though unfortunately, Kowet's detachment tends to keep Hume away from us. From the slightly dubious "News Analysis" file, Kowet gives us "But How Long Does it Take to Say Goodbye to Ben?" 8-2, apparently thinking the coverage of the *Post*'s editor Ben Bradlee's retirement is excessive, but these sour grapes don't really prove it. While Kowet raises cogent points about individuals and their reporting of the BCCI scandal in "In the Web of the BCCI," 9-17, his unashamed partisanship here doesn't sit well as he attacks the media in this complicated story.

Kurtz, Howard. *The Washington Post.* (★ ★ ★)
Media. A fine reporter and colorful writer, Kurtz's first full year on the media beat did not disappoint. He engages with his trim overviews, and enlightens with his insight. His "Style" section profile of CNN anchorman "Bernard Shaw, Under Siege," 1-22, poignantly brings home the reporter's disciplined professionalism which saw him through the bombardment of Baghdad. "My attitude was, this was not the end of the world," he says. In "The Media Bombardment," 2-6, Kurtz writes an interesting comparison of the war coverage of the *Los Angeles Times* and NBC News. Unsurprisingly, print comes out ahead. His mildly amusing "The Pace of Peace," 3-25, is a kind of 'what next?' column for the media. Kurtz correctly perceives the problem with political reporting: "political reporters are all dressed up for '92 with nowhere to go." Kurtz' *Magazine* cover story; "How to Succeed in Washington by Going on Television," 5-19, acutely assesses why the same experts and pundits appear on local and national TV news and public affairs shows: "the overriding lust is not for money or power but for *recognition* as a serious opinion-maker." In "Too Much Sununu News?" 6-28, Kurtz crisply responds to an accusation by L. Brent Bozell of the Media Research Center that the *Post* was ignoring travel abuses of various Democrats while skewering the Republican Sununu. He supplies an interesting "Outlook" piece on the reticence of otherwise aggressive journalists to take a critical look at institutions such as publishing because of career concerns in "Inside Stories," 7-21. Though he offers no solution, it's still worthwhile. In his trim review of television coverage of the coup "Live from Moscow, The Rush of History," 8-22, Kurtz wryly notes: "The Soviet right-wing takeover had turned into a perfect three-day miniseries, and with any luck it would all be wrapped up in time for the weekend talk shows." Kurtz provides a well-constructed, yet relatively unsubstantial, "Democratic Hopefuls Find News Coverage Is Scarce," 9-23, a nice breakdown

of how the networks aren't coping with the party because there isn't a clear front-runner. His 10 Best selection, "Cuomo Sapiens: The Thinking Man's Non-Candidate," 11-14, is an effervescent, diabolically clever treatment of Mario Cuomo's open-minded presidential indecision.

Lauter, David. *Los Angeles Times.* (★)
White House. Lauter is ever cautious in avoiding the bias we'd criticized a few years back, but we can see him straining to do so in spots. Perhaps this is why his sweeping overviews still tend toward the conventional, with few exceptions. His "Column One" "High-Tech War Hopes Overdrawn," 2-5, is a slightly condescending overview of the limitations of technology via the Persian Gulf War. Fortunately, the tone moderates into an intelligent discussion of the limitations of some technologies. Lauter takes his turn at bat in the *LAT* lineup on the "front" from the White House and handles himself quite well in "Iraq Accepts Cease-Fire Talks: U.S. Wants Quick POW Release, Formal End of War," 3-1. A broad, accurate overview of events leading up to the first step in signing of the cease-fire. He borders on the editorial in "White House Will Not Reveal Portion of Bush's Political Travel Paid For by GOP," 4-27, as Lauter debates the costs of piggybacking "official" and "political" business. His "U.S. Weighs Implications of 'Tragedy,' " 5-22, is less on the "implications" of the assassination of Rajiv Gandhi than an immediate reaction from Washington. Some light appraisal of the situation but not much; finding out this isn't going to facilitate democracy in India is not really news. Lauter disappoints in "Summit Seen as Middle East Springboard," 7-27, where he relies mostly on a press conference with Scowcroft, who, as the NSC chief is his primary source, a rehash of what each side hopes to accomplish. He solidly handles the feature "Babi Yar Death Site Moves Bush, Survivors to Tears," 8-2, focusing on Bush's speech at the ravine, and winding up with some statistics on the Jewish population in the Ukraine today, but we don't get a strong sense of their plight. "Thomas' Views Don't Fit Orthodox Right," 9-14, begins strongly on Clarence Thomas and his testimony before the Senate Judiciary Committee, but he ends up rambling about Thomas seeing busloads of criminals and saying, "there but for the grace of God go I." He provides a nice history in the sensitively done "When Sex Talk Goes Too Far," co-written by Stuart Silverstein 10-8, a more probing report than many of the other rather titillating stories of how the lines drawn on sexual harassment have become blurred.

Lewis, Neil A. *The New York Times.* (★ ½)
Legal affairs. Lewis was uncharacteristically superficial in appraising the politics of legal issues from Thornburgh's Justice Department to Thomas' Supreme Court nomination. While his work remains respectable, it shows little of the enterprising quality we'd liked so much last year. He gives a cosmetic but still interesting look at the life and trial of Henry Barr, who used to work for Richard Thornburgh, in "How Cocaine Brought Low a Soaring Law Career," 2-27, but Lewis never directly quotes anyone involved. His "Police Brutality Under Wide Review by Justice Dept." 3-15, is an acceptable review of Thornburgh's announcement of the investigation for wide patterns of police abuse, but seems to lack specificity — what kind of broad patterns will they be looking for? In "Clark Clifford, Symbol of the Permanent Capital, Is Faced With a Dilemma," 4-5, Lewis pens an extremely uncritical profile of Clark Clifford, whose bank is now under investigation by the Federal Reserve, a shallow portrait of the ultimate Washington insider. The haphazardly written "Navy Court Hears Appeal of a Marine Convicted of Spying," 5-13, makes little sense unless you know the finer background points on the case of Private Clayton Lonetree, convicted of having an affair with a Soviet woman at the U.S. embassy. While Lewis manages to impart some information about the new Supreme Court nominee Clarence Thomas in "From Poverty to U.S. Bench," 7-2, it's clear where the *Times* stands: "It was the sense that he had earned everything, and that nothing was given him because of his race, that has made him an impassioned opponent of affirmative action." In "Thomas Hearings Viewed as Test for Bush and Civil Rights Groups," 9-10, Lewis pens a neatly drawn and well tied together article. Though we've heard these themes on race and "natural law" before, the encompassing nature of this piece makes it worthwhile. Lewis's "Law Professor Accuses

Thomas of Sexual Harassment in the 1980s," 10-7, is a dignified and unsensationalized account of Anita Hill's accusations of Clarence Thomas although we still felt he treated Democratic Senators involved with kid gloves.

Marcus, Ruth. *The Washington Post.* (★ ½)
Supreme Court. Marcus sometimes seemed more preoccupied with the politics of the High Court, particularly after the resignation of Thurgood Marshall. Although her overviews are regularly satisfying in detail, her constant attempts to fit her information into this context can grate. Marcus gathers all the pieces in a finely balanced overview of Jeffrey Mason suing Janet Malcolm in "Misquotation Is Issue in Freud Researcher's High Court Libel Appeal," 1-13. Her "Courts Strain to Define Sex Harassment," 2-19, is a solid but surface discussion of different cases which have helped to define sexual harassment laws. She rather intuitively perceives the deep and divisive nature of the issue in "Court Splits on Coerced Confessions," 3-27, yet, seems lost in some of the more complex aspects of this, such as "harmless error." In the poorly organized "Supreme Court Agrees to Rule on Desegregation of Colleges," 4-16, she waits until the ninth paragraph to tell us what the court will be deciding in this case, getting all the implications before we know the question at hand in United States vs. Mabus. She supplies a broad overview of how conservativism is now shaping the rulings of the court in her detailed but loose "Energized Conservativism Rules High Court," 6-30, trying to be more analytic, but she seems only to be listing cases. Her "Self-Made Conservative," 7-2, is a well-done biography of Clarence Thomas, Marcus adroitly portraying his background and the major influences on his character: "Thomas's career is pervaded by an insistence that he be judged on his own merits and a seeming horror at the thought of special treatment because of his race." In "How Thomas, Conservatives Are at Odds," 8-14, she gives an adequate update in which the most important bit of information concerns further discussion of original intent, from documents written by Clarence Thomas. Marcus's "Divided Committee Refuses to Endorse Judge Thomas," 9-28, a satisfying breakdown of who voted which way and why, focuses on Joe Biden, chairman of the committee and, coincidentally, the swing vote. Marcus calmly and professionally related the events of the hearings, losing none of the drama, with "Supreme Court Nominee Calls Judiciary Process a Lynching," 10-12, and "Attacks on Thomas's Accuser Intensify," 10-13.

Martz, Larry. *Newsweek.* (★)
Contributing editor. As in previous years, Martz has all the earmarks of being a quite competent reporter, but he can't seem to stop interjecting his own small asides; sometimes snide, sometimes poignant. In "What Happened in Palm Beach?" with Peter Katel 4-15, the team chalks up one more Kennedy scandal, an overview as good as can be expected, though closing with "But it's hard to see any happy ending. Once again, the patriarch has no trousers." Martz's "Legal Sleaze in Palm Beach," 4-22, debates the press accusing the alleged victim of the William Kennedy Smith rape case as being loose, with this update spreading the sleaze around some more, but thankfully not adding to it. He provides a surprisingly balanced report on the conspiracy theory of the "October surprise" in "A Reagan Bargain With Iran?" with Jane Whitmore 4-29. Martz doesn't indict, but appropriately notes that perhaps this is a question which should be examined. Martz details the chief of staff's airline junkets in "The 'Air Sununu' Flap," 5-6, never mentioning that Sununu was following procedure according to the current White House rules. Staying with the story, "Headed for the Exit," with Ann McDaniel and Thomas DeFrank 7-1, the team looks at the situation as if Sununu were gone already. This is a vivid insider peek at the "Air Sununu" ruckus, with all parties, from *The Washington Post* to *Los Angeles Times,* getting their nod in the chief of staff's forthcoming downfall. His subdued "Who Says There's No Free Lunch?" with Eleanor Clift 10-14, avoids the cynical tone that he's so famous for in this overview of the House banking flap, detailing the check-kiting and Foley's attempt to head off other potential ethics problems. He offers a haphazard dispatch on the press and how times have changed in the perfunctory "Toppling the Last Taboos," with Paul McKelvey 10-28, just tapping the vein with a listing of forbidden words and issues over the years.

Massing, Michael. *Columbia Journalism Review.* (★★★)
Contributing editor to *CJR* and contributor to a host of other publications, Massing's globetrotting gives a wide-ranging perspective to his reports that others only dream about. Although he drops from sight from time to time, we're always pleased when his byline resurfaces. His "Is the Most Popular Evening Newscast the Best?" *CJR* 3/4-91, is a perceptive comparison/contrast of the big three network news programs, where Massing goes behind the camera to bring us the personalities off-screen who shape the news. A little perspective might have helped "A Harvard Man's Crimson Record," *The Washington Post* 6-2, this "Outlook" essay calculated to provoke outrage over the presence of Gen. Hector Gramajo, a former Guatemalan defense minister, in this year's graduating class at Harvard University's Kennedy School of Government. Massing portrays him as the first official with blood on his hands to study at the behest of the U.S. government. His "The Salvation of Panama?" *The New York Review of Books* 6-13, is a review of Kevin Buckley's book *Panama: The Whole Story,* and is essentially a critique of U.S. policy toward that country both before and after the '89 invasion, with Massing caustically contending that "In a sense, the invasion cut short Panamanians' apprenticeship in democratic practice." In "Sitting on Top of the News," *NYRB* 6-27, Massing gives a dead-on critical review of Bob Woodward's *The Commanders,* sharply zeroing in on a growing defect exhibited by the media in the book: "The road from Watergate to the Gulf War is marked by ever greater cautiousness, and opportunism, on the part of the press." Massing journeys to Iraq in "Can Saddam Survive?" *NYRB* 8-15, following in the footsteps of Milton Viorst of *The New Yorker,* (Baghdad, Kurdish territory, Karbala), and disagrees with Viorst's assessment of Saddam's ability to stay in power. Massing tries to avoid sweeping judgments, basing his conclusions on firsthand observations, including his observations that much of the pro-American feeling in the immediate aftermath of the war is dissipating as the sanctions continue.

Mathews, Jay. *The Washington Post.* (★★★)
West Coast. Mathews seems rejuvenated by the competition Lou Cannon's move to California has brought to the Los Angeles bureau. Back to doing the weighty and detailed features which first caught our eye, Mathews provides vigorous and vivid pictures of West Coast life. His lively "Escape From L.A.: Antelope Valley Towns Surge," 1-29, is a marvelous feature on Antelope Valley growth with the lead drawing us in: "On one side of Lancaster Boulevard is utter desolation. . .On the other side of this narrow road is a shiny, bustling Wal-Mart. . .This is how California grows." Mathews scripts a lively and informative profile of the new Governor of Alaska, Walter Joseph Hickel in "Independent and Unconventional," 2-23, bringing this unorthodox and no-nonsense character to life. He writes a baroque "Outlook" essay on California's decline as a trendsetter for other state governments and Washington in "Golden State in Dry Dock," 3-10, blaming it on the state's growing tendency to govern through ballot initiative. Mathews provides a well-flavored slice of life in the absorbing feature, "The Soviet Balladeer's Inhospitable Treatment," 5-31, which recounts the Soviet Bob Dylan, Bulat Okudzhava, and his brush with U.S. hospitals and their billing system — pay up front. His delightful "For Math Teacher Jaime Escalante, A Calculated Move," 6-14, is a vivid and detailed portrait of the teacher from "Stand and Deliver" who moved from Sacramento to Santa Barbara because, among other things, his wife liked "the cleaner air and the absence of malathion-spraying against the Mediterranean fruit fly." He provides a smart unsensationalized dissection of a report on force used by the LAPD "L.A. Police Probe Cites Bias, Misuse of Force," 7-10, Mathews professionally detached over this hot issue. He recounts the wild story of gunman Richard Worthington who held a nursery hostage in "Nurse Tells of Terror in Utah Hospital Siege," 9-23, and though strange stuff for the front page, Mathews tells it breathlessly. He reports on more trouble at the LAPD in "4 Slayings by L.A. Police Officers Create Little Public Furor," 10-2, but doesn't offer enough detail on these horribly descriptive cases for the article to be compelling.

Matlack, Carol. *National Journal.* (★ ½)
Staff correspondent. Although Matlack keeps Beltway inhabitants in the know with her reliable coverage of the lobbyists, she seldom probes the deeper ethical issues inherent in many of her subjects. She sharply questions the possibility of real campaign finance reform in "Congressional Slush," 1-12: "In the roughly 15 years that House & Senate candidates have been filing campaign finance reports with the FEC, public attention has focused mostly on the sources of campaign cash, not on how it is spent." Matlack details in "New Lobbying Team at Home Builders," 2-3, that the National Association of Home Builders has expanded its congressional affairs staff to six lobbyists to "forge stronger links between association members and their state congressional delegations," but unfortunately she doesn't delve too deeply into the implications of such a maneuver. She dutifully notes in "Massachusetts Plots Another Miracle," 4-6, that Paul Tsongas, the former Mass. senator who quit politics six years ago after learning he had cancer, expects to declare his candidacy for the Democratic presidential nomination, a perfunctory report telling us very little about the nature of his candidacy. In "Marketing Ideas," 6-22, she writes that the approximately 100 non-profit policy research groups, or think tanks, are shedding the role of dispassionate scholar and coming to the table with detailed policy agendas and strong ideological stands. She never raises the question as to whether new marketing plans force them to take a stand their donors want to hear. Matlack provides a good balance on the pros and cons of being a congressional wife in the D.C. job market with "Connected Couples," 7-20, but never addresses the ethical issues of being a paid lobbyist for NYNEX, when a spouse is a "powerful" member of the subcommittee deciding telecommunications legislation. Her "Animal Rights Furor," 9-7, is a haphazard treatment in which Matlack really only provides a list of who's doing what on both sides of the equation, animal-rights groups and the National Association for Biomedical Research.

McGee, Jim. *The Washington Post.* (★ ★)
Investigations. Unlike many in the press who were intimidated by the byzantine nature of the BCCI/First American scandal, McGee got on the story early and stayed with it, offering clear, credible updates. His "Who Controls First American Bankshares?" 2-3, is a broad overview of the beginnings of BCCI and its relationship with D.C.'s First American, but his uncorroborated information is a bit suspect, leaving us wondering what he culled from earlier *Post* interviews. He does provide new information on the scandal in his sweeping overview, "Allegations About 1st American Lay Dormant for Years," 3-31, providing a good history of what happened, where the press fell short, and where it shined. The *Post* conspicuously comes off clean. His "Regulators Chastise 1st American of D.C.," co-written with Jerry Knight 4-19, is a well-developed summary of the report by federal banking regulators rating First American, with some trim background included. In "Fed Seeks to Expand Its Power Over Foreign Banks in the U.S.," 5-10, he provides an enlightening breakdown of the Riegle-Garn proposal to close some of the loopholes which came to light in the BCCI case, but his lack of specificity isn't repaired until the close of the piece. His solid update, "Fed Rejects Foreign Bank's Slow Stock Sell-Off Plan," 6-10, is as much on the future of BCCI as that of First American, and despite the title, it's First American about which McGee is most concerned. McGee turns "Regulators in 5 Nations Seize BCCI," 7-6, into a conventional listing of the First American story, rather than concentrating on the repercussions for BCCI or world banking and detailing the specifics on the fraud involved. He highlights shortcomings in international banking communications in "BCCI's Stake in First American Known in '88," 9-13, retelling how the Bank of England knew of BCCI's secretly financed stock purchases in First American in 1988, but never getting to why this miscommunication occurred. His "FBI Checks: 'Thorough, Impartial,' " 10-8, is occasioned by the Anita Hill-Clarence Thomas flap with the FBI defending its ability to do an investigation, but McGee tells us nothing we didn't know from previous dispatches.

McGurn, William. *National Review.* (★ ★)
Washington bureau chief. McGurn provides serviceable congressional updates, but doesn't seem to have the same high level sources at the White House that Fred Barnes of *The New Republic*

does. He generally tints his reports with more strictly conservative analysis than we'd like to see. His "Beltway Battles," 2-25, an unsurprising survey of the domestic political impact of the Gulf War, is a nice summation on the decline of Sam Nunn following his vote against the use of force: ". . .Nunn showed he was as much a Democrat as Howard Metzenbaum or Teddy Kennedy, which is to say someone good for getting an outmoded tank contract or new jobs program for his district but not to be trusted with the more critical responsibilities of Executive office." In "New American Order," 4-1, he writes one more roll call of the politicians and pundits who turned out to be wrong about the Gulf War, from liberal Democratic congressmen to conservative columnists, with nothing really new, but it is one of the livelier efforts we've seen from McGurn in a while. He churns out a bland report on the controversy over NYU professor Carol Iannone's nomination to the National Endowment for Humanities in "Borking the Humanities," 6-10, typical of the second and third tier topics on which McGurn seems to concentrate and in which conservatives apparently are interested. He tries to predict what Robert Strauss's nomination as ambassador to Moscow portends for U.S. policy toward the Soviet Union in "Bush Democrats," 7-8, one of McGurn's more interesting efforts. There is little new in "The Trials of Clarence Thomas," 8-12, though his perfunctory report on the political fallout of the Thomas nomination does pass along one telling vignette from Thomas's courtesy calls on the Hill, where "legions of black secretaries and working people [came] out of their offices to shake his hand and offer encouragement — many coming out of liberal offices." His critical "Bush's Slow Reaction," 9-23, documents the Bush administration's support for Gorbachev and its lack of support for Soviet democrats and nationalist leaders, with McGurn worried that the pattern is still holding.

McQueen, Michel. *The Wall Street Journal.* (★)
White House. Although much of McQueen's portfolio remains simplistic and superficial, we saw more signs of promise, leading us to believe she may simply be on the wrong beat. Her terrific leder, "A Little Boost: Kinder and Gentler? Bush Policies Do Help at One Family Shelter," 7-22, profiles a shelter helped by Bush policy, Holy Family in Indiana, McQueen offering a detailed and moving glimpse into the lives of the inhabitants. In "Polled Americans Strongly Support Gulf War, Even Beyond Goals of U.N. Mandate on Kuwait," 1-25, she provides a relatively lifeless breakdown of a *WSJ*/NBC News poll. Her "Americans, More Optimistic About the Economy, Have Become Less Eager for Federal Remedies," 3-22, gives simplistic detail to a *WSJ*/NBC News poll on the economy, little of what is presented here supporting her title. McQueen recounts the apparent flip-flops by President Bush over civil rights legislation in "Besides Congress's Fight Over a Civil-Rights Bill, There's a Battle of the Bushes: George vs. George," 4-18, with little new information here to make it necessary. Her "Critique of Sununu's Plane Use Draws Audience From Among Many Enemies," 4-24, is a well-written piece on Sununu's free rides, but late, coming Wednesday following the weekend stories, and McQueen equivocates when assessing Sununu's chances of recovery. In "A Heartbeat Away: Has Quayle Learned Enough in Two Years? The Public Is Skeptical," co-written by Gerald F. Seib 5-7, the pair lists the things the Vice President's done in a useful overview of Quayle's accomplishments, but says little of the "public" mentioned in the title. Her "Polled Voters Say Quayle Could Grow Into Job of President and Is Not a Drag on GOP Ticket," 5-16, is a split-personality piece between the public and the strategists who "say the wide-spread anxieties about his qualifications and skill won't be calmed overnight," with all this contrary to public opinion polls. McQueen teams up with Andy Pasztor for "Slimming Down," 9-30, an early and cohesive appraisal of Bush's arms-reduction plan, but it seems apparent Pasztor handled the sophisticated information on defense and McQueen simply reported on a poll.

Moore, W. John. *National Journal.* (★ ½)
Law. Moore is still incisive on the war on drugs, giving us his best work in that arena, though on strictly legal issues, he's become uncharacteristically dry. Moore begins the year with "Bush's Most Improved Player?" 1-12, where he neatly displays how then-Attorney General Dick Thornburgh recovered from a slow start to become the rising star of the administration and his

precise examples contribute to the report's fluidity. He is adept at sensing and categorizing the shift at the margin in the war against drugs from the casual to the hard-core user in "Rethinking Drugs," 2-2, yet the big picture, including political infighting, is blurred. His "Dueling by Telephone," 2-23, simply reports how Fleet Call Inc.'s melee with the cellular telephone industry at the FCC was a battle of Washington heavyweights, but he never properly states the issue at hand and only lists a "who's who" of those involved. Moore takes a focused look at the sophisticated, multi-million dollar lobbying business involved in the issue of abortion in "Abortion Wars," 3-16, providing a good example of the National Abortion Rights Action League's power in the fight against Bork's nomination. His "Prosecutor, Heal Thyself," 3-23, is a penetrating analysis of Jeffrey Tobin's kiss-&-tell book on the Iran-contra investigation, *Opening Arguments.* As a young member of Walsh's prosecutorial team, Tobin says, "Prosecutors thinking broadly put all of us at peril. . .jeopardized the whole edifice of the law." Moore accurately notes in "Court's Right Turn Shakes Congress," 7-6, that the Supreme Court does follow election returns: "In the long-run, public opinion registers itself in the election of Presidents. And they appoint Justices." This precise analysis concurs with the prevailing conservativism of the Bush administration. He provides a nice evaluation of the general council's office on certain bits of legislation in "The True Believers," 8-17, but since no one would talk to him from C. Boyden Gray's office, the article, on the whole, is rather limp. His "In Whose Court?" 10-5, has states overturning some Supreme Court decisions as the mood of the High Court becomes more federalist, a compendium of cases that's rather mindnumbing.

Moss, J. Jennings. *The Washington Times.* (★)
Congress. While Moss does occasionally exhibit an eye for detail that we appreciate, he rarely digs beneath the surface of an issue. His quick year-opener "Iraq Crisis Overshadows Other Concerns on Hill," 1-2, was merely a serviceable overview of the agenda for 1991 in Congress. The information-lacking dispatch "Jockeying Begins on Civil Rights Bill," 2-7, has a dry press release feel as it reports party maneuvering for the upper hand on civil rights. Moss delivers a credible recap of the Moynihan social security vote, "Senate Defeats Moynihan Bill," 4-25, and though he notes the "unusual alliances" produced by the particulars of Moynihan's plan, he never explains in detail the reason for the alliances. Moss gets some good quotes from the floor debates in "House Rejects Bush's Civil Rights Measure," 6-5, but this accounting of the fight over the different versions of the civil rights bill still lags from little detailed analysis. His tepid "Liberals Fear Future Court," 7-1, culls most of its information from other sources, such as CNN, ABC and *The New York Times,* with Moss filching from the rich and giving it to us poorly. Another report that barely rises above press release level is "Skinner Wants Drug Testing for Transit Workers," 8-29, with the lack of attention to detail hampering this piece on the N.Y. Dept. of Transportation and the question of random drug testing. He adequately recounts the events at a freshmen congressional news conference in "Bad Checks: Foley Asked to List Names," 9-27, noting the freshmen are clearly not subservient to the incumbents, but he short-circuits the article by failing to fully explore why Democrat Tom Foley wanted to keep the congressional check bouncers secret. His micro look at voter discontent, via New Hampshire, "Democrats Hunt Down Right Path in New Hampshire," 10-8, has Moss saying the populous is open to anything non-Bush, primarily on economic issues, an atmospheric report, but vague on serious complaints.

Murray, Frank J. *The Washington Times.* (★ ½)
White House. While Murray is beginning to probe a bit deeper, as he did when covering the Reagan White House, he still seldom gets to the meticulous detail. At the close of many of his dispatches, we note the qualifier that wire service reports are used as sources, leading us to believe he just doesn't have the contacts in this administration. Marlin Fitzwater's assertion that Saddam Hussein was fighting a PR battle rings true in Murray's "Saddam Winning War of Words," 2-12, one of the few places we saw this report played up, particularly in context of the Gorbachev and subsequent Soviet peace initiatives. His "Bush, Mitterrand Deadlock on PLO," 3-15, skillfully utilizes an appropriate selection of quotes to convey a sharp sense of how Bush

diplomatically checked the French President on the PLO and a Palestinian state. Murray gives us more inside information on the 30-minute phone call during the Gulf War in "Bush Rebuffs ANC Leader," 3-19. While the official line was that Bush "indicated areas of disagreement with ANC views," Murray reports that the President delivered a long, angry and sharp rebuff to Mandela. He recounts a golf course news conference in which Bush defends himself on U.S. failure to aid the rebel factions within Iraq in "Bush Insists He Didn't Mislead Iraqi Dissidents," 4-5. Murray's "Bush Seeks to Keep China Trade Status," 5-27, previews the President's message to Congress on reasons for extending most-favored-nation trading status to China again, competently presenting the White House position on the issue despite routine reporting. Although he shies away from the analytic in "Bush Appoints Democrat," 6-5, he still provides a vivid account of the Strauss appointment to the Moscow ambassadorship, Murray really capturing the mood: "an added plus was Mr. Strauss' expertise in trade, likely to be a growing issue in U.S.-Soviet relations." He offers some substantive detail on a forthcoming Bush speech to the U.N. in "U.N to Hear Bush Views on Realigned World," 9-23.

Muwakkil, Salim. *In These Times.* (★ ★ ½)
A senior editor at the trim socialist tabloid out of Chicago, Muwakkil fashions taut, intriguing dispatches on various racial issues. Always intelligent and original, he is quickly becoming the Joe Klein of the left on this topic. His "Fashion Fatalities and Other Deadly Legacies," 1-23/29, is a socio-economic dissection of the killing of black, inner-city kids for clothing and jewelry, where Muwakkil presents some intriguing analyses and includes preliminary mechanisms for a solution. He scripts a pensive examination of the divisions of the Black Muslims in the U.S. over action in the Persian Gulf in "Peaceful Desires Unite Religious Blacks," 2-6/12, his cautious tone avoiding a diatribe, and probing the issues carefully. In "The Racist Reality of Police Culture," 3-27/4-2, he writes less about Rodney Glen King and the endemic use of brute force in the police departments across the nation than radical reaction to it, but his lack of cohesion leaves too many stray threads. His "PUSHing for Survival Without Jesse Jackson," 4-3/9, is a stylishly-written dispatch on the latest upheaval at People United to Serve Humanity, but we would have liked the policies and personnel at PUSH more deeply explored. He provides a forthright, resilient criticism from the left of the left-liberal orthodoxy for having "stifled debate on racial issues" in "Race, Class & Candor," 5-22/28. Muwakkil is not throwing in the towel to conservatives, but instead declaring the necessity for the left to eschew "political correctness" and seek new approaches — "even if they are called 'new paradigms.' " A shimmering "New Trends in Brutality from Chicago's Finest," 7-10/23, details an Amnesty International issues report on the Chicago police, where, after an investigation by the city's Office of Professional Standards and documentation of electroshock, little has been done. His perceptive and informative "Thomas Nomination Resuscitates Dialectic," 8-7/20, views the Thomas nomination to the Supreme Court through the prism of his earlier discussion on the politics of race and the growing gap between self-help and handouts.

Mydans, Seth. *The New York Times.* (★ ★)
Los Angeles. Much of Mydans's time this year was devoted to pursuing the Rodney Glen King case, where he provided clear, if not always timely coverage. He tended to take credited material from the hometown *Los Angeles Times,* which had better access to police reports and officials involved in the investigation. Mydans provides sufficient detail in "Tape of Beating by Police Revives Charges of Racism," 3-7, pulling together quotes from a variety of sources to indicate a problem endemic to the LAPD, but he doesn't concretely prove it. A well-organized "News Analysis" essay, "In Los Angeles, Gridlock at the Top," 4-11, on the Bradley-Gates confrontation, has Mydans noting that "In this city where the Mayor is by charter politically limited in his ability to hire and dismiss department heads like the police chief, all parties to the political struggle have come up against the limits of their power." Mydans's features remain compelling, moving without being maudlin, although he seldom attempts to make his subjects universal. He quills a lackluster "One Last Deadly Crossing for Illegal Aliens," 1-7, on Mexicans crossing California highways in this P. 1, below-the-fold feature. His atmospheric "Civics 101

on Tape in Arizona, Or, 'We All Have Our Prices,' " 2-11, has legislators taking bribes on camera, the sting netting seven lawmakers and eleven others, with still more indictments on the way. His "As Cultures Meet, Gang War Paralyzes a City in California," 5-6, supplies little of substantive value in a them-vs.-us story involving the Cambodians and Mexicans in Long Beach. In "Reports Put Twist on Motorist Saga," 6-7, Mydans gets much of his information from police reports from the *LAT* and other press accounts, but he pulls together well this serviceable piece on Rodney King trying to run down some undercover cops. He writes an intriguing article on how private sponsors have created Biosphere 2 in "8 Seek Better World in 2-Year Ecology Project," 9-27, yet Mydans doesn't quite get the reasoning behind the project. His delightfully tongue-in-cheek "Taylor's 8th: Familiar Role, New Lead," 10-7, makes the most of covering Liz Taylor's wedding, especially the guest list where he notes how many times each guest has been married.

Nazario, Sonia L. *The Wall Street Journal.* (★ ★)
Social issues, healthcare and education. Nazario has yet to match the work she did on affirmative action two years ago, for which she received a 10 Best in Business Reporting. Her beats are so varied that she seems wearied by the unrelated streams of information she must monitor to stay on top of each. Good background on the campaign by state health department director Kenneth Kizer urging state universities to divest holdings in tobacco companies "California Widens Attack on Cigarettes," 1-30, is a nicely rounded piece that even features the future plans of the campaign. In "LA Law: A Videotaped Beating Highlights Problems of Los Angeles Police," co-written by David Jefferson 3-12, the couple details strong-arm tactics of the LAPD, pre-and post-Rodney Glen King, assertively written, well-structured and cohesive on the many allegations. Nazario isn't given enough space to fully explore the novelty of "It Comes Too Late for Most of Us to Get Even for Those Ds in Math," 3-19, on an imaginative program featuring Professor Richard B. Chase who will teach you Management of Service Operations at USC or your money back. She provides a nice history of California's program to spark debate and discussion on religions in "Religion Is Returning to Public Schools," 5-1, Nazario carefully walking the line between reporting and advocacy, but never crossing it. Her "Report on Los Angeles Police Department Finds Racism, Suggests Changes, Gates's Resignation," co-written by David J. Jefferson 7-10, is a good breakdown of the commission report which outlines the problems of the LAPD. In her B1 feature, "Swimming Pools Do Attract Pests You Can't Tell Easily to Buzz Off," 8-28, she bemoans the overabundance of bees in pools in Scottsdale, Arizona and leaves us wondering what this piece is doing in the *Journal.* She effectively covers the medical merger in "Health-Care Firms to Be Purchased in $77 Million Deal," 9-4, in which Community Psychiatric Centers acquires Healthcare International Inc. and HealthVest Inc. In "Relaxation Classes Rile Many Parents," 10-7, she mulls over the pros and cons of teaching kids how to relax via New Age techniques, though Nazario never explores other methods that she mentions here.

Nelson, Jack. *Los Angeles Times.* (★ ★)
Washington bureau chief. Nelson drifts in and out of our purview, some years accumulating a substantial body of work, others hardly appearing on the paper's pages. We see little of the carelessness of earlier days as Nelson provided crisp evaluations and rounded overviews in one of his more prolific years, certainly the best since we have been reviewing his material. He delivers a balanced report in "Yeutter's Attack on Democrats Stirs Up Political Firestorm," co-written by William J. Eaton 1-25, but doesn't have anything more than Yeutter saying that Democrats will have to run for cover come election time because of the Persian Gulf War. His update, "Land War Timing Up to Military, Bush Says," 2-6, is surprisingly rounded on Bush's leaving the ground war up to the generals. Nelson supplies a nice breakdown as to voters identifying themselves as either Democrats or Republicans in "GOP Preferred by 36% to 29%, New Poll Finds," 3-22, though unfortunately there's little of any analytic value. He doesn't delve deep enough in "Cuomo to Challenge Bush Policies on Domestic Issues," 4-26, there being so much more he could have pursued in the interview to clarify Cuomo's thinking on a host of

issues, from economic policy to foreign affairs. His article, "Bush to 'Go for Excellence' in Filling High Court Seat," 6-29, is a sharply-defined and clearly-written piece on the options, politically and legalwise, in choosing Thurgood Marshall's successor. He presents a solid discussion of the Soviet suggestion of U.S.-U.S.S.R. participation in setting up a Middle East peace conference in "Soviets Offer Joint Mideast Peace Trip," co-written by Jim Mann 7-30, Nelson giving a good roundup on the fragile peace conference. In "Bush Praises Union Treaty in Restive Ukraine," 8-2, he gives plenty of detail on the itinerary and the speech to the Supreme Soviet of the Ukrainian Soviet Socialist Republic, but we don't find out precisely the terms and conditions of the Unity agreement. Nelson provides no smoking gun in "Boren's Role in Efforts for Gates Questioned," co-written by Michael Ross 10-9, where they report there is some question as to whether David Boren was behind the campaign to drum up support for CIA nominee Robert Gates or if it was Brent Scowcroft's idea.

Noah, Timothy. *The Wall Street Journal.* (★ ★)
Housing, urban affairs and civil rights. Noah had his best year yet, now clearly settled into the daily grind of the Washington bureau. He shows none of the snideness we saw during his tenures at *Newsweek* and *The New Republic,* his reports cleanly and articulately presented, though less analytic than we'd like. Noah seems to accentuate the negative in "Bush 'Empowerment' Self-Help Plans for the Poor Could Prove as Costly as Any Proposal by Liberals," 1-30. His "Governors, Harried by Medicaid Costs, Point Their Fingers at Rep. Waxman," 2-4, discusses governors dealing with Medicaid as the fastest growing single item in the state budget, Noah doing a fine job of balancing, with no liberal or conservative bias noticeable. He provides a good, though light, portrait in "Connecticut's Gov. Weicker Aspires to Initiate an Income Tax and Revels in the Sound and Fury," 3-26, a nice political appraisal marred only by Noah not tackling the economic implications involved in the tax. The debate in "Job Tests Scored on Racial Curve Stir Controversy," 4-26, is outlined well as he tries to clear up the idea of "race-norming" as "ranked on a percentile basis in comparison only with the performance of others in the same ethnic group." In "Washington Riots Spotlight Tensions Between District Hispanics and Blacks," 5-9, Noah highlights the problems that have plagued N.Y. and Miami for ages, which now hit D.C. He supplies decent background, but the lack of a feasible solution detracts from this adequately reported piece. He provides sharp census analysis in "U.S. Population Grew Less White in the '80s as Hispanics, Asians Boosted Presence," 6-12, with all you really need to know, although the title seems a peculiar angle from which to approach this topic. In "Mosbacher, While Admitting Undercount of Minorities, Won't Adjust 1990 Census," 7-16, Noah presents a broad range of views here on Commerce Secretary Mosbacher's decision, but he doesn't tell us what led up to it. In his leder "Throttling Down: Instead of Tax Rises, Michigan Tries to Cure Deficit With Cutbacks," 10-30, Noah gives a strong analysis of Michigan Gov. John Engler's attempts to break a tradition of "big government" by reining in spending.

O'Rourke, P. J. *The American Spectator, Rolling Stone.* (★ ★ ½)
O'Rourke's book, *Parliament of Whores: A Lone Humorist Attempts to Explain the Entire U.S. Government,* released this year, spent numerous weeks on the best-seller list. He spent most of the year sarcastically chewing up liberals and taking focus on major topics, including the Gulf War. O'Rourke does an admirable job of covering the war, miles from the front in "Club Scud: Cheap Gas and Sober Journalists," *RS* 3-7. He details the essence of the conflict as ". . .the Gog and Magog of hacker networks, the devil's own personal core dump." He offers more hilarious dispatches from Saudi Arabia in "No Sex, No Drugs, Only Rock & Roll," *RS* 3-21, accenting it with his own brand of wry humor: "The dirty little secret of this war is that we all privately hoped the Israelis would get fed up with being Scud-whipped and drop the big one, fusing the sands of Iraq into one vast sheet of glass so we could go in there and finish this thing with Windex." O'Rourke's best work out of the Gulf War "Hoo-Ah!" *RS* 5-2, features his observations on the liberation of Kuwait and the chaotic aftermath, including a look at Iraq's defensive strategy which led to its defeat. "In Defense of Defense," *TAS* 5-91, an adaption from O'Rourke's new book, has O'Rourke defending U.S. defense spending, drawing on the U.S.

invasion of Panama and his two-day visit aboard a guided-missile cruiser: "But the best and final argument against cutting defense [is] the involuntary smile that comes across the face of every male when he has a weapon in hand." His cover story "Commies-Dead But Too Dumb to Lie Down," *TAS* 11-91, has P.J. back with *TAS*'s 3rd annual "Joe McCarthy Memorial New Enemies List," once again based on reader submissions, though in his introduction, O'Rourke snidely insists on kicking liberals when they're down.

Ostrow, Ronald J. *Los Angeles Times.* (★ ★)
Justice/FBI. Ostrow seemed revitalized, reporting the myriad issues with a vigor that had been absent for the past few years. He regularly provides well-focused detail, and at least gives us a sense of the broader picture. The unnamed sources are excusable in "Israel Lacked U.S. Codes to Protect Its Jets," co-written by Robin Wright 1-22, where they explain: "The withholding of the codes indicates that the Bush Administration may have used more than pleas and promises. . .to persuade the Israelis not to strike back. . ." His informative "Column One" piece, "The Mob Against the Ropes," 2-9, gives us much on La Cosa Nostra that we've read before, but the topic always keeps us until the end. In "Bush Calls for Quick Passage of Bill That Expands Death Penalty, Limits Appeals," 3-12, he gives a neatly defined account of what's in the bill, who's for it and who's going to give it trouble, but we never really know the bill's chances for success. Ostrow doesn't adequately cover the big picture in "Colombia Seen Weakening Its Judiciary," 5-24, with his article featuring Martinez worrying about decisions of the National Assembly that will hamper the drug war. His "Ex-CIA Official Pleads Guilty in Iran-Contra Case," co-written by Michael Ross 7-10, is more official and efficiently reported than the *NYT* account, with Ross and Ostrow meticulously avoiding pointing accusing fingers at Gates, as the *NYT*'s Johnston has done consistently. In "Drug War Looks Like a Long One," co-written by Paul Richter 8-5, the team produces a strong, though quite lengthy, update on the War on Drugs, asking the right questions, but making no recommendations: interdiction or treatment? Ostrow and Richter do sketch some answers on international spying in "Economic Espionage Poses Major Peril to U.S. Interests," 9-28, where they keenly note: "Because of U.S. law and customs, American intelligence agencies do not pass on information they inadvertently come across to domestic companies that might stand to gain or lose from it." Ostrow gets the chronology down in "Doubts Raised on Quality of Thomas Investigation," 10-9, particularly in detailing Joe Biden's role, but he never asks the big question of who leaked the FBI report to the press.

Pear, Robert. *The New York Times.* (★ ★ ★)
Domestic policy. Always distinguished by his fine reporting skills, Pear has settled into this beat nicely after years of covering the State Department. We now turn to him first for intelligent reporting and discussion of health care policy issues that's sure to be a hot topic in the next year. He provides solid detail pulling State of the Union Address together in "Bush Speech to Urge Bank Law Changes," 1-29, hours before it occurs. Bills in both houses to protect the status of soldiers fighting in the Gulf are detailed in his solid "Congress Rushes to Pass Benefits for Gulf Veterans," 2-19, with accompanying graphics providing the detail, augmenting the political angles Pear covers. He writes as though Congress were doing the poor a favor in "Spurning Bush, Congress Provides New Money to Fight Infant Deaths," 3-26, detailing how Congress allotted $25 million for infant programs, without specifying "where the money would come from." He gives a sharp evaluation of the reasons behind the Medicaid-Medicare-private insurers gap in "Low Medicaid Fees Seen as Depriving Poor of Care," 4-2, and "Higher Fees for Doctors May Not Help Medicaid," 4-3, yet some topics were left unanswered, especially on how to develop a better system. He stays on the story and delivers a superlative breakdown of the Democratic plan to put a cap on health care costs in "Senate Democrats to Offer Plan to Restrain Health Care Costs," 5-25, though never addressing the more subtle problems inherent in the proposal. He isn't convincing portraying Clarence Thomas's go-with-the-flow attitude as indecision in "Court Nominee Defied Labels as Head of Job-Rights Panel," 7-16, Pear mainly reviewing the record of his chairmanship of the Equal Employment Opportunity Commission over eight years. In "Study Says Fees Are Often Higher When Doctor Has Stake in Clinic," 8-9, Pear reports

that a Florida study seems to confirm that his earlier dispatch on limiting the referrals doctors can make to clinics in which they have invested is right on target, rightly including doctors' defenses and qualifiers. The AMA gives in on the doctors' financial investment in clinics and labs and then recommending patients to them in "Doctors Warned on Conflicts of Interest," 9-4, a smart follow-up to his previous medical reports.

Perry, James M. *The Wall Street Journal.* (★ ★)
Washington. A long-time veteran of Washington politics, we appreciate Perry's experience and value his writing skill and reporting abilities, particularly as he gears up for the election year. His "Virginia's Wilder to Base Run for White House on Blend of Fiscal Conservatism and Compassion," 12-19-90, is a keen report on the hopes of likely Democrat VP candidate, Douglas Wilder. Though carefully reported, "When It Comes to Big Guns, Iraq Has Bigger, Better and More Than Allies," 2-5, seems to find Perry uncomfortable and out of his realm, talking to the established experts on the military to pull this piece on Iraqi artillery together. His "Congress Faces a Vote on Gun Control, Fearing Retaliation From Both Sides," 3-21, is tuned into the highly-charged atmosphere in Congress over the Brady bill, though he unfortunately meanders toward the end where he gives a lopsided example of NRA smear tactics. In "What Publishers Call Quoting, Computer Firms Call Piracy as Industries Face Off on Capitol Hill," 4-23, Perry details the fight over legislation pertaining to the use of unpublished sources, never quite managing to link the literary and software abuses within this question. Both Dems and Reps opine in "Pundits Give Democrats Little Chance of Winning the White House in 1992," 5-15, with Perry allowing them to attach an over-abundant amount of significance to the Gulf War instead of the economy and its direction. He provides an informative and well-written piece on term limitation in "Movement to Limit Lawmakers' Terms Revs Up and Heads Toward Congress," 7-17, yet Perry never focuses on the question of the effectiveness of term limitation as a solution to the corruption in Congress and the power of the lobbyists. His "Harkin, Wilder Join Presidential Race, Both Promising Challenges to the Status Quo," co-written by David Shribman 9-16, is a focused campaign kickoff piece that doesn't give an appraisal of the overall field, except as a list of candidates. He delivers a memorable opening in the short "As Cuomo Denies Publicly He Will Run, Many Think He's Privately Preparing," 10-14: "The patter of little feet on the Democratic presidential campaign trail may soon be joined by the crunching sound of Big Foot."

Piccoli, Sean. *The Washington Times.* (★ ★)
"Life!" writer. Piccoli hasn't yet developed his descriptive talents enough to provide a sense of the atmosphere in his features. His lively, bright snapshots show promise, but need fleshing out with background and color. His light "Quick-Sketch Titians Draw on Tourists to Florence," 1-2, is a jaunty piece on the street artists in Florence, where we get some sense of ambience, but Piccoli's lack of colorful description mars the article. He has tremendous fun with "I Dreamed I Saw Elvis Last Night," 2-12, in which he provides a hilarious vignette on the continuing fascination with Elvis Presley. In "GOP Glee," 3-26, Piccoli consults the usual GOP conservatives to make a case that Republicans are generally gloating over the outcome of the Persian Gulf War. He is careful to note, though, that Newt Gingrich told *Congressional Quarterly* that "If this victory is something that we try to stand pat on. . .frankly, we'll get killed in '92." His "The Ad Game," 5-6, is a good-natured feature on different promotions and contests companies use in order to promote their products, but rather light due to the absence of substantial economic data. Piccoli takes a quick look at what Clarence Thomas's neighbors think of the judge in "Neighbors Say Thomas Just Your 'Average' Guy," 7-8. He provides an atmospheric and lively profile of Alexandria banker Taylor Berke in "Birdman of Alexandria Is No Bird-Brained Banker," 9-24, the article's charm coming in part from Berke who travels to work and even testifies before Congress with his parrot.

Pisik, Betsy. *The Washington Times.* (★ ★ ½)
"Life!" writer. Pisik's consistently well-developed and sprightly features are a welcome addition to this section, which has languished long in the shadow of the *Post*'s "Style" section. Pisik lacks depth in "Gonzalez, the Fighting Pacifist," 1-25, perhaps due to space limitation, though otherwise, this quick, bright profile touches on both the personal and professional, pro and con, distilling enough information for an in-depth impression. She supplies an entertaining "life!" feature on Matthew Lesko in "Info Man," 2-13, a lively article on the man who compiles information disseminated free by the government, but which is not put together anywhere, except by him. Her "Jose Cuervo, You Sure Are a Friend to Local Charity," 3-8, is a civic-minded feature on Jose Cuervo tequila sponsoring a "Barcathlon" to benefit D.C.'s Multiple Sclerosis Society, a fluff piece, but nicely detailed on the clean events — thumb wrestling, etc. She provides an intriguing "Beach Magazine Making New Waves," 5-28, on a new beach publication *Beach Culture,* which addresses the intellectual and social life within the community and Pisik's description of it certainly lends weight to it being called the MTV of magazines. She delivers a charming feature on the creator of "Brenda Starr, Reporter," in "Glamorous Granny Recalls Her Famous, Daring Strip," 8-2, the piece delightfully vivid: "Back in 1940, women cartoonists were plenty desirable but not on the comics page. 'I would bring my drawings in,' Miss Messick remembers, 'and the editors would toss them aside and say [wolfishly] Let's have lunch.' " In "They Shoot Bosses, Don't They?" 9-31, Pisik sharply highlights incidences of workplace violence to draw a graphic portrait of the disgruntled worker who may turn dangerous. This becomes more compelling, as two weeks later another incident in northern New Jersey took the lives of four people by a fired co-worker.

Price, Joyce. *The Washington Times.* (★ ★)
General assignment. Price shows a rather impressive versatility because of the broad range of her beat. As she doesn't often have the chance to follow through with her dispatches, she makes every dispatch as complete and detailed as possible. The highly readable "American Sinners Pay Bigger Price Starting Today," 1-1, is a half tongue-in-cheek report on the new sin taxes, well detailed, though there's little on its economic impact. Price does a fine job of collecting details in "Law Seen Decreasing Teen Abortions, Births," 3-15, a story that others ignored or downplayed, by keeping the article balanced and soliciting and securing dissenting points of view from Planned Parenthood in regard to this Minnesota law. Her "NEA Film Flap Gets Brushoff," co-written by George Archibald 4-3, has too many unnamed aides in this quick dispatch on the National Endowment of the Arts support of the controversial film "Poison," though one named aide, Kerry Knott of Rep. Richard Armey's office, wryly notes: "If the NEA would be honest with people, they'd change their name to National Endowment for Bad Art." She delivers another sterling report on the abortion issue in "Clinics to Enforce Ban on Abortion Counseling," 5-30, eminently professional, never tipping her hand as to the pro-life, or pro-choice groups. In "Pro-Life Bills Gain in States," 6-10, she uses the latest anti-abortion bill to go to the governor's office, this time in Louisiana, as a springboard to launch into a discussion of where the pro-life movement is now. We found this valuable information that no one else seemed to be covering. In "Schools' War on Drugs Pays Homage to Drag Queens," co-written by George Archibald 7-25, the pair gets solid information on allegations that a N.Y. program called Youth Enrichment Services has used federal funds to have gay social events. She never moves into the economic realm, instead solely exploring the demographics in "Study Cites Gain in Affluent Blacks," 8-9, Price painstakingly fair in examining both the gains and the shortfalls of blacks via the Population Reference Bureau. The abundant detail in "Pro-Lifers See Hope in State Hoppers," 9-16, never really fleshes out this recount of which states may return to pre-Roe v. Wade status, or have bills pending along those lines.

Putka, Gary. *The Wall Street Journal.* (★)
Education. At a time when so many large issues are being debated on this beat, Putka seldom gets beyond the multitude of statistics on various aspects of the education system. He continues to provide trim, but impersonal, reports which break no new ground. He writes a comparison

of the NYC public and Catholic school systems in "New York Archdiocese Begins Campaign to Save 140 Catholic Schools in City," 1-30, leaving us wondering how its outcome fits into the larger issues facing national education. He follows up the story giving us an eye-opening report on how the Catholic schools get better results in "Back to Basics: Education Reformers Have New Respect for Catholic Schools," 3-28, supplying sharp detail, but an odd choice for a leder. Putka's unfocused "Combatting Gangs: As Fears Are Driven From the Classroom, Students Start to Learn," 4-23, is a scattershot leder on how the Compton, California, school is dealing with gang violence. He makes no judgment of Chris Whittle's plan to operate schools for profit in "Whittle Develops Plan to Operate Schools for Profit," 5-15, the details of the plan too nebulous for us to decide as the specifics hadn't yet been announced. His densely written "Academic Barter: A Professor Swapped Degrees for Contracts, University Suspects," 7-12, presents Prof. Frost at U. of Texas, which is intertwined with his research firm and contracts with NASA. In "Concern Goes Up as SAT Scores Go Down," 8-27, Putka provides appalling detail on what today's students don't know, with little questioning of the methods of reform possible, either of the tests themselves or with the system. His "Florida Schools to Put Cultural Literacy to Test," 9-5, is curiously sterile as it discusses E. D. Hirsch's book, and its application in Florida schools. We never get a sense of being in the classroom where it's put to the test, but do get a good outline of the updating of Hirsch's ideas.

Reinhold, Robert. *The New York Times.* (★ ★ ★)
Los Angeles bureau chief. Although not a California native, Reinhold has a sharp grasp of state politics and important issues, such as water rights, that he developed over the past three years in this post. No other reporter at an East coast daily can match his coverage of the Golden State. In "State of States, 1991: Rocky Almost Everywhere," 1-14, Reinhold assembles a sharp picture of the pressures within various states to deal with economic recession: ". . .even liberal Democrats like Gov. Mario Cuomo of New York. . .talk like fiscal conservatives." Reinhold offers "Drought Forces Cutoff of Water to Vast Farmlands in California," 2-5, where we get information solely on what this will do to the alfalfa crop and projections of farmers about further planting and spring irrigation. In "Charges Sought in Los Angeles Beating," 3-8, Reinhold presents a dignified, taut dispatch on L.A. Police Chief Daryl Gates seeking a felony charge against the cops who beat up Rodney Glen King. He pens a neat profile cum appraisal of Gates's ability to stay in office in "Fate of Police Chief in Los Angeles Is Vigorously Debated After Beating," 3-14, Reinhold probing all the angles, with no attempt at a definitive conclusion. His "Battle Lines Drawn in Sand as Las Vegas Covers Water," 4-23, a richly detailed report on the conflict over dwindling water resources and rapid growth, is finely balanced as Reinhold resists bashing the resort industry, noting 90% of water goes to agriculture, with only 6000 people employed and $168 million in revenues. Reinhold uses the budget situation in California as a springboard for examining the conditions in eight other states in "California Misses Deadline on Budget," 7-2, the peripheral information adding little to our knowledge, but providing a useful update. He provides an intriguing article on Jerry Brown and his announcement to form an exploratory committee for his candidacy for president in "Ex-California Governor to Seek the Presidency," 9-4. Reinhold details the changing demographic patterns in California in "They Came to California for the Good Life; Now They're Looking Elsewhere," 10-16, but he places too many dry statistics up front, leaving good anecdotes for the windup too many readers never reach.

Richardson, Valerie. *The Washington Times.* (★)
West coast, out of San Francisco, general assignment. Richardson persists in filing quirky offerings of moderate interest, though she still remains in need of stricter supervision from the home office, as her talents for organization are unimproved. The non-informational "Wilson Picks Seymour to Succeed Him in Senate," 1-3, has Richardson viewing Seymour's defeat for the GOP nomination for lieutenant governor of California last year due to his switching, according to Richardson, to a pro-choice stance. Her colorful "California Farmers Face Fifth Year of Drying Times," 2-12, focuses solely on farmer Chris Hurd, never directly citing or

quoting anyone else. Richardson offers too many broad generalizations: "What worries him and other growers more than the drought is the politics." In "Bradley Won't Cry If Chief Gets Gate," 3-28, Richardson supplies some interesting background which gives insight into the Tom Bradley-Daryl Gates relationship, but she gives us little solid detail in terms of Gates' chances for survival. Staying with one of the major California stories this year, she pens "Resignation Call Splits LA Further," 4-4. This rounded overview highlights the deepening split between Gates and Bradley, who calls for Gates' resignation, with some detail, but most of it was suspiciously similar to CNN. Her "Frisco Mayor's Race Tests Family Loyalties," 8-9, is a strange and unappealing story of Angela Alioto, the liberal daughter of San Fran's "elder statesman," announcing her candidacy for mayor, against her father's support. Richardson doesn't flesh out the characters well, never indicating their stance on issues. She scripts an ineffective comparison/contrast of California Gov. Pete Wilson and Massachusetts Gov. William Weld in "GOP Governors Take Different Tacks on Taxes," 9-23. While she gets much opinion and writes on the media coverage of each, Richardson provides almost no hard information. Her sufficient roundup, "California's Term-Limit Vote Survives Test in State Court," 10-11, is a quick but solid overview of the California Supreme Court upholding Prop. 140, which limits terms of state legislators and governor.

Riddell, Peter. *Financial Times.* (★ ½)
Washington bureau chief. Riddell serves up Beltway politics with a typically British flair, irredeemably blunt but never nasty. Though his writing can be dense and his appraisals off-target, we continue to make the effort, as he often brings new information to the mix. In "Washington Coming Round to an Acceptance of War," 1-11, Riddell overplays, somewhat inappropriately, Bush's willingness to negotiate up to the wire on Iraq. His "Bush Regains the Initiative," 2/23-2/24, is a poorly conceived and executed dispatch on the U.S. response to the Soviet peace plan during the Gulf War, Riddell focusing erroneously on U.S. actions over the preceding six weeks rather than either the Soviet peace plan or Bush's response. The smart appraisal of the World Bank, "US Establishment Types Who Go Native," 3-8, reports on the passing of the baton from Barber Conable to Lewis Preston, though Riddell doesn't pursue the claim that "internal and external critics. . .argue that the bank lacks direction." His "Bush 'Stung' by Criticism Over Iraq," 4-8, is characteristically to the point: "The sureness of touch which Mr Bush showed up to the end of the Gulf War has deserted him in the past five weeks." In "US Keeps Up Pressure for Soviet Reforms," 5-29, he delivers a preliminary dispatch as Gorbachev vies for a place at the table at the G-7 summit. His short evaluation, "Bush Attack on Congress Falls Flat," 6-14, is a conventional look at Bush's speech deriding Congress for not passing the anti-crime and highway legislation which Riddell uses as a springboard to look at how Bush may campaign in '92. "Outward, Onward and Upward," co-written by Lionel Barber 7-29, is a careful probing of the debate over the U.S. role in the world and at home, the team offering a balanced appraisal of Bush in the national and international rings. Riddell's perceptive delving into the American political scene in "Paradox Pervades the Body Politic," 8-30, is unfortunately undercut by his conclusion that George Bush doesn't need to take a new tack, and therefore a risk, to win a second term, equating him with John Major.

Rodriguez, Paul M. *The Washington Times.* (★ ★)
Congress. Rodriguez seems to be constantly digging, probing until he hits paydirt. The *Post* had the John Sununu travel story, but Rodriguez and the *Times* caught Congress's checks uncovered and the members most chagrined. In "Foley Admits 1 Float, Orders Ethics Probe," 10-4, catching Speaker of the House Foley flat-footed, after having bounced one of his own checks at the now-closing House bank, Rodriguez draws clean lines over who's involved. "DeConcini Tells Panel He Broke No Senate Rules," 1-10, is a straight, uncomplicated report and presentation on DeConcini's defense as a member of the Keating 5. Rodriguez outlining his testimony that he stayed within the rules of the Senate. He provides a good wrap-up on the Senate Ethics Committee's recommendations in "Keating 5 Legacy Will Be Clearer Ethic Rule," 2-20, noting: "tougher standards of conduct that will affect all 100 senators." Rodriguez also

supplies a useful selection of quotes from observers as well as Senators. In the unfocused "Keating Five Decision Was Sure to Displease," 3-7, he discusses the difficulties the Senate Ethics Committee had in dealing with the Keating Five case, but he never details what the decision was. "Congressmen Digging Up Their Own Travel Records," co-written by J. Jennings Moss 4-26, is solidly detailed on congressmen running scared after the John Sununu story hit the front pages. He avidly pursues the topic and turns in a scoop for the *Times,* "Girlfriend Gets Discount on Air Aspin," 5-7, Rodriguez pointedly chronicling Les Aspin taking a military aircraft that cost $4,000 an hour to fly from Colorado with his girlfriend, who reimbursed the government $178.50. He breaks the story of how the Hill Dems have been investigating the October surprise conspiracy theory for 18 months in "Hill Democrats Hid 'October Surprise' Probe," 7-26, Rodriguez supplying bombshell information that's compactly detailed. His follow-up, "Carter's Hostage Try Could Draw GOP Eye," 7-30, is a satisfactory report on GOP response to a *WT* story that the Democrats are conducting a secret investigation into the October surprise.

Rogers, David. *The Wall Street Journal.* (★ ½)
Congress. Rogers is beginning to break out of the rut he's been in, now giving us serviceably detailed roundups of events on the Hill. After years on this beat, though, he still has not developed the political sophistication necessary to raise his work much above the ordinary. In "The Keating 535: Five Are on the Grill, But Other Lawmakers Help Big Donors Too," co-written by Jill Abramson 1-10, the pair provides a sharp overview of the Keating 5, as changing tactics in Congress and rising campaign costs continue to exacerbate problems of this nature. He delivers little insight into the bigger picture of the economy, "Deficit Law Turns the Budget Debate Into Process of Cutting and Spending," 2-7, a good roundup of how lawmakers and Bush are trying not to look like deficit makers, though it is little more than a compendium of examples. His "Congress Clears Pay-Benefits Package of $655 Million for Gulf War Veterans," 3-22, is a satisfactory summary of the day's events in Congress, focusing on the spending bills. In "Fascell, Who Broke Ranks Over the Gulf War, Now Plays Key Role in Reuniting the Democrats," 4-22, a quasi-profile, political assessment of Rep. Dante Fascell (D-Fla.) who sponsored the Gulf War resolution, Rogers writes a memorable lead: "In their own postwar hell, Democrats are rediscovering Dante." His "Congressional Appropriations Panels Fight Caps and 'Sharks' as They Slice Up the Spending Pie," 5-23, is an insightful overview of how appropriations now work, interesting but his anecdotes don't quite come together despite their colorful character. He writes a murky story of Gates and Fiers in "Senate Panel Delays Action on CIA Post," 7-17, that adds clearer detail than the *NYT* account, but this article merely keeps us posted, with nothing substantial reported. His "The Lives of 2 Insiders Turned Outsiders Reflect a Hunger to Find New Answers to Old Problems," 8-21, is a light but intriguing profile of reformers Donald Ryan and Robin Britt, with Rogers precisely handling this neat diversion, though without much feeling or empathy. In "Bloc of Democrats Swing Votes May Decide Confirmation in the Senate," 10-14, he merely provides an ephemeral roundup of the swing votes.

Rohter, Larry. *The New York Times.* (★ ★)
Miami bureau chief. Rohter changed posts again, moving from his Hollywood beat to Florida midway through the year. Though not always consistent, he usually covers his topics evenly, giving us a broad overview of the subjects. He does a respectable job in "Pop-Music Fashion Becomes a Sales Hit," 1-8, on the greening of rock-and-roll: "Giant entertainment conglomerates, including MCA Inc.,. . .are becoming a major force in an industry that was once limited to hippie entrepreneurs." His "Tactics in the Annual Campaign for Oscars," 2-28, is little more than the annual article on the Academy Awards and update on the latest tactical techniques, but is as unsurprising as an Oscar telecast. He takes an interesting angle in "Police Beating Unsettles World of Make-Believe," 3-26, a well-played report on how television and film might be affected by the Rodney Glen King case. His "Advertising's Antic Upstarts," 3-31, a fun article on the precarious new advertising campaigns and their young copywriters, is more

a profile of the advertising business than real news, but there still seems to be more beneath the water on which to report. He gives a fairer view of the former first lady after the Kitty Kelley book in "Nancy Reagan: Mending a Frayed Image," 5-11, seemingly an apology for the earlier scathing piece the *Times* ran, but it doesn't address any allegations made against her. His "New Influx of Cuban Refugees Is Creating Strains for Florida," 7-27, the first of many stories on the subject, not only brings us the news, but reports it sharply, drawing clear demographic lines. In his detailed and crisply written "More Than an Ex-Dictator's Future at Stake as Trial of Noriega Begins," 9-5, he meticulously takes us through the plot and casting of the Noriega trial, but he misses most of the high drama. Rohter's "In Florida, Gators and Humans Vie for Same Turf," 10-9, is a delightful feature on the increasing Florida close encounters between human beings and alligators, giving us plenty of information while never being alarmist.

Romano, Lois. *The Washington Post.* (★ ★ ½)
"Style" writer. Romano progressed to penning weightier Hill features and profiles that no longer shy away from the political angles, as her talents as a portraitist are becoming finely honed. Romano writes on security measures in Washington in "Battening Down and Buttoning Up as Deadline Looms," 1-15, going from the serious to the anecdotal, quoting a police officer: "If you want to strike a blow against the United States of America, you don't go to Des Moines and blow up a cow." In "Lawrence Eagleburger, The Calm Amid the Storm," 2-5, a profile of Deputy Secretary of State Eagleburger, just back from a high-level mission to Israel, she doesn't reveal much backstage diplomacy but does give readers a valuable look at this 30-year career diplomat. Her "Ron Dellums, Waging Peace," 2-20, a serviceable, if antiseptic portrait of Rep. Ron Dellums, charts how the radical from Berkeley came to Washington 20 years ago crusading against the Vietnam war, and now finds him opposing another war. She acidly notes on controversial Sen. Alan Simpson in the wake of the Arnett affair, "Simpson, on Second Thought," 2-27: "His humor, some now say, is beginning to sound like a borscht belt comedian's overused shtick." Her "Congressman Natcher, Present on All Counts," 4-17, is a sweet thumbnail sketch of Rep. William Natcher, Democrat of Kentucky, 81 years old, 37 years in Congress, and has *never* missed 16,883 votes and roll calls in that time. In "The Past and Paradox of Steve Solarz," 5-29, she gives a revealing and three-dimensional profile of the N.Y. Democratic congressman, unfortunately marred by the ubiquitous portrait of "a man who could some day be ready for the White House." Romano never really gets inside Bernard Sanders in "Vermont's Man From Left Field," 7-9, sketching this inherently interesting Socialist congressman from Vermont rather tepidly. In "Food Fight: The Man in the Middle," 10-4, she reports on Rep. Charlie Rose who runs the House Administration Committee, but despite all his accomplishments and anecdotes, Romano can't tell us how he manages to get his complex job done, or what he thinks.

Rosenberg, Howard. *Los Angeles Times.* (★ ½)
Television. Rosenberg had fewer astute insights this year, apparently worn out from almost daily coverage of television's handling of the Persian Gulf War. Though we saw flashes of wit and wisdom, his observations often seemed tired and unoriginal. In "Enough of This Shoot-From-the-Lip Coverage, Already," 1-22, a half-hearted critique of CNN, as the pressures of covering the war make for fast news and errors, he only vaguely makes the connection with TV news in general: "TV's war correspondents of today are known for being their stories," instead of reporting them. From "Sanitized Gap Separates Americans From War," 2-6, comes the ubiquitous complaint that pack journalism from the war zone isn't fair to the American people, though he doesn't strongly make his point that the viewers have to see the carnage to be informed. The unimaginative "There's Little TV News Without a Spin," 2-15, has Rosenberg noting that TV news always has a spin. "Minicamwitness News — Welcome to the Revolution," 3-8, views the Rodney Glen King case as minicam revolution, making anyone who owns one a potential newsman, but Rosenberg doesn't address the implications, only the newsworthiness of true events captured on film. His " 'Hollywood': The Naked Truth," 7-26, is as much a review of Hollywood tactics as it is of the BBC's "Naked Hollywood" documentary series about to

debut on A&E: "The real Hollywood sign is a dollar sign." In "Smith vs. Courtroom TV," 8-2, he provides a concise argument for allowing television at the trial of William Kennedy Smith; "that charge [of distorted coverage, i.e. sound bites] is just as applicable to print reporters, who have no space to regurgitate entire trial transcripts." His " 'LBJ' Class Act on a Double History Bill," 9-30, reviews of PBS's new bio of "LBJ" and TNT's "Days of Crisis" on the Iran hostage drama, provides poignant episodes from the shows that capture the times succinctly. In the disappointing "The Talk of the Electronic Town," 10-10, he fires scattershot information about the Hill-Thomas hearings, including raving about mixed messages and miniskirts.

Rosenstiel, Thomas B. *Los Angeles Times.* (★ ★)
Media. Rosenstiel continues to be assigned to report superfluous surveys, which distracts him from the real task at hand: covering the media with precision and insight. His clipped, crisp wordsmithing and detailing combine to provide sharp evaluations. Rosenstiel's "Information on War Key to Public Trust," 1-24, is a surprisingly balanced report on the unfairness of pools during war coverage; "Nonetheless, few journalists think the Pentagon is deliberately deceiving them." He pulls together worldwide opinion in the short "Images of Death Give Iraq a Boost in Propaganda War," 2-14, but it still falls short of being a concrete story. His "Mysterious Media Baron Brings His Road Show to the Big Apple," 3-21, begins colorfully, by quoting the code message that employees use to signify Robert Maxwell's arrival, "The ego has landed," then degenerates into a substandard profile of Maxwell. He remains distant to the core controversy in "Use of Woman's Name in Kennedy Case Reports Sparks Debate on Rape Coverage," 4-18, compiling numerous quotes but never assessing how revealing the name of the alleged victim helps or hurts the story. He supplies a moderately engaging article on the results of a survey of what interests Americans in, "Bush Illness, Kurds Top Public Interest," 5-23. His "End of a Paper Trail," 6-24, is a solid news report on the retirement of *The Washington Post*'s Ben Bradlee, Rosenstiel talking to Bradlee, former *Post* staffers, current employees and different editors to add spice to what otherwise might be an obituary. The obvious "Networks Seek New Approach to Campaigns," 7-11, limits his approach to the wisdom of NBC director of political coverage, Bill Wheatley: the media should identify what issues are important and then which candidates are most able to address those issues. His "UPI Again Files for Bankruptcy," 8-29, is a cursory look at United Press International's going down for the second time, with a history of important dates for the service that doesn't supply the full story of this debacle. In "Clash Between Thomas, Accuser May Be Settled on TV," 10-9, Rosenstiel insightfully observes that the bottom line is this: ". . .the American public's gut judgment about which of these two comes across on television as more believable."

Rosenthal, Andrew. *The New York Times.* (★ ★)
White House. Though still not as detached from the conventional Beltway view as we'd like, Rosenthal is beginning to cull new insights on this beat, finding more original angles upon which to frame his stories. He pens a neatly rounded "Bush Leaves Open Timing of Assault on Iraq's Forces," 1-6, on Bush's statements on the eve of war with Rosenthal's overview of the day's events rather pessimistic. His "Scowcroft and Gates; A Team Rivals Baker," 2-21, has a memorable lead on NSC adviser and deputy, Brent Scowcroft and Robert Gates, respectively: "twins of the White House, 'fused at the hip,' " Rosenthal providing an astute assessment of how the team conducts business. In his intriguing appraisal "In Reagan's Cool Shadow," 3-30, Rosenthal probes the advantages of having Reagan back gun control legislation for Bush, as Bush can now soft-pedal his own view while keeping it on the table, as "the Gipper made [him] do it." The curt update, "Bush Not Pressing Kuwait on Reform," 4-3, finds Rosenthal covering Bush's fishing trip in Islamorada, Florida, with too little news here on Bush simply "prodding" the Emir on political reform as "the issue is so sensitive." In "Sununu Is Ordered to Clear Flights With Bush Lawyer," 5-10, he sharply notes that Sununu's wings being clipped "would be especially stinging to the imperious chief of staff since it puts him under the authority of a less senior official." Though neatly done, "Bush Returns to Prepare for Moscow," 7-23, is merely a detailed dispatch on the Moscow summit and Bush's itinerary. His bemused article, "A Spy's

Bequest: Riddles He Might Love," 8-15, on former CIA Director William Casey wryly notes, "In a city where many former officials linger in that category called Forgotten But Not Gone, Mr. Casey has accomplished the opposite trick." His precise delineation, "Thomas's Edge Steady, Vote Due Today," 10-15, is impressively detailed, with Rosenthal apparently having talked to quite a few senators on the vote. Rosenthal offers little new information and few quotes in the standard "Economic Ills Cast Shadow Over Bush Re-election Plans," 10-24. The *Times* and the White House finally catch on to the fact that Bush can no longer avoid the economy.

Ross, Michael. *Los Angeles Times.* (★ ★)

Capitol Hill. Ross moved to Washington after a career spent on the foreign desk, most recently as Cairo bureau chief for the *Times.* His obvious forte is foreign relations, penning intelligent discussions of foreign issues facing the different agencies on the Hill. He admirably captures Egypt's fear about Iraq's lack of air resistance, the result of bigger plans in "Egyptians Feel Iraqis Plan Chemical Attacks," 1-24. In "The Arabs: Divisions Beyond the Stereotype," 2-12, Ross makes a game attempt at defining the divisions behind the facade of Arab brotherhood, doing quite a nice job, but his conclusion of widespread post-war unrest in the Middle East is a little off. His "Democrats Plan to Study Alleged Hostage Deal," 5-3, simply tells of a Gary Sick meeting with Democrats on the House Foreign Affairs Committee, where they may or may not decide to review the "October surprise." Though somewhat of a rehash, "CIA Nominee Faces New Iran-Contra Questions," 6-30, is still a good overview of the lingering questions on Gates' knowledge of the Iran-contra affair clouding the nomination. In "Ex-CIA Official Pleads Guilty in Iran-Contra Case," co-written by Ronald Ostrow 7-10, the team efficiently reports while avoiding finger-pointing: "Fiers gave no indication that he would contradict testimony by Robert M. Gates." Staying on the story, "Some in Agency Oppose Gates as CIA Chief," co-written by Douglas Jehl 8-2, the pair discusses allegations that go from within the CIA to the Senate Intelligence Committee, but they never explain how precisely Gates may have "politicized" his office. In "Boren's Role in Efforts for Gates Questioned," co-written by Jack Nelson 10-9, Nelson and Ross provide the smoke, but no smoking gun in this report that questions whether Senate Intelligence Committee chairman David Boren was behind a letter-writing campaign to drum up support for CIA nominee Robert Gates.

Savage, David G. *Los Angeles Times.* (★ ★)

Supreme Court. Savage has retreated from covering cases that the Court doesn't hear, making exceptions only when it will have a wide-ranging effect. Much improved at providing background material, he is becoming adept at the broad overviews so important in reporting on the Court. His "Forbidden Words on Campus," 2-12, is an intelligent column about the political correctness movement on college campuses, though despite its length, we get little depth and only a smattering of the legal and political aspects. He concentrates more on the feminist side of the issue in "Court Rejects Limiting Jobs to Protect Fetuses," 3-21, although he does make effective use of excerpts from Blackmun's decision. His focus, however, is clearly on the woman's rights. Savage candidly notes in "Justices OK Ban on Abortion Advice in U.S.-Aided Clinics," 5-24, that Judge Souter hasn't yet voted against the Chief Justice nor written an opinion, concurrence or dissent of importance and may be overwhelmed by the workload. His "Vanishing Voice of Liberalism," 6-29, is a fairly standard "Column One" on the changing face of the Supreme Court. In "Thomas Hearings Likely to Focus on Abortion Issue," 7-14, he gives us a well-balanced article on the discovery that Clarence Thomas once praised an article by Lewis Lehrman that was decidedly anti-abortion, Savage properly not blowing this out of proportion as did other reporters. His "Panel Deadlocks, 7 to 7, on Thomas Nomination," co-written with William Eaton 9-28, is a good breakdown of who voted which way on the Senate Judiciary Committee. In "Thomas, Backers Try to Make Him Seem Victim," 10-13, Savage presents an otherwise respectable and acceptable account save for his omniscient: "Diplomatically, Thomas aimed his criticism at 'the process,' but he really had in mind the senators, their staffs and the liberal interest groups that oppose him." His "Bush Confident on Key Vote," 10-15, sharply notes that no one reached their Thomas decision with ease, as well as presenting the breakdown of the fury of women's groups.

Seper, Jerry. *The Washington Times.* (★ ★)
Investigations and Justice Department. Seper has honed his organizational skills, and cut the cloak-and-dagger feel to provide clearly penned and well-documented dispatches. Although he doesn't often hit paydirt, he keeps digging. Seper provides key details of the upgrading of training and technology by the new Mexican anti-drug czar, Jorge Carrillo Olea, "Mexico Invests in Arms to Fight War on Drugs," 1-28, an important news item on the war on drugs handled admirably. In the plausible "Justice Targets INS Chief for Ouster," 2-25, he uncovers an operation by high-ranking Justice Dept. officials "to paint U.S. Immigration and Naturalization Service Commissioner Gene McNary as inept in an effort to run him out of office." His "Thornburgh to Probe Complaints of Brutality," 3-15, is a solid overview of the Justice Department's widening investigation of police brutality to review complaints nationwide from '85 onward. Seper unearths a communications problem between Thornburgh and the INS in "Thornburgh Urged to Speak to INS," 4-25. The attorney general hasn't met with the head in six months, yet critiques it regularly, adding another piece to the puzzle. In "Yale Alumni Come Full Circle in Race," 6-10, an interesting comparison of the two candidates for John Heinz's Senate seat, Harris Wofford and Richard Thornburgh, Seper highlights the parallels, and includes a brief political history of both. Seper doesn't prove conclusively in "Role of Gray's Staff in City Race Probed," 7-1, that former Rep. William Gray's staff, or Gray himself, was involved in a fraudulent letter on Justice Dept. stationery which the writer thought would propel George Burrell Jr. ahead of the competition in the Philadelphia mayoral primary. His "Writer's Death Draws Interest of FBI, DEA," 8-13, is a strange story of the death of freelancer Daniel Casolaro, who was researching a book on Inslaw. Seper alleges it was his knowledge of the BCCI scandal, not the "October surprise," that caused his untimely demise. He writes a taut, concise dispatch in "11 Indicted in BCCI-Medellin Case," 9-6, on those indicted on racketeering charges for drug money laundering through BCCI, Seper never straying far from the facts in this effective snapshot.

Shales, Tom. *The Washington Post.* (★ ★ ★)
Television. Year after year, we look to Shales for consistently sharp observations and eloquently dry wit on the state of television. His trenchant commentary is never overbearing or obnoxious, as Shales critiques his targets with great care and precision. He takes a critical look at the way CBS and NBC gave a higher priority to NFL play-off games than to two Presidential news conferences in "Fumbling the Ball on Bush," 1-14, Shales contending that sports has the upperhand over the money-losing news divisions. "The Endangered NBC Peacock," 3-29, has Shales reporting that GE is slashing costs drastically at NBC, with the resulting loss in news coverage quality. The article rambles and is repetitive at times, but it does capture a U.S. institution apparently on its last legs. His "Hollywood Hype and the Jaws of Victory," 5-21, is an amusing effort that offers pungent observations on Hollywood's three-hour televised salute to the returning Persian Gulf troops. "Implicit in this hype is the notion. . .that all the problems facing the country, foreign and domestic, fade into insignificance." Shales delivers a cheery, bouncy profile in "Leslie Nielsen, Licensed Nut," 6-28, of "Naked Gun" fame, where we come away enriched by Nielsen's infectious lunacy, both on and off screen, that Shales captures so well. In "TV's Sinking Net Worth," 7-31, he takes a bemused look at the death throes of the three major TV networks: "Should one be optimistic or pessimistic about the wrenching changes?. . .The first law of TV probably applies: Whatever comes next will likely be worse." Shales charges "One Day That Shook the World," 8-20, with his characteristic wit, in an on-the-spot review of the television coverage of the coup. In "The Senators' Final Say and Television's Blinking Eye," 10-16, Shales seems almost saddened by the savage silliness of the Senate proceedings over Anita Hill and Clarence Thomas. His review of ABC News's "Town Meeting" with Gorbachev and Boris Yeltsin in "Gorbachev and Yeltsin: Worth the Wait," 9-7, strikes a curious mixture of cynicism and awe: "The two Russian leaders acted. . .as if they might be an unusually stiff and proper morning deejay team."

Shapiro, Walter. *Time.* (★ ★)

Senior writer. An essayist for the newsweekly, Shapiro continues to tone down the stridency of his voice, opting for a more pensive style that has elevated the quality of his material considerably. He delivers a finely drawn "A Whole Greater Than Its Parts?" 2-25, a pensive essay on communitarianism, or the idea that one needs "to temper the excesses of American individualism with the strong assertion of the rights of the larger society." Shapiro's "The Birth and — Maybe — Death of Yuppiedom," 4-8, is a goofy article on the evolution of the yuppie, and its possible death due to recession. This would have been much more interesting if he'd viewed, and thus skewered, yuppies as the creation of a marketer's or producer's fantasy. Shapiro celebrates the joys of baseball in mini-reviews of several books on the subject, from Hank Aaron's memoir, *I Had a Hammer,* to sociologist Alan M. Klein's *Sugarball,* in "The Seventh-Inning Stretch," 6-17. Shapiro notes James Fiskin's idea of political polling in the clearly-detailed "Vaulting Over Political Polls," 7-22, which will be aired on PBS: ". . .whatever happens in Austin [the site of the convention], the novel event itself will be an affirmation that grass-roots democracy can still flourish in a television age." In the slightly bizarre "The Glory and the Glitz," 8-5, he details turning the Lorraine Motel in Memphis, where Martin Luther King was assassinated, into a National Civil Rights Museum, Shapiro oddly muted here, where one would expect he would shred the tackiness of this. His intriguingly written cover, "Tough Choice," 9-16, is a perceptive dissertation on the choice issue in education, Shapiro only getting editorial in the end, calling for a state to run a real free choice school system and let the chips fall where they may.

Shribman, David. *The Wall Street Journal.* (★ ★ ½)

Special projects and politics. Shribman focused more on politics, his strong suit, than special projects, producing a body of work improved over last year, but still rarely on the margin. In the somber "An Anti-War Effort Emerges This Time Even Before the War," 1-16, Shribman takes anecdotal notes on protest rallies and prayer meetings of the anti-war movement in Columbus, Ohio. Shribman's "In New York, and Other States Where the Census Has Cut Seats, Congressmen Prepare for Battle," 2-27, is a detailed microcosmic look at the redistricting in upstate New York, sharply chronicling the respective records of three House members as one seat is to be eliminated. His "Abortion-Rights Activists, Fearing More Setbacks in States, Hope to Make the Issue National Again," 3-20, is an exceptionally good overview of the state of abortion rights country-wide in which Shribman avoids a mere listing of different states. He scripts an intuitively evil interpretation of dark motives on the GOP end for participating in redistricting in "Republicans, Often Hoping for More Than Good Government, Help Minority Redistricting Efforts," 4-2. His "Tsongas Kicks Off '92 Presidential Race, Vowing to Start 'Economic Renaissance,' " 5-1, is a colorful dispatch on former Sen. Paul Tsongas throwing his hat into the presidential candidacy ring. He widens his scope to capture "The Democratic Race for 1992 Nomination Gets Off to Slow Start," 7-8. This P. 1 political update makes one good point — late starts reduce the time-frame to make early errors. The focused snapshot "Harkin, Wilder Join Presidential Race, Both Promising Challenges to the Status Quo," co-written by James M. Perry 9-16, is a campaign kickoff piece combining the messages of Sen. Harkin and Gov. Wilder, although we get no appraisal of the overall field, except as a list of candidates. We never get the full portrait of Harris Wofford, running for the Pennsylvania Senate seat, in "Wofford, Campaigning as Outsider vs. Insider, Pulls Even With Thornburgh in Pennsylvania," 10-31, yet it does pit him forcefully against the "insider" Dick Thornburgh: "The Wofford campaign 'is the guinea pig for 1992.' "

Smothers, Ronald. *The New York Times.* (★ ★)

Special correspondent. Smothers regularly turns out sprightly, enjoyable features that could be improved by better organization. He now is beginning to venture more into the politics of the southern states, although he will need a year or two of experience before competing on a par with Peter Applebome. The history/profile works well in "Left Behind in Murder Inquiry but Still Behind Bars," 2-3, on how the criminal justice system treated Edward Lewis Humphrey, once a murder suspect in the U. of Florida mass killings of five students, now semi-exonerated. In the poorly organized "On Second Thought, Forget Lunch," 3-14, Smothers gives us a snapshot of the ethics scandal in S.C. legislature that flicks back and forth between legislators and public response. He presents an interesting report on alligator farms in "Louisiana Farmers, Finding Gold in Alligator Skins, Face a Changing Market," 4-1, noting that "although alligator farming is no means universally endorsed, it has generally been accepted and even applauded by many environmentalists." His "Airplane in Crash Carried Recorder," 7-12, is a moderately useful article on the FCC requiring most small commercial planes to carry flight recorders after one crashed in Alabama. Solid detail raises the investigative "Seized Bank Helped Atlanta's Ex-Mayor and Carter Charities," 7-15, from the ubiquitous BCCI scandal stories, his fine background linking the BCCI to Andrew Young and Jimmy Carter's housing project. Smothers rightly avoids sensationalism in "Lawyers Trade Allegations at Child-Abuse Trial," 8-20, on the drama in a McMartin-like trial in North Carolina. In the disorganized "North Carolina Examines Inspection Lapses in Fire," 9-5, Smothers tries unsuccessfully to relate a current fire to a national safety agenda, ignoring that this was merely a tragic, but isolated incident, unrelated to government cutbacks. Smothers's "Racially Divisive Campaign in Memphis," 10-2, insightfully examines the political and racial issues between white conservative incumbent Richard C. Hackett and black challenger Willie W. Herenton.

Solomon, Burt. *National Journal.* (★)
White House. More often than not, Solomon is the least satisfying reporter on this important beat, so few and far between are the insights he offers. He's surely valuable to inside-the-Beltway politicos for his insider feel and perspective, but for news and information in a timely fashion we turn more to the mainstream press. Solomon unfairly compares Bush to the last several presidents in "Making Foreign Policy in Secret May Be Easy, But it Carries Risks," 1-12, and finds him wanting badly, though he provides less about Bush's foreign policymaking as such, than what's wrong with it. He delivers a fairly good wrap-up of the domestic issues that will divide the parties in "Bush, Congressional Democrats May Be Spoiling for a Fight," 2-9: "War has put the mutual disdain between conservatives and the White House 'on the back burner right now'. . .but it is still 'bubbling beneath the surface.' " Solomon provides plenty of gossip mixed with good analysis in "As Reelection Time Grows Closer, Bushmen Become Like Brothers," 3-16, on who's "in" at the White House. He focuses on the new education secretary, Lamar Alexander, in "Politically Punctual President Launches His Education Agenda," 4-20, with Bush hoping to set an agenda for this domestic policy, but Solomon doesn't define Alexander's proposal that pointedly. His convincing "Even for a President on a Roll There Is a Worst-Case Scenario," 7-20, supplies good examples of the precedent set in state elections following abortion rulings, as well as the larger message of how the Supreme Court has played a pivotal role in the presidential elections of FDR and Nixon, showing that Bush is not invincible. Solomon provides a brief glimpse of the press and public reaction at the White House in the unnecessary "For Bush's Staff, Discretion Is the Better Part of Power," 8-3. Another disappointing piece, "A Pair of Dominant Grandfathers Shape a Presidential Persona," 9-7, chronicles the history of the Bush and Walker families, but he doesn't get around to explaining how this has contributed to Bush's sense of noblesse oblige and its effect on policy. Solomon notes on Bush's appearances as everyman at Disney World, the Grand Ole Opry and so on in "Bush Evokes All the Right Feelings Without Rolling in the Flag," 10-12, useful only to Beltway types.

Specter, Michael. *The New York Times.* (★ ★)
Now on the metro desk, Specter left his *Washington Post* slot as NY bureau chief in the fall to file atmospheric and colorfully written dispatches on the tri-state area for the *Times.* His "New York City Budget Woes May Get Messy," *WP* 2-9, is a marvelously malodorous report on the likely impact of deep budget cuts in the sanitation department: "City streets now merely dirty could be overflowing with refuse when the warm weather arrives this spring." He provides a sympathetic profile of Connecticut Governor Lowell Weicker and his effort to deal with the state's fiscal crisis with a mixture of budget cuts and a state income tax in the face of ferocious

opposition in "A Familiar Trip From Frying Pan to Fire," *WP* 3-3. His humorous report "Skull and Bones at Yale: First No Woman, Now No Club," *WP* 4-16, reports on the decision that "caused the alumni board, the most anonymous part of this furtive organization, to crush the rebellion with a speed unseen since Soviet tanks rolled into Prague in 1968." Specter revels in the strengths of New York City in "Through It All, Why I Love New York," *WP* 5-26, that seems to be an antidote to the apocalyptic coverage the city has been receiving recently during its budget crisis. He provides an eye-opening report on a New York outrage, the rise of Medicaid mills, in "Medicaid's Malady," 7-8, where unscrupulous physicians "grind routinely through dozens of patients in a single hour," billing Medicaid and often receiving kickbacks. His "One State Lawmaker, One Vote and Political Wrath of the NRA," *WP* 7-25, is a disturbing report on the efforts of the NRA to unseat New Jersey state senator William Gormley, the only Republican state senator to vote for the ban on assault weapons. Anecdotes bring the blustery and atmospheric "Hurricane Rakes New England, Loses Some Force," *WP* 8-20, to life as Specter details Hurricane Bob blowing through New England, doing major damage to Rhode Island and other states. Specter hooks a bit of the controversy surrounding the potential release of photographic negatives of the scrolls in "Library to Release Dead Sea Scrolls," *WP* 9-22, but, considering all the infighting over intellectual rights to the scrolls, this is oddly lifeless.

Stanfield, Rochelle L. *National Journal.* (★ ★)
Demographics, education and immigration. The powers that be at *NJ* moved Stanfield midyear from the foreign affairs beat to her current territory. She turns in an acceptable year's work despite the switch, her efforts thorough and often insightful. The perceptive "The Other War Zone," 2-2, probes the relationship Gorbachev will have with the U.S. after the Gulf War, Stanfield providing a good discussion of the U.S. need to deal with the republics, that proves its worth in hindsight after the coup. Her "In the New Game, Moscow's a Wild Card," 3-23, miscalls the situation: "There's a new ambivalence within the Bush Administration about what role the Soviet Union should play in the postwar Middle East." It didn't prove to be ambivalence, but instead caution. In "Ignoring Pretoria," 3-16, she notes that South Africa seems to be completing its long climb to democracy — or is close to sliding into civil war — yet, she doesn't ask when sanctions should be lifted or why some members of Congress are holding up money for the nation. She reports on the plethora of government officials, economists, business executives, etc. who feel the method of census taking is out-of-date in "Statistics Gap," 4-13. Stanfield supplies interesting ideas for alternatives, but never touches on a solid solution. She provides a very thorough investigation of the divisive issue of Bush's education agenda in "Shirking Job 1," 5-4. This piercing report details corporate and education leaders who are among the most vocal boosters of getting youngsters ready to enter school, and they are starting to wonder whether Bush has overlooked this top priority. In "Cracking *el Sistema*," 6-1, Stanfield supplies solid information and background on how unfriendly naturalization processes are contributing to Hispanic discontent: without naturalization they cannot vote, and without a vote, they have no voice and no clout. Continuing on the education improvement story, she highlights different approaches business would take to reforming schools in the interesting but overly long, "School Business," 7-27. Stanfield's "Strains in the Family," 9-28, is the lead item in a special report featured on the cover "America in the '90s" though she tries to cover too much in this extended exercise on demographics, economics, immigration and the family.

Steinfels, Peter. *The New York Times.* (★ ½)
Theology. It always amazes us that Steinfels covers religion from a distinctly agnostic perspective, rarely mentioning God or Jesus, Allah or Buddah outside of his Saturday "Beliefs" column. He walks the line carefully, but his caution makes him less a correspondent of theology than a reporter of the hierarchy and mechanisms inherent in organized religions. In his 1-19 "Beliefs," we find Steinfels as personal as we've seen over the question: "Must a loving God be persuaded to take action on the world's behalf?" via the Persian Gulf. He collects a body of opinions, which debate, but never fully answer the question. He provides an obituary, "Pedro Arrupe, Jesuit Chief for 18 Years, Dies at 83," 2-6, on the head of the Jesuit order from 1965

to 1983, an insightful piece on the vast hierarchy and tension between the branches of the Catholic Church, without being judgmental. His "Catholic Study Finds Press Tilting Against the Church," 3-27, is a fairly standard report, undoubtedly occasioned by *Newsweek*'s unveiling of this bias that cited the *NYT,* among others. Steinfels provides a look at how exorcism fits into the church in the straightforward "Exorcism, Filmed With Priest's Consent, to Be Shown on TV," 4-4, also supplying a survey of the reactions of various church officials to the filming, noting "how the decision was arrived at remained unclear." His "Papal Encyclical Urges Capitalism to Shed Injustices," 5-3, is a balanced interpretation of John Paul II's encyclical on the market economic system, accompanied by a full half-page of excerpts of the document itself. He chronicles the split between conservatives and moderates in "Southern Baptists: Facing a Deep Rift," 5-14, the issue curtly defined and dissected, yet it doesn't seem like quite the deep rift described in the title. In his 7-6 "Beliefs," he gives a discussion of the Presbyterian brief statement on beliefs that was accepted by the General Assembly, but he seems strangely disconnected as he assesses more than the liberal sexual statement that was trumpeted by the press. His "Lutherans Say Choosing Abortion Can Be Morally Responsible Move," 9-4, is an interesting but esoteric discussion of the issue that avoids the mention of religion at all.

Taylor, Paul. *The Washington Post.* (★ ★ ½)
Family affairs. Taylor moved from politics to family affairs at his own request, apparently tired of the grind of covering national issues and personalities. His dispatches on family issues are surprisingly insightful, although they lack the heady sophistication of his reports from the campaign trail. Taylor provides us plenty of data and detail, which is digested and organized in "Nonmarital Births: As Rates Soar, Theories Abound," 1-22: "fewer young expectant parents feel the tug of social conventions pulling them toward matrimony." He provides adequate treatment to speeches by Rep. Rostenkowski and Sen. Rockefeller in "Two Hill Leaders Stress Need to Address Poor Children's Plight," 3-19, where both urge increased attention to the problems of poor children, yet the piece lacks the political sophistication we expect from Taylor. His facile " 'One-Stop' Prenatal Care System Urged," 4-24, expands upon the assertion that the U.S relies on "high-cost medical technology rather than low-cost expansion of prenatal care" and then details the fight between Congress and the administration over this issue. In "Milwaukee's Controverisal Private School Choice Plan Off to Shaky Start," 5-25, he writes a point-counterpoint overview of the town's voucher experiment, Taylor giving us neatly defined background but making no predictions as to whether it will succeed. His " 'Two Faces of Fatherhood,' " 6-16, is sensitive without being sappy, on how fatherhood, particularly after divorce, doesn't match the ideal image portrayed in commercials. He provides a survey of Jewish leaders on various topics in "U.S. Jewish Leaders Hopeful, Wary About Bush's Peace Offensive," 7-22, this trim report offering little appraisal of the situation. His unimaginative "Huge Gap Showing in the Safety Net," 8-29, uses New Hampshire as a case in point to argue that the welfare safety net is torn and battered: "Federal welfare programs have hit their highest level in history." Taylor takes a he-said, she-said approach in "Thomas's View of Harassment Said to Evolve," 10-11, in this light review of Thomas's EEOC experience with sexual harassment, including the Earl Harper case.

Thomas, Evan. *Newsweek.* (★ ½)
Washington bureau chief. Thomas reenters our sights for the first time in several years, toning down his strident style to bring us neatly documented overviews. The "Impact!" quality that we'd complained about in 1987 resurfaces occasionally, but is more palatable with less frequency. His "Saddam and Bush: The Words of War," co-written by Howard Fineman 1-21, teeters between silliness and meaness as it discusses the rhetoric of Hussein and Bush and how it affects diplomacy. A quick and pensive examination of where the military might want to go with its hardware is given in the smartly analyzed "War's New Science," co-written by John Barry 2-18. Thomas's input is questionable here as this is Barry's specialty. The tautly penned "A Textbook Victory," co-written by John Barry 3-11, delivers a sharp overview of where Saddam went wrong and Stormin' Norman went right. His neat dissection of Bush's non-commital course on the

Kurds and Shiite rebels, "Where Was George This Time?" co-written by Ann McDaniel 4-15, falters at the end: "And if Saddam is still in power a year from now, Bush could have blood on his hands." He provides a clearly Democratic perception of the Veep in "The Quayle Handicap," with Ann McDaniel and Thomas M. DeFrank 5-20, and though the team observes that he's "not quite been the stumblebum the comics make him out to be," the article never delivers any new goods. The lack of cohesion in "Where Did All the Money Go?" co-written by Rich Thomas 7-1, is due to the plethora of statistics cited in this article on governors trying to hold state budgets together as federal funds shrink. The overview of "Playing Chicken in Iraq," co-written by Ann McDaniel with Clara Bingham 9-30, doesn't provide much more than the daily papers on the alleged hidden arsenal that the U.N. is looking for in Iraq. His " 'There Is Always Something,' " 10-21, is quite strong and perceptive, taking his cue from Suzanne Garment's book *Scandal: The Culture of Mistrust in American Politics*: "The problem with the scandal machine is that it's all-consuming. It cannot distinguish between human foibles, and true outrages that harm the public interest."

Tolchin, Martin. *The New York Times.* (★ ½)
Public policy. Tolchin continues to specialize in clear, crisp snapshots of various issues and bills. Although he always includes salient detail, we get little sense of continuity either within his dispatches or in his overall body of work. Tolchin doesn't quite supply the answer in "Legislation and Crises, Illusions and Realities," 1-11, asking if bills just slip through the cracks or, as he quotes Steven Ross, counsel for the House, do they reflect "the inability to close a deal?" The report is thick on the way Washington does business. There's little depth in "White House Reassures Hard-Pressed Governors," 2-3, a dry article on federal "flexibility" for state funds for items such as Medicaid. Tolchin details the shifts in thinking about state fiscal problems as most governors face an unprecedented gap between revenue and expenditures in "Cuts After Decade of Cuts: Governors Grim at Meeting," 2-4. His reporting doesn't propel the story forward, but does conveys a strong sense of how governors are treating this serious dilemma. In the sharply detailed and cleanly presented "Congress Withholds $55 Million in Aid to Jordan," 3-23, Tolchin covers Congress, detailing the foreign aid bill and various other measures involved in the compromise actions to get the bill passed. He provides little more that a snapshot in "Bush Seeks Review of Policy that Allowed Sununu Trips," 4-25, but does get into who will review policy and why, plus detail on the policy itself. His "Senator Who Hunted Bank Scandal Is Watching Doubters Take His Path," 7-29, is a surprisingly balanced piece on Kerry's persistence with BCCI. He reports on uncovered checks at the House bank in "Legislators Seek Exoneration in House Bank Controversy," 10-1, Tolchin seeming to have got most of this out of *Congress Daily,* a Capitol Hill sheet published by *National Journal.*

Toner, Robin. *The New York Times.* (★ ½)
National political correspondent. Towards the close of the year Toner began to seem worn out, providing fewer fresh insights and surprises in her reporting. She seems in over her head for this critically important posting, still unseasoned. Her "Bush's Luck in War Confers an Aura of Invincibility in '92," 2-27, doesn't shed any new light on the accepted notion "that Mr. Bush has set the stage for a re-election campaign that draws a stark and brutal contrast between a party willing to use American force to counter aggression and a party that flinched." Toner transforms a poll on the first signs of real vulnerability for Bush on domestic issues into a highly readable article in "Poll Finds Postwar Glow Dimmed by the Economy," 3-8. She also sharply appraises Democratic strategies for 1992 only days after the end of the war. Her well-written "1992 Election Is Far Off, But Not Far Enough for Some," 4-7, takes a look at difficulties Democrats are having in fielding presidential candidates: "the Democratic party has not been kind, in recent years, to those who won the nomination but lost the election." Toner's "Louisiana Is Bracing for Politics With Gusto," 5-29, a light survey of the field in the gubernatorial race in Louisiana, never comes to life, despite Toner's talk of "Louisiana's flamboyant standards." She provides an adequate profile of John D. Rockefeller as he positions himself for a possible run at the '92 Democratic nomination in "Rockefeller's Assets," 7-21. Despite having covered him in the

late-70s, or maybe because of it, Toner seems less than impressed with him. Her "As Presidential Field Shrinks, Democrats' Distress Grows," 8-8, could have been the definitive appraisal of the Democrats, but Toner merely amplifies her themes of yesterday, pondering the dearth of candidates, rather than the dearth of ideas and enthusiasm within the party. She gives us a nice conglomeration of information and anecdotes on Doug Wilder in "Wilder Ponders a Role Quixote Would Love," 9-4, but offers little in the way of appraising his candidacy, especially in areas other than fiscal responsiblity. There's little to hold "Space for All in Abortion Debate, Quayle Says," 10-9, together as it rambles on about what Quayle thinks of abortion and the GOP platform.

Waldman, Steven. *Newsweek.* (★ ½)
Washington. We see Waldman now as frequently in other publications as we do in the newsweekly. His utilitarian dispatches still show signs of his quick wit, and he brings a freshness to all his subjects. His "Days of Whine and Poses," *The Washington Monthly* 3-91, is an excellent review of John Tower's *Consequences: A Personal and Political Memoir* that is just as much political evaluation of Tower, the press and the confirmation process as the book itself. Waldman makes some perceptive points, despite "Tower can barely go a page without hissing at Nunn." He provides an interesting and entertaining "Watering the Grass Roots," 5-6, on how lobbying and PR firms are orchestrating grass-roots campaigns by manipulating the public. The brevity of "Consumer News Blues," 5-20, hampers this piece on TV self-censorship to keep advertisers happy. This article on consumer reporting is helpful on the local level, but we are left unaware how widespread the practice has become. He supplies solid reporting in the cover "Lead and Your Kids," 7-15, on lead poisoning, an eye-opening dispatch that's almost a public service piece, with Waldman carefully avoiding alarming his audience by emphasizing that health officials aren't sure what kind of damage lead poisoning causes. His " 'A Perfect Combination of Chutzpah and Soul,' " *The Washington Post Magazine* 8-18, is a fine profile of Jean and Edgar Cahn, whose contributions to social issues, such as helping to make legal aid available to the poor, are outlined well. This moving article takes care to highlight the struggle and the humanity of a black woman and Jewish man, married in 1957, who fought for rights for the poor. "The Mentor and the Protegee," co-written by Marcus Mabry, Clara Bingham and Marc Levinson 9-23, is a lightweight examination of the relationship between Clark Clifford and Robert Altman.

Walsh, Edward. *The Washington Post.* (★ ★ ½)
Chicago. Arriving at his new post late last year, Walsh settled in nicely at his Midwest beat, giving us adept coverage of pertinent national issues as well as compelling regional news. His "A Year Before Caucuses, Presidential Campaign Activity in Iowa Is 'Zippo,' " 2-17, is a perfunctory report from Des Moines on the complete and total lack of presidential politicking a year before the caucuses, listing the reasons but offering little insight. He scribes a non-sensationalist account of one of the most publicized footnotes to the Gulf War, the alleged murder of a returning soldier by his wife and brother-in-law in "Wife, In-Law of Gulf Soldier Charged With His Slaying," 3-27. Walsh's "Wellstone Faces Fallout of Anti-War Offensive," 4-7, is an organized profile of controversial Sen. Paul Wellstone (D-Minn.),who is unpopular because of his strong opposition to the Gulf War: "His liberal views and intense personal style attract some and repel others but leave few neutral." He pens a delightful little article on the opening day at the new Comisky Park in Chicago, "Amid Rubble at 'Old Comisky,' " 4-19, an "American Journal" feature christening the new while remaining respectful of nostalgia. Walsh's brief but evocative "Chicago Savors a Rare Title," 6-14, details the celebratory mood in Chicago following the Bulls' victory in the NBA championships, neatly capturing the town's elation. His "Dentist's AIDS Death Shakes Tiny Town," 7-20, is a sober report on the ramifications following the disclosure that a dentist in a small Illinois town died of AIDS: "the debate here centers on the conflict between the privacy rights of health care workers and the rights of patients." Walsh serves up a good profile, with an insider's feel, of national security advisor Brent Scowcroft and his key role in fashioning hard line responses to crises in the Gulf and the Soviet Union in "Bush's Man With the Hawk's Eye View," 10-7.

Wattenberg, Daniel. *Insight.* (★ ★)
Domestic politics. Like most *Insight* writers, Wattenberg ably covers a plethora of topics, but his forte continues to be domestic politics. His probing "Hill Democrats Are Trying to Set Stakes in Political Stand," 1-14, compiles opinion on what each party's stand on military action in the Gulf will do for them, though he offers very little of his own interpretation. Wattenberg's "Making Noise, Not War," 2-11, is an acerbic report on the anti-war protest movement that is cleverly written but far too slanted to be passed off as a straight news report, which it is here as part of *Insight*'s cover on the Persian Gulf War. He supplies a solidly informative article on the state of South Africa's black schools and the results of the "liberation before education" movement in the detailed "ANC Joins Chorus Heralding Back-to-School Movement," 3-4. In his thickly written "The GOP Divides to Conquer," 6-3, he notes how the GOP is using their voting rights strategy to apportion racial quotas in the government. An interesting discussion, but his outrage at GOP "hypocrisy" comes through too strongly. Wattenberg's cover "Ronald and the Reagan Bashers," 7-22, is an unapologetic defense of the Reagan Administration in the face of recent attacks. Instead of Reagan giving substantial answers, we read more of the standard generalities, such as on the federal deficit, "the president can't spend a penny. The Congress is all that can spend money." His "Kevin Costner Dances with the GOP," 8-5, is an amusing "Film" entry, marred by some overly-cute writing, "outing" Kevin Costner, star of "politically correct" movies, as a Republican. He files a report on the violence between African-Americans and Hasidic Jews in Crown Heights "A Venomous Tree Grows in Brooklyn," 10-7, Wattenberg able to capture the demogoauery on both sides and touch on the underlying issues which divide the community.

Wermiel, Stephen. *The Wall Street Journal.* (★ ½)
Supreme Court. For the first time in several years, Wermiel drops from a three-star rating. His work this year simply lacked the microscopic insight and clarity we've come to expect. His "Scalia's Criticism of Journalists Misses the Target, Apparently on Purpose," 2-11, is surprisingly self-serving on Justice Scalia's complaints of Supreme Court reporters who, Scalia says, focus on the results of the decisions reached, not the legal paths which took them to the decision. Wermiel writes a snide comment on fumbling over victim's rights decisions in "Supreme Court's Conservative Majority Again Stumbles on Victim-Rights Issue," 2-25, his tone marring the piece, considering he is the premier SCOTUS reporter. In "Justices Bar 'Fetal Protection' Policies," 3-21, Wermiel gets good reactions from many sides in the UAW v. Johnson Controls case, though he misses many of the basics, and we don't find out what the judges, media and advocacy groups were reacting to. He cites the two recent cases of fetal protection and SCOTUS refusal to limit punitive damage awards against businesses as his reasoning behind "Business Still Finds Its Struggle Is Uphill Despite High Court's Conservative Slant," 3-25. The use of only two examples does not really prove his thesis. Wermiel never quite gets to the heart of the matter over habeas corpus rulings in "Supreme Court Conservatives Play Role of Legislators on Death Penalty Issue," 4-22, although he does put a clear focus on the debate and the party lines. He limits his "Controversy Brews Behind High Marks Given to Bush Nominees for Judgeships," 5-13, solely to the political impact, which is astute enough, yet we'd have liked to have seen the ABA process of approval more defined. The neatly penned but obvious "The Marshall Seat: Bush's Court Nominee, A Black Republican, Is a Deft Political Choice," co-written by Paul M. Barrett 7-2, is an acceptable roundup on Clarence Thomas, although there's little on why Thomas is such a bold nomination. "Mystery Man: Judge Thomas, Billed as Conservative, May Prove Unpredictable," co-written by Paul M. Barrett 7-19, sounds distanced, as if they they merely repeated others' press clippings and press releases.

Whalen, Bill. *Insight.* (★ ★ ½)
Politics. Whalen adeptly focuses his lens on the Washington fray as well as combing through the list of Democratic presidential contenders giving us fine profiles. Though one of the magazine's brightest writers, he left this autumn. A rare look at the Democratic side of the aisle by Whalen, "Gore May Be Maneuvering for Another Presidential Run," 2-11, results in a well-

rounded report on the place occupied by Gore in the Democratic presidential constellation following his pro-war vote in the Senate. His "Governor Builds a Reputation as Pee-wee Herman of Politics," 3-25, is an entertaining article on Maryland Governor William Donald Schaefer, "one of America's most colorful and puzzling heads of state." In "Tsongas Ready to Make His Run," 4-8, he delivers an acute profile: ". . .Tsongas faces two potential drawbacks. One is that a portion of the electorate automatically will compare him to Dukakis. The other is that his fellow Democratic candidates will make the connection for any voters unwilling to do so themselves." Whalen delivers a multi-faceted profile of Commerce Committee Chairman John D. Dingell in "D.C.'s Big Game Hunter," 5-27, seemingly carried away by Dingell's forceful personality, at one point labeling Energy and Commerce "the most powerful committee on Capitol Hill." His "Packing a Wallop for the Conservatives," 7-15, is an informative if dull profile of Malcolm Wallop, leader of conservative Republicans in the Senate, who has stood up to President Bush on such issues as the budget agreement. Whalen provides an adequate summary of the troubled speakership of Tom Foley in "Mr. Nice Guy Under Fire," 8-19. He begins in a peculiar manner, with criticism of Foley's wife: "In a chamber full of micromanagers, Mrs. Foley is perhaps the ultimate buttinsky." Whalen's opinions of Jerry Brown in "A Flash in the Pan?" 9-30, are slightly askew: "It was not clear from Brown's high-decibel, 45-minute discourse on politics whether he was running for president, practicing Gestalt therapy or auditioning for the lead role in *The Last Angry Man*." In "'92 Race Gets Wilder," 10-14, he pens one of the best reports we've seen this year that places Douglas Wilder's candidacy in the context of internal Democratic racial politics, a 10 Best selection for Political Reporting.

Wilkerson, Isabel. *The New York Times.* (★ ★)
National correspondent. Wilkerson's delightful features and news items from the Rustbelt glow with color. Whether it's the ambiance and romance of riverboat gambling or a stark examination of the inner cites, we come away satiated. Her political astuteness surprises in "With Chicago Calm, Daley Glides Toward Primary," 2-19, as the calmest race in years "glides" to its conclusion in the Democratic primary, Wilkerson capturing the mood here, effectively contrasting it to uglier past contests. She offers a delightful report on the comeback of riverboat gambling, "Gambling Returns to the Mississippi," 4-2, though, unfortunately, there's little hard information here on how much revenue the port cities in Iowa hope to gain, and why it might spread to the eastern shore. Wilkerson offers no solutions in her P. 1 "Ravaged City on Mississippi Floundering at Rock Bottom," 4-4, where she draws a stark portrait of all the problems of East St. Louis, IL. Her "Michigan Judges' Views of Abortion Are Berated," 5-3, focuses on the judges who must decide if minors may have abortions instead of the law itself, the sketchy quality detracting from the relation to broader issues involved. She takes a bemused look at the "Premier Dan Quayle Memorabilia Exhibit" in the fluffy "Quayle's Hometown Gets a Jump on History," 5-14: "It's all very 50's, very Middle American, almost surreal in its innocence." Her "Hoosiers Glimpse a Bit of Byzantium," 7-8, is a rather colorless dispatch on stolen mosaics, from a sixth century Byzantine church, depicting Christ and the Gospels, and in spite of international intrigue, this piece never takes off. Wilkerson gets most of the picture in "A.T.&T. Settles Bias Suit for $66 Million," 7-18, about 13,000 workers with unpaid maternity leave, but the legalese detracts from the article's liveliness. She makes a compelling argument that something needs to be done in "To Save Its Men, Detroit Plans Boys-Only Schools," 8-14, but she isn't quite sure if this last-ditch experiment to open three all-male academies in inner-city Detroit is the solution.

Williams, Juan. *The Washington Post.* (★ ★ ★ ½)
Staff writer. Williams peppers his hard-hitting essays with canny observations that cannot easily be discounted. We continue to be impressed by both his eloquence and his ability to carve out unique angles in his writings. His "Double Talk From War Protesters," 2-7, is a sharp op-ed piece demolishing protesters' claims that they oppose the Persian Gulf War while supporting the troops. Williams' scalding "Donkeys and Windmills: Democrats Look at '92," 3-10, summarizes Democratic presidential hopes and fears for 1992: "The best chance for Democrats

will come if Bush is unable to capitalize on the promise of his triumph in the Persian Gulf." His "How to Pick 'Em," 4-28, a straightforward *Book World* review of *Los Angeles Times* political correspondent Robert Shogan's new book, *The Riddle of Leadership,* with Williams offering mostly a summation and little in the way of criticism or analysis. He writes an over-long profile of Virginia Governor Doug Wilder in action, "One-Man Show," 6-9, Williams documenting how Wilder has assumed his position in politics while alienating everyone around him: "He acts independently and demands respect for this integrity, but he doesn't necessarily reward others for acting in the same manner." Williams, in Japan for 3 months on a U.S.-Japan Society Fellowship, writes on how the Japanese are worried over such perceived symptoms of Japan-bashing as the 50th anniversary of Pearl Harbor in his superb article "Fear and Remembrance in Japan," 7-2. Williams projects the potential for black conservatives to "overwhelm" the liberal establishment in "Thomas and the Isolation of the Liberal Establishment," 9-15, believing that the old orthodoxy is cracking under the weight of its own bankrupt ideas. His "Open Season on Clarence Thomas," 10-10, is an important column detailing the extra-legal efforts of the liberal establishment to derail the Clarence Thomas nomination, a 10 Best selection for Commentary. Williams adds: "To listen to or read some news reports on Thomas over the past month is to discover a monster of a man, totally unlike the human being full of sincerity, confusion, and struggles whom I saw as a reporter who watched him for some 10 years."

Williams, Marjorie. *The Washington Post.* (★ ★ ½)
Staff writer. Williams spent much of the year writing features on the slow political death of Clark Clifford, her trim, elegant prose carrying us through the saga. Much of her work, however, lacked the kind of solid information that made "The Long and Short of Richard Darman," 7-29-90, for example, the talk of the town. In "Wounds of Long-Ago Battles," 1-16, Williams goes to a veteran's hospital and plies stark tales from various vets, both pro-and anti-military action in the Gulf, not only from Vietnam. She provides a sharp, scathing portrait in "Clark Clifford: The Rise of a Reputation," 3-8: "Through his intermittent work as adviser and problem-solver to presidents, he has made himself appear a lifelong public servant who only incidentally practices hardball Washington law." Her "Lee Atwater: American Original," 3-30, is a barbed op-ed column on the late political consultant, which looks through the controversies and contradictions to find a deeply cyncial man whose only virtues were a lack of hypocrisy and self-delusion. Her windy second part profile, "Clark Clifford: On the Tightrope of Virtue," 5-8, again stars the beleaguered Washington icon and examines the BCCI scandal, with Williams reporting that Clifford really has no one to blame but himself. She provides an amusing "The Brains Behind Headaches," 7-4, on the Fifth International Headache Congress at the J.W. Marriott, with Williams wandering about and making discoveries about the different kinds of headaches and their treatments. Her light touch just borders on the sarcastic in "Hot Line to Heaven?" 8-13, on Dial-the-Pope, a 900 number on which you can hear recorded messages from John Paul II, but she's careful to include the views of some Catholic commentators, such as Michael Novak, to offset this. The colorful "The Performance of a Lifetime," 9-12, is a vivid account of Clark Clifford's testimony before the House Banking Committee that, while atmospheric, doesn't really give us much hard information.

Yang, John. *The Washington Post.* (★ ★)
White House. Yang's eye for detail and subtlety is as sharp as ever, particularly when he does his own reporting. When he uses secondary sources from time to time, he's less effective. He takes "How Budget Cutters Worked Up a $60,000 Appetite," 1-23, on the expenses at the budget summit for food and drink, from the January issue of *Armed Forces Journal International,* and scripts it into a reasonable rehash. The generous detail colors "Lawmakers Pledge Funds Needed to Conclude War," 2-23, in this snapshot look at the budgetary considerations of the Persian Gulf War. Yang provides a good smattering of costs in "Bush Unveils Education Plan," 4-19, with a slightly different angle propelling this solid outline of Bush's education "crusade," to use Sec. of Education Lamar Alexander's term. In the nice follow-up "Ski Industry Lobby Paid Expenses for Sununu, Wife in Aspen," co-written by Charles Babcock 4-30, the pair culls the

story of John Sununu's skiing escapade from several different sources, including *Time* magazine. His "For Bush's Speech, A New Word Order," 6-22, is an interesting report on new chief White House speechwriter Tony Snow, with Yang wryly noting, "It remains the central fact of any speechwriter's life, however, that he is only as effective as the speechgiver." He provides a sharp outline of Bush's communique and rationale for getting Gorbachev and his team to move faster on START in "Bush Urges Gorbachev to Conclude Strategic Arms Treaty," 7-7, the comprehensive background giving us a sense of the importance of Bush taking the lead. Yang uses Bush's vacation as a starting point to analyze his character's dichotomy of the elitest and entrepreneur in "Bush Relaxes With His Contradictions," 8-16, though unfortunately, he fails to probe deeper than the mere impressions of the President. His "Guarantees Would Be Costly Only If Israel Were to Default," 9-14, supplies generous details on how the loan guarantees to Israel would work, who would pay for it, and how it would be accounted for in the budget. Yang's itelligent report leads us to believe he should be covering similar stories.

APPENDIX

INDEX OF JOURNALISTS

The following appendix lists journalists who are rated in this edition of *MediaGuide* grouped according to assignment as of December 15, 1991. An evaluative review of each can be found in the *MediaGuide* section indicated in the third column. Asterisks indicate a pending assignment for 1992. An index of abbreviations immediately follows this section.

Journalist	Publication/Syndicate	Section

ADVERTISING/MARKETING

Journalist	Publication/Syndicate	Section
Deveny, Kathleen	*WSJ*	FR
Farhi, Paul	*WP*	FR
Horovitz, Bruce	*LAT*	FR
Kanner, Bernice	*NY*	FR
Lipman, Joanne	*WSJ*	FR
McCarthy, Michael J.	*WSJ*	FR
Pereira, Joseph	*WSJ*	FR
Rothenberg, Randall	*NYT*	FR

AGRICULTURE/FOOD AND BEVERAGE INDUSTRY

Journalist	Publication/Syndicate	Section
Freedman, Alix M.	*WSJ*	FR
Ingersoll, Bruce	*WSJ*	FR
Schneider, Keith	*NYT*	SHE

AIRLINES/TRANSPORTATION

Journalist	Publication/Syndicate	Section
Brown, David A.	*AWST*	NSDIP
Cushman, John H., Jr.	*NYT*	FR
Hamilton, Martha A.	*WP*	FR
McGough, Robert	*FW*	FR
Nomani, Asra Q.	*WSJ*	FR
O'Brian, Bridget	*WSJ*	FR
Ott, James	*AWST*	FR
Salpukas, Agis	*NYT*	FR

AUTOMOTIVE

Journalist	Publication/Syndicate	Section
Flint, Jerry	*Forbes*	FR
Ingrassia, Paul	*WSJ*	FR
Levin, Doron P.	*NYT*	FR
Taylor, Alex, III	*Fortune*	FR
Treece, James B.	*BW*	FR
White, Joseph	*WSJ*	FR

AVIATION

Journalist	Publication/Syndicate	Section
Hughes, David	*AWST*	NSDIP
Lenorovitz, Jeffrey M.	*AWST*	NSDIP
Nordwall, Bruce D.	*AWST*	NSDIP
Vartabedian, Ralph	*LAT*	NSDIP

BANKING/S&Ls/INSURANCE

Journalist	Publication/Syndicate	Section
Bacon, Kenneth	*WSJ*	FR
Freudenheim, Milt	*NYT*	FR
Labaton, Stephen	*NYT*	FR
Lohr, Steve	*NYT*	FR
McNamee, Mike	*BW*	FR
Quint, Michael	*NYT*	FR
Rosenblatt, Robert A.	*LAT*	FR
Schmidt, Susan	*WP*	FR
Thomas, Paulette	*WSJ*	FR
Truell, Peter	*WSJ*	FR

BUSINESS

Journalist	Publication/Syndicate	Section
Ansberry, Clare	*WSJ*	FR
Banks, Howard	*Forbes*	FR
Barrett, William P.	*Forbes*	FR
Bartlett, Sarah	*NYT*	FR
Berg, Eric N.	*NYT*	FR
Berss, Marcia	*Forbes*	FR
Bleiberg, Robert M.	*Barron's*	FR
Byrne, John A.	*BW*	FR
Byron, Christopher	*NY*	FR
Carley, William M.	*WSJ*	FR
Chambliss, Lauren	*FW*	FR
Charlier, Marj	*WSJ*	FR
Commins, Kevin	*JC*	FR
Cook, James	*Forbes*	FR
Cowan, Alison Leigh	*NYT*	FR
Crossen, Cynthia	*WSJ*	FR
Dentzer, Susan	*USNWR*	FR

Journalist	Publication/Syndicate	Section
Dobrzynski, Judith H.	*BW*	FR
Donlan, Thomas G.	*Barron's*	FR
Feder, Barnaby J.	*NYT*	FR
Ferguson, Tim W.	*WSJ*	FR
Flanigan, James	*LAT*	FR
Greenwald, John	*Time*	FR
Gupta, Udayan	*WSJ*	FR
Hayes, Thomas C.	*NYT*	FR
Ivey, Mark	*BW*	FR
Jenkins, Holman, Jr.	*Insight*	FR
Johnson, Robert	*WSJ*	FR
Kleinfield, N. R.	*NYT*	FR
Knight, Jerry	*WP*	FR
Lelyveld, Michael S.	*JC*	FR
Loomis, Carol J.	*Fortune*	FR
Mahar, Maggie	*Barron's*	FR
Morgenson, Gretchen	*Forbes*	FR
Nutly, Peter	*Fortune*	FR
Ramirez, Anthony	*NYT*	FR
Richter, Paul	*LAT*	FR
Rudnitsky, Howard	*Forbes*	FR
Saporito, Bill	*Fortune*	FR
Shapiro, Eben	*NYT*	FR
Stern, Richard L.	*Forbes*	FR
Stevenson, Richard	*NYT*	FR
Warsh, David	*BG*	FR
Yang, Dori Jones	*BW*	FR

COMPUTERS/ HIGH TECHNOLOGY/ TELECOMMUNICATIONS

Journalist	Publication/Syndicate	Section
Andrews, Edmund L.	*NYT*	FR
Asker, James R.	*AWST*	NSDIP
Bulkeley, William L.	*WSJ*	FR
Burgess, John	*WP*	FR
Carey, John	*BW*	FR
Carroll, Paul B.	*WSJ*	FR
Elmer-DeWitt, Philip	*Time*	SHE
Kandebo, Stanley W.	*AWST*	NSDIP
Lazzareschi, Carla	*LAT*	FR
Lewis, Peter	*NYT*	FR
Markoff, John	*NYT*	FR
Pollack, Andrew	*NYT*	FR
Proctor, Paul	*AWST*	NSDIP
Schrage, Michael	*LAT*	FR
Verity, John	*BW*	FR
Victor, Kirk	*NJ*	FR
Wiegner, Kathleen K.	*Forbes*	FR
Zachary, G. Pascal	*WSJ*	FR

CONGRESS

Journalist	Publication/Syndicate	Section
Birnbaum, Jeffrey H.	*WSJ*	SPR
Calmes, Jackie	*WSJ*	SPR

Journalist	Publication/Syndicate	Section
Clymer, Adam	*NYT*	SPR
Cohen, Richard E.	*NJ*	SPR
Dewar, Helen	*WP*	SPR
Eaton, William J.	*LAT*	SPR
Fritz, Sara	*LAT*	SPR
Gilmartin, Patricia A.	*AWST*	NSDIP
Holmes, Steven A.	*NYT*	SPR
Houston, Paul	*LAT*	SPR
Kenworthy, Tom	*WP*	SPR
Rodriguez, Paul	*WT*	SPR
Rogers, David	*WSJ*	SPR
Ross, Michael	*LAT*	SPR

CULTURE

Journalist	Publication/Syndicate	Section
Bering-Jensen, Helle	*Insight*	SPR
Fleming, Thomas	*Chronicles*	SPC
Grenier, Richard	*WT*	SPC

DEFENSE

Journalist	Publication/Syndicate	Section
Baker, Caleb	*DN*	NSDIP
Broder, John M.	*LAT*	NSDIP
de Briganti, Giovanni	*DN*	NSDIP
Fialka, John J.	*WSJ*	NSDIP
Finnegan, Philip	*DN*	NSDIP
Fulgham, David A.	*AWST*	NSDIP
Gellman, Barton	*WP*	NSDIP
Gold, Philip	*Insight*	NSDIP
Healy, Melissa	*LAT*	NSDIP
Henderson, Breck W.	*AWST*	NSDIP
Hitchens, Theresa	*DN*	NSDIP
Holzer, Robret	*DN*	NSDIP
Leopold, George	*DN*	NSDIP
Mecham, Michael	*AWST*	NSDIP
Morrison, David	*NJ*	NSDIP
Morrocco, John D.	*AWST*	NSDIP
Munro, Neil	*DN*	NSDIP
Opall, Barbara	*DN*	NSDIP
Pasztor, Andy	*WSJ*	NSDIP
Polsky, Debra	*DN*	NSDIP
Schmitt, Eric	*NYT*	NSDIP
Shifrin, Carole A.	*AWST*	NSDIP
Silverberg, David	*DN*	NSDIP
Smith, Bruce A.	*AWST*	NSDIP
Smith, R. Jeffrey	*WP*	NSDIP
Wartzman, Rick	*WSJ*	NSDIP
White, David	*FT*	NSDIP

DIPLOMATIC AFFAIRS

Journalist	Publication/Syndicate	Section
Greenberger, Robert S.	*WSJ*	NSDIP
Lewis, Paul	*NYT*	NSDIP
Mauthner, Robert	*FT*	NSDIP

Journalist	Publication/Syndicate	Section

ECONOMICS/FISCAL & MONETARY POLICY

Journalist	Publication/Syndicate	Section
Berry, John M.	WP	FR
Boyd, John	JC	FR
Brittan, Samuel	FT	FR
Dentzer, Susan	USNWR	FR
Gleckman, Howard	BW	FR
Haas, Lawrence J.	NJ	FR
Hershey, Robert D., Jr.	NYT	FR
Johnston, Oswald	LAT	FR
Kuttner, Robert	TNR	FR
Moberg, David	ITT	FR
Mufson, Steven	WP	FR
Murray, Alan	WSJ	FR
Nasar, Sylvia	NYT	FR
Norman, Peter	FT	FR
Passell, Peter	NYT	FR
Prowse, Michael	FT	FR
Risen, James	LAT	FR
Rosenbaum, David E.	NYT	FR
Rowen, Hobart	WP	FR
Silk, Leonard	NYT	FR
Srodes, James L.	FW	FR
Starobin, Paul	NJ	FR
Thomas, Rich	NW	FR
Uchitelle, Louis	NYT	FR
Wessel, David	WSJ	FR

EDUCATION

Journalist	Publication/Syndicate	Section
Innerst, Carol	WT	SPR
Nazario, Sonia L.	WSJ	SPR
Putka, Gary	WSJ	SPR

ENERGY/OIL

Journalist	Publication/Syndicate	Section
Kriz, Margaret	NJ	SHE
Lippman, Thomas W.	WP	FR
Solomon, Caleb	WSJ	FR
Sullivan, Allanna	WSJ	FR
Tanner, James	WSJ	FR
Wald, Matthew L.	NYT	FR

ENGINEERING

Journalist	Publication/Syndicate	Section
Dornheim, Michael A.	AWST	NSDIP
Scott, William B.	AWST	NSDIP

ENTERTAINMENT INDUSTRY

Journalist	Publication/Syndicate	Section
Grover, Ronald	BW	FR
Gubernick, Lisa	Forbes	FR
Harris, Kathryn	Forbes	FR
Landro, Laura	WSJ	FR

ENVIRONMENT

Journalist	Publication/Syndicate	Section
Abramson, Rudy	LAT	SHE
Chase, Alston	WT	SPC
Holusha, John	NYT	SHE
Lancaster, John	WP	SHE
Satchell, Michael	USNWP	SHE
Taylor, Ronald A.	WT	SHE
Weisskopf, Michael	WP	SHE

FEATURES

Journalist	Publication/Syndicate	Section
Allen, Henry	WP	SPR
Borger, Gloria	USNWR	SPR
Donohoe, Cathryn	WT	SPR
Hall, Carla	WP	SPR
Piccoli, Sean	WT	SPR
Pisik, Betsy	WT	SPR
Romano, Lois	WP	SPR
Williams, Marjorie	WP	SPR

FINANCE

Journalist	Publication/Syndicate	Section
Day, Kathleen	WP	FR
Henriques, Diana B.	NYT	FR
Light, Larry	BW	FR
Wayne, Leslie	NYT	FR

FINANCIAL MARKETS

Journalist	Publication/Syndicate	Section
Crudele, John	NYP	FR
Forsyth, Randall W.	Barron's	FR
Fuerbringer, Jonathan	NYT	FR
Herman, Tom	WSJ	FR
Laderman, Jeffrey M.	BW	FR
Liscio, John	Barron's	FR
Lowenstein, Roger	WSJ	FR
McCartney, Robert	WP	FR
Mitchell, Constance	WSJ	FR
Norris, Floyd	NYT	FR
Platt, Gordon	JC	FR
Power, William	WSJ	FR
Salwen, Kevin G.	WSJ	FR
Weiss, Gary	BW	FR

FOREIGN AFFAIRS

Journalist	Publication/Syndicate	Section
Ajami, Fouad	USNWP	SPC
Bernstein, Jonas	Insight	FNCR
Black, George	TN	SPC
Borowiec, Andrew	WT	FNCR
Gelb, Leslie H.	NYT	SPC
Geyer, Georgie Anne	UPS	SPC
Hoagland, Jim	WP	SPC
Kamen, Al	WP	NSDIP
Kirk, Donald	Freelance	FNCR

Journalist	Publication/Syndicate	Section
Kirkpatrick, Jeane	LATS	SPC
Lewis, Anthony	NYT	SPC
Madison, Christopher	NJ	NSDIP
Melloan, George	WSJ	FNCR
Meyer, Cord	NAS	SPC
Mortimer, Edward	FT	SPC
Nelan, Bruce	Time	NSDIP
Rosenfeld, Stephen S.	WP	SPC
Sciolino, Elaine	NYT	NSDIP
Sieff, Martin	WT	FNCR
Simpson, John	TS	FNCR
Tanzer, Andrew	Forbes	FNCR

FOREIGN CORRESPONDENTS

Abidjan
Noble, Kenneth B.	NYT	FNCR

Addis Ababa
Parmelee, Jennifer	WP	FNCR

Bangkok
Shenon, Philip	NYT	FNCR
Wallace, Charles P.	LAT	FNCR

Beijing
Holley, David	LAT	FNCR
Kristof, Nicholas D.	NYT	FNCR
McGregor, James	WSJ	FNCR
Sun, Lena H.	WP	FNCR
WuDunn, Sheryl	NYT	FNCR

Beirut
Boustany, Nora	WP	FNCR

Berlin
Marshall, Tyler	LAT	FNCR
Tagliabue, John	NYT	FNCR

Bogota
Farah, Douglas	WP	FNCR

Bonn
Fisher, Marc	WP	FNCR
Jones, Tamara	LAT	FNCR
Kempe, Frederick	WSJ	FNCR
Kinzer, Stephen	NYT	FNCR
Peel, Quentin	FT	FNCR
Protzman, Ferdinand	NYT	FNCR

Brussels
Barnard, Bruce	JC	FNCR
Buchan, David	FT	FNCR
Havemann, Joel	LAT	FNCR

Budapest
Bohlen, Celestine	NYT	FNCR
Kamm, Henry	NYT	FNCR
Williams, Carol J.	LAT	FNCR

Buenos Aires
Long, William R.	LAT	FNCR
Nash, Nathaniel C.	NYT	FNCR
Robinson, Eugene	WP	FNCR

Cairo
Hedges, Chris	NYT	FNCR
Murphy, Caryle	WP	FNCR

Journalist	Publication/Syndicate	Section
Murphy, Kim	LAT	FNCR
Walker, Tony	FT	FNCR

Caribbean
de Cordoba, Jose	WSJ	FNCR
French, Howard W.	NYT	FNCR
James, Canute	FT	FNCR

Europe
Bering-Jensen, Henrik	Insight	FNCR
Dempsey, Judy	FT	FNCR
Fuhrman, Peter	Forbes	FNCR
Marsh, David	FT	FNCR
Newman, Barry	WSJ	FNCR
Porter, Janet	JC	FNCR
Reier, Sharon	FW	FNCR

Germany
Meyer, Michael	NW	FNCR

Hong Kong
Bangsberg, P. T.	JC	FNCR
Worthy, Ford S.	Fortune	FNCR

Jerusalem
Carnegy, Hugh	FT	FNCR
Diehl, Jackson	WP	FNCR
Haberman, Clyde	NYT	FNCR
Williams, Daniel	LAT	FNCR

Johannesburg
Contreras, Joseph	NW	FNCR
Davidson, Joe	WSJ	FNCR
Kraft, Scott	LAT	FNCR
Ottaway, David B.	WP	FNCR
Wren, Christopher	NYT	FNCR

Latin America
Asman, David	WSJ	FNCR
Robinson, Linda	USNWR	FNCR

London
Forman, Craig	WSJ	FNCR
Frankel, Glenn	WP	FNCR
Marcom, John, Jr.	Forbes	FNCR
Prokesch, Steven	NYT	FNCR
Rockwell, Keith M.	JC	FNCR
Schmidt, William E.	NYT	FNCR
Tuohy, William	LAT	FNCR
Whitney, Craig R.	NYT	FNCR

Managua
Boudreaux, Richard	LAT	FNCR
Cody, Edward	WP	FNCR

Manila
Branigin, William	WP	FNCR
Drogin, Bob	LAT	FNCR

Mexico City
Baker, Stephen	BW	FNCR
Darling, Juanita	LAT	FNCR
Fraser, Damien	FT	FNCR
Golden, Tim	NYT	FNCR
Miller, Marjorie	LAT	FNCR
Moffett, Matt	WSJ	FNCR

Middle East
Beyer, Lisa	Time	FNCR

Journalist	Publication/Syndicate	Section
Brooks, Geraldine	*WSJ*	FNCR
Chesnoff, Richard Z.	*USNWR*	FNCR
Church, George J.	*Time*	FNCR
Horwitz, Tony	*WSJ*	FNCR
Kelly, Michael	*TNR*	FNCR
Mallet, Victor	*FT*	FNCR
Miller, Judith	*NYT*	FNCR
Pletka, Danielle	*Insight*	FNCR
Randal, Jonathan C.	*WP*	FNCR
Montreal		
Ryan, Leo	*JC*	FNCR
Moscow		
Bogert, Carol	*NW*	FNCR
Boulton, Leyla	*FT*	FNCR
Clines, Francis X.	*NYT*	FNCR
Dahlberg, John-Thor	*LAT*	FNCR
Dobbs, Michael	*WP*	FNCR
Gumbel, Peter	*WSJ*	FNCR
Keller, Bill	*NYT*	FNCR
Lloyd, John	*FT*	FNCR
Parks, Michael	*LAT*	FNCR
Remnick, David	*WP*	FNCR
Schmemann, Serge	*NYT*	FNCR
Nairobi		
Henry, Neil	*WP*	FNCR
Hiltzik, Michael A.	*LAT*	FNCR
Ozanne, Julian	*FT*	FNCR
Perlez, Jane	*NYT*	FNCR
New Delhi		
Coll, Steve	*WP*	FNCR
Fineman, Mark B.	*LAT*	FNCR
Gargan, Edward A.	*NYT*	FNCR
Housego, David	*FT*	FNCR
Nicosia		
Williams, Nick B., Jr.	*LAT*	FNCR
Paris		
Davidson, Ian	*FT*	FNCR
Dickey, Christopher	*NW*	FNCR
Drozdiak, William	*WP*	FNCR
Greenhouse, Steven	*NYT*	FNCR
Ibrahim, Youssef M.	*NYT*	FNCR
Lawday, David	*USNWR*	FNCR
Lewis, Flora	*NYT*	FNCR
Revzin, Philip	*WSJ*	FNCR
Riding, Alan	*NYT*	FNCR
Tempest, Rone	*LAT*	FNCR
Rio de Janeiro		
Brooke, James	*NYT*	FNCR
Kamm, Thomas	*WSJ*	FNCR
Lamb, Christina	*FT*	FNCR
Rome		
Cowell, Alan	*NYT*	FNCR
Montalbano, William D.	*LAT*	FNCR
San Salvador		
Christian, Shirley	*NYT*	FNCR

Journalist	Publication/Syndicate	Section
Freed, Kenneth	*LAT*	FNCR
Hockstader, Lee	*WP*	FNCR
Sao Paulo		
Bruce, James	*JC*	FNCR
Southeast Asia		
Erlanger, Steven	*NYT*	FNCR
Magnier, Mark	*JC*	FNCR
Seoul		
Darlin, Damon	*WSJ*	FNCR
South Africa		
Waldmeir, Patti	*FT*	FNCR
Tokyo		
Blustein, Paul	*WP*	FNCR
Brauchli, Marcus	*WSJ*	FNCR
Cullison, A. E.	*JC*	FNCR
Helm, Leslie	*LAT*	FNCR
Holden, Ted	*BW*	FNCR
Impoco, Jim	*USNWP*	FNCR
Jameson, Sam	*LAT*	FNCR
Lehner, Urban C.	*WSJ*	FNCR
Neff, Robert	*BW*	FNCR
Nelian, Ed	*WT*	FNCR
Powell, Bill	*NW*	FNCR
Reid, T. R.	*WP*	FNCR
Sanger, David E.	*NYT*	FNCR
Schlesinger, Jacob	*WSJ*	FNCR
Sterngold, James	*NYT*	FNCR
Wagstyl, Stefan	*FT*	FNCR
Watanabe, Teresa	*LAT*	FNCR
Weisman, Steven R.	*NYT*	FNCR
Toronto		
Claiborne, William	*WP*	FNCR
Farnsworth, Clyde H.	*NYT*	FNCR
Symonds, William C.	*BW*	FNCR
Walsh, Mary Williams	*LAT*	FNCR
Vienna		
Thurow, Roger	*WSJ*	FNCR
Warsaw		
Battiata, Mary	*WP*	FNCR
Bobinski, Christopher	*FT*	FNCR
Engelberg, Stephen	*NYT*	FNCR
Harden, Blaine	*WP*	FNCR
Powers, Charles T.	*LAT*	FNCR
Sikorski, Radek	*NR*	FNCR

HEALTH

Journalist	Publication/Syndicate	Section
Bishop, Jerry	*WSJ*	SHE
Cimons, Marlene	*LAT*	SHE
Hilts, Philip J.	*NYT*	SHE
Kosterlitz, Julie	*NJ*	SHE
Rich, Spencer	*WP*	SHE
Winslow, Ron	*WSJ*	SHE

Journalist	Publication/Syndicate	Section

HUMOR

Baker, Russell	*NYT*	SPC
Barry, Dave	*TMH*, TMS	SPC
Buchwald, Art	*LATS*	SPC
Royko, Mike	*CT*, TMS	SPC

INVESTIGATIONS

Babcock, Charles R.	*WP*	SPR
Gerth, Jeff	*NYT*	SPR
Hedges, Michael	*WT*	SPR
Lardner, George	*WP*	NSDIP
McGee, Jim	*WP*	SPR
Seper, Jerry	*WT*	SPR

JUSTICE DEPARTMENT

Barrett, Paul M.	*WSJ*	SPR
Isikoff, Michael	*WP*	SPR
Johnston, David	*NYT*	SPR
Ostrow, Ronald J.	*LAT*	SPR

LABOR

Bernstein, Aaron	*BW*	FR
Bernstein, Harry	*LAT*	FR
Kilborn, Peter T.	*NYT*	FR

LAW

Allen, Charlotte	*Insight*	SPR
Crovitz, L. Gordon	*WSJ*	SPC
Hentoff, Nat	*WP*	SPC
Lewis, Neil A.	*NYT*	SPR
Moore, W. John	*NJ*	SPR

LOBBYING

Abramson, Jill	*WSJ*	SPR
Matlack, Carol	*NJ*	SPR

MANAGEMENT

Bennett, Amanda	*WSJ*	FR
Deutsch, Claudia H.	*NYT*	FR

MEDIA

Alter, Jonathan	*NW*	SPR
Diamond, Edwin	*NY*	SPR
Eastland, Terry	*TAS*	SPC
Fabrikant, Geraldine	*NYT*	FR
Jones, Alex	*NYT*	FR
Kowet, Don	*WT*	SPR
Kurtz, Howard	*WP*	SPR

Journalist	Publication/Syndicate	Section
Landro, Laura	*WSJ*	FR
Rosenstiel, Thomas B.	*LAT*	SPR
Shales, Tom	*WP*	SPR

MEDICINE

Altman, Lawrence K., M.D.	*NYT*	SHE
Chase, Marilyn	*WSJ*	SHE
Waldholz, Michael	*WSJ*	SHE

NATIONAL AFFAIRS

Applebome, Peter	*NYT*	SPR
Archibald, George	*WT*	SPR
Ayres, B. Drummond	*NYT*	SPR
Barringer, Felicity	*NYT*	SPR
Bennet, James	*WM*	SPR
Berke, Richard L.	*NYT*	SPR
Bond, David F.	*AWST*	NSDIP
Cannon, Lou	*WP*	SPR
Carlson, Margaret	*Time*	SPR
Chapman, Stephen	*CT*, CS	SPC
Charen, Mona	CS	SPC
Cohen, Richard	*WP*	SPC
DeParle, Jason	*NYT*	SPR
Egan, Timothy	*NYT*	SPR
Farney, Dennis	*WSJ*	SPR
Fields, Suzanne	*WT*	SPC
Fineman, Howard	*NW*	SPR
Francis, Samuel	*WT*, Chronicles	SPC
Garrett, Major	*WT*	SPR
Gergen, David	*USNWR*	SPC
Goodman, Ellen	*BG*, WPWG	SPC
Greenberg, Paul	FS	SPC
Greenfield, Meg	*NW*, *WP*	SPC
Gross, Jane	*NYT*	SPR
Hinds, Michael deCourcy	*NYT*	SPR
Ifill, Gwen	*NYT*	SPR
Ivins, Molly	*MJ*, TP	SPC
*Jehl, Douglas	*NYT*	SPR
Kilpatrick, James J.	UPS	SPC
Krauthammer, Charles	WPWG	SPC
Kristol, Irving	*WSJ*	SPC
Leo, John	*USNWR*	SPC
Lerner, Max	*NYP*, LATS	SPC
Lindberg, Tod	*Insight*	SPC
Martz, Larry	*NW*	SPR
Massing, Michael	*CJR*	SPR
Mathews, Jay	*WP*	SPR
Matthews, Christopher	*SFE*, KFS	SPC
McCarthy, Colman	WPWG	SPC
Muwakkil, Salim	*ITT*	SPR
Mydans, Seth	*NYT*	SPR
Noah, Timothy	*WSJ*	SPR
Novak, Michael	*Forbes*	SPC
O'Rourke, P. J.	*TAS*, RS	SPR

Journalist	Publication/Syndicate	Section
Page, Clarence	*CT,* TMS	SPC
Pear, Robert	*NYT*	SPR
Peirce, Neal R.	*NJ*	SPC
Perry, James M.	*WSJ*	SPR
Postrel, Virginia	*Reason*	SPC
Price, Joyce	*WT*	SPR
Quindlen, Anna	*NYT*	SPC
Raspberry, William	*WP*	SPC
Reinhold, Robert	*NYT*	SPR
Richardson, Valerie	*WT*	SPR
Roberts, Paul Craig	*WT*	SPC
Rohter, Larry	*NYT*	SPR
Rosenthal, A. M.	*NYT*	SPC
Rusher, William A.	NEA	SPC
Seligman, Dan	*Fortune*	SPC
Shapiro, Walter	*Time*	SPR
Shribman, David	*WSJ*	SPR
Sidey, Hugh	*Time*	SPC
Smothers, Ronald	*NYT*	SPR
Sobran, Joseph	*NR,* UPS	SPC
Sowell, Thomas	SHNS	SSPC
Specter, Michael	*NYT*	SPR
Stanfield, Rochelle L.	*NJ*	SPR
Taylor, Paul	*WP*	SPR
Tolchin, Martin	*NYT*	SPR
Tyrrell, R. Emmett, Jr.	*TAS,* KFS	SPC
Waldman, Steven	*NW*	SPR
Walsh, Edward	*WP*	SPR
Wattenberg, Ben	NEA	SPC
Weisberg, Jacob	*TNR*	SPC
Wicker, Tom	*NYT*	SPC
Wilkerson, Isabel	*NYT*	SPR
Wilkins, Roger	*MJ*	SPC
Williams, Walter	CS	SPC
Yoder, Edwin	WPWG	SPC
Zuckerman, Mortimer	*USNWR*	SPC

NATIONAL SECURITY

Journalist	Publication/Syndicate	Section
Adelman, Kenneth	TMS	SPC
Beichman, Arnold	*WT*	SPC
Gaffney, Frank	Freelance	SPC
Gertz, Bill	*WT*	NSDIP
Gordon, Michael R.	*NYT*	NSDIP
Kempster, Norman	*LAT*	NSDIP
Mann, Jim	*LAT*	NSDIP
McManus, Doyle	*LAT*	NSDIP
Mossberg, Walter S.	*WSJ*	NSDIP
Pincus, Walter	*WP*	NSDIP
Scarborough, Rowan	*WT*	NSDIP
Summers, H. G. (Harry), Jr.	LATS	SPC
Talbott, Strobe	*Time*	SPC
Toth, Robert C.	*LAT*	NSDIP
Tyler, Patrick E.	*NYT*	NSDIP
Wines, Michael	*NYT*	NSDIP
Wright, Robin	*LAT*	NSDIP

Journalist	Publication/Syndicate	Section

OMBUDSMAN

Journalist	Publication/Syndicate	Section
Harwood, Richard	*WP*	SPR

PERSONAL FINANCE

Journalist	Publication/Syndicate	Section
Quinn, Jane Bryant	*NW*	FR

POLITICS

Journalist	Publication/Syndicate	Section
Apple, R. W., Jr.	*NYT*	SPR
Balz, Dan	*WP*	SPR
Barber, Lionel	*FT*	SPR
Barnes, James A.	*NJ*	SPR
Barone, Michael	*USNWR*	SPC
Bethell, Tom	*TAS*	SPC
Blumenthal, Sidney	*TNR*	SPC
Broder, David	*WP*	SPC
Brownstein, Ronald	*LAT*	SPR
Buchanan, Patrick	TMS	SPC
Buckley, William F., Jr.	*NR,* UPS	SPC
Canham-Clyne, John	*ITT*	SPR
Clift, Eleanor	*NW*	SPR
Cockburn, Alexander	*TN, ITT*	SPC
Dionne, E. J., Jr.	*WP*	SPR
Easterbrook, Gregg	*NW*	SPR
Edsall, Thomas B.	*WP*	SPR
Evans, Rowland	*CST,* CS	SPC
Germond, Jack	*NJ*	SPC
Gigot, Paul	*WSJ*	SPC
Hallow, Ralph Z.	*WT*	SPR
Hitchens, Christopher	*TN,* *Harper's*	SPC
Kinsley, Michael	*TNR*	SPC
Klein, Joe	*NY*	SPR
Kondracke, Morton	*TNR*	SPC
Kramer, Michael	*Time*	SPC
Lambro, Donald	*WT*	SPC
McGrory, Mary	*WP*	SPC
McGurn, William	*NR*	SPR
Moss, J. Jennings	*WT*	SPR
Nelson, Jack	*LAT*	SPR
Novak, Robert	*CST,* CS	SPC
Pruden, Wesley	*WT*	SPC
Riddell, Peter	*FT*	SPR
Safire, William	*NYT*	SPC
Schneider, William	*NJ*	SPC
Shields, Mark	*WP*	SPC
Thomas, Evan	*NW*	SPR
Toner, Robin	*NYT*	SPR
Wattenberg, Daniel	*Insight*	SPR
Whalen, Bill	*Insight*	SPR
Will, George F.	*NW,* WPWG	SPC
Williams, Juan	*WP*	SPR
Witcover, Jules	*NJ*	SPC

Journalist	Publication/Syndicate	Section

PUBLISHING

Journalist	Publication/Syndicate	Section
Cohen, Roger	*NYT*	FR
McDowell, Edwin	*NYT*	FR
Reilly, Patrick M.	*WSJ*	FR

RELIGION

Steinfels, Peter	*NYT*	SPR
Thomas, Cal	LATS	SPC

RETAIL

Barmash, Isadore	*NYT*	FR
Schwadel, Francine	*WSJ*	FR
Trachtenberg, Jeffrey A.	*WSJ*	FR

SCIENCE

Angier, Natalie	*NYT*	SHE
Booth, William	*WP*	SHE
Broad, William J.	*NYT*	SHE
Browne, Malcolm W.	*NYT*	SHE
Bylinski, Gene	*Fortune*	SHE
Gladwell, Malcolm	*WP*	SHE
Kolata, Gina	*NYT*	SHE
Stipp, David	*WSJ*	SHE
Wilford, John Noble	*NYT*	SHE

SPACE

Covault, Craig	*AWST*	NSDIP
Kolcum, Edward H.	*AWST*	NSDIP
Sawyer, Kathy	*WP*	NSDIP

STATE DEPARTMENT

Friedman, Thomas L.	*NYT*	NSDIP
Goshko, John M.	*WP*	NSDIP
Hoffman, David	*WP*	NSDIP
Krauss, Clifford	*NYT*	NSDIP
Oberdorfer, Don	*WP*	NSDIP
Strobel, Warren	*WT*	NSDIP

SUPREME COURT

Ceol, Dawn	*WT*	SPR
Gest, Ted	*USNWR*	SPR
Greenhouse, Linda	*NYT*	SPR
Marcus, Ruth	*WP*	SPR
Savage, David	*LAT*	SPR
Wermiel, Stephen	*WSJ*	SPR

Journalist	Publication/Syndicate	Section

TELEVISION

Journalist	Publication/Syndicate	Section
Goodman, Walter	*NYT*	SPR
Rosenberg, Howard	*LAT*	SPR
Shales, Tom	*WP*	SPR

TRADE

Armbruster, William	*JC*	FR
Auerbach, Stuart	*WP*	FR
Bradsher, Keith	*NYT*	FR
Lawrence, Richard	*JC*	FR
Maggs, John	*JC*	FR
Mongelluzzo, Bill	*JC*	FR
Rachid, Rosalind	*JC*	FR
Shear, Jeff	*Insight*	FR
Stokes, Bruce	*NJ*	FR
Tumulty, Karen	*LAT*	FR

WHITE HOUSE

Barnes, Fred	*TNR*	SPC
Bedard, Paul	*WT*	NSDIP
Devroy, Ann	*WP*	SPR
Dowd, Maureen	*NYT*	SPR
Gerstenzang, James	*LAT*	SPR
Lauter, David	*LAT*	SPR
McQueen, Michel	*WSJ*	SPR
Murray, Frank J.	*WT*	SPR
Rosenthal, Andrew	*NYT*	SPR
Seib, Gerald	*WSJ*	NSDIP
Solomon, Burt	*NJ*	SPR
Yang, John	*WP*	SPR

WALL STREET

Abelson, Alan	*Barron's*	FR
Cohen, Laurie P.	*WSJ*	FR
Eichenwald, Kurt	*NYT*	FR
Paltrow, Scot J.	*LAT*	FR
Smith, Randall	*WSJ*	FR

INDEX OF ABBREVIATIONS

AWST	Aviation Week & Space Technology	NYER	The New Yorker
BG	The Boston Globe	NYP	New York Post
BW	BusinessWeek	NYT	The New York Times
CJR	Columbia Journalism Review	PR	Policy Review
CS	Creators Syndicate	RD	Reader's Digest
CST	Chicago Sun Times	RS	Rolling Stone
CT	Chicago Tribune	SHE	Science, Health & Environmental Reporters
DN	Defense News		
FA	Foreign Affairs	SHNS	Scripps-Howard News Service
FEER	Far Eastern Economic Review	SFE	San Francisco Examiner
FNCR	Foreign Correspondents	SPC	(Social/Political) Commentators
FP	Foreign Policy	SPR	Social/Political Reporters
FR	Financial Reporters and Columnists	TA	The Atlantic
FS	Freelance Syndicate	TAS	The American Spectator
FT	Financial Times	TE	The Economist
FW	Financial World	TMH	The Miami Herald
HBR	Harvard Business Review	TMS	Tribune Media Services
HE	Human Events	TN	The Nation
ID	Investor's Business Daily	TNI	The National Interest
ITT	In These Times	TNR	The New Republic
JC	The Journal of Commerce	TNYRB	The New York Review of Books
KFS	King Features Syndicate	TP	The Progressive
LAT	Los Angeles Times	TPI	The Public Interest
LATS	Los Angeles Times Syndicate	TS	The Spectator
MJ	Mother Jones	UFS	United Features Syndicate
NAS	North America Syndicate	UPS	Universal Press Syndicate
NEA	Newspaper Enterprise Association	UR	Utne Reader
NJ	National Journal	USNWR	U.S.News & World Report
NPQ	New Perspectives Quarterly	WM	The Washington Monthly
NR	National Review	WP	The Washington Post
NSDIP	National Security/Diplomatic Correspondents	WPWG	Washington Post Writers Group
		WSJ	The Wall Street Journal
NW	Newsweek	WT	The Washington Times
NY	New York		

INDEX